THE MODERN LAW
OF
REAL PROPERTY

First Edition	.	.	.	September 1925
Second Edition	.	.	.	September 1927
Third Edition	.	.	.	February 1933
Fourth Edition	.	.	.	May 1937
Fifth Edition	.	.	.	July 1944
Second Impression	.	.		August 1945
Third Impression	.	.		January 1947
Fourth Impression	.	.		December 1947
Sixth Edition	.	.	.	September 1949
Second Impression	.	.		July 1952
Seventh Edition	.	.	.	September 1954
Second Impression	.	.		September 1956
Eighth Edition	.	.	.	March 1958
Second Impression	.	.		January 1961
Ninth Edition	.	.	.	March 1962
Second Impression	.	.		February 1964
Third Impression	.	.		August 1966
Tenth Edition	.	.	.	May 1967

THE MODERN LAW

OF

REAL PROPERTY

TENTH EDITION

BY

G. C. CHESHIRE

D.C.L., LL.D., F.B.A.

Of Lincoln's Inn, Barrister-at-Law
Sometime Vinerian Professor of English Law in the University of Oxford
and Fellow of All Souls College

With the material relating to the Rent Acts and Security
of Tenure, Registered Conveyancing and Town
and Country Planning

REVISED BY

J. D. DAVIES, B.C.L., M.A., LL.B.

Of Lincoln's Inn, Barrister-at-Law
Fellow of St. Catherine's College, Oxford

LONDON
BUTTERWORTHS
1967

ENGLAND: BUTTERWORTH & CO. (PUBLISHERS) LTD.
LONDON: 88 KINGSWAY, W.C.2

AUSTRALIA: BUTTERWORTH & CO. (AUSTRALIA) LTD.
SYDNEY: 20 LOFTUS STREET
MELBOURNE: 473 BOURKE STREET
BRISBANE: 240 QUEEN STREET

CANADA: BUTTERWORTH & CO. (CANADA) LTD.
TORONTO: 1367 DANFORTH AVENUE, 6

NEW ZEALAND: BUTTERWORTH & CO. (NEW ZEALAND) LTD.
WELLINGTON: 49/51 BALLANCE STREET
AUCKLAND: 35 HIGH STREET

SOUTH AFRICA: BUTTERWORTH & CO. (SOUTH AFRICA) LTD.
DURBAN: 33/35 BEACH GROVE

PRINTED IN GREAT BRITAIN BY
SPOTTISWOODE, BALLANTYNE AND CO. LTD.
LONDON AND COLCHESTER

PREFACE TO THE TENTH EDITION

THE preparation of successive editions of any law book is attended by many hazards, but it becomes unusually arduous if the relevant legislation continually fluctuates or if it tends to be revolutionary rather than evolutionary.

Fluctuations in legislative policy, due to the divergent views of the political parties upon the respective merits of landlord and tenant, are especially prominent in the context of the Rent Acts. In 1962, when the ninth edition of this book was published, the Conservative Government, confident that the scales of justice had become too heavily weighted in favour of the tenant, freed so many houses from the control of these Acts, that it seemed justifiable to reduce from seventy-two to nine pages the account of the subject that Mr. J. B. Butterworth contributed to the eight edition. Now, however, there has been a violent swing in the opposite direction. No great affection is felt in ruling circles for the landlord, and the Rent Act 1965, a ghastly example of legislation by reference, has strengthened and expanded the former statute law. This has made it necessary to restore Mr. Butterworth's account in a modernized but shortened form, an unenviable task that Mr. J. D. Davies, M.A., LL.B., B.C.L., of St. Catherine's College, Oxford, has been good enough to undertake. That he has accomplished it in twenty-four pages is no mean feat.

There is further leasehold legislation to come—this time of a revolutionary nature. What is now considered objectionable is the long lease at a ground rent, which for a century or more has contributed so successfully to the development of large estates. The property market has long been familiar with the transaction by which a freeholder grants a lease of land for, say, 99 years at a nominal rent in consideration that the tenant will erect thereon a house of a specified value and character. Thus at the end of the term the freeholder becomes the absolute owner of a house that he has not built. Yet, economically the transaction is fair to both parties. For 99 years the landlord receives no benefit from the ever-expanding value of the site, but he holds a long-term investment that will slowly though surely increase in value to the advantage of his successors. The increment is not unearned. On the other hand, the tenant gains the means of making an immediate profit from a site that he has acquired for a long period at a negligible cost. Having constructed the house according to contract, its sale should bring him a handsome return upon his expenditure of capital. The leasehold may perhaps be resold several times, and at first sight it may seem unjust that the one who buys it in the closing years of its life should receive no compensation for the loss of his home. In fact, however, there is no hardship, for the imminence of this loss will have been, or should have been, reflected in the purchase price.

Such are the realities of the transaction. But realism is not always the language of politics. Though the analysis might not perhaps have amused Lord Nottingham, the new principle is said to be that "the land belongs in equity to the landowner and the house belongs in equity to the occupying tenant"; Cmnd. 2916 (1966). Therefore, it is proposed to give the latter, if he has been continuously in occupation for the last five years, the right of compulsory enfranchisement, *i.e.* the right to buy out the lessor and thus to convert the leasehold into freehold at a price which "will completely disregard the value of the buildings on conversion", Cmnd. 2916 (1966). All that he will pay is the value of the freehold interest in the site subject to the lease.

Legislative effect has not yet been given to the proposal, and therefore no elaboration of this new political "equity" will be found in the following pages.

A more welcome intervention by the legislature since the last edition has been the reform of the rule against perpetuities by the Perpetuities and Accumulations Act 1964, which has required a substantial change in the former treatment of this subject. The fact that the Act does not affect instruments taking effect before 14th July, 1964, has raised a tantalizing problem. Is it better, first to state the common law and then to deal separately with the statutory alterations; or to weave the alterations into the progressive statement of the common law? For better or for worse, I have adopted the first alternative. One of my fears is that in the incessant struggle for brevity I may have given too condensed an account, only three pages longer than formerly, of this difficult part of the law.

The arrangement of the book remains unaltered, except that the former section on the right of a tenant to security of tenure now appears at the end of the chapter on leaseholds under the title "Security of Tenure and Control of Rent". It has been brought up to date by Mr. J. D. Davies.

The chapter on restrictive covenants has been recast and I hope improved, and short accounts have been added of tenancy by estoppel and also of the equitable doctrine of laches.

The labour of producing this edition has been lightened by Mr. J. D. Davies, to whom I express my gratitude. In addition to the work that he has done on security of tenure, he has revised the sections on land registration and planning law. He has also given me sound advice on various other parts of the book, especially that which treats of the rule against perpetuities.

This edition purports to state the law as it was on October 1st, 1966, but more recent developments have been noted when space allowed.

As always in the past, the staff of the publishers, and particularly on this occasion Mr. S. H. W. Partridge, Mr. R. N. G. Harrison and Miss Jennifer Cemm, have borne with patience my frequent intrusions upon their time and have never failed to dispel the anxieties of a hesitant mind.

Finally, it is of some interest to record that this book, in the forty-two years of its life, has grown in length by 15 per cent and the cost of living has increased by 211 per cent, but the price has increased by only 114 per cent.

G. C. C.

January 1, 1967.

PREFACE TO THE FIRST EDITION

MY classical friends assure me that the principles which every author should observe were laid down for all time by Horace. Compose, submit the result line by line to Maecius, consult the judgment of two friends, and preserve to yourself a *locus poenitentiae* by withholding publication for nine years. Such rules are no doubt of inestimable value, but unfortunately the real property legislation of the last few years has been too rapid to permit of an author profiting by the wisdom of Horace in the particular matter of delay. Despite his awful warning,

nescit vox missa reverti,

which never seemed so impressive to me as it does now on the eve of publication, I felt, in view of the representations of colleagues and pupils, that some attempt should be made to publish with as little delay as possible an account of the new system of real property law.

As the lack of adequate time is the only excuse that I can offer for the shortcomings of this book, it may be in point to indicate why I have thought it advisable to publish as soon as possible. The old system of real property law was described with such lucidity and fullness in several works of repute that it would have been presumptuous to offer another book had the law remained unaltered. It is, however, to be profoundly modified on January 1st, 1926. The process of modification was begun by the Law of Property Act, 1922. This was originally designed to come into operation on January 1st, 1925, but a closer examination of the Act showed that it would not lead to a simplification of the law, especially in the matter of accessibility, unless it were cast into a different form. Its greatest defect was that while it introduced a number of new rules and brought about a number of abolitions, both in the existing common law and the existing statutes, it did not repeal and re-enact the latter in a manner calculated to render the search for the law the simple task it should be. To avoid, therefore, what might have been chaos, the legislature set to work in 1924 to consolidate a great part of the statute law bearing on real property, and to incorporate the principles and alteration of the Act of 1922 in the consolidating statutes. Such of the provisions of the Act of 1922 as were not of a merely transitional character were repealed and re-enacted in the consolidating statutes, while the date at which the transitional provisions were to come into operation was postponed to January 1st, 1926. Six consolidating bills were drafted and

*a**

appeared in print during the late summer of 1924, but it was not until April, 1925, that they were passed by Parliament.

The position was, then, that only in April, 1925, did the new legal rules which, for the moment at any rate, are destined to regulate rights of property in the land, become known, and though they were postponed from coming into operation until January 1st, 1926, the result was that a student had but eight months within which to master the new system. Examinations wait for no man, and when it is remembered that the King's Printer's copies of the new Acts cover more than six hundred pages, it will be realised that the prospect with which a student was faced was not a happy one.

When it was known in January, 1924, what the intentions of the legislature were, I therefore felt justified in attempting to prepare a book which would not merely record the changes, but would present the law as a composite whole. Despite the short time available, I felt that something was required, before the new era dawned in January, 1926, to enable students to envisage a legal system which is, in many respects, widely different from that described in existing books. The present book represents an attempt to supply the want. It has many defects, but it is hoped that they are defects which can be readily eradicated should sufficient support be forthcoming to justify the publication of a second edition.

One of these defects is a somewhat excessive length, though something may be said in palliation of what, to a student, is perhaps the worst vice known to the law. In the first place the number of pages has been greatly increased owing to the manner in which the text has been set out. The subject is complicated, and the design has been to space the text out and to add numerous headings and indentations, so that the subject matter may easily catch the eye of a reader. Secondly, the book contains a number of repetitions which are due partly to the speed at which it has been written and partly to the intervals which, owing to other calls upon my time, have separated the composition of its various parts. Thirdly, it must be admitted that the bulk of real property law is greater now than it formerly was. At the beginning of my labours I was imbued with the idea that the task of a student had been lightened. So much had disappeared. The old rules relating to remainders, the old canons of descent, the rule in Shelley's Case, copyholds, gavelkind—they were all gone, and one's first impression was that the amount of law which a book on real property need deal with had been diminished. This will be true in twenty or thirty years' time, but unfortunately it is far from the truth at the present moment. Quite apart from the fact that a knowledge of the old law remains necessary for the purpose of investigating title, it is also a fact that a great many of the new rules can neither be understood nor explained unless the former rules are known. The Administration Act, 1925, for instance, abolishes curtesy, but the Law of Property Act, 1925, retains it in the case of entailed interests.

So much may be said by way of excuse. The Horatian requirement of time has been lacking, but not the other essentials. The rôle of Maecius has been filled by Mr. T. K. Brighouse, M.A., a former colleague of mine in the University College of Wales, Aberystwyth, who, though not a lawyer, has been an experienced and valuable critic on the literary side. Despite what must be a distinctly repellent subject to a layman, he has read every word of this book at least twice, and has not only saved me from some of the worst mistakes of a naturally defective style, but has advised and procured alterations in many passages where my proposed treatment would have obscured the lucidity of statement. The extent of my obligation to him is immeasurable.

On the legal side, the help I have received has been equally considerable. The main task has fallen on Mr. P. H. L. Brough of the Equity Bar, who has sacrificed a great deal of his time to reading and advising on the manuscript before it has been submitted to others. Moreover, he has given me the benefit of his practical experience in the initial stages of the book by helping to arrange the form in which some of the more difficult parts of the new legislation might be set out. His clearness of vision and his natural aptitude for realising the object of an obscure enactment have been of inestimable value to me.

I owe a debt of deep gratitude to Sir John Miles, B.C.L., M.A., Fellow and Tutor of Merton College, Oxford, who, besides encouraging me to begin the preparation of this book, has always been anxious at the sacrifice of his own time to afford me the benefit of his mature knowledge and sound advice.

To Professor J. D. I. Hughes, B.C.L., M.A., of Leeds University, to Mr. Ernest A. Steele, LL.B., of Halifax, and to Mr. L. E. Salt, M.A., Fellow and Bursar of Pembroke College, Oxford, I am under a deep obligation. They have each done me the honour of reading the whole of the book in proof form, and when I recall the number of their suggestions and criticisms to which I have paid heed, I realise the extent of my indebtedness to them. Their unselfish labours have prevented the appearance of innumerable sins, both of omission and commission, and their judgment has frequently kept me from straying into an unwise method of treatment.

Mr. Harold Potter, LL.B., of Birmingham University, and Mr. John Snow, M.A., of New College, Oxford, have very kindly read the chapter on conveyancing and have suggested several practical improvements which have been of the utmost value to me. It is, however, only fair to Mr. Potter to say that he would have elaborated the introductory note to Book III in a manner which would have greatly increased its usefulness and value, had not his proposals unfortunately reached me too late to permit of their inclusion.

The above is an inadequate acknowledgment of the services which have been rendered to me, but at the same time it must be recorded that none of the gentlemen who have so willingly extended me their aid is responsible in the slightest degree for the mistakes and failings which no doubt will be found to characterise this book. For these I am wholly responsible, while only partially responsible for anything which may be worthy of approval.

Lastly, I must acknowledge the help, of a different character, but no less valuable, which I have received from my wife. From the moment when this book was begun she abandoned a great part of her leisure and, having mastered for the occasion the unattractive art of typing, converted an almost illegible manuscript into a form which made the task of all those who had to deal with it a task of ease instead of a burden.

G. C. C.

OXFORD,
Sept. 1925.

TABLE OF CONTENTS

BOOK I.

INTRODUCTION TO THE STUDY OF THE MODERN LAW.

BOOK II.

ESTATES AND INTERESTS IN LAND.

PART I.

THE ESTATE IN FEE SIMPLE ABSOLUTE IN POSSESSION.

PART II.

INTERESTS ARISING UNDER A STRICT SETTLEMENT OR TRUST FOR SALE.

PART III.

COMMERCIAL INTERESTS.

A. INTERESTS CONFERRING A RIGHT TO THE LAND ITSELF.

B. INTERESTS CONFERRING A RIGHT ENFORCEABLE AGAINST THE LAND OF ANOTHER.

BOOK III.

THE TRANSFER AND EXTINCTION OF ESTATES AND INTERESTS.

PART I.

PART II.

TRANSFER *INTER VIVOS* BY ESTATE OWNERS.

PART III.

TRANSFER BY OPERATION OF LAW.

PART IV.

TRANSFER ON DEATH.

PART V.

EXTINCTION OF ESTATES AND INTERESTS.

PART VI.

REGISTERED CONVEYANCING.

PART VII.

INCAPACITIES AND DISABILITIES WITH REGARD TO THE HOLDING AND TRANSFER OF ESTATES AND INTERESTS.

BOOK IV.

TOWN AND COUNTRY PLANNING.

INDEX.

TABLE OF CASES

PAGE

*b**

TABLE OF STATUTES

In the following Table references are given to Halsbury's Statutes of England Second Edition showing the volume and page numbers at which the annotated Act is printed.

b**

Table of Statutes.

BOOK I.

INTRODUCTION TO THE MODERN LAW.

SUMMARY.

INTRODUCTION TO THE STUDY
OF THE MODERN LAW.

SECTION I. INTRODUCTORY NOTE.

The early editions of this work suggested that the English Merits of English land law.
land law offers no intellectual entertainment and that it is scarcely
a subject worthy of study for its own sake.   Further reflection
and the rebukes of critics, however, show that this lament,
momentarily justifiable though it may have been in 1925 (the
date of the first edition), after trying conclusions with some seven
hundred pages of new legislation, is less than fair and that it
underrates the virtues and accomplishments of this department of
English law.   It may, indeed, be difficult to agree with the Real
Property Commissioners of 1829 that it is a department which
" appears to come almost as near to perfection as can be expected
in any human institutions,"[1] but, nevertheless, whether it is regarded as a mirror of one aspect of English life over a period of
nearly a thousand years or as a body of law that has adapted itself
without undue strain to a succession of political and social up-
heavals, culminating in the calamity of the welfare state, it is no
mean contribution to the legal thought of the world.

It would not be wise in the opening pages of the book to
develop this theme fully, but three illustrations may be given, the
force of which should become clearer in the course of reading.

Perhaps the most vivid is the invention and development by the
common law of the doctrine of an estate in the land as something
distinct from the land itself, a distinction which has enabled
proprietary rights to be moulded with a flexibility wholly unknown
to the legal systems that derive from Rome.   One learned com-
mentator, indeed, has gone so far as to say that :—

> " Our law of property is, on this side at least, far richer, far more
> " practical, and at the same time far more generalized and more
> " logical than any other."[2]

---

[1] First Rep. p. 6.
[2] Lawson, *The Rational Strength of English Law*, p. 97.

3

Moreover, the development of the doctrine was accompanied by a precision of technical language that made it possible to reduce the most intricate set of dispositions to comparative simplicity. The old rules that governed future interests, for instance, were not unlike a series of mathematical formulæ. Superficially they seemed shrouded in mystery and they brought little pleasure to the average student, but to one who applied them in the light of the technical vocabulary no problem presented undue difficulty.

Another outstanding contribution to legal institutions, described by Maitland as the most distinctive feature of English law, has been the conception of the trust, a conception that not only attained the object for which it was introduced—the modification of the feudal land law—but which in the course of its development has become the axis round which revolve so many activities of the English-speaking people.

Nevertheless, the public importance of the land law in the feudal society of its origin eventually brought its troubles. When the country settled down after the upheaval of the Norman Conquest, the social bond which, both on the public and on the private side of life, united men together in a political whole was the land. Broadly speaking, land constituted the sole form of wealth, and it was through its agency that the everyday needs of the governing and the governed classes were satisfied. The result of this was that from an early date a complicated system of law, founded on custom and developed by the decisions of the courts, began to grow up, and we may call it for convenience the common law system.

In its origin this system was eminently suitable for a society that was based and centred on the land, and appropriate to the simple notions prevailing in a feudal population, but in several respects it gradually came to outlive the reason for its existence.

Tendency of the law to become static.

It tended to become static. Rules that were in harmony with their early environment lived on long after they had become anachronisms. Law will wither unless it expands to keep pace with the progressive ideas of an advancing community, but in this particular context the rigidity and formalism of the common lawyers retarded the process, and, though equity intervened to great effect in several directions, the few reforms attempted by the legislation before the first quarter of the nineteenth century served to complicate rather than to simplify the law. Statutory reform, however, began in earnest after the report of the Real

Legislative reforms of early nineteenth century.

Property Commissioners in 1829. Though lavishing, as we have seen, extravagant praise upon the substantive rules of law, the commissioners went on to express their opinion that the modes by which interests in land were created, transferred and secured had become unnecessarily defective and that they demanded substantial alteration. The result of this view was that on their recommendation a number of statutes were passed between 1833 and 1837 which swept away many impediments to the smooth operation of the law. The chief of these were :—

> Prescription Act, 1832 ;
> Fines and Recoveries Act, 1833 ;
> Real Property Limitation Act, 1833;
> Dower Act, 1833 ;
> Inheritance Act, 1833 ;
> Wills Act, 1837.

Between 1837 and 1922 the legislature became more and more active in the sphere of real property law, but most of the enactments were directed towards the simplification of conveyancing and the extension of the landowners' powers of enjoyment. No comprehensive effort was made to smooth the path by abolishing the substantive defects that had settled on the main body of the law like barnacles on the hull of a ship. Then came the war of 1914, and with it a general desire to set the social life of the nation in order. One of the results of this desire was to give an impetus to land legislation, and it will be as well to state at the outset the main idea which lay at the back of the legislation that resulted. It was nothing more than a desire to render the sale of land as rapid and simple a matter as is the sale of goods or of shares. A layman knows that if he desires to transfer to another the ownership of a chattel, such as a motor car or a picture, the only requirement is the making of a contract which names the parties, records their intention, describes the article to be sold and states the price to be paid. The moment that such a contract is concluded, the ownership of the article, in the absence of a contrary intention, passes to the buyer. At first sight it is difficult to appreciate why the same simple expedient cannot be adopted in the case of land, and not unnaturally a layman grows impatient of the long and expensive investigation attendant upon the conveyance of a piece of land worth perhaps one half of the car which can be effectively sold in a quarter of an hour.

But the difference is inevitable, and the reason is that in the great majority of cases the possessor of personal goods is their absolute owner, and therefore able to pass a title which will confer upon their deliveree an equally full and unencumbered ownership. If A. is in possession of a piano, it is probable that he is its owner, and in most cases a buyer is safe in paying its value and taking delivery of possession. No doubt the maxim of the law is *nemo dat quod non habet*, and if it should happen that A., instead of being the owner, is a thief or is merely holding the piano under a hire purchase agreement, then a buyer from him will not acquire ownership. But the fact remains that despite risks of this nature a buyer is generally justified in assuming that the possessor of goods is also the owner, and as a rule there is no need to go to trouble and expense in order to ascertain whether some person other than the possessor has any interest in them.

Tendency towards simplification of conveyancing.

Main object of legislation of 1925.

Contrast between land and goods.

It is a legitimate risk to take. But for a purchaser of land to be content with the word of the vendor and with the appearance of ownership that flows from his possession would be an act of sheer folly.

Permanence of land causes multiplicity of rights.

Land and goods are and must ever be on a different plane. Land is fixed, permanent and vital to the needs of society, and a subject-matter in which rights may be granted to persons other than the ostensible owner. A. is in possession of land and is obviously exercising all the powers of enjoyment and management which amount to the popular idea of ownership, but none the less it is by no means certain that he is in fact entitled to dispose of the interest that he may have agreed to sell. He may be merely in possession under a lease for any period from one to 999 years or more, or he may be a mere life tenant holding under a family settlement ; and even though he holds the fee simple—the largest interest known to the law and one that approximates to the absolute ownership of goods—it is likely that he or his predecessors have granted to third parties rights, such as mortgages, restrictive covenants and rights of way, which continue to be enforceable against the land regardless of any transfer to which it may have been subjected. So long as third parties can in this way have legally enforceable rights against land which outwardly appears to belong absolutely to the possessor, it is difficult, in the absence of compulsory registration of title, to devise a system under which conveyances of land can be conducted with the facility of sales of goods, and it will always be incumbent on a purchaser to make careful searches and inquiries in order to see that the land is unburdened.

Difficulties attending reform of English land law.

We may start, then, with the assumption that no effort of legislative genius can, from the point of view of simplicity and rapidity, put conveyances of land on an equal footing with sales of goods. But when the question of reforming the law came before Parliament in 1922, the result of 600 years of development from a feudal origin was that the law of real property contained so many antiquated rules and useless technicalities that additional and unnecessary impediments had arisen to hinder the facile transfer of land. The real property law as it existed in 1922 might justly be described as an archaic feudalistic system which, though originally evolved to satisfy the needs of a society based and centred on the land, had by considerable ingenuity been twisted and distorted into a shape more or less suitable to a commercial society dominated by money. The movement of progressive societies has been from land to money, or rather to trade, and a legal system which acquired its main features at a time when land constituted the major part of the country's wealth can scarcely be described as suitable to an industrial community. To borrow the words of Bagehot directed to a different subject, the 1922 real property law might be likened to " an old man who still wears with attached fondness clothes in the fashion of his youth ; what you see of him is the same ; what you do not see is wholly altered."

To take any structure, whether it be a system of law, a constitution or a house, and for a period of 600 years to patch it here and there in order to adapt it to new conditions, cannot fail to lead to complications of a bewildering character.

The Legislation of 1925. Confirmed in the views just mentioned, the legislature began in 1922 to reform the law on a far more ambitious scale than had been attempted in the earlier legislative changes, for, though the main purpose was to simplify conveyancing, yet this was pursued not merely by a simplification of the machinery of land transfer, but also by a free use of the pruning knife.   In the official view, reforms were needed as a prelude to the simplification and extension of the system of registration of title.[1]

Simplification of law of real property.

The first Act to be passed was the Law of Property Act, 1922, which was described in its preamble as

Law of Property Act, 1922.

> " An Act to assimilate and amend the law of Real and Personal
> " Estate, to abolish copyhold and other special tenures, to amend
> " the law relating to commonable lands and of intestacy, and to
> " amend the Wills Act 1837, the Settled Land Acts 1882 to 1890,
> " the Conveyancing Acts 1881 to 1911, the Trustee Act 1893 and
> " the Land Transfer Acts 1875 and 1897."

The all-important fact that emerges from this descriptive title is that one main object was to " assimilate . . . the law of real and personal estate."

We shall see as we proceed that a comparison of the law relating to real and personal property respectively is, from the point of view of convenience and reason, very much to the advantage of the latter.   Part I of the Act therefore put the two forms of property as nearly as possible upon the same footing, a result which was obtained partly by abolishing the chief differences that formerly existed between the two, and partly by eliminating many of the technical anachronisms that had grown up in the land laws.   In addition, the law of personal property, which thus became the dominating system, was itself amended in several particulars.

Assimilation of real and personal property by the Act of 1922.

The date at which the Act of 1922 was appointed to come into operation, however, was postponed, for the changes it made were sufficiently drastic to necessitate the re-drafting and consolidation of the real property statute law from the year 1285. The Law of Property (Amendment) Act, 1924, was therefore passed to facilitate the task of consolidation, and then all but the

Necessity for further legislation.

---

[1] Wolstenholme and Cherry, *Conveyancing Statutes* (12th Edn.), p. 166.

transitional provisions of this Act and of the Act of 1922 were absorbed into the following seven statutes, passed in 1925.

1925
legislation.

Law of Property Act ;
Settled Land Act ;
Trustee Act ;
Land Charges Act ;
Administration of Estates Act ;
Land Registration Act ;
Universities and College Estates Act.[1]

Practical results of the legislation.

The practical result at the present day is that the whole law of real property is contained partly in these statutes, partly in older statutes, partly in subsequent legislation, such as the various Landlord and Tenant Acts, the Town and Country Planning Acts and the Rent Acts, and partly in the mass of judge-made rules so far as these, which still form the bulk of the law, have not been abolished or modified by statute.

Three-fold historical division of Real Property Law.

Real property law, like most of the other branches of our jurisprudence, falls into three divisions, which are due to the order of its historical development :—

First of all we get the purely common law system, which was designed to meet the needs of a feudal society.

Secondly in order of time we have the equitable system which, though not comprehensive, was gradually evolved in certain directions with a view to adapting the common law rules to a society moved by different ideals and possessing a more commercial outlook on life.

And finally we come to the various legislative enactments by which the judge-made law of land was rendered more adequate to the needs of society.

We will now sketch in its barest outline the common law system, then describe at somewhat greater length certain conceptions that were introduced into the law by the Chancellor in the exercise of his equitable jurisdiction, and finally discuss the legislative changes of 1925.

SECTION II.   THE COMMON LAW SYSTEM.
(1) THE DOCTRINE OF TENURE.[2]

Feudalism.

Feudalism in Europe. The outstanding feature of the English land law and one that explains many of its peculiarities is that, at least from the time of the Norman Conquest, it fell into line with the continental systems and became and remained for several centuries intensely feudalistic. *Feudalism* itself is a word of some vagueness and ambiguity, and one that was certainly

---

[1] These Acts of 1925 are not consolidating Acts in the true sense of the term, since the Acts of 1922 and 1924 with which they are concerned were amending Acts ; *Grey* v. *Inland Revenue Commissioners,* [1960] A. C. 1 ; [1959] 3 All E. R. 603.   This point is important in regard to the rules of interpretation ; *ibid.*
[2] For the history of this doctrine, see Simpson, *An Introduction to the History of Land Law,* pp. 1 *et seq.*

unknown to the peoples to whom it is applied. It is often expected to represent the history of Western Europe from the eighth to the fourteenth century,[1] and, like the modern use of the word *capitalism*, to describe the social characteristics of the period.[2] To a lawyer, however, it represents :—

> " A state of society in which the main social bond is the relation
> " between lord and man, a relation implying on the lord's part
> " protection and defence ; on the man's part protection, service
> " and reverence, the service including service in arms. This personal
> " relation is inseparably involved in a proprietary relation, the
> " tenure of land—the man holds of the lord, the man's service is a
> " burden on the land, the lord has important rights in the land."[3]

Thus it is the negation of independence. It implies subordination, it means that one man is deliberately made inferior to another.

In pre-feudal days the land of Europe was owned absolutely, though subject to custom, by persons who were grouped together in village communities, and it therefore becomes a matter of interest to discover why it was that a great part of the world lapsed from a state of comparative freedom into one of servility, why landownership disappeared and land tenure took its place. The change represented a retrogressive step in the history of man, but in Europe it was one of the necessary consequences of the disruption of the Roman Empire by the Barbarian invaders. The overthrow of that Empire caused chaos and disorganization in Europe and produced conditions in which it was necessary for private persons to procure for themselves a higher degree of protection than could be furnished by their own unaided efforts. In those days interference with personal freedom or with the ownership of property might come from several different quarters, such as a revolt of peasants, the arrogance of a powerful neighbour, the extortion of a government or the hostility of some tribe. The only method of obtaining security was mutual support, and so it came to pass that men deliberately subordinated themselves to the strong hand of some magnate versed in the arts of war, and were compensated for the diminution of personal independence and the loss of landownership by acquiring the protection afforded by the forces of which he disposed. This process involved both a personal and a proprietary subordination, but it is only on the latter that we need dwell.

One of the effects of the feudalization of Europe was that from a legal aspect land became the exclusive bond of union between men. Individual or communal landownership was destroyed. The ownership of the whole of the land in any given district was vested in the overlord, and the persons who had formerly owned it in their own right now held it from the overlord. In return

Reason for introduction of feudalism.

Disruption of Roman Empire.

Feudalism resorted to for security.

Growth of feudalism on Continent.

---

[1] Pollock and Maitland, *History of English Law*, vol. i. p. 44.
[2] Plucknett, *A Concise History of the Common Law* (5th Edn.), p. 506.
[3] Maitland, *The Constitutional History of England*, p. 143.

B*

for the land which they held they were bound to render services, chiefly of a military nature, to the overlord, while the latter in his turn was bound to protect his tenants. Feudalism implied a reciprocity of rights and duties. The lord gained in dignity and consequence and became entitled to personal services, while the tenant obtained security.

Reasons for spread of feudalism. This conversion from ownership to tenure began in the lower ranks of society, but quickly spread upwards until it finally embraced the greater part of the land of Western Europe. Various reasons contributed to this extension. The general anarchy of the times, the lack of a central government sufficiently strong to ensure a well-ordered and peaceful existence, and the natural ambition of magnates to increase the extent of their possessions induced even the large landowners to put themselves and their land under the protection of someone greater than themselves.

Government based on feudalism. This development took place under the Franks, and in the time of the Carolingians a still further impetus was given to the movement, for the government itself—if such a term can be applied to those times—was obliged to resort to the principle of feudalism. Administration had to be carried on somehow and taxes were difficult to collect. The solution was to farm out Crown lands to great men who paid a sum of money to the government and who in return became lords of the lands (which were called benefices) and of the persons who dwelt thereon. A little later, when military pressure from the east and the south made it imperative that society should be organized on a basis that would afford protection to the State, the device of granting benefices in return for military services, a device that was gradually failing owing to the scarcity of Crown lands, was widened in scope by an act of confiscation.

Church lands feudalized. The Church had become the greatest landowner in Europe. Charles Martel, who was Mayor of the Frankish Empire in the first part of the eighth century, deliberately carried out wholesale seizures of Church property, but in A.D. 751 some sort of amicable arrangement was made whereby vast tracts of Church lands were granted by the ecclesiastical corporations to laymen at the request of the King. The Church ownership of the lands was recognized by the payment of an uneconomic rent to the corporations, while the tenants—and this was the significance of the transaction—became liable by virtue of their holdings to render services to the King.[1] Thus did the net of feudalism spread everywhere. In this way life and government were made to depend upon the land.[2]

Social and administrative unit. **The Manor.** This can be seen by an examination of that unit of society which is called the Manor. The grant of benefices

---

[1] Vinogradoff, *Cambridge Medieval History*, vol. ii. p. 646.
[2] See generally, *Encyclopædia Britannica, sub nom.* Feudalism.

led to the creation of great estates or manors vested in the grantees from the Crown. Topographically a manor denoted a certain area of land consisting of a number of houses, strips of arable and pasture land and waste lands, all of which were within the domain of the lord of the manor. The waste, in proportion to the cultivated land, formed by far the greater part of the manor, a fact which serves to explain the inclosures of later centuries. But we shall miss the significance of this system unless we realize that the manor was both a social and an administrative unit through the agency of which a whole country was governed. Each manor was, as it were, a small government in itself.

The central government required soldiers and money, but instead of approaching its subjects directly it looked no further than the lord of the manor. His obligation *vis-à-vis* the government was to supply a fully equipped fighting force, and the right which he obtained in return was that of holding his manor or group of manors immune from the legal and administrative control of the government. Thus, when the power of a central government was on the wane, it became customary to grant immunities to powerful men, which meant nothing more nor less than that the functions of government were handed over to feudal lords.

VINOGRADOFF has said :—

" As in the later Empire, the Government is obliged to have recourse
" to great landlords in order to carry out its functions of police,
" justice, military and fiscal authority. Great estates had become
" extra-territorial already under Roman rule in the 4th and 5th
" centuries, and it would be superfluous to point out how much more
" the governments of the barbarians stood in need of the help of great
" landowners." [1]

One of the most important features of the administrative side of a Continental manor was the lord's right of jurisdiction. As the royal writ did not run within the territorial limits of a manor, the lord set up local courts of his own, and it was only in the manorial court of the defendant that a plaintiff was entitled to sue. Thus, to use the expressive language of Stubbs,[2] there was

Lord's right of jurisdiction.

" a graduated system of jurisdiction based on land tenure in which
" every lord judged, taxed and commanded the class next below
" him, . . . in which private war, private coinage, private prisons
" took the place of the imperial institutions of the Government."

Summary. By way of summary we may say that the characteristics of feudalism are the relation of lord and vassal; the principle that every person interested in land is a mere holder thereof, a tenant and not an owner ; the condition that this tenure shall continue to exist only so long as the tenant performs the particular services imposed upon him at the beginning of the

Characteristics of feudalism.

---

[1] Vinogradoff, *op. cit.* p. 651.   [2] *Constitutional History*, vol. i. p. 278.

tenure ; and lastly the recognition of a reciprocity of rights and duties. The foundation of the whole system is the fief—that is to say, the land which the inferior holds as tenant of the superior. The word *fief* becomes *feudum* in Latin, and *feud*, and later *fee* in English.

Feudalism
established
in England.

Feudalism in England. We now come to consider the effect which this Continental feudalism had upon the land law of England. As the scope of this book makes it undesirable to elaborate particular questions of legal history, it is not proposed to discuss the extent to which feudalism existed in England prior to the Conquest. That a system was in vogue which bore similarities to Continental feudalism cannot be doubted, but the only fact that we need notice here is that the Normans applied their own ideas to the conditions prevalent in this country, and succeeded in establishing an English variety of feudalism which, though differing in many respects from that of the Continent, became a striking and universal feature of the land law. The policy of William left England, whatever it may have been before, a highly feudalized state. He took the line that, since the English landowners had denied his right to the Crown of England and had compelled him to assert it by force, their landed possessions became his to dispose of as he chose.[1] What he did was not so much to seize land and parcel it out among his Norman followers, as to allow all Englishmen who recognized him as King to redeem by money payments the estates which by right of conquest had momentarily passed to him.

This process of confiscation and redistribution flowed on evenly, and though it cannot be said that the redistributions amounted to direct feudal grants, there is no doubt that they came to be regarded as such when the idea of Norman feudalism took hold of men's minds. As STUBBS says :—

" After each effort the royal hand was laid on more heavily ; more and
" more land changed owners, and with the change of owners the title
" changed. The complications and irregularities of the Anglo-Saxon
" tenures were exchanged for the simple and uniform feudal theory.
" The 1500 tenants in chief of Domesday took the place of the countless
" landowners of Edward's day. . . . It is enough for our purpose to
" ascertain that a universal assimilation of title followed the general
" changes of ownership. The King of Domesday is the supreme
" landlord ; all the land of the nation, the old folkland, has become
" the King's, and all private land is held immediately or mediately
" of him ; all holders are bound to their lords by homage and fealty,
" either actually demanded or understood to be demandable in every
" case of transfer by inheritance or otherwise." [2]

---

[1] Stenton, *William the Conqueror*, pp. 494–5.
[2] Stubbs, *Constitutional History*, vol. i. pp. 282–3.

This English feudalism differed from the Continental variety in that all freemen were bound by the Salisbury Oath of 1086 to swear allegiance directly to the King instead of to the immediate lord from whom they held their lands ; and again in the fact that William, instead of setting up great territorial jurisdictions, organized administration in such a way that he governed the country through sheriffs who were directly responsible to him. Though the Frankish system of tenure displaced the Anglo-Saxon system, the establishment of a feudal mode of government was deliberately avoided. But in respect of tenure the result was much the same as on the Continent. By a certain date, which we need not attempt to define, the doctrine of land tenure became universal in England.

Every acre of land in the country was held of the King. As POLLOCK and MAITLAND have said :—

" The person whom we might be inclined to call the owner, the person
" who has the right to use and abuse the land, to cultivate it or leave
" it uncultivated, to keep all others off it, holds the land of the King
" either immediately or mediately." [1]

If a tenant held immediately of the King, he was said to hold of him in chief or *in capite*. But the position might be less simple. Instead of a tenant holding directly of the King he might hold mediately, as for instance where C. held of B. who held of A. who held of the King. C., who stood at the bottom of the scale, and who to a layman would look more like an owner than anybody else, was called the *tenant in demesne—tenet terram in dominico suo*. The persons between him and the King were called *mesne lords*, and their lordships were called *seignories*. A. held the land, not *in demesne* but in service, since he was entitled to the services of B., and B. was in a similar position, since he was entitled to the services of C. The services due from these tenants would not necessarily be of the same nature, for A. might hold of the King by military service, B. of A. in return for a money rent, and C. of B. in return for some personal service. In such a case each grantee owed to his immediate grantor the service that he had agreed to render, and from this point of view the service was called *intrinsec*. Services were not merely personal, but charged on the tenement, so that if A. failed in the performance of his military duties the King could distrain upon the land in the hands of C., as could A. if B. fell into arrear with the rent. B. could agree to perform the military service in place of A., but no private arrangement of this kind could free the land from the burden. From this point of view the service was called *forinsec*, *i.e.* foreign to any bargain between other parties.[2] Of course, if, for example, A. failed to perform his military service and the King proceeded

---

[1] *History of English Law*, vol. ii. p. 211.
[2] Pollock and Maitland, *History of English Law*, vol. i. p. 216.

against the land in C.'s occupation, the latter had a remedy against A., called the writ of *mesne*. A tenant came under an obligation, confirmed by the oath of fealty, to serve his lord faithfully, and the price of infidelity in this respect was the forfeiture of his fief. In particular, forfeiture ensued if he did anything to the disinherison of his lord, as, for example, if he deliberately failed to defend an action for the recovery of land brought against him by a third party.[1]

Universality of tenure in England.

Perhaps the most striking fact about English feudalism was the universality of this doctrine of land tenure. On the Continent tenure applied only to those who held lands in return for military services,[2] but in England it applied to every holder whatever the nature of the duties that he had agreed to perform might be. Moreover a movement began by which the number of mesne lordships was increased to a bewildering extent. As each year passed, more and more sub-tenancies were created. A., who held of the King, would transfer his land or part of it to B., and B. to C., and so on, but each transfer, instead of being an out and out grant by which the transferor got rid of his entire interest, would operate as a grant of land to be held by each transferee as tenant of his immediate transferor. As a result " innumerable petty lords sprang up between the great barons and the immediate tenant of the soil." [3]

Sub-infeudation.

This process, which was termed subinfeudation, was carried to such lengths that Maitland was able to discover a case where there were as many as eight sub-tenancies in the same piece of land. One explanation of this reluctance to part with one's entire interest was the economic significance of land in the centuries immediately succeeding the Conquest. Apart from cattle, land was practically the only form of wealth. Money was scarce, and something had to take its place as a medium of exchange. This can be illustrated by the recompense usually given for services rendered.

Sub-infeudation spreads because land was main form of wealth.

Domestic servants in a manor were paid by a crude method of profit-sharing. As Vinogradoff has stated, " The swine-herd of Glastonbury Abbey, for instance, received one sucking pig a year, the interior parts of the best pig and the tails of all the others which were slaughtered in the Abbey. The chief scullion had a right to all remnants of viands—but not of game—to the feathers and the bowels of geese." [4]

But the form which payment took in the case of labourers on the manorial estate, and also in the case of servants who rendered non-domestic services for a great lord, was a grant of land to be held only so long as the services were properly performed. Thus

---

[1] For a discussion of this defunct principle, see the judgment of DENNING. L.J., in *Warner* v. *Sampson*, [1959] 1 Q. B. 297, 312–6 ; [1959] 1 All E. R, 120, 123–126.

[2] Holdsworth, *History of English Law*, vol. ii. p. 199.

[3] Hayes, *Introduction to Conveyancing*, p. 9.

[4] Vinogradoff, *Villainage*, pp. 321–2.

it was through one of the forms of tenure, known as tenure by sergeanty, that most of the wants of men were satisfied. The persons who severally acted as president of a lord's court, carried his letters, fed his hounds, cared for his horses and found him in bows and arrows, generally held land as tenants in sergeanty of the lord.[1] They would continue to hold the land as long as they served faithfully and no longer.

In other words, the importance of land as a means of payment made it advisable for tenants to keep as tenacious a hold upon it as possible, and, when a transfer was contemplated, to sub-infeudate rather than dispose of it outright. But for reasons into which we need not enter,[2] the practice of subinfeudation was obnoxious to the great lords, and was finally stopped in 1290 by the Statute *Quia Emptores*.[3]

Sub-infeudation stopped by Quia Emptores.

This important statute altered the law in two respects.

First, it set at rest a controversy by enacting that every free man should be at liberty to alienate the whole or part of his land without the consent of his lord. If part only were conveyed, the services were to be apportioned.

Secondly, it enacted that every alienee should hold the land of the same lord of whom the alienor previously held. The effect of this was to prevent the creation of new tenancies. The alienor dropped out, the alienee stepped into his shoes for all purposes, and thus instead of a new sub-tenancy there was the substitution of one tenant for another. If, therefore, the existence of a mesne lordship is proved at the present day, it follows that it must have been created before 1290. The statute, however, extended only to land held for a fee simple estate, *i.e.* the largest interest known to the law,[4] and it has never prevented the creation of a new tenure by the grant of a lesser estate, such as a fee tail or a life interest.

The statute did not bind the Crown. This had two consequences.

Crown not bound by Quia Emptores.

In the first place, the privilege of unrestricted alienation did not avail tenants *in capite*. In their case the consent of the Crown remained necessary and in practice this was given only on the payment of a fine.[5]

Secondly, the Crown was unaffected by the abolition of sub-infeudation and was therefore still able to create new tenancies in respect of the fee simple.

Quia Emptores was indeed a landmark in the history of real property. Its chief virtue was that it led to the gradual dis-

Importance of Quia Emptores.

---

[1] Pollock and Maitland, *History of English Law*, vol. i. p. 265.
[2] See Challis, *Law of Real Property* (3rd Edn.), pp. 18–19.
[3] 18 Ed. 1, c. 1; Holdsworth, *History of English Law*, vol. iii. p. 79.
[4] The meaning of " fee simple " will appear later ; *infra*, pp. 33 ; 110.
[5] Challis, *op. cit.*, pp. 14, 15. Such fines were abolished by the Tenures Abolition Act, 1660.

appearance of the numerous petty lordships that had arisen between the Crown and the tenant *in demesne.* Blackacre might no doubt have been held before 1290 by B. of A., but if in course of time it passed into the hands of a succession of alienees, each one being substituted for his predecessor, it would ultimately become extremely difficult to prove the existence of A.'s original lordship. Thus, there was a constant tendency for seignories to become vested in the Crown, and to this extent the law was simplified.

Plurality of forms of tenure.

Forms of Tenure. A feature of English feudalism, and one that complicated the law of land, was that there was not one common kind of tenure. We have seen how in early days, if a man wanted work of a regular nature done for him, he would generally get it done in exchange for land granted by him to the workman. Considering the diversity of personal needs which require to be satisfied, it is obvious that the services due from tenants would vary considerably in nature, importance and dignity. One tenant had to fight; another to look after a household, or to provide arms, or to pray for the soul of his overlord, or to do such agricultural work as might be demanded of him. There were

Variety of services.

vast differences between the possible services. It was considered an honourable thing to fight, but not to plough, and thus it came to pass that there gradually arose different forms of tenure based upon the differences in the nature of the services. The following table shows the state of affairs in the time of Edward I, when the tenures had become stabilized.

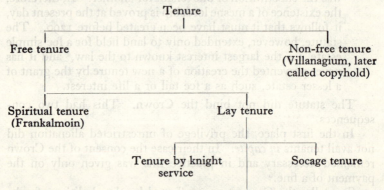

Divergent methods of land holding.

In addition to these regular tenures there also existed in certain districts a few customary methods of landholding under which land was subject in various respects to a number of abnormal incidents. Instances are gavelkind, borough-English and ancient demesne.

Gavelkind is a word which denotes the customs that have applied since the Conquest to socage land situated in Kent.[1]

---

[1] Pollock and Maitland, *History of English Law,* vol. ii. pp. 269 *et seq.*; Blackstone, vol. ii. p. 84 ; Challis, *Law of Real Property* (3rd Edn.), p. 14.

Such land was in certain particulars subject to different legal rules from those obtaining in other parts of the country. Thus,

> (*a*) the land descended upon intestacy to all the sons equally;
> (*b*) a husband who survived his wife was entitled until his re-marriage to a life estate in one-half of her land although issue of the marriage might not have been born [1];
> (*c*) a widow was entitled until her re-marriage to dower in one-half of her husband's land;
> (*d*) an infant could alienate his land by the form of conveyance known as a feoffment when he reached 15 years of age; and
> (*e*) the land was devisable.

Borough-English was a custom, found in certain parts of the country, under which the land descended to the youngest son to the exclusion of all the other children.[2]

Ancient demesne land was land held by freehold tenants in any manor which had belonged to the Crown in the time of Edward the Confessor or William the Conqueror.[3] The tenants in ancient demesne were subject to certain restraints and entitled to certain immunities.[4]

Knight Service.[5] The most important of the regular tenures in early days was knight service, or the tenure by which a man was obliged to render military services in return for the land that he held. Soon after the Conquest a process set in whereby the military needs of the country were satisfied in this manner. All the land of the country was held directly of the King, and it was a practically universal rule that the tenants in chief—that is, those men who held directly of the King as distinct from sub-tenants who owed their position to the practice of subinfeudation—held by knight service. Each tenant in chief had to produce for forty days in each year a definite number of fully armed horsemen. The number required in any particular case did not depend upon the extent of the tenant's land, but was arbitrarily fixed when the grant of the land was made, and, as the unit of the feudal host was a constabularia consisting of ten knights, it appears always to have been some multiple of 5 or 10.[6] For about a hundred years after the Conquest the army—to the strength of about 5000 knights—was actually raised in this way, but it was soon discovered that such a short service as forty days scarcely promoted the success

Nature of knight service.

---

[1] *Re Howlett, Howlett* v. *Howlett,* [1949] Ch. 767; [1949] 2 All E.R. 490.
[2] Littleton, ss. 165, 211; Blackstone, vol. ii. p. 83.
[3] Co. Inst. 542; Blackstone, vol. ii. p. 99; Holdsworth, *History of English Law,* vol. iii. pp. 263-9; Challis, *Law of Real Property* (3rd Edn.), p. 29; *Merttens* v. *Hill,* [1901] 1 Ch. 842.
[4] Real Property Commissioners' Third Report, pp. 12 *et seq. Merttens* v. *Hill, supra; Iveagh (Earl)* v. *Martin,* [1961] 1 Q. B. 232; [1960] 2 All E. R. 668.
[5] See Holdsworth, *History of English Law,* vol. iii. pp. 37-46.
[6] Round, *Feudal England,* pp. 259-60.

Scutage.

of military operations, and the King began about 1166 to exact money payments called scutage from the tenants in chief instead of requiring the production of the fixed quota of knights. But by the time of Edward I even scutage had become useless as a means of providing an army, and it can be said that thenceforth the tenure ceased to be military in the sense that it no longer served to supply forces for the defence of the realm.[1]

Survival of tenure by knight service.

What at first sight seems remarkable is that knight service, instead of falling into oblivion after it had ceased to fulfil its original function, continued to develop, and ended by hardening into a legal system far stricter and more onerous than it had hitherto been. The explanation of this inopportune survival was that, quite apart from the duty of military service, the tenure carried with it certain feudal incidents which had such a high financial value for the lords of whom the lands were held that to foster and develop it became a matter of great personal interest. Subinfeudation led to the extension of knight service, and though the military sub-tenant had neither to fight nor to pay scutage, yet, being a military tenant, he was subject to a number of onerous claims from which he would have been free had his tenure been one of the other forms. As the matter is now merely of anti-quarian interest, we must confine ourselves to the barest statement of the most valuable of the rights enforceable against a military tenant, namely :—

Incidents of knight service

1. RELIEF. The lord was entitled to the payment of a certain sum, called a relief, when a new tenant succeeded to the land on the death of the old tenant. Payment of the relief entitled the heir to immediate possession, but this was not so where the land was held of the King. In this case the official escheator took possession and held an inquest as to who was next heir. It was only when the heir had done homage and paid the relief that he was entitled to enter the land. This royal privilege of first possession was called *primer seisin*.[2]

2. AIDS. The lord was entitled to demand in three special cases that his tenants should pay him a certain sum of money called an aid. The three cases arose when the lord was imprisoned and required a ransom ; when he desired to make his eldest son a knight ; and when he was obliged to supply his eldest daughter with a dowry on her marriage.

3. ESCHEAT *PROPTER DELICTUM TENENTIS*. The com-mission by the tenant of a felony caused the land to escheat, that is to pass to the lord of whom it was held. Felony originally meant a breach of that faith and trust which ought to exist between lord and vassal, *e.g.* where the tenant laid violent hands on his lord. At an early date, however, felony lost its exclusively feudal signification and came to mean in effect any serious crime such as murder. The result of this was to benefit

---

[1] Pollock and Maitland, *History of English Law*, vol. i. p. 231.
[2] Pollock and Maitland, vol. ii. p. 292.

the lords, and though it would seem incompatible with the interests of the Crown as custodian of the public peace that the land of a murderer or a thief should pass to a subject, the right of escheat was expressly confirmed by Magna Carta in 1215, subject to the proviso that the land should be held by the Crown for a year and a day. Forfeiture of the land was now said to occur because the felon's blood was attainted or corrupted.[1]

4. WARDSHIP. The most profitable right of the lord was that of wardship. If an existing tenant died leaving as his heir a male under 21 or a female under 14, the lord was entitled to the wardship of the heir, and as a consequence was free to make what use he liked of the lands during the minority without any obligation to render an account of his stewardship. Upon reaching the prescribed age the ward might sue for *livery* or *ousterlemain, i.e.* might enforce delivery of the land. For this privilege half a year's profits had to be paid, though relief was not exigible.

5. MARRIAGE. Another privilege which the lord enjoyed in respect of infant tenants was the right of marriage. As Blackstone has said :

" While the infant was in ward, the guardian had the
" power of tendering him or her a suitable match, without
" disparagement or inequality : which if the infants refused,
" they forfeited the value of the marriage, *valorem maritagii*, to
" their guardian : that is, so much as a jury would assess, or
" anyone would *bonâ fide* give to the guardian for such an
" alliance : and if the infants married themselves without the
" guardian's consent, they forfeited double the value, *duplicem
" valorem maritagii.*" [2]

Tenure by Sergeanty [3] was in early times, and from an economic point of view, of considerable importance, but it soon ceased to be anything more than a peculiarly dignified method of holding land. All tenures imply service of one kind or another, but the characteristic of sergeanty was that it required the tenant to perform services of an essentially personal nature. It was that particular form of landholding which was designed to supply the necessities of life. In the first place the great officials of the realm were sergeants, and as such might be required " to carry the banner of the king, or his lance, or to lead his army, or to be his marshall, or to carry his sword before him at his coronation, or to be his sewer at his coronation or his carver or his butler, or to be one of his chamberlains at the receipt of his exchequer or to do other like services."[4]

Sergeanty services essentially personal.

Duties of this nature came to be regarded as conferring honour and dignity, and for this reason outlasted the tenure itself, but

[1] Pollock and Maitland, vol. i. p. 284 ; Digby, *History of Real Property,* p. 132 ; Holdsworth, *op. cit.,* vol. iii. p. 62.
[2] Blackstone, vol. ii. p. 70.
[3] Holdsworth, *History of English Law,* vol. iii. pp. 46 *et seq.*
[4] Littleton, s. 153.

they did not exhaust the forms of personal services that might be demanded from sergeants. A great lord would require that his accounts should be kept, his letters carried, his estates managed, armour provided, his food cooked, and so on, and he would in most cases grant lands to various sergeants to be held by them so long as the duties were faithfully performed. However, as time went on, it was realized that this was scarcely a convenient method of supplying the needs of life, and tenure by sergeanty began to decay as early as the fourteenth century. It died out altogether except in the case of those great men who performed honourable services for the King, or of humbler persons whose duty it might be to perform some small military duty, such as to supply transport. Moreover, the idea took root, and was fixed law by Littleton's day, that the tenure could exist only between the King and his immediate tenants in chief. The tenure of the great men who performed what were regarded as honourable services came to be called *grand sergeanty*, while that of the lesser military tenants was termed *petit sergeanty*. Grand sergeanty came to be similar to knight service, while petit sergeanty, after the time of Littleton, was practically equivalent to socage.[1]

Decay of sergeanty. (margin note)

Abolition of Military Tenures. It is not necessary to describe these tenures further, because in 1660 a considerable simplification of the forms of landholding was effected by the legislature. The Statute for the abolition of Military Tenures,[2] which was passed in that year, practically destroyed all the *free* lay tenures except socage. Tenure by knight service was destroyed altogether, and sergeanty was allowed to continue only in an emasculated form. Formerly it had rendered the tenant liable to onerous duties similar to those that might be exacted from a knight service tenant, but the effect of the Act was to abolish it as a separate tenure, and, where it existed, only to leave the privilege of performing those honorary services which, as we have seen, were peculiar to the higher ranks of sergeants. In other words, sergeanty was converted into socage,[3] the exceptional feature of the converted land being that the tenant might in some cases substantiate his right to perform certain honorary and dignified services.

Conversion of military tenures into Socage. (margin note)

Frankalmoin was the tenure by which a man made provision for the repose of his soul, and it arose where lands were granted to an ecclesiastical body on the implied understanding that as tenant it would say prayers and masses for the souls of the grantor and his heirs. For various reasons the tenure fell into desuetude, and,

Frank-almoin. (margin note)

---

[1] Holdsworth, History of English Law, vol. iii. p. 51.
[2] Tenures Abolition Act, 1660.
[3] Challis, *Law of Real Property* (3rd Edn.). p. 9.

though it was not formally abolished by the Act of 1660, it was seldom encountered in practice.[1]

The Act of 1660 was, then, a move in the right direction, since it simplified the system of landholding by practically reducing the former tenures to two, that is to say, to socage and copyhold, though the simplification was not quite so complete as this, owing to the retention of those divergent customary methods of holding land known as gavelkind, ancient demesne and borough-English.[2] Yet even apart from these peculiar cases it is obvious that the existence from 1660 to 1925 of two separate and quite different methods by which a man might hold land, tended to increase the complexities of conveyancing and to render real property law unnecessarily difficult.

1660 Act simplified landholding.

We must now briefly describe the two tenures of socage and copyhold which held the field until the legislation of 1925 abolished the latter.

Socage.[3] As distinguished from knight service, socage was that species of tenure which represented the new aspect that the economic life of the country gradually assumed. It was essentially non-military and free from the worst features of knight service. At first it could not be defined in positive terms, but was described negatively as being that form of tenure which was neither spiritual, military, sergeanty nor villeinage.

Socage a non-military tenure.

In early days the services due in respect of the land varied considerably. The tenant might pay a nominal rent sufficient to record the fact that the lands were held of the lord, or a substantial rent equal to the economic value of the land, while sometimes his obligation would extend to the performance of agricultural services. Originally, no doubt, the socmanni, as they were called, belonged to the lower orders of society, but the tendency was for this mode of landholding to extend upwards, since it was free from the worst of the feudal burdens incidental to knight service, and to escape those even the greater landowners were willing to sacrifice something of their dignity.

Early history.

The next step was that it became usual to commute services, whatever these might have been, into money payments, and though these, when they were originally fixed, no doubt represented the economic value of the land, yet with the gradual fall in the value of money they became in course of time so

Commutation of services.

---

[1] The chief reason for the decline of frankalmoin tenure was that upon alienation of the land, even to another ecclesiastical body, or upon escheat of the lordship to a superior lord, the tenure was converted into socage. Moreover, no fresh grant in frankalmoin, except by the Crown, has been possible since *Quia Emptores* ; Challis, *Law of Real Property* (3rd Edn.), p. 11. Ecclesiastical bodies more frequently held land by one of the other tenures; Maitland, *Constitutional History*, p. 25.

[2] *Supra*, pp. 16–17.

[3] Holdsworth, *History of English Law*, vol. iii. pp. 51 *et seq.*

insignificant in amount as scarcely to merit the trouble of collection.[1]   Thus at the present day it is practically impossible to prove that A. holds of B. in socage tenure, for the payment of rent which would have revealed the existence of the tenure has in most cases not been made for centuries.   B. does not lose much, for the rent is generally of little pecuniary value, and the only other event which might have benefited him before the doctrine of escheat was abolished in 1926—namely, the death of the tenant intestate and without heirs, whereby the land would pass to B. by escheat—is normally of rare occurrence.   Of course the land must be held of somebody, and the rule is that, where no private person can prove his lordship, it is deemed to be held of the Crown.

So socage became the great residuary tenure.   It included every tenure which was not knight service, sergeanty, frankalmoin or villeinage, and its outstanding characteristic came to be that it involved some service which was absolutely certain and fixed, and which in the vast majority of cases took the form of a money payment.[2]   Though subject to aids and to relief, it was free from the obnoxious rights of wardship and marriage that characterized knight service.   The guardian of an infant socage tenant was the nearest relative who was incapable of inheriting the land.   It was enacted by the Statute of Marlborough, 1267, that a guardian in socage must account for the profits of the land at the end of his stewardship, and must not give or sell the ward in marriage.

Copyhold tenure.

Copyhold Tenure.[3]   The other tenure to which as late as 1925 English land might be subject was copyhold, the modern name for the old villeinage.   Although this tenure was abolished as from January 1st, 1926, something must be said about its origin and peculiar characteristics.

Origin of copyholds.

We see in this tenure a system of land holding which represented in modern times customs far older than feudalism, and which dated back to the primitive method of agriculture called the open field system.   In remote days the actual tillers of the English soil were almost certainly members of free village communities who owned in common the land that they farmed; but after the Conquest, although they still continued to follow those precepts and habits of agriculture that had been customary for generations, they were gradually absorbed into the feudal system. An overlord had appeared, a new concept in the shape of the manor had been established, and by imperceptible degrees the humble tillers found themselves part of the manorial organization; no longer free owners, but instead subservient to an overlord upon

---

[1] Pollock and Maitland, *History of English Law*, vol. i. p. 271.
[2] Littleton, s. 117.
[3] Holdsworth, *History of English Law*, vol. iii. pp. 491 *et seq.*;   vol. vii. pp. 296 *et seq*;   Simpson, *An Introduction to the History of Land Law*, pp. 145 *et seq.*

whose will, according to the strict letter of the law, they were absolutely dependent. BLACKSTONE thought that the modern copyholders were merely serfs who by continual encroachments on their superiors had gradually established a customary right to estates which strictly speaking had always been held at the will of the lords,[1] but in fact the truth is the exact reverse, for the lords had gradually induced the belief that only by their will were these ancient owners permitted to enjoy their customary rights and estates.[2]

To understand the character of copyhold tenure we must refer once more to the feudal manor which was the unit of society in mediaeval England. *(margin: Importance of the manor.)*

A typical manor consisted of

(*a*) the land belonging to the lord, which was called his demesne,

(*b*) the land held of the lord by free tenants whether in socage or knight service,

(*c*) the land held of the lord by persons called villein tenants,

(*d*) rights of jurisdiction exercisable by the lord over the free tenants in the Court Baron, and over the villeins in the Court Customary,

(*e*) waste land on which the tenants were entitled to pasture their cattle.

The first point that emerges about the villeins is that it was they who cultivated the lord's demesne, a practice which originated in what has been termed the farm system. " Farm " in Anglo-Saxon times meant food, and the system in vogue was for the tenant, in return for his holding, to produce a farm—that is, enough food to sustain his lord for some given period, say a night, a week or a fortnight.[3] *(margin: Farm system.)*

In the thirteenth century this primitive system gave way to the labour service system,[4] which meant that the villein tenant came under an obligation, often specified in the greatest detail,[5] to cultivate by his own labour his lord's demesne. But the mere obligation to perform agricultural services does not alone suffice to distinguish a villein from a socage tenement, since it was by no means impossible for a socage tenant to be subject to the same liability. What, then, was the test of villein tenure ? *(margin: Labour service system.)*

One fact which might be thought at first sight to provide this test is that the villeins received no protection in the King's courts. If they were unjustifiably ejected by the lord, they *(margin: Test of villein tenure.)*

---

[1] Blackstone, vol. ii. p. 95.
[2] See Pollock, *The Land Laws*, pp. 43–52 ; and Appendix, Note D.
[3] Vinogradoff, *Villainage*, pp. 301–2.
[4] *Ibid.*, p. 304.
[5] See, for example, Pollock and Maitland, *History of English Law*, vol. i. p. 349.

could recover neither possession nor damages in the royal courts, for in the view of the latter they were nothing more than tenants at the will of the lord.[1] But though superficially the tenure seemed precarious to the last degree, it was saved from being so in actual fact because the tenants were entitled to protection from the lord's manorial court, where those rules which had been hallowed by immemorial custom within the manor were recognized and enforced. These manorial customs gradually grew into legal systems under which the rights and the duties of the tenants were defined, and the everyday events of marriage, succession, alienation and the like were regulated.[2] But the lack of a remedy in the royal courts was not a sufficient test of villeinage or no villeinage since it also affected an ordinary tenant for years.

Test of villein tenure found in nature of services.   That test is to be found, however, in the nature of the services rendered by a tenant. If a man was bound to perform agricultural services it could not be said that he was necessarily a villein tenant, but if he did not know from day to day *what* kind of work would be assigned to him, then he was looked upon as a villein tenant. In other words, the test was the uncertainty of the nature of the work. As POLLOCK and MAITLAND have said :—

" When they go to bed on Sunday night they do not know what
" Monday's work will be ; it may be threshing, ditching, carrying ;
" they cannot tell. This seems the point that is seized by law and that
" general opinion of which law is the exponent. Any considerable
" uncertainty as to the amount or kind of the agricultural services
" makes the tenure unfree. The tenure is unfree, not because the
" tenant holds at the will of the lord in the sense of being removable
" at a moment's notice, but because his services, though in many
" respects minutely defined by custom, cannot be altogether defined
" without constant reference to the lord's will."[3]

So then in the thirteenth century villeinage was that tenure in which the return made by the tenant for his holding was the performance on his lord's demesne of agricultural services uncertain in nature.

Money payment system.   But in the fourteenth and fifteenth centuries this labour service system gave way to a money payment system under which the tenant in villeinage paid a rent to his lord instead of giving personal services, and the lord cultivated his demesne by hired labour.[4] This was an example of the general movement from natural husbandry to the money system, which was fostered in England by several causes, such as the growth of the woollen trade with Flanders and the great increase of trade with the

---

[1] See, for example, Pollock and Maitland, *History of English Law*, vol. i. p. 341.
[2] Vinogradoff, *Villainage*, p. 172.
[3] *History of English Law*, vol. i. p. 354.
[4] Holdsworth, *History of English Law*, vol. iii. p. 204.

Continent as a result of the English occupation of Normandy and Aquitaine.[1]

The result of the change as regards villeinage was to benefit the tenant, because the rents remained stabilized despite the gradual fall in monetary values. This transition from labour services to money payments corresponded with the transition in nomenclature from villeinage to copyhold tenure.

Villeinage becomes copyhold.

" With the completion of the transition from praedial services to " money rents, tenure in villeinage may be said to have come to an " end. . . . The essence of villein tenure had consisted in the un- " certainty of the tenant's services, and when the old agricultural " services were commuted for a fixed money payment, this uncertainty " passed away." [2]

The derivation of the word " copyhold " is this : the copyhold tenant, like his predecessor the villein, held at the will of the lord; but yet at the same time he held on the conditions which had become fixed by the customs of his particular manor. The lord's will could not be exercised capriciously, but only in conformity with custom. He still held a court, and that court kept records of all transactions affecting the lands. These records were called the rolls of the court. When, for instance, a tenant sold his interest to a third party, the circumstances of the sale would be recorded, and the buyer would receive a copy of the court rolls in so far as they affected his holding. Inasmuch as he held his estate by copy of court roll, he came to be called a copyholder.

Meaning of term " copy hold."

The change from villeinage to copyhold was of far-reaching importance to the tenant. He was rid of all traces of servility; he acquired an interest which in essentials was on all-fours with interests in land held by socage tenure, and above all he obtained recognition and protection from the King's courts. This protection was assured by the end of the fifteenth century. COKE summed up the position in expressive language :—

Importance of change to tenant.

" But now copyholders stand upon a sure ground, now they weigh not " their lord's displeasure, they shake not at every blast of wind, they " eat, drink and sleep securely ; only having an especial care of the " main chance, viz., to perform carefully what duties and services " soever their tenure doth exact and custom doth require : then let " lord frown, the copyholder cares not, knowing himself safe and not " within any danger. For if the lord's anger grow to expulsion, the " law hath provided several weapons of remedy ; for it is at his election " either to sue a *subpœna* or an action of trespass against the lord. " Time hath dealt very favourably with copyholders in divers " respects." [3]

---

[1] Vinogradoff, *Villainage*, p. 180.
[2] Page, *The End of Villeinage*, p. 83, cited Holdsworth, vol. iii. p. 206.
[3] *Compleat Copyholder*, s. 9.

Defects of
copyhold
tenure.

Despite the possibility of enfranchisement, a process by which copyhold might be converted into socage tenure, a great proportion of English land, even in 1925, was still copyhold. The tenure was distinguished by several defects. For instance, the customs, which represented the local law governing land of this tenure, varied considerably from manor to manor, so that it was impossible to determine the law applicable to a disputed matter without an examination of the manorial records ; the form of conveyance was far different from that required in the case of socage ; copyhold and socage lands were often intermixed in so confusing a fashion as to make it difficult to discriminate between them, a dilemma from which the only escape in the event of a sale was the execution of two conveyances, one appropriate for copyhold, the other for a socage holding ; certain rights of the land were so burdensome to the tenant that they caused strife and ill-will ; and finally, it was impossible for either the lord or the tenant, without the assent of the other, to exploit the minerals under the land.

This bare summary of the history of copyhold tenure should be enough to show that from about the beginning of the seventeenth century it was nothing more nor less than an outmoded and exceedingly inconvenient form of ordinary tenure. It served no particular social need and it certainly impeded a simplified system of conveyancing because of its frequent diversity from socage tenure. It has been rightly described by a lecturer as " an anachronism and a nuisance." [1]

Abolition of
all tenures
except
socage.

Summary of Tenures in 1925. If we now take stock of the feudal tenures as they existed in 1925 we shall find the position to have been as follows : the greater part of English land was held by socage tenure, a considerable part was subject to copyhold tenure, while the remainder was held either in grand sergeanty or in frankalmoin, or was affected by the peculiar customs of gavelkind, borough-English or ancient demesne. Here was room for at least one form of simplification, and we shall see later [2] that the Law of Property Acts, 1922 and 1925, seized the opportunity. They converted copyhold and ancient demesne into socage tenure ; they abolished gavelkind, borough-English, and all other customary modes of descent ; and they purported to abolish frankalmoin.[3] The honorary services incident to sergeanty were retained. Escheat *propter defectum sanguinis*, which was the right of a lord to take the land of his tenant who had died intestate without leaving heirs, was abolished and replaced by a right in the Crown to take the land as *bona vacantia* in the same way that it takes goods.

Present
position of
doctrine of
tenure.

The result is that though the general theory of tenure is still a part of English law in the sense that all land is held of a superior

[1] Underhill, *A Century of Law Reform*, p. 310.   [2] *Infra*, p. 82.
[3] As to frankalmoin, see *infra*, p. 83.

and is incapable of absolute ownership, yet the law of tenure is both simpler and of less significance than it was before 1926. It is simpler because there is now only one form of tenure—namely, socage. It is of less significance because all the tenurial incidents (including escheat) which might in exceptional cases have brought profit to a mesne lord have been abolished, so that there is no inducement for a private person to prove that he is the lord of land. We can, in fact, now describe the theory of tenure, despite the great part that it has played in the history of English law, as a conception of merely academic interest. It no longer restricts the tenant in his free enjoyment of the land.

(2) THE DOCTRINE OF THE ESTATE.[1]

Tenure signifies the relation between lord and tenant, and what it implies is that the person whom we should naturally call the owner does not own the land, but merely holds it as tenant of the Crown or of some other feudal superior. But if he is not owner of the land, what is the nature of the interest that he holds? In statutes, in judicial decisions and in common speech he is always described as a " landowner," but we may well ask what it is that he owns.

What is the nature of the tenant's interest?

It may be said at once that the doctrine of tenure as developed in England made it difficult, if not impossible, to regard either him or his lord as the owner of the land itself. The land could not be owned by the tenant, since it was recoverable by the lord if the tenurial services were not faithfully performed; it could not be owned by the lord, since he had no claim to it as long as the tenant fulfilled his duties.[2]

Quite apart from this practical difficulty, however, the truth is that English law has never applied the conception of ownership to land. " Ownership " is a word of many meanings, but in the present context we can take it to signify a title to a subject-matter, whether movable or immovable, that is good against the whole world. The holder of the title, such as the owner of a motor-car, has a real as opposed to a personal right—he is the absolute owner. This position is illustrated by the Roman doctrine of *dominium*, under which the *dominus* was entitled to the absolute and exclusive right of property in the land. Nothing less in the way of ownership was recognized. A man had either absolute ownership or no ownership at all. Possession was regarded as fundamentally different—*nihil commune habet proprietas cum possessione*—and, though it was adequately protected, the remedies available were personal, not real.

No doctrine of ownership in English land law.

---

[1] Holdsworth, *History of English Law*, vol. iii. pp. 101–37; Pollock and Maitland, *History of English Law*, vol. ii. pp. 2–29; Hargreaves. *Introduction to Land Law* (3rd Edn.), pp. 20–25; 44–53; Simpson, *An Introduction to the History of Land Law*, pp. 44 *et seq.*

[2] Hargreaves, *Introduction to Land Law* (3rd Edn.), p. 44.

English law concentrates on possession, not on ownership.

In sharp contrast to this attitude, English law, in analysing the relation of the tenant to the land, has directed its attention not to ownership, but to possession, or, as it is called in the case of land, *seisin*. All titles to land are ultimately based upon possession in the sense that the title of the man seised prevails against all who can show no better right to seisin. Seisin is a root of title, and it may be said without undue exaggeration that so far as land is concerned there is in England no law of ownership, but only a law of possession.

> " . . . ' seisin ' . . . is an enjoyment of property based upon title, and " is not essentially distinguishable from right. In other words, the " sharp distinction between property and possession made in Roman " law did not obtain in English law ; seisin is not the Roman " possession and right is not the Roman ownership. Both of these " conceptions are represented in English law only by seisin, and it " was the essence of the conception of seisin that some seisins " might be better than others."[1]

This unfailing emphasis upon the concrete and obvious fact of possession will be apparent if we consider for a moment the following three topics :—the remedies that lie for the recovery of land, the position of a tenant who is wrongfully dispossessed, and the long established mechanism of conveyancing.

Possessory nature of early actions for the recovery of land.

The English actions for the recovery of land, called in early days *real actions*, have consistently and continuously turned upon the right to possession. Moreover, their object throughout has been not to enquire whether the title to possession set up by the defendant is an absolute title good against all persons, but whether it is relatively better than any title that the plaintiff can establish. English land law is committed to the doctrine of relative titles to possession. Thus, the issue raised in the most ancient and solemn remedy, the *writ of right*, was not whether the demandant (plaintiff) could prove an absolute title good against third parties, but whether he or the defendant could establish the earlier and therefore the better seisin.[2] Similarly, the possessory assizes, simpler remedies introduced by Henry II to supplement the writ of right and to rectify a recent invasion of possession, merely considered the specific question whether the demandant or his ancestor had been unjustly disseised of his free tenement by the defendant. The assize of *novel disseisin*, *i.e.* recent dispossession, enabled A. to recover land from B. on proof that he had been ejected by B. The assize of *mort d'ancestor* availed him if he could show that he was the heir of his deceased ancestor, X., and that X.'s seisin had been usurped by the defendant.

The sole question in these actions was one of fact relating to seisin. Did B. disseise A.? Did B. take the seisin held by A.'s

---

[1] Plucknett, *A Concise History of the Common Law* (5th Edn.), p. 358.
[2] Lightwood, *Possession of Land*, pp. 73–4 ; Plucknett, *A Concise History of the Common Law* (5th Edn.), p. 358; Simpson, *op. cit.* pp. 34 *et seq.*

ancestor ? [1] If so, the court ordered restoration of the seisin, but it did not adjudge that A. held an absolute title good against all adversaries. If the defendant wished to agitate the question of title further, he would be driven to issue a writ of right. [2]

At a later date the various *writs of entry* met the case where the disseisin of which the demandant complained was not so immediate, as, for example, where B., after disseising the demandant, had granted the land to Y., who had granted it to the defendant. These actions, no less than the possessory assizes, merely decided whether the better right to seisin lay in the demandant or in the defendant.

Finally, it must be observed that this mediaeval principle of relativity of titles dominated the later action of ejectment and still dominates the modern action for the recovery of land as it is now called. [3] All that the plaintiff need do is to prove that he has a better right to possession than the defendant, not that he has a better right than anybody else. If, for instance, he is ejected by the defendant, he will recover by virtue of his prior possession, notwithstanding that a still better right may reside in some third person. [4]

Possessory nature of modern action for recovery of land.

The effects that flow from a disseisin of the tenant afford a further illustration of the crucial part played by possession in English law. It was established at an early date that the seisin wrongfully taken by the disseisor was the commencement of a fresh title and that it gave him a real though tortious interest, valid against all but the disseisee and his successors in title.

Effect of loss of seisin on proprietary rights.

"Possession being once admitted to be a root of title, every "possession must create a title which, as against all subsequent "intruders, has all the incidents and advantages of a true title." [5]

The disseisor has full beneficial rights over the land. He holds a fee simple estate which is transmissible either *inter vivos* or by will, and which the disseisee cannot defeat unless he takes proceedings within twelve years after the wrongful entry. [6] Moreover, although the disseisee had a right of action to recover the land, for a long period in our legal history his lack of possession confronted him with serious and ever-increasing difficulties as against the disseisor and his successors in title. In mediaeval days and for long afterwards, the effect of the disseisin was to deprive him of most of his beneficial rights over the land until he had vindicated his claim to seisin in the appropriate real action. His

---

[1] Holdsworth, *History of English Law* (1st Edn.), vol. iii. p. 80 ; Maitland, *Forms of Action* (1st Edn.), p. 322.
[2] Plucknett, *op. cit.*, p. 359.
[3] 56 L. Q. R. 376 *et seq.*, article by Professor Hargreaves, replied to by Holdsworth in 56 L. Q. R. 479–82.
[4] *Asher* v. *Whitlock* (1865), L. R. 1 Q. B. 1.
[5] Pollock and Wright, *Possession in the Common Law*, p. 95.
[6] Limitation Act, 1939, *infra*, pp. 805 *et seq.*

former rights were reduced to a right of entry, a reduction that entailed certain important consequences.

> Thus, he lost the power of alienation, for, being dispossessed he was unable to make the delivery of seisin essential for a conveyance of land, and a right of entry could neither be devised until 1837,[1] nor conveyed *inter vivos* until 1845.[2]
>
> Circumstances might well occur which would deprive him of his right of entry and leave him with a mere right of action—a *chose in action* that was equally inalienable, though it would descend to his heirs.[3] For instance, where the disseisor died while still in possession, the land passed to his heir by operation of law with the result that the interest held by him was no longer regarded as tortious. The right of entry was said to be " tolled," *i.e.* taken away, by descent cast.[4]
>
> Again, if the disseisee failed to recover seisin, his widow had no right to dower ;[5] if he died heirless, the land did not in all cases escheat to his lord ;[6] and if he died leaving an infant heir, his lord was not entitled to wardship.[7]

The position may be summarized in the words of HOLDSWORTH : " The person seised has all the rights of an owner ; the person disseised has the right to get seisin by entry or action ; but till he has got it he has none of the rights of an owner.   In other words, the common law recognizes not *dominium* and *possessio*, but seisin only."[8]

Possession is a root of title for conveyancing purposes.

The third illustration of the emphasis laid by English land law upon possession, not upon ownership, is afforded by the practice of conveyancers.   A vendor must prove to the satisfaction of the purchaser, not only that he is entitled to the land which he has agreed to sell, but also that his title is not subject to adverse claims vested in third parties.   He can scarcely be expected to prove that he has a title good against the whole world, for, since land is permanent and indestructible, it may well be that there exists a competing and better title created many years ago and still existing.

English land law has no doctrine akin to that of Roman law by which possession for a definite but short period had the positive effect of investing the possessor with *dominium*.   As one writer has observed, the absolute ownership of a perishable chattel, such as a motor-car, is a comparatively easy matter to prove, but " if we were to insist upon the same fulness of ownership with regard to land we should have to trace back our title to the original grant of Paradise to Adam."[9]   What the vendor can do, however, and

---

[1] Wills Act, 1837, s. 3.   [2] Real Property Act, 1845, s. 6.
[3] Hayes, *Introduction to Conveyancing*, p. 231.
[4] The doctrine of descent cast was abolished by the Real Property Limitation Act, 1833, s. 39.
[5] Maitland, *Collected Papers*, vol. i. p. 366.   [6] *Ibid.*, pp. 368–9.
[7] *Ibid.*, p. 369.   On the subject generally, see Holdsworth, *History of English Law* (1st Edn.), vol. iii. pp. 81–2.
[8] *Ibid.*, p. 84.
[9] Hargreaves, *Introduction to Land Law* (3rd Edn.), p. 44.

what he does in practice is to rely upon the fundamental principle that seisin is evidence of his title to the land.

> " With very few exceptions, there is only one way in which an
> " apparent owner of English land who is minded to deal with it can
> " show his right so to do ; and that way is to show that he and those
> " through whom he claims have possessed the land for a time suffi-
> " cient to exclude any reasonable probability of a superior adverse
> " claim." [1]

What, then, emerges so far is that land cannot be the subject-matter of ownership, though the person in whom its seisin is vested is entitled to exercise proprietary rights in respect of it. But again the question recurs—what is the nature of the interest held by the person seised ? Is there nothing that he can be said to own ? The answer made by English law is unique. The person entitled to seisin owns an abstract entity, called an *estate*, which is interposed between him and the land.[2] " The English lawyer . . . first detaches the ownership from the land itself, and then attaches it to an imaginary thing which he calls an estate."[3]

Only subject-matter of ownership is an estate in the land.

The estate represents the extent of his right to seisin. Thus the correct description of a tenant entitled to immediate seisin for his life is that he is *seised of Blackacre for an estate for life*. This estate entitles its owner to exercise proprietary rights over the land for the prescribed period, subject to observance of the tenurial duties, and it may be disposed of as freely as any other subject-matter of ownership. This doctrine, as will be explained later,[4] is not confined to the case where a man is entitled to immediate seisin. If he is definitely entitled to it at some future time, he is equally the owner of an estate.

Two phenomena of great significance have emerged during the development of this doctrine by the common law.

Features of the doctrine of the estate.

> First, estates vary in size according to the time for which they are to endure. On this basis they are classified as estates of freehold and estates less than freehold.

> Secondly, several different persons may simultaneously own distinct and separate estates in the same piece of land.

These matters will now be discussed in more detail.

The main classification of estates depends upon their quantification and their quantification depends upon their duration. The estate will vary in size according to the time for which it is to continue. " Proprietary rights in land are, we may say,

Estates classified according to their duration.

---

[1] Pollock and Wright, *Possession in the Common Law*, pp. 94–5.
[2] Lawson, *The Rational Strength of English Law*, p. 87.
[3] Markby, *Elements of English Law*, s. 330.
[4] *Infra*, p. 35.

projected upon the plane of time."[1] Thus a person may be entitled to seisin for ever or for a lesser period.

Meaning of freehold estate.

Estates are sub-classified into those of freehold and those less than freehold. Into which of these categories they fell depended in the earliest days upon the quality of the tenure by which the estate owner held his land. A tenant in knight service, sergeanty, socage or frankalmoin was called a "freeholder," since the services due from him were free from servile incidents. He was said to have a frank tenement or freehold estate to distinguish him from a villein tenant.[2] Such was the original meaning of the expression "freehold estate."

But one of the characteristics of these free tenants was that the time for which they were entitled to hold the land was not fixed and certain. They invariably held either for life or for some other space of time dependent upon an event that might not happen within a lifetime, and it was this uncertainty of duration, not the quality of the services to be rendered, that gradually came to be regarded as the essential feature of a freehold estate.[3] Thus, even at the present day, an estate is freehold if its duration is uncertain; it is less than freehold if the time of its termination is fixed or capable of being fixed. The life tenant is a freeholder, but not so the tenant holding under a lease for a definite period, even though he holds for as long a period as 999 years.[4]

Freeholds and non-freeholds distinguished in respect of seisin.

Freehold and non-freehold estates were further distinguished in respect of seisin. At first the word "seisin" was used to denote possession both of land and of chattels, but this usage did not last long and by the fifteenth century a man was said to be seised of land, but possessed of chattels. Later the subject-matter of seisin became even further restricted. The real actions that lay for the recovery of land, the possessory assizes and the writs of entry, were available only to freeholders, *i.e.* to tenants in fee simple, in tail and for life. These actions, as we have seen, were based entirely upon seisin and since they availed only free-holders it is not unnatural that the word "seisin" was reserved exclusively to describe the possession of a freehold estate. Since mediaeval days it has been correct, for instance, to describe a life tenant as seised, but a tenant for years as possessed, of the land.

On the basis of duration common law has classified estates in the manner set out in the following table.

---

[1] Pollock and Maitland, *op. cit.*, vol. ii. p. 10. Compare the language used in the course of argument in *Walsingham's Case* (1579), 2 Plowd. 547, at p. 555 : "The land itself is one thing and the estate in the land is another thing, for an estate in the land is a time in the land, or land for a time, and there are diversities of estates which are no more than diversities of time, for he who has a fee simple in land has a time in the land without end."

[2] Pollock and Maitland, *op. cit.*, vol. ii. p. 78 ; Holdsworth, *History of English Law*, vol. ii. p. 351.

[3] Co. Litt. 43*b*.

[4] See, generally, Preston, *An Elementary Treatise on Estates*, c. 1.

Estates classified according to their duration.

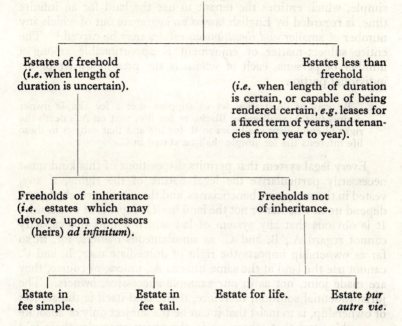

| Estates of freehold (*i.e.* when length of duration is uncertain). | Estates less than freehold (*i.e.* when length of duration is certain, or capable of being rendered certain, *e.g.* leases for a fixed term of years, and tenancies from year to year). |

| Freeholds of inheritance (*i.e.* estates which may devolve upon successors (heirs) *ad infinitum*). | Freeholds not of inheritance. |

| Estate in fee simple. | Estate in fee tail. | Estate for life. | Estate *pur autre vie.* |

As regards duration, the three freehold estates may be distinguished as follows :

The fee simple is the largest estate in point of duration, for, being one that is granted to a man *and his heirs*, it will last as long as the person entitled to it for the time being dies leaving an heir, and therefore it may last for ever in the sense that it may never pass to the Crown for want of an heir. The word *fee* denotes its inheritability, and the word *simple* indicates that it is inheritable by the general heirs of the owner for the time being whether they be ascendants, descendants or collateral.

The estate tail, which is the only other estate of inheritance, is less in quantum than the fee simple since it is inheritable only by the specified descendants of the original grantee and never by his ascendants, and also because it is descendible only to his lineal issue and not to his collateral relatives. Thus it is inferior to the fee simple in the sense that it has not as great a capacity for perpetual existence. The classic formula for its creation is—to A. and the *heirs of his body*.

Life estates include an estate which A. holds for his own life and also one that he holds during the lifetime of B., this second species being called an estate *pur autre vie.*

Apportionment of fee simple allowed by English law.

The second phenomenon mentioned above is that the fee simple, which entitles the tenant to use the land for an infinite time, is regarded by English law as an aggregate out of which any number of smaller *and simultaneous* estates may be carved.[1] The entire subject-matter of enjoyment is apportionable among a number of persons, each of whom is the present owner of his individual portion.

> By way of illustration let us suppose that a fee simple owner desires that A. shall enjoy Blackacre for life, that on A.'s death the right of enjoyment shall pass to B. for life and that subject to these life interests the fee simple shall be vested in C.

Every legal system that permits dispositions of this kind must necessarily particularize the legal nature of the rights, if any, vested in the successive beneficiaries, and the solution reached must depend upon whether or not the land itself is capable of ownership.

No apportionment possible if land itself capable of ownership.

It is obvious that any system of law which admits this capacity cannot regard A., B. and C. as simultaneous owners, for, in so far as ownership imports the right of immediate user, B. and C. cannot use the land at the same time as A., unless, of course, they are made joint, not as in our example successive, owners. The jurisprudential solution, therefore, if the land itself is the subject of ownership, is to insist that it can be the subject only of absolute ownership, and that where, as in the above example, there is a limitation to a succession of persons the entire and absolute ownership shall pass from one beneficiary to another upon the happening of the prescribed events. This is what is called *substitution*. Under this doctrine, if land is limited to A., then to B. and then to C., the legal result is that : " These persons in their turn become owners of the property, each taking by substitution for the one who preceded him ; each in his turn being complete owner ; but each taking nothing until his turn comes." [2]

B., for instance, is not even a limited owner of the land during the life of A., but on the death of the latter he becomes the absolute owner of the land for a limited time. Until his turn comes he has no proprietary interest that he can alienate or otherwise dispose of.

The rule in Roman law.

This is the solution of Roman law and of certain modern legal systems which regard *dominium* as the exclusive and unlimited right to the land itself, not merely to its user.

By Roman law, A., the owner, might indeed let the land to X. by *locatio conductio* or grant it to him for life by way of *usufruct*, but his ownership was affected by neither transaction. In the former case, X., if evicted, had merely a contractual right enforceable against A. alone ; in the latter, he acquired only a *jus in re*

---

[1] Digby, *History of Real Property*, p. 270.
[2] Markby, *Elements of Law*, s. 330.

aliena, i.e. a right to use for his life land the ownership of which remained vested in A.

English law, however, having divorced ownership from the land itself and attached it to an imaginary thing called an *estate*, which entitles the owner to use the land for a longer or a shorter period of time, has been able to take a bolder course. Having decided that estates may vary in size according to their duration, it goes a step further and concedes that any estate, whether its duration is long or short and whether it confers a right to immediate or to future seisin, is capable of a present existing ownership.

Why apportionment possible in English law.

Two results flow from this view.

First, there may be different degrees or gradations of estate ownership. The tenant in tail and the tenant for life, no less than the tenant in fee simple, are owners of their estates.[1] As compared with the tenant in fee simple, they must, indeed, be described as *limited* owners, since their estates have not the same capacity of infinite duration. None the less they are owners, and their ownership differs from that of the tenant in fee simple only in degree—in quantity. There is no difference in kind or quality.[2]

English law recognizes different degrees of ownership.

The same remedies for the recovery of the land and the same powers of dealing with the estate by way of alienation are available, irrespective of the size of the estate. The different freehold estates, in other words, represent various grades in the hierarchy of ownership.

The second result of the English doctrine is that an estate may be the subject of a present existing ownership, even though the right of the owner to seisin is postponed to a future time. This is explicable in elementary terms.

Futurity of right to seisin not incompatible with present ownership.

> An estate is the right to possess and use the land for the period of time for which it has been granted. In the case of the fee simple the period is infinite, since the estate is capable of perpetual existence. The entire ownership, in other words, resides in the person holding the fee simple, since he and his successors are entitled to use the land for ever. But time is divisible, and this right of perpetual user may be divided into successive periods of limited duration or, as one writer put it, into successive intervals of time.[3] One slice of the perpetual time, one slice of the entire ownership, may be given to A., another to B., and so on.

Therefore, if the fee simple owner makes a grant

> to A. for life, then to B. for life and then to C. in tail,

each grantee receives at once a portion of the one uniform subject-matter, namely the right to use the land. A., B. and C.

---

[1] It will be seen later that since the legislation of 1925 it is no longer correct to describe them as " estate owners."

[2] Pollock and Maitland, *History of English Law*, vol. i. p. 7.

[3] 1 *Jurid. Soc.* p. 535, a paper read to the society by Stephen Martin Leake.

each hold a distinct and separate share of the identical thing. The only difference between them lies in the periods for which the user is to be enjoyed. Moreover, there is no futurity about the *ownership* of B. and C. Upon the execution of the grant they become the immediate and absolute owners of an estate. It is not the right of ownership, but the right to actual seisin of the land that is future. Indeed, by virtue of their power of disposition they may exchange their property for money and so make it immediately available.[1]

Advantages of the English doctrine.

In conclusion, it may be said that this doctrine of the estate has given an elasticity to the English law of land that is not found in countries outside the area of the common law.[2] This is particularly true in respect of settlements, *i.e.* dispositions of property designed to provide for a succession of persons, such as the present and future members of a family. The desire to do this has dominated English real property law throughout its long history; for land, with its virtue of permanency, is an ideal source of endowment and its use for this purpose has been favoured by the courts. The aims of a settlor will be more effectively attained if he is permitted to vest a definite right of ownership in certain persons upon the occurrence of certain prescribed events in the future, as for example by directing that if a son is born to the present tenant of Blackacre, he shall, on reaching his majority, immediately acquire a definite proprietary interest, even though the present tenant is still alive. If the land itself is the subject-matter of ownership, the simultaneous existence of two or more owners, unless they are to take jointly, is, as we have seen, impossible, and therefore in countries where that concept of ownership prevails the power to create successive interests stretching into the future is necessarily restricted. But once admit that what is owned is an imaginary thing called an estate, then it immediately becomes possible to frame elaborate and subtle schemes for the passing of the beneficial enjoyment of the land to one person after another in certain prescribed eventualities. There is room " to deal with ownership in a more fanciful way than if it were attached to the soil." [3]

We will now conclude with a short description of the term of years which, quantitatively considered, is the smallest proprietary interest recognised by English law.

Term of years not a freehold interest.

Leasehold Interest.[4] This interest, generally referred to as a term of years, arises where land has been demised, *i.e.* leased,

---

[1] 1 *Jurid. Soc.* p. 538.
[2] It has been described by a distinguished writer as " one of the most brilliant feats of the English mind "; Lawson, *The Rational Strength of English Law*, p. 97.
[3] Markby, *The Elements of Law*, s. 330.
[4] Holdsworth, *History of English Law*, vol. iii. 213–7; vol. vii. 238–96; Simpson, *An Introduction to the History of Land Law*, pp. 87–9; 229–38.

to a man for a definite number of years. It thus lacks the requirement of an uncertain duration, and though the period for which
it is to last may be very great, as for instance 999 years, yet it is
not a freehold estate, and in the eye of the law is a smaller interest
than a life estate.

Moreover it is not even real property. At an early period Meaning of
" Real
Property."
English law arrived at the general principle that, while land
could be recovered specifically by a dispossessed tenant from
a man who had ejected him, yet a person who was deprived of
personal chattels could not enforce their actual recovery, but had to
content himself with compensation in the shape of pecuniary
damages. Broadly speaking, actions fell into two classes. The
real actions lay for the restitution of some object, and the *personal
actions* for the recovery of damages. As land was the only object
of which restitution *in specie* could be enforced, it followed that
it formed the only subject matter of a real action, and it is not
surprising to find the ancient lawyers seizing upon this fact and
defining land as real property. Property which could be recovered in a real action was itself called real property, and thus
it resulted that real property consisted solely of interests in land.

But not every interest in land could be specifically recovered, Leasehold
not real
property.
for, as we have seen, the real actions were available only to free-
holders, *i.e.* only to tenants who were seised of the land. A
tenant for years was possessed, not seised, and if dispossessed
he could originally bring only a personal action for the recovery
of damages. It is true that by the close of the Middle Ages a
remedy had been introduced whereby he might recover the term
itself, but nevertheless he was still regarded, and has ever
since been regarded, as a non-freeholder. The doctrine of seisin
was never extended to his interest, and the *possessory assizes* and
the *writ of right*, which were the real actions properly so called,
were never made available to him. He continued to hold merely
personal property because originally his sole remedy was to bring
a personal action.

At first sight this refusal of the law to regard a leaseholder's Reason why
terms of
years not
freehold.
interest as real property is curious. It was not due to the unim-
portance or insignificance of terms of years. Such interests were
on the contrary exceedingly valuable. The cause of their segrega-
tion, the reason why they were dissociated from the real actions and
from feudal doctrine, was none other than economic pressure.[1]

At a time when investments in the modern sense of the term Original
advantages
of leaseholds.
were unknown, one of the few methods by which a man might
increase his income was to purchase a beneficial lease and take
the profits of the land as interest on the money expended. Again,
one of the ordinary methods of exacting security for a debt was
for the debtor to lease his lands at a nominal rent to the creditor, so

---

[1] Pollock and Maitland, *History of English Law*, vol. ii. pp. 113 *et seq*.

that the latter could obtain interest at the agreed rate out of the profits of the land without coming into conflict with the usury laws.[1]   Another familiar form of investment was to purchase a wardship, which was the right to administer for one's own benefit the lands of an infant tenant in Knight Service.   But if terms of years and wardships were to be effective investments, it was necessary that they should not be regarded as freehold estates in land carrying seisin, or, in more general terms, it was convenient to exclude them from the domain of strict real property law.   There were several considerations that made this line of action advisable, but none more potent than the fact that freehold estates as distinct from chattels could not be left by will.   It may have been a matter of sound policy that an estate in lands should inevitably descend to the heir of the deceased tenant, but it would be poor comfort to tell a man who had invested his money in the purchase of a term of years that he had lost the right of bequeathing his money because he had converted it into land. After showing that as early as 1200 there was a large speculative traffic in wardships, MAITLAND says :—

" And then as to the term of years; we believe that in the twelfth
" century and even later this stands often if not generally in the same
" economic category.   It is a beneficial lease bought for a sum of
" ready money ; it is an investment of capital, and therefore for testa-
" mentary purposes it is a *quasi-catallum.*" [2]

Chattels classified as real and personal.   Thus the position reached by the common law was that estates of freehold represented real property law in the strict sense of that term, and as such were subject to all the consequences of feudal tenure ; while on the other hand leaseholds (together with some other rights in land) were not so subject, and for this reason were neither affected by the incidents of feudalism, nor governed by the same legal rules as freeholds.

This position soon gave rise to a difficulty, for a term of years, no matter how it might be treated by the technique of the law, was obviously a valuable interest in land, and one which it was appropriate to bring within the province of the land laws.   To sever its connection with the law of land merely because it was outside the scope of the real actions would have been absurd, and so the law was obliged to surmount the difficulty by the invention of a new terminology.

It was already a commonplace that the subject-matter of proprietary interests was either real property or chattels.   Chattels were personal property, since they were not specifically recoverable in a real action.   Leaseholds were thus subject to the law of chattels, but since they lacked the attribute of movability the

---

[1] Holdsworth, *History of English Law*, vol. iii. pp. 128, 215.
[2] Pollock and Maitland, *History of English Law*, vol. ii. p. 116.

obvious solution was to regard them as a *tertium quid*—interests partly real and partly personal. Thus it was that personal property was sub-divided into chattels real and chattels personal.

"Chattels real," saith Sir Edward Coke, "are such as concern or savour "of the realty; as terms for years of land, wardships in chivalry, . . . "the next presentation to a church, estates by a statute merchant, "statute staple,[1] *elegit* [2] or the like. And these are called real chattels, "as being interests issuing out of or annexed to real estates; of which "they have one quality, viz. immobility, which denominates them *real*, "but want the other, viz. a sufficient legal indeterminate duration, and "this want it is that constitutes them *chattels*."[3]

Chattels real.

Thus there are two classes of chattels known to English law— chattels real as described by COKE, and chattels personal, which originally were confined to movable things, but which are now taken to comprise many forms of wealth, such as negotiable instruments, copyright, patents, trade marks, shares in a company and so on.

Chattels personal.

We see, therefore, that the Law of Property as a whole falls into the following three divisions :

The Law of Property classified.

The *law of real property* strictly so called, *i.e.* the rules that govern freehold interests in land—the fee simple, the entailed interest and the life interest.
The *law of chattels real, i.e.* the rules that govern leaseholds.
The *law of pure personalty.*

Of these three departments of law the first and the last stand furthest apart, for the law of real property has been constructed on feudal principles, while the law of pure personalty has drawn its inspiration from a variety of non-feudal sources, such as Roman and Canon law and the customs of merchants. Midway between the two comes the law of chattels real, which BLACKSTONE describes as having a " mongrel amphibious nature," since it has derived its rules partly from real property law and partly from the law of pure personalty. The tendency, however, for several centuries has been to bring freeholds into conformity with chattels real, and the process of assimilation has been carried to such lengths, especially by the legislation of 1925, that we now have substantially a common and uniform system of law for real property and chattels real.[4]

---

[1] A tenancy by statute merchant or statute staple arose when a merchant creditor by taking advantage of the Statutes Merchant and Staple (Edward I and III) obtained seisin of his debtor's lands ; see Digby, *History of the Law of Real Property*, p. 282.

[2] *Infra*, pp. 726–7.

[3] Blackstone, vol. ii. p. 386.

[4] *Infra*, pp. 85 *et seq.*

SECTION III.   MODIFICATION OF THE COMMON LAW BY EQUITY.

SUMMARY.

Introductory Note. Our next task is to show how equity modified and tempered the feudal principles of the common law by its introduction of the " use " and the consequent establishment of the trust concept, which is probably the most outstanding characteristic of English law.   It is this concept that has produced the peculiarly English distinction between the legal and the equitable estate that forms the basis of modern conveyancing.

(1) DISADVANTAGES INCIDENTAL TO THE COMMON LAW TENURES.

Stagnating effect of doctrine of seisin.

To understand the origin of uses it is necessary to examine the position of a tenant of land under the common law. That his position was not without its troubles can be realized by a glance at some of the disabilities and burdens which weighed upon him, several of which were due to the important part played by seisin in the feudal system.   The feature of that system was its immaturity, as regards both the interests which might be created in land and the methods by which the interests could be dealt with.   Possession is an obvious fact, and in early days it was the dominating fact upon which most of the repressive rules that came into being were founded.

Importance of seisin.

Two fundamental principles which in themselves were sufficient to establish the importance of seisin were that the feudal services which in the early history of tenure were of such consequence to the lord were enforceable against the person seised and only against him; and again that it was only against the same person that an action for the recovery of land could be brought. It was necessary that there should always be some person capable of meeting adverse claims and preserving the seisin for successors.[1] The effect of not knowing who was actually seised of land would be the loss of public and private rights therein,[2] and therefore two inviolable rules that became established were that there must never be an abeyance of seisin, or in other words that there must be an uninterrupted tenancy of the freehold ; and that every transfer of a freehold estate must be effected by an open and public delivery of seisin. Any disposition that would cloud the title to the seisin was forbidden at common law.

The following were some of the fetters laid on the free enjoyment of a freehold estate at common law :—

(A) Conveyances were required to be public and formal.

In a feudal society it was imperative that there should be no uncertainty as to the identity of the freehold tenant of any piece of land. A question might arise regarding the title to the land or the right of a lord to enforce the feudal dues to which he was entitled, and as both these matters could be settled only if it was known who was seised, common law ordained that every transfer of a freehold estate must be effected by an open and public delivery of seisin, either upon or within view of the land conveyed. The merit of this was that in the event of a dispute the actual freehold tenant would be well known to the neighbourhood. The method itself was called *feoffment with livery of seisin*, but the operative part of the transaction was the delivery, and a charter of feoffment, which only served to authenticate the transaction, was not strictly necessary.[3]

There were other kinds of common law assurances, but it may be said of them all that they were open and notorious, though, when the feudal vigour began to abate, they gradually ceased to bear this characteristic.[4] It often happens that a man, instead of publishing his dealings with land to the world at large, prefers to resort to some transaction which is secret and free from ceremony, but at common law this was a desire that was unattainable, at any rate in the early days.

Conveyances made cumbrous.

Feoffment with livery of seisin.

---

[1] See Co. Litt. 342*b*, Butler's note (1).
[2] Challis, *Law of Real Property* (3rd Edn.), p. 100.
[3] Co. Litt., 271*b*, note 1.
[4] Hayes, *Introduction to Conveyancing*, pp. 29–30. For the history of the subject see Holdsworth, *History of English Law*, vol. iii. pp. 220–46 ; vol. vii. pp. 353 *et seq.*

c*

(B) THE TYPES OF INTERESTS WERE STRICTLY LIMITED.

Power of disposition restricted.

As it was essential that the seisin should not be in abeyance for an instant, but should always be vested in a freehold tenant, it followed that every conveyance of freehold had to be made to take immediate effect, so that the seisin passed at once to the grantee. This meant that many dispositions which a tenant might legitimately desire to make were rendered impossible. For instance, a gift of a freehold interest which was to vest in the donee if and when he attained 21 years of age was void, since such a gift had to be completed by delivery of seisin, and if seisin were delivered at once, it would, having been parted with by the donor, be vested in nobody until the donee attained 21. If a grant were made to A. for life and after his death to B. when he attained 21, the grant to the latter failed unless he had reached that age at the death of A., because otherwise an abeyance of seisin would have occurred. Again, under a grant to A. for life and after his death to the future children of B., only children who were in existence at A.'s death could take, for to allow later children to come in would have broken still another general principle, namely, that a transfer of a freehold interest had to be carried out by a public transaction.

Thus it is clear that the concentration of the common law upon the simple fact of possession led to extreme simplicity in the interests that might be created, and restricted within narrow bounds the limitation of future interests.[1]

(C) A TENANT AT COMMON LAW COULD NOT DEVISE HIS FREEHOLD ESTATE.

No wills of freeholds.

Whatever may have been the rule in Anglo-Saxon days, one of the effects of the introduction of feudal tenures into this country was to abolish the right of leaving freeholds by will, except in a few particular localities and boroughs. To have allowed such wills would not only have diminished the lord's right of taking the land by escheat and have been a hardship to the heir, but it would have run counter to a feudal policy which demanded that every transfer should be notorious and public.[2]

(D) A TENANT AT COMMON LAW WAS LIABLE TO CERTAIN ONEROUS FEUDAL INCIDENTS.[3]

Blackstone's account of military tenures.

This is no place to elaborate the burdensome nature of the tenurial dues that have already been briefly described. It must

---

[1] *Infra*, pp. 215 *et seq.*
[2] Holdsworth, *History of English Law*, vol. iii. pp. 75–6.
[3] See *supra*, pp. 18–19.

suffice to cite an expressive passage in which BLACKSTONE sums up the position of one who held his lands in Knight Service :—

" In the meantime the families of all our nobility and gentry groaned
" under the intolerable burthens, which (in consequence of the fiction
" adopted after the Conquest) were introduced and laid upon them by
" the subtlety of the Norman lawyers. For, besides the scutages
" to which they were liable in defect of personal attendance, which
" however were assessed by themselves in parliament, they might be
" called upon by the king or lord paramount for aids, whenever his
" eldest son was to be knighted or his eldest daughter married ; not
" to forget the ransom of his own person. The heir, on the death of
" his ancestor, if of full age, was plundered of the first emoluments
" arising from his inheritance, by the way of relief and primer seisin ;
" and, if under age, of the whole of his estate during infancy. And
" then, as Sir Thomas Smith very feelingly complains, ' when he came
" ' to his own, after he was out of wardship, his woods decayed, houses
" ' fallen down, stock wasted and gone, lands let forth and ploughed to
" ' be barren,' to reduce him still further, he was yet to pay half a year's
" profit as a fine for suing out his livery ; and also the price or value of
" his marriage, if he refused such wife as his lord and guardian had
" bartered for, and imposed upon him ; or twice that value, if he
" married another woman. Add to this, the untimely and expensive
" honour of Knighthood, to make his poverty more completely splendid.
" And when by these deductions his fortune was so shattered and
" ruined that perhaps he was obliged to sell his patrimony, he had
" not even that poor privilege allowed him, without paying an
" exorbitant fine for a licence of alienation." [1]

There were additional disadvantages that resulted directly from the important part played by the feudal services. Thus, for instance, several of the feudal dues consisted of payments which were made by the newcomer upon the death of a tenant, and, as these would never be enforceable if the lands were granted to a body which never died, the rule soon became established that lands granted to an association such as a monastery without the licence of the King and the lord paramount, were forfeited. Such a grant was called a *grant in mortmain*, and statutes were passed from time to time maintaining the rule as to forfeiture.[2]

Grants in Mortmain forbidden.

Enough has now been said to show that the position of a free-hold tenant at common law, as regards freedom of disposition, was not enviable.

Rigidity of common law.

" Large deductions must therefore be made from the praise lavished
" on the ancient common law, when its provisions are said to have
" promoted security of enjoyment, simplicity of title and notoriety of
" transfer. As civilisation advanced, it proved less and less sufficient
" to attain those favourite objects of its founders, while it was mani-
" festly ill-adapted to meet the growing demands of freedom and
" commerce. The rules of ownership and modes of assurance which

---

[1] Blackstone, vol. ii. p. 76.
[2] *Ibid.*, vol. ii. p. 268 ; *infra*, pp. 872–4.

" we have endeavoured to explain, composed an unbending and
" oppressive code, utterly inadequate to the extended view and com-
" plicated interests of an intelligent and wealthy community. The
" progress of society called for a more pliant and liberal policy." [1]

(2) DISADVANTAGES OF COMMON LAW TENURES AVOIDED BY THE DEVICE OF PUTTING LANDS IN USE.

Influence of the Chancellor.

History shows us that whenever a grievance presses hardly
on the greater part of the population, it is not long before a
remedy is discovered, and it was certainly not long before a
" more pliant and liberal policy " was introduced with regard to
the rights and powers of landowners in general. But the new
policy did not come from the common law. It was the sole
work of the Chancellor, who made it possible by means of the protection which he gave in his court of equity to the new conception
called the *use* of lands. It was due to this alone that a tenant was
enabled to retain the ordinary advantages of landholding which
were assured to him by the common law while escaping some of
the worst disabilities of that system.

(A) ORIGIN AND EFFECT OF PUTTING LANDS IN USE.

Derivation of word " use."

Origin. The word " use " is derived not from the Latin
usus but from *opus*.[2] Maitland has shown us that before
Domesday it was a common practice for one man to deal with land
ad opus—on behalf of—another, as, for instance, where the sheriff
seized lands *ad opus domini Regis*, where a knight about to go to
the Crusades conveyed his property to a friend on behalf of his
wife and children, or where the vendor of an unfree tenement
surrendered it to the lord to hold on behalf of the purchaser.[3]
The word *opus*, which was in such connections commonly
adopted, became gradually transformed into *oes*, *ues*, and thence
into *use*. Now, if one person could deal with land on behalf of
or to the use of another for a particular purpose, the question that
inevitably occurred to men was why one person should not in a
general way be allowed to hold land to the use of another. This,
as a matter of fact, is exactly what was done in course of time.
The tenant A. would transfer his land by a common law conveyance to B., who undertook to hold it on behalf of, or, adopting
the correct expression, to the use of, A. In such a case B. was
called the *feoffee to uses*, that is, the person to whom the feoffment

---

[1] Hayes, *Introduction to Conveyancing*, vol. i. pp. 30–1.

[2] Maitland, *Collected Papers*, vol. ii. p. 403 ; Pollock and Maitland, *History
of English Law*, vol. ii. p. 226. For the origin and history of uses, see Holdsworth, *History of English Law*, vol. iv. pp. 407 *et seq.*; 81 L.Q.R. 562 *et seq.*
(J. L. Barton); Simpson, *An Introduction to the History of Land Law*, pp. 163
et seq.

[3] Maitland, *supra.*

had on certain conditions been made; while A. went by the name of the *cestui que use*, which being interpreted meant the person on whose behalf the land was held.

The practice did not spring into life all at once, and Maitland believed that 1230 was the earliest time at which one man was holding land permanently and generally to the use of another.

First example of uses.

" In the second quarter of the thirteenth century came hither the
" Franciscan Friars. The rule of their order prescribes the most perfect
" poverty : they are not to have any wealth at all. . . . Still, despite
" this high ideal, it becomes plain that they must have at least some
" dormitory to sleep in.   They have come as missionaries to the towns.
" The device is adopted of having land conveyed to the borough
" community to the use of the friars." [1]

By the fourteenth century this device had become more extensive and there is evidence that it was a common practice for a land-holder to convey his land to two or more friends *ad opus suum*— to his own use[2]—or to the use of a third person.

Practice of putting land in use spread.

Legal Effect of putting Lands in Use. The important point to observe is the legal effect of this practice.   It was to cut off the *cestui que use* in the eyes of *the common law* from all connection with the land.   By an assurance operating at common law he had conveyed his estate to the feoffees to uses, and was therefore deprived of all common law rights over the land. He was nothing, the feoffees were everything; he had exchanged an actual estate for an intangible right, for instead of keeping seisin he had decided to rely upon the confidence that he had reposed in the feoffees.

Cestui que use lost his rights in the eye of common law.

" If therefore B. (the feoffee) refused to account to his *cestui que use*
" A. for the profits, or wrongfully conveyed the estate to another, this
" was merely a breach of confidence on the part of B., for which the
" common law gave no redress ; much less did that law acknowledge
" any right in A. to the possession or enjoyment of the land.   The
" ordinary judicature knew no other proprietor than B. ; to him and to
" him alone attached the privileges and liabilities of a landholder ;
" for he it was to whom the possession was legally delivered.   To
" have regarded A. in any other light than that of a mere stranger to
" the soil would have been to subvert a system raised upon in-
" vestiture and tenure.   It was accordingly decided at a very early
" period [3] that the common law judges had no jurisdiction whatever
" in regard to the use." [4]

If the feoffees failed or refused to carry out the directions imposed upon them,[5] or if they deliberately alienated the land for their

---

[1] Maitland, *Equity* (ed. Brunyate), p. 25 ; and see *Collected Papers*, vol. ii. p. 408.   A Papal Bull ordained in 1279 that a use was not property.
[2] Maitland, *Equity*, pp. 25–6.
[3] 4 Edw. 4.
[4] Hayes, *Introduction to Conveyancing*, vol. i. p. 33.
[5] 3 Rot. Parl. 511, No. 112, cited Ames ; 21 *Harvard Law Review*, p. 265 ; *Select Essays in Anglo-American Legal History*, vol. ii. p. 741.

own purposes,[1] there was no common law action by which they could be rendered liable, and as a *cestui que use* who was let into possession of the land was regarded as a mere tenant at will of the feoffees to uses, he could be turned out by the latter at any moment, and in the event of contumacy could be sued in trespass.[2]

This absence of all remedy seems at first sight to stultify the practice of putting lands in use, and it would have been fatal had no alternative means been discovered for protecting the *cestui que use*. But an adequate form of protection was ready to hand. From about the year 1400 the Chancellor, in the first blush of his growing jurisdiction, stepped in and interceded on behalf of the *cestui que use*. He could not interfere with the jurisdiction of the common law courts by proceeding in a direct fashion against the land itself, because the absolute title to the land was vested in the feoffees by operation of the immutable principles enforced in those courts, but his rôle was to see that men acted honestly according to the precepts of good morality, and, in accordance with the principle that equity acts *in personam*, he did not hesitate to proceed against feoffees who disregarded the moral rights of the *cestui que use*. He was in a stronger position than the common law courts, for not only could he order a person to perform some definite act under pain of attachment, but his power of *viva voce* examination enabled him to discover breaches of good faith.

" The spectacle of feoffees retaining for themselves land which they " received upon the faith of their dealing with it for the benefit of " others was too repugnant to the sense of justice of the community " to be endured. The common law could give no remedy, for by " its principles the feoffee was the absolute owner of the land. A " statute might have vested, as the Statute of Uses a century later did " vest, the legal title in the *cestui que use*, but in the absence of a statute " the only remedy for the injustice of disloyal feoffees to uses was to " compel them to convey the title to the *cestui que use* or hold it for his " benefit. Accordingly the right of the *cestui que use* was worked out " by enforcing the doctrine of personal obedience." [3]

In other words, the wrong which an unfaithful feoffee committed was breach of contract, but it was a breach for which at that time no remedy lay in the ordinary courts, since the general principle of the enforceability of contracts was still undeveloped. Further, it was common for a use to be declared in favour of a third party, and even if the modern doctrine of contract had been perfected, the rules as to privity of contract would have precluded the grant of a remedy to the *cestui que use*.

---

[1] Sanders, *Uses*, vol. i. p. 67.
[2] Preston on Estates, vol. i. p. 145.
[3] Ames, *Select Essays*, vol. ii. p. 741.

(B) Creation of the Distinction between the Legal and the Equitable Estate.

Thus we find that from the year 1400 the Chancellor began to build up a comprehensive jurisdiction over uses, but it is especially important to observe that his intervention in this field led to the introduction into English law of what is generally described as a duality of landownership. He did not deny that the *feoffee* was entitled at common law to the exclusion of the *cestui que use*, since the land had been conveyed to him by a conveyance effective at common law. That fact was inescapable, but what the Chancellor insisted upon was that the *feoffee* should scrupulously observe the directions imposed upon him by the *feoffor*. The feoffment had not been made to him for his own benefit.

Attitude of equity.

In other words, while the feoffee was regarded as owner by the common law, the *cestui que use* was considered to be the true owner by equity : the former had the legal ownership, the latter the equitable ownership of the same piece of land. Thus we get the essentially English distinction between the legal and the equitable estate—the legal estate recognized and protected by the common law courts, and the equitable estate recognized and protected only by the Chancellor. This is what is meant by duality of ownership. Starting with the assumption that A. had conveyed land to B. to be held to the use of A., or to the use of C., Hayes, writing in 1840, described the position that arose, in a passage the lucidity of which justifies citation [1] :—

Duality of ownership.

" But, under the auspices of an ecclesiastical chancellor, the use, though
" alien to the soil, took root in our civil jurisprudence, and attained
" to a degree of influence and importance which at length almost
" superseded the ancient polity. Means were soon devised for com-
" pelling B., the owner in point of law, to keep good faith towards A.
" or C., the owner in point of conscience. The king, in his Court of
" Chancery, assumed jurisdiction to extort a disclosure upon oath of
" the nature and extent of the confidence reposed in B., and to enforce
" a strict discharge of the duties of his trust. Hence Equity arose.
" From this period, when the right of A. (or C.) became cognizable in
" the Court of Chancery, we may speak of him as the equitable or
" beneficial owner, and of B. as the legal owner. But in order to pre-
" serve a clear perception of the twofold character of the system, we
" must keep steadily in view the fact that B. had still the *real* right, to
" be enforced on one side of Westminster Hall, by judgment of law *in*
" *rem*, which went at once to the possession of the land itself; while A.
" A. (or C.) had nothing more than a mere right *in personam*, to be enforced
" on the other side of the Hall, by subpœna, directed against the
" individual trustee. The Chancery, in assuming jurisdiction over

---

[1] Hayes, *Introduction to Conveyancing*, vol. i. pp. 33–4.

" the use, left untouched and inviolate the ownership at common law.
" It exercised no direct control over the land, but only coerced and
" imprisoned the person of the legal owner who obstinately resisted
" its authority.   It usurped none of the powers or functions of a court
" of law, but, leaving to the latter the redress of wrongs done to the
" realty, confined its jurisdiction to matters of trust and confidence,
" which could not be reached by the arm of ordinary justice."

**Tenurial
burdens
avoided
by uses.**

Advantages of putting Lands in Use.   Before we proceed
any further it is desirable to notice how some of the worst burdens
incidental to tenure at common law might be avoided by the device
of a use.

There were at least six substantial advantages that might
accrue to the *cestui que use*.

(i) LANDS BECAME DEVISABLE.

The very natural desire that the power of testamentary disposition, which already applied to goods and chattels, should be
extended to land, contributed more largely than any other factor
to the rapid establishment of the use.   The obligation of the
feoffees to administer the legal estate according to the wishes of
the *cestui que use* was not confined to the lifetime of the latter, and
from an early date it was the usual practice for the beneficial
owner to specify what the destination of the use should be after
his death.   In this indirect way, by making a testamentary disposition of the equitable as distinct from the legal estate, men
were accustomed to provide for their younger sons, daughters and
other relatives, to ensure the payment of their debts and to
make charitable gifts.[1]

(ii) CONVEYANCES OF LAND FACILITATED.[2]

The common law principle that a conveyance should be open
and notorious could easily be evaded by means of the use, for just
as the *cestui que use* could direct what dispositions of the land
should be made after his death, so he could give similar directions
that would be operative during his life.   A transfer of the use
required no formality ; the one essential was that the intention of
its owner should be clearly manifested.   Moreover, the system
of conveyancing was radically affected as the result of an equitable
doctrine which applied even where land had not deliberately been
put in use.   This was that a mere contract to sell a legal estate
raised a use in favour of the purchaser immediately on payment
of the purchase money.   Such a contract was called a *bargain and
sale*, and though at first it passed merely an equitable estate to
the purchaser, it gained a far wider operation after the Statute

---

[1] Holdsworth, *History of English Law*, vol. iv. pp. 438–9.
[2] Holdsworth, *supra*, vol. iv. pp. 424–7.

of Uses in 1535 and developed into the normal method of conveying *legal* estates.[1]

(iii) Settlements of Land Facilitated.

We have already mentioned,[2] and indeed shall have occasion to explain more fully later,[3] that the power of a landowner at common law to create future interests was so severely restricted that only the simplest forms of settlements of a legal estate were possible. This stringency was relaxed upon the introduction of uses. The use, to which the restrictive rules of common law were wholly inapplicable, conferred upon its owner an almost unrestrained liberty to specify who the future beneficiaries should be, upon what events their interests should arise, and in what order the interests should take effect. The equitable estate was, in fact, a pliable instrument, a subject-matter that could be moulded by its owner into such forms as might appear desirable to him. Thus arose what were called shifting and springing uses. [4]

(iv) Avoidance of Feudal Burdens.

The most oppressive of the feudal burdens to which a tenant was liable at common law[5] were those that became exigible at his death, namely, wardship, marriage, reliefs and primer seisin. No relief from these would be gained by the appointment of a sole feoffee to uses, for the latter, in his capacity as tenant at law,

---

[1] For the history of the matter, see Holdsworth, *History of English Law,* vol. vii. pp. 356–60. The process of development may be briefly described as follows :

(1) A., having bargained and sold land to B. for a fee simple estate and having received the purchase money, was implicitly seised to the use of B.

(2) The Statute of Uses provided that when A. stood seised to the use of B., the latter should acquire the *legal* estate (*infra*, p. 53). Had this been the only enactment, therefore, a bargain and sale after the statute would have provided a secret method of conveying *legal* estates.

(3) The Statute of Enrolments, however, passed at the same time, enacted that no estate of *inheritance or freehold* should pass, nor should any use be raised, by a bargain and sale, unless the bargain and sale was made by deed and enrolled in one of the King's Courts of Record.

(4) The last statute applied only to sales of freehold or inheritable estates. Therefore a bargain and sale of a leasehold might be made privately without enrolment. This fact was quickly appreciated (certainly before 1620), and it became usual to transfer a fee simple as follows : A. bargained and sold Blackacre to B. *for one year*. On payment of the purchase money A. became seised to the use of B. The Statute of Uses operated upon this state of affairs and passed the legal possession to B., leaving the reversion in A. Next day A. executed a deed of *release* which extinguished his reversion and consequently enlarged B.'s leasehold into the fee simple. This form of conveyance, which was called a *lease and release*, remained the normal method of conveyance until 1841, when it was enacted that a release alone should be as effectual as a lease and release. A simple deed of grant was substituted for a release in 1845.

[2] *Supra*, p. 42. [3] *Infra*, pp. 214 *et seq*
[4] *Infra*, pp. 219 *et seq*. [5] *Supra*, pp. 18–19.

would be caught in the feudal net and *his* death would entitle the lord to exact such dues as might be demandable. The usual practice, therefore, was to enfeoff, not one, but several, persons as joint tenants. The rule of joint tenancy is that the share of a tenant who dies does not pass to his heir but accrues to the surviving tenants.[1] He leaves nothing for which his heir can be made to pay a relief, he leaves nobody over whom the lord can claim the right of wardship or of marriage. The one essential, therefore, was to ensure that the number of feoffees never fell below two. The death of the *cestui que use* himself, despite his position as the true beneficial owner, created no right to feudal dues, since they were the consequence of tenure, and the use " being the creature of conscience, the offspring of moral obligation could not be the subject of tenure."[2] " The lord could not look behind the feoffees ; they were his tenants : it was nothing to him that they were allowing another person to enjoy land which was by law theirs."[3]

(v) Avoidance of Forfeiture and Escheat.

Land held by tenure at common law was forfeited to the Crown if the tenant committed high treason, and upon his conviction or outlawry for felony it passed to the Crown for a year and a day and then escheated to the lord.[4] These unpleasant consequences, however, were avoided, if a tenant, before embarking upon some doubtful enterprise, had the prescience to vest his lands in a few confidential friends. The delinquent might possibly suffer the extreme penalty, but at least his family would not be destitute.

(vi) Evasion of the Mortmain Statutes.

We have noticed that, since those feudal dues that became exigible at the death of a tenant would be lost to the lord if land came into the hands of a body that might never die, such as a corporation, a series of Acts, generally called the Mortmain Statutes, were passed from an early date providing that land granted to a corporation without the licence of the King and lord paramount should be forfeited.[5] Uses, however, provided an obvious means of evading this prohibition, and, until the practice was finally stopped in 1392,[6] it was a common plan for a donor to enfeoff a number of persons to hold to the use of a monastery or other corporation.

---

[1] *Infra*, p. 300.
[2] Hayes, *Introduction to Conveyancing*, vol. i. p. 34.
[3] Maitland, *Equity*, p. 27.
[4] See Challis, *Law of Real Property* (3rd Edn.), pp. 33 *et seq.*
[5] *Infra*, pp. 872-4.   [6] 15 Ric. 2, c. 5.

Influence of common law doctrines on the use. We should next notice how the Chancellor dealt with this new form of ownership called the use or equitable estate. It was his own creation. He had invented something hitherto unknown to the law. He was free to do what he liked with his own. In the quaint language of an old judge, the use was as clay in the hands of the potter,[1] and, as the owner of a use was in theory allowed to give any imaginable directions as to its enjoyment, the Chancellor might have allowed it to be moulded into forms entirely subversive of common law principles. There were, in fact, several forms of landed interests, unattainable at common law, which he did permit to be carved out of the use, but they were mostly confined to the realm of future interests. Thus, for instance, the dispositions mentioned on page 42, which would have been void at common law, were open to a landowner if he was content to create them by way of use.

Development of equitable estates by Chancellor.

It may be said in general, indeed, that in framing rules for the governance of the use the Chancellor refused to be bound, or to let the development of the use be hampered, by any of the common law rules connected with tenure. And yet it was certainly not his policy to encourage wide deviations from the established tenets of law. The exact contrary was the case. Having begun by affording an adequate protection to the use, he then to some extent allowed the fact that its basis rested on personal confidence to fade into the background, and proceeded to regard it as a kind of interest in land, " a sort of immaterialized piece of land," in which actual estates might be created just as they might be created at common law.[2]

In general equity followed the law.

In other words, the general policy of the Chancellor in his development of the use was to adopt the accepted rules of common law. When necessary he was prepared to depart from those rules on the ground of convenience, but he usually took them as his guide. It can, indeed, be said " that there scarcely is a rule of law or equity of more ancient origin, or which admits of fewer exceptions, than the rule that Equity followeth the law."[3]

Thus upon the death of the *cestui queuse*, Equity applied the common law rules of descent ; the common law rights of a husband to the wife's property after her death were extended to the equitable interest, though a wife was not dowable out of her husband's equitable estates until 1833 ; and estates, similar in extent to those possible at law, might be created in the use. " There is the same division in Equity as there is at law, of estates of freehold and inheritance, of estates of freeholds only, and of estates less than freehold ; of estates in possession, remainder or reversion ; and of estates several and of estates undivided."[4]

---

[1] *Brent's Case* (1575), 2 Leon. 14, 16. [2] Maitland, *Equity*, p. 31.
[3] Butler's note to Co. Litt., 250*b*, xvi.
[4] *Ibid.*

Definition
of use.

Summary. To sum up this part of the discussion we may say that a use of lands existed where the legal estate was vested in A. in such circumstances that he was subject to a trust enforceable in Equity to convey the legal estate to such persons, and in the meantime to apply the rents and profits in such manner, as the *cestui que use* should direct; and, failing directions, should hold the land and pay the profits to the use of the *cestui que use* himself.[1]

(C) The Later History of Uses and the Rise of the Modern Trust Estate.

Later history
of uses.

What, then, is the essential difference between the legal and the equitable estate? It is clear at first sight that the legal estate carries the bare technical ownership, while its equitable counterpart gives the *cestui que use* beneficial ownership. One is the nut the other the kernel. If land is conveyed to

A. and his heirs to the use of B. and his heirs,

there is no doubt that A. is the true *legal* owner. But it is an unprofitable ownership, for unless he succeeds in some fraudulent enterprise he will be compelled to deal with the land as B. desires. In truth, the difference goes much deeper than this, but before stating wherein it lies we should say something of the subsequent history of uses.

Object of
Statute of
Uses.

Statute of Uses, 1535. The equitable estate, which was the greatest achievement of the Chancellor, was not allowed to pursue its course of development undisturbed. It was assailed by the legislature under Henry VIII, who, with a view to the " extirping and extinguishment of all such subtle practised feoffments, fines, recoveries, abuses," procured the passing of the Statute of Uses in 1535.[2] Many reasons were alleged in justification of this statute, but the real object of the King's action was to restore to something like their ancient buoyancy and dimensions those feudal dues of which the collection had been rendered so much less fruitful by the practice of conveying land to uses. The simplest remedy was to abolish uses altogether, and this the King essayed to do. Holdsworth has shown how Henry, pursued by the spectre of poverty, made his grand attack on this popular institution.[3] The feudal revenues had undoubtedly declined, and whatever indulgence Parliament showed the King in other respects, it refused to vote him a permanent and adequate income. For

---

[1] Sugden's *Gilbert on Uses*, p. 1 ; Fearne, *Contingent Remainders*, p. 291, note *h*.

[2] 27 Hen. 8, c. 10.

[3] 26 *Harvard Law Review*, pp. 108–27 ; Holdsworth, *History of English Law*, vol. iv. pp. 450–61.

some six years Henry was engaged upon his design. In 1529 a Bill was drafted so drastic in its proposals that, had it ever become a statute, it would have changed the face of the land law and struck a death-blow at uses. But opposition arose from two quarters : from the majority of landowners, who saw themselves deprived of the power to make family settlements, secret conveyances and wills, and from the lawyers, who dreaded the loss of profitable business. In no way daunted Henry set to work on a new scheme, and proceeded to remove the opposition of the legal profession by threatening to institute a stringent inquiry into the abuses of the common law, an inquiry which was pretty certain to be fruitful in disclosures, and one which was to be followed by a reform of those abuses. In 1535 there were three draft bills before Parliament, and out of these the final Act, the Statute of Uses, emerged. *Opposition to Statute.*

The Act contained a very long preamble, the general object of which was to denigrate as grievances the advantages which uses conferred upon the landowning class as a whole, while keeping in the background the real purpose of the statute, which was to replenish the royal coffers. The preamble made the Statute look as if it were a highly popular measure, but MAITLAND put the matter in its true historical setting when he said :— *Final draft.*

" A long preamble states the evil effects of the system [of uses], and
" legal writers of a later day have regarded the words of the preamble
" as though they stated a generally admitted evil. As a matter of
" historical fact this is not true. The Statute of Uses was forced upon
" an extremely unwilling parliament by an extremely strong-willed
" King. It was very unpopular and was one of the excuses, if not one
" of the causes, of the great Catholic Rebellion known as the Pilgrimage
" of Grace. It was at once seen that it would deprive men of that
" testamentary power, that power of purchasing the repose of their
" souls, which they had long enjoyed. The King was the one person
" who had all to gain and nothing to lose by the abolition of uses." [1]

Effect of the Statute of Uses. The statute was passed, however, and its effect was to abolish the distinction between the legal and the equitable estate in the case of the passive use, that is to say where the feoffees stood seised to the use of B. and were the mere passive instruments for carrying out the directions of B. A conveyance to *The temporary abolition of Uses.*

A. and his heirs to the use of B. and his heirs,

which before the statute would have carried only the equitable estate to B., operated after 1535 to pass the legal estate to him. This was so because the statute provided in effect that, when any person was seised of lands to the use of any other person, the *cestui*

---

[1] Maitland, *Equity*, p. 34 ; and see Froude, *History of England*, vol. iii. pp. 91, 105, 158.

que use should be deemed to have lawful seisin of the land to the extent of his interest in the use, and the seisin, that prior to the Act would have been in the feoffee to uses, A., should be deemed to be in the *cestui qui use* B.   In other words, the statute brought about two results :—

> First, to adopt a technical expression, it executed the use, that is to say, it turned B.'s former equitable estate into a legal estate carrying common law seisin ; and
> Secondly, the common law seisin, which would normally have been vested in A. as a consequence of the conveyance, was taken away from him entirely.[1]

A. was a mere nonentity, and as a general rule nothing was to be gained by conveying to A. to the use of B. instead of making a direct conveyance at common law to B., since in both cases B. was seised of the legal estate, and by reason of that fact was in both cases subject to the dues, burdens and incapacities that had always affected an estate at common law.

Advantages and disadvantages of the statute. The advantages of the statute lay with the common lawyers and with the King, its disadvantages with the general class of land-owners.   The common lawyers profited because not only did they escape from the far-reaching scheme of law reform with which they had been threatened six years earlier, but they also acquired a profitable jurisdiction over the uses that had been turned into legal estates.   The King profited because the conversion of uses into legal estates involved the abolition of the power to devise lands, and this, in itself, increased very considerably the value of the tenurial incidents.[2]

Unpopularity of the statute. The statute was a real grievance in many ways.   For one thing the common belief was that it prevented wills of land, and, though this was a misapprehension,[3] it caused such irritation[4] that it was found necessary in 1540 to pass the Statute of Wills which permitted a tenant to devise all his socage lands and two-thirds of his lands held in Knight Service.

It would seem then, if we proceeded no further with the history of uses, as if Lord COKE was right when he said that

> " the makers of the statute at last resolved that uses were so subtle
> " and perverse, that they could by no policy or provision be governed
> " or reformed ; and therefore as a skilful gardener will not cut away
> " the leaves of the weeds, but extirpates them by the roots, and as
> " a wise householder will not cover or stir up the fire, which is secretly
> " kindled in his house, but will utterly put it out ; so the makers of
> " the said statute did not intend to provide a remedy and reformation
> " by the continuance or preservation, but by the extinction and ex-

---

[1] Fearne, *Contingent Remainders*, p. 273, Butler's note.
[2] Holdsworth, *History of English Law*, vol. iv. pp. 463–4.
[3] See an article by R. E. Megarry, 7 *Cambridge Law Journal*, pp. 354 *et seq.*
[4] Froude, *History of England*, iii. p. 89.

" tirpation of uses ; and because uses were so subtle and ungovern-
" able, they have with an indissoluble knot coupled and married them
" to the land, which, of all elements, is the most ponderous and
" immovable." [1]

This, however, was to go too far, for the Act did not entirely abolish uses. There were at least two cases in which the grantees to uses retained the legal estate and were still compelled by the Chancellor to fulfil the intention of the grantor.

Exceptions to applica- tion of the statute.

First, since the statute applied only where a feoffee was seised to the use of another, it was necessarily inoperative where a term of years, as distinct from a freehold estate, was given to A. to the use of B., for A. was possessed, not seised, of the subject-matter.

Uses of leaseholds.

Secondly, the exclusion of the statute was admitted where an active duty was imposed upon the feoffees to uses, as for instance where they were directed to collect the rents and profits and to pay them to B. In these circumstances it was recognized that the legal estate must remain with the feoffees, for otherwise they could not justify their right to the rents.

Active uses.

In both these instances, the conscience of the feoffees to uses was affected and they came under a moral duty to deal with the legal estate on behalf of the beneficiary—in the one case to transfer the term to him, in the other to secure the rents for him—and it was a duty that was enforceable only by the Chancellor. As regards terminology, however, it became usual to describe the person whose conscience was affected in these cases as being under a *trust* to carry out the directions of the grantor.[2] The uses were not those which the statute could execute, yet they were trusts which in conscience ought to be performed.[3] The statutory abolition of the passive use, of course, was in no way affected by this exercise of the Chancellor's jurisdiction. It long remained true that if the fee simple were granted to A. to the use of B., A. was divested of the legal estate and deprived of his former functions. Nevertheless, the principle that a moral duty must be performed was developed with such insistence that the passive use was ultimately restored in the shape of the passive trust, for the courts of equity gradually extended the circum- stances in which the person upon whom the statute conferred the legal estate was bound in conscience to hold it in trust for some other person in accordance with the intention of the grantor.[4]

Ultimate restoration of the passive use.

A striking example of this enduring concern of Chancery with the problem of conscience is furnished by the ancient rule that there could be no use upon a use. The rule established before the statute was that if land were conveyed to

The use upon a use.

---

[1] *Chudleigh's Case* (1595), 1 Co. Rep. 124a.
[2] Plucknett, *Concise History of the Common Law* (5th Edn.), pp. 598–9.
[3] Blackstone, vol. ii. p. 336.
[4] Plucknett, *op. cit.*, p. 599.

A. and his heirs to the use of B. and his heirs to the use of C. and his heirs,

it was only the use in favour of B. that took effect. He acquired the equitable estate, and the second use in favour of C. was ruled out as being repugnant to the first.[1] This was confirmed at common law soon after the statute in *Jane Tyrrel's Case*,[2] the result of which was that B., not A., acquired the legal estate and the limitation in favour of C. was still nugatory. The repugnancy of his use with that of B. was, of course, apparent, for as was said in another case,

" the use is only a liberty to take the profits, but two cannot severally
" take the profits of the same land, and therefore there cannot be
" a use upon a use." [3]

Passive use finally restored.

Although it was equally obvious, as Blackstone remarks,[4] that B. was never intended by the parties to have any beneficial interest in the land, the Chancery court at first came to the same conclusion and repudiated the second use.[5] Ultimately, however, and certainly by 1700, it reversed this view and restored the passive use by holding that B. must be regarded as holding the legal estate in trust for C. It was against conscience for one man to retain what was clearly intended for another. The exact stages by which this result was reached are not discernible. It was long thought that *Sambach* v. *Dalston* (or *Daston*)[6] in 1634 was the decisive authority, but recent researches have shown that this is to go too far.[7] The importance of that decision was the refusal of the court to ignore the grantor's intention. In the actual circumstances of the case he intended to benefit not only C., but also an infant after the death of C. and therefore the court directed B. to make such dispositions of the land as would fulfil the whole of the grantor's design. This direction, however, did not involve

---

[1] (1952), Bro. Ab., Feoff. al Uses, 40 ; cited Ames, *Select Essays*, vol. ii. p. 748.

[2] (1557), 2 Dyer, 155a ; Digby, *History of Real Property*, p. 375.
Jane bargained and sold land (*supra*, p. 48) to her son, G. and his heirs, upon the understanding that G. was to hold to the use of Jane for life and thereafter to the use of himself in tail. The purchase money was paid, and therefore by implication of law (*supra*, p. 49) Jane was seised to the use of G. The statute operated upon this use, and gave G. the legal fee simple. But further uses had been declared, namely, to Jane for life and then to G. in tail, and the question was whether these were valid or not. It was held that they were void.

[3] *Daw* v. *Newborough* (1716), 1 Comyns 242 ; cited Ames, *Select Essays*, vol. ii. p. 748.

[4] Vol. ii. p. 336.

[5] *Girland* v. *Sharp* (1595), Cro. Eliz. 382 ; Digby, *History of Real Property*, p. 375.

[6] Tothill, 188 ; Nelson 30, *sub. nom. Morris, Lambeth et Margery* v. *Darston*; see 74 *L.Q.R.*, p. 550.

[7] 74 *L.Q.R.*, pp. 550–60 (J. E. Strathdene); Simpson, *An Introduction to the History of Land Law*, p. 180; see further 82 *L.Q.R.*, pp. 215–25 (J. L. Barton).

the restoration of the passive use or any recognition of the modern passive trust, for B.'s obligation was to divest himself of the legal estate, not to retain it and hold it on behalf of C.[1]

Eventually, however, a change in the political situation facilitated the restoration of the passive use. The passive use had been abolished in 1535 for the sole reason that the King laid the loss of his feudal revenue at its door. But towards the end of the seventeenth century a complete revolution had occurred in the political sphere. Owing to the abolition of the military tenures in 1660 and to the gradual fall in the value of money, the feudal dues had become of little consequence and, indeed, the royal finances had been put on a more satisfactory footing. This fact, coupled with an almost universal desire for the old liberty of action, enabled the Chancellor once more to recognize the former distinction between the legal and the equitable estate whenever the intention was that B. should hold land on behalf of C. The device eventually adopted by conveyancers to make this intention effective was merely to limit a use upon a use.[2]

Rise of the modern passive trust.

> If it was desired to create an equitable estate in favour of C., instead of adopting the pre-statute method of a conveyance to A. to the use of C., all that was necessary was to add a second use and make the conveyance run to A. to the use of B. to the use of C.

The effect of this was that the statute divested A. of his interest and passed the legal estate to B., with the result that, since the second use was not executed by the statute, C. was left with a mere equitable estate corresponding with the equitable estate that existed in the pre-statute days under the name of the use.

Thus the old distinction was retained in spite of the statute, but both the method of creating the distinction and the terminology adopted to describe it were changed. The first use in favour of B., which was executed by the statute, was still called a use, but the second one in favour of C., on which the statute did not operate, was for greater clearness always designated a " trust." [3]

The trust.

The practice ultimately adopted was to leave A. out altogether and to create the equitable estate by conveying the land

> *unto and to the use* of B. and his heirs in trust for C. and his heirs.

The effect of this was that B., called the *trustee*, acquired the legal estate by virtue of the common law ; but he also obtained the use, and though he was deemed to take the legal estate at common law and not under the statute, for there was no other person seised

---

[1] Plucknett, *op. cit.*, pp. 601–2.   [2] *Ibid.*, p. 602.
[3] Hayes, *Introduction to Conveyancing*, vol. i. p. 54. See Holdsworth, *History of English Law*, vol. v. 307–9 ; vol. vi. 641–4.

to his use,[1] yet, since a use had been declared in his favour, the rule that there could be no use upon a use prevented the statute from operating upon the second use and passing the legal estate to C.[2]

Thus, despite the complacent optimism of Lord COKE, the old distinction between the legal and the equitable estate was fully restored by at any rate the early eighteenth century. In 1738, Lord HARDWICKE stated the position in these words :—

> " Yet [after 1535] the judges still adhered to the doctrine that
> " there could be no such thing as *an use upon an use,* but where the
> " first use was declared, there it was executed and must rest for
> " that estate : therefore on a limitation to A. and his heirs to the use of
> " B. and his heirs, in trust for D., B.'s estate was held there to be
> " executed by the statute, and D. took nothing.
> " Of this construction equity took hold and said that the intention
> " was to be supported. It is plain B. was not intended to take,
> " his conscience was affected. To this the reason of mankind
> " assented, and it has stood on this foot ever since and by this means
> " a statute made upon great consideration, introduced in a solemn
> " and pompous manner, by this strict construction has had no other
> " effect than to add at most three words to a conveyance." [3]

The last remark of the Lord Chancellor, however, though picturesque and arresting, was scarcely accurate, for, as we shall see, the statute had a vital and a lasting effect in so far as it enabled a class of future interests (springing and shifting uses), hitherto unknown to the common law, to be carved out of the legal estate.[4]

(D) THE ESSENTIAL DIFFERENCE BETWEEN THE LEGAL AND THE EQUITABLE ESTATE.

Nature of the trust estate.

The position with regard to equitable estates remained as indicated above until January 1st, 1926. If, that is to say, it was desired to create a trust estate, all that was necessary was to convey land *unto and to the use of* trustees in fee simple, in trust for the *cestui que trust*—or beneficiary, as we will designate him in future.

The questions that now require answering are :—

1. What is the nature of trust estates, and
2. What is the exact point of difference between them and legal estates ?

---

[1] " The statute ought to be expounded that when the party seised to the use and the *cestui que use* is one person, he never taketh by the statute, except there be a direct impossibility for the use to take effect by the common law " : Bacon, *Uses,* 47.

[2] *Samme's Case* (1609), 13 Co. Rep. 54 ; *Doe d. Lloyd* v. *Passingham* (1827), 6 B. & C. 305 ; *Orme's Case* (1872), L. R. 8 C. P. 281 ; *Hadfield's Case* (1872), L. R. 8 C. P. 306 ; *Cooper* v. *Kynoch* (1872), 7 Ch. App. 398 ; *Sanders on Uses,* 5th Edn., p. 89 ; Hargreaves, *Introduction to Land Law* (3rd Edn.), pp. 99–101.

[3] *Hopkins* v. *Hopkins* (1738), 1 Atk. 581, 591.

[4] *Infra,* pp. 218–22.

1. In the first place it may be said in a general way that the old uses which continued, after and in spite of the statute, to have their old effect were simply the same original uses appearing under the different name of trusts.[1] But this is not the whole story. As Lord MANSFIELD said in *Burgess v. Wheate* [2] :—

> " An use and a trust may essentially be looked upon as two " names for the same thing ; but the opposition consists in the " difference of practice of the Court of Chancery."

Trusts more highly developed than Uses.

As is inevitable in the development of any legal conception equitable interests became much more elaborate and were adapted to many more purposes than in the days before the Statute of Uses. Lord Keeper HENLEY said in the same case :—

> "Geometry was the same in the time of Euclid as in that of " Sir Isaac Newton, though he applied the principles and rules " to effect greater discoveries and more important demon-" strations. An use, say the older books, was neither *jus in re*, " nor *ad rem*, but a confidence resting in privity of person and " estate, without remedy but in a court of equity. What else " is a trust ? what other definition can be given of it ? no other " is attempted. But it is said since the existence of trusts (since " the statute), equity has modelled them into the shape and " quality of real estates, much more than it did in earlier times " when they were called uses. It has made tenants by the " curtesy, permitted tenants in tail to suffer common recoveries " etc. And why ? Because equity follows the law. And " between *cestui que trust* and those claiming by, from and " under him, it is equity that he should be considered as " formally possessed of that estate of which he is and appears " substantial owner. But this is only the effect of the equitable " jurisdiction's growing to maturity, and was an accident that " to a degree accompanied uses as well as trusts. Lord Bacon " observes that they grew to strength and credit by degrees and " as the Chancery grew more eminent."

Thus uses required that the feoffee to uses should have the fee simple estate, but trusts could be declared upon the estates of tenants in tail, for life or years ; uses were generally passive, that is, the feoffee was a dormant instrument compelled by equity to obey the directions of the *cestui que use*, but later development allowed the creation of special trusts under which the trustee might be directed to perform such duties as the sale of land, the accumulation of profits, the managements of estates and so on. Again, the use applied only to land, but the subject-matter of trusts has expanded to such a degree that at the present day it includes, not only every conceivable kind of property, but even objects unconnected with property. The

Expansion of subject-matter of trusts.

---

[1] *Lloyd* v. *Spillet* (1740), 2 Atk. 150, *per* Lord HARDWICKE.
[2] (1757–9), 1 Eden. 177.

trust, for instance, has enabled unincorporated associations, such as clubs, trade unions and nonconformist bodies, which, owing to the indefinite and fluctuating character of their personnel, are not persons in the legal sense, both to own property and to fulfil the objects of their formation. The ownership of premises cannot reside in an unincorporated club, but it may be vested in a few persons, who, in the capacity of trustees, will not only have a legally protected ownership but will be amenable to the jurisdiction of the court if they fail to administer the property on behalf of the members and in accordance with the rules.[1] Then again the trust is not the only form of equitable interest known to the law. The interest in land retained by a person before 1926 who mortgaged the land in return for a loan of money; the interest that arises in favour of a person who has made a valid contract for the purchase of land or a valid agreement for a lease; the right which an owner possesses to enforce certain restrictive covenants—these are all equitable interests and exhibit the one great characteristic that distinguishes trust from legal estates.

Difference
between
legal and
equitable
estates.

2. That brings us to the second point. What is that characteristic, or, in other words, what is the difference between the legal and the equitable estate ?

As we have said, the difference is not adequately defined by the statement that the legal estate confers an empty title, while the equitable estate amounts to beneficial ownership of the land. The fundamental distinction is this :—

> A legal estate is a right *in rem*, an equitable estate a right *in personam*, that is to say, the former confers a right enforceable against the whole world, the latter one which can be enforced only against a limited number of persons.

If A. is entitled to the legal estate in Blackacre, then as a general rule it is true to say that, apart from some voluntary act of his own, he cannot be deprived of his rights in the land by the fraud of some third person. If, for instance, the owner of a fee simple grants a term of years in the land to A. and then sells and conveys the fee simple to X., fraudulently concealing the existence of the lease, the rights of A. as the owner of a legal estate are entirely unaffected by the transaction.

Legal estate
a right
in rem.

Exactly the same principle applies to all legal as distinct from equitable interests. For instance, a landowner may allow his neighbour to enjoy some right over his land such as a right of way. If the right which is so enjoyed exhibits

---

[1] See Maitland, *Collected Papers*, vol. ii., *The Unincorporate Body*, pp. 271–84 ; *Trust and Corporation*, pp. 321–404

certain characteristics (to be described in a later chapter),[1] it is known as an easement, and an easement is a legal interest properly so called, and moreover is permanently enforceable against all subsequent owners of the land over which it is exercisable. That land may very well be bought by a person who does not know of the right and has no reason to know of it, but nevertheless it will be binding upon him. The person entitled to enjoy the right has a legal interest which can be enforced against all persons whether they know of it or not.

So then the legal estate, or in fact any legal interest however small, is binding against all people, no matter how they have obtained what seem to be absolute and unrestricted rights over the land. But the rights conferred upon the owner of an equitable estate are not and never have been so extensive as this, though they are enforceable against so many people that they come to look very like *jura in rem*. The general principle is that they are enforceable only against those persons who, owing to the circumstances in which they have acquired the land, ought in conscience to be held responsible. This principle derives from the consistent refusal of the Chancellor to enforce the use against a person who acquired the land from the feoffee to uses unless he was affected by the confidence that had been reposed in the original feoffee.

Equitable estate a jus in personam.

"As the use had its beginning in personal confidence, so its " continuance, as a binding obligation on the legal owner of the " land, was measured by the continuance of that confidence."[2]

The number of persons who were deemed to be affected by this confidence gradually grew in number.

The starting point was of course that the trustee himself, or the *feoffee to uses* as he was originally called, was permanently bound to observe the trust. The first extension of this was made in 1465, when it was held that a person who bought the land from the trustee with notice of the conditions upon which the land was held was bound by the trust.[3] The next stage, reached in 1522, was that all those who came to the trustee's estate by way of succession, such as his heir or doweress, were held responsible for carrying out the trust.[4]

Enforceability of equitable estates gradually extended.

---

[1] *Infra*, pp. 465 *et seq.*

[2] Hayes, *Introduction to Conveyancing*, vol. i. p. 42. See also Sandars, *Uses and Trusts*, vol. i. pp. 55–6.

[3] Y.B. 5 Ed. IV, Mich. pl. 16, fo. 7. For the whole of this subject see the account given by Jenks in his *Modern Land Law*, pp. 141 *et seq.*

[4] Y.B. 14 Hen. VIII, Mich. pl. 5, fo. 8, cited Jenks, *op. cit.*; Maitland, *Equity*, p. 117.

The law, which had reached this point at the time when the Statute of Uses was passed, was adopted and carried further by the courts when equitable estates reappeared under the name of trusts. Thus it was decided by *Chudleigh's Case* in 1595 [1] that a voluntary alienee from the trustee, that is to say, a person who had acquired the estate without giving valuable consideration for it, was bound by the trust even though he had no notice of its existence. Therefore a trust was enforceable both against a man who bought the land *with notice* of the trust, and against one who received it by way of gift but without notice. Again, at some date after 1660 [2] trusts were made enforceable against creditors of the trustee who had seized the trust estate with a view to obtaining satisfaction for the debts due to them.

The one person, therefore, whose conscience was unaffected and against whom the equitable estate became unenforceable was the purchaser for value of the legal estate *without notice* of the rights of the *cestui que use*. If the feoffee to uses fraudulently sold the land to an unsuspecting purchaser, the equity of the *cestui que use* was gone so far as the land was concerned and he could not claim relief against the purchaser. Nevertheless his equity remained in full force against the fraudulent trustee.

> " The *very* land was irrecoverably gone, but the use remained ;
> " and while the conscience of the person *to* whom the possession had
> " passed was unaffected, the person from whom it had passed was
> " still liable, as before, to fulfil the equities tacitly included in the
> " use." [3]

Equitable doctrine of notice.

Doctrine of Notice. The only other point to observe is the policy adopted by the court with regard to the vital question of notice. A person who bought the land for valuable consideration from the trustee was not liable to carry out the trusts provided that he had no notice of them at the time of purchase, but it is obvious that, unless a careful watch had been kept on the conduct of such a purchaser, he would have taken care not to have notice. The definition of notice was therefore made elastic. If a purchaser was diligent enough and acted in a reasonable and sensible manner, making all those investigations which the purchaser of land normally did make, then he was affected only by actual notice of trusts. If, however, he omitted to make the usual investigations then he might be affected by constructive notice.

---

[1] 1 Co. Rep at 122*b* ; *Mansell* v. *Mansell* (1732), 2 P. Wms. 678.
[2] See Maitland, *Equity*, p. 112.
[3] Hayes, *Introduction to Conveyancing*, vol. ii. p. 43.

Constructive Notice. It has always been regarded as impossible to frame a satisfactory definition of constructive notice,[1] but it is generally taken to include two different things [2] :—

1. The notice which is implied when a purchaser omits to investigate the vendor's title properly or to make reasonable inquiries as to deeds or facts which come to his knowledge.

2. The notice which is imputed to a purchaser by reason of the fact that his solicitor or other legal agent has actual or implied notice of some fact. This is generally called " imputed notice."

Now the question is : what ought a prudent, careful man to do when he is purchasing an estate ? The answer will afford us an insight into the equitable doctrine of notice, and at the same time will show us in what circumstances a purchaser takes an estate free from any trust or other equitable interests to which it may be subject.

It is not necessary to go back further than the Conveyancing Act, 1882 (now re-enacted by the Law of Property Act, 1925 [3]), which contained a section designed to protect purchasers against a doctrine that had been refined to the point of unfairness. The Act provides that no purchaser is to be affected by notice of any instrument, fact or thing unless he actually knows of it, or unless he would have known of it had such inquiries and inspections been made, as ought reasonably to have been made, or unless his solicitor, while carrying out that particular transaction, actually obtains knowledge of that instrument, etc., or would have obtained it had he made reasonable inquiries and inspections. What it comes to, then, is that a purchaser is deemed to have notice of anything which he has failed to discover either because he did not investigate the title properly or because he did not inquire for deeds relating to the property.

We will take these cases separately :—

(i) NOTICE FROM NOT INVESTIGATING TITLE. For centuries it has been regarded as essential that a man who is purchasing land should investigate the title of his vendor, that is to say, should require the vendor to " prove his title " by producing evidence to show that the interest which he has contracted to sell is vested in him, and that it is unencumbered by rights and interests enforceable against the land by third parties. Except in those parts of the country where the system of registration of title is in force,[4] proof of the title[5] takes the form of requiring the vendor to set out the history of the land in what is called an

---

[1] Sugden, *Vendor and Purchaser*, p. 71.
[2] White and Tudor, vol. ii. p. 172.
[3] S. 199 (1) (ii).
[4] For registered conveyancing, see *infra*, p. 837 *et seq.*
[5] For a fuller account of investigation of title see *infra*, pp. 837 *et seq.*

abstract of title with a view to showing how the interest he has contracted to sell became vested in him, so as to prove that for a given number of years he and his predecessors have rightfully exercised dominion over the land consistent with that interest. The old rule both at law and in equity was that, if a vendor could adduce evidence of acts of ownership for a period of not less than sixty years, he had satisfied the obligation which lay upon him, and, unless anything appeared to the contrary, had proved a title which the purchaser was bound to accept. But there was no rigid rule about the length of this period, for it was useless to trace the title for sixty years unless the result was to show that the vendor was entitled to convey that interest which he had agreed to sell.[1] For instance, a vendor might very well show sixty years' possession in himself, but if this possession was held under a long lease, something more was obviously required to substantiate a right to sell the fee simple. The vendor's proof must always begin with a " good root of title," *i.e.* with some instrument transferring the interest that the purchaser now seeks to obtain.

Length of
title.

The Vendor and Purchaser Act, 1874, provided that in an open contract of sale, that is, where no express stipulation had been entered into fixing a precise date from which title should be traced, forty years should be substituted for the old period of sixty years. Thus under the law as it existed in 1925 a vendor who failed to persuade the purchaser to accept a shorter title was obliged to adduce evidence of acts of ownership stretching over a period of at least forty years. This obligation was satisfied by the vendor showing what conveyances of the estate—whether *inter vivos* or as a result of death—had been effected, for, to take a simple illustration, if documents could be produced showing that forty-five years earlier X. had bought the estate for valuable consideration and then left it by will to the vendor, it was pretty clear that the latter could make a good title.

" If, then, on the sale of a freehold in fee, the vendor produces the title-
" deeds for the last 40 years, and these show that the fee simple in the
" land sold has been conveyed to him free from incumbrances, and if
" there be satisfactory evidence that the deeds produced relate to the
" land sold, and the vendor be in possession of the lands and the deeds,
" he has shown a good title to the land." [2]

The general obligations of a vendor are the same under the modern law, except that the period for which title must be traced under an open contract has been further reduced from forty to thirty years.[3]

Abstract of
title.

The first duty of the vendor is to prepare an abstract of title, that is, a statement of the material parts of all deeds and other

---

[1] Williams, *Vendor and Purchaser* (1st Edn.), p. 76.
[2] *Ibid.*, p. 84.
[3] Law of Property Act, 1925, s. 44 (1).

instruments by which the property has been disposed of during the period in question, and also of all facts, such as births, deaths and marriages, which affect the ownership of the land. But in addition to producing this abstract the vendor is required to verify its contents by producing either the actual documents abstracted or the best possible evidence of the contents of those which he is not in a position to produce, and by proving facts, such as births and deaths, which are material to the title.

We can now understand what is meant by constructive notice. One object of investigating title is to discover whether the land is subject to rights vested in persons other than the vendor, and the equitable doctrine of notice ordains that a purchaser is bound by any right which he would have discovered had he made the ordinary investigations as sketched above. Again, if he fails to make inquiries of third persons who happen to be in possession of the land, he is affected with notice of all equitable interests held by them, as, for example, an option to purchase the fee simple that has been granted to a lessee already in possession.[1] Moreover, if the vendor has imposed conditions requiring a purchaser to accept a title shorter than thirty years, the doctrine of notice is extended to rights which would have been disclosed had title been shown for the normal period.[2] *Connection between notice and investigation of title.*

In general, then, it may be said that a purchaser will be bound by equitable interests of which he may in fact be ignorant but whose existence he would have discovered had he acted as a prudent man of business, placed in similar circumstances, would have acted.[3]

(ii) NOTICE FROM NOT INQUIRING FOR DEEDS. As we have just seen, the conveyancing practice of this country demands that a person who is buying land should examine the vendor's deeds, in order both to ascertain whether a good title can be made and to ensure that no third person possesses rights enforceable against the land. It follows from this that, if a purchaser makes no inquiries for the title-deeds, and allows them to remain in the possession of a third person, he will be deemed to have notice of any equitable claims which the possessor of the deeds may have against the land.[4] If he makes inquiry but fails to secure their production, his liability for any equity that they would have disclosed depends upon whether or not his failure was due to his own gross negligence. If he is satisfied with an unreasonable excuse for their non-production, he is liable[5]; but if the excuse *Omission to inquire for deeds may constitute notice.*

---

[1] *Daniels* v. *Davison* (1809), 16 Ves. 249.
[2] *Re Cox and Neve's Contract*, [1891] 2 Ch. 109, pp. 117–18.
[3] *Bailey* v. *Barnes*, [1894] 1 Ch. 25, 35.
[4] *Walker* v. *Linom*, [1907] 2 Ch. 104.
[5] *Oliver* v. *Hinton*, [1899] 2 Ch. 264, 274.

C.R.P.—D

is reasonable, he may successfully shelter behind the plea of purchaser for valuable consideration without notice.[1]

Legal and Equitable Estate finally contrasted. We are now in a position to return to our explanation of the essential difference between the legal and the equitable estate. We have said that a legal interest is enforceable against all the world, while an equitable interest can be enforced only against a limited number of persons. To be more precise, if an equitable interest in Blackacre is created in favour of X., the following are the persons who, if they subsequently acquire an interest in the land, will take that interest subject to X.'s right :

1. a person who acquires Blackacre as the heir, devisee or personal representative of the trustee ;
2. a person who has acquired the legal estate in Blackacre *without the payment of valuable consideration*, even though he has no actual or constructive notice of the equitable interest ;
3. a creditor of the trustee, whether with or without notice of the trust ; or
4. a person who has given valuable consideration for the legal estate in Blackacre, but who is affected by actual or constructive notice of the equitable interest.

An equitable interest such as a trust is, then, if we put the matter with strict regard to historical accuracy, one that can be enforced only against those particular persons, but a definition which is almost equally accurate [2] is that an equitable interest is one that is enforceable against the whole world *except a purchaser for valuable consideration of the legal estate which is subject to the equitable interest, provided that, when the purchaser acquired the legal estate, he had no notice, either actual or constructive, of the equitable interest.* In the case of such a person there is no reason why equity should not allow the common law to run its normal course. Equity follows the law, and will not interfere with law unless there is some very strong equitable ground for doing so. Where a person has paid for the interest which is secure at law, and moreover has acted honestly and diligently, there is no equitable reason for postponing him to somebody who from the point of view of equity is in no stronger position, and from the point of view of law is in a far inferior position.

The position was put very forcibly by JAMES, L.J., in *Pilcher v. Rawlins* [3] :—

" I propose simply to apply myself to the case of a purchaser
" for valuable consideration without notice, obtaining, upon the

---

[1] *Hewitt* v. *Loosemore* (1851), 9 Hart 449 ; on the subject generally see *infra*, pp. 615 *et seq.*
[2] But see Maitland, *Equity*, pp. 120–21.
[3] (1871), L. R. 7 Ch. App. 259, 268.

" occasion of his purchase and by means of his purchase deed, some
" legal estate, some legal right, some legal advantage ; and according
" to my view of the established law of this court, such a purchaser's
" plea of a purchase for valuable consideration without notice is an
" absolute, unqualified, unanswerable plea to the jurisdiction of this
" court. Such a purchaser may be interrogated and tested to any
" extent as to the valuable consideration which he has given in order
" to show the *bona fides* or *mala fides* of his purchase, and also the
" presence or the absence of notice, but when once he has gone
" through that ordeal and has satisfied the terms of the plea of
" purchase for valuable consideration without notice, then this court
" has no jurisdiction whatever to do anything more than to let him
" depart in possession of that legal estate, that legal right, that legal
" advantage which he has obtained. In such a case the purchaser is
" entitled to hold that which, without breach of duty, he has had
" conveyed to him."

Apparently, the only exception to this immunity enjoyed by
the purchaser for value without notice arises where in fact the
vendor's only title to convey the fee simple is that he is tenant for
life under a settlement, but he fraudulently conceals the existence
of the settlement.[1]

In brief, then, an equitable estate is not so safe as a legal
estate. An equitable owner may find himself, without any fault
or negligence on his part, postponed to a third person who has
obtained the legal estate in the same lands, and his remedy will be
reduced to that of recovering the value of the estate from the
fraudulent or negligent trustee. The facts of *Pilcher* v. *Rawlins*
will serve to illustrate this proposition.

> Pilcher, who was the sole surviving trustee of £8,373, which he
> held in trust for X. for life and after his death for X.'s children,
> lent the money to Rawlins on a legal mortgage of Blackacre. This
> was a perfectly legitimate transaction, the effect of which was to
> vest the legal estate of Blackacre in Pilcher as trustee for X., so that
> until the mortgage was redeemed by Rawlins, Pilcher acquired the
> legal and X. the equitable estate in the lands.
> Rawlins then arranged to grant a legal mortgage of Blackacre
> to Z. in return for a loan of £10,000. As things stood this was
> impossible because a legal mortgage before 1926 necessitated the
> transfer to the lender of the legal fee simple, and this was vested in
> Pilcher. Pilcher, however, decided to abet Rawlins in the fraudulent
> scheme. First of all Rawlins (who was a solicitor) prepared an abstract
> of title to Blackacre which stopped short of and excluded the mortgage
> to Pilcher and thus made it appear that the legal fee simple was still
> vested in himself. Of course it was not, but at this point Pilcher came
> into the plot by re-conveying his legal estate in Blackacre to Rawlins
> in consideration of a repayment of X.'s trust moneys. This repay-
> ment was never in fact made, but Rawlins, having thus attained the
> legal estate, was enabled to transfer it to Z., who paid over the
> £10,000. The deed of re-conveyance was suppressed. When the
> fraud was discovered, the question was, which of the two innocent
> parties, X. or Z., had the better right to Blackacre.
> It was held that, as Z. had acted reasonably and honestly, the
> legal interest which had passed to him must prevail over the mere

---

[1] *Weston* v. *Henshaw,* [1950] Ch. 510 ; see *infra*, p. 715.

equitable interest vested in X. Pilcher was the sole trustee and as such had the legal estate and the title-deeds. That being so, the effect of his reconveyance was to give the legal estate to Rawlins, and, as the whole mortgage transaction was concealed, there was no document to put Z. on inquiry.

Other forms of equitable interests.

Throughout the preceding account we have principally considered one form of equitable interest, the trust, but though this is the most important species, we must observe that it is not the only one. The trust, already described, is an interest which corresponds with a legal interest in the sense that just as there may be a legal fee simple, entailed interest or life interest, so also may there be equitable counterparts possessing the same incidents, for equity follows the law.[1] But other equitable interests may exist which have no analogy at common law. The more important of these, which will require a more detailed discussion later, are the following:—

1. **The Restrictive Covenant,** *i.e.* a covenant by which the use of the covenantor's land is restricted for the benefit of the covenantee's adjoining land, *e.g.* where it is agreed that it shall not be used for the purposes of trade. The effect of such a covenant, if the necessary conditions are satisfied,[2] is that the covenantee acquires an equitable interest in the burdened land in the sense that he is entitled to an injunction preventing a breach of the agreement by the covenantor or by his successors in title except a purchaser for value of the legal estate without notice of the covenant.

2. **The Equity of Redemption,** *i.e.* the right of a mortgagor to redeem the mortgaged property upon payment of all that is due by way of capital or interest.[3]

3. **The Equitable Charge,** which arises where, without the transfer of any definite estate, land is designated as security for the payment of a sum of money. In such a case, the chargee acquires an equitable interest that entitles him to take judicial proceedings for the sale of the land.[4]

4. **The Equitable Lien.** This is similar in effect to the equitable charge, and most generally arises when the vendor conveys the land to the purchaser before he has been paid. If so, he becomes entitled by operation of law to an equitable lien on the land for the amount of the unpaid purchase money which is enforceable by a sale under the direction of the court.[5]

---

[1] We shall see later (*infra,* pp. 94–5) that by the legislation of 1925 it is now impossible for entailed and life interests to subsist as *legal* as distinct from equitable estates.
[2] *Infra,* p. 539.   [3] *Infra,* p. 584.
[4] *Infra,* p. 582.   [5] *Infra,* p. 651.

5. **The Estate Contract.** This arises where the owner of a legal estate either agrees to convey it to the other contracting party or to create a legal estate out of it in favour of that other. Thus, if A., the owner of the fee simple absolute in Blackacre, agrees to sell it to B. or to create a term of years absolute out of it in favour of B., the equitable interest in the land as measured by the terms of the contract passes at once to B., although the legal estate remains with A. until an actual conveyance or lease has been executed.[1]

An equitable interest is distinguishable from what is generally called an *equity* or a *mere equity*. This is a concept that defies precise definition, but it includes a right to enforce an equitable remedy, such as specific performance, or to set aside or rectify a conveyance for fraud, undue influence, mistake and similar reasons.[2]

Equitable interest distinguished from a "mere equity."

The distinction between such an equity and an equitable interest emerges if we consider their binding effect upon third parties. The purchaser for value of a legal estate, as we have seen, takes it free from equitable interests of which he had no notice. But the purchaser of an equitable interest in land is subject to existing equitable interests in the same land whether he has notice of them or not. The reason is that every conveyance of an equitable interest is an innocent conveyance in the sense that it conveys only that which the assignor is entitled to convey. Hence, the purchaser of an equitable interest is bound by an earlier equitable interest whether he has notice of it or not. *Qui prior est tempore potior est jure.*[3] On the other hand, the purchaser of an equitable interest is not bound by a mere equity, though prior in point of time, unless he had notice of it when he took his assignment.[4]

To state the distinction in another way: the defence of purchaser for value without notice avails the purchaser of an equitable interest against the owner of an earlier equity, but not against the owner of an earlier equitable interest.

SECTION IV.   SETTLEMENTS.[5]

The desire of the upper classes to order the future destiny of their land and to prevent its sale out of the family, which has been a feature of English social life for many centuries,

Historical importance of settlements.

---

[1] *Infra*, p. 669.

[2] *Phillips* v. *Phillips* (1862), 4 De G. F. & J. at p. 218, *per* Lord WESTBURY; *National Provincial Bank Ltd.* v. *Ainsworth*, [1965] A.C. at pp. 1238, *per* Lord UPJOHN; at 1252–3, *per* Lord WILBERFORCE; 71 *L.Q.R.* 480–3 (R. E. Megarry).

[3] *Phillips* v. *Phillips, supra*, at p. 215; *Cave* v. *Cave* (1880), 15 Ch.D. 639. But see *infra* pp. 637–9, for the modification of this principle by the Law of Property Act, 1925, s. 137 (1).

[4] *Garrard* v. *Frankel* (1862), 30 Beav. 445.

[5] Simpson, *An Introduction to the History of Land Law*, pp. 218–24.

requires attention in any historical survey, since it has decisively affected the form and substance of real property law. The inclination of a fee simple owner, an inclination deeply rooted in parental anxiety and distrust, is to make what is called a *settlement* by which he retains the benefit of ownership during his own life, but withholds the entire ownership in the shape of the fee simple from his descendants for as long as possible by reducing them, one after the other, to the position of mere limited owners. The English doctrine of estates is ideally adapted to the achievement of this object. The fee simple of infinite duration is divisible into shorter periods of time each of which may be allotted successively to a number of persons, with the result that while these periods are running there is no person able to dispose of the entire ownership.

The strict settlement. Settlements in one form or another have been common since at any rate the early thirteenth century,[1] and indeed for some 200 years after the statute *De Donis Conditionalibus* in 1285,[2] it was possible to grant an estate tail that would perforce descend from heir to heir and would permanently remain inconvertible into a fee simple. Although by the end of the fifteenth century means had been contrived to cut short such an impolitic tying-up of the land, by allowing any tenant in tail in possession and of full age to bar the entail and so to acquire the fee simple,[3] the urge to keep the land in the family for as long as the law would permit still persisted, and by the time of the Restoration the general form that the *strict settlement* now assumes had been established. The form of this will be described in detail later, but it is desirable to appreciate its general design even at this early stage in the book if the significance of much of the existing legislation is to be grasped. Suppose, for instance, that a fee simple owner, A., a widower, has decided to use the land as a source of endowment for his only son B., who is about to be married, and for B.'s issue. In such a case the practice for several centuries has been for A. to execute a deed of settlement by which he limits the land

> to himself for life, then to B. for life and then, after making provision for B.'s widow and younger children, to the first and every other son of B. successively in tail.

Under such a settlement the desire of A. to keep the land in the family is at least partly achieved, for the first person able to acquire complete control over the land is the eldest son of B., who may bar the entail and so convert it into a fee simple as soon as he attains his majority. To create a fee simple absolute, however, the disentailment must either be effected by him after he has become entitled

---

[1] *Infra*, p. 154, gifts to a person and a special class of heirs.
[2] *Infra*, p. 155. For the effect of this statute, see Plucknett, *The Legislation of Edward I*, pp. 125–35.
[3] *Infra*, p. 157, common recovery.

in possession on the deaths of A. and B. or, if he desires to act earlier, it must be effected with the collaboration of the present possessor. There is no difficulty, therefore, if he waits until the successive life tenants, A. and B., are dead, for in that case he is tenant in tail in possession and free to act independently. But even while, say, B. is tenant for life in possession, he may join as party to the disentailment and thus enable his son to acquire the fee simple absolute.

This collaboration of life tenant in possession and tenant in tail in remainder—usually of father and son—has consistently been utilized by conveyancers as part of the scheme to prolong the retention of the land in the family. That scheme will, of course, succeed automatically if the eldest son or other heir in each generation refrains throughout his life from barring the entail, for in that event the entailed interest will descend in due course to his own heir. But the danger is that he will wait until he becomes entitled in possession and will then acquire and sell the fee simple. Hence the long established practice of making what is called a *resettlement* by which the eldest son, on the attainment of his majority, is in most cases persuaded to bar the entail with the concurrence of his father and then voluntarily to settle the fee simple thus acquired upon himself for a mere life interest with a further limitation in favour of his own sons successively in tail. This ensures that the land will remain in the family for yet another generation. If, therefore, a resettlement is effected in each generation, the land is held by a succession of limited owners and there is nobody who can claim to be owner of the fee simple.[1]

The device of a re-settlement.

Settlements, as we have said, are of respectable antiquity, but at common law the opportunities of carving up the *legal* fee simple so as to anticipate events that might affect the family in the future were severely restricted, for limitations only of the simplest nature were allowed. The Chancellor, on the other hand, had never imposed restrictions upon limitations of the *equitable* estate. The use might be moulded into any form congenial to its creator and adapted to solve the riddles of the future. The Statute of Uses, therefore, played an important part in the evolution of the strict settlement, an evolution that was complete towards the end of the seventeenth century. The flexibility of the use was imparted to the legal estate by the statute. What was impossible at common law might now be achieved by a single assurance, either a grant to uses or a will. The simple expedient of vesting the legal estate in feoffees with a declaration of the uses to which they were to hold, entitled the beneficiaries to legal interests in the land, as and when their rights matured. The opportunities of a settlor were now greater.

Importance of the Statute of Uses.

For instance, common law did not permit a man to convey a

---

[1] The process of a re-settlement is described *infra*, at p. 127.

freehold estate to himself, nor did it recognize any estate limited to take effect after the grant of a fee simple.[1]

Neither of these rules affected the use and they ceased to affect the legal estate into which the use was converted by the Statute of Uses, if the limitation were made by a grant to uses or by will. The normal method of creating a marriage settlement was for the settlor to grant his fee simple to feoffees to the use of himself in fee simple until the intended marriage, and thereafter to the use of himself for life with remainder to such uses in favour of his wife and issue as his fancy might dictate. Thus, after the statute he acquired a determinable fee simple during the interval between the settlement and the marriage, but on his marriage it was displaced in favour of the subsequent limitations, which were themselves legal.[2]

Again, at common law a freehold estate could not be given to a man to begin at some future date,[3] nor was it permissible to annex to a grant a condition that the freehold should shift from the donee to another person upon the happening of a prescribed event.[4]

Yet, the Chancellor had always protected such limitations of the equitable estate and therefore when uses were statutorily converted into legal estates, a limitation to feoffees to the use of X. when he married (springing use) or to the use of Y. for life, but if he became insolvent then to the use of Z. for life (shifting use), operated to vest a legal estate in X. and Z. upon the occurrence of the prescribed events.

Another innovation of the Chancellor that greatly increased the pliability of settlements was the *power of appointment.* The normal procedure upon the creation of a use was for the feoffor to declare then and there the exact uses to which the land should be held. But such a definitive declaration was not essential. The feoffor might reserve to himself or to a third person a power to declare in the future what uses should arise or to revoke existing uses and substitute new ones in their place. The donee of such a power, who might be a stranger having no proprietary interest, present or future, in the land, was thus enabled before the Statute of Uses to give fresh directions as to the enjoyment of the equitable estate. If, for example, in place of an existing use in favour of A. for life, he *appointed* to the use of B. in tail, the original feoffees immediately stood seised to the use of B. who consequently acquired an equitable estate tail. If the appointment were made after the statute, B. would take a legal estate tail.

Thus, through the machinery of powers, an appointor was able to dispose of an estate that he did not own, and the legal ownership might at his instance be freely shifted and modified to suit exigencies occurring after the date of the settlement.

---

[1] *Infra,* p. 218.   [2] Digby, *History of Real Property,* pp. 357-8.
[3] *Infra,* p. 215-6.   [4] *Infra,* p. 217.

A settlement of land, though it afforded a convenient means of providing for descendants and, when followed by periodic re-settlements, of keeping the land in the family, suffered from three particular disadvantages. It tended to render land inalienable, it might have an adverse effect upon the prosperity of the family and it complicated conveyancing.

Disadvantages of settlements.

Inalienability of Land.—The first of these dangers was inherent in the pliability that the legal estate had inherited from the use. It soon became obvious that, unless some limit of time was imposed upon the power to create future interests, an astute employment of a series of springing and shifting clauses might well render the fee simple inalienable for an unreasonable period. Thus, the general employment in settlements of such devices to create a series of merely limited interests, enduring far into the future, would have starved the market of land to the detriment of the community. The courts have always fought against the creation of inalienable interests and they ultimately destroyed this particular form of the evil by developing what is now called the *rule against perpetuities*. This rule, which will require detailed treatment later, allows a settlor to provide that an estate shall shift to a person or spring up in his favour upon the occurrence of a prescribed contingency, but it ordains that the estate shall be void unless the contingency, if it ever happens at all, will necessarily happen not later than twenty-one years from the death of some person or persons alive when the settlement takes effect.

(i) Might render land inalienable.

Settlements Tended to Impoverish Families. The chief defect inherent in a system of strict settlements and of periodic re-settlements is that at no point of time is there any beneficiary competent to exercise many of the powers of a fee simple owner, unless indeed a right to do so is reserved by the settlement or granted by some statute. The person who under this system has every appearance of being owner is the life tenant in possession, but since his beneficial interest must necessarily determine with his death it follows that any interest granted by him must also determine at that moment. A conveyance by him purporting to pass the fee simple will at common law pass to the grantee nothing more than an estate *pur autre vie*, and a lease for any number of years will automatically determine on his death unless saved by statute or permitted by the settlement. The grave effects resulting from this limited power of alienation in the days when the strict settlement was the foundation of landed society can easily be realized. Given a system whereby it is usual for a fee simple owner, in view of his approaching marriage, to limit the land to himself for life and then to his eldest son in tail, and given further the inclination to re-settle the land in each generation on the eldest son for life, with remainder in tail to *his* eldest son, a moment's reflection will show what a prejudicial

Effect of settlement upon power of alienation.

(ii) Adverse effect on the prosperity of the land.

D*

effect such a perpetual series of life tenants, each devoid of the power to convey the fee simple estate, must have not only on the supply of land available for purposes of trade, but also on the prosperity of the settled land itself.

The common practice, by which the eldest son under a strict settlement was persuaded on reaching his majority to convert his estate tail into a fee simple and then to re-settle the fee simple upon himself for a mere life estate with remainder to his own issue in tail, was stigmatized as follows by a critic some hundred years ago.[1]

" It is commonly supposed that a son acts with his eyes open and with
" a special eye to the contingencies of the future and of family life.
" But what are the real facts of the case ?   Before the future owner of
" the land has come into possession, before he has any experience of
" his property, or of what is best to be done, or what he can do with
" regard to it, before the exigencies of the future or his own real posi-
" tion are known to him, before the character, number and wants of
" his children are learned, or the claims of parental affection and duty
" can make themselves felt, while still very much at the mercy of a
" predecessor desirous of posthumous greatness and power, he enters
" into an irrevocable disposition by which he parts with the rights of
" a proprietor over his future property for ever, and settles its devolu-
" tion, burdened with charges, upon an unborn heir."

No absolute owner under a system of settlement and re-settlement.
Under such a system there never exists, apart from statute, a beneficial owner capable of selling or dealing with the fee simple.   In the words of Sir FREDERICK POLLOCK :—

" The lord of this mansion is named by all men its owner ; it is said
" to belong to him ; the park, the demesne, the farms are called his.
" But we shall be almost safe in assuming that he is not the full and
" free owner of any part of it.   He is a ' limited owner,' having an
" interest only for his own life.   He might have become the full
" owner . . . if he had possessed the means of waiting, the inde-
" pendence of thought and will to break with the tradition of his order
" and the bias of his education, and the energy to persevere in his dissent
" against the counsels and feelings of his family.   But he had every
" inducement to let things go their accustomed way.   Those whom
" he had always trusted told him, and probably with sincere belief,
" that the accustomed way was the best for the family, for the land, for
" the tenant and for the country.   And there could be no doubt that
" it was at the time the most agreeable to himself." [1]

It is clear, in fact, that an uncontrolled system of settlements and re-settlements is an evil—both social and economic—to any country which tolerates it, though it was not one that was apparent to the lawyers of the early nineteenth century.   Thus we find the Real Property Commissioners in their report of 1829 stating:

---

[1] Cliffe Leslie, *Fraser's Magazine*, Feb. 1867, cited Scrutton, *Land in Fetters*, p. 135.
[1] *Land Laws*, p. 9.

" The owner of the soil is, we think, vested with exactly the dominion
" and power of disposition over it required for the public good, and
" landed property in England is admirably made to answer all the
" purposes to which it is applicable. Settlements bestow on the
" present possessor of an estate the benefits of ownership, and secure
" the property to his posterity. . . . In England families are pre-
" served and purchasers always find a supply of land in the market."

This language is specious. It is true in the sense that settled
land could usually be sold in fee simple, because a settlement
might contain, and a well-drawn settlement would contain, powers
enabling the tenant for life to deal with the land by way of sale,
lease, mortgage and so on.[1] If he took advantage of such a power
and for instance sold the land to X., the fact that he was a mere
life tenant was no obstacle to the transfer of the fee simple, for the
feoffees had been directed by the settlement to hold to such uses
as might be appointed by the donee of the power and therefore
they now held to the use of the appointee X. Thus under the
Statute of Uses, X. acquired a legal fee simple. But although the
land could be rendered manageable and saleable by this device, it
happened only too often that powers were either omitted altogether
or were too restricted in character. Speaking broadly, land was
kept in families only at the expense of removing it from commerce
and too often starving it of money necessary for its development
and improvement. No doubt the evil was not so great under the
rural conditions prevalent until the early nineteenth century,
but it became urgent when the vast spread of industrialism produced a demand for coal and other minerals, and converted
England from an agricultural to a trading community. To
appreciate the nature of the problem it is only necessary to
examine the position of a life tenant of settled land in, say, 1835.
This was admirably summed up by UNDERHILL :— [2]

" Unless the will or settlement . . . contained express powers (which
" was frequently not the case) a tenant for life could neither sell, ex-
" change, nor partition the settled property, however desirable it might
" be. If the estate consisted of a large tract of poor country, fruitful
" in dignity but scanty in rent, and specially if the portions of younger
" children charged on it were heavy, he too often found it a *damnosa*
" *hereditas* ; the rents, after payment of interest on the portions,
" leaving a mere pittance for the unfortunate life tenant to live on, and
" quite disabling him from making improvements, or even keeping
" the property in a decent state of repair. Nay more, if he did spend
" money in improvements the money was sunk in the estate to the
" detriment of his younger children. He could not pull down the
" mansion-house however old or inconvenient it might be, nor even
" strictly make any substantial alterations in it. Unless expressly
" made unimpeachable for waste he could not open new mines. But
" in addition to these disabilities, what pressed still more hardly upon

---

[1] For a seventeenth-century precedent, see Holdsworth, *op. cit.*, vol. vii
p. 547
[2] *Century of Law Reform*, pp. 284-5.

" him and on the development of the estate generally, was his in-
" ability to make long leases.[1] Consequently when valuable minerals
" lay beneath a settled property, or the growth of the neighbouring
" town made it ripe for building sites (the rents for which would
" greatly exceed the agricultural rents), nothing could lawfully be
" done. The tenant for life could not open mines himself, even if
" he had the necessary capital for working them, nor, even if unim-
" peachable for waste, could he grant leases of them to others for a
" term which would repay the lessees for the necessary expenditure
" in pits and plant, nor could he grant building leases or sell for building
" purposes at fee farm rents. In some settlements powers were ex-
" pressly inserted, enabling the trustees to grant such leases and to
" sell, exchange and partition. But frequently, especially in wills,
" such powers were omitted, and in such cases the only means of doing
" justice to the land was to apply for a private Act of Parliament
" authorizing the trustees or life tenant to sell, exchange, partition or
" lease. But such Acts were expensive luxuries, only open to the
" rich, and beyond the means of most country gentlemen of moderate
" means."

Statutory Reform. When, however, the modern industrial
era set in, the legislature took the matter in hand, and in a tentative
manner began to pass a series of public Acts of Parliament which
enabled settled land to be dealt with in a manner likely to enhance
its prosperity.   A start was made in the 'forties with statutes
which empowered tenants for life to borrow money for the
purpose of carrying out permanent drainage improvements and
to charge the loan on the inheritance.   Then the Improvement
of Land Act, 1864, enabled a tenant for life to raise money with
the consent of the Ministry of Agriculture in order to execute
certain specified improvements, and to charge the loan on the
corpus of the property.[2]   Further examples were the Limited
Owners Residences Acts, 1870 and 1871, which allowed money
to be raised for completing or adding to a mansion-house ; and
the Limited Owners Reservoir Act, 1877, which sanctioned the
same method for the construction of permanent waterworks.

But in 1856 the much more important Settled Estates Act had
been passed which contained the germ of all the future legislation on the subject.   Its object was to facilitate leases and sales
of settled estates, and after being amended by several statutes in
the succeeding generation, it was replaced in 1877 by the Settled
Estates Act of that year.   This allowed the Chancery Division
of the High Court to sanction the sale, exchange or partition
of the settled land, and the grant of leases of 21 years for an
agricultural or occupation lease, 40 years for a mining lease,
and 99 years for a building lease.   It also allowed the tenant
for life without resorting to the court to make a valid lease up

Disad-
vantages
gradually
eliminated
by statute.

Early Acts.

Settled
Estates Act,
1877.

---

[1] A tenant *in tail*, however, was empowered by the Fines and Recoveries
Act. 1833. s. 41, to grant a lease for a term not exceeding 21 years.
[2] *Infra*, p. 560.

to a period of 21 years. So this Act made great strides towards permitting all opportunities for the proper development of the land to be seized, but its weakness was that, except in the case of short leases, its enabling powers could not be exercised without an order of the court. It had in truth facilitated dealings, since it substituted an order of the court for a private Act of Parliament, but it stopped short of placing the powers unreservedly in the hands of the tenant for life.

About this time an agitation sprang up for the total abolition of life estates and the restriction of grants to the creation of a fee simple, the argument being that settlements, besides making conveyances difficult and costly, deprived a father of a much-needed power of control over his eldest son, and prevented an estate from being thrown on the market when its poverty made such a course desirable. For better or for worse the argument did not prevail. It was realized that settlements enabled a fair and reasonable provision to be made for all the members of a family, and therefore, while the general features of the time-honoured system were retained, a plan was evolved to prevent settled land from becoming an inert mass through lack of capital or of adequate powers of management.[1] *Agitation to abolish settlements.*

The Settled Land Act, 1882. The principle adopted by Lord Cairns and incorporated in the famous Settled Land Act of 1882 was to put the entire management of the land into the hands of the tenant for life for the time being, and to give him, at his own sole discretion and without asking the permission of the court or the trustees of the settlement, wide powers of selling, leasing, mortgaging and otherwise dealing with the property. These powers were independent of, and could not be restrained by, the settlement itself, but they were subject to certain statutory provisions designed to protect the interests of all persons entitled under the settlement, and to prevent the tenant from acquiring more than a life interest in the income or profits. *New era opened with Settled Land Act, 1882.*

The objects of the Act were lucidly explained by CHITTY, L.J., in the following words [2] :—

> " The object is to make land a marketable object notwithstanding
> " the settlement. Its main purpose is the welfare of the land itself
> " and of all interested therein, including the tenants and not merely
> " the persons taking under the settlement. The Act of 1882 had
> " a much wider scope than the Settled Estates Act. The scheme
> " adopted is to facilitate the striking off from the land of fetters im-
> " posed by settlements ; and this is accomplished by conferring on
> " *tenants for life in possession* and others considered to stand in a like
> " relation to the land large powers of dealing with it by way of sale,
> " exchange, lease and otherwise, and by jealously guarding those
> " powers from attempts to defeat them or to hamper their exercise.

---

[1] *Century of Law Reform,* pp. 287–90.
[2] *Re Mundy and Roper's Contract,* [1899] 1 Ch. 275, 288.

" At the same time the rights of persons claiming under the settle-
" ment are carefully preserved in the case of a sale by shifting the
" settlement from the land to the purchase money, which has to be
" paid into court or into the hands of the trustees."

The Act of 1882 was amended in small particulars by further
statutes passed in 1884, 1887, 1889, and 1890, but its policy has
stood the test of time, and though it has now been repealed and
replaced by the Settled Land Act, 1925, its general principles still
continue to govern the rights and the liabilities of a tenant for life
under a strict settlement.

(iii) Settle-
ments
raised a con-
veyancing
difficulty.

Complication of Conveyancing. The third disadvantage
of a settlement—its aggravation of the complexity of conveyancing
—became evident when a tenant for life, by virtue of a power
conferred upon him, had agreed to sell the fee simple to a purchaser. In this event, he would prove the title down to the date
of the settlement in the normal fashion by tracing the history of
the land back to a good root of title, in order to show that the fee
simple was owned by the original settlor. So far there was nothing
abnormal, but at this point arose the difficulty that the vendor
himself did not own the estate that he had contracted to sell. His
case would be, of course, that as tenant for life under a settlement
he possessed a power, conferred upon him either by the settlement itself or after 1882 by the Settled Land Act, to convey the
fee simple. The general rule on this matter is that the exercise
of a power, whether it is given by act of parties or by statute, is
void unless all the conditions imposed by the instrument or statute
from which it derives are literally observed. If attention is concentrated on a sale after 1882, the governing factors in this
respect were that the Act of that year empowered a tenant for
life under a settlement to convey a good title to the fee simple,
provided that the purchase money was paid to the trustees. In
other words, before the statutory power of sale or any other
statutory power was validly exercisable, it was essential that, *within
the meaning of the Act,*

the instrument under which the vendor held was a " settlement " ;
the vendor himself was a " tenant for life " or one of the persons to
whom the statutory powers were given ;
the trustees were properly constituted.

In order, therefore, to verify that these conditions were
satisfied, it was necessary for the original deed of settlement and,
in fact, several further deeds if there had been one or more
re-settlements, to be abstracted by the vendor and investigated by
the purchaser. Moreover, the family rights, which in the normal
form of settlement were legal, not equitable,[1] came on the title

---

[1] After the re-introduction of the use in the form of the trust (*supra*,
pp. 55-8) it was, of course, possible to create a strict settlement by the
alternative method of a grant unto and to the use of trustees to hold the legal
estate upon the requisite trusts, in which case the beneficiaries would be
entitled to merely equitable interests.

to the fee simple, and in his own protection the purchaser would be concerned to ascertain whether any member of the family had assigned his beneficial interest to a third party, for if so no valid title to the fee simple could be transferred without the concurrence of the assignee. Thus, in order to satisfy himself that a good title would be made, the purchaser was confronted with the formidable task of scrutinizing a series of transactions and documents stretching back perhaps for very many years.

Trust for Sale.—So far we have concentrated attention upon the strict settlement, but an entirely different way of apply-ing the principle of the settlement to land was by means of a trust for sale, a method that has been common in wills for some 500 years and in deeds since the early nineteenth century.[1] This transac-tion, which has now almost supplanted the strict settlement, falls into two parts and, though not strictly necessary, it is usually effected by two separate deeds. If, for instance, it precedes the marriage of the settlor: The trust for sale.

> The first deed in its opening clause conveys the fee simple to the trustees upon trust (with the consent of the husband until the intended marriage, and after the marriage with the consent of the husband or wife or of the survivor, and after the death of the survivor at the discretion of the trustees), to sell the said fee simple. Conveyance to the trustees.
>
> The second clause of the deed directs the trustees to hold the money arising from the sale and the rents and profits accruing prior to the sale upon such trusts as are declared by a deed already engrossed and made between the same parties and on the same date as the present deed.[2]

According to the equitable doctrine of conversion the effect of the execution of this deed is that in the eyes of equity the land is immediately converted into money, for that doctrine, based on the principle that equity looks on that as done which ought to be done, insists that an imperative direction to turn land into money shall impress the land with the quality of money no matter how long the sale may [be postponed.[3] The important point to notice, therefore, is that a trust for sale relating to the fee simple and containing a succession of beneficial limitations is a settlement of personalty, not of realty.

> The second deed sets out the beneficial trusts of the personalty into which the realty has already been notionally converted. It will usually provide in the first place that the income, whether arising from the invested purchase money or from the rents and profits prior to the sale, shall be held in trust for the husband during his life and after his death in trust for his wife if she survives him. Secondly, it will provide that after the death of the husband and wife the capital shall be divided among the children or remoter issue of the marriage in such shares as the husband and wife or the survivor shall appoint, and, failing appointment, among the children equally.[4] Declaration of the beneficial interests.

---

[1] 3 *Cambridge Law Journal*, p. 63.
[2] See Burnett, *Elements of Conveyancing* (8th Edn.), pp. 455–6.
[3] *Fletcher* v. *Ashburner* (1779), 1 Bro. C. C. 497. The reverse is also true.
[4] Burnett. *op. cit.*, pp. 456–8.

The investigation of title upon a sale by the trustees raises none of the exceptional difficulties that, as we have already seen, formerly attended a sale by a tenant for life under a strict settlement. According to the long established conveyancing practice, the beneficial trusts of the money are kept off the title to the fee simple in the sense that they are not disclosed to the purchaser, whose main preoccupation is merely to ascertain that the settlor was entitled to the fee simple that was conveyed to the trustees. He is not responsible for the proper application of the money, provided that he pays it to at least two trustees. The beneficiaries must now look to the trustees and to them alone. This was not always so. In earlier days it was considered that the purchaser, since he had notice of the existence of beneficial limitations, was bound to see that the money was applied in accordance with the trust,[1] and it therefore became the usual practice to insert a clause in the first deed authorizing the trustees to give the purchaser a receipt exonerating him from liability in this respect. This has been made unnecessary, however, by a series of statutes dating from 1859,[2] which are now represented by the following:

> The receipt in writing of a trustee for any money . . . payable to him under any trust or power shall be a sufficient discharge to the person paying . . . the same and shall effectively exonerate him from seeing to the application or being answerable for any loss or misapplication thereof.[3]

Device of trust for sale extended in 1925. It will be seen later that in 1925, the legislature, impressed by the advantages that this form of settlement imparted to the practice of conveyancing, made it the basis of several of the reforms introduced in that year. In particular, it was by extending the machinery and principle of the trust for sale that the law relating to strict settlements[4] and to tenancies in common[5] was strikingly simplified.

SECTION V. THE SIMPLIFICATION OF THE LAW IN 1925.

SUMMARY.

---

[1] Vaizey, *The Law of Settlements of Property*, pp. 1409–12.
[2] Law of Property Amendment Act, 1859, s. 23 ; Conveyancing Act, 1881, s. 36 ; Trustee Act, 1893, s. 20.
[3] Trustee Act, 1925, s. 14 (1).
[4] *Supra*, pp. 79–80 ; *infra*, p. 705 *et seq.*   [5] *Infra*, p. 312

Introductory Note.—Even as late as the conclusion of the war of 1914 there were many features of the land law which seemed unnecessarily cumbrous and antiquated to a generation that, for the moment at any rate, considered itself destined to effect a general simplification of life.　There was certainly much in the fundamentals of the subject that would seem strange to an impartial critic.　Thus land was the subject of tenure, not of ownership, but instead of there being one common form of tenure with incidents of universal application, there were the two distinct forms of socage and copyhold, with various divergent offshoots such as gavelkind and borough-English.　This division of tenures, which led to differences in the ordinary incidents of ownership and in the modes of conveyance, was complicated by a cross-division under which estates were classified as being either freehold or leasehold.　The main object of the legislation of 1925 was the simplification of conveyancing, and the committee that was appointed to suggest alterations was instructed by its terms of reference " to consider the present position of land transfer, and to advise what action should be taken to *facilitate and cheapen the transfer of land.*"　It was found, however, that a necessary preliminary to the attainment of this object was the simplification of the law of real property.　It is scarcely possible to modernize a system of transfer if the subject-matter of the transfer is itself governed by effete and antiquated rules.　An analysis of the legislation of 1925, therefore, requires us to consider how it simplified, first the law of real property, and then the system of conveyancing.

Complications resulting from tenures.

A. SIMPLIFICATION OF THE LAW OF REAL PROPERTY.

In 1925 land was subject, not to one system, but to three systems of law.　This surprising result was caused by the distinction between freeholds and chattels real,[1] and by the existence of two forms of tenure—socage and copyhold.　The law of real property strictly so-called, which governed freehold interests in land, was still different in several respects from that which governed chattels real.　Furthermore, whether the interest enjoyed by a proprietor were a freehold or a chattel real, the land affected would be held either by socage or by copyhold tenure.　This was an added complication, since in several important respects the rules governing socage and copyhold lands were divergent.　There was thus a law of freeholds, a law of leaseholds and a law of copyholds.　The obvious solution, therefore, and the one adopted by the legislature, was first to institute one common form of tenure by the abolition of copyhold ; then to assimilate as far as practicable the law of real property and of chattels real ;

Three systems of land law before 1926.

---

[1] *Supra,* pp. 36–9.

finally, to abolish certain anachronisms of the common law—irritating survivals that were inimical to a simplified legal system. We will consider these three improvements separately.

(1) THE REDUCTION OF TENURES TO ONE COMMON FORM.

Classes of tenure gradually reduced.

History of Simplification of Tenures.—The account that we have already given of tenure shows that for a long period there has been a gradual but continuous reduction in the number of possible tenures. This process was far advanced before 1926, but in that year uniformity was at last attained.

Six hundred years ago the law on this subject was complicated. In the time of Edward I there were four distinct and important varieties of tenure, distinguished from each other by the different kinds of services due and each exhibiting fundamental differences in the substantive rule of law to which they were subject.[1]   This led to the growth of a mass of confused and intricate law, and it was only by slow degrees that simplification began to emerge.

Statute *Quia Emptores*.

The Statute *Quia Emptores*, 1290, though it was not concerned with the actual reduction of the several varieties, at least stemmed the increasing confusion, since it forbade the creation of any further tenures within each variety. The introduction of the doctrine of *uses* led indirectly to a decline in the importance of tenures, for the relationship of lord and tenant would lose much of its value and significance if it was freed from those tenurial incidents the avoidance of which was one of the chief inducements to put land in use.

Statute of Uses.

The Statute of Uses, on the other hand, was a retrograde step in the process of simplification, though it was only for a time that it restored the importance of tenures. Before another century had passed the King no longer looked to the feudal incidents for a revenue, while the country as a whole evinced a desire to regain the advantages which had disappeared with the abolition of uses, and to be rid of the burdensome incidents that were a feature of the law of tenures.

Statute 12 Car. II, c. 24.

In fact, even before the ultimate re-establishment of uses in the seventeenth century the first direct simplification of tenures was effected by the Statute for the Abolition of Military Tenures in 1660.   The effect of this Act was the reduction of tenures to socage, copyhold and frankalmoin, though the honorary incidents of grand sergeanty were retained, and various customary modes of holding land, such as gavelkind, borough-English and ancient demesne, continued to exist in certain parts of the country.   In effect only two important tenures remained—namely, socage and copyhold.

Copyhold tenure a hindrance to conveyancing.

The position, then, long before 1925, showed a vast improvement upon that of the time of Edward I, but, as we have already seen, the continued existence of copyhold as a distinct tenure not

---

[1] *Supra*, pp. 16 *et seq*.

only disturbed the simplicity of conveyancing, but also tended to embarrass the full exploitation of the land.[1] Not only did the form of conveyance vary according as the land was socage or copyhold, but, what was a far more serious blemish, such legal incidents as the mode of descent and the types of interest creatable often differed from those recognized by the general law. In this respect, indeed, there was not even a system of law common to all copyholds, for the actual customs upon which the legal incidents were dependent frequently varied from manor to manor. There was thus room for reform in this particular field of law, and the opportunity was seized by the legislature.

All previous modes of descent, whether operating by the general law or by the custom of gavelkind or borough-English or by any other custom of any county, locality or manor, were abrogated.[2] Escheat[3] *propter defectum sanguinis* was discarded and replaced by the right of the Crown to take as *bona vacantia* the interest of a tenant who died intestate and heirless.[4] The honorary services incident to tenure by sergeanty, where they still existed, were expressly reserved, but the tenure itself had already disappeared.[5] An attempt was also made to abolish frankalmoin, though whether it succeeded is doubtful. The Statute of 1660, which by its first section abolished knight service, provided in s. 7 that nothing in the first section was to affect frankalmoin. The Administration of Estates Act, 1925, instead of abolishing frankalmoin by express language, merely repealed s. 7 of the Statute of 1660.[6] This repeal, however, would appear to be fruitless, for even if the seventh section had been omitted from the Statute, frankalmoin would have been unaffected by an enactment that merely abolished knight service. The matter is indeed of little importance, for no land can be held by frankalmoin at the present day unless it has been continuously so held by the same ecclesiastical tenant since before *Quia Emptores*, 1290.[7] Finally and at long last, the decisive step was taken of abolishing copyhold tenure. As from January 1st, 1926, every parcel of copyhold land was enfranchised and converted into freehold land held by socage tenure.[8]

[margin note: Abolition of all tenures except socage.]

Extinguishment of Manorial Incidents. It was realized, of course, that copyhold tenure could not be dismissed in this peremptory manner, for certain manorial incidents had long been associated with it, and to extinguish without compensation such of those as possessed a money value would obviously be unjust

[margin note: Features of old law of copyholds. Manorial incidents.]

---

[1] *Supra*, p. 26
[2] Administration of Estates Act, 1925, s. 45 (1) (a).
[3] *Supra*, p. 26.
[4] Administration of Estates Act, 1925, s. 45 (1) (d).
[5] Law of Property Act, 1922, s. 136.
[6] 2nd Schedule. [7] *Supra*, p. 21, note 1.
[8] Law of Property Act, 1922, Part V, ss. 128–137, and 12th Schedule as amended by Law of Property (Amendment) Act, 1924, s. 2 and 2nd Schedule ; Law of Property Act, 1922, s. 189.

to the beneficiary, whether lord or copyholder. The solution adopted was based upon a tripartite classification of these incidents.

The first class, consisting of those that had become anachronisms were extinguished immediately without compensation.[1]

Manorial incidents of pecuniary value. The second class consisted of those incidents that still possessed a money value. These were temporarily saved,[2] but it was provided that they should be extinguished upon the payment of compensation, the amount of which was to be determined either by agreement or by the Minister of Agriculture and Fisheries at the instance of either party. The final date of extinction was to be December 31st, 1935, though if by then no agreement upon the amount of compensation had been reached either party might apply to the Minister requiring the amount to be determined, provided that the application was made before December 31st, 1940. Owing to the war, this was later extended to November 1st, 1950.[3]

Manorial incidents that still continue. The following incidents, falling within the third class, were permanently saved and they continue to attach to the land, unless the parties agree to their extinction upon payment of compensation.[4]

(a) Any commonable rights to which the tenant is entitled.[5]

(b) Any right of the lord or the tenant to mines, minerals, gravel, pits or quarries, whether in or under the land.[6]

(c) Any rights of the lord in respect of fairs, markets or sporting.[7]

(d) Any liability for the construction, maintenance, cleansing or repair of any dykes, ditches, canals, sea or river walls, bridges, levels, ways, etc.[7]

Unimportance of doctrine of tenure. Thus, after some 800 years of development the doctrine of tenure still characterizes the English law of real property. Land is still incapable of ownership by a subject. Every acre is held by a tenant, not owned, though by a gradual process of extermination the various forms of tenure that complicated the law in former days have at last been reduced to the one type—socage. But what are the practical effects of the doctrine? Are the rights that the English tenant in fee simple enjoys any less

---

[1] Law of Property Act, 1922, 12th Schedule (1); forfeiture for an alienation without the lord's licence; liability of the copyholder to customary suits and to do fealty; customary modes of descent or any custom relating to dower (*infra*, p. 792), curtesy (*infra*, p. 161) or freebench (Blackstone, II. p. 337).

[2] Law of Property Act, 1922, s. 128 (2): *rents*; *fines* payable to the lord in certain circumstances, *reliefs* payable to the lord upon descent of the land; *heriots*, the right of the lord to seize the best beast or best chattel upon the tenant's decease; *forfeitures* for a variety of acts by the tenant; the right of the lord to fell *timber* trees.

[3] S.I. 1949, No. 836.

[4] Law of Property Act, 1922, s. 138 (12).   [5] *Ibid.*, 12th Schedule (4).

[6] *Ibid.*, 12th Schedule (5).   [7] *Ibid.*, 12th Schedule (6).

valuable, for instance, than those of an absolute owner of land in the State of New York where all feudal tenures have been expressly abolished ? Is tenure a mere name, a reminder only of the pomp and splendour of former days ? The truth is, of course, that it is a mere historical survival that now has little practical effect. To have styled the tenant a landowner some centuries ago would have been inaccurate, since his very right to retain the land was conditioned on his performance of the tenurial liabilities. But in course of time these liabilities have almost entirely disappeared, and it is only on the rarest occasion that anything of value can now be claimed by virtue of tenure. Until 1926, indeed, a lord, if he were still able to establish his lordship, might be fortunate enough to derive an unearned increment under the doctrine of escheat, but he lost even this vague *spes successionis* when the Administration of Estates Act provided that the land of a tenant who dies intestate without leaving near relatives shall pass to the State. Even in such a non-feudal State as New York it is difficult to see to whom else it can pass. The feudal doctrine of tenure has no doubt impressed an indelible mark upon the framework of the law, but it no longer affects the tenant's rights of enjoyment, though the modern tendency to stress the rights of the community at large has resulted in the imposition of restrictions upon him that were unknown to earlier ages. The living results of feudalism must be sought, not in the realm of tenures, but in that classification of estates which is a peculiarity of English law. Apart from this " wonderful calculus of estates," as Maitland expressed it, perhaps the sole feudal incident that is a living force at the present day consists of those rights of common which the successors of the copyhold lord and tenant may still hold in the manorial waste. To quote Maitland again :—

Few living results of tenure.

> " Everyone knows that this doctrine [of tenure], however indis-
> " pensable as an explanation for some of the subtleties of real pro-
> " perty law, is in fact untrue. ' The first thing the student has to
> " do is to get rid of the idea of absolute ownership.' So says Mr.
> " Williams [1] ; but we may add with equal truth, that the second
> " thing he has to do is to learn how, by slow degrees, the statement
> " that there is no absolute ownership of land has been deprived of
> " most of its important consequences." [2]

If this was true in 1880 when Maitland wrote, how unsubstantial must the doctrine of tenure be after the abolition of copyholds.

(2) The Assimilation of Real and Personal Property Law.

Originally, as we have seen, there were wide distinctions between the law of real and of personal property, but there has

Tendency to unify law of realty and personalty.

---

[1] Williams, *The Law of Real Property* (12th Edn.), p. 17.
[2] Maitland, *Collected Papers*, vol. i. p. 196. See also Challis, *Law of Real Property* (3rd Edn.), p. 3.

been a tendency ever since an early age to make both these departments of the law subject to the same legal rules, and in the main the rules that have been adopted are those that govern personal property. Thus the legislation of 1925 essayed to complete a process of assimilation that was already far advanced. We shall perhaps gain a greater clearness of view if we first consider in what particulars a common body of legal rules had been created before 1926, and then review the contents of the statutes designed to procure as complete a unification as possible.

(i) Matters in which Assimilation had been effected prior to 1926.

(*a*) **Remedies for Dispossession.** The original rule that leaseholds, unlike freeholds, were not specifically recoverable [1] ceased to be true towards the middle of the fifteenth century, by which time the action *ejectione firmae* was available to the termor. The actions that lay for recovery were still, indeed, different according as the demandant's interest was freehold or leasehold, but complete assimilation in this particular was attained in the seventeenth century, by which time the *ejectione firmae* had been borrowed from the law of chattels real and, under the name of the action of ejectment, had been adapted to the recovery of freeholds. [2]

Remedies assimilated in 17th century.

(*b*) **The Power of Testamentary Disposition.** It was always possible to bequeath leaseholds and other forms of personal property, but the feudal law would not admit a will of freeholds. A partial power of testamentary disposition over real property was obtained, however, in 1540, when the Statute of Wills permitted tenants to devise all their socage lands and two-thirds of their land held in knight service. This testamentary power was completed by the Statute for the Abolition of Military Tenures in 1660,[3] which converted knight service tenure into free and common socage.

Assimilation in 1660.

(*c*) **Availability of Property for Creditors.** The history of this is given below,[4] but we may state here that while at an early date leaseholds and other forms of personal property belonging to a deceased debtor constituted assets available for all creditors, the general rule was that a fee simple estate passed directly to the heir or devisee of a deceased tenant and could not be seized by his creditors. Gradual inroads upon this immunity of real property were, however, made by statute and by equity, and assimilation was almost attained in 1833, when the Adminis-

Original immunity of realty.

Deceased debtor.

---

[1] *Supra*, p. 37.
[2] Holdsworth, *History of English Law*, vol. vii. pp. 4 *et seq.*
[3] 12 Car. II, c. 24.   [4] *Infra*, pp. 740–5.

tration of Estates Act made all land belonging to a deceased debtor available as assets for the one class of creditors—namely, simple contract creditors—who had not already obtained a remedy against freeholds. There was, however, still a difference in respect of remedies, for to render personal property available a creditor had to proceed against the personal representatives, while to satisfy his claim against real property, which did not vest in the personal representatives, he had to bring a suit in equity for administration. Assimilation on this point came with the Land Transfer Act, 1897, which provided that realty should vest in the personal representatives, as had always been the practice with personalty.

The law that regulated the right of a creditor to seize the land of his *living* debtor was also assimilated before 1926. At common law all the chattels, real and personal, of a judgment debtor might be seized, but there was no right to satisfaction out of his freeholds. The Statute of Westminster, 1285, made half the debtor's land available for creditors, and this was extended to the whole of the land by the Judgments Act of 1838.[1]

Living debtor.

(ii) Matters in which Assimilation was effected by the Legislation of 1925.

The process of assimilation was carried further by the legislation of 1925 in the following respects.

(a) The Size and Nature of Estates and Interests.
Before 1926 there was a fundamental distinction between realty and personalty with regard to the interests that might be created.

In the case of real property it has been possible for many centuries to create not only legal and equitable estates of different sizes—namely, the fee simple, the estate tail and the life estate— but also to split the full fee simple up into a series of partial and successive legal or equitable interests, as for example by a grant to A. for life, then to B. in tail, and then to C. in fee simple.

Interests in real property.

The position with regard to personal property was different. Pure personalty (goods and money) and chattels real (such as an unexpired lease for 20 years) were *at common law* the subjects of absolute ownership only. They were outside the doctrine of estates altogether and they could not be divided into successive interests. A grant of an existing term of years to A. for life or in tail made A. at common law the owner of the entire term. A gift for an hour was a gift for ever. The position *in equity* was slightly

Interests in personal property at common law.

Interests in personal property in equity.

---

[1] *Infra*, pp. 726–7.

different, for to a limited extent equity did permit successive interests to be created in personalty if the device of a grant to trustees was adopted. If the owner of a leasehold for 30 years granted it to trustees

upon trust for A. for life and then upon trust for B. for life,

A. did not become absolute owner of the whole term as he would have done at common law, but held merely for life, while on his death B. similarly became entitled to a life estate. The interests both of A. and of B. were of course equitable. There was one method, however, though it was seldom used, by which even at common law an effective life estate might be given in personalty— namely, by will. Without adopting the instrument of a trust a testator might make a direct bequest of a leasehold

to A. for life with a further gift to B. for life,

and the bequests would be upheld. But it is important to observe that under the old law it was impossible to create an estate tail in leaseholds either by a direct bequest or through the instrumentality of trustees. A term of years, not being an estate of inheritance, could not be entailed.[1]

Summary of old law. A summary of the old law of the subject is, then, that in real property there might be legal or equitable fees simple, estates tail or life interests, either alone or in succession, but that in personal property there was normally only absolute ownership, though there might be equitable and, exceptionally, legal life interests.

Assimilation in 1926. Assimilation, as regards both the size of the interests creatable and their nature when created, was, however, effected in 1925 by the Law of Property Act. In the first place, this provides that personalty may be entailed.[2] The result is that the nature of the subject-matter no longer affects the quantitative interest that may be carved out of it. In realty there may be a fee simple estate, in personalty absolute ownership; while in both cases either entailed interests or life interests may validly be created. Secondly, as we shall see later,[3] entailed and life interests, whether in real or in personal property, can no longer exist as legal estates, but must always be equitable. Moreover, it is no longer possible to have a future *legal* estate in freeholds.

Realty and personalty subject to different intestacy rules. (b) **Descent on Intestacy.** Perhaps the most striking difference between realty and personalty in 1925 lay in the rules that regulated their descent or distribution upon the death of

---

[1] *Leventhorpe* v. *Ashbie* (1635), 1 Roll. Abr. 831.
[2] Law of Property Act, 1925, s. 130 (1) ; *infra*, p. 174.
[3] *Ibid.*, s. 1 (1), (2), (3), *infra*, p. 94.

the owner intestate. The old canons of descent, based upon feudal doctrines as amended by statute, governed the descent of fee simple and entailed estates, while the Statutes of Distribution contained a different set of rules prescribing what relatives were entitled to share the leaseholds and personal chattels of the deceased. Both these systems, together with various customary modes of descent, have been abolished and new distributive rules have been introduced which apply to both real and personal property.[1] The old canons of descent have, however, been retained for entailed interests.

(*c*) **The Order in which Assets were applied in payment of debts.** It is essential that definite rules shall prescribe the order in which the beneficiaries under a will must be deprived of their interests for the benefit of the unpaid creditors of the testator. The old rules on this matter represented another difference between real and personal property, for they required the exhaustion of the general personal estate before recourse was had to the realty. The old rules have now been replaced by fresh statutory provisions which, from this point of view, have put realty and personalty on the same footing.[2]

(*d*) **The Necessity for Words of Limitation.** A conveyance which was intended to pass the whole fee simple had under the old law to contain technical words of limitation, namely, to A. *and his heirs* or to A. *in fee simple*, otherwise it operated to pass only a life estate. Such words were not necessary in the case of a transfer of leaseholds ; a simple grant to A., without more, was sufficient to transfer the whole interest of the grantor. Assimilation on this point, however, was effected by the Law of Property Act, 1925,[3] which provides that a conveyance of freehold land without words of limitation shall pass the whole interest held by the grantor unless a contrary intention appears in the conveyance.

(*e*) **The Method of creating Legal Mortgages.** The method of creating a legal mortgage of the fee simple before 1926 was by a conveyance of the legal fee simple to the mortgagee with a proviso that he should re-convey the estate upon repayment of the loan ; but where the subject-matter of the mortgage was a leasehold interest, the almost universal practice was for the mortgagor to grant a sub-lease of the property to the mortgagee.

---

[1] Administration of Estates Act, 1925, ss. 45, 46, as amended by the Intestates' Estate Act, 1952 ; *infra*, p. 772.
[2] Administration of Estates Act, 1925, s. 34 (3) ; 1st Schedule, Part II ; *infra*, p. 729.
[3] S. 60 (1) ; *infra*, p. 115.

This particular difference between freeholds and leaseholds has now disappeared, for the practice of conveying the fee simple is forbidden, and it is enacted that a legal mortgage of freeholds must be made by the grant of a lease or its equivalent.[1]

(*f*) **The Application of the Rule in Dearle *v.* Hall.**   If successive assignments or mortgages of an *equitable* interest in property were made before 1926, the order in which the several assignees or mortgagees were entitled to repayment out of the property depended upon the nature of the property.   If it was land, whether freehold or leasehold, they ranked for payment according to the order of time in which they had taken their assignment or mortgage; but if it was pure personalty, the rule in *Dearle* v. *Hall*[2] applied, and the priorities were governed by the order of time in which the assignments or mortgages had been notified to the trustees of the personalty.   This rule now applies to equitable interests in land, so that a later assignee who is the first to notify the estate owner of the land affected ranks prior to an earlier assignment of which he had no notice when he took his own assignment.[3]

Rule in Dearle v. Hall.

Conclusion.   The above review of those differences between realty and personalty that were eradicated by the legislation of 1925 shows that the law relating to the two forms of property has been assimilated as far as is possible.   Certain differences must, of course, inevitably persist.   For instance, easements and profits may subsist in land, but not in pure personalty ; time under the Limitation Act varies according as the subject-matter is realty or personalty ; the forms of alienation are different ; so is the procedure on alienation, for investigation of title, though not usual in the case of personalty, is essential upon the transfer of an interest in land ; but it would seem that most of the divergences which industry may still detect must always in the nature of things continue to exist, since they result inevitably from the physical difference between the two forms of property.

Remaining differences between realty and personalty.

(3) THE ABOLITION OF CERTAIN ANACHRONISMS.

Anachronisms abolished.

A subsidiary part of the simplification of land transfer was the abolition of certain real property rules and doctrines which, though they had originally been introduced to preserve principles of importance in feudal days, were nothing more than obstructive anachronisms in 1925.   The abolitions and alterations of this

---

[1] *Infra,* pp. 551 *et seq.*
[2] *Dearle* v. *Hall* (1828), 3 Russ. 1.
[3] Law of Property Act, 1925, s. 137 ; *infra,* pp. 637 *et seq.*

character effected by the various Acts will be fully described later, and we shall therefore content ourselves for the moment with a mere enumeration of those that are the most important.

(i) The abolition of the rule in *Shelley's Case.*[1]

(ii) The indirect abolition of the old contingent remainder rules.[2]

(iii) The abolition of the rule in *Whitby* v. *Mitchell.*[3]

(iv) The almost complete abolition of the old canons of descent.[4]

(v) The final abolition of the doctrine of *Dumpor's Case* so far as it related to leases.[5]

(vi) The reversal of the rule that husband and wife were not always two persons for the purposes of the acquisition of land.[6]

(vii) The abolition of special occupancy.[7]

B. THE SIMPLIFICATION OF CONVEYANCING: THE CULT OF THE ESTATE OWNER

Until the present system of private conveyancing is replaced by State registration of title, a purchaser must rely on his own exertions to satisfy himself on two matters—first, that the vendor is entitled to convey the estate which he has contracted to sell; secondly, that there are no incumbrances in favour of third parties that will continue to affect the land after the conveyance. The legislation of 1925 made no fundamental alteration in the practice relating to the former matter, but devoted its main attention to the question of incumbrances. In the normal case there will be no undisclosed incumbrances, but nevertheless the doctrine of constructive notice exists and a purchaser dare not do otherwise than institute an expensive inquiry. His danger is obvious. Land is different from such subjects of ownership as goods, since more often than not it is affected by rights vested in parties other than the ostensible owner.

Peter may appear to be absolute unincumbered tenant in fee simple of Blackacre, but investigation may disclose that James has an easement of way over the land, that John is

---

[1] *Infra,* p. 169.
[3] *Infra,* pp. 236–7; 239–40
[5] *Infra,* pp. 383–4
[7] *Infra,* p. 185, note 1.

[2] *Infra,* pp. 230–3.
[4] *Infra,* pp. 787–9.
[6] *Infra,* pp. 865–6

entitled to a yearly rentcharge of £50 out of it, that Matthew has a right to prevent the erection of buildings upon it, or that Paul, having lent £500 to Peter, has taken an equitable charge upon Blackacre as security for repayment of the loan.

The power to create rights of this description in favour of third parties, and enforceable primarily against the land itself rather than against its owner, is a valuable, in fact an inevitable, feature of our social life. For the sake of brevity, we will describe them in future as third party rights.

Classifica-
tion of
third party
rights.

In some cases (as for instance in the case of easements, profits and restrictive covenants), third party rights are a necessary local complement of landownership ; in others they originate in the financial requirements of owners ; while in others (as for instance in the rights given to children by a settlement), they are due to the social traditions of family life. They may be conveniently divided into two classes—

> first, those arising either under a settlement or a trust for sale, as for instance financial provisions made for children by a marriage settlement ;
>
> secondly, those arising under some other transaction connected with the tenant's activities as a landowner or business man. Examples of this second class are easements, restrictive covenants, annuities, rentcharges, pending actions and deeds of arrangement.

But whatever their origin or character, it is obvious that the possibility of their existence and the risk that they may continue to bind the land after its sale, must cause a purchaser to walk warily and with no undue haste.

> " None of these things," says an expert writer, referring to a number of liabilities not imposed by deed, such as orders of court, pending actions, rent charges and easements, " may appear in the abstract of title presented by a vendor to a purchaser, yet they may cause the purchaser to be ejected from the land for which he has paid, or, if he remains in possession, thrust payments or other liabilities on him, of which had he known, he would not have bought the land." [1]

Extent to
which
purchaser
bound by
third party
rights.

The extent to which a purchaser is affected by them depends upon the fundamental distinction between the legal and the equitable estate.[2] A purchaser for value of the legal fee simple which is subject to third party rights is absolutely bound by them if they amount to legal estates or interests, the question of his actual knowledge or ignorance of their existence being irrelevant.

---

[1] J. S. Stewart Wallace, 41 *L.Q.R.*, pp. 176–7.
[2] *Supra*, pp. 60 *et seq.*

On the other hand, he is not bound by rights that are merely equitable in nature, unless he has actual or constructive notice of their existence. Thus:

> An easement or a profit in perpetuity, a rentcharge or a lease for a definite number of years will be enforceable against an innocent purchaser because each is a legal interest, *i.e.* a right *in rem* enforceable against the whole world. On the other hand, if a fee simple owner has made an " estate contract " with X. (*e.g.* has agreed to grant him a lease or to sell him the legal fee simple), or if he has subjected the land to a restrictive covenant in favour of Y. (as for instance by covenanting that he will erect no business premises), the rights thus vested in X. and Y. since they are merely equitable in nature, will not bind a subsequent purchaser who takes a conveyance of the legal estate, unless he is affected with notice.

The outstanding facts then, are that a purchaser has more to fear from legal than from equitable third party rights, and conversely that the third party himself is less secure with an equitable than a legal right.

The following is a bare sketch of how the legislation attempted to simplify the problem of third party rights.

Outline of statutory alterations in 1925.

1. It drastically curtailed the category of legal estates and legal third party rights. The result is that under the modern law most of the latter are equitable.

2. It made the legal estate the basis of conveyancing. The principal effect of this is that the legal estate can be conveyed only by its owner, not as frequently occurred under the former law by a person, called an *appointor*, who had no estate in the land at all.

3. The existing system by which in certain circumstances the conveyance of a legal estate by way of sale overreached equitable third party rights, *i.e.* encumbered the purchase money instead of the land with their payment and disburdened the purchaser of the duty to investigate them, was considerably extended. In the result,

> (a) these rights are cleared off the land altogether if they can equally well be satisfied out of the purchase money ; but

> (b) if this is not possible, then they can be registered as *land charges* in a public register, so that their owners are protected and a purchaser is warned.

This sketch now requires a little elaboration.

Legal
estates
reduced to
one in case
of freeholds
and one in
case of
leaseholds.

1. **Reduction in the number of Legal Estates.** Under the former law any recognized interest in land, regarded quantitatively, might be either legal or equitable. The Law of Property Act, 1925, however, reduces the possible legal estates to the fee simple absolute in possession in the case of freeholds, and the term of years absolute in the case of leaseholds.

The person in whom such an estate is vested is called the *estate owner.* All other estates, interests and charges in or over the land can exist only as equitable interests,[1] with the exception of those interests permitted to exist at law by section 1 (2) of the Act. [2]

In the case of freeholds, for instance, the

> determinable fee simple,[3]
> entailed interest,[4]
> life interest,[5]
> future interest of whatever size,[6]

can subsist only in equity, not at law. Each one must be created behind a trust, *i.e.* the legal estate in the land affected must be held by an *estate owner* whose function it is to give effect to the equitable interest. The very terminology, indeed, is changed. The correct expression now, for instance, is " entailed interest " not " estate tail," and " life interest " instead of " estate for life."

This statutory change radically affects third party rights, for it means that with the reduction in the number of legal estates the risk to a purchaser is correspondingly diminished. Thus a purchaser for value of Blackacre is unaffected by a right of way held only for life unless he has notice of it, since a life interest is no longer legal, but equitable.

The first section of the Law of Property Act runs as follows :

(1) The only estates in land which are capable of being conveyed or created at law are—

    (a) An estate in fee simple absolute in possession ;

    (b) A term of years absolute.

(2) The only interests or charges in or over land which are capable of subsisting or of being conveyed or created at law are—

    (a) An easement, right, or privilege in or over land for an interest equivalent to an estate in fee simple absolute in possession or a term of years absolute ;

    (b) A rentcharge in possession issuing out of or charged on land being either perpetual or for a term of years absolute ;

---

[1] S. 1 (1), (2), (3).   [2] *Infra.*   [3] *Infra*, p. 282.
[4] *Infra*, p. 154.   [5] *Infra*, p. 182   [6] *Infra*, p. 234

(c) A charge by way of legal mortgage ;

(d) Land tax,[1] tithe rentcharge,[2] and any other similar charge on land which is not created by an instrument ;

(e) Rights of entry exercisable over or in respect of a legal term of years absolute, or annexed, for any purpose, to a legal rentcharge.

(3) All other estates, interests, and charges in or over land take effect as equitable interests.

It will be observed that in referring in the first sub-section to *estates* and in the second to *interests* the Act invented a new terminology that depends upon the difference between a right to the land itself and a right to some claim against the land of another person.

To be entitled to a legal as distinct from an equitable interest in the land itself it is necessary to hold an estate, and the only estate that qualifies for this purpose is either the fee simple absolute in possession or the term of years absolute according as the subject-matter is freehold or leasehold.[3]

On the other hand, a claim against the land of another, if falling within the five items in sub-section (2) is termed an *interest* in that land, but to constitute a *legal* interest it must correspond in duration to one of the two legal estates. A person entitled in perpetuity or for 21 years to an easement, such as a right of way over Blackacre, owns a legal interest in Blackacre. If he is entitled to it for life, he is a mere equitable owner.

Thus, the ancient doctrine of estates under which the fee simple, the entail and the life interest were recognized as estates at common law, has been drastically abridged. There is only the one freehold estate at law—the fee simple absolute in possession. The doctrine, however, has only been " as it were, pushed back into equity"[4] in the sense that the interests that were formerly estates at law still subsist with equal vigour as equitable interests.

2. **The Legal Estate as the Basis of Conveyancing.** This may be illustrated by two observations. First, we have seen that it was a common practice before 1926 to limit land to A. and B. in fee simple to such uses as X. might appoint, with the result that if X., who had no proprietary interest in the land, " appointed " to the use of Y. and his heirs, A. and B. thereupon stood seised to the use of Y. and he took a *legal* fee simple under the Statute of Uses.[5] This is no longer possible. The Statute

Powers of appointment now equitable.

---

[1] Land tax has been abolished by the Finance Act, 1963, s. 68 as regards properties that were still chargeable to it on March 24th, 1963.

[2] Extinguished by the Tithe Act, 1936, and replaced by a sixty years' redemption annuity payable to the Crown.

[3] Rivington, *Law of Property in Land* (2nd Edn.), p. 32.

[4] Lawson, *Rational Strength of English Law*, p. 94.

[5] *Supra*, p. 72.

of Uses has been repealed[1] and, though land may still be limited to A. and B. upon such trusts as X. shall appoint, this merely empowers X. to dispose of the equitable interest. With very few exceptions powers are now equitable.[2]

Title to legal estate alone investigated.

Secondly, if a legal estate that is held in trust for beneficiaries is offered for sale, the purchaser's sole concern in the normal case is to trace the title of the vendors to the legal estate. He is entirely unaffected by the beneficial interests, for these are overreached and are no longer binding on the land once the legal estate has been conveyed.[3]

Former difficulties attending conveyance of settled land.

3. **Overreaching and Investigation of Title.** The policy of freeing the title to the legal estate from beneficial interests to which it may be subject, that had long been a feature of the trust for sale, was simplified by the 1925 legislation in the case of settled land. Before 1926 a settlement was created by a single deed which conferred legal estates and interests upon the successive beneficiaries, so that for instance the husband acquired a legal estate for life and the eldest son a legal estate tail. When the tenant for life exercised, say, his statutory power of sale, his conveyance did, indeed, overreach these legal interests, but, as we have seen, the conveyancing difficulties were not inconsiderable.[4] These derived mainly from the fact that, since the fee simple was not vested in the tenant for life, his right to convey it rested solely upon the statutory powers. The whole settlement required investigation, and before the purchaser was relieved from liability in respect of the beneficial limitations, it was incumbent upon him to make sure that the statutory conditions for the exercise of the power had been satisfied.

Difficulties removed in 1925.

These difficulties, however, were removed by the Settled Land Act, 1925. Owing to the reduction in the number of legal estates, the limited and beneficial interests arising under a settlement are now necessarily equitable, and the legal fee simple out of which they have been carved must, in accordance with the statutory provisions, be vested in the first tenant for life and be transferred to each subsequent life tenant as and when he becomes entitled to possession.[5]

Dual position of tenant for life.

Thus the life tenant occupies a dual position. He is a mere tenant for life as regards beneficial enjoyment, but the owner in fact of the legal fee simple for conveyancing purposes. This means that within the scope of his statutory powers he can dispose of the legal estate, whether it be the fee simple absolute in possession or the term of years absolute, so as to pass to the purchaser a title free from the settlement rights; but it does not mean that he becomes

---

[1] Law of Property Act, 1922, s. 207, Sched. VII.
[2] *Infra*, pp. 199–200.   [3] *Infra*, pp. 718–9.
[4] *Supra*, pp. 78–9.   [5] *Infra*, p. 705–14.

entitled to the capital money arising from the transaction. It is, in fact, a condition of the purchaser's immunity that the money should be paid to the trustees.

In order to emphasize this separation of the legal estate from the beneficial and equitable interests and to facilitate conveyancing, a new method of creating a settlement, framed on the pattern of the trust for sale, was introduced by the Settled Land Act, 1925. Every settlement *inter vivos* must now be made by two deeds. One (the *vesting deed*) vests the legal fee simple in the tenant for life, describes the property and names the trustees ; the other (the *trust instrument*) declares the beneficial interests of the tenant for life and the other persons entitled under the settlement.[1]

Modern method of creating a settlement.

The effect of a conveyance made by the life tenant in his capacity as estate owner is to overreach the equitable interests of the beneficiaries, *i.e.* it clears them off the title to the legal fee simple and converts them into equivalent interests in the purchase money. Their fate is of no concern to the purchaser, provided that he pays the purchase money to the trustees, not to the tenant for life. His sole object is to investigate the title to the *legal* estate. He must, therefore, trace that title down to the first vesting deed, *i.e.* he must require the vendor to show that the person who purported to vest the legal estate in the first tenant for life was in fact entitled to do so. He does not see, nor in general may he demand to see, the trust instrument. That instrument is the sole charter of the beneficiaries. The rights that it grants to the beneficiaries are still intact, still secure, but they are now purely pecuniary in character. The whole operation set in motion upon a conveyance by the tenant for life is an illustration of what is called the *curtain* principle. The vesting deed is, as it were, a curtain that masks the equitable interests.[2]

Over-reaching of equitable interests.

In the case, then, of a trust for sale and strict settlement, the beneficial trusts are cleared altogether off the title to the legal estate and, since they may equally well be engrafted on the purchase money, no harm is done to their owners. Family rights and incumbrances in the nature of pecuniary claims do not impede a conveyance of the legal estate. There are, however, other equitable third party rights to which the doctrine of overreaching is necessarily inapplicable, since they are incapable of being attached to money. For instance, an estate contract or a restrictive covenant of which a purchaser has had notice must continue to affect the land after conveyance to him of the legal

Rights incapable of attaching to money protected by registration.

---

[1] Settled Land Act, 1925, s. 4 ; *infra*, pp. 705-14. In the case of a settlement made by a testator, the legal estate devolves upon his executors who hold it upon trust to convey it to the life tenant. The will itself constitutes the trust instrument and the executors make a *vesting assent*, corresponding to the vesting deed, in favour of the life tenant ; *infra*, p. 710.

[2] For a more detailed account of these matters, see *infra*, pp. 131-7 (the statutory powers) ; pp. 705-9 (the vesting deed and trust instrument) ; pp. 712-4 (conveyance by tenant for life under his statutory powers).

estate.   In such cases the obvious method of simplifying the task of the purchaser and at the same time of protecting the equitable owner is to require rights of this nature to be publicly recorded if they are to remain binding against purchasers.   This was the policy adopted by the legislature in 1925.

Extension of system of registration

Legislation enabling rights against land to be registered has long been in force, but it has appeared in successive and somewhat slow stages.   Thus life annuities charged upon land were made registrable as far back as 1777, and the system was extended to judgments in 1838, to *lites pendentes* in 1839, to deeds of arrangement in 1887, and to what are called land charges in 1888.   These several topics are the subject of full discussion later,[1] but what should be observed at once is that a great extension of the system of registration was made by the Land Charges Act, 1925.   Without going into details, it may be said that practically all equitable rights against land, except those which arise under a trust for sale or a settlement, may be entered in one of the registers kept at the Land Registry in London.   Registration of a registrable right constitutes notice of it to the whole world; failure to register it carries the penalty that it is void against a purchaser for value of the legal estate.   Therefore the owner of a third party right that falls within the provisions of the Act can secure complete protection for himself by registration, while a purchaser need do no more than search at the Registry to discover whether the land is incumbered or not.   With the one exception of the puisne mortgage,[2] *legal* third party rights, such as a right of way held in perpetuity, are not registrable.

Summary of alterations made in 1925.

By way of summary, it may be said, then, that one of the principal objects of the 1925 legislation was to simplify and clear the title to the legal fee simple, which is the estate that the majority of purchasers wish to obtain.   As a result of the legislation the general position is now as follows :

The only legal freehold estate in Blackacre is the fee simple absolute in possession.

In all cases this will be vested in a definite person or body of persons called the *estate owner*.

According to the circumstances the estate owner will be one of the following :

A beneficial owner entitled in his own right.
Trustees for sale.
The tenant for life or " statutory owners "[3] in the case of settled land.

---

[1] *Infra*, pp. 665 *et seq*.
[2] *Infra*, p. 668.
[3] These are the trustees, who take the legal fee simple in settled land when there is no person entitled to take it as tenant for life, *infra*, p. 715.

Personal representatives.
A mortgagor.[1]
A bare trustee.[2]

A conveyance of the legal fee simple must be made by or in the name of the estate owner, not by anybody else.   Thus the exercise of a power of appointment can no longer affect the legal estate,[3] and in the case of a settlement the tenant for life conveys the legal fee simple because it is vested in him, not as formerly because he was statutorily entitled to convey what he had not got.   The conveyance of a legal fee simple that is subject to equitable third party rights is considerably simplified :

Rights which arise under a settlement or a trust for sale are overreached by the conveyance and cleared off the title, for no injury is done to their owners by converting them into rights against the purchase money.

If the rights do not arise in that way but are nevertheless convertible into rights against the money, the estate owner may clear them off the title by creating a settlement or a trust for sale for that particular purpose.[4]

If the rights do not arise under a settlement or a trust for sale and are not convertible into money rights, such as a restrictive covenant, their continued enforcement depends in general on registration.

One aspect of the clear-cut distinction between the legal estate and the equitable interest deserves attention.   Land is employed to satisfy at least two requirements, one affecting the family of its owner, the other affecting its commercial exploitation. It must be subject to rules that facilitate its employment as a continuing source of income for the present and future members of a family, but at the same time it must be under effective administration and above all be readily transferable by way of sale, lease, mortgage and similar transactions if good estate management so demands.   These two requirements, at first sight contradictory, have been reconciled by English law.   The estate owner, despite the existence of family trusts, is given full powers of management and disposal in respect of the land, but he holds them as trustee for such equitable beneficiaries as may exist.   In this way the well-being of the land, the needs of the market and the prosperity of the family are harmonized.[5]

Reconciliation of family and commercial needs.

---

[1] In a mortgage of a legal fee simple, the mortgagor remains the estate owner of the legal fee simple, but nevertheless the mortgagee is entitled by virtue of his power of sale to convey it to a purchaser.

[2] A bare or naked trustee is one who holds property for the absolute benefit of beneficiaries of full age, and who himself has no beneficial interest in the property and no duty except to transfer it to its owner; *Christie* v. *Ovington* (1875), 1 Ch. D. 279.   See 38 Halsbury's *Laws of England* (3rd Edn.), para. 1495.

[3] Save in a few exceptional cases, *infra*, pp. 199–200.

[4] *Infra*, pp. 719–21.

[5] Lawson, *The Rational Strength of English Law*, pp. 91–2.

SECTION VI.   THE DEFINITION OF *LAND.*

As we are about to discuss the interests that may subsist in land, it is obviously appropriate that we should first gain a clear idea of the meaning attributed by law to the word " land."

Distinction between corporeal and incorporeal hereditaments.

Law is at one with the layman in agreeing that " land " includes the surface of the earth, together with all the sub-jacent and super-jacent things of a physical nature such as buildings, trees and minerals,[1] but it also gives the word a far wider meaning, and one which would not occur to those unversed in legal terminology.   Using the word " hereditament " to signify a right that is heritable, *i.e.* capable of passing by way of descent to heirs, our legal ancestors reached the remarkable[2] conclusion that hereditaments are either corporeal or incorporeal.   Let BLACK-STONE himself tell the dismal tale:

" Hereditaments, then, to use the largest expression, are of two " kinds, corporeal and incorporeal.   Corporeal consist of such as " affect the senses ; such as may be seen and handled by the body ; " incorporeal are not the object of sensation, can neither be seen " nor handled, are creatures of the mind and exist only in contem-" plation.   Corporeal hereditaments consist of substantial and " permanent objects." [3]

The distinction is unwarranted.

What this comes to is that the subject-matter of estate ownership may consist either of corporeities or of incorporeities.   There is nothing remarkable in this, for it is obvious that an incorporeity such as a right of way may, equally with a house or a piece of land, be held in fee simple or for life.   What is remarkable, however, is a terminology which declares that an interest in a corporeity, *i.e.* a physical thing capable of carrying seisin, is itself a corporeal *interest*, but that an interest in an incorporeity is an incorporeal *interest*.   This nomenclature will not bear a moment's examination, for no proprietary interest can be other than a mere *right* of ownership, and no matter what the nature of its subject-matter may be, it must always be incorporeal.

" All property of whatever kind is an *incorporeal* right to the *cor-" poreal* use and profit of some *corporeal* thing." [4]

It is difficult to answer the following criticism of AUSTIN :

" With us *all* rights and obligations are not *incorporeal things* ; but " certain rights are styled *incorporeal hereditaments*, and are opposed " by that name to *hereditaments corporeal*.   That is to say, *rights of* " a certain species . . . are absurdly opposed to the *things* (strictly " so called) which are the *subjects* or *matter* of rights of another " species.   The word *hereditaments* is evidently taken in two senses " in the two phrases which stand to denote the species of heredita-" ments.   A corporeal hereditament is the thing itself which is the

---

[1] As to waste products dumped on land, see *Rogers* (*Inspector of Taxes*) v. *Longsdon*, [1966] 2 All E. R. 49.; [1966] 2 W. L. R. 861.
[2] Co. Litt. 6*a* ; *Lloyd* v. *Jones* (1848), 6 C. B. 81, 90
[3] *Commentaries*, vol. ii. p. 17.
[4] 1 *Jurid. Soc.*, p. 542.

" subject of the right ; an incorporeal hereditament is not the
" subject of the right, but the right itself." [1]

The continued use to the present day of this unscientific
terminology need not, however, disturb us. The two facts to
bear in mind are: first, that whether an interest, such as a fee
simple estate, exists in a corporeity or an incorporeity, it is an
interest in *land* ; secondly, that the number of incorporeities
recognized by English law is considerable. BLACKSTONE described
no fewer than ten *incorporeal hereditaments* some of which are
no longer of practical importance.[2] The most important now
are easements,[3] profits[4] and rents.

Land has an extensive meaning in law.

There is one class of corporeal things, namely *fixtures*, which
are regarded as " land " and which are sufficiently important to
merit a somewhat extensive treatment.

" Land " includes fixtures.

FIXTURES

The primary meaning from a historical point of view of
" fixtures " is chattels which are so affixed to land or to a building
on land as to become in fact part thereof.[5] Such chattels lose the
character of chattels and pass with the ownership of the land,
for the maxim of the law is, *quicquid plantatur solo, solo cedit.*

Meaning of fixtures.

This question whether a chattel has been so affixed to land
as to become part of it is sometimes exceedingly difficult to
answer. It is a question of law for the judge,[6] but the decision in
one case is no sure guide in another, for everything turns upon the
circumstances and mainly, though not decisively, upon two
particular circumstances, namely, the *degree of annexation* and
the *object of annexation.*[7] We will take these considerations
separately.

The legal test.

1. **Degree of Annexation.** The general rule is that a chattel
is not deemed to be a fixture unless it is actually fastened to or
connected with the land or building. Mere juxtaposition or the
laying of an article, however heavy, upon the land does not
primâ facie make it a fixture, even though it subsequently sinks into

Degree of annexation an important element.

---

[1] *Jurisprudence*, i. p. 372 ; but see Sweet's answer in Challis, *Law of Real
Property* (3rd Edn.), pp. 48–58. The Law of Property Act, 1925, s. 1 (2), *supra*,
pp. 94–5, perpetuates the confusion in describing a right to, for instance, an
easement as an interest in land, notwithstanding that in s. 205 (ix) it includes
an easement in the definition of " land." The truth is that an incorporeity,
such as an easement, is neither an estate nor an interest, but something in
which an estate or an interest can exist.

[2] *Commentaries*, vol. ii. c. iii. The list is : advowsons, tithes, commons,
ways, offices, dignities, franchises, corodies (a right to receive victuals for
one's maintenance), annuities and rents.

[3] *Infra*, p. 466.   [4] *Infra*, p. 511.

[5] Leake, *Uses and Profits of Land*, p. 103.

[6] *Reynolds* v. *Ashby*, [1904] A. C. 466.

[7] *Holland* v. *Hodgson* (1872), L. R. 7 C. P. 327, 334 ; BLACKBURN, J.

the ground. If a superstructure can be removed without losing its identity, it will not in general be regarded as a fixture. Examples are a Dutch barn, consisting of a roof resting upon wooden uprights, the uprights being made to lie upon brick columns let into the ground[1]; or a printing machine weighing several tons, standing on the floor and secured by its own weight.[2] The case is the same if the posts that support the roof of a corrugated iron building are not embedded in the concrete floor, but are held in position by iron strips fixed into the floor. The concrete foundation, which is of course a fixture, is regarded as a separate unit from the superstructure.[3] Again, a printing machine that stands by its own weight upon the floor is not a fixture, even though the driving apparatus is attached to the building at certain points.[4] On the other hand a chattel that is attached to land, however slightly, is *primâ facie* to be deemed a fixture. Thus, a verandah connected with a house is a fixture,[5] as also are doors, windows, chimneypieces, ovens and other similar things.

Nevertheless the extent of annexation is not a decisive test.

" Perhaps the true rule is, that articles not attached to the
" land otherwise than by their own weight are not to be considered
" as part of the land, unless the circumstances are such as to show
" that they were intended to be part of the land, the onus of showing
" that they were so intended lying on those who assert that they
" have ceased to be chattels ; and that, on the contrary, an article
" which is affixed to the land even slightly is to be considered as
" part of the land, unless the circumstances are such as to show
" that it was intended all along to continue a chattel, the onus
" lying on those who contend that it is a chattel." [6]

It is for this reason that the second consideration mentioned above is material, namely, the :

Purpose of annexation an important element.

2. **Object of Annexation.** The test here is to ascertain whether the chattel has been fixed for its more convenient use as a chattel, or for the more convenient use of the land or building.[7]

---

[1] *Elwes* v. *Maw* (1802), 3 East, 38, at p. 55 ; *Wiltshear* v. *Cottrell* (1853), 1 E. & B. 674.

[2] *Hulme* v. *Brigham*, [1943] K. B. 152 ; [1943] 1 All E.R. 204.

[3] *Webb* v. *Bevis, Ltd.*, [1940] 1 All E. R. 247 ; distinguish *Jordan* v. *May*, [1947] K. B. 427 ; [1947] 1 All E. R. 231 (electric lighting engine and dynamo bolted to a concrete bed. These were held to be fixtures, *aliter* the batteries). The degree of affixation is not necessarily the same in every type of case ; see, *e.g.*, *London County Council* v. *Wilkins*, [1955] 2 Q. B. 653 ; [1955] 2 All E. R. 180 ; affd. [1956] 3 All E. R. 38 (whether a wooden sectional hut is exempt from rateability).

[4] *Hulme* v. *Brigham*, [1943] K. B. 152 ; [1943] 1 All E. R. 204.

[5] *Buckland* v. *Butterfield* (1820), 2 Brod. & Bing. 54.

[6] *Holland* v. *Hodgson* (1872), L. R. 7 C. P. 328, 334, *per* BLACKBURN, J. ; *Bradshaw* v. *Davey*, [1952] 1 All E. R. 350 (yacht mooring in the Hamble River held intended to be a chattel).

[7] *Wake* v. *Hall* (1883), L. R. 8 App. Cas. 195, 204.

For example, stones laid one upon another without any mortar for the purpose of forming a wall become fixtures, but if stones are deposited in a builder's yard and for the sake of convenience stacked one on top of another they are not fixtures.[1]

Again, a comparatively durable method of affixation will not render a chattel a fixture, if the method of annexation is necessary to its proper enjoyment as a chattel. Thus in the well-known case of *Leigh* v. *Taylor* : [2]

> A tenant for life, the owner of some valuable tapestry, laid strips of wood over the drawing-room paper and fixed them to the walls with two-inch nails. Canvas was stretched over these strips, and the tapestry was fastened by tacks to the strips. It was held that the tapestry had not become a fixture.

VAUGHAN WILLIAMS, L.J., said :

" In my judgment it is obvious that everything which was done " here can be accounted for as being absolutely necessary for the " enjoyment of the tapestry, and when one arrives at that con- " clusion there is an end of the case." [3]

The principle of this decision was adopted in a case where a tenant had erected oak and pine panelling and a chimney-piece.[4]

On the other hand, chattels may be annexed to or placed on land in circumstances which show an obvious intention to benefit the use of the land, and if this is so they become fixtures. Examples are, seats secured to the floor of a cinema hall,[5] and such objects as statues, stone seats and ornamental vases, held in position merely by their own weight, which are part of the architectural design of a house and its grounds.[6]

It is useful to note even at this early stage the principal trans- actions in which the question whether particular chattels are fixtures or not requires decision. The question arises as between the following parties.

Persons be- tween whom a question of fixtures may arise.

(1) As between Landlord and Tenant.

In the course of time, the rule that an article becomes part of the land to which it has been affixed has been relaxed in favour of the tenant for years, and he is now allowed to remove three particular classes of articles notwithstanding that they are fixtures in the strict sense of the term.

Certain fixtures removable.

First, it has long been the rule that during the term the tenant may remove fixtures that have been attached to the land for the purpose of carrying on his particular trade, since it is in the public

Trade fixtures.

---

[1] *Holland* v. *Hodgson, supra,* at p. 335.
[2] [1902] A. C. 157.
[3] See the same case in C. A. *sub nom. In re De Falbe,* [1901] 1 Ch. 523, 537.
[4] *Spyer* v. *Phillipson,* [1931] 2 Ch. 183.
[5] *Vaudeville Electric Cinema Co.* v. *Muriset,* [1923] 2 Ch. 74.
[6] *D'Eyncourt* v. *Gregory* (1866), L. R. 3 Eq. 382.

interest that industry should be encouraged. Thus in *Poole's Case*[1] in 1703 it was held by Lord HOLT " that during the term the soap-boiler might well remove the vats he set up in relation to trade and that he might do it by the common law (and not by virtue of any special custom), in favour of trade and to encourage industry. But after the term they became a gift in law to him in reversion, and are not removable."

Engines for working collieries,[2] salt pans,[3] coppers and pipes erected by a brewing tenant,[4] the fittings of a public house[5] and petrol pumps installed at a wayside garage[6] have been held to come within the description of trade fixtures.

Ornamental and domestic fixtures.

Secondly, it is now well established that during the term a tenant may remove such chattels as he has affixed to a house for the sake either of ornament or of convenience, but this relaxation of the strict rule is not supported by such strong reasons as apply in the case of trade fixtures and it will not be extended. Examples of objects which have been held removable on this ground are ornamental chimney-pieces, wainscot fixed to the wall by screws, fixed water-tubs, stoves and grates, ranges and ovens.[7]

But any fixture which partakes of the nature of a permanent improvement and which cannot be removed without substantial damage to the house, such as a conservatory connected by a door with one of the living rooms, does not come within the exception of an ornamental fixture.[8]

Trade, ornamental and domestic fixtures must be removed before the end of the tenancy, otherwise they become a gift in law to the reversioner,[9] but a further period of grace is allowed when the tenant continues in possession after the term under a reasonable supposition of consent on the part of the landlord.[10]

Agricultural fixtures.

The third exception relates to agricultural fixtures. Formerly, a farmer was in an unfavourable position with regard to chattels that he had fixed to his holding, for it was held in *Elwes* v. *Maw*[11] in 1803 that, though the sole purpose of their affixation was to further and improve his agricultural operations, yet they could not be regarded as trade fixtures. In that case, the tenant farmer had built at his own cost a beast-house, a carpenter's shed, a fuel house, a wagon-house and a fold-yard, each of which he removed before the end of the lease, leaving the premises in the same

---

[1] (1703) 1 Salk. 368.
[2] *Lawton* v. *Lawton* (1743), 3 Atk. 13.
[3] *Mansfield* v. *Blackburne* (1840), 6 Bing. N. C. 426.
[4] *Lawton* v. *Lawton, supra.*
[5] *Elliott* v. *Bishop* (1854), 10 Ex. 496.
[6] *Smith* v. *City Petroleum Co.,* [1940] 1 All E. R. 260.
[7] From Woodfall, *Landlord and Tenant* (24th Edn.), p. 758 *q.v.*
[8] *Buckland* v. *Butterfield* (1820), 2 Brod. & B. 54.
[9] *Poole's Case* (1703), 1 Salk. 368, *supra.*
[10] *Ex parte Brook* (1878), 10 Ch. D. 100, 109 ; *Leschallas* v. *Woolff,* [1908] Ch. 641.
[11] (1802), 3 East, 38 ; Smith's *Leading Cases,* vol. ii. p. 188.

state as when he first became tenant. He was held liable to pay damages to the landlord.

The only mitigation at common law of this rigour came in 1901, when it was decided that, though buildings put up by a farmer are not trade fixtures, yet glasshouses built by a market-gardener for the purposes of his trade do come within this description and may be removed before the end of the tenancy against the will of the landlord.[1]

This particular matter has, however been put upon a more equitable footing by a succession of statutes and the position now is as follows :—

Any engine, machinery, fencing, *or other fixture* affixed to a holding by a tenant and any building erected by him thereon, for which he is not otherwise entitled to compensation, becomes his property and is removable by him during the tenancy or within two months after its termination. After the expiration of this period the property in fixtures is no longer vested in him.[2]

Within at least a month before the termination of the tenancy notice of removal must be given to the landlord, who thereupon acquires an option to purchase the fixture.[3] There is no right of removal until the tenant has paid all rent and satisfied his other obligations under the tenancy.

The result of these developments is that if a landlord disputes the right of his tenant to remove a certain chattel from the premises, there are two separate questions to be answered. First, has the chattel become a fixture by reason of its affixation to the land ? If not, *cadit quaestio.* If, however, the answer is in the affirmative, the further question arises whether it is a landlord's or a tenant's fixture, and this of course depends upon whether the chattel falls within one of the three categories already described.[4]

(2) As between Mortgagor and Mortgagee.

Fixtures pass with the land to the mortgagee even though not mentioned in the deed,[5] as also do those which are added later by the mortgagor himself while in possession. Moreover, a mortgagor in possession is not entitled to remove " tenant's " fixtures, whether they have been annexed to the land before or after the mortgage transaction.[6] These rules apply whether the mortgage is legal or equitable, and whether it affects freehold or leasehold premises. Where, however, fixtures have been annexed to land by a *third party* under an agreement between him and the mortgagor which permits him to remove them in certain circumstances,

Fixtures belong to mortgagee.

---

[1] *Mears* v. *Callender*, [1901] 2 Ch. 388.
[2] Agricultural Holdings Act, 1948, s. 13 (1).   [3] *Ibid.*, s. 13 (2), (3).
[4] *Bain* v. *Brand* (1876), 1 App. Cas. 762, at p. 767, *per* Lord Cairns.
[5] *Vaudeville Electric Cinema, Ltd.* v. *Muriset*, [1923] 2 Ch. 74. Law of Property Act, 1925, s. 62 (1).
[6] *Longbottom* v. *Berry* (1869), L. R. 5 Q. B. 137.

E*

his right of removal cannot in general be defeated by the mortgagee. The mortgagee, by allowing the mortgagor to remain in possession, implicitly authorizes him to make agreements usual and proper in his particular trade.[1]

(3) AS BETWEEN VENDOR AND PURCHASER.

Fixtures belong to purchaser.

A conveyance of land, in the absence of express reservation, passes the fixtures to the purchaser without special mention,[2] and they cannot be removed by a vendor who remains in possession between the contract of sale and the completion of the transaction, even though they consist of articles which, as between landlord and tenant, would be " tenant's fixtures." [3] The fixtures are deemed to have been paid for by the price fixed for the land, and if the vendor desires to remove them or to receive an additional sum in respect of them a clause to that effect must be inserted in the contract.

(4) AS BETWEEN TENANT FOR LIFE AND REVERSIONER OR REMAINDERMAN.

The general rule obtains that chattels annexed by a tenant for life so as to become part of the land belong to the owner of the fee simple. Nevertheless the personal representatives of a deceased tenant for life are entitled to remove " such fixtures as are removable by a tenant for years," *i.e.* objects affixed for purposes of trade, ornamentation or domestic use.[4]

(5) AS BETWEEN THE EXECUTOR OF A FEE SIMPLE OWNER AND A DEVISEE.

If A., the tenant in fee simple of Blackacre, devises Blackacre to B., it might be argued that A.'s executors are entitled to remove, at any rate, " tenant's fixtures." The rule, however, is well established that all fixtures, no matter of what description, pass with the land to the devisee.[5]

Statutory definition of land.

In conclusion, the following is the definition of *land* for the purposes of the Law of Property Act, 1925 :

> " ' Land ' includes land of any tenure, and mines and minerals,
> " whether or not held apart from the surface, buildings or parts of
> " buildings (whether the division is horizontal, vertical or made in
> " any other way), and other corporeal hereditaments ; also a manor,
> " an advowson, and a rent and other incorporeal hereditaments,
> " and an easement, right, privilege, or benefit in, over, or derived
> " from land. . . ." [6]

---

[1] *Gough* v. *Wood & Co.*, [1894] 1 Q. B. 713.
[2] Law of Property Act, 1925, s. 62 (1).
[3] *Gibson* v. *Hammersmith Ry. Co.* (1863), 32 L. J. Ch 337. *Phillips* v. *Lamdin*, [1949] 2 K. B. 33 ; [1949] 1 All E. R. 770.
[4] *Lawton* v. *Lawton* (1743), 3 Atk. 13 ; *supra*, pp. 103–5. There is some question whether the power of removal by the personal representative is not more restricted than in the case of a tenant for years.
[5] *Re Whaley*, [1908] 1 Ch. 615.
[6] Law of Property Act, 1925, s. 205 (1) (ix).

BOOK II.

ESTATES AND INTERESTS IN LAND.

SUMMARY.

After this brief historical survey, the next task is to describe the estates and interests that may subsist in land. The general arrangement of the following account of this matter is based upon the distinction between family interests arising under a settlement or a trust for sale and what, for want of a better title, are called " commercial interests," *i.e.* interests such as leaseholds, mortgages and easements, that arise in the ordinary routine of business and for the most part are not inevitable parts of family endowment schemes. What deserves to be emphasized is that the propensity of the upper classes to distribute portions of the fee simple among a succession of descendants or other relatives, a propensity that has been a feature of English social life for many centuries, though far less pronounced now in this age of crippling taxation, has left an indelible mark upon the law of real property. To this sentiment is due the continued employment in conveyancing practice of entailed, life and future interests and of powers of appointment, interests that are never found except as cogs in the wheel of a settlement.

Before the proposed dichotomy of interests can be elaborated, however, it is necessary to describe the fee simple absolute in possession. This is the axis round which any account of landed interests must revolve, for it represents the subject-matter out of which lesser proprietary rights, whether family or commercial, may be carved.

PART I.

THE ESTATE IN FEE SIMPLE ABSOLUTE IN POSSESSION.

SUMMARY.

SECTION I. DEFINITION.

Meaning of "fee simple." The first essential is to investigate the precise meaning of the statutory expression fee simple absolute in possession, which as we have seen is the only *freehold* interest capable of existing as a legal estate.[1] The word *fee* had by Littleton's day come to denote that the estate was inheritable, that is to say, that it would endure until the person entitled to it *for the time being*—whether the original donee or some subsequent alienee—died intestate and left no heir.[2] The word *simple* showed that the fee was one which was capable of passing to the heirs *general* and was not restricted to passing to a particular class of heirs.[3] This last fact therefore distinguishes a fee simple from another kind of fee which used to be called a fee tail and is now called an entailed interest, for this is a freehold that passes, on the intestacy of its owner, only to the particular class of lineal descendants specified in the instrument of creation.[4]

Thus

> if a tenant in fee simple died intestate before 1926, his estate passed to his nearest heir, who according to the circumstances might be a descendant or an ascendant, a lineal or a collateral relative.[5]

---

[1] Law of Property Act, 1925, s. 1 (1) (a) ; *supra*, pp. 94–5.
[2] Pollock and Maitland, *History of English Law*, vol. ii. p. 14.
[3] Co. Litt. 1a, b, 18a ; Blackstone, vol. ii. 105.
[4] *Infra*, pp. 160–1.   [5] *Infra*, pp. 789–92.

An entailed interest, on the other hand (and this is still the law), was capable of passing only to lineal descendants, and these might, according to the terms of the instrument of gift, be either lineal descendants in general or a restricted class of descendants, such as male heirs or the issue of the tenant by a specified wife. The characteristic of general inheritability is still the attribute of a fee simple, but the significance of this is now modified, as will be explained later, by the abolition of the doctrine of heirship except in the case of the entailed interest. The land itself no longer passes to the nearest heir but upon the death of the owner intestate is held by the administrators on trust for sale, the proceeds of the sale being distributed among the nearest relatives according to a scheme introduced by the Administration of Estates Act, 1925, as amended by the Intestates' Estates Act, 1952 and the Family Provision Act, 1966.[1] The relatives specified by the Act, however, comprise descendants and ascendants, both lineal and collateral, and it is therefore still true to say that a fee simple is an estate which, though in the converted form of money, is the subject of general inheritability. *(Fee simple distinguished from fee tail.)*

But it is not every fee simple that is a legal estate, for the Law of Property Act confines that attribute to a fee simple absolute in possession. Postponing for the moment the consideration of the last two words, we must inquire what is meant by the word " absolute." This is not defined in the Act, but it clearly excludes an estate that is defeasible either by the breach of a condition or by the possibility that it may pass to some new owner upon the happening of a specified event. More than a hundred years ago Preston explained the purport of *absolute* in the following words [2] :— *(Meaning of " absolute.")*

> " The epithet *absolute* is used to distinguish an estate extended " to any given time, without any condition to defeat or collateral " limitation to determine the estate in the mean time, from an " estate subject to a condition or collateral limitation. The term " absolute is of the same signification with the word pure or simple, " a word which expresses that the estate is not determinable by " any event besides the event marked by the clause of limitation."

Thus a fee simple absolute is distinguished from a *determinable* fee simple, *i.e.* one which according to the express terms of its limitation may determine by some event before the completion of the full period for which it may possibly continue.[3] *(Determinable fee.)*

If, for instance, premises are limited in fee simple to an incorporated golf club "so long as the premises are used for the purposes of the Club,"

---

[1] *Infra*, p. 793.
[2] *An Elementary Treatise on Estates*, pp. 125–6.
[3] See " Determinable Interests," *infra*, pp. 282–4.

the interest is a fee simple because it may possibly continue for ever, but it is not a fee simple absolute since it will cease and will return to the grantor or his successors if at some time in the future the premises are put to other uses.

Fee liable to be divested. Again, the limitation of a fee simple may be accompanied by what is called a shifting clause which provides that if a certain event happens the estate shall pass from the grantee to another person. As, for instance, where there is a grant of Whiteacre,

> to A. in fee simple, but if he becomes entitled to Blackacre, then to B. in fee simple.

Here the fee simple given to A. is not absolute, since it is liable to be divested from him on the occurrence of the specified event. There is one exception to this rule, for it is provided that a fee simple which is liable to be divested under the provisions of the " Lands Clauses Acts, the Schools Sites Acts or any similar Statute " shall nevertheless be a fee simple *absolute*.[1] Statutes of this type, which enable land to be acquired compulsorily by a local authority for certain public purposes, generally provide expressly that if the purpose fails or is not carried out the land shall revert to the original owner or shall vest in some other person. An express provision to this effect is not, however, essential to bring a statute within the exception. It is sufficient if the implication is that the local authority shall be divested of its interest upon the fulfilment or failure of the purpose for which the land was acquired.[2]

Fee simple vested in corporation. The Law of Property Act, 1925, also provides that a fee simple vested in a corporation shall be regarded as absolute notwithstanding its liability to determine upon the dissolution of the corporate body.[3]

Fee simple on condition. If a condition is annexed to the limitation of a fee simple providing that the grantor shall be entitled to re-enter and recover his interest if a certain event happens or does not happen, it is equally clear on general principles that the estate is not a fee simple absolute within the meaning of the description given by Preston.

Fee simple liable to be defeated on non-payment of perpetual rent. Nevertheless the provision of the Law of Property Act, 1925, which denied the character of a legal estate to an interest of this nature caused considerable difficulty. In certain parts of England

---

[1] Law of Property Act, 1925, s. 7 (1).

[2] *Tithe Redemption Commission* v. *Runcorn Urban District Council,* [1954] Ch. 383 ; [1954] 1 All E. R. 653 (highway vested in the local highway authority).

[3] S. 7 (2). As to whether the lands of a corporation upon its dissolution reverted to the donor or escheated to the lord, see Co. Litt. 13*b* ; Gray, *Perpetuities,* ss. 44–51A ; Challis, *Law of Real Property* (3rd Edn.), pp. 35–6, 467–8 ; *Hastings Corporation* v. *Letton,* [1908] 1 K. B. 378 ; *In re Woking U.D.C.,* [1914] 1 Ch. 500 ; *In re Thomas Spencer Wells, Swinburne-Hanham* v. *Howard,* [1933] 1 Ch. 29 ; 49 L. Q. R. 240 ; 50 L. Q. R. 33 ; 51 L. Q. R. 347, 361.

and especially in Manchester it has been a common practice for a purchaser of a fee simple, instead of paying the purchase money in a lump sum, to enter into a covenant to pay a perpetual annual rentcharge, often called a fee farm rent. The payment of the rent is secured to the vendor and his successors by the reservation of either a right of entry or a right of re-entry. The former permits the vendor and his successors to enter the land at any time in the future if the annual payment falls into arrear and to hold the land *as a leasehold interest* until the arrears are paid.[1] The right of re-entry (which is more common in the case of a lease [2]) arises where the conveyance contains a condition that the purchaser and his successors will pay the rent and that the vendor shall be entitled to re-enter if this condition is broken. In this case the person entitled to the rent may either re-enter upon the land or bring proceedings for its recovery, whereupon the interest of the purchaser is forfeited and the vendor *re-acquires his old estate*.[3]

The fact that a fee simple liable to interruption in either of these ways was not a legal estate within the meaning of the Law of Property Act, 1925, operated to the prejudice of a landowner, for not only did it seem to make the land subject to the Settled Land Act and thus to require the execution of a vesting deed, but it made it difficult to discover where the legal estate resided.[4]

In view of this inconvenience it was later enacted that

" a fee simple subject to a legal or equitable right of entry or re-entry is for the purposes of this Act a fee simple absolute." [5]

The word " absolute " does not imply freedom from incumbrances. Thus a fee simple, though subject to a lien or a mortgage, whether legal or equitable, or to a mere charge, is none the less absolute.

Estate absolute though incumbered

Finally, to have the character of a legal estate, a fee simple absolute must be *in possession*. " Possession " is not here confined to its popular meaning, for it includes receipt of rents and profits or the right to receive the same.[6] Therefore a tenant in fee simple who has leased the land to a tenant for years is the owner of a legal estate even though he is not in physical possession of the land. If, however, he is entitled to the fee simple only at some time in the future, as for instance in the case of a limitation

Meaning of " in possession."

to A. for life and then to B. in fee simple,

he has a mere equitable interest.

---

[1] Littleton, s. 327; Co. Litt. 202*b*; *ibid.*, note 93 by Hargrave and Butler.
[2] *Infra*, pp. 392; 397.   [3] Littleton, s. 325.
[4] See an article in the Law Journal Newspaper, January 16th, 1926.
[5] Law of Property (Amendment) Act, 1926, Schedule. The rentcharge, being perpetual, is a *legal* interest under the Law of Property Act, 1925, s. 1 (2) (b), *supra*, p. 95 ; and under *ibid.*, s. 1 (2) (e), the right of entry, being " annexed to a legal rentcharge," is also a *legal* interest.
[6] Law of Property Act, 1925, ss. 205 (1) (xix) ; 95 (4).

SECTION II. MODE OF CREATION.

Quantum of an estate shown by words of limitation.

Words of Limitation. Whether a fee simple passes to a grantee or a devisee of land depends upon the words of limitation contained in the deed or will. Words of limitation are those whose purpose it is to indicate the exact estate that is to pass. In the case of deeds the law was in former times exceedingly strict upon this point. If certain expressions were adopted the effect was to create a fee simple; if others, a fee tail or life estate. Thus before 1882 the only way of creating a fee simple by a direct grant *inter vivos* was by a limitation to the grantee *and his heirs*. This expression has been common form since the birth of English law, and perhaps its original implication was that the tenant could not alienate his interest without first consulting the apparent heirs. In the thirteenth century, however, all restraints of that kind on alienation disappeared and it became settled that the expression did not confer rights of any sort upon the heir, but was used merely to show that the tenant had an estate that would endure at least as long as his heirs endured.[1]

Position before 1882 in deeds.

If in a *deed* there was for instance a grant to

" A. and his assignees,"
" A. for ever,"
" A. and his descendants,"
" A. and his successors,"[2]

Position after Conveyancing Act, 1881.

then, however indefinite the expression might be, and however obvious the intention of the parties might be to convey the fee simple, the only effect was to pass a life estate to A. This strictness was mitigated and an alternative form of words was permitted by the Conveyancing Act, 1881, which provided that in deeds executed after December 31st, 1881, the fee simple should pass if the expression " in fee simple " was adopted.

Devises of land.

In the case of land *devised by will* the law was more liberal in its definition of words of limitation than it was in the case of deeds. Thus in addition to the technical expression " and his heirs," any informal words which clearly showed that the testator intended to give the fee simple were allowed to have that effect,[3] but notwithstanding this more lenient attitude the fact remained that laxity in the use of words of limitation frequently defeated intention. The Wills Act, 1837, therefore provided that

Wills Act, 1837.

" where any real estate shall be devised to any person without any
" words of limitation, such devise shall be construed to pass the fee
" simple, or other the whole estate or interest which the testator had
" power to dispose of by will in such real estate, unless a contrary
" intention shall appear by the will."[4]

---

[1] Pollock and Maitland, *History of English Law*, vol. ii. p. 13.
[2] *Bankes* v. *Salisbury Diocesan Council of Education Incorporated*, [1960] Ch. 631 ; [1960] 2 All E. R. 372.
[3] Jarman on Wills (7th Edn.), p. 1781.   [4] S. 28.

The effect of this enactment was to reverse the former law.

Before 1837 the effect of using a non-technical expression was to pass only a life estate, unless an intention to pass the whole fee simple could be clearly deduced ; but since 1837 the effect is to pass the entire interest which the testator happens to have in the lands, unless his intention clearly is to give some smaller interest. The burden of proving that a smaller interest passes lies on those who maintain that hypothesis.

The rule thus introduced for wills by the Act of 1837 was extended to deeds by the Law of Property Act, 1925. It provides that [1]

Present position for deeds and wills.

> " a conveyance of freehold land to any person without words of " limitation or any equivalent expression, shall pass to the grantee " the fee simple or other the whole interest which the grantor had " power to convey in such land, unless a contrary intention appears " in the conveyance."

It will be noticed that the language of this section corresponds closely with that of the Wills Act.

The position, then, at the present day, both for deeds and for wills, is that, if it is desired to confer a fee simple upon X., the wisest plan is to limit the land to "X. in fee simple" or to "X. and his heirs"; but that, if any other expression is used, as for instance "to X.", or "to X. for ever," the fee simple, if owned by the alienor, will pass unless the instrument clearly shows that there was no such intention.[2]

A limitation before 1926, not *to A. and his heirs*, but

Rule in Shelley's Case.

to A. for life remainder to his heirs

would have conferred a fee simple estate upon A. under the rule known as the *Rule in Shelley's Case.* This rule, which is described below at page 169, has, however, been abolished, and the effect of such a limitation now is to give a life interest to A. and a fee simple estate to his heir.

Where it was desired to grant a fee simple to a corporation sole, *i.e.* a body politic having perpetual succession and consisting of a single person, such as a bishop, a parson, the Crown or the Postmaster-General, the old law was that the grant must be made to the person in question *and his successors*, otherwise it merely operated to confer an estate for life on the actual holder of the office.[3] This rule has, however, been altered,[4] and a conveyance of freehold land in which the word " successors " has been omitted passes to the corporation the fee simple or other the whole interest which the grantor has, unless a contrary intention appears in the conveyance.

Corporation sole.

---

[1] Law of Property Act, 1925, s. 60 (1).
[2] See, for example, *Quarm v. Quarm*, [1892] 1 Q. B. 184.
[3] Co. Litt. 8*b*, 94*b*.
[4] Law of Property Act, 1925, s. 60 (2).

Corporation aggregate.
In the case of a corporation aggregate, *i.e.* a collection of several persons united into one body under a special name and having perpetual existence, such as a limited liability company, it is sufficient to grant to the corporation under its corporate name.[1]

Voluntary conveyances.
If a feoffment were made before the Statute of Uses to a stranger in blood without the receipt of a money consideration (*i.e.* a voluntary conveyance), and *without declaring a use* in favour of the feoffee, the rule was that the land must be held by the feoffee to the use of the feoffor.[2] The equitable interest that thus returned by implication to the feoffor was called a resulting use. The effect of the enactment by the Statute of Uses that a *cestui que use* should have the legal estate was, of course, that the legal estate resulted to the feoffor.[3] In order to prevent this it became the practice in the case of such a conveyance to declare in the *habendum*[4] of the deed that the land was granted " unto and to the use of " the grantee. The repeal of the Statute of Uses by the legislation of 1925 would, in the absence of a further enactment, have restored the original rule, and it might have led practitioners to believe that the expression " to the use of " was still necessary in order to render a voluntary conveyance effective. It is, however, enacted that

" in a voluntary conveyance a resulting trust for the grantor shall " not be implied merely by reason that the property is not expressed " to be conveyed for the use or benefit of the grantee "[5]

SECTION III. THE LEGAL POSITION OF A TENANT IN FEE SIMPLE.

Extent of Ownership. The legal position of a tenant in fee simple may be considered from two points of view—the subject-matter of his interest and the proprietary rights exercisable by him in that subject-matter.

Subject-matter of his interest.
The fee simple is the largest estate in *quantum* known to the law, since it may continue for ever. Moreover, a comprehensive meaning is given by the law to the expression *corporeal hereditaments* as used in the definition of land. In accordance with the maxim *cujus est solum, ejus est usque ad caelum et ad inferos*, it may be said in general that a tenant in fee is owner of everything attached to or lying below the surface. For instance, all minerals that lie beneath the soil belong absolutely to the tenant in fee, and although **Things on or below the land.** he does not acquire the ownership of anything that overhangs

---

[1] Co. Litt. 94*b*.
[2] Sanders, *An Essay on Uses and Trusts*, p. 60.
[3] *Ibid.*, p. 97 ; *Beckwith's Case* (1589), 2 Co. Rep. 56*b*.
[4] *Infra*, p. 686.
[5] Law of Property Act, 1925, s. 60 (3).

his land, such as a cornice, an illuminated advertisement, telephone wires or the bough of a tree, he can maintain an action of nuisance or of trespass against the person who allows it to be there,[1] unless it has been acquired by that person as an easement.[2] Moreover, in the absence of trustworthy evidence of ownership, there is a legal presumption that the fee simple owner, if in possession, is *primâ facie* owner of chattels found on the land.[3]

The proprietary rights of the tenant, however, do not extend to treasure trove. Treasure trove.

" Treasure trove is where any gold or silver in coin, plate, or bullion
" is found concealed in a house or in the earth, or other private place,
" the owner thereof being unknown, in which case the treasure belongs
" to the King or his grantee having the franchise of treasure trove ; but
" if he that laid it be known or afterwards discovered, the owner and
" not the King is entitled to it ; this prerogative right only applying in the
" absence of an owner to claim the property. If the owner, instead
" of hiding the property casually lost it, or purposely parted with it,[4] in
" such a manner that it is evident he intended to abandon the property
" altogether, and did not purpose to resume it on another occasion, as
" if he threw it on the ground or other public place, or in the sea, the
" first finder is entitled to the property as against every one but the
" owner, and the King's prerogative does not in this respect obtain. So
" that it is the hiding and not the abandonment of the property that
" entitles the King to it." [5]

The owner's rights in respect of wild animals, such as game, depend upon the circumstances. Such animals are not within the absolute ownership of any particular person. There are two exceptions, for wild animals which have been tamed belong to the person who has tamed them, and animals too young to escape belong to the occupier of the land on which they are until they gain their natural liberty.[6] In other cases the tenant in fee or, indeed, the occupier of the land, has not an absolute, but a qualified, right of ownership over the animals within the confines of his property in the sense that the exclusive right to catch and appropriate them belongs to him *ratione soli*.[7] Thus, game which is killed by a Wild creatures.

---

[1] *Wandsworth Board of Works* v. *United Telephone Co.* (1884), 13 Q. B. D. 904 ; *Lemmon* v. *Webb*, [1895] A. C. 1 ; *Gifford* v. *Dent*, [1926] W. N. 336; *Kelsen* v. *Imperial Tobacco Co. (of Great Britain and Ireland), Ltd.*, [1957], 2 Q. B. 334; [1957] 2 All E. R. 343. No such action arises from the mere fact that an aeroplane passes through the air over land; Civil Aviation Act, 1949, s. 40 (1).

[2] *Simpson* v. *Weber* (1925), 541 T. L. R. 302.

[3] *South Staffordshire Water Co.* v. *Sharman*, [1896] 2 Q. B. 44 ; *Hannah* v. *Peel*, [1945] K. B. 509 ; *Hibbert* v. *McKiernan*, [1948] K. B. 142 ; *Re Cohen, National Provincial Bank Ltd.* v. *Katz*, [1953] Ch. 88; [1953] 1 All E. R. 378; *City of London Corporation* v. *Appleyard*, [1963] 2 All E. R. 834; [1963] 1 W. L. R. 982.

[4] *Quaere*, however, whether a possessor can divest himself of possession of a thing by its deliberate abandonment ; Pollock and Wright on Possession, p. 124 ; *Haynes' Case* (1613), 12 Co. Rep. 113 ; *Arrow Shipping Co.* v. *Tyne Improvement Commissioners*, [1894] A. C. 508, at p. 532.

[5] Chitty on the Prerogative, p. 152, cited *A.-G.* v. *Moore*, [1893] 1 Ch. 676, 683 ; *A.-G.* v. *Trustees of British Museum*, [1903] 2 Ch. 598.

[6] *Case of Swans* (1592), 7 Co. Rep. 15*b*.

[7] *Blades* v. *Higgs* (1865), 11 H. L. Cas. 621, *per* WESTBURY, L.C.

trespasser belongs to the occupier of the land on which it is killed. The only exception to this principle and one not altogether free from doubt is that if A. starts game on the land of B., and hunts it on to the ground of C. and kills it there, the ownership of the game belongs to A. the hunter, though of course he is liable in trespass both to B. and to C.[1]

Ponds and lakes.

Rights over Water. Again, the tenant in fee possesses certain valuable rights over water that may run through or be situated on his land. Water standing upon his land in a lake or pond is part of the land and belongs to him. If it stands partly upon his land and partly upon that of another, each is probably entitled to such part as lies opposite his own bank, but only up to a point half way between his and the opposite bank.[2]

Percolating water.

Water percolating underneath the land and not contained in a defined and contracted channel is a common supply in which nobody has any property, but it becomes the absolute property of any occupier by whom it is appropriated.[3] Thus if by drainage or mining operations on his own land an occupier draws off all such subterranean water from beneath neighbouring lands, he becomes the owner of it and will not be liable to his neighbours, though the effect of his operations may have been to dry up a spring or a well on their land.[4]

Streams and rivers.

The next type of case is where a river or stream runs in a *definite channel*, whether above or below the surface, though it must be noted that an underground stream does not come within this category until it is established that it follows a definite course.[5] Underground water, the course of which cannot be ascertained without excavation, ranks as percolating water. Two questions arise where a stream follows a definite course ; first, the rights of the riparian owner or owners in the *bed*, secondly, their rights in the *water*.

Rights in the bed.

The bed of a *non-tidal* river belongs, when there is no evidence of acts of ownership to the contrary, to the owner of the land through which it flows, but when the lands of two proprietors are separated by a running stream, each proprietor is *primâ facie* owner of the soil of the bed of the river *ad medium filum aquae*. The soil of the bed is not the common property of the two proprietors, but the share of each belongs to him separately, so that, if from any cause the stream becomes diverted, each owner may use his share of the bed in any way he chooses.[6] On the other

---

[1] *Sutton* v. *Moody* (1697), 1 Ld. Raym. 250, criticized by Lord CHELMSFORD in *Blades* v. *Higgs* (1865), 10 H. L. Cas., at p. 639.

[2] See *Mackenzie* v. *Bankes* (1878), L. R. 3 App. Cas. 1324.

[3] *Ballard* v. *Tomlinson* (1885), L. R. 29 Ch. D. 115, 121, *per* BRETT, M.R.

[4] *Acton* v. *Blundell* (1843), 12 M. & W. 324 ; *Chasemore* v. *Richards* (1859), 7 H. L. Cas. 349.

[5] *Bleachers' Assocn. Ltd.* v. *Chapel-en-le-Frith Rural Council*, [1933] Ch. 356.

[6] *Bickett* v. *Morris* (1866), L. R. 1 Sc. & Div. 47 (especially at p. 58).

hand, the bed of a *tidal* river, up to a point where the water flows and reflows regularly, belongs to the Crown unless it has been granted to a subject.[1]

But the water as distinct from the bed of a river is not the subject of absolute ownership, and, though subject to certain rights exercisable by the owners of the lands through which it flows, it does not belong to them in the ordinary sense of the term. Such a riparian owner has, as a natural incident of his ownership, certain riparian rights, which have been authoritatively described as follows :—

> "A riparian proprietor is entitled to have the water of the stream, "on the banks of which his property lies, flow down as it has been "accustomed to flow down to his property, subject to the ordinary "use of the flowing water by upper proprietors, and to such further "use, if any, on their part in connection with their property as may "be reasonable under the circumstances."[2]

The law, as thus stated, may be elaborated into three propositions [3] :—

1. A riparian owner may take and use the water for ordinary purposes connected with his riparian tenement (such as domestic purposes or the wants of his cattle), even though the result may be to exhaust the water altogether.

2. A riparian owner may take the water for extraordinary purposes, provided, first that such user is connected with the riparian land, and secondly that he restores the water substantially undiminished in quantity and unchanged in value. Common examples are where water is employed in the irrigation of the adjoining land or the working of a mill, for in such cases practically the same amount of water ultimately returns to the stream.[4] Manufacture, in the present connection, is *primâ facie* an extraordinary purpose, though the ultimate solution of this question depends upon local trading conditions, and on the use to which the water of rivers is put in the adjoining district.[5]

3. A riparian owner has no right whatever to take the water for purposes unconnected with the riparian tenement.[6] Thus it has been held that the mere possession of a mill on the bank of a stream does not entitle a waterworks company to collect the water in a reservoir for the benefit of a neighbouring town.[7]

Rights in the water.

Riparian rights classified.

---

[1] *A.-G.* v. *Lonsdale* (1868), L. R. 7 Eq. 377, at p. 288.

[2] *John Young & Co.* v. *Bankier Distillery Co.*, [1893] A. C. 691, at p. 698, *per* Lord MACNAGHTEN ; *Provender Millers (Winchester), Ltd.* v. *Southampton C.C.*, [1940] Ch. 131 ; [1939] 4 All E. R. 157.

[3] *Attwood* v. *Llay Main Collieries*, [1926] Ch. 444, 458.

[4] *Embrey* v. *Owen* (1851), 6 Ex. 353; Dist. *Rugby Joint Water Board* v. *Walters*, [1966] 3 All E. R. 497.

[5] *Ormerod* v. *Todmorden Mill Co.* (1883), 11 Q. B. D. 155, at p. 168, *per* Lord ESHER ; see 22 *Modern Law Review*, pp. 35–40 (A. H. Hudson).

[6] *McCartney* v. *Londonderry and Lough Swilly Ry. Co.*, [1904] A. C. 301 ; *Attwood* v. *Llay Main Collieries*, *supra*.

[7] *Swindon Waterworks Co.* v. *Wilts. and Berks. Canal Navigation Co.* (1875), L. R. 7 H. L. 697.

Public rights in a river.

The public have a common law right to navigation in a tidal river up to the point where the tide ebbs and flows,[1] but the non-tidal part of a river is in exactly the same position as a road running between two properties, and though the public may by dedication acquire the right of navigation thereon, it must be proved in case of dispute that this has been established by long enjoyment or by Act of Parliament.[2] Such a right of navigation if once established prevails over the ordinary rights of a riparian owner, and he cannot make any use of the bed of the river or of its water which will prejudice enjoyment by the public; he is not, for instance, entitled to abstract an excessive quantity of water, or to erect a wharf or other building on the bed so as to obstruct to the smallest extent the passage of boats.[3]

Land adjoining sea.

A tenant in fee of lands adjoining the sea is also entitled to the sea-shore down to a point which is reached by an ordinary high tide, but all the shore below that is vested in the Crown or its grantee.[4]

No right to fish in non-tidal river.

Rights over Fish. As regards the person who possesses the right of fishing in a river, a distinction must again be drawn between tidal and non-tidal rivers, for, while all members of the public are entitled to fish in the former up to the point where the tide ebbs and flows, the right in the case of a non-tidal river belongs to the owner of the bed of the stream, or to any person who has acquired a right from or against him. It is often thought that if a river is navigable the public have a right to fish in it, but this is not true in respect of that part of a river which lies above the flow of the tide, for the privilege of navigation no more confers a right to fish than the right to pass along a public highway entitles a member of the public to shoot upon it.[5] BOWEN, L.J., said :—

> "There is another most important matter to be recollected as
> "regards such streams as the Thames, viz. that although the public
> "have been in the habit, as long as we can recollect, and as long as our
> "fathers can recollect, of fishing in the Thames, the public have no
> "right to fish there—I mean they have no right as members of the
> "public to fish there. That is certain law. Of course they may fish
> "by the licence of the lord or the owner of a particular part of the bed
> "of a river, or they may fish by the indulgence, or owing to the
> "carelessness or good nature of the person who is entitled to the soil,
> "but right to fish themselves as the public they have none, and
> "whenever the case is tried the jury ought to be told this by the
> "judge in the most emphatic way, so as to prevent them from doing
> "injustice under the idea that they are establishing a public right.
> "There is no such right in law. . . ."[6]

---

[1] *A.-G.* v. *Tomline* (1880), 14 Ch. D. 58.
[2] *Orr-Ewing* v. *Colquhoun* (1877), L. R. 2 App. Cas. 839.
[3] *A.-G.* v. *Terry* (1874), L. R. 9 Ch. App. 423.
[4] *Lowe* v. *Govett* (1832), 3 B. & Ad. 863.
[5] *Smith* v. *Andrews*, [1891] 2 Ch. 678, 696. It is a misdemeanour to fish in such a river even though the fish are returned alive to the water; *Wells* v. *Hardy*, [1964] 1 Q. B. 447; [1964] 1 All E. R. 953.
[6] *Blount* v. *Layard*, [1891] 2 Ch. 681 note, at p. 689

The position is, then, that the owner of the bed of a river is presumptively entitled to the fishing, and if, for instance, the opposite banks are in different hands, each proprietor is owner of the fishing *usque ad medium filum aquae.*[1] But this fishing may become separated from the ownership of the bed and be vested as an incorporeal right in the hands of another person, and when this has been done it exists either as a several fishery or as a common of fishery. Both these rights are instances of what is called a *profit à prendre.* A several fishery is, as was said by Lord COLERIDGE, *(margin: Fishing right as an incorporeal right.)*

" a right to take fish *in alieno solo* and to exclude the owner of the
" soil from the right to take fish himself."[2]

A right to fish in the river of another in common with the owner, or in common with others to whom the same right has been granted, is called a " common of fishery," or " common of piscary."[3]

Rights of Ownership. In his account of the fee simple estate, written in 1885, Challis was able to give a comforting description of the extensive powers of enjoyment available to its owner. *(margin: Restrictions to which a landowner is subject.)*

" It confers," he said, " and since the beginning of legal history it
" always has conferred, the lawful right to exercise over, upon and
" in respect to the land, every act of ownership which can enter into
" the imagination, including the right to commit unlimited waste."[4]

Challis would, no doubt, have agreed with Samuel Johnson that a man cannot be allowed by society to be complete master of what he calls his own, and that he must submit to the restrictions placed by the law upon the exercise of his proprietary rights.[5] There is little doubt, however, that the restrictions now imposed by statute upon a landowner's right to enjoy what at common law is his own would have passed the understanding of both those writers. Even in Challis' time, of course, statutory interference with the freedom of a landowner was not unknown. He was obliged, for instance, to erect new buildings in conformity with local bye-laws, and he might be compelled to demolish houses that were unfit for habitation. Later he became subject to legislation passed in the interests of the poorer sections of the community, such as the Housing Acts[6] and the Rent Restriction Acts,[7] which further increased his burdens and circumscribed his proprietary rights.

But the most vigorous attack upon the right of a man to do what he likes with his own has been made by the various Town *(margin: Planning Control.)*

[1] *Hanbury* v. *Jenkins,* [1901] 2 Ch. 401.
[2] *Foster* v. *Wright* (1878), L. R. 4 C. P. D. 438, 449.
[3] Leake, *Uses and Profits,* p. 176.
[4] *The Law of Real Property* (3rd Edn.), p. 218.
[5] In a letter to Boswell, February 3rd, 1776.
[6] *Infra,* pp. 367–9.   [7] *Infra,* pp. 422 *et seq.*

and Country Planning Acts, which seek to prevent the evils that inevitably arise if no public control is placed upon the development of land. That building operations need to be controlled in the interests of the community is, of course, obvious. Land is scarce, the demand for houses increases with a rapidly rising population, the profit instinct is no weaker than formerly, and unless something is done to curb the activities of the speculative builder certain unfortunate results must inevitably ensue. Too often, uncontrolled development sacrifices agricultural land and places of natural beauty, defaces the countryside with unco-ordinated buildings sprawling along the main roads and causing embarrassment to the sanitary and educational authorities, and in general it is effected with little thought for the amenities of the neighbourhood or for the problems that it will raise in the future. Nevertheless, there is a need to preserve a just balance between the rights of landowners and the interests of the community. To give an adequate account of planning control in the present chapter would upset the balance of the book and divert the attention of the reader from fundamental principles, but the subject is of such importance in the modern law that it is dealt with in a separate account and at a later stage.[1]

---

[1] *Infra*, p. 879.

BOOK II.

ESTATES AND INTERESTS IN LAND.

PART II.

INTERESTS ARISING UNDER A STRICT SETTLEMENT OR TRUST FOR SALE.

SUMMARY.

CHAPTER I.

THE GENERAL FRAMEWORK AND EFFECT OF A STRICT SETTLEMENT AND A TRUST FOR SALE.

SUMMARY

Introduction. The interests to be discussed in this Part usually arise under a settlement. The general meaning of a " settlement " is any disposition of real or personal property, made either by deed or will, that establishes a series of beneficial trusts in favour of a succession of persons. The two different methods by which land may be subjected to such succession trusts are either to make a disposition within the meaning of the Settled Land Act, 1925, or to settle the land upon trust for sale. Moreover, the definition of a settlement given by the Settled Land Act is so wide[1] that any instrument which creates a succession of limited interests will inevitably fall within that statute unless it clearly satisfies the narrower definition of a trust for sale contained in the Law of Property Act, 1925.[2]

It is of vital importance to distinguish these two assurances. They are mutually exclusive. The first is governed by the Settled

Meaning of a settlement.

Importance of distinction between

---

[1] *Infra,* pp. 696-9.   [2] *Infra,* pp. 150-1.

settlement
and trust
for sale.

Land Act, the second by the Law of Property Act. Indeed, it is expressly enacted that the statutory definition of a settlement contained in the Settled Land Act shall not apply to land held on trust for sale.[1] The chief practical importance of the distinction is that upon the occasion of a conveyance title to settled land must be made by the tenant for life, since the legal estate is vested in him, while title to land held upon trust for sale must be made by the trustees. The result of a mistake in this regard is troublesome and expensive, for a purchaser who takes a conveyance from the trustees when the instrument is a settlement or from the tenant for life in the reverse case, does not thereby acquire the legal estate.

SECTION I.   THE STRICT SETTLEMENT.

1. The General Framework.

Object of a
strict
settlement.

A settlement is best illustrated by a description of what is called the " strict settlement "—the classic method devised by conveyancers for ensuring, so far as the law permits, the retention of a family estate by the descendants of the settlor. It is proposed now to sketch in the barest outline the beneficial limitations that are adopted to bring this end about, without troubling for the moment to describe the actual form in which the settlement must be made.

Settlement in
contempla-
tion of
marriage :
list of bene-
ficial in-
terests.

If H., the owner of a fee simple absolute in possession, is about to marry W., and if he desires to provide for her and for the future children of the marriage out of the land, he will carve a succession of equitable interests out of the fee simple. These interests in the order in which they take effect are generally as follows :—

(i) A determinable fee simple to H. until his marriage.

(ii) A life interest to H. after his marriage.

(iii) A rentcharge to W. for life if she survives H.

(iv) A provision that a certain capital sum shall be charged on the land and distributed by the trustees after the death of the husband among the younger children of the marriage by way of what are called *portions.*[2]

(v) An entailed interest to the first and other sons successively according to seniority.

Function of
entailed
interest.

The ultimate limitation of an entailed interest to the first and other sons is the method best suited for keeping the land in the

---

[1] Settled Land Act, 1925, s. 1 (7).

[2] When the time for payment comes, the trustees may invoke the Settled Land Act, 1925, s. 16 (1) (iii), and call upon the life tenant to raise the money by a mortgage of the fee simple. The former practice of securing payment by the grant of a long term of years (a *portions term*) to trustees is now seldom followed.

family for at any rate a limited period. There are three stages in the legal life of a person to whom such an interest is granted by a marriage settlement.

First, there is a *contingent* interest, *i.e.* one that awaits the contingency of the son's birth before it arises.

Secondly, as soon as he is born, the son becomes entitled to a *vested interest in remainder*, *i.e.* an interest that, though definite, does not carry possession of the land until the death of the life tenant.

While in this stage he is entitled on his own initiative, upon the attainment of majority, to effect a disentailment which defeats the rights of his own descendants, but does not defeat the ulterior limitations to his brothers and their issue. The interest thus acquired by him is called a *base fee* and is described later.[1] If he takes this course he defeats the design of the settlor to tie up the land.

Thirdly, he becomes entitled upon the death of the life tenant to a vested interest in possession.

While in this final stage the eldest son, without consulting any other person, may acquire a fee simple which, though still subject to the prior beneficial interests settled upon his mother and the younger children of the marriage, will prevail not only against his own descendants, but also against all other persons, such as his brothers, who are entitled in remainder upon the determination of his entailed interest. He may do this by barring the entail either by deed[2] or by will.[3] If, however, he adopts neither of these dispositions, and dies leaving issue, the entailed interest descends to his heir. If he dies without issue, the interest passes to his next brother, and while unbarred, will descend to the brother's heir.

Subject, therefore, to a number of hazards there is at least a chance that the land will descend from son to son, a chance that would not exist if the ultimate limitation in a strict settlement were to the eldest son in fee simple. If this plan were adopted and if the eldest son were to die while still a minor, the fee simple would be sold and the proceeds divided amongst his relatives, collateral as well as lineal.[4] If he were to die after attaining his majority, he would be free to dispose of the fee simple by deed or will, but in the absence of such a disposition it would be sold and the proceeds divided as above.

Resettlement. The large landed proprietors who flourished under a less exacting Exchequer in the more spacious days of the past were not prepared, however, to allow the fate of the family

Modern practice of resettlement.

---

[1] *Infra*, p. 178. [2] *Infra*, p. 176.
[3] *Infra*, p. 181. [4] *Infra*, pp. 793 *et seq.*

property to depend upon the vagaries of the tenant in tail. They therefore evolved the process of resettlement that is still a feature of modern conveyancing, by which the tenant in tail in each generation, upon the attainment of his majority, is persuaded voluntarily to reduce his entailed interest to a life interest, and, by thus relinquishing his power of disentailment, to tie up the land for yet another generation.[1] Advantage is taken of the acquisitive side of human nature. The son, who is now entitled to a vested remainder in tail, requires a competence wherewith to face the pleasures and perils of this world. He possesses a ready means of raising money, since, presuming that he survives his father, he will succeed to the estate, and all that he need do is to come to an agreement with the moneylenders whereby, in return for a lump sum of money, he executes a partial disentailment by acting without the consent of his father, and conveys to them the base fee.[2] If this transaction is carried out, it may ultimately result in the estate being lost to the family—a disaster that is obviously repugnant to the father's wishes. Perhaps the position can be accurately, if cynically, summed up by saying that the father desires to keep the property in the family at the lowest cost to himself, while the son is anxious to place his pecuniary affairs on as prosperous a footing as possible. If, as usually happens, the two parties come to an amicable understanding, what takes place is a resettlement of the property. The lines of a resettlement are as follows [3] :—

Objects of re-settlement.

We will presume that the father is tenant for life under a strict settlement, that his wife is alive, and that the eldest son, being about to marry, is desirous, not only of acquiring an immediate allowance for himself, but also of making provision for his own wife and future children. It must also be presumed that, in consideration of the son cutting down his entail to a life interest, the father is prepared to consent to a disentailment and to charge his own life interest with the payment during the remainder of his life of a yearly rentcharge to the son.

Though one instrument may be employed, the transaction is generally carried out by two deeds—a disentailing assurance followed by a deed of resettlement.

Disentailing assurance.

The disentailing assurance, to which the father and the son are both parties, conveys the settled land to a third person, X. in fee simple,

subject to all the interests ranking before the entailed interest, with the exception of the father's life interest,

---

[1] *Supra*, p. 71.   [2] *Infra*, pp. 177–9.
[3] For a clear account see Elphinstone, *Introduction to Conveyancing*, pp. 638 *et seq*.

but freed from the father's life interest, the son's entail, and all the estates, rights and interests limited to take effect after the determination or in defeasance of the entailed interest.

It is then declared that the fee simple shall be held upon such trusts as the father and son shall jointly appoint, and in default of and until appointment upon the trusts of the existing settlement.[1]

The father and son as settlors, in the exercise of their joint power of appointment then fulfil their common design by a declaration of the appropriate trusts in the deed of resettlement. The first three of these, which are of course subject to the existing limitations in favour of the father's wife and younger children, are generally as follows :—

Deed of resettlement.

First an annuity of £x to the son during the life of his father if the son shall so long live.

Secondly, a life interest to the father in restoration of the life interest that he held under the old settlement.

The father thus regains the right to exercise the powers incident to his former life interest, and in addition becomes entitled to exercise any other powers that may be given by the resettlement deed.

Thirdly, a life interest to the son to take effect on the death of the father.[2]

The beneficial limitations, therefore, stand as follows :—

(a) a yearly rentcharge of £x to be paid to the eldest son during his father's life ;

(b) a life interest to the father ;

(c) a jointure to the father's widow ;

(d) portions for the younger children ;

(e) a life interest to the son ;

(f) entailed interests to the sons of the son ;

(g) a life interest (in case the first son's line fails) to the second son of the father ;

(h) entailed interests to the second son's sons ;

(i) similar interests for life and in tail to the father's other sons ;

(j) remainder in fee simple to the original settlor.

Then the deed empowers the son to provide a jointure for *his* wife and portions for his younger children, and finally declares that nothing in the resettlement shall prejudice

---

[1] For a precedent, see *Encyclopædia of Forms and Precedents* (4th Edn.), vol. vii, p. 618.

[2] *Ibid.*, vol. xvi. p. 470.

C.R.P.—F

the power of the father to appoint portions to his younger children under the original settlement, if this has not already been done. The documents which record the original settlement, the disentailment and the resettlement together constitute what is called a *compound* settlement.

Effect of re-settlement.
This process of resettlement, the outstanding feature of which is the reduction of the son's entailed interest to a life interest and the consequent loss of his power to obtain a fee simple absolute by executing a disentailing deed after his father's death, is generally repeated once in every generation when the prospective heir attains his majority, though the modern practice is to disentail at majority and to postpone the resettlement until his marriage. It is a process that affords the only method whereby land can be kept in a family. A man who is about to marry may desire to tie up the land in this manner for the longest period possible. His power in this respect, however, is limited by the Rule against Perpetuities [1] which precludes him from tying it up for longer than a life or lives in being plus a further period of 21 years. The utmost he can do, therefore, at the time of the marriage is to settle the land upon himself for life with remainder to his unborn children successively in tail, but when his eldest son reaches 21 and thus becomes competent to deal with the entailed interest, an opportunity presents itself of utilising this new life in being, if the son consents, to tie up the property for another generation. Even so, however, there is no certainty that the land will remain in the family even for this period, for the statutory power of sale given by the Settled Land Act enables any tenant for life at any moment to dispose of the legal fee simple. [2]

Effect of the Settled Land Act.
Such, then, is the outline of a strict settlement. Let us now state in a summary form, leaving the conveyancing details to be discussed later, [3] the manner in which it is affected by the Settled Land Act. The general position is as follows :—

Legal estate kept separate from equitable interests.
The legal estate transferred to the tenant for life by the vesting deed is kept rigorously separate from the equitable interests of the beneficiaries, such as those sketched above, which are contained in the trust instrument. [4] Throughout the duration of the settlement and however long that duration may be, the legal estate must and will be vested in a person or persons competent to deal with it as permitted by the Act. Normally, it will remain with the first tenant for life until his death, though in certain exceptional circumstances, as for example where his equitable life interest is forfeited under the terms of the settlement, it will pass to the trustees. On his death it will devolve on the trustees who will as soon as practicable convey it by a vesting deed or a vesting assent to the person next entitled. [5]

---

[1] *Infra,* pp. 240 *et seq.*   [2] *Infra,* pp. 131–2.   [3] *Infra,* p. 712.
[4] *Supra,* p. 97; *infra,* pp. 705–12.   [5] *Infra.* p. 710.

There are, however, several exceptional circumstances in which land is regarded as *settled*, though the equitable interest or interests to which it is subject are not those usually created by a settlor on the occasion of his marriage. The statutory definition of a settlement, indeed, is so wide[1] that land becomes settled within the meaning of the Act in a number of cases where the person entitled to immediate possession is far from being a life tenant in the normal sense, as for instance where he is a tenant in tail in possession or an infant to whom a fee simple has been devised. Nevertheless, the principle that the legal estate must be kept separate from the equitable interests is inflexibly maintained, and the statutory provisions are so framed that whenever a settlement exists there is always a person invested with the legal estate and therefore entitled to perform the functions of a tenant for life,[2] and there are always persons qualified to act as trustees.[3]

Person with powers of tenant for life always available.

2. The Statutory Powers of a Tenant for Life.

In accordance with the policy that has prevailed since the Settled Land Act, 1882, the person invested with the legal estate, normally the tenant for life in actual possession, is empowered by the Settled Land Act of 1925 to manage and even to dispose of the fee simple, an aspect of his position that must now be developed in some detail. The general policy is that he shall have many of the powers of dealing with the land that are available to an estate owner entitled beneficially in his own right, but subject to this overriding proviso, that any gain accruing from the exercise of a power shall be held on trust for the equitable beneficiaries according to the limitations of the settlement. To this end the Act confers upon the tenant for life the right to exercise any of the following powers:—

Tenant for life as manager of the land.

(A) **Power of Sale or Exchange.** The tenant for life may sell the settled land or any part thereof, or any easement, right or privilege of any kind over or in relation to the land.[4] Every sale must be made for the best consideration in money that can reasonably be obtained,[5] but instead of being made in return for a lump sum it may be made in consideration, wholly or partly, of a rent payable yearly or half-yearly and secured upon the land sold. Such a rent may be perpetual or terminable, and in the latter case—that is to say, when it will cease to be payable after a certain number of years—it must be treated partly as principal and partly as interest, and the part constituting principal must be dealt with as capital money. The interest accruing on the principal sum must be accumulated by way of compound interest and added each year to capital.[6] The rent must be the best obtainable, though for a period not exceeding five years from the

Rent as consideration.

---

[1] *Infra*, p. 697.   [2] *Infra*, pp. 699–701.   [3] *Infra*, pp. 701–4.
[4] Settled Land Act, 1925, s. 38 (i).   [5] *Ibid.*, s. 39 (1).   [6] *Ibid.*, s. 39 (2).

sale it may be nominal.[1]   The statutory remedies for the recovery of a rentcharge given by the Law of Property Act, 1925,[2] lie for recovery of the rent.[3]

Fully-paid securities as consideration.

It is also provided that where the land is sold to any company incorporated by special Act of Parliament or by any order having the force of an Act of Parliament, the purchase money may consist, either wholly or partially, of fully-paid securities of any description of the purchasing company.[4]

Exchange.

The tenant for life may make an exchange of the whole or part of the land, or of any easement or privilege over it, for other land or for an easement or privilege over other land, and he may pay or accept money in order to render the exchanges equal in value.[5]

Exception of mines and minerals.

When a sale or exchange is made, the tenant for life is permitted to except the mines and minerals, and in such a case to reserve for the settled land all proper rights and powers incidental to mining operations.[6]

Mansion-house.

The powers of sale and exchange are exercisable with regard to any principal mansion-house which stands on the settled land, but in two cases mere notice to the trustees of the proposed transaction [7] does not suffice, and the tenant for life must first obtain either the consent of the trustees or an order of the court, namely :

(i) where the settlement existed prior to January 1st, 1926, and does not expressly dispense with the necessity for such consent ; and

(ii) where the settlement came into operation after 1925, but contains a provision that such consent is necessary.

The court must determine as a fact whether any particular house is a principal mansion-house,[8] but it is enacted that a house which is usually occupied as a farmhouse, or which, together with its pleasure and park grounds, does not exceed 25 acres in extent, is not a principal mansion-house within the meaning of the Act and can in all cases be disposed of without the consent of the trustees.[9]

Leasing powers.

(B) **Power to Grant Leases.** The tenant for life may lease the whole or part of the land or any easement or privilege incidental thereto for any purpose whatever, whether involving waste or not, for any of the following maximum periods :—

(a) 999 years for a building lease,

(b) 100 years for a mining lease,

---

[1] Settled Land Act, 1925, s. 39 (3).   [2] S. 121 ; *infra*, p. 561.
[3] Law of Property (Amendment) Act, 1926, Schedule.
[4] Settled Land Act, 1925, s. 39 (5).   [5] *Ibid.*, s. 39 (1)
[6] *Ibid.*, s. 50   [7] *Infra*, p. 138.
[8] *Re Feversham Settled Estate*, [1938] 2 All E. R. 210.
[9] Settled Land Act, 1925, s. 65.

(c) 999 years for a forestry lease,

(d) 50 years for any other kind of lease.[1]

When any of the above leases is made,

(i) the tenant for life must give one month's notice in writing to the trustees,[2]

(ii) he must procure the best rent reasonably obtainable, and

(iii) the lease must be by deed and must contain a covenant by the lessee for payment of the rent, and a condition allowing the tenant for life to re-enter in case the rent is in arrear for thirty days.

Duties of tenant in granting leases.

The deed must be so framed that the lessee will take possession within twelve months, but if the land is already leased to a third person, then, provided that such existing lease has no more than seven years to run, it is lawful to grant what is called a reversionary lease to take effect in possession when the existing one determines.[3]

Without any notice to the trustees, a lease may be granted for a term not exceeding twenty-one years at the best rent that can reasonably be obtained without a fine, provided that the lessee is made impeachable for waste. If the lease does not exceed three years, it may be made by writing without a deed, but the lessee must enter into a written agreement to pay the rent.[4]

Lease without notice to trustees.

As in the case of the power of sale, the tenant for life may lease the land and reserve the minerals,[5] and if he desires to lease the principal mansion-house, he must obtain the consent of the trustees in the cases which have been specified above.[6] He may confer upon the tenant an option to purchase the fee simple, provided that the option is not made exercisable after ten years.[7]

Special provisions are inserted in the Act with regard to building, mining and forestry leases:—

(i) A building lease is resorted to when it is desired to develop land without burdening the settled estate with an immediate outlay of money. The procedure is to grant a long lease to a builder at a low ground rent on condition that he erects buildings of a specified nature to the satisfaction of the lessor and expends upon them a stipulated sum of money. Both sides obtain advantages. The builder will be able to sub-let the houses on their completion at a rack rent, while the lessor, though receiving only a small rent during

Building leases.

---

[1] Settled Land Act, 1925, s. 41.   [2] *Ibid.*, s. 101.
[3] *Ibid.*, s. 42 (1) (i).   [4] *Ibid.*, s. 42 (5).
[5] *Ibid.*, s. 50.   [6] *Ibid.*, s. 65, *supra*, p. 132.
[7] *Ibid.*, s. 51

the tenancy, will, subject to the Landlord and Tenant Act, 1954,[1] become the absolute owner of the buildings upon the determination of the term.[2] In order to guard against the danger that the builder may not erect houses of the stipulated character and cost, the usual practice is, in the first place, to enter into an executory agreement whereby the builder is given a mere licence permitting him to enter into and build upon the land, and then later, when the buildings are properly completed, to grant him a definite lease for the agreed period.

Every building lease must be made partly in consideration of the lessee or some other person erecting new or additional buildings or improving or repairing buildings, and partly in consideration of the payment of rent. A peppercorn or nominal rent may be reserved for the first five years of the term.[3] A lease is valid although it does not specify a definite time within which the building or rebuilding shall begin.[4]

Mining leases.

(ii) As regards minerals the rule is that a tenant unimpeachable for waste[5] can *open* and work mines and retain the whole profits, though this right can no longer be exercised without the permission of the local planning authority, since it involves a material change in the user of land within the meaning of the Town and Country Planning Act, 1962. A tenant impeachable cannot *open* mines, but he can continue to work to his own profit those that have already been lawfully opened by a predecessor.[6] These rules have been varied by statute. If the tenant is impeachable for waste in respect of minerals, three-quarters of the rent arising from a mining lease becomes capital; if unimpeachable, one-quarter becomes capital and the residue goes to him as income.[7] A tenant for life who is impeachable for waste under the settlement is not impeachable in respect of mines that have been lawfully opened by a predecessor, and therefore he is entitled to three-fourths of the rents.[8] These rules with regard to minerals have lost much of their importance since the passing of the Coal Industry Nationalization Act, 1946, but they are still material, for " minerals " include " all sub-

Part of rent is capital.

---

[1] *Infra*, p. 460.
[2] This will cease to be true and building leases will no longer be granted if the proposed Leasehold Enfranchisement Act is passed.
[3] Settled Land Act, 1925, s. 44.
[4] *Re Grosvenor Settled Estates*, [1933] Ch. 97.
[5] For the meaning of waste, see *infra*, p. 186.
[6] *Re Hall, Hall* v. *Hall*, [1916] 2 Ch. 488.
[7] Settled Land Act, 1925, s. 47. These provisions may be displaced by the settlement; s. 48.
[8] *Re Chaytor*, [1900] 2 Ch. 804; *Re Fitzwalter, Wright* v. *Plumptre*, [1943] Ch. 285; [1943] 2 All E. R. 328.

stances in, on or under the land, obtainable by underground or by surface working."[1]

(iii) A forestry lease is defined by the Act as a " lease to the Forestry Commissioners for any purpose for which they are authorized to acquire land by the Forestry Act, 1919,"[2] but this is now to be construed as a reference to the Minister of Agriculture, Fisheries and Food, in whom the former powers of the Commissioners to acquire land are now vested.[3] In a forestry lease the rent may be nominal for any period not exceeding the first ten years or may be made to vary according to the value of the timber cut in any one year, and any other provisions may be made for the sharing of the profits of the user of the land between the tenant for life and the Minister.[4]

Forestry lease.

(C) **Power to raise Money by the Grant of a Legal Mortgage of the Settled Land.** It is occasionally expedient to raise a capital sum of money by mortgage in order to meet some expense that is connected with the settled land or desirable in the interests of its prosperity. There are nine different purposes specified by the Act for which a tenant for life may raise money in this manner, but as five of these are connected with the conversion of copyhold into socage and of perpetually renewable leases into long terms, it is only necessary to notice that a mortgage is permissible when the object is[5]:

Power to borrow money.

(i) The discharge of an incumbrance on the settled land.

Purposes for which money may be borrowed.

If, for instance, different parts of the land are subject to three separate mortgages, the tenant for life may grant a new mortgage of the entire land to another mortgagee and use the money to pay off the three original debts.[6]

(ii) Payment for any improvement authorized by the Settled Land Act or by the settlement.

This is a valuable power that was introduced in 1925. A tenant for life may spend existing capital money on carrying out any of the improvements authorized by the Act,[7] but he had no power under the old Settled Land Acts to borrow new money on mortgage for the purpose, though he could raise a loan under the Improvement of Land Acts with the approval of the Ministry of Agriculture and Fisheries.

(iii) Equality of exchange.

(iv) Payment of the costs of any transaction effected under (i) to (iii) above.

---

[1] Settled Land Act, 1925, s. 117 (1) (xv).
[3] Forestry Act, 1945, s. 4 (1), (2), (10) (b).
[4] Settled Land Act, 1925, s. 48.
[6] *Re Clifford, Scott* v. *Clifford,* [1902] 1 Ch. 87.
[7] Settled Land Act, 1925, s. 83; *infra,* p. 136.

[2] *Ibid.,* s. 117 (x).

[5] *Ibid.,* s. 71.

A legal mortgage may take the form of a long lease, and a tenant for life who grants a mortgage term for any of the above four purposes is not subject to those provisions of the Settled Land Act [1] which in a normal case restrict the length of lease that may be made.[2]

(D) **Power to effect improvements.** The tenant for life is empowered to effect certain authorized improvements on the land and to have the cost defrayed out of capital.[3] Moreover, his right to this payment, unlike the practice prevailing before 1926, is no longer conditional on his submitting a scheme of operations to the trustees before the work is done.[4] The Act authorizes thirty-one specific improvements which are classified into three categories according to the permanence or impermanence of their results.[5]

Part I improvements comprise twenty-five different works that clearly increase the permanent capital value of the land, such as drainage, irrigation, bridges, defences against water, the provision of farmhouses and cottages for labourers and the rebuilding of the mansion house.

Part II improvements are those, the lasting value of which is more doubtful, such as the erection of houses for agents, the repair of damage due to dry rot or boring for water.

Part III improvements are those whose value is transitory, as, for example, the installation of a heating or electric power apparatus for buildings, the wiring of a house for electricity or the purchase of motor lorries for farming purposes.

Power to accept leases.

(E) **Power to accept Leases of other Land.** A new power was introduced by the Act of 1925 allowing the tenant for life to accept a lease of any other land or of mines, easements and privileges " convenient to be held or worked with or annexed in enjoyment to the settled land," and there is no limit to the length of the term which he may so accept.[6]

Miscellaneous powers.

(F) **Miscellaneous Powers.** There are several miscellaneous powers which the tenant for life is entitled to exercise, and of these the following may be mentioned :—

Surrender of leases.

(i) power to accept, with or without consideration, a surrender of any lease of settled land ; [7]

---

[1] *Supra*, pp. 132–3.   [2] Settled Land Act, 1925, s. 71 (3).
[3] *Ibid.*, s. 83.   [4] *Ibid.*, s. 84 (1).
[5] *Ibid.*, 3rd Schedule.   For the significance of this classification, see, *infra* p. 145.
[6] *Ibid.*, s. 53.   [7] *Ibid.*, s. 52 ; 23.

(ii) power to sell or lease to a waterworks company either gratuitously or at a nominal rent any water, streams, or springs upon the settled land if the effect will be for the general benefit of the settled land ; [1]

Powers relating to water.

(iii) power, if the result will be for the general benefit of the settled land, to make grants or leases at a nominal price or rent for certain public and charitable purposes, *e.g.* the grant of land not exceeding one acre for a village institute or a public library.[2]

Powers for benefit of public.

(iv) power to grant or lease a restricted amount of land at a nominal price or rent for the purpose of providing allotments or dwellings for the working classes ; [3]

Allotments, etc.

(v) power *with the consent of the trustees* or *under an order of the court* for a tenant for life who is impeachable for waste to sell timber that is ripe and fit for cutting, provided, however, that three-quarters of the net proceeds become capital money and one-quarter becomes income ; [4]

Timber.

(vi) power *under an order of the court* to sell heirlooms, but in such a case the money arising from the sale becomes capital money, which in this case may be spent on the purchase of other heirlooms.[5]

Heirlooms.

Finally "any transaction" within the powers of an absolute owner may be sanctioned by the court if this will be for the benefit of the land or the beneficiaries, even though it is a transaction not otherwise authorized by the Act.[6]

Cases where more than notice is required. As a general rule a tenant for life need not obtain the consent of the trustees to his exercise of a power, but if he intends to sell, exchange, mortgage or charge the land, to make a lease exceeding twenty-one years or to grant an option to purchase or to take a lease of the land, he must notify the trustees of his intention at least one month before he completes the transaction.[7] Except in the case of a proposed mortgage or charge, it is permissible, indeed usual, to give a general notice, *i.e.* one which states his intention to grant, for example, leases from time to time, without mentioning any specific lease already arranged.[8] There are, however, as we have

---

[1] Settled Land Act, 1925, s. 54.   [2] *Ibid.*, s. 55.
[3] *Ibid.*, s. 57 (2).   [4] *Ibid.*, s. 66.
[5] *Ibid.*, s. 67.
[6] *Ibid.*, s. 64 (1). "Transaction" is defined in s. 64 (2). *Re White-Popham Settled Estates*, [1936] Ch. 725; [1936] 2 All E. R. 1486; *Re Mount Edgecumbe (Earl)*, [1950] Ch. 615; [1950] 2 All E. R. 242; *Re Simmons*, [1956] Ch. 125; *Re Downshire's Settled Estates, Downshire (Marquess)* v. *Royal Bank of Scotland*, [1953] Ch. 218; [1953] 1 All E. R. 103, but the authority of this last case is weakened, if not destroyed, by *Chapman* v. *Chapman*, [1954] A. C. 429; [1954] 1 All E. R. 798, see *per* Lord MORTON at p. 462.
[7] *Ibid.*, s. 101 (1).   [8] *Ibid.*, s. 101 (2).

F*

seen, not a few cases in which something more than notice is required, and it may be helpful to restate these in summary form :

Powers requiring order of court.

First, an order of the court must be obtained before the tenant for life may :

(*a*) grant more than the amount of land specified in the Act for providing allotments or dwellings for the working classes ; [1]

(*b*) buy or sell heirlooms ; [2]

(*c*) grant building or mining leases for terms longer than those specified in the Act.[3]

Powers requiring order of court or consent of trustees.

Secondly, *either* an order of the court *or* the consent of the trustees must be obtained before the tenant for life may :

(*a*) sell or lease the principal mansion-house in the cases specified above ; [4]

(*b*) sell the timber in the event of his being impeachable for waste.[5]

Powers requiring consent of trustees.

Thirdly, there are two cases in which the tenant for life must obtain the consent in writing of the trustees, namely, before he

(*a*) compromises or otherwise settles any claim or dispute relating to the settled land ; [6]

(*b*) releases or modifies a restrictive covenant imposed on other land for the benefit of the settled land.[7]

Settlement may grant additional powers.

Additional Powers and Restriction of Powers. Such, then, are the powers conferred upon the tenant for life by the Act, but it must be remembered that there is nothing to prevent additional powers being given to him by the settlement, for it is expressly provided[8] that when a settlor authorizes the exercise of any powers additional to or larger than those enumerated above, they shall operate in exactly the same manner and with the same results as if they had been permitted by the Act. Thus a settlement may allow the tenant for life :

1. to apply capital money for the financing of builders who have agreed to take building leases on the settled land,[9]

2. to use as income the whole of the rent reserved on a mining lease,[10] or

3. to raise money on mortgage for the purchase of a dwelling-house.[11]

---

[1] Settled Land Act, 1925, s. 57 (2).   [2] *Ibid.*, s. 67.
[3] *Ibid.*, s. 46.   [4] *Ibid.*, s. 65, *supra*, p. 132.   [5] *Ibid.*, s. 66.
[6] *Ibid.*, s. 58 (1).   [7] *Ibid.*, s. 58 (2).   [8] *Ibid.*, s. 109.
[9] *Ibid.*   [10] *Ibid.*   [11] *Ibid.*, s. 108 (2).

In fact all the powers given by a settlement are expressly preserved, for it is provided that nothing in the Act shall take away or abridge any power under the settlement which is exercisable by the life tenant or by the trustees with the consent of the life tenant.[1]   If, however, there is any conflict between the Act and the settlement, the Act prevails, and any power (not being a mere power of revocation and appointment[2]), conferred on the trustees becomes exercisable by the life tenant as an additional power.[3]

Such a conflict occurs, for instance, if the settlement empowers the life tenant to sell with the consent of a third person, for such a conditional power is inconsistent with the unfettered power of sale given by the Act.[4]

But though a settlor is allowed to confer upon the tenant for life the right to exercise powers additional to those permissible under the statute, it is enacted in no uncertain terms that any provisions inserted in the settlement with a view to cutting down the statutory powers shall be absolutely void. The enactment runs as follows :— *Prohibition against exercise of powers void.*

" If in a settlement, assurance, will or other instrument . . . a provision is inserted—

(a) purporting or attempting, by way of direction, declaration or otherwise, to forbid a tenant for life or a statutory owner to exercise any power under this Act, or his right to require the settled land to be vested in him ; or

(b) attempting, or tending or intended, by a limitation, gift or disposition over of settled land, or by a limitation, gift or disposition of *other* real or any personal property, or by the imposition of any condition, or by forfeiture, or in any other manner whatever, to prohibit or prevent him from exercising, or to induce him to abstain from exercising, or to put him into a position inconsistent with his exercising any power under this Act, or his right to require the settled land to be vested in him ;

that provision, as far as it purports or attempts, or tends, or is intended to have, or would or might have, the operation aforesaid, shall be deemed to be void." [5]

A condition, that is sometimes inserted in settlements requiring the tenant for life to reside in the mansion-house will serve to illustrate the application of this section. *Exemplified by conditions as to residence.*

---

1 Settled Land Act, 1925, s. 108 (2).
2 As, for example, where land is limited upon such trusts as T. shall appoint, and subject thereto to A. for life. Here, T.'s power to revoke the life interest and to appoint new interests remains exercisable by him : Wolstenholme and Cherry, vol. ii, p. 1167.
3 Settled Land Act, 1925, s. 108 (2).
4 *Re Jefferys*, [1939] Ch. 205 , 55 L. Q. R. 22.
5 Settled Land Act, 1925, s. 106, *Re Orlebar*, [1936] 1 Ch. 147.

Suppose that land is settled on X. for life with a proviso that if he does not reside in the mansion-house for at least three months in each year he shall forfeit his interest.

Such a clause is void so far as it " tends " to hinder or obstruct the exercise by X. of his statutory powers. This, of course is its natural tendency, for if he sells or leases the estate he must necessarily infringe the condition as to residence. It is a deterrent of this nature that is within the mischief of the section, and the rule therefore is that, notwithstanding a disposition of the land under his statutory powers, his life interest in the income remains intact.[1] If, on the other hand, there is no question of the exercise of the powers, his failure to satisfy the condition operates as a forfeiture of his interest.[2] If it has never been his intention to exercise the powers, it cannot be said that the condition has in any way hampered his freedom of action.

Another example of the operation of the section is this :—

If the settlor vests a fund of money in the trustees, with authority to apply the income thereof upon the maintenance of the estate and to pay any surplus not required for that purpose to the life tenant, X., the prospect of losing this income might tend to dissuade X. from exercising his power of sale. As a general rule, therefore, if he sells the land he still remains entitled to the income for life.[3]

Powers not assignable.

Again, as long as the land remains settled, the powers of a tenant for life are indestructible in the sense that they are not capable of assignment or release, but remain exercisable by him notwithstanding any assignment by operation of law or otherwise of his beneficial interest under the settlement.[4] Thus :

If lands stand settled on A. for life, remainder to B. for life with remainder over, and B. sells his reversionary life estate for value to X., the statutory power to grant leases after the death of A. is exercisable by B., for the design of the Act is to enable a life tenant to exercise his powers whether he has disposed of his beneficial interest or not.[5]

In such a case as this the former rule was that B. could not exercise his powers without the consent of his assignee for value, X., but the necessity for such consent has now been removed by the Act.[6] The rights of the assignee are, however, protected, for whatever interest he had in the property originally assigned

---

[1] *Re Paget* (1885), 30 Ch. D. 161 ; *Re Patten*, [1929] 2 Ch. 276. (An excellent example of the principle.) *Re Aberconway's Settlement Trusts, McLaren* v. *Aberconway (Baron),* [1953] Ch. 647 ; [1952] 2 All E. R. 981.
[2] *Re Acklom,* [1929] 1 Ch. 195. *Re Haynes, Kemp* v. *Haynes* (1887), 37 Ch. D. 306 ; *Re Trenchard, Trenchard* v. *Trenchard,* [1902] 1 Ch. 378.
[3] *Re Ames, Ames* v. *Ames,* [1893] 2 Ch. 479 ; *Re Herbert, Herbert* v. *Bicester (Lord)* [1946] ; 1 All E. R. 421 ; dist. *Re Burden, Mitchell* v. *St. Luke's Hostel Trustees,* [1948] Ch. 160 ; [1948] 1 All E. R. 31.
[4] Settled Land Act, 1925, s. 104 (1).
[5] *Re Barlow's Contract,* [1903] 1 Ch. 382 ; *Earl of Lonsdale* v. *Lowther,* [1900] 2 Ch. 687.
[6] Settled Land Act, 1925, s. 104 (4).

to him he has a corresponding interest in any money, securities or land into which that property may have been converted as a result of the exercise of some power.[1] Moreover, notice of an intended transaction must be given to him.[2]

If, however, it is shown to the satisfaction of the court that a tenant for life has by reason of bankruptcy, assignment, or otherwise ceased to have a substantial interest in the settled land, and has unreasonably *refused* to exercise the statutory powers, an order may be made authorizing the trustees of the settlement to exercise the powers in his name.[3] The mere fact that he has grossly neglected the land and has allowed it to become derelict does not justify the making of an order. The court must be satisfied that there has been an unreasonable refusal to exercise the powers.[4]

Position where life tenant has no substantial interest in the settled land.

Although any attempted assignment of the powers by the tenant for life is void, it is provided that if the life interest, with the intention of causing its extinction, is surrendered to the remainder-man or reversioner next entitled under the settlement, the statutory powers shall cease to be available to the life tenant and shall be exercisable as if he were dead.[5] For instance :

Effect of a surrender of a life interest.

if a tenant for life becomes bankrupt and the trustee sells his life interest to the tenant in tail in remainder,[6] or if a father surrenders his life interest to the tenant in tail in remainder with the object of avoiding death duties, the statutory powers become exercisable by the tenant in tail.

Exercise of the Powers of a Tenant for Life in Favour of Himself. When a tenant for life exercises his statutory powers, he is normally dealing with persons who have no connection with the estate, but it may happen that in his private capacity and not as life tenant he wishes to exercise one of the powers in favour of himself. The possibility of such a dealing between him and the settled estate was first allowed to a restricted extent by the Settled Land Act, 1890, but his freedom in this respect has been extended by the Act of 1925, and it is now provided that any disposition of the settled land may be made to him, that capital money may be advanced on mortgage to him, and that land may be bought from or exchanged with him.[7]

Provisions enabling dealings with tenant for life.

---

[1] Settled Land Act, 1925, s. 104 (4) (*a*).
[2] *Ibid.*, s. 104 (4) (*c*).
[3] *Ibid.*, s. 24 (1). This section does not apply to a statutory owner, *Re Craven's Settled Estates*, [1926] Ch. 985.
[4] *Re Thornhill's Settlement*, [1940] 4 All E. R. 83 ; affirmed, [1941] Ch. 24 ; [1940] 4 All E. R. 249.
[5] Settled Land Act, 1925, s. 105 (1). Law of Property (Amendment) Act, 1926, Schedule.
[6] *Re Shawdon Estates Settlement*, [1930] 1 Ch. 217 ; affirmed, [1930] 2 Ch. 1.
[7] Settled Land Act, 1925, s. 68 (1).

Since a person can scarcely negotiate a transaction with himself, it is provided that in all such cases the trustees shall have all the powers of a tenant for life in reference to negotiating and completing the transaction, and the right to enforce any covenants entered into by the tenant for life.[1]

Position of tenant for life as trustee.

Tenant for Life is Trustee for the Beneficiaries. Finally, it must be observed that the tenant for life, though he is given an almost unfettered liberty to exercise the statutory powers, is at the same time constituted trustee for all interested parties. The Act provides that :

" A tenant for life or statutory owner shall, in exercising any power
" under this Act, have regard to the interests of all parties entitled
" under the settlement, and shall, in relation to the exercise thereof
" by him, be deemed to be in the position and to have the duties
" and liabilities of a trustee for those parties."[2]

Several judicial pronouncements have placed those duties on a high level. It has been said that the duty to " have regard to the interests of all parties " requires the life tenant to consider all the interests in the widest sense, not merely pecuniary interests, but even the aspirations and sentiments of the family.[3]

" He must " [said Lord Esher] " take all the circumstances of the
" family, and of each member of the family who may be affected
" by what he is about to do ; he must consider them all carefully,
" and must consider them in the way that an honest outside trustee
" would consider them ; then he must come to what, in his judg-
" ment, is the right thing to do under the circumstances—not the
" best thing, but the right thing to do."[4]

Nevertheless, having regard to the deliberate policy of the Act in conferring upon the life tenant virtually the status of absolute owner, this superimposed trusteeship is somewhat abnormal, for in the nature of things it must inevitably be " a highly interested trusteeship."[5] The mere imposition of a trust is insufficient to ensure that powers, so freely confided to the judgment of the life tenant, will not be exercised from motives of selfishness and personal aggrandizement. A tenant who, with the object of securing a larger income wherewith to meet his debts or to indulge expensive tastes, or in order to relieve himself from the cares of management, or because he is hostile to the remainderman, sells land that will obviously be of far greater

---

[1] Settled Land Act, 1925, s. 68 (2).
[2] *Ibid.*, s. 107 re-enacting s. 53 of the 1882 Act. *In re Pelly's Will Trusts,* [1957] Ch. 1, 18 ; [1956] 2 All E. R. 326.
[3] *Re Marquis of Ailesbury's Settled Estates,* [1892] 1 Ch. 506, 536 ; *per* LINDLEY, L.J. ; and see BOWEN, L.J., *passim.* " He must act as an upright, independent and righteous man would act in dealing with the affairs of others," *per* FRY, L.J., at p. 546.
[4] *Re Earl of Radnor's Will Trusts* (1890), 45 Ch. D. 402, 417.
[5] *Re Stamford and Warrington,* [1916] 1 Ch. 404, 420, YOUNGER, J.

value in a few years' time, owing perhaps to rapidly changing conditions in the neighbourhood, can scarcely be described as acting " as an upright, independent and righteous man would act in dealing with the affairs of others," [1] and yet none of these facts alone is sufficient to render him liable, provided that he obtains the best price and otherwise observes the requirements of the statute. [2]

The tenant for life, however, will be personally liable upon clear proof that he has exercised a power with the sole object of conferring some benefit upon himself or upon some relative other than the remainderman, as, for example, where he accepts a bribe from a lessee, [3] where he makes an unsuitable investment, [4] or where a widow entitled for life *durante viduitate* makes a lease to her second intended husband in order to ensure her continued occupation of the premises. [5]

Disposal of Capital Money. It is obvious that in several cases the exercise of a statutory power will result in the payment of money to the trustees ; this is called *capital money*. Thus, for instance,

What is capital money.

1. money which becomes due on the sale of the land or of heirlooms ; [6]
2. fines paid by lessees in consideration of obtaining a tenancy ; [7]
3. three-quarters or one-quarter (as the case may be) of a mining rent ; [8]
4. three-quarters of the money arising from the sale of timber by a tenant impeachable ; [9]
5. consideration paid by a lessee for an option to purchase the freehold ; [10]
6. damages received by the tenant for life in respect of a breach of covenant by his lessee ; [11] and
7. money raised by a mortgage of the land for the purposes authorized by the Act. [12]

are all examples of capital money. [13] The expression also covers money arising otherwise than under the Act which ought to be

---

[1] See p. 142, note 3.
[2] Cp. the remarks of PEARSON, J., in *Wheelwright* v. *Walker* (1882), 23 Ch. D. 752, at pp. 761-2.
[3] *Chandler* v. *Bradley*, [1897] 1 Ch. 315.
[4] *Re Hunt's Settled Estates*, [1906] 2 Ch. 11.
[5] *Middlemas* v. *Stevens*, [1901] 1 Ch. 574.
[6] Settled Land Act, 1925, s. 67 (2).
[7] *Ibid.*, s. 42 (4).
[8] *Ibid.*, s. 47 ; *supra*, p. 134.
[9] *Ibid.*, s. 66 (2).
[10] *Ibid.*, s. 51 (5).
[11] *Ibid.*, s. 80 (1).
[12] *Ibid.*, s. 71 ; *supra*, pp. 135-6.
[13] And see Settled Land Act. 1925, ss. 52 ; 54 (4) ; 55 (2) ; 56 (4) ; 57 (3); 58-61.

treated as capital,[1] as for example money paid under a fire insurance policy which the life tenant was under an obligation to maintain.

Application of capital money.

As regards the manner in which capital money must be disposed of, the first point is that if raised for some particular purpose, it must be applied accordingly. Thus, money that has been borrowed on mortgage in order to carry out some specific improvement on the land must be so spent. If, however, the money has not been raised for some particular object, but is due, for instance, to the sale of the land, it must be applied in one or more of the modes set out in the Settled Land Act.[2] In addition to any special mode permitted by the settlement itself there are twenty different modes indicated by the Act. It would be inappropriate in a book of this nature to set out the whole list, but a few of the more important methods will be noted :—

Investment.

(a) The most usual destination of capital money is investment in what are called *trustee securities*—that is to say, investments in which the Trustee Investments Act, 1961, authorizes trustees to invest trust funds. Money which thus requires to be invested is paid to the trustees or into court at the option of the tenant for life, and the investment is made according to his direction. It cannot afterwards be altered without his consent. The money, either before or after investment, represents the land from which it originated, and it is held in trust for the same persons for whom the land was held under the settlement and for the same interests, so that, for instance, the income arising from the investments is paid to the tenant for life in the same way as the annual profits of the land would have been paid prior to its sale.[3]

Loan on mortgage.

(b) Provided that a report of the value of the property is first obtained, capital money may be lent on legal mortgage of land in Great Britain or Northern Ireland up to two-thirds of the value of the property;[4] and when the settled land is sold in fee simple or for a term having at least 500 years to run, it is now enacted that a tenant for life may allow a sum not exceeding two-thirds of the purchase money to remain on mortgage of the land sold.[5]

Purchase of land.

(c) Capital money may also be expended in the purchase of land or of mines convenient to be worked with the settled land, provided that the interest so bought is either the fee simple or a leasehold having at least sixty more years

---

[1] Settled Land Act, 1925, s. 81.　　　　　　[2] *Ibid.*, s. 73.
[3] *Ibid.*, s. 75.
[4] Trustee Act, 1925, ss. 1 (1) (b) ; 68 (20).　　[5] *Ibid.*, s. 10 (2).

to run.[1] Again, it may be used to finance a person who has agreed to take a building lease of the settled land, advances being made to him on the security of an equitable mortgage of his building agreement.[2]

(*d*) Lastly capital money may be used in payment for any improvement authorized by the Settled Land Act.

Expenditure on improvements.

The procedure that governs payment varies according as the capital money is in the hands of the trustees or in court. In the former case the trustees, unless ordered by the court, must not pay for the improvement until they have obtained from a competent engineer or a practical surveyor, acting independently of the tenant for life, a certificate certifying that the improvement has been properly executed and declaring the amount that ought to be paid.[3] Where the capital money is in court, the court may, on a report of the Minister of Agriculture, Fisheries and Food, or of a competent engineer or surveyor, or *on such other evidence as it may think sufficient*, make what order it thinks fit for the application of the money in payment of the improvement.[4]

Where capital money is with trustees.

Where capital money is in court.

In cases where the work done is not of lasting value it is economically sound that the life tenant should ultimately restore the amount expended to capital by the creation of a sinking fund out of income, and it is with this object in view that the Act classifies the authorized improvements into the three categories that have already been mentioned.[5] The position is this :—

Rules to repayment of cost.

Part I improvements. The tenant for life cannot be required to set up a sinking fund.

Part II improvements. Before meeting the cost out of capital, the trustees *may* if they think fit, and must if so directed by the court, require that the money shall be repaid to them out of the income of the settled land by not more than fifty half-yearly instalments.[6]

Part III improvements. The trustees *must* require the whole cost to be paid out of income in the manner mentioned above.[7]

The court, when in possession of the capital money, is in the same position as the trustees with regard to requiring repayment of the money, except that it is not bound to require repayment in twenty-five years.

The effect of an order requiring repayment by instalments is that the settled land becomes subject to a yearly rentcharge which

---

[1] Settled Land Act, 1925, s. 73 (1) (xi and xii).
[2] *Ibid.*, s. 73 (1) (xviii).   [3] *Ibid.*, s. 84 (2).
[4] *Ibid.*, s. 84 (3).   [5] *Ibid.*, 3rd schedule ; *supra*, p. 136.
[6] *Ibid.*, s. 84 (2) (*a*).   [7] *Ibid.*, s. 84 (2) (*b*).

takes effect as if it were limited by the settlement prior to the estate of the tenant for life.[1] If, however, the subject-matter of the settlement is agricultural land used as such for the purposes of a trade or business,[2] capital money may be applied in the execution of any improvements specified in the Agricultural Holdings Act, 1948,[3] without any provision being made for the replacement of the cost out of income.[4] How prejudicial this may be to remaindermen is evident from the inclusion in the specified improvements of the execution of running repairs other than those which the tenant is under an obligation to carry out.[5] This power to pay for improvements out of capital, however, is not available to trustees holding land under a trust for sale.[6]

Decay of the strict settlement. Such, then is the strict settlement—the method by which for nearly three centuries the man of property was accustomed to provide for his wife and issue. The exactions of the tax-collector, however, stepped-up by two world wars and increasing annually with the prodigality of the Welfare State, have rendered this practice impracticable and almost obsolete, though of course many settlements executed in the past are still operative and will remain so for some years to come. It is, indeed, obvious that the present level of taxation may spell disaster to an estate that has been settled in the traditional manner. Where there has been a succession of life estates consequent upon the periodical re-settlement of the estate, the payment of sur-tax may leave insufficient income for the proper maintenance of the land and its buildings. Again, although the beneficial rights of each tenant are confined to the receipt of the annual income arising from the property, estate duty is payable at his death on the full capital value of the settled property, with the result that it will probably be necessary to sell part of the land in each generation in order to meet the demands of the Treasury. Thus, property strictly settled is likely to be a rapidly diminishing entity.

Effect of high taxation upon settlements. It is scarcely surprising, therefore, that the man of property now concentrates his thoughts not upon the retention of the land in the family but upon mitigating the rigour of taxation, and it is to this end that the art of the conveyancer is largely directed. Settlements can be devised that will considerably reduce the amount payable by way of income tax, sur-tax and estate duty, so long as the settlor is prepared to renounce all claim over and interest in the settled property. He must be a man of some

---

[1] Settled Land Act, 1925, s. 85.
[2] Agricultural Holdings Act, 1948, s. 1 (2).
[3] *Ibid.*, Third Schedule.   [4] *Ibid.*, s. 81 (1) ; 94 (1).
[5] *In re The Duke of Northumberland, Halifax* v. *Northumberland*, [1951] Ch. 202 ; [1950] 2 All E. R. 1181 ; *In re Sutherland Settlement Trusts*, [1953] Ch. 792 ; *In re Lord Brougham's and Vaux's Settled Estates*, [1954] Ch. 24.
[6] *In re Wynn, Public Trustee* v. *Newborough*, [1955] 2 All E. R. 865 ; [1955] 1 W. L. R. 940. *In re Boston's Will Trusts, Inglis* v. *Boston*, [1956] Ch. 395 ; [1956] 1 All E. R. 593.

wealth and content to sacrifice part of his income for the good of the family. As has been well said in a leading treatise on the subject :—

> " If the property is retained in the hands of the head of the family
> " until his death, a high rate of tax and death duty is likely to be
> " incurred, and the family will suffer a financial loss. If, however,
> " the property vested in the head of the family is regarded as the
> " property of the family, it is a normal step for him to spread his
> " property over the whole family during his life, and if this is done
> " the tax and duty imposed upon the property will thereby be
> " reduced."[1]

To explain what can be done in this direction is a matter for the specialist,[2] but by way of illustration the possibilities of the discretionary trust may be adumbrated.[3] Such a trust is one under which the disposition of property is left to the discretion of the trustees within the limits prescribed by the donor.[4] A settlor, for instance, may establish a trust to endure for a fixed number of years under which the trustees are given an absolute discretion to apply the income or capital of the settled property as they think fit in favour of one or more members of a prescribed class of persons, such as his children, grandchildren and great grandchildren. Thus the income arising from the trust property is no longer the settlor's, provided that he survives for five years after the formation of the trust. Moreover, in view of the absolute discretion vested in the trustees, a member of the family has no enforceable right to a share of capital or income and therefore his liability for estate duty will not be increased by the fact that he was a potential beneficiary of the trust property. During the continuance of the trust, indeed, no estate duty whatsoever will be payable in respect of property still retained by the trustees, provided that no one of them is a potential beneficiary.

Importance of the discretionary trust.

SECTION II. THE TRUST FOR SALE.

An alternative method of settling land is to adopt the device of a trust for sale.

It will facilitate the understanding of this if we first consider a settlement of personalty, the beneficial limitations of which are usually similar to those found in a trust for sale of land. Such a settlement generally takes the following form.

Personalty settlement.

The subject-matter of the settlement, which in most cases consists of stocks, shares and other investments, is transferred to the trustees as legal owners to be held by them upon certain trusts. These beneficial trusts vary according as the property has been provided by the husband or by the wife.

---

[1] Potter and Monroe, *Tax Planning* (3rd Edn.), p. 71.
[2] See especially the book mentioned in the previous note.
[3] *Ibid.*, pp. 170–205.
[4] For a fuller description, see 21 Conv. (N.S.), p. 55 (L. A. Sheridan).

(i) Wife's
fund.

If the property is provided by or on behalf of the wife, the first trust is usually for the wife during her life, the second for her husband during his life if he survives her.

Protective
trust.

But in order to guard against the possible extravagance of the husband, it is a common practice to attach a *protective* trust to the property brought into the settlement by the wife, by which the husband is given, not an absolute life interest, but an interest determinable on his bankruptcy. This is called a *protected life interest.* It is followed by discretionary trusts stating how the trustees may deal with the income of the property if the interest of the husband is determined by his bankruptcy. These trusts were formerly set out in detail, but this is no longer necessary for it has been enacted that a mere declaration directing income to be held on *protective trusts* shall confer certain discretionary powers upon the trustees.[1] The statutory effect of using the expression is that the interest of the husband automatically determines if he attempts to alienate or charge it or if he becomes bankrupt,[2] and the trustees at their discretion may then apply the income during the rest of his life for the maintenance or support, or otherwise for the benefit, of any one or more of the following persons:

the husband,[3] the wife and the issue of the marriage, or, if there is no wife or issue, the persons who, if the husband were dead, would be entitled to the settled property or its income.

Trust for
children.

The property brought into the settlement by the wife is then limited in trust, after the death of the survivor of the husband and wife, for such issue of the marriage and in such shares as the husband and wife or the survivor shall appoint, and in default of appointment for such children of the marriage as attain 21, or being daughters marry under that age.

Thus, after the death of the parents, the capital of the trust fund is divided among the children according to the shares fixed by any appointment, or equally between them if there has been no appointment.

Trusts in
default of
children.

Lastly, trusts are declared with the object of making a final disposition of the property should there be no issue of the marriage. The usual practice now is to declare that the wife's fund, after the death of the husband, shall be held in trust for the wife absolutely

---

[1] Trustee Act, 1925, s. 33. As to protective trusts, see 21 Conv. (N.S.) pp. 110 *et seq.*; 323 *et seq.* (L. A. Sheridan).

[2] If, by virtue of a power contained in the settlement, the husband makes an advancement to an infant beneficiary, this is not a disposition that will cause his life interest to be forfeited, *Re Shaw's Settlement, Shaw* v. *Shaw,* [1951] Ch. 833; [1951] 1 All E.R. 656.

[3] In most cases the income will be paid to the husband. This is not an infringement of the bankruptcy law, for the income, since the husband has no *right* to it, is not property belonging to him that must pass to the trustee in bankruptcy; *infra,* pp. 291–2.

if there is no child who attains a vested interest under the settlement.[1]

Corresponding trusts are declared of the property brought into the settlement by the husband. The first trust is for the husband for life ; the second for the wife during her life if she survives him ; the third, in favour of the children, is the same as that declared of the wife's fund ; and the fourth, to take effect upon the failure of issue and if the wife is dead, is to the husband absolutely. (ii) Husband's fund.

In accordance with the rule that a person cannot limit his *own* property to himself until bankruptcy and then over to another,[2] a protective trust appended to the life interest in the property contributed by the husband, is void against his general creditors in the event of his subsequent bankruptcy. But there is a distinction in this context between alienation on bankruptcy and other forms of alienation, and he may guard against his own improvidence in these latter respects by taking a life interest that is to determine upon any attempt to alienate it, whether the alienation is voluntary by himself, as for example, a mortgage,[3] or involuntary by process of law in favour of a particular creditor, provided, however, that this is followed by a gift over in favour of his wife or some other person.[4]

It is now possible to appreciate the nature of a settlement by way of trust for sale of land. This is generally called a *trader's settlement*, since the object is not to pass the land in its entirety to the eldest son on the death of the settlor, but to distribute the value of the land, in the shape of money, among the children of the marriage when both parents are dead. Trust for sale.

In general a trust for sale arises where land is transferred by deed or will to trustees with an imperative direction that they are to effect a sale and to hold the proceeds thereof upon certain specified trusts. The manner of its formation has already been sufficiently described,[5] though it should be recalled that owing to the doctrine of conversion it constitutes a settlement not of land, but of money, and that therefore the beneficial limitations in the second deed usually correspond to those of a personalty settlement. How effected.

An instrument does not create a trust for sale unless it contains a peremptory direction imposing a duty upon the trustees to sell. A *trust* to sell must always be distinguished from a *power* to sell. A trust is obligatory upon the trustee, a power leaves it to his Trust distinguished from power.

---

[1] Before 1926 a more elaborate limitation was necessary because of the rule, then obtaining, that if property were given to the wife absolutely it would pass to the husband absolutely in the event of his survival. Under the new rules that govern the distribution of property on intestacy, the husband no longer becomes absolute owner of his wife's property unless she leaves no near relatives ; *infra*, pp. 793–4.

[2] *In re Pearson* (1876), 3 Ch. D. 807.

[3] *Brooke* v. *Pearson* (1859), 27 Beav. 181.

[4] *Re Detmold, Detmold* v. *Detmold* (1889), 40 Ch. D. 585.

[5] *Supra*, pp. 79–80 ; 147–51.

discretion whether he will sell or not. It has, indeed, been enacted that a disposition coming into operation after 1925 which directs that the trustees shall *either retain or sell* land shall constitute a trust for sale,[1] but, apart from this statutory provision, whether an instrument creates a trust or confers a power is a question that can be answered only by construing its terms. What is in form a trust for sale may be nothing more than a discretionary power ; what is in form a power may, when properly construed, be an imperative trust.[2] The distinction is of great importance in conveyancing, for if what is given to the trustees is a mere power of sale, it is exercisable not by them but by the tenant for life.[3] The trustees become trustees within the Settled Land Act, the land is settled land within the meaning of the same Act and is not subject to a trust for sale, and the proper person to make title is the tenant for life.[4]

Statutory definition of " trust for sale."

A trust for sale for the purposes of the Law of Property Act is required to be an " immediate binding " trust,[5] but the conveyancing view is that these two words do not alter the meaning hitherto attributed to the expression " trust for sale." [6]

Must be " immediate."

The word " immediate " does not mean that the land must be sold at once, for complete power to postpone the sale is implied in every case, unless a contrary intention appears.[7] Its significance is to distinguish a trust for sale from a *future* trust for sale. A future trust is not immediately effective, and it is enacted that where it is imposed upon land, the trustees are to be trustees for the purposes of the Settled Land Act, not trustees for sale.[8] Thus, if land is devised to a wife for life and after her death upon trust for sale, the land *during her life* is settled land and is governed by the Settled Land Act.[9]

Must be " binding."

" Binding " imports that the trust is imperative and irrevocable. An imperative trust is one which is obligatory upon the trustees in the sense that, according to the language of the instrument, the land must be sold ultimately, though the actual time of sale is a

---

[1] Law of Property Act, 1925, s. 25 (4).
[2] *Re Newbould, Carter* v. *Newbould* (1913), 110 L. T. 6, *per* SWINFEN EADY, L. J. ; compare *Re White's Settlement, Pitman* v. *White*, [1930] 1 Ch. 179. For the distinction between a power and a trust, see *infra*, pp. 196-8.
[3] Settled Land Act, 1925, s. 108.
[4] *Ibid.*, ss. 30 (1) (i) ; 108 ; 109 ; *infra*, p. 702. The position before 1926 involved a conflict of powers, since the tenant for life had a statutory, the trustees an express, power of sale. The Settled Land Act, 1882, s. 56, provided that in such a case the tenant for life should be unfettered in the exercise of the power, and that the trustees should not sell without his consent.
[5] Law of Property Act, 1925, s. 205 (1) (xxix).
[6] *Re Parker's Settled Estates, Parker* v. *Parker*, [1928] Ch. 247, dissenting from *Re Leigh's Settled Estates*, [1926] Ch. 852. See also *Re Leigh's Settled Estates* (No. 2), [1927] 2 Ch. 13 ; *Re Norton, Pinney* v. *Beauchamp*, [1929] 1 Ch. 84 ; *Re Sharpe's Deed of Release, Sharpe and Fox* v. *Gullick*, [1939] Ch. 51, 70 ; [1938] 3 All E. R. 449, 457.
[7] Law of Property Act, 1925, s. 25 (1).
[8] Settled Land Act, 1925, s. 30 (1) (iv).
[9] *Re Jackson's Settled Estates*, [1902] 1 Ch. 258.

matter of discretion. An instrument which imposes a duty upon the trustees, as distinct from one which gives them a mere power, may rightly be described as creating a binding trust.

The power of postponement may lead to the land remaining unsold for a considerable period, and it is essential that during the interval between the creation of the trust and the actual sale, the trustees should possess powers of disposition and management. These are given to them in abundance by the Law of Property Act, 1925. *(margin: Powers of trustees pending sale.)*

Despite the fundamental distinction between a settlement and a trust for sale, it is provided in the first place that the trustees, in relation to the land and the proceeds of sale, shall have all the powers given to a tenant for life and his trustees by the Settled Land Act, 1925.[1] Thus, for example, they may grant leases, raise money on mortgage for improvements and, after a sale of all or part of the land, may invest the proceeds in the purchase of other land.[2] It is further provided by the same section that they shall have the powers of management that are exercisable by trustees under section 102 of the Settled Land Act during the minority of a tenant for life of *settled* land. These include powers to

> erect, rebuild and repair houses ;
> continue the working of quarries ;
> drain or otherwise improve the land ;
> make allowances and arrangements with tenants ; and
> generally to deal with the land in a proper and due course of management.

Although, in the case of settled land these powers given by section 102 are exercisable only during the minority of the tenant for life, they may be exercised by trustees for sale whether there is a minority or not.[3]

In most cases the trustees will not have that close interest in the welfare of the land, that is desirable if the most provident use is to be made of these powers. It is, therefore, enacted that while the land remains unsold they may revocably delegate from time to time the *powers of leasing, of accepting surrenders of leases, and of management* to any person of full age (not being merely an annuitant), who is beneficially entitled in possession to the rents and profits for his life or for any less period.[4] Thus, pending sale, *(margin: Right of trustees to delegate certain powers.)*

---

[1] Law of Property Act, 1925, s. 28 (1), as amended by Law of Property (Amendment) Act, 1926, s. 7.

[2] *Re Wellsted's Will Trusts, Wellsted* v. *Hanson,* [1949] Ch. 296 ; [1949] 1 All E. R. 577.

[3] *Re Gray, Public Trustee* v. *Woodhouse,* [1927] 1 Ch. 242.

[4] Law of Property Act, 1925, s. 29 (1). Formerly, the law was different. While the land remained unsold the powers of leasing and of management were not possessed by the trustees. Instead, they were given to the person beneficially entitled to the income (Settled Land Act, 1882, s. 63), though they were not exercisable by him without the leave of the court (Settled Land Act, 1884, s. 7). If the powers are now delegated to him, he is in the same position as if before 1926 he had obtained the above leave.

the welfare of the land may be entrusted to the person most anxious to promote it.

How the law of settlements might be simplified.

This right of delegation, introduced by the legislation of 1925, points the way to a possible and much needed simplification of the law.

There are at present two methods open to a landowner who desires to provide for a succession of beneficiaries. He may create a settlement or a trust for sale. These are diametrically opposed in their objects. The first is designed to keep the land in the family as long as possible, the second is directed to the conversion of the land into money. In fact, as soon as a trust for sale comes into operation, the land is regarded by equity as already being money. It followed, therefore, under the old law, that the normal strict settlement limitations could not be employed in a trust for sale, for these hinge on the entailed interest given to the eldest son, and before 1926 such an interest could not be carved out of money. Now, however, any species of property may be entailed. There is, therefore, no longer any reason why the beneficial limitations of a trust for sale should not follow the pattern of a strict settlement.

> The trustees may, for example, be directed to hold the rents and profits until sale, and the ultimate proceeds of sale, upon trust for the settlor for life, and then, after provision of a rentcharge for his widow and of portions for his younger children, upon trust for his sons successively in tail.

If this were done and if advantage were taken of the power to postpone the sale indefinitely, the rights of the beneficiaries would be the same as if the land had been " settled " by a vesting deed and a trust instrument in accordance with the Settled Land Act.

Trust for sale might be made the one mode of settle- ment.

Thus, if it were enacted that all settlements of land must be created by way of trust for sale, nothing of value would be lost. Any ambition to keep the land in the family could still be satisfied, in fact even more effectively than by employing a strict settlement, since there would be no tenant for life with a statutory and un- fettered power of sale. The merit of such an enactment would lie in the further simplification of conveyancing, since, for one thing, the occasional difficulty of deciding whether land is settled or held on trust would no longer arise.[1] It would never be doubtful whether the trustees or the tenant for life were the appropriate parties to make title. It would always be made by the trustees.

It would seem, indeed, that the task of the conveyancer would be facilitated and unnecessary expense avoided if the Settled Land Act

---

[1] As to this difficulty, see 54 L. Q. R. p. 576 *et seq.* For a modern example, see *In re Herklot's Will Trusts, Temple* v. *Scorer,* [1964] 2 All E. R. 66; [1964] 1 W. L. R. 583.

were repealed and replaced by a short statute amplifying the provisions of the Law of Property Act with regard to trusts for sale.[1]

---

[1] For another suggestion see the proposal of Professor Malcolm M. Lewis, 54 L. Q. R., pp. 580–2. For a critical examination of the respective merits of the settlement and trust for sale, see Potter in 8 *Conveyancing and Real Property Lawyer*, pp. 147 *et seq.*

CHAPTER II.

ENTAILED INTERESTS.

SUMMARY.

SECTION I. HISTORY.

Conditional fee precursor of estate tail.   **Introductory Note.** The estate known to the common law as a conditional fee was the precursor of the estate tail. About the year 1200 it was becoming a common practice to limit lands to a man and a special or restricted class of his heirs, as for instance :—

1. to a man and " the heirs of his body " ; or
2. to a husband and wife and the heirs springing from their marriage ; or
3. to a woman and the heirs of her body—a form of gift that was called a *maritagium*.[1]

As the object of such a gift was to provide for a man's descendants, it was an understood thing that if the donee or one of his issue to whom the land descended died without leaving any heirs of the class specified in the instrument of creation, the estate, being no longer required for the maintenance of the family, should revert to the donor, and should not, like a fee simple, pass to the general heirs of the donee.[2] The courts, however, animated probably by a desire to render land freely alienable and to this end to prevent it from being irrevocably ear-marked for a particular family, took an entirely different view of the matter, for they held that if a grant were made to A. and the heirs of his body, or to him and any similarly restricted class of heirs, A. could make an out-and-out alienation of his estate, binding on his own heirs and on the donor, as soon as a child of the class indicated was born to him.   They said that the effect of such a gift was to confer upon A. a conditional fee, that is to say, an absolute fee simple, conditional however upon the birth of issue capable of inheriting the estate according to the terms of the original gift.   When once that condition was satisfied, even though the child died the next minute, A. was in as favourable a position as if the lands had originally been granted to him in fee simple, for at common law a condition once performed is utterly gone; but if the condition was not fulfilled by the birth of issue, then on A.'s death the estate reverted to the donor and his heirs.[3]

Meaning of conditional fee.

Statute *De Donis*.   But this rule, which meant in effect that the donee could alienate the land and thus defeat both the right of his issue to succeed to the estate and the right of the donor to take the estate back if issue already born became extinct, was not popular.   As early as 1258 there was an outcry against a doctrine that ran so contrary to the expressed intention of donors, and the result of this feeling was the passing in 1285 of the famous statute *De Donis Conditionalibus*.[4]   This enacted that the intention of the donor according as it was manifestly expressed in the original gift, should thenceforth be

Statute De Donis.

---

[1] Holdsworth, *History of English Law*, vol. iii. pp. 74, 111 ;   Plucknett, *Legislation of Edward I*, pp. 125–131.

[2] If the gift took the form of what was called *liberum maritagium*, the rule was that after the land had descended three times there should no longer be any reverter to the donor and his heirs.   Thus, the third heir became entitled in fee simple ; Plucknett, *Legislation of Edward I*, pp. 126–9.

[3] Pollock and Maitland, *History of English Law*, vol. ii. pp. 16–19 ;   Co. Litt. 19a ;   Challis, *Law of Real Property* (3rd Edn.), pp. 263–8.

[4] Statute of Westminster II. (1285), set out in full, Digby, *History of Real Property*, p. 226.

observed, so that those to whom the land was given should have no power to alienate it, but that it should pass to their issue, or to the giver or his heirs if such issue failed, either by an absolute default of issue or, after the birth of issue, by its subsequent extinction.[1]

Origin of fee tail.

The result of this statute was the appearance of a new kind of fee or inheritable estate, called a fee tail, or in Latin *feodum talliatum*, and so called because the quantum of the estate was " cut down " in the sense that, unlike the case of the fee simple, the right to inherit was restricted to the class of heirs specially mentioned in the gift, and was not available to the heirs-general of the donee.[2]

The land could not be disposed of by the tenant in tail, it could not be seized in satisfaction of his debts after it had come into the hands of his successors, and it was not forfeitable for treason or felony—a fact which, in those disturbed times, was regarded by the Crown as a serious defect.[3]

Remedies of donor and issue.

Special remedies were given to the issue and to the donor for the recovery of the land in case the form of the original gift was not observed, and these were called respectively the *writ of formedon* in the descender and the *writ of formedon* in the reverter.[4]

There was thus set up an entailed interest in the true and proper sense of that term, that is to say, an interest in land that was bound to descend from one generation to another to the issue of the tenant, and which could not by any means whatsoever be removed from the family so long as any lineal heirs of the class specified were in existence. It was an unbarrable entail, since neither the right of the issue to succeed, nor the right of the donor and his heirs to take on failure of issue, could be barred or taken away.[5] This state of affairs continued for some 200 years after the Statute *De Donis*, but the statute, instead of being a blessing calculated to ensure the stability of families, proved to be one of the most mischievous institutions in the realm. In a famous passage Blackstone has described some of its effects :[6]

Blackstone on the evils of unbarrable entails.

" Children grew disobedient when they knew they could not be set " aside ; farmers were ousted of their leases made by tenants in tail, " for, if such leases had been valid, then, under colour of long leases, " the issue might have been virtually disinherited ; creditors were " defrauded of their debts, for if tenant in tail could have charged his " estate with their payment, he might also have defeated his issue, by

---

[1] See Challis, *Law of Real Property* (3rd Edn.), p. 228.
[2] Litt., s. 18 ; Challis, *op. cit.* (3rd Edn), p. 60.
[3] 1st Rep. of Real Property Commission, 1829, p. 22.
[4] Holdsworth, *History of English Law*, vol. ii. p. 350.
[5] This apparently was not the intention of the draftsman of the statute. What was intended was that the land should be inalienable only until the third heir had entered, after which it could be alienated out of the family ; Pluck-nett, *Legislation of Edward I*, pp. 131–5.
[6] Blackstone, vol. ii. p. 116.

" mortgaging it for as much as it was worth ; innumerable latent
" entails were produced to deprive purchasers of the lands they had
" fairly bought, of suits in consequence of which our ancient books
" are full ; and treasons were encouraged, as estates tail were not
" liable to forfeiture longer than for the tenant's life. So that they
" were justly branded as the source of new contentions and mis-
" chiefs unknown to the common law, and almost universally con-
" sidered as the common grievance of the realm. But as the nobility
" were always fond of this statute, because it preserved their family
" estates from forfeiture, there was little hope of procuring repeal by
" the legislature . . ."

Methods of barring Estates Tail. Although the *Statute evaded.*
legislature did not step in to remedy a grievance that appears to
have borne so heavily upon the community, the ingenuity of
lawyers finally—and at least as early as 1472—contrived to discover means whereby estates tail could be barred and converted
into estates in fee simple, free from the succession rights of heirs
and from the rights of those persons who were entitled to take
upon a failure or extinction of heirs. The actual methods invented
are now a matter of ancient history, and it must suffice here to
state their names and their general effect.

1. **Common Recovery.** The most usual method was *to* *Evasion by common recovery.*
suffer a common recovery. In the earliest days of its history
a common recovery was a collusive real action which a
collaborator (called the *demandant*) brought against the tenant
in tail for the recovery of the land entailed. The tenant in
tail did not raise a substantial plea to the claim preferred
against him, but stated, contrary to the truth, that he had
obtained the land by conveyance from one X., who, at the
time of the conveyance, had warranted for himself and his
heirs that the title granted to the tenant in tail was a good one.
X., who was an accomplice of the parties, admitted the
warranty by disappearing from court. The court thereupon
proceeded to deliver judgment, that on the one hand the
demandant should recover the entailed lands for an estate
in fee simple, and that on the other the tenant in tail should
recover lands of equal value from X.

Now the effect of this collusive action was to defeat the *Effect of common recovery.*
rights both of the tenant's issue and of the persons entitled
on failure of issue, because if lands of equal value had
actually been recovered from X., which they never were, they
would have replaced the original entailed estate and would
have descended in the same manner. Ostensibly this was so,
but none of the untrue allegations made in the course of the
proceedings was traversable, and therefore all that the
persons entitled after the death of the tenant acquired was
a judgment enforceable against a man of straw. The court

was not prepared to tolerate a plea that a judgment, solemnly pronounced, was in effect nugatory.[1]

After delivery of judgment the demandant would convey either the fee simple or its value to the former tenant in tail.

Evasion by fine.

2. **Levy of a Fine.** The second method was to levy a fine. A fine, which from the earliest times had been regarded as the most sacred and efficacious form of conveyance known to the law,[2] was in substance a conveyance of land but in form an action.[3] It was an amicable composition or agreement of an action, made with the leave of the court, whereby the lands in question were acknowledged to belong to one of the parties, and it derived its name from the fact that it put an end (Lat. *finis*) to the action.[4] One of the purposes for which it was used was to bar an estate tail. The tenant in tail covenanted to sell the fee simple to a collaborator, and when he was sued by the latter in an action of covenant he decided to capitulate, and with the leave of the court a concord was drawn up acknowledging that the lands belonged to the plaintiff.

Difference between fine and common recovery.

From one point of view the levying of a fine was not so effective as the suffering of a recovery, since it barred the rights only of the tenant's issue, while a recovery barred not only the issue, but also everybody who became entitled to the estate on failure of issue. On the other hand, a fine, which was a personal action, enabled a tenant in tail who was not for the moment tenant in possession, *e.g.*

> where there was a grant to A. for life and after his death to B. in tail,

to bar his own issue without the necessity of obtaining the possessor's collaboration. In such circumstances, a *common recovery* was impossible unless the aid of the life-tenant, A., was obtained, because the proceedings reproduced the stages of a genuine action, and one of the fundamental rules of procedure was that a real action could be brought only against the person actually seised of the land.

Abolition of recoveries and fines.

Recoveries and fines, which even in their origin were collusive actions, gradually became wholly fictitious. Only formal matters

---

[1] For a full account see Blackstone, vol. ii. pp. 357 *et seq.* ; Cruise, vol. v. pp. 282, 493 ; Burton, *Real Property*, pp. 231–9 ; Pollock, *The Land Laws*, pp. 80–9 ; Digby, *History of Real Property*, pp. 251–4 ; 1st Report of Real Property Commission, 1829, pp. 21–3 ; Holdsworth, *History of English Law*, vol. iii. pp. 118 *et seq.*

[2] Holdsworth, *History of English Law*, vol. iii. p. 239.

[3] Pollock and Maitland, *History of English Law*, vol. ii. p. 94.

[4] Blackstone, vol. ii. p. 349 ; Challis, *Law of Real Property* (3rd Edn.). p. 304.

were transacted in court. If a tenant in tail desired to bar his entail, all that he did was to instruct his solicitor to suffer a common recovery. But the solicitor, in carrying out the instructions, did not simply frame a deed expressing the tenant's intention, but was obliged to prepare a long and complicated document that recited all the stages and events of an action which was supposed, contrary to fact, to have been litigated. Moreover, the fees that would have been payable had the action been actually brought were still payable. The result was that to convert a fee tail into a fee simple was a tedious and expensive transaction, and one which, owing to the complicated and exceedingly difficult state of the law, required an expert for its completion, and even then often failed to produce a sound title. The Real Property Commissioners, in their Report issued in 1829, stated :

" there is no object, however complicated, that could not be effected
" by a simple instrument, expressing in clear and intelligible language
" the intentions of the parties,"

and the result of their recommendations was the passing of the Fines and Recoveries Act, 1833, which abolished both recoveries and fines, and introduced a simple and straightforward method by which an estate tail might be barred.[1]

SECTION II. DIFFERENT CLASSES OF ENTAILED INTERESTS.

SUMMARY.

Introductory Note. We have already seen that an entailed interest is one that is given to a person and after his death to a specified class of that person's heirs. The different classes of entailed interests depend upon the terms of the instrument of gift and vary according as the estate is descendible to the heirs of the donee by any spouse or by a particular spouse, and also according as the heirs are restricted as to sex or not.

---

[1] *Infra*, p. 175.

In this way we get six different classes of entailed interests.

(1) Interests in tail general.
      (A) Interests in tail male general.
      (B) Interests in tail female general.
(2) Interests in tail special.
      (A) Interests in tail male special.
      (B) Interests in tail female special.

We will deal with each of these separately.

(1) INTERESTS IN TAIL GENERAL.

Estate tail general.

How they arise. An interest in tail general is the widest type of entailed interests. Such an interest arises when land is limited to

A. and the heirs of his body begotten,

without any restriction either as to the wife upon whose body the heirs are to be begotten, or as to the sex of the heirs who are to take.[1] It matters not how many times A. marries, for any child by any wife is eligible to succeed. If the entailed interest is not barred by the tenant during his lifetime nor left by his will it still descends according to the old canons of descent which were formerly applicable to all inheritable fees,[2] but which were abolished by the Administration of Estates Act, 1925, so far as regards the fee simple.

Subject to old canons of descent.

The canons of descent that concern an entailed interest are the following[3]:—

1. DESCENT IS TRACED FROM THE LAST PURCHASER, *i.e.* from the original donee in tail.[4] *Purchaser* in this context is a law term denoting anyone who acquires an estate by act of parties as distinct from act of law.[5] In this sense of the word an owner of land is a purchaser unless he has inherited it—or, in other words, unless it has descended upon him as a result of the last owner's intestacy. Practically the one and only way in which a person acquires an entailed interest nowadays is by virtue of a family settlement, and if by deed or will lands are settled upon X. for life and after his death on his son and the

---

[1] Litt., ss. 14, 15; Blackstone, vol. ii. p. 113.
[2] Law of Property Act, 1925, s. 130 (4).
[3] The canons are those that affected the descent of a fee simple before 1926 (*infra*, pp. 789–92), except those that relate to ancestors and collaterals.
[4] Blackstone. vol. ii. p. 222.
[5] It is a term, however, that has no uniform meaning; see *Inland Revenue Commissioners* v. *Gribble*, [1913] 3 K. B. 212, where at p. 218, BUCKLEY, L.J., said : " ' Purchaser,' as it seems to me, may mean any one of four things. First, it may bear what has been called the vulgar or commercial meaning ; purchaser may mean a buyer for money. Secondly, it may also include a person who becomes a purchaser, for money's worth, which would include the case of an exchange (see, *e.g., infra*, p. 649). Thirdly, it may mean a purchaser for valuable consideration, which need not be money or money's worth, but may be, say, a covenant on the consideration of marriage. Fourthly, it may bear that which in the language of real property lawyers is its technical meaning, namely a person who does not take by descent." See *infra*, p. 171.

heirs of his body, the son is a purchaser with regard to the entailed interest. When the son (A.) dies intestate, this first rule of descent requires us to look for *his* nearest lineal heir : and if A.'s eldest son B. takes the estate by descent and then himself dies intestate, the rule demands that we should look for the nearest heir not of B., but of A., because B., having himself taken by descent, is not a purchaser. Of course the son of B., if he has one, will be entitled as heir.

2. PRIORITY OF MALES. An entailed interest must descend to the lineal issue of the last purchaser, and the males of this issue rank before females of equal degree.[1]

3. PRIMOGENITURE. Where there are two or more males of the same degree, the eldest takes the entire interest to the exclusion of the rest ; but if there are no males, but two or more females of the same degree, all the females inherit together and are called coparceners.[2]

4. REPRESENTATION. Lineal descendants, *ad infinitum*, of any person deceased represent their ancestor, that is, occupy the same position as he himself would have occupied had he been living. Suppose, for instance, that A., who is tenant in tail, has two sons, X. the elder and Y. the younger, and X. dies before A., but leaves a son Z. On the death of A. the interest will pass to the grandson Z. and not to the son Y.[3]

So where there is an interest in tail general limited to

A. and the heirs of his body,

and A. dies intestate having failed to bar the entail, his eldest son by his first wife will take first. If the eldest son has predeceased A. leaving no children, the second son of A., or such son's representative if he is dead, will take, and so on through the sons in the order of their seniority. Failing sons or children of sons, the daughters of A. will share equally as coparceners.

Curtesy. Under the old law a husband was entitled in certain circumstances to a life interest in the whole of the land of which the wife died seised in fee simple or in tail. He became what was called a " tenant by the curtesy." Curtesy has been abolished with regard to all interests except an entailed interest,[4] and therefore the subject can only now be of importance when a female *tenant in tail* dies intestate.

Curtesy still applies to entailed interests.

The pre-requisites of this life interest are that the wife should have been actually [5] and solely [6] seised of the entailed interest, and

Modern position.

---

[1] Blackstone, vol. ii. pp. 212–14.

[2] *Ibid.*, vol. ii. p. 214. As to coparceners see *infra*, pp. 309–10.

[3] *Ibid.*, vol. ii, pp. 216–20.

[4] Administration of Estates Act, 1925, s. 45 (1) (*b*) ; Law of Property Act, 1925, s. 130 (4). But curtesy in respect of a fee simple may still, though rarely, arise under the Administration of Estates Act, 1925, s. 51 (2). This provides that the old rules of descent shall apply to realty (excluding chattels real) to which a lunatic, living on January 1st, 1926, and dying after that date without having recovered testamentary capacity, is entitled.

[5] *I.e.* by actual occupation or by receipt of rents and profits. This was seisin in deed as distinct from seisin in law. *Parks* v. *Hegan*, [1903] 2 I. R.643.

[6] Co. Litt. 29*a* ; *Doe d. Neville* v. *Rivers* (1797), 7 Term. Rep. 276.

that issue of the marriage capable of inheriting the land should have been born alive within her lifetime.[1] To satisfy the last requirement it is sufficient that a child should have been actually born alive though it may have died the next moment,[2] but it is essential that the child should be a person capable of succeeding to the land. Thus if there is a limitation to a woman and the heirs male of her body, and she bears a daughter only, her husband cannot take by curtesy.[3]

At common law once the requirements had been satisfied and an estate by the curtesy had vested in the husband, it could not be divested without his concurrence, for a wife could not alienate her freeholds except by a fine to which her husband was a party. The recognition, first by equity and in 1883 by statute, that a married woman could freely dispose of what was called her *separate property*,[4] revolutionized the position, for curtesy could be claimed only in non-separate property or in separate property that had not been alienated. At the present day non-separate property is extinct, and a new power of leaving entailed interests by will was introduced by the Law of Property Act, 1925. Hence it is only in the one case where a married woman dies intestate in respect of an entailed interest that her husband will become tenant by the curtesy.[5]

(A) **Interests in tail male general.** This arises where lands are limited to

> A. and the heirs *male* of his body begotten,
>
> the factor in which this species of estate differs from an interest in tail general being that only male heirs are to succeed.[6] Sons by any wife are capable of inheriting, and so are any other male issue claiming continuously through male issue, but daughters and their issue, whether male or female, can never inherit.

(B) **Interests in tail female general.** This is analogous to the last interest except that the only heirs entitled to take are females. Though this is a possible form of limitation, it never arises in practice.[7]

(2) INTERESTS IN TAIL SPECIAL.

Character- istic of special entails.

The characteristic of the remaining entailed interests is that by the words of the instrument of creation their descent is restricted to the heirs of the body of two specified persons, and not

---

[1] Litt. ss. 35–52.
[2] Blackstone, vol. ii. p. 127.
[3] Co. Litt. 19a. As to curtesy in general, see Blackstone, vol. ii. pp. 126 *et seq*.
[4] *Infra*, pp. 865–6.
[5] *Hope* v. *Hope*, [1892] 2 Ch. 336. Law Reform (Married Women and Tortfeasors) Act, 1935, s. 4 (1) (a).
[6] Litt. s. 2 ; Blackstone, vol. ii. p. 114.
[7] Co. Litt. 25a. ; Hargrave's note.

to the heirs of one, as in the cases described above. Such an estate may be limited either to one donee, *e.g.*:

> to H. and the heirs begotten by him on the body of W.,

or to two donees, *e.g.*:

> to H. and W. and the heirs of their two bodies begotten.[1]

In both cases it will be seen that it is not the heirs of H. by any wife who are capable of inheriting the interest, but only the children and their issue who can trace their descent from the particular wife W. If the limitation is to

> H. and the heirs begotten by him on the body of his wife W.,

H. has an interest in tail special and the wife has nothing.[2] But the effect of a limitation to H. and W. and the heirs of their two bodies begotten varies according to the relative positions of H. and W. If W. is the wife of H. or a person whom he may lawfully marry, the effect is to vest a joint interest in tail special in H. and W.;[3] but if H. and W. are persons who may not lawfully intermarry, by reason, for instance, of consanguinity, the limitation makes them joint tenants for life with separate inheritances.[4] That means that if H. dies first and has issue, W. becomes sole tenant for life, but that on the death of W. the issue of H. take one half and the issue of W. the other half as tenants in common in tail.[5] The result will be the same if, though capable of intermarrying, H. and W. do not actually intermarry.

After what has been said it will be sufficient to give the appropriate words of limitation for granting the remaining species of entailed interests :—

(A) **Interests in tail male special.** Grant to

> A. and his heirs male which he shall beget on the body of his wife X. ;

or to

> A. and X. and the heirs male of their two bodies begotten. [6]

(B) **Interests in tail female special.** This arises from the same limitation as that just described, with the substitution of female for male.[7]

Interest in tail after possibility of issue extinct. An entailed interest special may by implication of law give rise to what is called an entailed interest after possibility of issue extinct. If lands are given to a man and his wife, or to the man or to the

[margin: Tenant in tail after possibility.]

---

[1] Litt. s. 16 ; Preston on Estates, vol. ii. p. 413.
[2] Litt. s. 29   [3] Co. Litt. 20*b* ; 25*b*.
[4] Litt. 283 ; Preston, vol. ii. p. 417.   [5] Co. Litt. 182*a*.
[6] Litt. 25.
[7] For the whole of this section see Challis, *Law of Real Property* (3rd Edn.), pp. 290–5.

wife solely, in special tail, and one of them, or the designated spouse, dies before issue has been born, the survivor is termed a *tenant in tail after possibility*; and likewise if one dies leaving issue, but the other survives the issue.[1]   In both these cases it will be seen that, owing to the premature death of one of the persons from whose body the appropriate heirs are to proceed, it is impossible that any person should become entitled to succeed to the interest in accordance with the terms of the original gift. The possibility of the right class of heirs coming into being no longer exists, and therefore the survivor is said to be a tenant after possibility.   Such a person is virtually in the position of a tenant for life and he is not entitled to bar the entail.[2]   He is given the statutory powers of a tenant for life by the Settled Land Act.[3]

(3) WORDS OF LIMITATION.

We have now to consider what expressions—or, to speak technically, what words of limitation—must be used in order to create an entailed interest.   Owing to the way in which the matter was dealt with by the Act of 1925, it is unfortunately necessary to discuss the rules which obtained under the previous law.   The examples that have been given above of the various classes of entailed interests indicate the general nature of the proper words of limitation, and a short treatment of the subject will suffice here.

(A) CREATION BY DEED UNDER THE OLD LAW.

Deeds before 1926.

The first point is to ascertain the proper words of limitation necessary under the old law for the creation of an entailed interest by *deed*.

Word "heirs" essential.

1. The requirement of common law here was that the word *heirs* must be used and not such analogous expressions as *seed, offspring, descendants, issue* and so on.[4]   The effect of a grant, for example, to " A. and his issue " was to confer upon A. a mere life estate.

Lineal heirs.

2. The next requirement was that some expression denoting that the inheritance was to pass to the direct descendants of A. should be used, and the surest phrase for this purpose was *of his body*.   A grant to " A. and the heirs of his body " always conferred an entailed interest on A., but common law, though insisting upon the use of the word *heirs*, was not so exacting with regard to this second requirement, and was

---

[1] Litt. 32.
[2] Fines and Recoveries Act, 1833, s. 18 ; see *infra*, p. 180.
[3] Settled Land Act, 1925, s. 20 (1) (i).
[4] Co. Litt. 20 *a, b* ; Blackstone, vol. ii. p. 115.

satisfied with any words which expressly or by implication showed that the heirs were to issue from the body of A. Thus such expressions as

" of his flesh,"
" from him proceeding," or
" which he shall beget of his wife "

were sufficient for the purpose.[1]

Before January 1st, 1882, if the appropriate words of limitation as set out above were not adopted in a deed, the result was to confer a life estate upon the grantee, but the Conveyancing Act of 1881 [2] provided that in deeds executed after that date it should be sufficient to use the words *in tail* instead of *heirs of the body*, and the words *in tail male* or *in tail female* instead of *heirs male* or *heirs female* of the body.[3]

(B) Creation by Will under the Old Law.

Greater latitude of terminology was, however, open to testa- Wills before
1926. tors. It is more difficult to lay down hard and fast rules as to what words would, and what words would not, have created a certain interest when they were used in a testamentary as distinct from an *inter vivos* instrument, because the general principle of construction for wills is that the intention of the testator must be ascertained and given effect to, no matter what language he may have adopted, and as the *indicia* of intention vary infinitely and do not always impress judges in an equal degree, it is often Greater
latitude
allowed. dangerous to dogmatize that this or that expression will raise any particular estate. But at any rate we are on sure ground in saying that less formal language would create an entailed interest in a will than in a deed, and in fact any expressions that indicated an intention to give the devisee an estate of inheritance, descendible to his lineal as distinct from his collateral heirs, conferred an entailed interest upon him.[4]

Thus devises to

" A. and his seed," [5]
" A. and his offspring," [6]
" A. and his family according to seniority " [7]
" A. and his issue," [8]
" A. and his posterity " [9]

---

[1] Co. Litt. 20b. [2] S. 51.
[3] For criticism see Challis, *Law of Real Property* (3rd Edn.), pp. 297–8.
[4] Jarman on Wills, (7th Edn.), p. 1800.
[5] Co. Litt. 9b.
[6] *Young* v. *Davies* (1863), 2 Dr. & Sm. 167.
[7] *Lucas* v. *Goldsmid* (1861), 29 Beav. 657.
[8] *Oxford University* v. *Clifton* (1759), 1 Eden 473.
[9] *Wild's Case* (1599), 6 Co. Rep. 17a.

have all, at one time and another, been held capable of passing an entailed interest when such a construction was consistent with the intention of the testator.

Executory instruments.   The same rule of construction was applied in the case of executory instruments *inter vivos*, that is, in instruments which do not finally express the limitations in technical language, but indicate their general nature and leave the settlor's intention to be carried out by apt phraseology. What are called " marriage articles " form the commonest example of an executory instrument. They constitute a contract by which an intending husband and wife specify in general the terms upon which they are willing to enter into a marriage settlement. Thus, if marriage articles provide for the limitation of an interest to the " issue " of the husband and wife, the presumed intention will be carried out in the formal settlement by the grant of an entailed interest to the first son of the marriage, with remainders in tail to the other children.[1]

The rule in Wild's Case.   A devise " to A. and his children," requires particular attention because of the *Rule in Wild's Case*[2] laid down in 1599.[3] The rule was that

> where realty was devised to 'A. and his children', and A. had no child *at the time of the devise*, the word children was *prima facie* construed as a word of limitation, with the result that A. acquired an estate tail.

There was some justification for this. The testator clearly intended children to take in any event, but since they were not in existence they could take nothing except through A. and he could transmit to them nothing unless he was given an estate of inheritance.[4]

The rule, however, was not inflexible and it was disregarded by the courts where it would operate to defeat the intention of the testator as gathered from other passages in the will.[5]

(C) Words of Limitation under the Modern Law.

Law of Property Act, 1925.   We are now left with this question :—what words are necessary and sufficient to create an entailed interest in the case of a deed or will that comes into operation after 1925. The Law of Property Act, 1925, enacts as follows:

> An interest in tail may be created by way of trust in any property, real or personal, but only by the like expressions as those by which before January 1st, 1926, a similar estate tail could have been created *by deed* (not being an executory instrument) in freehold land.[6]

---

[1] *A.-G.* v. *Bamfield* (1703), 2 Freeman 268.   [2] (1599), 6 Co. 17*a*.
[3] See *infra*, p. 169 n. 5.
[4] *Radcliffe* v. *Buckley* (1804), 10 Ves. 195, 202, *per* Sir William Grant, M.R.
[5] *Byng* v. *Byng* (1862), 10 H. L. Cas. 171, 178 ; *Grieve* v. *Grieve* (1867), L. R. 4 Eq. 180.
[6] Law of Property Act, 1925, s. 130 (1).

The result is that the law on the subject is more inflexible Effect of
the Act. now than it was before 1926. The strict requirements of the common law applicable to deeds have been extended to wills. Thus, in both instruments the limitation must be to "A. in tail," or to "A. and the heirs of his body," except that in the last case any expressions will suffice that without expressly saying "of the body" indicate that the heirs are to issue from the body of A. The only exception to this rule is that a direction that personal property shall be enjoyed with land in which an entailed interest has already been created is sufficient to create a corresponding entailed interest in the personal property.[1]

On the other hand, informal expressions contained in the instrument which would not have been sufficient in a deed under the old law to create an entailed interest, though they would have been sufficient in a will or executory instrument, no longer suffice to create an entailed interest.[2] If, for instance, a testator who dies after 1925 devises land to " A. and his issue," an interest in tail does not pass to A.

The question that then arises is—what interest does pass to Effect of
instrument
not con-
taining
formal words
of limitation. A. when informal expressions such as " issue," " seed," " descendants " or " children " are contained in a conveyance or in a devise of land ?[3] The Act purports to provide an answer in a sub-section which in effect runs as follows :

> Expressions contained in an instrument coming into operation on or after January 1, 1926, which in a will made before that date would have created an entailed interest in freehold land, but would not have been effectual for that purpose in a deed, shall operate in equity, in regard to property either real or personal, to create absolute, fee simple or other interests corresponding to those which, *if the property affected had been personal estate*, would have been created therein by similar expressions before 1926.[4]

The first point to notice is that this sub-section is not concerned with those formal expressions that would have been Effect is
what it
would be if
the subject
matter were
personalty. effectual in a deed before 1926 to create an estate tail in land. A gift of personalty to A. and the heirs of his body or to A. in tail formerly gave A. the absolute ownership of the property,[5] but now, by virtue of the sub-section quoted on page 166,[6] it gives him an entailed interest. What we are concerned with here

---

[1] Law of Property Act, 1925, s. 130 (3).
[2] *Re Brownlie*, [1938] 4 All E. R. 54.
[3] The article by Mr. S. J. Bailey in 6 *Cambridge Law Journal*, pp. 67–82, should be consulted by all who desire to obtain a clear idea of this difficult matter. His article, however, has raised a controversy ; see 9 *Cambridge Law Journal*, pp. 46–55 ; 185–91. Reference should also be made to Jarman on Wills (7th Edn.), chapter xxxiii.
[4] Law of Property Act, 1925, s. 130 (2).
[5] *Chatham* v. *Tothill* (1771), 7 Bro. P. C. 453 ; *Portman* v. *Portman* (*Viscount*), [1922] 2 A. C. 473 ; Hawkins on Wills, p. 231.
[6] Law of Property Act, 1925, s. 130 (1).

are informal expressions, and we are told that if they appear in a grant or a devise of land operating after 1925, the donee is to acquire in the land the interest that he would have acquired in personalty had the same expression been contained in a gift of personalty. The question then is, what interest passes under a gift, for instance, of £5,000 Consolidated 4 per cent. Stock, in the following typical cases :

> To A. and his issue.
> To A. for life and then to his issue.
> To A. and his descendants.
> To A. and his children.

Find this and we know what interest is taken if the same expressions are adopted in a grant or devise of land.

The primary difficulty is that, since the effect of such informal expressions has always varied according as they appear in deeds or in wills, it is not obvious whether the rules for deeds or for wills are to be adopted. Presumably the solution is that a devise containing informal expressions is to have the effect that has always been allowed to a bequest containing the like expressions, and that a grant *inter vivos* is to have the effect that has always been attributed to a corresponding gift by deed of personalty.

The effect is that which the testator intended. Let us examine only *bequests* of personalty, for it is unlikely in practice that any but formal expressions will be found in a conveyance *inter vivos* of land.[1] It must be realized at once, however, that no unqualified rule can be laid down with regard to the *quantum* of interest that passes under this or that expression, for since the object in each case is to ascertain and to implement the intention of the testator, what always has to be done is to construe the will as a whole. Strictly speaking, the only correct answer to make to the question, " What interest is taken under a gift of personalty to A. and his issue ? " is, " That interest which the testator intended to give." Certain canons of construction have, however, become established that cover most of the expressions found in practice.

Gift to A. and his issue. The primary canon of construction is that a gift of personalty *to A. and his issue* shows an intention on the part of the testator that the issue alive when the will comes into operation shall take the property jointly with A.[2]

> " Thus, if the gift be immediate, A. and his issue (if any) living at
> " the testator's death would take in joint tenancy ; and if the gift
> " be deferred, issue subsequently born before the period of distribu-
> " tion would be admitted along with them ; and if no issue had come

---

[1] For the effect of gifts by deed containing informal expressions, see 6 *Cambridge Law Journal*, p. 81.

[2] *Re Hammond*, [1924] 2 Ch. 276.

" into existence before the period of distribution, A. would take the
" whole." [1]

Again, if there is a bequest to A. for life and after his death to
his issue, A. takes merely a life interest and the property is ultimately divided among the issue born during his life.[2]

Gift to A. for life and then to his issue.

Nevertheless this principle of construction which admits issue
as beneficiaries in the instances given is displaced if it appears
from the will as a whole that the testator meant to make A. sole
and absolute owner.

The word " issue " has consistently been held to mean
primâ facie descendants of every degree,[3] and it therefore seems
to follow that a gift of personalty *to A. and his descendants* is construed, in the absence of a contrary intention, in the same way
as a gift to A. and his issue.[4] The descendants alive at the death of
the testator take the absolute ownership jointly with A.

Gift to A. and his descendants.

A gift of personalty to *A. and his children* is *primâ facie* regarded
as a gift to A. and the children concurrently, so that A. and his
children alive at the testator's death take the property as joint
tenants, or, if there are no children living at that time, A. takes
the whole absolutely.[5]

Gift to A. and his children.

Rule in Shelley's Case.[6]—It is necessary to conclude this
account with an explanation of the *Rule in Shelley's Case*,[7] which,
though it has now been abolished by the Law of Property Act,
1925,[8] still remains of importance in the investigation of titles.

This rule, which was a rule applicable to deeds and to wills,
ordained that if in the same instrument an estate of *freehold* was
limited to A., with remainder, either immediately or after the
limitation of an intervening estate, to *the heirs* or to the *heirs of
the body* of A., the remainder, though importing an independent
gift to the heirs as original takers, conferred the fee simple in the
first case, and the fee tail in the second case, upon A., the ancestor.[9]
Thus the effect of a grant

Statement of the Rule.

to A for life, remainder to his heirs,

was to give A. the fee simple ; and the effect of a grant

to A. for life, remainder to the heirs of his body,

was to give A. an estate tail.

---

[1] Hawkins on Wills, pp. 241–2 ; the words quoted are those of Hawkins
himself.

[2] *Knight* v. *Ellis* (1789), 2 Br. C.C. 570 ; Jarman on Wills (6th Edn.),
p. 1200.

[3] Hawkins on Wills, p. 113.

[4] 6 *Cambridge Law Journal*, p. 75.

[5] Hawkins on Wills, p. 243. The rule in *Wild's Case* as stated above,
supra, p. 166, never applied to personalty.

[6] See Challis, *Law of Real Property* (3rd Edn.), pp. 52 *et seq.*

[7] (1581), 1 Co. Rep. 93b.

[8] S. 131.

[9] Hayes, *Introduction to Conveyancing*, vol. i. p. 542 ; Preston on Estates,
vol. i, 263–4.

G*

The interest which in terms was given to the heirs and which in most cases the donor, especially when he was a testator, meant the heirs to have, was in the eye of the law given to A. So A. could dispose of the estate and thereby defeat his heir, who would take only if A. died intestate still owning the estate.

Thus the operation of the rule was two-fold : it denied to a remainder the effect of a gift to the " heirs," and it attributed to the remainder the effect of a gift to A.[1] In fact, the legal effect of such a limitation was the direct opposite of what would naturally be expected, and it nearly always operated to defeat the intention of a testator. There was, however, some justification for the rule in the feudal conditions that attended its introduction. For one thing, the feudal lord would have lost some of the most valuable of the tenurial incidents if the heir, instead of coming in by descent, had been entitled *in his own right* to the land, as would have been the case if A. had taken a mere life estate.[2] Again, the rule facilitated free alienation, for, since a living person can have no heir, the alienation of the fee simple would have been impossible until after A.'s death if he had been regarded as a mere life tenant.

Another and more accurate way of stating the rule is as follows :

> Where the ancestor by any gift or conveyance takes an estate of freehold, and in the same gift or conveyance an estate is limited, either mediately or immediately to his heirs, in fee or in tail, in such cases " the heirs " are words of limitation of the estate and not words of purchase.

Words of purchase and words of limitation distinguished. This requires us to distinguish words of purchase from words of limitation. Words of purchase (*perquisitio*) point out, by name or description, the person who is to acquire (*perquirit*) an interest in land ; words of limitation indicate the size of the interest given by some instrument. A " purchaser " in this technical sense does not denote a person who buys land, but one to whom land is expressly transferred by *act of parties*, as for instance by conveyance on sale, by gift or by will. If land is given " to A. and his heirs," A. is a purchaser since he is personally designated as the transferee, but the words " and his heirs " are words of limitation. They merely indicate the *quantum* of interest that A. is to take, and give the heirs nothing by direct gift. The lands may, of course, descend to them as heirs if A. dies intestate, but they will not be purchasers since the land comes to them by operation of law and not by act of parties.[3] Thus, if land was given

to A. for life, remainder to the heirs of his body,

---

[1] Hayes, *op. cit.*, p. 534.
[2] Preston on Estates, vol. i, pp. 295–6.
[3] " Words of purchase are those which designate the first purchaser or

what the *Rule in Shelley's Case* declared was that the words " heirs of his body " were not words of purchase pointing out the heir as a person entitled to a definite interest in the land, but were words of limitation employed to mark out the extent of the interest given to A. Had the words " heirs of his body " been regarded as words of purchase, they would have indicated that the estate was given to the person who was found to be heir on the death of A. In other words, this person would have claimed the estate as having been given to him by the original conveyance. The result, in fact, was the same as if the grant had been

to A. and the heirs of his body,

but it is essential to notice that the *Rule in Shelley's Case* operated only where there were in terms two estates given, *i.e.* a freehold to the ancestor, A., and then a remainder to the heirs, *e.g.*

to A. for life and after his death to the heirs of his body.

It is true that a limitation *to A. and his heirs* or *to A. and the heirs of his body* gives A. a fee simple in the first case and a fee tail in the second case, but these results do not ensue from *Shelley's Case*. The law had been so established at a far earlier date.[1]

A mass of complicated rules was gradually erected around the rule,[2] but the chief difficulty that was encountered in its application occurred in the case of gifts by will, for it might operate in cases where the testator had used informal expressions such as *children, issue* and *descendants*. Moreover, although the rule was a rule of law in the sense that it could not be controlled by the intention of the testator once he had used words intended to be descriptive of heirs or heirs of the body of the ancestor, it was nevertheless necessary to construe the words that the testator

A rule of law.

person who is to take, and which cause an interest to attach in him originally. Words of limitation are words which serve to mark out the limits or quantity of an estate, and its course of devolution, and under which, in the case of an estate in fee or in tail, the heirs do not take originally but derivatively by descent from their ancestor "—Smith, *An Original View of Executory Interests* (1844), sections 403–4. Fearne, *Contingent Remainders*, pp. 79–80. " The word ' purchase ' (*perquisitio*) is applied in law to any lawful mode of acquiring property by the person's own act or agreement, as distinguished from acquisition by act of law, as descent, escheat and the like. A purchase in the above sense includes acquisition, not only under contract of sale for a valuable consideration, but also by gift or without consideration, and by devise."— Leake, *Property in Land*, p. 117. See also, *supra*, p. 160, note 5.

[1] If, for example, lands had been given " to W. and her heirs for her and their use absolutely and for ever," the *Rule in Shelley's Case* would not have applied, *Re McElligott, Grant* v. *McElligott*, [1944] Ch. 216 ; [1944] 1 All E. R. 441 ; 54 *L. Q. R.*, pp. 70 *et seq.* One of the commonest mistakes of examinees is to give as an illustration of the *Rule in Shelley's Case* a limitation *to A. and his heirs.*

[2] For clear statements of the essentials required to bring the rule into operation, see 32 Halsbury's Laws of England (3rd Edn.) para. 490. Challis, *Law of Real Property* (3rd Edn.), pp. 162 *et seq.*

Wills had
to be
construed
before rule
could be
applied.

had actually used in order to ascertain whether they were intended
to express what the law has always meant by the word " heirs,"
i.e. a man's whole inheritable issue. If the testator had meant
the words to bear that meaning, the *Rule in Shelley's Case* was
applied without exception; but if he had not used them in such a
wide sense, as for instance where he intended to designate some
individual person or some particular class of persons, the rule
was excluded and the particular donee or donees took an estate
by way of purchase,[1] as for example in the case of a strict settlement.[2] Thus the word *children*, aided by the context, might have
the force of the technical word *heirs* so as to let in the rule; while
the word *heirs*, restrained by the context, might have only the force
of the word *children*, and then the rule was irrelevant.[3] The rule
itself was a rule of law, but before the premises for its application
could arise there was a preliminary question of construction.
This was made clear by Lord DAVEY in the course of his speech
in the leading case of *Van Grutten* v. *Foxwell* [4] :—

> " In my opinion the rule in *Shelley's Case* is a rule of law and
> " not a mere rule of construction, *i.e.* one laid down for the purpose
> " of giving effect to the testator's expressed or presumed intention.
> " The rule is this : that wherever an estate for life is given to the
> " ancestor or *propositus* and a subsequent gift is made to take effect
> " after his death, in such terms as to embrace, according to the
> " ordinary principles of construction, the whole series of his heirs,
> " or heirs of his body, or heirs male of his body, or whole inheritable
> " issue taking in a course of succession, the law requires that the
> " heirs, or heirs male of the body, or issue shall take by descent,
> " and will not permit them to take by purchase, notwithstanding
> " any expression of intention to the contrary. Wherever, therefore,
> " the Court comes to the conclusion that the gift over includes
> " the whole line of heirs, general or special, the rule at once applies,
> " and an estate of inheritance is executed in the ancestor or tenant
> " for life, even though the testator has expressly declared that the
> " ancestor shall take for life and no longer, or has endeavoured to
> " graft upon the words of gift to the heirs, or heirs of the body,
> " additions, conditions or limitations which are repugnant to an
> " estate of inheritance, and such as the law cannot give effect to.
> " The rule, I repeat, is not one of construction, and, indeed, usually
> " overrides and defeats the expressed intention of the testator :
> " but the question always remains, whether the language of the gift
> " after the life estate properly construed is such as to embrace the
> " whole line of heirs or heirs of the body or issue, and that question
> " must be determined apart from the rule, according to the ordinary

---

[1] *Van Grutten* v. *Foxwell*, [1897] A. C. 658.
[2] *Re Williams Will Trusts, Pitts-Tucker* v. *Williams*, [1952] Ch. 828 ; [1952]
2 All E. R. 502, where the surprising claim was made that a devise " to the use of
my son William during his life with remainder to the use of his first and other
sons successively according to seniority in tail male " gave William an estate
tail under the rule. It seems a little difficult to conceive of a clearer case
where the intention of the remainder was to designate particular persons as
individuals to take in their own right, *i.e.* to take as purchasers.
[3] Hayes, *Introduction to Conveyancing*, vol. i. p. 543.
[4] [1897] A. C. 658, at p. 684.

" principles of construction, including those which I have already
" referred to."

There were in fact two separate questions, the blending of
which inevitably caused confusion. The first was, whether the
testator, by the expressions that he had used, had meant to describe heirs. This was the preliminary question of construction.
Given an affirmative answer, the second question was whether
the other conditions for the application of the rule were satisfied.[1]

The *Rule in Shelley's Case* was, however, abrogated, as from
January 1st, 1926, by the following section of the Law of Property
Act, 1925 [2] :—

Abrogation
of the Rule.

> " Where by any instrument coming into operation after the
> " commencement of this Act an interest in any property is expressed
> " to be given to the heir or heirs or issue or any particular heir or
> " any class of the heir or issue of any person in words which, but for
> " this section, would, under the rule of law known as the Rule in
> " Shelley's Case, have operated to give to that person an interest in
> " fee simple or an entailed interest, such words shall operate in equity
> " as words of purchase and not of limitation, and shall be construed
> " and have effect accordingly, and in the case of an interest in any
> " property expressed to be given to an heir or heirs or any particular
> " heir or class of heirs, the same person or persons shall take as would
> " in the case of freehold land have answered that description under
> " the general law in force before the commencement of this Act."

This section, which applies to personal as well as to real
property, has a two-fold effect upon a limitation that under the
old law would have been caught by the *Rule in Shelley's Case,*
as for instance a limitation to

Effects of
abrogation.

A. for life and then to his heirs ; or to
A. for life and then to the heirs of his body.

The first effect is to restrict A.'s interest to a life interest, and
the second is to appropriate a definite interest to the heir or to
the heir of the body of A. The heir is ascertained in accordance
with the canons of descent that obtained under the old law,[3] and
he takes the interest by way of purchase. What interest he takes
is perhaps a little doubtful, but presumably in all cases he takes
the fee simple or other the whole interest which the donor had
power to convey, unless a contrary intention appears in the deed
or will.[4]

Ancestor
takes a life
interest.

Heir takes
by purchase.

The result, then, of the abolition of the *Rule in Shelley's Case*

[1] Jarman on Wills (7th Edn.), p. 1823.   [2] S. 131.
[3] *Infra*, pp. 789–92.
[4] Law of Property Act, 1925, s. 60 (1) ; Wills Act, 1837, s. 28 ; *supra,*
pp. 114–5. The rule before the Wills Act, 1837, was that a devise to the *heirs of
the body* of a person conferred an estate tail (*Mandeville's Case* (undated),
Co. Litt. 26*b*), and the question whether the fee simple could pass under s. 28
of the Wills Act does not seem to have arisen

upon the expressions which are now essential to create an entailed interest, seems to be this :—

> (*a*) A gift to A. for life, remainder to the heirs of his body will no longer vest an entailed interest in A., despite the enactment that such an interest may be created by the like expressions as those by which before January 1st, 1926, a similar estate tail could have been created by deed.[1]
>
> (*b*) A gift to A. for life, remainder to the heirs of his body will be effectual to vest a definite interest in the *heir*, although such would not have been the result of a similar conveyance by deed under the old law.

SECTION III.   ENTAILED INTERESTS UNDER THE MODERN LAW.

SUMMARY

Entailed interest must be created by settlement. An entailed interest cannot subsist as a legal estate. It is necessarily an equitable interest [2] and the only possible methods by which it can be created are (1) a settlement by deed or will, and (2) an agreement for a settlement in which the trusts upon which the land is to be held are sufficiently declared.[3]

(1) ENTAILED INTERESTS MAY NOW BE CREATED IN ANY FORM OF PROPERTY.

Personalty can now be entailed. One of the radical changes introduced by the Law of Property Act, 1925, is that any form of property, whether real or personal, may be limited in tail. At common law an estate tail could not be carved out of chattels or other personal property, but it appeared to the Legislature that there was no reason why entailed interests should not be allowed in the case of such forms

---

[1] *Supra*, p. 166.   [2] Law of Property Act, 1925, ss. 1, 130.
[3] *Ibid.*, s. 130 (6).

of property as stocks and shares and long leaseholds. It was therefore enacted that :

" an interest in tail or in tail male or in tail female or in tail special
" (in this Act referred to as ' an entailed interest ') may be created
" by way of trust in any property, *real or personal*, but only by the
" like expressions as those by which before the commencement of
" this Act a similar estate tail could have been created by deed (not
" being an executory instrument) in freehold land, and with the like
" results, including the right to bar the entail either absolutely or
" so as to create an interest equivalent to a base fee, and accordingly
" all statutory provisions relating to estates tail in real property shall
" apply to entailed interests in personal property." [1]

One effect of these words is that an entail in personalty becomes subject to all rules, whether at common law or equity, which governed and still govern estates tail in realty.[2]

Before the Act it sometimes happened that when freeholds were limited by settlement to a series of legal tenants for life and in tail, it was desired to give the persons who for the time being were entitled to the land the enjoyment of certain family heirlooms such as valuable pictures and the like. As the heirlooms, being chattels, could not be carved into estates in the same way as the land, the only mode of carrying out the intention was to vest them in trustees upon trust that they should go along with the land so far as the rules of law and equity would permit. In such a case law and equity permitted any legal life tenant of the land for the time being to have an equitable life interest in the heirlooms, but required that the absolute ownership should vest in the first person to get an estate tail in the land. The Act now provides that when personal estate is directed to be held upon trusts corresponding with the trusts of land in which an entailed interest has been created, such direction shall create a corresponding entailed interest in the personal property.[3]

Heirlooms settled to go with land.

(2) ENTAILED INTERESTS MAY BE BARRED.

The Fines and Recoveries Act, in a general enabling section, provides that every " actual tenant in tail," *i.e.* the tenant of an entailed interest that has not been barred,[4] whether entitled in possession, remainder, contingency[5] or otherwise shall have full power to dispose of the land for an estate in fee simple or for any lesser estate.[6] This right of the tenant to disentail and so enlarge his equitable interest into a legal fee simple is absolute, and it

Indefeasible right of tenant to bar interest.

---

[1] Law of Property Act, 1925, s. 130 (1). A will is not within this section unless it takes effect after 1925 ; *Re Hope's Will*, [1929] 2 Ch. 136.
[2] *Re Crossley's Settlement Trusts, Chivers* v. *Crossley*, [1955] Ch. 627 ; [1955] 2 All E. R. 801.
[3] Law of Property Act, 1925, s. 130 (3).
[4] Fines and Recoveries Act, 1833, s. 1.
[5] *See*, for example, *Re St. Alban's (Duke) Will Trusts, Coutts & Co.* v. *Beauclerk*, [1963] Ch. 365 ; [1962] 2 All E. R. 402.
[6] Fines and Recoveries Act, 1833, s. 15.

cannot be restricted by any device on the part of the grantor; so, for instance, a clause inserted in the instrument of creation providing that the interest shall not be barred, or that it shall pass from the owner upon disentailment, is null and void.[1] The present mode of disentailment, however, falls to be considered under two heads according as the tenant is or is not entitled to actual possession.

(A) MODE OF DISENTAILMENT WHERE THE TENANT IS ENTITLED IN POSSESSION.

Interest must be barred by deed.

Disentailing Assurance. A tenant in tail in possession and of full age may, without the concurrence of any other person, effectually bar the entailed interest and thereby enlarge it into a legal fee simple by adopting any form of conveyance which is sufficient to dispose of a fee simple estate in lands, provided, however, that in the case of an *inter vivos* disentailment the conveyance is effected by deed.[2] So the estate must be barred by a deed, called a disentailing assurance, and no disentailment can be effected by contract.[3]

Effect of disentailing assurance.

The effect of a disentailing assurance which enlarges the fee tail into a fee simple is to defeat entirely the rights both of the tenant's issue and of the persons whose estates are to take effect after the determination or in defeasance of the entailed interest. Suppose, for instance, that :

> There is a grant of Blackacre to A. in tail, remainder to B. in tail, with a proviso that, if A. becomes entitled to White-acre, his entailed interest in Blackacre shall cease and shall vest in C. If A., before he becomes entitled to Whiteacre, executes a disentailing deed of Blackacre for an estate in fee simple, the result is that he takes a fee simple estate which defeats,
>> first, his own issue,
>> secondly, B., who was entitled to take on the determination of the entailed interest, and
>> finally, C., whose estate was in defeasance of A.'s entailed interest.[4]

But, on the other hand, no disentailment can defeat interests that rank prior to the entailed interest.[5]

(B) MODE OF DISENTAILMENT WHERE THE TENANT IS NOT ENTITLED IN POSSESSION.

Old law.

Under the normal strict settlement, by which land is limited to A. for life and then to his sons successively in tail, the eldest

---

[1] *Dawkins* v. *Lord Penrhyn* (1878), 4 App. Cas. 51, 64
[2] Fines and Recoveries Act, 1833, ss. 15, 40.
[3] Registration of the deed is no longer required ; Law of Property Act, 1925, s. 133.
[4] See *Milbank* v. *Vane*, [1893] 3 Ch. 79.
[5] Fines and Recoveries Act, 1833, ss. 15, 19.

son upon birth becomes entitled to an entailed interest in remainder. During the lifetime of his father he is not entitled to possession. The only method under the law prior to the Fines and Recoveries Act by which a tenant placed in this situation could effect a complete disentailment was to suffer a common recovery. If he adopted this course, he obtained an absolute fee simple in remainder which defeated the rights both of his own issue and of the persons who were entitled to take on failure of issue. But the difficulty from his point of view was that a recovery could be suffered only if the collaboration of the tenant in actual possession of the land—that is, in the case of settled land, his father—were obtained. This was a beneficial rule of law, since it enabled the father to influence his son and gave him considerable power to check a disentailment that might be undesirable. The son, however, if he failed to obtain the collaboration of his father, was free to levy a fine, and though this did not, like a recovery, convert the entailed interest into an absolute fee simple, it did produce the effect of creating in its place what is called a base fee that was unassailable by the issue, but of no avail against the remainderman and reversioner if the issue became extinct. The base fee is described below.[1] When fines and recoveries were abolished in 1833, it seemed desirable to the legislature to retain in a different form this doctrine of the old law of recoveries, and thus to empower the father to check an ill-advised disentailment. To this end a new functionary called the Protector of the Settlement was instituted, in order to prevent a tenant in tail who was entitled only in remainder from effecting a complete disentailment.

Protector of the Settlement.

The distinction between a tenant in tail *in possession* and a tenant in tail *in remainder*, therefore, is that the former can effect a complete bar without anyone's concurrence, while the latter can effect only a partial disentailment unless he obtains the consent of the Protector.

The position at the present day is as follows :—

Present position.

(i) A tenant in tail in remainder can effect a complete bar by executing a disentailing deed with the consent of the Protector. The protector of a settlement functions only where there is an entailed interest in remainder, preceded by one or more beneficial life interests. In this case, the Fines and Recoveries Act, 1833, provides in effect that the protector shall be the owner of the prior life interest or of the first of several life interests, or who would have been the owner had he not disposed of his beneficial interest.[2] Until there has been a resettlement,

Disentailment with protector's consent.

---

[1] *Infra*, pp. 178–80.
[2] Fines and Recoveries Act, 1833, s. 22. The Act in s. 32, however, allowed a settlor to appoint any persons up to the number of three to act as protector

there is usually only one life interest under a marriage settlement, namely that given to the husband.

Thus, if there is a limitation to H. for life with remainder to his eldest son in tail, the father, H., is the protector, and the son will not be able to acquire a fee simple in remainder, valid against persons whose interests are to take effect after the determination or in defeasance of the entailed interest, unless the consent of his father is expressed in the disentailing assurance itself or in a separate deed executed on or before the day on which the assurance is executed.[1]

The effect of a resettlement, however, is that life interests stand limited first to the father, then to the son, with the result that the son succeeds to the protectorship on the death of his father.

If there is no resettlement, the office of protector ceases on the death of the father, and the son, as tenant in tail in possession, can dispose of the land as his fancy dictates.

Disentailment without protector's consent creates base fee.

(ii) **A tenant in tail in remainder can effect a partial bar by executing a disentailing deed without the consent of the Protector.** When lands are subject to a strict settlement, family dissension may cause the eldest son to bar his entailed interest in remainder against the wishes of his father. The father may be niggardly or the son contumacious, and in that unfortunate event the probability is that the son will effect the partial disentailment that is within his power and will then dispose of the resultant base fee upon the best terms obtainable. The Fines and Recoveries Act [2] specifically enacts that a tenant in tail who is not for the moment entitled to actual possession of the land may execute a disentailing deed without the consent of the Protector, but that the effect of such a disentailment shall be merely to set up a base fee—that is to say, a fee simple that will defeat the tenant's own issue, but will not defeat persons who are entitled to take estates in the land upon the determination of the entailed interest by failure of issue or otherwise. Suppose, for instance, that:

Lands stand limited to A. for life, remainder to A.'s eldest son in tail, remainder to A.'s second son in tail, and so on. If the eldest son of A. disentails during his father's life and without his father's consent, he

---

in place of the person described in the text above. This power of nominating a special protector has been abolished as regards settlements made after 1925; Law of Property Act, 1925, 7th Schedule, repealing Fines and Recoveries Act, s. 32.

[1] Fines and Recoveries Act, 1833, ss. 34, 42.   [2] S. 34.

will acquire a fee simple which cannot be defeated by any of his own issue, but which nevertheless will go over to his brother's family if at any time in the future his own issue fails. In other words, the eldest son acquires a fee simple that will not fail, *i.e.* will not pass to somebody else, unless and until his descendants fail.

There may be other base fees than the one now under consideration,[1] but these are beside the present point, and as regards entailed interests the Fines and Recoveries Act provides that :

> " The expression ' base fee ' shall mean exclusively that estate " in fee simple into which an estate tail is converted where " the issue in tail are barred, but persons claiming estates " by way of remainder or otherwise are not barred." [2]

It is a less valuable fee simple than a fee simple absolute, since it will last only as long as there are in existence descendants who would have inherited the entailed interest had it never been barred; while a fee simple absolute continues as long as there exist any persons who are heirs, whether lineal or collateral, of the owner. In the example given above, if the eldest son of A., having barred the entail in his father's lifetime, conveys the interest so acquired to X. and then dies without having issue, the base fee held by X. ceases, and passes to the second son by way of remainder. On the other hand, had the interest conveyed to X. been a fee simple absolute, the death of the eldest son without issue would have made no difference to the perpetual nature of X.'s interest.

A base fee, however, may be converted, or will automatically become enlarged, into a fee simple absolute in any one of the following ways :— *Conversion of base fee into fee simple absolute.*

(*a*) UNION OF BASE FEE WITH REMAINDER OR REVERSION IN FEE. Suppose there is a limitation to *Union of base fee with remainder in fee.*

A. for life, remainder to B. in tail, remainder to C. in tail, remainder to B. in fee simple.

B. creates a base fee in himself by executing a disentailing deed during the life of A. and without his consent. The remainderman C. dies in the lifetime of B. without having issue. The position now is that both the base fee and the fee simple absolute in remainder are united in B. without

---

[1] Challis, *Law of Real Property* (3rd Edn.), pp. 325 *et seq.*   [2] S. 1.

there being any intermediate estate between them, and whenever this occurs the Fines and Recoveries Act enacts that the base fee shall be enlarged into as great an estate as the tenant in tail could have created had he been in possession at the time of disentailment.[1] In plain language, it is enlarged into a fee simple absolute.

Fresh disentailment assurance.

(*b*) FRESH DISENTAILING DEED. If a tenant in tail in remainder creates a base fee, he can convert it into a fee simple absolute by executing a fresh disentailing deed with the consent of the Protector.[2] But if the Protector no longer exists, as for instance where the life tenant under a strict settlement dies, the tenant can enlarge the base fee, whether he has parted with it or not, by himself executing a fresh disentailing deed.[3]

Lapse of time.

(*c*) BY LAPSE OF TIME. A base fee becomes valid against remaindermen and reversioners if any person takes possession under the disentailing assurance, and if he or any other person remains in possession by virtue of that assurance [4] for twelve years from the time when the tenant in tail would have been entitled to possession and therefore free to effect a complete bar of his own accord.[5]

(*d*) BY DEVISE. The owner of a base fee *in possession* is now permitted to enlarge the base fee into a fee simple absolute by will.[6]

Some entailed interests unbarrable.

Tenants unable to disentail. Two classes of tenants in tail are unable to disentail their estates namely a tenant in tail after possibility[7] and a tenant in tail to whom or to whose ancestors an estate has been granted by Parliament as a reward for services rendered, if the statute by which the grant is made has expressly prohibited the right of disentailment.[8] Examples are the Marlborough and the Bolton estates.[9]

---

[1] Fines and Recoveries Act, 1833, s. 39.

[2] *Ibid.* s. 35.

[3] *Ibid.*, s. 19 ; *Bankes* v. *Small* (1887), 36 Ch. D. 716.

[4] *Mills* v. *Capel* (1875), L. R. 20 Eq. 692.

[5] Limitation Act, 1939, s. 11 ; replacing and extending the Real Property Limitation Act, 1833, s. 23, and the Real Property Limitation Act, 1874, s. 6. This section also applies to a disentailing assurance which, owing to some defect such as the lack of a deed, fails to bar the tenant's *issue*.

[6] Law of Property Act, 1925, s. 176 (1), (3); *infra*, p. 181.

[7] Fines and Recoveries Act, 1833, s. 18 ; *supra*, p. 163.

[8] For example, statute (1814), 54 Geo. 3, c. 161, s. 28 ; (Duke of Wellington): and see Settled Land Act, 1925, s. 23 (2).

[9] Former examples were the Abergavenny, Shrewsbury and Arundel estates, but these have now been statutorily freed from restraints upon alienation.

(3) ENTAILED INTERESTS MAY BE DISPOSED OF BY WILL.

Prior to 1926 a tenant in tail could not devise his estate, and if he died without having disentailed, it passed by descent to the appropriate class of heirs. The Law of Property Act, 1925, however, provides that in a will *executed* on or after January 1st, 1926, a testator of full age may devise or bequeath all property of which he is tenant in tail *in possession* at the time of his death, and all money subject to be invested in the purchase of property, of which if it had been so invested he would have been tenant in tail in possession at his death.

Entailed interests may now be devised.

The tenant has power to dispose of the estate

" in like manner as if after barring the entail he had been tenant in fee simple or absolute owner thereof for an equitable interest at his death," [1]

and therefore the effect produced by the will is similar to that produced by a disentailing deed. But to guard against a disentailment by inadvertence, it is enacted that no will shall be sufficient to dispose of the estate unless it refers specifically either to the property entailed, or to the instrument creating the entail or to entailed property generally, and therefore a mere general devise or bequest is useless for the purpose.[2]

Effect of devise.

This power of disposition is also conferred by the Act [3] upon the owner of a base fee *in possession* provided that he is in a position to enlarge the base fee into a fee simple absolute. This position arises where a tenant in tail in remainder, having barred the entail without the consent of the life tenant as Protector, becomes entitled to possession upon the death of the life tenant. In such a case, as we have already seen, the owner of the base fee may bar the entail and enlarge the base fee into a fee simple absolute in possession by executing a fresh disentailing assurance. The extension of this principle made by the Law of Property Act, 1925, is that the owner may *devise* the base fee so as to pass a fee simple absolute to the devisee provided that the will refers specifically either to the base fee or to the instrument by which it was acquired. But he has no such testamentary power unless he is in possession of the base fee or of its rents and profits.[4] It will thus be seen that the power to execute a fresh disentailing assurance given by the Fines and Recoveries Act is wider than the power of testamentary disposition given by the Law of Property Act, for the former can be exercised by the tenant in tail even after he has conveyed the base fee to a purchaser and has lost all right to possession of the land.[5]

Base fee.

---

[1] Law of Property Act, 1925, s. 176 (1).
[2] *Ibid.*, s. 176 (1). The word *specifically* was interpreted in a liberal sense by VAISEY, J., in *Acheson* v. *Russell*, [1951] Ch. 67 ; [1950] 2 All E. R. 572. For a criticism of the decision, see 66 *L. Q. R.*, p. 449.
[3] S. 176 (3).   [4] Law of Property Act, 1925, s. 176 (3).
[5] *Bankes* v. *Small* (1887), L. R. 36 Ch. D. 716.

CHAPTER III.

LIFE INTERESTS.

SUMMARY.

SECTION I. THE GENERAL NATURE OF LIFE INTERESTS.

Distinction between the ancient and modern life interest.

History of Life Interests. The modern life interest differs fundamentally from that found in the days of feudalism. In those days, when lands were granted not in return for a rent nor by way of settlement, but on the condition that the tenant should render services of a military nature to the grantor, the tenant was given an interest merely for his life, because, although he was known to the lord and was presumably a man upon whose fidelity and courage reliance might be placed, yet the character of his eldest son was an unknown factor, and it would have been folly for a grantor to have tied his hands by pledging himself in advance to accept the son as a new tenant on his father's death. So in the twelfth century the life estate was the greatest interest that any one could have in land, and it arose when a feudal grant was made by a lord to a tenant. At first the grantee of such a feud did not possess the free power of alienation, for to have permitted this would have prejudiced the lord's right to make the new tenant on the death of the old pay a fine (or relief, as it was called), for the privilege of obtaining the feud ; and again, a tenant possessed of a free power of alienation might cause irreparable injury by granting the land to a personal enemy of the lord. But the restraints on alienation gradually disappeared, and it was recognized by the Statute *Quia Emptores* at the end of the thirteenth century that a feudal tenant could grant his interest to whom he pleased.[1] By degrees it was also recognized that the feud was an inheritable interest that would descend to the heirs-general of the tenant, and which therefore would endure as long as there were any such heirs in existence. It thus came to pass that an estate greater than a life estate became known to the law, and an interest which could endure only for life, as distinguished from a fee simple which might endure for ever, was added to the list of possible estates. In the words of Hayes :—

" Some time elapsed after the feudal relation began to be known in
" Europe before the right of inheritable succession was fully conceded.
" In its primitive state the possession was held at pleasure, or for a short
" term only : afterwards the tenure was for life, the lord resuming the
" land on the death of the tenant, and granting it out anew. But at
" length the son of the tenant was permitted to succeed : an indulgence
" which was followed by the extension of the grant, first to the tenant
" and his issue (*i.e.* in fee tail) and finally to him and his heirs (*i.e.* in
" fee simple, expressed in legal phraseology by the word fee without
" more), the law marking out a course of descent, which, enlarging
" by degrees, embraced his relations, lineal and collateral, male and
" female." [2]

But though after the establishment of the fee simple it became possible and indeed common to create a life estate with peculiar incidents of its own, the object of this practice was materially different from that which underlies the life interest found in present-day conveyancing. The estate in those days was granted, generally by the rich ecclesiastical corporations, in return for an annual rent, and was the result of a purely business transaction analogous to the modern lease for a term of years. The tenant resembled the modern tenant farmer, except that he held for life instead of from year to year or for a fixed number of years, and although he was said to have a *lease*, the interest vested in him was a freehold interest and not a term of years. But nowadays a lease for life at an economic rent is rarely if ever made, and in common with an entailed interest it always arises by virtue of a settlement. The modern life tenant is frequently a former fee simple owner who, by way of making provision for the children of his approaching marriage, deliberately cuts down his interest to a life interest, but who, notwithstanding this reduction, continues by virtue of the Settled Land Act to exercise as wide powers of enjoyment, short of disposing of the fee simple for his own exclusive benefit, as he formerly possessed.

Modern life interest generally originates in a settlement.

A life interest is a freehold interest—generally called a *mere freehold* to distinguish it from fees simple and entails, which are

Classes of life interests.

---

[1] For the growth of the power of alienation, see Holdsworth, *History of English Law*, vol. iii. p. 73 *et seq.* ; Plucknett, *A Concise History of the Common Law*, pp. 523 *et seq.*; Simpson, *An Introduction to the History of Land Law*, pp. 48–53.
[2] *Introduction to Conveyancing*, vol. i. pp. 7–8.

estates of inheritance—and under the modern law it is necessarily equitable in nature. It may be limited to endure for the life either of the tenant himself or of some other person, in which latter case it is called an interest *pur autre vie.*

Interest for the life of the tenant himself.

An interest for the life of the tenant himself, though normally created expressly by a settlement, made either by deed or by will, may also arise by implication of law in the case of the tenant in tail after possibility,[1] or by operation of law where a husband becomes tenant by the curtesy in the entailed lands of his deceased wife.[2]

Tenant *pur autre vie.*

The interest *pur autre vie* is the lowest estate of freehold known to the law, and is not so great as an interest for the life of the tenant himself. It arises in two ways :

The first is where there is an express limitation to A. for the life of B. Such a limitation may be made, like an ordinary lease for years, in return for a rent, or as part of a settlement of lands. A. is called the tenant *pur autre vie*, and B. the *cestui que vie*.[3]

Secondly, if a person, B., who is entitled to an estate for his own life assigns his interest to A., the effect is that A. becomes the tenant *pur autre vie*.[4]

Rights and liabilities of tenant *pur autre vie.*

From the point of view of rights and liabilities a tenant *pur autre vie* is in the same position as an ordinary tenant for life.

Thus, he is entitled to the rents and profits of the land during the continuance of his interest and to cut timber within the limits of estovers, while on the negative side he is liable for waste to the same extent as if he were holding for his own life.[5] Unless holding merely under a lease at a rent, he may exercise any of the wide powers conferred by the Settled Land Act.[6] No matter how the interest arises, he possesses an absolute power of alienation during his life,[7] and after his death his alienee is entitled to hold for the rest of the *cestui que vie's* life.[8] In the absence of such alienation the interest passes on the death of the tenant to his devisee,[9] or, if he has made no will, to the persons who are entitled to take his property under the rules that govern intestacy.[10] Prior to the legislation of 1925 there were certain peculiar rules which

---

[1] *Supra*, p. 163.
[2] *Supra*, p. 161.
[3] Litt., 56 ; Co. Litt., 41*b*.
[4] *Ibid.*, 41*b*.
[5] *Infra*, p. 186 (waste) ; p. 188 (estovers).
[6] Settled Land Act, 1925, s. 20 (1) (v) ; he is not so entitled if he is the assignee of a tenant for life holding under a settlement, *supra*, p. 140.
[7] Co. Litt., 41*b*.
[8] *Utty Dale's Case* (1590), Cro. Eliz. 182.
[9] Wills Act, 1837, s. 3.
[10] Administration of Estates Act, 1925, s. 46.

governed the devolution of an interest *pur autre vie*, but these have been abolished.[1]

In view of the danger that a tenant *pur autre vie* may be tempted to conceal the death of the *cestui que vie*, it is enacted by a statute of Anne that a person entitled to the land upon the termination of the life interest may, after swearing an affidavit that he believes the *cestui que vie* to be dead, obtain an order from the Lord Chancellor for the production of the *cestui que vie*. If the order is not complied with, the *cestui que vie* is taken to be dead and the person next entitled to possession may enter upon the lands.[2]

Cestui que vie Act.

SECTION II. THE RIGHTS AND OBLIGATIONS OF A LIFE TENANT.

The rights and obligations of a tenant for life entitled in possession may be summed up by saying that he may take the annual profits, but must not take or destroy anything that is a permanent part of the inheritance. He is entitled to fruits of all kinds, but must leave unimpaired the source of the fruits. He has certain positive rights, and one negative duty which is prescribed by the doctrine of *waste*.

Rights in general of a life tenant.

There is little that need be said of his positive rights. The profits that arise from the land, whether they arise continuously, periodically or occasionally, belong to him. A particular hazard, however, that confronts him is that after he has sown crops his

Emblements,

---

[1] Administration of Estates Act, 1925, s. 45 (1) (*a*); for the old law, see Challis, *Law of Real Property*, (3rd Edn.), pp. 358 *et seq.* A tenant *pur autre vie* could not at common law devise his interest, and the question that arose was—what was to happen to the land if he died in the lifetime of the *cestui que vie* ? This depended upon the form of the grant. If it were *to B. during the life of A.*, the land went on the death of B. to the person who first took possession. This person was called the *general occupant* (Blackstone, vol. ii. p. 259). Neither the general occupant nor the land that he held was liable for the debts of B. If the grant were *to B. and his heirs during the life of A.*, the land went on the death of B. to his heir, who took, not by descent, for title by descent can arise only in the case of an estate of inheritance, but as an occupant specially marked out and appointed by the original grant. He was called a *special occupant*, and again neither he nor the land was liable for the debts of B.

The Statute of Frauds (s. 3) made estates *pur autre vie* devisable and liable for debts. This section was repealed and re-enacted by the Wills Act, 1837, after which the position was as follows : (*a*) an *estate pur autre vie* was devisable ; (*b*) if it was not devised and if there was no special occupant (*i.e.* if the grant was merely " to B. during the life of A."), the estate passed to the personal representatives of B. and was treated as personalty as regards its liability for the debts of B. ; (*c*) if it was not devised and if there was a special occupant (*i.e.* if the grant was " to B. and his heirs during the life of A."), the estate went to the heirs and was treated as realty as regards liability for debts. General and special occupancy are now abolished by the Administration of Estates Act, 1925, s. 45, and if B. dies in the lifetime of A. his interest in all cases passes to his personal representatives.

[2] (1707), 6 Anne, c. 72.

tenancy may end unexpectedly before they are ripe as, for instance, by the death of a *cestui que vie*.   In this event, he is entitled to re-enter the land at harvest time and to reap what he has sown.   This is known as the right to *emblements*.[1]   It is enforceable, however, only in respect of crops such as corn, hemp, flax and potatoes, which bear an annual fruit.[2]   One crop only can be taken,[3] and the right does not extend to seeds that do not produce a crop within a year of sowing, such as young fruit-trees or the second crop of clover.[4]

The right can be exercised only if the estate comes to an end unexpectedly without any fault on the part of the tenant, and therefore, if it is forfeited in his lifetime owing to the breach of some condition, or if, being a determinable interest, it is brought to an end by the happening of the terminating event—as for instance by the re-marriage of a woman who is tenant *durante viduitate*—the crops belong to the reversioner.[5]

Liability for waste.   The position of the tenant for life on the negative side is governed by the common law doctrine of waste as enlarged by statute and equity, a doctrine that also affects a tenant for years.[6]

Definition of waste.   Waste means in general such damage to houses or land as tends to the permanent and lasting loss of the person entitled to the inheritance, and it falls into two main classes :—

Voluntary waste.   (i) **Voluntary Waste.**   This is a wrong of commission consisting of a positive act of injury to the inheritance.   It generally takes one of the following forms :—

    1. PULLING DOWN OR ALTERING HOUSES.[7]   Thus if glass windows be broken or carried away, it is waste, though they may have been put in by the tenant himself, and so also in the case of benches, doors, furnaces and other things fixed to the land.

    2. OPENING PITS OR MINES.[8]   It is waste to dig for gravel, lime, clay, stone and the like, unless for the reparation of buildings ; also to open a new mine, but not to work one that is already open.

    3. CHANGING THE COURSE OF HUSBANDRY.   To convert wood, meadow or pasture into arable land, or to turn arable or woodland into meadow or pasture, is technically waste.   The old writers state that such acts are waste, not only because

---

    [1] Co. Litt. 55*b*.   The right of the tenant for years to emblements has been replaced by a statutory right, *infra*, p. 371.

    [2] Co. Litt. 55*b* ;   Blackstone, vol. ii. p. 122.

    [3] *Graves* v. *Weld* (1833), 5 B. & Ad. 105.

    [4] *Graves* v. *Weld, supra.*

    [5] Co. Litt. 55*b* ;   *Oland's Case* (1602), 5 Co. Rep. 116*a*.

    [6] *Infra*, p. 363.   For the history of " waste," see Holdsworth, *History of English Law*, vol. ii. 248–9 ;   vol. iii. 121–3 ;   vol. vii. 275–81.   For a fuller account of the substantive law, see Leake, *The Law of Uses and Profits in Land*, pp. 18 *et seq.*

    [7] Co. Litt. 53*a*.   *Marsden* v. *Edward Heyes, Ltd.*, [1927] 2 K. B. 1.

    [8] Co. Litt. 53*b*, 54*b*.

they change the course of husbandry, but also because they destroy the owner's evidence of title, for if an estate which had been conveyed as pasture were found on the next conveyance to be arable, it might cause confusion.[1] This, of course, is no longer in itself a reason for regarding such an act of conversion as waste. In fact it is obvious that to change the system of husbandry must often have the effect of enhancing the value of land, as, for example, where a farm situated near a large town is tilled intensively as a market garden, and though such conversion is technically waste, the rule, established since at least 1833,[2] is that it will not entitle the owner of the inheritance to recover damages unless it causes an injury to the inheritance.[3] This kind of waste is known as ameliorating waste. In *Doherty* v. *Allman*,[4]

Ameliorating waste.

> a tenant for 999 years of land and buildings was proceeding to convert some dilapidated store buildings into dwelling houses when the lessor filed a bill for an injunction.

The injunction was refused on the ground that acts which improve the inheritance cannot constitute actionable waste. A similiar decision was reached where the tenant of an agricultural lease for 21 years converted part of the land into a market garden and erected glass-houses thereon for the cultivation of hot-house produce for the London market.[5]

4. CUTTING TIMBER. Timber trees are regarded as part of the inheritance and not part of the annual produce, and therefore it is waste to cut them, even though they are blown down by accident and have thus become what are called *windfalls*.[6] Sir GEORGE JESSEL, M.R., furnishes us with a definition of the term " timber " [7] :

What trees are timber.

> " The question of what timber is depends, first on general
> " law, that is, the law of England ; and secondly, on the special
> " custom of a locality. By the general rule of England, oak, ash
> " and elm are timber, provided they are of the age of 20 years
> " and upwards, provided also they are not so old as not to have
> " a reasonable quantity of useable wood in them, sufficient,
> " according to a text writer, to make a good post. Timber, that
> " is, the kind of tree which may be called timber, may be varied
> " by local custom. There is what is called the custom of the
> " country, that is, of a particular county or division of a county,
> " and it varies in two ways. First of all you may have trees
> " called timber by the custom of the country—beech in some
> " counties, hornbeam in others, and even whitethorn and black-
> " thorn and many other trees are considered timber in peculiar
> " localities—in addition to the ordinary timber trees.[8] Then
> " again, in certain localities, arising probably from the nature of

---

[1] Blackstone, vol. ii. p. 282.
[2] *Doe d. Grubb* v. *Burlington (Earl)* (1833), 5 B. & Ad. 507.
[3] *Jones* v. *Chappell* (1875), L. R. 20 Eq. 539, 541.
[4] (1877), 3 App. Cas. 709.
[5] *Meux* v. *Cobley*, [1892] 2 Ch. 253. Although this case and that referred to in the previous note concerned a tenant for years, there would be even stronger reasons for adopting the same attitude towards a tenant for life.
[6] *Garth* v. *Cotton* (1753), 3 Atk. 751.
[7] *Honeywood* v. *Honeywood* (1874), L. R. 18 Eq. 306, 309.
[8] *E.g.* beech in Buckinghamshire, *Dashwood* v. *Magniac*, [1891] 3 Ch. 306 ; birch in Yorkshire, *Countess of Cumberland's Case* (1610), Moore, 812 ; willows in Hampshire, *Layfield* v. *Cowper* (1694), 1 Wood, 330.

" the soil, the trees of even 20 years old are not necessarily timber,
" but may go to 24 years or even to a later period, I suppose, if
" necessary ; and in other places the test of when a tree becomes
" timber is not its age but its girth." [1]

When timber may be cut.

A tenant, whether for years or life, may cut and keep trees
that do not fall within this definition of timber, such as larch,
willows and chestnut, provided that they are ripe for felling and
have not been planted for ornament, shelter or shade.[2] But only
in three cases may he fell timber trees:—

First, where the land is a timber estate, that is, where it is
cultivated merely for the produce of saleable timber and where
the timber is cut periodically.[3] In such a case it is obvious that to
cut the trees does not injure the inheritance, because the total
value of the timber on the estate remains, roughly speaking, the
same throughout, though new trees take the place of old.[4]

Secondly, where there is a local custom to cut timber periodically according to the normal and ordinary course of husbandry
practised in the neighbourhood.[5]

Thirdly, every tenant for life is entitled to cut timber or other
trees for three specific purposes, namely, for the fuelling or repair
of a house (*housebote*), for making and repairing agricultural
implements (*ploughbote*) and for repairing existing walls, fences
and ditches (*haybote*). These are called *estovers*.[6] He will be
liable for waste, however, if he exercises these rights in an unreasonable manner, as for instance if he fells growing trees for
fuel when there is dead wood sufficient for the purpose.

Permissive waste.

(ii) **Permissive Waste.** Permissive waste arises from a
mere act of omission, not of commission, and it is generally the
result of allowing the buildings on an estate to fall into a state
of decay.[7]

Distinction between tenant impeachable and tenant unimpeachable.

Extent of Liability for Waste. At common law, tenants
for life or years whose tenancies arose by operation of law, such
as the doweress or tenant by the curtesy, were liable for waste;
but no liability arose in the case of tenancies, whether for life or
years, created by act of parties, for the courts were disinclined to
excuse the folly of the lessor in not imposing an express restraint

---

[1] If timber trees are blown down, they belong to the owner of the inheritance, but if they are dotards, *i.e.* decayed, they may be appropriated by
the tenant, Co. Litt. 53*a* ; *Herlakenden's Case* (1589), 4 Co. Rep. 62, 63*b*;
Newcastle (Duke) v. *Vane* (undated), 2 P. Wms. 241.
[2] *Re Harker's Will Trusts, Harker* v. *Bayliss,* [1938] Ch. 323 ; [1938]
I All E. R. 145.
[3] *Honeywood* v. *Honeywood* (1874), L. R. 18 Eq. 306, 309.
[4] *Lloyd-Jones* v. *Clark-Lloyd,* [1919] I Ch. 426, 436.
[5] *Dashwood* v. *Magniac,* [1891] 3 Ch. 306 ; *In re Trevor-Batye's Settlement,*
[1912] 2 Ch. 339
[6] Co. Litt. 41*b*.
[7] Co. Litt. 53*a*, 54*b*.

upon the tenant.[1] This, however, was altered by the Statute of Marlborough[2] 1267, which provided as follows :—

> "Fermors, during their terms, shall not make waste, sale nor exile
> "of houses, woods nor of anything belonging to tenements that they
> "have to ferm, without special licence had by writing of covenant
> "making mention that they may do it."[3]

This reference to a "special licence" recognized therefore, that a tenant for life might be expressly permitted to do acts that would normally constitute waste without incurring liability,[4] and from this point of view it led to the emergence of two classes of life tenants, namely those impeachable for waste, and those unimpeachable for waste.

(i) The law is that a tenant who is impeachable is liable for the commission of voluntary waste,[5] but is not liable for permissive waste[6] unless the settlor has imposed upon him an obligation to keep the property in repair.[7] *Tenant impeachable.*

Where such an obligation is imposed, an action lies against the tenant or against his personal representative, on the general equitable principle that a person who accepts a benefit must take the benefit *cum onere*.[8]

Where, however, the property which is settled upon the tenant consists of leaseholds, he is bound to perform any covenants, such as a covenant to repair, contained in the lease under which the property is held. Thus, if a house which is held by a testator on a long lease is bequeathed to A. for life, A. must take the *onus* with the *commodum*, and instead of throwing the financial burden upon the testator's estate must meet the cost of performing the covenants out of his own pocket.[9]

(ii) If, as is nearly always the case under a settlement, a tenant for life is unimpeachable, he is not liable either for voluntary or for permissive waste, and at common law may fell timber or open new mines and deal with the produce as absolute owner.[10] *Tenant unimpeachable.*

Equity, however, has consistently set its face against an abuse of this immunity and the rule has long been that *Equitable waste.*

---

[1] *Shrewsbury's (Countess) Case* (1600), 4 Co. Rep. 13*b*.
[2] 52 Hen. 3. c. 23.
[3] "Fermor" includes everybody holding for life or years.
[4] *Woodhouse v. Walker* (1880), 5 Q. B. D. 404, 406–7.
[5] Co. Litt. 53*a*.
[6] *Re Cartwright* (1889), 41 Ch. D. 532 ; *Re Parry and Hopkins*, [1900] 1 Ch 160 ; *Woodhouse v. Walker, supra.*
[7] *Woodhouse v. Walker, supra.*
[8] *Jay v. Jay*, [1924] 1 K. B. 826.
[9] *Re Betty*, [1899] 1 Ch. 821 ; *Woodhouse v. Walker* (1880), 5 Q. B. D. 404.
[10] *Lewis Bowles's Case* (1615), 11 Co. Rep. 79*b* ; Tudor, *Leading Cases on Real Property*, p. 153.

any tenant who commits wanton or extravagant acts of destruction, will be restrained by injunction and ordered to rehabilitate the premises. Examples of the application of this rule occur where the tenant dismantles a mansion or other house,[1] cuts saplings at unseasonable times,[2] or fells timber that has been planted for the ornament or shelter of the mansion-house and its grounds.[3] It is obviously difficult to decide whether timber is ornamental or not, but the question depends upon whether the person who carried out the planting intended the trees to be ornamental and not upon the personal opinion of the court or anybody else.[4]

Wanton acts of destruction of the kinds specified are said to constitute equitable waste because prior to the Judicature Act they could be remedied only in a court of equity ; but it is now expressly enacted that a tenant for life has no right to commit equitable waste unless an intention to confer such right appears in the instrument of creation.[5]

Tenant after possibility.

A tenant *pur autre vie* is liable for waste to the same extent as a tenant for his own life,[6] but a tenant in tail after possibility of issue extinct incurs no liability by the commission of voluntary or of permissive waste.[7]

Rights of remainder-man.

Where an act of waste has been committed, the remainder-man may sue for an account in the Chancery Division, or bring an action in the Queen's Bench Division, either for trover in respect of any things that may have been severed,[8] or for money had and received as a result of their sale,[8] or for the recovery of damages ; and he may sue in either Division for an injunction.

---

[1] *Vane* v. *Barnard* (1716), 2 Vern. 738.
[2] *Brydges* v. *Stephens* (1821), 6 Madd. 279.
[3] *Downshire* v. *Sandys* (1801), 6 Ves. 107.
[4] *Weld-Blundell* v. *Wolseley*, [1903] 2 Ch. 664.
[5] Law of Property Act, 1925, s. 135.
[6] Co. Litt. 41*b*, *Seymor's Case* (1612), 10 Co. Rep. 95*b*, 98*a*.
[7] *Williams* v. *Williams* (1810), 12 East, 209.
[8] *Seagram* v. *Knight* (1867), 2 Ch. App. 628, at p. 632.   See generally Tudor, *Leading Cases on Real Property*, p. 156.

CHAPTER IV.

EQUITABLE POWERS.[1]

SUMMARY.

SECTION I. NATURE AND CLASSIFICATION.

The principal object of this chapter is to describe the doctrine [Definition.] of powers under which the right of alienation may be divorced from the ownership of the estate or interest to which it relates. In this sense a power may be defined as an authority given by one person called the donor to another person called the donee entitling the latter to deal with or dispose of realty or personalty, either absolutely or partially and either for his own benefit or for the benefit of others, and whether or not he is already beneficially interested in the subject-matter before he exercises the authority.

Powers are of various classes, but they can conveniently be [Classification of powers.] divided as follows, namely, according to

(1) the purposes for which they are created ;

---

[1] See Holdsworth, *History of English Law*, vol. vii. pp. 149–93.

(2) the relation of the donee to the land ;

(3) the nature of the interests which their exercise creates.

(1) POWERS CLASSIFIED ACCORDING TO THE PURPOSES FOR WHICH THEY ARE CREATED.

The purpose and object of a power may be to authorize the donee either to manage and administer the property within certain limits, or to dispose of its ownership by the creation of interests. A familiar example of an administrative power is furnished by the Settled Land Act, which authorizes a tenant for life to manage the settled land in the interests of all concerned, as for instance by compromising claims, varying leases, modifying restrictive covenants or cutting timber. The same Act, by permitting the tenant for life to sell or to lease the land, also affords an example of the second class of powers whereby a person is enabled to dispose of an interest to which he is not beneficially entitled.

Power of appointment.
But the most important example of a dispositive, as distinct from an administrative, power arises where a person is authorized to appoint or to create actual interests in the land for the benefit, in some cases of himself, and in others of third persons. This is best illustrated from a settlement. A settlor, instead of declaring with finality what persons shall take interests in the land, what the extent of those interests shall be and in what circumstances they shall arise, may prefer to wait upon events and either to reserve to himself or to confer upon another a *power of appointment, i.e.* a power to make final dispositions at some time in the future.

Powers of appointment unknown at common law.
Such a power of appointing future interests was unknown to the common law.

" Simplicity was the striking feature of the common law in regard as " well to the estates which might be created, as to the modes by " which they might be raised." [1]

If a feoffment of land was once made, it was impossible to provide at common law that the feoffor might revoke the conveyance and make a new disposition of the land, for the essence of the feoffment was that it transferred his whole interest and right of disposal.[2] It was indeed possible to annex a condition to a feoffment providing that the estate delivered should cease on a given event, but the efficacy and usefulness of this was diminished by the rule that only the feoffor and his heirs could re-enter upon the happening of the event, and that the effect of such entry was to render nugatory all estates passing under the feoffment.[3]

Originated with uses.
But upon the establishment of uses there was, according to the view of equity, no repugnancy in reserving to oneself or to

---

[1] Sugden's *Gilbert on Uses*, p. 1.
[2] Co. Litt. 237a ; Sugden's *Gilbert on Uses*, p. 158, note.
[3] *Infra*, p. 289.

somebody else a power to revoke the uses that had been raised in the first instance and to replace them by the declaration of new uses. Thus :

> A. might convey to B. to such uses as A. the grantor, or as C. a stranger, should appoint, and in default of appointment to the use of D.

In other words, equity allowed the power of alienation to be detached from the ownership of the estate granted to B. and to be either retained by the grantor himself or vested in a stranger.[1] Under such a power the use might be appointed to E. subject to a right of revocation, and if this right of revocation were exercised, the use already given to E. might be withdrawn and superseded by one granted to F.[2] Originally the interests taken by E. and F. upon the exercise of the power were equitable, but they acquired the status of legal estates when the Statute of Uses enacted that where B. stood seised to the use of E., the latter was to have the legal estate.

Suppose for instance that :

> In contemplation of a marriage to be solemnized between H. and W. land is given by a settlement to H. for life with remainder to W. for life, and after the death of the survivor to such one or more of the children of the said H. and W. for such estates and in such shares and subject to such restrictions as H. and W. shall at any time by a deed revocable or irrevocable jointly appoint.
>
> H. and W., having two children—a son and a daughter—appoint the fee simple to the son subject to their own life interests. When exercising the power, however, they expressly reserve to themselves authority during their lives to vary or absolutely to revoke the estate so given, and to replace it by another estate granted under the power of appointment. For some reason or other H. and W. have decided to deprive the son of the fee simple already given to him, and therefore they first of all revoke and make void that estate, and then, still subject to their own life interests, limit and appoint the fee simple to the daughter.

Example of exercise of power of appointment.

Thus the fee simple that had been given to the son, subject to the life interests of his parents, is destroyed and is replaced by a similar interest in favour of the daughter.

As regards terminology, when X. gives B. the right to exercise a power of appointment, X. is called the *donor* ; B. the *donee* or *appointor* ; the person in whose favour the appointment is made

Terminology.

---

[1] Markby, *Elements of Law*, p. 170.
[2] Hayes, *Introduction to Conveyancing*, p. 70.

is termed the *appointee* ; and when the donee exercises the power he is said to make an appointment.

These powers of appointment may be either general, or special.

General and special powers. If the appointor is authorized to appoint the interest in favour of anybody in the world, including himself, without being required to obtain the consent of another person, he is said to have a *general power*, but if he may appoint only to the members of a restricted class, as for instance, "amongst the children of A.," he has a *special power*, and the persons whom he may select to take the property are called the *objects* of the power. Thus, the outstanding feature of a general, as distinct from a special power, is that the donee is the virtual owner of the property affected since he can appoint to himself at any moment during his life. Indeed, it is treated by the law as equivalent to ownership for certain defined purposes. For instance, property over which a testator has a general power passes under a general devise or bequest, as when the words of the will are:—

"I devise and bequeath all my real and personal estate, except "what I otherwise dispose of by this my will, to X."[1]

In such a case the property is distributable among the donee's creditors in the event of his bankruptcy; it is liable for estate duty on his death; and for the purposes of the rule against perpetuities it is treated as being at his free disposal.[2]

Nevertheless, the two conceptions of power and property are fundamentally distinct, and save in exceptional cases an unexercised power is in no sense the "property" of the donee.[3] Thus, a covenant to settle after-acquired property does not bind property over which the covenantor acquires a general power of appointment unless, of course, he exercises it in his own favour.[4]

Hybrid powers. The classification of powers into two classes, however, is not exhaustive, for there is an intermediate class consisting of powers that are hybrid in the sense that they are congruous neither with special nor with general powers.[5] They are treated by the courts as general for some purposes, but special for others.[6] The following are examples of this class:—

(i) A power given to X. to appoint to anybody in the world except himself.

---

[1] Wills Act, 1837, s. 27; *infra*, p. 775.

[2] *Infra*, p. 249.

[3] *Re Armstrong, ex parte Gilchrist* (1886), 17 Q. B. D. 521; see especially at p. 531, *per* FRY, L. J. See also 58 L. Q. R. p. 404, note 19.

[4] *Tremayne* v. *Rashleigh*, [1908] 1 Ch. 681. Again the exercise of a general power of appointment by a person who later becomes bankrupt is not a settlement of property within the meaning of the Bankruptcy Act, 1914, s. 42; *infra*, p. 733; *Re Mathieson*, [1927] 1 Ch. 288.

[5] For an account, see Morris and Leach, *The Rule against Perpetuities* (2nd Edn.) pp. 136–8; 4th Report of Law Reform Committee, 1956, Cmnd. 18, paras. 44–6.

[6] So far as concerns the rule against perpetuities, the Perpetuities and Accumulations Act, 1964, s. 7 has now imposed a test for determining which of these hybrid powers are general, which special; *infra*, p. 274.

This is neither general, since X. himself is excluded; nor special, since no restricted class of objects has been designated.[1]

(ii) A power given to X. to appoint to any person or persons alive at his death.[2]

This is not general, since X. cannot appoint to himself or to persons who predecease him; yet it is not special in the normal sense, since the objects include the whole human race living at his death.

(iii) A general power given to X. to be exercised with the consent of Y.[3]

Although not restricted in respect of objects, this is not properly speaking a general power, for X.'s right of alienation is not unrestricted and therefore he is not in the position of an absolute owner.

(iv) A general power exercisable jointly by two or more persons.[4]

Again, although the objects are not restricted, there is no person who can be regarded as absolute owner of the property to which the appointment relates.

(v) A general power exercisable only by will.

This, though traditionally called a *general testamentary power*, is more akin to a special power, for the donee cannot appoint to himself and is therefore far from being the absolute owner of the property affected.[5]

(2) POWERS CLASSIFIED ACCORDING TO THE POSITION OF THE DONEE WITH REGARD TO THE LAND.

Powers may be appendant, in gross, or simply collateral.

Power appendant.

(1) *A power appendant* or, as it is sometimes called, *appurtenant*, is one reserved to a person who already has an interest in the land to which the power relates, so that, when he exercises it his enjoyment of the interest will be affected. An example is where a tenant for life is authorized to grant leases in possession, or where land is conveyed to a person in fee simple with power to revoke such interest and make a new appointment.[6]

---

[1] *Re Park, Public Trustee v. Armstrong*, [1932] 1 Ch. 580, where it was held to be valid.
[2] *Re Jones, Public Trustee v. Jones*, [1945] Ch. 105.
[3] *Re Watts, Coffey v. Watts*, [1931] 2 Ch. 302.
[4] *Re Churston Settled Estates*, [1954] Ch. 334, [1954] 1 All E. R. 725.
[5] Gray, *The Rule against Perpetuities*, s. 526 (b); Morris and Leach, *op. cit.* pp.147–9; *infra*, p. 250.
[6] *In re Mills*, [1930] 1 Ch. 654.

Power in gross.

(2) If the owner of a power has an interest in the land, but one that will not be affected when the authority is exercised, the power is *in gross*. Thus :

> if a tenant for life under a settlement is authorized to appoint a jointure to his widow or to allocate portions to his children, the interests which arise upon exercise of the power take effect upon the determination of his interest and do not affect its enjoyment.

Power simply collateral.

(3) *A power simply collateral* is a bare power reserved to a stranger who has no interest in the property affected, and which he can exercise only on behalf of others, as for instance where an executor is authorized to pay to such friends as the testator's wife may nominate a sum not exceeding £25 in each case.[1]

This particular classification will be of importance when we consider the extinction of powers, and in this connection it is desirable to notice another form of authority called a *power in the nature of, or coupled with, a trust.*

Power in the nature of a trust.

Power in the nature of or coupled with a trust. In the first place it is necessary to distinguish between a power and a trust. A trust exists wherever a person comes under an obligation to deal with property in a specified manner : a power exists where a person is authorized to dispose of property. The former involves an obligation, the latter a discretion. The distinction has an important bearing upon the rights of the beneficiaries or potential beneficiaries. The court will itself perform a trust that the trustees have failed to carry out. The beneficiaries have rights and can insist that the trustees do their duty. But the court will never compel the exercise of a power. It will not interfere in a matter that is left to the free will of a party.[2]

Another distinction is that a trust to distribute property among a class of persons is void for uncertainty, unless all the possible beneficiaries are definitely ascertainable ; but a power to the same effect is valid even though the possible beneficiaries are indeterminate, provided that it can be determined with certainty whether a person whom the appointor wishes to select is a member of the specified class.[3]

In some cases, however, that which on the surface appears to be a mere power is construed to be a trust, and in this event,

---

[1] *In re Coates, Ramsden* v. *Coates*, [1955] Ch. 495 ; [1955] 1 All E. R. 26.

[2] *Brown* v. *Higgs* (1803), 8 Ves. 561, 574 ; see generally White and Tudor, *Leading Cases in Equity*, vol. ii. p. 261.

[3] *In re Gestetner Settlement, Barnett* v. *Blumka*, [1953] Ch. 672 ; [1953] 1 All E. R. 1150 ; *In re Coates, Ramsden* v. *Coates*, [1955] Ch. 495 ; [1955] 1 All E. R. 26 ; *In re Sayer, MacGregor* v. *Sayer*, [1957] Ch. 423 ; [1956] 3 All E. R. 600.; *Re Saxone Shoe Co.'s Trust Deed*, [1962] 2 All E. R. 904; [1962] 1 W. L. R. 943.

though subject to the rules governing trusts, it is generally called " a power in the nature of a trust."

Lord ELDON in *Brown* v. *Higgs* [1] said :—

> " There are not only a mere trust and a mere power, but there is also
> " known to this court a power which the party to whom it is given is
> " required and entrusted to execute ; and with regard to that species
> " of power, the court considers it as partaking so much of the nature
> " and qualities of a trust, that if the person who has that duty imposed
> " upon him does not discharge it, the court will, to a certain extent,
> " discharge the duty in his room and place."

Brown v. *Higgs.*

Whether a trust has been created depends upon the intention of the donor of the power as gathered from the terms of the relevant instrument. If he has specified an ascertainable class of persons, such as children and grandchildren, and if it is clear that he intended the members of that class to take the property in any event, though he has left to the donee the selection of the particular beneficiaries, then the inference is that he intended to create a trust.

Harding v. *Glyn.*

> " When there appears a general intention in favour of a class and
> " a particular intention in favour of individuals of a class to be
> " selected by another person, and the particular intention fails from
> " that selection not being made, the court will carry into effect
> " the general intention in favour of the class." [2]

In other words, the court will distribute the property equally among the members of the class *per capita*.[3] If the donor has provided that in default of appointment the property shall go over to other persons, it is clearly impossible to infer that he intended to benefit the class in any event.[4] Even though there is no gift over upon failure of appointment, however, there is no hard and fast rule that a trust must be implied. It is imperative that the general intention in favour of the class should be disclosed by the terms of the instrument.[5] This test was satisfied in *Harding* v. *Glyn*[6] upon the following facts :

> A testator gave his leasehold house, furniture and goods to his wife
> but " *did desire her* " at her death to give the same " *unto and amongst
> such of his own relations as she should think most deserving and approve
> of.*" The wife gave the furniture and goods to a person who was not
> a relative of her husband, and it was held that the court must distribute
> that property among the statutory next-of-kin, since the will
> imposed upon the wife a trust " *by way of power of naming and
> apportioning.*"

An illustration to the opposite effect is afforded by *In re Weeke's Settlement*,[7] where a testatrix devised to her husband a

Re Weekes' Settlement.

---

[1] (1803), 8 Ves. 561.
[2] *Burrough* v. *Philcox* (1840), 5 My. & Cr. 72, at p. 92, *per* Lord COTTENHAM.
[3] *In re Llewellyn's Settlement, Official Solicitor* v. *Evans*, [1921] 2 Ch. 281.
[4] *Goldring* v. *Inwood* (1861), 3 Giff. 139.
[5] *In re Weekes' Settlement*, [1897] Ch. 289.   [6] (1739), 1 Atk. 469.
[7] [1897] Ch. 289. See also *In re Combe*, [1925] Ch. 210 ; *In re Perowne, Perowne* v. *Moss*, [1951] Ch. 785 ; [1951] 2 All E. R. 201.

life interest in certain real property and gave him " *power to dispose of such property by will amongst our children,*" and there was no gift over in default of appointment. It was held that the power conferred upon the husband was a mere power and not one coupled with a trust.[1] There were no words in the will which could possibly justify the inference that the testatrix intended the children to take if her husband made no appointment.

(3) Powers Classified according to the Nature of the Interests which their Exercise Creates.

Under the old law one of the classifications of powers was into :

(1) common law powers,
(2) statutory powers,
(3) equitable powers, and
(4) powers to appoint uses.

Common law powers. The significance of a common law power was that it enabled the donee to deal with the legal estate, so that if for instance a testator authorized his executors to sell his land, but did not actually devise the land to them, they acquired the right at common law to pass the *legal* estate to a purchaser.[2]

Statutory powers. Statutory powers, such as the powers conferred by the Settled Land Acts, operated in a similar manner, so that a tenant for life could convey a legal estate by the exercise of his power of sale or leasing.

Equitable powers. Equitable powers were those that permitted the creation only of equitable interests. These were and still are the commonest examples of powers found in practice, and they arise, for instance, where personal property is vested in trustees with a power reserved to some person to appoint among the children of a marriage.

Powers to appoint interests in land. But the powers that concern us most are the old powers to appoint uses. We have seen that where A. stood seised to the use of B., the Statute of Uses operated to pass the legal estate to B.; and further that it was possible, not only to make a final declaration of the uses binding upon A., but also to reserve a power permitting the grantor or some other person to replace these by a fresh use that would carry the legal estate to the appointee. The donee of a power was thus enabled to dispose of a *legal* estate held by another person. But the legislation of 1925 shifted the basis of conveyancing from powers to estates. The legal estate must now be conveyed only by the person in whom it is vested. The Law of Property Act, 1925, provides, therefore,

---

[1] Dist. *In re Llewelyn's Settlement*, [1921] 2 Ch. 289.
[2] Holdsworth, *History of English Law*, vol. vii. pp. 153 *et seq.*

that with a few exceptions an appointor shall be restricted to the disposition of the equitable interest in the land affected.

The Statute of Uses has been repealed and it is now enacted that the provisions in any statute or other instrument requiring land to be conveyed to uses shall take effect as directions that the land shall be conveyed to a person of full age *upon the requisite trusts*.[1]

Now, in general, lead to creation of equitable interests.

In short all powers, with a few exceptions, are now equitable in the sense that they affect and dispose of the equitable interest only, and therefore they do not concern, nor do the interests arising under them concern, a purchaser who takes a conveyance from the estate owner. Thus in the very forefront of the Act it is provided that :—

" Every power of appointment over, or power to convey or charge
" land or any interest therein, whether created by a statute or other
" instrument or implied by law, and whether created before or after
" the commencement of this Act (not being a power vested in a legal
" mortgagee or an estate owner in right of his estate and exercisable
" by him or by another person in his name and on his behalf)
" shall operate only in equity."[2]

In the next sub-section the Act distinguishes between *legal* and *equitable* powers, and later defines the two types in this way :

Distinction between legal and equitable powers.

" Legal powers " includes the powers vested in a chargee by way of
legal mortgage or in an estate owner under which a legal estate
can be transferred ; and " equitable powers " means all the powers
in or over land under which equitable interests or powers only can be
transferred or created.[3]

The Acts also contain provisions which compel the owner of the legal estate concerned to give effect to equitable interests created by the exercise of the power.[4]

So the essential classification of powers under the modern law is into legal and equitable powers, and the following are the only legal powers that exist :—

(a) the powers of sale and leasing etc. possessed by a legal mortgagee or chargee ;[5]

List of legal powers.

(b) the powers vested in an estate owner in right of his estate, *e.g.* the powers of a tenant for life under the Settled Land Act ;

(c) certain powers of a miscellaneous nature. Examples are :

the power of a receiver to dispose of a legal estate vested in a person suffering from mental disorder, if authorized to do so by a nominated judge or the Court of Protection.[6]

---

[1] Law of Property Act, 1925, s. 1 (9).
[2] *Ibid.*, s. 1 (7).
[3] *Ibid.*, ss. 3, 205 (1) (xi).
[4] *Ibid.*, s. 3 ; Settled Land Act, 1925, s. 16.
[5] *Infra*, pp. 541 ; 575 ; 577.
[6] Mental Health Act, 1959, 7th Sch.

the power of a public utility company, if compulsorily acquiring land, to vest the legal estate in itself in certain circumstances, *e.g.* where the owner refuses or is unable to execute the necessary deed.[1]

SECTION II. EXECUTION OF POWERS.

(A) OBSERVANCE OF FORMALITIES.

Specified formalities must be observed.

The instrument that creates a power may require that its exercise shall be attended by special formalities, and the general rule on this matter is that all such formalities, no matter how trivial and unessential, must be strictly observed.[2] Thus in the case of *Hawkins* v. *Kemp* [3] :

It was required by the settlor that the appointment should be made by deed or instrument in writing, executed in the presence of and attested by three credible witnesses, enrolled in one of the courts at Westminster, and executed with the consent of the donee's wife, father, and father-in-law, and also of several trustees. It was held that all these arbitrary demands must be literally performed.

Statutory exceptions.

Not unnaturally, this led to the frequent failure of appointments, and therefore the legislature has provided that in three cases an execution shall not be defective owing to the breach of a technicality. The three cases are as follows :

Leasing powers.

(a) **Leasing powers.** It is provided by the Law of Property Act, 1925 [4] (re-enacting the Leases Acts of 1849 and 1850), that where in the intended exercise of a power of leasing, whether given by an Act of Parliament or by some instrument, a lease is actually granted, but is not binding upon the reversioners by reason of some deviation from the terms of the power, such lease shall, if it has been made in good faith and if the lessee has entered, take effect in equity as a contract for the grant of a valid lease. The effect is that the lessee can require the reversioners either to grant a new lease which complies with the requisite formalities, or to confirm the void lease, and it is provided that a confirmation may be either by memorandum signed by each of the parties or by memorandum signed by the party who accepts rent from the lessee. Such is the effect, for instance, where a mortgagor makes an oral lease under his statutory power of leasing, but omits to reserve a power of re-entry on non-payment of rent as required by the Law of Property Act, 1925.[5]

---

[1] Law of Property Act, 1925, s. 7 (3) ; Lands Clauses Consolidation Act, 1845, s. 77.

[2] Sugden on Powers (6th Edn.), p. 264.

[3] (1803), 3 East 410.   [4] S. 152.

[5] *Pawson* v. *Revell*, [1958] 2 Q. B. 360 ; [1958] 3 All E. R. 233, C. A. As for the reservation of a power of re-entry, see Law of Property Act, 1925, s. 99 ; *infra*, pp. 391 ; 397.

The lessee under such a void lease is bound on his side to accept a confirmation if the reversioner is willing to give one.

(b) Powers exercised by will. In the case of powers to be exercised by will, trouble frequently arose through donors requiring the will to be attested by a given number of witnesses. The Wills Act of 1837, therefore enacts, first, that no testamentary appointment shall be valid unless the will is in writing and signed by the testator ; and unless the signature is acknowledged by the testator in the presence of two or more witnesses present at the same time ; and unless the witnesses attest and subscribe the will in the presence of the testator. These are the necessary formalities for all ordinary wills. Secondly, the Act provides that every will executed in the above manner shall, so far as respects the *execution and attestation* thereof, be a valid execution of a testamentary power of appointment, notwithstanding any express requirement that the will should be executed with some additional or different form of execution or solemnity.[1] Powers exercised by will.

(c) Powers exercised by deed. A similar provision was made for deeds by Lord St. Leonards Act, 1859, in a section that is now incorporated in the Law of Property Act, 1925.[2] This provides that a deed executed in the presence of and attested by two or more witnesses and signed by the person by whom it is executed[3] shall, so far as respects the *execution and attestation* thereof, be a valid execution of a power of appointment, provided that the donee has not been required by the donor to make the appointment by will. It is expressly enacted that such an execution is valid even though the donor required that the deed should be executed or attested with some additional or other form of execution or solemnity. On the other hand nothing in the Act is to relieve the donee from obtaining any consent or from doing anything having no relation to the mode of execution and attestation which may have been prescribed by the donor. Moreover, unlike the rule laid down in the Wills Act, there is no provision that an appointment *inter vivos* must be made by deed, and therefore a direction by the donor that the power shall be exercisable by a mere written instrument is effective. Powers exercised by deed.

It should be stressed that the operation of these two statutory rules is restricted to the mode of executing and attesting the instrument. The rule *at law* still is that any other act which the Formalities, apart from statutory exceptions, must be observed *at law.*

---

[1] Wills Act, 1837, ss. 9, 10.
[2] S. 159. [3] S. 73.

H*

donor of the power may have specified must be performed. Thus if a deed is required, the power cannot be exercised either by mere writing or by will, and if a will is required a deed is not sufficient.

Rule in equity.

Non-execution.

Defective execution.

But at this point equity intervenes, and although it will not compel a donee to exercise a power [1] (except one which is coupled with a trust),[2] it is prepared to aid a defective execution in favour of the following persons—charities, creditors of the donee, purchasers for value from him, and his wife and legitimate children.[3] The court, however, will not grant its aid unless the donee has shown a clear intention to exercise the power and has indicated the proposed beneficiaries and the extent of their interests.[4] Further, it must be clear that the defect is of a formal character, not the failure to comply with what the donor regarded as essential. Thus relief will be given,

> if a power exercisable by deed or will is in fact exercised by a signed but unattested paper,[5] or
> if a power exercisable by deed is exercised by will,[6] unless the formality of a deed was regarded as essential by the donor.[7]

But relief will not be given,

> if a power exercisable by will is exercised by an irrevocable deed, for the donor intended that the donee should be free throughout his life to revoke an appointment should he so desire.[8]

(B) EXCESSIVE EXECUTION.

Forms of excessive appointments.

If in the exercise of a special power the appointor transgresses the limits that have been imposed upon him, he acts in excess of the power and is said to make an excessive appointment. Such an excess may take any one of three forms, for if the appointor :

(1) appoints to persons who are not objects of the power, that is, who are not within the class of appointees designated by the donor [9] ; or

(2) grants interests larger than those permitted by the power ; or

(3) annexes to the appointed interest, conditions and qualifications not authorized by the power,

in each case he makes an excessive execution.

---

[1] *Tollett* v. *Tollett* (1728), 2 P. Wms. 489 ; White and Tudor's *Leading Cases on Real Property*, p. 249.
[2] *Supra*, p. 196.
[3] For a discussion of the whole subject see White and Tudor, *Leading Cases in Equity*, vol. ii. pp. 255-9.
[4] *Garth* v. *Townsend* (1869), L. R. 7 Eq. 220.
[5] *Kennard* v. *Kennard* (1872), 8 Ch. App. 227.
[6] *Tollett* v. *Tollett* (1728), 2 P. Wms. 489.
[7] *Cooper* v. *Martin* (1867), 3 Ch. App. 47, 57-8 ; *Re Hambro's Marriage Settlements, Hambro* v. *Hambro*, [1949] Ch. 484.
[8] *Coffin* v. *Cooper* (1865), 13 W. R. 571 ; *Re Parkin*, [1892] 3 Ch. 510, 517.
[9] *In re Boulton's Settlement Trust*, [1928] Ch. 703.

The principle of law applicable to any kind of excessive appointment is that where there is a proper and complete execution followed by an improper excess, the execution is valid and the excess void ; but where it is impossible to distinguish between what is proper and what is improper, then the whole appointment falls to the ground.[1]

Excess alone generally void.

Thus, to take an example of excess in the objects :

> if the donee is authorized to appoint among *the children of A.*, he is not permitted to appoint in favour of A.'s grandchildren, and therefore, if he makes a grant to a child for life with a gift over to the issue of the child, the first gift is valid and the second void.[2]

In other words, if it is possible to separate the good from the bad, the separation will be made.[3] So, for instance :

> When property is appointed equally to an object and a stranger, the object will take one-half, but the other half, instead of going to the stranger, is divided among the persons who are entitled in default of appointment.
>
> But if a donee has a power of appointment among the children of A., and appoints to A.'s son X. and to X.'s wife and children (without specifying any shares), the whole gift fails, for it is quite impossible to sever the gifts and say what share is to go to the object X., and what to the strangers, the wife and children.[4]

(C) Fraud upon a Power.

An appointment is bad as being a fraud on the power unless it is made *bonâ fide* and in order to carry out the design intended by the donor.[5] But fraud in this connection is used in a technical sense and is not necessarily confined to moral turpitude.

Meaning of " fraud " in connection with powers.

Lord PARKER said in *Vatcher* v. *Paull*[6] :—

> " The term fraud in connection with frauds on a power does not
> " necessarily denote any conduct on the part of the appointor amount-
> " ing to fraud in the common law meaning of the term or any conduct
> " which could be properly termed dishonest or immoral. It merely
> " means that the power has been exercised for a purpose, or with an
> " intention, beyond the scope of or not justified by the instrument
> " creating the power. Perhaps the most common instance of this is
> " where the exercise is due to some bargain between the appointor and
> " appointee, whereby the appointor, or some other person not an
> " object of the power, is to derive a benefit. But such a bargain is
> " not essential. It is enough that the appointor's purpose and inten-

[1] *Alexander* v. *Alexander* (1755), 2 Ves. Sen. 640, 644 ; *Re Cohen,* [1911] 1 Ch. 37 ; *In re Farncombe's Trusts* (1878), 9 Ch. D. 652 ; Farwell on Powers, 298 ; *In re Holland,* [1914] 2 Ch. 595.
[2] *Brudenell* v. *Elwes* (1801), 1 East 442.
[3] *In re Kerr's Trusts* (1877), 4 Ch. D. 600, 604.
[4] *Re Brown's Trust* (1865), L. R. 1 Eq. 74.
[5] *Portland* v. *Topham* (1864), 11 H. L. C. 32, *per* WESTBURY, L.C.
[6] [1915] A. C. 372, 378, P. C.

" tion is to secure a benefit for himself, or some other person not an
" object of the power. In such a case the appointment is invalid
" unless the Court can clearly distinguish between the quantum of
" the benefit *bonâ fide* intended to be conferred on the appointee, and
" the quantum of the benefit intended to be derived by the appointor
" or to be conferred on a stranger." [1]

Bargain between appointor and appointee.

It is clear, of course, that an appointment is vitiated if it is
made upon a bargain or understanding which fetters the appointed
interest in the appointee's hands in favour either of the appointor
himself or some stranger, or which is intended to benefit the
appointor or a stranger. [2]

Thus in the leading case of *Aleyn* v. *Belchier* [3] :

a power of jointuring which was executed in favour of a wife with
an agreement that the wife should receive only part of the appointed
fund, and that the residue should go to pay the husband's debts,
was held to be a fraud on the power

In another case : [4]

A wife obtained against her husband, who was the donee of a special
power to appoint £50,000 among his children or remoter issue, a
decree nisi for the dissolution of their marriage. The husband,
being desperately anxious that the decree should be made absolute
in order that he might marry again, settled his wife's demands
respecting alimony and so induced her to press the divorce proceedings to a conclusion, by agreeing, *inter alia*, to appoint more
than half of the £50,000 to the only child of the marriage. It was
held, ten years later, that this appointment was void as a fraud on
the power since it was made for the purpose of securing freedom to
re-marry. If allowed to stand it would have meant that he could
appoint less than £25,000 among the children of his second marriage,
of whom there were three.

Power to select.

But an appointment may be stigmatized as fraudulent even
though no actual bargain has been struck. Thus, in the case of
a power to select from a class of persons, such as children, the
duty of the appointor is to make a *bonâ fide* and fair distribution
among the objects, and he obviously fails in this respect if his
appointment is directed to the achievement of some collateral
purpose. The true test is whether he exercised the power *bonâ
fide* for the end designed. [5] What was his purpose ? If it was
merely to select the appropriate beneficiaries, his decision, how-

---

[1] The revocation of an appointment already made is not within the
doctrine of fraud, since it cannot injure those who are entitled in default of
appointment ; *In re Greaves, Public Trustee* v. *Ash,* [1954] Ch. 434 ; [1954]
1 All E. R. 771.
[2] *Duggan* v. *Duggan* (1880), 8 L. R. Ir. 152 ; White and Tudor, p. 269.
In re Nicholson's Settlement, [1939] Ch. 11, at p. 18 *per cur.* ; [1938] 3 All
E. R. 532, at p. 534.
[3] (1758), 1 Eden, 132 ; White and Tudor, *Leading Cases in Equity,* vol. ii.
p. 263 ; which see generally.
[4] *Cochrane* v. *Cochrane,* [1922] 2 Ch. 230.
[5] *Re Wright, Hegan* v. *Bloor,* [1920] 1 Ch. 108, at p. 119, *per* P. O.
LAWRENCE, J.

ever capricious, stands. If it was to benefit, directly or indirectly, a non-object, the purpose is foreign to the power, and the appointment will be set aside as fraudulent, irrespective of whether his design succeeds or whether it was known to the appointee. In the well-known case of *In re Marsden's Trusts*,[1] for instance :

> A married woman appointed the whole property to her daughter to the exclusion of the other children, but an arrangement made between her and her husband, to which the daughter was not a party, showed that her motive was to benefit him, not to act fairly towards the children. According to the arrangement the hope of the wife that some provision out of the appointed property should be made for the husband, in the event of his survival, was discreetly to be conveyed to the daughter.

Although the daughter was not privy to the scheme the appointment was held to be void.

An appointment made subject to an unauthorized condition affords a good example of the attitude adopted by the courts.

Position where unauthorized condition annexed.

> Suppose that a testator, X., having a power exercisable in favour of his children, appoints the property to his daughter, but subject to the condition that she settles it on her own children.

This condition is excessive and must in any event be struck out, for otherwise non-objects would benefit, but whether the whole appointment is void as being fraudulent depends upon the true purpose and intention of the appointor.

If X. genuinely intended to benefit his daughter, the appointment stands good, freed from the condition.[2] If, on the other hand, what prevailed with him was not a genuine desire to benefit his daughter, but a determination to accomplish some object beyond the purpose of the power, the whole appointment is rejected as fraudulent.[3]

The position is different where the power is to appoint in favour of one person only, as for instance a wife or husband. Here, if there is no bargain between the appointor and appointee which fetters the enjoyment of the appointed property, the fact

---

[1] (1859), 4 Drew 594 ; *Topham* v. *Duke of Portland* (1869), 5 Ch. App. 40 ; *Re Crawshay, Hore-Ruthven* v. *Public Trustee*, [1948] Ch. 123 ; [1948] 1 All E. R. 107 ; *Re Dick, Knight* v. *Dick*, [1953] Ch. 343 ; [1953] 1 All E. R. 559 ; See 64 L. Q. R., pp. 221 *et seq*.

[2] *In re Holland*, [1914] 2 Ch. 595. If the condition is annexed not to the appointed share, but to the appointor's own property, as, for example, where he bequeaths £5,000 to his daughter, an object of the power, with a condition attached that she shall forfeit this unless she settles her appointed share on a non-object, the condition is not treated either as excessive or fraudulent. The daughter is put to her election, *i.e.* she can either retain the appointed share free from the condition and forfeit the £5,000, or retain the £5,000 upon the terms of settling the appointed share ; *In re Burton's Settlements*, [1955] Ch. 82 ; [1954] 3 All E. R. 193.

[3] *In re Dick, Knight* v. *Dick*, *supra* ; *In re Burton's Settlements*, *supra*, where the whole question is reviewed at pp. 96–101 ; 201–204 respectively.

that the appointor hoped to achieve a collateral purpose is immaterial and does not invalidate the appointment. The reason is that no detriment is caused to other possible beneficiaries, for there are no other objects of the power. The terms of the power are that the appointee shall be benefited if the appointor so decides, and, there being no bargain to fetter him, he is free to enjoy the property as he thinks fit. A striking illustration of this principle is afforded by *In re Nicholson's Settlement*.[1]

Effect of fraud.

The general rule is that an appointment made in fraud of a power is void *in toto*, and that the property goes as in default of appointment, unless indeed a new and valid appointment is made. Nevertheless, if the honest and dishonest parts can be severed, effect may be given to that which is lawful.[2]

Thus in the case of a power to appoint to children, the fraudulent exercise in favour of one child does not disturb the shares that have properly been appointed to the others.[3]

Protection of purchasers claiming under void appointments.

An important question, that has received attention from the legislature, arises when a purchaser takes a conveyance of property from an appointee whose title depends upon a fraudulent appointment. The question is whether such a purchaser acquires a good title.

The old law.

The answer to this question under the law in force before 1926 depended upon the nature of the interest taken by the purchaser, that is to say, upon whether he obtained the legal or the equitable estate. A fraudulent appointment made under a common law power, or a power operating under the Statute of Uses, so that the legal estate passed to the appointee (as for instance where there was a grant to A. to such uses as B. should appoint and B. appointed to C.) was not void, but voidable, and a purchaser who could show that he had given value and had had no notice of the fraud on the power obtained a good and indefeasible title. On the other hand an appointment in fraud of an equitable power, that is, a power the exercise of which passed only the equitable estate, was void, and a person who took from the appointee could not avail himself of the plea that he was purchaser for value without notice. The exercise of an equitable power has no direct effect upon the legal ownership. The legal estate in the property is vested in some other person, and that person must convey the legal estate to the appointee in order to give legal effect to the appointment.

These rules were laid down in *Cloutte* v. *Storey*[4]:

A father appointed the property to his son with a secret arrangement that it should be held for the father's benefit, and later the son sold

---

[1] [1939] Ch. 11, [1938] 3 All E. R. 532.
[2] *Whelan* v. *Palmer* (1888), 39 Ch. D. 648. See White and Tudor, *Leading Cases in Equity*, vol. ii. p. 274.
[3] *Harrison* v. *Randall* (1852), 9 Hare 397.
[4] [1911] 1 Ch. 18.

his interest to X., who gave value and had no notice of the fraud. As the property in question was personal property vested in trustees, it followed that the power was equitable and its exercise absolutely void.

When, therefore, practically all powers became equitable under the legislation of 1925 new provisions for the protection of purchasers were required. The Law of Property Act, 1925, enacts that : The modern law.

> " An instrument purporting to exercise a power of appointment over " property, which, in default of and subject to any appointment, is " held in trust for a class or number of persons *of whom the appointee* " *is one* shall not be void on the ground of fraud on the power as " against a purchaser in good faith." [1]

In the present context, however, a *purchaser in good faith* is defined as a person dealing with an appointee not less than 25 years old, for valuable consideration in money or money's worth, and without notice of the fraud or of any circumstances from which the fraud might with reasonable care have been discovered.[2] Even so, the protection is not complete, for if the appointee's interest exceeds what he would have got had no appointment been made, the title of the purchaser in good faith does not extend to the excess.[3]

To illustrate the rule and the qualification :

> Suppose that there is power to appoint, subject to a life interest, a fund of £1000 among the children of A., and that in default of appointment the fund is to be divided equally among the children. If there are four children and a fraudulent appointment during the life interest is made to one of the children, a purchaser of this appointed interest will be unable to claim the protection of the Act unless he can prove that he had no notice of the fraud, and that the child was over 25 at the time of the purchase, and even then his right will not extend to more than £250.

SECTION III. DETERMINATION OF POWERS.

The normal way in which a power is determined is for the donee to execute a deed of release.[4] It has always been the law that powers appendant and powers in gross can be released,[5] but it was not until 1882 [6] that the same procedure was made applicable to powers simply collateral.[7] It is now enacted [8] that Release.

---

[1] S. 157 (1).   [2] S. 157 (2)   [3] S. 157 (1), proviso.
[4] *Encyclopædia of Forms and Precedents* (3rd Edn.), vol. xiii. (Title Releases), p. 660.
[5] *Re Radcliffe*, [1892] 1 Ch. 227, 231. *In re Mills*, [1930] 1 Ch. 654.
[6] Conveyancing Act, 1881, s. 52.
[7] For definition, see *supra*, p. 196.
[8] Law of Property Act, 1925, s. 155.

all powers, except those in the nature of or coupled with a trust,[1] may be released either by deed or by a contract not to exercise the power. Thus, although the donee of a power exercisable only by will cannot make a valid appointment by an irrevocable deed, yet a release under seal of the power, or a covenant not to exercise it, is binding.[2]

Inconsistent dealing.

Apart from express release the rule is that any dealing with the estate by the donee of the power which is inconsistent with its further exercise puts an end to the power, so that if a husband appoints one-fourth of the property to his wife and the residue to his children, and the wife dies, he cannot appoint her fourth to a second wife.[3]

Settled Land Act powers.

A power appendant, such as the power of leasing enjoyed by a tenant for life under the Settled Land Act, is not extinguished by being exercised, and as we have seen, a tenant for life under that Act cannot release his statutory powers.[4]

Disclaimer.

Any power other than a Settled Land Act power or one coupled with a trust can be disclaimed by deed, and can then be exercised by the other person or the survivor of the other persons to whom it was given.[5]

---

[1] *Re Somes, Smith* v. *Somes,* [1896] 1 Ch. 250. *Re Wills' Trust Deeds, Wills* v. *Godfrey,* [1964] Ch. 219; [1963] 1 All E. R. 390.

[2] *In re Brown's Settlement,* [1939] Ch. 944; [1939] 3 All E. R. 391.

[3] *In re Hancock,* [1896] 2 Ch. 173; *Foakes* v. *Jackson,* [1900] 1 Ch. 807.

[4] *Supra,* p. 140.

[5] Law of Property Act, 1925, s. 156.

CHAPTER V.

FUTURE INTERESTS.[1]

SUMMARY.

---

[1] For the history of this subject see Holdsworth, *History of English Law*, vol. vii. pp. 81 *et seq.* ; and generally, see Gray, *The Rule against Perpetuities* (4th Edn.).

SECTION I. THE POSITION BEFORE 1926.

Old law simplified.

The law affecting future interests was greatly simplified by the legislation of 1925, though this simplification was incidental rather than due to any direct enactment. There is now in consequence less justification for Blackstone's dictum that " the doctrine of estates in expectancy contains some of the nicest and most abstruse learning of the English law."[1] But we cannot appreciate the extent or the effect of the simplification unless we know something of the old law, and we must therefore attempt in the following pages to give a short account of the difficulties that formerly beset the subject. The historical stages in the evolution of the law have been described with great particularity and clearness by Holdsworth,[2] but in the present brief account, in order to diminish the complexity of the subject as far as possible, we shall not keep to the strictly historical method, but attempt merely to bring into relief the various classes

Knowledge of old law still necessary.

---

[1] Blackstone. vol. ii. p. 163.
[2] *History of English Law*, vol. vii. pp. 81-149.

of future interests that might subsist under the old law. The arrangement we shall adopt, then, will be to describe, first, the future legal interests called *remainders*, secondly, the future legal interests called *executory interests*, and thirdly, the future equitable interests which might correspond either to remainders or to executory interests.

Before an explanation is given of these three classes it is advisable to develop a theme that pervades the whole of the present subject, namely, the meaning given by the law to the words " vested " and " contingent." Estates are either vested or contingent. The former may be vested either in possession or in interest.

An estate is vested in possession when its owner is entitled to present possession; it is vested in interest when there is a present unqualified right of taking possession as soon as it becomes vacant. If, for example, there is a limitation :

To A. for life and after his death to B. for life,

A. has an estate which is vested in possession, B. one which is vested in interest.[1] As Preston demonstrated over a hundred years ago, an estate vested in interest is always a present right in the sense that the owner is clothed with an immediate power of alienation, though it is not always present in the sense that he is entitled to the actual physical enjoyment of the land at the moment.[2] There is nothing conditional about it, *i.e.* there is nothing that must happen before the owner can establish his title. The test is always the same—is the owner absolutely entitled at the present moment to assume possession whenever it may fall vacant ? If so, he owns a vested interest—he is invested with a portion of the fee simple—even though in fact he may never obtain possession. In the example given above, for instance, it is obvious that B. may predecease A. and therefore may never enjoy the fruits of ownership, but this does not alter the fact that during his lifetime he continues to have an absolute and unqualified right to take possession upon the determination of the preceding estate. In the words of Fearne :

" The present capacity of taking effect in possession, if the possession " were to become vacant, and not the certainty that the possession " will become vacant before the estate limited in remainder deter- " mines, universally distinguishes a vested remainder from one that " is contingent." [3]

An estate is contingent if the accrual of the owner's title depends upon the occurrence of some event. If, for instance, there is a limitation :

---

[1] Hawkins on Wills, p. 263 ; Hayes, *Introduction to Conveyancing*, **vol.** i. p. 17 ; Gray, *op. cit.*, s. 794.
[2] Preston on Estates, vol. i. p. 65.
[3] Fearne, *Contingent Remainders*, p. 216.

> To X. and Y. for their lives, and then to the survivor of them in fee simple,[1]

the fee simple stands contingently limited while X. and Y. are still alive, for during that period neither of them can establish his claim to the estate. It is only the survivor who will be entitled, and at the moment it is dubious which of them will be the first to die. Again, if there is a gift

> To A. for life and then to B. at 21,

B, if still an infant, has a mere contingent interest, for he has not yet satisfied the condition upon which the acquisition of a definite interest depends. He is not yet qualified to take possession whenever it falls vacant.[2]

Before it can be said that a beneficiary is entitled to a portion of the ownership as having a vested interest, three things must concur:

(a) his identity must be established;
(b) the size of his interest must be ascertainable;[3] and
(c) his right to the interest (as distinguished from his right to possession) must not depend upon the occurrence of some event.

Until these conditions are satisfied the beneficiary has nothing more than a contingent interest.

We will now consider the three types of future interest under the old law.

Remainders.

Legal Remainders. Common law permitted future interests, called remainders, to be carved out of a legal estate, though, as we shall see presently, there were several restrictive rules which had to be observed. If a settlor decided to create two or more successive estates in his land, and drafted the desired limitations in one instrument, as for instance by a feoffment

> to A. for life and then to B. for life and then to C. in fee simple,

the first estate which preceded the next following remainder was called the " particular estate "[4] and those which followed were denominated " remainders."

Such an estate was called a remainder, not because it was the remnant that was left after the grant of the particular estate, but

---

[1] *Whitby* v. *Von Luedecke*, [1906] 1 Ch. 783; *In re Legh's Settlement Trusts, Public Trustee* v. *Legh*, [1938] Ch. 39; [1937] 3 All E. R. 823.
[2] On the distinction between " vested " and " contingent " see Fearne, *Contingent Remainders*, p. 74; Gray, *op. cit.*, s. 9 and chapter iii.
[3] Strictly speaking, this is not true in the case of a *class gift*, *e.g.*, a limitation to A. for life, remainder to his children in fee simple. The moment that a child is born he takes a vested interest, since he is entitled to possession when it becomes vacant. Yet, the size of his share is not ascertainable until A.'s death, for it will diminish each time another child is born. The truth is, as Gray shows, *op. cit.*, ss. 110, 110. 1, that it is artificial to regard a remainder of this kind as vested.
[4] So called because it is a *particular*, or small part, of the estate of inheritance.

because the land was to stand over or continue for the remainder-man after the particular estate had determined.[1]

A remainder should not be confused with a reversion, which is an interest that arises by operation of law, as distinct from act of parties, whenever the owner of an estate grants a particular estate, but does not dispose of the whole of his interest. If, for instance, a tenant in fee simple makes a conveyance of the land in tail, for life or for a term of years, there continues in him an estate which is called a reversion because the land will revert into his possession upon the determination of the particular estate.

Reversions distinguished.

" A reversion is where the residue of the estate always doth con-
" tinue in him that made the particular estate." [2]

Remainders fall into two classes, being either vested or contingent. It follows from what has already been said that a person has a vested remainder if he or his representatives are continually entitled and ready to take actual possession of the land whenever the particular estate ends. This implies that he must be a living ascertained person and that his title as owner does not depend upon the happening of some uncertain event. A simple example is a grant

Vested remainder.

to A. for life, remainder to B. in fee simple.

As opposed to this, a remainder is contingent if the grantee is not an ascertained person, or if, though ascertained, his title awaits the occurrence of some event, for in neither case is there a person ready to enter the land as soon as it is vacant. Grants

Contingent remainder.

to a bachelor for life, remainder to his son ; and
to A. for life, remainder in tail to his first son to attain 21,

are examples of contingent remainders.

A contingent remainder becomes a vested remainder when the person to whom it is limited is ascertained, or when the event upon which it is dependent happens. A contingent remainder may be so limited that it can vest only *eo instanti* with the determination of the particular estate, as for instance where the grant is to A. during the life of B., remainder to the heirs of B. In this case the death of B. terminates the particular estate and at the same time enables the person who is heir of B. to be ascertained,[3] for *nemo heres est viventis.*

Vesting of contingent remainder.

The result of the distinction between vested and contingent interests is that reversions and vested remainders, despite the element of futurity of possessory enjoyment that characterizes them, have always been regarded as *estates* in the true sense of the word, though, with the reduction in 1925 of legal estates to the fee simple absolute in possession and the term of years

Vested remainders are present estates.

---

[1] Pollock and Maitland, *History of English Law,* vol. ii. p. 21.
[2] Co. Litt. 22b.
[3] Co. Litt. 298a ; see *Boraston's Case* (1587), 3 Co. Rep. 19 ; Fearne, *Contingent Remainders,* p. 5, note (d).

absolute, the more appropriate word is now "interests." More-over, they are present, not future, interests. A future interest properly so called is one which cannot be the subject-matter of ownership until something happens that may never happen. This is not the position with regard to reversions and vested remainders, for although they may be described as future *interests* inasmuch as they do not at the moment carry immediate possession of the land, they are nevertheless present existing interests in the sense that they confer upon their holders a portion of the actual owner-ship of the land.

"The fee simple being supposed to be carved out into parts or
"divisions by the creation of particular estates, a grant to any person
"of one of these portions of the fee vested him with, or vested him
"in, an estate in the land." [1]

Aliter contingent remainders.

They are classified as future interests merely because the right of possessory enjoyment is postponed, but they are present in the sense that they may be disposed of as freely as an estate carrying a right to immediate possession. On the other hand, a contingent remainder does not become an estate, but continues as a mere possibility of acquiring an estate, until the contingency upon which it depends has occurred. [2]

Rules for remainders before 1926.

After this preliminary description of remainders we are in a position to examine those restrictive rules of the common law that furnished the limits within which a settlor could create interests of this type, though we may note that they were not finally established until the beginning of the seventeenth century. [3] The exceeding strictness of these rules indicates the reluctance with which common law permitted the existence of future interests, and it is well at the outset of our inquiry to realize the main object which the law had in view. That object was to preserve the continuity of seisin. Seisin meant the possession of land by a freeholder, *i.e.* by a tenant in fee simple, in fee tail or for life, and it was a feudal rule of the greatest antiquity that there should be an uninterrupted tenancy of the freehold, or, in more technical language, that the seisin should always be full. Every feoffment had to convey an estate that would at once carry the freehold to the feoffee. [4] This rule was required in the early days of the law for two distinct reasons. In the first place, those profitable feudal incidents which, as we have seen, [5] explained the survival of the military tenures, were due from the person who was seised of the land in question, and therefore it was of the utmost importance that an estate of freehold should never be without a known owner, for otherwise a lord might be prejudiced in the enforcement of his

Importance of seisin.

---

[1] Hawkins on Wills, p. 263.
[2] Hargreaves, *Introduction to Land Law* (3rd Edn.), pp. 50–3 ; 106.
[3] Holdsworth, *History of English Law*, vol. vii. p. 81 *et seq.*
[4] Preston on Estates, vol. i. pp. 217, 249.   [5] *Supra*, pp. 18 *et seq.*

rights. Secondly, it was a rule of procedure that a real action lay only against the actual freeholder, so that if the identity of the person seised was in any way doubtful, a dispossessed owner of land might be prevented from taking proceedings for its recovery. For these reasons, therefore, it was an inviolable principle of the common law that any disposition of land calculated to produce an abeyance of the seisin was void.[1]

By way of preface it is well to appreciate that the following restrictive rules imposed upon the creation of legal remainders constituted the whole foundation of the old law relating to future interests, and that unless they are constantly kept in mind it is impossible to arrive at a correct understanding of that law. On the other hand, if they are thoroughly grasped, the abstruseness asserted by Blackstone need occasion no fear to the reader.

Importance of the rules.

(a) The limitation of a remainder was void unless it was preceded by the limitation of a particular estate of freehold.

It was impossible at common law to limit a freehold remainder in such a way that it would arise of its own strength at some time in the future. A feoffment, for instance made

No freehold in futuro.

> to B. for life when he attains the age of 21 years

was void. The rule which forbade a limitation of this nature depended upon two principles, viz. : that the seisin must not be in abeyance, and that a conveyance which divested the freehold from the feoffor must at the same time vest it in the feoffee.[2]

The classic conveyance of the old law was the feoffment with livery of seisin, and as the operative part of this assurance was the actual delivery of possession and not the charter of feoffment,[3] it was clear that the seisin must pass from the feoffor. If, however, the seisin departed from him, it must of necessity vest in some definite person, for otherwise an abeyance of seisin would ensue. An alienor, therefore, who desired to confer a life estate upon B. at 21 was confronted with a difficulty. There could be no immediate delivery to B., for he was to take an interest in the land only if he attained 21, and that event would remain uncertain for some time. Again, the feoffment could not be made at one date to take effect later, for it was essential that the feoffor should immediately be divested of the seisin.[4]

Reason for the rule.

---

[1] Co. Litt. 342b ; *Freeman d. Vernon v. West* (1763), 2 Wils. 165 ; Hayes, *Introduction to Conveyancing*, vol. i. p. 14 ; Challis, *Law of Real Property* (3rd Edn.), p .100.

[2] Fearne, *Contingent Remainders*, p. 281.

[3] Co. Litt. 271b, note.

[4] *Per curiam, Barwick's Case* (1597), 5 Co. Rep. 93b.

The only method, then, of making an effective feoffment and of providing for continuity of seisin when it was desired to give B. a freehold estate at 21 was immediately to vest the seisin in some other person (called the particular tenant), who could answer the feudal requirements of the common law. Thus it came to be a rule that every freehold remainder which was to take effect upon the happening of a future contingency had to be supported by a particular estate of freehold,[1] so that the limitation which we are considering, instead of merely being to B. for life at 21, would be

to A. for life, remainder to B. for life when he attains 21.

This feudal rule outlived its reasons, but it continued to affect the limitation of remainders at common law until 1925, long after the feoffment had given way to other methods of conveyance.[2] It was a legacy of the Middle Ages which ceased to operate only with the inauguration of the new system on January 1st, 1926.

(b) A contingent remainder had to be so limited as to be capable of vesting either during the continuance of the particular estate or *eo instanti* that it determined.[3]

No abeyance
of seisin
after ter-
mination of
particular
estate.

The particular estate of freehold that was required by the first rule to support all freehold contingent remainders had to be one which was capable of enduring until the contingency happened. Thus a limitation which contemplated an interval of time between the termination of the particular estate and the vesting of the remainder rendered the remainder void. If, for example, there was a grant

to A. for life and one year after A.'s death to B. for life ; or
to A. for life, remainder to such of his children as either before *or after* his death attained 21,[4]

the remainder was in the first example void, and in the second void *as regards the children attaining 21 after A.'s death.* If the first limitation had been allowed to stand, the effect would obviously have been to cause an abeyance of the seisin for one year; and a like result might have ensued in the second case, since the very terms of the limitation contemplated the accrual of an estate to the remaindermen even if they, or any of them, did not reach the age of 21 until after the particular estate had determined.

---

[1] Blackstone, vol. i. p. 118 ; *Buckler's Case* (1597), 2 Co. Rep. 55*a.*
Barwick's Case, supra ; Fearne, *op. cit.*, p. 281 ; Sanders on Uses, vol. i ;
p. 141 ; Holdsworth, *History of English Law*, vol. vii. p. 84 ; Challis, *Law of
Real Property* (3rd Edn.), p. 104.
[2] *Savill* v. *Bethell*, 1902] 2 Ch. 523, 540.
[3] Fearne, *Contingent Remainders*, p. 307.
[4] *In re Lechmere and Lloyd* (1881), 18 Ch. D. 524 ; *Dean* v. *Dean*, [1891]
3 Ch. 150 ; *Miles* v. *Jarvis* (1883), 24 Ch. D. 633.

It followed as a logical result of this requirement that, even though a contingent remainder had been so limited as to be capable of becoming vested at the latest when the particular estate determined, yet it would fail unless it did actually vest (*i.e.* unless the contingency had actually happened) at the time of that determination. Thus, the weakness of remainders at common law was their liability to destruction by reason of the premature determination of the particular estate. In the case, for instance, of a limitation to

Remainder must have vested when particular estate ended.

> A. for life, remainder to the first son of B. to attain 21,

the remainder failed unless B.'s son had attained his majority at the time of A.'s death,[1] while in a limitation to

> X. for life, remainder to his children at 21,

those children who attained 21 in X.'s lifetime took estates to the exclusion of children who reached the prescribed age afterwards.[2] We shall see later that remainders might also fail owing to the artificial destruction of the particular estate before the occurrence of the contingency.[3]

(c) A contingent remainder was void if it was limited to take effect by cutting short the particular estate.[4]

Common law required that a contingent remainder should be so limited that it would take effect upon the natural determination of the particular estate of freehold, and not by breaking in upon it or by bringing it to an abrupt termination. There could be no remainder by proviso, *i.e.* it was impossible to terminate an estate by a proviso so as to make the estate which was to arise after the occurrence of the proviso a remainder.[5] Thus if the limitation was

No remainder by proviso.

> to a widow for life, but if she re-married, to X. for life ; or to B. for life on condition that when Y. married, B.'s estate should cease and remain to Y.,

the interests limited to X. and to Y. were void.

A limitation of this kind which attempted to defeat a prior estate was in effect a limitation upon condition, and had it been permitted it would have infringed the common law maxim that no one could take advantage of a condition (*i.e.* no one could enter and terminate the estate to which the condition was attached), except the grantor and his heirs, executors or administrators.[6]

---

[1] *White* v. *Summers*, [1908] 2 Ch. 256.
[2] *Festiug* v. *Allen* (1843), 12 M. & W. 279.
[3] *Infra*, p. 227.
[4] Fearne, *Contingent Remainders*, p. 10, note (*h*), 261 ; *Cogan* v. *Cogan* (1596), Cro. Eliz. 360 ; Holdsworth, *History of English Law*, vol. vii. p. 84.
[5] *Blackman* v. *Fysh*, [1892] 3 Ch. 209, 220.
[6] Fearne, *op. cit.* p. 261 ; Challis, *Law of Real Property* (3rd Edn.), p. 81. It would also have infringed the maxim that an entry for condition broken destroyed all the estates given by the original limitation ; *infra*, p. 289.

(d) No remainder could be limited after a fee simple estate.[1]

A fee could not be mounted on a fee.

Since a fee simple estate is the largest interest that can be enjoyed in land, it was a rule of the common law that a future estate could not be limited to take effect as a remainder expectant upon the determination of a preceding fee simple. A fee could not be mounted on a fee. Thus if a grant had been made in fee simple with a proviso that it should determine upon the payment of a certain sum or upon failure of the grantee to do a certain act, and go over to a stranger,

the gift over was void.

Definition of "remainder."

Summary. To summarize the law that has been stated above, we see that one class of future *legal* interests permitted by the common law consisted of remainders, which may be defined briefly as interests so limited as to be immediately expectant upon the natural determination of a particular freehold estate less in quantum than a fee simple. Only the simplest kinds of future interests could be created by way of remainder because, for various feudal reasons, their validity depended upon the observance of the four strict rules that we have specified.

Inadequacy of Common Law. It is evident from what has been said that in the matter of future limitations the common law fell short of what was required by society. In the nature of things there are three possible classes of future interests :

First, one that is to take effect in possession upon the determination of a previously limited estate, *e.g.* to A. for life and then to B. for life.

Secondly, one that is to take effect in possession by cutting short a previously limited estate, *e.g.* to A. for life, but as soon as B. is called to the Bar, then to B. for life.

Thirdly, one that arises of its own strength and has no support from or connection with a previously limited estate, *e.g.* to A. for life at 21.

Common law admitted the first class, but the overriding importance that it ascribed to seisin, together with its rules concerning feoffments and conditions, precluded altogether the recognition of the last two classes. Yet, feudal doctrines apart, there is no reason why these prohibited classes should not be available to a settlor, and we now have to see how they came to be recognized under the name of *executory interests* through the medium of equity.

---

[1] Fearne, *op. cit.* p. 12 ; Co. Litt. 18a ; *Musgrave* v. *Brooke* (1884), 26 Ch. D. 792.

Executory Interests. Executory interests were formerly purely equitable in nature, and their origin is to be found in the protection which the Chancellor afforded to the *use* of lands. The governor of the use was the intention of its owner, and though the Chancellor generally followed the rules of common law in regulating the equitable estate, his chief object was to give effect to the wishes of the owner. In the sphere of future interests, he attained the object by refusing to extend to limitations of the use those restrictions that common law imposed in the case of the legal estate. His general policy was to permit a man to create any form of future interest that seemed desirable to him provided that he was content to carve the interest out of the equitable estate and not out of the legal estate. In other words, a settlor had liberty of action if he took advantage of the machinery of uses. A grant to A. at 21 was void, but a grant to X. and his heirs *to the use of* A. at 21 was valid, for the common law rule requiring the support of a particular estate had no application to the equitable interest to which alone A. was entitled, and the Chancellor saw no reason why he should not compel X. to hold the land in favour of A. when the latter reached 21. The use in the hands of its owner was as clay in the hands of the potter,[1] and though in the case of the legal estate a fee could not be mounted on a fee, and though a freehold could not be made to spring up in the future nor to shift to another before its regular termination, there was no objection in principle to these dispositions being made of the equitable estate.

Thus even before the Statute of Uses it became possible, though not indeed common, to create future equitable interests of a kind that would have been impossible at common law. In course of time, when these interests were firmly established in our jurisprudence, they were classified either as *shifting* or as *springing uses* according as they displaced a prior estate or not.

A springing use was an interest limited by way of use to take effect at a future time without affecting any previously limited freehold estate.[2] Simple illustrations would be :

> feoffment to A. and his heirs to the use in fee simple of any wife whom B. may marry, or
> feoffment to A. and his heirs to the use in fee simple of C. at 21.

In both these cases the wife and C. became entitled to the equitable estate as soon as the respective events occurred.

A shifting use was an interest limited by way of use to take effect at some time in the future, in defeasance of and by way of substitution for some prior freehold interest, and before such prior interest had lasted its full measure of duration.[3] Examples would be

Marginal notes: Executory interests equitable in origin. Equitable future interests free from restrictions. Springing uses. Shifting uses.

---

[1] *Brent's Case* (1575), 2 Leonard 14, 16, *per* Manwood, J.
[2] Smith, *An Original View of Executory Interests* (1844), s. 117; Sugden's *Gilbert on Uses.*, pp. 152-3.
[3] Smith, *op. cit.*, s. 149.

feoffment to F. and his heirs to the use of A. and his heirs, but if A becomes entitled to Blackacre, to the use of B. and his heirs ; or, feoffment to F. and his heirs to the use of C. and his heirs, but if C. marries D., to the use of E. and his heirs.

It will be observed that the limitations in favour of B. and of E., if they had been contained in a direct feoffment instead of in a feoffment to uses, would have been in conflict with the third rule for remainders [1] and would therefore have been void.[2]

Effect of the Statute of Uses.

The critical event in the history of executory interests was the Statute of Uses. The statute had converted most uses into legal estates, and it therefore fell to the common law courts to decide what effect it had upon these equitable springing and shifting uses. There were two possible courses, either to hold them void altogether or to permit their continued existence, but to adopt the second course would require fortitude, since it would enable future *legal* estates to be created of a kind quite impossible of creation by way of remainder. As we have seen, a feoffment to B. for life at 21 was void as a remainder, though a feoffment to A. and his heirs to the use of B. for life at 21 was valid in equity as a springing use. If this latter form of limitation were still to be permissible, then it would be the *legal* estate, not as formerly the equitable estate, that would spring up in B. at 21, for the statute had enacted in effect that when A. was seised to the use of B., the latter was to have the legal estate.[3] In other words, by adopting the machinery of a feoffment to uses future limitations of the legal estate could be framed without regard to the rules laid down for remainders.

Executory interests became legal interests.

Fortunately for the development of settlements it was the latter course that was adopted. It was held as early as 1538 that springing and shifting interests, if contained in a feoffment to uses, vested in the beneficiaries as legal estates upon the happening of the specified events, and about 1555 the same conclusion was reached with regard to similar interests limited by will.[4] If, for instance,

A. conveyed land *before the statute* to B. and his heirs to the use of X. and his heirs, but unless X. adopted the name and arms of A. within two years, then to the use of Y. and his heirs,

it was out of the equitable, not out of the legal, estate that a future interest had been created in favour of Y. The legal estate was throughout vested in B. But *after the statute* the legal estate would shift from X. to Y. if there were no compliance with the name and arms clause, for in that event the terms of the original

---

[1] *Supra*, p. 217.
[2] It was said in the argument in *Hopkins* v. *Hopkins* (1734), Cas. *temp.* Talbot, 45, 51, that " springing uses are as old as uses themselves." For a case between 1417 and 1424 in which the aid of the Chancellor was supplicated, see 10 Selden Society, *Select Cases in Chancery*, 1364–1471, p. 114.
[3] *Supra*, pp. 53–4.
[4] Holdsworth, *History of English Law*, vol. vii. pp. 122 *et seq.*

grant required B. to stand seised to the use of Y. Thus the use was allowed to retain its mercurial attributes despite its statutory transformation into the legal estate.

Thus side by side with legal remainders there grew up legal springing and shifting uses, the two last differing from the first in the fact that they could be limited without regard to those four rules that restricted the limitation of remainders. It must, however, be observed—for this was a technical rule that obtained until 1925—that the one way by which a grantor could create a valid executory interest by an instrument *inter vivos* was to adopt the expression *to the use of*, or some other expression contained in the statute. A grant to B. at 21 was void ; a grant to A. to the use of B. at 21 was valid.

Executory uses required technical words.

On the other hand, a *testator* was not subject to the same restriction. He could, by a direct devise, and without adopting the expression *to the use of*, create exactly the same springing and shifting dispositions as he might have created by a grant *inter vivos* to uses.

Executory devises required no technical words.

The subject of springing and shifting interests created by will, which came to be called *executory devises*, requires a little elaboration. The position before the Statute of Uses was that though the power of testamentary disposition was for feudal reasons withheld from the tenant of the *legal* estate, it was exercisable in respect of the equitable estate. A landowner who put his land in use could specify the persons who were to fill the position of *cestuis que uses* after his death. The immediate effect of the Statute of Uses, which converted the equitable into the legal estate, was to abolish this indirect power of will making, but the abolition was felt to be such a grievance that in 1540 the Statute of Wills partially restored the power of testamentary disposition by enacting that all land held in socage and two-thirds of land held in knight service should be devisable. In 1660 tenure in knight service was abolished, so that from that time an owner enjoyed complete power of devising all his land by a direct will and was not compelled to employ the machinery of a devise to uses. In other words, the power of testamentary disposition was for the first time extended to the legal estate. The question that arose after the Statute of Wills was whether a testator could employ this power to create future interests analogous to the springing and shifting uses created by a grant *inter vivos* to uses, or whether he was obliged to limit the future interests in conformity with the rules that had been laid down for remainders. This question of the applicability of the Statute of Uses to a devise to express uses was much debated, since it was difficult to see how the earlier statute could affect a form of disposition that was not introduced until a later date. But though the subject roused many learned controversies,[1] no decision was ever given on

Executory devises.

---

[1] See opinion of Booth, Collect. Jur., V. i. 427 ; Sanders on Uses, vol. i. p. 250, and note ; Co. Litt. 272*a*, note (1) VIII. i ; Cruise, vol. i. p. 397.

the point, and it soon came to be considered a matter of no importance, for either by virtue of the Statute of Uses or with a view to carrying out the intention of testators, the courts consistently held that future limitations contained in wills were capable of producing exactly the same effect as if they had been made in a deed by a grant to uses. When once it was clear that a testator intended to create springing and shifting interests analogous to the interests that might be created by a grant to uses, then, despite the lack of the technical expression " to the use of," effect was given to that intention. Thus :

a grant by deed to A. at 21

was void ;

a grant to X. and his heirs to the use of A. at 21

was valid ; and

a devise to A. at 21

was valid.

Executory interests distinguished from remainders. We see, then, that after the Statute of Uses a second class of future *legal* interests was added to the older class which consisted of remainders. The second class comprised springing and shifting uses created by an instrument *inter vivos*, called generically *executory uses*, and springing and shifting interests limited by will, called *executory devises*. *Executory interests* was an expression which included both executory uses and executory devises. A remainder, as we have seen, was a future estate so limited as to be immediately expectant upon the natural determination of a particular freehold estate less than a fee simple. An executory interest was a future estate which, inasmuch as it infringed one or more of the rules laid down by the original common law for remainders, would have been invalid if it had been contained in an assurance at common law, but which was valid *provided that it was limited either by will or by a conveyance to uses.*[1] If a settlor desired to travel outside the remainder rules, that is to say, if he desired to

create a freehold *in futuro* unsupported by a particular estate,[2] or to

enable beneficiaries to take, although their rights became vested after the termination of the particular estate,[3] or to

make the particular estate shift on a given event to another donee,[4] or to

---

[1] Challis, *Law of Real Property* (3rd Edn.), p. 172.

[2] *E.g.*, grant to X. and his heirs to the use of A. at 21 ; or devise to A. at 21.

[3] *E.g.*, grant to X. and his heirs to the use of A. for life and then to the use of such of A.'s children as before or after his death attain 21.

[4] *E.g.*, grant to X. and his heirs to the use of A. for life, but immediately B. is called to the Bar, then to the use of B. and his heirs.

add a shifting clause to the limitation of the fee simple,[1]
he was at liberty to do so, but he must have made the limitation
either in a will or in a conveyance to uses.

Relation between Contingent Remainders and Exe- Difficulties
cutory Interests. We must now consider the relation between caused by
existence of
contingent remainders and executory interests. The law as two types
sketched above appears at first sight to be shrouded in mystery. of future
There were two types of future legal interests, interests.

> one (the remainder), subject to strict rules which might
> operate to defeat the interest contrary to the settlor's
> intention,
> the other free from such rules and free from that liability to
> destruction which attended remainders.

The question that this dichotomy naturally suggests is whether
a remainder could be saved from destruction by framing it as an
executory interest.

> Suppose, for example, that a feoffment were made to X. and his
> heirs *to the use of* A. for life and then *to the use of* B. and his heirs
> at 21, and that A. died before B. reached the required age.

As a remainder B.'s interest failed altogether, since it had not
vested at the determination of the particular estate, but it would
be saved from destruction if it could be construed as an executory
use.

But in reality such questions did not admit of any reasonable Rule in
doubt, for there was a sacred rule of common law, later known as *Purefoy* v.
the Rule in Purefoy v. *Rogers*, dating back to the sixteenth century *Rogers.*
and finally established in 1671,[2] which directed that a limitation
that was capable of taking effect as a remainder must never be
treated as an executory interest. The justification for this rule
was that contingent remainders, unlike executory interests, were
destructible, and therefore did not tend to a perpetuity, *i.e.* they
did not so easily enable a settlor to create a succession of limited
interests that would render the land inalienable for an unduly
long period.

Thus, the maxim was *once a remainder always a remainder.*
This meant that if the future limitation, whether contained in a
direct grant or in a grant to uses or in a will, was framed in
accordance with the rules for remainders, it had to be read as a
remainder, even though the result would be the destruction of the
interest limited. Thus, if there were a grant to the use of A. for

---

[1] *E.g.*, grant to X. and his heirs to the use of A. and his heirs; but if he does
not adopt the name and arms of the settlor within six months, then to the
use of B. and his heirs.

[2] *Purefoy* v. *Rogers* (1671), 2 Wms. Saunders, 380.

life and then to the use of B. in fee simple upon the attainment of his majority, the gift to B. would fail if he were still an infant when the particular estate ended.[1] The fact that the incantation " to the use of " had been adopted did not alter the nature of what in essence was a remainder. This remained the law until it was altered by statute in 1877 with reference to instruments coming into operation after that date.[2]

The operation of this fundamental rule, to which there were no exceptions, is well illustrated by *White* v. *Summers*,[3] where the facts were these :

A testator who died in 1847 devised land :

(1) to the use of A. for life ; and then

(2) to the use of A.'s sons successively in tail ; but in default of such issue

(3) to the use in tail of the first son of J. S. to attain 21 ; but in default of such issue

(4) to the use of F. S. for life ; and then

(5) to the use of the sons of F. S. successively in tail male.

A. died childless and therefore the second limitation failed to operate. At the time of A.'s death, X., the eldest son of J. S., was only ten years old, but, nothing daunted, J. S. took possession as guardian of X. who himself assumed possession at his majority. F. S. throughout her life failed to contest the legality of J. S.'s entry, but upon her death 47 years later her eldest son claimed the land under the fifth limitation as tenant in tail.

The plaintiff's case was that the third limitation created a contingent remainder which had failed to take effect, since no son of J. S. had attained 21 years of age upon the determination of the particular estate limited to A. The entry of J. S., therefore, was unlawful. As against this it was argued that the third limitation should be construed as an executory devise, for the testator evidently intended that the son of J. S. should take the land at 21, even though he did not attain this age until after A.'s death. Judgment was given for the plaintiff, PARKER, J., holding that the interest given to the son of J. S. must be construed as a contingent remainder.

Importance of the common law rules for remainders.

The common law rules for remainders, therefore, were of vital importance whenever the validity of a future limitation was questioned. No interest could be treated as an executory interest unless its limitation infringed one or more of those rules, as for instance by providing that a fee simple should shift from X. to

---

[1] *Purefoy* v. *Rogers* (1671), 2 Wms. Saunders, 380 ; *Goodright* v. *Cornish* (1694), 4 Mod. Rep. 255 ; *Brackenbury* v. *Gibbons* (1876), 2 Ch. D. 417, 419 ; *White* v. *Summers*, [1908] 2 Ch. 256.

[2] *Infra*, p. 227.   [3] [1908] 2 Ch. 256, at pp. 262-3.

Y. on a given contingency; and even so it would not be valid unless contained either in a grant to uses or in a will.

Equitable Future Interests under the Old Law.

We have seen that prior to the Statute of Uses equity allowed a settlor who carved future interests out of the equitable estate to disregard the rules which common law was in process of building up for remainders. We have also seen that the springing and shifting uses thus established, which were at that time purely equitable in nature, were converted into legal estates by operation of the statute, and that they came to occupy a position side by side with those other future legal interests called remainders. But the rôle played by equity in this department of the law was not exhausted, for in the first place there were from the start certain limitations to which the Statute of Uses did not apply (uses of chattels real and personal, uses of copyholds, uses where the grantee to uses was obliged to perform active duties); and secondly, the old equitable estate (called the use), despite its formal abolition by the statute, was ultimately restored under the new name of " trust " to its old position of an equitable estate.[1] From at least as early a date as 1700 Equity resumed the part that she had played in the realm of future interests before the Statute of Uses, and permitted settlors to carve out of trust estates future interests which were analogous to the contingent remainders and executory interests that might be carved out of the legal estate. There thus emerged a third and distinct class of future interests, which we may denominate *future trusts*, differing from legal contingent remainders and legal executory interests in the fact that they entitled the beneficiaries to call for an equitable instead of a legal estate.

In order to create future trusts it was necessary to vest the legal estate in trustees and then to declare the future trusts upon which the land was to be held. Suppose for instance that a settlor desired to vest the fee simple in A. as soon as the latter attained the age of 21 years. If, before the Statute of Uses, he made a feoffment

> to X. and his heirs *to the use of* A. and his heirs at 21,

the *equitable* estate sprang up in favour of A. when he reached the necessary age. If a similar limitation were made after the statute, then, as we have seen, the *legal* estate would spring up in A. But if after the re-establishment of the use under the new name of trust, a settlor granted land

> *unto and to the use of* X. and his heirs in trust for A. and his heirs at 21,

---

[1] *Supra,* pp. 55–8.

the position was just what it was before the Statute of Uses, in that A. was entitled to call for the equitable estate as soon as he attained his majority.

Future trusts corresponding to legal contingent remainders.

These future trusts might correspond either to legal contingent remainders or to legal executory interests. Thus if, after vesting the legal estate in trustees, a settlor granted a future equitable interest which was to take effect upon the natural determination of a particular freehold estate also equitable in nature, as for instance by a limitation

> unto and to the use of T.₁ and T.₂ and their heirs in trust for A. for life and then in trust for the eldest son of A. at 21,

the interest given to the eldest son was termed an equitable contingent remainder. But though an interest of this kind corresponded to a legal contingent remainder in the sense that it was made to await the termination of a prior estate, it differed from its legal counterpart in a most important respect. This was

Not affected by termination of prior estate.

that the rule requiring a legal contingent remainder to be vested by the time at which the particular estate ended did not apply to the limitation of an equitable contingent remainder.[1] The reason for this immunity was that, as the legal estate in the trustees fulfilled all feudal necessities concerning seisin, there was no reason why the interest should fail merely because the contingency was not satisfied until after the determination of the preceding interest.[2]

Thus while a grant

> to A. for life and then in fee simple to such of his children as attain 21

would, as we have seen,[3] vest the entire fee simple in the children who were over 21 at A.'s death to the exclusion of those who were still infants, a grant or devise

> unto and to the use of T.₁ and T.₂ and their heirs in trust for A. for life and then in trust for such of the children as attain 21

would entitle each child who reached the required age to share in the estate no matter whether he reached it before or after A.'s death.[4]

Future trusts corresponding to legal executory interests.

Finally, a future trust shared to the full the mercurial attributes that had always been a feature of the future use. Springing and shifting trusts were just as free from the restrictive rules of the common law as were springing and shifting uses.

---

[1] Fearne, *Contingent Remainders*, p. 304 ; *Berry* v. *Berry* (1878), 7 Ch. D. 657 ; *Re Finch, Abbiss* v. *Burney* (1881), 17 Ch. D. 211 ; *Astley* v. *Micklethwait* (1880), 15 Ch. D. 59.
[2] *Re Finch, Abbiss* v. *Burney* (1881), *supra*, per JESSEL, M.R.
[3] *Supra*, p. 216.   [4] *Re Averill*, [1898] 1 Ch. 523.

We will conclude this account of the old law with a short statement of the characteristics by which legal contingent remainders differed from executory interests.

(i) **Mode of Creation.** Executory interests, unlike contingent remainders, required either a grant to uses or a devise.

(ii) **Type of Interest that could be created.** By means of a will or a grant to uses it was possible to disregard the restrictive rules applicable to legal contingent remainders.

(iii) **Destructibility.** An executory interest was indestructible in the sense that it took effect when it was ready to do so, being entirely unaffected by the destruction of any precedent estate after which it was limited. On the other hand a legal contingent remainder failed altogether unless it became vested during the continuance of the particular estate. This premature determination of the particular estate might occur naturally by the death of the particular tenant before the specified contingency had been fulfilled, as where in a limitation

to A. for life, remainder to B. at 21,

A. died during the infancy of B. In addition, there were certain methods by which it might be deliberately and artificially brought about.[1] Without going into details,[2] it is enough to say that this artificial destruction of the particular estate was usually avoided in settlements by a conveyancing device invented during the time of the Commonwealth,[3] and was finally rendered ineffective by the Real Property Act, 1845. Moreover, the Contingent Remainders Act, 1877, enacted that a contingent remainder should take effect despite even the natural and premature determination of the particular estate, provided that it had been limited in conformity with the rule against perpetuities. There were, indeed, a few cases in which this Act would not operate, but it is sufficiently accurate to say that after 1877 contingent remainders were just as indestructible as executory interests.

(iv) **Subject Matter.** Neither remainders nor executory *uses* could be carved out of chattels real or personal, but it was possible to create executory interests in such chattels by will. These gifts were called executory bequests.

" The third sort of executory devises, comprising all that relates
" to chattels, is where a term for years or any personal estate is
" devised (more properly bequeathed) to one for life or otherwise,
" and after the decease of the legatee for life, or some other con-
" tingency or period, is given over to somebody else." [4]

---

[1] *I.e.* by the forfeiture, surrender or merger of the particular estate.
[2] For a full account, see 7th edition of this book, pp. 254–9.
[3] *I.e.* by the appointment of trustees to preserve contingent remainders.
[4] Fearne, *Contingent Remainders*, p. 402.

(v) **Rules relating to Remoteness of Limitations.** One of the most urgent problems that agitated the courts was whether any restriction as to the time within which contingent interests must become vested should be imposed upon settlors. If no check were imposed, it would be possible for a settlor to " tie up " the land, *i.e.* to prevent there being a vested estate, for an indefinite period. The modern rule on this subject is described in detail below.[1] The following is a summary of the law as it stood in 1925 :

(A) *Legal* contingent remainders were subject to the following separate rules :

(*a*) The rule, already noticed, that the remainder must have vested at the time when the particular estate ended, except after 1877 in those cases where the limitation was saved by the Act of that year.[2]

(*b*) The rule in *Whitby* v. *Mitchell.*[3]

(*c*) The rule against perpetuities.[4] There was seldom room for the application of this rule to legal contingent remainders, since at common law such remainders had to vest at the expiration of the particular estate, *i.e.* within a period that was shorter than that permitted by the rule. But a legal contingent remainder might be limited after another legal contingent remainder in such terms that the second remainder, though innocuous under (*a*) and (*b*) above, was an infringement of the rule against perpetuities. It was in such cases as these that the rule was held to be applicable.

(B) *Executory interests* were subject only to the rule against perpetuities.

(C) *Future trusts*, if they corresponded to legal contingent remainders, *e.g.*

> unto and to the use of T.₁ and T.₂ in fee simple in trust for A. for life and then in trust for such of the children as attain 25,

were subject both to the rule in *Whitby* v. *Mitchell* and to the rule against perpetuities[5] ; while if they corresponded to legal executory interests, *e.g.*

> unto and to the use of T.₁ and T.₂ in fee simple in trust for A. at 25,

they were subject only to the rule against perpetuities.

---

[1] *Infra*, p. 237 *et seq*.   [2] *Supra*, pp. 216–7; 227.
[3] *Infra*, pp. 236–7.   [4] *Re Nash*, [1910] 1 Ch. 1.
[5] *Re Finch, Abbiss* v. *Burney* (1881), 17 Ch. D. 211.

SECTION II. FUTURE INTERESTS UNDER THE MODERN LAW.

(1) ALL FUTURE FREEHOLD INTERESTS ARE EQUITABLE, AND CORRESPOND TO THE OLD EQUITABLE REMAINDERS AND EXECUTORY INTERESTS.

Introductory Note. The radical alteration resulting from the legislation of 1925 was that future freehold interests were reduced in all cases to an equitable status. This was the inevitable result of the new rule that the only *legal* freehold estate is the fee simple absolute in possession. Entailed and life interests cannot subsist as legal estates, whether limited *in praesenti* or *in futuro* ; a fee simple absolute cannot subsist as a legal estate unless it carries the right to present possession. *All future interests now equitable.*

Furthermore the Statute of Uses has been repealed, and therefore those future limitations to uses under which the *legal* estate could be made to spring up in a person, or to pass from one person to another on the occurrence of a future event, are no longer possible. Executory interests, as *legal* interests, vanished with the repeal of the statute upon which their validity depended, but the purposes they were formerly designed to serve can still be attained through the medium of a trust. *Repeal of Statute of Uses.*

Let us now see how these changes have simplified the law relating to future interests.

Present position of Future Interests. Before the legislation of 1925, it was possible, as we have seen, for a future interest to be either a legal remainder, an executory interest, or a future trust. The first two have ceased to exist in the sense that they no longer give the beneficiary a legal estate. We are left, therefore, with what may be called future trusts, *i.e.* future equitable interests which, under the old law, might correspond either to legal remainders or to executory interests. It was always possible, by a limitation operating on the equitable estate, to create the same types of future interests as could be created by way of legal remainder, but such equitable remainders had this advantage over their legal counterparts, that they were free from the restrictive rules of the common law. It was likewise possible to create springing and shifting interests which, except that they were equitable, were on all fours with executory interests. *Limitations formerly possible by way of future trusts still possible.*

What could be done under the old law by means of these future trusts represents exactly the position under the modern law. A settlor can create those future interests which it was possible to create at equity before 1926, but he cannot so frame his limitations as to confer legal estates or interests upon the future beneficiaries. In this latter respect the law is more stringent than formerly. In other respects, however, a settlor possesses complete freedom. Future trusts were, indeed, subject to the rule against perpetuities and in exceptional circumstances to the rule in *Whitby* v. *Mitchell*; but the creation both of legal remainders and of executory interests was subject to technical rules which were of rigid application. Thus there were certain limitations which were outside the scope of a legal remainder, such as a grant to A. for life at 21, while the adoption of the expression " to the use of," or its equivalent was necessary to the validity of an executory use. But these technical rules have disappeared as a necessary consequence of the new principle that all future freehold interests must be equitable. Furthermore, the rule in *Whitby* v. *Mitchell* has been abolished.

Abolition of technicalities.

Latitude under the New Law. Under the modern law, then, a person who keeps within the limits prescribed by the rule against perpetuities has complete liberty of action in the creation of future interests, both as regards the kinds of interests he can grant and the manner in which he can frame their limitation. It was, indeed, possible under the old law to create what estates were required, but, unless the originating instrument was a will, certain particular kinds, such as springing and shifting limitations, could be effectually created only by a grant to uses. But now, whatever estates a settlor creates and whatever expressions he adopts, the legal fee simple must vest in an estate owner, who will hold such legal estate upon trust to give effect to the future equitable interests. If, for instance, a series of future interests is created by settlement, the legal fee simple will vest in the tenant for life in trust for the beneficiaries entitled under the settlement ; but if the future interests owe their origin to a will, the legal fee simple will vest in the personal representatives of the testator on trust to convey it to the life tenant, whereupon the latter will become trustee for the future beneficiaries.

As one distinguished writer said :

> " Just the same interests can be created in future as have hitherto
> " been possible—just the same life estates and remainders and
> " shifting and springing interests—but they will be equitable. The
> " legal estate is one and indivisible and is in the estate owner. To
> " the world he represents the property ; all other interests are
> " behind his estate."[1]

Reversionary terms.

We have said that all future freehold interests are necessarily equitable in nature at the present day. This is strictly true, but the qualifying effect of the word *freehold* must be noticed, for, if the future interest which is limited to the donee is not a fee simple, an entailed interest or a life interest, but consists of a

---

[1] *The Law Journal*, vol. lx. p. 319. Article by J. M. Lightwood.

term of years absolute, it will vest in the donee as a legal estate. The Law of Property Act, 1925, provides that a term of years absolute shall be capable of subsisting *at law*,[1] and it defines such a term as meaning one that takes effect either in possession or in reversion.[2]

Thus,

> if land is leased to A. on March 1st for seven years dating from September 29th, this is a term of years absolute, and A. acquires a future legal estate which will become effective on the day fixed for its commencement.

On the other hand, a future leasehold interest *may* be equitable, as,

> when A., possessing a term of 99 years, assigns it to trustees to hold on trust for B. when the latter attains the age of 21 years.

(2) EXAMPLES AND CLASSIFICATION OF FUTURE INTERESTS.

Since a donor is allowed full liberty with regard to the different kinds of future interests he may create, it is perhaps superfluous to select examples of the different classes, but a glance at the types found in practice may elucidate the subject. *{Vested and contingent future interests.}*

All future interests fall into two great classes, those which are vested and those which are contingent.

This distinction has already been discussed,[3] but it may be useful to give a few examples of gifts by way of trust which are conditional on the occurrence of some event not certain to happen and which, therefore, create contingent interests :

to A. for life and then to his children now unborn ;
to A. for life and then to the first of his sons to attain 21 ;
to A. for life and then to the children of B. alive at B.'s death;
to A. for life and then to the heir of B.[4];
to B. at 21.

Classification of contingent future interests. Contingent future estates can be classified according as they are or *{Springing interests.}*

---

[1] Law of Property Act, 1925, s. 1.
[2] *Ibid.*, s. 205 (1) (xxvii). But see Law of Property Act, 1925, s. 149 (3), *infra*, p. 340, which provides that a term limited to take effect more than 21 years from the date of the instrument of creation shall be void.
[3] *Supra*, pp. 211-2.
[4] In the eyes of the law B. cannot have an heir until he dies.

are not preceded by a prior estate limited to another person. A gift

> to A. for life and then to his children who attain 21

is an example of the former class ; a gift

> to C. in tail at 21

is an example of the latter.   In this latter case C.'s right is denominated a springing future interest, and it arises of its own force, independently of any other estate, when C. reaches the required age.   Until that event happens the legal estate will remain in the grantor, but when it does happen, he will be obliged to execute a vesting deed transferring it to C.   If a similar estate arises, not by virtue of a deed of grant, but under a will, and if C. is not 21 when the testator dies, the legal estate meanwhile passes to the personal representatives, who will pay the rents and profits either to the persons entitled on intestacy or to the residuary devisee of the testator.

Shifting interests.   Again, contingent future interests that are preceded by a prior estate fall into two classes according as they do or do not defeat that estate when they take effect in possession.   When there is a limitation

> to A. for life and then to B. in fee simple when he attains 21,

the future interest given to B. does not affect A.'s interest in any way, since it takes effect in possession only upon the regular determination of the prior estate by the death of A.   But a future interest may be so framed that it can take effect only by defeating or displacing a prior estate, in which case it is known as a shifting future interest.   The following may be cited as examples :

> to A. for life, but if he neglects within five years to take the name and arms of the testator, to B. for life ; [1]
> to A. in fee simple, but if he becomes entitled to Blackacre, then to B. in fee simple ; [2]
> to A. for life, but if he does not make the manor-house his principal place of residence, to B. for life ; [3]
> to B., a woman, in fee simple, but if she marries without the donor's consent, then to her for life. [4]

Table of future interests.   The following table indicates the various species of future interests :—

---

[1] *Langdale* v. *Briggs* (1855), 8 De G. M. & G. 391.
[2] *Nicolls* v. *Sheffield* (1787), 2 Br. C. C. 215 ; *Harrison* v. *Round* (1852), 2 De G. M. & G. 190.
[3] *Dunne* v. *Dunne* (1856), 3 Sm. & Giff. 22.
[4] *Wright* v. *Wright* (1750), 1 Ves. Sen. 409.

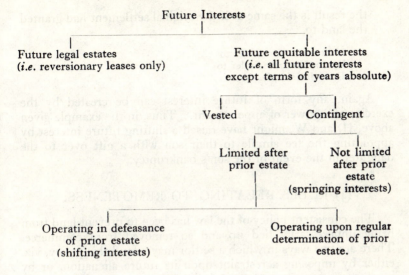

(3) CREATION OF FUTURE INTERESTS.

Any species of future interest can now be created by deed or will, and there is no longer any necessity to adopt the formal expression *to the use of* in order to raise springing and shifting interests by deed.

Powers of Appointment. It is open to a settlor either to declare the future interests finally and completely in the instrument of settlement, or, by the reservation of a power of appointment, to postpone their final declaration to some later date. Except as regards the application of the rule against perpetuities,[1] there is no difference between future interests that are finally declared by the original settlement, and those that are subsequently raised by the exercise of a power of appointment reserved in the original settlement. Interests brought into existence as the result of such an exercise take effect in exactly the same manner as if they had been designated by the original settlement, and they are generally construed as if they were contained in that instrument. The only difference is one of form.[2]

Creation by exercise of power.

For example, if lands are settled

> on H. for life, remainder to W. for life, remainder to such persons as H. and W. may appoint,

and if H. and W. appoint to their daughter in fee simple,

---

[1] *Infra,* pp. 249–52.   [2] Sugden on Powers (8th Edn.), p. 470.

I*

the result is the same as if the original settlement had granted the land to

H. for life, remainder to
W. for life, remainder to
D. in fee simple.

Again, any form of future interest can be created by the exercise of a power of appointment. Thus, in the example given above, H. and W. might have raised a shifting future interest by appointing the fee simple to their son with a gift over to the daughter in the event of the son's bankruptcy.

(4) RULES RELATING TO REMOTENESS.

The consistent policy of the law has been to prevent land from being unnecessarily tied up and so removed from commerce. There are two ways in which a settlor may offend this policy, viz. either by imposing a restraint upon its future alienation, or by creating a succession of partial future interests and so postponing to a remote period the time when the land will vest in somebody for an absolute interest. The law has attacked the first evil by invalidating most conditions against alienation,[1] and it has restrained the power of creating future interests by providing in the rule against perpetuities that such interests must arise within certain limits. It is with this rule that we are for the moment solely concerned.

(A) THE RULE AGAINST PERPETUITIES.[2]

(i) General Nature and History of the Rule.

Desire of owners to restrain future generations. The history of the rules whereby settlors have been prevented from limiting remote interests, is the history of a conflict between two antagonistic ideas. On the one hand there is the desire of the man of means to regulate the future enjoyment of his property for as long a period as possible. The right of making a settlement or a will is a potent weapon in the hands of a declining man, and unless human nature is transformed, the opportunity it offers of fixing the pecuniary destinies of the coming generations will not be neglected. A landowner, unless he gives thought to the fiscal consequences, is not always content to leave a large estate at the free disposal of a son. Old age especially, satisfied with its own achievements and often irritated by the apparent follies of a degenerate time, is inclined to restrain each generation of beneficiaries within close limits, and to provide for a series of limited

---

[1] *Infra*, pp. 290–1.
[2] For a full account of this difficult subject, reference should be made to Morris and Leach, *The Rule against Perpetuities*.

interests. A landowner views the free power of alienation with complacency when it resides in his own hand, but he does not feel the same equanimity with regard to its transfer to others.

> " But the freedom of alienation and devise was not congenial to the
> " spirit in which great landowners viewed their land. To preserve
> " their family name and position, ' to keep the land in the family,'
> " seemed to them a desirable and even laudable object, to restrain
> " any individual holder of the land from dealing with it so as to
> " interfere with the interest of subsequent generations of the family
> " in the family land was a necessary means to this end. To contrive
> " restraints on alienation and succession which the law would enforce,
> " to ascertain the furthest limits up to which the law would allow
> " the grasp of the dead hand to be kept on the hand of the living,
> " was the task set by the great landowners before their legal
> " advisers." [1]

This aspiration, however, soon aroused the antagonism of the courts. The law is moved, and from the earliest times always has been moved, by a deep-seated antipathy to this human love of power. It is one thing to permit the free power of alienation, another to allow it to be exercised to its own destruction. The view of the law is that no disposition should be allowed which tends to withdraw land from commerce, and in pursuance of this policy two rules have emerged which have successfully prevented the particular evil of " perpetuities," though they are essentially different from each other in nature. The first, directed against inalienable interests and often called the *old rule against perpetuities*, forbids the creation of any form of unbarrable entail; the second, the *modern rule against perpetuities*, invalidates an interest that may vest at too remote a date in the future.

Desire of law to remove restraints.

The Old Rule against Perpetuities. The antagonism of the law to an unbarrable entail became apparent at an early date in its doctrine of the conditional fee.[2] The purpose of a grant to a man and a specified class of heirs of his body was that the land should serve the necessities of each generation and pass from heir to heir ; but, as we have seen, the common law held that the grantee obtained a fee simple with an absolute power of alienation as soon as an heir of the prescribed class was born.[3] Irritated by such a decisive defeat of their intention, the great landowners procured the passing of the Statute *De Donis*, 1285, which enacted in effect that the intention of a donor was to prevail, and that an estate given to a man and the heirs of his body was perpetually to be reserved to the appropriate class of heir. Thus for the moment the power to grant an inalienable interest in the shape of an unbarrable entail came within the powers of a grantor, but

Conditional fee.

Statute De Donis.

---

[1] Scrutton, *Land in Fetters*, p. 108.
[2] *Supra*, p. 155. For the history of the old and new rules, see Holdsworth, *History of English Law*, vol. vii. pp. 81–144 ; 193–238.
[3] *Supra*, p. 155.

Estates tail become barrable.

the right was soon lost, for at any rate by the fifteenth century the law had recognized recoveries as methods by which entails could be barred and converted into fees absolute by tenants in tail in possession.

Attempts to create unbarrable entails.

When it had thus become impossible to ensure the maintenance of land in a family by the simple means of a grant to a man and the heirs of his body, settlors began to cast about for some device whereby they could attain their desire by a more indirect but equally effectual means. One plan was to insert in settlements

Clause of perpetuity.

a *clause of perpetuity*, that is, a condition to the effect that the interest of any tenant in tail who attempted to bar his entail should be forfeited. Such conditions were, however, held void in three cases decided between 1600 and 1613.[1]

Successive contingent remainders.

For the next series of attempts contingent remainders were pressed into service. At first, probably about 1556,[2] it became usual to prolong the period during which the land should be inalienable by making a grant to a son for life with contingent remainders to his unborn children, instead of granting him an immediate estate tail. This form of settlement, however, did not fulfil even the limited purpose for which it was designed, since, owing to the common law rules relating to seisin, it was possible for the life tenant to deal with his estate in such a way as to cause the destruction of the contingent remainder to the children before their birth.[3] Such a premature destruction was, however, prevented at a later date by the appointment of trustees to preserve contingent remainders. Another attempt took the form of the limitation of a perpetual freehold, by which successive estates for life were granted to the unborn issue of a person *ad infinitum*. A settlor, A., would limit the land to his son for life, remainder to every person that should be his heir one after the other for the life of such heir ; but it was held by the courts that all the contingent remainders after the life estate to the first unborn heir (*i.e.* A.'s son) were void.[4] This particular rule was generally, though incorrectly,[5] described as the rule against double possibilities, for it was said that the law would never countenance a possibility upon a possibility,[6] and in the limitation indicated one possibility was that A. would not have a son, another that the son, if born, would himself not have a son. The rule enforced by the courts was not, however, based on any

---

[1] *Corbet's Case* (1600), 1 Co. Rep. 83*b* ; *Mildmay's Case* (1605), 6 Co. Rep. 40*a* ; *Mary Portington's Case* (1613), 10 Co. Rep. 35*b*.

[2] Joshua Williams, Jurid. Soc. i. 47 ; cited Scrutton, *Land in Fetters*, pp. 116–17.

[3] *Supra*, p. 227.

[4] Fearne, *Contingent Remainders*, p. 502.

[5] Challis, *Law of Real Property* (3rd Edn.), pp. 116–18 ; Jarman on Wills (7th Edn.), p. 257 ; Holdsworth, *Historical Introduction to Land Law*, p. 222, note 6.

[6] Co. Litt. 184*a*.

such narrow ground. It was really a particular application of the parent rule that the grant of an unbarrable entail is void, and it was reaffirmed in 1890 in the case of *Whitby v. Mitchell*,[1] where the Court of Appeal decided once more that where lands were limited to a living person, and then to his unborn child, and then to the child of such unborn child, the last remainder was absolutely void. A settlor could exercise control up to a point but not beyond. He could withhold the fee simple from the grasp of his son by granting him a mere life estate, and he could, by the grant of an estate tail to his son's heir, prevent the acquisition of a fee simple until his son's son attained 21 ; but nothing that he could do could prevent his son and grandson from collaborating to bar the entail when the grandson attained 21.

Whitby v. Mitchell.

Still another device adopted by settlors was to carve a species of estate tail out of a term of years by the bequest of a long term to a person and his heirs one after the other *ad infinitum*. But such a limitation after the term to the first unborn heir was held void.[2]

Bequests of long terms.

Pausing here for a moment we see that the attempts which were constantly being made by settlors to keep their land within the family, although they varied in details, all had one object in common, namely, by a combination of estates tail and contingent remainders or executory bequests to set up unbarrable entails, and it was this particular species of inalienable estate that was regarded by the lawyers of the seventeenth century as a perpetuity.

Early meaning of " perpetuity."

"A perpetuity is the settlement of an estate or interest in tail, with " such remainders expectant upon it as are in no sort in the power " of the tenant in tail in possession to dock by any recovery or " assignment." [3]

Thus at an early date contingent remainders ceased to endanger the free alienability of land, for they failed altogether unless they had vested when the particular tenant died ; they were easily destructible ; and, if they were nothing more than unbarrable entails in disguise, they were void on the ground that virtually they created an inalienable interest.

The Modern Rule against Perpetuities. What ultimately led to the emergence of a new rule against perpetuities was the decision in the early seventeenth century that executory interests, unlike contingent remainders, were indestructible,[4] for this meant that land might be tied up to an almost indefinite extent by the adoption of a number of shifting uses under which the land

Inadequacy of Old Rule against Perpetuities.

Emergence of modern rule.

---

[1] (1890), 44 Ch. D. 85.
[2] *Sanders v. Cornish* (1630), Cro. Car. 230 ; Jarman (7th Edn.), p. 254.
[3] *Duke of Norfolk's Case* (1681), 3 Ch. Ca. ; *per* Lord NOTTINGHAM.
[4] *Pells v. Brown* (1620), 1 Cro. Jac. 590.

would pass from one person to another on the occurrence of given events. If, for instance, there were a devise :

> to A. and his heirs, but if the heirs ever fail then over to B and his heirs,

the successive occupants of the land under the first limitation would have been continually liable to lose their interest upon the occurrence of a contingency that might never happen or might not happen for generations. The courts, therefore, unaided by the legislature, undertook and succeeded in the task of finding some rule which would confine these executory interests within reasonable limits, and the principle upon which they proceeded was to restrict the remoteness of the date at which the executory interest might be made to vest.[1] They specified the latest moment at which this kind of future interest might be made to begin; or, to put it in another way, they said that though a settlor might fix a contingency upon which a vested interest was to spring up or to shift to a person, yet the contingency chosen must be one which, if it ever happened at all, would necessarily happen within a defined period of time. They ultimately held that no interest was to be valid unless it was bound to vest, if at all, within the compass of existing lives and twenty-one years after the extinction of the last life.

The two rules concerning perpetuities. Thus, English law has evolved two rules concerning perpetuities. Their common object is to promote the free circulation of property, but they accomplish this purpose by different means. The first and older rule, already discussed, looks to the character of the limitations and holds them to be void as constituting a perpetuity if their effect would be to set up an unbarrable entail ; the later and modern rule looks to the date at which the contingent interests will vest, if they vest at all, and holds them to be void as a perpetuity if this date is too remote.[2] Though invariably called the "rule against perpetuities," a better name would be the "rule against remoteness of vesting."[3]

History of modern rule The modern rule began to emerge about 1660,[4] and it was finally completed by the House of Lords in *Cadell* v. *Palmer* in 1833.[5] The main stages in its development may be shortly stated.[6] In *The Duke of Norfolk's Case*, 1681-85,[7] there was a

---

[1] Holdsworth, *History of English Law*, vol. vii. p. 225.
[2] Gray, *op. cit.*, ss. 2, 118a ; Fearne, *Contingent Remainders*, p. 429 ; Jarman on Wills (6th Edn.), p. 296, note *s* ; Challis, *Law of Real Property* (3rd Edn.), pp. 205-7.
[3] Gray, *op. cit.*, s. 2.
[4] *Snowe* v. *Cuttler* (1664), 1 Lev. 135 ; *Wood* v. *Saunders* (1669), 1 Ch. Cas. 131 ; Holdsworth, *History of English Law*, vol. vii. pp. 222 *et seq.*
[5] (1833), 1 Cl. & F. 372.
[6] Pollock, *Land Laws*, Appendix Note G ; Gray, *op. cit.*, ss. 123 *et seq.*; Holdsworth, *Historical Introduction to Land Law*, p. 224 ; Morris and Leach, *op. cit.*, pp. 8-10.
[7] (1681-85), 3 Ch. Cas. 1.

grant of a term of 200 years to trustees upon trust for the grantor's second son Henry and the heirs male of his body, but if his eldest son Thomas died without issue male *in Henry's lifetime,* then in trust for Charles, his third son.

Lord NOTTINGHAM held that the last limitation was good, since the shifting to Charles must take place, if it ever took place at all, upon the dropping of a life in being, namely that of Thomas. Thus the case did not fix the maximum period during which vesting might be suspended, but decided that an interest that must vest if ever within lives in being was valid. *Stephens* v. *Stephens,*[1] 1736, held that an executory devise to the unborn child of a living person upon the attainment of his majority was good, and thereby in effect extended the maximum period to lives in being plus a further twenty-one years. In *Thellusson* v. *Woodford,*[2] 1805, Lord ELDON was of opinion that the persons whose lives were chosen need have no connection with the settled property, but might be strangers chosen at random. This opinion was endorsed by *Cadell* v. *Palmer,*[3] which also decided that a term of twenty-one years without any reference to minorities might be added to existing lives, *e.g.* devise in fee simple to my eldest descendant alive twenty-one years after the death of my son Peter. This case, which finally settled the law, had to consider the following limitations:

Land was devised to trustees for 120 years from the testator's death, *if* twenty-eight *persons named in the will should so long live,* and for twenty years from the determination of the term or from the death of the last life. Out of this long term a number of smaller estates were created, some of which (*e.g.* a limitation to the son of an unborn person) would have been invalid under the old rule had they stood by themselves. — *Cadell* v. *Palmer.*

The House of Lords held that the limitation of the long term was valid, since, though it suspended the vesting of a fee simple absolute for a considerable period, yet the period, being confined to existing lives and a further space of twenty years, was not obnoxious as a perpetuity.

Position after 1925. Under the law as it stood prior to January 1st, 1926, the rule in *Whitby* v. *Mitchell* applied to all future estates limited by way of contingent remainders, whether legal or equitable. The rule against perpetuities applied to executory interests and to equitable contingent remainders, and in certain cases it had been extended by the courts, though without any historical or doctrinal justification, to legal contingent remainders.[4] — Abolition of old rule.

The Law of Property Act, however, abolished the rule in *Whitby* v. *Mitchell* in the following words:

---

[1] (1736), Ca. *temp.* Talbot. 228.
[2] (1798), 4 Ves. Jun. 227: (1805), 11 Ves. Jun. 112.
[3] (1833), 1 Cl. & F. 372.   [4] *Supra,* p. 228.

" The rule of law prohibiting the limitation, after a life interest to
" an unborn person, of an interest in land to the unborn child or other
" issue of an unborn person is hereby abolished, but without pre-
" judice to any other rule relating to perpetuities.

" This section only applies to limitations or trusts created by an
" instrument coming into operation after the commencement of this
" Act."[1]

Thus the rule against perpetuities, fortified by the rules
against accumulations,[2] is now the sole determinant of whether
an interest is too remote. It applies both to realty and personalty
out of which future contingent interests have been carved.

**Amendment
of the rule
in 1964.**

In the course of its development the rule against perpetuities
as laid down in *Cadell* v. *Palmer*, though based on sound policy
and designed to be flexible, gradually became encumbered with
complex and at times absurd interpretations that provided dangerous traps for the unwary practitioner.[3] Most of the anomalies,
however, by which it was disfigured were removed for the future by
the Perpetuities and Accumulations Act, 1964, which gave substantial effect to the recommendations of the Law Reform Committee made in 1956.[4] The Act came into operation on July
16th, 1964, and it applies only to instruments taking effect on or
after that date. In giving the details of the rule, therefore, it will
be simpler to deal first with the position at common law and then
under a separate heading to show in what respects that position
has been altered for instruments taking effect after the commencement of the Act.

(ii) The Rule Applicable to Instruments taking Effect before July 16th, 1964.

(a) Statement of the Rule.

**Length of
the period.**

(1) The perpetuity period.

At common law, the vesting of an interest may be postponed
during the lives of persons in being at the time when the instrument of creation takes effect, plus a further period of twenty-one
years after the extinction of the last life.[5] Any interest so limited
that it may possibly vest after the expiration of this period is
totally void.

---

[1] S. 161. A limitation to the unborn issue of an unborn taker is of course
void under the modern rule, unless it is expressly confined within due limits
as in *In re Nash*, [1910] 1 Ch. 1. As to the meaning of "coming into operation
after" the Act, see *Re Leigh's Marriage Settlement, Rollo* v. *Leigh*, [1952]
2 All E. R. 57.

[2] *Infra*, p. 277.

[3] For a devastating exposure of the "superfluous technicalities and complexities of the rule," see Leach, 68 *L.Q.R.* pp. 35–39.

[4] Fourth Report, 1956, Cmnd. 18.

[5] The lives must be those of human beings, not those of corporations or
animals.

For the purposes of the rule, conception is treated as equivalent to birth.[1] Thus a child, whether a beneficiary or not, who is *en ventre sa mère* at the time when the instrument of gift takes effect may constitute a life in being;[2] and a child *en ventre sa mère* at the end of the perpetuity period may qualify as a beneficiary under the limitation.[3] — Conception treated as equivalent to birth.

A settlor need not choose persons who have interests in the settled property or a connexion with the family, and he has full liberty of action with regard to the number of persons he may select.[4] If it is substantially practicable to ascertain the extinction of the last life, the gift is good, although the lives may be so numerous that it may be a difficult and expensive matter to ascertain the date of the survivor's death. Thus a not uncommon practice is to prolong the period to the utmost limit by the use of a *royal lives clause*, which selects the living descendants of some modern English sovereign as the lives in being.[5] In one case, for instance, a will that took effect in 1925 directed that the distribution of certain shares among the beneficiaries should be postponed until the expiration of twenty-one years (less the last two days thereof) from the death of the last survivor of the descendants of her late Majesty Queen Victoria alive at the testator's death. Since there were 134 descendants scattered among at least ten countries in Europe alone, it was obvious that the difficulty of proving the fact and date of death of each descendant might be almost insuperable. Nevertheless, the direction was held to be valid.[6] — No restriction on number of lives.

If, however, the number of the selected lives is so great as to render it impossible to ascertain the death of the survivor, as for instance where a testator defined the period as "twenty-one years from the death of the last survivor of all persons who shall be living at my death,"[7] the gift, though not an infringement of the rule against perpetuities, is void for uncertainty.

The lives in being must be designated either expressly, as in *Cadell* v. *Palmer*,[8] or by implication. Lives are designated by implication only if, according to the terms of the instrument of gift, they serve to measure the time within which the vesting contingency must occur. They must form a possible part of the apparatus for determining the moment at which the interest is to vest. — What constitutes a life in being.

---

[1] *Re Stern's Will Trusts, Bartlett* v. *Stern* [1962] Ch. 732 at p. 737; [1961] 3 All E. R. 1129 at p. 1132.

[2] *Long* v. *Blackall* (1797), 7 Term Rep. 100; *Re Wilmer's Trusts, Moore* v. *Wingfield*, [1903] 2 Ch. 411.

[3] Gray, *op. cit.* s. 220; Challis, *op. cit.* p. 182.

[4] *Cadell* v. *Palmer* (1833), 1 Cl. & Fin. F. 372.

[5] *Re Villar, Public Trustee* v. *Villar*, [1928] 1 Ch. 471; [1929] 1 Ch. 243.

[6] *Re Leverhulme, Cooper* v. *Leverhulme* (No. 2), [1943] 2 All E. R. 274. Such a clause if contained in an instrument taking effect at the present day would raise even greater difficulty and would no doubt be held void; *ibid.*, pp. 280–1.

[7] *Re Moore, Prior* v. *Moore*, [1901] 1 Ch. 936.

[8] *Supra*, p. 239.

"No lives can be of the slightest use unless they somehow restrict
"the period of time within which the gift is to be capable of vesting
"according to the conditions laid down by the donor."[1]

If, for instance, there is a

> bequest to A. for life, remainder to the children of B. alive
> at B's death,

B. is implicitly a life in being, for, though not himself a beneficiary,
the time of his death forms part of the vesting contingency. Again,
if a testator bequeaths a fund to such of his grandchildren as
attain the age of twenty-one years, the children who survive him
are effective lives in being, since the ascertainment of the beneficiaries requires a reference to their parents. The gift, therefore,
is good, for the grandchildren "must all become of age within
twenty-one years after the death of their parents, and the parents
must all have been born (or begotten) in the testator's lifetime".[2]

*Period where
no lives
chosen.*

If the settlor does not select lives by which to measure the perpetuity period, he is allowed an absolute period of twenty-one
years, and no longer.[3]

(2) **The Rule affects only contingent gifts.**

*The rule
forbids
remote
vesting.*

It must be emphasized that the object of the rule is to prevent
the vesting of an interest from being suspended for an excessive
period. It strikes only at contingent limitations. Thus it has
been epitomized as follows by the leading authority on the subject:

> "No interest subject to a condition precedent is good unless the
> "condition must be fulfilled, if at all, within twenty-one years after
> "some life in being at the creation of the interest."[4]

*The three
essentials
of vesting.*

We have already seen that the legal meaning of *vested* is vested
in point of interest, and that a person has a vested interest when he
is unconditionally entitled to a portion of the actual ownership of
the subject-matter. If, therefore, the beneficiaries are not yet
ascertained, or if the *quantum* of their interests is not yet definitely
fixed, or if some other event is still to happen before they can claim
their interests, they have nothing that can be called "vested", for
something more than the cessation of a preceding estate must occur
before they are entitled to possession. Speaking generally, *the
three essentials of vesting are ascertained beneficiaries, interests
definitely fixed from the point of view of quantum, and the occurrence
of what may perhaps be called qualifying events.*

By *qualifying events* are meant all those events and conditions
that must happen before a beneficiary becomes entitled to take

---

[1] 80 *L. Q. R.* p. 496 (J. H. C. Morris and H. W. R. Wade). For a contrary view, which it is respectfully submitted is not sustainable, see 81 *L. Q. R.*
pp. 105–15 (Professor David E. Allan).

[2] Gray, *op cit.*, s. 376.

[3] *Palmer* v. *Holford* (1828), 4 Russ 403.

[4] Gray, *op. cit.*, s. 376.

possession of property when the preceeding interest in it terminates. If, for instance, there is a grant

to A. for life, remainder to B. in fee simple when B. marries,
an event, namely marriage, must happen before B. obtains an
indestructible right to take possession.

The vesting of an interest must not, however, be confused with
its duration, for the rule deals with the *commencement* of interests,
not with their duration.[1] This means that an interest is validly
limited if it begins within the period though it may terminate after
the period has ended, for otherwise, as Gray remarks, all fee
simple estates would be bad.[2] Thus, a devise to the unborn son
of A. for life is valid, though obviously it may continue for longer
than 21 years after the death of A., the life in being.[3] Equally
valid is a further gift in fee simple to take effect on the determination of such life interest, provided that the donee will be ascertained within the perpetuity period.[4] Again, in *Wainwright* v.
Miller,[5]

> a settlement limited land in 1847 to W. for life with remainder
> to such of her children as she should appoint. She appointed
> to her daughter X., for life *until she should become a member
> of the Roman Catholic Church.*

The validity of this gift was contested on the ground that the event
of X.'s conversion to Roman Catholicism might not occur within
21 years from the death of W., the life in being. It was held,
however, that X.'s life interest was valid, since it was limited to
begin within the perpetuity period.

So the rule against perpetuities may be re-stated in this way:

> The limitation of future interests must be so framed that the bene-
> ficiaries and the quantum of their interests will necessarily be
> ascertained, and all qualifying events will necessarily have happened,
> within the perpetuity period.

All limitations void for remoteness will be found to be void
because there is a chance either of the beneficiaries remaining
unascertained, or of their interests being still unfixed or of certain
events not having occurred, when the perpetuity period is
exhausted.

(3) The facts upon which the question of remoteness depends.

At common law, whether these pre-requisites of vesting are
satisfied is settled in the light of the facts existing at the time when

Marginal notes:
The rule is directed against remoteness of com-mencement, not of deter-mination.

Re-state-ment of rule in connexion with vesting.

Whether limitation void depends upon the facts exist-ing when it took effect.

---

[1] *Re Chardon, Johnston* v. *Davies*, [1928] Ch. 464; *Re Cassel, Public Trustee*
v. *Mountbatten*, [1926] Ch. 358; dist. *Re Johnson's Settlement Trusts, McClure* v.
Johnson, [1943] Ch. 341; [1943] 2 All E. R. 499; Morris and Leach, *op. cit.*,
pp. 89–94.
[2] Gray, *op. cit.*, s. 232.
[3] *Stuart* v. *Cockerell* (1869), L. R. 7 Eq. 363.
[4] *Evans* v. *Walker* (1876), 3 Ch. D. 211.
[5] [1897] 2 Ch. 255.

the instrument of gift took effect. The relevant time is the date
of the testator's death in the case of a testamentary gift; but the
date of the execution of the deed if the limitations are made *inter
vivos.*[1]

Limitation void if it could possibly have vested beyond the perpetuity period.
In estimating whether a limitation is too remote, the common
law applies a ruthless test. No matter when the question arises,
the mind must be cast back to the time when the instrument of
creation took effect, and if at that time it would have been possible
to have conceived of circumstances in which the vesting of the
property would be postponed for longer than the perpetuity
period, the gift is void.

> "Unless it is created in such terms that it *cannot* vest after the
> "perpetuity period, it is not valid, and subsequent events cannot make
> "it so."[2]

Thus, at the time when the instrument of gift takes effect it must be
clear that the beneficiaries will necessarily be ascertained, if at all,
within the perpetuity period; and that any vesting contingency
specified by the donor will necessarily be satisfied, if at all, within
the same period.

According to this test, it is obvious, for instance, that a gift is
too remote if made to take effect

> when a candidate for the priesthood "comes forward from St.
> Saviour's Church, St. Albans;"[3]

or,

> when a house ceases to be maintained as a dwelling place.[4]

Application of the rule to class gifts.
Moreover, in the particular case of a class gift, the test requires
that the exact quantum of the share in the subject-matter to be
taken by each member of the class must be ascertainable within
the perpetuity period. This calls for some elucidation before we
proceed further.

Meaning of "class gift."
"A gift is said to be to a class of persons when it is to all those
who shall come within a certain category or description defined by
a general or collective formula, and who, if they take at all, are to
take one divisible subject in certain proportionate shares."[5] Thus
in a gift of a fund

> to all the children of A. who attain the age of twenty-one years,

---

[1] *Vanderplank* v. *King* (1843), 3 Hare 1.

[2] *Lord Dungannon* v. *Smith* (1846), 12 Cl. & Fin. 546 at p. 563.

[3] *Re Mander, Westminster Bank Ltd.* v. *Mander*, [1950] Ch. 547; [1950]
2 All E. R. 191.

[4] *Kennedy* v. *Kennedy*, [1914] A. C. 215. Other examples of remote contingencies are: *Re Lord Stratheden and Campbell*, [1894] 3 Ch. 265 ("on the
appointment of the next lieutenant colonel" of a volunteer corps); *Edwards* v.
Edwards, [1900] A. C. 274 (when the coal under certain land is exhausted);
Re Wood, Tullet v. *Colville*, [1894] 3 Ch. 381 (when a gravel pit is worked out);
Re Engels, National Provincial Bank v. *Mayer*, [1943] 1 All E. R. 506 (after
termination of the present war with Germany); *Re Fry, Reynolds* v. *Denne*,
[1945] Ch. 348 at p. 352; [1945] 2 All E. R. 205 at pp. 206, 207 (when an
unborn person, ascertainable within the perpetuity period, takes the testator's
surname.)

[5] *Pearks* v. *Moseley* (1880), 5 App. Cas. 714 at p. 723, *per* Lord Selborne.

the exact amount that each beneficiary will take depends upon the number of children that satisfy the condition as to age. The donor intends that the share of each shall be augmented or diminished in amount according to the number of other members of the class who eventually answer the description.[1]

In determining whether a class gift is valid on the score of remoteness, the fundamental principle, as we have said, is that the share of each member of the class must be definitely and finally ascertainable within the perpetuity period. If even one member may possibly fail to satisfy the vesting contingency within the period the *whole* gift fails for remoteness, and those who have already qualified take nothing.[2] "The vice of remoteness affects the class as a whole if it may affect an unascertained number of its members."[3] In other words, a class gift cannot be partially good, partially bad.

Whole gift void unless all members of class necessarily ascertainable within the period.

> Suppose, for instance, that a testator bequeaths his residuary estate to such of the grandchildren of his only son X., as attain twenty-one years of age.

If, at the death of the testator, X. is also dead leaving three daughters, the bequest is valid. The only lives in being are the daughters. It is, therefore, certain at the time when the will takes effect that if any of the grandchildren of X. qualify for a vested share they must do so within the perpetuity period. Their individual shares will be quantified within that period.

On the other hand, if X. survives the testator, the whole gift is void at common law for remoteness. X. may have further children, and the offspring of such children may not even be born, or if born may not attain their majority, until more than twenty-one years after the survivor of X. and his three daughters have died.[4]

---

[1] *Cattlin v. Brown* (1853), 11 Hare, 372 at p. 377, *per* Page Wood, V.C.

[2] *Leake v. Robinson* (1817), 2 Mer. 363.

[3] *Pearks v. Moseley, Re Moseley's Trusts* (1880), 5 App. Cas. 714 at p. 723 *per* Lord Selborne.

[4] *Re Mervin, Mervin v. Crossman*, [1891] 3 Ch. 197. But the principle that a class gift cannot be partially good, partially bad, may be affected by the class-closing rules derived from *Andrews v. Partington* (1791), 3 Bro. C. C. 401. These are rules of convenience designed to promote early vesting, and they do this by peremptorily closing the class at a specified moment though physically it is still susceptible of increase. In the case of a bequest to the grandchildren of X. at 21, for instance, suppose that X. and his three daughters, together with three infant grandchildren survive the testator. The closing-rule applicable to these facts is that the class closes when the first infant reaches 21. Other grandchildren alive at that time are also entitled to a share of the bequest provided that they reach 21; grandchildren born later are excluded; *Gimblett v. Purton* (1871), L. R. 12 Eq. 427. Thus, the first grandchild to satisfy the vesting contingency is immediately entitled to his minimum share and the requirements of convenience are satisfied. But in the instant example, the further, though indirect, effect of closing the class is to save a gift that would otherwise be totally void. For a full discussion of the closing rules, see 70 *L. Q. R.* pp. 61 *et seq.*, (J. H. C. Morris); Morris and Leach, *The Rule against Perpetuities*, pp. 109–25.

Not per-
missible to
wait and see
whether
perpetuity
period in
fact
exceeded.
The rule that a limitation is void *ab initio* unless it is clear at the time when the instrument of gift takes effect that it cannot vest beyond the perpetuity period, precludes any question of waiting to see what will probably happen in the future or even what in fact has happened since the gift was made. Attention must be concentrated solely on possibilities.

Thus a bequest to take effect "upon the realization of my foreign estate" is void, though it may be a confident assumption that the executors will have accomplished their task within a few years of the testator's death.[1]

Again, a limitation that might possibly have been too remote is not saved by the fact that in the events which have happened since the instrument of gift became effective the perpetuity period cannot now be exceeded.[2] Thus in *Proctor* v. *Bishop of Bath and Wells*:[3]

> An advowson was devised in fee simple to the first or other son of A. that should take Holy Orders, but in case A. should have no such son, then the advowson was given over to B. in fee simple. A. died without ever having a son.

The first limitation failed, for at the time of the testator's death, it could not be said that if any son became a clergyman he would necessarily do so within twenty-one years from the death of A., the life in being. The gift over to B. also failed. Had the facts occurring after the testator's death been relevant, B. would have vindicated his right to the fee simple. He could have shown that the contingency upon which his interest was to vest had in fact occurred within the perpetuity period, for at the death of the life in being it was established that A. could never have a clerical son.[4]

Possibilities
alone
considered:
example of
possibly
unborn
spouse.
A particular limitation upon which the rule that possible, not actual, events must be considered, occurs in what the Law Reform committee has called the case of the *possibly unborn spouse*.[5] Suppose, for instance, that there is a limitation

> To John, a bachelor, for life, remainder for life to the first wife he may marry, remainder in fee simple to the children of the marriage who reach the age of twenty-one years and who are alive at the death of the survivor of John and such wife.

If this limitation is contained in a deed, the gift to the children is void. John is the only life in being; it is possible that he may marry a woman not yet born; if so, it is possible that she may

---

[1] *Re Jones, Midland Bank Executor and Trustee Co. Ltd.* v. *League of Welldoers*, [1950] 2 All E. R. 239.
[2] *Re Wilmer's Trusts, Moore* v. *Wingfield*, [1903] 2 Ch. 411 at p. 422.
[3] (1794), 2 Hy. Bl. 358.
[4] In the case of instruments taking effect after 15th July, 1964, the facts occurring since the instrument of creation took effect are relevant; *infra*, pp. 264–70.
[5] *Re Frost, Frost* v. *Frost* (1889), 43 Ch. D. 246; *Re Garnham, Taylor* v. *Baker* [1916] 2 Ch. 413; *Re Deloitte, Griffiths* v. *Deloitte*, [1926] Ch. 56; criticized in 13 *The Conveyancer*, pp. 289–91.

survive him for longer than twenty-one years. It is immaterial that he may later marry a woman alive at the time when the deed took effect, for since she did not then answer to the description of his wife she cannot constitute a life in being for the purposes of the limitation.

If the same limitation is contained in a will, it is necessary to investigate the state of affairs at the testator's death. If John is not then married, the gift to the children is void for the reasons given above; but if he is married to Jane, the gift is valid, since Jane is a life in being, and therefore the children qualified to take must be ascertained within the perpetuity period.[1]

In applying the rule that possible, not actual, events must be considered, the common law courts have been perversely indifferent to the facts of nature. They have established a presumption that no person, male or female, is too old to beget children. The effect of this is well illustrated by *Re Dawson, Johnston* v. *Hill.*[2] In that case there was in effect a devise by T. in trust for his daughter D. for life, then for such of her children as should attain twenty-one, and for such of her grandchildren attaining twenty-one as should be born of any of her children dying under twenty-one.

Presumption of fertility a further example.

The gifts to D. and to her *children* did not infringe the rule, but if we put a hypothetical case, and consider what might have happened, we shall see how the limitation to the *grandchildren* might have taken effect after the perpetuity period.

D. might have had an only child X. born after T.'s death, and X. might himself have died under 21 leaving a child Z. The will directed that Z. was to take only if he attained 21; the rule against perpetuities required that he must necessarily attain that age, if at all, within 21 years from the dropping of the last life in being. Clearly, Z. might not have satisfied this condition. X. was not a life in being when the will took effect; D., the only remaining life in being might have died before the birth of Z. and if so the latter could not attain the required age within the perpetuity period. It was therefore held that the limitations subsequent to D.'s life interest were void for remoteness.[3]

But the interest of the case lies in the fact that when T. died, D. was over 60 years of age, and all her children had attained 21; and with a view to upholding the will it was argued that as she was past child-bearing, and consequently could have no child born after T.'s death, all grandchildren would in fact be ready to take within 21 years after the dropping of the last life in being. That was true, but it was equally true that the rule against perpetuities is applied in accordance with what might happen, and since in the eyes of the law men and women are capable of having children, no matter how great their age may be, the devise to the grandchildren was held void.[4]

---

[1] The principle applicable to this type of case has been amended so far as concerns instruments taking effect after July 15th, 1964; see *infra,* p. 270–1.

[2] (1888), 39 Ch. D. 155.

[3] It might be thought that despite the invalidity of the limitation to the grandchildren, the gift to the children should have been allowed to stand. The limitations in this case, however, constituted a "class gift," and we have seen (pp. 244–5) that a class gift cannot be partly good and partly bad.

[4] See also *Jee* v. *Audley* (1787), 1 Cox, Eq. Cas. 324; *Ward* v. *Van der Loeff,* [1924] A. C. 653.

Fertility of young persons.

Logically, the presumption of fertility attributed to the old should equally affect the young. Whether it must be presumed that no person can be too young to beget children was indeed canvassed in *Re Gaite's Will Trusts, Banks* v. *Gaite*[1] but was not determined. On the facts of that case, the argument in favour of such a presumption rested upon the possibility that within the short space of five years after the settlor's death a child might be born to his widow, already sixty-five years of age, and might then marry and have issue. The judge evaded the question of physical impossibility by holding that such a hypothetical marriage, contracted by a person under sixteen years of age contrary to the Age of Marriage Act, 1929,[2] was a legal impossibility.[3]

(4) Statutory modification of age contingencies.

Statutory reduction of age specified in limitation.

Prior to 1926, probably the commonest example of a gift that failed for remoteness and which in its downfall destroyed ulterior gifts was one that postponed the vesting of the beneficiary's interest until he reached an age greater than twenty-one years. The Law of Property Act, 1925, however, met this situation by providing that where a limitation makes the absolute vesting of capital or income, or the ascertainment of a beneficiary or class of beneficiaries, dependent upon the attainment by the beneficiary or members of the class of an age exceeding twenty-one years, with the result that the gift or any gift over is rendered void for remoteness, the limitation shall take effect for the purposes of such gift or ulterior gift as if it had specified the age of twenty-one years.[4]

Thus, if there is a

> devise for life to the first son of X. (a bachelor at the time of the testator's death) to attain the age of thirty years

the first son to reach twenty-one is entitled to take under the devise, and any further interests dependent upon his death and not themselves obnoxious to the perpetuity rule take effect according to their limitation.

The Act applies only where the gift would be too remote at common law. Thus, if there is a devise

> to the first son of X. to attain thirty

and if, when the testator dies, X. is also dead leaving sons, the sons are lives in being and the limitation is valid at common law. If a

---

[1] [1949] I All E. R. 459. For its full discussion see Morris and Leach, *op. cit.*, pp. 84–6.

[2] Now the Marriage Act, 1949, s. 2.

[3] As to the new statutory rule concerning fertility, see *infra*, p. 263.

[4] Law of Property Act, 1925, s. 163 (1). The section applies to any instrument executed after 1925 and to any testamentary appointment, devise or bequest contained in the will of a testator dying after 1925. But it has been repealed and replaced by a new provision in the case of wills or instruments *inter vivos* that became effective after 15th July, 1964; Perpetuities and Accumulations Act, 1964, s. 4; *infra*, pp. 271–2.

son satisfies the vesting contingency he must do so within his own lifetime.

Moreover, the statute applies only where the vesting contingency is the *attainment* by a beneficiary of a given age. It will not, for instance, save a bequest

> to my eldest grandchild alive twenty-one years after my death.[1]

(b) *Application of the Rule to powers of appointment.*

A power of appointment may offend the rule against perpetuities in two respects, for either its *creation* or its *exercise* may be too remote. Before stating the law on these two matters, however, it is useful to stress once more the significance of the distinction between general and special powers.

Distinction between general and special powers.

To give a person a general power is in effect to give him the absolute fee, for it entitles him to vest the whole fee in any person in the world, including himself, and therefore it does not tend to the creation of remote interests.

> "He has an absolute disposing power over the estate, and may bring "it into the market whenever his necessities or wishes may lead him "to do so. . . . The donee may sell the estate the next moment."[2]

On the other hand, the grant of a special power has an immediate tendency to be a perpetuity, for, since the objects in whose favour it is exercisable are restricted, it imposes from the moment of its creation a fetter upon the free disposability of the land.[3] It is important to notice, however, that a general power exercisable jointly by two or more persons or by one person with the consent of another is a special power for the purposes of the rule against perpetuities, the view taken by the law being that a power which cannot be exercised without the concurrence of two minds is not equivalent to property.[4]

General powers. A general power to appoint by deed, or either by deed or will, is void unless it will become effectively exercisable, if at all, within the perpetuity period. At the date when the instrument of creation takes effect, it must be possible to say that within that period the donee will be ascertainable, the event upon which the power is to arise will have occurred and any condition precedent to the right of exercise will have been satisfied.

Validity of creation. Power to appoint by deed, or either by deed or will.

On this basis, each of the following powers is void:

---

[1] The gift, however, would be valid at common law, if at the time of the testator's death, all his children were dead leaving children alive.

[2] Sugden, *Powers* (8th Edn.), pp. 395–6, cited Morris and Leach, *op. cit.*, (1st Edn.), p. 139.

[3] Co. Litt. 272a, Butler's note.

[4] *Re Churston Settled Estates,* [1954] Ch. 334; [1954] 1 All E. R. 725. See also *supra,* pp. 194–5.

A power given to the survivor of two living persons and their children.[1]

A power to arise upon the general failure of the issue of a marriage.[2]

A power given to an unborn person upon his marriage.[3]

If a general power to appoint by deed, or either by deed or will, is exercisable within the perpetuity period, it is not rendered objectionable by the fact that it may possibly be exercised after the period has expired, as may well happen, for instance, if it is given to the unborn child of a living person. By virtue of the power, such a donee ascertained within due limits acquires an unrestricted right of alienation, and as in the case of any absolute owner he is free to decide when he will exercise that right.[4]

General testamentary power.

On the other hand, a general testamentary power, *i.e.* one that is exercisable only by will, though it will vest in the donee, if at all, within the perpetuity period, is void if it may be exercised beyond that period. The reason is that the property is tied up during the lifetime of the donee in the sense that he possesses no right of alienation until his death. Therefore, such a power is void if, as in the case of one given to the unborn child of a living person, it may be exercisable at too remote a time.[5]

Validity of appointment.

The donee of a general power, since he can appoint to anybody in the world, including himself, has complete and absolute freedom of disposition, and therefore for the purpose of testing the validity of his appointments the perpetuity period is reckoned from the exercise of the power, not from its creation.

Moreover, the irrational rule has prevailed that this is so even in the case of a general testamentary power,[6] though here, as we have just seen, the donee is not in the position of an absolute owner.

Validity of creation.

Special powers. As regards the validity of its creation, a special power is subject to the following rule:

"A special power which, according to the true construction of the "instrument creating it, is capable of being exercised beyond lives in "being and twenty-one years afterwards is, by reason of the rule "against perpetuities, absolutely void."[7]

As in the case of a general power, a special power is too remote in

---

[1] *Re Hargreaves, Midgley v. Tatley* (1889), 43 Ch. C. 401.

[2] *Bristow v. Boothby* (1826), 2 Sim. & St. 465. *Prima facie*, "Issue" includes descendants of every degree.

[3] *Morgan v. Gronow* (1873), L. R. 16 Eq. 1 (in the case of the original appointment).

[4] *Re Fane, Fane v. Fane*, [1913] 1 Ch. 404 at p. 413.

[5] *Wollaston v. King* (1868), L. R. 8 Eq. 165; *Morgan v. Gronow* (1873), L. R. 16 Eq. 1.

[6] *Rous v. Jackson* (1885), 29 Ch. D. 521. See *infra*, pp. 274-5.

[7] *Re De Sommery, Coelenbier v. De Sommery*, [1912] 2 Ch. 622 at p. 630, *per* PARKER J.

its creation if the donee may not be ascertained or if the condition precedent to its exercise may not have occurred within lives in being and twenty-one years afterwards. But in the case of a special power there is the further requirement that the objects must be ascertainable within the same period. The difference in this respect between the two classes of powers may be illustrated by a power, to be exercised by deed, given to an unborn person.

A special power to this effect, as for instance, one conferred by settlement upon the eldest son of X., a bachelor, to appoint to his children, is void *ab initio*.[1] At the time of the settlement, it can no doubt be said that the appointor will be ascertained, if at all, within twenty-one years from the death of the life in being, X; but it cannot be said that the children in whose favour alone the appointment may be made will be ascertainable, if at all, within the same period. In other words, the occasion upon which the power is to become operative may be too remote.[2]

Example of power given to unborn person.

On the other hand, as we have seen, a general power to the same effect exercisable by deed is valid. The donee, being ascertainable within the perpetuity period has complete control over the property, and once ascertained is in the same position as if he were already its absolute owner.[3]

Provided that a special power is so limited that it cannot be *exercised* beyond the perpetuity period, it is immaterial that under its terms an appointment may possibly be made that will be too remote, as in the case, for instance, of a devise

Power validly created not void merely because admits of remote appointments.

to X. for life, remainder to such of his issue as he shall by will appoint.[4]

At the date of such a devise, it is impossible to say whether the perpetuity rule will be transgressed or not, but this uncertainty does not invalidate the power. The appointments will fail only if in fact they are too remote.[5] The question is not what may be done, but what in fact is done. In other words this is an exceptional case at common law where it is necessary to wait and see what happens.

Presuming now, that the power itself is valid in the sense that it is exercisable only within the perpetuity period, it remains to consider the test that governs the validity of appointments in fact made. It differs radically from that applicable to a general power, a fact that has been clearly explained by high authority in the following passage:—

Test of validity of appointment.

---

[1] *Wollaston* v. *King* (1868), L. R. 8 Eq. 165.
[2] Gray, *op. cit.*, ss. 475, 477.
[3] *Bray* v. *Hammersley* (1830), 3 Sim. 513; S. C. *sub. nom. Bray* v. *Bree* (1834), 2 Cl. & Fin. 353.
[4] *Slark* v. *Dakyns* (1874), 10 Ch. App. 35. *Re Vaux, Nicholson* v. *Vaux*, [1939] Ch. 465 at p. 472; [1938] 4 All E. R. 297 at p. 302.
[5] *Re Fane, Fane* v. *Fane*, [1913] 1 Ch. 404 at pp. 413–4.

"If a person be given a general power of appointment over certain
"property he is virtually the owner of that property. If and when he
"exercises the power the interests of his appointees come to them by
"virtue of and are created by the deed of appointment. In the case
"of a special power it is very different. If, for example, property be
"settled on trust for A. for life and after his death on trust for such of
"A.'s children or remoter issue and is such proportions as B. shall by
"deed appoint, B. has no interest in the property whatsoever. He
"has merely been given the power of saying on behalf of the settlor
"which of the issue of A. shall take the property under the settlement
"and in what proportions. It is as though the settlor had left a blank
"in the settlement which B. fills up for him if and when the power of
"appointment is exercised. The appointees' interests come to them
"under the settlement alone and by virtue of that document."[1]

Perpetuity period reckoned from the date of the instrument of creation.

It follows from this that the limitations made in pursuance of
the power must only be such as would have been valid in point of
perpetuity had they been contained in the instrument that created
the power.[2]   In short, the perpetuity period is reckoned from the
time when that instrument came into operation.

Thus in one case:

> A settlement made in 1844, upon the marriage of H. and W., limited
> land to W. for life and after her death to such of her children as she
> should appoint. The terms of her appointment were that the income
> of the land should be divided equally between her two daughters, X.
> and Y., during their respective lives, but that upon the death of one
> it should pass in its entirety to the survivor.

It was held that the gift to the survivor was void. It was a contingent gift, and the event upon which it was to vest—the death of
one of the daughters—would not necessarily occur within twenty-
one years from the deaths of H. and W. who constituted the sole
lives in being when the special power was created in 1844.[3]

Re Brown and Sibly's Contract.

A further example of the rule is afforded by *Re Brown and
Sibly's Contract*,[4] in which the facts were as follows:

> By a marriage settlement made in 1821 land was limited to the use of
> W. M. for life, and after his death to the use of all or any exclusively
> of the children, grandchildren or other issue of W. M. (to be born
> before the appointment was made), as he should by deed or will
> appoint.
> By his will, which took effect in 1868, W. M. appointed to his
> son W. E. M. in fee, but in case W. E. M. had no child who should
> attain 21, then in fee simple to W. M. B., who was the grandson of
> W. M.

---

[1] *Muir (or Williams)* v. *Muir*, [1943] A. C. 468 at p. 483, *per* Lord ROMER.
[2] *Ibid.*, at p. 481; Farwell on Powers (5th Edn.), p. 325.
[3] *Whitby* v. *Von Luedecke*, [1906] 1 Ch. 783; *Re Legh's Settlement Trusts,
Public Trustee* v. *Legh*, [1938] Ch. 39; [1937] 3 All E. R. 823. W., however,
might have achieved her object by making the interest in the entire income
vested instead of contingent. An appointment of one-half to X. for life with
remainder to Y. for life, and of one-half to Y. for life with remainder to X. for
life, would have been valid. The rule against perpetuities is, indeed, of a highly
technical nature, see 68 *L. Q. R.*, pp. 47-9.
[4] (1876), 3 Ch. D. 156.

If these limitations are set out in the 1821 deed, the position is this:—

W. M. for life (alive in 1821);
W. E. M. in fee (not a life in being in 1821);
W. M. B. in fee (not a life in being in 1821).

When viewed in this manner the invalidity of the last limitation is apparent, for whether any child of W. E. M. failed to attain majority, which was the condition precedent to the vesting of a title in W. M. B., would not necessarily be known within 21 years from the death of the life in being, W. M.

The rule, that the appointment ultimately made must be regarded as having been made in the original instrument of creation, merely ensures that the donee of the power shall not grant interests that the donor himself could not have granted. It follows, therefore, that the appointments must be read and construed in the light of the circumstances existing at the time when they are intended to take effect, not at the time when the power was created.[1]

> Suppose that a deed of settlement, executed in 1936, limits land to A., a bachelor, for life, remainder to such of his issue as he shall by will appoint. A. makes a will appointing to his eldest daughter, X. *on her marriage.* A. dies in 1966.

If X. is unmarried when the will takes effect in 1966, the gift to her is void, for she might not marry until more than twenty-one years after the death of A., the only life in being at the time of the deed of creation.

> The settlor in 1936 could not have validly limited land to A., a bachelor, for life remainder to A.'s eldest daughter on her marriage.

If, in the other hand, X. is already married in 1966, the gift to her is valid.[2]

> The settlor in 1936 could have validly limited land to A., a bachelor, for life, remainder to A.'s eldest daughter, *on condition that she was married at the time of her father's death.*

What is read into the instrument of creation is not the precise language of the appointment, but the precise appointment.[3]

(c) Effect of an infringement of the Rule upon subsequent interests.

A future interest dependent upon a vesting contingency that is too remote is struck out of the disposition, together with all

Marginal notes: Facts existing at date of appointment relevant to its validity. Remote interest, and later interests dependent thereon, extinguished.

[1] Gray, *op. cit.,* s. 523 (c) (d); *Wilkinson* v. *Duncan* (1861,, 30 Beav. 111; *Von Brockdorff* v. *Malcolm* (1885), 30 Ch. D. 172; *Re Thompson, Thompson* v. *Thompson,* [1906] 2 Ch. 199; *Re Paul, Public Trustee* v. *Pearce,* [1921] 2 Ch. 1.
[2] *Morgan* v. *Gronow* (1873), L. R. 16 Eq. 1.
[3] *Re Thompson, Thompson* v. *Thompson, supra* at p. 205, *per* JOYCE J.

subsequent interests that depend upon the same contingency. Thus, in *Proctor* v. *Bishop of Bath and Wells*,[1] a

> devise in fee simple to the first son of A. that should be bred a clergyman

was void, since this contingency might not occur, if it ever occurred at all, until more than twenty-one years after the death of A. Moreover, the subsequent gift

> to B. in fee simple if no son of A. ever became a clergyman

was equally void, since its vesting depended upon precisely the same event that had invalidated the prior limitation. Its vesting hinged upon the identical remote contingency. Where such is the position, the subsequent limitation is aptly described as intrinsically void.[2]

Position where subsequent interest is intrinsically valid. The difficulty arises where the subsequent limitation is not associated with the prior contingency, but is intrinsically valid in the sense that it is already vested in interest, though not in possession, or will necessarily become so, if at all, within the perpetuity period. That a valid interest should be adversely affected by the remoteness of a prior interest is a strange suggestion, but it is implicit in the prevailing doctrine, which is that any limitation that is *dependent or expectant* upon a prior remote limitation is itself invalid, since it is not intended to take effect until the prior limitation has been exhausted.[3] The range of this doctrine and the exact meaning of the vague expression "dependent and expectant" have never been judicially defined, and whether a limitation is affected by an earlier limitation contained in the same instrument is a question of some obscurity.[4] That the doctrine may defeat a settlor's intention is evident from the decision of Eve, J. in *Re Backhouse, Findlay* v. *Backhouse*,[5] where a testator bequeathed a picture

> to his son Jonathan for life; next
> to his second son Charles for life; next
> to his daughter Millicent for life; next
> after her death to the first and every other
> son then living of Jonathan, successively for
> their lives according to seniority; next
> on similar trusts to the sons of
> Charles *then living*; next
> on similar trust to the sons of Millicent,
> but not restricted to those then living; lastly
> to the testator's right heirs.

---

[1] (1794), 2 Hy. Bl. 358; *supra*, p. 246.
[2] Morris and Leach, *op. cit.* p. 173.
[3] *In re Abbott, Peacock* v. *Frigout*, [1893] 1 Ch. 54 at p. 57.
[4] Sir John Romilly, for instance, said that a testamentary limitation was void if it was *ulterior* to remote limitations, even though made in favour of a person living at the testator's death; *In re Thatcher's Trusts* (1859), 26 Beav. 365 at p. 370.
[5] [1921] 2 Ch. 51.

The first four limitations were valid, but the fifth—to the sons of Charles *then living*—was too remote. It was restricted to those living after all the sons of Jonathan were dead, and therefore whether the sons of Charles, some of whom might be born after the will took effect, would satisfy this condition would not necessarily be ascertained within the perpetuity period.

Moreover, the learned judge held that this remote gift broke the chain of limitations and invalidated the gifts to the sons of Millicent and the ultimate gift to the testator's right heirs, though each of these was vested.

It is a question of construction in each case whether, according to the intention of the settlor, a limitation is dependent on a prior remote limitation, as in *Re Backhouse*, or is independent and valid, presuming that taken by itself it satisfies the rule against perpetuities. The relevant decisions do not make easy reading, but they have been reduced by BUCKLEY, J. to the following three categories:[1]

Question of construction whether a limitation is intended to be dependent or independent.

(1) If a series of successive interests is created, each intended to take effect upon and only upon the exhaustion or termination of all antecedent interests in the chain, and one of them is void for remoteness, every subsequent interest fails, even a life interest given to a living person.[2]

(2) Where an interest is created which will not take effect in possession until a future date, but must vest in interest within the perpetuity period, and its possessory enjoyment is not dependent on the exhaustion of the precedent interests, it will be unaffected by remoteness in any of the antecedent interests.[3] This is illustrated by *Re Coleman, Public Trustee* v. *Coleman*.[4]

> A testator left his residuary estate on discretionary trusts to H. for life; after H.'s death upon similar discretionary trusts for any widow who might survive him; and after the death of such widow upon trust (not discretionary) for the children of H. at 21 in equal shares.

By virtue of the discretionary trusts, the trustees were empowered to confer an interest in any part of the income upon H. or his widow. But this trust in the widow's case was void, for H. might marry a woman born after the testator's death, and if so the discretion of the trustees, which was a condition precedent to her right to an interest, might be

---

[1] *In re Hubbard's Will Trusts*, [1963] Ch. 275 at pp. 284–8.
[2] *Beard* v. *Westcott* (1822), 5 B. & Ald. 801; *Re Buckton's Settlement Trusts, Public Trustee* v. *Midland Bank Executor and Trustee Co., Ltd.*, [1964] Ch. 497.
[3] *Re Hubbard's Will Trusts, supra*, at pp. 285–7. *Re Backhouse, supra*, p. 254, however, is inconsistent with this proposition.
[4] [1936] Ch. 528; followed in *Re Allan's Will Trusts, Curtis* v. *Nalder*, [1958] 1 All E. R. 401; [1958] 1 W. L. R. 220.

exercisable beyond the perpetuity period. Nevertheless, it was held that the limitation to the children was valid. By the terms of the will, they were to acquire shares in the residuary estate that were to vest both in interest and in possession on the death of H.'s widow, an event that would not be too remote. The will did not direct that the right to possession should be deferred until the discretionary trusts failed or were exhausted.

(3) The third category is, in the words of BUCKLEY, J.:

" Where a testator or settlor gives property to A. either im-
" mediately or at some future date which is not too remote, but
" so frames his trusts that the interest of A. may be displaced by
" the exercise of some power or discretion, the interest of A.
" will be unaffected by any invalidity of the power or discretion
" on the ground of its remoteness."[1]

In one case, for instance, a testator allocated a fund to be used at the discretion of trustees upon the maintenance of a mansion house so long as any person entitled to the house under a strict settlement shall be under twenty-one years of age, "and subject thereto" upon trust for A. absolutely. The discretionary trust for the maintenance of the house was admittedly too remote, but it was held that the trust in favour of A. was an independent limitation and was valid.[2]

Destination of property remotely limited.

The destination of the property affected by a remote limitation differs according as the disposition is made by deed or by will. In the former case it results to the settlor. In the case of a will, it goes to the residuary legatee or devisee, but to the persons entitled as on an intestacy of the testator if there is no residuary gift or if the residue itself is the subject matter of the limitation. If the void limitation is effected by the exercise of a special power of appointment, the property concerned passes to the persons entitled in default of appointment.

Contingencies with a double aspect.

Alternative limitations. Where a settlor makes the vesting of a future gift dependent upon two alternative events, one of which is too remote and the other not, the gift is allowed to take effect if the event which is not too remote is the one that actually happens.[3] This doctrine provides an exception to the rule that possible, not actual, events are alone considered, for the court waits to see which of the two events in fact occurs.[4] Thus in the early case of *Longhead* v. *Phelps*[5] a marriage settlement declared that certain trusts should arise

---

[1] *In re Hubbard's Will Trusts,* [1963] Ch. 275 at p. 287, *per* BUCKLEY, J.
[2] *In re Canning's Will Trusts,* [1936] Ch. 309; see also *In re Abbott,* [1893] 1 Ch. 54. The difficulties arising from this doctrine of dependency no longer affect instruments taking effect after July 15th, 1964; Act of 1964, s. 6; *infra,* pp. 275–6.
[3] *Longhead* v. *Phelps* (1770), 2 Wm. Bl. 704; *Leake* v. *Robinson* (1817), 2 Mer. 363; *Re Curryer's Will Trusts, Wyley* v. *Curryer,* [1938] Ch. 952; [1938] 3 All E. R. 574; Gray, *op. cit.,* Chap. ix.
[4] Morris and Leach, *op. cit.,* pp. 181–4.   [5] *Supra.*

if H. should die without leaving issue male *or* if such issue male should die without leaving issue.

The latter contingency was obviously too remote, for whether H.'s male issue died without themselves leaving issue would not necessarily be known within 21 years from his death, but in fact he died without male issue and it was held that the trusts were valid. In a more recent case a testator created a trust to take effect

"upon the decease of my last surviving child *or* the death of the last "surviving widow or widower of my children as the case may be "whichever shall last happen."

Here again the last contingency was too remote, since one or more of the children might marry a person born after the testator's death, but it was held that the trust would be valid if the first contingency in fact happened, *i.e.* if all the widows and widowers were dead when the last surviving child died.[1]

The courts, however, have consistently held that this indulgence will not be shown to the valid gift unless the settlor has himself expressly and distinctly designated the two alternative contingencies.[2] If vesting is in terms made dependent upon a single event which in fact includes two contingencies, one too remote the other not too remote, the future gift is void, although the contingency which actually happens is the one that satisfies the perpetuity rule. The court will not split the expression used by the settlor, *i.e.* will not separate and state in an alternative form the two events that the expression in fact includes. By way of illustration we may refer once more to *Proctor* v. *Bishop of Bath and Wells.*[3] In that case the fee simple was devised

Alternative contingencies must be expressed.

to the first or other son of A. who should be in Holy Orders, but in case he should have no such son then over to B. in fee simple.

It is clear on analysis that the event upon which the gift to B. was dependent included two contingencies, namely,

(a) failure of A. to leave sons;
(b) failure of any son to take Holy Orders.

A gift to B. to take effect if A. left no sons would obviously be valid, but though A. did in fact die childless, it was held that B. was not entitled to the fee simple. If the description of the event had been alternative, instead of single, in point of expression, all would have been well; *i.e.* if the testator had expressly stated that the fee simple was to vest in B.,

if A. had no son *or* if he had no son who should take Holy Orders,

---

[1] *In re Curryer's Will Trusts, Wyly* v. *Curryer*, [1938] Ch. 952; [1938] 3 All E. R. 574.
[2] *Re Bence, Smith* v. *Bence*, [1891] 3 Ch. 242; *Miles* v. *Harford* (1879), 12 Ch. D. 691 at p. 702, *per* JESSEL, M.R.
[3] (1794), 2 Hy. Bl. 358; *supra*, pp. 246; 254.

B.'s claim would have been upheld, since it was the first contingency that in fact happened. What the court refused to do was to redraft in an alternative form the single expression appearing in the will. In cases of this kind the court does not concentrate upon implementing the testator's intention, for a man who says that an estate is to go over to B. if none of A.'s sons becomes a clergyman obviously means it to go over if A. never has a son. Whether the intention will prevail is purely a question of words.

> "You are bound to take the expression as you find it, and if, by
> "giving the proper interpretation to that expression, the event may
> "transgress the limit, then the gift over is void."[1]

(d) *Exceptions to the Rule against Perpetuities.*

(1) **Limitations after entailed interests.**

Limitations after entailed interests.

A tenant in tail can bar his own and all subsequent interests. The rule, therefore, is that no limitation after an entailed interest is void for remoteness.[2] No perpetuity exists.

(2) **Contracts.**

Personal contracts not affected.

"It is settled beyond argument that an agreement merely personal, not creating any interest in land, is not within the rule against perpetuities."[3] Therefore, it is not void simply because the obligation it creates may last for an indefinite time.[4] For instance, in *Walsh* v. *Secretary of State for India*,[5]

> the East India Company entered into a covenant in 1770 whereby
> they promised to pay a certain sum of money if, at any time after
> 1794, they should cease to have a military force in their pay and
> service in the East Indies. It might have been centuries before such
> a state of things occurred, and in point of fact it was nearly a century,
> but nevertheless the court upheld the validity of the obligation.

Privity of contract excludes the rule.

It is equally well settled at common law that even a contract which creates an interest in land remains binding upon the parties themselves, notwithstanding that it may be enforceable beyond the perpetuity period. So long as privity of contract exists, there is no room for the rule against perpetuities. Thus in *Hutton* v. *Watling*[6]:—

> A written agreement by which X. sold his business to Y. stipulated
> that Y. should have the option, exercisable at any time in the future,
> to purchase the premises in which the business was carried on.

An action by Y. for specific performance brought seven years later

---

[1] *Miles* v. *Harford* (1879), 12 Ch. D. 691 at p. 702, *per* Jessel, M.R.
[2] *Nicolls* v. *Sheffield* (1787), 2 Bro. C.C. 215; *Heasman* v. *Pearse* (1871), 7 Ch. App. 275.
[3] *South Eastern Ry. Co.* v. *Associated Portland Cement Manufacturers, (1900) Ltd.*, [1910] 1 Ch. 12 at p. 33, *per* Farwell J.
[4] *Witham* v. *Vane* (1883), Challis, *Law of Real Property* (3rd Edn.), p. 440.
[5] (1863), 10 H.L. Cas. 376.
[6] [1948] Ch. 26.

was met by the plea that the stipulation was void for remoteness. The plea failed. In such a case, Y. is entitled not only to recover damages from X.,[1] but also to a decree of specific performance if the land is still retained by X., for "specific performance is merely an equitable mode of enforcing a personal obligation with which the rule against perpetuities has nothing to do."[2]

But once the promisee seeks to enforce the promise against a third person, the position is changed. We now pass from the law of contract to the law of property, with the result that such an option as that in *Hutton* v. *Watling* or an option given to a lessee to purchase the reversion, since it creates an executory interest in land, cannot be enforced against third persons who later acquire the promisor's land unless it is confined within the perpetuity period.[3] Thus where a railway company sold land to one Powell subject to a right of repurchase if at any time thereafter the land was required for the railway, it was held that the right was unenforceable against the appellant, to whom Powell's heir had sold the land.[4]

Rule affects contracts binding land, if no privity of contract.

JESSEL, M.R. said:

"If then the rule as to remoteness applies to a covenant of this "nature, this covenant clearly is bad as extending beyond the period "allowed by the rule. Whether the rule applies or not depends upon "this as it appears to me—does or does not the covenant give an "interest in the land? If it is a bare or mere personal contract it is of "course not obnoxious to the rule, but in that case it is impossible "to see how the present appellant can be bound. He did not enter "into the contract, but is only a purchaser from Powell, who did. "If it is a mere personal contract it cannot be enforced against the "assignee. Therefore, the company must admit that it somehow "binds the land. But if it binds the land it creates an equitable "interest in the land. The right to call for a conveyance of the land "is an equitable interest or equitable estate."

Thus, an option to call for a lease of land exemplifies this principle and is void if it is exercisable beyond the perpetuity period, but it has long been recognized that an option given to a tenant to *renew* his existing lease is entirely unaffected by the rule against perpetuities.[5]

A further illustration of the principles laid down by JESSEL, M.R., is that the grant of an easement to arise *in futuro* may be void on the ground of remoteness, as for example where it entitles

---

[1] *Worthing Corpn.* v. *Heather*, [1906] 2 Ch. 532.
[2] *Hutton* v. *Watling*, [1948] Ch. 26, *per* JENKINS J. This rule has been reversed in the case of instruments taking effect after July, 15th 1964; *infra*, p. 275.
[3] *Woodall* v. *Clifton*, [1905] 2 Ch. 257; *London and South Western Ry. Co.* v. *Gomm* (1882), 20 Ch. D. 562; *Griffith* v. *Pelton*, [1958] Ch. 205; [1957] 3 All E. R. 75.
[4] *London and South Western Ry. Co.* v. *Gomm, supra.*
[5] *Weg Motors, Ltd.* v. *Hales*, [1961] Ch. 176; [1960] 3 All E. R. 762; *affirmed*, [1962] Ch. 49; [1961] 3 All E. R. 181.

the grantee to use the drains and sewers "now passing *or hereafter to pass*" under a private road.[1]

The rule against perpetuities has no application to mortgages, and therefore a postponement of the right of redemption for longer than the perpetuity period is not void for remoteness,[2] though it may be void on other grounds[3]

(3) Certain rights of entry.

The rule affects certain rights of entry, but not others.

First, the right usually reserved to a lessor to enter upon the land and to terminate the lease if the tenant commits a breach of covenant[4] is not subject to the rule.[5]

Secondly, the owner of a rentcharge, *i.e.* a person, other than a reversioner, entitled to the payment of an annual sum of money out of land,[6] is empowered by the Law of Property Act, 1925,[7] in the event of non-payment to enter upon the land and to recover the money due either by levying distress or by leasing the land to a trustee until all arrears have been paid. The Act puts this right of entry, together with its attendant remedies, outside the rule against perpetuities.[8]

If the instrument creating the charge expressly empowers the creditor to enter the land and to determine the fee simple estate of the debtor for non-payment of rent, or to enter and enforce some covenant other than that to pay the sum due, it is doubtful whether such a power is excluded from the perpetuity rule by virtue of the Act.[9]

Thirdly, a rentcharge is sometimes created merely by way of indemnity against another rentcharge.[10] If, for instance, an estate which as a whole is subject to a rentcharge is being sold off in lots, it is a common practice to throw the burden of the charge entirely upon one lot. In practice the purchaser of that lot then gives the purchasers of the other lots an indemnity rentcharge issuing out of his land, so that if they as purchasers of parts of the whole land are compelled by the rent-owner to pay the charge, they will have a right to reimburse themselves out of the lot on which it has been thrown.

---

[1] *Dunn* v. *Blackdown Properties Ltd.*, [1961] Ch. 433; [1961] 2 All E. R. 62.
[2] *Knightsbridge Estates Trust Ltd.* v. *Byrne*, [1940] A.C. 613; [1940] 2 All E. R. 401.
[3] *Infra*, pp. 585–6.   [4] *Infra*, pp. 391; 397.
[5] *Re Tyrrell's Estate*, [1907] 1 I.R. 292 at p. 298, *per* WALKER L.C.
[6] *Infra*, p. 535.
[7] Law of Property Act, 1925, s. 121.
[8] *Ibid.*, s. 121 (6).
[9] See Morris and Leach, *op. cit.* p. 218. The doubt has been removed by the Perpetuities and Accumulations Act, 1964, s. 11, which, however, is not retrospective; see *infra*, p. 276.
[10] *Infra*, p. 562

The former doubt whether the law of remoteness applied to such cases was dispelled by the Law of Property Act, 1925, which provides that rentcharges created only by way of indemnity against other rentcharges, and powers to distrain or to take possession of land affected by such rentcharges, shall be excluded from the operation of the rule against perpetuities.[1]

Fourthly, a right of entry for condition broken attached to a fee simple is void if it is exercisable beyond the perpetuity period.[2]

Fifthly, if a fee simple is sold in return for a perpetual annual rentcharge, the right of entry or re-entry that accrues to the vendor in the event of non-payment,[3] although exercisable for an unlimited period, does not withdraw the land from commerce and therefore is unaffected by the rule against perpetuities.[4]

Right of entry for condition broken.

Right of entry in case of fee farm rent.

(4) Accumulative trust of income for the purpose of paying debts.

The rule does not apply to a trust directing that income shall be accumulated with a view to the payment of the settlor's debts, or for the discharge of incumbrances charged upon the land, for such a trust, though capable of enduring for an indefinite time, may be determined at any moment either by the beneficiaries paying the debts and freeing the land, or by the creditors enforcing their claims by the seizure of the land.[5] Neither does the rule apply to a trust under which money is to be accumulated for the reduction of the National Debt.

Provision for payment of debts.

(5) Administrative powers of trustees.

The former rule was that administrative powers given to trustees, such as a power to sell or lease land, or to receive remuneration for their services, were void if they were capable of being exercised at too remote a time, notwithstanding that they were attached to a trust which itself was not too remote.[6] This may be illustrated by *Re Allott, Hanmer* v. *Allott.*[7]

> A testator left his mines to trustees upon trust to pay annuities to his daughters out of the profits. He directed that if a daughter married, and was survived by her husband, such survivor should be entitled for his life to her annuity.
>
> After the testator's death, a deed of family arrangement was entered into which incorporated the trusts of the will and which *inter alia* gave the trustees powers to grant leases not exceeding 99 years.

---

[1] Law of Property Act, 1925, s. 162 (1) (a).

[2] *Re Hollis' Hospital Trustees and Hague's Contract,* [1899] 2 Ch. 540; Law of Property Act ,1925, s. 4 (3) *infra,* p. 282.

[3] *Supra,* pp. 112-3.

[4] Compare the remarks of Lord BROUGHAM in *Keppell* v. *Bailey* (1834), 2 My. & K. 517, at pp. 528-9.

[5] *Tewart* v. *Lawson* (1874), L. R. 18 Eq. 490; *Lord Southampton* v. *Marquis of Hertford* (1813), 2 Ves. & B. 54.

[6] Such powers do not include powers of distribution under a discretionary trust or powers of maintenance and advancement.

[7] [1924] 2 Ch. 498.

The life interest given to any surviving husband was valid despite the fact that he might be a person not born at the date of the execution of the deed. His life interest would necessarily arise, if it ever arose at all, immediately on the death of his wife. Nevertheless, the power of leasing was void, since it might be exercised, and so create a fresh interest, more than twenty-one years after the dropping of the lives in being if the husband lived so long.

The effect of administrative powers is not to tie up the property, but to facilitate its management, and therefore the Law Reform Committee recommended that they should be excluded from the perpetuity rule provided that the trusts to which they are ancillary are valid and subsisting. This recommendation has been accepted by the Perpetuities and Accumulations Act, 1964, in the only section that is retrospective. It provides that:—

> The rule against perpetuities shall not operate to invalidate a power conferred on trustees or other persons to sell, lease, exchange or otherwise dispose of property for full consideration, or to do any other act in the administration (as opposed to the distribution) of any property, and shall not prevent the payment to trustees or other persons of reasonable remuneration for their services.[1]

(6) Certain limitations to charities.

An interest given to a charity is void unless it will vest within the perpetuity period,[2] but a limitation transferring property from one charity to another upon a certain contingency is valid, although the contingency may not occur until some indefinite time in the future. Provided that the interest of the first charity will begin within the perpetuity period, it is immaterial that the second charity may not take until a remote date. Thus in one case, where

> a testator bequeathed £42,000 to the London Missionary Society with a gift over to the Blue Coat School if the Society failed to keep his family vault in repair,

it was held that the gift over was valid.[3] Had the gift over been, not to another charity, but to private persons, it would have been void.[4]

A gift to a charity is not void as a perpetuity merely because

---

[1] Act of 1964, s. 8 (1). If a power has been created before the commencement of the Act, *i.e.* 16th July, 1964, this section is applicable, provided that the exercise is effected after that date: s. 8 (2).

[2] *Chamberlayne* v. *Brockett* (1872), 8 Ch. App. 206; *Re Lord Stratheden and Campbell*, [1894] 3 Ch. 265; *Re Mander, Westminster Bank, Ltd.* v. *Mander*, [1950] Ch. 547; [1950] 2 All E. R. 191.

[3] *Re Tyler, Tyler* v. *Tyler*, [1891] 3 Ch. 252; following *Christ's Hospital* v. *Grainger* (1849), 1 Mac. & G. 460. For a criticism of this decision see Gray, *op. cit.*, s. 600.

[4] *Re Talbot, Jubb* v. *Sheard*, [1933] Ch. 895; *Re Bland-Sutton's Will Trusts, National Provincial Bank, Ltd.* v. *Middlesex Hospital*, [1951] Ch. 485; [1951] 1 All E. R. 494; reversed in part, [1952] A. C. 631; 1 All E. R. 984.

it creates an interest that may remain subject to the charitable trust for an indefinite period.[1]

(iii) The Rule Applicable to Instruments that take Effect after July 15th, 1964.

In the case of a disposition contained in an instrument that takes effect after July 15th, 1964, the rules obtaining at common law with regard to remoteness have been modified and rationalized as follows by the Perpetuities and Accumulations Act, 1964.[2]

Statutory modifications of the common law.

(a) The perpetuity period.

As an alternative to the common law period during which it is permissible to suspend the vesting of interests, a settlor is empowered by the Act to specify a fixed period of years not exceeding eighty.[3] This is an alternative choice that may perhaps lead to the disappearance of royal lives clauses,[4] but to be effective the fixed period must be expressly designated as the perpetuity period. A limitation, for instance, to such of the issue of X. as may be living at the expiration of eighty years after his death, would not satisfy this requirement.

A fixed period of years may be chosen.

The donor of a special power may provide that the perpetuity period applicable to the limitations shall be a fixed number of years not exceeding eighty. Such period will, of course, begin to run from the effective creation of the power, and it cannot be extended by the donee when he makes an appointment.[5]

Special powers of appointment.

(b) Presumption as to fertility.

The rule at common law that a person of whatever age must be regarded as capable of having children[6] has been abolished in the case of instruments taking effect after 15th July, 1964.

Presumed ages of parenthood.

Under the Act it is to be presumed in any proceedings that a male can beget a child at, but not under, the age of fourteen years; and that a female can have a child at, but not over, the age of fifty-five years.[7] In the case of a living person, however, evidence may be given to rebut these presumptions.[8]

The Act extends these presumptions to the possibility that a

Adopted and legitimated children.

---

[1] *Chamberlayne* v. *Brockett* (1872), 8 Ch. App. 206, at p. 211; *Goodman* v. *Saltash Corpn.* (1882), 7 App. Cas. 633, at pp. 650, 651; *Re Bowen, Lloyd Phillips* v. *Davis*, [1893] 2 Ch. 491, at p. 494.

[2] The following account owes much to the article, *Perpetuities Reform at Last* by J. H. C. Morris and H. W. R. Wade, 8 *L. Q. R.* pp. 486–534.

[3] Perpetuities and Accumulations Act, 1964, s. 1 (1). This provision does not apply to certain options to acquire an interest in land; s. 9 (2), *infra*, p. 267. The Act is hereinafter referred to as "the 1964 Act".

[4] *Supra*, p. 241.

[5] 1964 Act, s. 1 (2).

[6] *Supra*, pp. 263–4.

[7] Perpetuities and Accumulations Act, 1964, s. 2 (1) (a).

[8] *Ibid.*, 2 (1) (b).

person will at any time have a child by adoption, legitimation or other means. If a person is adopted or legitimated under English legislation, he ranks as a "child" for the purpose of taking under a gift to "children" contained in a disposition that comes into effect *after* he has been adopted or legitimated.[1] The difficulty in this context, however, is that in certain circumstances English law recognizes the status and rights conferred upon a person adopted or legitimated in a foreign country even though one of these rights may be to take as a child under a disposition coming into effect *before* he changed his status.[2] It is, therefore, enacted that where a person adopts or legitimates a child evidence shall not be admissible to rebut the statutory presumption.[3] It is an irrebuttable presumption, for instance that a woman over fifty-five years will not adopt a child.

Effect on perpetuity rights if presumption falsified. If, in accordance with these presumptions, property is distributed on the footing that a person is incapable of having a child and the presumption is later falsified, the question arises whether the disposition should be nullified or modified. The statutory solution is to empower the High Court to make such order, "so far as may be just," for placing the beneficiaries in the position they would have held had the presumption not been applied.[4] This power will avail a person, for instance, who has been adopted by a woman over fifty-five years of age.

(c) *Uncertainty as to remoteness.*

Position at common law. We have already seen that at common law a limitation is void if, in the light of the circumstances existing at the time of its effective creation, it may conceivably fail to vest within the perpetuity period. Its fate depends upon possible events in the future, not upon what in fact happens.[5] The Law Reform committee recommended that the validity of a limitation should no longer be tested *ab initio* by reference to what may be within the bounds of possibility, but that instead a "wait and see" principle should be adopted under which validity would be determined on the basis of actual events.[6] This recommendation has been accepted and **Statutory amendments.** in the case of instruments taking effect after 15th July, 1964, the "wait and see" principle applies to three distinct situations.

(1) Interests capable of vesting beyond the perpetuity period.

A disposition that is capable of vesting beyond the perpetuity

---

[1] Adoption Act, 1958, s. 16; Legitimacy Act, 1926, s. 3.
[2] *Re Hurll, Angelini* v. *Dick*, [1952] Ch. 722; [1952] 2 All E. R. 322 (legitimation). It is not clear, however, whether this is true of foreign adoptions; see the conflicting opinions expressed in *Re Valentine's Settlement, Valentine* v. *Valentine* [1965] Ch. 831; [1965] 2 All E. R. 226.
[3] Perpetuities and Accumulations Act 1964, s. 2 (4).
[4] 1964 Act, s. 2 (2).
[5] *Supra*, pp. 243–8.
[6] Cmnd. 18, para. 10 (3) 1956.

period (*i.e.* the common law period or the fixed period not exceeding eighty years if this has been expressly specified) is to be treated as valid until such time as it becomes established that its vesting must occur, if at all, after the end of that period.[1] As soon as events show that it can never vest within the period, it becomes void; as soon as events show that it can never vest outside the period, it becomes immune from the doctrine of remoteness.[2]

The effect of this amendment may be illustrated by the old case of *Proctor* v. *Bishop of Bath and Wells*,[3] where there was

> a devise in fee simple to the first son of X. that should be bred a clergyman and take Holy Orders. X. had no son born at the time of the testator's death.

The devise was void at common law. If a son were born he might not take Holy Orders, if at all, within twenty-one years from the death of X., the only life in being when the will took effect. But, under the Act of 1964, the devise is presumptively valid, not void *ab initio*. There must be a pause to see what happens. The gift will be valid if in fact a son is born who satisfies the vesting contingency within twenty-one years after X.'s death.

In the application of this "wait and see" principle, each distinct part of a limitation is treated by the Act as a separate disposition. For instance: *Waiting period differs for different parts of a disposition.*

> A testator devises land to A. for life, remainder to his widow for life, remainder to such of the children of A. as are alive at the death of the widow; but if there be no such children, then to the first son of X. to marry.

In such a case, the gift to the children of A. and the gift to the first son of X. to marry are distinct dispositions subject to different waiting periods.

The "wait and see" principle applies equally to the validity of appointments made by the exercise of a special power. *Exercise of special power of appointment.*

> Suppose that a testator, who dies in 1965, devises land to A., a bachelor, for life, remainder to such of his issue as he shall by will appoint. A. appoints in favour of his infant daughter, X. *on her marriage.* A. dies in 1970.

At common law the appointment is too remote.[4] Under the Act, it is valid provided that the daughter marries within twenty-one years after A's death.

One problem raised by these provisions is the destination of the intermediate income during the waiting period.[5] The general rule, subject to certain exceptions, is that a contingent gift carries *Intermediate income.*

---

[1] 1964 Act, s. 3 (1).
[2] Cmnd. 18, para. 17 (1956).
[3] (1794), 2 Hy. Bl. 358.
[4] Compare the example discussed *supra*, p. 253.
[5] See Morris and Leach, *op. cit.*, pp. 93–5.

K*

the income arising from the corpus although the vesting contingency may ultimately never be satisfied, except so far as such income has been otherwise disposed of by the donor.[1] Suppose, for example, that a testator bequeaths the residue of his estate to his grandchild, X., upon her marriage and that she is an infant and unmarried at the time of the testator's death. In these circumstances, the income is accumulated during her infancy and the trustees may use it for her maintenance and education,[2] and may make advances to her out of capital,[3] but at her majority the income becomes and remains payable to her even though she may never marry.[4]

The rights of the beneficiaries in such a case, however, are subject to the perpetuity rule, the effect of which varies according as the disposition falls to be determined by the common law or by the Act of 1964.

Suppose, for instance, that a will bequeaths the residue of the estate to the daughters of X. when they marry, and that X. is childless at the time of the testator's death.

At common law the bequest is void *ab initio*. It is impossible to say at the time when the will takes effect that if any children born to X. marry, they will do so within twenty-one years from her death.

Payments out of income permitted during waiting period.

But under the statutory "wait and see" provisions the gift is not void *ab initio*. It is void only if at the end of twenty-one years from X.'s death none of his daughters, if any, has married. The destination of the income of the corpus during this waiting period therefore presents a problem. If a daughter is born to X., is she to receive the benefit of the income although the bequest may ultimately become void for remoteness? The recommendation of the Law Reform Committee that such should be the rule[5] is accepted by the Act of 1964, which provides that when it becomes established that the vesting of a gift must occur, if at all, after the end of the perpetuity period, " the validity of anything previously done in relation to the interest disposed of by way of advancement, application of intermediate income or otherwise" shall not be affected.[6]

(2) General powers capable of exercise beyond the perpetuity period.

A general power of appointment that may possibly be exercised beyond the perpetuity period and which is therefore void

---

[1] See, for example, Law of Property Act, 1925, s. 175 (2).
[2] Trustee Act, 1925, s. 31 (1) (i); 31 (2).
[3] *Ibid.*, s. 32.
[4] *Ibid.*, s. 31 (1) (ii).
[5] Cmnd. 18, para. 22 (1956)
[6] Section 3 (1).

at common law,[1] is to be treated as valid until it is established that it will not in fact be exercised at too remote a time.[2] If, for instance, it is exercisable only by will and is given to the unborn child of X., it will be valid if the donee is born and dies within twenty-one years after X.'s death; if it is exercisable by deed, or either by deed or will, but only on the marriage of the unborn child, it will be valid if the marriage occurs within the same period.

(3) "Any power, option or other right" capable of exercise beyond the perpetuity period.

In a more comprehensive section, the Act deals separately with the remote exercise of "any power, option or other right". It provides that a power, option or other right is no longer to be rendered void merely because it may possibly be exercised at too remote a time. It will be void only if it is not in fact fully exercised within the perpetuity period.[3]

> For instance, a special power granted by a deed of settlement to the eldest son of X., a bachelor, is void *ab initio* at common law;[4] but under the Act it is not void unless exercised beyond the perpetuity period calculated from the date of the settlement.

On the other hand, if the exercise of a special power satisfies the test of remoteness prescribed by this sub-section, the question whether the appointed interests are too remote is governed, as we have seen, by an earlier subsection.[5]

The reference in this enactment to an "option" means *inter alia*, that a right conferred by contract upon one person to purchase the land of another at some unspecified time in the future is no longer void *ab initio*,[6] but void only if it is not in fact exercised within the perpetuity period. *(margin: Option to purchase land.)*

But, except where the option is one that entitles a tenant to purchase his landlord's reversion, which is exercisable throughout the continuance of the lease however long this may be,[7] the only period applicable to an option to acquire for valuable consideration any interest in land is twenty-one years.[8]

Duration of the waiting period. In considering whether the wait and see provisions are applicable, the first step is to ascertain whether the disposition satisfies the common law rule against *(margin: Permissible time of waiting.)*

---

[1] *Supra*, p. 249.
[2] Act of 1964, s. 3 (2).
[3] Section 3 (3). It will be noticed that a general power is caught by this sub-section as well as by sub-section (2).
[4] *Supra.*, p. 251.
[5] Section 3 (1); see the example given *supra.*, p. 265.
[6] As under the common law, *London and South Western Ry. Co.* v. *Gomm* (1882), 20 Ch. D. 562; *supra*, p. 259; *Dunn* v. *Blackdown Properties Ltd.*, 1961] Ch. 433; [1961] 2 All E. R. 62; *supra*, pp. 259–60.
[7] Act of 1964. Section 9 (1); *infra*, p. 276.
[8] *Ibid.*, s. 9 (2).

perpetuities. If the contingent interests that it grants must vest, if at all, within the period fixed by that rule, there is no need to invoke the statutory provisions. The Act of 1964 operates only where the vesting contingency may possibly occur after that period has expired. Where this is the case, the Act prescribes the period during which it is permissible to wait and see whether in the light of future events the limitations are or are not too remote. In the result the waiting period is as follows:—

> The period of years not exceeding eighty if this has been specified by the settlor.
> Failing such a specification, a period based on the common law formula of lives plus twenty-one years, but restricted so far as lives are concerned to the individual persons defined by the Act itself. These, which may conveniently be called the "statutory lives", must be in being and ascertainable at the time when the disposition takes effect.[1]

It is important to realize the consequence of this last requirement. If, for instance, the limitations of a will include a gift "to the widow of X.," she becomes a statutory life only if X. has predeceased the testator. If he survives the testator, his widow will not be ascertainable when the will takes effect. If there are no statutory lives and no specified term of years, the period of waiting is twenty-one years.[2]

"Statutory lives"
(a) Creator of the disposition.
(b) Certain beneficiaries.

The statutory lives are defined as follows:[3]

(a) The person by whom the disposition is made, if made by deed, even though he himself takes no interest in the property.[4]
(b) Any of the following persons in whose favour the disposition is made, namely—

> (i) In the case of a class gift, any member or potential member of the class.[5]

A person is a member of the class if he has satisfied all the conditions that entitle him to an interest; he is a potential member if he has satisfied only some of the conditions but may in time satisfy the remainder.[6] If, for instance, there is a gift by will to such of the daughters of X. as may marry and if at the time of the testator's death X. has an unmarried daughter, she constitutes a life in being. She has satisfied the condition relating to birth and there is a possibility that she may later marry.

---

[1] Act of 1964, s. 3 (4) (a). The object of this sub-s. is merely to qualify the common law period so far as the relevant lives are concerned. It implies the retention of the additional twenty-one years.
[2] Act of 1964, s. 3 (4) (b).
[3] *Ibid.*, s. 3 (5) criticized, 80 *L. Q. R.*, pp. 495–508.
[4] *Ibid.*, s. 3 (5) (a).
[5] *Ibid.*, s. 3 (5) (b) (i).
[6] *Ibid.*, s. 15 (3).

(ii) In the case of an individual disposition to a person subject to certain conditions, any person as to whom some of the conditions are satisfied and the remainder may in time be satisfied.[1]

This would be the position, for instance, if in the last illustration the gift had been to the first granddaughter of X. to marry, and if at the time of the testator's death a granddaughter had been born but was not yet married.

(iii) The above two provisions apply equally to special powers of appointment.[2]

If, for instance, the power is conferred by will and is exercisable in favour of any of the issue of X., descendants of X. alive at the testator's death constitute statutory lives.

(iv) The person on whom any power, option or other right is conferred.[3]

Trustees who possess a special power of appointment, for instance, fall within this category.

(c) In certain circumstances, the parents and grandparents of the designated beneficiaries also constitute persons whose lives are relevant in the present context. The Act provides that:

> The persons capable of ranking as "statutory lives" shall include a person having a child or grandchild who would be a life in being under the rules (b) (i to iv) given above; and also a person whose children or grandchildren, if subsequently born, would by virtue of descent be a life in being under the same rules.[4]

(c) Parents and grandparents of certain beneficiaries.

Suppose, for instance, that a bequest is made to such of X.'s daughters as may marry, and that at the testator's death a daughter has been born to X. but has not yet married. In these circumstances, as we have seen in dealing with rule (b) (i),[5] the daughter ranks as a life in being. Under the instant rule, therefore, X. is equally qualified in that respect.

Again, suppose that there is a bequest to the first granddaughter of X. to marry, and that at the testator's death X. has one unmarried son. In these circumstances, X. ranks as a life in being under the concluding words of the instant rule, since any granddaughter subsequently born will similarly qualify under rule (b) (ii). The unmarried son is also a life in being under the instant rule, for if a daughter is subsequently born to him she will qualify as such by virtue of rule (b) (ii).

It is enacted, however, that the lives of the persons designated in (b) and (c) above shall be disregarded if their number is

---

[1] Act of 1964, s. 3 (5) (b) (ii).
[2] *Ibid.*, s. 3 (5) (b) (iii) and (iv).
[3] *Ibid.*, s. 3 (5) (b) (v).
[4] *Ibid.*, s. 3 (5) (c).
[5] *Supra*, p. 268.

such as to render it impracticable to ascertain the death of the survivor.[1]

(d) Owner of precedent interest.

(*d*) Any person on the failure or determination of whose prior interest the disposition is limited to take effect constitutes a life being.[2]

A simple illustration of this is that under a limitation to A. for life remainder to the first grandchild of X. to marry, A. ranks as a life in being. It would seem, however, that he will not qualify as such under a limitation to A. for life, remainder to B. for life, remainder to the first grandchild of X. to marry, for it is on the determination of B.'s interest that the gift to the grandchild is to take effect.[3] It is this subsection which shows most clearly how the duration of the "wait and see" periods varies for different parts of one disposition.[4]

(*d*) *Special provisions designed to save remote interests.*

The Act of 1964 contains three additional provisions designed to cure the vice of remoteness, but it is essential to bear in mind that these are not to be invoked until it has become clear that the limitations in question will not be saved by the "wait and see" rule.[5] The provisions are as follows:

(1) **Provisions concerning the death of a surviving spouse.**

The case of the possibly unborn spouse.

This deals with the case of the possibly unborn spouse. Suppose for instance that the limitations contained in a will are

> to X., a bachelor, for life, remainder to his future wife for life, remainder to such of his children as are living at the death of X. and such wife.

Position at common law.

As we have seen, the limitation to the children is void at common law.[6] It is possible that X. may marry a woman not yet born, and therefore it cannot be affirmed at the time of the testator's death that the vesting contingency will necessarily occur within the perpetuity period.

Wait and see provisions not a complete remedy.

If X. marries a woman who is alive at the date of the will, the gift to the children will not be saved by the "wait and see" rule unless she dies not later than twenty-one years after X.'s death. The wife cannot qualify as a "statutory life", though possibly and most probably she is alive at the date of the testator's

---

[1] *Act of 1964, s. 3 (4) (a).*
[2] *Ibid.*, s. 3 (5) (d).
[3] See 80 *L. Q. R.*, p. 505 (J. H. C. Morris and H. W. R. Wade).
[4] *Supra.*, p. 265.
[5] Because s. 3, which introduces the "wait and see" rule is expressed to operate "apart" from ss. 4 and 5 which contain these three additional provisions.
[6] *Supra*, pp. 246–7.

death, for under the Act of 1964 lives in being for the purposes of the "wait and see" rule must be ascertainable at the commencement of the perpetuity period.[1]

It is therefore provided by the Act of 1964 that a disposition such as that given above, which fails for remoteness, shall be treated for all purposes as if it had been limited to take effect immediately before the end of the perpetuity period, if to do so will save it from being void for remoteness.[2] *Position under the Act of 1964.*

If, then, in the case of the above example, X. marries, and his wife dies within twenty-one years of his death, the limitation to the children is saved under the "wait and see" rule. If she survives beyond that time, the "wait and see" rule is impotent, but the limitation is none the less saved, since by virtue of the above enactment it vests at the end of twenty-one years from X.'s death in the children then living and will take effect in possession on the death of the wife.

(2) Age reduction provisions.

An interest whose vesting is postponed until the attainment by the beneficiary of an age exceeding twenty-one years is void *ab initio* at common law, but as we have already seen it was provided by section 163 of the Law of Property Act, 1925, that in such a case the age of twenty-one years should be substituted for that specified by the donor.[3] *Former law.*

Such a disposition contained in an instrument taking effect after 15th July, 1964, may well be saved by the "wait and see" provisions of the Act of 1964.[4] *Effect of "wait and see" provisions.*

> Suppose, for instance, that a gift is made by will to the first son of X., a bachelor, to attain the age of thirty years; and that X. is survived by a son aged ten.

If the son satisfies the prescribed contingency, he will have done so within twenty-one years from the death of X., the life in being.

On the other hand, the wait and see rule may be ineffective. If, for instance, in the example just given the eldest son is only five years of age at X.'s death, the vesting contingency cannot be satisfied within the perpetuity period, though if section 163 were applicable the gift to him would be saved by the reduction of the vesting age from thirty to twenty-one years.

It was felt, however, that instead of mechanically reducing the age to twenty-one years in every case, it would be preferable to conform more closely with the donor's wishes and to reduce it only to whatever age would suffice to prevent the limitation from being *Extent of reduction under Act of 1964.*

---

[1] Act of 1964, s. 3 (4) (a); *supra*, p. 268.
[2] Act of 1964, s. 5.
[3] *Supra*, pp. 248–9.
[4] Owing to the drafting of the Act, however, the exact operation of the "wait and see" provisions in the present context is far from clear; see 81 *L. Q. R.* pp. 346–7 (J. D. Davies).

too remote. The Act of 1964, therefore, repeals section 163 of the Law of Property Act, 1925,[1] though not retrospectively,[2] and replaces it by the following provision:—

> "Where a disposition is limited by reference to the attainment by
> "any person or persons of a specified age exceeding twenty-one
> "years, and it is apparent at the time the disposition is made or
> "becomes apparent at a subsequent time—
>
> > "(a) that the disposition would, apart from this section be void
> > for remoteness, but
> > "(b) that it would not be so void if the specified age had been
> > twenty-one years,
>
> "the disposition shall be treated for all purposes as if, instead of
> "being limited by reference to the age in fact specified, it had been
> "limited by reference to the age nearest to that age which would, if
> "specified instead, have prevented the disposition from being so
> "void."[3]

Let us suppose once more than a will limits land to the first son of X., a bachelor, to attain thirty years of age and that at X.'s death his only son is four years old. In these circumstances it has become apparent that the "wait and see" rule cannot save the ultimate limitation. The son cannot attain the prescribed age within the perpetuity period. Hence the above section operates, and the qualifying age is reduced from thirty to twenty-five years.

Disposition in favour of two or more persons. If the disposition is in favour of two or more persons, as for example to the children of X. at 30 years of age, and if at X.'s death his son is four, his daughter five years old, the reduction of the specified age to twenty-five, necessary to save the son's interest, affects the daughter also.[4]

Two or more different ages. If the disposition specifies different ages for distinct classes of beneficiaries, as for instance thirty for sons twenty-five for daughters, the classes are segregated for the purpose of estimating the extent of the reduction. The reduction must be such as is necessary in each separate class.[5]

(3) Class-closing provisions.

Modification of rule that class gift cannot be partly good, partly bad. We have already seen that at common law a class gift cannot be partly good, partly bad. If some members of the class may possibly fail to satisfy the vesting contingency within the perpetuity period, the whole gift fails even in respect of those members whose interests are already vested.[6]

The Act however abolishes this rule and in its place provides that the disposition shall take effect in favour of those members

---

[1] Act of 1964, s. 4 (6).
[2] *Ibid.*, s. 15 (5).
[3] Section 4 (1).
[4] The reason is that there is only one "disposition", not several "dispositions" to cover all members of the class; 80 *L. Q. R.* p. 509 (J. H. C. Morris and H. W. R. Wade).
[5] Act of 1964, s. 4 (2).
[6] *Supra*, pp. 244–5.

who acquire vested interests within the perpetuity period to the exclusion of those who fail to qualify within that time. This policy applies to two distinct cases.

First, where the only cause of failure at common law is that some members of the class may not be ascertainable within the perpetuity period. (i) Where no question of age reduction.

In such a case, the Act provides that, unless their interests are saved by virtue of the "wait and see" provision, those members shall be excluded from the class.[1]

> Suppose, for instance, that a disposition is made by will to X., a bachelor, for life, remainder to such of his children as may marry. Suppose further that X. dies leaving a married son and an unmarried daughter.

If the daughter marries within twenty-one years after X.'s death, her interest is saved by the "wait and see" provisions; if she is still a spinster at the expiry of that time, she is excluded from the class. In the latter event, the gift, which would have been wholly void at common law, takes effect in favour of the son.

The second case is where neither the "wait and see" principle nor the age reduction provisions will save the gift, as may occur if the attainment by the members of the class of an age exceeding twenty-one years is part of the vesting contingency. The following is an example of such a case. (ii) Question of age reduction arises.

> Bequest to X., a bachelor, for life, remainder to such of his children as marry and attain the age of twenty-five years.
> X. dies leaving a married daughter aged nineteen and a son aged three.

The inability of the son to reach the prescribed age within the perpetuity period which ends twenty-one years from the death of X., the only life in being, may no doubt be rectified under the age reduction provisions.[2] But the marriage contingency remains, for whether this is satisfied may not be established until too remote a time. If in fact he marries within twenty-one years of X.'s death, the "wait and see" rule will operate to validate the whole gift. If not, then the daughter becomes the sole beneficiary, for the effect of the Act of 1964 is to exclude the son from the class of designated beneficiaries.[3]

(e) General and special powers of appointment.

We have already discussed the importance of the distinction between general and special powers of appointment in the context of the doctrine of remoteness.[4] We have also seen that it is some- Statutory definition of "special power."

---

[1] Section 4 (4).
[2] *Supra*, pp. 271–2.
[3] Act of 1964, s. 4 (3).
[4] *Supra*, pp. 249 *et seq.*

times difficult to determine whether a so-called "hybrid" power is to be classed as general or special.[1]   This difficulty is removed by the Act of 1964 which defines what powers shall be treated as special powers for the purposes of the rule against perpetuities, but only for those purposes.   By virtue of this enactment:

A power is to be treated as a special power, unless:—

> (*a*) in the instrument of creation it is expressed to be exercised by one person only, and
>
> (*b*) it could, at all times during its currency when that person is of full age and capacity, be exercised by him so as immediately to transfer to himself the whole of the appointable interest without the consent of any other person or compliance with any other condition, not being a formal condition relating to the mode of exercise.[2]

The result is that the only general power is one under which "there is a sole donee who is at all times free without the concurrence of any other person to appoint to himself."[3]

Hybrid powers.   Thus, for instance, a power, is to be regarded as a special power if it is exercisable by the donee jointly with other persons or only with the consent of other persons; or exercisable in favour of any persons alive at the donee's death; or exercisable in favour of any person except the donee.   On the other hand, a power to appoint to any person in the world except X. should be classified as general.[4]

General testamentary power.   But the general testamentary power, *i.e.* one unrestricted in respect of objects but exercisable only by will,[5] is treated as exceptional by the Act.

Under the existing case law, such a power is regarded as special so far as the validity of its creation is concerned;[6] but as general when the question is whether an appointment is too remote.[7]   The perpetuity period runs from the date of the instrument of creation in the former case, in the latter from the date of the appointment. To classify such a power as general in respect of the appointments is illogical for, unlike the case where exercise by deed is permissible, the donee is in no sense the virtual owner of the property. Any transfer of the ownership to himself is necessarily ineffective until after his death.   Nevertheless, it was felt to be unwise to revise a rule that has obtained for some seventy years, and one upon which conveyancing precedents in constant use have been based.   Therefore, the distinction between the validity of the

---

[1] *Supra*, pp. 194–5.
[2] Act of 1964, s. 7.
[3] Fourth report of Law Reform Committee, 1566, Cmnd. 18, para. 47.
[4] Morris and Leach, *op cit.* p. 137.
[5] *Supra*, pp. 195; 250.
[6] *Wollaston* v. *King* (1868), L. R. 8, Eq. 165; *Morgan* v. *Gronow* (1873), L. R. 16 Eq 1; *supra*, p. 250.
[7] *Rous* v. *Jackson* (1885), 29 Ch.D. 521.

power itself and the validity of appointments is retained by the Act.[1]

The expression "power of appointment" includes any discretionary power to transfer a beneficial interest in property without the furnishing of consideration.[2] It ranks as a special power.

Discretionary trusts.

(f) *Extended scope of the Rule.*

The scope of the rule against perpetuities is enlarged in two respects by the Act of 1964. It is extended to possibilities of reverter and analogous possibilities, a matter that is dealt with in a later chapter;[3] and its effect upon certain contracts for the purchase of land is expanded.

Possibilities of reverter.

We have seen that at common law a contract for the purchase of land, since it creates an equitable interest in favour of the promisee, is not enforceable by or against third parties if it is too remote; but that it remains enforceable without any limit of time between the parties themselves, since the rule against perpetuities is not concerned with personal obligations.[4]

Contract for purchase of land, if too remote, no longer binding upon the parties.

The second limb of the common law rule, however, is now abolished. The Act provides in effect that:

> where a disposition, made *inter vivos* and creating proprietary rights capable of transfer, would be void for remoteness as between persons other than the original parties, it shall be void as between the person by whom it was made and the person in whose favour it was made or any successor of his.[5]

(g) *Effect of an infringement of the Rule upon subsequent interests.*

The Law Reform Committee, after castigating the doctrine of dependency, recommended that

Common law doctrine of dependency abolished.

> "no limitation which itself complies with the rule should be in-"validated solely by reason of being preceded by one or more "invalid limitations whether or not it expressly or by implication "takes effect after or subject to, or is dependent upon, any such "invalid limitation."[6]

The Act of 1964 deals with this recommendation in the following terms:

> "A disposition shall not be treated as void for remoteness by reason "only that the interest disposed of is ulterior to and dependent upon "an interest under a disposition which is so void, and the vesting "of an interest shall not be prevented from being accelerated on "the failure of a prior interest by reason only that the failure arises "because of remoteness."[7]

---

[1] Section 7, proviso. [2] Act of 1964, s. 15 (2). [3] *Infra*, pp. 288–9.
[4] *Supra*, pp. 258–60. [5] S.10 [6] Cmd. 18, para. 33 (1956).
[7] S. 6.

Thus each limitation in a chain of limitations must be considered separately according to its own intrinsic validity and without regard to the remoteness of its predecessors. An interest which is already vested or which will necessarily vest, if at all, within the perpetuity period takes effect according to its individual terms. If, for instance, the facts of *Re Backhouse*[1] were to recur in a modern instrument, the gifts to the sons of Millicent and the ultimate gift to the testator's heirs would be accelerated by the elimination of the gift to the sons of Charles. The chain of limitations would be shortened, not broken as it was held to be in that case.

On the other hand, if the facts of *Proctor* v. *Bishop of Bath and Wells*[2] were to recur, the ultimate gift to B. in fee simple would still fail as being itself intrinsically void.

Acceleration.   It will be noticed that the concluding words of the enactment do not direct that the ulterior interest *shall* be accelerated, *i.e.* allowed to take effect immediately upon the failure for remoteness of the prior interest, but that such failure shall not prevent acceleration. The reason for this negative approach is that there may be other obstacles to acceleration. If, for example, the interest that fails is followed by a contingent interest, which in turn is followed by a vested interest, the latter is not accelerated until it is established whether, or not, the contingent interest will take effect.[3]

(h) *Exceptions to the Rule.*

The exceptions to the rule recognized by the common law have been affected in three respects.

Administrative powers.   First, as we have already seen, the administrative powers of trustees are excluded from the rule even in respect of instruments taking effect before 16th July, 1964.[4]

Option to buy leasehold reversion.   Secondly, an option to acquire for valuable consideration the freehold interest expectant upon a lease, is wholly exempted from the rule regardless of the length of the lease, provided that it is exercisable only by the lessee or his successors in title, and provided that it is not exercisable later than one year after the end of the lease.[5]

Remedies for the recovery of a rentcharge.   Thirdly, the former doubt as to the ambit of section 121 of the Law of Property Act, 1925,[6] has been removed. It is provided by the 1964 Act that the perpetuity rule shall not apply to any powers or remedies for recovering or compelling the payment of an annual sum to which that section relates, or otherwise becoming exercisable on the breach of any condition or other requirement relating to that sum.[7]

---

[1] *Supra*, p. 254.   [2] *Supra*, p. 254.
[3] *Re Townsend's Estate, Townsend* v. *Townsend* (1886), 34 Ch. D. 357.
[4] Act of 1964, s. 8 (1); *supra*, pp. 261–2.   [5] *Ibid.*, s. 9 (1).
[6] *Supra*, p. 260.   [7] Act of 1964, s. 11 (1).

(B) THE RULES AGAINST ACCUMULATIONS OF INCOME.

At common law, the rule against perpetuities governs not only the right to suspend the vesting of an estate, but also the right to direct the accumulation of income arising from an estate. Therefore, before the law was altered by statute in 1800 it was held that a direction for the accumulaion of income for a period which did not exceed the perpetuity period was valid.[1] This was decided in the famous case of *Thellusson* v. *Woodford*,[2] where the facts were these:—

At the end of the eighteenth century a certain Mr. Thellusson, a man of great wealth, took advantage of the rule and made a will the object of which was to accumulate an enormous fortune for the benefit of certain future and unascertained members of his family. Keeping well within the limits imposed by law, he directed that the income arising from his land should be accumulated during the lives of all his sons and grandsons living at his death, and that, at the dropping of the last life, the capital sum so produced should be divided amongst the male representatives of his sons' families. At the time of the controversy engendered by this will it was calculated that the accumulation would endure for about 80 years, and produce an amount of approximately 100 million pounds.[3] It was held that these trusts for accumulation were valid, but a statute, generally called the Thellusson Act,[4] was subsequently passed in order to prevent further examples of what has been called posthumous avarice.

Thellusson v. Woodford

This statute has been re-enacted and amended by the Law of Property Act, 1925,[5] as well as by the Perpetuities and Accumulations Act, 1964, and the position now is that a settlor who desires the income of his property to be accumulated is restricted to choosing *one* only[6] of the following periods for the duration of the accumulation:

Modern law.

(1) the life or lives of the settlor or settlors;

(2) a term of 21 years from the death of the settlor;

(3) the minority or respective minorities of any persons living or *en ventre sa mère* at the death of the settlor;

(4) the minority or respective minorities only of any person or persons who, under the limitations of the settlement, would, if of full age, be entitled to the income directed to be accumulated;[7]

(5) a term of twenty-one years from the date of the settlement;

---

[1] Fearne, *Contingent Remainders*, p. 537, note.

[2] (1790), 4 Ves. 227; affirmed (1805), 11 Ves. 112.

[3] Challis, *Law of Real Property* (3rd Edn.), p. 201. Holdsworth, *History of English Law*, vol. vii, pp. 228 *et seq.*

[4] Accumulations Act, 1800 (39 & 40 Geo. III, c. 98).

[5] Sections 164–6. The Act affects not only an express direction to accumulate income, but also a power of accumulation, *Re Robb's Will Trusts, Marshall v. Marshall*, [1953], Ch. 459; [1953] 1 All E. R. 920.

[6] *Jagger* v. *Jagger* (1883), 25 Ch. D. 729.

[7] Law of Property Act, 1925, s. 164 (1) (a) (b) (c) (d).

> (6) the duration of the minority or respective minorities of any person or persons in being at the date of the settlement.[1]

The last two periods were added by the Act of 1964 with the object of giving a wider choice to persons who make an *inter vivos* settlement. They apply only to instruments taking effect after 15th July, 1964.

Difference between (3) and (4).

The difference between the third and fourth periods is that while the third period is for the minority of a person living at the death of the settlor, the fourth includes the minority of any person who may *afterwards* become entitled to an interest in the land.[2] Thus by the choice of the fourth period an accumulation may lawfully be directed for the minorities of persons who are not alive at a testator's death. This is illustrated by the case of *Re Cattell, Cattell* v. *Cattell*,[3] where

> a testator vested property in trustees upon trust for the children of his sons and daughters. He directed that the income of the property should be accumulated during the minorities of any of the children. The testator died in 1880. Gladys was born to one of his sons in 1885 and Frederick to another of his sons in 1912. It was argued that it was inadmissible to accumulate the income during these minorities, since the infants were not alive at the testator's death.

The Court of Appeal held that accumulation during both minorities was warranted by the statute. Lord PARKER said:

> "In my opinion the fourth alternative covers not only children who "are born or *en ventre sa mere* at the death of the settlor, but children "who are subsequently born, and I think that the fact that the fourth "alternative comes immediately after and in contrast with the third "alternative, which refers only to born children and children *en* "*ventre sa mère* at the time of the death of the settlor, points strongly "to this conclusion."[4]

This interpretation necessarily admits of accumulations during successive minorities, and is open to the objection that income may be withdrawn from use for a very considerable time; but, as Challis points out,[5] this latitude of choice is set off by the fact that the minorities chosen must be those of persons who are prospectively entitled to the income.

Accumulations for purpose of buying land.

A settlor sometimes directs an accumulation of income to be made, not for the purpose of dividing the capital among children, but for the purchase of land. It is provided by the Accumulations Act, 1892, in a section that has been re-enacted by the Law of Property Act, 1925,[6] that an accumulation for this particular purpose may be made to endure only for the fourth statutory period.

---

[1] Perpetuities and Accumulations Act, 1964, s. 13 (1).
[2] Fearne, 537, Butler's note citing Preston.
[3] [1914] 1 Ch. 177.
[4] *Per* Lord PARKER, [1914] 1 Ch. 177 at p. 188.
[5] *Op. cit.*, p. 202.
[6] Section 166.

Where an excessive accumulation has been directed, the effect differs according as the direction violates the general perpetuity period or one of the six statutory periods. A direction for accumulation which transgresses the rule against perpetuities, by designating a period longer than a life or lives in being and 21 years afterwards, is void *in toto* and no income can be accumulated;[1] but a direction which, while it exceeds the statutory periods yet keeps within the general perpetuity period, is good *pro tanto*, and is void only in so far as it exceeds the appropriate statutory period.[2] The excess alone is void. So if accumulation is ordered for the life of a person other than the settlor (which is not one of the statutory periods), it will be good for 21 years.[3]

Effect of excessive accumulation.

If the person entitled to property under a trust is an infant, there is a statutory duty imposed on the trustees to maintain the infant out of the income, and to accumulate any surplus income during the remainder of the minority.[4] Where, in accordance with the directions of a settlor, income has been accumulated for one of the statutory periods, and at the termination of that period the beneficiary is an infant, so that a further accumulation may be necessary, it is enacted that the two accumulations shall not be counted together and so held to amount to an infringement of the Act.[5]

Accumulations during minorities.

The right to stop accumulations. In the case of instruments taking effect after 15th July, 1964, the presumption that no woman over fifty-five years of age can have a child, introduced by the Act of 1964,[6] applies to the right of beneficiaries to put an end to accumulations.[7] That right is defined in *Saunders* v. *Vautier*[8] and later cases and is as follows: Where there is a gift of capital and income to a beneficiary absolutely, but subject to a trust that the income is to be accumulated until he attains an age exceeding twenty-one years, he may, on reaching his majority, stop the accumulation and insist that the capital and accumulated income be paid to him forthwith. Once the property belongs to him absolutely, his free enjoyment of it cannot be fettered. This

The rule in *Saunders* v. *Vautier.*

---

[1] *Curtis* v. *Lukin* (1842), 5 Beav. 147.

[2] What is the appropriate period raises a difficult question of construction that must be determined according to the language of the instrument and the facts of the case; *Re Watt's Will Trusts, Watt* v. *Watt* [1936] 2 All E. R. 1555 at p. 1562, a test described by Upjohn J. as "artificial and difficult"; *Re Ransome's Will Trusts, Moberly* v. *Ransome* [1957] Ch. 348, at p. 361; [1957] 1 All E. R. 690 at p. 696.

[3] *Longden* v. *Simson* (1806), 12 Ves. 295; *Griffiths* v. *Vere* (1803), Tudor's *Leading Cases*, 618. See also *Re Ransome's Will Trusts, Moberly* v. *Ransome,* [1957] Ch. 348; [1957] 1 All E. R. 690.

[4] Trustee Act, 1925, s. 31; *infra*, p. 864.

[5] Law of Property Act, 1925, s. 165. *Re Maber, Ward* v. *Maber* [1928] Ch. 88.

[6] *Supra*, pp. 263–4.

[7] Perpetuities and Accumulations Act, 1964, s. 14.

[8] (1841), 4 Beav. 115; *Wharton* v. *Masterman*, [1895] A. C. 186. Morris and Leach, *op. cit.*, pp. 289–95; 4th Report of Law Reform Committee. Cmnd. 18 (1956) para. 14.

right, however, will not avail existing beneficiaries if it is possible that further beneficiaries may come into existence, and before 1964 the possibility that a woman over fifty-five years of age might have children sufficed to exclude the rule in *Saunders* v. *Vautier*.[1]

Exceptions to Act.

Exceptions. There are certain exceptions to the Act. If a settlor directs income to be accumulated for any of the following purposes, the direction will be valid although it may exceed the statutory periods:

Provisions for payment of debts.

(*a*) **Accumulations for payment of debts.** Provisions for the payment of the debts, whether of the settlor or of any other person, need not be confined within one of the six periods.[2]

Portion provisions.

(*b*) **Accumulation for raising portions.** Provisions for raising portions for any children or remoter issue of the settlor, or for any children or remoter issue of a person taking an interest under the settlement, or of a person to whom any interest is limited,[3] are excepted from the Act.[4]

The reason appears to be that unless such accumulations were permissible, it would be necessary for large owners to sell part of the estates in order to provide fortunes for their younger children; but at the same time it must be recognized that this particular exception admits of a latitude that may be productive, in a great degree, of all the inconveniences that were felt or apprehended under the rules of the common law, because, by a will artfully prepared, every purpose aimed at by Mr. Thellusson may be accomplished.[5]

But on the whole the courts have construed this enactment (which repeats the corresponding section of the Thellusson Act) in

Meaning of "portion."

such a way as to render a flagrant evasion of the spirit of the statute impossible. Thus, an accumulation for the purpose of creating a fund out of which it would be possible to pay portions is not within the exception.[6] Again, an accumulation of the whole of a testator's property with a view to swelling a portions fund has been held void.[7]

As Lord CRANWORTH said, in *Edwards* v. *Tuck*,[8]

"a direction to accumulate all the person's property to be handed "over to some child or children when they attain 21 can never be "said to be a direction for raising portions for the child or children: "it is not raising a portion at all, it is giving everything. 'Portion'

---

[1] *Re Deloitte, Griffiths* v. *Deloitte* [1926] Ch. 56.
[2] Law of Property Act, 1925, s. 164 (2) (i).
[3] *I.e.*, the interest need not be carved out of the precise property the income of which is to be accumulated.
[4] Law of Property Act, 1925, s. 164 (2) (ii).
[5] Fearne, *Contingent Remainder*, (10th Edn.), p. 541, note by Preston.
[6] *Re Bourne's Settlement Trusts, Bourne* v. *Mackay*, [1946] 1 All E. R. 411.
[7] *Wildes* v. *Davies* (1853), 1 Sm. & G. 475.
[8] (1853), 3 De G.M. & G. 40.

"ordinarily means a part or share, and though I do not know that
"a gift of the whole might not in some circumstances come under the
"term of a gift of a portion, yet I do not think it comes within the
"meaning of a portion in this clause of the Act, which points to the
"arising of something out of something else for the benefit of some
"children or class of children. . . . If every direction for accumula-
"tion for a child was a portion, the intention of the legislature, which
"was to prevent accumulations, such accumulations being most
"frequently directed for the benefit of children, would be entirely
defeated."

(c) **Accumulation of timber.** The Act does not apply to
any provision respecting the accumulation of the produce
of timber or wood.[1]

Timber accumulation.

The probable explanation of this exception is that timber is not
usually regarded as annual income, but merely as a resource for
some particular occasion, so that a direction concerning its accumulation, provided that it conforms to the rule against perpetuities,[2] does not in effect withdraw income from the owner of the
estate.[3]

---

[1] Law of Property Act, 1925, s. 164 (1) (iii).
[2] *Ferrand* v. *Wilson* (1845), 4 Hare, 344.
[3] Fearne, *Contingent Remainders*, p. 537, Butler's note.

CHAPTER VI.

DETERMINABLE INTERESTS.

Definition of determinable interest.

A DETERMINABLE interest is one that may come to an end before the completion of the maximum period designated by the grantor. For instance, the first clause in a deed of strict settlement, made by a man in view of his approaching marriage, provides that the settlor shall hold the land in trust for himself in fee simple *until the solemnization of the intended marriage*.[1] In such a case the maximum interest taken by the settlor is a fee simple, but it is a modified, not an absolute fee, since it will not run its full course if the terminating event—the marriage—supervenes.

" A *direct* limitation marks the duration of estate by the life of a
" person, by the continuance of heirs, by a space of precise and
" measured time ; making the death of the person in the first
" example, the continuance of heirs in the second example, and the
" length of the given space in the third example, the boundary of
" the estate or the period of duration.
   "A *collateral* [*i.e.* determinable] limitation, at the same time that
" it gives an interest which may have continuance for one of the
" times in a direct limitation, may, on some event which it describes,
" put an end to the right of enjoyment *during the continuance of that
" time*."[2]

Terminology.

Much confusion of terminology is apparent among the writers on this subject. Thus Preston, in the above quotation, speaks of *collateral* limitations ; Littleton describes the terminating event as a *condition in law*, while most of the other early writers adopt the expression *conditional limitations*. The words *collateral* and *conditional*, however, besides being obscure, are used in many different senses, and the modern practice is to describe this particular species of modified interest as a determinable interest, and the limitation by which it is created as a determinable limitation.[3]

Dwindling importance of determinable interests.

The older writers deal fully with determinable fees simple, and the classic example is that given by Blackstone, who states that the effect of a grant to A. and his heirs, *tenants of the manor of*

---

[1] See the precedent of a Trust Instrument, *infra*, p. 707.
[2] Preston on Estates, vol. i. p. 42, cited Challis, *Law of Real Property* (3rd Edn.), pp. 252–3.
[3] Challis, pp. 253–4.

Dale, is to give A. and his heirs a fee simple which will be defeated as soon as they cease to be tenants of that manor.

In such a case there resides in the grantor and his heirs what is called a *possibility of reverter,*[1] since there is a possibility that the terminating event will occur and so cause the estate to revert.[2]

Another example of a determinable fee is afforded by *In re Leach,*[3] where freeholds were devised

> upon trust to pay the rents to Robert until he should assign, charge or otherwise dispose of the same, or become bankrupt.

It was held that Robert took an equitable fee simple which would determine if one of the specified events occurred in his lifetime, but which would become absolute if he died without their having occurred.

Determinable fees, however, disappeared from practical conveyancing (and gave way to shifting future estates operating under the Statute of Uses) when it was once decided that the fee simple in the case of a determinable limitation could not be made to pass to a stranger on the occurrence of the terminating event. The common law has never allowed a fee to be limited after a fee simple. As was said by Lord CAIRNS in the *Buckhurst Peerage Case*[4]:

> " There is no instance in the books that we are aware of in which
> " a fee simple or a fee tail qualified in the way that I have mentioned,
> " as by the addition of the words ' lords of the manor of Dale,' is
> " followed by a remainder to other persons upon the first takers
> " ceasing to be lords of the manor."

Thus at the present day, if it is desired to make a fee simple pass from the grantee to some other person when a given event does or does not happen, the limitation will take the form of the grant of an equitable future interest.

The uncertain duration of a determinable fee does not impede its effective disposition, for the instrument by which it is limited constitutes a settlement for the purposes of the Settled Land Act, 1925.[5] The person entitled to possession is a tenant for life within the meaning of the same Act, and as such he may convey the land by way of sale, mortgage or lease under his statutory powers.[6] *(margin: Determinable fee is settled land.)*

The matter aroused considerable controversy, but, in one case it was decided that the possibility of reverter arising on the grant of a determinable fee simple was subject to the rule against perpetuities.[7] This view has now been adopted by the *(margin: Possibility of reverter subject to rule against perpetuities.)*

---

[1] Blackstone, vol. ii. p. 109.
[2] Co. Litt. 18a.
[3] [1912] 2 Ch. 422.
[4] (1876), 2 App. Cas 1, at p. 23.
[5] S. 1. (i), (ii) (c); *infra.,* p. 700.
[6] *Supra,* p. 131 *et seq.*
[7] *Hopper* v. *Liverpool Corporation* (1944), 88 Sol. Jo. 213 (limitation of a house in fee simple so long as it shall be used as a news room and coffee room). On the subject generally, see Morris and Leach, *op. cit.,* pp. 209–18.

Perpetuities and Accumulations Act, 1964.[1] Thus, if the terminating event in fact occurs within the perpetuity period (*i.e.* twenty-one years, unless the instrument of creation refers to lives in being or specifies a fixed term of years not exceeding eighty), the reverter will take effect by virtue of the "wait and see" provisions of the Act. Otherwise, it will be void and the determinable fee will become absolute.[2]

Resulting trust also subject to the rule.

An interest analogous to a possibility of reverter arises where a testator gives personalty to trustees upon trust to pay the income to a corporation or other body until some event occurs that may not occur within the perpetuity period. In such a case, the occurrence of the event raises a resulting trust in favour of the person entitled to the undisposed residue of the testator's estate. Formerly, a resulting trust of this nature was exempt from the rule against perpetuities,[3] but it has been subjected to the rule by the Act of 1964.[4]

Determinable life interests.

There may be a limitation of a determinable *life* interest.

"If a man grant an estate to a woman *dum sola fuerit*, or *durante*
"*viduitate* or *quamdiu se bene gesserit*, or to a man and woman during
"the coverture, or so long as such a grantee dwell in such a house, . . .
"or for any like uncertain time, which time as Bracton says is
"*tempus indeterminatum*, in all these cases if it be of lands or tene-
"ments, the lessee hath in judgment of law an estate for life deter-
"minable."[5]

The *protective trust*[6] is a common example of a determinable life interest.

In such cases the grantee takes an interest that may endure for life, or may determine sooner by the occurrence of the terminating event. It differs from a determinable fee in that it may be followed by a gift over to a third party which may validly take effect when the event occurs.[7]

A tenant for life whose estate is liable to cease on some event during that life has the powers of an ordinary tenant for life as provided by the Settled Land Act.[8]

Term of years.

Lastly, a *term of years* may be made determinable upon some event liable to occur before the period of the term has expired, as for instance where there is a lease for 50 years if A. shall so long live, or a lease for 20 years until B. marries. Such leases are now converted into leases for 90 years.[9]

---

[1] S.12 (1) (a).
[2] Cmnd. 18 p. 20 (1956).
[3] *Re Randall, Randell* v. *Dixon* (1888), 38 Ch. D. 213; *Re Blunt's Trusts, Wigan* v. *Clinch*, [1904] 2 Ch. 767; *Re Chardon, Johnston* v. *Davies*, [1928] Ch. 464; *Re Chambers' Will Trusts*, [1950] Ch. 267.
[4] S.12 (1) (b).
[5] Co. Litt. 42*a*.
[6] *Supra*, p. 148.   [7] Blackstone, vol. ii. p. 155.
[8] Settled Land Act, 1925, s. 20 (1) (vi).   [9] *Infra*, p. 338.

CHAPTER VII.

INTERESTS UPON CONDITION.

SUMMARY.

SECTION I. GENERAL NATURE AND EFFECT.

Conditions subsequent. An interest upon condition sub- Definition.
sequent arises where a qualification is annexed to a conveyance,
whereby it is provided that, in case a particular event does or
does not happen, or in case the grantor or the grantee does or
omits to do a particular act, the interest shall be defeated.[1]
Examples of such interests taken from the Reports are :

Grant to trustees in fee simple on condition that, if the land granted
shall ever be used for other than hospital purposes, it shall revert
to the heirs of the grantor ; [2]
conveyance in fee simple to the council of a school on condition that
the council shall publish annually a statement of payments and
receipts ; [3]
devise of land to J. " on condition that he never sells out of the
family " ; [4]
grant of a life interest to A. provided that he makes the mansion-
house his principal place of residence ; [5]

---

[1] Litt. s. 325 ; Cruise, Digest, Tit. xiii. c. 1.
[2] *Re Hollis' Hospital*, [1899] 2 Ch. 540.
[3] *Re Da Costa*, [1912] 1 Ch. 337.
[4] *Re Macleay* (1875), L. R. 20 Eq. 186.
[5] *Wynne* v. *Fletcher* (1857), 24 Beav. 430.

285

devise to A. for life on condition that he assumes the name and arms of the testator within 12 months.[1]

Right of entry for condition broken.

In all cases of this type there vests in the grantor, his heirs and assignees a right of re-entry, the exercise of which determines the estate of the grantee. On principle, therefore, a fee simple subject to a condition subsequent should be classified as an equitable interest, not as a legal estate, for since it may be defeated by a re-entry before its full course is run it can scarcely be described as "absolute." Nevertheless, for reasons already explained,[2] it has been given the status of a legal estate by the Law of Property Act (Amendment) Act, 1926,[3] in words that are wide enough to include any right of re-entry. They state that

> a fee simple subject to a legal or equitable right of entry or re-entry is for the purposes of the Law of Property Act, 1925, a fee simple absolute.

Distinction between limitations on condition and determinable limitations.

Distinction between condition and limitation.

There is a fundamental and somewhat subtle distinction between limitations upon condition and determinable limitations. Some writers contend that the distinction is a mere matter of words. On this basis the effect of such expressions as *until, so long as, whilst,* is to create a determinable interest; while such phrases as *on condition, provided that, if, but if it happen,*[4] will raise an interest upon condition.

But the distinction goes deeper than this. We must differentiate between a limitation properly so called, and a condition.

Meaning of "limitation."

A limitation is a form of words which creates an estate and denotes its extent by designating the event upon which it is to commence and the time for which it is to endure.[5] It marks the utmost time for which the estate can continue. It appears in two forms. A direct limitation marks the time by denoting the size of the estate in familiar terms, *e.g.* by using such expressions as " for life " or " in fee simple " ; a determinable limitation gives an interest for one of the times possible in a direct limitation, but also denotes some event that may determine the estate during the continuance of that time. In the simple example of a grant to A. and his heirs, tenants of the Manor of Dale, the terminating event is incorporated in, and forms an essential part of, the whole limitation, and if the estate expires because the tenancy of

---

[1] *In re Evans' Contract,* [1920] 2 Ch. 469.
[2] *Supra,* p. 113.
[3] Schedule, amending Law of Property Act, 1925, s. 7 (1).
[4] See Sanders on Uses, vol. i. p. 156 ; Shep. Touchstone, 122 ; Bac. Abr. " Condition " (A) ; Challis, *Law of Real Property* (3rd Edn.), p. 283.
[5] Shep. Touchstone, 117 ; Blackstone, vol. ii. p. 155. Preston on Estates, vol. i, pp. 40 *et seq.*

Dale is no longer in A.'s family, it is none the less considered to have lasted for the period originally fixed by the limitation. So in general the province of a limitation is to fix the period for the commencement and the duration of an estate, and to mark its determinable qualities.[1]

A condition, on the other hand, specifies some event which, if it takes place during the time for which an estate has already been limited to continue, will defeat that estate.

Meaning of
"condition."

" And here is condition because there is not a new estate limited " over, but the estate to which it is annexed is destroyed." [2]

In short, if the terminating event is an integral and necessary part of the formula from which the size of the interest is to be ascertained, the result is the creation of a determinable interest ; but if the terminating event is external to the limitation, if it is a divided clause from the grant, the interest granted is an interest upon condition.[3]

Outwardly a condition resembles a determinable limitation, for the difference between a grant

> to a woman for life, but if she remarries then her life interest shall cease,

and a grant

> to a woman during widowhood

is not apparent at first sight. The natural inference is that the legal effect must be the same in each case. Nevertheless, certain practical distinctions between the two limitations existed at common law and to a diminished degree still exist.[4] The present position appears to be as follows.

(1) A determinable interest comes to an end automatically upon the occurrence of the terminating event, as for example upon the remarriage of a woman to whom an estate has been granted during her widowhood. This is inevitable, for according to the limitation itself, *i.e.* according to the words fixing the space of time for which the widow's right of enjoyment is to continue, her interest ceases with her remarriage and nothing remains to be done to defeat her right. There can, indeed, be no question of defeating what has already come to an end.[5]

Automatic termination of determinable interest.

---

[1] Fearne, p. 11, Butler's note.

[2] *Rudhall's Case,* (1596), *Savile* 76, cited *Re Hollis' Hospital,* [1899] 2 Ch. 540, 549.

[3] Fearne, *Contingent Remainders,* p. 11, note (*h*) ; vol. ii. s. 36 (Smith, An Original View of Executory Interests); Challis, *Law of Real Property* (3rd Edn.), p. 260.

[4] "Although in some respects a condition and a limitation may have the same effect, yet in English law there is a great distinction between them"; *Re Moore, Trafford* v. *Machonochie* (1888), 39 Ch. 8. 116, at p. 129, *per* COTTON, L. J.

[5] Preston on Estates, p. 47 ; Challis, *Law of Real Property* (3rd Edn.), p. 219 ; *Re Evans' Contract,* [1920] 2 Ch. 469, 472.

No automatic termination of interest upon condition.

The effect of a condition operating by way of re-entry, on the other hand, is to defeat an interest *before* it has reached the end of the period for which it has been limited. The interest becomes voidable upon the breach of the condition. It does not become void unless and until the grantor, his heir or assignee re-enters upon the land.[1]

Applicability of the rule against perpetuities. Conditions subsequent.

(2) The rule against perpetuities applies both to conditions subsequent and to a possibility of reverter arising on the grant of a determinable fee.

The position as regards common law conditions was established long before the rule came into existence, and the old authorities never doubted that a right of entry was enforceable at any distance of time by the grantor or his heirs.[2] But, after several dicta in favour of subjecting conditions to the rule,[3] the point was finally decided to that effect [4] and was later confirmed by the Law of Property Act, 1925.[5]

Possibilities of reverter.

As we have already seen, a possibility of reverter appertaining to a determinable fee simple has been subjected to the rule by the Perpetuities and Accumulations Act, 1964.[6]

Assignability

(a) Right of entry for condition broken.

(3) At common law, a right of entry affecting a fee simple was neither devisable nor alienable *inter vivos*, and availed only the grantor and his heirs.[7] This, however, is no longer the position. The Wills Act, 1837 allows a testator to devise "all rights for condition broken and other rights of entry";[8] and the Law of Property Act, 1925, deals with their assignment *inter vivos* by providing that:

All rights and interests in land may be disposed of, including—

a right of entry into or upon land whether immediate or future, and whether vested or contingent.[9]

(b) Possibility of reverter.

Whether a possibility of reverter is on the same footing in both these respects is not so clear. It has, indeed, been held that it may be disposed of by a testator since it is covered by the words of the Wills Act cited above.[10] But its assignment *inter vivos*

---

[1] Co. Litt. 218a. At common law, the seisin transferred by livery cannot be divested without its actual resumption by re-entry, Co. Litt. 214b.

[2] Challis, *op. cit.*, pp. 187 *et seq.*

[3] *Re Macleay* (1875), L. R. 20 Eq. 186 ; *London & South Western Rly. Co.* v. *Gomm* (1882), 20 Ch. D. 562, 582 ; *Dunn* v. *Flood* (1883), 25 Ch. D. 629.

[4] *Re Hollis' Hospital Trustees and Hagues' Contract,* [1899] 2 Ch. 540; *in re Da Costa,* [1912] 1 Ch. 337. A contrary view was expressed by PALLES, C.B., in *A.-G.* v. *Cummins,* [1906] 1 I. R. 406, and his view has prevailed in Northern Ireland, *Walsh* v. *Wightman,* [1927] N. I. 1.

[5] S. 4 (3).

[6] S. 12 (1) (c); *supra*, p. 275.

[7] Fearne, *Contingent Remainders*, Butler's note, p. 386 (7th Edn.).

[8] S. 3.

[9] Law of Property Act, 1925, s. 4 (2); replacing the Law of Property Act, 1845, s. 6.

[10] *Pemberton* v. *Barnes,* [1899] 1 Ch. 544; where it was held that the possibility of reverter arising upon the grant of a determinable fee in copyholds was within the Act.

presents some difficulty. In the view of the common law, what was left in the grantor of a determinable interest was not an estate but a possibility that he might acquire an estate at a future time. Such a *bare possibility*, as it was called, was not assignable at common law,[1] but it seems a reasonable assumption that it now falls within the wide language quoted above from the Law of Property Act, 1925.

(4) As will be seen in the next section, a condition attached to any limitation of property may prove to be void for a variety of reasons. A condition subsequent that is thus invalidated is totally cancelled, and the limitation takes effect as if it had not been imposed;[2] but a determinable interest fails altogether if the possibility of reverter is invalidated, for to treat it as absolute would be to alter its quantum as fixed by the limitation.[3]

Void conditions.

(5) At common law, a remainder might be limited to take effect after a determinable life estate, but not after a life estate that was defeasible by a condition subsequent. If, for instance, there were a feoffment

Determinable interest, but not interest upon condition, might be followed by remainder.

to A. during widowhood and then to B. for life

the remainder to B. was valid, since by force of the limitation itself it took effect upon the natural determination of the particular estate. But had the limitation been

to A., a widow, for life on condition that if she remarried the land should remain to B. for life,

B.'s remainder would have come into conflict with three rules of ancient origin: a remainder was not allowed to cut short a particular estate;[4] none but the grantor and his heirs could exercise a right of re-entry; and in any event, the effect of re-entry was to defeat all the estates that depended upon the original livery of seisin.[5]

The matter has long been of only historical interest, for a settlor, minded to impose such a condition upon a widow's interest, could at an early date frame his limitation as a shifting use, and can now effect the same result by way of a future trust.

---

[1] As to the three different meanings of the word *possibility*, see Challis, *Law of Real Property* 3rd Edn., p. 76, note.

[2] *Re Wilkinson, Page* v. *Public Trustee,* [1926] Ch. 842, 846; *Re Croxon, Croxon* v. *Ferrers,* [1904] 1 Ch. 252. If the illegal condition is *precedent*, the gift fails entirely.

[3] *Re Moore, Trafford* v. *Maconochie* (1888), 39 Ch. D. 116. If, however, a possibility of reverter or a condition subsequent is void under the rule against perpetuities, the interest of the grantee becomes absolute; Perpetuities and Accumulations Act, 1964, s. 12.

[4] *Supra,* p. 217.

[5] Fearne, *op. cit.,* pp. 261–2, p. 386, note; Preston, *op. cit.,* pp. 50 *et seq.*

SECTION II. VOID CONDITIONS.

There are four types of conditions subsequent that are void when annexed to the grant of an estate or interest :—

(1) CONDITIONS REPUGNANT TO THE INTEREST GRANTED.[1]

Meaning of repugnancy.

A condition that is repugnant to the interest to which it is annexed is absolutely void.[2] For instance, a condition attached to the grant of a fee simple that the grantee shall always let the land at a definite rent, or cultivate it in a certain manner or be deprived of all power of sale, is void on the ground of its incompatibility with that complete freedom of enjoyment, disposition and management that the law attributes to the ownership of such an estate.[3] It is not permissible to grant an interest and then to provide that the incidents attached to it by law shall be excluded. The most important examples of repugnant conditions that arise in practice are those designed to prohibit alienation or to exclude the operation of the bankruptcy laws.

Total restraints void.

Conditions against alienation. In accordance with the cardinal principle that the power of alienation is necessarily and inseparably incidental to ownership, it has been held in a long line of decisions that if an *absolute* interest is given to a donee—whether it be a fee simple, a fee tail, a life interest or any other interest, and whether it be in possession or *in futuro*—any restriction which *substantially* takes that power away is void as being repugnant to the very conception of ownership. Therefore, a condition that the donee

> shall not alienate at all,[4] or
>
> shall not alienate during a particular time, such as the life of a certain person,[5] or during his own life,[6] or
>
> shall alienate only to one particular person,[7] or to a small and diminishing class of persons, such as his brothers,[8] or
>
> shall not adopt some particular mode of assurance such as a mortgage,[9] or

---

[1] For a trenchant criticism of this doctrine, see 59 *L. Q. R.* 343.

[2] *Re Dugdale, Dugdale* v. *Dugdale* (1888), 38 Ch. D. 176 ; *Bradley* v. *Peixoto* (1797), 3 Ves. 324.

[3] Jarman on Wills (7th Edn.), p. 1462.

[4] Litt. s. 360 ; Co. Litt. 206b, 223a ; *Re Dugdale, Dugdale* v. *Dugdale,* (1888), 38 Ch. D. 176.

[5] *Re Rosher* (1884), 26 Ch. D. 801.

[6] *Corbett* v. *Corbett* (1888), 14 P. D. 7.

[7] *Muschamp* v. *Bluet* (1617), Bridg. J. 132 ; *In re Cockerill,* [1929] 2 Ch. 131.

[8] *In re Brown, District Bank Ltd.* v. *Brown,* [1954] Ch. 39.

[9] *Ware* v. *Cann* (1830), 10 B. & C. 433.

shall not bar an entail,[1]
is void.

A restraint that is partial, however, and which therefore does
not substantially deprive the owner in fee of his power of alienation, is valid. Thus it has been held that a condition is valid
which restrains the owner from alienating to a specified person,[2]
or to anyone except a particular class of persons, provided, however, that the class is not too restricted.[3] But when does a
restraint cease to be total ? Great minds may differ on the
question. In the case of *In re Macleay*,[4] where there was a
devise

" to my brother J. on the condition that he never sells out of the
" family,"

the condition was held by JESSEL, M.R., to be valid, though
some doubt has been thrown on the correctness of this decision
by a later case.[5]

The difficulty, indeed, is to ascertain the principle upon which
such restraints have been permitted, for they would seem to be
just as repugnant to ownership as a total restraint. Perhaps the
truth is that the courts, losing sight of the fundamental doctrine
of repugnancy, have, unintentionally and unwittingly, allowed the
necessities of public policy to engraft certain exceptions on the
main rule.[6]

**Conditions excluding the operation of the bankruptcy
laws.** Just as the donee of property cannot be deprived of
the normal rights of ownership, so also is it impossible to render
his interest immune from involuntary alienation for insolvency or
bankruptcy.[7] It is not permissible, for instance, to annex to the
grant of a life interest a condition that it shall not be liable to
seizure for debt. Thus in *Graves* v. *Dolphin* [8] :

a testator directed his trustees to pay £500 a year to his son for
life, and declared that it should not on any account be subject
or liable to the debts, engagements, charges or incumbrances
of his son, but that it should always be payable to him and
to no other person. The son became bankrupt, and it was held
that the annuity became the property of his creditors.

But, as we have seen in discussing the protective trust,[9]
there is no objection to the grant by one person to another of

Marginal notes:
Partial restraints valid.
Conditions excluding insolvency laws void.
Contrast determinable limitation.

---

[1] *Sir Anthony Mildmay's Case* (1584), 6 Rep. 40a ; *Mary Portington's Case*
(1613), 10 Rep. 35a ; *Dawkins* v. *Lord Penrhyn* (1878), 4 App. Cas. 51.
[2] Co. Litt. 223a.
[3] *Doe d. Gill* v. *Pearson* (1805), 6 East 173
[4] (1875), L. R. 20 Eq. 186.
[5] *Re Rosher* (1884), 26 Ch. D. 801. But the restriction was placed only
on a sale, and it was to endure only for the life of J.
[6] *Ibid*, at p. 813.
[7] *Re Machu* (1882), 21 Ch. D. 838 ; *Re Dugdale* (1888), 38 Ch. D. 176.
[8] (1826), 1 Sim. 66.
[9] *Supra*, p. 149.

an interest which is to determine upon the bankruptcy of the grantee. Lord ELDON, adverting to the distinction between a determinable limitation and a limitation upon condition, made this clear over a hundred years ago :—

> " A disposition to a man until he becomes bankrupt and after
> " his bankruptcy over, is quite different from an attempt to give
> " to him for his life with a proviso that he shall not sell or aliene
> " it. *If that condition is so expressed as to amount to a limitation*
> " reducing the interest short of a life interest, neither the man nor
> " his assignees can have it beyond the period limited." [1]

The distinction at first sight seems fine and far from obvious, but in fact it is fundamental. In one case the only interest passing under the limitation is an interest *until* the donee becomes bankrupt ; in the other, an absolute interest is first limited for life, and then an attempt is made to remove one of the incidents, namely liability for debts, to which all absolute interests are subject.

Thus, if husband and wife both bring property into a marriage settlement, the wife's property may be limited to the husband until he becomes bankrupt and then over to the trustees. But the husband cannot settle his own property upon himself in the same manner, for this would be a fraud on the bankruptcy laws.[2] On the other hand, it has long been recognized that a man may settle his own property upon himself until he attempts to assign, charge or encumber it, or until he does something that makes it liable to be taken in execution by a particular creditor, and if so over to another person. The limitation over, once it has taken effect, is not avoided by the subsequent bankruptcy of the settlor.[3]

(2) CONDITIONS IN RESTRAINT OF MARRIAGE.

Personalty.

The law as to the validity of conditions in restraint of marriage differs according as the gift is of real or of personal property.

The rules governing personalty have come to us from the Roman Law through the ecclesiastical courts and the Court of Chancery. It is marked by numerous and fine distinctions, and, in the words of a learned judge, is " proverbially difficult " [4] ; but it is sufficient for our purposes to say that a condition in total restraint of marriage is void, while one in partial restraint is good, provided that it is reasonable from the point of view of public policy.[5]

For instance, a condition that a person shall not marry a

---

[1] *Brandon* v. *Robinson* (1811), 18 Ves. 429, at pp. 432, 433–4. See the Trustee Act, 1925, s. 33, as to these protected life interests.
[2] *Mackintosh* v. *Pogose*, [1895] 1 Ch. 505, 511 ; *Re Brewer's Settlement*, [1896] 2 Ch. 503.
[3] *Brooke* v. *Pearson* (1859), 27 Beav. 181. *In re Detmold* (1889), 40 Ch. D. 585; *supra*, p. 149.
[4] YOUNGER, J. : *Re Hewett*, [1918] 1 Ch. 458, 463.
[5] *In re Lanyon* [1927] 2 Ch. 264.

named person,[1] a Papist,[2] a Scotchman,[3] or a domestic servant[4] is valid, but a condition that he shall not marry at all is void. But a partial restraint is not upheld unless there is a bequest over to another person in default of compliance with the condition. In the absence of such a bequest, the condition is treated as in-effectual on the ground that it has merely been imposed *in terrorem, i.e.* as an idle threat calculated to secure compliance by the donee.[5] A condition, however, is valid which restrains a *second* marriage, either of a man or of a woman.[6]

The rules relating to real estate, on the other hand, are both few and simple. While a condition in general restraint of marriage if attached to a gift of personalty is void *per se*, in the case of realty it is not void *per se*, but only if there is an intention to promote celibacy. Thus in *Jones* v. *Jones* [7]

> a man after devising land to three women during their lifetime added :

> " provided the said Mary . . . shall remain in her present
> " state of single woman, otherwise . . . if she shall bind herself
> " in wedlock she is liable to lose her share of the said property
> " immediately and her share to be possessed and enjoyed by the
> " other mentioned parties share and share alike."

It was held that the condition was valid since its object was not to prevent her from marrying but to provide for her whilst unmarried.

The *in terrorem* doctrine does not apply to realty,[8] and it may be said that a condition in partial restraint of marriage attached to real estate is always good,[9] and that one in total restraint *may* be good. However, a general restraint cannot be imposed upon a tenant in tail, since it is incompatible with and repugnant to an interest that is expressly made descendible to the heirs born of the marriage of the donee.[10]

(3) CONDITIONS CONTRARY TO PUBLIC POLICY.

Any condition that has a tendency to conflict with the general interest of the community, even though it will not necessarily do so, is void.[7] Thus in *Egerton* v. *Brownlow* :[11]

Realty.

Meaning of public policy.

---

[1] *Re Bathe*, [1925] Ch. 377.
[2] *Duggan* v. *Kelly* (1848), 10 Ir. Eq. Rep. 473.
[3] *Perrin* v. *Lyon* (1807), 9 East 170.
[4] *Jenner* v. *Turner* (1880), 16 Ch. D. 188. *Quaere*, however, whether this example and those given in the preceding two notes would not nowadays be treated as void for uncertainty ; see *infra*, pp. 294-5.
[5] *Re Whiting's Settlement*, [1905] 1 Ch. 96 ; *Re Hewett*, [1918] 1 Ch. 458; *Leong* v. *Chye*, [1955] A.C. 648 ; [1955] 2 All E. R. 903.
[6] *Allen* v. *Jackson* (1876), 1 Ch. D. 399.   [8] (1876), 1 Q. B. D. 279.
[7] *Jenner* v. *Turner* (1880), 16 Ch. D. 188, at p. 196, *per* BACON, V.-C.
[8] *Re Bathe*, [1925] Ch. 377.
[9] *Earl of Arundel's Case* (1575), 3 Dyer, 342b.
[10] *Egerton* v. *Brownlow* (1853), 4 H. L. Cas. 1 ; *Re Wallace*, [1920] 2 Ch. 274.
[11] (1853), 4 H. L. Cas.

Lands were devised to Lord Alford for 99 years if he should so long live, and then to the heirs male of his body, with a proviso that if Lord Alford should not in his lifetime acquire the dignity of Marquis or Duke of Bridgewater, the estates should pass from his heirs male immediately on his decease.

After great conflict of opinion the condition was held invalid by the House of Lords as being contrary to public policy. But there were special considerations applicable to that case. For instance, since the rank to be obtained was among the highest in the peerage, and one that conferred legislative rights and imposed legislative duties upon the holder, there was a danger that efforts to obtain the qualifying position would be pushed so far as to come into conflict with the general interests of the community. These special considerations were recognized in a later case, where a limitation that property should go to a certain person provided that he acquired the title of baronet was held to be capable of taking effect upon the fulfilment of the condition.[1]

" A baronetcy is a barren title involving on the part of its holder the
" performance of no duties to the State or the public, except those
" which are cast upon every good citizen. In this respect it differs
" most materially from a peerage, the subject of discussion in *Egerton*
" v. *Brownlow*. The public neither gains nor loses by the title being
" conferred. . . . In fact the possession of such a title by an individual
" is a matter of indifference, so far as the welfare of the State or of
" the public at large is concerned."

Again, a condition whose object is to restrain a man from doing his duty,[2] or to cause the separation of a husband and wife who are at present unseparated, is contrary to public policy and void [3]; but where in this latter case the parties are already separated, a limitation to a woman with a condition that the interest shall cease if she and her husband live together again, is valid as constituting a maintenance of the wife while she is unprovided for, unless there is evidence showing that the donor's object is to induce her not to return to her husband.[4]

(4) UNCERTAIN CONDITIONS.

Examples of uncertain conditions.

A condition subsequent, designed to defeat a vested estate, is void if it is uncertain either in expression or in operation. It

---

[1] *Re Wallace*, [1920] 2 Ch. 274. The condition here was precedent, but a condition, if contrary to public policy, is invalid whether precedent or subsequent. The *effect* of invalidity, however, is different ; *infra*, p. 297.

[2] *In re Sandbrook*, [1912] 2 Ch. 471 (condition held void which divested property if the donees " should live with or be or continue under the custody, guardianship or control of their father "). *In re Borwick*, [1933] Ch. 657 (condition held void which divested a gift if the infant donee during minority became a Roman Catholic, for this tended to influence the parent in the discharge of his duty of religious instruction).

[3] *Re Moore* (1888), 39 Ch. D. 116 ; distinguished, *Re Thompson*, [1939] 1 All E. R. 681. *In re Caborne, Hodge and Nabarro v. Smith* [1943] 1 Ch. 224 ; [1943] 2 All E. R. 7.

[4] See *Re Lovell*, [1920] 1 Ch. 122.

must be possible, not only to affirm with precision exactly what the words imposing the condition mean, but also to ascertain with certainty the circumstances that will cause a forfeiture.[1] In a well-known passage Lord CRANWORTH stated the position as follows :

" I consider that from the earliest times one of the cardinal rules
" on the subject has been this : that when a vested estate is to be
" defeated by a condition on a contingency that is to happen after-
" wards, that condition must be such that the court can see from
" the beginning, precisely and distinctly, upon the happening of what
" event it was that the preceding vested estate was to determine." [2]

Several cases have been concerned with conditions designed to secure the observance by a donee of a particular religion, as for example by requiring him " to be a member of " or " to conform to " [3] the Church of England, or not to marry any person " not of Jewish parentage and of the Jewish faith." [4] Such phrases are shrouded in uncertainty and are generally held to be ineffective. Of those, for instance, who profess membership of the Church of England, many are devout observers of its practice and doctrines, but the conduct of countless others affords little evidence of any religious conviction. Faith varies infinitely in degree, and, even if it were possible to do so, a donor does not normally specify the exact degree that will satisfy his anxiety.[5] Again, whether a person " conforms to " a particular religion defies any certain answer.[6] Does, for instance, conformity to the Church of England necessitate attendance at religious services ? If so, how regular must the attendance be ? On the other hand, a condition for the forfeiture of an interest if the donee should " become a convert to the Roman Catholic faith " has been upheld, for such a conversion requires the performance of certain definite acts.[7] The court can, therefore, say with certainty what has to be done and whether it has in fact been done.

Many other examples might be given of uncertain conditions. For instance, provisions that an interest should be forfeited if the donee " in any way associated, corresponded or visited with any of my present wife's nephews or nieces," [8] or " have social or

---

[1] *In re Sandbrook, Noel* v. *Sandbrook*, [1912] 2 Ch. 471, at p. 477, *per* PARKER, J.; *In re Murray, Martins Bank, Ltd.* v. *Dill*, [1955] Ch. 69, at pp. 77–8 ; [1954] 3 All E. R. 129, at pp. 132–3, *per* Lord EVERSHED, M.R. Different considerations apply in the case of a condition precedent ; *In re Allen, Faith* v. *Allen*, [1953] Ch. 810; [1953] 2 All E. R. 898; *Re Selby's Will Trusts, Donn* v. *Selby*, [1965] 3 All E. R. 386; [1966] 1 W. L. R. 43.
[2] *Clavering* v. *Ellison* (1859), 7 H.L. Cas. 707, 725.
[3] *Re Tegg, Public Trustee* v. *Bryant*, [1936] 2 All E. R. 878
[4] *Clayton* v. *Ramsden*, [1943] A.C. 320; [1943] 1 All E. R. 16; *Re Moss's Trusts, Moss* v. *Allen*, [1945] 1 All E. R. 207. *In re Tarnpolsk*, [1958] 3 All E. R. 479; [1958] 1 W. L. R. 1157; *In re Krawitz's Will Trusts*, [1959] 3 All E. R. 793; [1959] 1 W. L. R. 1192.
[5] *In re Donn, Donn* v. *Moses*, [1944] Ch. 8.
[6] *Re Tegg, supra.*
[7] *Re Evans, Hewitt* v. *Edwards*, [1940] Ch. 629.
[8] *Jeffreys* v. *Jeffreys* (1901) 84 L.T. 417.

other relationship with " a named person,[1] have been held void, since it is impossible to say with reasonable certainty which of the many connections included in the words " association " or " relationship " offend the prohibition.

Again, a condition that property shall be enjoyed by a bene-fisiary " only so long as she shall continue to reside in Canada " is too vague to be enforced, for there are many forms and degrees of residence and it is impossible to say precisely which of them fall under the ban.[2] But the law does not exact too high a standard of certainty. The condition need not be clear beyond a peradventure. So in one case a requirement of " permanent residence in England" was held to be sufficiently certain, since the word " permanent " postulates an intention to live in a place for life as opposed to living there temporarily or for a fixed period.[3]

Name and arms clauses.

In several cases decided between 1945 and 1960, courts of first instance, in disregard of what had been conveyancing practice for at least a century, showed a surprising tendency to stigmatize as void for uncertainty clauses in a will or settlement providing for the forfeiture of an interest given to X. upon his failure to assume the surname and arms of Y. It has been held more than once, for instance, that to decree forfeiture if X. "disuses" the surname Y. does not show with sufficient precision what degree of disuser he must avoid.

> "What percentage short of 100 per cent. of the disuser of the name
> "would amount to a disuser of it within the meaning of the clause."[4]

The Court of Appeal, however, has now overruled these decisions on the ground that they imposed an unreasonably rigorous test of certainty.[5]

> "It seems to me altogether fanciful to suggest that there is any real
> "ambiguity in a requirement that I should adopt and use a surname
> "in place of that which I already have: for the requirement does no
> "more nor less than postulate that I should thereafter use the new
> "surname, just as I at present use my existing name. Equally, as

---

[1] *Re Jones, Midland Bank Executor and Trustee Co. Ltd.* v. *Jones,* [1953] Ch. 125; [1953] 1 All E. R. 357.

[2] *Sifton* v. *Sifton,* [1938] A.C. 656; [1938] 3 All E. R. 425. See also *In re Brace, Gurton* v. *Clements,* [1954] 2 All E. R. 354, when a condition requiring the donee " to provide a home for " X. was held to be so vague as to be unintelligible.

[3] *Re Gape's Will Trusts, Verey* v. *Gape,* [1952] Ch. 743; [1952] 2 All E. R. 579. Compare *Bromley* v. *Tryon,* [1952] A.C. 265, when it was held that a condition for forfeiture if a beneficiary became entitled to specified settled land " or the bulk thereof" was not void for uncertainty, since " bulk " meant anything over half.

[4] *Re Bouverie, Bouverie* v. *Marshall,* [1952] Ch. 400, at p. 404, *per* VAISEY, J.

[5] *Re Neald, Carpenter* v. *Inigo Jones,* [1962] Ch. 643; [1962] 2 All E. R. 335 overruling *In re Fry, Reynolds* v. *Denne,* [1945] Ch. 348; [1945] 2 All E. R. 205; *In re Lewis's Will Trusts, Whitelaw* v. *Beaumont* (1951) 2 T. L. R. 1032; *In re Kersey, Alington* v. *Alington,* [1952] W. N. 541; 96 Sol. Jo. 851; *In re Bouverie, Bouverie* v. *Marshall,* [1952] Ch. 400; *In re Wood's Will Trusts, Wood* v. *Donnelly,* [1952] Ch. 406; The Court of Appeal also held that a name and arms clause is not contrary to public policy.

"it seems to me, there is no real ambiguity in a divesting provision
"expressed to take effect if I should at any time 'disuse' or 'dis-
"continue to use' the surname which I have adopted."[1]

Effect of void conditions. If realty is conveyed to a
person on a condition which is void, then, in the case of a condition precedent, the conveyance is void, and the interest does not
arise[2]; but in the case of a condition subsequent the condition
alone is void, and the donee takes an absolute interest in the
property free from the restrictive clause.[3]

---

[1] *Re Neald, supra,* at p. 667, *per* Lord EVERSHED. See also p. 679, *per*
UPJOHN, L. J., and p. 682, *per* DIPLOCK, L. J., as to disuser.

[2] A bequest of *personalty* subject to an illegal condition precedent is void
if the condition is *malum in se, i.e.* wrong in itself, but if the condition is only
malum prohibitum, i.e. indifferent in itself but contrary to a human law, the
bequest takes effect unfettered by the condition; *Re Elliott, Lloyds Bank,
Ltd.* v. *Burton on Trent Hospital Management Committee,* [1952] Ch. 217;
[1952] 1 All E. R. 145.

[3] Co. Litt. 206a; *Re Croxon,* [1904] 1 Ch. 252; *In re Turton,* [1926] Ch.
96 (impossible condition).

L*

CHAPTER VIII.

CONCURRENT INTERESTS.

SUMMARY

Distinction
between
several and
concurrent
ownership.

Introductory. Several and concurrent ownership now require to be distinguished. The owner of an interest in land may be entitled to possession either alone or in conjunction with other persons, and in both cases he may be entitled to take possession either now or at some time in the future.

If he is entitled in his own right without having any other person joined with him in point of interest, he is said to hold in severalty ; but where he and other persons have simultaneous interests in the land, they are said to hold concurrently, or in co-ownership, and to have concurrent interests. In other words, land may be the subject of several, that is, separate ownership, or of co-ownership. The former does not require explanation, but we are obliged to deal with the various forms of co-ownership which the law recognizes.

SECTION I. THE OLD LAW.

Such a fundamental change in the principles applicable to concurrent interests was effected by the legislation of 1925 that we need do little more than enumerate the various forms that such interests might take under the old law, and the methods by which they might be converted into several interests. At common law there are four possible forms of co-ownership, one of which, tenancy by entireties, is now defunct;[1] while another, coparcenary, seldom arises.[2] The two found in practice are joint tenancy and tenancy in common.

(A) JOINT TENANCY.

A joint tenancy arises whenever land is conveyed or devised to two or more persons without any words to show that they are to take distinct and separate shares, or, to use technical language, without words of severance.[3] If an estate is given, for instance, to

A. and B. in fee simple,

without the addition of any restrictive, exclusive or explanatory words, the law feels bound to give effect to the whole of the grant, and this it can do only by creating an equal estate in them both.[4] From the point of view of their interest in the land they are united in every respect. But if the grant contains words of severance showing an intention that A. and B. are to take separate and distinct interests, as for instance where there is a grant to

A. and B. equally,

the result is the creation not of a joint tenancy, but of a tenancy in common.

The two essential attributes of joint tenancy which must be kept in mind if the true inwardness of the legislation of 1925 is to be grasped are the absolute unity which exists between joint tenants, and the right of survivorship.

(1) There is, to use the language of Blackstone,[5] a thorough and intimate union between joint tenants. Together they form one person. This unity is fourfold, consisting of unity of title, time, interest and possession. All the titles are derived from the same grant and become vested at the same time;[6] all the interests are identical in size; and there is unity of possession, since each tenant *totum tenet et nihil tenet.* Each, holds the whole in the sense that in conjunction with his co-tenants he is entitled to present possession and enjoyment of the whole; yet he holds nothing in the sense that he is not entitled to the exclusive possession of any individual part of

Definition of joint tenancy.

Charac-teristics.

Unity between joint tenants.

---

[1] *Infra*, p. 310. [2] *Infra*, p. 309.
[3] Litt. s. 277; Blackstone, vol. ii. p. 179.
[4] *Ibid.*, p. 180. [5] *Ibid.*, p. 182.
[6] In the case of a grant to uses, the fact that the interests vested at different times did not prevent the creation of a joint tenancy, *e.g.* under a grant to X. and Y. to the use of all the sons of A. born within the lifetime of the settlor, sons born after the time of the grant became joint tenants with those alive at the time of its execution.

the whole.[1] Unity of possession is a feature of all forms of co-ownership.

For this reason one joint tenant cannot, as a general rule, maintain an action of trespass against the other or others, but can do so only if the act complained of amounts either to an actual ouster, or to a destruction of the subject matter of the tenancy.[2]

Right of survivorship.

(2) The other characteristic that distinguishes a joint tenancy is the right of survivorship, or *jus accrescendi*, by which, if one joint tenant dies without having obtained a separate share in his lifetime, his interest is extinguished and accrues to the surviving tenants whose interests are correspondingly enlarged.[3] For example:

A. and B. may be joint tenants in fee simple, but the result of the death of B. is that his interest totally disappears and A. becomes owner in severalty of the land.

There are cases, however, where the right of survivorship does not benefit both tenants equally, for if there is (say) a grant to

A. and B. during the life of A.

and A. dies first, there is nothing that can accrue to B.[4]

Cases where a tenancy in common is preferred to a joint tenancy.

Preference of equity for tenancy in common.

From early times the right of survivorship caused a divergence of views between common law and equity.   Common law favoured joint tenancies because they inevitably led to the vesting of the property in one person through the operation of the doctrine of survivorship, and thus facilitated the performance of those feudal dues that were incident to the tenure of land. But a tenancy in common never involved this right of survivorship, and equity, which was not over-careful of the rights of the lord, soon showed a marked inclination, in the interests of convenience and justice, to construe a joint tenancy as a tenancy in common.[5]

Equity aims at equality, a feature that is conspicuous for its absence if the survivor becomes the absolute owner of the land.

---

[1] By Littleton's time the expression *totum tenet et nihil tenet* had become *per my et per tout*, which in Blackstone's view (vol. ii, p. 182) meant that each tenant was seised "by the half or moiety and by all." *My*, however, did not mean half, but was an early form of the French word *mie*.
[2] Blackstone, vol. ii. p. 183 ; *Martyn* v. *Knowllys* (1799), 8 Term Rep. 145 ; *Murray* v. *Hall* (1849), 7 C. B. 441 ; *Stedman* v. *Smith* (1857), 8 E. & B. 1 ; *Wilkinson* v. *Haygarth* (1847), 12 Q. B. 837.
[3] Litt. s. 280. Co. Litt. 181*a*; Blackstone, vol. ii. p. 183.
[4] Co. Litt. 181*b*.
[5] Burton on Real Property, p. 63.

This preference of equity for a tenancy in common has been shown in three cases :—

(a) **Where money is advanced on mortgage by two or more persons.** Where two or more persons advance money, either in equal or in unequal shares, and take a mortgage of land from the borrower to themselves jointly, the rule *at law* is that they are joint tenants, so that the land and the right to the money belong absolutely to the survivor. The rule *in equity*, however, which prevails over the rule at law, is that they are tenants in common, and that the survivor is a trustee for the personal representatives of the deceased mortgagees.[1]

Joint loan on mortgage.

This equitable rule caused difficulty in those cases where trustees advanced trust money on mortgage. In practice a conveyance of land to trustees is always made to them as joint tenants, for the very nature of their office requires that the death of one shall not disturb the administration of the trust or deprive the survivor of power to execute conveyances and to give binding receipts for money. These advantages, however, will be lost if the trustees are to be regarded as tenants in common, for in that case each of them is entitled to a separate, though at present an unidentifiable, share of the land that passes on his death to his personal representatives. To avoid this inconvenience, it soon became the practice to insert a *joint account clause* in a mortgage to trustees. This declares that upon the death of one of the mortgagees the receipt of the survivor shall be a sufficient discharge for the money, and that the survivor shall be able to re-convey the land without the concurrence of the personal representatives of the deceased trustee.

Loans on mortgage by trustees.

Joint account clause.

The position has been made clearer by the Law of Property Act, 1925,[2] which (re-enacting the Conveyancing Act, 1881) provides that where there is a mortgage for the payment of money and either the sum advanced is expressly stated to be advanced by more persons than one on a joint account, or the land is *conveyed to them jointly and not in shares*, the money lent shall, *as between the mortgagees and the mortgagor*, be deemed to belong to the mortgagees on a joint account, and the survivor shall be able to give a complete discharge for the money. Trustees always advance money on a joint account, and the fact that they are trustees is never disclosed in the mortgage.[3]

---

[1] *Petty* v. *Styward* (1632), 1 Eq. Cas. Abr. 290 ; *Steeds* v. *Steeds* (1889), 22 Q. B. D. 537 ; White and Tudor, *Leading Cases in Equity*, vol. ii. pp. 882–5.
[2] Law of Property Act, 1925, s. 111.
[3] *Encyclopædia of Forms and Precedents* (3rd Edn.), vol. x, p. 170.

It will be noticed that the Act is not confined to loans of money made by trustees, but applies generally to all joint mortgages coming within the provisions of the section ; and in a case where there is no question of trustees, it is important to remember that the joint account rule just stated applies only as between the mortgagor and the mortgagees, and not even between them if a contrary intention is shown in the deeds. As between the mortgagees themselves evidence is admissible to show that, despite the presence of a joint account clause, it was intended that the money should belong to them as tenants in common.[1]

Joint purchase of land.

(b) **Where joint purchasers of land provide the purchase money in unequal shares.** The invariable rule *at law* is that when purchasers take a conveyance to themselves in fee simple, they become joint tenants, and upon the death of one of them the whole estate passes to the survivor. Equity adopts the same attitude and does not treat the purchasers as being tenants in common, unless it can be inferred that they did not intend to take jointly.[2]

Money contributed in unequal shares.

Thus, though this is not the only circumstance that will raise the inference, it is established that purchasers who contribute the money in unequal proportions are to be regarded as tenants in common of the land conveyed.[3]

Partnership land.

(c) **Where land is bought by partners.** In the leading case of *Lake* v. *Craddock*,[4] where five persons joined in buying some waterlogged land with a view to its improvement by drainage, the court laid down the general rule that persons who make a joint purchase for the purposes of a joint undertaking or partnership, either in trade or in any other dealing, are to be treated in equity as tenants in common. The right of survivorship is incompatible with a commercial undertaking—*jus accrescendi inter mercatores pro beneficio commercii locum non habet.*[5] Thus :

> If two partners take a grant or a lease of a farm and one dies, the survivor will be a trustee not only of the stock, but also of the land, for the personal representatives of the deceased partner.[6]

When once it is clear that property is partnership property, the rule in equity is that it is held by the partners as tenants

[1] *Re Jackson* (1887), 34 Ch. D. 732.
[2] *Lake* v. *Gibson* (1729), Eq. Cas. Ab. 294, *pl.* 3 ; *Lake* v. *Craddock* (1732), 3 P. W. 158 ; White and Tudor, *Leading Cases in Equity*, vol. ii. p. 881.
[3] *Robinson* v. *Preston* (1858), 4 K. & J. 505; *Lake* v. *Craddock, supra*; White and Tudor, *Leading Cases in Equity*, vol. ii. p. 882.
[4] *Supra.*
[5] Co. Litt. 182a.
[6] *Elliot* v. *Brown* (1791), 3 Swan. 489.

in common, and it has been enacted by the Partnership Act, 1890, that all property brought into the business, or subsequently bought for the purposes of the business, or bought with money belonging to the business, is *primâ facie* partnership property.

Despite these exceptional cases, the fundamental rule is that whenever land is granted or devised to two or more persons simply and without words of severance, the donees become joint tenants holding a single title, interest and possession, and when one dies his interest is extinguished and passes to the survivors.

Nature of
joint
tenancy
summarized.

Determination of Joint Tenancy.

Since "each joint tenant stands in all respects in exactly the same position as each of the others,"[1] it follows that anything which creates a distinction between them severs the tenancy and converts it into a tenancy in common. Stated in more detail, its determination may be effected by,

    (i) alienation by one joint tenant ;
    (ii) acquisition by one tenant of a greater interest than that held by his co-tenants ;
    (iii) partition ;
    (iv) sale ; and
    (v) mutual agreement.[2]

The first four of these methods require discussion.

(i) Although during the continuance of the tenancy one joint tenant holds nothing separately from his fellows, there is a general rule to the effect that *alienatio rei praefertur juri accrescendi* and in accordance with this doctrine it has long been the law that one joint tenant can alienate his share to a stranger. The effect of such alienation, whether by way of sale or mortgage, is to convert the joint tenancy into a tenancy in common, since the alienee and the remaining tenant or tenants hold by virtue of different titles and not under that one common title which is essential to the existence of a joint tenancy.

Alienation
by a joint
tenant.

    If A. and B. are joint tenants in fee and A. makes a grant in fee to X., the result is that B. and X. hold the lands as tenants in common, in equal undivided shares. If A., B. and C. are joint tenants in fee and A. makes a grant to X. in fee, X. is tenant in common with B. and

---

[1] Challis, *The Law of Real Property*, p. 367.
[2] *Williams* v. *Hensman* (1861), 1 John & H. 546, 557.

C., though as between themselves the latter continue to hold as joint tenants.[1]

Again, the effect of the bankruptcy of a joint tenant is to sever the tenancy and to pass his interest to his trustee in bankruptcy.[2]

Owing to the doctrine of survivorship, no severance results from a disposition by will—*jus accrescendi praefertur ultimae voluntati.*[3]

Acquisition of a larger interest by a joint tenant.

(ii) A joint tenancy is also severed if one of the joint tenants acquires an interest greater in quantum than that held by his co-tenants. This destruction of the unity of interest may result from the act of the parties or by operation of law. As an instance of the former :

> If A. and B. are joint tenants for life and A. purchases the fee simple in reversion, the jointure is severed; A. holding an undivided half in fee simple and B. an undivided half for life. When B. dies, the fee simple in the entirety of the land vests in A.[4]

Again, A. may release his interest to B. and so terminate the tenancy by vesting the whole ownership in B.[5]

A case in which a greater interest than that held by his fellows is cast upon a joint tenant by operation of law occurs where the reversion in fee descends to one of the joint tenants.[6]

If the joint tenants agree deliberately to put an end to the tenancy, the two methods open to them, in addition to a mutual agreement that henceforth they shall hold as tenants in common, are (iii) partition and (iv) sale.

Partition.

(iii) Partition is a method whereby the joint *possession* is disunited, and its effect is to make each former co-tenant separate owner of a specific portion of the land, and thus to terminate the co-ownership for ever. Instead of holding an undivided share in the whole, each person will hold a divided share in severalty. If 50 acres are held by A. and B. as joint tenants in fee, the effect of the destruction of the unities of title or interest is, as we have seen, to create a tenancy in common ;

---

[1] Litt. s. 292.

[2] *Bedson* v. *Bedson*, [1965] 2 Q. B. 666, at p. 690; [1965] 3 All E. R. 307, at p. 319, *per* RUSSELL, L. J.

[3] Blackstone, vol. ii. pp. 185–6.

[4] Co. Litt. s. 182*b* ; *Wiscot's Case* (1599), 2 Co. Rep. 60*b*.

[5] *Re Schär, Midland Bank Executor and Trustee Co., Ltd.* v. *Damer*, [1951] Ch. 280 ; 1950 2 All E. R. 1069.

[6] Cruise, Digest, Tit. xvii. c. 117. Contrary to the view of the majority of the Court of Appeal, it is submitted that the two methods of severance already discussed avail a husband or wife in respect of the matrimonial home; *Bedson* v. *Bedson*, [1965] 2 Q. B. 666, at p. 688–91; [1965] 3 All E. R. 307, at pp. 318–20, *per* RUSSELL, L. J., *dissenting.*

but the effect of partition is that each becomes absolute owner of 25 acres.

Partition is either voluntary, or compulsory.

(*a*) Voluntary partition. Co-owners may agree between themselves to divide the property into separate shares to be held in individual ownership. The actual amount or position of the land that is to be allotted to each party may be settled by the co-owners themselves, or by an arbitrator selected by them, or even by the drawing of lots.[1] The usual practice is first to enter into a preliminary agreement whereby the co-owners consent to the land being partitioned into allotments convenient to be held in separate ownership and as nearly as possible of equal values, provision being made for the payment of a sum of money to secure equality of partition where it is impossible to give each party land of equal value.[2] When the division has been settled, the last step is for the co-owners to execute that form of conveyance which is appropriate to the interest involved. A deed is necessary in the case of land, but joint tenants must execute a deed of release, while the proper form for tenants in common is a deed of grant.

How voluntary partition effected.

(*b*) The subject of compulsory partition is one that needs no discussion, since it was abolished by the legislation of 1925.[3] It will suffice to say that, though at common law joint tenants and tenants in common were not allowed to compel partition, the right to do so by action was given to them by a number of Partition Acts ranging from 1539 to 1868, the last of which empowered the court to order a sale instead of a physical partition if it thought fit to do so. There could, however, be no compulsory partition if the land was subject to a trust for sale under which it was converted into money according to the equitable doctrine of conversion.[4] The Partition Acts have now been repealed, for under the new law, as we shall see, land held by co-owners is always subject to a trust for sale.

Compulsory partition now abolished.

(iv) The normal and the simplest method of bringing a joint tenancy to an end is by sale. If all the joint tenants agree to sell, the joint title can be passed to the purchaser and the land

Sale of entire land.

---

[1] Litt. ss. 55, 243–6.

[2] For a precedent see *Encyclopædia of Forms and Precedents* (3rd Edn.), vol. xi. p. 383.

[3] *I.e.* by the repeal of the Partition Acts ; Law of Property Act, 1925, 7th Schedule.

[4] *Biggs* v. *Peacock* (1882), 22 Ch. D. 284.

will vest in him as single owner. Prior to 1926, if one joint tenant was obstructive, the others could compel a sale by the indirect method of bringing a partition action.

(B) TENANCY IN COMMON.

A tenancy in common arises

Creation of tenancy in common.

    (i) where land is limited to two or more persons with words of severance showing an intention, even in the slightest degree,[1] that the donees are to take separate shares, or

    (ii) where equity reads what is at law a joint tenancy as a tenancy in common,[2] or

    (iii) where one joint tenant disposes of his interest to a stranger, or acquires an interest greater than that of his co-tenants.[3]

Limitation with words of severance.

The following expressions have at one time and another been construed as words of severance sufficient to create a tenancy in common :

" equally to be divided " ;
" to be divided " ;
" in equal moieties " ;
" equally " ;
" amongst " ;
" share and share alike."

So also, if land is devised to A. and B. on condition that they pay in equal shares ten shillings a week to X. during his life, this imposition of an equal burden on both donees shows that what would normally be a joint tenancy is to be a tenancy in common.[4]

Differences between joint tenancy and tenancy in common.

There is a fundamental distinction between tenancy in common and joint tenancy.

In the first place, that intimate union which exists between joint tenants does not necessarily exist in a tenancy in common.

(i) Unity.

In the latter case the one point in which the tenants are united is the right to possession.[5] They all occupy promiscuously, and if there are two tenants in common, A. and B., A. has an equal right with B. to the possession of the whole land. But their union may stop at that point, for they may each hold different interests, as where one has a fee simple, the other a life interest ; and they may each hold under different titles, as for instance where one has bought and the other has succeeded to his share.[6] Each has a *share* in the ordinary meaning of that word. His share is

---

[1] *Robertson v. Fraser* (1871), 6 Ch. App. 696, 699.
[2] *Supra*, pp. 301–3.
[3] *Supra*, pp. 303–4
[4] *Re North, North v. Cusden*, [1952] Ch. 397 ; [1952] 1 All E. R. 609.
[5] Co. Litt. 189 a.   [6] Blackstone, vol. ii. p. 191.

undivided in the sense that its boundary is not yet demarcated, but nevertheless his right to a definite share exists.

The second characteristic, and it is really the complement of the first, is that the *jus accrescendi* has no application to tenancies in common, so that, when one tenant dies, his share passes to his personal representatives, and not to the surviving tenant.[1]

" A tenancy in common, although it is an ownership only of an " undivided share, is, for all practical purposes, a sole and several " tenancy or ownership ; and each tenant in common stands " towards his own undivided share in the same relation that, if he " were sole owner of the whole, he would bear towards the whole."[2]

Although the tenancy thus possesses certain advantages over a joint tenancy, it suffers from this disadvantage that, since the shares are distinct, it becomes necessary on a sale of the whole land to make a separate title to each separate share.

Tenancy in common is not a form of landholding that is likely to arise as the result of a direct deed of grant, but it is found in practice in the case of partnership land (unless one partner is made sole owner as trustee for his co-partners); it frequently arises under a will, as for instance where a testator leaves land to his children equally; and it may be advantageously employed in a strict settlement.

Limitations of tenancies in common are adopted in strict settlements when it is desired to provide that, if there are no sons, the land shall pass to the daughters. The further object is to secure that if there are several daughters and one of them dies without issue, her share in the land shall go to the other daughters instead of passing under the limitation to the ultimate remainderman. The .future interests so limited between the daughters are called cross remainders.

Thus :

A settlement made in view of the approaching marriage of H. and W. (after limiting a life estate to H., a rentcharge to W., and portions to the younger children) grants the land to the first and other sons of the marriage successively in tail male, with remainder to the sons in tail general. It then provides that, should there be no sons and no issue of sons, the land shall go to all the daughters of H. and W. *in equal shares as tenants in common in tail.* The effect of this is to give each daughter a separate undivided share in the land, which she will possess as tenant in common with her sisters. So far the full design of the settlor has not been attained, for if one of the daughters were to die a spinster her interest would pass, not to her sisters, but to the ultimate

Marginal notes:
(ii) Survivorship.

How tenancy in common arises in practice.

Its place in strict settlements.

Cross remainders.

---

[1] Blackstone, vol. ii. p. 194
[2] Challis, *Law of Real Property* (3rd Edn.), p. 368.

remainderman in fee, since only issue can succeed to an entailed interest.

The limitation of the cross remainders is therefore inserted at this point.   It runs as follows :

> " And if and so often as there shall be a failure of issue of
> " any such daughter, then, as well as to her original share as
> " to any share or shares which shall have accrued to her or
> " her issue by virtue of this present limitation, to the others
> " of such daughters in tail in equal shares as tenants in
> " common."

The effect of the limitation so far is that if there are four daughters, A., B., C. and D., then A., for instance, takes an immediate share in one-fourth undivided part of the land, while B., C. and D. are entitled as tenants in common to a future estate in A.'s part should she die without issue. If, then, A. dies without issue, B., C. and D. each remain possessed of their original one-fourth share and each acquires one-third of A.'s share.   Thus B., C. and D. will each be holding an original and an accrued share.   If B. dies later without issue, C. and D. each retain their original fourth together with the third of the fourth acquired from A., and further they share between them not only B.'s original fourth, but also the share which had accrued to B. from A.

The final limitation in this part of a settlement provides that if all the issue of all the daughters except one fail, the whole of the land shall pass to that one in tail.[1]

It does not follow, of course, that these cross remainders will take effect as intended by the settlement, for if a daughter either bars the entail or, under the new rule introduced in 1926, disposes of her entailed interest by will, the effect is to defeat the future interests which might pass to the other daughters under the cross remainders.

Cross remainders implied in wills but not in deeds.   Where lands are limited to several persons as tenants in common in tail, with a limitation over upon failure of issue of *all* the beneficiaries, it was well established before 1926 that in gifts by will, but not by deed, cross remainders might be implied between the tenants in common.[2]   In view of the rule that entailed interests can now be created only by formal expressions,[3] it is perhaps doubtful whether such implication is now possible.[4]

---

[1] Authorities are : Preston on Estates, vol. i. p. 94 *et seq.* ; Challis, *Law of Real Property* (3rd Edn.), pp. 370–3 ; Elphinstone, *Introduction to Conveyancing*, pp. 490–1.

[2] Hawkins, *Construction of Wills* (3rd Edn.) p. 247.

[3] Law of Property Act, 1925, s. 130 (1) ; *supra*, pp. 166–7.

[4] Cross remainders are implied where realty or personalty is left to two or more persons as tenants in common during their respective *lives*, with a gift over on the decease of the survivor. Thus, when one dies, his share passes to the survivor or survivors ; *Re Davies, Public Trustee* v. *Davies*, [1950] 1 All E. R. 120.

The three methods by which a tenancy in common is deter- Determina-
mined and converted into separate ownership are (i) partition, tion of
(ii) sale, and (iii) the acquisition by one tenant, whether by grant common.
or by operation of law, of the shares vested in his co-tenants.

(C) Coparcenary.

Coparcenary arose at common law wherever land descended
to two or more persons who together constituted the heir. This
occurred if a tenant in fee simple or a tenant in tail died intestate
leaving only female heirs. In each case the females succeeded
jointly to the estate and were called coparceners. Coparcenary
also arose under the custom of gavelkind, according to which the
land descended to all the sons equally, failing them to all the
daughters equally, and failing them to all the brothers equally.[1]
Gavelkind, however, has been abolished ; the rules regulating
the disposition of a fee simple estate upon the intestacy of its
owner have been altered by the Administration of Estates Act,
1925 ; [2] and coparcenary can now arise only in the case of entailed
interests.

If the owner of an entailed interest (other than an interest in Coparcenary
tail male) dies without having either barred the entail or disposed confined to
of the interest by will, and if he leaves no male heirs who are entails.
entitled to succeed *per formam doni*, the interest passes to the
female heirs of the appropriate class. For instance:

Where the owner of an entailed interest general dies intestate
leaving no sons, but three daughters, the interest descends
to all the daughters jointly.[3] The daughters are called coparceners because, in the words of Littleton,

" by the writ which is called *breve de participatione facienda* the law
" will constrain them that partition shall be made among them." [4]

Coparceners constitute a single heir, and they occupy a Distinction
position intermediate between joint tenants and tenants in between
common.[5] Like joint tenants they have unity of title, interest and other
and possession ; like tenants in common their estate is un- concurrent
affected by the doctrine of survivorship, and if there are three interests.
coparceners and one dies, her share passes separately to her heirs
or devisee, not to the survivors, though the unity of possession
continues. It follows that unity of time is not necessary to constitute coparcenary, for if a man has two daughters to whom his

---

[1] *Supra*, pp. 16–17.   [2] *Infra*, pp. 793 *et seq.*
[3] Litt., ss. 55, 241, 254, 265 ; Blackstone, vol. ii. p. 187.
[4] Litt. s. 241. As distinct from the case of joint tenancy and tenancy in
common, partition may be compelled at common law, since the co-tenancy
arises, not by act of parties, but by operation of law.
[5] Challis, *Law of Real Property* (3rd Edn.), p. 374.

estate descends and one dies leaving a son, such son and the surviving daughter will be coparceners.[1]

Determination of coparcenary.

Coparcenary is converted into separate ownership (i) by partition, or (ii) by the union in one parcener of all the shares ; and it is converted into a tenancy in common if one parcener transfers her share to a stranger.[2]

Coparcenary under the modern law.

The present position with regard to coparcenary is that interests held by coparceners are necessarily equitable, since for the most part they consist of entailed interests,[3] and these arise only under a settlement or a trust for sale. Therefore, it would seem that when a tenant in tail dies intestate, leaving female heirs, the legal fee simple vests in the trustees in the case of a settlement and is held by them on trust for sale and to give effect to the equitable rights of the coparceners.[4]

(D) TENANCY BY ENTIRETIES.

Prior to 1883.

Under the law prior to 1883, where land was granted to a husband and wife in such a way that, had they not been married, they would have taken as joint tenants, the effect, owing to the doctrine that husband and wife are one person in the law, was to make them tenants by entireties, unless a contrary intention could be inferred from the grant. Each was tenant of the whole land and no less, and they were not able to sever their interests so as each to take a separate half.[5] When one died the estate passed absolutely to the survivor.

After 1883.

After the Married Women's Property Act, 1882, had made it possible for a wife to own property separately from her husband, a joint limitation to husband and wife without words of severance made them ordinary joint tenants.[6] But though the effect of this Act was to make husband and wife two persons *vis à vis* each other, they remained one person in regard to strangers. Therefore, if after 1882, land were granted or devised equally between a husband, wife and a stranger, X., the old common law rule still applied that, failing a contrary intention, one moiety went to X., the other to the husband and wife, though no longer of course as tenants by entireties.[7]

---

[1] Co. Litt. s. 164a.   [2] Litt. s. 309.

[3] If a person who was a lunatic on January 1st, 1926, and was therefore incapable of making a will, dies without recovering his testamentary capacity, his beneficial interest in land devolves according to the old canons of descent— Administration of Estates Act, 1925, s. 51 (2). Coparcenary, therefore, may still arise under this provision in the case of a fee simple estate.

[4] Settled Land Act, s. 36 (1) (2).

[5] Co. Litt., s. 187a, b ; Blackstone, vol. ii. p. 182 ; Challis, *Law of Real Property* (3rd Edn.), p. 376.

[6] *Thornley* v. *Thornley*, [1893] 2 Ch. 229, 234.

[7] *Re Jupp* (1888), 39 Ch. D. 148. This decision was not followed in *In re Jeffery*, [1914] 1 Ch. 375. where it was pointed out, following earlier cases, that it was a pure question of construction whether husband and wife were to be regarded as one person for this purpose, and that any indication to the contrary, however slight, would suffice to displace the doctrine.

This is, however, no longer the case, for it is now enacted by the Law of Property Act, 1925, that

> " A husband and wife shall, for all purposes of acquisition of any
> " interest in property, under a disposition made or coming into
> " operation after the commencement of this Act, be treated as two
> " persons." [1]

Any tenancy by entireties existing immediately before January 1st, 1926, was converted on that date into a joint tenancy, though without prejudice to existing rights.[2] If, therefore, land stood limited on December 31st, 1925, to a husband and wife and a third person, the effect of this conversion was to vest the legal estate in the three parties as trustees for sale, upon trust to hold one moiety of the proceeds on behalf of the husband and wife jointly and the other moiety on behalf of the third person.[3]

Conversion of pre-1926 tenancies.

SECTION II. THE MODERN LAW.

The object of the legislation of 1925 was to simplify conveyances of land, and where this simplicity could not otherwise be attained, to make radical alterations in the old law. The law relating to concurrent interests was a subject that called for considerable alteration. If conveyancing is to be a simple matter, one primary essential is that the legal estate to be acquired by a purchaser should be vested in an easily ascertainable person and not distributed among a number of persons whose titles will each require to be investigated.

Old law of concurrent interests hindered conveyancing.

Joint tenancy. Joint tenancy does not raise difficulties in this respect, for although several persons are interested in the land, yet there is but one title to be deduced, and if the purchaser is satisfied as to the validity of the deed or the will under which the tenancy stands limited, he is not concerned further with the tenants except to see that they are all parties to the deed of sale.

Tenancy in common. In tenancy in common, however, the case is different, for the existence of a number of persons interested in the land, each of whom, as we have seen, is entitled to a separate share, raises a serious hindrance to simplicity of transfer. An analogous difficulty occurs in the case of a settlement where the beneficial title is distributed among a number of persons *in succession*, but we have seen that this plurality of interests is not allowed to hinder conveyancing, since the tenant for life is treated as the fee simple owner for purposes of transmission, and the interests of the various beneficiaries are not allowed to affect a purchaser. The conveyancing problem raised by a number of successive interests is in fact comparatively simple, because the

Especially tenancy in common.

---

[1] S. 37.   [2] Law of Property Act, 1925, 1st Schedule, Part VI.
[3] For the explanation of this trust for sale, see *infra*, pp. 312–4.

tenant for life is obviously marked out as the person to act as an intermediary for passing the legal estate.

But where land is held by tenants in common, there is no one person in whom the legal estate can appropriately be vested, for all the tenants have the equal right to present enjoyment, so that tenancy in common is a greater hindrance to simplicity of transfer than a settlement. The complication here is that the separate title of each tenant must be investigated.

" Lastly, all this confusion is ' worse confounded ' by concurrent
" ownership in tenancy in common. Here is an example which
" recently came before me in my official capacity. A man by his
" will devised his freeholds to the use of his wife for life, and after
" her death to the use of his children in fee simple. He had ten
" children ; one of them died during the widow's life, leaving a
" similar will, seven children, and a widow. This is quite a simple
" example ; yet the result is that a house worth about £150 per
" annum is (the widow being dead) now vested (not merely in equity
" but at law) in seventeen persons in the following proportions :

" Each of the nine living children of testator or their assigns $\frac{7}{70}$

" Each of the seven children of the deceased child, subject
   to the prior life interest of their mother ...   . $\frac{1}{70}$

" Moreover, several of the parties have mortgaged their shares, and
" in the result when the great expense of proving the title of each of
" the seventeen has been paid, a very small balance will remain for
" distribution. Thus, tenancy in common is (having regard to the
" Settled Land Acts) a far greater detriment to the proper manage-
" ment of land than settlements (which are popularly debited with
" this sin), and introduces infinitely greater difficulty with regard to
" its sale, as not only must the parties be unanimous, but the title
" of each of them has to be deduced."[1]

Tenancies in common of *legal* estate abolished.

To end all such confusion the Law of Property Act revolutionized the law relating to tenancies in common.

The object was to enable land which is subject to such tenancies to be sold without casting upon the purchaser any obligation to consider the titles or the beneficial rights of the tenants. The first step in the attainment of this object is the enactment that

" a *legal* estate is not capable of subsisting or of being created in an
" undivided share in land."[2]

What this particular enactment means is that there can never again be a *legal* tenancy in common, *i.e.* a tenancy in common of a legal estate.

Trust for sale now arises in all cases.

It is then enacted that an undivided share in land shall not be created except behind a trust for sale.[3] This involves two consequences :—

First, the legal estate must be held by *joint* tenants upon trust for sale.

---

[1] Sir Arthur Underhill in Fourth Report, 1919, p. 30.
[2] Law of Property Act, 1925, s. 1 (6).
[3] Settled Land Act, 1925, s. 36 (4).

Secondly, the subject-matter of the tenancy in common is converted from land to money, for, as we have already seen, land directed to be sold is regarded by equity as having already been sold.[1]

The corner stone of this new edifice is the vesting of the legal estate in joint tenants upon trust for sale, and since it is essential to the success of the scheme that this legal joint tenancy should remain invulnerable until terminated by sale, the old rules as to severance[2] have been abolished for *legal* joint tenancies. It is enacted that

Joint tenancy of legal estate cannot be severed

" no severance of a joint tenancy of a *legal* estate, so as to create a " tenancy in common in land, shall be permissible."[3]

If, therefore, it is desired to vest a fee simple absolute in possession or a term of years absolute in tenants in common, the correct method is to create an express trust for sale by conveying the legal estate to trustees upon trust to sell the land and to hold the rents and profits until sale and the ultimate proceeds of sale upon such trusts as the grantor may see fit to create.[4] He may provide, for instance, that the beneficiaries shall be entitled to the proceeds in unequal shares.

An alternative method is merely to convey the legal estate to trustees upon *the statutory trusts*, an expression which is defined by the Act to mean,

upon trust to sell the land, with power to postpone the sale, and to hold the rents and profits until sale and the ultimate proceeds of sale upon trust to give effect to the beneficial and equitable rights of the persons to whom the land was limited.[5]

If the correct method of a conveyance upon trust for sale is not adopted, the Law of Property Act contains a number of

Effect of failure to create a trust for sale.

---

[1] Nevertheless, this principle that the equitable tenants in common hold interests in personalty, not in the land, is not free from exceptions. Thus, pending the sale, they have the same right to possession of the land as legal tenants in common had before 1926, *Bull* v. *Bull*, [1955] 1 Q. B. 234 ; [1955] 1 All E. R. 253 ; and an agreement by one tenant to sell his share to the other or others is a contract for the sale of land within the meaning of the Law of Property Act, 1925, s. 40 (*infra*, p. 648), and therefore requires a note or memorandum signed by the vendor ; *Cooper* v. *Critchley*, [1955] Ch. 431 ; [1955] 1 All E. R. 520. See 18 *M.L.R.* pp. 408–12.

The doctrine of conversion proved troublesome where a legal estate had been granted before 1926 to tenants in common in tail. The effect of the 1925 legislation was to make them equitable tenants in common of personalty, but as a result of this they became absolute owners, since before 1926 personalty could not be entailed and the new rule making this possible (*supra*, pp. 174–5) applied only to instruments executed after 1925. Hence the Law of Property (Entailed Interests) Act, 1932, s. 1, overruling *Re Price*, [1928] Ch. 579, provides that in such a case the entail shall continue to exist in the personalty arising under the trust for sale.

[2] *Supra*, pp. 303–4.
[3] Law of Property Act, 1925, s. 36 (2).
[4] See *Encyclopædia of Forms and Precedents* (3rd Edn.), vol. xv, p. 776, Form 145.
[5] Law of Property Act, 1925; s. 35 (1).

provisions designed to ensure that, no matter what form the transaction may have taken, the effect shall be exactly the same as if the tenancy in common had been properly limited behind a trust for sale. There appear to be three normal cases, namely:

> a direct conveyance of the legal estate to tenants in common ;
> a devise to tenants in common ;
> a contract to convey an undivided share.

(i) Conveyance.
L. P. A.
s. 34 (2).

With regard to a conveyance, the Law of Property Act, 1925, provides that,

> where land is expressed to be conveyed to any persons of full age in undivided shares, the conveyance shall operate as if the land had been expressed to be conveyed to the grantees, or if there are more than four than to the first four named, as joint tenants upon the statutory trusts.[1]

Thus, if land is conveyed in fee simple to A., B., C., D. and E. in equal shares, A., B., C. and D. become joint tenants of the legal estate, while all five are entitled equitably to the proceeds of sale and the rents and profits until sale.

(ii) Devise.

A devise to two or more persons in undivided shares operates to vest the legal estate in the trustees (if any) of the will for the purposes of the Settled Land Act, or, if there is none, in the personal representatives, but in either case the land is held on the statutory trusts and not as settled land.[2]

(iii) Contract to convey.

A contract to convey an undivided share in land is deemed to be fully performed by a conveyance of a corresponding share in the proceeds of sale arising under a trust for sale.[3]

Settlement.
S. L. A.
s. 36 (4).

As regards settlements, the Settled Land Act, 1925, provides that a tenancy in common shall not be capable of creation except under a trust instrument or under the above provisions of the Law of Property Act, and shall then take effect under a trust for sale.[4] Thus if it is desired to settle land on A. and B. for their lives in equal shares, with remainder to C. in fee simple, the legal estate must be vested in the trustees upon trust for sale, and the disposition merely operates to give the beneficiaries a corresponding share of the net proceeds of sale and the rents and profits until sale.

---

[1] Law of Property Act, 1925 s. 34 (2).
[2] *Ibid.*, s. 34 (3). For an example, see *Re House, Westminster Bank* v. *Everett.* [1929] 2 Ch. 166.
[3] Law of Property Act, 1925, s. 42 (6). Elaborate provisions are made in the Law of Property Act, 1925, 1st Schedule, Part IV, for the conversion into equitable interests of tenancies in common that were in existence on December 31st, 1925. These transitional provisions have given rise to a number of important decisions, but owing to the necessity of keeping this book within reasonable limits they are not dealt with here: See further: Gibson's *Conveyancing* (16th Edn.), pp. 687–96; Rivington, *Law of Property in Land* (3rd Edn.), pp. 248–54.
[4] S. 36 (4).

If beneficiaries under an existing settlement become entitled in possession to the land, *e.g.* where in a

> devise to X. for life, remainder to X.'s children equally during their lives,

X. dies leaving three children, the legal fee simple that was formerly held by X. as tenant for life must be vested in the trustees of the settlement and held by them upon the statutory trusts.[1] The settlement within the meaning of the Settled Land Act comes to an end and is replaced by a trust for sale.

It seems doubtful, however, whether the language of these enactments covers all cases in which a tenancy in common may arise, as for example when two persons buy land and contribute the purchase price in unequal shares.[2] This was the position in *Bull* v. *Bull*,[3] where a mother and son bought a house as a dwelling place for themselves, the conveyance being made to the son only, who had provided the greater part of the purchase price. In an action in which the issue was the validity of a notice to quit served on the mother, the Court of Appeal, citing s. 36(4) of the Settled Land Act, held that the parties were tenants in common in equity, and that the legal estate vested in the son upon the statutory trusts for sale. *Quaere whether the legislation embraces all tenancies in common.*

This decision, though expedient, is difficult to fit into the words of the legislation. There was nothing that could constitute a trust instrument within the meaning of the Settled Land Act; and the land was not "expressed to be conveyed" to persons in undivided shares as required by the Law of Property Act. It would seem, then, that the courts will readily impose a trust for sale if this will fulfil the intention of the parties.

Let us examine the effect of the statutory trust for sale that arises in these various cases from the point of view, first, of a purchaser of the land, secondly, of the beneficiaries. *Advantage of new scheme.*

The advantage to the purchaser is that he is no longer compelled to investigate the title of each tenant in common. He is concerned only with the legal estate held by the joint tenants upon trust for sale, since the rights of the persons beneficially entitled exist merely as equitable interests behind the trust for sale, and they are overreached upon a conveyance of the land by the trustees. It is a matter of indifference, therefore, that some of the tenants in common are infants, or that some of them are unwilling to acquiesce in the sale. Although it is true that in the case of a statutory, as distinct from an express, trust for sale the trustees are required, so far as practicable, to consult, and give *Advantage to purchaser.*

---

[1] Settled Land Act, 1925, s. 36 (1), (2), (3).
[2] *Supra*, p. 302.
[3] [1955] 1 Q. B. 234; [1955] 1 All E. R. 253 followed in *Cook* v. *Cook*, [1962] p. 181; [1962] 2 All E. R. 262; affd. [1962] p. 235; [1962] 2 All E. R. 811 (C. A.).

effect to the wishes of the beneficiaries entitled in possession,[1] yet it is expressly enacted that it shall be no concern of a purchaser to see that this requirement has been complied with.[2]

Advantage to tenants in common.

The advantage to the tenants in common is that, no matter how numerous they may be, a sale of the land affected is always possible without difficulty or undue expense. Neither are they prejudiced by the loss of their rights in the land itself, for they have corresponding rights in the money arising from the sale. Thus if A. is entitled under the tenancy in common to a half share in the land, and B. and C. are entitled to a quarter share each, the duty of the trustees is to ensure that A., B. and C. receive the purchase money in the same proportions. They need not sell at once, nor indeed at any time, for they are statutorily empowered to postpone the sale,[3] or, instead of selling, to partition the land among the persons beneficially entitled.[4] The tenants in common can still deal with their equitable interests as freely as they could formerly have dealt with their legal interests. If A., B. and C. are tenants in common and C. sells his equitable interest to D., the legal joint tenancy remains vested in the trustees upon the statutory trusts for A., B. and D.

Changes in joint tenancies.

Joint Tenancies. Certain consequential changes have also been effected in joint tenancies, and the law relating to this matter varies according as the land is, or is not, settled within the meaning of the Settled Land Act.

Settled land.

The position with regard to settled land is what it was before 1926. If two or more persons are beneficially entitled for their lives under a settlement, as for example where land is devised to X. and Y. for their lives with remainder to Z. in fee simple,[5] they together constitute the tenant for life within the meaning of the Settled Land Act and there is no question of any trust for sale.[6] They are invested with the legal estate, and it is their function to make title upon a sale or other disposition of the land.

Joint tenants beneficially entitled.

In the second case, however, where the land is not settled, but is *beneficially* limited for a legal estate to joint tenants, *e.g.*

> where a father conveys Blackacre to his two sons in fee simple without words of severance.

it is enacted that the *legal* estate shall be held upon trust for sale in like manner as if the persons beneficially entitled were

---

[1] Law of Property Act, 1925, s. 26 (3); as amended by Law of Property (Amendment) Act, 1926, Sched.

[2] Law of Property Act, 1925, s. 26 (3); as amended by Law of Property (Amendment) Act, 1926, Sched.

[3] *Ibid.*, s. 25.

[4] *Ibid.*, s. 28 (3).

[5] See also *In re Gaul and Houlston's Contract*, [1928] 1 Ch. 689, devise to X. and Y. in fee simple, subject to a charge, created voluntarily, of £1,000 in favour of Z. Thus, the land was settled by virtue of the Settled Land Act, s. 1 (1) (v); *infra*, p. 698, note 7.

[6] Settled Land Act, 1925, s. 19 (2).

tenants in common.[1]   This means, not that they become equitable tenants in common, but equitable joint tenants of the proceeds of sale and of the income until sale.   Thus if land is granted to A., B. and C. jointly in fee simple, A., B. and C. become joint tenants of the legal estate upon trust for sale.   A legal and an equitable joint tenancy are automatically and inescapably brought into existence.   A., B. and C. are trustees for sale of the legal estate and can therefore make title with facility, but they are joint beneficiaries with regard to the equitable interest.   They may postpone the sale of the land, indefinitely, but if the date at which it should be effected becomes a matter of dispute, any one of them may apply to the court which then has an absolute discretion to make such order as seems right and proper.[2]   The number of persons holding the legal estate must not exceed four.[3]

This change in the law is unintelligible unless we remember that a *legal* joint tenancy can no longer be severed.   It is essential to the success of the new rules for tenancies *in common* that the legal joint tenancy which must necessarily arise should continue undisturbed and should not be convertible into a tenancy in common by some transaction or event amounting to a severance, for otherwise the legal title would be split up into a number of separate titles and the old troubles incidental to a conveyance of the legal estate would return.   Hence the new rule that a *legal* joint tenancy cannot be severed.[4]   The object of the introduction of an equitable tenancy is to preserve to each tenant his right to sever his interest and thus to avoid the danger of his premature death and the consequent operation of the *jus accrescendi.* *Why trusts for sale necessary.*

We have already considered the methods by which a joint tenancy may be severed and converted into a tenancy in common,[5] but it is important to notice with some particularity the course open to a beneficial joint tenant who desires to prevent the survivorship of his equitable interest to the other tenants. *Modern position of beneficial joint tenant.*

> If land has been conveyed to A. and B. as joint tenants, what is the effect upon A.'s beneficial interest if he predeceases B. ?   The answer, of course, is that it survives absolutely to B. to the detriment of A.'s successors.   The further question then arises, what can A. do in his lifetime to avoid this possible loss ?   In other words, how can the legal or the equitable joint tenancy, or both, be determined ?

The solution is, either to determine the joint tenancy altogether, or, while retaining the legal joint tenancy, to sever it on its equitable side.   Let us consider the two cases separately.

A joint tenancy is determined altogether by any one of the following methods :

---

[1] Law of Property Act, 1925, s. 36 (1).
[2] Law of Property Act, s. 30.   For example, see *Jones* v. *Challenger*, [1961] 1 Q. B. 176 ; [1960] 1 All E. R. 785, and authorities there cited.
[3] Law of Property Act, 1925, s. 34 (2).
[4] *Ibid.*, s. 36 (2), *supra*, p. 313.
[5] *Supra*, pp. 303–6.

Determina-
tion of the
legal and the
equitable
joint
tenancies.

(a) **Sale of the Legal Estate.** If A. and B. sell in their capacity as trustees for sale, their conveyance passes the legal fee simple to the purchaser freed from their rights as joint tenants. The purchaser is not concerned with these rights, since they exist behind the trust for sale and are merely equitable in nature.

A trust for sale cannot be exercised unless there are at least two trustees, but it is enacted by the Law of Property (Amendment) Act, 1926, that a surviving joint tenant, who is solely and *beneficially* entitled to the land, may deal with the legal estate as if it were not held on a trust for sale.[1] Thus if land is devised in fee simple to a husband and wife jointly, the wife, on the death of her husband, can pass a good title to a purchaser of the legal estate without appointing another trustee in place of her husband.[2]

Such a conveyance, however, is not without its dangers, for a deceased tenant, without the knowledge of the survivor, may have severed his interest, a fact that will not appear on the vendor's abstract of title to the legal estate. It was formerly felt, therefore, that the only sure method of overreaching the equitable interest arising by virtue of the severance was for the survivor to reconstitute the trust for sale by appointing a new trustee. But this is no longer necessary. The Law of Property (Joint Tenants) Act, 1964, which is retrospective to January 1st, 1946, provides that

> the survivor of two or more joint tenants shall, in favour of the purchaser of the legal estate, be deemed to be solely and beneficially interested if he conveys as beneficial owner[3] or if the conveyance includes a statement that he is so interested.[4]

This provision, however, is not to apply if a memorandum of severance has been endorsed on or annexed on the conveyance by which the legal estate was vested in the joint tenants; or if a receiving order, or a petition for such an order, has been registered under the Land Charges Act, 1925.[5]

(b) **Voluntary partition.** If all the joint tenants are of full age it is clear that as beneficial owners they may partition the land between themselves, whereupon the legal

---

[1] Schedule, amending Law of Property Act, 1925, s. 36.

[2] According to *Re Cook, Beck* v. *Grant*, [1948] Ch. 212 ; [1948] 1 All E. R. 231 ; this would be the position apart from the Act of 1926, since, on the death of the husband the entire interest in the land, both legal and equitable, vests in the wife. The trust for sale ceases, since she is now owner and cannot be trustee for herself.

[3] As to the effect of conveying as beneficial owner, see *infra*, p. 684.

[4] S. 1, (1). The Act does not apply if the title to the land has been registered; *ibid.*, s. 3.

[5] *Ibid.*, s. 1 (1), proviso. Registration constitutes notice of the order or petition to the purchaser.

joint tenancy will be converted into separate ownership. Apart from this, however, the Act provides, as we have seen, that where a legal estate is beneficially limited to persons as joint tenants it shall be held on trust for sale *in like manner as if the persons beneficially entitled were tenants in common.* Then, another section provides that where the proceeds of sale have become absolutely vested in tenants in common of full age, the trustees may, with the consent of the persons (if any) of full age interested in possession to the profits of the land until sale,

    (i) partition the land in whole or in part, and

    (ii) provide by way of mortgage or otherwise for the payment of any equality money.[1]

(c) **Release.** Where land is held by A. and B. as joint tenants it is open to either of them to release his interest to the other, whereupon the alienee will become sole and several owner.[2] An agreement for such a release is unenforceable by action unless it is evidenced by a written memorandum signed by the vendor or his agent.[3]

Severance. It remains to be seen how it is possible to sever the equitable joint tenancy between A. and B. without disturbing the joint tenancy of the legal estate. This result is achieved if either of the tenants enters into any transaction which severs the tenancy and converts it into a tenancy in common, as for example where he alienates his share to a stranger[4]; or if one of the tenants acquires an interest greater in quantum than that held by the other.[5] *(margin: Determination of the equitable joint tenancy only.)*

Alienation, however, is not always practicable, and therefore a new and exceedingly useful method of severance has been introduced by statute. *(margin: Notice of desire to sever.)*

It is provided in effect that :

If any tenant desires to sever the joint tenancy in equity, he may give to the other joint tenants a written notice of such desire, whereupon he becomes entitled as tenant in common to his share of the profits of the land and of the purchase money after the land is sold.[6]

Suppose, for instance, that land is limited to A., B. and C. as joint tenants.

---

[1] Law of Property Act, 1925, s. 28 (3). See *Re Gorringe and Brayton's Contract*, [1934] Ch. 614n ; *Re Brooker*, [1934] Ch. 610.
[2] Law of Property Act, 1925, s. 36 (2).
[3] *Cooper* v. *Critchley*, [1955] Ch. 431 ; [1955] 1 All E. R. 520.
[4] *Supra*, p. 303.   [5] *Supra*, p. 304.
[6] Law of Property Act, 1925, s. 36 (2), proviso.

We know that this creates both a legal and an equitable joint tenancy. If C. dies without having dealt with his interest, A. and B. retain the legal estate as trustees for sale, and hold the equitable interest under the doctrine of survivorship, freed from the interest of C. But if in his lifetime C. gives notice of his desire to sever, his equitable joint tenancy becomes an equitable tenancy in common, and A. and B. hold the legal estate upon trust to sell and to divide the proceeds between themselves and the personal representatives of C. The equitable tenancy in common will continue to exist until either the sale is carried out, or the shares become vested in one person, or a voluntary partition is effected.

Meaning of "party-wall." **Party-Walls.** We must finally examine the effect of the legislation of 1925 upon party-walls. According to FRY, J., the term " party-wall " may mean [1]:

(*a*) a wall of which two adjoining owners are tenants in common ; or

(*b*) a wall divided vertically into two strips, one half of the thickness belonging to each of the neighbouring owners ; or

(*c*) a wall belonging entirely to one owner, but subject to an easement in the other to have it maintained as a dividing wall ; or

(*d*) a wall divided vertically into two equal strips, each strip being subject to a cross easement in favour of the owner of the other.

It may be said that *most* of the party-walls in this country come within the first class, that is, are held by the adjoining owners as tenants in common, and in view of this it is clear that the effect of the statutory alterations relating to concurrent interests would have been absurd had special provisions for party-walls not been added. The effect would have been to render the majority of such walls subject to a trust for sale !

It is therefore enacted [2] that a wall which under the old law would have been held by tenants in common shall be regarded as severed vertically as between the respective owners, and that the owner of each part shall have such rights to support and user over the other part as he would have had *qua* tenant in common under the old law. In other words, most party-walls now fall within the last class enumerated by FRY, J.

---

[1] *Watson* v. *Gray* (1880), 14 Ch. D. 192, 194–5.
[2] Law of Property Act, 1925, s. 38, Schedule I, Part V, see also s. 187 (2).

CHAPTER IX.

TRUSTS.

SUMMARY.

The history and nature of the trust have already been de- Scope of
scribed,[1] but something more must be said of the various forms it discussion.
may take, the requirements essential for its express creation, and
the general position of trustees.

SECTION I. DEFINITION AND CLASSIFICATION OF TRUSTS.

A trust arises where any person, called the trustee, who Definition.
is the legal owner of property, is bound to hold and administer
that property on behalf of another person called the beneficiary,
or *cestui que trust*, whether the obligation is created expressly,
or by implication or by operation of law.[2]

It is clear from this definition that trusts may arise in several
different ways, and it becomes necessary, therefore, to show how
they may be classified. It must be admitted, however, that no
classification is entirely satisfactory, since a trust may sometimes
be accurately described as arising either by act of parties or by
operation of law.[3]

---

[1] *Supra*, pp. 44 *et seq.*
[2] *Wilson* v. *Bury (Lord)* (1880), 5 Q. B. D. 518, 530–1.
[3] *In re Llanover Settled Estates*, [1926] Ch. 626, 636–8.

321

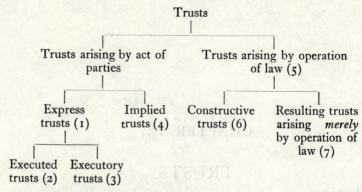

(1) **Express trusts.**   An express trust is one which has been intentionally and deliberately created by some person, either in an instrument such as a deed or a will, or even, where the subject of the trust consists of personal chattels, by an oral declaration. It differs from other forms of trust because, in the words of Lord CAIRNS, it " arises upon the construction of a written instrument, " not upon the inference of law imposing a trust upon the conscience ; [it is] a trust arising upon the words of the instrument itself." [1]

(2) **Executed trusts.**   An executed trust is one in which the terms of the trust are finally declared by the settlor in the will or deed in such a complete manner that no further instrument is required to define the limitations to which he intends to subject the property.   An example with which we are already acquainted occurs in the case of a strict settlement.

(3) **Executory trusts.**   An executory trust arises where the person who creates it gives general instructions as to what limitations it shall contain, but directs that these shall be stated with legal precision in a later formal instrument.   If, for instance, a testatrix devises land to trustees and directs that it shall be held on certain limitations which are indicated in non-technical and informal language, the effect is to create a trust that, in the words of Lord CAIRNS, " is to be executed by the preparation of a complete and formal settlement, carrying into effect, through the operation of an apt and detailed legal phraseology, the general intention indicated by the testatrix."[2]

Such a trust is generally found in connection with what are called marriage articles, which constitute a contract made in consideration of marriage to settle property on terms that are to be embodied later in a formal marriage settlement.[3]

---

[1] *Cunningham* v. *Foot* (1878), 3 App. Cas. 974, 984.
[2] *Sackville-West* v. *Viscount Holmesdale* (1870), L. R. 4 H. L. 543, 571.
[3] Sanders, *Uses and Trusts,* vol. i. p. 335–7.

(4) **Implied trusts.** An implied trust is one that is enforced by the court as a result either of the language of the parties or of the circumstances surrounding some transaction, and which gives effect to what, in the opinion of the court, must have been the intention of the parties. Its existence is an inference from the circumstances and it would be much more appropriately called an " inferred " trust. Instances of such trusts are numerous.[1] If, for instance, a person agrees for valuable consideration to settle an estate, he immediately becomes a trustee of it;[2] or if he contracts to sell his estate to another, he implicitly declares himself a trustee for the purchaser and is accountable to him for the rents and profits.[3] In general, it has been said that :—

> " Wherever a person having a power of disposition over property
> " manifests any intention with respect to it in favour of another, the
> " court, where there is sufficient consideration, or in a will where
> " consideration is implied, will execute that intention through the
> " medium of a trust, however informal the language in which it
> " happens to be expressed." [4]

(5) **Trusts arising by operation of law.** Trusts arising by operation of law do not depend upon the declarations or the supposed intention of the person in whom the legal ownership of the property resides, but are imposed upon the owner by equity upon the ground that he ought to hold the property for the benefit of some other person.

In dealing with trusts arising by operation of law we are met with some confusion of language, for the term " implied trusts " is often included in this category and used synonymously with " constructive trusts " and " resulting trusts," but since implied trusts are dependent upon presumed intention, while those that arise by operation of law are not, it seems better to follow the classification which has been given above.

(6) **Constructive trusts.** A constructive trust in the strictest sense is one which is enforced against a person who, occupying a fiduciary position with regard to property, obtains some personal advantage by reason of that position. A person, for instance, who has expressly been appointed trustee occupies a fiduciary position, and the leading case of *Keech* v. *Sandford*[5] affords an illustration of how he may also become a constructive trustee. The facts were these:—

> A testator who was possessed of a term of years bequeathed it to *Keech* v.
> B. in trust for an infant. Before the term came to an end, B. in his *Sandford.*

---

[1] See Lewin on Trusts, (15th Edn.) pp. 80 *et seq.*
[2] *Finch* v. *Winchelsea* (1715), 1 P. Wms. 277.
[3] *Infra*, p. 650.   [4] Lewin on Trusts, (15th Edn.) p. 80.
[5] (1726), Cas. *temp.* King, 61 ; White and Tudor, *Leading Cases in Equity*, vol. ii. p. 648.

capacity as trustee applied to the lessor to renew the lease for the benefit of the infant. The lessor refused to grant a new lease to the infant, and therefore B. obtained a renewal for his own benefit. It was held that, although there was no fraud and although B. had showed a proper regard for the interests of his beneficiary, yet he must be held accountable in respect of the renewed lease as trustee for the infant.

The principle, however, is not confined to the case of persons who are already express trustees, but affects everyone who is in a fiduciary position and who, as such, acquires some personal advantage.[1]

(7) Resulting trusts. A resulting trust may arise in two ways :—

(i) Conveyance in the name of another. The first is where, upon a purchase of land, A. provides the money, but the legal estate is conveyed to B., a stranger in blood. In this case there is a resulting trust that arises by operation of law in favour of A. unless there are some circumstances connected with the transaction which show that A. intended to make a gift to B.

> " The clear result of all the cases, without a single exception, is
> " that the trust of a legal estate, whether freehold, copyhold or lease-
> " hold ; whether taken in the names of the purchaser and others
> " jointly, or in the names of others without that of the purchaser ;
> " whether in one name or several ; whether jointly or successive,
> " results to the man who advances the purchase money." [2]

But this presumption in favour of a resulting trust will be rebutted if it can be shown that the person who advanced the money intended that the person to whom the property was conveyed should take it beneficially.

(ii) Failure of express trust. The second kind of resulting trust arises where an express trust that is already in existence has failed, either wholly or partially. In such a case the trust results, to the extent of its failure (*e.g.* where one of the expressed objects cannot be carried out), to the settlor or his representatives, unless a contrary intention is indicated in the instrument of disposition.[3] Though for convenience this species of trust is here classed with trusts arising by operation of law, we must note that perhaps its true nature is that of an express trust since a trust arises on the face of the settlement or will.[4]

---

[1] See especially White and Tudor, *Leading Cases in Equity*, vol. ii. p. 558 *et seq.*

[2] *Dyer* v. *Dyer* (1788), 2 Cox, 92 ; *ibid.*, II. 756, *per* Eyre, C.B.

[3] *Re Boyes, Boyes* v. *Carritt* (1884), L. R. 26 Ch. D. 531.

[4] *Salter* v. *Cavanagh* (1838), 1 Dr. & Wal. 668.

SECTION II. CREATION OF EXPRESS TRUSTS.

There are very few rules restricting the mode in which a trust must be created. The trust is the successor of the old use, and for the raising of a use no formalities were necessary. Spoken words were as effectual as written instruments, and according to the preamble to the Statute of Uses bare signs and gestures seem to have been sufficient. The one guiding principle was that effect should be given to the intention of the settlor, no matter how it had been indicated by him. So in general is it with the modern trust. *(margin: Early Law.)*

A trust may be created either by an instrument *inter vivos* or by will. *(margin: Summary of modern law.)*

If it is created *inter vivos* and if it relates to land, it must conform to the Law of Property Act, 1925, which requires a writing.[1] *(margin: Inter vivos trusts.)*

If it is created by will, then, whether it relates to real or to personal property, the instrument of creation must be made in accordance with the Wills Act, 1837, which prescribes the manner in which all wills must be made.[2] *(margin: Testamentary trusts.)*

This last requirement is, however, subject to one important modification in the case of what are generally called *secret trusts.* If a testator gives property to A. " on trust " without specifying what the trusts are, or if he gives it to him absolutely without any mention of a trust, then, provided that the trusts upon which he desires the property to be held have been communicated to A. and assented to by him in the testator's lifetime, the court allows the trust to be proved by parol or other evidence after the will has taken effect.[3] In such a case, *(margin: Secret testamentary trusts.)*

> " what is enforced is not a trust imposed by the will, but one arising
> " from the acceptance by the legatee of a trust, communicated to him
> " by the testator, on the faith of which acceptance the will was made
> " or left unrevoked, as the case might be." [4]

The underlying principle is that it would be fraudulent for the legatee to claim the property for himself in repudiation of a trust that he had agreed to observe.

The essential preliminary to the validity of these secret trusts is that the testator's purpose should have been communicated to and accepted by A.[5] In the words of Lord SUMNER :

> " The necessary elements on which the question turns are in-
> " tention, communication and acquiescence. The testator intends

---

[1] *Infra,* p. 327.
[2] *Infra,* pp. 762 *et seq.*
[3] *Blackwell* v. *Blackwell,* [1929] A. C. 318 ; *Re Williams,* [1933] Ch. 244.
[4] *Blackwell* v. *Blackwell,* [1929] A. C. 318, at p. 342, *per* Lord WARRINGTON.
[5] *Re Keen, Evershed* v. *Griffiths,* [1937] Ch. 236 ; [1937] 1 All E. R. 452.
In re Jones, Jones v. *Jones,* [1942] Ch. 328 ; [1942] 1 All E. R. 642 ; 53 L. Q. R. 501 ; 12 *The Conveyancer* (N. S.), p. 28.

" his absolute gift to be employed as he and not as the donee desires ;
" he tells the proposed donee of this intention, and, either by the
" express promise or by the tacit promise which is signified by
" acquiescence, the proposed donee encourages him to bequeath
" the money in the faith that his intention will be carried out." [1]

The communication to and acquiescence by the donee must
be made *before or at the time of the execution of the will* when the
gift in the will is to him " on trust " without the details being
specified in the will,[2] though it is sufficient if made at any time
before the testator's death when the gift is to A. absolutely without
any mention of a trust.[3]

Completely secret trusts not enforced. Failing communication and acquiescence in the testator's
lifetime, no trust undisclosed in the will is enforceable. Thus,
for example, there can be no question of enforcement if the
testator names X. as trustee, but neither states the details of the
trust in the will nor declares them before his death[4] ; or if he
leaves property to X. absolutely, warning him that this is to be
held on trusts to be revealed later, but never in fact revealed.[5] In
both cases the property must be held by X. on trust for the testator's
next-of-kin. It makes no difference that an unattested paper
showing how the property is to be held is discovered after the
testator's death, for to act on this evidence would be an evasion of
the formal requirements of the Wills Act.

Trusts of personalty. If neither the Law of Property Act nor the Wills Act
applies, if, that is to say, the trust relates neither to freeholds
nor to leaseholds, and if it is not contained in a will, it may be
created by word of mouth or by some other indication of intention,
and without any kind of formality. A clear oral declaration by
the owner of personalty that he is a trustee of that property for
another person constitutes a valid trust and can be enforced by
the volunteer in whose favour it was declared.[6]

Thus in *Peckham* v. *Taylor*[7] :

A lady refused to make a will, but told X. that she desired to dispose
of all her personal property in her lifetime according to a scheme
which she indicated to him. She then gave him a certain amount
of money in order that he might carry out her instructions. X.
actually distributed some of the money in accordance with her
instructions, but she died before the total distribution was made
and no written evidence of her intention could be produced. It
was held, however, that a valid trust, proved by parol evidence, had
been constituted and must be enforced. The Master of the Rolls
in giving judgment said : " It is immaterial for the purpose of
" establishing a trust of personal property whether it be declared
" orally or in writing; the only question is as to the evidence of its
" existence. . . . I am clear there was a gift [of the property] to X.

---

[1] *Blackwell* v. *Blackwell*, [1929] A. C. 318, at p. 334.
[2] *Johnson* v. *Ball* (1851), 5 De G. & Sm. 85 ; *Re Gardner, Huey* v.
Cunnington, [1920] 2 Ch. 523, at p. 532.
[3] *Re Gardner, Huey* v. *Cunnington, supra.*
[4] *In re Boyes, Boyes* v. *Carritt* (1884), 26 Ch. D. 531, at p. 535.
[5] *Ibid.*
[6] *Jones* v. *Lock* (1865), L. R. 1 Ch. App. 25.   [7] (1862), 6 L. T. 487.

"upon the trusts of it declared by her. It was a gift without the
"reservation of any power of revocation, and I think if she had
"subsequently recovered . . . she could not have claimed that
"property again."

But it was found in the case of land that parol declarations Trusts of land.
of trusts led to disputes and inconveniences, and therefore the
Statute of Frauds in 1677 required for the first time that the
creation of a trust of real estate should be manifested and proved
by some writing signed by the settlor.[1] This provision has now
been re-enacted by the Law of Property Act, 1925, in the following words [2] :—

"A declaration of trust respecting any land or any interest therein Formalities under Law of Property Act.
"must be manifested and proved by some writing signed by some
"person who is able to declare such trust, or by his will."

There are several points that should be noticed about this
enactment. Thus it is confined to land and does not interfere
with the rule that a trust of pure personalty may be constituted
by oral declarations.

It does not require a deed, but only a writing, and even so it
does not require that the trust should have been declared by
writing in the first place. The statute uses the words "manifested and proved," and it is sufficient if the trust can be proved
by some writing signed by the settlor no matter what the date of
the writing may have been.[3] To constitute an express trust, the
settlor must indicate :

(i) the property that is subjected to the trust,
(ii) the persons who are to be benefited, and
(iii) the interests that they are to take,

but a trust will be sufficiently constituted if these three essentials
can be gathered from some writing, even though it has been
executed subsequently to the transfer of the property to the
trustee.[4]

The writing is to be signed by "some person who is able to
declare such trust," that is, the person who is the owner of the
property in respect to which the trust is declared.[5] No provision
is made for signature by an agent.

The statutory provisions apply only to express trusts, and
not to resulting, implied or constructive trusts.[6]

SECTION III. THE VARIATION OF TRUSTS.

The general principle is that apart from statute the Court of Variation of Trusts Act, 1958.
Chancery has no jurisdiction to remodel the limitations contained
in a trust instrument. It will ensure that the trustees carry out

---

[1] S. 7.   [2] S. 53 (1) (b).
[3] *Rochefoucauld* v. *Boustead*, [1896] 1 Ch. 196, 208.   [4] *Ibid.*
[5] *Tierney* v. *Wood* (1854), 19 Beav. 330.
[6] Law of Property Act, 1925, s. 53 (2).

the intention of the settlor as there expressed, but it will not sanction any attempt by them to administer the trust in a manner not authorized by the instrument.[1]

In accordance with this view, it was held by the House of Lords in *Chapman* v. *Chapman*[2] that the Court of Chancery has no inherent jurisdiction to authorize the variation of a trust designed to confer upon infant beneficiaries a benefit that they would not enjoy if the limitations framed by the settlor were to continue undisturbed. This decision made it impossible to rearrange the limitations of a settlement with the object of reducing the amount of estate duty that would ultimately fall upon the infants, although a rearrangement to this end may be made by the Court of Protection in the interest of mental patients[3] and, on the dissolution of a marriage, by the Divorce Court in the interests of children.[4] It was felt that such an innocuous method of saving what might be a very considerable sum of money should be generally available, and therefore it was legalized by the Variation of Trusts Act, 1958. This provides that where real or personal property is held on trusts under any will, settlement or other disposition, whether made before or after the passing of the Act, the court may order any arrangement varying or revoking all or any of the trusts, or enlarging the powers of the trustees of managing or administering any of the property subject to the trusts.[5]

Such an arrangement, however, is permissible only if it is made on behalf of one or more of the following beneficiaries :—

(a) Any person having an interest, vested or contingent under the trust, who by reason of infancy or other disability is incapable of assenting.

(b) Any person, whether ascertained or not, who may at a future date become entitled under the trust.

(c) Any unborn person.

(d) Any person who might take as a discretionary beneficiary under a protective trust if the interest of the principal beneficiary were to be determined.[6]

If an application to the court is made on behalf of a person in

---

[1] *Re New*, [1901] 2 Ch. 534, at p. 544, *per* ROMER, L.J.
[2] [1954] A. C. 429 ; [1954] 1 All E. R. 798.
[3] *In re C.W.M.* [1951] 2 K. B. 714 ; [1951] 2 All E. R. 707, C. A.
[4] *Thomson* v. *Thomson and Whitmee*, [1954] P. 384 ; [1954] 2 All E. R. 462.
[5] Variation of Trusts Act, 1958, s. 1. (1). As to the extent of the jurisdiction thus given to the court, see *In re T's Settlement Trusts*, [1964] Ch. at pp. 160–2, *per* WILBERFORCE, J.
[6] As to protective trusts see *supra*, p. 148; and see *In re Bristol's Settled Estates, Bristol* v. *Jermyn*, [1964] 3 All E. R. 939; [1965] 1 W. L. R. 469.

classes (a), (b) or (c) no order must be made unless it will be for the benefit of that person. As was demonstrated by one learned judge, the court must be satisfied in the case of each individual infant that on balance the proposed variation is for his benefit and also for the benefit of any individual person who may hereafter be born and become interested under the trusts. It need not be shown that the proposed variation will make each individual infant better off, but it must be a reasonable one and one that an adult would be prepared to accept.[1] This requirement that what is proposed must be for the benefit of each infant, however, does not apply to persons in class (d). Thus an arrangement may be allowed even though the court is not satisfied that a benefit will thereby accrue to the potential beneficiaries under a protective trust contained in the settlement. This does not mean that these interests are to be disregarded. The applicants must still convince the court that the proposed arrangement taken as a whole, is one that ought to be sanctioned.[2]

SECTION IV. THE OFFICE OF TRUSTEE.

Trustees are either ordinary or statutory trustees, but we are not concerned to describe the position of the latter.

Ordinary trustees are in the majority of instances appointed by the settlor in the instrument which creates the trust and in such a case are then called original trustees. Prior to 1926 there was no limit upon the number of persons who might be so appointed, but it is now enacted that in the case of settlements of land and dispositions of land on trust for sale the number of trustees shall not in any case exceed four, and that if more than four are appointed, then the four first named (who are able and willing to act) shall alone be the trustees.[3] This provision applies only to trusts of land, and not then if the land is vested in trustees for charitable, ecclesiastical or public purposes. Again, it does not apply to portions trustees in whom a term of years has been vested, or to trustees in whom a term has been vested in order that they may provide for the payment of a rentcharge.[4] *Original trustee.*

Appointment of new trustees. One of the periodical troubles in the history of any trust is the appointment of a new trustee (called a substituted trustee) in place of one who by reason of death or some other event has ceased to function. Formerly it was usual to take power in the instrument of creation to appoint new trustees in certain circumstances, but there is no longer any *New trustees.*

---

[1] *In re Cohen's Settlement Trusts, Eliot-Cohen* v. *Cohen,* [1965] 3 All E. R. 139; [1965] 1 W. L. R. at p. 1236, *per* STAMP, J.
[2] *In re Burney's Settlement Trusts,* [1961] 1 All E. R. 856 ; [1961] 1 W. L. R. 545.
[3] Trustee Act, 1925, s. 34 (2).
[4] *Supra,* p. 126, note 2.

M*

necessity to do this in view of the Trustee Act, 1925, which (re-enacting and extending similar provisions in the Trustee Act, 1893) attaches such a power to trusts in general.   This provides [1] that where a trustee, either original or substituted,

> is dead, or
>
> remains out of the United Kingdom for more than twelve months, or
>
> desires to be discharged, or
>
> refuses or is unfit to act, or
>
> is incapable of acting, or
>
> is an infant, or
>
> has been removed under a power contained in the trust instrument, or
>
> (if a corporation trustee) has been dissolved,

then the person nominated by the trust instrument for the purpose of appointing new trustees or, if there is no such person, then the surviving trustees or the personal representatives of the last surviving trustee may by writing appoint one or more new trustees.

Appointment of additional trustee. — Even if none of the above events has occurred so as to justify the appointment of a new trustee, it is provided that an *additional trustee* may be appointed for any trust where a sole trustee (not being a trust corporation) has been originally appointed, or where there are not more than three trustees, whether original or substituted, none of them being a trust corporation.   The number must, however, never be increased beyond four.[2]

Retirement of trustee. — Apart from statutory provisions a trustee cannot retire from his office unless all the beneficiaries, being of full age, consent, or unless a substituted trustee is appointed to take his place, but since the Conveyancing Act of 1881 it has been permissible in certain circumstances for a trustee to retire even though he is not replaced by another.   The rule now is [3] that where a trustee is desirous of being discharged from the trust, and where after his discharge there will be *either a trust corporation or at least two individuals* to act as trustees, then, if the trustee by deed declares that he desires to be discharged and his co-trustees consent, he shall be deemed to have retired from the trust.

Powers of new trustees. — Every new trustee who is appointed under the statutory provisions has the same powers, authorities and discretions, and may in all respects act, as if he had been originally appointed a trustee by the trust instrument.[4]   But before 1881 the mere appointment of a new trustee did not operate to vest the legal estate of the trust property in him, and it was necessary that he should take a conveyance from the retiring trustees.   Such a conveyance, however, ceased to be necessary after 1881, for the Conveyancing Act of that year made a " vesting declaration "

Vesting of property in new trustees.

Express vesting declaration.

---

[1] Trustee Act, 1925, s. 36.   [3] *Ibid.*, s. 36 (6).
[2] *Ibid.*, 1925, s. 39.   [4] *Ibid.*, s. 36 (7).

sufficient, that is, a declaration made by the appointor in the deed of appointment to the effect that the estate which is subject to the trust shall vest in the new trustee. Even an express declaration of this kind is not necessary now, for the Trustee Act, 1925, provides that [1]:

> " if the deed [appointing the new trustee] is made after the com- Implied
> " mencement of this Act and does not contain such a declaration, the vesting
> " deed shall, subject to any express provision to the contrary therein declaration.
> " contained, operate as if it had contained such a declaration by the
> " appointor extending to all the estates, interests, and rights with
> " respect to which a declaration could have been made."

These provisions relating to an express or an implied declaration do not, however, apply to land held by the trustees as mortgagees ; or |to land held under a lease which contains a covenant against assignment without consent, unless the consent is obtained before the execution of the deed [2]; or to any share, stock, annuity or property which is only transferable in books kept by a company or other body.

So far we have dealt with what may be called the private Power of appointment of new trustees, that is, with their appointment by court to the person upon whom the power is conferred by the trust appoint instrument. But there are cases in which, though desirable, it trustees. may be difficult or impossible for the power of appointment to be exercised within the statutory limits, as for instance where a trustee is convicted of felony, or absconds, or is made bankrupt, or when the trustees appointed by will all die in the testator's lifetime. To provide for such cases the Trustee Act, 1925 [3] (replacing earlier enactments) empowers the court,

> " whenever it is expedient to appoint a new trustee or new trustees,
> " and it is found inexpedient, difficult or impracticable so to do
> " without the assistance of the court,"

to appoint new trustees either in substitution for or in addition to any existing trustee, or even though there is no existing trustee.

Devolution of trustee's estate. The ordinary practice is to appoint two or more trustees of land as joint tenants, so that when one dies his estate and interest pass to the surviving trustee or trustees in accordance with the doctrine of survivorship applicable to joint tenancy. The old rule, however, was that in the event of the death of a sole or sole surviving trustee the trust estate passed to his heir or to his devisee, according as he died testate or intestate. This was altered by the Conveyancing Act, 1881,[4] under which the estate was made to pass to the *personal representatives of the sole surviving trustee* in the case of

---

[1] Trustee Act, 1925, s. 40 (1) (b). [2] *Ibid.*, s. 40 (4).
[3] *Ibid.*, s. 41. [4] S. 30.

deaths occurring on or after January 1st, 1882, and this has now been re-enacted by the Administration of Estates Act, 1925.[1] Until a new trustee is appointed, such personal representatives are capable of exercising any power or trust which was given to or which might have been exercised by the sole trustee.[2]

Devolution of trustee's powers.

---

[1] Administration of Estates Act, 1925, ss. 1 (1), 3 (1) (ii).
[2] Trustee Act, 1925, s. 18.

BOOK II.

ESTATES AND INTERESTS IN LAND.

PART III.

COMMERCIAL INTERESTS.

SUMMARY.

A. INTERESTS CONFERRING A RIGHT TO THE LAND ITSELF

CHAPTER I.

LEASEHOLD INTERESTS.

SUMMARY.

SECTION I. MEANING OF TERM OF YEARS ABSOLUTE.

A leasehold is a legal estate if it is created in the manner required by the law[1] and if it satisfies the definition of a " term of years absolute " contained in the Law of Property Act, 1925.[2] Otherwise it is an equitable interest.[3] A term of years absolute means a term that is to last for a certain fixed period, even though it may be liable to come to an end before the expiration of that period by the service of a notice to quit ; the re-entry of the landlord[4] ; operation of law[5] ; or a provision for cesser on redemption, as in the case of a mortgage term.[6] It includes a term for less than a year, or for one year, or for a year or years and a fraction of a year, and also the tenancy from year to year that is common in the case of agricultural leases.

Meaning of terms of years.

The Act provides that[7]

Concurrent legal estates.

" A legal estate may subsist concurrently with or subject to any other " legal estate in the same land in like manner as it could have done " before the commencement of this Act,"

and it therefore follows, for instance, that the owner of a legal term may by sub-lease grant a legal sub-term to another person. In such a case two legal estates exist at once in the same land.

Reversionary leases.

A term of years absolute is a legal interest notwithstanding that it does not entitle the tenant to enter into immediate possession, but is limited to begin at a future date.

Perpetually renewable leases.

There is no limit of time for which a lease may be made to endure ; periods of 99 or 999 years are common, and longer periods are possible, but all leases for unspecified or for indeterminate periods, such as leases in perpetuity or until war breaks out, are void for uncertainty.[8] The nearest approach to a perpetual lease under the old law was one which was perpetually renewable, that is one in which the lessor covenanted that he would from time to time grant a new lease on the determination of the one then existing, if the lessee should so desire and should pay a fine for the privilege. Leases of this nature were inconvenient[9] and were abolished as from January 1st, 1926.

Their abolition and conversion into leases for 2,000 years.

Perpetually renewable leases existing on January 1st, 1926,

[1] *Infra,* pp. 352 *et seq.*
[2] Law of Property Act, 1925, s. 205 (1) (xxvii).
[3] *Ibid.,* s. 1 (1) (*b*).
[4] *Infra,* pp. 391 ; 397.
[5] For example, where the purposes for which a portions term (*supra,* p. 126, note 2) has been created are satisfied, the term merges in the reversion and ceases accordingly ; Law of Property Act, 1925, s. 5 (1) (2).
[6] *Infra,* p. 571.
[7] Law of Property Act, 1925, s. 1 (5).
[8] *Sevenoaks, Maidstone and Tonbridge Ry. Co.* v. *London, Chatham and Dover Rly.* (1879), 11 Ch. D. 625, 635.
[9] See remarks by JESSEL, M.R., *In re Smith's Charity* (1882), 20 Ch. D. 516.

were converted into leases for 2,000 years calculated from the date at which the existing term began ; and any perpetually renewable sub-lease granted by the tenant out of his interest was converted into a term of 2,000 years less one day.[1] Any fine that was due on renewal became payable as additional rent.[2]

If a contract is made after 1925 which, when properly construed, provides for the grant of a lease with a covenant for perpetual renewal it operates as an agreement to grant a lease for 2,000 years, but the lessor is not entitled to convert into additional rent any fine that may have been reserved.[3] Thus a lessor may find to his discomfiture that a lease, though not expressly made renewable, is converted, by reason of the language used, into a term that will endure for 2,000 years unless the tenant chooses to determine it sooner. This will be the case, for instance, if a lease for three years certain contains a covenant that,

> the lessor will on the request of the tenant grant him a tenancy at the same rent containing the like provisions as are herein contained including the present covenant for renewal.[4]

Such a clause contains the seeds of its own reproduction[5] in the sense that a lease granted for a second period of three years would also contain a covenant for renewal, and so on *ad infinitum*.

The result, then, of the legislation is that there may be a valid contract for renewal, but not for perpetual renewal. In order to keep permissible renewals within reasonable bounds, however, it is enacted that an agreement to renew for a longer period than 60 years from the end of the lease in question shall be void.[6]

A term for 2,000 years that arises as a result of this legislation is in general subject to the covenants, conditions and provisions of the original lease, but the following special incidents have been attached to it by statute :— *Special incidents of the 2,000 years term.*

(*a*) The lessee or his successor in title may terminate the lease by giving at least ten days' written notice before any date at which, but for its conversion, it would have expired if no renewal had taken place.[7]

(*b*) The lessee is bound to register with the lessor every assignment or devolution of the term within six months of its taking place.[8]

(*c*) A lessee who assigns the term to another, thereafter ceases to be liable on the covenants contained in the lease.[9]

---

[1] Law of Property Act, 1922, s. 145, 15th Sched., para. 1.
[2] *Ibid.*, para. 12.
[3] *Ibid.*, para. 5.
[4] *Parkus* v. *Greenwood*, [1950] Ch. 644 ; [1950] 1 All E. R. 436 ; *Northchurch Estates, Ltd.* v. *Daniels*, [1947] Ch. 117 ; [1946] 2 All E. R. 524.
[5] An expression used by counsel in the court below, [1950] Ch. 33, at p. 34.
[6] Law of Property Act, 1922, 15th Sched., para. 7 (2).
[7] Law of Property Act, 1922, 15th Sched., para. 10 (1) (i).
[8] *Ibid.*, para. 10 (1) (ii).
[9] Law of Property Act, 1922, 15th Sched., para. 11 (1).

This applies even to the original lessee, and is therefore an exception to the general rule that despite an assignment he remains liable on his contractual obligations.[1]

Abolition of leases for lives, etc. There were certain other leases of a somewhat peculiar nature that have been disturbed by legislation.

A lease *at a rent, or in consideration of a fine,*[2] made

(i) for life or lives, *e.g.* to T. during the lives of A. and B. ; or
(ii) for a term of years determinable on a life or lives, *e.g.* to T. for 99 years if X. shall so long live ; or
(iii) for a term of years determinable on the marriage of the lessee, *e.g.* to T. for 20 years until T. marries,

now takes effect as a lease for 90 years.[3] This lease may be terminated upon the death or the marriage, as the case may be, of the original tenant, for after these events have occurred a month's notice in writing to terminate the tenancy upon one of the usual quarter days may be given by either side.[4]

SECTION II. THE NATURE OF A TERM OF YEARS.

A term of years arises and the relation of landlord and tenant is created whenever one person, called the landlord or lessor, confers upon another, called the tenant or lessee, the right to the exclusive possession of certain land for a period that is definite or capable of definition. The lessor retains an interest which is called a reversion.

Distinction between licence and lease. **Exclusive Possession.** A necessary feature of a lease is that the lessee shall acquire the right of possession to the exclusion of the lessor.[5] This does not mean, however, that whenever a person is let into exclusive possession he necessarily becomes a lessee. It may well be that he obtains only a personal privilege in the shape of a licence which may be revoked according to the explicit or implicit terms of the contract.[6] Whether a transaction creates a lease or a licence, whatever label the parties may have used, is a question of intention to be inferred from the circumstances. Although a person who is given exclusive possession of

---

[1] *Infra*, pp. 412 *et seq.*
[2] A fine is usually the single payment of a lump sum made by the tenant, and is additional to the rent. By statute the word includes " a premium or foregift and any payment, consideration or benefit in the nature of a fine, premium or foregift " ; Law of Property Act, 1925, s. 205 (1) (xxiii).
[3] Law of Property Act, 1925, s. 149 (6).
[4] *Ibid.*
[5] *L. and N. W. Rly.* v. *Buckmaster* (1874), 10 Q. B. 70, 76. For a modern example of a licence as distinct from a lease, see *Appah* v. *Parncliffe Investments, Ltd.*, [1964] 1 All E. R. 838; [1964] 1 W. L. R. 1064.
[6] *Infra*, pp. 477–81.

land is *prima facie* to be regarded as a tenant, yet he will be nothing more than a licensee if the inference from the circumstances and the conduct of the parties is that he shall have a mere personal privilege of occupation but no definite interest in the land.[1]

> " In all cases where an occupier has been held to be a licensee " there has been something in the circumstances such as a family " arrangement, an act of friendship or generosity or such like to " negative any intention to create a tenancy." [2]

Thus licences rather than leases were created where an employer allowed his retiring servant to remain in his cottage rent free for the rest of his life [3] ; where a father, wishing to provide a home for his son and daughter-in-law, allowed them to occupy a house that he had bought in return for their promise to pay the instalments still due to a building society [4] ; where a landlord allowed the daughter of his deceased employee to remain in her father's cottage rather than evict her immediately [5] ; where a woman bought a house and allowed her brother to occupy it, rent free [6] ; and where a company allowed their former managing director to continue in occupation of a flat on the business premises.[7]

The Period must be Definite. Though a lease may be limited to endure for any specified number of years, however many, it cannot be limited in perpetuity.[8] The term must be for a definite period in the sense that it must have a certain beginning and a certain ending.

There must be certain beginning and ending.

This does not necessarily mean that the parties must immediately fix the exact date of commencement, for it is open to them

Date for commencement of term must be fixed.

---

1 *Booker* v. *Palmer*, [1942] 2 All E. R. 674, at p. 677 ; *Errington* v. *Errington and Woods*, [1952] 1 K. B. 290, and authorities cited *ibid.* at p. 297 ; [1952] 1 All E. R. 149 ; *Cobb* v. *Lane*, [1952] 1 All E. R. 1199 ; *Murray, Bull & Co., Ltd.* v. *Murray*, [1953] 1 Q. B. 211 ; [1952] 2 All E. R. 1079 ; *Isaac* v. *Hotel De Paris, Ltd.*, [1960] 1 All E. R. 348 ; [1960] 1 W. L. R. 239. *Finbow* v. *Air Ministry*, [1963] 2 All E. R. 647 ; [1963] 1 W. L. R. 697.
2 *Facchini* v. *Bryson*, [1952] 1 T. L. R. 1386, 1390, *per* DENNING, L.J.
3 *Foster* v. *Robinson*, [1951] 1 K. B. 149. Also where an evacuee was given the same privilege, *Webb Ltd.* v. *Webb*, Oct. 24, 1951, unreported, but referred to, [1952] 1 K. B. at 297.
4 *Errington* v. *Errington & Woods*, *supra*; but see *infra*, pp. 480–1.
5 *Marcroft Wagons Ltd.* v. *Smith*, [1951] 2 K. B. 496.
6 *Cobb* v. *Lane*, [1952] 1 All E. R. 1199.
7 *Murray, Bull & Co.* v. *Murray*, [1953] 1 Q. B. 211 ; [1952] 2 All E. R. 1079. On the recent development of the law relating to licences, see *infra*, pp. 477–81 ; 68 *L. Q. R.*, pp. 379 *et seq.* ; 69 *L. Q. R.*, pp. 466 *et seq.* ; 16 *M. L. R.*, pp. 1 *et seq.* ; 16 *The Conveyancer*, pp. 323 *et seq.* ; 17 *The Conveyancer*, pp. 440 *et seq.*
8 *Sevenoaks, Maidstone and Tunbridge Ry. Co.* v. *London, Chatham and Dover Ry. Co.* (1879), 11 Ch. D. 625, at pp. 635–6. The effect of an instrument purporting to create a perpetual lease at a rent may perhaps be either to create a yearly tenancy or to pass the fee simple to the lessee subject to the payment of an annual rentcharge in perpetuity ; *Doe d. Roberton* v. *Gardiner* (1852), 12 C. B. 319, 333.

to agree that the lease shall *begin* upon the occurrence of an uncertain event, as for example,

upon the declaration of war by Great Britain[1] ; or
upon possession of the premises becoming vacant.[2]

Such an agreement, though at first conditional, becomes absolute and enforceable as soon as the event occurs.[3]

Reversionary leases.

A term expressed to begin from a past date or, as is more usual, from the date of the lease is called a lease *in possession*. But a term of years, since it is not a freehold estate, does not invest the tenant with seisin, and therefore it has always been possible to make a *reversionary* lease, by which the term is limited to commence at some future date. Formerly such a term might be granted so as to commence at any time in the future, as, for instance, where a lease was made in 1917 to commence in 1946,[4] but a restriction has now been imposed upon this right by the Law of Property Act, 1925, which provides that

" A term, at a rent or granted in consideration of a fine, limited
" after the commencement of this Act to take effect *more than* 21
" *years* from the date of the instrument purporting to create it,
" shall be void, and any contract made after such commencement
" to create such a term shall likewise be void."[5]

The first limb of this enactment nullifies the creation of a reversionary lease limited to take effect more than 21 years from the date of the lease, *e.g.* a lease executed in 1960 for a term of ten years to run from 1985. The second limb nullifies a contract to create *such a term, i.e.* a term that will commence more than 21 years from the date of the lease by which it will eventually be created. For example, a contract made in 1960 to grant a lease for ten years in 1962, the term to run from 1985 is void.[6]

Thus, the Act relates the period of 21 years to the date of the lease, not to the date of the contract. Therefore a contract in a lease for 35 years giving the tenant an option to renew it for a further period of 35 years by making a written request to this effect twelve months before the expiration of the current term, is not void, since the contractual option, if exercised, will result in a term to begin upon the execution of the second lease. It is immaterial that it will be more than 21 years before the contractual right is exercised.[7]

---

[1] *Swift* v. *Macbean*, [1942] 1 K. B. 375 ; [1942] 1 All E. R. 126.
[2] *Brilliant* v. *Michaels*, [1945] 1 All E. R. 121. In this case, however, it was held that no final agreement had been made.
[3] *Ibid.*, at p. 126, citing Fry, *Specific Performance* (6th Edn.), p. 458.
[4] *Mann, Crossman and Paulin* v. *Land Registry*, [1918] 1 Ch. 202.
[5] S. 149 (3). This restriction does not affect terms, such as portions terms, taking effect in equity under a settlement.
[6] *In re Strand and Savoy Properties, Ltd. D.P. Development Co., Ltd.* v. *Cumbrae Properties, Ltd.*, [1960] Ch. 582 ; [1960] 2 All E. R. 327 ; *Weg Motors, Ltd.* v. *Hales*, [1961] Ch. 176; affd. [1962] Ch. 49; [1960] 3 All E. R. 762; affd. [1961] 3 All E. R. 181; see 76 *L. Q. R.* pp. 352–4 (R.E.M.).
[7] *In re Strand and Savoy Properties, Ltd., supra.*

The date upon which a lease is to terminate is generally expressed specifically, but in accordance with the maxim—*id certum est quod certum reddi potest*—it is sufficient if made to depend upon some uncertain event, provided that the event occurs before the lease takes effect; as for example where lands are let to

A. for so many years as B. shall fix.

Date for termination of lease.

On the other hand a lease is void if the date of its termination remains uncertain after it has taken effect. It was accordingly held in *Lace* v. *Chantler*,[1] for instance, that an agreement to let a house

for the duration of the war

did not create a valid tenancy.[2]

There was a troublesome doctrine of the common law which established, in the case of a lease not operating under the Statute of Uses, that the lessee acquired no estate in the land until he actually entered into possession. Until that time he was said to have a mere right to take possession, and this right was called an *interesse termini*. This requisite of entry to perfect a lease was, however, swept away by the Law of Property Act, 1925, and all terms of years absolute, whether created before or after the commencement of the Act, take effect from the date fixed for the commencement of the term without actual entry.[3]

Interesse termini abolished.

SECTION III. CREATION OF TERMS OF YEARS

SUMMARY.

(1) INTRODUCTORY NOTE.

A term of years may be brought into existence either by a lease or by an agreement for a lease.

---

[1] [1944] K. B. 368 ; [1944] 1 All E. R. 305.

[2] A conveyancing device by which the difficulty may be surmounted is to grant a lease for a fixed period determinable upon the happening of the uncertain event, *e.g.* to A. for 99 years terminable on the cessation of hostilities. In *Great Northern Ry. Co.* v. *Arnold* (1916), 33 T. L. R. 114, ROWLATT, J., managed even to construe a lease similar to that in *Lace* v. *Chantler* as a lease for 999 years terminable on the cessation of the 1914 War. The effect of *Lace* v. *Chantler* was to defeat so many leases made before and during the war of 1939 that it was found necessary to save them by a temporary measure, the Validation of War-time Leases Act, 1944.

[3] Law of Property Act, 1925, s. 149 (1), (2).

Lease.

A lease is a conveyance by which the lessor grants to the lessee an interest less than a freehold and less than that to which he himself is entitled. By its own force, if made in the form required by law, it creates the legal relation of landlord and tenant—either at once in the case of an immediate letting or at the agreed future date in the case of a reversionary lease—and it exposes the parties to all the legal consequences of that relation. Thus, for instance, the fact that a tenant holds under a lease confers upon the landlord the right to distrain upon the premises for rent in arrears.

Agreement for lease.

An agreement for a lease, on the other hand, does not operate as an actual conveyance, but is a contract that binds the parties, the one to grant and the other to accept a term of years or a tenancy at will.[1] Such an agreement does not directly and immediately create the relation of landlord and tenant, and so the person who has agreed to let cannot, for instance, distrain *at common law* for arrears of rent, even though the other party has gone into possession.[2]

A lease which is framed in formal and technical language will state that

" The landlord hereby demises unto the tenant all that messuage or " dwelling house, etc.,"

but the mere fact that an instrument is drafted as an agreement does not preclude it from taking effect as an actual demise. Whether the contract operates as a lease or as an agreement depends upon the intention of the parties, which must be collected from all the circumstances.

We will now deal separately with these two modes of creation, beginning with the agreement for a lease.

(2) AGREEMENT FOR A LEASE.

Constituents of enforceable agreement.

No agreement for a lease is enforceable by action unless the following requirements have been satisfied :—

Parties must be *ad idem*.

(i) **A final and complete agreement must have been reached.** An agreement for a lease is an ordinary contract, and in accordance with the general principles of contract law it will not be binding upon the parties until their minds are at one, both upon matters that are cardinal to every agreement for a lease and also upon matters that are part of the particular bargain.[3]

Agreement must be complete.

In the first place the parties must be beyond the stage of negotiation. The contract must be complete, and the question whether it is so or not frequently causes difficulty in cases where

---

[1] *Borman* v. *Griffith*, [1930] 1 Ch. 493.
[2] *Dunk* v. *Hunter* (1822), 5 B. & Ald. 322. But see *infra*, pp. 356–9, as to his position in equity.
[3] *Rossiter* v. *Miller* (1878), 3 App. Cas. 1124, at p. 1151, *per* Lord BLACKBURN.

the parties have agreed that a completed bargain shall be put into some more formal shape. When they have concluded their bargaining and have finally reached agreement, the normal practice is for their solicitors to embody the result in a formal instrument couched in technical legal phraseology and known as a formal contract. There is, of course, no necessity for this. Very often the negotiations are contained in a number of letters which have passed between the intending lessor and lessee, and provided that these show complete agreement upon the terms of the tenancy, the contract is as binding upon them as if it had been drafted by conveyancing counsel. But the difficulty comes when the parties have distinctly agreed that their informal though complete agreement shall be replaced by a formal contract to be drawn up by a solicitor. In such a case the parties, having just made what purports to be a contract, proceed to refer to another contract, and the question is whether they are already finally bound or whether they are free from all liability until they have executed the formal contract. If the latter is the true position, then either can with impunity refuse to execute the formal contract when it has been drawn up.

The principle which governs this case has been thus stated by PARKER, J. : [1]

Agreement to make a contract is not enforceable.

" It appears to be well settled by the authorities that if the docu-
" ments or letters relied on as constituting a contract contemplate
" the execution of a further contract between the parties, it is a
" question of construction whether the execution of the further
" contract is a condition or term of the bargain or whether it is a
" mere expression of the desire of the parties as to the manner in
" which the transaction already agreed to will in fact go through.
" In the former case there is no enforceable contract either because
" the condition is unfulfilled or because the law does not recognize
" a contract to enter into a contract.[2] In the latter case there is a
" binding contract and the reference to the more formal document
" may be ignored."

If, in other words, the parties have made a firm contract, though in a form that probably would not commend itself to a lawyer, they are bound, even though they may have gone on to say that the agreement shall be put into proper form by a solicitor. But if their intention is that the efficacy of the document they have signed shall be conditional upon the execution of a later and more formal contract, no obligation is created until the formal contracts are exchanged.[3] Until that has been done, either party is free to repudiate the bargain.

---

[1] *Von Hatzfeldt-Wildenburg* v. *Alexander*, [1912] 1 Ch. 284, 288–9.
[2] See a criticism of this statement by SARGANT, L. J., in *Chillingworth* v. *Esche*, [1924] 1 Ch. 97, 113–14.
[3] *Trollope & Sons* v. *Martyn Bros.*, [1934] 2 K. B. 436, 455 ; *Eccles* v. *Bryant and Pollock*, [1948] Ch. 93 ; [1947] 2 All E. R. 865. If the exchange takes place by post the earliest date at which the contract is concluded is the date when the later of the two documents is posted ; *ibid.*

In *Winn* v. *Bull*,[1]

> a written agreement was entered into whereby the defendant agreed
> to take from the plaintiff a lease of a house for a certain time at a
> certain rent," subject to the preparation and approval of a formal
> " contract," and it was held that there was no contract.

In fact, it may now be said that the words " subject to
contract " or " subject to formal contract," which are so freely
used by house agents in the drafting of agreements, render
unenforceable any agreement into which they are introduced, unless there are some very exceptional circumstances necessitating
a different construction.[2] An offer is something that by acceptance
creates a bargain, but an offer subject to contract lacks that
essential characteristic.[3] Parties who wish to be bound by an
agreement until it is superseded by another and more formal
document should include in their agreement some such statement
as : " This is a provisional agreement until a fully legalized agreement is signed." This constitutes an immediately binding
obligation and is in no sense conditional.[4]

(ii) There must be a sufficient Memorandum or a sufficient Act of Part Performance.

The Law of Property
Act, 1925, re-enacting[5] in almost identical terms a section of
the Statute of Frauds,[6] contains the following provision which
mutatis mutandis is equally applicable to a contract for a lease of
land :—

Sufficient
memoran-
dum.

> " No action may be brought upon any contract for the sale or
> " other disposition of land or any interest in land, unless the agreement
> " upon which such action is brought, or some memorandum or note
> " thereof, is in writing and signed by the party to be charged or by
> " some other person thereunto by him lawfully authorized."

It follows, therefore, that even when the parties are in complete
accord upon all the terms of the tenancy their agreement will
not be enforceable by either side in the absence of a sufficient
memorandum or of an act of part performance as described
later.[7]

It will be noticed that this particular section of the Act is
worded differently from section 54,[8] which, dealing *inter alia* with
a lease as distinct from an agreement for a lease, provides as we

---

[1] (1877), 7 Ch. D. 29.

[2] *Chillingworth* v. *Esche*, [1924] 1 Ch. 97. On the subject generally, which is
equally relevant to a sale of land, *infra*, pp. 649–50, see *Rossiter* v. *Miller* (1878),
3 App. Cas. 1124 ; *Lockett* v. *Norman-Wright*, [1925] 1 Ch. 56 ; *Raingold*
v. *Bromley*, [1931] 2 Ch. 307 ; *Berry, Ltd.* v. *Brighton and Sussex Building
Soc.*, [1939] 3 All E. R. 217 ; *Spottiswoode, Ballantyne & Co., Ltd.* v. *Doreen
Appliances, Ltd.*, [1942] 2 K. B. 32 ; [1942] 2 All E. R. 65 ; *Brilliant* v.
Michaels, [1945] 1 All E. R. 121 ; 48 *L.Q.R.* pp. 310–16; *Graham and Scott
(Southgate), Ltd.* v. *Oxlade*, [1950] 2 K. B. 257; [1950] 1 All E. R. 856.

[3] *Bennett, Walden & Co.* v. *Wood*, [1950] 2 All E. R. 134.

[4] *Branca* v. *Cobarro*, [1947] K. B. 854; [1947] 2 All E. R. 101.

[5] S. 40.　　　　　　　　　　[6] 29 Car. II, c. 3, s. 4.

[7] *Infra*, p. 349–51.　　　　　[8] *Infra*, p. 353.

shall see that a lease not " put in writing " shall create only a tenancy at will. The present section requires evidence of a completed contract, and it will be satisfied if that evidence can be gathered from a document or from documents signed by the defendant or his agent, and in existence at the time when the action is brought.[1]

There cannot in the nature of things be a completed contract of this kind until final agreement has been reached upon what may be called the cardinal terms of a lease, namely, the parties, the premises, the duration of the lease, and the rent or other consideration, if any, to be paid for the premises.

What the memorandum must contain.

It is essential that there should be written evidence of at least these matters. But this is not necessarily sufficient. There must also be written evidence of the contract actually made, and therefore the memorandum will be insufficient unless it refers to every material term that forms a substantial part of the oral bargain.[2] There is this qualification, however, that

" if a term is exclusively for the benefit of one party, that party may " sometimes waive the benefit of it and sue on the contract for " enforcement, even though the memorandum contain no evidence " of that term." [3]

But if the oral term omitted from the memorandum is beneficial to the defendant as well as to the plaintiff, the latter cannot concede it and then enforce the contract with the term added.[4]

Evidence of cardinal terms necessary.

The memorandum must either name the parties or describe them in such a manner that they can be identified without fair and reasonable dispute, and without resorting to parol evidence directly connected with the contract. If, for instance, the intending lessor is not named, but is referred to in the memorandum as the " proprietor " of the premises,[5] or as " executor "[6] or " trustee "[7] or " personal representative," [8] such description will suffice to satisfy the statute, since the identity of the person described can be easily ascertained ; but if he were merely described as " lessor," the memorandum would be useless,

Description of parties.

---

[1] *Lucas* v. *Dixon* (1889), 22 Q. B. D. 357.

[2] *Hawkins* v. *Price*, [1947] Ch. 645 ; [1947] 1 All E. R. 689 ; *Burgess* v. *Cox*, [1951] Ch. 383 ; [1950] 2 All E. R. 1212. These cases concerned contracts for the sale of land, but the same principle applies to an agreement for a lease.

[3] *Hawkins* v. *Price*, [1947] Ch. 645, at p. 659 ; [1947] 1 All E. R. 689, at p. 690, *per* EVERSHED, J. The learned judge advisedly said " may *sometimes*," since it has been suggested (Fry, *Specific Performance* (6th Edn.), p. 243) that to be capable of waiver a term must be " of no great importance." If this vague test represents the law the result will surely be chaotic uncertainty.

[4] *Burgess* v. *Cox*, [1951] Ch. 383 ; [1950] 2 All E. R. 1212. This is perhaps difficult to reconcile with *Martin* v. *Pycroft* (1852), 2 De G. M. & G. 785 ; *cf. Preston* v. *Luck* (1884), 27 Ch. D. 497.

[5] *Rossiter* v. *Miller* (1878), 3 App. Cas. 1124, at p. 1140.

[6] *Hood* v. *Barrington* (*Lord*) (1868), L. R. 6 Eq. 218.

[7] *Catling* v. *King* (1877), 5 Ch. D. 660.

[8] *Fay* v. *Miller, Wilkins & Co.*, [1941] Ch. 360 ; [1941] 2 All E. R. 18.

for the court would be driven to require parol evidence on the very point on which the statute requires written evidence.[1]

Description of property. The same principle applies to the description of the property, which is the second point upon which the memorandum must furnish evidence. It is impossible to lay down beforehand what is a sufficient description of property, for, however detailed the expressions and even the plans may be, there is more often than not room for controversy,[2] but the general principle is—*id certum est quod certum reddi potest*,[3] and, provided that the memorandum furnishes something definite to go on, extrinsic evidence will be admitted to explain such descriptions as

" Mr. Ogilvie's house," [4]

or

" 24 acres of land, freehold . . . at Totmonslow in the parish of " Draycott in the county of Stafford." [5]

Statement of rent and period of tenancy. Lastly, a statement of the rent and of the dates at which the tenancy is to begin and to end must appear in writing.

"It is settled beyond question that, in order for there to be a valid "agreement for a lease, the essentials are not only for the parties "to be determined, the property to be determined, the length of the "term and the rent, but also the date of its commencement."[6]

The courts will not infer a stipulation that it is to commence within a reasonable time after the agreement.

Effect of non-compliance with statute. The Law of Property Act does not make a parol agreement for a lease void, but merely renders written evidence indispensable to the successful institution of proceedings.[7] The parol agreement is a valid subsisting contract, but nevertheless one of imperfect obligation since it cannot be enforced in one particular way, *i.e.* by action. As we shall see when we discuss the doctrine of part performance its terms may be indirectly enforced in another way.

Form of memorandum. The memorandum need not be in any particular form, but may, for example, consist of a letter written by one of the parties to the other or to a third person, or of an affidavit or a will [8]; it need not be made contemporaneously with the completion of the parol agreement, but is effective if it comes into existence at any time before action brought [9]; and it may also consist of a document that has been drawn up with the express intention of repudiating the parol agreement.[10] If, for instance,

---

[1] See *Sale* v. *Lambert* (1874), L. R. 18 Eq. 1 ; *Potter* v. *Duffield* (1874), L. R. 18 Eq. 4.
[2] *Shardlow* v. *Cotterell* (1881), 20 Ch. D. 90, 93, JESSEL, M.R.
[3] *Plant* v. *Bourne*, [1897] 2 Ch. 281, 288.
[4] *Ogilvie* v. *Foljambe* (1817), 3 Mer. 53.
[5] *Plant* v. *Bourne, supra* ; *Auerbach* v. *Nelson*, [1919] 2 Ch. 383.
[6] *Harvey* v. *Pratt*, [1965] 1 W.L.R. 1025, at p. 1027, *per* Lord DENNING, M. R.; [1965] 2 All E. R. 786.
[7] *Maddison* v. *Alderson* (1883), 8 App. Cas. 467, 488.
[8] *Re Holland*, [1902] 2 Ch. 360, 383.
[9] *Ibid.*
[10] *Bailey* v. *Sweeting* (1861), 9 C. B. (N. S.) 859.

A. orally agrees to take a lease of premises from B. for five years at £100 a year, it is impossible (in the absence of part performance) for either party to enforce the contract ; but if either party writes to the other intimating that he does not intend to carry out the parol undertaking, he will render that undertaking enforceable against himself, should it happen that his letter of repudiation refers to the essential terms.

In fact any kind of signed document which contains the terms that have been settled will satisfy the statute.

The signature must be that of " the party to be charged or his agent," or, in other words, of the defendant in the action. If, therefore, in an agreement between A. and B. the memorandum is signed by A. only, it follows that B. can enforce the contract, but that A. cannot.[1] The signature need not be a subscription written at the foot of the agreement, but may appear anywhere, provided that it was written with the view of governing the whole instrument.[2] Indeed, the signature may consist merely of the defendant's initials [3] or of his printed name,[4] provided that the intention clearly is to authenticate the document. *Signature.*

An agent is " lawfully authorized " to sign the memorandum on behalf of his principal if his authority to do so has been conferred upon him in writing or orally, or if it is reasonably inferable from the attendant circumstances[5] and especially from his instructions. For instance, *Authority of agent to sign.*

"the mere appointment by an owner of an estate agent to dispose
"of a house confers no authority to make a contract; the agent is
"solely employed to find persons to negotiate with the owner; but,
"if the agent is definitely instructed to sell at a defined price, those
"instructions involve authority to make a binding contract and to
"sign an agreement."[6]

When the terms of the agreement are contained not in one, but in several documents, the difficult question often arises whether parol evidence is admissible to connect one document with another. Suppose, for instance, that *Memorandum contained in several documents*

an intending lessee A. has signed a document containing all the terms of the agreement and has paid a quarter's rent in advance. The other party, B., has not signed the written agreement, but has signed a receipt for the rent in the following terms :

---

[1] *Cf. Reuss* v. *Picksley* (1866), L. R. 1 Exch. 342.

[2] *Cf. Johnson* v. *Dodgson* (1837), 2 M. & W. 653 ; distinguish *Caton* v. *Caton* (1867), L. R. 2 H. L. 127.

[3] *Hill* v. *Hill*, [1947] Ch. 231 ; [1947] 1 All E. R. 54.

[4] *Cf. Cohen* v. *Roche*, [1927] 1 K. B. 169 ; *Leeman* v. *Stocks*, [1951] Ch. 941 ; [1951] 1 All E. R. 1043.

[5] *Davies* v. *Sweet*, [1962] 2 Q. B. 300, at p. 305; [1962] 1 All E. R. 92.

[6] *Keen* v. *Mear*, [1920] 2 Ch. 574, at p. 579, *per* ROMER, J.

"Received of A. £30, being payment of one quarter's "rent in respect of the house at Hammersmith."

A. cannot sue on the first document alone since it does not contain B.'s signature; nor on the receipt, because for one reason, though implicitly referring to a lease, it does not state when it is to begin and end.[1]   But if A. is allowed to adduce parol evidence with a view to showing that the receipt is connected with and should be read with the memorandum, then taking the two together he will have a complete memorandum containing all that the statute requires.

When parol evidence admitted to connect documents.

In such a case, it has long been established that, if one document expressly refers to another, the latter can be put in evidence, but as the authorities now stand an implicit reference is also regarded as sufficient.[2]

The present rule may be stated in this way :—

> If you can spell out of the instrument *signed by the party to be charged* a reference in it to some other transaction, you are at liberty to give parol evidence as to what that other transaction is, and if it is evidenced by a document, you can enforce the contract by showing that the two documents contain all the terms of the agreement.[3]

Suppose, for instance, that two parties to an agreement for a lease insert a carbon paper into a typewriter and type the following :

> "I agree to take a lease of 50 High Street for five "years at £100 a year from December 25, 1962, and "to pay £25 by way of rent in advance."

"I," *i.e.* the tenant, signs the top paper ; the landlord signs the carbon copy and also signs a receipt for £25.   If, now, the tenant sues for specific performance he is met by a difficulty, for he cannot rely upon the carbon copy signed by the defendant, since it contains no description of "I."   If, however, there is an implicit reference in the carbon copy to some document which describes "I," there is sufficient written evidence of the necessary terms.   It is clear that the implicit reference exists in at least two forms, since the carbon copy indicates that there is (*a*) the original writing of which the carbon is a duplicate, and (*b*) a transaction connected with the payment of £25.   This transaction may be represented

---

[1] *Cf. Long* v. *Millar* (1879), 4 C. P. D. 450.
[2] *Baumann* v. *James* (1868), 3 Ch. App. 508; *Hill* v. *Hill*, [1947] Ch. 231; [1947] 1 All E. R. 54.
[3] The rule as stated is meant to express the words of RUSSELL, J., in *Stokes* v. *Whicher*, [1920] 1 Ch. 411, at p. 418 ; *Cf. Fowler* v. *Bratt*, [1950] 2 K. B. 96 ; [1950] 1 All E. R. 662 ; *Turner* (*L.D.*) *Ltd.* v. *Hatton* (*R.S.*) (*Bradford*), *Ltd.*, [1952] 1 All E. R. 1286.

by a document, *e.g.* a cheque signed by the plaintiff, and it is open to the plaintiff to show that it is so in fact.[1]

Under this rule the hypothetical agreement suggested above would be enforceable by the tenant against the landlord.

Doctrine of Part Performance. It now remains to be noticed that even though there is no memorandum under the Law of Property Act, yet, if there has been an oral contract followed by a sufficient act of part performance, the result in equity is in effect to exclude the operation of the statute. The attitude adopted by equity is that it would be fraudulent for a defendant to take advantage of the absence of a signed memorandum if he has stood by and allowed the plaintiff to alter his position for the worse by carrying out acts in performance of the contract.

If, for instance, B. has orally agreed to let premises to A., and if A. goes into actual possession of and improves the premises, it would be fraudulent, or at least inequitable, for B. to refuse to implement his bargain on the ground that a sufficient memorandum was lacking.[2] Equity therefore grants a decree of specific performance of the contract against B. In doing this, however, it does not charge him on the contract itself, but holds him liable upon the equities arising from the changed position in which A. finds himself.[3] A. has prejudiced himself by acting on the assumption that B. would carry out the bargain, and the fact that he has been allowed to do this gives him an undoubted equity against B. Upon proof of his act of part performance, therefore, he is allowed by equity to give parol evidence of an agreement that would otherwise require written evidence. If he satisfies the court in these two respects, he is entitled to a decree ordering the other party to execute a formal lease to include the terms which have been agreed upon.

The crucial question is—What is an act of part performance in the eyes of equity? Although one of the parties may have done several things towards performing his side of the agreement, it does not at all follow that they will amount to part performance as defined by law. The mere payment of rent in advance under a parol agreement, for instance, is not sufficient to ground an action by the tenant for specific performance, even though there is no doubt that the payment was made on the understanding that the agreement would be carried out.[4]

As Lord SELBORNE pointed out in the leading case of *Maddison*

Basis of the doctrine of part performance.

What acts amount to part performance.

---

[1] This hypothetical case is based upon *Stokes* v. *Whicher, supra,* which was distinguished in *Timmins* v. *Moreland Street Property Co. Ltd.,* [1958] Ch. 110; [1957] 3 All E. R. 265.

[2] *Caton* v. *Caton* (1866), 1 Ch. App. 137, 148, Lord CRANWORTH.

[3] *Chaproniere* v. *Lambert,* [1917] 2 Ch. 356.

[4] *Thursby* v. *Eccles* (1900), 49 W. R. 281 ; *Chaproniere* v. *Lambert,* [1917] 2 Ch. 356.

v. *Alderson*,[1] no act done in furtherance of the agreement will
satisfy the legal requirements of part performance unless it is one
which unequivocally and in its own nature demonstrates that
some contract relating to the land has been made. It need not
refer to the particular agreement upon which the plaintiff relies.
It must be an act which is intelligible only on the assumption that
some such contract has been made, and if it is explicable on some
other equally good ground, it does not satisfy the test. If, for
instance, A. is found to be in actual possession of land which has
hitherto been owned and occupied by B., the only reasonable
explanation of this change of possession is that the parties have
entered into some contract, either of sale or lease, with regard to
the land. Entry into possession, therefore, is an act of part performance, and if B. resists a suit for specific performance by
relying upon the absence of a written memorandum, A. will be
permitted to show by parol evidence what the actual contract was.[2]

**Why pay-
ment of
money not
an act of
part per-
formance.**

There are at least two reasons why the mere payment of rent
in advance is not a sufficient act of part performance :—

First, payment of money is an equivocal act and, unlike entry into
   possession, does not, in itself, clearly demonstrate that the
   parties must have entered into a contract relating to land.[3]

Secondly, specific performance in a suit founded on part performance is decreed because the relative position of the parties has
   been irremediably altered, with the result that the party who
   has acted acquires an equity against the other, but there
   is nothing irremediable or prejudicial in the payment of
   money. The payer has no equity except the right to recover
   his money, and upon repayment he is in the same position
   as before.[4]

A change of possession is, in the majority of cases, associated
with the doctrine of part performance. Entry into possession is
clearly sufficient. On the other hand, remaining in possession,
unless there are additional circumstances, is not sufficient.

**Distinction
between
entering
into and
remaining in
possession.**

If A. is tenant in possession of lands under a lease which
expires on December 25th, the mere fact that he is still in
possession on January 1st is not sufficiently unequivocal to
found a suit for specific performance of a parol agreement
to grant him a new lease.

The possibility that the landlord has entered into a new contract relating to the land is certainly one explanation of A.'s continuance in possession, but it is not the only explanation. There

---

[1] (1883), 8 App. Cas. 467.
[2] *Morphett* v. *Jones* (1818), 1 Swan. 172 ; *Brough* v. *Nettleton*, [1921]
2 Ch. 25. *Kingswood Estate Co., Ltd.* v. *Anderson*, [1963] 2 Q. B. 169; [1962]
3 All E. R. 593.
[3] *Maddison* v. *Alderson* (1883). 8 App. Cas. 467, at p. 479.
[4] *Chaproniere* v. *Lambert*, [1917] 2 Ch. 356.

are others equally good, as, for instance, that he refuses to go or that he has been given a few days' grace. But if, in addition to remaining in possession after the proper date, A. begins to pay rent at a higher rate than under the old lease,[1] or if he spends money with the approval of the landlord on the improvement of the premises,[2] the requirement of part performance is satisfied, for what he has done is explicable only on the assumption that the landlord has agreed to grant a new lease. If the act relied upon by the plaintiff clearly refers to the type of contract that he seeks to prove, the fact that some ingenious mind might suggest a different explanation will not avail the defendant.[3]

Although possession generally forms the basis of a claim under the doctrine, this is not necessarily so, and to decide whether the act of the plaintiff constitutes part performance in the eyes of the law the practical method of applying Lord SELBORNE'S test is to consider whether a stranger, after learning what had been done, would inevitably conclude that the land in question had been the subject-matter of some agreement between those parties. Thus: *Part performance not inseparable from possession.*

> The defendant entered into an oral contract with the plaintiff to take a lease of a flat, part of the contract being that certain alterations should be made by the plaintiff. During the progress of the alterations the defendant frequently visited the flat and made suggestions as to the manner in which the work should be done. Her suggestions were carried out, and when, on the completion of the work, she repudiated the contract, she was adjudged liable in a suit for specific performance. The submission of the plaintiff to interference by the defendant and the adoption of her suggestions were plainly referable to a contract relating to the premises.[4]

Since the basis of the doctrine of part performance is that the plaintiff, having altered his position on the faith of the contract, acquires an equity against the defendant, it follows that the part performance must be by the plaintiff. *Party who has acted can alone sue.*

It is provided by the Law of Property Act, 1925, that nothing therein contained with regard to formalities shall affect the operation of the law relating to part performance.[5]

It is important to observe that a person who is compelled to base his action on part performance is not in such a favourable position as one who can produce a memorandum satisfying all the requirements of the statute. In the latter case he may recover damages at common law if for some reason, such as undue delay in seeking relief, he cannot obtain a decree for specific performance ; but if he relies solely on part performance he cannot recover damages and he will therefore be remediless if, in the circumstances, specific performance is impossible.[6] *Distinction between contract enforceable at law and one enforceable in equity.*

---

[1] *Miller and Aldworth* v. *Sharp,* [1899] 1 Ch. 622.
[2] *Nunn* v. *Fabian* (1865), L. R. 1 Ch. App. 35.
[3] Cf. *Broughton* v. *Snook,* [1938] Ch. 505 ; [1938] 1 All E. R. 411.
[4] *Rawlinson* v. *Ames,* [1925] 1 Ch. 96 ; *Dickinson* v. *Barrow,* [1904] 2 Ch. 339.
[5] S. 55 (*d*).   [6] *Lavery* v. *Pursell* (1888), 39 Ch. D. 508.

(3) LEASES.

(A) FORMALITIES.

Deed un-
necessary for
leases not
exceeding
three years.

At common law a parol lease was sufficient to create the
relation of landlord and tenant in the case of corporeal hereditaments, and there was no necessity to employ either a deed or a
writing. This is still the law with regard to leases *not exceeding
three years*, for the Law of Property Act, 1925,[1] re-enacting in
effect the Statute of Frauds, 1677, provides that

" the creation by parol of leases taking effect in possession for a
" term not exceeding three years (whether or not the lessee is given
" power to extend the term) at the best rent that can reasonably be
" obtained without taking a fine "

shall be valid.

Meaning of
" lease not
exceeding
three years."

Thus a mere oral lease suffices to create a *legal* term of years,
provided that it is to take effect in possession, that it reserves the
best rent obtainable, and that it is not to last for longer than three
years. A lease exceeds three years within the meaning of the
Act only if it is for a definite term longer than that period. It is
immaterial in such a case that it contains a provision allowing its
earlier determination by notice. On the other hand, a periodic
tenancy for an indefinite period, such as one from year to year or
week to week, may be validly created by a parol lease, for, though
it may endure for much longer than three years, it may equally
well be determined at an earlier date.[2]

Leases
exceeding
three years.

Necessity of Deed. A lease, however, which exceeds three
years will not pass a legal estate immediately and directly to the
tenant unless it is made by deed. The history of this requirement
is as follows. The Statute of Frauds, section 1, enacted[3] that

" All leases . . . or terms of years . . . made or created by
"parol, and *not put in writing and signed by the parties* so making
" or creating the same, or their agents thereunto lawfully authorized
" by writing, shall have the force and effect of leases or estates *at
" will* only."

The second section excepted leases not exceeding three years
at a rent of two-thirds at least of the full improved value of the
land.

The next enactment was the Real Property Act, 1845,[4] which
demanded a further formality by providing that

" A lease required by law to be in writing of any tenements or
" hereditaments . . . made after the first day of October, 1845, shall
" be *void at law* unless also made by *deed.*"

Thus it was only in the case of leases exceeding three years
that a deed became necessary, since it was these alone that had

---

[1] S. 54 (2).
[2] *Kushner* v. *Law Society*, [1952] 1 K. B. 264; [1952] 1 All E. R. 404.
[3] 1677. 29 Car. II, c. 3, s. 1.   [4] S. 3.

previously been " required by law to be in writing." An unsealed lease exceeding three years had and still has a greater effect than is indicated by the language of the two statutes cited, but since 1845 it has never sufficed to pass to the tenant an immediate legal interest equivalent to that which the parties intended to create. The Statutes of 1677 and 1845 have been in effect re-enacted by the Law of Property Act, 1925, in the two following sections :— *Law of Property Act, 1925.*

" 54.—(1) All interests in land created by parol and not put in writing
" and signed by the persons so creating the same, or by their
"agents thereunto lawfully authorized in writing, have, not-
" withstanding any consideration having been given for the
" same, the force and effect of interests at will only.

" (2) Nothing in the foregoing provisions . . . shall affect the
" creation by parol of leases taking effect in possession for a
"term not exceeding three years . . . at the best rent which
" can be reasonably obtained without taking a fine. "

" 52.—(1) All conveyances of land or of any interest therein are
" *void for the purpose of conveying or creating a legal estate*
" unless made by deed.

" (2) This section does not apply to—
" (*d*) leases or tenancies or other assurances not required by law
" to be in writing "

On the surface, therefore, it appears that a parol lease exceeding three years merely creates an equitable tenancy at will, while a written but unsealed lease, though creating an interest in land, does not create a legal estate. This, however, is not an accurate statement, and we must now attempt to define the exact effect of a lease exceeding three years which fails to satisfy the statutory requirements.

(B) Effect of Leases exceeding Three Years which are not made in accordance with the required Formalities.

The scope of the following inquiry is to ascertain, first what was the legal effect between 1677 and 1845 of a lease not put into writing as required by the Statute of Frauds; secondly, what has been the effect since 1845 of a lease not made by deed as required by the Real Property Act of that year. Inasmuch as both these Statutes have been re-enacted by the Law of Property Act, 1925, the result of this inquiry will be a statement of the modern law on the subject. *Scope of inquiry.*

(i) **Effect at Common Law.** The Statute of Frauds said that a lease which was not put in writing should create a mere tenancy at will, and this was the view taken by the common law when a tenant did nothing more than enter into possession of the premises under a parol lease. But common law went further and presumed that a tenant who had not merely gone into possession, but had *Lease not in writing might create a yearly tenancy.*

C.R.P.—N

also paid rent on a yearly basis, became tenant from year to year, and that he held this yearly tenancy subject to such of the terms and conditions of the unwritten lease as were consistent with a yearly tenancy.[1]

Thus in *Richardson* v. *Gifford*[2] in 1834 there was a written agreement by which defendant took certain premises for three and a quarter years and engaged to keep them in good repair while they were in his occupation. The agreement was not signed by both parties and therefore did not satisfy the requirements of the Statute of Frauds.

When the defendant was sued for failure to repair, it was held that though there was no legal contract for a term of three and a quarter years, yet he was liable on the covenant because he became tenant at will upon entry into occupation subject to the terms of the agreement, and afterwards tenant from year to year and still subject to the terms of the agreement.

In the view of the eighteenth-century lawyers, the well-established presumption that possession accompanied by payment of a yearly rent shows an intention in the parties to create a yearly tenancy was not rebutted merely because possession had been taken under a lease that infringed the statute.

Unsealed lease might create yearly tenancy.

The provision of the Real Property Act, 1845, that an unsealed lease should be *void at law* was construed in the same manner. The document was void as a lease in the sense that it did not create the agreed term of years, but if the intended tenant entered into possession and paid rent at a yearly rate, he was presumed to be a yearly tenant.[3]

Position to-day at common law.

Moreover the above represents the legal position at the present day *if we confine our attention to the common law.* A conveyance of land, and this includes a lease,[4] is void under the Law of Property Act, 1925, for the purpose of creating a legal estate unless made by deed (except of course in the case of a lease not exceeding three years), but nevertheless, if the tenant enters into possession and pays a yearly rent, he will become a yearly tenant. Again, by the same Act a term exceeding three years which is not put in writing is to have the force and effect of an equitable interest at will only, but, given the same two facts of possession and payment of rent, it also will be converted into a legal yearly tenancy. It is expressly provided that the requirements of the Act with regard to formalities shall not " affect the right to acquire an interest in land by virtue of taking possession."[5]

---

[1] *Doe d. Rigge* v. *Bell* (1793), 2 S. L. C. 119 ; *Mann* v. *Lovejoy* (1826), Ry. & M. 355 ; *Clayton* v. *Blakey* (1798), 8 Term Rep. 3 ; *Richardson* v. *Gifford* (1834), 1 Ad. & El. 52 ; *Hamerton* v. *Stead* (1824), 3 B. & C. 478, at p. 483, *per* LITTLEDALE, J.

[2] (1834), 1 Ad. & El. 52.

[3] *Martin* v. *Smith* (1874), L. R. 9 Exch. 50. *Rhyl U.D.C.* v. *Rhyl Amusements, Ltd.*, [1959] 1 All E. R. 257 ; [1959] 1 W. L. R. 465, where the lease was void for lack of compliance with the Public Health Act, 1875, s. 177.

[4] S. 205 (1) (ii).   [5] S. 55 (c).

(ii) **Effect in Equity.** Equity, however, took a very different view of the effect of a lease for more than three years which was not put in writing as required by the Statute of Frauds, or which, after 1845, was not made by deed. While admitting that the statutes rendered such a lease incapable of passing the term agreed upon by the parties, courts of equity held that the abortive lease must be regarded as an *agreement for a lease*, provided, of course, that the constituents of an enforceable agreement, as described above, were present. In other words, an *oral* lease followed by an act of part performance, and a *written* lease signed by the party to be charged and constituting a sufficient memorandum of the terms of the bargain, were both allowed to have the same effect as an agreement for a lease. It becomes necessary, therefore, to ascertain what the effect has always been at equity of such an agreement.

An agreement for a lease is a contract to which the equitable remedy of specific performance is peculiarly appropriate. If a party can prove to the satisfaction of the court that such an agreement has been entered into, he can bring a suit for specific performance requiring the other party to execute a deed in the manner required by statute so as to create that legal term which the parties intended to create. One effect, therefore, of such a specifically performable contract is that the prospective tenant immediately acquires an equitable interest in the land in the sense that he has an equitable right to a legal estate.[1]
As was said in a case prior to 1845,[2]

> " The defendant was let into possession under an agreement which
> " gave the parties a right to go into equity to compel the execution
> " of it by making out a formal lease."

The same view was upheld even when the Real Property Act, 1845, had enacted that a lease exceeding three years made otherwise than by deed should be void at law. As Lord CHELMSFORD said in *Parker* v. *Taswell*,[3]

> " The legislature appears to have been very cautious and guarded
> " in language, for it uses the expression ' shall be void at law.' If
> " the legislature had intended to deprive such a document of all
> " efficacy, it would have said that the instrument should ' be void to
> " ' all intents and purposes.' There are no such words in the Act.
> " I think it would be too strong to say that because it is void at law
> " as a lease it cannot be used as an agreement enforceable in Equity,
> " the intention of the parties having been that there should be a lease,
> " and the aid of Equity being only invited to carry that intention into
> " effect."

The effect of this divergence between the views of common law and equity was that, prior to the passing of the Judicature

Marginal notes: Void lease equivalent to agreement for lease. Effect at equity of agreement for lease. Effect of divergence between common law and equity.

[1] *Palmer* v. *Carey*, [1926] A. C. 703, 706 (P.C.).
[2] *Doe d. Thomson* v. *Amey* (1840), 12 Ad. & El. 476.
[3] (1858), 2 De G. & J. 559.

Act, 1873, an unsealed lease and an agreement for a lease resulted in the creation of two entirely different interests, according as the common law or the equitable doctrine was invoked. At common law the tenant acquired the interest of a tenant from year to year if he paid rent and entered into possession : in equity he was entitled to call for the execution of a legal lease and to have inserted therein all the provisions of the void lease or of the agreement.

Effect of Judicature Act.

The Judicature Act, however, materially affected the position. It provides in effect that, whenever an action is brought in any court, the plaintiff may set up equitable claims and the defendant may raise equitable defences, and that, whenever the rules of law and equity are at variance on some particular point, the rule of equity shall prevail.

Doctrine of *Walsh* v. *Lonsdale*. The particular point of variance which existed in the case of an unsealed lease fell to be considered in the leading case of *Walsh* v. *Lonsdale*,[1] decided in 1882. In that case

Walsh v. *Lonsdale*.

> the plaintiff agreed to take a lease of a mill for seven years, and part of the agreement was that a deed should be executed containing *inter alia* a provision that *on any given day* the lessor might require the tenant to pay one year's rent in advance. No deed was executed, and the plaintiff, who was let into possession, paid rent quarterly, but not in advance, for a year and a half. The landlord then demanded a year's rent in advance and upon refusal distrained for the amount. The plaintiff brought the action to recover damages for illegal distress, and for specific performance of the agreement for a lease.
>
> The main ground upon which he rested his claim was that, as he had been let into possession and had paid rent under an agreement which did not operate as a lease, he was in the position of a tenant from year to year and held the mill upon such of the agreed terms as were consistent with a yearly tenancy. The condition making a year's rent always payable in advance was obviously inconsistent with a yearly tenancy which could be determined by half a year's notice, and for this reason it was argued that the distress was illegal.

Agreement for lease may be as efficacious as a lease.

This argument did not prevail. It was decided that a tenant who holds under an agreement for a lease of which specific performance will be decreed occupies the same position *vis a vis* the landlord, as regards both rights and liabilities, as he would occupy if a formal lease under seal had been executed.

If a lease by deed had been executed in this case on the lines of the agreement, the defendant would have been entitled to distrain for rent not paid in advance, and the mere fact that the formal lease had not been actually made was not to prejudice his rights. Sir GEORGE JESSEL, M.R., put the matter thus :—

> " There is an agreement for a lease under which possession has been
> " given. Now since the Judicature Act the possession is held under
> " the agreement. There are not two estates as there were formerly

---

[1] (1882), 21 Ch. D. 9.

" —one estate at common law by reason of the payment of the rent
" from year to year, and an estate in equity under the agreement.
" There is only one court and the equity rules prevail in it. The
" tenant holds under the same terms in equity as if a lease had been
" granted, it being a case in which both parties admit that relief is
" capable of being given by specific performance. That being so he
" cannot complain of the exercise by the landlord of the same rights
" as the landlord would have had if a lease had been granted. On
" the other hand, he is protected in the same way as if a lease had
" been granted ; he cannot be turned out by six months' notice as a
" tenant from year to year. He has a right to say : ' I have a lease
" ' in equity and you can only re-enter if I have committed such a
" ' breach of covenant as would, if a lease had been granted, have
" ' entitled you to re-enter according to the terms of a proper proviso
" ' for re-entry.' That being so, it appears to me that being a lessee in
" equity he cannot complain of the exercise of the right of distress
" merely because the actual parchment has not been signed and
" sealed."

Such, then, is the doctrine of *Walsh* v. *Lonsdale.* It is one
example of the principle that equity regards as already done what
the parties to a transaction have agreed to do—a principle that is by
no means confined to an agreement for a lease, for it applies to any
agreement for valuable consideration for the transfer of a proprietary interest to another, whether by way of sale, mortgage or
other disposition.

In the context of landlord and tenant, *Walsh* v. *Lonsdale* has
been followed[1], qualified[2] and explained[3] in later cases and is now
the governing rule whenever it is necessary to ascertain the effect
of a lease or agreement which is not made by deed as required by
the Law of Property Act, 1925. It goes perilously near to
neutralizing the effect of that section[4] of the Act which provides
that all conveyances of land

" are void for the purpose of transferring or creating a legal estate   *Agreement*
" unless made by deed,"   *may not be*
  equivalent
for if a tenant has an enforceable right to call for a deed, he is, as   *to lease.*
far as his rights and liabilities in relation to the landlord are
concerned, in practically the same position as if he actually had
a deed.

It must not, however, be concluded that an agreement for a
lease is as effective in all respects and against all persons as a lease.
This is not so.[5] What JESSEL, M.R., meant was that if, in litigation between the parties, the circumstances would justify a

---

[1] *Lowther* v. *Heaver* (1889), 41 Ch. D. 248 ; *Coatsworth* v. *Johnson* (1886)
55 L. J. Q. B. 220.
[2] *Cornish* v. *Brook Green Laundry, Ltd.,* [1959] 1 Q. B. 394 ; [1959] 1 All
E. R. 373, where it was held that it cannot be invoked if the agreement to
grant a term of years is subject to a condition precedent performable by the
proposed tenant and not yet performed.
[3] *Manchester Brewery Co.* v. *Coombs,* [1901] 2 Ch. 608 ; *Gray* v. *Spyer,*
[1922] 2 Ch. 22.
[4] S. 52 (1); *supra,* p. 353.
[5] *Manchester Brewery* v. *Coombs,* [1901] 2 Ch. 608, 617.

decree for the execution of a sealed lease, then both in the Queen's Bench Division and in the Chancery Division, the case must be treated as if such a lease had been granted. There are at least three facts which illustrate the limitations of the doctrine, and the advantages of a lease as compared with a mere agreement for a lease.

First, the doctrine stands excluded if the agreement is one of which equity will not grant specific performance.

Specific performance is still a discretionary remedy and will not be granted in all cases, as for instance where a lessee who seeks the aid of the court will be unable to perform the covenants in the lease owing to his insolvent state or where he has already committed a breach of a covenant that would have formed part of the lease. Thus, in *Coatsworth* v. *Johnson* [1] :—

> The plaintiff entered into possession under an agreement that the defendant would grant him a lease for twenty-one years. Before any rent was due or had been paid, the defendant gave him notice to quit and evicted him on the ground that he had done that which amounted to a breach of a covenant contained in the agreement and intended to be inserted in the lease.

The plaintiff sued in trespass, but failed. At common law, having paid no rent, he was a mere tenant at will and as such could be evicted at the pleasure of the defendant; in equity he was precluded from obtaining a decree for specific performance, since he had broken a covenant into which he had entered.

Secondly, the statutory definition of " conveyance " [2] includes a lease but not an agreement for a lease.

Thus, a tenant under a mere agreement cannot claim those privileges which are granted by section 62 of the Law of Property Act, 1925,[3] to one who takes a " conveyance " of land.[4]

Thirdly, the doctrine does not in all cases affect the rights of third parties.[5]

Agreement for a lease not always enforceable against third parties.

For instance, privity of estate exists between a landlord and an assignee from a tenant holding *under a lease*, so as to make the covenants enforceable by and against the assignee,[6] but no such privity exists in the case of an assignee from a person "whose only title to call himself a lessee depends on his right to specific performance of the agreement." [7] But a more important fact is that, since an agreement confers a mere equitable right upon the lessee, it will not on general principles be enforceable against a purchaser of a legal estate (including a lessee under a sealed

---

[1] (1886), 55 L. J. Q. B. 220.
[2] Law of Property Act, 1925, s. 205 (1) (ii).
[3] *Infra*, pp. 485-7.
[4] *Borman* v. *Griffith*, [1930] 1 Ch. 493.
[5] *Manchester Brewery* v. *Coombs*, [1901] 2 Ch. 608 ; *Purchase* v. *Lichfield Brewery Co.*, [1915] 1 K. B. 184.
[6] *Infra*, pp. 404 *et seq.*
[7] *Purchase* v. *Lichfield Brewery Co.*, *supra*, at p. 188, *per* LUSH, J.

lease) in the land to which the agreement relates. To quote the words of MAITLAND :

> " Between the contracting parties an agreement for a lease may be as
> " good as a lease ; just as between the contracting parties an agree-
> " ment for the sale of land may serve as well as a completed sale and
> " conveyance. But introduce the third party and then you will see
> " the difference. I take a lease ; my lessor then sells the land to X. ;
> " notice or no notice, my lease is good against X. I take a mere
> " agreement for a lease, and the person who has agreed to grant the
> " lease then sells and conveys to Y., who has no notice of my merely
> " equitable right. Y. is not bound to grant me a lease." [1]

It must be observed, however, that an agreement for a lease is now an *estate contract* within the meaning of the Law of Property Act, 1925,[2] and that therefore it will be enforceable against third parties who acquire the land from the lessor, if it has been registered as a *land charge* at the Land Registry.[3] Registration constitutes notice to the whole world, lack of registration renders the agreement void against a later purchaser of the legal estate for money or money's worth,[4] even though in actual fact he may have known of its existence. Thus

Agreement for a lease may be registered.

> if A. takes such an agreement from B. and then B. wrongfully sells
> and conveys the land to an unsuspecting purchaser, Y., the contract
> of A. *if registered* will prevail against Y. in any court, but *if not
> registered* will be defeated by the conveyance, even though Y., far
> from being unsuspecting, actually knew that it had been made.

If, however, in the case given A. goes into possession of the land before the sale to Y. and pays rent on a yearly basis, he acquires a yearly tenancy which will be binding upon Y. The failure of A. to register presumably does not affect the *legal* estate that arises in him at common law under the rules already discussed. If this is so, Y. can, of course, determine the tenancy by half a year's notice.[5]

Summary. We have now reviewed the methods whereby the relation of landlord and tenant may be constituted, and it may be helpful in conclusion to summarize the present state of the law.

Summary statement of how relation-ship of land-lord and tenant arises.

1. A parol, written or sealed lease not exceeding three years confers a legal term of years upon the tenant.

2. A sealed lease exceeding three years has the same effect.

3. A written lease exceeding three years confers an equitable term upon the tenant by virtue of the doctrine of *Walsh* v. *Lonsdale*, provided that there is a sufficient memorandum as required by the Law of Property Act, 1925. Where there is such a memorandum there will be no occasion,

---

[1] Maitland, *Equity*, p. 158.
[2] S. 2 (3) (iv); *infra*, p. 669.
[3] Land Charges Act, 1925, ss. 10 (1), C. (iv) ; 13 (2) ; *infra*, p. 648.
[4] *Sharp* v. *Coates*, [1948] 1 All E. R. 136 ; on appeal, [1949] 1 K. B. 285 ; [1948] 2 All E. R. 871.
[5] *Infra*, p. 419.

owing to the superior efficacy of the *Walsh* v. *Lonsdale* doctrine, to rely upon the common law rule that possession plus payment of a yearly rent may raise a yearly tenancy. The agreement should, however, be registered as a land charge.[1]

4. A parol lease exceeding three years will confer an equitable term of years upon the tenant under the doctrine of *Walsh* v. *Lonsdale* if a sufficient act of part performance is proved ; but if there is no act of part performance and therefore no enforceable contract, the parol lease will create a yearly tenancy if followed by possession and the payment of a yearly rent.

Suppose, for instance, an oral agreement between A. the landlord and B. the tenant, who already holds under a lease expiring on December 25th, that B. shall have a new lease on the same terms as the present one. B. is in possession, but, as we have already seen, the mere fact of *remaining on* in possession does not constitute an act of part performance, and therefore, if A. repudiates his agreement, the want of an enforceable contract will debar B. from relying on the equitable doctrine of *Walsh* v. *Lonsdale*. There will be nothing, however, to prevent him from relying on the common law doctrine and claiming a yearly tenancy.

SECTION IV. TENANCIES FROM YEAR TO YEAR, AT WILL AND AT SUFFERANCE.

A tenancy from year to year differs from a tenancy for a fixed number of years, in that, unless terminated by a proper notice to quit, it may last indefinitely ; and from a tenancy at will, in that the death of either party or the alienation of his interest by either party does not effect its determination. It is practically the universal form of letting in the case of agricultural lands.[2]

It may arise either by express agreement, or by operation of law.

Yearly tenancy by express creation.

1. Where the tenancy is created by express agreement, the phrase best adapted for carrying out the intention of the parties is "from year to year," since this enables the tenancy to be determined at the end of the first or any subsequent year.[3] But it sometimes happens that the parties by inadvertence use expressions which have the effect of creating a tenancy for at least two years, as for example:

" for one year and so on from year to year,"

in which case the tenancy can be determined only by notice in the second or any later year.[4]

---

[1] *Infra*, p. 669
[2] It is greater than a tenancy for one year, *Bernays* v. *Prosser*, [1963] 2 Q. B. 592.
[3] *Doe d. Clarke* v. *Smaridge* (1845), 7 Q. B. 957.
[4] *Brooke* v. *Searle*, [1912] 1 Ch. 610 ; *Cannon Brewery* v. *Nash* (1898), 77 L. T. 648.

2. A tenancy from year to year will arise by operation or pre- | Implied
sumption of law whenever a person is in occupation of land | yearly
with the permission of the owner, not as a licensee nor for an | tenancy.
agreed period, and he pays rent measured by reference to a
year. The two important cases where this occurs are where
either a tenant at will or a tenant at sufferance pays a yearly
rent.

(a) **Where a Tenant at Will pays a Yearly Rent.** | Tenancy
Generally speaking, a tenancy at will exists when A. | at will.
occupies the land of B. on the understanding that A.
may go when he likes and that B. may terminate A.'s
interest when he likes. LITTLETON says :—

> " Tenant at will is where lands or tenements are let by one
> " man to another, to have and to hold to him at the will of
> " the lessor, by force of which lease the lessee is in possession.
> " In this case the lessee is called tenant at will, because he
> " hath no certain or sure estate, for the lessor may put him
> " out at what time it pleaseth him." [1]

But such a tenancy equally arises when possession is held at the will of the lessee, and indeed it is
important to notice that, even though a lease is made
determinable at the will of the lessor only, it is also by
implication determinable at the will of the lessee. In
other words, every tenancy at will must be at the will of
both parties.[2] In the words of Lord SIMONDS :—

> " A tenancy at will though called a tenancy is unlike any
> " other tenancy except a tenancy at sufferance to which it is
> " next of kin. It has been properly described as a personal
> " relation between the landlord and his tenant : it is determined
> " by the death of either of them or by one of a variety of acts,
> " even by an involuntary alienation, which would not affect
> " the subsistence of any other tenancy."[3]

The express creation of a tenancy at will is a rare | Implied
phenomenon, but where a person has been given ex- | tenancies
clusive possession of premises for an indefinite period | at will.
without a declaration of the exact interest that he is to
hold and without anything to explain why he has been
allowed into occupation, he is presumed to be a tenant at
will. Nevertheless, his true position depends at bottom
upon the intention of the parties, and the presumption is
rebutted if the circumstances negative an intention to
create a tenancy at will. It may well appear that he was
let into possession as a licensee.[4]

The courts, indeed, have altered their attitude to-

---

[1] Litt., s. 68.
[2] Co. Litt. 55*a* ; *Fernie* v. *Scott* (1871), L. R. 7 C. P. 202.
[3] *Wheeler* v. *Mercer*, [1957] A. C. 416, at p. 427; [1956] 3 All E. R. 631,
at p. 634.
[4] *Supra,* pp. 338–9; *infra,* pp. 477 *et seq.*

N*

wards implied tenancies at will in modern times, being partly moved perhaps by a desire to temper the severity of the statutory rule that the lessor loses his right to recover the land if the tenant remains in occupation for thirteen years from the commencement of the tenancy without a written acknowledgment of the lessor's title.[1] It was formerly held, for instance, that a person allowed to occupy a house rent free was a tenant at will, not a licensee, on the ground that his right to exclusive possession was incompatible with the position of a mere licensee.[2] But in the modern view, no incompatibility exists,[3] and therefore the presumption that such an occupier is a tenant at will may well be rebutted by the surrounding circumstances.[4]

Tenancies at will disfavoured.

Despite the termination of his tenancy, a tenant at will has always been allowed a right to emblements, *i.e.* a right to re-enter the land at harvest and recover the crops that he has sown. This situation, in which the land reverted to the lessor but the right to enjoyment remained in effect with the tenant, seemed unsatisfactory to the common law courts and if the circumstances warranted it they were disposed to treat a tenancy at will as having been converted into one from year to year.[5]

Tenant at will may become yearly tenant.

Thus, it has been the law from an early date that the payment and acceptance of rent is presumptive evidence of an intention by the parties to establish a yearly tenancy, provided that the rent is contractually assessed on a yearly basis.[6] CHAMBRE, J., said:—

" If he accepts yearly rent, or rent measured by any aliquot " part of a year, the courts have said that is evidence of a taking " for a year." [7]

The assessment of rent on a yearly basis is evidence of an intention to create a yearly tenancy, even though payment may fall due at more frequent intervals such as every quarter or month. This is not so, however, if rent is fixed by reference to some period less than a year.[8] Where, for example, a lease for one year reserves a rent of £3 weekly, the tenant holds under a weekly tenancy if he remains in possession after the end of the year.[9] But, the presumption in favour of a yearly tenancy raised by the payment and acceptance of rent may be rebutted by contrary evidence, as for instance by proof that, unknown to the lessor, the

---

[1] Limitation Act, 1939, s. 9 (1) ; *infra*, p. 819.
[2] *Lynes* v. *Snaith*, [1899] 1 Q. B. 486.   [3] *Supra*, pp. 338–9.
[4] *Cobb* v. *Lane*, [1952] 1 All E. R. 1199 ; contrast *Buck* v. *Howarth*, [1947] 1 All E. R. 342.
[5] Smith's *Leading Cases*, notes to *Clayton* v. *Blakey*, vol. ii. p. 130.
[6] *Clayton* v. *Blakey*, *supra*.
[7] *Richardson* v. *Langridge* (1811), 4 Taunt. 128.
[8] *Ladies' Hosiery & Underwear, Ltd.* v. *Parker*, [1930] 1 Ch. 304.
[9] *Ibid.*, at pp. 327–9 ; *Adler* v. *Blackman*, [1953] 1 Q. B. 146 ; [1952] 2 All E. R. 945.

payments have been made by a squatter who disseised the original occupier.[1]

(b) Where a Tenant at Sufferance pays a Yearly Rent.

This is the second case in which a tenancy from year to year may arise by presumption of law. Lord COKE said :—

Tenancy at sufferance.

> " Tenant at sufferance is he that at first comes in by lawful " demise and after his estate ended continueth in possession " and wrongfully holdeth over." [2]

A man, for example, becomes a tenant at sufferance if having an estate *pur autre vie*,[3] he continues to hold after the death of the *cestui que vie*; or if being tenant for a fixed term, he " holds over," *i.e.* remains in possession without the consent of the landlord, after the term has come to an end.

Such a person differs from a tenant at will because his holding over after the determination of the term is a wrongful act, and he differs from a disseisor in that his original entry upon the land was lawful.[4]

A tenant at sufferance, unless he is a tenant of premises within the Rent Restriction Acts,[5] is in a precarious position. He may be ejected at any moment and has no right to emblements, while he becomes liable to statutory penalties for the sin of remaining in occupation after he should have departed. In the view of the common law tenants at sufferance came under no liability to pay rent, since it was the folly of the owners that suffered them to continue in possession after their estate had ended,[6] but the Landlord and Tenant Act, 1730,[7] enacts that any tenant (or any other person getting possession under or by collusion with him) who shall wilfully hold over after the determination of the term, and after demand made and written notice given for delivery up of possession, shall pay double the yearly value of the lands for the time the premises are detained. A tenant is not deemed to hold over " wilfully " unless he is well aware that he has no right to retain possession.[8]

Liabilities of tenant at sufferance.

Similarly, by the Distress for Rent Act, 1737, a tenant holding under a periodic tenancy who gives notice to quit and who does not give up possession in accordance with his notice is liable to pay double the rent for the time he remains

---

[1] *Tickner* v. *Buzzacott*, [1965] Ch. 426; [1965] 1 All E. R. 131. In this case, the original occupier was not a tenant at will but was holding under a lease for an unexpired period of 75 years.

[2] Co. Litt. 57*b*. [3] *Supra*, p. 184.

[4] Co. Litt. 57*b*, and Butler's note to 270*b*. [5] *Infra*, p. 423.

[6] Cruise, Digest, Tit. ix., c. ii. 5.

[7] S. 1. Distinguish the statutory tenant, *i.e.* one who holds over under the Rent Restriction Acts.

[8] *French* v. *Elliott*, [1959] 3 All E. R. 866 ; [1960] 1 W. L. R. 40.

in possession.[1] Such a person is not a tenant at sufferance, but his tenancy is statutorily prolonged at double rent.

On the other hand, a tenant at sufferance, since he is in possession, may maintain trespass against a third party or recover in ejectment against a mere wrongdoer,[2] and if he remains in possession for twelve years without paying rent, he defeats the right of the landlord and of those claiming under the landlord to recover the land.[3]

How ten-
ancy at
sufferance
becomes a
yearly
tenancy.

Our present task, however, is to see how a tenancy at sufferance may be converted by implication of law into a tenancy from year to year. In brief this conversion takes place if the landlord waives the tort of the tenant.[4]

A. L. SMITH, L.J., explained this in *Dougal* v. *McCarthy*[5] :

" If the landlord consents to such holding over by the
" tenant, and the tenant consents to remain in possession as
" tenant, then the implication of law is, unless there is evidence
" to rebut it, that the tenant holds over as tenant from year to
" year on the terms of the old tenancy so far as they are not
" inconsistent with a tenancy from year to year."

The best evidence of this consent is the payment and acceptance of rent on a yearly basis. Thus in *Dougal* v. *McCarthy*[5]

premises were let at an annual rent of £140 for one year ending February 1st. The tenants remained in possession after February 1st and on February 25th they received a demand from the landlord for £35, being one quarter's rent due in advance. The tenants did not answer this demand, but wrote on March 26th intimating their intention to discontinue the tenancy.

It was held that under the circumstances the parties must be taken to have consented to a tenancy from year to year on the terms of the original lease.

A. L. SMITH, L.J., said :—

" In the present case there is a direct statement by the land-
" lord to the tenants that he consents to their holding over,
" because on February 25th, three weeks after the expiration of
" the tenancy, he writes asking for a quarter's rent as on a fresh
" tenancy. For a whole month the tenants do nothing, but hold
" over with notice that the landlord is demanding rent from them
" as tenants on the terms of the agreement which expired on
" February 1st. Speaking for myself, I should say that the
" proper inference from that was that the tenants consented to
" hold over on the terms of the old agreement."

If, however, the contractual tenant who " holds over " occupies premises that are within the Rent Restriction Acts, the landlord has no alternative but to accept the rent, for the

[1] S. 18.
[2] *Asher* v. *Whitlock* (1865), L. R. 1 Q. B. 1.
[3] *Re Jolly,* [1900] 2 Ch. 616.
[4] *Right d. Flower* v. *Darby and Bristow* (1786), 1 Term Rep. 159.
[5] [1893] 1 Q. B. 736, at p. 743 ; *Lowther* v. *Clifford,* [1926] 1 K. B. 185, affd., [1927] 1 K. B. 130.

tenant becomes a " statutory tenant " and not a tenant holding under a new contractual agreement.[1]

It will have been observed that where a yearly tenancy arises by implication of law there is often some instrument of agreement under which the premises were formerly held, or under which it was intended that they should be held. For instance, there is the old lease when a tenant holds over with the consent of the landlord and, as in *Walsh* v. *Lonsdale*,[2] there is the void lease or the mere agreement for a lease where the formalities for the creation of the strict relationship of landlord and tenant are wanting. The problem that arises in these cases is whether the covenants and the terms of the instruments in question continue to bind the parties after they have changed their former position and the tenant holds from year to year. Strictly speaking, this is a matter of evidence to be decided by the jury, but the general principle is that the yearly tenant holds the land subject to all the terms of the old or the void lease or the agreement, as the case may be, where they are not inconsistent with the general nature of a yearly tenancy.

Terms upon which implied tenancy held.

Examples of terms which in this way will be read into an implied yearly tenancy are agreements to pay rent,[3] to keep a house in repair,[4] to keep the premises open as a shop and to promote its trade as far as possible.[5]

On the other hand, covenants by the tenants to build,[6] or to paint every three years,[7] and a covenant by the lessor giving the tenant an option to purchase the freehold at a certain price[8] are incompatible with a yearly tenancy and will not be enforced.

SECTION V. RIGHTS AND LIABILITIES OF LANDLORD AND TENANT.

SUMMARY.

---

[1] *Morrison* v. *Jacobs*, [1945] 1 K. B. 577; [1945] 2 All E. R. 430; *infra*, P 432.

[2] *Supra*, p. 356.   [3] *Lee* v. *Smith* (1854), 9 Exch. 662.

[4] *Cole* v. *Kelly*, [1920] 2 K. B. 106.

[5] *Sanders* v. *Karnell* (1858), 1 F. & F. 356.

[6] *Bowes* v. *Croll* (1856), 6 E. & B. 255, 264.

[7] *Pinero* v. *Judson* (1829), 6 Bing. 206.

[8] *Bradbury* v. *Grimble*, [1920] 2 Ch 548.

In the majority of cases the rights and the liabilities of a landlord and a tenant are fixed by the express covenants that, having been settled by the parties, are incorporated in the lease or the agreement under which the premises are held. But an agreement may be silent on several matters of importance, or there may be no agreement at all, and therefore it is necessary to consider, first, what the position of the parties is where there are no express covenants, and then to notice shortly the usual covenants common to all ordinary leases.

(1) POSITION WHERE THERE ARE NO EXPRESS COVENANTS OR CONDITIONS.

(A) IMPLIED OBLIGATIONS OF THE LANDLORD.

Implied covenant for quiet enjoyment.

(i) Quiet Enjoyment. A covenant that the lessee shall have quiet enjoyment of the premises is implied in every lease that does not expressly deal with the matter.[1] The meaning of this is that the lessee shall be put into possession and that he shall be entitled to recover damages if his enjoyment is substantially disturbed by the acts, either of the lessor or of somebody claiming under the lessor.[2] Instances are, where the lessor, having reserved the right to work minerals under the land, so works them as to cause the land to subside[3]; or where, in a lease of shooting rights, he erects buildings so as substantially to reduce the area over which the rights are exercisable[4]; or where, with a view to getting rid of the tenant, he removes the doors and windows of the demised premises,[5] or subjects him to persistent and prolonged intimidation;[6] or where he erects scaffolding which obstructs access to the premises.[7] There is no liability under the covenant, however, if the act of disturbance is committed by a person claiming not under the lessor, but under a title paramount to his.[8]

---

[1] *Markham* v. *Paget*, [1908] 1 Ch. 697. In early days there was no such implication unless the word *demise* had been used in the lease ; *ibid.*

[2] *Jones* v. *Lavington*, [1903] 1 K. B. 253 ; *Sanderson* v. *Berwick-upon-Tweed Corpn.* (1884), 13 Q. B. D. 547, 551 ; *Matania* v. *National Provincial Bank*, [1936] 2 All E. R. 633.

[3] *Markham* v. *Paget*, [1908] 1 Ch. 697.

[4] *Peech* v. *Best*, [1931] 1 K. B. 1 (a case, however, of an express covenant).

[5] *Lavender* v. *Betts*, [1942] 2 All E. R. 72.

[6] *Kenny* v. *Preen*, [1963] 1 Q. B. 499; [1962] 3 All E. R. 814.

[7] *Owen* v. *Gadd*, [1956] 2 Q. B. 99; [1956] 2 All E. R. 28, a case of an express covenant, but equally applicable to an implied covenant.

[8] *Jones* v. *Lavington, supra.*

(ii) **Fit for Habitation.** Again, upon the letting of a furnished house, there is an implied warranty, in the nature of a condition, that the premises shall be reasonably fit for habitation at the date fixed for the commencement of the tenancy.[1] Thus,

> if the house is infested with bugs,[2] if its drainage is defective,[3] or if it has been lately occupied by a person suffering from tuberculosis,[4]

the tenant is entitled to repudiate the tenancy and to recover damages. But provided that the house is fit for habitation at the beginning of the tenancy, the fact that it later becomes uninhabitable imposes no liability upon the landlord.[5]

The implied condition just noticed is confined to furnished houses. If a landlord lets an unfurnished house or flat, or if he leases land, there is in general no implied covenant by him that the house is fit for habitation,[6] or that the land is suitable for the purpose for which it has been let,[7] or that it is safe from dangerous trees situated on his own adjoining property,[8] or that it can be lawfully used in the manner desired by the tenant,[9] or that it is free from dangerous defects.[10] In fact, it is well established that, in the absence of an express contract, the landlord is not liable for defects rendering an unfurnished house dangerous, even though they are due to his own acts.[11]

This principle, however, is subject to an important exception introduced by statute for the protection of persons taking houses at a low rental. The Housing Act, 1957, provides that in any contract made after 6th July, 1957, for letting for human habitation a house or part of a house at a rent not exceeding £80 in the administrative county of London and £52 elsewhere, there shall be implied a condition, notwithstanding any condition to the contrary, that the landlord will keep the house fit for human habitation throughout the tenancy.[12] There is no such implication, however, if the letting is for at least three years upon the terms

Implied warranty in the case of a furnished house.

Unfurnished houses.

Housing Act, 1957.

---

[1] *Collins* v. *Hopkins*, [1923] 2 K. B. 617.
[2] *Smith* v. *Marrable* (1843), 11 M. & W. 5.
[3] *Wilson* v. *Finch-Hatton* (1877), 2 Ex. D. 336.
[4] *Collins* v. *Hopkins, supra.*
[5] *Sarson* v. *Roberts*, [1895] 2 Q. B. 395.
[6] *Hart* v. *Windsor* (1843), 12 M. & W. 68 ; *Robbins* v. *Jones* (1863), 15 C. B. (N. S.) 221 ; *Cruse* v. *Mount*, [1933] Ch. 278 ; *Bottomley* v *Bannister*, [1932] 1 K. B. 458.
[7] *Sutton* v. *Temple* (1843), 12 M. & W. 52.
[8] *Shirvell* v. *Hackwood Estates Co.*, [1938] 2 K. B. 577; [1938] 2 All E. R. 1.
[9] *Edler* v. *Auerbach*, [1950] 1 K. B. 359, at p. 375 ; [1949] 2 All E. R. 692, at p. 700. *Hill* v. *Harris*, [1965] 2 Q. B. 601; [1965] 2 All E. R. 358; 81 L. Q. R. pp. 334-7 (R. E. M.).
[10] *Sleafer* v. *Lambeth Metropolitan Borough Council*, [1960] 1 Q. B. 43 ; [1959] 3 All E. R. 378.
[11] *Davis* v. *Foots*, [1940] 1 K. B. 116 ; [1939] 4 All E. R. 4.
[12] Housing Act, 1957, s. 6 (1), (2). In the case of a contract made before 6th July, 1957, and after 31st July, 1923, the equivalent figures are £40 for London and £26 elsewhere ; *ibid.*

that the tenant will put the house into a state fit for human habitation, and if the lease is not determinable by either party before the expiration of three years.[1]

Whether the statutory condition has been broken is a question of fact and one not always easy to determine, but the Act provides that a house shall be deemed to be unfit for human habitation if and only if it is unreasonably defective in respect of one or more of the following matters—repair, stability, freedom from damp, natural lighting, ventilation, water supply, drainage and sanitary conveniences, facilities for storage, preparation and cooking of food and for the disposal of waste water.[2]

In the event of a breach of the implied condition, the tenant may repudiate the tenancy and also recover damages,[3] provided that the landlord had notice of the existence of the defect and failed to remedy it.[4] Moreover, the landlord is liable in damages to any other person, such as the tenant's wife, who or whose goods may be injured while lawfully on the defective premises.[5]

Housing Act, 1961.

The statutory obligations of the landlord have been further increased by the Housing Act, 1961, if he has let a dwelling-house after 24th October, 1961, for a term of less than seven years. In the case of such a lease, he is subjected to an implied covenant—

(a) to keep in repair the structure and exterior of the house (including drains, gutters and exterior pipes); and

(b) to keep in repair and proper working order the installations in the house—

(i) for the supply of water, gas and electricity and for sanitation (including basins, sinks, baths and sanitary conveniences), and

(ii) for space heating or heating water.

Moreover, it is enacted that any covenant to repair by the tenant shall be of no effect in so far as it relates to the above matters.[6]

These obligations do not require the landlord to reinstate the premises if they are damaged by fire or by tempest, flood or other inevitable accident; or to effect repairs necessitated by the tenant's failure to use the premises in a tenant-like manner.[7]

The parties cannot contract out of the Act,[8] but with their

---

[1] Housing Act, 1957, s. 6 (2) proviso.

[2] S. 4. As to the test of unfitness in the case of disrepair, see *Summers* v. *Salford Corpn.*, [1943], A. C. 283, *per* Lord ATKIN at p. 289 ; [1943] 1 All E. R. 68, at p. 70. The other Law Lords accepted Lord ATKIN's statement.

[3] *Walker* v. *Hobbs & Co.* (1889) 23 Q. B. D. 458.

[4] *McCarrick* v. *Liverpool Corpn.*, [1947] A. C. 219 ; [1946] 2 All E. R. 646.

[5] Occupiers' Liability Act, 1957, s. 4 (1).

[6] Housing Act, 1961, s. 32 (1). A lease is treated as one for less than seven years if, though made for that period or longer, it is determinable at the lessor's option within seven years; *ibid.*, s. 33 (2). As to what is a "house" within the meaning of the Act, see *Okereke* v. *Borough of Brent Council*, [1966] 1 All E. R. 150.

[7] *Ibid.*, s. 32 (2).

[8] *Ibid.*, s. 33 (7).

consent the County Court may exclude or modify the repairing obligations of the landlord if it is considered reasonable to do so.[1]

(iii) **No Derogation from Grant.**[2] The only other covenant to which a landlord becomes implicitly subject is one that he shall not derogate from his grant. He must not frustrate the use of the land for the purposes for which it was let ;[3] or, as BOWEN, L.J., put it, having given a thing with one hand, a grantor must not take away the means of enjoying it with the other.[4] WOOD, V.-C., in one case said :— Implied covenant not to derogate from grant.

> " If a landlord conveys one of two closes to another, he cannot
> " afterwards do anything to derogate from his grant, and if the con-
> " veyance is made for the express purpose of having buildings erected
> " upon the land so granted, a contract is implied on the part of the
> " grantor to do nothing to prevent the land from being used for the
> " purpose for which, to the knowledge of the grantor, the conveyance
> " is made."[5]

This general principle of law becomes particularly applicable when the lessor makes an inconsiderate use of land adjacent to the tenant's holding. Thus where lands were leased to a tenant for the purpose of carrying on the business of a timber merchant, and the landlord proceeded to erect buildings on adjoining land in such a way as to interrupt the free flow of air to the tenant's drying sheds, it was held that damages were recoverable for breach of the implied covenant.[6] Again, where a flat is leased in a building, the whole of which is clearly intended to be used solely by residential tenants, the landlord commits a breach of the covenant if he subsequently lets the greater part of the premises for business purposes.[7]

(B) IMPLIED OBLIGATIONS AND RIGHTS OF THE TENANT.

(i) Obligations.

Obligation to Repair. A tenant, including one from year to year,[8] is subject to an implied obligation to keep and to deliver

---

[1] Housing Act, 1961, s. 33 (6).
[2] For a comprehensive discussion, see 80 *L. Q. R.* pp. 244–78 (P. W. Elliott). criticized in part, 81 *L. Q. R.* pp. 28–31 (Michael A. Peel).
[3] *Browne* v. *Flower*, [1911] 1 Ch. 219, at pp. 225–7, where illustrations are given by PARKER, J.
[4] *Birmingham, Dudley & District Banking Co.* v. *Ross* (1888) 38 Ch. D. 295, 313.
[5] *North Eastern Rly. Co.* v. *Elliot* (1860), 1 J. & H. 145, 153.
[6] *Aldin* v. *Latimer Clark*, [1894] 2 Ch. 437 ; *Harmer* v. *Jumbil Tin Areas*, [1921] 1 Ch. 200. The principle is also applicable if the tenant is prevented from entering the lessor's land in order to execute essential repairs to the demised premises; *Ward* v. *Kirkland*, [1966] 1 All E. R. 609, at p. 617; [1966] 1 W. L. R. 601, at p. 619.
[7] *Newman* v. *Real Estate Debenture Corpn.*, [1940] 1 All E. R. 131 ; distinguished in *Kelly* v. *Battershell*, [1949] 2 All E. R. 830.
[8] *Marsden* v. *Edward Heyes, Ltd.*, [1927] 1 K. B. 1.

up the premises in a tenant-like manner and to keep the fences in a state of repair.[1]

Further, tenants are subject to the doctrine of waste,[2] though in varying degrees.

Permissive waste.

A tenant for a fixed number of years is liable for voluntary and also for permissive waste,[3] though perhaps a doubt still lingers with regard to the latter question.[4]

Tenant from year to year.

A tenant from *year to year* is liable for voluntary waste, but otherwise his only obligation, it would seem, is to use the premises in a "tenant-like" manner.[5] This expression is obscure if not unintelligible, and all that it means apparently is that the tenant must do such work as is necessary for his own reasonable enjoyment of the premises.[6] There is some authority for the view that he must keep the premises wind and water tight in the sense that, although he is not bound to do anything of a substantial nature, he must carry out such repairs as are necessary to prevent the property from lapsing into a state of decay.[7] The existence of this obligation, however, has been doubted by the Court of Appeal.[8]

Tenant at will.

A tenant *at will* is not liable for either kind of waste, though the effect of the commission by him of any act of voluntary waste is to terminate his tenancy and to render him liable to an action of trespass.[9]

(ii) Implied Rights of the Lessee.

Meaning of estovers.

A. **Estovers.** A tenant for years, notwithstanding the doctrine of waste, is entitled to take estovers from the land, that is to say, wood, even though it be timber,[10] for the purpose of carrying out certain repairs. Estovers fall into three classes, namely: 1. house-bote (wood to be used either as fuel or for building purposes); 2. plough-bote (wood for making and repairing agricultural implements); and 3. hay-bote (wood for repairing hedges).[11]

---

[1] *Cheetham v. Hampson* (1791), 4 Term Rep. 318; *Goodman v. Rollinson* (1951), 95 Sol. Jo. 188. For the tenant of an agricultural holding, see *Wedd v. Porter*, [1916] 2 K. B. 91.

[2] *Supra*, pp. 186–9.

[3] *Yellowly v. Gower* (1855), 11 Exch. 274.

[4] See cases collected in Hill and Redman, *Law of Landlord and Tenant* (14th Edn.) p. 208.

[5] *Warren v. Keen*, [1954] 1 Q. B. 15; [1953] 2 All E. R. 1118.

[6] See the illustrations given by DENNING, L.J., in *Warren v. Keen, supra*, at p. 20. The expression is an extension to tenants generally of the rule that the agricultural tenant must farm the land in a " husbandlike " manner. In this context, " husbandlike " has a perfectly definite meaning. The tenant must observe the custom of the country, *i.e.* the local usages of husbandry.

[7] *Ferguson v. ———* (1797), 2 Esp. 590; *Wedd v. Porter, supra*, at p. 100.

[8] *Warren v. Keen, supra.*

[9] *Countess of Shrewsbury's Case* (1600), 5 Co. Rep. 13b.

[10] For the definition of " timber ", see *supra*, p. 187.

[11] Co. Litt. 41b.; *cf. infra*, p. 519.

This right is limited by immediate necessity : a tenant cannot cut and store wood with a view to future requirements.

B. **Emblements.** A tenant for years is entitled at common law to emblements.[1] It is obvious that a tenant for a fixed term of years cannot be entitled to this right, because he knows when his tenancy will end, and it is his own fault if he sows crops which will not come to maturity until after that date.   But there may be cases where a tenancy comes to an end unexpectedly, as for instance upon the sudden determination of a tenancy at will or upon the determination of the estate out of which the term has been created, in which the common law right to emblements exists.   The right is obviously inconvenient to both parties, and in one type of case, *i.e.* where the lessor's estate ended prematurely, it was modified by the Landlord and Tenant Act, 1851. This provided that a tenant for years at a rack rent (*i.e.* a rent which represents the full annual value of the land),[2] whose lease expired owing to the failure of his lessor's estate, should in lieu of emblements be entitled to remain in occupation until the end of the current year of tenancy.

Common Law rule as to emblements.

This Act has, however, in the case of agricultural tenancies been replaced by the Agricultural Holdings Act, 1948,[3] which provides that a tenant at a rack rent, whose term ceases by the death, or the cesser of the estate, of a landlord entitled only for life or for any other uncertain interest, shall continue to hold and occupy the holding until the occupation is determined by a twelvemonth's notice to quit, expiring at the end of a year of the tenancy.

Agricultural Holdings Act, 1948.

C. **Right to remove Certain Fixtures.**   The extent of this right of removal has already been discussed.[4]

(2) POSITION WHERE THERE ARE EXPRESS COVENANTS AND CONDITIONS.

In the majority of cases the rights and the liabilities of a lessor and a lessee are regulated by express covenants inserted in the lease, but, as the number of matters that may be the subject of agreement is infinite, and as the agreed terms will naturally vary widely in different cases, it is obvious that in a treatise of this limited scope we cannot do more than notice shortly the more important covenants that find a place in a normal lease.

Nature of covenants generally entered into.

Generally speaking, and where no exceptional circumstances exist, a lessee will enter into covenants with regard to the payment

---

[1] See *supra*, pp. 185-6.
[2] *Re Sawyer and Withall*, [1919] 2 Ch. 333.
[3] S. 4 (1).
[4] *Supra*, pp. 101-5.

of rent, rates and taxes, and the maintenance, repair and insurance of the premises; while the lessor will undertake to keep the lessee in quiet enjoyment, and may perhaps take upon himself part of the burden of repairs. The following covenants require special mention :—

(A) COVENANT BY TENANT TO PAY RENT.

Rent-service.

The rent payable by a tenant for years is called a rent-service,[1] and though it generally consists of the payment of money, it may equally well take the form of the delivery of personal chattels,[2] as corn, or the performance of personal services.[3] The covenant should state precisely the dates at which rent is payable, but if no mention is made of the matter, payment is due at the end of each period by reference to which the rent has been assessed. Thus in the case of a yearly rent nothing need be paid until the end of each year of the term.[4] If a day for payment is fixed, it becomes due on the first moment of that day and is held to be in arrear if it is not paid by midnight.[5]

Payment of rent not excused by subsequent events.

The liability to pay rent is unaffected by the subsequent occurrence of some unforeseen event which operates to the detriment of the tenant. This is consonant to the general principle that if a man deliberately assumes an absolute obligation, he cannot escape liability by proof that subsequent events have made performance a matter of hardship, for he might have expressly guarded against what has happened.[6] Thus a tenant must continue to pay his rent notwithstanding that the premises are utterly destroyed by fire,[7] or by a hostile bomb,[8] or are requisitioned by the Crown acting under statutory powers or under the prerogative,[9] even though the Crown itself is the lessor.[10]

Doctrine of frustration inapplicable.

The present rule, though doubts have been cast upon its soundness by high authority,[11] is that in such cases a tenant cannot rely upon the contractual doctrine of frustration, under which a

---

[1] *Infra*, p. 385.
[2] Co. Litt. 142a.
[3] *Marlborough* v. *Osborn* (1864), 5 B. & S. 67.
[4] *Coomber* v. *Howard* (1845), 1 C. B. 440; *Collett* v. *Curling* (1847), 10 Q. B. 785.
[5] *Dibble* v. *Bowater* (1853), 2 E. & B. 564.
[6] *Jacobs, Marais & Co.* v. *Crédit Lyonnais* (1884), 12 Q. B. D. 589, 603; *Atkinson* v. *Ritchie* (1809), 10 East 530, 533.
[7] *Matthey* v. *Curling*, [1922] 2 A. C. 180.
[8] See *Redmond* v. *Dainton*, [1920] 2 K. B. 256 ; *Denman* v. *Brise*, [1949] 1 K. B. 22 ; [1948] 2 All E. R. 141.
[9] *Whitehall Court* v. *Ettlinger*, [1920] 1 K. B. 680. But see the Landlord and Tenant (Requisitioned Land) Act, 1942, which allows a tenant to disclaim a lease if the land is requisitioned by the Crown.
[10] *Crown Land Commissioners* v. *Page*, [1960] 3 Q. B. 274 ; [1960] 2 All E. R. 726.
[11] Lord SIMON and Lord WRIGHT in *Cricklewood Property & Investment Trust, Ltd.* v. *Leighton's Investment Trust, Ltd.*, [1945] A. C. 221 ; [1945] 1 All E. R. 252.

contract is discharged if the common venture of the parties is frustrated by the occurrence of some unexpected event that strikes at the root of the agreement.[1] When the doctrine applies, the contractual rights and obligations cease automatically upon the occurrence of the frustrating event. But a lease creates more than a contract. It creates an estate. Indeed, it is the transfer of this estate to the tenant that represents the common venture of the parties. Whatever may be the effect of extraneous circumstances upon the contractual side of the lease, the estate remains vested in the tenant and the land remains available to him. Therefore, the rule is that the estate does not cease merely because it has become burdensome or even because the performance of one or more of the contractual obligations has become impossible.

If, for example, the tenant is entitled and bound to erect houses on the demised land, which it is his design to sub-let at profitable rents, and then before he begins the work all building operations are forbidden by the Ministry of Public Building and Works, the rule is that the impossibility of performing this particular term of the contract does not cause the cessation of the estate to which it is incident.[2]

The landlord's remedies for the recovery of rent will be considered later.

(B) COVENANT TO REPAIR.[3]

Various expressions are used by practitioners to describe the extent of the obligation imposed by a covenant to repair the premises. The following are typical examples :—

" good tenantable repair " ;
" good and tenantable order and repair " ;
" well and substantially repair ";
" perfect repair."

By the use of appropriate language, the parties can, of course, settle the standard of repair as high or as low as they choose, but it is generally admitted that such epithets as " good," " perfect " or " substantial " do not increase the burden connoted by the

Covenant to repair.

---

[1] *London and Northern Estates Co.* v. *Schlesinger*, [1916] 1 K. B. 20 ; *Whitehall Court, Ltd.* v. *Ettlinger*, [1920] 1 K. B. 680 ; *Matthey* v. *Curling*, [1922] 2 A. C. 180 ; *Swift* v. *Macbean*, [1942] 1 K. B. 375; [1942] 1 All E. R. 126; *Denman* v. *Brise*, [1949] 1 K. B. 22; [1948] 1 All E. R. 141 ; *Cricklewood Property and Investment Trust, Ltd.* v. *Leighton's Investment Trust, Ltd., supra,* per Lord RUSSELL of KILLOWEN and Lord GODDARD.

[2] See the opinions of Lord RUSSELL of KILLOWEN and Lord GODDARD in the *Cricklewood Case, supra ;* and the decision of the Court of Appeal in *Denman* v. *Brise*, [1949] 1 K. B. 22. For a fuller discussion, see Cheshire and Fifoot, *The Law of Contract* (6 Edn.), pp. 488–91.

[3] It must be borne in mind that, whether the matter has been dealt with by covenant or not, the lessor is under a statutory obligation to repair a dwelling-house that has been let for less than seven years; *supra* p. 368.

simple word " repair." [1] By way of caution, it should be noticed that, if the premises are in a state of disrepair at the beginning of the lease, a covenant by the tenant to " keep " them in repair obliges him to put them in the required state at his own expense. [2]

Extent of obligation.
The extent of the obligation assumed by a covenantor who has agreed to repair the premises is this :—

> After making due allowance for the locality, character and age of the premises at the time of the lease, he must keep them in the condition in which they would be kept by a reasonably minded owner. [3]

Locality is material.
The locality is a material consideration, for the state of repair suitable for a house, say, in Grosvenor Square, differs from that which is appropriate to a house in Spitalfields.

Character of premises is material.
The character of the premises is also material. Thus the standard of repairs will vary according as the premises are the mansion house or a labourer's cottage on the estate. The essential fact to notice, however, is that it is the character of the premises at the beginning, not at the end, of the lease that is material in this context.

> Thus in one case a new house, situated in what was then a fashionable part of London was let in 1825 to a good class of tenant on a 95 year lease. In course of time the character of the neighbourhood deteriorated to such an extent that the only persons willing to occupy the house expected nothing more than that the rain should be kept out.

The covenantor, therefore, argued that the standard of repair required of him was to be measured by the needs and expectations of prospective tenants in 1920. The argument failed. The obligation of a covenantor is neither increased nor diminished in extent by a change in the character of the neighbourhood. [4]

Age of premises is material.
The age of a house is also material, though only in the sense that the covenantor's obligation is not to bring it up to date, but to keep it in a reasonably good condition for a building of that age. He cannot escape liability by the allegation that to keep so old a building in the covenanted condition requires renewal, not mere repairs. Repair always involves renewal. The covenant must be fulfilled, even though this necessitates the replacement of part after part until the whole is renewed. [5] The correct antithesis is between renewal and reconstruction. The former is required, the latter not. Whether the work necessary for the maintenance

---

[1] *Anstruther-Gough-Calthorpe* v. *McOscar*, [1924] 1 K. B. 716 ; at pp. 732–733, 729 ; but see pp. 731–2.
[2] *Payne* v. *Haine* (1847), 16 M. & W. 541.
[3] *Proudfoot* v. *Hart* (1890), 25 Q. B. D. 42 ; *Lurcott* v. *Wakely and Wheeler*, [1911] 1 K. B. 905 ; *Anstruther-Gough-Calthorpe* v. *McOscar*, [1924] 1 K. B. 716 ; *Lloyd's Bank Ltd.* v. *Lake*, [1961] 2 All E. R. 30 ; [1961] 1 W. L. R. 884.
[4] *Anstruther-Gough-Calthorpe* v. *McOscar, supra.*
[5] *Lurcott* v. *Wakely and Wheeler*, [1911] 1 K. B. 905, at pp. 916–17, *per* FLETCHER-MOULTON, L. J.

of a building is renewal or reconstruction is a question of degree, the test being whether the replacement affects a subordinate part or substantially the whole of the building.[1]

> Thus the tenant of a house is not bound to replace defective foundations by foundations of an entirely different character;[2] but he must demolish and replace a dangerous wall if it is but a subsidiary part of the whole building.[3]

It is usual to qualify the covenant to repair by a clause to the effect that the covenantor shall not be liable for " fair wear and tear," or, what signifies the same thing, for " reasonable wear and tear." The effect of these words is to exempt the covenantor from liability for damage that is due to the ordinary operation of natural causes, always presuming that he has used the premises in a reasonable manner.[4] As TINDAL, C.J., put it in a case where a tenant had invoked such a clause :

Exception of fair wear and tear.

> " What the natural operation of time flowing on effects, and all
> " that the elements bring about in diminishing value, constitute a
> " loss which, so far as it results from time and nature, falls upon the
> " landlord."[5]

But where the defect, though initially due to natural causes, will obviously cause further and lasting damage unless rectified, the clause will not continue to avail a covenantor who stands idly by and allows the ravages of time and nature to take their course. TALBOT, J., made this clear in a passage later adopted by the House of Lords.

> " The tenant," he said, " is bound to do such repairs as may be
> " required to prevent the consequences flowing originally from wear
> " and tear from producing others which wear and tear would not
> " directly produce. For example, if a tile falls off the roof, the
> " tenant is not liable for the immediate consequences ; but if he does
> " nothing and in the result more and more water gets in, the roof
> " and walls decay and ultimately the top floor or the whole house
> " becomes uninhabitable, he cannot say that it is due to reasonable
> " wear and tear. . . . On the other hand, take the gradual wearing
> " away of a stone floor or staircase by ordinary use. This may in
> " time produce a considerable defect in condition, but the whole
> " defect is caused by reasonable wear and tear, and the tenant is not
> " liable in respect of it."[6]

---

[1] *Ibid. Sotheby* v. *Grundy,* [1947] 2 All E. R. 761.

[2] *Lister* v. *Lane and Nesham,* [1893] 2 Q. B. 212 ; *Sotheby* v. *Grundy, supra ;* *Pembery* v. *Lamdin,* [1940] 2 All E. R. 434 (landlord's covenant).

[3] *Lurcott* v. *Wakely and Wheeler,* [1911] 1 K. B. 905.

[4] *Haskell* v. *Marlow,* [1928] 2 K. B. 45, 59.

[5] *Gutteridge* v. *Munyard* (1834), 1 Mood. & R. 334, 336. The words quoted do not appear in the report 7 C. & P. 129.

[6] *Haskell* v. *Marlow, supra,* at p. 59. This decision was overruled by the Court of Appeal in *Taylor* v. *Webb,* [1937] 2 K. B. 283 ; [1937] 1 All E. R. 590, but the principles laid down in this second case, after being stigmatized by a later Court of Appeal as inconsistent with earlier authorities, *Brown* v. *Davies,* [1958] 1 Q. B. 117 ; [1957] 3 All E. R. 401, were finally overruled by the House of Lords in *Regis Property Co. Ltd.* v. *Dudley,* [1959] A. C. 370 ; [1958] 3 All E. R. 491, and the authority of *Haskell* v. *Marlow* restored.

Covenant not to make improvements without consent.

A covenant against the making of improvements without consent is statutorily subject to a proviso that consent shall not unreasonably be withheld, though the landlord is entitled to demand the payment of a reasonable sum for any damage or loss of value that may be caused to the premises or to neighbouring premises belonging to him.[1] The word " improvements " refers to improvements from the point of view of the tenant, and the statute applies even though what he proposes to do, *e.g.* the demolition of part of the main structure of a building, will temporarily diminish the value of the premises.[2] In such a case no injury is, in theory, suffered by the landlord, since he is permitted by the statute to demand an undertaking from the tenant that the premises will be reinstated.

Covenant to repair imposes absolute obligation.

As in the case of a covenant to pay rent,[3] a covenant to repair imposes an absolute obligation for the non-performance of which the covenantor remains liable, notwithstanding that owing to some extraneous cause beyond his control, such as the refusal of the authorities to grant him a building licence [4] or the requisitioning of the premises,[5] he is unable to execute the necessary work.

Measure of damages under Landlord and Tenant Act.

The measure of damages *at common law* for breach of a contract to repair varies according as the breach occurs during the tenancy or at the end of the tenancy. In the first case the measure is the amount by which the value of the reversion has diminished; but in the second case, where the premises are delivered up in disrepair, it is the amount that it will cost to carry out the repairs required by the covenant.[6] If, for instance, a tenant converts into flats a house which he has covenanted to keep suitable for single occupation, the first rule applies and the measure of damages is not necessarily the full cost of reinstatement, but the sum that represents the loss which the lessor has sustained.[7] It was found that the second rule might inflict unnecessary hardship upon an outgoing tenant, since it enabled a landlord to recover substantial damages even though the performance of the covenant would have been entirely useless, as, for instance, where the premises were to be demolished, or where the want of repair would not diminish by one penny the rent obtainable on a re-letting. It is, therefore, provided by the Landlord and Tenant Act, 1927,[8] that

---

[1] Landlord and Tenant Act, 1927, s. 19 (2). The tenant may apply to the High Court or the County Court for a declaration that the lessor has unreasonably withheld his consent ; Landlord and Tenant Act, 1954, s. 53 (1) (b).

[2] *Lambert* v. *Woolworth & Co.*, [1938] Ch. 883 ; [1938] 2 All E. R. 664.

[3] *Supra*, pp. 372–3.

[4] *Eyre* v. *Johnson*, [1946] K. B. 481 ; [1946] 1 All E. R. 719.

[5] *Smiley* v. *Townshend* [1950] 2 K. B. 311 ; [1950] 1 All E. R. 530. But the Landlord and Tenant (Requisitioned Land) Act, 1944, relieves the tenant of liability for damages to the land during the period of requisition.

[6] *Joyner* v. *Weeks*, [1891] 2 Q. B. 31.

[7] *Westminster (Duke)* v. *Swinton*, [1948] [1 K. B. 524 ; 1948] 1 All E. R. 428. See also *James* v. *Hutton and J. Cook & Sons, Ltd.*, [1950] 1 K. B. 9 ; [1949] 2 All E. R. 243.

[8] S. 18 (1) ; *Haviland* v. *Long*, [1952] 2 Q. B. 80 ; [1952] 1 All E. R. 463.

whether the breach is of a covenant to repair during the currency of a lease or to leave premises in repair at the termination of a lease,

> the damages shall in no case exceed the amount by which the value of the reversion (whether immediate or not) is diminished.

The diminution in the value of the reversion is the amount that it will cost within the terms of the covenant to make the house reasonably fit for the class of tenant likely to take it. The fact that the landlord has been able to relet it, though spending less than that amount on repairs, is an irrelevant consideration.[1] In other words the primary test of the measure of damages still seems to be the cost of doing the covenanted repairs. There are many cases where the sale of the property unrepaired will fetch as high a price as its sale in a state of good repair, so that in one sense the value of the reversion as a whole is undiminished, as, for example, where the tenancy relates only to a few rooms in a large building and they cannot be made fit for occupation unless the covenanted repairs are done. In such a case it is now recognized that the cost of the necessary repairs *prima facie* represents the diminution in value of the reversion.[2]

In one particular case the landlord is denied any right to damages. The Act provides that :— *No damages recoverable if premises to be demolished.*

> If it is shown that the premises, in whatever state of repair they may be, will at or shortly after the termination of the tenancy, be pulled down, or such structural alterations made as will render repairs valueless, no damages shall be recoverable for breach of the covenant.[3]

Thus the Act requires the tenant to prove that the landlord had decided to demolish the premises and that this decision still held at the end of the lease. If this be shown, it is immaterial that the decision is later changed. Damages are irrecoverable.[4] The onus, therefore, that lies upon the tenant is to show that the demolition or structural alteration of the premises was firmly intended, not merely contemplated, by the landlord and also that the achievement of the plan was reasonably possible.[5]

> "An ' intention ' to my mind connotes a state of affairs which the " party ' intending '—I will call him X.—does more than merely " contemplate : it connotes a state of affairs which, on the contrary,

---

[1] *Jaquin* v. *Holland,* [1960] 1 All E. R. 402 ; [1960] 1 W. L. R. 258 ; *Hanson* v. *Newman,* [1934] 1 Ch. 298.
[2] *Jones* v. *Herxheimer,* [1950] 2 K. B. 106 ; [1950] 1 All E. R. 323 ; *Smiley* v. *Townshend,* [1950] 2 K. B. 311, at pp. 322–3 ; [1950] 1 All E. R. 530, at p. 534.
[3] Landlord and Tenant Act, 1927, s. 18 (1).
[4] *Salisbury* v. *Gilmore,* [1942] 2 K. B. 38 ; [1942] 1 All E. R. 457.
[5] *Cunliffe* v. *Goodman,* [1950] 2 K. B. 237 ; [1950] 1 All E. R. 720.

" he decides, so far as in him lies, to bring about and which, in point
" of possibility, he has a reasonable prospect of being able to bring
" about, by his own volition." [1]

It has been held that, if a tenant covenants to spend a stated yearly
sum on repairs or in default to pay to the landlord the difference
between this sum and the amount actually expended, an action to
recover the difference is an action for debt and is not governed by
the statute, since the money must be spent or paid whether there
is a breach of the covenant to repair or not.[2]

(C) COVENANT BY TENANT TO INSURE AGAINST FIRE.

Covenant to
insure.

By the Fires Prevention (Metropolis) Act, 1774,[3] no action
may be brought against any person in whose house a fire shall
accidentally begin, though it is expressly enacted that this provision
shall not defeat an agreement made between landlord and tenant.
The result is that, when the property has been burnt, a landlord
can maintain an action against his tenant in two cases :—

first, where the tenant has covenanted to repair, for his
contractual liability is not excluded by the happening of an
inevitable accident against which he might have expressly
protected himself [4] ; and

secondly, where the fire has begun owing to the negligence of the tenant or of those for whom he is responsible.[5]

But, in addition, it is usual for a tenant to covenant that he will
insure the demised buildings to their full value and will keep them
insured during the term.   It has been held in such a case that the
omission to keep the premises insured for any period, no matter
how short, and even though no fire breaks out during the period,
constitutes a breach of the covenant,[6] a fact that may have serious
consequences if the landlord chooses to enforce his remedies.[7]

If the landlord himself takes out a policy without having
agreed to do so, he is not liable to expend the insurance money
on the reinstatement of the premises in the event of their destruction, unless the cost of the premiums is reflected in the rent.[8]

(D) COVENANT BY TENANT NOT TO ASSIGN OR UNDERLET.

Covenant
not to
assign.

Unless there is a special agreement to the contrary, a tenant
is free to grant his interest to a third party either by assignment

---

[1] *Ibid.*, at pp. 253, 724, respectively, *per* ASQUITH, L.J.
[2] *Moss' Empires Ltd.* v. *Olympia (Liverpool), Ltd.,* [1939] A. C. 544 ; [1939]
3 All E. R. 460.
[3] S. 86.   The Act applies to the whole of England.   As to its interpretation,
see *Goldman* v. *Hargrave,* [1966] 2 All E. R. 989 (P. C.).
[4] *Redmond* v. *Dainton,* [1920] 2 K. B. 256.
[5] *Musgrove* v. *Pandelis,* [1919] 2 K. B. 43.
[6] *Penniall* v. *Harborne* (1848), 11 Q. B. 368.
[7] *Infra,* pp. 397–401.
[8] *Mumford Hotels, Ltd.* v. *Wheler,* [1964] Ch. 117; [1963] 3 All E. R. 250.

or by underlease,[1] but as it is undesirable from the landlord's point of view that the premises should fall into the hands of an irresponsible person, it is usual to provide for the matter by express covenant.

The courts, however, have always construed this covenant with great strictness and have insisted that the restraint imposed upon the tenant shall not go beyond the letter of the express agreement.[2] Thus, a covenant *not to assign or underlet* is not broken by an equitable mortgage accompanied by deposit of the deeds,[3] nor by a deed of arrangement whereby the tenant constitutes himself trustee for his creditors,[4] nor by permitting another person to have the use of the premises without giving him legal possession,[5] nor in general by any transfer which is involuntary, as, for instance, one which results from the bankruptcy of the tenant.[6] A provision that "this lease shall be non-assignable" does not embrace a sub-lease of the premises.[7] An agreement *not to sublet* is not broken by a sub-lease of part of the premises.[8] A covenant *not to part with the possession of the premises or any part thereof* is not broken by the grant of a licence to place an advertisement hoarding on the wall of the demised premises, since the tenant is not thereby deprived of legal possession.[9] It would seem that the letting of lodgings is no breach of a covenant *not to underlease the premises*.[10]

What is a breach of the covenant?

The result of a tenant's breach depends upon the nature of the covenant by which he has bound himself. A covenant is either absolute or qualified.

Two classes of covenant.

An absolute covenant is one which imposes an unconditional prohibition upon the tenant, there being no provision for its relaxation at the will of the lessor. In this case any assignment contrary to the terms of the covenant renders the tenant liable, notwithstanding that it is in no way prejudicial to the lessor's interest.

Absolute covenant.

A qualified covenant, which is far more common in practice, is one which merely prohibits an assignment *without the consent of the lessor*. It has long been usual to qualify this type of covenant even further by a provision that the lessor's *consent shall not be*

Qualified covenant.

[1] *Keeves* v. *Dean*, [1924] 1 K. B. 685, 691.

[2] *Church* v. *Brown* (1808), 15 Ves. 258, 265, *per* Lord ELDON; *Grove* v. *Portal*, [1902] 1 Ch. 727, 731.

[3] *Doe d. Pitt* v. *Hogg* (1824), 4 Dow. & Ry. 226.

[4] *Gentle* v. *Faulkner*, [1900] 2 Q. B. 267.

[5] *Chaplin* v. *Smith*, [1926] 2 K. B. 198.

[6] *Re Riggs, Ex p. Lovell*, [1901] 2 K. B. 16. As to whether a bequest of a leasehold interest breaks a covenant not to assign, see 27 *The Conveyancer* (N. S.), p. 159 *et seq.* (D. G. Barnsley).

[7] *Sweet and Maxwell, Ltd.* v. *Universal News Services, Ltd.*, [1964] 2 Q. B. 699; [1964] 3 All E. R. 30.

[8] *Cook* v. *Shoesmith*, [1951] 1 K. B. 752.

[9] *Stening* v. *Abrahams*, [1931] 1 Ch. 470.

[10] *Doe d. Pitt* v. *Laming* (1814), 4 Camp. 73, 77; *Greenslade* v. *Tapscott* (1834), 1 Cr. M. & R. 55, doubting the last case; *Victoria Dwellings Association, Ltd.* v. *Roberts*, [1947], L. J. N. C. C. C. R. 177; *Phillips* v. *Woolf*, [1953] C. L. Y. 1966; *Re Smith's Lease, Smith* v. *Richards*, [1951] 1 All E. R. 346.

unreasonably withheld, and the Landlord and Tenant Act, 1927, in a section that is retrospective, now makes this qualification inevitable by providing that :—

> A covenant against " assigning, underletting, charging or parting with the possession of demised premises without licence or consent," shall, despite any contrary agreement, be subject to a proviso that " such licence or consent is not to be unreasonably withheld." [1]

Thus, the Act requires that the grounds for the refusal of consent shall in fact be reasonable, and therefore its operation cannot be curtailed by a provision in the lease that certain specified grounds shall not be deemed unreasonable.[2]

It is enacted by another statute that the lessor may not require the payment of a fine in return for his consent, unless express provision for such a payment is contained in the lease.[3]

Effect of breach of qualified covenant.

If the tenant disregards a qualified covenant of this nature and assigns the premises without the consent of the lessor, the result is a little peculiar.

> If he omits to apply for consent, he is liable in any event to the payment of damages, and also at common law to the forfeiture of his interest if a right of re-entry [4] is contained in the lease.[5] He may, however, apply to the court for relief against such forfeiture.[6]
>
> If on the other hand he makes a formal request for consent and meets with a refusal, then, provided that the refusal is in fact unreasonable, he incurs no liability whatsoever for his breach of covenant. But he has no right to recover damages.[7]

The distinction was well put by NEVILLE, J., in a case where the lessor had agreed not to withhold his consent to an assignment to *a respectable and responsible person.*

> " It is obviously a formality to apply for the consent of the land-
> " lord in a case where under the terms of the covenant he has no
> " power to prevent the assignment by withholding his consent. It
> " matters not, where the proposed assignee is a respectable and
> " responsible person, whether the landlord gives or does not give

---

[1] S. 19 (1) (a) ; this section does not apply to the lease of an agricultural holding.

[2] *In re Smith's Lease, Smith* v. *Richards,* [1951] 1 All E. R. 346; dist. *Adler* v. *Upper Grosvenor Street Investment, Ltd.,* [1957] 1 All E. R. 229; [1957] 1 W. L. R. 227.

[3] Law of Property Act, 1925, s. 144 ; *Gardner & Co., Ltd.* v. *Cone,* [1928] Ch. 955 ; *Comber* v. *Fleet Electrics, Ltd.,* [1955] 2 All E. R. 161.

[4] *Infra,* p. 397.

[5] *Barrow* v. *Isaacs & Son,* [1891] 1 Q. B. 417 ; *Creery* v. *Summersell and Flowerdew & Co., Ltd., supra.*

[6] *House Property and Investment Co., Ltd.* v. *Walker (James), Goldsmith and Silversmith, Ltd.,* [1948] K. B. 257 ; [1947] 1 All E. R. 789 ; *i.e.* relief under the Law of Property Act, 1925, s. 146 (2), *infra,* p. 401.

[7] *Treloar* v. *Bigge* (1874), L. R. 9 Exch. 151 ; *Fuller's Theatre and Vaudeville Co.* v. *Rofe,* [1923] A. C. 435; *Wilson* v. *Fynn,* [1948] 2 All E. R. 40. As to joinder of parties if the assignee sues the landlord for a declaration that the assignment is effective, see *Theodorou* v. *Bloom,* [1964] 3 All E. R. 399; [1964] 1 W. L. R. 1152.

" his consent. The cases show that if, on the one hand, . . . the
" landlord has been asked and has withheld his consent, the lessee
" retains his interest under the lease, whereas if he has not been
" asked and so is unable to give the consent that he should give, the
" withholding of which is inoperative if the request be made, then
" the whole of the property of the lessee becomes the property of
" the lessor.[1] It certainly seems strange that so small and perfectly
" indifferent a matter should make such a difference, but so stands
" the law." [2]

The onus of proving that consent has been unreasonably refused lies on the tenant,[3] but the crucial question is—What does the law regard as a reasonable refusal? It was suggested by Tomlin, J., that the question is capable of submission to a precise test, namely, the reason for which consent is withheld must be connected either with the personality of the assignee or with the manner in which he proposes to use the premises.[4]

> In conformity with this opinion, Tomlin, J., held that it was unreasonable for a landlord, who had let Blackacre to X. and Whiteacre to Y., to forbid an assignment of Blackacre by X. to Y., on the ground that Y. might terminate his tenancy of Whiteacre.[5]

Grounds on which lessor is justified in withholding consent.

This proposed test, after being doubted by Lord Dunedin and Lord Phillimore,[6] and never consistently followed,[7] has now been disapproved by the Court of Appeal.[8] In forming his opinion the landlord need not confine his attention to matters arising during the currency of the lease. Whether an act is reasonable must be determined not on abstract considerations, but in the light of the particular circumstances.[9] It is safer, therefore, to be content with the somewhat elusive statement that the lessor must have some fair, solid and substantial cause for disallowing an assignment.[10] To give a few instances, it has been held that a landlord has a valid reason for withholding his consent,

if he considers that other property belonging to him will be

---

[1] *I.e.* at common law and if the lease contains a right of re-entry. But see *supra*, p. 380, note 6.

[2] *Lewis and Allenby (1909), Ltd.* v. *Pegge*, [1914] 1 Ch. 782, 785.

[3] *Shanley* v. *Ward* (1913), 29 T. L. R. 714.

[4] *Houlder Bros. & Co.* v. *Gibbs*, [1925] Ch. 198, at p. 209. The suggestion was approved by Evershed, J., in *Re Swanson's Agreement, Hill* v. *Swanson*, [1946] 2 All E. R. 628, but all that he said on the matter was *obiter*; see the remarks of Tucker, L.J., in *Lee* v. *Carter (K.), Ltd.*, [1949] 1 K. B. 85, at p. 96; [1948] 2 All E. R. 690, at p. 695.

[5] *Houlder Bros.* v. *Gibbs*, *supra*. The decision was affirmed at p. 575.

[6] *Tredegar* v. *Harwood*, [1929] A. C. 72, at pp. 78, 81.

[7] *Premier Confectionery Co.* v. *London Commercial Sale Rooms, Ltd.*, [1933] Ch. 904; *Wilson* v. *Fynn*, [1948] 2 All E. R. 40; *Lee* v. *Carter (K.), Ltd.*, *supra*; *In re Town Investments Ltd.*, [1954] Ch. 301; [1954] 1 All E. R. 585.

[8] *Swanson* v. *Forton*, [1949] Ch. 143; [1949] 1 All E. R. 135.

[9] *Houlder Bros. & Co.* v. *Gibbs*, [1925] Ch. 575, at p. 584, *per* Warrington, L.J.; *In re Greater London Properties Ltd.'s Lease, Re Taylor Bros. (Grocers), Ltd.* v. *Covent Garden Properties Co., Ltd.*, [1959] 1 All E. R. 728; [1959] 1 W. L. R. 503.

[10] *Treloar* v. *Bigge* (1874), L. R. 9 Exch. 151, 155; *Barrow* v. *Isaacs & Son*, [1891] 1 Q. B. 417, 419; *Mills* v. *Cannon Brewery Co.*, [1920] 2 Ch. 38, 45.

injured by the use that the assignee intends to make of the demised premises [1]; or

if, where the lease is of a tied public-house, he fears that the value of the trade will depreciate because the assignee is a foreigner who does not intend to reside on the premises [2]; or

if the effect of the assignment will be to nullify a collateral agreement made at the time of the lease [3]; or

if the sole or substantial object of the parties is that the assignee shall acquire a statutory tenancy protected by the Rent Restriction Acts [4]; or

if the rent reserved in a proposed sub-lease is well below that obtainable in the open market, but the sub-lessee agrees to pay a large sum by way of premium[5]; or

if the assignment will embarrass the future development of the property of which the demised premises form part.[6]

Is the test of reasonableness objective or subjective?

No decisive answer has yet been given to the fundamental question whether the test of reasonableness is objective, not subjective, as some affirm[7] but others deny.[8] Must the court merely enquire whether the landlord's refusal of consent is in fact unreasonable? Or, must it also consider what influenced his mind in reaching his decision? This difference of opinion is not purely academic, for if the state of his mind is relevant, certain difficult problems will inevitably arise.

For instance, if the landlord has justified his refusal on some insupportable ground he will presumably be unable at the date of the trial to rely upon an alternative and better ground.[9] Again, a refusal will apparently be ineffectual if, though justifiable in the circumstances, it is justified on inadmissible grounds, as for instance where the proposed assignee is in fact an undischarged bankrupt, but the landlord's only declared objection is to his religion.

It is submitted that the question must be approached objectively, and that, as it has been aptly put, the landlord's " mental processes or uttered words," are irrelevant.

---

[1] *Bridewell Hospital (Governors)* v. *Fawkner and Rogers* (1892), 8 T. L. R. 637.
[2] *Mills* v. *Cannon Brewery Co., supra.* Distinguish *Parker* v. *Boggon,* [1947] K. B. 346 ; [1947] 1 All E. R. 46.
[3] *Wilson* v. *Fynn,* [1948] 2 All E. R. 40.
[4] *Lee* v. *Carter (K.), Ltd., supra ; Swanson* v. *Forton, supra ; Dollar* v. *Winston,* [1950] Ch. 236 ; [1949] 2 All E. R. 1088, n. ; dist. *Bookman (Thomas) Ltd.* v. *Nathan,* [1955] 2 All E. R. 821; [1955] 1 W. L. R. 815.
[5] *In re Town Investments, Ltd.,* [1954] Ch. 301; [1954] 1 All E. R. 585.
[6] *Pimms, Ltd.* v. *Tallow Chandlers Co.,* [1964] 2 Q. B. 547; [1964] 2 All E. R. 145.
[7] *Re Smith's Lease, Smith* v. *Richards,* [1951] 1 All E. R. 346, at p. 349, *per* ROXBURGH, J.
[8] *Lovelock* v. *Margo,* [1963] 2 Q. B. 786, at p. 789; [1963] 2 All E. R. 13 at p. 15, *per* Lord DENNING, M. R.
[9] *Parker* v. *Boggon,* [1947] K. B. 346; [1947] 1 All E. R. 46 where MAC-NAGHTEN, J. was prepared to allow a better ground to be put forward.

"In short, what must be tested for unreasonableness is the with-
"holding and not the landlord, the act and not the man."[1]

It is provided by statute that in the case of a lease for more
than 40 years made in consideration of the erection or the substantial improvement, alteration or addition of buildings, the
tenant may, notwithstanding a prohibition of assignment without
the lessor's consent, assign the premises without such consent,
provided that the assignment is made more than seven years
before the end of the term, and provided that within six months
after its completion it is notified in writing to the lessor.[2] *Special case of certain long leases.*

The rule at common law as laid down in *Dumpor's Case*[3] is
that a condition is an entire and indivisible thing and therefore
incapable of enforcement if once the person entitled to enforce
it has allowed it to be disregarded. The effect of this doctrine
was that, if a lease from A. to B. contained a covenant or condition
against assigning without licence, and A. permitted B. to assign to
C., A.'s right to stop further assignments was utterly gone. When
once consent had been given to an assignment, the term became
freely assignable. Again, and as a result of the same doctrine,
if a lease was made to several lessees, upon condition that neither
they nor any one of them should assign without a licence, a
licence given to one of the lessees destroyed the condition with
regard to the others. Again, if a tenant was allowed to assign
part of the land leased, the condition ceased to apply to the
whole of the land. *Doctrine of Dumpor's Case.*

This absurd doctrine was, however, abrogated by statute[4] in
1859 so far as conditions contained in leases were concerned, and
the present position is regulated by the Law of Property Act, 1925.[5]
This provides that, *Present position.*

"where a licence is granted to a lessee to do any act, the licence,
unless otherwise expressed, extends only—

    (*a*) to the permission actually given ; or

    (*b*) to the specific breach of any provision or covenant referred
        to ; or

    (*c*) to any other matter thereby specifically authorized to be
        done ;

and the licence does not prevent any proceeding for any subsequent breach unless otherwise specified in the licence."

Moreover, it is enacted that where a lease contains a covenant
or condition against assigning or doing any other act without
licence, and a licence is granted to one or more of several lessees,

---

[1] 79 *L. Q. R.* pp. 479–82, at p. 482 (R. E. M.).

[2] Landlord and Tenant Act, 1927, s. 19 (1) (b). This section does not
apply if the lessor is a Government department, a local or public authority, or
a statutory or public utility company.

[3] (1601), Smith's *Leading Cases*, vol. i, p. 35. Holdsworth, *History of
English Law*, vol. vii, p. 282.

[4] Law of Property Amendment Act, 1859, s. 1.

[5] S. 143 (1).

or is granted in respect only of part of the property, it shall not operate to extinguish the lessor's remedy in case the covenant is broken either by the other lessees or with regard to the rest of the property.[1]

The result is that the rule in *Dumpor's Case* no longer applies to leases.

"Usual covenants."

Although there are many other covenants which may figure in a lease, those that are normally found have been mentioned. But it frequently occurs in practice that an agreement for a lease provides for the inclusion in the latter of the *usual covenants*. It was generally considered, on the authority of *Hampshire* v. *Wickens*,[2] that the only covenants by a tenant which could be described as " usual " were :—

to pay rent ;
to pay tenant's taxes ;
to keep and deliver up the premises in repair ;
to allow the lessor to enter and view the state of repair ;

and that the covenant for quiet enjoyment was the only usual covenant binding the lessor.

It has now been decided, however, that the list is neither fixed nor closed. The question whether particular covenants are usual is a question of fact dependent upon the circumstances of each case, which can be resolved only after considering the evidence of conveyancers, the practice in the particular district and the character of the property.[3]

SECTION VI.   REMEDIES OF THE LANDLORD FOR THE ENFORCEMENT OF THE COVENANTS.

SUMMARY.

From the point of view of remedies, the covenant to pay rent must be distinguished from all other covenants entered into by the tenant.   These two classes will now be treated separately.

---

[1] Law of Property Act, 1925, s. 143 (3).
[2] (1878), 7 Ch. D. 555, 561, *per* JESSEL, M.R.
[3] *Flexman* v. *Corbett*, [1930] 1 Ch. 672.

(1) THE COVENANT TO PAY RENT.

A rent is either a rent-service or a rentcharge.

1. **Rent-Service** consists of an annual return, made by the tenant in labour, money or provisions, in retribution for the land that passes,[1] and this is the rent which is due whenever a tenant holds his lands of a reversioner.[2] A reversion is an estate that arises by operation of law whenever the owner of an estate carves a smaller estate, called a *particular estate*, out of it in favour of another. The residue of the estate continues in him that made the particular estate.[3]

Rent due from tenant is a rent-service.

Thus, where lands are leased at a rent for a term of years, the lessor is the *reversioner* and the rent payable by the tenant is called a *rent-service*.

Exactly the same position would arise if a rent were reserved on the grant by an owner in fee simple of an entailed or a life interest, but in fact rent is not reserved in such a case at the present day, for these interests practically always owe their creation to family settlements, the object of which is to provide fortunes for the settlor's family and not to exact an economic rent from those who will occupy the land.

Since rent-service is that rent which is due from a tenant who holds of a reversioner, it follows that rent which is reserved on the grant of an estate in fee simple cannot be a rent-service, for since *Quia Emptores* such a grantee no longer holds of the grantor, but is substituted for him. There is no reversion, no residue left in the grantor.

The origin of the term rent-service lies far back in legal history. Originally the services due from a tenant took many forms, but in course of time they were commuted into fixed money payments called rents service, since they represented the services that formerly issued out of the land. If the tenant failed to perform the services or to pay the rent into which they had been commuted, the lord enjoyed of common right, *i.e.* independently of statute or agreement, the remedy of distress, a feudal institution of very ancient origin, which entitled him to seize cattle and other chattels found upon the land. This remedy existed of common right only where the distrainor had an interest in the shape of a reversion in the land upon which the chattels lay, for otherwise it could scarcely be said with justice that there was anything he was entitled to seize.[4]

Why called rent-service.

---

[1] Gilbert on Rents, p. 9. For the history of the subject, see Holdsworth, *History of English Law*, vol. vii., pp. 262 *et seq.*

[2] Litt., s. 213.

[3] Co. Litt. 22b.

[4] Litt., s. 213; Gilbert, p. 9; Co. Litt. 78b, 142b; Bac. Abr. tit. Rent (A) 1.

C.R.P.—O

2. **Rentcharge.** From a rent-service must be distinguished a rentcharge. This differs from rent-service in that its owner has no tenurial interest in the land out of which it is payable, and having no such interest, is not entitled as of common right to the remedy of distress. It is, then, any rent *expressly* made payable out of land, other than rent payable by a tenant to a reversioner. For instance, if A. sells land to B. in fee simple, he may agree to accept an annual sum of money from B. in perpetuity instead of a lump sum down, and if it is expressly agreed that the fee simple estate shall be charged in favour of A. with a power of distress should the rent fall into arrears, the rent (whatever name may be given to it by local usage, such as quit rent, ground rent, chief rent, etc.) is a rentcharge.

" It is called a rentcharge because the land for payment thereof
" is charged with a distresse." [1]

Formerly, if a rent was made payable out of a fee simple and for some reason an express power of distress was not reserved, the rent was called a *rent-seck* or dry rent—*dry* because it did not confer the power to distrain.[2]

Thus, at common law the three kinds of rent are rent-service, rentcharge and rent-seck. But rents-seck have long ceased to exist, for the inability of their owners to distrain was removed by the Landlord and Tenant Act, 1730,[3] which enacted that the owners of rents-seck, rents of assize and chief rents should have the same remedy by distress as was available to the owner of a rent-service.

LINDLEY, L.J., said :—

" Bearing in mind what was done by the Act of Geo. II, which
" by section 5 gave a power of distress for all rents, there is now no
" magic in the word rentcharge. Whether you speak of a rentcharge
" or only of a rent, if it is a rent and not merely a sum covenanted to
" be paid, seems to me to be utterly immaterial, because under the Act
" of Geo. II you have a power of distress in respect of it." [4]

The same remedy is given by the Law of Property Act, 1925.[5] For the purpose of this Act, " rent "

" includes a rent-service or a rentcharge, or other rent, toll, duty,
" royalty, or annual or periodical payment, in money or money's
" worth, reserved or issuing out of or charged upon land, but does
" not include mortgage interest." [6]

---

[1] Co. Litt. 144a.
[2] Litt., s. 218.
[3] 4 Geo. 2 c. 28, s. 5.
[4] *Re Gerard (Lord) and Beecham's Contract,* [1894] 3 Ch. 295, at p. 314.
[5] S. 121.   [6] S. 205 (I) (xxiii).

This is not the place to elaborate the subject of rentcharges. The historical difference between them and rent-service has been demonstrated, and we may now proceed to set out the remedies that are available to a landlord for the recovery of the rent service due to him.

(A) DISTRESS.

The right of distress which has existed in England since the Conquest was originally allowed for the enforcement of a great number of services that in feudal days might be incident to tenure, such as rent-service, suit-service, heriot-service, aids, reliefs and so on, but most of these are now obsolete, and practically the only purposes for which common law distress is exercisable are the recovery of rent in arrear, and the recovery of compensation for damage done to land by trespassing cattle taken damage feasant.

Nature of distress.

The value of the remedy to a landlord is that he can seize and sell the chattels found on the land and thus procure the rent without the necessity of taking legal proceedings. At common law, indeed, his right was limited to the retention of the goods, but he was ultimately given a power of sale by a statute passed in 1689.[1]

Value of distress.

It is essential that the reversion should be vested in the distrainor at the time when the rent falls due and also when the distress is levied.

Reversion must be in distrainor.

Thus if L. has assigned the reversion to X. at a time when rent is due, L. cannot distrain, since he no longer holds the reversion; and X. is under the same disability, since he was not the reversioner at the critical moment.

Distress cannot be made until the rent is in arrears, which does not occur until the day after it is due,[2] and it can be levied neither between sunset and sunrise,[3] nor on a Sunday.[4]

When it may be made.

As a general rule the right of seizure is confined to chattels upon the actual land out of which the rent issues, but it may be extended by agreement to other premises, and by the Distress for Rent Act, 1737, goods which have been fraudulently and secretly removed by a tenant after the rent became due, in order to avoid distress, may be seized by the landlord within 30 days wherever found.

Where it may be made.

---

[1] Distress for Rent Act, 1689, s. 1.
[2] *Duppa* v. *Mayo* (1670), 1 Wms. Saund. 287 ; 31 Digest (Repl.) 253, *3885.* *In re Aspinall,* [1961] Ch. 526; [1961] 2 All E. R. 751.
[3] *Tutton* v. *Darke* (1860), 29 L. J. Ex. 271.
[4] *Werth* v. *London and Westminster Loan Co.* (1889), 5 T. L. R. 521 ; but see *Child* v. *Edwards,* [1909] 2 K. B. 753 (special agreement).

Involves a right of entry.

A distrainor may enter the demised premises and may commit in so doing what in any one else would be a trespass,[1] as for example by entry through an unlocked door;[2] but he may neither break open a door whether of the living house or of an outhouse,[3] nor effect an entrance through a closed but unfastened window.[4]

What may be seized.

The general rule of the common law is that all personal chattels found upon the premises out of which the rent issues, whether they belong to the tenant or to a stranger, can be distrained, but this extensive power is cut down in two ways :—

Privileged things.

1. SOME THINGS ARE PRIVILEGED FROM DISTRESS.

It is outside the scope of this work to deal with this question in detail, and the reader is referred to the notes given in Smith's *Leading Cases* to *Simpson* v. *Hartopp*.[5]   It will suffice here to

Absolutely privileged.

say that the following articles are absolutely privileged in the sense that they can never be seized :—

machinery belonging to a third person which is on an agricultural holding under a contract of hire [6] ;
livestock belonging to a third person which is on an agricultural holding solely for breeding purposes [7];
animals *ferae naturae* ;
things delivered to a person in the way of his trade, such as cloth given to a tailor to be made into a suit ;
things in actual use, such as a horse drawing a cart ;
things in the custody of the law, such as property already taken in execution ;
clothes, bedding and tools up to the value of £5.

Conditionally privileged.

The following things are conditionally privileged, that is to say, they can be seized only if there is not a sufficiency of other distrainable goods to be found upon the premises :

beasts of the plough ;
sheep and instruments of husbandry ;
the instruments of a man's trade or profession, such as the text-books of a solicitor ;
the live-stock of a third person found on the land of an agricultural tenant as a result of a contract of agistment.[8]

Lodger's goods.

2. GOODS BELONGING TO AN UNDER-TENANT OR A LODGER ARE PROTECTED. BLACKBURN, J., said :—

" The general rule at common law was that whatever was found " upon the demised premises, whether belonging to a stranger " or not, might be seized by the landlord and held as a distress " till the rent was paid or the service performed.   This state of

---

[1] *Long* v. *Clarke*, [1894] 1 Q. B. 119, 122.
[2] *Southam* v. *Smout*, [1964] 1 Q. B. 308; [1963] 3 All E. R. 104.
[3] *American Concentrated Must Corp.* v. *Hendry* (1893), 62 L. J. Q. B. 388.
[4] *Nash* v. *Lucas* (1867), L. R. 2 Q. B. 590.
[5] (1744) : Willes 512 ; Smith's *Leading Cases*, vol. i. p. 137.
[6] Agricultural Holdings Act, 1948, s. 20.   [7] *Ibid.*
[8] Agricultural Holdings Act, 1948, s. 19 (1).   If distrained because of an insufficiency of other goods the landlord cannot thereby recover more than the amount due and unpaid under the contract of agistment.

" things produced no harm, because at common law the land-
" lord, not being able to sell the distress, generally gave up the
" goods as soon as he found they were not the tenant's, as his
" continuing to hold them would not induce the tenant to pay.
" But in the reign of William and Mary a very harsh and un-
" just law was passed, by which the right was given to the land-
" lord to sell any goods seized and to apply the proceeds to the
" payment of the rent unless the tenant or the owner of the
" goods first paid it, and this held out a great temptation to a
" landlord to take the goods of a stranger although he knew
" they were not the tenant's." [1]

This has gradually been put on a more equitable footing, and
at the present day the Law of Distress Amendment Act, 1908,[2]
except in the case of certain specified goods,[3] provides a means
by which a lodger or under-tenant or indeed any person not
being a tenant of the premises and not having any beneficial
interest in the tenancy, may avoid the seizure of his belongings.
Suppose for instance that

> L. has leased premises to T., and that X. is the lodger or
> the under-tenant of T. If in such a case L. levies a
> distress on any goods belonging to X. for arrears of rent
> due from T., X. may serve L. with a notice declaring that
>
> > T. has no right of property in the goods ;
> > the goods are not goods excepted from the Act ;
> > so much rent is due from X. to T. ;
> > future instalments will become due on stated days ;
> > he will pay such rent to L.

With this notice, which is of no effect unless it contains the
requisite statements,[4] X. must also send an inventory of his
goods. If L. distrains on the goods of X. after receipt of this
notice and inventory, he is guilty of an illegal distress, and X.
may apply to a justice of the peace or to a magistrate for the
restoration of his goods. The protection afforded by the Act
applies only to a tenant whose rent equals the full annual
value of the premises.

How Distress is Levied. No person can distrain for rent
unless he is a certificated bailiff, that is, unless he has been
authorized to levy distress (either in the one particular case or in
general cases) by a certificate in writing under the hand of a
county court judge.[5] *Procedure.*

Such a bailiff should be provided by the landlord with a
distress warrant authorizing him to make the levy. The first
step is to seize and impound the goods. At common law the
impounding had to take place off the premises, but now it is *Impounding.*

---

[1] *Lyons* v. *Elliott* (1876), 1 Q. B. D. 210, 213.
[2] S. 1.
[3] *I.e.,* goods belonging to the husband or wife of the tenant ; goods
comprised in a bill of sale, hire purchase agreement or settlement made by
the tenant.
[4] *Druce & Co.* v. *Beaumont Property Trust,* [1935] 2 K. B. 257.
[5] Law of Distress Amendment Act, 1888, s 7.

lawful to secure the goods in some part of the premises themselves.[1]

The usual practice is to leave a man in possession, but this is
not essential, for goods are deemed to be impounded if what is
called " walking possession " is taken of them, *i.e.* if they are left
on the premises but periodically inspected by the bailiff.[2] Anyone
who interferes with goods after they have been impounded is
liable in treble damages for pound breach.[3] As soon as the seizure
is complete, the landlord is bound to give the tenant [4] notice of the
distress and of the place, if any, to which the goods have been
removed,[5] and he is not at liberty to sell them until five days have

The sale.   elapsed since the service of the notice. Thus a tenant is allowed
five days within which to pay what is due, but he is entitled to an
extension of this period to 15 days if he makes a request in writing
to this effect to the landlord and gives security for any additional
expense that the delay may involve.[6] The sale is generally
though not necessarily by auction, and it usually takes place on
the premises unless the tenant has requested in writing that the
goods shall be removed to a public auction-room   If it does not
produce sufficient proceeds, no second sale is as a general rule
permissible.[7]

Only six years' arrears of rent may be recovered by the remedy
of distress, whether or not the lease is under seal.[8]   When the
demised premises consist of an agricultural holding only one year's
arrears are recoverable by this method.[9]

(B) ACTION FOR ARREARS OF RENT.

What arrears   Whether a lease is made by deed or not, only six years' arrears
recoverable.   of rent are recoverable by action.[10] Thus a landlord must bring
his action within six years after the rent has become due or has
been acknowledged in writing to be due, or after some payment
has been made by the tenant.[11] A payment of part of the rent
does not entitle the landlord to sue for the remainder more than
six years after it became due.[12]

But while the relation of landlord and tenant continues under
a lease for a fixed term of years, the right of the landlord to recover

---

[1] Distress for Rent Act, 1737, s. 10.
[2] *Lavell* v. *O'Leary*, [1933] 2 K. B. 200.
[3] Distress for Rent Act, 1689, s. 3 (1).   [4] *Ibid.*, s. 1.
[5] Distress for Rent Act, 1737, s. 9.
[6] Law of Distress Amendment Act, 1888, s. 6.
[7] *Rawlence and Squarey* v. *Spicer*, [1935] 1 K. B. 412.
[8] Limitation Act, 1939, s. 17.
[9] Agricultural Holdings Act, 1948, s. 18.
[10] Limitation Act, 1939, s. 17.   This is an alteration of the old law which
permitted 20 years' arrears to be recovered upon the personal covenant contained in a deed.
[11] Limitation Act, 1939, s. 23 (4).
[12] *Ibid.*, proviso.

rent is not *totally* barred by non-payment no matter how long the rent is in arrear.[1]   Suppose, for instance, that

A. holds lands of B. for 99 years at £100 a year, and that A. has not paid rent for 25 years.   B.'s right to recover rent is not extinguished, but is limited to the recovery of the last six years' arrears.

The only case in which the right of a landlord is extinguished altogether occurs where for a period of 12 years the rent has been paid to a third person who wrongfully claims to be entitled to the reversion.[2]

The rule is that a landlord cannot pursue the two remedies of action and distress at one and the same time.   If he has levied a distress, he cannot bring an action for recovery until he has sold the distrained articles and found the purchase money insufficient to satisfy his demand.[3]   If he has sued to judgment first, then, even though the judgment remains unsatisfied, he loses his remedy of distress altogether for that particular rent.[4] *Inter-relation of remedies.*

(C) EXPRESS PROVISO FOR RE-ENTRY.

The breach of a covenant by a tenant does not entitle the lessor to resume possession by a re-entry upon the premises, unless the right to do so is expressly reserved in the lease.   On the other hand, an undertaking by the tenant which is framed not as a mere covenant, but as a condition, carries with it at common law a right of re-entry if the condition is broken.   Whether a stipulation amounts to a covenant or a condition is sometimes a question of considerable nicety, but it depends entirely upon the intention of the parties.   A condition is a clause which shows a clear intention on the part of the landlord, not merely that the tenant shall be personally liable if he fails in his contractual duties, but that the lease shall determine in the event of such a failure.   The tenancy is to remain conditional upon the fulfilment by the tenant of his obligations.   In an early case, BAYLEY, J., said : *Distinction between covenant and condition.*

" In a lease for years no precise form of words is necessary to make a condition.   It is sufficient if it appear that the words used were intended to have the effect of creating a condition.   They must be the words of the landlord, because he is to impose the condition." [5]

In this case it was " stipulated and conditioned " in the lease that the tenant should not assign or underlet the premises, otherwise

---

[1] *Grant* v. *Ellis* (1841), 9 M. & W. 113 ; *Archbold* v. *Scully* (1861), 9 H. L. C. 360.
[2] *Lehain* v. *Philpott* (1875), L. R. 10 Ex. 242 ; *infra*, pp. 818–9
[3] *Archbold* v. *Scully, supra.*
[4] *Chancellor* v. *Webster* (1893), 9 T. L. R. 568.
[5] *Doe d. Henniker* v. *Watt* (1828), 8 B. & C. 308.

than to his wife or children, and it was held that these words were sufficient to create a condition. Mere words of agreement, however, as for example when the tenant " agrees that he will not assign the premises without the consent of the landlord," create nothing more than a covenant.[1]

Express proviso for re-entry and forfeiture of lease.

It is, however, the usual practice for a lease to contain, in clear and unmistakable language, an express clause which reserves to the lessor the right of re-entry if one or more of the covenants are broken, and which provides that upon re-entry the lease shall be forfeited. The virtue of this is that the lessor, if he finds himself saddled with an impecunious tenant who is a persistent defaulter in the payment of rent, may regain possession instead of being driven to constant litigation.

The following is a precedent of a proviso for forfeiture :—

" Provided always that if any part of the said rent shall be in arrears
" for 21 days, whether lawfully demanded or not, the lessor or his
" assigns may re-enter upon the said premises, and immediately
" thereupon the said term shall absolutely determine."

Breach of condition renders lease voidable.

In such a case the effect of allowing the rent to fall into arrears for more than 21 days is to render the tenant's interest liable to forfeiture, and not *ipso facto* to cause a forfeiture. However clearly the proviso may state that the lease shall be void on breach of condition, it has been held in a long series of decisions that its only effect is to render the lease voidable.[2] It is at the option of the landlord whether the tenancy shall be determined or not, and it is only if he does some act which shows his intention to end it that the lease will be avoided.[3] Thus an actual entry by the landlord or the grant of a lease to a new tenant works a forfeiture, but the usual practice at the present day is to sue for the recovery of possession instead of making a re-entry, for, as WILLES, J., said,

" The bringing of an action of ejectment is equivalent to the ancient
" entry. It is an act unequivocal, in the sense that it asserts the right
" of possession upon every ground that may turn out to be available
" to the party claiming to re-enter."[4]

Condition of forfeiture may be waived.

Waiver. The question whether the landlord has by some unequivocal act elected to treat the lease as forfeited is an important one from the point of view of waiver. Common law dislikes conditions of forfeiture, and it will always treat such a condition as waived and therefore unenforceable if, after the act of forfeiture has been committed, the landlord clearly shows that he regards the tenancy as still existing. The two essentials for waiver are that,

1. the landlord must be aware of the commission of an act of forfeiture by the tenant, and

---

[1] *Crawley* v. *Price* (1875), L. R. 10 Q. B. 302.
[2] *Davenport* v. *R.* (1877), L. R. 3 App. Cas. 115, 128.
[3] *Toleman* v. *Portbury* (1871), L. R. 6 Q. B. 245, 250.
[4] *Grimwood* v. *Moss* (1872), L. R. 7 C. P. 360, 364.

2. he must do some positive act which is a recognition of the continuance of the tenancy.[1]

Thus a merely passive attitude on his part has no effect,[2] but on the other hand (and this applies to all conditions of forfeiture, whether in respect of the non-payment of rent or of the non-performance of other covenants),

1. if, after the act of forfeiture has been committed, he demands or sues for rent,[3] or accepts payment of it notwithstanding that his acceptance is stated to be "without prejudice";[4] or
2. if he distrains for rent whether due before or after the breach;[5] or
3. if he grants a new lease to the defaulting tenant;[6] or
4. if he or some person authorized by him unequivocally demands the rent that is due,[7]

each of these acts is strong evidence that he has elected not to avoid the lease.[8] At bottom, however, the question always is *quo animo* was the act done.[9]

The waiver of a covenant or of a condition does not operate as a general waiver, but extends only to the particular breach in question.[10] An important distinction should be noticed between continuing and non-continuing breaches of covenant, for acceptance of rent or the levy of distress after the breach of a continuing covenant, *e.g.* to insure the premises or to keep them in repair, waives the forfeiture only up to the date of distress or payment of rent. The proviso for re-entry may be enforced if the breach subsequently continues.[11]

But when once a landlord unequivocally and finally elects to treat a lease as void, as, for instance, where he serves a writ for recovery of the land, no subsequent receipt of rent or other act will amount to waiver so as to deprive him of his right to enforce the clause of re-entry.[12]

What Constitutes a Demand of Rent. In the precedent Demand of rent.

---

[1] *Dendy* v. *Nicholl* (1858), 4 C. B. (N. S.) 376.
[2] *Perry* v. *Davis* (1858), 3 C. B. (N. S.) 769.
[3] *Dendy* v. *Nicholl, supra. Dist. Clarke* v. *Grant,* [1950] 1 K. B. 104; [1949] 1 All E. R. 768.
[4] *Segal Securities, Ltd.* v. *Thoseby,* [1963] 1 Q. B. 887; [1963] 1 All E. R. 500. It is a question of fact whether money has been tendered and accepted as rent; if answered affirmatively, the consequences as regards waiver raise a question of law; *Windmill Investments (London), Ltd.* v. *Milano Restaurant, Ltd.,* [1962] 2 Q. B. 373; [1962] 2 All E. R. 680.
[5] *Doe d. David* v. *Williams* (1835), 7 C. & P. 322.
[6] *Ward* v. *Day* (1864), 5 B. & S. 359.
[7] *Creery* v. *Summersell and Flowerdew & Co., Ltd.,* [1949] Ch. 751.
[8] *Ibid.,* at p. 761.
[9] *Ibid.*
[10] Law of Property Act, 1925, s. 148.
[11] *Doe d. Hemmings* v. *Durnford* (1832), 2 Cr. & J. 667; *Doe d. Baker* v. *Jones* (1850), 5 Exch. 498.
[12] *Civil Service Co-operative Society* v. *McGrigor's Trustee,* [1923] 2 Ch. 347; *Evans* v. *Enever,* [1920] 2 K. B. 315.

o*

which is set out above it will be noticed that the landlord reserves a power of re-entry for non-payment of rent *whether lawfully demanded or not*. The object of inserting these words is to avoid the strictness of the common law which requires the landlord, failing a contrary agreement, to make a formal demand upon the premises themselves for the exact amount of rent due, and to make it between the hours of sunrise and sunset so as to afford the tenant an opportunity of counting out the money while light remains.[1] This common law rule has, however, been partly abrogated by a statute which enacts that, even though the formal demand has not been dispensed with in the lease, yet, if one-half year's rent is in arrear and there are not sufficient distrainable goods upon the premises and a power of re-entry has been reserved, the landlord can recover the premises by action at the end of the period fixed in the proviso for re-entry without making any formal demand of rent.[2] The restricted nature of this statutory modification makes it desirable, in the interests of a sure and speedy remedy, to obviate by express words the necessity for a formal demand.

Common Law rule.

Relief against Forfeiture. One of the aims of the old Court of Chancery was to prevent the enforcement of a legal right from producing hardship, and therefore, since the sole object of a right of re-entry was to give a landlord security for the rent, it was always prepared to relieve the tenant against the forfeiture, provided that he paid all that was due by way of arrears of rent, together with costs and interest. In this way, the landlord obtained all that the right of re-entry was intended to secure to him, and it would be inequitable for him to take advantage of the forfeiture.[3]

Relief granted against forfeiture for non-payment of rent.

Originally a tenant might petition for and obtain this relief at any time after he had been ejected under the power of re-entry, but his right has been restricted by statute. The present position depends upon the Common Law Procedure Act, 1852[4] (which re-enacted in this particular the Landlord and Tenant Act of 1730), and upon the Judicature Act, 1925. The result of these Acts is as follows:—

Time within which relief must be sought.

> If the lessor sues for possession and the tenant at any time before the trial pays or tenders to the lessor or pays into court the rent and arrears and costs, all further proceedings are stayed and he regains possession under the old lease.[5]

[1] Notes to *Duppa* v. *Mayo* (1668), 1 Wms. Saund. 282, 287.
[2] Common Law Procedure Act, 1852, s. 210.
[3] *Howard* v. *Fanshawe*, [1895] 2 Ch. 581 ; and authorities there cited.
[4] Ss. 210–12.
[5] Common Law Procedure Act, 1852, s. 212. For a " trial " to come within the meaning of this section, it must be an effective trial binding on all the necessary parties ; *Gill* v. *Lewis*, [1956] 2 Q. B. 1 ; [1956] 1 All E. R. 884, where judgment was signed against only one of two joint tenants.

It has now been held, however, that there is no case for such a stay of proceedings unless six months' rent is in arrear.[1]

If the tenant does not, or cannot, take this opportunity and judgment is given against him, he is barred from all relief in law or equity unless he applies for relief within six months after execution of the judgment.[2] If he applies within this period, the court is empowered by the Act of 1925 to relieve him from the forfeiture subject to such terms and conditions as to payment of rent, costs and otherwise, as could formerly have been imposed by the old Court of Chancery. The effect of a grant of relief is that he holds the land according to the terms of the original lease without the necessity of a new lease.[3]

The grant of relief within this extended time of six months, however, is a matter of discretion, the general principle being that, so far as rent is concerned, the landlord can claim nothing more than to be restored to the position that he would have occupied had the forfeiture not been incurred. The position has been stated in the following authoritative passage:

"The function of the court in exercising this equitable jurisdiction "is to grant relief when all that is due for rent and costs has been "paid up, and (in general) to disregard any other causes of complaint "that the landlord may have against the tenant. The question is "whether, provided all is paid up, the landlord will not have been "fully compensated, and the view taken by the court is that if he "gets the whole of his rent and costs, then he has got all that he is "entitled to so far as rent is concerned, and extraneous matters of "breach of covenant, are, generally speaking, irrelevant."[4]

Even so, however, exceptional circumstances may justify the refusal of relief, such as the inordinate conduct of the tenant himself or the fact that the landlord has altered his position in the belief that the forfeiture is effective. Thus, for instance, relief was refused to a tenant who did not apply until just before the six months had elapsed, by which time the landlord, after incurring expenditure upon the maintenance of the property, had "made an arrangement" to let another party into possession.[5]

If relief is granted upon conditions to be performed within a limited time, the court has jurisdiction to extend the time if it is just and equitable to do so.[6]

Relief may be granted to the tenant where the landlord, instead of bringing an action for recovery of the land, enters into

---

[1] *Standard Pattern Co., Ltd.* v. *Ivey,* [1962] Ch. 432; [1962] 1 All E. R. 452 criticized, 78 *L. Q. R.* pp. 168–71 (R. E. M.).

[2] Common Law Procedure Act, 1852, s. 210–212.

[3] Supreme Court of Judicature (Consolidation) Act, 1925, s. 46.

[4] *Gill* v. *Lewis,* [1956] 2 Q. B. 1, at p. 13, [1956] 1 All E. R. 844, at p. 853, *per* Jenkins, L. J. See also *Belgravia Insurance Co., Ltd.* v. *Meah,* [1964] 1 Q. B. 436; [1963] 3 All E. R. 828.

[5] *Stanhope* v. *Haworth* (1886), 3 T. L. R. 34.

[6] *Chandless-Chandless* v. *Nicholson,* [1942] 2 K. B. 321 ; [1942] 2 All E. R. 315.

peaceable possession, though in such a case it is likely that the court, acting by analogy to the statute, would require the action for relief to be brought within six months from the resumption of possession by the landlord.[1]

Relief to under-lessees.

Relief to Under-lessees. The old rule was that, if the lease contained a proviso for re-entry, an under-lessee from the original tenant could be evicted if the original tenant committed an act of forfeiture, but the Law of Property Act, 1925,[2] re-enacting the Conveyancing Act, 1892, provides that where a head lessor proceeds by action or otherwise to enforce a forfeiture, the court may, on the application of an under-lessee, vest the property in the under-lessee for part or the whole of the remainder of the term and upon such conditions as are thought fit. The general principle here is that the landlord is entitled to be restored to his former position, but only in respect of the part of the premises occupied by the under-lessee. It would not be equitable, for instance, that the latter should be required to pay the rent due to the landlord in respect of the whole of the premises.[3] The proper way of giving effect to the statute is to create a new lease in favour of the sub-tenant, but one that is implicitly subject to the terms and conditions contained in the original lease.[4] In no case, however, may he be granted a lease for any longer term than he is entitled to under the sub-lease.[5]

Mortgagees and squatters.

Relief is available to the mortgagee of a leasehold interest holding under a sub-demise or under a charge by way of legal mortgage.[6] It is not available to a squatter who has dispossessed a lessee.[7]

(2) COVENANTS OTHER THAN THE COVENANT TO PAY RENT.

A. ACTION FOR DAMAGES.

Damages and injunction.

If the tenant fails to observe any of the covenants contained in the lease, it is open to the lessor either to sue for damages for

---

[1] *Howard* v. *Fanshawe*, [1895] 2 Ch. 581; *Lovelock* v. *Margo*, [1963] 2 Q. B. 786; [1963] 2 All E. R. 13. For the special rules that govern the jurisdiction of the County Court to grant relief, see the County Courts Act 1959, s. 191, as amended by the County Courts (Jurisdiction) Act, 1963, s. 1 (1) (a).
[2] S. 146 (4).
[3] *Chatham Empire Theatre* (1955) *Ltd.* v. *Ultrans Ltd.*, [1961] 2 All E. R. 381 ; [1961] 1 W. L. R. 817.
[4] *Chelsea Estates Investment Trust Co., Ltd.* v. *Marche*, [1955] Ch. 328; [1955] 1 All E. R. 195.
[5] *Factors (Sundries), Ltd.* v. *Miller*, [1952] 2 All E. R. 630.
[6] *Belgravia Insurance Co., Ltd.* v. *Meah*, [1964] 1 Q. B. 436; [1963] 3 All E. R. 828. As to these forms of mortgage, see *infra*, p. 574.
[7] *Tickner* v. *Buzzacott*, [1965] Ch. 426; [1965] 1 All E. R. 131.

breach or to obtain an injunction to restrain the breach.[1]   This
remedy is available, for instance, notwithstanding the Agricultural
Holdings Act, 1948, where a tenant farmer fails to observe the
rules of good husbandry.[2]

In the one case of a covenant to *repair*, however, a statutory
restriction has been imposed upon this right of action which applies
wherever the premises, other than an agricultural holding, have
been let for a period of not less than seven years.   In such a case,
if at least three years of the tenancy remain unexpired, the landlord, as a preliminary to his action to recover damages for breach
of covenant, must serve on the tenant not less than one month
before the commencement of the action a notice,

> specifying the particular breach in question ; and
> requiring it to be remedied, if it is capable of remedy ; and
> demanding compensation.[3]

Statutory restriction on enforcement of repairing covenants.

Within 28 days of receipt of this notice the tenant may serve a
counter-notice on the landlord claiming the benefit granted to him
by the Act.   The nature of this benefit is described below.[4]

B. Enforcement of Forfeiture.

As a further safeguard to the landlord it is the common
practice, just as in the case of the covenant to pay rent, to ensure
the observance of all other covenants by inserting an express
proviso for re-entry and forfeiture in the event of their breach.
The following is a typical clause in a lease :—

Condition of forfeiture.

> " If there shall be any breach or non-observance of any of the
> " lessee's covenants hereinbefore contained, then and in any of the
> " said cases it shall be lawful for the lessor, at any time thereafter,
> " into and upon the said demised premises, or any part thereof, to
> " re-enter and the same to have again, repossess and enjoy in his
> " former estate."[5]

In two respects, what has already been said above about
forfeiture for non-payment of rent applies equally to these other
covenants, namely, the effect of a breach is to render the lease

No relief against forfeiture.

---

[1] *Coward* v. *Gregory* (1866), L. R. 2 C. P. 153.
[2] *Kent* v. *Conniff*, [1953] 1 Q. B. 361 ; [1953] 1 All E. R. 155.
[3] Leasehold Property (Repairs) Act, 1938, ss. 1 (2), 7 (1) ; as amended by
Landlord and Tenant Act, 1954, s. 51 (1).
[4] *Infra*, pp. 400–1.
[5] In this case forfeiture is provided for by the act of the parties, but it
also occurs by operation of law if the tenant asserts a title in himself adverse
to the landlord (*e.g.* by a written declaration that he, not the landlord, is
entitled to the freehold), or if he lets a stranger into possession with the
intention of enabling him to set up such an adverse title.   But in all cases,
it is a question of fact whether the tenant's act shows an intention to deny the
landlord's title ; *Wisbech St. Mary Parish Council* v. *Lilley*, [1956] 1 All
E. R. 301 ; [1956] 1 W. L. R. 121 ; *Warner* v. *Sampson*, [1959] 1 Q. B. 297 ;
[1959] 1 All E. R. 120.   See generally, Hill and Redman, *Law of Landlord
and Tenant* (13th Edn.), p. 485.

voidable, not void ; and the right of avoidance is lost by any act on the part of the lessor which amounts to a waiver of the condition.[1] But until the legislature intervened, the jurisdiction of the court to relieve the tenant varied according as the forfeiture was due to non-payment of rent or to the breach of a covenant relating to some other matter. The question soon arose whether equity would protect a tenant against the loss of his interest under such a clause if, having incurred a forfeiture by breaking one of the covenants, he was prepared to put the matter right by paying all costs and compensation. To cite the words of KAY, L.J. :—

" At first there seems to have been some hesitation whether this
" relief " [grantable in the case of non-payment of rent] " might not be
" extended to other cases of forfeiture for breach of covenants, such
" as to repair and the like, where compensation could be made ; but it
" was soon recognized that there would be great difficulty in estimating
" the proper amount of compensation, and since the decision of Lord
" ELDON in *Hill* v. *Barclay*[2] it has always been held that equity would
" not relieve, merely on the ground that it could give compensation,
" upon breach of any covenant in a lease except the covenant for
" payment of rent. But, of course, this left unaffected the un-
" doubted jurisdiction to relieve in case of breach occasioned by
" fraud, accident, surprise or mistake."[3]

This denial of relief was maintained even though the breach, instead of causing loss to the landlord, operated to his advantage by restoring to him, at a much earlier date than he had a right to expect, premises upon which the tenant in the expectation of continued tenure might have already expended large sums of money. The strongest example of this was where a tenant failed to re-insure for a short time after the previous year's policy had run out. If in such a case no fire had occurred in the uninsured period the landlord had obviously lost nothing, and yet it was held in several cases that such a breach was sufficient to produce a forfeiture against which no relief could be given.[4] This particular case of forfeiture (by failure to insure) received legislative attention in 1859,[5] when relief was made possible on certain conditions, but it still remained true that the merely technical and innocuous breach of any other covenant inevitably led to the loss of his interest by the tenant if the landlord chose to take advantage of a proviso for re-entry.

Changes by Conveyancing Act, 1881. The law, however, was fundamentally changed in two respects by the Conveyancing Act of 1881,[6] which first required certain conditions to be satisfied before forfeiture could be enforced, and then gave the tenant the right to petition for relief.

---

[1] *Supra.*, pp. 392–3.
[2] (1810), 16 Ves. 402.
[3] *Barrow* v. *Isaacs & Son*, [1891] 1 Q. B. 417, 425.
[4] See, *e.g.*, *Doe d. Muston* v. *Gladwin* (1845), 6 Q. B. 953.
[5] Law of Property Amendment Act, 1859, ss. 4–9 ; later repealed by the Conveyancing Act, 1881.
[6] S. 14.

These provisions were re-enacted by section 146 of the Law of Property Act, 1925, and amended by three further Acts in 1927, 1938 and 1954.[1] The law now stands as follows :—

1. **The Statutory Restriction on the Landlord's Right to Enforce a Forfeiture.** The Act of 1925 forbids a lessor to re-enter or to bring an action for the recovery of the premises until he has served on the tenant a notice specifying the particular breach complained of, and, if the breach is capable of remedy, requiring him to remedy it and in any case requiring him to make compensation in money. Then, if the tenant fails within a reasonable time after service of this statutory notice to remedy the breach if it is remediable, and to make reasonable compensation in money, the landlord can proceed to enforce the forfeiture.[2] A period of three months is normally regarded as a " reasonable time," but in special circumstances it may be much less.[3] This statutory rule is designed to afford the tenant an opportunity of considering the matter before an action is brought against him and of making up his mind whether he can admit the breach and whether he ought to offer compensation.[4]

Notice to tenant required.

L.P.A.,s.146.

To eliminate the risk of the notice not reaching the occupying tenant, it is enacted by the Landlord and Tenant Act, 1927,[5] that *in the case of a covenant to repair* a right of re-entry shall not be enforceable unless the lessor proves that service of the notice was known either—

(a) to the lessee ; or
(b) to an under-lessee holding under a sub-lease which reserves only a nominal reversion to the lessee ; or
(c) to the person who last paid the rent,

and that a reasonable interval had elapsed since the time when the fact of service was *known to* such person. The sending of a registered letter to a person is, however, to be regarded *primâ facie* as good service.

It is now established that the statutory notice need not contain a demand for compensation if the lessor does not desire to be indemnified.[6] Whether, in the case of a negative covenant, the statutory notice will be ineffective if it omits to require a breach to be remedied has occasioned some difficulty. If, for instance, the tenant has agreed not to permit the premises to be used for illegal or immoral purposes and he is convicted of using them for habitual prostitution, it

Position where negative covenant not remediable.

---

[1] Landlord and Tenant Act, 1927 ; Leasehold Property (Repairs) Act, 1938 ; Landlord and Tenant Act, 1954.
[2] Law of Property Act, 1925, s. 146 (1).
[3] *Civil Service Co-operative Society* v. *McGrigor's Trustee*, [1923] 2 Ch. 347.
[4] *Horsey Estate, Ltd.* v. *Steiger*, [1899] 2 Q. B. 79, 91.   [5] S. 18 (2).
[6] *Lock* v. *Pearce*, [1893] 2 Ch. 271.

may be that the landlord is already branded locally as the owner of a brothel. If so, the tenant may no doubt discontinue his immoral use of the premises, his only mode of redemption, but mere cesser will not wipe out the past and remove the stigma on the landlord's reputation. In this sense the breach is not capable of remedy. If, therefore, the landlord can show that he has suffered lasting damage of this nature, his statutory notice need not require the breach to be remedied.[1]

But it has been held that the position is different where the action for forfeiture is brought against the original tenant in respect of immoral uses permitted not by him, but by his sub-tenant or assignee. In these circumstances, it is the duty of the original tenant to take immediate steps to stop the wrongful user and also to enforce the foreiture against the wrongdoer. It is only if he fails to do so within a reasonable time after learning the facts that the breach will be regarded as incapable of remedy.[2]

Notice to be distinct.

As regards the details which must be brought to the knowledge of the tenant, the rule has been laid down that the notice must be sufficiently precise to direct his attention to the particular things of which the landlord complains, so that he may understand with reasonable certainty what he is required to do and may be in a position to put matters right before the action is brought.[3]

If, for instance,

> the tenant holds half a dozen houses from the landlord and he is merely notified that he has broken his covenant to repair, the notice will be bad as not indicating which of the houses are involved.

Exceptional case of the covenant to repair.

Where a landlord wishes to enforce a forfeiture in respect of a covenant to keep or put the premises in repair, he is subject to a further statutory restriction. In the case of this particular covenant it is provided that if the lease is for seven years or more, and if at the date of the service of the notice under section 146 three years or more of these remain unexpired, the tenant may within 28 days of that date serve a counter-notice on the landlord claiming the benefit of the Leasehold Property (Repairs) Act,

---

[1] *Rugby School* v. *Tannahill*, [1935] 1 K. B. 87; *Egerton* v. *Esplanade Hotels London, Ltd.*, [1947] 2 All E. R. 88; *Hoffman* v. *Fineberg*, [1949] Ch. 245; [1948] 1 All E. R. 592.

[2] *Glass* v. *Kencakes, Ltd.*, [1966] 1 Q. B. 611; [1964] 3 All E. R. 807. These difficulties will be avoided if the statutory notices requires the tenant to remedy the breach *if it is capable of remedy*. The landlord can then claim in his action (1) that the breach is incapable of remedy, or (2) if it is capable of remedy that it has not been remedied; *ibid.*, pp. 629–30.

[3] *Fletcher* v. *Nokes*, [1897] 1 Ch. 271, 274 ; approved *Fox* v. *Jolly*, [1916] A. C. 1.

1938.[1] Moreover, in the notice served upon him, the tenant must be expressly informed of his right to serve a counter-notice.[2]

The effect of a counter-notice is that no proceedings what- soever may be taken by the landlord for the enforcement of any right of re-entry or forfeiture, or for the recovery of damages, in respect of a breach of the repairing covenant, unless he first obtains the leave of the County Court.[3] But as soon as the lease has less than three years to run, there is no longer any need to apply for this leave.[4] The circumstances in which leave is to be given are specifically enumerated by the statute.[5] At this stage of the proceedings the landlord need only show a *prima facie* case of a breach by the tenant.[6] Effect of counter-notice.

The Act applies to leases created and to breaches occurring before or after June 23, 1938, when it came into operation.[7]

2. The Right of the Tenant to Claim Relief. After requiring the above preliminaries from a lessor before he can enforce a forfeiture the Act of 1925 then provides that, when the lessor is proceeding by action or entry to recover the premises, the lessee may apply to the court for relief, and the court may, after reviewing the circumstances of the case and the conduct of the parties, refuse such relief, or grant it upon such terms as to costs, expenses, damages, compensation, penalty, etc., as seem fit.[8] This application must be made by all the tenants if the premises are held by joint lessees.[9] Power of court to grant or refuse relief.

Attempts have been made to specify the principles upon which this relief should be granted or withheld,[10] but the House of Lords has held that though such statements are useful and may reflect the judicial view for normal cases, yet the discretion given by the statute is so wide that it is better not to lay down rigid rules for its exercise.[11] It is established,

---

[1] Leasehold Property (Repairs) Act, 1938, s. 1 (1) ; as amended by the Landlord and Tenant Act, 1954, s. 51 (1).

[2] Leasehold Property (Repairs) Act, 1938, s. 1 (4). [3] *Ibid.*

[4] *Baker* v. *Sims*, [1959] 1 Q. B. 114 ; [1958] 3 All E. R. 326.

[5] Leasehold Property (Repairs) Act, 1938, s. 1 (5) ; (a) where substantial damage has been caused, or will be caused if breach not remedied ; (b) where an immediate remedy is required for giving effect to any enactment, byelaw or order of a local authority respecting the safety, repair, maintenance or sanitary condition of the house; (c) where the tenant does not occupy the whole of the house and the breach is injurious to the other occupant; (d) where the cost of repair is relatively small as compared with the much greater expense that a postponement will involve; (e) or where it is " just and equitable " that leave should be given. It is sufficient to give the court jurisdiction if the landlord proves any one of these five facts, *Phillips* v. *Price*, [1959] Ch. 181 ; [1958] 3 All E. R. 386.

[6] *Sidnell* v. *Wilson*, [1966] 2 Q. B. 67; [1966] 1 All E. R. 681.

[7] Leasehold Property (Repairs) Act, 1938, s. 5.

[8] Law of Property Act, 1925, s. 146 (2).

[9] *T. M. Fairclough & Sons, Ltd.* v. *Berliner*, [1931] 1 Ch. 60.

[10] *E.g. Rose* v. *Hyman*, [1911] 2 K. B. 234.

[11] *Hyman* v. *Rose*, [1912] A. C. 623.

however, that the discretion will not be exercised in favour of a lessee who knowingly suffers premises to be used for immoral purposes.[1]

Limitation of time.

The result is that, even after the statutory notice under section 146 has been served, and even though there has been no compliance with its requirements after a reasonable interval, the tenant may still apply for relief. As regards the time within which he must apply, however, he is in a worse position than in the case of a covenant to pay rent.[2] The particular section of the Act which deals with forfeiture opens with the words :

" Where a lessor is proceeding . . . to enforce such a right of " re-entry or forfeiture,"

and it has been held that the lessor cannot be said to be *proceeding* where he has sued to judgment and has obtained possession of the premises by way of execution.[3]   In other words, a tenant will irretrievably lose his right to relief unless he makes application before the landlord has actually re-entered.

Exceptions to the statutory requirements.

The particular sub-sections of the Act already considered are general in nature and would, without more, apply to every covenant contained in a lease, but there are three covenants for the breach of which a lessor need not serve the statutory notice as a preliminary to enforcing the forfeiture, and in respect of which relief is not grantable.[4]   The covenants so excepted are the following :—

1. THE COVENANT TO PAY RENT.[5]

2. THE COVENANT FOR INSPECTION IN A MINING LEASE.   If a mining tenant, under obligation to pay royalties according to the quantity of minerals gotten, breaks the covenant by which he has agreed to give access to his books and accounts, forfeiture may be enforced without service of the statutory notice and no relief is grantable.[6]

3. THE CONDITION OF FORFEITURE ON THE BANK-RUPTCY OF THE TENANT *IN CERTAIN CASES*.   It is common to provide in a lease that the premises shall be forfeited to the lessor if the tenant becomes bankrupt or if his interest is taken in execution.   There are certain classes of property in which it is vital to the landlord that he should recover his property in either of these events, and where the lease relates to such property the Act provides that the statu-

---

[1] *Borthwick-Norton* v. *Romney Warwick Estates, Ltd.,* [1950] 1 All E. R. 798; *Borthwick-Norton* v. *Dougherty,* [1950] W. N. 481.
[2] *Supra,* pp. 392-3.
[3] *Rogers* v. *Rice,* [1892] 2 Ch. 170.
[4] It is no longer necessary to consider the further exception, *i.e.* a covenant not to assign the premises where the breach occurred before January 1st, 1926.
[5] Law of Property Act, 1925, s. 146 (11) ; *supra,* pp. 391 *et seq.*
[6] *Ibid.,* s. 146 (8) (ii).

tory provisions shall be excluded. The following are the leases concerned [1] :—

Leases of

    (a) agricultural or pastoral land,
    (b) mines or minerals,
    (c) a public house or beer-shop,
    (d) a furnished house,
    (e) any property with respect to which the personal qualifications of the tenant are of importance for the preservation of the value or the character of the property, or on the ground of neighbourhood to the lessor or to any person holding under him.

In such a lease, then, the lessor can proceed to enforce a forfeiture as soon as the bankruptcy occurs, and the tenant has no claim to relief.

If the demised land is not within one of the classes enumerated above, the extent to which the statutory provisions concerning notice and relief apply depends upon whether the lessee's interest is sold, or is not sold, for the benefit of his creditors within one year from the bankruptcy or taking in execution. The two rules on the matter, which are designed to enable the trustee in bankruptcy to decide whether he will disclaim the lease or use it for the benefit of the creditors, are as follows [2] :—

    (a) If the interest is sold within the year, the statutory provisions apply without any limit of time. This means, in the case of bankruptcy, that if the trustee in bankruptcy is able to sell the tenant's interest under the lease within the year for the benefit of the creditors, then, despite proceedings for forfeiture, he can apply for relief even after the year has elapsed, and the court may grant the application and confirm the title of the purchaser.[3]

    (b) If the interest is not sold within the year, the statutory provisions apply only during that year, *i.e.*, although the landlord cannot take steps to regain possession during that period without serving the statutory notice and without the risk of defeat by a successful application for relief, yet, after the year has elapsed, his right to recover the premises is absolute. No notice need be served, no relief can be granted.[3]

Relief in case of decoration covenants.

In practice, however, leases do not usually contain a proviso for forfeiture on the bankruptcy of the tenant, except in the five cases enumerated above, since it is troublesome for the landlord to be deprived of his rent until a decision has been reached by the trustee, and if he accepts rent falling due after the date of bankruptcy the forfeiture is thereby waived.[4]

---

[1] Law of Property Act, 1925, s. 146 (9).
[2] *Ibid.*, s. 146 (10).
[3] *Civil Service Co-operative Society* v. *McGrigor's Trustee*, [1923] 2 Ch. 347, 355 ; *Horsey Estate, Ltd.* v. *Steiger*, [1899] 2 Q. B. 79 ; *Gee* v. *Harwood*, [1933] 1 Ch. 712 ; affd., [1934] A. C. 272.
[4] *Doe d. Gatehouse* v. *Rees* (1838), 4 Bing (N.C.) 384.

Internal Decorative Repair. A special rule has been introduced by the Act for covenants relating to the internal decorative repair of a house. It is provided that where a statutory notice has been served by the landlord indicating a breach of such a covenant, the court, after reviewing all the circumstances and in particular the length of the term, may wholly or partially relieve the tenant from liabilities for such repairs. But this power to set a covenant aside is not exercisable when a tenant, having expressly agreed to put the property in a decorative state of repair, has never performed the covenant, nor is it to apply to anything which is necessary for keeping the property in a sanitary condition or in a state which makes it fit for human habitation.[1]

Protection of under-lessees.

Under-lessees. The jurisdiction of the court to relieve an under-lessee, or a person deriving title under him,[2] against a forfeiture due to the under-lessor's failure to pay rent[3] is equally exercisable where the failure relates to some other covenant.[4] This is so, even though the nature of the breach, *e.g.* the bankruptcy of a publican, precludes the under-lessor from applying for relief.[5] It is a jurisdiction that should be sparingly exercised.[6]

SECTION VII. COVENANTS WHICH RUN WITH THE LAND AND WITH THE REVERSION.[7]

Scope of inquiry.

Introductory Note. A covenant in a lease is *primâ facie* a contract binding only on the lessor and the lessee—the actual contracting parties. But it was early seen that to enforce this doctrine of privity of contract was highly undesirable in the case of leases, since both parties had transmissible interests the value of which depended largely upon the obligations that each had assumed. Thus the mediæval land law, although it never lost sight of the general principle that a stranger to a contract cannot sue or be sued upon it, did recognize that covenants contained in a lease might have a wider operation than ordinary contracts. As HOLDSWORTH remarked,

" they were regarded in a sense as being annexed to an estate in the " land, so that they could be enforced by anyone who took that estate " in the land." [8]

The scope, then, of our present inquiry is to ascertain in what circumstances persons other than the original lessor and lessee

---

[1] Law of Property Act, 1925, s. 147.
[2] *In re Good's Lease*, [1954] 1 W. L. R. 309 ; as, for example, a mortgagee by way of sub-demise ; *Grand Junction Co., Ltd.* v. *Bates*, [1954] 2 Q. B. 160 [1954] 2 All E. R. 385.
[3] *Supra*, pp. 394–6.
[4] Law of Property Act, 1925, s. 146 (4).
[5] Law of Property (Amendment) Act, 1929, s. 1 ; restoring the old law as laid down in *Hurd* v. *Whaley*, [1918] 1 K. B. 448 ; *Imray* v. *Oakshette*, [1897] 2 Q. B. 218 ; *Ewart* v. *Fryer*, [1901] 1 Ch. 499.
[6] *Creery* v. *Summersell and Flowerdew & Co., Ltd.*, [1949] Ch. 751.
[7] Holdsworth, *History of English Law*, vol. vii. pp. 287–92.
[8] Holdsworth, *History of English Law* (1909 Edn.), vol. iii. p. 131.

can sue or be sued upon the covenants. Two events may occur—
an assignment of the term by the tenant or an assignment of the
reversion by the lessor. In each case the two questions that arise
are whether the benefit and burden of the covenants pass to the
assignee. In short, do the covenants run with the land and with
the reversion. Four cases, therefore, fall to be considered :— Four cases to be con- sidered.

1. The lessee assigns his interest to A. Can A. enforce the
   covenants inserted in the lease in favour of the lessee ? Does
   the benefit of these covenants run with the land ?
2. The lessee assigns his interest to A. Can A. be sued on the
   covenants inserted in the lease in favour of the lessor ? Does
   the burden of the covenants entered into by the lessee run
   with the land ?
3. The lessor assigns his interest, *i.e.* the reversion, to Z. Can
   Z. enforce the covenants inserted in the lease in favour of the
   lessor ? Does the benefit of the covenants run with the
   reversion ?
4. The lessor assigns his reversion to Z. Can Z. be sued upon
   the covenants inserted in the lease in favour of the lessee ?
   Does the burden of the lessor's covenants run with the
   reversion ?

In this section we are concerned only with the rules laid down
by common law and by statute. It must be realized, however,
that these rules may in certain limited circumstances be modified
by the doctrine of *Tulk* v. *Moxhay*, under which a covenant
between landlord and tenant is sometimes enforceable by and
against third parties in cases where this would be impossible
either at common law or under the statutes that we shall presently
consider.[1] Limits of presents discusion.

It will simplify our task if, before dealing separately with the
four divisions of the subject given above, we describe what is
meant by covenants that *touch and concern the land demised*, for it is
only these, as distinct from those merely affecting the person, that
are capable of running either with the reversion or with the land. Covenants touching and con- cerning the land.

From the present point of view all covenants fall into one
or other of two classes, being either personal to the contracting
parties, or such as touch and concern the land.

The time-honoured expression " touching and concerning the
land " has been replaced in the most recent statute dealing with
the matter by the phrase *having reference to the subject-matter*.[2]
This affords a clue to the meaning of what is at first sight a little
vague. If the covenant has direct reference to the land, if it lays
down something which is to be done or is not to be done upon
the land, or, and perhaps this is the clearest way of describing the
test, *if it affects the landlord in his normal capacity as landlord or the*

---

[1] *Infra*, pp. 537 *et seq.*   [2] Law of Property Act, 1925, ss. 141, 142.

tenant in his normal capacity as tenant, it may be said to touch and concern the land.

Lord RUSSELL, C.J., said :—

> "The true principle is that no covenant or condition which affects
> "merely the person, and which does not affect the nature, quality, or
> "value of the thing demised or the mode of using or enjoying the
> "thing demised, runs with the land" ;[1]

and BAYLEY, J., at an earlier date asserted the same principle :

> "In order to bind the assignee, the covenant must either affect the
> "land itself during the term, such as those which regard the mode of
> "occupation, or it must be such as *per se*, and not merely from col-
> "lateral circumstances, affects the value of the land at the end of the
> "term."[2]

If a simple test is desired for ascertaining into which category a covenant falls, it is suggested that the proper inquiry should be whether the covenant affects either the landlord *qua* landlord or the tenant *qua* tenant. A covenant may very well have reference to the land, but, unless it is reasonably incidental to the relation of landlord and tenant, it cannot be said to touch and concern the land so as to be capable of running therewith or with the reversion.[3] Tested by this principle the following covenants have been held to touch and concern the land :—

Examples of covenants touching and concerning the land.

Covenants by the tenant—

to pay rent or taxes ;[4]

to repair or leave in repair ;[5]

to spend a stated yearly sum on repairs, or in default to pay to the landlord the difference between this sum and the amount actually expended ;[6]

to lay dung on the land annually ;[7]

to renew tenant's fixtures ;[8]

to reside on a farm during the term ;[9]

by a publican tenant to buy all beer from the lessor ;[10]

not to assign or under-let ;[11]

not to allow a third party, X., to be concerned in the conduct of the business carried on at the demised premises.[12]

---

[1] *Horsey Estate, Ltd.* v. *Steiger*, [1899] 2 Q. B. 79, 89.
[2] *Mayor of Congleton* v. *Pattison* (1808), 10 East, 130, 138 ; cited Behan, *Covenants affecting Land*, p. 52, *q.v*
[3] Approved in *Breams Property Investment Co., Ltd.* v. *Stroulger*, [1948] 2 K. B. 1, at p. 7 ; [1948] 1 All E. R. 758, at p. 759.
[4] *Parker* v. *Webb* (1700), 3 Salk. 5.
[5] *Martyn* v. *Clue* (1852), 18 Q. B. 661.
[6] *Moss' Empires, Ltd.* v. *Olympia (Liverpool), Ltd.*, [1939] A. C. 544.
[7] *Sale* v. *Kitchingham* (1713), 10 Mod. 158.
[8] *Williams* v. *Earle* (1868), L. R. 3 Q. B. 739.
[9] *Tatem* v. *Chaplin* (1793), 2 H. Bl. 133.
[10] *Clegg* v. *Hands* (1890), 44 Ch. D. 503.
[11] *Goldstein* v. *Sanders*, [1915] 1 Ch. 549.
[12] *Lewin* v. *American and Colonial Distributors, Ltd.*, [1945] Ch. 225, 236; [1945] 2 All E. R. 271, n.

Covenants by the lessor—

  to renew the lease ; [1]

  to supply the demised house with good water ; [2]

  not to build on adjoining land so as to depreciate the amenity of the demised land ; [3]

  to erect a new building in place of an old one ; [4]

  to keep a housekeeper to act as servant of the lessee ; [5]

  not to serve a notice to quit for three years, unless he requires the premises for his own occupation. [6]

On the other hand personal, or collateral, covenants do not touch and concern the land, since they have no direct reference to the subject-matter of the lease. The word *collateral*, admittedly ambiguous, in this context indicates a covenant relating to a matter not normally relevant to the relationship of landlord and tenant. For instance, a covenant by either party to pay a sum of money to the other is merely collateral,[7] unless it is inextricably bound up with other covenants that touch and concern the land.[8]

> Thus a covenant by a lessee, in furtherance of his express undertaking to repair, to expend £500 yearly upon repairs, or to pay the lessor the difference between this amount and what is actually expended, is not a bare obligation personal to the contracting parties. It touches and concerns the land, since it is part and parcel of the repairing covenant.[9]

In *Thomas* v. *Hayward* [10] :—

> Where the lessor of a public house had covenanted that he would not open another beer or spirit house within half a mile of the demised premises, the question arose whether this covenant could be enforced by an assignee of the lessee.

It was held that it could not, because it was collateral in the sense that it did not oblige the lessor to do or to refrain from doing anything on the demised premises. On the other hand a covenant by the tenant of a public house to conduct the business in such a manner as to afford no ground for the suspension of the licence, was held to touch the land, since it concerned the manner in which the covenantor was to use the premises as tenant.[11]

---

[1] *Muller* v. *Trafford*, [1901] 1 Ch. 54; *Weg Motors Ltd.* v. *Hales*, [1961] Ch. 176 ; [1960] 3 All E. R. 762; affd. [1961] 3 All E. R. 181; [1961] 3 W. L. R. 558.

[2] *Jourdain* v. *Wilson* (1821), 4 B. & Ald. 266.

[3] *Ricketts* v. *Enfield Churchwardens*, [1909] 1 Ch. 544.

[4] *Easterby* v. *Sampson* (1830), 6 Bing. 644.

[5] *Barnes* v. *City of London Real Property Co.*, [1918] 2 Ch. 18.

[6] *Breams Property Investment Co., Ltd.* v. *Stroulger*, [1948] 2 K. B. 1 ; [1948] 1 All E. R. 758.

[7] *Re Hunter's Lease, Giles* v. *Hutchings*, [1942] Ch. 124; [1942] 1 All E. R. 27.

[8] *Moss' Empires, Ltd.* v. *Olympia (Liverpool), Ltd.*, [1939] A. C. 544 ; [1939] 3 All E. R. 460 ; *Boyer* v. *Warbey*, [1953] 1 Q. B. 234 ; [1952] 2 All E. R. 976.

[9] *Moss' Empires, Ltd.* v. *Olympia (Liverpool), Ltd.*, *supra*.

[10] (1869), L. R. 4 Ex. 311.

[11] *Fleetwood* v. *Hull* (1889), 23 Q. B. D. 35.

Option to purchase the fee simple.

A covenant that entitles the tenant to purchase the fee simple at a given price at any time during the term, affects the parties *qua* vendor and purchaser, not *qua* landlord and tenant. It is collateral to the lease and as such it cannot run as a matter of course with the land or with the reversion as being one that touches and concerns the land. Nevertheless, if it does not infringe the rule against perpetuities,[1] its effect is to confer upon the tenant an equitable interest in the land[2] which, like any other piece of property, is freely assignable unless the terms of its grant show that it is personal to him. Therefore, the option, will pass on an assignment of the demised land and will be enforceable against the landlord; and if registered as an estate contract[3] it will be enforceable against an assignee of the reversion.[4]

Running of covenants at common law and by statute.

We can now take up the four cases that have been indicated above and determine in what circumstances the covenants will run in each case. The rules depend partly upon the common law as finally enunciated in *Spencer's Case*, 1583,[5] and partly upon statutes. The statutes that formerly regulated the matter were the Graunties of Reversions Act,[6] passed in 1540 after the dissolution of the monasteries, and the Conveyancing Act, 1881,[7] but both these were repealed and replaced by the Law of Property Act, 1925.[8]

Benefit of covenant runs with land.

1. *The lessee assigns his interest to A. Can A. enforce the covenants which were inserted in the lease in favour of the lessee?* The rule even at common law is that the benefit of the covenants runs with the land, enabling an assignee (A.) from the lessee to sue the lessor on any covenants which touch and concern the land demised and which enure for the benefit of the lessee, such as a covenant by the lessor to supply the demised premises with pure water. The authority for this rule is *Spencer's Case*, in the fourth resolution of which the court, dealing with a covenant for quiet enjoyment, said :—

" for the lessee and his assignee hath the yearly profits of the land,
" which shall grow by his labour and industry, for an annual rent ;
" and therefore it is reasonable when he hath applied his labour and
" employed his cost upon the land, and be evicted (whereby he loses
" all) that he shall take such benefit of the demise and grant as the
" first lessee might. . . ."

Burden of covenant runs with land.

2. *The lessee assigns his interest to A. Can A. be sued upon the covenants which were inserted in the lease in favour of the*

---

[1] *Supra*, p. 267.
[2] *London and South Western Rail Co.* v. *Gomm* (1882), 20 Ch.D. 562; *supra*, pp. 259–60.
[3] *Infra*, p. 669.
[4] *Griffith* v. *Pelton*, [1958] Ch. 205; [1957] 3 All E. R. 75, explaining *Woodhall* v. *Clifton*, [1905] 2 Ch. 257; *Re Button's Lease, Inman* v. *Button*, [1964] Ch. 263; [1963] 3 All E. R. 708, see generally, 74 *L. Q. R.* pp. 242–58 (W. J. Mowbray).
[5] (1583), 5 Co. Rep. 16.   [6] 32 Hen. 8, c. 34, s. 1.
[7] Ss. 10, 11.   [8] Ss. 141, 142.

lessor ? The common law answers this also in the affirmative, provided that the covenant touches and concerns the land, for it is said in *Spencer's Case* that :—

> " When the covenant extends to a thing *in esse*, parcel of the demise,
> " the thing to be done by force of the covenant is *quodammodo*
> " annexed and appurtenant to the thing demised, and shall go with
> " the land and shall bind the assignee, although he be not bound by
> " express words."

It is true that the judgment then proceeded to draw a distinction between a covenant which referred to something already in existence (such as to repair an existing wall), and one which related to a thing not in existence at the time of the lease (such as a covenant to build a new wall), and laid down that though the former would bind assignees in all cases, yet the latter would not do so unless the original lessee had covenanted for himself *and his assigns*. This distinction rested upon no solid basis, but, though adversely criticized,[1] it remained law until 1926. It has been abolished by the Law of Property Act, 1925, which provides that [2] :— *Distinction between thing in esse and in posse.*

> " A covenant relating to any land of a covenantor or capable of being
> " bound by him, shall, unless a contrary intention is expressed,[3] be
> " deemed to be made by the covenantor on behalf of himself, his
> " successors in title and the persons deriving title under him or them,
> " and subject as aforesaid shall have effect as if such successors and
> " other persons were expressed.
>   " This subsection extends to a covenant to do some act relating
> " to the land, notwithstanding that the subject matter may not be in
> " existence when the covenant is made."

This section, however, applies only to covenants made on or after January 1st, 1926, and therefore the distinction between a covenant relating to something *in esse* and one relating to something *in posse* will remain of importance for several years. In the case of a lease executed before 1926, the burden of a covenant relating to something not in existence will not run with the land unless it was expressly imposed upon the lessee *and his assigns*.

    3. *The lessor assigns his interest, i.e. the reversion, to Z. Can Z. enforce the covenants which were inserted in the lease in favour of the lessor ?* The rule at common law is that the grantee of a reversion can sue upon an implied covenant, that is, one which automatically results from the relationship of landlord and tenant (such as a covenant to pay rent), but he cannot sue upon express covenants contained in the lease.[4] The difficulty is said to be that in the case of a reversion there is no corporeal thing to which the covenant can be regarded as annexed, such as there is where the land is assigned.[5] *Benefit of covenant runs with reversion.*

---

    [1] *Minshull* v. *Oakes* (1858), 2 H. & N. 793. See Behan, *Covenants affecting Land*, pp. 75 *et seq.*   [2] S. 79.
    [3] *In re Royal Victoria Pavilion, Ramsgate*, [1961] 3 All E. R. 83; [1961] Ch. 581.
    [4] Platt on Covenants, p. 530 ; *Wedd* v. *Porter*, [1916] 2 K. B. 91, 100–101.
    [5] *E.g.* Smith, *Leading Cases*, vol. i. pp. 61–2.

A mitigation of this strict rule of the common law became urgent when the monasteries were dissolved by Henry VIII in 1539, because, if the law had not been altered, it would have precluded the grantees of the monastic lands from enforcing against existing lessees the express covenants in leases granted by the monasteries before their dissolution. Hence the Statute 32 Henry VIII, which, though designed merely to accommodate grantees of monastic lands, soon came to be regarded as having universal application and as laying down the law for assignees of reversions in general. This statute, which remained the only law on the subject until the Conveyancing Act of 1881, enacted that assignees of reversions should have the same right of enforcing forfeitures, and the same right of suing for a breach of any covenant, as the original lessors.[1]

Provisions of the Law of Property Act, 1925. Both these statutes have been repealed, and the right of an assignee of a reversion to enforce the covenants now rests upon the Law of Property Act, 1925,[2] which, in a section that applies to all leases whether made before 1926 or after 1925, provides that :

(1) " Rent reserved by a lease, and the benefit of every covenant or " provision therein contained, having reference to the subject-matter " thereof,[3] and on the lessee's part to be observed or performed, and " every condition of re-entry and other condition therein contained, " shall be annexed and incident to and shall go with the reversionary " estate in the land, or in any part thereof, immediately expectant on " the term granted by the lease, notwithstanding severance of that " reversionary estate, and without prejudice to any liability affecting " a covenantor or his estate.

(2) " Any such rent, covenant or provision shall be capable of being " recovered, received, enforced and taken advantage of by the person " from time to time entitled, subject to the term, to the income of the " whole or any part, as the case may require, of the land leased.

(3) " Where that person becomes entitled by conveyance or otherwise, " such rent, covenant or provision may be recovered, received, " enforced or taken advantage of by him notwithstanding that he " becomes so entitled after the condition of re-entry or forfeiture has " become enforceable, but this subsection does not render enforceable " any condition of re-entry or other condition waived or released " before such person becomes entitled as aforesaid."

Lease must be in writing. One result of this enactment, which provides, in repetition of the Conveyancing Act, 1881, that " rent reserved by a lease,[4] and the benefit of every covenant or provision therein contained " shall pass with the reversion, is to abolish the old construction put upon 32 Henry VIII, viz. that the assignee of a reversion could not sue upon the covenants unless the original lease was under seal. The rule now is that the assignee can sue if the lease is in writing or if the tenancy is the result of a written

---

[1] S. 10.   [2] S. 141.
[3] *I.e.*, touching and concerning the land demised.
[4] " Lease " includes " an under-lease or other tenancy " ; s. 154.

agreement for a lease,[1] even though in the latter case the agreement is signed by the landlord only.[2] The same is the case if a parol lease is made for a period not exceeding three years, or if a parol agreement for a lease of any length is followed by a sufficient act of part performance.

The Court of Appeal has held that under this section of the Act, the assignee of the reversion is the only person entitled to sue the tenant for any breach of covenant, whether of a continuous nature or not and even though committed before the date of the assignment.[3]

Breach of covenant committed before assignment.

> " The expression 'go with' must be intended to add something to
> " the concept involved in the expression 'annexed and incident to'
> " and in my view connotes the transfer of the right to enforce the
> " covenant from the assignor to the assignee with the consequent
> " cessation of the right of the assignor to enforce the covenant
> " against the tenant."[4]

4. *The lessor assigns his reversion to Z. Can Z. be sued upon the covenants which were inserted in the lease in favour of the lessee?* There was no right of action against Z. at common law, but a right was given by the same Statute 32 Henry VIII, which enacted that a lessee and his assigns should have the same remedy against the assignees of the lessor as the original lessee would have had against the lessor. This enactment was attended by certain difficulties, which are no longer of interest, since they were removed by the Conveyancing Act, 1881,[5] in a section now replaced by the Law of Property Act, 1925, and applicable to all leases whenever made.[6] This section runs as follows :—

Burden of covenant runs with reversion.

> " The obligation under a condition or of a covenant entered into
> " by a lessor with reference to the subject-matter of the lease shall, if
> " and as far as the lessor has power to bind the reversionary estate
> " immediately expectant on the term granted by the lease, be annexed
> " and incident to and shall go with that reversionary estate, or the
> " several parts thereof, notwithstanding severance of that reversionary
> " estate, and may be taken advantage of and enforced by the person
> " in whom the term is from time to time vested by conveyance,
> " devolution in law, or otherwise, and, if and as far as the lessor has
> " power to bind the person from time to time entitled to that reversion-
> " ary estate, the obligation aforesaid may be taken advantage of and
> " enforced against any person so entitled."

The word " covenant " as used in this section is not confined to its strict meaning of a contract under seal, but includes any promise touching and concerning the land[7] that is contained in a tenancy agreement made otherwise than by deed.[8]

---

[1] *Rickett* v. *Green*, [1910] 1 K. B. 253 ; *Boyer* v. *Warbey*, [1953] 1 Q. B. 234 ; [1953] 1 All E. R. 269.
[2] *Rye* v. *Purcell*, [1926] 1 K. B. 446.
[3] *Re King, Robinson* v. *Gray*, [1963] Ch. 459; [1963] 1 All E. R. 781.
[4] *Ibid.*, at p. 497, *per* DIPLOCK, L. J.
[5] S. 11.   [6] S. 142 (1).
[7] *Davis* v. *Town Properties, etc.*, [1903] 1 Ch. 797.
[8] *Weg Motors Ltd.* v. *Hales*, [1961] Ch. 176 ; [1960] 3 All E. R. 762.

**Apportion-
ment of con-
ditions on
severance.**

One particular difficulty which arose under 32 Henry VIII was that, owing to its indivisible nature,[1] a condition could not be enforced by an assignee of *part* of the reversion. If the reversion was severed, the condition could not be apportioned. The statutory rule, however, now is that, where such a severance has taken place, every condition contained in the lease is apportioned and remains annexed to the severed parts of the reversion.[2]   If the owner of a severed part of the reversion determines the tenancy by a notice to quit,[3] the lessee is permitted within one month to determine the whole tenancy by serving notice on the owner in whom the rest of the reversion is vested.[4]

**Essentials
of enforce-
ability.**

Before we conclude the subject of covenants that run with the land or the reversion, there are two general observations of considerable importance to be made :—

**Privity of
estate or
contract
essential.**

1. First, there can be no question of the enforcement of covenants between two parties unless there exists between them either privity of estate or privity of contract. *Privity of contract* denotes that relationship which exists between the lessor and the lessee—and between them only—by virtue of the covenants contained in the lease. This relationship is created by the contract itself and continues to subsist between the lessor and lessee despite an assignment of their respective interests. *Privity of estate* describes the relationship between two parties who respectively hold the same estates as those created by the lease. This is the position where one holds the original reversion and the other the original term, or rather, the whole of what is now left of the original term. Thus there is privity of estate between the lessor and an assignee from the lessee of the residue of the term ; also between the lessee and an assignee of the reversion ; also between an assignee of the reversion and an assignee of the residue of the term. In the absence of assignment, therefore, there is privity both of contract and of estate between the lessor and lessee.[5]

There are certain important rules that flow from this general principle. Thus :

**Original
lessee always
liable to
original
lessor.**

" It is perfectly settled by a multitude of decisions that, notwith-
" standing an assignment of his lease, the lessee continues liable on
" the personal privity of the contract to the payment of the rent
" and the performance of the covenants during the whole term ;

---

[1] *Supra*, pp. 383–4.
[2] Law of Property Act, 1925, s. 140 (1) ; replacing Law of Property Amendment Act, 1859, s. 3, and Conveyancing Act, 1881, s. 12.
[3] See, *e.g.*, *Smith* v. *Kinsey*, [1936] 3 All E. R. 73 ; [1936] W. N. 294.
[4] Law of Property Act, 1925, s. 140 (2).
[5] *Bickford* v. *Parson* (1848), 5 C. B. 920, 929. See also Platt on Leases, vol. ii., p. 351 : " Privity of estate is the result of tenure ; it subsists by virtue of the relation of landlord and tenant, and follows alike the devolution of the reversion and of the term."

" although the lessor concur in the assignment, or, by acceptance
" of rent or otherwise, recognize the assignee as his tenant. " [1]

Again, as the liability of an assignee of the tenant is
based upon the privity of estate between him and the lessor
or the latter's assignee,[2] it follows that the tenant's assignee
cannot be liable for a breach of covenant committed before
he took the estate under the assignment,[3] and cannot sue
the lessor for breaches committed prior to that time. Lastly,
and consistently with the same principle, an assignee ceases
to be liable for breaches occurring after he has assigned his
interest to a third party, for such a re-assignment obviously
destroys the privity of estate which previously existed.[4] He
is liable, however, even for these subsequent breaches, if he
expressly covenants with the landlord at the time of taking the
assignment that he will perform the terms of the lease.[5]
Moreover, in any event, he remains liable after re-assignment
for any breaches which occurred while the tenancy was vested
in him.[6]

Assignee liable and entitled only in respect of matters occurring while he holds the land.

It will thus be seen that, where one of the lessee's
covenants has been broken after an assignment of the term,
the lessor has the option of suing either the original lessee
on the privity of contract or the particular assignee who
had the estate when the breach occurred, but although this
joint liability undoubtedly exists, the rule is that the assignee
in possession is the principal debtor, while the lessee occupies
the position of a surety.[7] Nevertheless the continuing liability of the original lessee is an obvious menace to him, and
it became the invariable practice for every assignee expressly
to covenant to indemnify his assignor against future breaches
of the provisions contained in the lease. This is no longer
necessary, for it is now enacted that every assignment for
valuable consideration shall be deemed to include a covenant
by the assignee that he will pay all rent falling due in the
future and will perform all the covenants, agreements and
conditions binding upon the original lessee. This implied
covenant of indemnity binds all persons, such as later
assignees, deriving title under the assignee.[8] To take an
example :

Implied indemnity by assignee

---

[1] *Ibid.*, pp. 352-3. Distinguish, however, the liability of a lessee who
acquires a statutory term of 2000 years under the provisions for converting
perpetually renewable leases ; *supra*, pp. 336-7.

[2] *Purchase* v. *Lichfield Brewery*, [1915] 1 K. B. 184.

[3] *Grescot* v. *Green* (1699), 1 Salk. 199.

[4] *Paul* v. *Nurse* (1828), 8 B. & C. 486.

[5] *Lyons (J.) & Co., Ltd.* v. *Knowles*, [1943] 1 K. B. 366 ; [1943] 1 All E. R.
477.

[6] *Harley* v. *King* (1835), 2 C. M. & R. 18 ; *cf. Richmond* v. *Savill*, [1926]
2 K. B. 530.

[7] *Humble* v. *Langston* (1841), 7 M. & W. 517, at p. 530, *per* PARKE, B.

[8] Law of Property Act, 1925, s. 77 (1) (*c*) ; 2nd Sched., Part IX.

L. leases land to T. Later successive assignments of the land are made first to U., then to V., and finally to W. If L. sues T. for the breach committed by W. of some condition contained in the lease, the implied covenant of indemnity entitles T. to make U. a party to the action. Similarly U. can join V., and V. can join W. as a party. In this way judgment can be given against the person who has actually committed the breach.[1]

There must be an "assignment."

2. The second observation is that the rules laid down above with regard to the running of covenants apply only where there has been an assignment in the true and proper sense of that term, for it is only then that privity of estate exists between the reversioner and the person who is in occupation of the land. The term " assignee " is very comprehensive : it applies to all persons who take the estate either by act of party or by act of law, such as the executors of a lessee or assignee, and persons taking the premises by way of execution for debt, but in the eyes of the law no person occupies the position of assignee of the land unless he takes the *identical term* which the lessee had, and also takes the *whole of that term.*[2]

Whole interest must be transferred.

Thus if the lessee, on making what purports to be an assignment of his term, reserves to himself a reversion, no matter how trifling it may be—as where he assigns the remainder of his lease less one day—the transaction amounts to an under-lease and not to an assignment. In such a case it is obvious that there is neither privity of contract nor privity of estate between the superior landlord and the under-lessee, and therefore neither of them can sue or be sued *at law* upon the covenants of the lease,[3] though as we shall see later the under-lessee may be liable under the equitable doctrine of *Tulk* v. *Moxhay* on purely negative covenants.[4] But there is no magic in words. If a man has acquired an interest in the tenancy and a question arises with regard to his position, the first point that falls to be considered is whether he has taken the whole of the tenant's interest. Thus where the tenant executes a deed couched in the form of an under-lease, which purports to sub-let the property for the whole of the remainder of his term or for a longer period, the transaction amounts to an assignment.[5]

Identical interest must be transferred.

The other point, as we have observed, is that if there is to

---

[1] As to the nature of this covenant see *Butler Estates Co.* v. *Bean*, [1942] 1 K. B. 1 ; [1941] 2 All E. R. 793.

[2] Platt on Leases, vol. ii. pp. 419–20.

[3] *South of England Dairies Co.* v. *Baker*, [1906] 2 Ch. 631.

[4] *Infra*, p. 540, note 4.

[5] *Beardman* v. *Wilson* (1868), L. R. 4 C. P. 57 ; *Hallen* v. *Spaeth*, [1923] A. C. 684 ; *Milmo* v. *Carreras*, [1946] K. B. 306 ; [1946] 1 All E. R. 288.

be an assignment, the alienee must take the identical interest which the alienor possessed. If, for instance, a tenant deposits his lease with X. by way of mortgage, X. obtains a mere equitable right to the land and not the legal term to which the tenant was entitled. Therefore, whether he goes into possession or not, he can neither sue nor be sued on the covenants.[1] A similar result again ensues where a person obtains a title under the Limitation Act against the lessee, as was decided in *Tichborne* v. *Weir*.[2] The facts of this case were as follows :—

Tichborne v. Weir.

> In 1802 D. leased land to B. for 89 years.
> In 1836 G. seized the land and remained in possession of it until 1876, paying D. the rent which had been fixed by the lease of 1802.
> In 1876 G. by deed assigned all his interest to the defendant, who remained in possession until 1891, paying the same rent to the plaintiff, who had succeeded to D.

> The original lease between D. and B. contained a covenant by B. to keep the premises in repair, and the plaintiff now sued the defendant for breach of that covenant. The right of the original covenantor B. to his tenancy of the land had been extinguished by lapse of time when the defendant came to the land in 1876, but the question that arose was whether the defendant was an assignee of B. through G. It was clear, if the identical lease which was vested in B. had passed to G. and from him to defendant, that the latter would be liable as assignee on the repairing covenant, and it was strenuously argued that the effect of the Real Property Limitation Act, which was the statute then in force, was to transfer the term from B. to G.
> But it was held that the only effect of the statute was to extinguish B.'s right of recovering the land and not to convey what he had to G. It therefore followed that the defendant was not liable on the repairing covenant, because, not possessing the very estate to which it was attached, he was not an assignee.

But the limits of the decision must be noted. It was said by a learned Irish judge [3] :—

O'Connor v. Foley, [1906].

> " It appears to me to decide only this, that the Statute of " Limitations operates by way of extinguishment, and not by " way of assignment of the estate which is barred; and that a " person who becomes entitled to a leasehold interest by adverse " possession for the prescribed period is not liable to be sued " *in covenant as assignee* of the lease, unless he has estopped " himself from denying that he is assignee."

So, in the first place, the decision will not apply where the occupier of the lands has estopped himself from denying

---

[1] *Cox* v. *Bishop* (1857), 8 De G. M. & G. 815 ; He may, however, be liable under the doctrine of *Tulk* v. *Moxhay, infra*, pp. 537 *et seq.*

[2] (1892) 67 L. T. 735 ; followed in *Taylor* v. *Twinberrow*, [1930] 2 K. B. 16.

[3] FitzGibbon, L. J., in *O'Connor* v. *Foley*, [1906] 1 I. R. 20, 26.

that he holds on all the terms of the original lease,[1] but although this point was pressed in *Tichborne* v. *Weir*, it was held that the terms under which the defendant paid rent did not warrant the conclusion that he stood for all purposes in the shoes of the original tenant B.[2]   But where a lease contains a proviso that the rent shall be reduced by a half if all the covenants are duly observed, and an adverse possessor avails himself of the privilege, he is estopped from denying that he is subject to the burden of the lease.[3]

Secondly, the case only goes to show that an adverse possessor cannot be sued in covenant as assignee, and when we come to deal with equitable doctrines, we shall see that he is liable on such negative covenants as create an equitable burden on the estate he takes.[4]

SECTION VIII. DETERMINATION OF TENANCIES.

SUMMARY.

1. TENANCIES FOR A FIXED PERIOD.

Modes of determination.   A tenancy for a fixed period may be terminated by forfeiture, surrender, merger, effluxion of time, or, where an agreement to that effect has been made, by a notice to quit given by either party.   There is no need to add to the account already given of forfeiture.[5]

Surrender.   Surrender occurs where the tenant yields up his estate to the lessor.   In the case of a joint tenancy, a surrender is not effective unless made by all the tenants.[6]

Express surrender.   The express surrender of a lease not exceeding three years may be effected by a written instrument,[7] but in terms for longer periods it must be made by deed.[8]

Surrender by operation of law.   If, however, the intention of the parties as inferred from their conduct is that the lease should be yielded up, surrender results by operation of law without the necessity either of a writing or a deed.[9]   This doctrine rests upon the principle of estoppel.   It

---

[1] As for instance in *Rodenhurst Estates, Ltd.* v. *Barnes, Ltd.*, [1936] 2 All E. R. 3.

[2] For another instance, see *Official Trustee of Charity Lands* v. *Ferriman Trust, Ltd.*, [1937] 3 All E. R. 85.

[3] *Ashe* v. *Hogan*, [1920] 2 I. R. 159.

[4] *Re Nisbet and Potts' Contract*, [1905] 1 Ch. 391, *infra*, pp. 530–1.

[5] *Supra*, pp. 391–6 ; 397–403.

[6] *Leek & Moorlands Building Society* v. *Clark*, [1952] 2 Q. B. 788 ; [1952] 2 All E. R. 492.

[7] Law of Property Act, 1925, ss. 53 (1) ; 54 (2).

[8] *Ibid.*, s. 52.   [9] *Ibid.*, s. 52 (2) (c).

operates where the owner of a particular estate, such as a tenant for years, is a party to some transaction that would not be valid if his estate continued to exist. If, for example, the lessor grants to him a new lease which is to begin during the currency of the existing lease, the latter is implicitly surrendered and the tenant is estopped from disputing the validity of the new lease.[1]

Other examples of implied surrender occur, if

possession is delivered by the tenant to the lessor and accepted by the latter [2];

the tenant is permitted to remain in occupation of the premises as a licensee paying no rent [3];

the lessor grants a new lease to a third party, or accepts a third party as the new tenant, with the assent of the existing tenant.[4]

Merger. The term of years and the reversion are concurrent interests that cannot be held by one and the same person at the same time. If, therefore, they become united in one person in the same right, as for example where the lessor conveys the fee simple to the tenant, the term is at common law immediately annihilated. It is said to be " merged," *i.e.* sunk or drowned in the greater estate.[5] It will be explained later, however, that in equity the union of a smaller and a greater estate in one person does not always result in merger.[6]

Union of term and reversion in one person.

Effluxion of time. In principle there is no need for a notice to quit in the case of a lease for a definite term, since the tenancy terminates automatically upon the expiration of the agreed period. The scope of this rule, however, has been drastically restricted by legislation, for there are several cases in which there is no automatic cessation of a tenancy upon the expiration of the period for which it was granted. These cases are the following :—

Special cases.

Leases of an agricultural holding.[7]
Business leases.[8]
Long leases of dwelling-houses at a low rent.[9]
Tenancies falling within the Rent Acts.[10]

In the result there are comparatively few cases in which effluxion of time has its normal effect.

Notice to quit. A notice to quit is necessary in the case of yearly and other periodic tenancies, and also in the case of a lease

When necessary.

---

[1] *Lyon* v. *Reed* (1844), 13 M. & W. 285 ; *Fenner* v. *Blake,* [1900] 1 Q. B. 426 ; *Knight* v. *Williams,* [1901] 1 Ch. 256. To produce a surrender, the new lease must be effective, not, for example, one which is beyond the powers of the lessor, *Barclays Bank, Ltd.* v. *Stasek,* [1957] Ch. 28 ; [1956] 3 All E. R. 439.
[2] *Dodd* v. *Acklom* (1843), 6 Man. & G. 672.
[3] *Foster* v. *Robinson,* [1951] 1 K. B. 149 ; [1950] 2 All E. R. 342.
[4] *Wallis* v. *Hands.* [1893] 2 Ch. 75 ; *Metcalfe* v. *Boyce,* [1927] 1 K. B. 758.
[5] Blackstone, II. p. 177.
[6] *Infra,* p. 832.
[7] *Infra,* p. 448.
[8] *Infra,* p. 452.
[9] *Infra,* p. 460.
[10] *Infra,* p. 432.

for a fixed period if a stipulation to that effect is made. In the case of a dwelling house, however, the Rent Act, 1957,[1] provides that no notice shall be valid unless it is given not less than four weeks before the date on which it is to expire. The common law rule applies in this context and the provision is satisfied by a notice given on one day to expire that day four weeks hence.[2]

Essentials of validity. Since the notice is a unilateral act performed in the exercise of a contractual right, it must conform strictly to the terms of the contract.[3] The onus of proving its validity lies upon the person by whom it is given.[4] Two matters in particular upon which its validity depends may be observed.

Must indicate the correct day. (i) First, it is void unless it either names the correct date for the termination of the tenancy [5] or uses a formula from which the correct date is ascertainable with certainty. A familiar example of the latter is when the notice requires the yearly tenant to quit the premises

" at the expiration of the year of your tenancy, which shall expire " next after the end of one half-year from the service of this notice." [6]

Must be un-conditional. (ii) Secondly, a notice to quit must be unconditional. It must be expressed in such decisive and unequivocal terms, that the person to whom it is directed can entertain no reasonable doubt as to its intended effect. In particular, although no precise form is required, " there must be plain unambiguous words claiming to determine the existing tenancy at a certain time." [7] Thus a notice given by a tenant would be ineffective if it expressed his intention to quit the premises on March 25, unless he was unable to obtain alternative accommodation.

Where, however, the naming of a certain day for the termination of the tenancy is followed by an intimation that the lease shall continue if the other party assents to certain terms, as for example to an increase [8] or diminution [9] of rent, the courts are inclined to treat the document as a valid notice accompanied by an offer of a new tenancy capable of acceptance or refusal by the other party. In *Dagger* v. *Shepherd*,[10] for instance, the question arose

---

[1] S. 16, *infra*, p. 464. This section only applies where the true relation between the parties is that of landlord and tenant; *Alliance Building Society* v. *Pinwill*, [1958] Ch. 788 ; [1958] 2 All E. R. 408.
[2] *Schnabel* v. *Allard*, [1966] 3 All E. R. 816; overruling *Thompson* v. *Stimpson*, [1961] 1 Q. B. 195 ; [1960]3 All E. R. 500.
[3] *Dagger* v. *Shepherd*, [1946] K. B. 215, 220 ; [1946] 1 All E. R. 133, 135 ; *Hankey* v. *Clavering*, [1942] 2 K. B. 326, 330 ; [1942] 2 All E. R. 311, 314.
[4] *Lemon* v. *Lardeur*, [1946] K. B. 613 ; [1946] 2 All E. R. 329.
[5] *Hankey* v. *Clavering, supra.*
[6] *Addis* v. *Burrows*, [1948] 1 K. B. 444 ; [1948] 1 All E. R. 177.
[7] *Gardner* v. *Ingram* (1889), 61 L. T. 729, at p. 730, *per* Lord COLERIDGE.
[8] *Ahearn* v. *Bellman* (1879), 4 Exch. D. 201 ; but Lord ESHER vigorously dissented.
[9] *Bury* v. *Thompson*, [1895] 1 Q. B. 696.
[10] [1946] K. B. 215 ; [1946] 1 All E. R. 133.

whether a notice, given on December 21, directing the tenant to quit the premises

" on or before the 25th March next "

was valid and effective. It was objected by the tenant that the notice was void for uncertainty, since he was left in doubt as to its intended effect. In his submission the document contained nothing more than a statement that the tenancy was to end on some unspecified date between December 21 and March 25. The court, however, rejected this submission. It construed the document as an irrevocable notice to quit on March 25 in any event, but followed by an offer to accept the termination of the tenancy at any earlier date at which the tenant might elect to give up possession.

(iii) A notice to quit given by a lessor must relate to the whole **Must relate** of the premises. It is void if it directs the tenant to surrender **to the whole** possession of part only of what he holds, unless this is permitted **premises.** by the lease itself or by statute.[1] Such a statutory power is vested in the lessor of an agricultural holding if he requires part of the land for certain purposes, such as the erection of cottages or the provision of allotments, specified by the Agricultural Holdings Act, 1948.[2] If, however, he takes advantage of this power, the tenant may treat the notice as a notice to quit the entire holding.[3]

2. YEARLY AND OTHER PERIODIC TENANCIES.

A tenancy from year to year does not expire at the end of the **Half a** first or any subsequent year, but continues until it is determined **year's notice** by a notice served either by the landlord or tenant. It has been **necessary.** the rule since the reign of Henry VIII that not less than half a year's notice is necessary, unless a different agreement has been made by the parties.

It is well established what is meant by " half a year." If the **Meaning of** tenancy began on one of the usual quarter days, it means the **" half a** interval between a quarter day and the next quarter day but one, **year."** notwithstanding that, measured by days, such a period may not amount to half a year.[4] Thus in a Lady Day tenancy notice to quit will be good if given on or before Michaelmas Day, though the actual period is five days short of 182. If the tenancy began at some day falling between two quarter days, then the length of notice must be 182 days at least.[5]

There are two exceptions to the rule requiring half a year's **Exceptions** notice. **to the rule.**

---

[1] *Re Bebington's Tenancy, Bebington* v. *Wildman*, [1921] 1 Ch. 559. The actual decision is now out of date owing to the Law of Property Act, 1925, s. 140 (1), (2) ; *supra*, p. 412.
[2] S. 31.   [3] S. 32.
[4] *Right d. Flower* v. *Darby* (1786), 1 Term Rep. 159
[5] 1 Wms. Saunders 276 C ; *Sidebotham* v. *Holland*, [1895] 1 Q. B. 378, 384.

Contrary agreement.

(i) First, where the parties have made a different arrangement.

> " I know of nothing which prevents parties, in entering into an
> " agreement from year to year, from stipulating that it should be
> " determinable by a notice to quit shorter than the usual six months'
> " notice ; or that the notices to quit to be given by the landlord and
> " tenant respectively should be of unequal length ; or that the ten-
> " ancy should be determinable by the one party only by notice to
> " quit, and by the other party either by notice to quit or in some
> " other way." [1]

Agricultural holding.

(ii) Secondly, it is provided by statute in the case of an agricultural holding, that, notwithstanding any express stipulation
to the contrary, a notice to quit shall be invalid if it purports to
terminate the tenancy before the expiration of twelve months
from the end of the current year of tenancy.[2]

Notice must be so given as to expire at end of current year.

A yearly tenancy is terminable only at the end of the current
year, and therefore a notice, given for example by the landlord,
must require the tenant to quit the holding on that date—no
earlier, no later. Literally interpreted, the end of the current
year is midnight of the day prior to the anniversary of the day on
which the tenancy began.

> For instance, if a yearly tenancy began on September 29, its
> current period ends each year on September 28. In strict-
> ness, therefore, a notice given, say, by the landlord, must
> direct the tenant to quit on September 28 and it must reach
> the tenant at least half a year before that day. A notice, for
> instance, that is not served upon him till after March 25,
> and which directs him to quit on the next ensuing
> September 28 is bad, and he will be entitled to remain until
> September 28 in the following year.

> The courts, however, after some hesitation, have extended
> the strict meaning of the expression " end of the current year "
> to include the anniversary of the day on which the tenancy began.
> " A notice to quit " at the first moment of the anniversary," said
> LINDLEY, L.J., " ought to be just as good as a notice to quit on
> the last moment of the day before." [3] A notice, therefore, given
> not later than Lady Day, will be good if it purports to terminate a
> Michaelmas tenancy on September 29.[4]

Other periodic tenancies.

Similar rules apply in the case of other periodic tenancies.
Subject to the statutory rule in the case of a dwelling house,[5] the
length of the notice must be not less than the length of the tenancy,
e.g. at least seven days' notice is necessary to terminate a weekly
tenancy, and the notice must purport to terminate the tenancy at

---

[1] *Allison* v. *Scargall*, [1920] 3 K. B. 443, at p. 449, *per* SALTER, J.
[2] Agricultural Holdings Act, 1948, s. 23, *infra*, p. 448.
[3] *Sidebotham* v. *Holland*, [1895] 1 Q. B. 378.
[4] *Sidebotham* v. *Holland*, *supra* ; *Crate* v. *Miller*, [1947] K. B. 946 ; [1947]
2 All E. R. 45 ; dealing with the analogous case of a weekly tenancy.
[5] Rent Act, 1957, s. 16; *supra*, p. 418; *infra*, p. 464.

the end of the current period,[1] *i.e.* either on the anniversary of the date of its commencement[2] or on the preceding day. In computing the period of seven days or other the appropriate period, the day of expiry but not the day of service is included. Thus, a tenancy that began on a Saturday may be terminated by a notice to quit given on a Saturday, notwithstanding that this does not give the tenant seven clear days' notice.

> In *Lemon* v. *Lardeur*,[3] a tenant who held on a four-weekly tenancy was given " a month's notice as from August 1, 1945, to vacate " the premises. No evidence was given of the date on which the tenancy began.

The notice was invalid, for, since it had not been shown that August 1, was the first day of one of the four-weekly periods, it was impossible to ascertain whether the month's notice would expire at the end of the current period.

These rules may be varied by the parties. Subject to the statutory rule that four weeks notice is necessary to terminate a lease of a dwelling-house the length of the notice and the date at which it may be given are matters upon which they may make what arrangement they like.[4]

3. TENANCIES AT WILL.

A tenancy at will may be expressly terminated at any time by either party. The strict rules that govern a notice to quit do not, however, apply in this case, for it has been said by high authority that : Express determination.

> " Anything which amounts to a demand of possession although not
> " expressed in precise and formal language, is sufficient to indicate
> " the determination of the landlord's will." [5]

Thus a declaration, that the landlord will take steps to recover possession unless the tenant complies with certain conditions, determines the tenancy if the conditions are not accepted.[6] Implicit determination : (i) by lessor.

The tenancy is also implicitly determined if the lessor does acts inconsistent with its continuance, as for instance if he alienates the reversion or removes material, such as stones from the land.[7]

Implicit determination also occurs if the tenant does acts (ii) by tenant.

---

[1] *Lemon* v. *Lardeur*, [1946] K. B. 613 ; [1946] 2 All E. R. 329 ; *Queen's Club Garden Estates, Ltd.* v. *Bignell*, [1924] 1 K. B. 117 ; *Bathavon R.D.C.* v. *Carlisle*, [1958] 1 Q. B. 461 ; [1958] 1 All E. R. 801.

[2] *Crate* v. *Miller, supra.*

[3] [1946] K. B. 613.

[4] *Land Settlement Association, Ltd.* v. *Carr*, [1944] K. B. 657 ; [1944] 2 All E. R. 126. As regards the actual decision in this case, see Agricultural Holdings Act, 1948, s. 2 (1).

[5] *Doe d. Price* v. *Price* (1832), 9 Bing. 356, 358, *per* TINDAL, C.J.

[6] *Doe d. Price* v. *Price, supra* ; *Fox* v. *Hunter-Paterson*, [1948] 2 All E. R. 813.

[7] *Doe d. Bennett* v. *Turner* (1840), 7 M. & W. 226.

incompatible with his limited rights, as for instance if he commits waste or assigns the land to a stranger.

The death of either party also determines the tenancy.

A premature determination is not allowed to prejudice the rights of either party. If the tenant quits before the day on which his rent is due, he does not escape liability;[1] while if he has sown crops he has a right at common law to re-enter and reap them if the lessor determines the tenancy before they are ripe.[2]

SECTION IX. SECURITY OF TENURE AND CONTROL OF RENT.

SUMMARY.

Introduction. The contractual aspect of leases and tenancies has in recent years been considerably modified. Various Acts place a limit on the rent which a landlord can obtain, and also restrict his right to recover possession of the premises at the end of the lease. The origin of these Acts lies in the acute housing shortage which began during the war of 1914 and which still persists.[3] But protection is now given to agricultural and business tenancies, and to furnished as well as unfurnished lettings of houses. Different policy considerations govern these various tenancies, hence varying degrees of protection are given and different methods employed by the legislature to secure that protection. Each type of tenancy will have to be considered separately.

The Rent Acts. Consideration of the Rent Acts is further complicated by two periods in which the legislature began to relax control of dwelling houses, one period beginning after the 1914-18 war and ending with the re-commencement of war in 1939, the other beginning in the middle nineteen-fifties (under a Conservative Government) and ending in 1965 (under a Labour Government). There has been no codification of these various Rent Acts, and the present law is to be found in various sections from all these Acts (many

---

[1] Cruise, *Digest*, Tit. ix., c. 1, s. 13.
[2] Co. Litt 55b ; see *supra* p. 371.
[3] The problem is not confined to the United Kingdom. See Willis (1950), 36 *Cornell L. Q.* 54 for an interesting survey of the problem.

sections taking effect as amended by later Acts). The resulting
statute-law is of formidable complexity; to which there has to be
added a very considerable case-law, for the Acts are silent on many
points of principle and detail.[1]

(1) THE RENT ACTS.

(A) Unfurnished lettings of houses for periods not in excess
of 21 years.

It is to this category of tenancy that what are called "The Rent Control and
Acts" apply.[2] A house let in this way may be either "controlled" regulation.
or "regulated." It will be controlled if it is within the ambit of the
Rent Acts 1920–1957; it will be regulated if within the ambit
of the Rent Act, 1965. The importance of this distinction will be
seen later, but it is first necessary to ascertain the basic requirements that must be satisfied before a house can be brought within
the Rent Acts at all. The Acts apply only where "a house or part
of a house is let as a separate dwelling."[3] This requirement needs
careful consideration. Sub-tenancies raise special problems,
which will be considered separately.[4]

(i) Requirements for the application of the Acts.

Only houses are within the Acts. House has a wide meaning Meaning of
but there must be some permanent structure involved; movable house.
structures such as caravans do not qualify nor, conversely, would
a permanent structure unsuitable for habitation such as a factory.
A part of a house or a flat (even if not a self-contained unit) may be
let as a separate dwelling, so that a house may contain several
separate Rent Act "houses."[5] On the other hand, two flats or a
house and cottage let together as a unit may constitute one Rent
Act "house."[6]

So long as there is a tenancy, its nature is immaterial; it may Meaning of
be periodic, or even at will or sufferance.[7] But a licensee, such as tenancy.
a lodger, is not protected.[8] The distinction between lease and

---

[1] See *per* Scrutton, L.J., in *Haskins* v. *Lewis*, [1931] 2 K. B. 1, at p. 9.
The most valuable and complete account is that by Megarry: *The Rent Acts*
(9th Edn. 1961).
[2] The principal Acts are: Increase of Rent and Mortgage Interest (Restrictions) Act, 1920; Rent and Mortgage Restrictions Act, 1923; Rent and
Mortgage Interest Restrictions (Amendment) Act, 1933; Increase of Rent and
Mortgage Interest (Restrictions) Act, 1938; Rent and Mortgage Interest
Restrictions Act, 1939; Rent Act, 1957; Rent Act, 1965.
[3] 1920 Act, s. 12 (2); 1933 Act, s. 16 (1).
[4] *Infra.*, p. 439.
[5] *Abrahart* v. *Webster*, [1925] 1 K. B. 563.
[6] *Langford Property Co., Ltd.* v. *Goldrich*, [1949] 1 K. B. 511; [1949] 1 All
E. R. 402; *Whitty* v. *Scott-Russell*, [1950] 2 K. B. 32; [1950] 1 All E. R. 884.
[7] *Artizans, Labourers and General Dwellings Co., Ltd.* v. *Whitaker*, [1919]
2 K.B. 301; *Remon* v. *City of London Real Property Co., Ltd.*, [1921] 1 K. B. 49.
But a mortgagor in possession, even one who attorns tenant to his mortgagee,
is outside the Acts: *Portman B.S.* v. *Young*, [1951] 1 All E. R. 191.
[8] *Barrell* v. *Fordree*, [1932] 2 K. B. 257, at p. 261, *per* Scrutton, L.J.

licence, difficult though it is,[1] is vital. Furthermore, the courts are wary of licences so-called in order to evade the Acts, and may construe them as leases.[2]

Employees. An employee occupying his employers's house may be a service tenant, in which case he will be protected by the Acts (though in a limited way[3]); or he may be a service occupier or only an ordinary licensee, in neither of which cases is he specially protected.[4] It is entirely a question of the parties' intentions whether in a case of this sort a tenancy or a licence has been created, but an intention to create a tenancy will not be inferred without good grounds. In particular, proximity to work is not conclusive.[5]

Let as a house. To be within the Acts, a house must also be *let as a house.* The important factor here is not the *de facto* use of the house but the purpose for which the house was let. Actual use is relevant evidence only if the lease is inconclusive.[6] A structure let as a barn, for instance, does not come within the Acts merely because the tenant chooses to live there.[7]

Variation in use. A change in user may take a house or part of it out of the Acts, as for instance when a tenant uses premises, let as a house, only for business purposes. Again, if a tenant of a house protected by the Acts sub-lets it furnished, it is its character after the sub-lease that is decisive, so that the only protection for both the sub-tenant *and* the tenant will be the limited protection given to furnished houses.[8] The original intended use of a house may of course be varied by agreement. In such cases the landlord's agreement to the variation must be clearly shown.[9] When the lease contemplates no specific use, or several possible uses, then the use at the time when the landlord sues for possession is the crucial one.[10]

A separate dwelling. The house must be let as a *separate* dwelling. The significance of this requirement escaped notice until 1945 when, in *Neale* v. *Del Soto*,[11] the Court of Appeal held that a tenant who shared accommodation with another did not occupy a separate dwelling

---

[1] *Supra*, pp. 338–9.

[2] *Samrose Properties, Ltd.* v. *Gibbard*, [1958] 1 All E. R. 502; [1958] 1 W. L. R. 235.

[3] *Infra*, p. 437.

[4] See *infra*, p. 464, for the limited protection that is available generally.

[5] *Torbett* v. *Faulkner* [1952] 2 T. L. R. 659; *Thompsons (Funeral Furnishers) Ltd.* v. *Phillips*, [1945] 2 All E. R. 49; *Ramsbottom* v. *Snelson*, [1948] 1 K. B. 473; [1948] 1 All E. R. 201.

[6] *Wolfe* v. *Hogan*, [1949] 2 K. B. 194 at p. 204–5; [1949] 1 All E. R. 570, at p. 575, *per* DENNING, L.J.; *Levermore* v. *Jobey*, [1956] 2 All E. R. 362; [1956] 1 W. L. R. 697. *British Land Co., Ltd.* v. *Herbert Silver (Menswear), Ltd.*, [1958] 1 Q. B. 530; [1958] 1 All E. R. 833.

[7] *Epsom Grand Stand Association* v. *Clarke*, [1919] W. N. 170, *per* BANKES, L.J.

[8] *Infra*, pp. 441–2. A licence involving exclusive occupation may have a similar effect: *Gee* v. *Hazleton*, [1932] 1 K. B. 179; but this is not true of residential licences generally: *E. Moss, Ltd.* v. *Brown*, [1946] 2 All E. R. 557.

[9] *Court* v. *Robinson*, [1951] 2 K. B. 60. [1951] 1 All E. R. 209.

[10] *Gidden* v. *Mills*, [1925] 2 K. B. 713; *Prout* v. *Hunter*, [1924] 2 K.B. 736; *Phillips* v. *Hallahan* [1925] 1 K. B. 756, at p. 760, *per* GREER, J.

[11] [1945] K. B. 144; [1945] 1 All E. R. 191 (C. A.).

and was therefore, not protected by the Acts. The problems of sharing were dealt with in the 1949 Act but before discussing the statutory provisions, it is necessary to consider the doctrine previously evolved by the courts.

A tenant who, *as a term of his tenancy*,[1] shared *living* accommodation, whether with his landlord or another tenant,[2] was not protected for the premises had not been *let* as a separate dwelling. However, no sharing would exclude a house from control unless it was a sharing of living rooms. For this purpose, a kitchen is a living room,[3] but a lavatory or bathroom is not. Therefore a tenant who shared a kitchen was unprotected before the 1949 Act, while a tenant who had the exclusive possession of a bedroom, kitchen and sitting room but who shared with others the use of a combined bathroom and lavatory and who could use the garden for drying clothes and storing coal was protected.[4] Nor did the complications end there for, to exclude the Acts, the sharing of a living room had to be *for living purposes*; and where, for instance, rooms were let together with the right to use the kitchen and scullery to draw water and boil the washing once a week, or with a right to the occasional use of another bedroom, the sharing was still not for living purposes, and the tenants were protected.[5]

The word " sharing " is in fact inaccurate.[6] It suggests that the parties enjoy an equality of rights in what is shared whereas this is very rarely the case. The tenant's right to use the kitchen will normally be a licence. The landlord remains in possession, controls the kitchen, and may allow others to use it.[7] The tenant can do none of these things. The situation may also be reversed. If a landlord lets rooms and a kitchen, and his tenant later gives the landlord a right or licence to use the kitchen in common with himself, it is the landlord who shares with the tenant. The tenant will be fully protected.[8] In sharing cases, the crucial question is, " Who enjoys the dominant position with regard to the shared accommodation? "[9]

The doctrine of sharing.

Ambiguity in the meaning of sharing.

---

[1] *Llewellyn* v. *Hinson*, [1948] 2 K. B. 385; [1948] 2 All E. R. 95 (C. A.); see especially ASQUITH, L.J., at p. 391.

[2] *Neale* v. *Del Soto* and *Llewellyn* v. *Hinson*, *supra*.

[3] *Rogers* v. *Hyde*, [1951] 2 K. B. 923; [1951] 2 All E. R. 79 (C. A.); *Baker* v. *Turner*, [1950] A. C. 401, at pp. 414, 420, 431; [1950] 1 All E. R. 834, at pp. 839, 842, 850.

[4] *Cole* v. *Harris*, [1945] K. B. 474; [1945] 2 All E. R. 146 (C. A.).

[5] *Hayward* v. *Marshall*, [1952] 2 Q. B. 89; [1952] 1 All E. R. 633 (C. A.) *Goodrich* v. *Paisner*, [1957] A. C. 65.

[6] *Baker* v. *Turner*, [1950] A. C. 401, at p. 415; [1950] 1 All E. R. 834 at p. 840, H. L. *per* Lord PORTER; *Rogers* v. *Hyde*, [1951] 2 K. B. 923, at p. 930; [1951] 2 All E. R. 79, at p. 81 (C. A.) *per* Lord ASQUITH.

[7] *Baker* v. *Turner*, [1950] A. C. 401, at p. 433; [1950] 1 All E. R. 834 at p. 851 *per* Lord MACDERMOTT; *Rogers* v. *Hyde*, [1951] 2 K. B. 923 at p. 933; [1951] 2 All E. R. 79 at p. 82 (C. A.) *per* Lord ASQUITH.

[8] *Rogers* v. *Hyde*, *supra*.

[9] It was at one time thought that a landlord could recover possession from a tenant who was sharing with a sub-tenant on the grounds that the tenant no longer occupied a separate dwelling, but this contention was rejected by the House of Lords in *Baker* v. *Turner*, [1950] A. C. 401; [1950] 1 All E. R. 834.

P*

The 1949 Act alters the law where a sharing results from the terms of the tenancy. The Act applies whenever a tenant has exclusive occupation of rooms and would be protected were it not for the fact that the tenancy between himself and his landlord provides that he is to share other living accommodation either (a) with his landlord or (b) with a third person.[1]

(a) If he is to share living accommodation with his landlord, the Rent Acts are still excluded. Hence to this situation the difficulties just discussed are still relevant. But though the Rent Acts are excluded, the tenant is given the limited protection which the Act of 1946 confers upon tenants of furnished houses.

(b) If he is to share living accommodation with persons other than the landlord his separate accommodation is deemed to be a dwelling house and is accordingly fully protected by the Rent Acts. In addition, the landlord is prevented from exercising any right he possesses under the tenancy agreement to terminate or modify the tenant's right to use the shared living accommodation.[2]

Premises used partly as living accommodation and partly as " a shop or office or for business, trade or professional purposes "[3] are covered by special provisions. Until 1965, such premises were within the protection of the Rent Acts. If *a* purpose of the letting was to enable the tenant to live on the premises, that was sufficient. The test was not one of dominant user, but of legitimate user.[4] This did not mean that premises obviously let as a shop came within the the Acts because someone occasionally slept there, but actual residence that was neither contrary to the terms of the tenancy nor incompatible with the nature of the business could have that effect. It was further necessary, if the Acts were to apply, for there to have been one letting of one entity; and this would be untrue of a single lease of a physically distinct shop and house, and also of separate leases of a physically joint shop and house, even if granted to the same tenant on the same day.[5]

This rule governing mixed user has to be distinguished however from another rule,[6] that land or other premises let together with a house are treated as one with the house. Save for " old control,"[7] this rule applies except where the land consists of agricultural land of more than two acres. Under this rule, both house and land are within the Rent Acts unless the combined rateable value takes both

---

[1] 1949 Act, ss. 7, 8; 1957 Act, Sched. VIII. See *infra*, p. 441, for shared sub-tenancies.

[2] There is provision for the county court to terminate or modify a tenant's right to shared accommodation other than living accommodation, and to modify his right to shared living accommodation: see generally, *Lockwood* v. *Lowe*, [1954] 2 Q. B. 267.

[3] 1920 Act, s. 12 (2) (ii); 1939 Act, s. 3 (3).

[4] *Vickery* v. *Martin*, [1944] K. B. 679; [1944] 2 All E. R. 167; *Levermore* v. *Jobey*, [1956] 2 All E. R. 362; [1956] 1 W. L. R. 697.

[5] *Cumbes* v. *Robinson*, [1951] 2 K. B. 83; [1951] 1 All E. R. 661.

[6] 1920 Act, s. 12 (2) (iii); see especially ROMER, L. J., in *Whiteley* v. *Wilson*, [1953] 1 Q. B. 77, at p. 85; [1952] 2 All E. R. 940, at p. 944.

[7] *Infra*, p. 428.

out of the Acts altogether. But for the rule to apply, the parties must have considered the two parts as subject to one letting, *and* the dominant purpose of that one letting must have been the letting of the house as a house. Thus, where a bungalow was let with a camping site, and the dominant purpose was held to be the letting of the site, the result was that neither was within the Rent Acts.[1]

The 1965 Act reverses the rule concerning business premises, but only in relation to tenancies regulated by that Act.[2] The present policy is to exclude premises let for business purposes from the Rent Acts, *even where there is a residential element in the letting*, and to apply to them the protection of the Landlord and Tenant Act, 1954.[3] Consequently the rule governing mixed user contained in section 12 (2) (ii) of the 1920 Act and section 3 (3) of the 1939 Act will not affect at all the regulated tenancies brought into being by the 1965 Act. But the rule governing premises let along with a house and contained in section 12 (2) (iii) of the 1920 Act will in general affect regulated tenancies though it will not have the particular effect of bringing within the 1965 Act any tenancies that come within the 1954 Act.[4] *Policy changed in respect of business tenancies.*

Houses let furnished are excluded from the Rent Acts[5] but only if *Exclusion of furnished houses.*

> "*bona fide* let at a rent which includes payment in respect of board, "attendance or use of furniture."[6]

A house is not so *bona fide* let unless the amount of the rent attributable to these three items is a substantial proportion of the whole rent.[7] The House of Lords considered the effect of these provisions in two cases[8] heard together in 1948, and as a result several difficulties of interpretation were solved.

The furniture must be for the use of the tenant in the house, so that furniture in the entrance hall of a block of flats, or on a staircase which is not included in the lease, does not qualify. Nor do articles which, if detached from the realty, would cease to be usable, for instance a fitted wardrobe without a back. But the fact that it is technically a fixture does not prevent an article being "furniture" if, when detached, it would be usable. Refrigerators, *Furniture.*

---

[1] *Feyereisel* v. *Turnidge*, [1952] 2 Q. B. 29; [1952] 1 All E. R. 728.

[2] See *infra*, pp. 429–30, on regulation.

[3] 1965 Act, ss. 1 (3), 11 (7), 13 (5); Sched. 1, paras 1 (1) and 3. S. 43 (1) (c) of the 1954 Act, Part II, which excluded from that Act premises protected by the Rent Acts, is not to affect regulated tenancies, so that premises caught by the 1954 Act are outside the 1965 Act.

[4] The effect of s. 1 (3) of the 1965 Act on sub-tenancies of regulated houses is complex and at present controversial: see Bramall: *The Rent Act 1965*, p. 6 and p. 105. For furnished sub-tenancies generally, see *infra*, p. 441.

[5] Lettings of furnished houses are protected by the Act of 1946, *infra*, p. 442.

[6] 1920 Act, s. 12 (2) (i); 1939 Act, s. 3 (2) (b).

[7] 1923 Act, s. 10 (1).

[8] *Palser* v. *Grinling, Property Holding Co., Ltd.* v. *Mischeff,* [1948] A. C. 291; [1948] 1 All E. R. 1.

medicine chests and bedding are among articles which have been held to be furniture for this purpose.

Attendance and board. Attendance must be personal to the tenant. Central services in a block of flats, such as hot water or a lift, are excluded. But the provision of a servant to clean interior premises or to carry coals or collect refuse constitute attendance, even if several tenants benefit. Board is not confined to full board; breakfast without other meals probably constitutes board, but a morning cup of tea does not. The ultimate test, however, is the substantiality of all these services *taken together*, not each service individually.

(ii) Control, decontrol and recontrol.

The limits of control. To be within the Rent Acts a house must not only comply with the various requirements we have specified; in addition it must come within certain financial limits. This subject is best discussed historically. The early Rent Acts applied to houses the rent of which or the rateable value of which did not on August 31st, **Old control.** 1914 exceed £105 in London or £78 elsewhere. But houses the rateable value of which in April, 1931 exceeded £35 in London or £20 elsewhere were later decontrolled. Also, although the basic principle is that a house that is within the relevant financial limits is controlled by the Acts whether or not a tenancy has been granted of it, provisions were made between the two wars for decontrol of houses not actually let and houses of which leases of a certain minimum length had been granted. This era of the Rent Acts is now referred to as "old control." It has not disappeared altogether since the "new control" which began in 1939 specifically excluded[1] from new control all premises still *actually* subject to old control. With this exception, the Act of 1939 brought within the ambit of new control all houses the rateable value of which did not in April, 1939 exceed £100 in London and £75 elsewhere. The **New control.** rateable value at that date was crucial, and control applied whether or not the house was then let. Control also applied to houses first assessed after that date. Where only part of a house was let, or there was one letting of two physical entities, there was an apportionment or addition, as the case might be, of rateable values.

Rent level. There was one further financial requirement for there to be control; the tenancy must have been at a rent which was at least two-thirds of the rateable value;[2] for old control the date was 1914, for new control 1939. Rent free tenancies were, therefore, not controlled. "Rent" is here used in a popular sense and means the sum which the tenant pays and not the net amount which the landlord receives after rates and taxes.[3] A house will remain controlled (if its rateable value is within the relevant limits) even

---

[1] 1939 Act, s. 3 (1).
[2] 1920 Act, s. 12 (7).
[3] *Mackworth* v. *Hellard*, [1921] 2 K. B. 755; *Sidney Trading Co.* v. *Finsbury Borough Council*, [1952] 1 All E. R. 460.

though a particular tenancy of it is free or at less than two-thirds of the rateable value. A sub-tenant in such a case for instance, will be protected if the rent due from him exceeds two-thirds of the rateable value of the premises.

Such was in general the extent of control until 1954. In that year section 35 of the Housing Repairs and Rents Act decontrolled houses erected after 30th August in that year, and also separate premises produced by conversion of other premises after that date.[1] In 1957 a much more extensive decontrol took place. The Rent Act[2] of that year decontrolled as from July 6th, 1957 all dwelling houses the rateable value of which, on November 7th, 1956, exceeded £40 in London and £30 elsewhere, irrespective of when a tenancy had been granted.[3] In addition all new lettings coming into operation after July 6th, 1957 were freed from control, even if the premises let would otherwise have been within control.[4]

Decontrol.

The Act of 1965 reverses this policy of decontrol. But its method of doing so is most complex. First of all, the Rent Acts are declared to govern — to " regulate " — houses the rateable value of which did not on March 23rd, 1965 exceed £400 in London and £200 elsewhere.[5] But this provision is then made applicable in the following cases only:

Recontrol and regulated tenancies.

(1) A tenancy of a house will be regulated by the new Act if it is not already controlled and if the reason for its not being controlled is the 1957 Act's limitation of control to houses the rateable value of which is £40/30 or less, according to where they are. In other words, if *apart from* this provision of the 1957 Act, a tenancy would have been controlled, it will now be regulated.[6]

(2) Similarly, a tenancy will be regulated by the new Act if it is not already controlled and if the reason for this is the 1957 Act's limitation of control to tenancies that came into operation after July 6th, 1957. Thus all tenancies entered into on or after that date are regulated, if they are of houses within the relevant financial limits.

(3) Lastly, a tenancy of a house is regulated by the new Act if it is not already controlled and if the only reason for this is that section 35 of the 1954 Act had decontrolled it. Thus, houses built after August 30th, 1954 can be regulated.

It can now be seen that to-day we have both controlled and

Control and Regulation.

---

[1] It also decontrolled lettings by local authorities, housing associations, etc.   [2] S. 11.

[3] Sched. V of the Act contains precise instructions as to the determination of rateable values in special cases. Apportionment can also take place, 1957 Act, s. 19 (4).   [4] S. 11 (1).

[5] Ss. 1 (1), 43; coupled, as under earlier Acts, with powers of apportionment.

[6] Houses let at less than two-thirds of their rateable value on March 23rd, 1965 are outside the Acts: 1965 Act, Sched. I, para. 1 (3).

regulated tenancies.[1] Control is not repealed, but remains an important part of the law for tenancies still subject to it. But no new controlled tenancies can come into existence. Where the 1965 Act re-imposes the Acts, it does so by introducing the concept of the regulated tenancy.[2] The effects of control and regulation must now be considered. First in relation to rent and then in relation to security of tenure.

(iii) Provisions affecting rent.

Control of rent.

Before 1957 every controlled house had a "standard rent" which, together with certain permitted increases, represented the total recoverable rent. But the standard rent was based on the rent at which a house had been let at a particular time, often when it was first let, and this rule was adhered to even if the rent had been preferential or uneconomic from the very beginning. The 1957 Act abolished the whole system of the standard rent and replaced it with a rent limit based on the gross rateable value as shown in the valuation list on 7th November, 1956. This figure, when multiplied by the "appropriate factor" (which varies according to the liability for repairs) and adjusted for rates, improvements, and some other payments (for services for instance), is a means of arriving at a rent limit which is supposed to bear a relation to the economic value of the house. The tenant cannot be asked to pay more than the rent limit and, if he has paid more, he can recover the excess.[3] Nor can these provisions be circumvented by indirect payments. Any pecuniary consideration which is demanded for the grant or renewal of a tenancy may be recovered as an illegal

Premiums.

premium.[4] For instance, in *Elmdene Estates Ltd.* v. *White*,[5] the X. Co. agreed to grant a tenancy of a flat in consideration that the tenant would sell his own house at £500 less than its admitted value to the Y. Co., in which X. Co. had a financial interest. The House of Lords held that this consideration constituted a premium, and that the tenant could recover the £500 he had paid. In the words of Lord Radcliffe ". . . the particular means adopted of passing the consideration from giver to taker is not significant."[6] The concept of a premium also extends to the requiring of an ex-

---

[1] It is not possible to consider, in an account of this size, the special rules applicable to parsonage houses, agricultural workers' houses, public houses, and lettings by local authorities, housing trusts, etc.

[2] Decontrolling provisions in the Act are (1) those enabling the Minister to convert, in respect of a particular area, controlled tenancies into regulated tenancies—this, *infra*, p. 431, is concerned only with rent levels, not total decontrol—and (2) s. 12, which enables the Minister to free from regulation any area in which there is no housing shortage.

[3] 1920 Act, s. 14 (1); 1957 Act, Sched. VI, para. I; 1923 Act, s. 8 (2); 1938 Act, s. 7 (2). There is a bar to recovery after 2 years.

[4] 1949 Act, esp. ss. 12 (2), 2 (5), 2 (6), 18 (2).

[5] [1960] A. C. 528; [1960] 1 All E. R. 306.

[6] [1960] A. C. 528, at p. 542.

cessive price for e.g. furniture or services,[1] and to the requiring of a loan.[2] These provisions have been strengthened by the 1965 Act and apply to both controlled and regulated tenancies. It is now illegal to "receive" as well as to "require" a premium.[3]

The 1965 Act does not affect the 1957 rent limit, for houses which remain controlled remain subject to the 1957 provisions. But section 11 of the 1965 Act makes provision for the eventual conversion of controlled tenancies to regulated tenancies. Such a conversion will affect not the whole country at once, but the country area by area, as the Minister of Housing (who may act only under an order that has been approved by Parliament) decides. The intention is that a rent review of controlled tenancies shall take place after the new scheme of rent control for regulated tenancies has been successfully brought into operation.

Eventual review of 1957 rents.

It is to this new scheme that we must now turn, for it is a wholly different departure. The attempt to relate a rent limit to the economic value of a house by means of a fixed formula has been abandoned and been replaced by a system of registered rents, determined as follows.

The whole country is divided into rent assessment areas and each area is provided with rent officers and a rent assessment committee.[4] Either the landlord or the tenant of a regulated tenancy can apply to the rent officer for the determination of a fair rent. Should the parties to the tenancy not be in agreement on what is a fair rent, the aim of the Act is that they should be brought together in consultation with the rent officer.[5] If agreement still proves impossible, the rent officer determines the fair rent, but either party may then refer the matter to the rent assessment committee, whose decision is final. Once the fair rent is determined, it is registered in a local public register. An application to vary the rent can be made, but not within three years of the date when registration took effect, unless in the meanwhile significant changes have occurred in the terms of the tenancy or the condition of the premises.[6]

Registered rents.

A person who wishes to build, convert, or let premises that will be subject to the Acts when let can apply beforehand to the rent officer for a certificate of fair rent, which is only provisional, but which is an indication of the economic return that will be available to him if he decides to proceed.[7]

---

[1] 1949 Act, s. 3 (1). *Eales* v. *Dale*, [1954] 1 Q. B. 539; [1954] 1 All E. R. 717.

[2] 1957 Act, s. 14.

[3] 1965 Act, s. 37 and Sched. 5.

[4] 1965 Act, s. 2 and ss. 21–9, Scheds. 2, 3, and 4; s. 1. 1965 No. 2151.

[5] It is not the intention of the Act that the rent officer should be a legal adviser or a mere public relations officer.

[6] 1965 Act, Sched. 3, para. 3.

[7] Ss. 3–9 contain transitional provisions whereby the rent of houses coming regulated under the Act are pegged, subject to various saving pro-

The register must contain specific entries of any sums payable by the tenant for services or of any provision in the tenancy agreement for variation in the rent.[1] However, the most controversial section is that which indicates the factors that determine a fair rent.[2]

"Regard shall be had . . . to all the circumstances (other than personal "circumstances), and in particular to the age, character and locality "of the dwelling-house and to its state of repair."

But the scarcity of houses in any area is to be wholly ignored. The rent is not to be higher because there is insufficient housing available. What is material is the house and where it is.[3] Improvements that a tenant has made voluntarily are to be ignored, as also are defects due to failure by a tenant to perform his covenants. It can be seen therefore that a fair rent is frequently less than the rent that could otherwise be obtained in the open market in an area where there is a shortage of housing.

The last point that falls to be made is that the system of fair rents, like the rent limit, is still subject to the basic rule of the Acts that during the contractual period of a tenancy (as distinct from the statutory period) the landlord cannot escape from his obligations by relying on the Acts. The terms of the lease are still significant. Accordingly, the fair rent is a rent limit during the contractual period so that, if the tenancy is for a fixed period at a lesser rent, the tenant can not be made to pay a higher rent. But during the statutory period, the fair rent is the rent which the landlord can actually recover—the recoverable rent.[4]

(iv) The statutory tenancy.

A basic principle of the Rent Acts is that, on the termination of a protected contractual tenancy (and this will include all, even weekly, tenancies, once duly terminated) a statutory tenancy arises and continues until it is brought to an end either by the tenant himself, or by the county court on the application of the landlord. The terms and conditions of the original contract of tenancy continue to apply in relation to the statutory tenancy, for instance a landlord's covenant to supply continuous hot water, but only in so far as they are not in conflict with the provisions of the Acts.[5] The statutory tenancy alters the common law rules of holding over. A tenant of a protected house who, on the termination of his contractual tenancy, continues in possession paying the rent as before,

---

visions, until the administrative system of registered rents is constituted. Under s. 21, the registration system is introduced, on the decision of the Minister, area by area.

[1] 1965 Act, s. 28.   [2] *Ibid.*, s. 27.
[3] *Cf Infra*, p. 446, note 5.
[4] *Kerr* v. *Bryde*, [1923] A. C. 16; 1965 Act, s. 3 (1) and (2), and s. 7.
[5] 1920 Act, s. 15 (1). *Engvall* v. *Ideal Flats, Ltd.*, [1945] K. B. 250; [1945] 1 All E. R. 230; *Boyer* v. *Warbey*, [1953] 1 Q. B. 234; [1952] 2 All E. R. 976.

will ordinarily be a statutory tenant not a contractual tenant[1] unless a new contractual tenancy has clearly been created.[2]

The statutory tenancy[3] is not a tenancy in a strict sense. It confers no estate or interest in land.[4] It can neither be assigned nor devised (though sub-tenants are protected),[5] and it will not pass to a trustee in bankruptcy.[6] Nevertheless, it confers a right against the whole world to remain in possession and enables the tenant to maintain trespass against anyone, even the landlord, entering without permission or authority.[7] It is more aptly called "a status of irremovability."[8]

Nature of a statutory tenancy.

"Protection of the home seems to be the whole policy and intention of the Acts."[9] Accordingly, a statutory tenancy arises and continues only in favour of a tenant who is in occupation of the house or intends to return to it. Vicarious enjoyment is not within the protection given. Hence, where a statutory tenant allowed his sister to reside in a rented house, and he himself neither resided there not intended to, there was no protection.[10] A rather curious application of this principle is that, when a house is let to a corporation, the letting is within the Act so that the corporation, as contractual tenant, can take advantage of rent limits, but can not hold over as statutory tenant as it can not "reside."[11]

Requirement of residence.

Difficult questions arise in cases where a statutory tenant absents himself from the house for long periods. "Non occupation" is a question of fact and degree. The sea captain who is absent for months but returns between voyages to his home does

Periodic absences.

[1] *Remon* v. *City of London Real Property Co., Ltd.,* [1921] 1 K. B. 49. Periodic tenancies do not, of course, terminate in this sense, but remain contractual until the expiry of due notice. See also *supra,* pp. 365 and 417–20.

[2] *Morrison* v. *Jacobs,* [1945] K. B. 577; *Marcroft Wagons, Ltd.* v. *Smith,* [1951] 2 K. B. 496; [1951] 2 All E. R. 271; *Abbey* v. *Barnstyn,* [1930] 1 K. B. 660; *Murray Bull* v. *Murray,* [1953] 1 Q. B. 211; [1952] 2 All E. R. 1079; *Dealex Properties* v. *Brooks,* [1966] 1 Q. B. 542; [1965] 1 All E. R. 1080, especially *per* RUSSELL, L.J., at p. 554, at pp. 1084–5.

[3] The phrase appears to have been invented by Lord COLERIDGE, J., in *Hunt* v. *Bliss,* [1919] 36 T. L. R. 74, and has since crept into the Acts.

[4] *Per* EVERSHED, M.R., in *Dudley and District Benefit Building Society* v. *Emerson,* [1949] Ch. 707, at p. 717, [1949] 2 All E. R. 252.

[5] *Infra,* p. 439 and see *Solomon* v. *Orwell,* [1954] 1 W. L. R. 629, at pp. 631, 633; [1954] 1 All E. R. 874, at pp. 875–6.

[6] *Keeves* v. *Dean,* [1924] 1 K. B. 685; *Lovibond & Sons, Ltd.* v. *Vincent,* [1929] 1 K. B. 687. But as to assignment now see 1957 Act, s. 17 (2).

[7] *Cruise* v. *Terrell,* [1922] 1 K. B. 664; *Keeves* v. *Dean (supra); Marcroft Wagons, Ltd.* v. *Smith,* [1951] 2 K. B. 496, at p. 501; [1951] 2 All E. R. 271. It will not of course avail against title paramount.

[8] *Keeves* v. *Dean, supra,* at p. 686, *per* LUSH, J.

[9] *Reidy* v. *Walker,* [1933] 2 K. B. 266, at p. 272 *per* GODDARD, L.J. and see also *per* GODDARD, L.J. in *Dando* v. *Hitchcock,* [1954] 2 Q. B. 317; [1954] 2 All E. R. 335.

[10] *Skinner* v. *Geary,* [1931] 2 K. B. 546, the first case to enunciate this principle. The Acts are silent on the point. It must be emphasized that the position during a contractual tenancy is different: see *British Land Co.* v. *Herbert Silver (Menswear), Ltd.,* [1958] 1 Q. B. 530, at p. 539; [1958] 1 All E. R. 833. The residence rule we are now considering has no application.

[11] *Hiller* v. *United Dairies (London), Ltd.,* [1934] 1 K. B. 57; *Carter* v. *S.U. Carburettor Co.,* [1942] 2 K. B. 288; [1942] 2 All E. R. 228.

not lose statutory protection; neither does a tenant who is forced to spend several years in a sanatorium.[1] But if such a long absence does occur, the onus is on the tenant to explain it. To retain protection, the tenant must prove an intention to return to the house as his home *and* that this intention is corroborated by some "outward and visible sign."[2] Furniture, or a caretaker to maintain the house, are sufficient evidence; but the house can become nonoccupied by the caretaker abandoning the premises, and in such a case the tenant's protection is lost.[3]

Two homes.   The notion of "*a* home" does not preclude the possibility of a person having two homes. But the courts are cautious in protecting "two-house men"; the second house must be more than one used only occasionally, as a matter of convenience rather than as a home.[4] A man may very well have two homes, however, while carrying out a move of homes.[5]

Doctrine of transmission.   An important exception to the personal nature of a statutory tenancy is the doctrine of transmission, which derives from the Act of 1920. This principle of transmission is that, if a statutory tenant dies, his statutory tenancy is continued in favour of "the widow of a tenant who was residing with him at the time of his death or, where a tenant leaves no such widow or is a woman, such member of the tenant's family so residing[6] as aforesaid as may be decided in default of agreement by the county court."[7] The effect of transmission is that the new statutory tenant steps into the shoes of the old tenant for all purposes.[8] But, apart from the Act of 1965, such a transmission can only occur once. When the tenant in possession by virtue of transmission dies, protection ceases.[9]

Moodie v. Hosegood.   Until 1951, when the contractual, as distinct from the statutory, tenant of a controlled house died, it was thought that no transmission could take place. This loophole was filled by judicial interpretation when, in *Moodie* v. *Hosegood*,[10] the House of Lords held that a statutory tenancy did arise by transmission in such circumstances. The interest of a person entitled to the tenancy

---

[1] *Skinner* v. *Geary*, [1931] 2 K. B. 546; *Wigley* v. *Leigh*, [1950] 2 K. B. 305; [1950] 1 All E. R. 73.

[2] *Per* ASQUITH, L.J., in *Brown* v. *Brash*, [1948] 2 K. B. 247, at p. 254; [1948] 1 All E. R. 922, the leading case on this topic, and which establishes this dual test.

[3] *Brown* v. *Brash*, [1948] 2 K. B. 247; [1948] 1 All E. R. 922.

[4] *Langford Property Co., Ltd.* v. *Tureman*, [1949] 1 K. B. 29; [1948] 2 All E. R. 722; *Beck* v. *Scholz*, [1953] 1 Q. B. 570; [1953] 1 All E. R. 814.

[5] *Herbert* v. *Byrne*, [1964] 1 All E. R. 882, at p. 886, *per* Lord DENNING, M.R.; [1964] 1 W. L. R. 519, at pp. 526–7.

[6] In all cases save that of the widow, the residence requirement is 6 months as a minimum: 1933 Act, s. 13.

[7] 1920 Act, s. 12 (1) (g) as amended by 1933 Act, s. 13, 1954 Act, s. 42 (2). The section is further amended by the 1965 Act, see *infra*, p. 435.

[8] *Sherrin* v. *Brand*, [1956] 1 Q. B. 403; [1956] 1 All E. R. 194.

[9] *Pain* v. *Cobb* (1931), 146 L. T. 12; *Summers* v. *Donohue*, [1945] K. B. 376; [1945] 1 All E. R. 599.

[10] [1952] A. C. 61; [1951] 2 All E. R. 582; overruling earlier decisions to the opposite effect.

under the contractual tenant's will is postponed to the termination of the statutory tenancy.

Family, in the context of transmission, is not a technical term.[1] It includes not only blood relations but anyone who has by law *or* by conduct been received into the family as a member. It thus includes, in appropriate cases, illegitimate children.[2] Again a niece by marriage who had taken upon herself the obligations of a daughter was held to be within the family;[3] but it is difficult to generalize. Where a lady who had been living with her two cousins of the same age died, the two cousins were held not to be within the notion of her "family."[4] Where two or more members of the "family" compete to be statutory tenant, the county court may be forced to make a selection, for transmission cannot be to more than one person.[5] *Meaning of family.*

A considerable addition to the law of transmission was made by the Act of 1965. Section 13 of that Act makes provision for a second (but only a second) transmission, which will occur on the termination of the first transmitted tenancy, whether that tenancy was controlled or regulated. The status of the first transmitted tenancy will be controlled or regulated according to the status of the tenancy from which it derived, but a tenancy on a second transmission will automatically become regulated.[6] *Second transmission.*

A statutory tenancy will cease on surrender[7] by the tenant, but he is not absolved from giving due notice of his intention to do so.[8] A statutory tenancy will also cease on being replaced by another arrangement,[9] or if the dwelling house ceases to exist,[10] or if the *Determination of statutory tenancies.*

---

[1] *Price* v. *Gould* (1930), 143 L. T. 333; *Brock* v. *Wollams*, [1949] 2 K. B. 388; [1949] 1 All E. R. 175.

[2] In some cases, either of the unmarried parents may become a statutory tenant. *Gammans* v. *Ekins*, [1950] 2 K. B. 328; [1950] 2 All E. R. 140; *Hawes* v. *Evenden*, [1953] 1 W. L. R. 1169; [1953] 2 All E. R. 737; *Perry* v. *Dembrowski*, [1951] 2 K. B. 420. The courts will not so hold if a man and woman merely live together, without having children.

[3] *Jones* v. *Whitehill*, [1950] 2 K. B. 204; [1950] 1 All E. R. 71; Cf. *Ross* v. *Collins*, [1964] 1 All E. R. 861; [1964] 1 W. L. R. 425.

[4] *Langdon* v. *Horton*, [1951] 1 K. B. 666; [1951] 1 All E. R. 60.

[5] *Trayfoot* v. *Lock*, [1957] 1 All E. R. 423; [1957] 1. W. L. R. 351; *Dealex Properties, Ltd.* v. *Brooks*, [1966] 1 Q. B. 542; [1965] 1 All E. R. 1080. But the court has a wider discretion, as a result of the different wording of s. 13 (2) of the 1965 Act, to make more than one member of the family the regulated tenant on a *second* transmission. The position is not wholly clear however—see 29 *Conveyancer* at p. 436.

[6] Save for a second transmission in respect of premises used partly for business; the tenant in this case becomes a continuation tenant under s. 24 of the 1954 Act, see *infra*, p. 453.

[7] See *per* UPJOHN, L.J., in *Fredco Estates, Ltd.* v. *Bryant*, [1961] 1 All E. R. 34, at p. 46; [1961] 1 W. L. R. 76, at p. 91.

[8] 1920 Act, s. 15 (1). *King's College, Cambridge* v. *Kershman* (1948), 64 T. L. R. 547. Cf. *infra*, p. 437, ground (iii).

[9] *Foster* v. *Robinson*, [1951] 1 K. B. 149; [1950] 2 All E. R. 342. *Bungalows (Maidenhead), Ltd.* v. *Mason*, [1954] 1 All E. R. 1002; [1954] 1 W. L. R. 769; *Kingswood Estates Co., Ltd.* v. *Anderson*, [1963] 2 Q. B. 169; [1962] 3 All E. R. 593.

[10] *Ellis & Sons Amalgamated Properties, Ltd.* v. *Sisman*, [1948] 1 K. B. 653; [1948] 1 All E. R. 44; *Phillips* v. *Barnett*, [1922] 1 K. B. 222, at p. 226, *per*

circumstances change so as to take the tenancy out of the Acts, for instance by the payment of a rent which is less than two-thirds of the rateable value.[1]   Otherwise, a statutory tenancy can only terminate as provided under the Acts.

(v) Security of tenure and grounds of possession.

General protection of tenants.

To obtain possession against an unwilling tenant, contractual or statutory, the landlord must obtain an order of the County Court.[2]   It is an overriding requirement that no such order must be made unless the judge satisfies himself that it is reasonable to do so having regard to the general interests of the landlord, the tenant, and the public,[3] a task that he must perform in "a broad common-sense way as a man of the world".[4]   In addition, he must be satisfied that there exists one of the specified grounds of possession laid down in the Acts.   Furthermore, during a contractual as distinct from a statutory tenancy, a landlord must show that he is entitled to possession under the Acts *and* under the terms of the tenancy.[5]

Inviolability of the Acts.

The parties cannot contract out of their rights under the Acts, in respect of rent or of security of tenure,[6] save where this is expressly provided for in the Acts.[7]   Nor can estoppel exclude the Acts.[8]

Grounds for possession.

The statutory grounds for claiming possession are as follows:—

(i) Failure to pay rent or breach of covenant.[9]   Acceptance of rent by the landlord after knowledge of breach may constitute waiver, but not necessarily.[10]

Scrutton, L.J.   This is an important point of distinction from a contractual tenancy; a contractual tenant's interest would cover any new house erected on the land demised.

[1] *J. and F. Stone, Lighting & Radio, Ltd.* v. *Levitt,* [1947] A. C. 209.

[2] 1965 Act, s. 35;   *Peachey Property Coop., Ltd.* v. *Robinson,* [1966] 2 All E. R. 981, showing that judgment by default in the High Court is not effective.

[3] 1933 Act, s. 3 (1).   *Williamson* v. *Pallant,* [1924] 2 K. B. 173;   *Cresswell,* v. *Hodgson,* [1951] 2 K. B. 92; [1951] 1 All E. R. 710;   *Regional Properties Co. Ltd.* v. *Frankenschwerth* [1951] 1 K. B. 631;   *Yelland* v. *Taylor,* [1957] 1 All E. R. 627; [1957] 1 W. L. R. 459.

[4] *Per* Lord Greene, M.R., in *Cumming* v. *Danson,* [1942] 2 All E. R. 653, at p. 655.

[5] *Wolmer Securities, Ltd.* v. *Corne,* [1966] 2 Q. B. 243; [1966] 2 All E. R. 691. It has been pointed out, *supra,* p. 433, that protection for statutory tenants is confined to those in occupation of a house as a home, while the protection of a contractual tenant is not limited by this rule.

[6] *Artizans, Labourers and General Dwellings Co., Ltd.* v. *Whitaker,* [1919] 2 K. B. 301;   *Barton* v. *Fincham,* [1921] 2 K. B. 291;   *Schmit* v. *Christy,* [1922] 2 K. B. 60.   But a tenant who has agreed to give up possession in consideration of the landlord paying him a sum of money can sue for payment: *Rajbenback* v. *Mamon,* [1955] 1 Q. B. 283; [1955] 1 All E. R. 12.   Cf. also *Foster* v. *Robinson,* [1951] 1 K. B. 149; [1950] 2 All E. R. 342.

[7] S. 14 of 1965 Act, *infra,* p. 439.

[8] *Welch* v. *Nagy,* [1950] 1 K. B. 455; [1949] 2 All E. R. 868.   It is commonly said that the acts operate in *rem,* but this is not always a helpful guide: see *Critchley* v. *Clifford,* [1962] 1 Q. B. 131, at p. 148, *per* Danckwerts, L.J.; [1961] 3 All E. R. 288.

[9] 1933 Act, Sched. I (a) and Landlord and Tenant Act, 1954, Sched. II (4).

[10] *Oak Property Co.* v. *Chapman,* [1947] K. B. 886; [1947] 2 All E. R. 1; *Carter* v. *Green,* [1950] 2 K. B. 76; [1950] 1 All E. R. 627.

(ii) Conduct which is a nuisance or an annoyance to adjoining occupiers; use of the premises for an immoral or illegal purpose; or allowing the premises to deteriorate.[1]

(iii) Notice to quit given by the tenant, followed by steps taken by the landlord (e.g. a contract to sell or let) which would be prejudicial to him if he could not obtain possession as expected.[2]

(iv) An assignment or a sub-lease, without the consent of the landlord, of the whole of the house or, part being already sublet, the remainder of the house.[3]

The effect of this provision is that the consent of the landlord is necessary in the cases referred to whether or not the lease contains a prohibition against assignment or sub-letting. The policy behind this rule is that the tenant shall be protected in the use of the house as a home, not that he shall make a financial gain out of his privileged position.[4]

(v) Conduct prejudicial to the continuance of an off-licence in licensed premises.[5]

(vi) When a house subject to a service tenancy is occupied by an employee who has ceased to be employed by the landlord and the house is needed for another servant (whether that servant is to be a tenant or a licensee).[6]

(vii) When a landlord requires a house as a home for himself,[7] or a son or daughter over 18, or his father or mother, or (in the case of regulated tenancies only) his father-in-law or mother-in-law, *and* the judge is satisfied that greater hardship would result from not granting the order for possession than from granting it.[8] This provision will not operate in favour of a landlord who has purchased the house after a certain date, namely November 7th, 1956 in the case of controlled tenancies,

---

[1] 1933 Act, Sched. I (b).

[2] 1933 Act, Sched. I (c). Cf. *supra*, p. 435; notice to quit given by the tenant is not therefore enough of itself.

[3] 1933 Act, Sched. I (d), and 1965 Act, Sched. I, para. 12 (1). *Regional Properties Co., Ltd.* v. *Frankenschwerth*, [1951] 1 K. B. 631; [1951] 1 All E. R. 178. Subsequent, even implied consent suffices; *Hyde* v. *Pimley*, [1952] 2 Q. B. 506; [1952] 2 All E. R. 102.

[4] Cf. *supra*, p. 433 and *infra*, p. 440.

[5] 1933 Act, Sched. I (e). This does not apply to regulated tenancies, as business tenancies are outside the 1965 Act: 1965 Act, Sched. I, para. 12 (2).

[6] 1933 Act, Sched. I (g); see *supra*, p. 424 for service tenants. Difficulties have been experienced in determining when a servant becomes " engaged in " employment: *Beninga (Mitcham), Ltd.* v. *Bijstra*, [1946] K. B. 58, *R. F. Fuggle, Ltd.* v. *Gadsden* [1948] 2 K. B. 236; [1948] 2 All E. R. 160. See also ss. 16 and 33 of the 1965 Act for the special position of agricultural cottages.

[7] A landlord may require the house for " himself " if he needs it for his children and a housekeeper: *Smith* v. *Penny*, [1947] K. B. 230; [1946] 2 All E. R. 672. But he can not claim space in which to instal a family just so that he can be looked after: *Richter* v. *Wilson*, [1963] 2 Q. B. 426; [1963] 2 All E. R. 335.

[8] 1933 Act, Sched. I (h) and 1965 Act, Sched. I, para. 12 (3).

March 23rd, 1965 in the case of regulated tenancies.[1] "Pur-chase" in this context has caused difficulties, but it is not a technical expression. It will cover the purchaser of a reversion only,[2] but it will not cover a devisee (unless the testator was himself a purchaser[3]). Moreover, only the tenant at the time of the purchase will be protected in this way.[4] The object of the disqualification is only

> "that people should not be able to buy houses over the heads of the "tenants and then remove them without giving them alternative "accommodation."[5]

The onus is on the landlord to bring himself within this ground of obtaining possession but, having done so, the burden of proving that greater hardship would result from a grant of possession than a refusal lies upon the tenant.[6] This is a question of fact[7] for the judge, who must take a wide variety of circumstances into account, including of course alternative accommodation.[8]

(viii) The provision of suitable alternative accommodation.[9] The onus here is on the landlord,[10] and he must show that the alternative accommodation (i) confers a reasonably equivalent security of tenure, by way of the Rent Acts or a lease of substan-tial length, and (ii) is convenient as regards proximity to place of work[11], and (iii) is

> "similar as regards rental and extent to the accommodation afforded "by dwelling-houses provided in the neighbourhood by any housing "authority[12] for persons whose needs as regards extent are, in the opin-"ion of the court, similar to those of the tenant and his family; or other-"wise reasonably suitable to the means of the tenant and to the needs "of the tenant and his family as regards extent and character."[13]

1957 Act, Sched. VI, para. 21; 1965 Act, Sched. I, para. 12 (3).

[2] *Wright* v. *Walford*, [1955] 1 Q. B. 363; [1955] 1 All E. R. 207; cf. *Powell* v. *Cleland*, [1948] 1 K. B. 262; [1947] 2 All E. R. 672.

[3] *Baker* v. *Lewis*, [1947] K. B. 186; [1946] 2 All E. R. 592; *Littlechild* v. *Holt*, [1950] 1 K. B. 1; [1949] 1 All E. R. 933.

[4] *Epps* v. *Rothnie*, [1945] K. B. 562; *Fowle* v. *Bell*, [1947] K. B. 242; [1946] 2 All E. R. 668. A sub-tenant at the time of the purchase is not pro-tected: *Cairns* v. *Piper*, [1954] 2 Q. B. 210.; [1954] 2 All E. R. 611.

[5] *Littlechild* v. *Holt*, [1950] 1 K. B. 1, at p. 7, *per* Denning, L.J.; [1949] 1 All E. R. 933.

[6] *Sims* v. *Wilson*, [1946] 2 All E. R. 261, especially *per* Morton, L.J., at p. 263.

[7] *Coplans* v. *King*, [1947] 2 All E. R. 393.

[8] See especially *Harte* v. *Frampton*, [1948] 1 K.B. 73, at p. 79, *per* Asquith, L.J.; [1947] 2 All E. R. 604.

[9] 1933 Act, s. 3 (1).

[10] *Nevile* v. *Hardy*, [1921] 1 Ch. 404, at p. 408, *per* Peterson, J.

[11] A business being carried on *in* a dwelling house raises different considera-tions; *Middlesex County Council* v. *Hall*, [1929] 2 K. B. 110; see also *Warren* v. *Austin*, [1947] 2 All E. R. 185, where the Court of Appeal held that space for lodgers was a relevant factor.

[12] Certificates may be given by a housing authority as to these matters and as to provision of housing by the authority itself: 1933 Act, ss. 3 (2) and 3 (4).

[13] 1933 Act, s. 3 (3) (b) (i) and (ii), conferring a wide discretion on the county court: *Creswell* v. *Hodgson*, [1951] 2 K. B. 92; [1951] 1 All E. R. 710. The alternative accommodation may be suitable although it is less attractive,

The specific reference to "family" is important. The alternative accommodation will normally only be suitable if the tenant and his family can live in it as a unit.[1] "Family", though it covers e.g., married children with their families, is confined to those who have made their home with the tenant.[2] It is not a technical term and even a lodger may, in the course of time, come to be a member of the family.

(ix) Sub-letting at an excessive rent.[3] In such a case possession may be given of part or all of the house.

(x) Overcrowding caused by the tenant.[4]

In very limited circumstances, and only in respect of regulated tenancies, it is possible under the 1965 Act[5] for the landlord to modify the tenant's statutory security of tenure. This power exists only where a landlord was formerly the owner-occupier of the house *and* where, *before* the commencement of *each* tenancy since granted in respect of that house, he gives to the tenant notice in writing that the house might in the future be required as a residence for the landlord "or any member of his family who resided with the owner-occupier when he last occupied the dwelling-house as a residence." If this circumstance should come about, the court must grant possession, irrespective of hardship or reasonableness.[6]

Limited power to modify security of tenure.

(vi) Sub-tenancies.

A sub-tenancy which comes within the Acts is protected even though the head tenancy is outside the Acts, as for instance when the latter is an agricultural holding. It is the letting to the occupying sub-tenant that is material.[7] But in such a case, protection lasts only so long as the head tenancy lasts.[8]

Unprotected head tenancy.

When a tenant protected under the Rent Acts lawfully creates a residential sub-tenancy[9] the operation of the Acts is affected, but not excluded. The house is still let to the head tenant so that he does not lose all protection, but the sub-tenant is protected

Protected head tenancy.

---

or although the rent is higher. It may also be suitable if it is part of the house already occupied: *Parmee* v. *Mitchell*, [1950] 2 K. B. 199; [1950] 1 All E. R. 872.

[1] *Sheehan* v. *Cutler*, [1946] K. B. 339; *Selwyn* v. *Hamill*, [1948] 1 All E. R. 70.

[2] *Standingford* v. *Probert*, [1950] 1 K. B. 377; [1949] 2 All E. R. 861, the leading authority; cf. *Darnell* v. *Milwood*, [1951] 1 All E. R. 88.

[3] 1933 Act, s. 4 (1). Cf. note 9, *infra*.

[4] Housing Act, 1957, s. 84, replacing 1933 Act, Sched. I (f).

[5] S. 14.

[6] It has been suggested that for s. 14 to apply, the original landlord must be the plaintiff, but there does not seem to be justification for this limitation in the section, nor does it accord with the protection being extended to the owner occupier *or* a resident member of his family: see 29 *Conveyancer* 429, at p. 442.

[7] *Critchley* v. *Clifford*, [1962] 1 Q. B. 131; [1961] 3 All E. R. 288.

[8] *Critchley* v. *Clifford*, *supra*, at p. 147 and 150: save under the operation of s. 41 of the 1954 Act, *infra*, p. 441.

[9] The tenant must inform the landlord of the terms of the sub-tenancy: 1933 Act, s. 4 (4), 1939 Act, Sched. 1. But it must be remembered that leases frequently contain stringent conditions relating to sub-letting.

against both his landlord and the head landlord. The requirements for the sub-tenancy to come within the Acts are the same as in the case of a head tenancy, but there are further rules to solve the particular problems created by sub-tenancies.

Sub-lease of the whole. Under the more recent Acts, "the tenant is given a reasonably free hand to deal with the premises as he thinks fit."[1] If he lets unfurnished, the position will depend on whether the sub-lease is of the whole or only a part and, in the case of a contractual tenancy, on the terms of the tenancy. A statutory tenant who sub-lets the whole so that he ceases to be resident, thereby loses the protection of the Acts.[2] But if he sub-lets a part or parts while continuing **Sub-lease of part.** to reside in the house, and without having abandoned the intention ever to re-occupy the parts sub-let, he remains protected in respect *of the whole.*[3] A sub-tenant in these cases is protected not only during, but also after the termination of, the head tenancy, whatever the cause, voluntary or hostile, of that termination;[4] provided only that the sub-tenancy is lawful and not in breach of covenant.[5] The sub-tenant is protected unless there is a distinct ground for giving possession against him. In effect, he steps into the shoes of the tenant, neither gaining nor losing by his change of position, a principle that holds good for contractual and statutory tenancies.[6] But the principle worked out by the courts is that, for the sub-tenant to secure this protection after the head tenancy (whether contractual or statutory) ceases, both the tenancy[7] *and* the sub-tenancy[8] must have been

---

[1] Per JENKINS, L.J., in *Shackleton* v. *Greenhalgh*, [1951] 1 K. B. 725, at p. 730; [1950] 2 All E. R. 1223. The importance of this is for statutory tenancies. The right of the contractual tenant to sub-let is inherent; but even in this case the sub-tenant has to be protected.

[2] *Haskins* v. *Lewis*, [1931] 2 K. B. 1; *Finkle* v. *Strzelczyk*, [1961] 3 All E. R. 409; [1961] 1 W. L. R. 1201. In effect, this is not distinguishable from an assignment. A landlord can of course assent to such a sub-lease. And see *supra*, pp. 433 and 437.

[3] *Roe* v. *Russell*, [1928] 2 K. B. 117; *Berkeley* v. *Papadoyannis*, [1954] 2 Q. B. 149; [1954] 2 All E. R. 409. *Baker* v. *Turner*, [1950] A. C. 401, at p. 433, [1950] 1 All E. R. 834, *per* Lord MACDERMOTT. The position may be different if parts *never* occupied by the tenant are sub-let; possession may be obtained against the tenant: *Crowhurst* v. *Maidment*, [1953] 1 Q. B. 23; [1952] 2 All E. R. 808.

[4] 1920 Act, s. 15 (3) and 15 (5), overlapping provisions. See also 1923 Act, s. 4. *Ward* v. *Larkins*, (1923), 130 L.T. 184; *Lewis* v. *Reeves*, [1952] 1 K. B. 19 (where at p. 26, DENNING, L.J., points out that the sub-tenant is better protected than the tenant's family—see *infra.*, p. 434).

[5] *Dobbs* v. *Linford*, [1953] 1 Q. B. 48; [1952] 2 All E. R. 827; *Drive Yourself Hire Co. (London), Ltd.* v. *Strutt*, [1954] 1 Q. B. 250; [1953] 2 All E. R. 1475. As to waiver by the landlord, see *Oak Property Co.* v. *Chapman*, [1947] K. B. 886; [1947] 2 All E. R. 1, and *Carter* v. *Green*, [1950] 2 K. B. 76; [1950] 1 All E. R. 627.

[6] *Stanley* v. *Compton*, [1951] 1 All E. R. 859 and see, generally, *Haskins* v. *Lewis*, [1931] 2 K. B. 1. *Quaere*, is the protection of the sub-tenant of a hitherto contractual tenant correctly described as a "statutory tenancy."

[7] *Cow* v. *Casey*, [1949] 1 K.B. 474; [1949] 1 All E. R. 197; *Knight* v. *Olive*, [1954] 1 Q. B. 514; [1954] 1 All E. R. 701; *Knightsbridge Estates Trust, Ltd.* v. *Deeley*, [1950] 2 K. B. 228; [1950] 1 All E. R. 577.

[8] *Stanley* v. *Compton*, [1951] 1 All E. R. 859, especially at p. 863, *per* DENNING, L.J.

within the Acts. In respect of sub-tenancies, this principle has been rigidly adhered to; for instance, in relation to furnished and to unfurnished but shared sub-tenancies, the courts have refused to allow the sub-tenant to acquire greater protection against the head landlord on the termination of the head tenancy.[1] But the legislature has relaxed this rule so far as the position of the head tenancy is concerned.[2] For instance, if the rateable value of the whole premises let to the head tenant takes the premises outside the Acts, but the rateable value of the part sub-let is within the limits of protection, section 41 of the Act of 1954 requires the head tenancy to be treated as if it were a separate tenancy of the part sub-let. Accordingly, the sub-tenant is brought within the protection given on the termination of the head tenancy. But section 41 only applies where the head tenancy is of "something in the nature of buildings",[3] and would not apply where the head tenancy was an agricultural holding.[4]

If a tenant of an unfurnished house protected by the Rent Acts lets the whole of it furnished, both tenant and sub-tenant will be protected by and only by the 1946 Act.[5] The whole house is regarded as furnished. The protection of the Rent Acts will however revive when the sub-tenancy ends if, in the meanwhile, the landlord has taken no action to recover possession.[6] If the furnished sub-tenancy is only of a part, the position is again different for, under section 9 of the Act of 1949, the tenant *and* sub-tenant enjoy the protection of the Rent Acts against the landlord even though, as against the tenant, the sub-tenant only enjoys the more limited protection of the 1946 Act. The sub-tenant is protected by the Rent Acts however only while the tenant retains his tenancy; thereafter his protection is under the 1946 Act.[7] *(Furnished sub-tenancies.)*

An order for possession granted against a tenant, even if it affects the whole premises, will not affect a sub-tenant, but will suffice only to deprive the tenant of protection.[8] To obtain *(Orders for possession.)*

---

[1] *Shackleton* v. *Greenhalgh*, [1951] 1 K. B. 725; [1950] 2 All E. R. 1223; *Solomon* v. *Orwell*, [1954] 1 All E. R. 874; [1954] 1 W. L. R. 629.

[2] Housing Repairs and Rents Act, 1954, s. 41 reversing the effect of the cases cited in note 7 on p. 440. Sub-tenants are also protected when the head tenancy is for a period exceeding 21 years; Landlord and Tenant Act, 1954, s. 2, s. 15 (1), 1957 Act, s. 21 (1).

[3] *Per* UPJOHN, L.J., in *Hobhouse* v. *Wall*, [1963] 2 Q. B. 124, at p. 132; [1963] 1 All E. R. 701. The Court of Appeal would not go beyond this rather elusive phrase. For a criticism, see 1963 Jo. Planning Law 330.

[4] See *Critchley* v. *Clifford*, *supra*, p. 439, for the limited protection available.

[5] *Glossop* v. *Ashley*, [1922] 1 K. B. 1; *Prout* v. *Hunter*, [1924] 2 K. B. 736; this is not ordinarily applicable to residential licences: *E. Moss, Ltd.* v. *Brown*, [1946] 2 All E. R. 557. But if the tenant ceases to reside, he may lose his protection on that ground.

[6] *Leslie and Co.* v. *Cumming*, [1926] 2 K. B. 417.

[7] By virtue of s. 7 of the 1949 Act. Similarly with a sub-tenant of unfurnished rooms who shares living accommodation with the tenant and the tenant's interest ceases: *Shackleton* v. *Greenhalgh*, [1951] 1 K. B. 725; [1950] 2 All E. R. 1223; *Solomon* v. *Orwell*, [1954] 1 All E. R. 874; [1954] 1 W. L. R. 629.

[8] *Haskins* v. *Lewis*, [1931] 2 K. B. 1; 1920 Act, s. 15; a sub-lease of the whole premises will lose the protection of the Acts, but may still be lawful.

possession against a protected sub-tenant, a landlord must show a ground of possession against the sub-tenant. The two cases must be considered independently of each other,[1] though it is common for them to be heard and decided in one action.

These complicated rules can be summed up, in general, in this way: If a tenant within the Acts sub-lets the whole house *unfurnished*, no statutory tenancy will arise in his favour, but if possession of the whole premises is awarded against him, the sub-tenant can step into his place; the sub-tenant will also step into his place if the tenancy determines on other grounds. If only part is sub-let, and the tenant remains in his part without abandoning the other parts altogether, the tenant is protected in respect of the whole; but in certain cases, he may remain protected only in respect of the part he lives in; the sub-tenant is protected as above. If the whole house is let *furnished*, the 1946 Act governs the whole: if only part is so let, the tenant can retain Rent Act protection, but the sub-tenant is not protected after the head tenancy ends; this principle also applies to shared sub-tenancies. If a head tenancy is outside the Acts, a sub-tenant may nevertheless be protected by the Acts; but after the head tenancy ends, the sub-tenant has to rely on the provisions of the Act of 1954.

(B) FURNISHED LETTINGS.

We have now seen that, in the case of unfurnished lettings for not more than 21 years, a tenant is protected during his contractual tenancy by the rent limit, and after its termination by the rent limit and the statutory tenancy; we have also seen that the 1965 Act introduces machinery for determining and registering fair rents on a regional basis.

1946 Act, and its relation to the Rent Acts.

For furnished lettings, a very limited degree of protection was provided for the tenant in 1920,[2] but it proved inadequate. A new system of controlling such lettings was introduced in 1946.[3] Its aim was to control rents rather than to give security of tenure, but the latter aspect of the system is developed in the Act of 1965. Rents under the 1946 Act are registrable in a public register; but the tribunals that determine the rents are not concerned, as the 1965 rent officers and panels are, with the general problems of rent levels in a district.[4] The 1946 Act and Rent Act systems co-exist as their functions are almost entirely[5] exclusive of each other's;

---

[1] *Enniskillen Urban District Council* v. *Bartley*, [1947] N. 1. 177.

[2] 1920 Act, ss. 9 and 10; these sections were repealed by the 1957 Acts.

[3] The Furnished Houses (Rent Control) Act, 1946. Its provisions also affect certain shared unfurnished tenancies; *supra*, pp. 426 and 441.

[4] *R* v. *Paddington and St. Marylebone Rent Tribunal, ex parte Bell London and Provincial Properties, Ltd.*, [1949] 1 K. B. 666, at p. 680, *per* Lord GODDARD, C.J.; [1949] 1 All E. R. 720. (The '*Bell*' Case').

[5] A partly furnished house can fall into both systems, since there may be enough furniture to attract the 1946 Act without excluding the Rent Acts. In such a case the principle of the '*Bedrock* Case' (see next note) applies; the rent of the premises furnished can not be reduced to less than the Rent Act limit.

but the rent of a furnished letting of a house for which a rent has been registered under the 1965 Act cannot be reduced, under the 1946 Act, to a figure less than the recoverable 1965 Act rent.[1] Obviously, it can be more.

The 1946 Act, which first made provision for rent tribunals to be set up throughout the country, now applies, as amended, to all houses or parts of houses the rateable value of which does not exceed £400 in London and £200 elsewhere; an apportionment of values where only part is let can be made either by the tribunal or by the county court.[2] As in the case of the Rent Acts, the Minister of Housing is given power to decontrol; it may be by the class of house or by the area.[3]

Jurisdiction based on rateable values.

For the Act to apply, two main conditions must be satisfied:[4] first, there must be a contract[5] granting the right to occupy[6] a house or part of a house as a residence. Such a contract is the basis of the tribunal's jurisdiction, and therefore it must be in existence[7] at the time when reference of a case to the tribunal is made. Indeed, if an existing contract is referred to a tribunal, the case must be heard even if the tenant surrenders his interest in the premises before the date of the hearing, unless the reference is withdrawn.[8] The contract need not amount to a tenancy in the strict sense, for lodgers as well as tenants are protected.[9] On the other hand the accommodation must be occupied "as a residence," hence neither ordinary hotel accommodation[10] nor a tenancy granted to a corporation is covered by the Act. The Acts specifically exclude lettings where the rent includes payment for board,[11] and "holiday-lets."[12]

Occupation as a residence.

---

[1] 1965 Act, s. 39 (5). The courts had previously evolved an analogous rule for houses within the ambit of Rent Act control. *R* v. *Paddington and St. Marylebone Rent Tribunal, ex parte Bedrock Investments, Ltd.*, [1947] K. B. 984; [1947] 2 All E. R. 15 (the '*Bedrock* Case'); *R* v. *Fulham, Hammersmith and Kensington Rent Tribunal, ex parte Marks*, [1951] 2 K. B. 694; [1951] 2 All E. R. 465 (*Marks'* Case). This rule continues to govern controlled houses.

[2] 1965 Act, ss. 39 (2), 39 (3) and 43.

[3] 1965 Act, ss. 39 (2) (b) and 39 (4).

[4] 1946 Act, s. 2 (1).

[5] By virtue of 1965 Act, s. 39 (10), successors in title to the original contracting parties are included; hence assignees can take advantage of the 1946 Act. Sub-lessees are not protected against the head landlord under the 1946 legislation.

[6] "Use in common with any other person of other rooms" (s. 2 (1)) does not matter, so long as there is exclusive occupation of at least one room.

[7] A notice to quit which has not yet come into effect does not prevent there being a referable contract; see *R* v. *London, etc., Rent Tribunal, ex parte Honig*, [1951] 1 K. B. 641, at p. 644, *per* Lord GODDARD, C.J.; [1951] 1 All E. R. 195.

[8] *R* v. *West London Rent Tribunal, ex parte Napper*, [1965] 3 All E. R. 734.

[9] *R* v. *Battersea, Wandsworth, Mitcham and Wimbledon Rent Tribunal, ex parte Parikh*, [1957] 1 All E. R. 352; [1957] 1 W. L. R. 410.

[10] *R* v. *Rent Tribunals for Bethnal Green and Paddington, ex parte Rowton Houses, Ltd.*, (1947), 91 Sol. J. 255.

[11] 1946 Act, s. 12 (3). The value of the board to the lessee must form a substantial proportion of the whole rent.

[12] 1965 Act, s. 39 (11).

Furniture
or services.

Secondly, the right to occupy the accommodation must be "in consideration of a rent which includes payment for the use of furniture or for services."[1] There being no specific requirement that the proportion of rent payable for the furniture must be substantial, the *de minimis* principle is applied. Thus, where the only furniture in a flat consisted of an electric clock and curtains in two rooms, the jurisdiction of the tribunal was excluded.[2] "Furniture" has the same meaning as under the Rent Acts,[3] but "services" includes not only attendance but also

> "the provision of heating and lighting, the supply of hot water and
> "any other privilege or facility connected with the occupancy of a
> "house, not being a privilege or facility requisite for the purpose of
> "access, cold water supply or sanitary accommodation."[4]

A tribunal, in deciding whether it has jurisdiction, will take into account any furniture provided by the landlord even though he is not contractually bound to provide it; it is presumed that the rent includes payment for the use of any furniture. The same is not true, however, of services which the landlord is under no obligation to provide, such as a porter at a block of flats; it cannot be presumed that payment for such voluntary services is included in the rent, and therefore they must be disregarded.[5] Moreover, the courts will not usually be prepared to imply a covenant to provide such services,

> "unless there is such a necessary implication that the court can have
> "no doubt what covenant or undertaking they ought to write into
> "the agreement."[6]

Hence, where a notice was displayed outside a block of flats saying "Flats to let, central heating, constant hot water" and each flat contained a radiator, a bathroom and kitchen utensils but no means of heating water, the court refused to imply a term to provide central heating and hot water in the tenancy agreement.[7] If the tenant maintains that the lease has omitted to provide services for which he bargained, the appropriate remedy is rectification and not an application to the rent tribunal, for a rent tribunal has no

---

[1] 1946 Act, s. 2 (1). Where separate sums are payable for premises, furniture and services, the rent is the total amount payable: 1949 Act, s. 12 (2).

[2] *R. v. Blackpool Rent Tribunal, ex parte Ashton*, [1948] 2 K. B. 277; [1948] 1 All E. R. 900.

[3] *R. v. Hampstead and St. Pancras Furnished Houses Rent Tribunal, ex parte Ascot Lodge, Ltd.*, [1947] K. B. 973; [1947] 2 All E. R. 12.

[4] 1946 Act, s. 12 (1).

[5] *R. v. Hampstead and St. Pancras Furnished Houses Rent Tribunal, ex parte Ascot Lodge, Ltd., supra; R. v. Blackpool Rent Tribunal, ex parte Ashton, supra.* Cf. *infra*, p. 445, note 5.

[6] *R. v. Paddington and St. Marylebone Rent Tribunal, ex parte Bedrock Investments, Ltd.*, [1947] K. B. 984, at p. 990; *per* Lord Goddard, C.J.; [1947] 2 All E. R. 15, at p. 17.

[7] *R. v. Croydon and District Rent Tribunal, ex parte Langford Property*, [1948] 1 K. B. 60.

power to rectify and can only consider the existing contract.[1]
Similarly, services which the landlord is contractually bound to
provide, but which in breach of contract he is not providing are
ignored, for breach of contract is no concern of the tribunals.[2]

Either party to a contract that is within the Act, or the local
authority,[3] can set the tribunal in motion. All that is required is a
written notice, which need not be in any particular form.[4] On a
first reference in respect of particular premises, the tribunal may
approve or reduce the contractual rent, but can only increase it if
the rent includes payment for services.[5] A rent so fixed will be
registered with the local authority and will constitute a rent limit
for all subsequent furnished[6] lettings of those premises.[7] If the
rent so fixed is different from the contractual rent, then the contract takes effect for the future, but not retrospectively,[8] in this
varied form.[9]

First
reference.

Only if there has been a relevant change of circumstances may
there be another reference to the tribunal.[10] But if there has been
such a change, in addition to its above powers, the tribunal now has,
on this second or subsequent reference, the power to increase the
rent. The tribunal, in estimating the proper alteration in rent in
respect of the new circumstances, must not however consider the
whole case afresh; the original determination of rent does not
cease to have relevance.[11] On registration of a new rent, the consequences are as on first registration.

Change of
circum-
stances.

Rent paid in excess of the amount entered in the register can

Con-
sequences
of registra-
tion.

---

[1] *R.* v. *Paddington and St. Marylebone Rent Tribunal*; *R.* v. *Croydon and District Rent Tribunal, supra*.

[2] *Bell* Case, [1949] 1 K. B. 666, at p. 684, *per* Lord GODDARD, C.J.; [1949] 1 All E. R. 720; *Bedrock* Case, [1947] K. B. 984, at p. 990, *per* Lord GODDARD, C.J.; [1947] 2 All E. R. 15. But in determing the fair rent, as distinct from determining jursidiction, the tribunal must take into account voluntary, i.e. non-contractual services, which "the landlord in fact is supplying and the tenant enjoying, and which there is every reason to suppose will be continued." *Bell* Case, [1949] 1 K. B. 666 at p. 684.,

[3] *Bell* Case, *supra*, followed in *R.* v. *West London Rent Tribunal, ex parte Napper*, [1965] 3 All E. R. 734.

[4] 1946 Act, s. 2 (1). *Francis Jackson Developments, Ltd.* v. *Hall*, [1951] 2 K. B. 488,; [1951] 2 All E. R. 74.

[5] 1946 Act, ss. 2 (2) and 2 (4); any such increase can only be in respect of the increased cost of providing those services.

[6] But it will not govern, for instance, a new letting with board. The land-lord may change the furniture, however!

[7] But it in no way governs a letting of part of those premises: *Gluchowska* v. *Tottenham Borough Council*, [1954] 1 Q. B. 439; [1954] 1 All E. R. 408.

[8] *Bowness* v. *O'Dwyer*, [1948] 2 K. B. 219, at p. 225, *per* EVERSHED, L.J.: [1948] 2 All E. R. 81.

[9] *Villa d'Este Restaurant* v. *Burton*, [1957] 2 Q. B. 214; [1957] 1 All E. R. 862, showing that this rule applies to a furnished letting for a period of years.

[10] 1946 Act, s. 2 (3); *De Jean* v. *Fletcher*, [1959] 1 All E. R. 602; [1959] 1 W. L. R. 341; note, however, that s. 2 (5) of the 1946 Act enables a tribunal to limit its decision to a specific future period of time.

[11] *R.* v. *Fulham, Hammersmith and Kensington Rent Tribunal, ex parte Gormly*, [1952] 1 K. B. 179; [1951] 2 All E. R. 1030; *R.* v. *Fulham, Hammersmith and Kensington Rent Tribunal, ex parte Hierowski*, [1953] 2 Q. B. 147; [1953] 2 All E. R. 4.

be recovered by the tenant; it is also an offence for a landlord to require such payment.[1] Premiums are also prohibited.[2]

Procedure and appeals.

In determining the fair rent, a tribunal can take a most wide variety of matters into account, even those based on its own knowledge.[3] "These tribunals act on all kinds of evidence which no court of law would look at for a minute."[4] The tribunal can also visit the premises concerned. The hearing, which is a public one, is most informal; the parties need not appear and only if they give notice that they desire to be heard need they be given notice of when and where the tribunal will meet. The tribunal should, however, have all the necessary facts before it; if, for instance, it has mistaken the identity of the landlord, its decision cannot stand.[5] The tribunal must give reasoned decisions, however, if so required, and there is now an appeal on points of law to the Divisional Court.[6] Prior to 1959, an aggrieved party could only proceed by writ such as *certiorari*; this jurisdiction must still be borne in mind, but is not of such crucial importance now that an appeal is possible.

Security of tenure.

Rent tribunals have a limited discretion to give tenants of furnished homes some security of tenure. This discretion exists where a tenancy can be determined only by a notice to quit, i.e., a periodic tenancy, and does not exist where the tenancy is for a fixed term and expires automatically.[7] But the discretion exists whether the notice to quit is served before or after the reference to the tribunal.[8] The effect of section 11 of the 1949 Act, as amended

---

[1] 1946 Act, ss. 4 and 9 as amended by the 1949 Act, s. 12 (4). A tenant who pays the excess aids and abets the offence.

[2] 1949 Act, s. 12.

[3] But this indulgence does not extend to issues never mentioned at the hearing which a party may have wished to rebut: *Bell* Case, [1949] 1 K. B. 666; [1949] 1 All E. R. 720.

[4] *R. v. London, etc., Rent Tribunal, ex parte Honig*, [1951] 1 K. B. 641, at p. 646, *per* Lord GODDARD, C.J.; [1951] 1 All E. R. 195.

[5] For his circumstances, commitments and expenses are vital; it is not just a matter of the rooms as rooms: *R. v. Paddington and St. Marylebone Rent Tribunal, ex parte Haines*, [1962] 1 Q. B. 388; [1961] 3 All E. R. 1047.

[6] Tribunals and Inquiries Act, 1958, ss. 9 and 12, Sched. I.

[7] As Megarry points out (*The Rent Acts*, (9th Edn.), p. 494), "The moral (if it can be called such) for tenants is to obtain by contract the desired security of tenure, if need be at an excessive rent, and then to refer the contract to a tribunal. The moral for landlords is to grant a tenancy for a short but fixed term." See also the comments of JENKINS, L.J., in *Mauray* v. *Durley Chine (Investments), Ltd.*, [1953] 2 Q. B. 433, at p. 448; [1953] 2 All E. R. 458. This situation is not materially affected by the restrictions on obtaining possession in the 1965 Act: s. 32 (1) (b).

[8] 1965 Act, s. 39 (6) (a), amending s. 11 of the 1949 Act. This is an important change for, hitherto, the reference had to precede the notice. S. 39 (6) (a) only affects s. 11 of the 1949 Act; the old position continues to govern a reference under s. 5 of the 1946 Act. [Under this section, on a reference by a local authority or a lessee being *followed* (within six months of the tribunal's decision) by a notice to quit, that six months' security is obtained, subject only to the power of the tribunal to substitute a lesser period, and to s. 39 (7) of the 1965 Act.] But s. 39 (6) (a) appears to qualify s. 11 (5) of the 1949 Act, which provided that s. 11 was to be construed as one with the 1946 Act, and overrules *R. v. Folkestone and Area Rent Tribunal, ex parte Sharkey*, [1952] 1 K. B. 54. S. 39 (6) (a) thus appears to make s. 11 into a new and independent power,

by section 39 (8) of the 1965 Act, is to postpone the operation of a
notice to quit for a period of up to six months.[1] This six months
is not the limit of possible security, however, as successive applications can be made, apparently without limit. The tribunals will
not however renew security indefinitely.[2] Moreover, under
section 39 (7) of the 1965 Act a tribunal can be asked by a lessor to
bring a letting to an end even before the end of a period of security
already obtained, if the tenant has broken a term of his contract,
or caused nuisances etc.

The security afforded under these provisions is obtained by
postponing the operation of a notice to quit. The effect of such a
postponement would appear to be the prolongation of the contractual letting. This was assumed to be so in the opinion of
Lord PORTER in *Preston and Area Rent Tribunal* v. *Pickavance*,[3] and
it is submitted that it is preferable to the view that a contractual
letting is replaced by a non-contractual statutory tenancy.[4] **Form of the security.**

Finally, under section 40 of the 1965 Act, there is a possibility
of excluding these provisions for security of tenure. This possibility
is open only to a landlord who, at or before the time when the contract of letting was made, was able to and did give notice to the incoming tenant that, either then or previously, he occupied the
house as his residence. Provided that he has not continued to
reside in part of the house, the effect of this notice will be to exclude the security of tenure provisions if, at the time the landlord's
notice to quit takes effect, the landlord requires the house either
for himself or **Exclusion of security.**

> "a member of his family, who resided with him when he last occupied
> "the dwelling as a residence."[5]

(2) AGRICULTURAL TENANCIES.

Before the war of 1914, the farming industry rested in effect
upon a friendly partnership between the landlord and tenant,
under which the former found the capital and the latter did the
work. After the war, however, economic pressure brought this
system to an end, and it is estimated that between 1919 and 1927
some 100,000 farmers became occupying owners, with the in- **The policy in the case of agricul- tural tenancies.**

---

by reversing the view of the Divisional Court in the *Sharkey* Case [1952] 1
K. B. 54, at p. 58; [1951] 2 All E. R. 921; that "section 11 is not intended to
create a power but is only extending a power which a tribunal would have had
when acting under section 5 of the earlier Act." And see generally *Preston
and Area Rent Tribunal* v. *Pickavance*, [1953] A.C. 562, [1953] 2 All E. R. 438.
  [1] *Alexander* v. *Springate*, [1951] 1 K. B. 803; [1951] 1 All E. R. 351; pre-
ferably to the expiry of the tenancy current at that time—see Megarry, *The
Rent Acts* (9th Edn.), p. 495.
  [2] And see 1949 Act, s. 11 (4).
  [3] [1953] A. C. 562, at pp. 572, 574; [1953] 2 All E. R. 438.
  [4] Nevertheless this was the ratio of the Court of Appeal in *Francis Jackson
Developments, Ltd.* v. *Hall*, [1951] 2 K. B. 488; [1951] 2 All E. R. 74. This
decision has been severely criticised: see Megarry, *The Rent Acts*, (9th Edn.),
pp. 499–500.
  [5] Cf. the slightly different provisions in the Rent Acts, *supra*, p. 437.

evitable result that the industry became seriously under-capitalized. The imposition of tariffs and the introduction of marketing schemes did little to cure this evil, and on the outbreak of war in 1939 the Government was compelled to introduce a national plan for agriculture, involving a vast expenditure of money, designed to stimulate the production of home-grown food. In order to prevent a waste of this public money, County War Agricultural Committees were established, which were entrusted with the task of promoting agricultural development and efficiency and were empowered *inter alia* to dispossess an inefficient farmer. After the war the national plan was put on a permanent footing by the Agriculture Act, 1947; the committees were retained under the title of County Agricultural Executive Committees, and by way of encouraging the efficient farmer a system of security of tenure was introduced. The policy introduced in 1947, and now expressed in later Acts in 1948 and 1958, is, broadly stated, that security is given to tenants (other than service tenants) in occupation of an "agricultural holding," which means land let for agricultural use *and* so used for business purposes.[1] There is no minimum size for an agricultural holding.[2] Notwithstanding that he has been served with a notice to quit the holding, a tenant is allowed to remain in occupation of the land unless he has been a bad farmer or has committed a breach of covenant contained in the lease. In the event of the parties being unable to agree on a rent, a rent will be fixed by an arbitrator.[3] The rent will be the full economic rent.

The fulfilment of this policy is based in the first place upon the rule that no agricultural tenancy shall automatically determine by mere effluxion of time, a rule that involves an alteration in the principles of the common law concerning a notice to quit the land.

It has, indeed, always been true at common law that a yearly or other periodic tenancy continues indefinitely until it is determined by a notice to quit. The statutory rule superimposed upon this in the particular case of an agricultural holding is that, with a few exceptions, a landlord's notice to quit is effective only if it is to take effect at least twelve months from the end of the current tenancy.[4] Since the expression "contract of tenancy" in this statutory context has always meant a letting "for a term of years or from year to year,"[5] it was held under the Act of 1923 that a letting for a succes-

---

[1] Agricultural Holdings Act, 1948, s. 1. "Land" can include buildings: *Blackmore* v. *Butler*, [1954] 2 Q. B. 171; [1954] 2 All E. R. 403.

[2] *Stevens* v. *Sedgman*, [1951] 2 K. B. 434; [1951] 2 All E. R. 33; and see Scammell, *The Law of Agricultural Holdings*, pp. 29–32.

[3] Agricultural Holdings Act, 1948, ss. 8 and 9.

[4] Agricultural Holdings Act, 1948, s. 23, replacing s. 25 of the 1923 Act, which reproduced s. 28 of the Agriculture Act, 1920. *Lower* v. *Sorrell*, [1963] 1 Q. B. 959; [1962] 3 All E. R. 1074. Among the exceptions are a notice given to a tenant against whom a receiving order in bankruptcy has been made; a notice given by a tenant to a sub-tenant; and a notice given by virtue of a provision in the contract of tenancy that the landlord may resume possession for some purpose other than agricultural.

[5] Agricultural Holdings Act, 1948, s. 94, reproducing s. 56 of the 1923 Act.

sion of periods each shorter than a year, as for example for successive periods of 364 days but terminable by three months' notice to quit given by either party,[1] was unaffected by the statutory obligation to give twelve months' notice. In order to close this loophole, therefore, the Agricultural Holdings Act, 1948, has now provided that,

> where after 1st March, 1948, land is let for agricultural purposes for an interest less than a tenancy from year to year, the agreement, unless previously approved by the Minister shall take effect, with the necessary modifications, as if it were an agreement for a yearly tenancy.[2]

This conversion into a yearly tenancy, however, does not affect an agreement " made in contemplation of the use of the land only for grazing or mowing during some specified period of the year."[3] Thus, an agreement to let pasture land for grazing purposes only for a period shorter than a year, is excluded from the Act, even though it has in fact been renewed on similar terms at the end of each period.[4]

As distinct from a periodic tenancy, at common law a lease of a farm for a fixed period terminates automatically by effluxion of time and, subject to any agreement the parties may make, no notice to quit is necessary. The statutory rule, however, is that a tenancy of an agricultural holding for *a term of two years or upwards* shall not terminate automatically at the end of the period for which it was granted, but shall continue as a tenancy from year to year on the terms of the original tenancy so far as applicable. It may, however, be determined at the end of the period for which it was granted or at the end of any succeeding year by a notice to quit, not shorter than one year nor longer than two years, given by either party.[5] This rule does not apply to leases granted before 1st January, 1921.[6]

Although the obvious design of the two enactments just considered is that no agricultural tenancy shall be determinable except by a notice to quit, there is one remarkable *casus omissus*. If the letting is for a definite period greater than one year but less than two years, it is caught by neither enactment and will, therefore, expire automatically by effluxion of time.[7] A tenancy for one year certain is protected, however, since it is regarded as an in-

---

[1] *Land Settlement Association* v. *Carr*, [1944] K. B. 657 ; [1944] 2 All E. R. 126.

[2] Agricultural Holdings Act, 1948, s. 2 (1); *Goldsack* v. *Shore*, [1950] 1 K. B. 708; [1950] 1 All E. R. 276.

[3] *Ibid*. Cf. *Verrall* v. *Farnes, infra*, p. 450.

[4] *Scene Estate Ltd.* v. *Amos*, [1957] 2 Q. B. 205 ; [1957] 2 All E. R. 325 ; distinguished in *Rutherford* v. *Maurer*, [1961] 2 All E. R. 775; [1962] 1 Q. B. 16.

[5] Agricultural Holdings Act, 1948, s. 3 (1), replacing s. 28 of the 1923 Act.

[6] *Ibid.*, s. 3 (3).

[7] *Gladstone* v. *Bower*, [1960] 2 Q. B. 384 ; [1960] 3 All E. R. 353.

terest that is less in quantum than a tenancy from year to year.[1] Contractual licences to occupy land for agricultural use are also within the protection of the legislation.[2]

Notice to quit not effective without consent of Agricultural Land Tribunal.

Having thus established the position that in practically all cases an agricultural tenancy does not expire until notice to quit is given by one of the parties, the Act then approaches the problem of security of tenure by providing that such a notice, if given by the landlord, shall not be effective without the consent of the Agricultural Land Tribunal, provided that within a month of its receipt the tenant serves a counter-notice on the landlord claiming this statutory privilege.[3] Such a counter-notice, however, is not available to the tenant in the following cases :[4]

Exceptions.

(a) Where the Tribunal has consented to the effectiveness of the notice to quit before it was given.

(b) Where the notice to quit states that it is given because the land is required for some non-agricultural use for which planning permission under the Town and Country Planning Acts has been given or is not necessary.[5]

(c) Where the Tribunal has certified within the preceding six months that the tenant has neglected the rules of good husbandry.

(d) Where, when the notice to quit is served, the tenant has failed to comply with a written notice requiring him within two months to pay rent that is due, or to remedy within a given[6] time a breach of some condition or term of the tenancy. To escape this ban upon a counter-notice, the tenant must be able to prove a complete compliance with the terms of the written notice. A partial compliance, though substantial, is not enough.[7]

(e) Where the landlord's interest has been materially prejudiced by a breach, not capable of remedy, of some term or condition binding the tenant.

(f) Where the tenant has become bankrupt at the time when the notice to quit is served.

---

[1] *Bernays* v. *Prosser*, [1963] 2 Q. B. 592; [1963] 2 All E. R. 321.

[2] *Verrall* v. *Farnes*, [1966] 2 All E. R. 808; [1966] 1 W. L. R. 1254; in this case a rent-free "trial tenant" became a tenant from year to year under s. 2 (1).

[3] Agricultural Holdings Act, 1948, s. 24 (1) as amended by Agriculture Act, 1958, s. 8. (1), Sched. I, para. 8; *Mountford* v. *Hodkinson*, [1956] 2 All E. R. 17; [1956] 1 W. L. R. 422.

[4] *Ibid.*, s. 24 (2).

[5] For the meaning of these last words, see *Ministry of Agriculture Fisheries and Food* v. *Jenkins*, [1963] 2 Q. B. 317; [1963] 2 All E. R. 147.

[6] Exception (d) takes effect as amended by s. 19 of the Agriculture (Miscellaneous Provisions) Act, 1963. A landlord's notice to repair must be in a specific form and must give reasonable time, which can not be less than six months; see generally S.I. 1964, No. 707. The tenant loses his protection through failure to comply with this notice, not for breach of covenant as such.

[7] *Price* v. *Romilly*, [1960] 3 All E. R. 429; [1960] 1 W. L. R. 1360; *Shepherd* v. *Lomas*, [1963] 1 W. L. R. 962.

(g) Where the tenant, or the last survivor of two or more joint tenants, with whom the contract of tenancy was made,[1] has died within three months before the date of the giving of the notice to quit.[2]

If the landlord wishes to prevent the service of an effective counter-notice, his notice to quit must state the reason for which it is given and that reason must be one of the seven prescribed by the Act.[3] But if the notice to quit is given for one of the reasons specified in (b), (d) or (e), the tenant may without one month require the question to be submitted to arbitration.[4] This provision for arbitration excludes the ordinary jurisdiction of the High Court,[5] but the arbitrator must give adequate reasons for his award[6] and, if he fails to do so, there is an error of law on the face of the award, which can be set aside in the High Court.[7]

If none of these reasons is applicable, the service of a counter-notice requires the Tribunal to decide whether it consents to the operation of the notice to quit. In the first place, no such consent can be given unless the landlord bases his application for the termination of the tenancy upon one or more of the following five grounds

(i) That the attainment of the purpose which he had in mind is desirable in the interest of good husbandry.

(ii) That the attainment of his purpose is desirable in the interest of the sound management of the estate.

(iii) That the attainment of his purpose is desirable in the interests of agricultural research, education, experiment or demonstration or the provision of smallholdings or allotments.

(iv) That greater hardship would be caused by withholding than by giving consent.[8]

(v) That the land is required for some non-agricultural use unconnected with the Town and Country Planning Acts.

If, and only if, the Tribunal is satisfied as to one or more of these grounds, then, subject to one qualification, it must consent to the termination of the tenancy. The qualification is that, even though satisfied it must withhold its consent if in all the circum-

---

[1] Even though the original tenant, now deceased, has assigned the tenancy ; *Clarke* v. *Hall*, [1961] 2 All E. R. 365; [1961] 2 Q. B. 331.

[2] Agricultural Holdings Act, 1948, s. 24 (2), as amended by the Agriculture (Miscellaneous Provisions) Act, 1954, s. 7.

[3] *Budge* v. *Hicks*, [1951] 2 K. B. 335 ; [1951] 2 All E. R. 245.

[4] S.I. 1959, No. 81; S.I. 1964, No. 706.

[5] *A.-G. of Duchy of Lancaster* v. *Simcock*, [1966] Ch. 1; [1965] 2 All E. R. 32.

[6] Tribunals and Inquiries Act, 1958, s. 12.

[7] *Re Poyser and Mills' Arbitration*, [1964] 2 Q. B. 467; [1963] 1 All E. R. 612.

[8] "Hardship" is a wide term in this context capable of including personal circumstances; *Bailey* v. *Purser*, [1967] 1 All E. R. 188; *sub nom. Purser* v. *Bailey*, [1967] W. L. R. 146.

stances it considers that a fair and reasonable landlord would not insist on possession.[1]

(3) BUSINESS TENANCIES.

History of business tenant's right to new lease.

Part I of the Landlord and Tenant Act, 1927 conceded for the first time that a tenant might be entitled, after his contractual tenancy had ended, to compel the grant of a new lease, for at any rate a limited period. This right, however, was granted to him in a somewhat indirect manner. The primary object of the Act was to entitle a business tenant to compensation at the end of his tenancy for the loss of the goodwill that he had built up on the premises if their letting value had been thereby increased. Only where he could show that the compensation would not adequately indemnify him for the loss of goodwill likely to ensue if he moved his business elsewhere, was the court given a discretion to grant him a new lease not exceeding fourteen years. It was difficult enough to prove that goodwill had attached to the premises by reason of his business activities, but infinitely more difficult to establish the amount by which these activities, divorced from other factors, had increased the letting value of the holding. This unsatisfactory method of dealing with the problem has now been abandoned. Under the fundamentally different scheme contained in Part II of the Landlord and Tenant Act, 1954, the question of goodwill is not crucial.[2]

Object of the Act of 1954.

The policy and method of this legislation is to prolong—"to continue"—a valid business tenancy until it is determined by a statutory notice of termination.[3] The contractual tenancy remains in existence but varied as to the method of termination.[4] But when notice is given by the landlord, the tenant becomes entitled, subject to specific grounds of opposition which the landlord can attempt to prove, to the grant by the court of a new lease in respect of the relevant "holding". The tenant may also force the issue by expressly requesting the grant of a new lease. Business tenancies, therefore, terminate neither automatically nor on the expiry of ordinary notices to quit.

Meaning of business premises.

"Business" bears a wide meaning in this context. It includes a trade, profession, and also "any activity carried on by a body of persons, whether corporate or incorporate".[5] This wide language

---

[1] Agricultural Holdings Act, 1948, s. 25, as amended by Agriculture Act, 1958, ss. 3, 8 (1), 10 (1), Sched. I, Part I, para. 9.

[2] It is still an object of the legislation of course: see *per* Lord DENNING, M.R., in *O'Callaghan* v. *Elliot*, [1966] 1 Q. B. 601, at p. 608; [1965] 3 All E. R. 111, distinguishing mining leases.

[3] For the relation of statutory and contractual notices to quit, see *Scholl Manufacturing Co., Ltd.* v. *Clifton (Slim-Line), Ltd.*, [1966] 3 All E. R. 16; [1966] 3 W. L. R. 575. *Weinbergs Weatherproofs, Ltd.* v. *Radcliffe Paper Mills Co., Ltd.*, [1958] Ch. 437.

[4] *Bowes-Lyon* v. *Green*, [1963] A. C. 420, at pp. 434–5, *per* Lord REID; [1961] 3 All E. R. 843.

[5] Landlord and Tenant Act, 1954, s. 23 (2).

must be taken literally and not construed *eiusdem generis*.[1] The
expression "business premises" also extends to land that is un-
built on.[2]

But to come within the Act, *occupation* of the premises by the
tenant for business purposes, from the time of application through
to the hearing in court, is vital; and the occupation must be
genuine, not spurious.[3] Where only part of the demised premises
remains so occupied, only that part constitutes the statutory
"holding" eligible for a new lease.[4] Thus in *Bagettes* v. *G. P.
Estates*,[5] a property company engaged in the business of sub-letting
flats failed in its claim for a new lease on the ground that it was not
in occupation of the sub-let flats, nor did its continuous occupation
of staircases and boiler rooms help as, once the tenancy of the flats
ended, there was no business for those central services to further.

Premises let for mixed business and living purposes were,
until 1965, regarded as houses to be protected by the Rent Acts.
This principle still applies to controlled houses[6] but does not
apply to the regulated tenancies created by the Act of 1965. Premises which otherwise come within the ambit of regulation, but
which contain a business element, are now within the 1954 Act.[7]
Tenants of such premises are thus not spared from having to pay
the economic rent.

"Tenancy" includes[8] an interest by way of lease or underlease

Meaning of "in occupation".

Mixed lettings.

Meaning of tenancy.

---

[1] *Addiscombe Garden Estates, Ltd.* v. *Crabbe*, [1958] 1 Q. B. 513, at p. 530;
per PARKER, L.J.; [1957] 3 All E. R. 563 (incorporated tennis club held a
"business' in this sense); *Hills (Patents), Ltd.* v. *University College Hospital
Board of Governors*, [1956] 1 Q. B. 90; [1955] 3 All E. R. 365 (hospital a
"business").

[2] *Bracey* v. *Read*, [1963] Ch. 88; [1962] 3 All E. R. 472 (racehorse gallops).

[3] *I. and H. Caplan, Ltd.* v. *Caplan (No. 2)*, [1963] 2 All E. R. 930; [1963]
1 W. L. R. 1247; *Teasdale* v. *Walker*, [1958] 3 All E. R. 307; [1958] 1 W. L. R.
1076; a notice to quit premises governed by a continuation tenancy, given
during a period of non-occupation may, under s. 24 (3) be of from 3–6 months'
duration, and is not affected by subsequent resumption of occupation.

[4] See especially *per* Lord REID in *I. and H. Caplan, Ltd.* v. *Caplan (No. 1)*,
[1961] 3 All E. R. 1174, at pp. 1175–6; [1962] 1 W. L. R. 55, at p. 58; although
the time of the hearing is the crucial time for determining the holding, earlier
occurrences are not irrelevant.

[5] [1956] Ch. 290; [1956] 1 All E. R. 729; if the property company had
retained occupation of a larger central core, for offices for instance, this might
have constituted an independent holding; see *per* JENKINS, L.J., at p. 303.

[6] *Supra*, p. 426. But not on a second transmission under s. 13 of the Rent Act,
1965; also, if the Minister converts control to regulation in a particular area,
mixed premises will come under the 1954 Act, not the Rent Acts; Rent Act,
1965, s. 11 (7).

[7] Rent Act, 1965, s. 1 (3), reversing (for regulated tenancies only) the exclusion from the 1954 Act (see 1954 Act, s. 43 (1) (c)) of premises capable of
coming within the Rent Acts. Residential sub-tenancies of business premises
are within the Rent Acts irrespective of the status of the head tenancy; in
excluding mixed tenancies from the Rent Acts, s. 1 (3) preserves the protection
given to residential sub-tenants by s. 15 (3) of the Act of 1920 and s. 41 of the
Housing Repairs and Rents Act, 1954, *supra*, pp. 427 and 440–1.

[8] 1954 Act, 69 (1): *Wheeler* v. *Mercer*, [1957] A. C. 416; [1956] 3 All E. R. 631;
(excluding from the Act tenants holding over at will). Agricultural and
mining tenancies, tenancies of public houses, service tenancies, and (with
exceptions) tenancies for 3 months or less are excluded: s. 43. See note 7,
supra, for the exclusion of the Rent Acts.

(or an agreement for one), and such an interest obtained by assignment, but special provisions are needed to determine the landlord who is "competent" for the purposes of the Act. When there is a chain of tenancies, it is necessary to know which landlord to treat with. The answer depends on the length of a landlord's interest: the "competent" landlord is the first person in the chain who is entitled either to the fee simple, or to a reversionary interest (whether immediate or not) which has at least 14 months to run.[1] But this statutory formula was considerably complicated by the decision of the House of Lords in *Bowes-Lyon* v. *Green*[2] that the 14 months could include the statutory continuation period of a mesne landlord in business occupation. Hence, in

> *Morris Marks* v. *British Waterways Board*[3] a company, B, in 1949 sub-let premises on a business tenancy to C. B.'s tenancy was contractually due to terminate on June 26th, 1963 and the sub-lease 12 days earlier. B. was a business tenant under the Act and there was the possibility of the tenancy being continued under the Act. Accordingly, during 1962, the statutory notices were properly served by C. on B. as competent landlord, not on the freeholder, although B.'s contractual tenancy had less than 14 months to run. B., in fact, surrendered his tenancy to the freeholder in December 1962, but the Court of Appeal held that B. could give notice to C. of the *freeholder's* intention to reconstruct at the end of the tenancy. This enabled the freeholder to prove this intention at the hearing of the application for a new lease. "I must say it takes a good gulp to swallow that", said HARMAN, L.J.,[4] but this is nevertheless what the Court of Appeal did, by emphasizing that the object of the landlord's notice was to inform the tenant of the case he would have to meet at the hearing.

Authority of competent landlord. Notices given to the tenant and agreements made with him by the competent landlord are binding upon the mesne landlords, but if their consent is not first obtained they are entitled to compensation for any loss that they may suffer.[5]

Cases where grant of new lease precluded. There will be no question of a tenancy being continued under the Act if the tenant's interest is forfeited for breach of covenant, if he voluntarily surrenders his interest to the landlord or if, in the case of a periodic tenancy, such as one from year to year, he himself gives notice to quit the holding.[6] Again, the possibility of a new lease is ruled out if the tenant, holding under a lease for a term of years certain, gives notice, not later than three months before the date on which the tenancy would normally end by effluxion of time, that he does not desire to continue occupation.[7] In each of these cases the tenancy is effectively and irretrievably determined, except that in the event of forfeiture the tenant may apply to the court for relief.

---

[1] 1954 Act, s. 44 (1).   [2] [1963] A. C. 420; [1961] 3 All E. R. 843.
[3] [1963] 1 W. L. R. 1008.   [4] [1963] 1 W. L. R. 1008, at p. 1018.
[5] 1954 Act, Sched. VI; see also s. 28 and *Bowes-Lyon* v. *Green*, [1963] A. C. 420; [1961] 3 All E. R. 843.
[6] Landlord and Tenant Act, 1954, s. 24 (2).
[7] *Ibid.*, s. 27. A term in a tenancy agreement obliging a tenant to surrender his interest or to give notice to quit in such a way as to prevent him being

Landlord's notice to terminate the tenancy.[1] The landlord may serve a notice on the tenant specifying the date at which the tenancy is to terminate, but he must serve it not more than twelve nor less than six months before the date specified. This date, however, cannot be earlier than that on which the tenancy, whether periodic or not, might have been terminated according to the contractual terms to which it is subject.

Essential contents of the notice.

The notice must be in the form prescribed by the Lord Chancellor,[2] and in particular it must satisfy two conditions: first, it must require the tenant to state in writing within two months whether he is willing to surrender possession at the specified date; secondly, it must state whether the landlord would oppose an application by the tenant for a new lease and, if so, upon which of the grounds permitted by the Act.[3]

"The landlord must *honestly and truthfully* state his ground in his "notice and he must establish it as *existing* at the time of the hearing."

The current tenancy is brought to an end at the date fixed for its termination in the landlord's notice.

Request by the tenant for a new lease.[4] If the landlord has not given notice to terminate the tenancy, the tenant may give a notice in the prescribed form requesting the grant of a new tenancy of the whole or part of the premises, and stating his suggestions with regard to the rent and the other terms of the proposed tenancy. A date must be specified for the commencement of the new tenancy and it must not be more than twelve nor less than six months after the date of the request. Neither must it be earlier than the date on which the current tenancy would normally end by effluxion of time or on which it could be ended by a notice to quit given by the tenant. The effect of the request is to terminate the current tenancy immediately before the date specified for the commencement of the new tenancy.

Right of tenant to take the initiative.

A request for a new lease, however, cannot be made unless the current tenancy is one granted for a term of years certain exceeding one year, or granted for a term of years certain and thereafter from year to year. If, therefore, the tenancy is periodic, as for example quarterly or yearly, the tenant cannot take the initiative. He must wait until the landlord serves a notice to

---

able to request a new lease is void: s. 38; *Joseph* v. *Joseph*, [1966] 3 All E.R. 486.

[1] 1954 Act, ss. 24, 25.

[2] S. I. 1957, No. 1157.

[3] *Per* Lord DENNING, in *Betty's Cafés, Ltd.* v. *Phillips Furnishing Stores, Ltd.*, [1959] A. C. 20, at p. 51; [1958] 1 All E. R. 607. But the landlord who gives this notice need not always be the landlord who contests the hearing: *Morris Marks* v. *British Waterways Board*, [1963] 1 W. L. R. 1008; but cf. *infra*, p. 458.

[4] Landlord and Tenant Act, 1954, s. 26 (1) (3). *Sidney Bolsom Investment Trust, Ltd.* v. *E. Karmios & Co., Ltd.*, [1956] 1 Q. B. 529.

terminate the tenancy, whereafter he will be at liberty to demand a new lease.

Interim continuance of tenancies.

The effect, therefore, of a notice given by the landlord in the prescribed form (even though followed by the refusal of the tenant to surrender possession), or of a request made by the tenant for a new lease, is that the current tenancy is ultimately brought to an end. It is obvious, however, that in most cases the tenant's application for a new lease will not be disposed of by the court until some time after the current tenancy has thus determined. If this proves to be the case the statutory rule is that the tenancy shall continue for a period of three months after the application is " finally disposed of." [1]

Landlord's grounds for opposing grant of a new lease.[2]

Breach of repairing covenants.

(a) That the tenant ought not to be granted a new tenancy in view of his failure to observe the contractual terms respecting the repair and maintenance of the holding.

Unpunctual payment of rent.

(b) That the tenant ought not to be granted a new tenancy in view of his persistent delay in the payment of rent.

Breach of contractual terms.

(c) That the tenant ought not to be granted a new tenancy in view of other substantial breaches of his contractual obligations or for any other reason connected with his use or management of the holding.

In the above three cases the landlord must show that the state of affairs of which he complains existed at the time of his notice of opposition and that it still exists at the date of the hearing of the court.[3]

Alternative accommodation available.

(d) That the landlord has offered to provide the tenant on reasonable terms with alternative accommodation that is suitable to his requirements, including the preservation of goodwill, having regard to the nature of his business and the facilities afforded by the holding.

Applicant a sub-tenant.

(e) That the applicant for a new tenancy is a sub-tenant of part only of the holding, and that when the reversion falls in to the landlord it will profit him more to let or otherwise dispose of the property as a whole.

This ground becomes relevant when the premises have been let as a single unit and the lessee has sub-let part of them, such as the ground floor of a house. In these circumstances, although the superior tenant may have no desire to retain possession at the end of the term, the sub-tenant is entitled to apply for a new tenancy of the ground floor. If, however, the landlord objects that the

---

[1] Landlord and Tenant Act, 1954, s. 64. As to the meaning of "finally disposed of," see *Austin Reed, Ltd.* v. *Royal Insurance Co., Ltd., (No. 2)* [1956] 3 All E. R. 490; [1956] 1 W. L. R. 1339.

[2] S. 30 (1).

[3] *Betty's Cafés Ltd.* v. *Phillips Furnishing Stores Ltd.,* [1959] A. C. 20 ; [1958] 1 All E. R. 607.

aggregate of the rents reasonably obtainable on separate lettings would be substantially less than that obtainable from a letting of the property as a whole, and that he requires possession for the purpose of letting or otherwise disposing of it as a whole, the decision whether a new tenancy shall be granted lies within the discretion of the court.

(f) That the landlord intends to demolish or reconstruct the whole or a substantial part of the premises and that he can not reasonably do so without obtaining possession of the holding. It must be noted that demolition *or* reconstruction will suffice (although the courts would be anxious to see a good reason for demolition without reconstruction),[1] and that a broad common sense view is taken of what constitutes a substantial reconstruction[2] needing possession of the premises.[3] Putting in a new shop front, for instance, would not suffice. But it is the issue of intention that has most exercised the courts. The intention must exist at the time of the hearing,[4] and it must be a genuine settled intention,[5] one that had

Demolition or reconstruction of premises.

> "moved out of the zone of contemplation—the sphere of the tenta-
> "tive, the provisional and the exploratory—and had moved into the
> "valley of decision."[6]

On the other hand, not everything can be arranged in advance, for instance the necessary planning consents; what the landlord must prove here is a reasonable case for obtaining them.[7]

Once the necessary intent is established, it is irrelevant that it is part of a wider intent which would, if relevant, raise further issues. The intent to incorporate a holding, when empty of buildings, into an agricultural holding is not relevant.[8] This rule is of great importance in keeping exclusive of each other the various grounds of opposition we are considering. A landlord who has purchased the freehold within five years may, for instance, suc-

---

[1] *Craddock* v. *Hampshire County Council*, [1958] 1 All E. R. 449; [1958] 1 W. L. R. 202; *Housleys, Ltd.* v. *Bloomer-Holt, Ltd.*, [1966] 2 All E. R. 966; [1966] 1 W. L. R. 1244.

[2] *Atkinson* v. *Bettison*, [1955] 3 All E. R. 340; [1955] 1 W. L. R. 1127; *Joel* v. *Swaddle*, [1957] 3 All E. R. 325; [1957] 1 W. L. R. 1094; *Bewlay (Tobacconists), Ltd.* v. *Bata Shoe Co., Ltd.*, [1958] 3 All E. R. 652; [1959] 1 W. L. R. 45.

[3] *Whittingham* v. *Davies*, [1962] 1 All E. R. 195; [1962] 1 W. L. R. 142.

[4] *Betty's Cafés, Ltd.* v. *Phillips Furnishing Stores*, [1959] A. C. 20; [1958] 1 All E. R. 607; *Morris Marks* v. *British Waterways Board*, [1963] 1 W. L. R. 1008; *supra*, p. 455.

[5] *Fisher* v. *Taylor's Furnishing Stores, Ltd.*, [1956] 2 Q. B. 78, especially at p. 84, *per* DENNING, L.J. It is possible, of course, for a landlord honestly to change his mind after successfully resisting a tenant's application. Cf. *Espresso Coffee Machine Co., Ltd.* v. *Guardian Assurance Co., Ltd.*, [1959] 1 All E. R. 458; 1 W. L. R. 250 (a case on ground (g), *infra*).

[6] *Per* ASQUITH, L.J., in *Cunliffe* v. *Goodman*, [1950] 2 K. B. 237, at p. 254; [1950] 1 All E. R. 720, at p. 725, a passage frequently cited with approval on this issue.

[7] *Gregson* v. *Cyril Lord, Ltd.*, [1962] 3 All E. R. 907; [1963] 1 W. L. R. 41 (a case on ground (g), *infra*).

[8] *Craddock* v. *Hampshire County Council*, [1958] 1 All E. R. 449; [1958] 1 W. L. R. 202.

Q*

ceed under ground (f) although his intention is to occupy the reconstructed premises himself; such a landlord would fail under ground (g). The courts will be very watchful to see that ground (f) is not being used to circumvent the 5 year rule in ground (g),[1] but as the law stands at present, a purchaser of the freehold within five years can resist a tenant's application for a new lease if he intends to reconstruct and occupy the premises himself.

Occupation required by landlord.

(g) That the landlord intends to occupy the premises wholly or partly for the purposes of his business or as his residence. Much of what has just been said about "intends" in ground (f) applies here, but there are further complications. Ground (g) is not available to a landlord who has acquired his interest[2] in the premises within the period of five years immediately preceding the date specified in the landlord's notice as the date for termination of the tenancy.[3] This principle is applied rigorously, even to the case of a transfer within five years from an individual to a private company controlled by him.[4] Furthermore, if a tenant can show that the landlord intends to occupy the premises himself for only a short time and then to transfer it, the landlord will not be able to resist the tenant's application, for the courts hold that the spirit of this ground is offended.[5]

This ground is, then, in the words of the Act, not to apply

Statutory provisions as to merger.

" if the interest of the landlord, or an interest which has merged in
" that interest and but for the merger would be the interest of the
" landlord, was purchased or created, after the beginning of the
" period of five years."

To illustrate the effect of merger, let it be supposed that,

A., the fee simple owner, lets the premises to B. for 21 years and a year later B. sub-lets them to C. If, two years before the sub-lease is due to end, B., the competent landlord of C., surrenders his interest to A. in return for £500, there is a merger of that interest in the fee simple held by A.

---

[1] *Fisher* v. *Taylor's Furnishing Stores, Ltd.*, [1956] 2 Q. B. 78; [1956] 2 All E. R. 78; *Betty's Cafés, Ltd.* v. *Phillips Furnishing Stores*, [1959] A. C. 20; [1958] 1 All E. R. 607; these cases rejected that much of the judgment of the Court of Appeal in *Atkinson* v. *Bettison*, [1955] 3 All E. R. 340; [1955] 1 W. L. R. 1127 as suggested that the landlord's dominant motive is relevant.
[2] A landlord's interest dates from the time of its *original* creation or purchase; for instance, a *renewal* of a mesne landlord's lease by the freeholder within 5 years of the date for the termination of a sub-tenant's lease does not bring the mesne landlord within this disability if, by successive tenancies, he has exceeded the 5 year period: *Artemiou* v. *Procopiou*, [1966] 1 Q. B. 878; see especially *per* SALMON, L.J. at p. 891; [1965] 3 All E. R. at p. 546.
[3] *Frederick Lawrence, Ltd.* v. *Freeman, Hardy and Willis, Ltd.*, [1959] Ch. 731; [1959] 3 All E. R. 77.
[4] *Tunstall* v. *Steigmann*, [1962] 2 Q. B. 593; [1962] 2 All E. R. 417; the emphasis in ground (f) on intent at the time of the hearing (*Morris Marks* v. *British Waterways Board, supra*, p. 455) is, therefore, not the whole issue under ground (g).
[5] *Willis* v. *Association of Universities of the British Commonwealth*, [1965] 1 Q. B. 140; [1964] 2 All E. R. 39.

Should C. subsequently move for the grant of a new lease, A. cannot object that he requires the premises for his own purposes, since the interest that he has purchased within the forbidden period would have been " the interest of the landlord " had it not been for the merger.

The word " purchased," as used in the sub-section, bears its popular meaning of buying for money, and if, therefore, in the instance just given, B. had surrendered his tenancy to A. without receiving any money consideration, A. would not be debarred from alleging that he required the premises for his own occupation at the end of C.'s sub-tenancy.[1]

Meaning of " purchased."

The word " created " is inserted in the sub-section in order to prevent an incoming landlord from avoiding the five-year restriction by taking a lease of the premises subject to an existing lease. If, for example, A., entitled in fee simple, lets a holding to T. for five years on March 25th, 1958, and on March 25th, 1961, leases it to X. for fifty years, an interest has been " created " in favour of X. after the beginning of the five-year period.[2]

Result of application for a new tenancy. If the landlord establishes one of the seven grounds upon which he is entitled to oppose the application, the court is precluded from granting a new tenancy.[3] But if the landlord fails in this respect, the court is bound to make the grant.[4]

Where, however, the ground which the landlord has failed to establish is that he has offered alternative accommodation, or desires to let as a single unit the whole of the land of which the tenant's holding forms part, or, that he has decided to demolish or reconstruct the premises, and it further appears that his opposition on that ground, though not justifiable at the moment, will become justifiable at some date not later than one year after the termination of the current tenancy, as for example where he is not ready to begin the reconstruction immediately, the court may order that the tenancy shall end at that date and, if it makes such an order, it may not grant a new tenancy.[5]

The rules that must govern the grant of a new tenancy are laid down by the Act.[6] Failing agreement by the parties, the court must grant a tenancy for such a period as it considers reasonable.[7] If, as is usual, it takes the form of a lease for a term certain, the

Duration of new tenancy.

---

[1] *Bolton (H. L.) (Engineering) Co., Ltd.* v. *T. J. Graham & Sons, Ltd.,* [1957] 1 Q. B. 159 ; *Frederick Lawrence Ltd.* v. *Freeman, Hardy & Willis Ltd., supra.*

[2] *Bolton (H. L.) (Engineering) Co. Ltd.* v. *T. J. Graham & Sons Ltd., supra,* at p. 170. Distinguish the different effect under the Rent Acts, *Powell* v. *Cleland,* [1948] 1 K. B. 262 ; [1947] 2 All E. R. 672.

[3] Landlord and Tenant Act, 1954, s. 31 (1).

[4] *Ibid.,* s. 29 (1).

[5] *Ibid.,* s. 31 (2).   [6] *Ibid.,* Ss. 32–5.

[7] *London and Provincial Millinery Stores, Ltd.* v. *Barclays Bank, Ltd.,* [1962] 2 All E. R. 163; [1962] 1 W. L. R. 510.

term must not exceed fourteen years.[1] The new tenancy will, of course, be subject to the Act and an application for its further renewal upon its termination will be open to the tenant.

Amount of rent.

In default of agreement, the new rent payable must be that which a tenant might reasonably be expected to pay if the holding were let in the open market by a willing lessor. The court, however, must disregard certain matters, such as the value of any goodwill attached to the premises by the tenant, or of any improvement that he or a predecessor in title has voluntarily made during the tenancy that is ending.[2]

Other terms of the lease.

The primary purpose of the Act is that the tenant should be protected in the way of his business and therefore, in fixing the other terms of the new tenancy, no restrictions should be allowed which tend to hinder him from carrying on his trade as before.[3] The court has the widest possible discretion in the matter.[4]

Compensation to tenant.

A tenant whose application for a new tenancy fails is entitled to compensation if, and only if, the failure is attributable to one of the grounds of opposition (e), (f) or (g) in the list given above.[5]

(4) LONG TENANCIES OF RESIDENTIAL PREMISES.

Policy in the case of long tenancies.

A long tenancy is commonly associated with a building agreement made between landlord and tenant under which a lease of land is granted, partly in consideration of the payment of a ground rent and partly in consideration that the tenant will erect a house or houses that will become the property of the landlord at the end of the term. Since the ground rent is practically always less than two-thirds of the rateable value of the premises, the protection afforded by the Rent Acts has seldom been available to the tenant. This was felt to be a grievance, and after much political agitation the matter was dealt with by Part I of the Landlord and Tenant Act, 1954.

The Act now applies to long tenancies of premises, the rateable value of which does not exceed £100 in London or £75 elsewhere,[6] and irrespective of the amount of the rent.[7] Sub-tenants

---

[1] Landlord and Tenant Act, 1954, s. 33. It is possible to grant a periodic tenancy or to insert a break clause.

[2] S. 34; *Re "Wonderland", Cleethorpes, East Coast Amusement Co., Ltd.* v. *British Transport Commission*, [1965] A. C. 58; [1963] 2 All E. R. 775.

[3] *Gold* v. *Brighton Corpn.*, [1956] 1 W. L. R. 1291; [1956] 3 All E. R. 442.

[4] *In re No. 1 Albemarle St.*, [1959] Ch. 531 ; [1959] 1 All E. R. 250.

[5] Landlord and Tenant Act, 1954, s. 37 (1). Where, however, the tenancy was current on October 1st, 1954, the date when the Act came into force, no compensation is payable unless, at the date when the tenant is to quit, he has continuously occupied the whole or part of the premises for his own business purposes for at least five years: Sched. IX, para. 5 (1), and see generally *Connaught Fur Trimmings, Ltd.* v. *Cramas Properties, Ltd.*, [1965] 2 All E. R. 382; [1965] 1 W. L. R. 892.

[6] Neither 1957 Act decontrol nor 1965 Act recontrol applies for this purpose to long tenancies, hence the earlier limits apply: Rent Act, 1957, s. 11 (4).

[7] 1954 Act, ss. 1, 2; Rent Act, 1957, s, 21 (2) and Sched. 8.

are also protected.[1] The Acts proceed by excluding residential tenancies for a longer period than 21 years from the operation of the Rent Acts, whether they are at a low rent or not; they then proceed to secure the tenant in his holding by providing that his tenancy shall automatically continue after the date on which it would normally expire until such time as the landlord *either* applies for possession on one of the grounds permitted by the Act *or* makes proposals for the creation of a statutory tenancy.[2]

The Act does not avail a tenant unless he holds a "long tenancy," *i.e.* one granted for a term of years certain exceeding twenty-one years, whether subsequently extended or not,[3] *and* unless what is called the "qualifying condition"[4] is satisfied. This means the tenancy must be one that would have been caught by the Rent Acts had it not been for its length and, as would commonly be the case, that the rent was less than two-thirds of the rateable value. In other words, the premises must consist of a house or part of a house that has been let as a separate dwelling for the purpose of use as a residence, and they must be in the residential occupation of the tenant *at the end of the term.* In *Herbert* v. *Byrne*,[5] Byrne bought for £100 the last five months of a 99-year lease of a house within the 1954 Act rateable limit and let at a ground rent of £2 a year. The lease was due to expire in December 1962 but by November Byrne had obtained possession of part of the house from unprotected sub-tenants. He thereupon installed a few pieces of furniture and began to sleep there, though his family continued to live elsewhere until March 1963. The Court of Appeal held that the 1954 Act protected Byrne in respect of the whole house, including those parts occupied by protected sub-tenants. His intention to move his family home there was genuine and he had acquired a sufficient degree of residence by December 1962; that he had had an eye to the Act from the beginning was to be discounted. This pre-occupation of the Act with the situation as the lease ends seems less than just to the landlord, but is inevitable on the wording.[6] As Lord DENNING, M.R., put it,

> "The 'qualifying condition' . . . comes to this: you are to look at the "position at the end of the lease, and ask yourself whether the lease- "holder would have been protected if it had been not a long lease at "a low rent, but a short lease at a rack-rent. If the leaseholder would "have qualified under the old Rent Acts for protection on the expiry

Only residential tenancies are protected.

---

[1] Landlord and Tenant Act, 1954, s. 15: *Herbert* v. *Byrne*, [1964] 1 All E. R. 882, at pp. 884–5, *per* Lord DENNING, M.R.; [1964] 1 W. L. R. 519, at pp. 524–5.

[2] 1954 Act, s. 3; 1957 Act, s. 21 (1).

[3] 1954 Act, s. 2 (4).

[4] *Ibid.*, s. 2 (1), as amended by Rent Act, 1957, s. 26 (1), (3).

[5] [1964] 1 All E. R. 882: see especially at pp. 884–6, *per* Lord DENNING, M.R.; [1964] 1 W. L. R. 519, at pp. 525–6.

[6] Landlord and Tenant Act, 1954, s. 22 (3). See also the comments of HARMAN, L.J., in *Haines* v. *Herbert*, [1963] 3 All E. R. 715, at pp. 717–5; [1963] 1 W. L. R. 1401, at pp. 1404–5.

"of such a short lease, he qualifies now, under the Act of 1954, for
"protection on the expiry of the long lease, but with this difference:
"In determining whether he qualifies or not, you do not look at the
"terms of the old long lease itself as you would look at the terms of a
"short lease. You look at the state of affairs not at the beginning of
"the lease, nor at the date of the hearing, but at the end of the lease."

Effect of tenant's notice to terminate tenancy.

There will be no automatic continuance of the tenancy if it is terminated at the " term date " (*i.e.* the contractual date for its expiration)[1] by at least one month's written notice given by the tenant.[2] If it continues after the term date, it may be terminated at any time if he gives at least one month's previous notice to that effect.[3]

Effect of landlord's notice.

If a tenant does not take this course, the tenancy continues as a contractual tenancy at the same rent and, so far as is compatible with the Act, on the same terms as heretofore,[4] but it may be brought to an end by what is called "a landlord's notice to resume possession."[5] This must state the date at which the tenant is to give up possession ("date of termination"), which must not be earlier than the term date; it must be served not more than twelve nor less than six months before the term date; and it must invite the tenant to state whether he is willing to give up possession.[6] Even so, however, it has no effect unless it either

(a) contains proposals for a statutory tenancy, or

(b) notifies the tenant that if he is unwilling to give up possession an application will be made to the court for an order for possession.[7]

Landlord's proposal for statutory tenancy.

Proposals for a statutory tenancy must state the amount and dates of payment of the standard rent ; whether any " initial repairs " are required to put the house into a good state of repair, and if so by whom they are to be executed ; the extent to which each party should be liable for repairs during the tenancy ; and any other terms that the landlord may suggest. Failing agreement between the parties, these matters must be settled by the court.[8]

The rent payable by the tenant is regulated in this manner : if the rateable value of the premises is not higher than £40 in London or £30 elsewhere in England or Wales, it is the amount equal to the rent limit specified by the Rent Act, 1957,[9] unless the parties agree to a smaller sum ; but if the rateable value is above £40 or £30, but below £100 or £75, according as the holding is situated

---

[1] Landlord and Tenant Act, 1954, s. 2 (6).
[2] *Ibid.*, s. 5 (1).   [3] *Ibid.*, s. 5 (2).
[4] *Ibid.*, s. 3 (1) (2). *Byrne* v. *Herbert*, [1966] 2 Q.B. 121; [1965] 3 All E.R. 705.
[5] *Ibid.*, s. 4 (5).
[6] *Ibid.*, s. 4 (1) (2) (4) (5).   [7] *Ibid.*, s. 4 (3).
[8] *Ibid.*, 1954, ss. 7, 8, 9.   [9] *Supra*, p. 430.

in London or elsewhere, the rent is the amount agreed to by the parties or determined by the court.[1]

Where the landlord has served a notice to resume possession *and has not* proposed a statutory tenancy, he may apply to the court for possession. The application will be heard if the tenant has elected to retain possession or if, two months from the service of the notice, the qualifying condition is fulfilled.[2] If neither of these facts is established, as for example if the tenant is no longer in occupation of the holding, the tenancy ends by virtue of the notice to resume possession.

Landlord's notice to resume possession without proposing statutory tenancy.

The grounds on which an order for possession may be made are, with certain modifications, those permitted by the Rent Acts,[3] If one of these is established the court is instructed to make the order for possession if satisfied that it is reasonable to do so.[4] But one further ground is that for purposes of redevelopment the landlord proposes to demolish or reconstruct the whole or a substantial part of the premises. In this case the court is bound to make the order if it is satisfied that the ground has been established, that possession of the particular premises will be required and that the landlord has already made reasonable preparations for proceeding with the work.[5]

Grounds upon which landlord may claim possession.

In a White Paper published in February 1966,[6] the Government announced proposals that, if they become law, will affect most considerably long tenancies of residential premises. The White Paper defines a "qualified leaseholder"; he is the holder of a lease originally granted, at a ground rent, for more than twenty-one years in respect of premises (excluding flats) now within the 1965 Rent Act rateable value limits of £400 in London and £200 elsewhere, who has been in continuous occupation of the premises or part thereof as his residence for at least the five years past. To such a leaseholder, whether a lessee or sub-lessee, it is proposed to give the right, at any time during the currency of the lease, to purchase the freehold, all intermediate titles being likewise extinguished: alternatively, at the end of the lease, he could demand a fifty year extension of the lease, though that would constitute the limit of his rights. The landlord will be able to oppose purchase of the freehold and the fifty year extension only on the ground that, when the lease expires, he will want the premises for occupation by himself or his family and hardship would be suffered if he could not so obtain them; but even when within this provision, the landlord would be liable to pay compensation to the leaseholder for his loss of rights. The landlord will be able to obtain possession during the

Prospective changes in the law.

---

[1] Landlord and Tenant Act, 1954, s. 9; Rent Act, 1957, Sched. VI, para. 8 (2).

[2] Landlord and Tenant Act, 1954, s. 13 (1).

[3] *Ibid.*, s. 12, and Sched. III.; *supra*, pp. 436–9.

[4] *Ibid,.* s. 13, (4).

[5] *Ibid.*, s. 13 (2).

[6] Cmnd. 2916.

fifty-year extension only on the ground that he intends to redevelop the property; again he will be liable to compensate the leaseholder. The White Paper bases its proposals, and its provisions for purchase and compensation prices, on the principle that, while the land and its development value as a site belong to the landlord, the buildings on the land already morally belong to the leaseholder. It is obvious that these proposals, if they become law, will require a complete reconsideration of the relationship of landlord and tenant in this type of lease.

(5) GENERAL PROVISIONS TO PROTECT TENANTS

We have now seen the extent to which tenants of certain types are protected both during and after the expiry of their contractual tenancies. Two more general points must now be added to this account. Firstly, a notice to quit a dwelling-house is effective only if given at least four weeks before it is to take effect; this applies, for instance, to weekly tenancies, and affects notice given by the tenant as well as by the landlord.[1] Secondly, a landlord must now always go to the court to obtain possession.[2] This crucial rule applies during and after the expiry of a tenancy and to all forms of residential tenancies, even if the tenancy has clearly come to an end without hope of statutory renewal or if the landlord possesses an undisputed right of entry. All lawful occupiers of residential premises are protected in this way.[3] This denial to the landlord of self-help is backed by a variety of criminal offences which a landlord may find he has committed if he takes matters into his own hands. In particular, the offence of "harassment"[4] includes far more than disturbing possession; it includes all acts "calculated to interfere with the peace or comfort" of the household, and extends to the withholding of services. But the tenant is not, under this part of the Act,[5] given any greater security of tenure than he otherwise possessed. The court *must* make the appropriate possession order, and the power to postpone its execution is very limited.[6]

---

[1] Rent Act, 1957, s. 16: *Schnabel* v. *Allard*, [1966] 3 All E. R. 816; [1966] 3 W. L. R.1295; *supra*, p. 418. The section does not apply to tenants at will or to licensees: *Crane* v. *Morris*, [1965] 3 All E. R. 77; [1965] 1 W. L. R. 1104.

[2] By the combined effect of ss. 30, 31 and 32 of the Rent Act, 1965: the court is, of course, the County Court; see generally *Borzak* v. *Ahmed*, [1965] 2 Q. B. 320; [1965] 1 All E. R. 808.

[3] But if an unlawful eviction occurs, there is no authority to re-instate the person evicted who may, however, succeed in trespass.

[4] S. 30.

[5] Save for argicultural employees, who are within s. 33.

[6] *Jones* v. *Savery*, [1951] 1 All E. R. 820. The court has greater powers of postponement where the order is being made consequent on non-payment of rent: Administration of Justice Act, 1965, s. 23.

B. INTERESTS CONFERRING A RIGHT ENFORCEABLE AGAINST THE LAND OF ANOTHER.

CHAPTER II.

EASEMENTS AND PROFITS.

SUMMARY.

SECTION I.   RIGHTS *IN ALIENO SOLO* GENERALLY.

Incorporeal interests:

Introductory Note.   In this chapter our concern is with rights *in alieno solo*, *i.e.* with the case where X. possesses some right that is enforceable against the land of another.   If the owner of Blackacre is entitled to an easement, such as a right of way, over Whiteacre, he is said, in the curious language of English law, to have an incorporeal interest.   Perhaps it is more intelligible to describe him as holding an interest in an incorporeity.[1]

Whether his interest is legal or equitable depends, as in the case of the so-called corporeal interests, upon the period for which it is to endure.

It is a legal freehold estate—a fee simple absolute in possession—if he is in actual enjoyment of a right that has been acquired by him or his predecessors in perpetuity.
It is a legal chattel interest if it satisfies the statutory definition of a term of years absolute.[2]
It is a mere equitable interest if it is to endure for any other period, such as the life of the owner.

Servitudes.

Servitudes.   As we have seen, the *jura in re aliena* which are known to English Law cover a very wide field and include such diverse subjects as advowsons, tithes, rentcharges and so on,[3] but our present concern is solely with what Roman lawyers called " praedial servitudes ".   Though servitude is a word that is occasionally adopted by the judges,[4] it is not admitted as a term of art in English Law, and yet it is a suitable expression to denote the particular legal interests which form the subject of this chapter.

Definition.

A praedial servitude in Roman Law meant a right *in rem*, annexed to a definite piece of land, the *praedium dominans*, which entitled the owner of that land to do something or to prevent the doing of something on another piece of land, the *praedium serviens*.[5]   This is a sufficiently accurate description of easements and profits which represent the praedial servitudes of English Law.

---

[1] *Supra*, pp. 100–1.   [2] *Supra*, pp. 336–7.   [3] *Supra*, p. 101, note 2.
[4] *E.g. Dalton* v. *Angus* (1881), L. R. 6 App. Cas. 740, at p. 796 ; *per* Lord SELBORNE.
[5] Moyle, *Justinian* (4th Edn.), p. 214.

An easement is a privilege without a profit,[1] that is to say, it is a right attached to one particular piece of land which allows the owner of that land either to use the land of another person in a particular manner (as by walking over or depositing rubbish on it) or to restrict its user by that other person to a particular extent, but which does not allow him to take any part of its natural produce or its soil.[2] Easements described.

Thus an easement may be either positive or negative.[3] It is positive if it consists of a right to do something upon the land of another, as, for example, to walk or to place erections such as signboards thereon. Positive and negative easements.

A negative easement, on the other hand, does not permit the execution of an act, but imposes a restriction upon the use which another person may make of his land. For instance, the easement of light signifies that the adjoining owner may not build so as unreasonably to obstruct the flow of light, and again an easement of support implies that the adjoining owner must not interfere with his own land or building so as to disturb his neighbour's.

An easement confers upon its owner no proprietary or possessory right in the land affected. It merely imposes a definite and limited restriction upon the proprietary rights of the owner of the land. A right which entitles one person to the unrestricted use of the land of another may be an effective right to ownership or possession, but it cannot be an easement.[4]

A *profit à prendre*, as defined by LINDLEY, L.J., is "a right to take something off another's land,"[5] and it is this participation in the produce of the soil or in the soil itself that principally distinguishes a profit from an easement. A right is a profit only if the thing to be taken is something that is capable of ownership. Thus the rights to pasture cattle on another's land, or to take sand or fish from another's river, or to take turf, stones or pheasants from another's estate are all examples of profits, for such things are capable of ownership; but a right to collect and carry away water from a spring on another person's land, or to water cattle in another's stream is an easement, since water is no part of the soil like sand, nor the produce of soil like grass, and unless stored in a tank or other receptacle is not capable of private ownership.[6] Definition of a profit.

---

[1] *Hewlins* v. *Shippam* (1826), 5 B. & C. 221 ; Termes de la Ley, *sub voce* " Easement."

[2] *Manning* v. *Wasdale* (1836), 5 A. & E. 758.

[3] *Dalton* v. *Angus* (1881), 6 App. Cas. 740, 821.

[4] *Copeland* v. *Greenhalf*, [1952] Ch. 488; [1952] 1 All E. R. 809.; dist. *Ward* v. *Kirkland*, [1966] 1 All E. R. 609; [1966] 1 W. L. R. 601.

[5] *Duke of Sutherland* v. *Heathcote*, [1892] 1 Ch. 484.

[6] Co. Litt. 4a ; Blackstone, vol. ii. 18 ; *Mason* v. *Hill* (1833), 5 B. & Ad. 1 ; *Race* v. *Ward* (1855), 4 E. & B. 702.

SECTION II. EASEMENTS.

SUMMARY.

(A) CHARACTERISTICS OF EASEMENTS.

Importance of distinguishing between easements and other rights.

Introductory Note. A question that not infrequently arises is whether some right exercisable over the land of another is an easement or a right of an inferior nature, and it is a question of capital importance. An owner may grant a multitude of different rights over his land to X., but it will make a world of difference to the legal position of X. whether they are easements or not. An easement held in perpetuity is a *jus in rem*, not a mere *jus in personam*; it permanently binds the land over which it is exercisable and permanently avails the land for the advantage of which it exists.[1] If X. acquires an easement either in perpetuity or for a term of years absolute, he becomes the owner of an actual legal interest in the land and can enforce it against anybody who comes to the land whether by way of purchase, lease, gift or as a squatter, and whether with or without notice of the easement.

Thus at common law the benefit of an easement passes with a transfer of the land to which it is annexed without being specially mentioned,[2] and it is now expressly provided that a conveyance of land shall be deemed to include and shall operate to convey all easements which are attached to the land conveyed.[3]

Personal rights distinguished from easements.

On the other hand, if X. is given some right over the land of another which is analogous to an easement but which nevertheless the law does not regard as an easement, he acquires a contractual

---

[1] *Leech* v. *Schweder* (1874), L. R. 9 Ch. App. 463, at p. 474.
[2] Co. Litt. 121*b*.
[3] Law of Property Act, 1925, s. 62 (1), re-enacting Conveyancing Act, 1881, s. 6 (1); *infra*, pp. 463–6.

right, not a definite interest in the land. It is a personal right whose infringement may give him a remedy in damages against the other party to the contract, and if negative in nature it may be enforceable in equity against a person who acquires the grantor's land with notice of its existence,[1] but it is not a real right enforceable irrespective of notice against all subsequent owners of that land. Neither can a right be given the status of an easement at the free will of contracting parties, for the rule is that no right over land will be regarded as an easement unless it possesses certain attributes which the law has determined.

This being the state of the law, the first task must be to obtain an exact knowledge of what those attributes and characteristics are, so that in all cases of uncertainty it may be possible to fix the legal status of any particular right.

Characteristics. If an interest is to be an easement it must possess the four following characteristics [2] :—

(1) **There must be a dominant and a servient tenement.**[3] The very nature of an easement, as being a right *in alieno solo*, requires that there shall be a tenement over which it is exercisable, the *servient tenement*, but in addition to this the law requires that there shall be another tenement, the *dominant tenement*, for the benefit of which the easement exists. To adopt legal phraseology an easement must be appurtenant or attached to land. *(Easement must be appurtenant to land.)*

If X., the owner of Blackacre, has acquired a right of way over the adjoining tenement Whiteacre, he possesses an easement of way not because he is X., but because he is the fee simple owner of Blackacre. The easement exists because Blackacre exists.[4]

It follows from this that there cannot be an easement *in gross*,[5] *i.e.* an easement that is independent of the ownership of land by the person who claims the right. Of course a person who does not own a yard of property may be granted a privilege to pass over Whiteacre, but though this may give him a contractual right it certainly does not entitle him to an easement. It amounts to a licence confined in its effect to the actual parties.

(2) **An easement must accommodate the dominant tenement.** It is a fundamental principle that an easement must not only be appurtenant to a dominant tenement, but *(Easement must accommodate dominant tenement.)*

[1] See the doctrine of *Tulk* v. *Moxhay, infra*, p. 537, *et seq.*
[2] *In re Ellenborough Park*, [1956] Ch. 131 ; [1955] 2 All E. R. 38.
[3] Holdsworth, *History of English Law*, vol. vii. pp. 324 *et seq.*
[4] *Rangeley* v. *Midland Ry.* (1868), 3 Ch. App. 306, 311 ; *Ackroyd* v. *Smith* (1850), 10 C. B. 164, 188 ; *Hawkins* v. *Rutter*, [1892] 1 Q. B. 668.
[5] *Ackroyd* v. *Smith, supra* ; *Weekly* v. *Wildman* (1698), Ld. Raym. 406, *per* TREBY, C.J. In the U.S.A. both easements and profits may be *in gross*.

must also be connected with the normal enjoyment of that tenement.[1] There must be a direct *nexus* between the enjoyment of the right and the user of the dominant tenement.[2] This requirement has been stated in various ways:—

"An easement must be connected with the enjoyment of the "dominant tenement and must be for its benefit."[3]

"It must have some natural connection with the estate as being "for its benefit."[4]

"The incident sought to be annexed, so that the assignee of the "land may take advantage of it, must be beneficial to the land in "respect of the ownership."[5]

To take a simple example, a right of way in order to rank as an easement need not lead right up to the dominant tenement, but it must at least have some natural connection with it.[6] You cannot, remarked BYLES, J., have a right of way over land in Kent appurtenant to an estate in Northumberland,[7] for a right of way in Kent cannot possibly be advantageous to Northumberland land.[8] We may expand the statement of the principle thus : a right enjoyed by one over the land of another does not possess the status of an easement unless it accommodates and serves the dominant tenement, and is reasonably necessary for the better enjoyment of that tenement, for if it has no necessary connexion therewith, although it confers an advantage upon the owner and renders his ownership of the land more valuable, it is not an easement at all, but a mere contractual right personal to and only enforceable between the two contracting parties.

Whether the necessary *nexus* exists depends greatly upon the nature of the dominant tenement and the nature of the right alleged.   If, for example, the dominant tenement is a residential house and if there is annexed to it by express grant a right to use an adjoining garden for purposes of relaxation and pleasure, this is a clear case where the right is sufficiently connected with the normal enjoyment of the house to rank as an easement.[9] The fact that the right enhances the value of the dominant tenement is a relevant, but not a decisive, consideration.[10] The principle is perhaps best illustrated by *Hill* v. *Tupper*,[11] where the facts were as follows :—

---

[1] *Ackroyd* v. *Smith* (1850), 11 C. B. 19.
[2] *In re Ellenborough Park*, [1956] Ch. 131, 174 ; [1955] 2 All E. R. 38, 42.
[3] *Clapman* v. *Edwards*, [1938] 2 All E. R. 507. Gale on Easements (12th Edn.), p. 20.
[4] *Bailey* v. *Stephens* (1862), 12 C. B. (N.S.) 91, 115, *per* BYLES, J.
[5] *Ibid.*
[6] *Todrick* v. *Western National Omnibus Co.*, [1934] Ch. 561.
[7] *Bailey* v. *Stephens* (1862), 12 C. B. (N.S.) 99.
[8] *Todrick* v. *Western National Omnibus Co.*, [1934] Ch. 561, 580, ROMER, L.J.
[9] *In re Ellenborough Park*, [1956] Ch. 131 ; [1955] 2 All E. R. 38.
[10] *Ibid.*, at pp. 173, 43 respectively.   [11] (1863) 2 H. & C. 121.

A canal company leased land adjoining the canal to Hill and gave him the " sole and exclusive right " to let out pleasure boats on the canal. Tupper, an innkeeper, disregarded this privilege by himself letting out boats for fishing purposes. Hill thereupon brought an action in his own name against Tupper, his alleged cause of action being a disturbance of his easement to put boats on the canal.

It was held that the right conferred upon Hill by the contract with the company was not an easement but a mere licence personal to himself, since it was acquired in order to exploit an independent business enterprise, not to accommodate the riparian land as such.[1] The right was not beneficial to the land as land ; rather, the land was required for the exploitation of the right.

The principle applies equally to profits appurtenant, and may be illustrated by the remark of Coke that the right of cutting turfs for fuel cannot be claimed as appurtenant to land, but only to a house, because the use of fuel has no connection with land as such. In the leading case of *Bailey* v. *Stephens*,[2]

> A., who was seised in fee of a piece of land called Bloody Field, claimed the right to enter an adjoining close for the purpose of cutting down, carrying away and converting to his own use the trees and wood growing thereon, but it was held that, as the wood was not employed for the beneficial enjoyment of Bloody Field, it was not connected therewith and so was not a valid profit.

(3) Dominant and servient owners must be different persons. If one person owns two adjoining properties which, physically speaking, are separate properties, any rights that he may have been in the habit of exercising over one or other of them, as, for example, by passing over one to reach the highway, are not easements (though they are often called " quasi-easements "), because they derive from his ownership not of the quasi-dominant land, but of the quasi-servient land itself.[3] FRY, L.J., in one case said :— *Owner cannot have easements over his own land.*

> " Of course, strictly speaking, the owner of two tenements
> " can have no easement over one of them in respect of the
> " other. When the owner of Whiteacre and Blackacre passes
> " over the former to Blackacre, he is not exercising a right of
> " way in respect of Blackacre ; he is merely making use of his
> " own land to get from one part to another."[4]

---

[1] *In re Ellenborough Park, supra,* at pp. 175, 45 respectively. Contrast the Pennsylvanian case of *Miller* v. *Lutheran Conference and Camp Association,* [1938] 331 P.A. 241; Aigler, Smith and Tefft, *Cases on Property* (1960), vol. ii, p. 212, where a somewhat similar right was treated as an easement *in gross* capable of assignment.

[2] (1862), 12 C. B. (N.S.) 91.

[3] *Bolton* v. *Bolton* (1879), 11 Ch. D. 968.

[4] *Roe* v. *Siddons* (1888), 22 Q. B. D. 224, at p. 236 ; and see *Metropolitan Ry.* v. *Fowler,* [1892] 1 Q. B. 165 ; *Derry* v. *Sanders,* [1919] 1 K. B. 223.

Thus, if X. is the owner of two separate tenements and he lets one of them to a tenant, the latter cannot acquire by prescription an easement over the other, for his occupation is in the eyes of the law the occupation of his landlord, a person who cannot acquire an easement against himself.[1] As will be seen later, however, the right to light is exceptional in this respect.[2]

If the principle were otherwise and if rights exercised by a man over one of two properties both owned by him were to be treated as easements, they would necessarily remain vested in him after a sale of the quasi-servient tenement. They would also pass without express mention to a purchaser of the quasi-dominant tenement. But these consequences do not ensue. To quote an ancient instance :—

> " J. S. had a close and a wood adjoining to it, and time out
> " of mind a way had been used over the close to the wood to
> " carry and re-carry. He granted the close to one and the
> " wood to another. The question was, if the grantee of the
> " wood shall have the way? And it was adjudged he should not,
> " for the grantor by the grant of the close had excluded himself
> " of the way, because it was not saved to him, and he himself
> " could not use it, no more can his grantee."[3]

The moral to be drawn from this rule is that, when a large estate is split up and sold to different purchasers, any quasi-easements which were enjoyed by the former owner should be expressly reserved to the purchaser of the quasi-dominant tenement.[4]

Right to easements depends upon grant, actual or presumed.

(4) **A right over land cannot amount to an easement unless it is capable of forming the subject-matter of a grant.** As we shall see, apart from statute, every easement must originate in a grant, either express, implied or presumed. It follows from this that no right can have the status of an easement unless it is the possible subject-matter of a grant.[5] This in turn requires that its nature and extent should be capable of exact description. Its sphere of operation must be precise and certain. If it is so vague or so indeterminate as to defy precise definition, it cannot rank as an easement.[6] This requirement, which is common to all forms of grant, is especially important in the present context, for a right over the land of another is allowed to ripen into an easement if it has been enjoyed for a long time without any inter-

---

[1] *Warburton* v. *Parke* (1857), 2 H. & N. 64; *Gayford* v. *Moffatt* (1868), L. R. 4 Ch. App. 133.

[2] *Infra*, pp. 508; 511.

[3] *Dell* v. *Babthorpe* (1593), Cro. Eliz. 300.

[4] *Wheeldon* v. *Burrows* (1879), 12 Ch. D. 31, 49; *infra*, pp. 489–92.

[5] *Potter* v. *North* (1669), 1 Wms. Saund. 347, *arguendo*; *Goodman* v. *Saltash Corpn.* (1882), 7 App. Cas. 633, 654; *Dalton* v. *Angus* (1881), 6 App. Cas. 740, 795; *Chastey* v. *Ackland* (1895), 11 T. L. R. 460; *Harris* v. *De Pinna* (1886), 33 Ch. D. 238, 262; *Bryant* v. *Lefever* (1879), 4 C. P. D. 172, 178, BRAMWELL, L. J.

[6] For a criticism of the statement in the text, see 30 *California Law Review*, pp. 133 *et seq.*

ruption by the servient owner, but this necessarily implies that there should be something definite capable of interruption.[1]

A right to the flow of light to a particular window satisfies the test of certainty, for not only does the light pass over the servient tenement along a defined channel, but it can be interrupted by an obstruction placed across its line of approach.[2] Again, it has been held that a *jus spatiandi*, *i.e.* a right to wander at large over the servient tenement, is sufficiently determinate to constitute an easement if it is limited to a particular house or group of houses and is exercisable over an adjoining garden.[3] So also the right to a flow of air can subsist as an easement if it is claimed in respect of some definite channel, such as a ventilator in a building,[4] but not if what is claimed is that the current of air flowing indiscriminately over the entire servient tenement shall not be interrupted.[5]

In *Harris* v. *De Pinna*,[6] where such a claim to the general flow of air was made, BOWEN, L.J., said :—

> " It would be just like amenity of prospect, a subject matter
> " which is incapable of definition.   So the passage of undefined
> " air gives rise to no rights and can give rise to no rights for
> " the best of all reasons, the reason of common sense, because
> " you cannot acquire any rights against others by a user which
> " they cannot interrupt."

It follows that a person is without remedy if his premises have been exposed to damp and frost owing to the demolition of an adjacent house, for there can be no easement of protection against the weather.[7]

Other practical consequences result from the general principle that an easement must originate in a grant.   For instance, a claimant to an easement must be a person capable of receiving a grant, that is, he must be a definite person or a definite body such as a corporation.   Thus a claim put forward by a vague fluctuating body of persons, such as the inhabitants of a village, will not be sustainable.[8] — *Must be a capable grantee.*

Again, the same principle demands that the servient owner should have been lawfully entitled to grant the right claimed to be an easement.   Thus a claim[9] against a company incorporated by statute will fail upon proof that the grant was *ultra vires*.[10] — *Must be a capable grantor.*

Such, then, are the essential characteristics of easements, and it — *Rights which lack the necessary characteristics not easements.*

[1] *Webb* v. *Bird* (1862), 13 C. B. (N.S.) 841, 843.
[2] *Harris* v. *De Pinna, supra,* at p. 259.
[3] *In re Ellenborough Park,* [1956] Ch. 131 ; [1955] 2 All E. R. 38.
[4] *Cable* v. *Bryant,* [1908] 1 Ch. 259.
[5] *Webb* v. *Bird, supra* ; *Bryant* v. *Lefever, supra.*
[6] (1886), 33 Ch. D. 238, at p. 262.
[7] *Phipps* v. *Pears,* [1965] 1 Q. B. 76; [1964] 2 All E. R. 35, see 27 M. L. R., pp. 614–5 (H. W. Wilkinson); 80 *L. Q. R.* pp. 318–21 (R.E.M.).
[8] *Infra,* pp. 482; 527 *et seq.*
[9] *Paine & Co., Ltd* v. *St. Neots Gas and Coke Co.,* [1939] 3 All E. R. 812.
[10] *Mulliner* v. *Midland Ry. Co.* (1879), L. R. 11 Ch. D. 611.

is important that they should be borne in mind, for otherwise certain judicial statements that new kinds of rights *in rem* cannot be created at will may be misunderstood. This principle has been asserted more than once. Thus Lord BROUGHAM said[1] :—

> " There are certain known incidents to property and its enjoyment,
> " amongst others certain burdens wherewith it may be affected, or
> " rights which may be created and enjoyed over it by parties other
> " than the owner. . . . But it must not therefore be supposed that
> " incidents of a novel kind can be devised and attached to property at
> " the fancy or caprice of any owner ; . . . great detriment would
> " arise and much confusion of rights, if parties were allowed to invent
> " new modes of holding and enjoying real property, and to impress
> " upon their land and tenements a peculiar character."

POLLOCK, C.B., in *Hill* v. *Tupper*,[2] said :—

> " A new species of incorporeal hereditament cannot be created at
> " the will and pleasure of the owner of property, but he must be con-
> " tent to accept the estate and the right to dispose of it subject to the
> " law as settled by decisions or controlled by Act of Parliament."

Again, CRESSWELL, J., in *Ackroyd* v. *Smith*,[3] said :—

> " Nor can the owner of land render it subject to a new species of
> " burden, so as to bind it in the hands of an assignee."

Unless such language is scrutinized with some care there is a danger that it may be taken to imply that the classes of easements are closed. For instance, one learned author has said that:—

> " The various kinds of easements which are recognized at common
> " law are strictly limited and defined ; nothing can amount to a valid
> " easement unless the subject matter of the claim is capable of being
> " referred to one or other of six definite heads—air, light, support,
> " water, ways and fences."[4]

List of easements not closed.

Although it may not make much real difference to the actual result, it is submitted that this interpretation of the doctrine laid down by certain judges is not correct. That doctrine means not that an easement of a kind never heard of before cannot be created, but that a new species of incorporeal hereditament or a new species of burden cannot be brought into being and given the status and legal effect of an easement. In other words, if a right exhibits the four characteristics described above, it is an easement that will run with the dominant and against the servient tene-ment, even though its object may be to fulfil a purpose for which it has not hitherto been used; but if it lacks one or more of those characteristics, it may, indeed, be enforceable between the con-

---

[1] *Keppell* v. *Bailey* (1834), 2 My. & K. 517, at p. 535.
[2] [1863], 2 H. & C. 121, at pp. 127–8.
[3] (1850), 10 C. B. 164, at p. 188. *Copeland* v. *Greenhalf*, [1952] Ch. 488.
See Holdsworth, *History of English Law*, vol. vii. pp. 331 *et seq.*
[4] Behan, *Covenants affecting Land*, p. 45.

tracting parties, but it cannot, like an easement, be enforceable by
or against third parties.[1] One of the main purposes of law is to
keep pace with the requirements of society and to adapt itself to
new modes of life and new business methods, a fact that was
present to the mind of Lord St. Leonards when he said that:—

> "The category of servitudes and easements must alter and expand
> "with the changes that take place in the circumstances of mankind."[2]

Thus in a case where an easement was claimed to place stores
and casks upon land reclaimed from the sea, the Privy Council
said:—

> "The law must adapt itself to the conditions of modern society and
> "trade, and there is nothing in the purposes for which the easement
> "is claimed inconsistent in principle with a right of easement as
> "such."[3]

The same [4] principle was recognized by Lord Herschell in
an earlier case when he said:—

> "Easements may be of various characters, and it is a fallacy to   *Simpson* v.
> "suppose that every easement must be brought within some particular *Godman-*
> "class which has been recognized, such as the class relating to water- *chester*
> "courses, or light or air or otherwise. If the right is granted by the *Corpn.*
> "owner of land to enter and do something on the grantor's land for
> "the benefit of the land of that other person, that *primâ facie* is an
> "easement. And I do not see any reason why there should not be
> "a perfectly valid easement in this right to go upon the land of the
> "owner of locks and sluices, and in times of flood raise those locks
> "or sluices to let the water down for the benefit of the land of the
> "person who exercises the right."[4]

Examples of Easements. The following list of ease-   Examples of
ments, which begins with the most important kinds and which,   easements.
of course, is not exhaustive, will afford some idea of how great
their variety is:—

(a) Rights of *way*, whether for general or special purposes, and   Way.
    whether exercisable in all modes or limited to a carriage way,
    bridle way, foot way or a way for cattle.

(b) A right that the *light* flowing over adjoining land to a window   Light.
    shall not be unreasonably obstructed.

(c) Rights in connection with *water*, such as a right to enter upon   Water.
    adjoining land to divert the course of a stream for irrigation
    purposes, or a right to pollute a river or to discharge water on
    to the land of another.

(d) A right to the *support* of buildings by adjoining land or buildings.   Support.
    (Though a landowner has a natural right to have his *land*
    supported by adjoining land, yet a right to have *buildings*
    supported can be claimed only if it has actually been
    acquired as an easement.)

---

[1] *In re Ellenborough Park*, [1956] Ch. 131, at pp. 140–1; [1955] 2 All E. R.
38, at pp. 42–3.
[2] *Dyce* v. *Hay* (1852), 1 Macq. 305.
[3] *A.-G. of Southern Nigeria* v. *John Holt & Co.*, [1915[A. C. 599, at 617.
[4] *Simpson* v. *Godmanchester Corpn.*, [1896] 1 Ch. 214, 219. Perhaps it
would be more accurate to say that the categories are closed, but not the
purposes for which each category may be used.

Fence.

(e) **Right to have a *fence* maintained by an adjoining owner.**

Strictly speaking, there can be no easement requiring X., the owner of Blackacre, to maintain his fences for the benefit of Y., the owner of the adjoining Whiteacre, since an easement connotes not activity, but mere passive sufferance on the part of the servient owner. Moreover, such an easement would for the most part be superfluous. The main purpose of a fence is to prevent cattle trespass, and, since the duty of a landowner is to keep his own cattle in, not to keep his neighbour's out, a remedy is always available to Y. if his land is invaded by X.'s stock.

Nevertheless, it is recognized that a specific obligation binding X. to maintain effective fences on his own land may arise by prescription, *i.e.* by immemorial conduct, which, as in the case of an easement, will be enforceable by the successive owners of the dominant Whiteacre against the successive owners of the servient Blackacre.[1] This will not be superfluous, since it will render Y. immune from liability for cattle trespass upon X.'s land. But to establish such a prescriptive obligation it must be proved that the owners of the servient tenement have not only consistently executed repairs, but have done so as a matter of duty, as and when required by the dominant owners.[2]

The law, however, does not recognize a prescriptive obligation of one owner to repair the fences on the land of another.

Miscellaneous easements.

Such are the only easements commonly found in practice, but we may add examples of some variations and extensions of these interests :—

(i) Right to hang clothes on a line passing over neighbouring soil.[3]
(ii) Right to run telephone lines over neighbouring land.[4]
(iii) Right to use a close for the purpose of mixing muck and preparing manure thereon for the use of an adjoining farm.[5]
(iv) Right to fix a signboard to the walls of another's house.[6]
(v) Right of a landowner to use a particular seat in a parish church.[7]
(vi) Right to nail trees to a wall.[8]
(vii) Right to lay stones upon adjoining land to prevent sand from being washed away by the sea.[9]
(viii) Right to use a lavatory situated on the servient tenement.[10]

It seems clear that several of these miscellaneous easements cannot well be referred to any of the definite heads—air, light, support, water, ways, and fences—unless considerable latitude is given to the conception of support.

Distinction between easements and other rights.

Having seen something of the nature of easements, we will

---

[1] *Jones* v. *Price,* [1965] 2 Q. B. 618; [1965] 2 All E. R. 625.
[2] Contrast *Hilton* v. *Ankesson* (1872), 27 L.T. 519, with *Lawrence* v. *Jenkins* (1873), L.R. 8 Q. B. 274; Bullen and Leake (3rd Edn.), p. 329.
[3] *Drewell* v. *Towler* (1832), 3 B. & Ad. 735.
[4] *Lancashire Telephone Co.* v. *Manchester Overseers* (1884), 14 Q. B. D. 267.
[5] *Pye* v. *Mumford* (1848), 11 Q. B. 666.
[6] *Moody* v. *Steggles* (1879), L. R. 12 Ch. D. 261.
[7] *Mainwaring* v. *Giles* (1822), 5 B. & Ald. 356 ; *Brumfitt* v. *Roberts* (1870), L. R. 5 C. P. 224.
[8] *Hawkins* v. *Wallis* (1763), 2 Wils. 173.
[9] *Philpot* v. *Bath* (1905), 21 T. L. R. 634.
[10] *Miller* v. *Emcer Products, Ltd.,* [1956] Ch. 304 ; [1956] 1 All E. R. 237.

conclude this part of the subject by adverting to other rights of a somewhat similar nature from which they must be distinguished.

1. **Licences.** A licence is created in favour of B. if, without being given any legal estate or interest, he is permitted by A. to enter A.'s land for an agreed purpose. It is an authority that justifies what would otherwise be a trespass. It is said to be *coupled with a grant* when the licensee, having been granted a definite proprietary interest in the land or in chattels lying on the land, is given permission to enter in order that he may enjoy or exploit the interest. Such a licence, as distinct from a *bare* licence, is of this nature if given to a man who is entitled to chattels,[1] or to growing timber [2] or to game on the land.[3] There are here two separate matters—the grant and the licence.

> " But a licence to hunt in a man's park and to carry away the deer
> " killed to his own use ; to cut down a tree in a man's ground and to
> " carry it away the next day after to his own use, are licences as to
> " the acts of hunting and cutting down the tree ; but as to the
> " carrying away of the deer killed and the tree cut they are grants." [4]

Such a licence is not effective at common law unless the grant is formally valid. Thus a grant by an unsealed writing of a right to shoot and carry away game, coupled with a licence to enter the land, is ineffective, since a deed is necessary at common law for the grant of a *profit à prendre*.[5] But the rule at equity, which now prevails and which is illustrated in another context by *Walsh* v. *Lonsdale*,[6] is that a contract to grant an interest is treated as if the formalities required by law had been observed. Thus a properly evidenced contract to grant a right of shooting over land is specifically enforceable and is as effective as an actual grant under seal.[7]

If not coupled with a grant a licence may be either gratuitous, as for instance where permission is given to play cricket on a field; or supported by consideration, as for instance where the licensee buys a ticket for a theatre or a race meeting,[8] or where he is contractually entitled to the exclusive privilege of supplying refreshments in a theatre.[9]

Effect of a Licence. At common law a bare licence may be revoked at any moment, whether it is part of a contract or a mere indulgent permission unsupported by consideration, as for

Side notes: Licence. — Licence coupled with a grant. — Effect at common law of a bare licence.

---

[1] *Wood* v. *Manley* (1839), 11 A. & El. 34.
[2] *Jones (James) & Sons, Ltd.* v. *Tankerville (Earl)*, [1909] 2 Ch. 440.
[3] *Frogley* v. *Lovelace (Earl)* (1859), John. 333.
[4] *Thomas* v. *Sorrell* (1673), Vaugh. 330, at p. 351, *per* VAUGHAN C.J.
[5] *Wood* v. *Leadbitter* (1845), 13 M. & W. 838.
[6] *Supra*, pp. 356–9.
[7] *Hurst* v. *Picture Theatres, Ltd.*, [1915] 1 K. B. 1 ; *Frogley* v. *Lovelace, supra*.
[8] *Wood* v. *Leadbitter, supra* ; *Hurst* v. *Picture Theatres, Ltd., supra*.
[9] *Warr (Frank) & Co., Ltd.* v. *London County Council*, [1904] 1 K. B. 713, 723.

example, a permission to practise golf in a park. Its only legal effect is that until revoked it precludes the licensor from maintaining an action of trespass.[1] If, however, a licensee remains on the land after his permission to be there has been withdrawn, he is treated by the common law as a trespasser, even though the withdrawal is in complete disregard of the contract.[2] He cannot enforce his contractual right to occupation, although it is conceded that he may recover damages.[3] It is immaterial that he has entered the land and has acted to his financial detriment in the belief that his right to occupation is legally secure.

The distinction made at common law between a bare licence and a licence coupled with a grant was stated as follows by Baron ALDERSON in *Wood* v. *Leadbitter*.[4]

> " A mere licence is revocable ; but that which is called a licence " is often something more than a licence ; it often comprises or is " connected with a grant, and then the party who has given it cannot " in general revoke it so as to defeat his grant to which it is incident. " It may further be observed that a licence under seal (provided it " be a mere licence), is as revocable as a licence by parol, and on the " other hand a licence by parol, coupled with a grant, is as irrevo- " cable as a licence by deed, provided only that the grant is of a " nature capable of being made by parol."

The judgment, indeed, contained dicta suggesting that the particular licence in issue, which was to enter a racecourse for the purpose of viewing the races, would have been irrevocable had it been made by deed. These dicta, however, must now be disregarded, since they reflected the view current in 1845 that an easement might be created in gross, a view that was not finally exploded until twenty-three years later.[5]

Effect in equity of a bare licence.

In 1915, the influence of the Judicature Act upon a bare licence was considered for the first time by the Court of Appeal,[6] but even as late as this the confusion evident in *Wood* v. *Leadbitter* concerning the effect of a deed still pervaded the reasoning of the Lords Justices.

> The plaintiff, who had been ejected from a cinema theatre for which he had bought a ticket, elected to sue the owners for assault rather than for breach of contract, since, if he could establish this cause of action, he would recover substantial, not merely nominal, damages.

This required proof that the licence was irrevocable during the

---

[1] *Thomas* v. *Sorrell* (1673), Vaugh. 330, 351. Any revocation must be clear and reasonable ; *Minister of Health* v. *Bellotti*, [1944] K. B. 298 ; [1944] 1 All E. R. 238 ; *Mellor* v. *Watkins* (1874), 9 Q. B. 400.
[2] *Wood* v. *Leadbitter* (1845), 13 M. & W. 838 ; *Thompson* v. *Park*, [1944] K. B. 408 ; [1944] 2 All E. R. 477.
[3] *Kerrison* v. *Smith*, [1897] 2 Q. B. 445.
[4] (1845), 13 M. & W. 838, at pp. 844-5.
[5] *Rangeley* v. *Midland Ry. Co.* (1868), L. R. 3 Ch. App. 306.
[6] *Hurst* v. *Picture Theatres, Ltd.*, [1915] 1 K. B. 1. See also *Cowell* v. *Rosehill Racecourse* (1937), 56 C. L. R. 605 (Australia).

continuance of the performance, but the Court of Appeal overcame the difficulty by holding that it was coupled with an interest and that despite the absence of a deed the plaintiff was entitled in equity to a decree for the specific performance of his contractual right to view the complete entertainment. The fatal defect in this reasoning, of course, was that there was no proprietary interest capable of being contained in a grant. . . .

"The right to see a spectacle cannot, in the ordinary sense of legal "language, be regarded as a proprietory interest. Fifty thousand "people who pay to see a football match do not obtain fifty thousand "interests to the football ground."[1]

A more successful way of softening the rigidity of the common law was indicated in the dicta of the House of Lords in *Winter Garden Theatre (London), Ltd.* v. *Millennium Productions, Ltd.,*[2] where their Lordships favoured the argument that if a contractual licence is given for value, though not coupled with a grant, its revocation in breach of the contract should be prevented where possible[3] by the grant of an injunction. In other words, equity does what it can by means of a decree of injunction to preserve the sanctity of a bargain[4] and by that remedy it is prepared to restrain a revocation that would derogate from the right of occupation conferred by the contract. If the contract does not expressly state the time for which the licence is to last, a promise by the licensor must be implied that he will not revoke the permission in a manner contrary to the intention of the parties.[5] The exact scope of the implied promise, if any, must be ascertained in each case, for it will, of course, vary with the circumstances. For instance a spectator who buys a ticket for a theatre is a licensee with a right to occupy his seat until the spectacle is over[6] ; a licence of the " front of the house rights " at a theatre cannot be revoked until a reasonable time has been afforded to the licensee for his withdrawal.[7] In those cases such as *Hurst* v. *Picture Theatres, Ltd.,* where there is no time or opportunity to obtain an injunction, the court will presumably give judgment on the basis of what the rights of the parties would have been, had the grant of this remedy been practicable.

As between the parties themselves, then, the effect of a licence is reasonably clear. Difficulties have arisen, however, when we travel further and ask whether the licensee acquires a personal right

Contractual licence does not bind successors in title of licensor.

[1] *Cowell* v. *Rosehill Racecourse Co., Ltd.,* [1937], 56 C. L. R. 605, *per* LATHAM, C.J., whose judgment is conveniently summarized by Lord EVER-SHED in 70 *L. Q. R.,* p. 333.

[2] [1948] A. C. 173 ; [1947] 2 All E. R. 331; distinguished, *Australian Blue Metal, Ltd.* v. *Hughes,* [1963] A. C. 74; [1962] 3 All E. R. 335.

[3] *Thompson* v. *Park,* [1944] K. B. 408 ; [1944] 2 All E. R. 477.

[4] *Winter Garden Theatre (London), Ltd.* v. *Millennium Productions, Ltd.,* [1948] A. C. 173, 202, *per* Lord UTHWATT ; [1947] 2 All E. R. 331, 343.

[5] *Errington* v. *Errington and Woods,* [1952] 1 K. B. 290; [1952] 1 All E. R. 149.

[6] *Hurst* v. *Picture Theatres, Ltd.,* [1915] 1 K. B. 1.

[7] *Winter Garden Theatre (London), Ltd.* v. *Millennium Productions, Ltd.,* [1948] A. C. 173 ; [1947] 2 All E. R. 331.

enforceable only against the licensor or a proprietary interest binding upon the licensor's successors in title except a purchaser for value of the legal estate. This problem may be considered by reference to the case of *Errington* v. *Errington and Woods*[1] where the facts were as follows:—

> A father bought a house for £750. He paid £250 in cash and borrowed £500 from a building society, the loan being secured by a mortgage of the house and repayable by instalments of fifteen shillings a week. He allowed his son and daughter-in-law to go into possession and told them that if they paid all the instalments he would convey the legal estate to them. He died nine years later having devised the house to his widow. The son then left his wife, but the latter remained in occupation of the house and continued to pay the instalments.

An action brought by the widow for possession against the daughter-in-law was dismissed. The Court of Appeal held that the son and daughter-in-law were neither tenants at will nor weekly tenants, but licensees entitled to occupy the house as long as they paid the instalments. This licence was binding upon the licensor's devisee.

Substantially, the reasoning adopted by the court was that, since the son and daughter-in-law were entitled in equity to restrain the revocation of the licence contrary to the terms of the implied contract, they acquired in effect an equitable interest, or at least an equity,[2] in the land that was capable of binding third parties, as in the case of a restrictive covenant.[3]

This reasoning must be considered afresh in the light of *National Provincial Bank, Ltd.* v. *Ainsworth*,[4] in which the House of Lords finally rejected the so-called 'deserted wife's equity'. It overruled the cases in which it had been held that a wife deserted by her husband had an equity, *qua* licensee, to continue in occupation of the matrimonial home subject to any order to the contrary that might be made by the court under section 17 of the Married Women's Property Act, 1882. But, though the decision is an authority only on this particular matter, the position of contractual licenses inevitably came under review, and it is a reasonable inference from the observations of their Lordships that if the occasion arises they will not accept the ground upon which *Errington* v. *Errington and Woods* was decided.

Lord UPJOHN, Lord WILBERFORCE and in the Court of Appeal, RUSSELL, L.J. associated themselves with the strictures on the decision made by Professor Wade[5] and, although they refrained from expressing a final opinion upon the position of a contractual

---

[1] [1952] 1 K. B. 290; [1952] 1 All E. R. 149.
[2] *Supra*, p. 69.
[3] This reasoning was defended by the present author in 16 M.L.R. pp. 1–13; but rejected by Professor H. W. R. Wade in 68 *L. Q. R.* pp. 337–52. For an attack on the decision from a different angle, see 69 *L. Q. R.* pp. 466–84 (A. D. Hargreaves).
[4] [1965] A. C. 1175; [1965] 2 All E. R. 472.
[5] See note 2 *supra*,

licensee let into occupation of land, their disinclination to regard him as possessing more than a personal right is reasonably evident. RUSSELL, L.J., in particular, resisted the view that this personal right is converted into some form of equitable interest binding on third parties merely because the licensor may be restrained from revoking his permission.[1] Moreover, there was an equal disinclination to temper the authority of *King* v. *David Allen & Sons,, Billposting, Ltd.*[2] and *Clore* v. *Theatrical Properties, Ltd.*,[3] which held that the rights of a contractual licensee cannot be enforced against third parties.[4]

It does not follow, however, that the actual decision in *Errington* v. *Errington and Woods* was wrong. In fact, the prevalent view seems to be that it is sustainable on the principle stated in *Ramsden* v. *Dyson*[5] and many other cases. The basis of this principle is the doctrine of estoppel by acquiescence.[6] Its operation in the case of licensees in occupation of land is as follows: If the licensee expends money on the land under an expectation, induced or encouraged by the licensor, that if he does so he will be allowed to remain in possession, a court of equity will not allow his expectation to be defeated. A supervening equity to be protected vests in him, though the exact nature and extent of the protection will vary with the circumstances. The circumstances may be such as to entitle him to call for a conveyance of the legal estate, as in *Dillwyn* v. *Llewellyn*,[7] or for the imposition upon the land of some encumbrance or burden, that will avail him against third parties other than a purchaser for value of the legal estate without notice.[8] Though the issue did not arise in *Errington* v. *Errington and Woods*, the court favoured the view that the payment by the licensees of all the instalments would entitle them to a conveyance of the house.[9]

Exception to the rule that successors in title of licensor not bound.

In any event, whatever may be the true nature of a licence, it is radically different from an easement. The two interests are distinguishable in at least three respects—an easement must be created by a deed of grant, whether actual, implied or presumed ; it is not a personal right, but is of necessity annexed to a dominant tenement ; once established, there can never be any question of its unilateral revocation by the servient owner.

Licence distinguished from easement.

---

[1] [1964] Ch. 665, at p. 698.
[2] [1916] 2 A. C. 54.   [3] [1936] 3 All E. R. 483.
[4] See [1964] Ch. at pp. 697–8; [1965] A. C. at pp. 1239; 1251.
[5] (1866), L. R. 1 H. L. 129, at pp. 170–1. *Inwards* v. *Baker*, [1965] 2 Q. B. 29; [1965] 1 All E. R. 446. (See *Re Solomon*, [1967] 2 W. L. R. 172, 179–80.
[6] In *Ward* v. *Kirkland*, [1966] 1 All E. R. 609, 111 at pp. 621–5; [1966] 1 W. L. R. 601, at pp. 626–30, UNGOED-THOMAS, J. discusses several of the cases in which the principle was enforced.
[7] (1862), 4 De G.F. & J.517; *Chalmers* v. *Pardoe*, [1963] 3 All E. R. 552; [1963] 1 W. L. R. 677.
[8] *Ives (E. R.) Investments Ltd.* v. *High*, [1967] 1 All E. R. 505.
[9] Presumably this would avail them against all successors in title of the licensor except a purchaser for value of the legal estate without notice; cf. *Ward* v. *Kirkland, supra.*

2. Local customary rights. Indefinite and fluctuating classes of persons, such as the inhabitants of a village, may be entitled to exercise over another's land rights which, if the matter rested between the servient owner and a definite dominant owner, would properly be termed easements. Common instances occur

(i) where the inhabitants of a village pass across another's land on their way to church.[1] or

(ii) where the fishing inhabitants dry their nets on certain property.[2]

Such rights are not easements, for an easement lies in grant, and a vague and fluctuating body of persons such as fishing inhabitants is incapable of taking under a grant. If, therefore, they are to be established, some other title than grant must be shown, and this, as we shall see later, is what the law calls *custom*.[3]

Natural rights of property. This is an expression often used to describe a right that is one of the ordinary and inseparable incidents of ownership, though its exercise requires an adjacent owner to forbear from doing something on his own land that otherwise he would be free to do. The epithet " natural " serves to distinguish such rights from easements, which do not automatically accompany ownership but must be acquired by grant, either actual, implied or presumed.[4] Thus *ex jure naturae*,

an owner has a right to so much support from his neighbour's land as will support his own land, unincumbered by buildings, at its natural level[5]; and a riparian owner is entitled to demand that other riparian owners shall not divert the natural course of the stream.[6] Such natural rights differ from easements in at least two respects—their existence does not depend upon some form of grant, and they cannot be extinguished by unity of seisin.[7]

(B) THE METHODS BY WHICH EASEMENTS MAY BE CREATED.

The basic principle is that every easement must have had its origin in grant.[8]

All the methods of acquisition except one are traceable to a grant which has been or which might have been made, and the one exception, namely statute, is not of frequent occurrence.

---

[1] *Brocklebank* v. *Thompson*, [1903] 2 Ch. 344.
[2] *Mercer* v. *Denne*, [1905] 2 Ch. 538.
[3] *Infra*, pp. 527.
[4] *Bonomi* v. *Backhouse* (1859), E. B. & E. 654 ; Sweet's *Law Dictionary, sub nom.* " Natural rights."
[5] *Bonomi* v. *Backhouse, supra.*   [6] *Supra*, pp. 119 *et seq.*
[7] Jenks, *Modern Land Law*, p. 166. For extinguishment of easements, see *infra*, p. 508.
[8] *Angus* v. *Dalton* (1877), 3 Q. B. D. 102, *per* COCKBURN, C.J.

It may facilitate exposition to set the subject out in the form of a genealogical table.

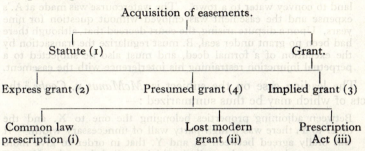

The figures in parentheses denote the order of treatment in the following pages.

(1) Acquisition by Statute. An example of statutory creation is an Inclosure Act. This is a statute that discharges land
from rights of common to which it has hitherto been subject and
distributes it in plots among a number of absolute owners.[1] As
part of the scheme of distribution easements of way over adjoining
plots are frequently reserved to the respective owners.[2]

Deed necessary at common law.

(2) Acquisition by express grant. An easement is an
incorporeal hereditament and therefore, in accordance with the
historic rule of the common law, it must be granted by deed, for

Effect of mere parol or written grant in equity.

" the deed of incorporeate inheritances doth equal the livery of cor-
" poreate." [3]

At common law, a grant of an easement made orally or by an
unsealed writing creates only a licence,[4] but courts of equity,
acting upon the principle that what ought to be done must be
regarded as actually done—a view which has given us the doctrine
of *Walsh* v. *Lonsdale* [5]—and expanding the doctrine of part performance,[6] are prepared to rectify the want of a deed when the
altered position of one of the parties gives him an equitable right
against the other party.[7] If a grantee under a parol grant of an
easement materially alters his position for the worse in reliance
on the grant, as for instance by the expenditure of money deliberately acquiesced in by the grantor, the latter will not be allowed
to say that there is a mere licence and no easement.

" This court will not permit a man knowingly though but passively
" to encourage another to lay out money under an erroneous opinion
" of title." [8]

---

[1] *Infra*, p. 515.
[2] For example, *Adeane* v. *Mortlock* (1839), 5 Bing. N. C. 236.
[3] Co. Litt. 9a, b ; Law of Property Act, 1925, s. 52 (1).
[4] *Wood* v. *Leadbitter* (1845), 13 M. & W. 838 ; *Fentiman* v. *Smith* (1803),
4 East, 107.
[5] *Supra*, pp. 356-9 *et seq.*   [6] *Supra*, pp. 349 *et seq.*
[7] *Cory* v. *Davies*, [1923] 2 Ch. 95, at p. 112.
[8] *Dann* v. *Spurrier* (1803), 7 Ves. 231, at p. 235.

Thus in *Duke of Devonshire* v. *Eglin* [1] :

> A. was given express permission to make a watercourse under B.'s land to convey water to a town. The watercourse was made at A.'s expense and the easement was enjoyed without question for nine years. Upon a dispute arising, the court decreed that, although there had been no grant under seal, B. must regularize the transaction by the execution of a formal deed, and must also be subjected to a perpetual injunction restraining his interference with the easement.

The leading case on the subject is *McManus* v. *Cooke*,[2] the facts of which may be thus summarized :—

> Between adjoining properties belonging the one to X. and the other to Y. there was a high party wall of unnecessary width. It was orally agreed between X. and Y. that in order to give more space to each owner the wall should be pulled down by X. and replaced by one which was lower and thinner, the work to be at their joint expense. It was also agreed orally that each of the parties should erect a lean-to skylight, and that both of these should rest on the new wall and incline upwards and outwards to the respective houses. X. duly carried out his part of the work, but Y., instead of building a lean-to skylight on his side, built one so shaped that part of it showed above the wall and in consequence obstructed the access of light to X.'s skylight. X. sued for an injunction to restrain Y. from maintaining an erection which infringed the agreement.

KAY, J., decided in favour of the plaintiff X. on the ground that the effect of the oral agreement was to give each party an easement of light over the other's land, and that despite the want of a deed this easement was enforceable by the party who had gone to expense in carrying out his side of the agreement, thereby giving to Y. all the advantages to which he was entitled under the contract.

Dominant tenement must be identified. If the dominant tenement has not been clearly described by the parties, the court will identify it by construing the instrument that created the easement, and for this purpose extrinsic evidence of the circumstances in which the instrument was executed is admissible.[3]

Easement could not formerly be excepted or reserved. If the owner of two adjoining properties desires, upon the sale of one of them, to retain an easement over that one, he cannot do so at common law either by way of *exception* from the grant or by way of *reservation*.[4] The only things that can be excepted are specific parts of the land, such as timber and minerals ; and the word " reservation " is only appropriate where services, such as the payment of rent, are to be rendered for the tenure of land.[5] It was formerly necessary, therefore, either that the conveyance of the land should be executed by the *grantee* (whereupon the easement would arise by way of re-grant from him),[6] or that the con-

---

[1] (1851), 14 Beav. 530.   [2] *McManus* v. *Cooke* (1887), 35 Ch. D. 681

[3] *Johnstone* v. *Holdway*, [1963] 1 Q. B. 601; [1963] 1 All E. R. 432; *The Shannon, Ltd.* v. *Venner, Ltd.*, [1965] Ch. 682; [1965] 1 All E. R. 590.

[4] *Durham and Sunderland Ry.* v. *Walker*, [1842], 2 Q. B. 940.

[5] Leake, *Uses and Profits of Land*, p. 265.

[6] *Wickham* v. *Hawker* (1840), 7 M. & W. 63.

veyance should be made to him *to the use* that the vendor should enjoy the easement and subject thereto *to the use* of the purchaser in fee simple.[1]

With the repeal of the Statute of Uses the latter method is now impossible, but the Law of Property Act, 1925, destroys the old objections by providing that a legal estate may be created by a reservation without any execution of the deed by the grantee.[2] Such a reservation, however, still operates as a re-grant and the rights of the parties must be ascertained on that footing.[3]

Finally, it is of the greatest practical importance to observe that, owing to section 62 of the Law of Property Act, 1925, which re-enacts the Conveyancing Act, 1881, a grant of land may have a far-reaching, and sometimes an unexpected, effect upon the creation of easements. This section provides that unless a contrary intention is expressed in the conveyance : *(margin: Statutory effect of a conveyance of a dominant tenement.)*

> "A conveyance of land shall be deemed to include and shall by
> " virtue of this Act operate to convey with the land, all buildings,
> " erections, fixtures, commons, hedges, ditches, fences, ways, waters,
> " watercourses, liberties, privileges, easements, rights, and advan-
> " tages whatsoever, appertaining or reputed to appertain to the land
> " or any part thereof, or, at the time of conveyance, demised,
> " occupied, or enjoyed with, or reputed or known as part or parcel
> " of or appurtenant to the land or any part thereof." [4]

The object of this section is to ensure that a purchaser, without inserting numerous descriptive terms, usually called *general words*, in the conveyance, shall automatically acquire the benefit not only of easements and other rights appurtenant to the land in the strict sense, but also of quasi-easements and other privileges which have hitherto been enjoyed in respect of the land. It is obvious that easements already appurtenant to the land conveyed continue in favour of the purchaser, but the statutory words are so sweeping and comprehensive that the conveyance, unless expressly limited in its operation, may have an effect far wider than the vendor intends. The effect indeed may be catastrophic in the sense that privileges which have hitherto been enjoyed by the permission of the vendor in respect of the land conveyed, a permission which could at any moment have been withdrawn, may acquire the status of permanent easements as a result of the conveyance.

Suppose, for example, that A., the owner of two adjoining closes, Blackacre and Whiteacre, leases Blackacre to X., and as a friendly act allows X. to use a path over Whiteacre as a short cut to the main road and also to store his coal in a

---

[1] Conveyancing Act, 1881, s. 62 (1).   [2] S. 65 (1).
[3] *Mason* v. *Clarke*, [1954] 1 Q. B. 460, at p. 467 ; [1954] 1 All E. R. 189, at p. 192. The decision of the Court of Appeal was reversed, [1955] A. C. 778 ; [1955] 1 All E. R. 914, but not on this point. *Johnstone* v. *Holdway, supra*, at p. 484.
[4] S. 62 (1) ; re-enacting Conveyancing Act, 1881, s. 6 (1).

shed on Whiteacre.   Later A. sells and conveys the fee simple of Blackacre to X.

In this case at the time of the conveyance there is a " privilege . . . enjoyed with the land " conveyed.   The statute therefore comes into operation, and the effect of the conveyance, unless it expresses a contrary intention, is that a right of way over Whiteacre and a right to use the shed become appurtenant to Blackacre.[1]

Again, if B., the owner of a mansion and park, allows Y., the tenant of the lodge at one of the gates, to use the main drive as a means of access to the neighbouring village, and later sells and conveys the fee simple of the lodge to him, a similar result follows.   Y. acquires an easement of way over the drive.[2]

The permissive nature of the privilege enjoyed prior to the conveyance is quite irrelevant in these cases.   The question is not whether the purchaser had an enforceable right to enjoy the privilege, but whether it was in fact enjoyed by him *qua* occupant of the land prior to the conveyance.[3]

The right must be one known to the law. Diversity of occupation before conveyance essential.

No right will be conveyed by virtue of the Act, however, unless it is one capable of being granted at law, or in other words unless it is a right known to the law.[4]

Neither will the Act operate unless, as in the examples given above, there has been some diversity of ownership or occupation of the two closes prior to the conveyance.[5]   If, for instance, the vendor, the common owner and occupier of Blackacre and Whiteacre, has been in the habit of passing over Blackacre in order to reach the highway, his conveyance of Whiteacre does not entitle the purchaser to invoke the statute and to establish a right of way over Blackacre.   What the vendor was accustomed to do was attributable to his general rights as the occupying owner of both closes, not to a privilege deriving from his occupation of Whiteacre, as distinct from his occupation of Blackacre.[6]   In order to substantiate his claim, the purchaser would have to bring himself within the doctrine of an implied grant.[7]

---

[1] *International Tea Stores* v. *Hobbs*, [1903] 2 Ch. 165 ; *Wright* v. *Macadam*, [1949] 2 K. B. 744 ; [1949] 2 All E. R. 565.
[2] *International Tea Stores* v. *Hobbs, supra,* at p. 172 ; *Goldberg* v. *Edwards*, [1950] Ch. 247.
[3] *Wright* v. *Macadam*, [1949] 2 K. B. 744, at pp. 750–1; [1949] 2 All E. R. 565, at pp. 570–1. *Phipps* v. *Pears*, [1965] 1 Q. B. 76; [1964] 2 All E. R. 35.
[4] *International Tea Stores* v. *Hobbs*, [1903] 2 Ch. 165, at p. 172; *Goldberg* v. *Edwards*, [1950] Ch. 247. *Ward* v. *Kirkland*, [1966] 1 All E. R. 609; [1966] 1 W. L. R. 601. *Green* v. *Ashco Horticulturist, Ltd.*, [1966] 2 All E. R. 232; [1966] 1 W. L. R. 889.
[5] *Long* v. *Gowlett*, [1923] 2 Ch. 177 ; 15 *M. L. R.* p. 265.
[6] *Ibid.*, at pp. 200–1.   The right to light, however, stands on a different footing ; *ibid.*, at pp. 202–3, citing *Broomfield* v. *Williams*, [1897] 1 Ch. 602.
[7] *Infra*, p. 487.

Neither does the statute operate unless there has been a Meaning of "convey-ance."
" conveyance " of land, a word which statutorily includes

> " a mortgage, charge, lease, assent, vesting declaration, vesting
> " instrument, disclaimer, release and every other assurance of
> " property or of any interest therein by any instrument except a
> " will."[1]

This definition does not comprise an oral lease.[2] Nor does it comprise an agreement for a lease or for the sale of land, since an assurance is " something which operates as a transfer of property "[3] and a mere agreement has no such operation, notwithstanding that under the doctrine of *Walsh* v. *Lonsdale* [4] it is for many purposes as effective as a lease.[5]

Enough has now been said to show that a vendor who retains property adjoining that sold, should be extremely vigilant to ensure that any advantages or privileges hitherto enjoyed in respect of the land sold are expressly excepted from the conveyance, unless he wishes them to continue.

If an intention is shown in the preliminary contract of sale that a certain privilege shall not pass to the purchaser, the vendor is entitled to insert a clause in the deed of conveyance restrictive of the operation of the statute. Moreover, in such a case he is entitled to have the conveyance rectified if, owing to the common mistake of the parties, it does not include a restrictive clause of this nature.[6]

(3) Acquisition by implied grant.

An owner, as we Depends upon pre-sumed in-tention of parties to grant.
have seen, cannot have an easement over his own land.[7] Where, however, he has been accustomed to use one part in a particular manner, as for example by crossing a field to reach the highway, his practice is conveniently described as the exercise of a *quasi-easement*. If he later severs his ownership by granting part only of the land to another, such a quasi-easement is capable of ripening by implication into an easement properly so called in favour either of the land granted or the land retained.

The principle of this mode of creation is that although there has been no express mention of an easement in the grant of the land, yet it may very well be that the common intention of the parties cannot be carried out unless some particular easement is deemed to arise by implication. For the purposes of the doctrine, however, a lease and a devise are on the same footing as a grant.

The premises for the application of the doctrine are, first, that A., the owner of two separate tenements, has been in the habit of enjoying certain quasi-easements over one of them ; and

---

[1] Law of Property Act, 1925, s. 205 (1) (ii).
[2] *Rye* v. *Rye*, [1962] A. C. 496; [1962] 1 All E. R. 146.
[3] *Re Ray*, [1896] 1 Ch. 468, 476.   [4] *Supra*, p. 356.
[5] *Borman* v. *Griffith*, [1930] 1 Ch. 493 ; *infra*, p. 491.
[6] *Clark* v. *Barnes*, [1952] 2 Ch. 368.   [7] *Supra*, p. 471.

secondly, that the common ownership of A. has been severed. That is, if A. sells the quasi-servient tenement, certain easements may be implied in his favour ; if he sells the quasi-dominant tenement, certain easements may be implied against him ; while the question of implication may also arise when he disposes of both the tenements to different persons.   We will now consider these three cases separately.

(*a*) THE COMMON OWNER SELLS THE QUASI-SERVIENT TENE-MENT.   WHAT QUASI-EASEMENTS OVER THAT TENEMENT WILL BE IMPLIED IN FAVOUR OF THE QUASI-DOMINANT TENEMENT RETAINED BY THE SELLER ?

Easements not implied in favour of grantor.

The law is disinclined to imply easements in favour of a grantor.   The reason is not far to seek.   In the case of a grant of land the law is guided by two principles: the words of a deed must be construed as far as possible in favour of the grantee,[1] and the grantor cannot derogate from his own absolute grant by claiming rights over the thing granted.[2]

Except in case of a way of necessity.

If the grantor intends to retain a right over the land, it is his duty to reserve it expressly in the grant.[3]   As a general rule there will be no implication in his favour.[4]   There are, no doubt, exceptions to this rule, the most obvious of which are the way of necessity and the mutual easements of support between two adjacent buildings.   A way of necessity arises where land which is entirely surrounded by other land is segregated by the common owner, and either retained by him or conveyed to another person.   In such a case a way is implied both in favour of the grantor and against him.

" Where a man having a close surrounded with his own land grants the close to another in fee, for life or for years, the grantee shall have a way to the close over the grantor's land, for without it he cannot derive any benefit from the grant."[5]   This rule applies where the landlocked close is devised,[6] and also where part of the surrounding land is owned by third persons.[7]

---

[1] *Per* Lord SELBORNE—*Neill* v. *Devonshire* (1882), 8 App. Cas. 135, at p. 149.

[2] *Per* Lord WESTBURY—*Suffield* v. *Brown* (1864), 4 De G. J. & S. 194.   The rule may be varied by contract, see, *e.g.*, the draft forms of standard contracts of sales of land published by the Lord Chancellor under the Law of Property Act, 1925, s. 46, which provide that a vendor who sells a house reserving adjoining land shall retain the right to build on such land.   This right may, of course, operate to the prejudice of the house sold.

[3] *Per* THESIGER, L.J.—*Wheeldon* v. *Burrows* (1879), 12 Ch. D. 31, at p. 49.

[4] *Wheeldon* v. *Burrows, supra.* ;   *Aldridge* v. *Wright,* [1929] 2 K. B. 117 ; *Liddiard* v. *Waldron,* [1934] 1 K. B. 435 ;   *Re Webb's Lease, Sandom* v. *Webb,* [1951] Ch. 808 ;   [1951] 2 All E. R. 131.

[5] Wms. Saund. 323 N (6) ;   *Union Lighterage Co.* v. *London Graving Dock Co.,* [1902] 2 Ch. 557, 573 ;   *Pinnington* v. *Galland* (1853), 9 Ex. 1.

[6] *Pearson* v. *Spencer* (1861), 1 B. & S. 571.

[7] *Barry* v. *Hasseldine,* [1952] Ch. 835 ;   [1952] 2 All E. R. 317.

The same doctrine also applies where the grantor disposes of the surrounding land and keeps that which is enclosed.[1]

The extent of the implied right is strictly limited and depends upon the mode of enjoyment of the surrounded land prevailing at the time of the grant. The way may be used for any purpose which is essential to maintain that mode of enjoyment : it may not be used for other purposes. Thus : *(margin: Extent of way of necessity.)*

> Where at the time of the grant the surrounded close was used only for agricultural purposes, it was held that the grantor was not entitled to carry over it timber and other materials.[2]

There are, perhaps, other cases in which easements will be implied in favour of a grantor without express reservation,[3] but they defy exhaustive enumeration and all that can be said is that the scales are heavily weighted against him. The necessary inference from the circumstances must be that he was intended to retain the precise easement that he claims.[4]

(b) THE COMMON OWNER SELLS THE QUASI-DOMINANT TENE-MENT. WHAT QUASI-EASEMENTS OVER THE PART RE-TAINED BY HIM WILL BE IMPLIED IN FAVOUR OF THE GRANTEE ?

The law is much more inclined to imply easements in favour of the grantee than in favour of the grantor, and the extent to which the implication goes is clearly indicated in the leading case of *Wheeldon* v. *Burrows*,[5] where THESIGER, L.J., said :— *(margin: Continuous and apparent easements implied in favour of grantee.)*

> " . . . on the grant by the owner of a tenement of part of
> " that tenement as it is then used and enjoyed, there will pass to
> " the grantee all those continuous and apparent easements (by
> " which, of course, I mean quasi-easements), or in other words
> " all those easements which are necessary to the reasonable en-
> " joyment of the property granted, and which have been and are
> " at the time of the grant used by the owner of the entirety for
> " the benefit of the part granted."

Thus, for instance, it has been law since 1663[6] that if a man grants a house in which there are windows, he cannot build on his own adjoining land so as to obstruct the light. The principle of such a case is that the grantor is assumed to have intended that his grant shall be effectual, and when two properties are severed, the parties to the severance, both the

---

[1] Wms. Saund., *supra* ; *London Corporation* v. *Riggs* (1880), 13 Ch. D. 798.
[2] *London Corporation* v. *Riggs, supra* ; *Serff* v. *Acton Local Board* (1886), 31 Ch. D. 679.
[3] *Re Webb's Lease, Sandom* v. *Webb*, [1951] Ch. 808, 816–7, 823 ; [1951] 2 All E. R. 131 136–7, 141.
[4] *Ibid.*, at p. 828.
[5] *Wheeldon* v. *Burrows* (1878), 12 Ch. D. 31, 49.
[6] *Palmer* v. *Fletcher* (1663), 1 Lev. 122 ; *Phillips* v. *Low*, [1892] 1 Ch. 47.

R*

man who gives and the man who takes, must be presumed to intend that such reasonable incidents shall go with the thing granted as will enable the person who takes it to enjoy it in a proper and substantial way.[1]

It will be noticed that the rule in *Wheeldon* v. *Burrows* is limited to continuous and apparent easements. Strictly speaking a continuous easement is one, such as the right to light, the constant enjoyment of which does not, as in the case of a right of way, require the active intervention of the dominant owner. The word " continuous," however, is not in this context to be taken in its strict sense but rather in the sense of permanence.[2] The two words "continuous" and "apparent" must be read together and understood as pointing to an easement which is accompanied by some obvious and permanent mark on the land itself, or at least by some mark which will be disclosed by a careful inspection of the premises.[3] Instances are :

    (i) watercourses consisting of some actual construction such as pipes [4] ;
    (ii) a made road [5] ;
    (iii) light flowing through windows [6] ;
    (iv) drains which can be discovered with ordinary care,[7] and so on.

When a way is implied.   A right of way is not necessarily such a quasi-easement as will pass under the rule in *Wheeldon* v. *Burrows*. To do so it must be apparent. There is no difficulty where there is a definite made road over the quasi-servient tenement to and for the apparent use of the quasi-dominant tenement. Such will clearly pass upon a severance of the common tenement.[8] But the existence of a formed road is not essential, and if there are other indicia which show that the road was being used at the time of the grant for the benefit of the quasi-dominant tenement and that it is necessary for the reasonable enjoyment of that tenement,[9] it will pass to a purchaser of the latter.[10] Thus :

---

[1] *Bayley* v. *G. W. R.* (1884), 26 Ch. D. 434, *per* Bowen, L.J., at p. 452 ; *Aldridge* v. *Wright*, [1929] 2 K. B. 117.
[2] Gale on Easements (12th Edn.), pp. 106 *et seq.*
[3] *Pyer* v. *Carter* (1857), 1 H. & N. 916, 922, adopting Gale on Easements. *Ward* v. *Kirkland*, [1966] 1 All E. R. 609; [1966] 1 W. L. R. 601.
[4] *Watts* v. *Kellson* (1871), 6 Ch. App. 166 ; *Schwann* v. *Cotton*, [1916] 2 Ch. 120 ; affd., [1916] 2 Ch. 459.
[5] *Brown* v. *Alabaster* (1887), 37 Ch. D. 490.
[6] *Allen* v. *Taylor* (1880), 16 Ch. D. 355.
[7] *Pyer* v. *Carter* (1857), 1 H. & N. 916.
[8] *Brown* v. *Alabaster* (1887), 37 Ch. D. 490 ; *Davies* v. *Sear* (1869), L. R. 7 Eq. 427.
[9] " Necessary " must not be confused with " necessity " (see " way of necessity," *supra*, p. 488. A way of necessity is one without which the property cannot be used at all, but " necessary " in the present connection indicates that the way conduces to the reasonable enjoyment of the property.
[10] *Hansford* v. *Jago*, [1921] 1 Ch. 322 ; *Borman* v. *Griffith*, [1930] 1 Ch. 493, 499.

A man built four cottages on his own land and left a strip between the rear of the cottages and the boundary of his land in order to afford a back means of access to the main highway. It was held that the quasi-easement of way was sufficiently continuous and apparent to pass under the present doctrine, for at the time of the grant the strip, though not formed into a made road, was worn and marked with rough tracks, so that no one seeing it could doubt that it was used as a way to the cottages.[1]

This doctrine of *Wheeldon* v. *Burrows* is of particular importance in those cases where section 62 of the Law of Property Act, 1925,[2] is inapplicable because there has been no diversity of occupation prior to a conveyance,[3] or because there has been no " conveyance " as defined by the Act.[4] Thus in *Borman* v. *Griffith* [5] :

Doctrine of *Wheeldon* v. *Burrows* of less import- ance now.

> X., who owned a large park containing two houses, The Gardens and The Hall, agreed in writing to lease the former to the plaintiff for seven years. A drive ran from the public road to The Hall, passing *en route* close to The Gardens. There was no separate drive for The Gardens, but at the time of the agree- ment X. was constructing, and he later completed, an un- metalled way which ran from the back door of the house to the public road. The agreement reserved no right of way to the plaintiff, but he constantly used The Hall drive in preference to the unmetalled way. Later, the defendant took a lease from X. of The Hall and the rest of the park, and began to obstruct the plaintiff in his use of the drive. In the ensuing action the plaintiff claimed to be entitled to a right of way over the drive.

The question, therefore, was whether the plaintiff had acquired the quasi-easement which the common owner of the whole land had exercised over the drive when passing from The Gardens to the public road. There was clearly no easement of necessity, since the unmetalled way provided a means of approach to the outside world. It was equally clear that section 62 was inapplicable to a mere agreement for a lease. Nevertheless it was held that an easement of way had arisen by implication in favour of the plaintiff accord- ing to the doctrine of *Wheeldon* v. *Burrows*. Thus, under that doctrine a grantee acquires only those easements to which he has an implied contractual right; but under section 62 of the Law of Property Act, 1925, the conveyance may vest in him an easement to which he has no contractual right whatsoever.[6]

In the normal case, the qusai-easement that passes by im- plication to the purchaser or lessee of the quasi-dominant tenement is already in existence at the time of the contract. But the law recognizes that one, not hitherto enjoyed, shall also

Fresh easement may be implied.

---

[1] *Hansford* v. *Jago, supra.*   [2] *Supra*, pp. 485-7.
[3] *Supra*, p. 486.   [4] *Supra*, p. 487.
[5] [1930] 1 Ch. 493.
[6] 15 M. L. R. pp. 265-6 (A. D. Hargreaves.)

be implied in his favour if this is necessary to effectuate the common intention of the parties.[1] In one case, for instance :—

> Three cottages were let for the purpose of being used as a restaurant. By certain statutory regulations no premises could be used for this purpose unless they were provided with a ventilation system. In the circumstances, it was impossible to do this without affixing a duct to the outside walls of the landlord's building.

The Court of Appeal granted a declaration that the tenant was entitled to construct and maintain the duct.[2]

(c) THE COMMON OWNER SEVERS HIS PROPERTY AND SELLS ONE PART TO X. AND THE OTHER PART TO Y. WHAT QUASI-EASEMENTS HITHERTO ENJOYED BY THE COMMON OWNER OVER THE QUASI-SERVIENT TENEMENT WILL PASS TO THE PURCHASER OF THE QUASI-DOMINANT TENEMENT ?

Contemporaneous sales.

Where, instead of a sale of part of the land and a retention by the common owner of the other part, there have been simultaneous sales effected by separate but *contemporaneous* conveyances to different persons, all those continuous and apparent quasi-easements which were in use at the time of the sales pass by implication with the respective parts.[3] In other words, when the sales are by the same vendor and take place at one and the same time, the rights of the parties are exactly the same as if the common owner had sold the dominant part and kept the rest of the land.

Thus in *Schwann* v. *Cotton,*[4]

> where a testator devised Blackacre to X. and Whiteacre to Y., it was held that a right to the free passage of water which flowed through an underground pipe running across Blackacre to Whiteacre passed by implication to the devisee of Whiteacre.

Separate sales.

If the sales are not simultaneous, the later purchaser is in the same position as his vendor. So if the vendor first sells the quasi-servient tenement, he will not, in the absence of an express reservation, be entitled to easements over the part sold, except a way of necessity where one exists, nor will a subsequent purchaser from him be in any better position[5] ; but if

---

[1] *Pwllbach Colliery Co., Ltd.* v. *Woodman*, [1915] A. C. 634, at p. 646.

[2] *Wong* v. *Beaumont Property Trust, Ltd.*, [1965] 1 Q. B. 173; [1964] 2 All E. R. 119. The court classified this as an easement of necessity, but this must have been *per incuriam*. "An easement is surely not an 'easement of necessity' merely because it is necessary to give effect to the intention"; 80 *L. Q. R.*, p. 322 (R. E. M.). An easement of necessity is based on public policy, not on presumed intention; 27 M. L. R., p. 721 (H. W. Wilkinson).

[3] *Allen* v. *Taylor* (1880), L. R. 16 Ch. D. 355 ; *Swansborough* v. *Coventry* (1832), 9 Bing. 305 ; *Barnes* v. *Loach* (1879), 4 Q. B. D. 494 ; *Schwann* v. *Cotton*, [1916] 2 Ch. 120 ; 459 (C. A.); *Hansford* v. *Jago*, [1921] 1 Ch. 322.

[4] *Supra.*

[5] *Murchie* v. *Black* (1865), 19 C. B. (N. S.) 190.

the vendor first sells the quasi-dominant tenement, the purchaser thereof can enforce quasi-easements against a subsequent purchaser of the quasi-servient tenement to the same extent as he could have done against the vendor.

(4) **Acquisition by presumed grant.** Proof of the existence of an easement may be, and usually is, based upon a mere presumption that at some time in the past it has been granted by deed. There are three possible methods by which a claimant may avail himself of this presumption, for he may plead,

(i) prescription at common law ; or
(ii) the doctrine of a lost grant ; or
(iii) the Prescription Act.

Each method is based upon identical reasoning. The established principle no doubt is that an easement must be created by deed of grant, since incorporeal hereditaments lie in grant.[1] On the other hand, it is obviously undesirable that a man should be deprived of an easement long and continuously enjoyed merely because its formal creation by deed is incapable of proof. Therefore, in accordance with the maxim—*omnia praesumuntur rite et sollemniter esse acta*—the law is prepared to infer from this long enjoyment that all those acts were done that were necessary to create a valid title.[2] In this way, a claim, founded upon factual enjoyment without interruption by the servient owner, is referred to a lawful origin.

Why grant is presumed.

" Every species of prescription . . . is founded on this presumption,
" that he who has had a quiet and uninterrupted possession of any-
" thing for a long period of years, is supposed to have a just right,
" without which he could not have been suffered to continue in the
" enjoyment of it.

Principle upon which grant presumed.

" For a long possession may be considered as a better title than can
" commonly be produced, as it supposes an acquiescence in all other
" claimants ; and that acquiescence also supposes some reason for
" which the claim was forborne." [3]

(i) **Prescription at Common Law.**[4] At common law, therefore, a man may assert a prescriptive title to an easement founded upon long enjoyment. This, however, immediately raises the question—how long must his enjoyment have lasted before a grant in his favour will be presumed ? The conclusion reached by the courts was that he must have enjoyed his right for *time immemorial*, that is to say, " during the time whereof the memory of man runneth not to the contrary." [5]

Enjoyment during time immemorial.

---

[1] *Supra*, p. 472.
[2] *Philipps* v. *Halliday*, [1891] A. C. 228, 231 ; *Foster* v. *Warblington Urban Council*, [1906] 1 K. B. 648, 679.
[3] Cruise, *Digest of Real Property*, vol. iii. Tit. xxi. para. 4.
[4] For the history of prescription, see Holdsworth, *History of English Law*, vol. vii. pp. 343 *et seq.*
[5] Co. Litt. 114*b*.

It is obvious that this designation of what is generally termed *legal memory* is vague and unsatisfactory, and so the courts soon solved the difficulty in a rough and ready fashion by fixing some date at which the memory of man was supposed to begin. They did not choose a date at random, but took as their guide the statutes that from time to time restricted the period within which actions for the recovery of land had to be brought. At first those statutes, instead of fixing a given number of years, adopted the singular expedient of making the period of limitation run from particular dates or events as, for example, from the last return of King John into England. The last statute which adopted this plan was the Statute of Westminster in 1275, which fixed the first year of the reign of Richard I, *i.e.* 1189, as the period of limitation for the recovery of land by a writ of right. These statutes were, of course, not concerned with prescription, but the courts, from time to time, adopted the various statutory dates as the time at which *legal memory* was to be taken as beginning. Thus after the Statute of Westminster, a prescriptive claim to an easement had to be based on an enjoyment carried back to 1189. Unfortunately, this policy of keeping in line with successive statutes of limitation was not maintained, for when the legislature set up a different principle in 1623[1] by enacting that actions for the recovery of land must be brought within a fixed number of years (20 years for the action of ejectment), the courts omitted to restrict *legal memory* to the same period.[2] So, absurd though it is, 1189 is at the present day still considered to be the time from which a claimant who is prescribing at common law must prove enjoyment of the easement. The result has been the adoption of what COCKBURN, C.J., described as a " somewhat startling rule,"[3] for, in order to lighten the burden of a claimant, the courts are willing to presume that enjoyment has lasted from 1189 if proof is given of an actual enjoyment from as far back as living witnesses can speak.[4] A lifetime's enjoyment or even a shorter period raises the presumption that the enjoyment has stretched back to the reign of Richard I.[5]

This principle that the court will be satisfied with something like a lifetime's enjoyment affords some alleviation to claimants who, in strict theory of law, should stretch their enjoyment back to 1189, but in the majority of cases it is ineffectual because of another difficulty that confronts a claim based on prescription. If it can be shown that there was a time subsequent to 1189 when for some reason or other the easement could not possibly have existed, it is obvious that user enjoyed even for several centuries

---

[1] Following 32 Henry VIII, c. 2.
[2] For the above see the judgment of COCKBURN, C.J.; *Bryant* v. *Foot* (1867), L. R. 2 Q. B. 161, at pp. 180–1.
[3] *Bryant* v. *Foot, supra*, at p. 181.
[4] First Report of Real Property Commissioners, p. 51.
[5] *Bailey* v. *Appleyard* (1838), 8 A. & E. 161, at p. 166.

will be of no avail, since despite its length it must have started after the removal of the impossibility, and that was after 1189. This almost precludes prescription at common law in the case of easements appurtenant to buildings, such as a right to light, for proof that the building did not exist in the time of Richard I must inevitably defeat the claim.[1]

Enjoyment of an easement for time immemorial is not in itself sufficient to raise the presumption of a grant. Certain conditions as to the nature of the enjoyment must also be satisfied.

Nature of the user.

All forms of prescription ultimately depend on the acquiescence of the servient owner. Why should long enjoyment confer a right protected by the courts ? The answer is, that if the servient owner has allowed somebody to exercise an easement over his land for a considerable period and if he has omitted to prevent such exercise when he might very well have done so, it is only reasonable to conclude that the privilege has been rightfully enjoyed, for otherwise some attempt to interfere with it would long ago have been made by any owner who possessed even a modicum of common sense. Fry, J., in one case said [2] :—

"In my opinion, the whole law of prescription, and the whole
"law which governs the presumption or inference of a grant or cove-
"nant, rests upon acquiescence. The courts and the judges have had
"recourse to various expedients for quieting the possession of persons
"in the exercise of rights which have not been resisted by the persons
"against whom they are exercised ; but in all cases it appears to me
"that acquiescence and nothing else is the principle upon which these
"expedients rest. It becomes, then, of the highest importance to
"consider of what ingredients acquiescence consists. . . . I cannot
"imagine any case of acquiescence in which there is not shown to be
"in the servient owner :

"(1) a knowledge of the acts done ;
"(2) a power in him to stop the acts or to sue in respect of
        them ; and
"(3) an abstinence on his part from the exercise of such power."

User as of right. This stress upon the element of acquiescence gives the clue to the kind of user required for a prescriptive title. In technical language, it must be *user as of right*,[3] or, to use the expression taken by Coke from Bracton,[4] *longus usus nec per vim, nec clam, nec precario.* The servient owner cannot be said to have acquiesced in an easement that has been enjoyed *vi, clam* or *precario.*

User must not be violent; nor secret; nor precarious.

---

[1] *Bury* v. *Pope* (1587), Cro. Eliz. 118 ; *Norfolk* v. *Arbuthnot* (1880), 5 C. P. D. 390 ; Real Property Commission, First Report, 1829, p. 51.

[2] *Dalton* v. *Angus* (1881), 6 App. Cas. 740, at p. 773. Lord Penzance was "in entire accord with" Fry, J. (p. 803), and Lord Blackburn (at p. 823) described it as "a very able opinion." Thesiger, L.J., has used very similar language to that of Fry, J., in *Sturges* v. *Bridgman* (1879), 11 Ch. D. 852, at p. 863.

[3] *Gardner* v. *Hodgson's Kingston Brewery*, [1903] A. C. 229 ; *Tickle* v. *Brown* (1836), 4 A. & E. 369.

[4] Co. Litt., 113b.

User
must not
be violent;

nor secret;

nor
precarious.

Thus, if the dominant owner has used coercion, or if his user is contentious in the sense that the servient owner continually and unmistakably protests against it, there is clearly no acquiescence, and the user, being *vi*, will not avail the claimant.[1]   Again, there is no acquiescence if the user has been *clam*, *i.e.* by stealth, for a man cannot assent to something of which he is ignorant, and the law allows no presumptive right to be acquired where there has been any concealment or where the enjoyment has not been open.[2]   It must always be found that the servient owner had actual or constructive knowledge of the enjoyment upon which the claimant relies.[3]   Lastly, where the user has been *precario*, that is, where it is enjoyed by the permission of the servient owner and the permission is one which he may withdraw at any moment, it cannot be said that he has acquiesced in the existence of the easement as a matter of right.   To ask permission is to acknowledge that no right exists.   In this case an explanation of the user is forthcoming, and an irrevocable right to the perpetual enjoyment of the easement is not consistent with the explanation. What a plaintiff must show is that he claims the privilege not as a thing permitted to him from time to time by the servient owner, but as a thing that he has a right to do.

For instance :

A woman relied upon sixty years' user of a cartway from her stables through the yard of an adjoining inn, but on it appearing that she had paid 15*s.* each year for this privilege, it was held by the House of Lords that the user, being *precario*, was not *as of right*.[4]

Thus a common method of preventing user from developing into a right is to exact a small periodical payment, and although in such a case there is in one sense a right to enjoy what has been paid for, yet it does not amount to a right to a permanent easement, but at the most to a right to damages for breach of contract.[5]

Continuous
user.

User must be continuous.   In addition to being *as of right*, user must also be continuous, though the continuity varies according to the nature of the right in question.   For instance, a right of way from the nature of the case admits only of occasional enjoyment, and therefore if it is used as and when occasion demands, the requirement of continuity is satisfied.[6]

---

[1] *Eaton* v. *Swansea Waterworks* (1851), 17 Q. B. 267 ; *Dalton* v. *Angus* (1881), 6 App. Cas. 740, at p. 786 ; *Hollins* v. *Verney* (1884), 13 Q. B. D. 304, at p. 307.

[2] *Union Lighterage Co.* v. *London Graving Dock Co.*, [1902] 2 Ch. 557, in which a dock-owner's claim to an easement of support by means of invisible rods sunk under the adjoining land was disallowed ; *Dalton* v. *Angus, supra*, at p. 827.   *Liverpool Corporation* v. *Coghill*, [1918] 1 Ch. 307 (injurious substances discharged into the public sewer at night for more than 20 years).

[3] *Lloyds Bank* v. *Dalton*, [1942] Ch. 466 ; [1942] 2 All E. R. 352 ; *Davies* v. *Du Paver*, [1953] 1 Q. B. 184 ; [1952] 2 All E. R. 991.

[4] *Gardner* v. *Hodgson's Kingston Brewery*, (1903) A. C. 229.

[5] *Ibid.*, at p. 231.   [6] *Dare* v. *Heathcote* (1856), 25 L. J. Ex. 245.

But so far as a discontinuous easement, such as a right of way, is concerned, it is impossible to define what in every case constitutes sufficient continuity of user. Every case must depend upon the exact nature of the right claimed, and all that can be said is that the user must be such as to disclose to the servient owner the fact that a continuous right to enjoyment is being asserted and that therefore it ought to be resisted if it is not to ripen into a permanent right.[1]

The right which is claimed on the ground of its continuous and uninterrupted exercise for a length of time need not have been exercised by the same person throughout its whole length : it is sufficient that it has been exercised by the successive owners of the estate in the dominant tenement to which the easement is appurtenant. *Continuous user by successive owners.*

Such prescription is called prescription in the *que estate.* The plaintiff claims the easement because it is annexed to a certain tenement which is vested in him for an estate in fee simple.[2] *Prescription in the que estate.*

There is another kind of prescription called prescription in gross or in the person, which is applicable to profits only, and which arises where the plaintiff, quite independently of the ownership of land, alleges that from time immemorial he and his ancestors have personally exercised a right to take something from the land of another. This kind of prescription, which we shall refer to later,[3] is inapplicable to easements, for easements cannot exist in gross, but must always be appurtenant to land [4] and prescribed for in the *que estate.* *Prescription in the person.*

(ii) **Lost Modern Grant.** The " lost modern grant," represents the second stage in the history of acquisition by presumed grant. If easements which were fortified by long enjoyment, but for the grant of which no deed could be produced, were to receive the protection they deserved, it was soon seen that something must be done to turn the flank of the rule that a prescriptive claim at common law failed if it was shown that the easement must have come into existence at some time later than 1189. Stimulated by a determination to support ancient user at all costs, judicial astuteness in course of time evolved the very questionable theory [5] of the lost modern grant. After actual enjoyment of an easement has been shown for a reasonable length of time, the court presumes that an actual grant was made at the time when enjoyment began, but that the deed has been lost. The justification for this attitude is that if a claimant, despite his inability to *Fiction of lost modern grant.* *Its justification.*

---

[1] *Hollins* v. *Verney* (1884), 13 Q. B. D. 304, at p. 315. In that case a right of way was claimed for the purpose of removing wood cut upon adjoining land, but the evidence showed that the right had been exercised only on three occasions at intervals of twelve years. The Court of Appeal held that there had not been sufficient continuity of enjoyment.

[2] Co. Litt., 113*b*, 121*a* ; Blackstone, vol. i. 265 ; *Austin* v. *Amhurst* (1877), 7 Ch. D. 689.

[3] *Infra*, p. 512.   [4] *Supra*, p. 469.

[5] *Bryant* v. *Foot* (1867), L. R. 2 Q. B. 161, 181, COCKBURN, C.J.

prove enjoyment back to 1189 or to produce a deed of grant, has clearly exercised the easement for (say) the last 60 years, it is possible that at some time an actual grant was made to him or his predecessor, and that it was subsequently lost. Therefore, since long enjoyment must be upheld, the only course open to the court is to leave it to the jury to presume that the grant was in fact made.

The virtue of this theory is that it avoids the disaster which overtakes common law prescription when it is shown that the easement could not have existed (say) in 1750, for it does not matter what the state of affairs was then if you rely on a grant made some years later.

COCKBURN, C.J., said [1] :—

> "Juries were first told that from user during living memory or
> "even during twenty years, they might presume a lost grant or
> "deed, [and here the courts did act by analogy to the Limitation
> "Act 21 James 1][2]; next they were recommended to make such
> "presumption ; and lastly, as the final consummation of judicial legis-
> "lation, it was held that a jury should be told not only that they might
> "but also that they were bound to presume the existence of such a
> "lost grant, although neither judge nor jury nor anyone else had the
> "shadow of a belief that any such instrument had ever really existed."

So the lost grant fiction rested and still rests upon the basis of long user, and though in theory the user is merely presumptive evidence, in practice and effect it is decisive. At the present day it is the last expedient of a claimant who finds himself unable to rely upon prescription at common law or upon the provisions of the Prescription Act.[3]

Period of enjoyment. The general rule is that twenty years' enjoyment is enough to raise the presumption,[4] but there is no rigid adherence to that period, and if we look at the more recent cases in which the plea has been successful we shall find that in no instance did the enjoyment shown run to less than forty years.[5] That does not necessarily mean that a shorter period would not suffice.

User as of right necessary. The same kind of user must be shown as in the case of pre-scription at common law, so that if it is *vi, clam* or *precario* the doctrine will not be invoked by the court.[6] Again, in accordance with general principles, it must be clear that there was some person or body of persons to whom the grant might have been

---

[1] *Bryant v. Foot* (1867), L. R. 2 Q. B. 161, 181.
[2] *Bright v. Walker* (1843), 1 Cr. M. & R. 211, 217, PARKE, B.
[3] *Hulley v. Silversprings Bleaching Co.*, [1922] 2 Ch. 268.
[4] *Bryant v. Foot* (1867), L. R. 2 Q. B. 161 ; *per* COCKBURN, C.J., at 181.
[5] *Leconfield v. Lonsdale* (1870), L. R. 5 C. P. 657 (*120 years*) ; *Bass v. Gregory* (1890), 25 Q. B. D. 481 (*40 years*) ; *Philipps v. Halliday*, [1891] A. C. 228 (*70 years*) ; *Haigh v. West*, [1893] 2 Q. B. 19 (*115 years*) ; *Simpson v. Godmanchester Corpn.*, [1897], A. C. 696 (*200 years*) ; *Hulbert v. Dale*, [1909] 2 Ch. 570 (*104 years*).
[6] *Hanna v. Pollock*, [1900] 2 Irish Reports, 664, 671 ; *407 b* ; *Partridge v. Scott* (1838), 3 M. & W. 220.

made [1] ; that there was a fee simple owner capable of executing the grant [2] ; and that the right claimed was one which might have been the subject-matter of a grant.[3]

Although there has been a difference of judicial view on the point, the better opinion seems to be that the presumption of a lost modern grant cannot be rebutted by evidence that no such grant was in fact made.[4]   If for instance a claim to an easement of support in respect of a house were made, it might be a simple matter to prove that no grant had ever been executed, but it would not be a good reason for refusing to apply the doctrine. The doctrine is plainly a fiction ; it is a means to an end, and the end is that some technical ground may be found for upholding a right that has been openly enjoyed.   A lost grant, however, will not be presumed when such a grant would have been in contravention of a statute.[5]

How claim may be defeated.

The extent of a prescriptive easement is commensurate with its user.   Once the purposes for which it has been used during the period of its acquisition have been determined by evidence, its use for purposes radically different in character is not permissible. In other words, the burden upon the servient tenement must not be increased by reason of a radical change in the character of the dominant tenement.[6]   For example, a right of way that has been used to carry agricultural produce to a farm cannot lawfully be used to meet the requirements of a factory into which the farm is later converted.[7]   But if the character or nature of the user remains constant, there is no objection to an increase in its intensity.[8] A right of way appurtenant to a golf club, for instance, is not misused merely because the membership of the club has greatly increased.[9]

Extent of prescriptive easement.

(iii) **Acquisition under the Prescription Act.** The two chief objects of the Prescription Act were to shorten the time of legal memory, and to make it impossible in actions brought under the Act for a claim to be defeated by proof that at some point of time later than 1189 the easement could not have existed. For these purposes the act separates the right to light from all other easements, and deals with each class in a different manner.

Object of the Act.

---

[1] *Tilbury* v. *Silva* (1890), 45 Ch. D. 98, at p. 122.
[2] *Daniel* v. *North* (1809), 11 East, 372.
[3] *Bryant* v. *Lefever* (1879), 4 C. P. D. 172.
[4] This view has been held by the following :—THESIGER, L.J., 4 Q. B. D. 172 ; COTTON, L.J., *ibid.* 187 ; LINDLEY, J., 6 App. Cas. 765.   The contrary view has been expressed by the following :—COCKBURN, C.J., 4 Q. B. D. 201 ; BRETT, L.J., 5 App. Cas. 783; also 17 Ch. D. 591; FARWELL, J., [1901] 2 Ch. 599.
[5] *Neaverson* v. *Peterborough Rural Council*, [1902] 1 Ch. 557.
[6] *Wimbledon and Putney Common Conservators* v. *Dixon* (1875), 1 Ch., D. 362.
[7] *Williams* v. *James* (1867), L. R. 2 C. P. 577, at p. 582, *per* WILLES, J.
[8] *British Railways Board* v. *Glass*, [1965] Ch. 538; [1964] 3 All E. R. 418; (Lord DENNING, M.R., dissenting).
[9] *Ibid.*, at p. 568, *per* DAVIES, L.J.

(a) **Easements other than the easement of light.**

Section 2 enacts in effect that

Effect of enjoyment for 20 years.

where an easement has been actually enjoyed without interruption for twenty years, it shall not be defeated by proof that it commenced later than 1189, but it may be defeated in any other way possible at common law.

Effect of enjoyment for 40 years.

Thus a claimant who relies on the Act is untroubled by the doctrine of legal memory, but he may still be met by the defences admissible in a case where common law prescription is pleaded, as for instance that the right is not the possible subject-matter of a grant[1]; or that the enjoyment has been contentious, secret or precarious.[2]

The same section goes on to enact that an easement which has been enjoyed without interruption for forty years shall be considered absolute and indefeasible unless it appears that it was enjoyed by some consent or agreement expressly given by deed or writing.

The advantage derived from enjoyment for the longer of these periods will be explained below.[3]

Enjoyment must immediately precede action.

The two periods specified do not mean *any* period of twenty or forty years, but the period *next before some suit or action* wherein the claim is brought into question.[4] Thus, the plaintiff must prove uninterrupted enjoyment for the period which immediately precedes and which terminates in an action.[5] For instance,

suppose that a claimant proves that he and his predecessors in title have enjoyed a right of way over adjoining lands for more than a hundred years, except for a short period of eighteen months twelve years ago, when he happened to be seised in fee of both tenements. Although this is a case where the court will still presume a lost modern grant,[6] it is not a good basis of a claim under the Act, because during part of the *last* twenty years he has enjoyed the privilege not as the owner of an easement over the land of another, but as the owner of the servient tenement.[7]

Meaning of interruption.

It is essential that the enjoyment for the period of twenty or forty years should be uninterrupted, but the Act provides

---

[1] *Staffordshire Canal Co.* v. *Birmingham Canal Co.* (1866), L. R. 1 H. L. 254, 278.

[2] See Gale on Easements (12th Edn.), p. 185, note (*d*).

[3] *Infra*, pp. 502–3.   [4] Prescription Act, 1832, s. 4.

[5] *Jones* v. *Price* (1836), 3 Bing. N. C. 52; *Parker* v. *Mitchell* (1840), 11 A. & E. 788; *Hyman* v. *Van den Bergh*, [1907] 2 Ch. 516; affd., [1908] 1 Ch. 167.

[6] *Cf. Hulbert* v. *Dale*, [1909] 2 Ch. 570.

[7] *Bright* v. *Walker* (1834), 1 Cr. M. & R. 211, 219; Gale on Easements (12th Edn.), p.190, note *u*.

that nothing is to be deemed a statutory interruption unless it has been submitted to or acquiesced in by the dominant owner for one year after he had notice of the interruption and of the person responsible therefor.[1]

" Interruption " means some overt act, such as the obstruction of a right of way, which shows that the easement is disputed.[2] Thus,

> if A. has regularly passed over a track on B.'s land for twenty-five years and is then sued in trespass by B., his user of the way for the twenty years next preceding the action will entitle him to judgment. If, however, before his right has been contested, he submits to or acquiesces in an interruption that continues for one year, his previous enjoyment for twenty-five years becomes unavailing to him and he must start it afresh in order to satisfy the statute.

The crucial question, therefore, is—what amounts to submission or acquiescence ? This is a question of fact dependent upon the circumstances, but the test that should be applied seems a little obscure.

> Suppose, in the case above, that B. erects a wall across the track over which A. has been passing for twenty-five years and that A., though he protests violently and threatens legal proceedings, lets thirteen months elapse without forcing the issue by a positive act of resistance.[3]

Does his protest suffice to negative his submission to or acquiescence in the interruption ? It has been held that he need not go so far as to remove the obstruction or to take legal proceedings. It is said to be enough that he communicate to the servient owner, with sufficient force and clarity, his opposition to the interruption.[4] This vague test is scarcely satisfactory. Strictly speaking, no doubt, submission or acquiescence is a state of mind, but if a dissident state of mind, unfortified by some positive act of resistance, is to nullify an aggressive act of interruption, what certainty will remain in the title to the servient tenement ? A single protest will remain effective after the year has elapsed and the statutory rule that interruption for a year shall defeat a claimant will be deprived of its intended force. The weight of judicial opinion, however, is disinclined to regard inactivity by the dominant owner for longer than a year after the interruption and after his protest as necessarily fatal to his claim.[5]

An interruption that occurs after the enjoyment of an ease-

---

[1] S. 4. [2] *Carr* v. *Foster* (1842), 3 Q. B. 581, *per* PARKE, B.
[3] *Cf. Davies* v. *Du Paver*, [1953] 1 Q. B. 184; [1952] 2 All E. R. 991.
[4] *Bennison* v. *Cartwright* (1864), 5 B. & S. 1 ; *Glover* v. *Coleman* (1874), 10 C. P. 108.
[5] *Davies* v. *Du Paver, supra,* (where, however, that view was not shared by SINGLETON, L. J.); *Ward* v. *Kirkland*, [1966] 1 All E. R. 609;[1966] 1 W. L. R. 601.

Effect of enjoyment for 19 years and a fraction.

ment has persisted for nineteen years and a fraction of a year will not avail the servient owner, provided that the dominant owner sues to vindicate his right within a year afterwards.[1] The interruption is not yet an interruption within the meaning of the statute. Nevertheless, the acquisition of an easement requires enjoyment for the full period of twenty years immediately preceding an action, and therefore if the servient owner brings an action before the period has elapsed he will be entitled to a declaration that no easement exists, notwithstanding the deficiency of the interruption.[2]

User must be as of right.

Difference between the two periods of 20 and 40 years.

The nature of the enjoyment necessary for the statutory periods, must be similar to that required at common law, that is to say, it must be *as of right*.[3] This is so even where user has been shown for the full period of forty years. The Act does not mean that easements enjoyed for forty years otherwise than by written permission are in all circumstances indefeasible, but only if their enjoyment has been open and notorious. Lord MACNAGHTEN gave a warning against reading too much into the Act :—

> " The Act was passed, as its preamble declares, for the purpose
> " of getting rid of the inconvenience and injustice arising from
> " the meaning which the law of England attached to the ex-
> " pressions ' time immemorial ' and ' time whereof the memory
> " of man runneth not to the contrary.' The law as it stood put
> " an intolerable strain upon the consciences of judges and jury-
> " men. The Act was an Act ' for shortening the time of pre-
> " scription in certain cases.' And really it did nothing more."[4]

This enables us to appreciate the significance of enjoyment for the longer period of forty years. A hasty reading of section 2 might induce the belief that a right enjoyed for forty years is indefeasible unless it can be proved that it was enjoyed by virtue of a written grant. But this is not so. In the case of enjoyment for the *shorter* period the claim cannot be met by the objection that enjoyment originated subsequently to 1189, but it can be met and defeated by any one of the common law defences, namely :—

(a) that the right claimed lacks one or more of the characteristics essential to an easement [5] ; or,

(b) that the right in question, though enjoyed for twenty years, is prohibited by law, as, for example, because a grant would have been *ultra vires* the grantor [6] or the grantee [7] ; or,

---

[1] *Flight* v. *Thomas* (1840), 8 Cl. & Fin. 231.
[2] *Reilly* v. *Orange*, [1955] 2 Q. B. 112; [1955] 2 All E. R. 369.
[3] *Tickle* v. *Brown* (1836), 4 A. & E. 369, at p. 382 ; *Bright* v. *Walker* (1834), 1 Cr. M. & R. 211 ; *Lyell* v. *Hothfield*, [1914] 3 K. B. 911.
[4] *Gardner* v. *Hodgson's Kingston Brewery Co.*, [1903] A. C. 229, 236.
[5] *Mounsey* v. *Ismay* (1865), 3 H. & C. 486.
[6] *Rochdale Canal Co.* v. *Radcliffe* (1852), 18 Q. B. 287, 315 ; *Staffordshire Canal Co.* v. *Birmingham Canal Co.* (1866), L. R. 1 H. L. 254, 278.
[7] *National Manure Co.* v. *Donald* (1859), 4 H. & N. 8.

(c) that the user was not *as of right*,[1] *i.e.* that it was
forcible, or secret, or enjoyed by permission *whether
written or oral*.[2]

Next, a claim to an easement based upon forty years' enjoyment can likewise be defeated upon the first two grounds, and
also by proof that the user was forcible or secret or enjoyed by
written permission. What is not sufficient to nullify a user
lasting for this longer period is the oral permission of the
servient owner. On general principles user that is precarious
in any sense cannot originate an easement, but the statute, by
enacting that user for forty years is not to be considered precarious unless enjoyed by written permission, has, in the case
of this longer period, given a special and restricted meaning to
" precarious " if the claim is based on statutory prescription.[3]
The difference, then, between the two periods is that an oral
consent will defeat enjoyment for twenty years, but not enjoyment for forty years. Another difference, as we shall see in a
moment, is that certain disabilities of the servient owner,
which obstruct a claim based on twenty years user, do not
affect a claimant who has enjoyed an easement for forty years.

The question what kind of permission prevents user from
being " as of right " under the statute is not free from difficulty. It is clear that permission of any sort, if it can be
proved, is fatal to a claim based upon prescription at common
law, however long the enjoyment may have lasted. The case
of a claim based on the statutory period of twenty years is not
so clear. On the one hand, it may perhaps be said that though
an oral permission given from time to time *during* the twenty
years is fatal, yet one which extends over the whole period
(*i.e.*, a permission given more than twenty years ago and not
since renewed) does not prevent the enjoyment from being
" as of right." [4] As against this, however, it has been said by
high authority that where at any rate the permission is intended to be temporary it would be surprising if it were to
result after the lapse of twenty years in the creation of an easement binding the servient tenement in perpetuity.[5] In the
case of the forty years period a written permission, even
though given more than forty years before the action, will
defeat a claim to an easement.

What
constitutes
permission.

---

[1] *Supra*, pp. 495–7.
[2] *Burrows* v. *Lang*, [1901] 2 Ch. 502.
[3] *Gardner* v. *Hodgson's Kingston Brewery Co.*, [1901] 2 Ch. 198, 214;
for the facts see *supra*, p. 496. The annual payment of 15/– had been orally
fixed some 60 years before the action. That was held, however, to be no
evidence that an oral agreement granting the easement had in fact been made.
[4] *Kinloch* v. *Nevile* (1840), 6 M. & W. 795, 806; *Gardner* v. *Hodgson's
Kingston Brewery*, [1901] 2 Ch. 198, 215, 217–8.
[5] *Reilly* v. *Orange*, [1955] 2 Q. B. 112, at p. 119, *per* JENKINS, L.J.; [1955]
2 All E. R. 369, at p. 372.

Disabilities. The Act provides that a right, even though enjoyed for the statutory periods, shall not ripen into a legal easement if the servient owner has been under certain disabilities. The time during which such person may have been an infant, idiot, *non compos mentis* or tenant for life, or during which an action has been pending and diligently prosecuted, is excluded from the period of twenty years,[1] though it begins to run again *at the point where it was interrupted* as soon as the disability is removed. Suppose, for instance, that

the claimant began to exercise the right in 1890, when the servient owner was the fee simple owner. In 1895 the latter became tenant for life under a settlement, but on his death in 1907 his successor came to the estate as tenant in fee simple. The claimant has exercised the right continuously from 1890 until 1924, when the action is brought. Five of these thirty-four years preceded the disability of a life tenancy and seventeen came afterwards. The twelve years during which the disability lasted must of course be excluded, but the question is whether the claimant may add the periods of five and seventeen years together and allege enjoyment for the statutory period ; or whether he will be defeated by his inability to show enjoyment for the last twenty years.

He will not be defeated, for the rule is that a claimant must show twenty years' enjoyment either

(i) wholly before the disability if it still exists at the time of the action, or

(ii) partly before or partly after, if the disability be ended.[2]

The above disabilities, however, do not affect a claim based on a forty years' enjoyment [3] ; that is to say, an uninterrupted user as of right for so long will confer an absolute title, no matter what the position of the servient owner may have been. One modification is, however, admitted by section 8, which provides that where the servient tenement has been held during the whole or any part of the forty years for a term of life or for a term of years exceeding three years, the period during which such term lasted shall be excluded in the computation, provided that the claim is resisted by the reversioner within three years of the determination of the term.[4]

A curious feature of these rules is that the deduction of the time during which the servient tenement has been held by a tenant for a term exceeding three years only affects the

---

[1] S. 7.
[2] *Cf. Clayton* v. *Corby* (1843), 2 Q. B. 813.　　　　　　　　　[3] S. 7.
[4] The section is in words restricted to ways and watercourses, but there is reason to believe that the word " convenient " has slipped into the section instead of " easement," see *Wright* v. *Williams* (1836), 1 M. & W. 77.

computation of the longer period of forty years. Thus an easement of way may be acquired by twenty years user, though for the greater part of that time the servient tenement has been in the hands of a tenant. [1]

None of the disabilities applies to the easement of light.

(*b*) **The easement of light.** As the Act treats this particular easement quite differently from all others, it is necessary to cite the section dealing with it in full [2] :— Light.

> " When the access and use of light to and for any dwelling-"house, workshop or other building, shall have been actually "enjoyed therewith for the full period of 20 years without "interruption, the right thereto shall be deemed absolute and "indefeasible, any local usage or custom to the contrary not-"withstanding, unless it shall appear that the same was enjoyed "by some consent or agreement, expressly made or given for that "purpose by deed or writing."

We have seen that where a claim to an easement is made under the Act, it must clearly appear that the enjoyment has been *as of right*, and the reason is that the statutory words *claiming right thereto*, have been construed as equivalent to the common law expression *as of right*. Since these words, however, are omitted from the section dealing with light, it follows that in the case of this particular easement a fresh mode of creation has been statutorily introduced.[3] All that the claimant need show, if he claims not at common law but under the Act, is actual user and absence of written agreement,[4] but the user must have continued for the period of twenty years next before the action in which the right is questioned. In other words, the right is not absolute and indefeasible after twenty years' user, but remains merely inchoate until it has been established in legal proceedings.[5] To defeat a claim to light, based upon user for the statutory period, the servient owner must produce an express agreement by deed or writing which shows that the user has been permissive during the last twenty years.[6] Thus, for instance, user of light for twenty years is not dismissed as precarious, merely because it has been enjoyed under an oral permission extending over the whole period.[7] Even the payment of rent by the dominant owner under an oral agree- *Its enjoyment need not be " as of right."*

---

[1] *Palk* v. *Shinner* (1852), 18 Q. B. 568.

[2] S. 3.

[3] *Per* Bowen, L.J.; *Scott* v. *Pape* (1886), 31 Ch. D. 554, at p. 571

[4] *Truscott* v. *Merchant Taylors* (1856), 11 Exch. 855; *Frewen* v. *Phillips* (1861), 11 C. B. (N. S.) 449; *Colls* v. *Home and Colonial Stores*, [1904] A. C. 179, at p. 205; *Kilgour* v. *Gaddes*, [1904] 1 K. B. 457.

[5] *Hyman* v. *Van Den Bergh*, [1907] 2 Ch. 516; affd., [1908] 1 Ch. 167. The reason is that the third section, cited above, must be read in connexion with the fourth section which requires the period to be *next before* some action.

[6] *Foster* v. *Lyons*, [1927] 1 Ch. 219; *Willoughby* v. *Eckstein*, [1937] Ch. 167, [1937] 1 All E. R. 257.

[7] *Mallam* v. *Rose*, [1915] 2 Ch. 222.

ment will not prevent the acquisition of the easement,[1] unless some receipt or acknowledgment has been given which can be construed as a written agreement.

The Act only supplements the common law.

Common law not displaced by the Act. The Act is only supplementary to the common law—it provides an additional method of claiming easements, but leaves the other two methods untouched. If, for instance, the claimant is unable to show enjoyment for the statutory period of the last twenty years, as will happen if there has been unity of possession for part of that period, he may either prescribe at common law or invoke the doctrine of a lost grant.[2] Normally, he will rely on the Act. Failing this, he will base his case on prescription at common law ; and failing that, he will plead a lost modern grant, but only if driven to it, for, as Lord LINDLEY said,

"that doctrine only applies where the enjoyment cannot be "otherwise accounted for." [3]

Although a plaintiff can succeed only on one ground, the modern practice is to plead alternative claims by statute, common law prescription and lost modern grant.[4]

Interruption of enjoyment.

A right to light cannot, of course, be acquired if its enjoyment has been effectively interrupted within the meaning of the Prescription Act, *i.e.* if there has been some adverse act by the servient owner which has lasted for at least one year.[5] In this type of easement, the adverse act must in the nature of things take the form of some physical structure, such as a hoarding, so sited as to obstruct the flow of light to the dominant tenement. An alternative to this cumbrous and unsightly method, however, has been introduced by the Rights of Light Act, 1959,[6] which enables the access of light to be notionally obstructed by the registration of a notice as a local land charge.

Notional interruption by registered notice.

A notice in the prescribed form must be submitted to the local authority by the servient owner,[7] and it must state that its registration is intended to represent the obstruction to the access of light that would be caused by an opaque structure of certain specified dimensions, whether of unlimited height or not, erected upon the

---

[1] *Plasterers' Co.* v. *Parish Clerks' Co.* (1851), 6 Exch. 630.

[2] See *Hulbert* v. *Dale*, [1909] 2 Ch. 570, argument of counsel at p. 573.

[3] *Gardner* v. *Hodgson's Kingston Brewery Co.*, [1903] A. C. 229, 240.

[4] See Bullen and Leake, *Pleadings* (4th Edn.), Part II., 518. The three alternative claims were pleaded together in *Bailey* v. *Stephens* (1862), 12 C. B. (N. S.) 91 ; *Norfolk* v. *Arbuthnot* (1880), 5 C. P. D. 590 ; *Wheaton* v. *Maple*, [1893] 3 Ch. 48 ; *Roberts* v. *James* (1903), 89 L. T. 282.

[5] *Supra*, p. 500.

[6] This Act embodies the recommendations of the Harman Committee; see Cmnd. 473 (1958).

[7] *I.e.* the owner of a legal fee simple or of a term of years absolute of which at least seven years remain unexpired, or the mortgagee in possession of such a fee or term; Rights of Light Act, 1959, s. 7 (1).

servient tenement.[1]   The notice must also be accompanied by a certificate from the Lands Tribunal certifying either that adequate notice of the proposed registration has been given to all persons likely to be affected, or that the case is one of exceptional urgency and that therefore registration for a limited time is essential.[2]   The notice, if not cancelled, expires one year after registration or, where accompanied by a certificate of exceptional urgency, at the end of the period specified in the certificate.[3]

For the purpose of determining whether a right to light has been acquired either at common law or under the Prescription Act, the access of light to the dominant tenement is to be treated as obstructed by a registered notice to the same extent and with the like consequences as if the structure specified in the application for registration had in fact been erected[4]; and any right of action that the dominant owner would have had in that event is available by reason of the notice.[5]   In order to obviate the difficulties that may arise where the right is interrupted after it has been enjoyed for nineteen years and a fraction,[6] the Act provides in effect that the enjoyment by the dominant owner of the flow of light shall be notionally prolonged for one year if he sues for cancellation of the notice.[7]

Effect of registration.

The first section of the Rights of Light Act contains temporary provisions designed to protect the owners of property damaged by enemy action in the 1939–45 war, for it would obviously be unjust that twenty years' enjoyment of the light that has flowed over the damaged area pending its rehabilitation should create easements in favour of adjacent owners.   The provision still relevant is that which extends the requisite period of enjoyment from twenty to twenty-seven years in the case of an action brought on or after January 1st, 1963, in so far as it raises the question whether the dominant tenement has acquired an absolute and indefeasible right to the light and whether anything done before that date has infringed the right.[8]

Rights of Light Act: temporary provisions.

Easements against fee simple only.   It must finally be remarked that, since the whole basis of a prescriptive claim is immemorial user, an easement can be prescribed for only in respect of a fee simple estate.   The rule is absolute that an easement claimed either by prescription at common law, or under the doctrine of a lost grant or under the Prescription Act must be claimed in favour of the fee simple estate in the dominant tenement as against the fee simple estate in the

No presumed grant except in respect of the fee simple in both tenements.

---

[1] Rights of Light Act, 1959 s. 2 (1), (2).
[2] *Ibid.*, s. 2 (3).   [3] Rights of Light Act, 1959, s. 3 (2).
[4] *Ibid.*, s. 2 (1).   [5] *Ibid.*, s. 3 (3).
[6] *Supra*, pp. 479–80.
[7] Rights of Light Act, 1959, s. 1 (1) (2).
[8] *Ibid.*, s. 1 (3).

servient tenement.[1]   An easement may be granted expressly for a lesser interest than a fee simple, but it cannot arise by virtue of a presumed grant.   A tenant for years, no matter what the length of his lease may be, cannot for instance acquire a right of way over the adjoining land of his lessor.   He may, however, acquire by prescription an easement against the land of a stranger, though if he does so it enures for the benefit of the fee simple and does not cease with the cessation of his leasehold interest.[2]

Exceptional case of light.

Owing, however, to the wording of the Prescription Act, the right to light is an exception to these rules.   It is peculiar in two respects :—

First, the fee simple estate of a landlord is bound by an easement of light acquired over the land while in the occupation of a tenant.[3]

> A., the fee simple owner of Blackacre, leases it to a tenant for 25 years.   During the tenancy, X., the owner of an adjoining house, builds a window overlooking Blackacre and enjoys access of light to it for twenty years.   A right to light is thereby acquired that is enforceable against A., his tenant and all successors in title of Blackacre.

Secondly, if two tenements are held by different lessees under a common landlord, and one lessee enjoys the use of light over the other tenement for the necessary period, he and his successors acquire an indefeasible right to the light not only against the other tenant, but also against the common landlord and all succeeding owners of the servient tenement.[4]

(C) EXTINGUISHMENT OF EASEMENTS.

Release.

An easement may be extinguished by release or as the result of unity of seisin.

Express release.

(1) **Release.**   An extinguishment may be effected by a release, either express or implied.

The dominant owner is free to execute a deed of release relieving the servient tenement from the burden of any easement to which it is subject.   At common law a deed is imperative,[5] but if

---

[1] *Bright* v. *Walker* (1834), 1 Cr. M. & R. 211, 221; *Wheaton* v. *Maple & Co.*, [1893] 3 Ch. 48; *Kilgour* v. *Gaddes*, [1904] 1 K. B. 457, 466.   So far as the doctrine of the lost grant is concerned, this rule would appear to be contrary to principle; see 74 *L. Q. R.* pp. 82–96 (V.T.H. Delany).

[2] *Wheaton* v. *Maple, supra*, at p. 63.

[3] *Simper* v. *Foley* (1862), 2 John. & H. 555.

[4] *Morgan* v. *Fear*, [1907] A. C. 425 ; *Willoughby* v. *Eckstein*, [1937] Ch. 167, at p. 170.

[5] Co. Litt., 264b.

the servient owner, in reliance on an agreement to release, has prejudiced his position to such an extent that it would be inequitable and oppressive to treat the easement as still in being, equity will disregard the absence of formalities and will hold the dominant owner to his bargain.[1] If, for instance, a person who is entitled to an easement of light orally agrees to an alteration in the servient tenement which must necessarily obstruct the flow of light to the window, he cannot, after expense has been incurred in making the alteration, bring an action in respect of the resulting obstruction.

But a more important and at the same time more difficult point is whether in any given case there has been an implied release or abandonment of the easement by the dominant owner. *Implied release.*

The general principle is that whether he intended to abandon his right depends upon the proper inference to be drawn from the circumstances.[2]

No one circumstance necessarily implies an abandonment, and thus, while Roman Law regarded a rural servitude as lost after two years non-user, it has been laid down again and again in English courts that mere non-user is not decisive of the question.[3] If the non-user is explicable only on the assumption that the dominant owner intended to give up his right, it will amount to an abandonment, but not if there are other circumstances which go to show that he regarded the right as still alive. In other words, a cessation may show either an abandonment or a mere abeyance of easement according to the particular circumstances of each case. *Non-user.*

The principle was re-stated in a modern case :—

" Non-user is not by itself conclusive evidence that a private right " of easement is abandoned. The non-user must be considered with " and may be explained by, the surrounding circumstances. If those " circumstances clearly indicate an intention of not resuming the " user, then a presumption of a release of the easement will, in " general, be implied and the easement will be lost." [4]

Thus in the leading case of *Moore* v. *Rawson*,[5]

a plaintiff, who had some ancient windows, pulled down the wall in which they were situated and rebuilt it as a stable with no windows. Some fourteen years later the defendant erected on his adjoining land a building which would have obstructed the flow of light to the windows had they still been there. After another three years the plaintiff made a window in the stable in the exact spot where one of the old windows had been, and then proceeded to bring an action against the defendant for obstruction of light.

    [1] *Davies* v. *Marshall* (1861), 10 C. B. (N. S.) 697 ; *Waterlow* v. *Bacon* (1866), L. R. 2 Ch. 514.
    [2] *Cook* v. *Bath Corpn.* (1868), L. R. 6 Eq. 177.
    [3] *R.* v. *Chorley* (1848), 12 Q. B. 515 ; *Ward* v. *Ward* (1852), 7 Exch. 838; *Crossley & Sons, Ltd.* v. *Lightowler* (1867), 2 Ch. App. 478.
    [4] *Swan* v. *Sinclair*, [1924] 1 Ch. 254, 266 ; affd., [1925] A. C. 227.
    [5] *Moore* v. *Rawson* (1824), 3 B. & C. 332.

It was held that he could not succeed, because, in erecting a building entirely different from the old one, he had shown an intention to abandon the enjoyment of his former right.

However, as was stated by HOLROYD, J.,

"If he had done some act to show that he intended to build "another in its place, then the new house, when built, would in effect "have been a continuation of the old house, and the rights attached "to the old house would have continued. If a man has a right of "common attached to his mill, or a right of turbary attached to his "house, if he pulls down the mill or the house, the right of common "or of turbary will *primâ facie* cease. If he shows an intention to "build another mill or another house, his right continues."

The same principle can be seen at work in the case of rights of way. So :

where the exercise of a right of way had been discontinued for many years because the dominant owner had a more convenient route over his own land, it was held that the non-user was adequately explained and did not constitute an abandonment.[1]

Non-user of way.

But any non-user of a right of way caused by something which is adverse to the enjoyment of the right will be regarded as an abandonment.[1]   In a modern case :

Certain houses were put up for sale in lots in 1871, one of the conditions being that a strip of land running at the back of the houses should be formed into a roadway, and that the purchaser of each lot should have a right of way along the road when made. At the time when the action was brought in 1923 the road had not been constructed, fences lay across its proposed site between each pair of lots, and in 1883 the then owner of lot 1 nearest the exit of the proposed road had levelled up the site, and by so doing had caused a sheer drop of 6 feet to occur between that lot and lot 2. The plaintiff was now desirous of building a garage on lot 2, and the question arose whether he was still entitled to a right of way over the strip of land at the back of lot 1.

The majority of the court dismissed his claim on the ground that, though as a rule mere non-user is insufficient to extinguish a right of way, yet in this case the continued existence of the dividing fences and the raising the level of lot 1 were circumstances adverse to a right of enjoyment, sufficient to show an intention on the part of the various owners to abandon the project.[2]

(2) **Unity of seisin.** Easements are also extinguished by unity of seisin, that is to say, if the fee simple of both the dominant and the servient tenements become united in the same owner, all easements properly so called come to an end, for the owner can do what he likes with his own land, and any right that formerly ranked as an easement because it was exercisable over another's land is now merely one of the ordinary incidents of his ownership.[3]   An easement which has been destroyed by this union of

[1] *Ward* v. *Ward* (1852), 7 Exch. 838.
[2] *Swan* v. *Sinclair,* [1924] 1 Ch. 254 ; affd., [1925] A. C. 227.
[3] Co. Litt., 313a.   *Lord Dynevor* v. *Tennant* (1888), 13 App. Cas. 279.

title in one hand does not revive if the property is again severed into its original parts.[1] A complete extinguishment occurs when both the tenements become united in one person for an estate in fee simple, but if he acquires only a particular estate in one of them, as for instance a life interest or a term of years, the easement is merely suspended and will revive again if upon the determination of his particular estate the tenements are once more in different hands.[2]

Unity of seisin without unity of possession does not extinguish an easement of light, as, for example, where the owner of the servient tenement acquires the fee simple in the dominant tenement while the latter is in the possession of a tenant for years.[3] It is doubtful, however, whether this is true in the case of easements other than light.[4]

SECTION III. PROFITS À PRENDRE.

SUMMARY.

(A) GENERAL NATURE OF *PROFITS À PRENDRE.*

Introductory Note. *Profits à prendre* differ from easements in the fact that they import the taking of some thing which is capable of ownership from the servient tenement. Such things are exceedingly numerous and diverse, as for instance, the soil itself, the grass growing on or the minerals lying below the soil, animals such as fish and fowl,[5] sand from the seashore, ice from a canal, heather, turf, acorns and so on.

Profits distinguished from easements.

But in addition to this fundamental distinction there are the following important differences between easements and profits :

Differences between easements and profits.

---

[1] Gale on Easements (12th Edn.), p. 452 ; except under the doctrine of implied grant, *supra*, p. 487.

[2] *Thomas* v. *Thomas* (1835), 2 Cr. M. & R. 34.

[3] *Richardson* v. *Graham*, [1908] 1 K. B. 39.

[4] In *Buckby* v. *Coles* (1814), 5 Taunt. 311, MACDONALD, C. B., was of opinion that a right of way was not extinguished by mere unity of seisin (at p. 315), but the Court of Common Pleas expressed a " decided opinion " to the opposite effect (pp. 315–6) and counsel abandoned the argument.

[5] *Peech* v. *Best*, [1931] 1 K. B. 1, 9.

Profits may exist in gross.

(*a*) Unlike an easement,[1] a profit may be granted in gross to be held independently of the ownership of lands.[2] From early times it was held that an express grant by deed to a man, his heirs and assigns of a perpetual right to a profit was a valid grant,[3] and as the possibility of a grant is the basis of all the methods whereby profits as well as easements may be acquired, it was later held that a profit in gross might be prescribed for at common law.[4] Such profits in gross are not common, but once established they may be sold or leased to a third party,[5] and they will pass under a will.

Different periods under Prescription Act, 1832.

(*b*) Profits as well as easements may be prescribed for under the Prescription Act, but the statutory periods of enjoyment are fixed at 30 and 60 years respectively instead of 20 and 40.[6]

Remedies different.

(*c*) Inasmuch as a profit imports the privilege of carrying away something from the servient tenement, the dominant owner enjoys such possessory rights as will enable him to maintain trespass or nuisance at common law for an infringement of his right, but the owner of an easement is restricted to the remedies of abatement or an action of nuisance.[7]

No quasi-profits.

(*d*) A right in the nature of an easement can be acquired by an indefinite and fluctuating class of persons such as the inhabitants of a village, while a *profit à prendre* cannot be directly claimed by such persons, for otherwise the result would be to exhaust the servient tenement,[8] though in exceptional cases it can be indirectly acquired, as we shall see later.[9]

Profit may be appendant.

(*e*) A profit may be *appendant* to land, that is annexed to the land by operation of law, but an easement may not. If before the passing of the Statute *Quia Emptores* in 1289 the lord of a manor granted *arable* land to be held of him by a freehold tenant, the common law automatically appended to the grant a right in the tenant to pasture upon the waste lands of the manor such cattle as were necessary to plough and manure the arable land.[10]

---

[1] *Supra,* p. 469.
[2] *Chesterfield* v. *Harris,* [1908] 2 Ch. 397, *per* BUCKLEY, L.J., at p. 421.
[3] 1495, Y. B. 11 Hen., fol. 8*a,* cited by PARKE, B., *Wickham* v. *Hawker* (1840), 7 M. & W. 63, at p. 79.
[4] *Welcome* v. *Upton* (1840), 6 M. & W. 536 ; *Johnson* v. *Barnes* (1872), L. R. 7 C. P. 592 ; 8 C. P. 527 ; *Shuttleworth* v. *Le Fleming* (1865), 19 C. B. (N S.). 687 ; *Goodman* v. *Saltash Corpn.* (1882), L. R. 7 App. Cas. 633, at p. 658.
[5] *Goodman* v. *Saltash Corpn., supra.*
[6] Prescription Act, 1832, s. 1.
[7] *Fitzgerald* v. *Firbank,* [1897] 2 Ch. 96 ; *Peech* v. *Best, supra* ; *Nicholls* v. *Ely Beet Sugar Factory,* [1936] 1 Ch. 343.
[8] *Infra,* pp. 530.
[9] *Infra,* pp. 531–3.
[10] Co. Litt. 122*a* ; Blackstone, vol. ii. p. 33. *Dunraven* v. *Llewellyn* (1850), 15 Q. B. 791, 810 ; Holdsworth, *History of English Law,* vol. iii. pp. 147 *et seq.*; Hall, *Law of Profits à Prendre and Rights of Common,* p. 224.

This right of pasture was held to be appendant, and necessarily appendant, to a grant of arable land within a manor, for the grantee obviously could not till the arable land without beasts of plough, and he would have no means of sustaining the animals unless he could pasture them on the manorial waste.[1] This right, therefore, arose of common right upon the grant of arable land within a manor and it must be distinguished from profits or easements appurtenant to land, which are opposed to common right and must be deliberately acquired by an actual or presumed grant.[2] Profits appendant are still possible, but they must have come into existence before 1289, for the effect of *Quia Emptores* is that all sales by the lord of a manor since that date take the land out of the manor altogether, so that the grantee does not hold of the manor in the waste of which he claims a right.

Apart from the differences indicated, the nature of a profit is in general similar to that of an easement. Thus, for instance, it is necessary that a profit which is *appurtenant* to land should be connected with the dominant tenement in the sense of increasing its beneficial enjoyment.[3] The law does not recognize an unlimited profit appurtenant, as for instance a right to cut turf [4] or to catch salmon[5] for sale, or to dig clay wherever it is required for making bricks.[6]

Similarities between easements and profits.

To be valid a profit appurtenant must be limited, and the limit is arrived at by estimating the needs of the dominant tenement.[7]

(B) CLASSES OF *PROFITS À PRENDRE.*

Historical origin. In order to realize the place of profits in modern law and in present-day society, it is necessary to glance at their historical origin. For this purpose it is essential to notice that profits fall into two classes, namely those enjoyed by their owner to the exclusion of everybody else, and those enjoyed by him in common with other persons including the owner of the servient tenement.

Two classes of profits.

The first are called " several " *profits à prendre*, and the latter *profits à prendre* in "common," or rights of common, or more often simply *commons*.

---

[1] Blackstone, vol. ii. p. 33.

[2] *Tyrringham's Case* (1584), 4 Co. Rep. 36b ; *Warrick* v. *Queen's College, Oxford* (1871), L. R. 6 Ch. App. 716.

[3] *Clayton* v. *Corby* (1843), 5 Q. B. 415, 419 ; *Bailey* v. *Stephens* (1862), 12 C. B. (N. S.) 91 ; *cf. supra,* pp. 469–71.

[4] *Valentine* v. *Penny* (1604), Noy. 145.

[5] *Chesterfield* v. *Harris,* [1908] 2 Ch. 397 ; [1911] A. C. 623.

[6] *Clayton* v. *Corby, supra.*

[7] See *infra,* p. 516–7, in reference to common of pasture.

C.R.P.–S

Distinction
between
profits and
commons.

" Common may be said to exist where two or more take, in common
" with each other, from the soil of a third person a part of the natural
" produce." [1]

Thus, while every common is a *profit à prendre*, it does not
follow that all *profits à prendre* are commons. The distinction
is one that should be appreciated, for commons not only form
the majority of profits found in modern times, but they give us the
clue to the history of this department of law. Broadly speaking,
profits à prendre in common came first and several profits second,
so that what we need to discover is the origin of commons.

Origin of
commons.

Two different views have been put forward on this matter.[2]
The older view was that commons began with feudalism and
originated in the grants that the lord of a manor usually made to
the manorial tenants. The later view, initiated by Joshua Williams
and shared by Vinogradoff, is that they derived from the Anglo-
Saxon method of land cultivation. That method, known as the
common or open field system, which was probably designed to
give everybody in the vill an equal share both of good and of bad
land, was somewhat as follows [3] :—

The open
field
system.

The arable land which belonged to the vill was divided into
three large and unfenced fields that were cultivated in rotation, *i.e.* wheat the first year, spring crops the second, while
for the third year the land lay fallow. Each of the three fields
was divided up into a number of strips measuring in most cases
about an acre each, and the strips were allotted to the various
landowners in the vill. An owner would have several strips,
not all adjacent to each other but scattered about the fields,
so that he would have a share in the soils of different quality.
In addition to the arable strips there were also meadows
situated in the lower lying districts, and what were called waste
lands, which consisted of the less valuable parts of the village
property. As the three fields in which the strips of the villagers
lay scattered were subjected to a triennial rotation of sowing,
it followed that there was always one which lay fallow. Each
strip owner had the right to pasture his cattle on this fallow,
but it is obvious that when the meadows were under hay, this
pasturage would be insufficient, and in consequence we invariably find a right in the landowners to pasture their cattle
on the waste parts of the common property.[4]

---

[1] Woolrych on Commons, p. 13.
[2] Holdsworth, *History of English Law*, vol. iii. p. 144.
[3] *Ibid.*, vol. ii. pp. 56 *et seq.*
[4] This system was still prevailing at Laxton in Nottinghamshire as lately
as 1925. The property, belonging to Earl Manvers, contained about 900 acres
and was divided into three large fields. Each field was subdivided into about
400 plots. The fields were cropped in rotation, one being reserved for wheat,
a second for spring crops, and the third lying fallow. After harvest the tenants
had a right of pasturage over the two fields that had been under crops.

So in the beginning of things the land of this country was owned and cultivated by village communities ; the non-arable part of the village land was owned in common by the villagers, and therefore, when they exercised rights such as pasturage, which we should now term *profits à prendre*, over those lands, they were individually using what belonged to them collectively.

But at some period or other an over-lord appeared, and though at first his appearance did not disturb the view that all the land of the village belonged to the villagers, yet, when the system of manors became established in this country and when the Norman lawyers had subjected every acre of land to the universal formula of tenure, that view underwent a complete change. The villager continued to exercise his right of common, but instead of exercising a right over something that belonged to himself in common with others, he was regarded as exercising it over the property of the manorial lord :— Manors.

" . . . the common or uncultivated land of the township was, in
" process of time, regarded as the sole property of the lord of the
" manor and was called the lord's waste, and the old customary
" rights of the villagers came . . . to be regarded as rights of user on
" the lord's soil—as *jura in re alienâ*." [1]

As time progressed various factors combined to strengthen this new theory. Statutes of the thirteenth century allowed the lord to appropriate the common land to himself, provided that he left the tenants sufficient pasturage in the waste ; the Black Death, by carrying off half the population, diminished the number of persons who were interested in keeping the old rights of common alive ; and lastly, in Tudor days, when the growth of the wool trade made pasture land more valuable than arable, the manorial lords succeeded in carrying out inclosures on a large scale. Inclosures.

It appears, then, that *profits à prendre* are rights which have existed from a very early date in the history of this country, and which in their origin were exercised by numbers of persons in common with each other. Moreover, that is the form in which they are most frequently found nowadays. It may of course happen that a man possesses the right to take something off the land of another without affecting the right of the owner to take similar things for his own use ; or he may be entitled to the exclusive right of taking something, as often occurs in the case of pasturage rights over the Sussex Downs ; but the type of profit that a practising lawyer will most likely have to consider is a right of common properly so called. We will complete this part of the subject by a short description of these commons.

Classification of rights of common. Rights of common are classified into

---

[1] Digby, *History of Real Property*, p. 192.

(i) rights appendant,
(ii) rights appurtenant,
(iii) rights in gross, and
(iv) rights *pur cause de vicinage*. A common *pur cause de vicinage*, which is the only one we have not explained, is restricted to the right of pasturage, and arises where adjacent commons are open and unfenced and there is a custom for the cattle to inter-common, that is, for the cattle rightfully put upon the common of one manor to stray and feed upon the common of the adjoining manor without being treated as trespassers.[1]

Rights of common may also be classified according to their subject-matter into four kinds, namely, common of pasture, of piscary, of turbary and of estovers.[2]

Common of pasture.

(1) **Common of pasture.** This, the most usual common, arises when the owner of cattle is, in common with others, entitled to put his cattle to feed on the land of another.[3]

Limited as to kind of animals.

In the case of a common *appendant* the right is limited to " commonable cattle," that is, horses and oxen to plough the land and cows and sheep to manure it.[4] A common *appurtenant* is not limited in this way, but depends upon the extent of the enjoyment proved or upon the terms of the grant if there is one, and so a right may well be established to pasture such animals as hogs, goats and geese.[5] Common

Limited as to number.

in gross may also be enjoyed in respect of any animal. Commons of pasture appendant and appurtenant are also restricted in another manner, as we have already had occasion to notice, for there is no right to pasture an unlimited number of commonable cattle. The rule at common law is that the right is exercisable only in respect of cattle *levant et couchant* on the land, *i.e.* the number that the dominant tenement is capable of supporting through the winter.[6] Again a right of pasturage in gross cannot be prescribed for unless it is restricted in the same manner.[7]

This doctrine of *levancy et couchancy* has, however, now

---

[1] Co. Litt. 122*a* ; *Tyrringham's Case* (1584), 4 Co. Rep. 37.
[2] Blackstone, vol. ii. p. 32 ; Co. Litt. 122*a*.
[3] *Tyrringham's Case* (1584), 4 Co. Rep. 36*b*, 37.
[4] *Ibid.* This pasture may be claimed for certain animals only, *e.g.* sheep (when it is called " sheep walk "), *Robinson* v. *Duleep Singh* (1879), L. R. 11 Ch. D. 798 ; or swine (called common of "pannage") *Chilton* v. *Corpn. of London* (1878), L. R. 7 Ch. D. 562.
[5] *Bennett* v. *Reeve* (1740), Willes 246 ; *Tyrringham's Case, supra.*
[6] *Robertson* v. *Hartopp* (1889), 43 Ch. D. 484, 517. Holdsworth, *History of English Law*, vol. vii. p. 320 and authorities there cited.
[7] *Mellor* v. *Spateman* (1669), 1 Saund 339.

been abolished by the Commons Act, 1965,[1] which requires all rights of grazing to be registered, but limits registration to a defined number of animals.[2] In the case of a common in gross there is no objection in principle to the existence of pasture without stint, or, in other words, to a right to put an unlimited number of cattle on the servient tenement, because, as it is not appurtenant to anything, there is no dominant tenement with reference to the needs of which the content of the right must be proportioned. Thus, as was said by BUCKLEY, L.J.,[3]

Common without stint.

> " it may well be that there can exist in law a right in gross
> " to enter and take without limitation—without stint—the profits
> " or proceeds of another's land commercially for the purpose of
> " sale."

Such an unstinted right might no doubt be granted expressly by deed, but though there is no objection to it in principle, the case of *Mellor* v. *Spateman* [4] clearly decided that it could not be prescribed for.

> " And the court did not dislike any part of the plea, but only
> " it was not said in the plea ' *levant et couchant* within the town.'
> " And KELYNGE, C.J., said positively that there cannot be any
> " common in gross without number."

The old expression *common sans nombre* which is met with in earlier cases is not inconsistent with this principle, for it merely meant that the right was for beasts *levant et couchant*, the point being in such a case that the number was not positively fixed at a definite figure.

(2) **Common of piscary.** A stranger may acquire a right to catch fish in inland waters, such as lakes, ponds and non-navigable rivers, belonging to private owners. This right takes two forms :

Common of piscary.

> (i) A " several fishery " or a " free fishery," which is not a right of common, is a right to take fish *in alieno solo* and to exclude the owner of the water from the right to take fish himself [5] ; while

Several fishery.

> (ii) A " common of fishery " is a liberty of fishing in another man's water in common with other persons.[4]

Common of fishery.

" Common of piscary being given for the sustenance of the tenant's family " [5] must, if appurtenant to a house, be limited to the needs of that house, and the fish cannot be caught for sale.[6] It should be noted that though the fishery

---

[1] *Infra*, p. 519. [2] S. 15.
[3] *Foster* v. *Wright* (1878), L. R. 4 C. P. D. 438, at p. 449.
[4] Blackstone, vol. ii. p. 34 ; *Seymour* v. *Courtenay* (1771), 5 Burr. 2817 ; MANSFIELD, C.J.
[5] Blackstone, vol. ii. p. 35.
[6] *Chesterfield* v. *Harris*, [1908] 2 Ch. 397.

in arms of the sea and in tidal rivers is open to all subjects of the realm,[1] yet a prescriptive right to a several fishery or a common of fishery therein may be established.[2] The presumption, however, is in favour of the public.

Turbary.

(3) **Common of turbary.** Common of turbary is the right of cutting turf or peat in another man's land to be expended as fuel in the house of the commoner.[3] For the last 400 years this right has always been treated as a common appurtenant, with the qualification that it must be appurtenant to an ancient house or to a new house erected in continuance of the ancient one.[4] It cannot be appurtenant to land,[5] for, as we have seen, a thing which is appurtenant must agree in nature and quality with the thing to which it is attached, and the idea of using fuel on land apart from a house is absurd.

Estovers.

(4) **Common of estovers.** BLACKSTONE has said :—

" Common of estovers, or estouviers, that is necessaries (from
" estoffer, to furnish), is a liberty of taking necessary wood, for
" the use or furniture of a house or farm, from off another's
" estate. The Saxon word *bote* is used by us as synonymous to
" the French estovers ; and therefore house-bote is a sufficient
" allowance of wood to repair or to burn in the house (which
" latter is sometimes called fire-bote) ; plough-bote and cart-
" bote are wood to be employed in making and repairing
" instruments of husbandry ; and hay-bote or hedge-bote is
" wood for repairing hays, hedges or fences." [6]

This right, which very closely resembles common of turbary, is generally appurtenant to a house,[7] though of course it may be attached to land for the purpose of repairing fences. When it is appurtenant to a house, the wood taken must be expended on that house, and cannot be used for the reparation of new buildings which may have been erected, or as fuel in new fireplaces which may have been built in the original house.[8] But when the old dominant house is demolished and replaced by another one, the right continues to exist according to its original extent :

" If an ancient cottage which had common be fallen down, and
" another cottage be erected in the place where the old cottage
" stood ; this is no new cottage, but it may claim common as
" an ancient cottage by prescription." [9]

---

[1] *Fitzwalter's Case* (1674), 1 Mod. 105 ; *Carter* v. *Murcot* (1768), 4 Burr. 2162, at p. 2164.
[2] *Carter* v. *Murcot, supra.*
[3] Blackstone, vol. ii. p. 34.
[4] *A.-G.* v. *Reynolds*, [1911] 2 K. B. 888 ; *Warrick* v. *Queen's College, Oxford* (1871), L. R. 6 Ch. App. 716, 730.
[5] *Tyrringham's Case* (1584), 5 Co. Rep. 37.
[6] Blackstone, vol. ii. p. 35.   [7] *A.-G.* v. *Reynolds*, [1911] 2 K. B. 888.
[8] *Luttrel's Case* (1602), 4 Co. Rep. 86a.
[9] *Bryers* v. *Lake*, cited Hall, *Law of Profits à Prendre and Rights of Common*, p. 322.

A right similar to the common of estovers and also called estovers is given at common law to a tenant for life or years enabling him to cut timber which would otherwise be waste.[1] The only difference between the common law right and that which we have just considered is that the former arises in the tenant by virtue of the possession of the land rented and is exercisable over that land, while the latter is a profit to be taken out of somebody else's land.

Rights of common will cease to be exercisable unless they are registered with a local authority in accordance with the Commons Registration Act, 1965.[2] The expression "rights of common" includes:—

Commons Registration Act 1965.

cattlegates or beastgates[3] and rights of sole or several vesture or herbage[4] or of sole or several pasture, but does not include rights held for a term of years or from year to year.[5]

(C) ACQUISITION OF *PROFITS A PRENDRE*.

It will not be necessary to consider this topic at any length for the methods by which easements may be acquired are applicable, with very few exceptions, to the acquisition of *profits à prendre*, whether rights of common or not. At the outset we can dismiss profits appendant because they have been impossible of acquisition since *Quia Emptores* in 1289, and a claimant will be required to prove that he holds arable land which was granted by the lord of a manor to a freehold tenant before that date.[6]

The six possible methods of acquiring easements are set out on page 483. We will take each one of these and show to what extent it applies to profits :—

(1) **Statute.** Profits may be acquired by statute, as frequently happens when Inclosure Acts confer new rights upon manorial lords by way of compensation for the interest lost by them in the soil itself.

Statute.

(2) **Express grant.** Profits, whether appurtenant or in gross,

Deed of grant.

---

[1] *Supra*, p. 370.
[2] S. 1. They must be registered at the end of a period, not less than three years, from the commencement of the Act, By virtue of S. I. 1965, No. 2000, ss. 2 (2) and 11 of the Act came into force on January 1st, 1966; by virtue of S. I. 1966, No. 971, s. 4 (7) came into force on October 1st, 1966; ss. 17 and 18 will come into force on January 1st, 1970, and the rest of the Act on January 2nd, 1967.
[3] Cattlegate or beastgate, sometimes called *stinted pasture*, is a right to pasture a fixed number of beasts on the land of another, generally for a part of the year only. See, *e.g.* *Rigg* v. *Earl Lonsdale* (1857), 1 H. & N. 923.
[4] The right of sole vesture, *vestura terras*, is not merely to graze cattle, but to take away the product of the land, such as grass, corn, underwood, turf, peat, and so forth.
[5] Commons Registration Act, 1965, 5s. 22 (1).
[6] Viner's Abridgement—Common C. p. 1; Comyns' Digest, Tit. Covenant B.

may be created by an express grant, which at common law must be made by deed.[1] The want of a deed, however, is not necessarily fatal to the grantee, for if he can prove a specifically enforceable agreement for the grant of the profit, *i.e.* an agreement that is either evidenced by a written memorandum or fortified by an act of part performance, he may invoke the familiar doctrine of equity that the grantor must be regarded as having already done what he ought to have done.

Thus in an early case [2] :

Position in Equity where no deed.

The defendant signed a written memorandum by which he agreed in return for valuable consideration that the plaintiff should have the exclusive right of sporting over and killing the game on defendant's lands, but some years later he revoked the agreement.

At the instance of the plaintiff, WOOD, V.-C., decreed specific performance by ordering the execution of a formal deed and meanwhile granting an injunction forbidding defendant to interfere with the enjoyment of the right.

Profits appurtenant pass under the general words.

Section 62 of the Law of Property Act, 1925, which, as we have already seen, provides that a conveyance of land shall operate to pass rights and advantages appertaining to the land at the time of the conveyance,[3] applies not only to easements but also to profits, such as a right of depasturing sheep on an adjoining mountain.[4]

Profits do not arise by implied grant.

(3) Implied grant. The next method whereby *easements* may be acquired is that of an implied grant under the doctrine of *Wheeldon* v. *Burrows*, but since this is confined to interests of a continuous and apparent nature, it can have no application to *profits*, which can scarcely possess either of these characteristics.

Prescription.

(4) Prescription at common law. Profits can be acquired by prescription at common law, and when this method of claim is adopted it must conform to all those general principles which obtain in the case of easements, so that

   (i) the possibility of a grant must be shown ;
   (ii) user is required to be *as of right* ; and
   (iii) the claim is liable to be defeated by proof of its origin since 1189.

There is this difference, however, between easements and profits, that although a man can only prescribe in a *que estate*

---

[1] Co. Litt. 9 *a, b* ; *Wood* v. *Leadbitter* (1845), 13 M. & W. 838, at pp. 842–3 ; *Mason* v. *Clarke*, [1954] I Q. B. 460 ; [1954] I All E. R. 189.
[2] *Frogley* v. *Lovelace* (1859), John. 333 ; *Mason* v. *Clarke*, [1955] A. C. 778 ; [1955] I All E. R. 914 (part performance).
[3] *Supra*, p. 485.
[4] *White* v. *Williams*, [1922] I K. B. 727.

tor an easement, he may prescribe in himself and his ancestors for a profit.[1] Examples of this personal prescription are rare,[2] since profits in gross themselves are rare, and such cases as are to be found in the Reports refer to *several* profits and not to rights of common.[3] Where a man does prescribe in the person, he must adduce evidence to show that either he and his ancestors, or some other person and *his* ancestors from whom the plaintiff acquired the title to the profit, have enjoyed the right from time immemorial.[4]

(5) **Lost modern grant.** *Profits à prendre* may be claimed Lost grant. by virtue of a lost modern grant, but instances are rarely found. If a claim is so made, it must conform to the rules and surmount the objections that apply where an easement is founded on a lost grant.[5]

(6) **Prescription Act, 1832.** The Prescription Act treats profits Prescription differently from easements in that it requires longer periods Act, 1832. of enjoyment. The periods fixed for profits are 30 years and 60 years instead of 20 and 40. But, for the purposes of the Commons Registration Act, 1965, the time during which the servient tenement has been requisitioned, or a right of grazing has been prevented by reason of animal health, must be ignored in computing the period of 30 or 60 years or in determining whether there has been an interruption within the meaning of the Prescription Act.[6] Otherwise the provisions of the Act of 1832 are exactly the same for both interests.

The Act applies only to profits appurtenant, not to those Applies in gross, for it requires the claimant to allege in his pleading only to that the right has been enjoyed " by the occupiers of the profits tenement in respect whereof the same is claimed. . . ."[7] As appurtenant MONTAGUE SMITH, J., said in the leading case :—

> " The whole principle of this pleading assumes a dominant
> " tenement and an enjoyment of the right by the occupiers of it.
> " The proof must of course follow and support the pleading. It
> " is obvious that the right claimed in gross cannot be so pleaded
> " or proved."[8]

(D) EXTINGUISHMENT OF *PROFITS À PRENDRE*.

Several profits and profits in common may be extinguished by any of the following methods :—

---

[1] Co. Litt. 122a.
[2] *Per* MONTAGUE SMITH, J.—*Shuttleworth* v. *Le Fleming* (1865), 19 C. B. (N. S.) 687.
[3] Cases are :—*Welcome* v. *Upton* (1840), 6 M. & W. 536 ; *Shuttleworth* v. *Le Fleming, supra* ; *Johnson* v. *Barnes* (1873), L. R. 8 C. P. 527.
[4] *Welcome* v. *Upton* (1839), 5 M. & W. 398.
[5] *Neaverson* v. *Peterborough R.D.C.*, [1902] 1 Ch. 557 ; *Mills* v. *New Forest Commission* (1856), 18 C. B. 60.
[6] Commons Registration Act, 1965, s. 16.
[7] Prescription Act, 1832, s. 5.
[8] *Shuttleworth* v. *Le Fleming* (1865), 19 C. B. (N. S.) 687.

S*

(1) **Unity of Seisin.** If the owner of the profit or common also becomes owner of the land over which the right is exercisable, the right is extinguished, provided that his estates in the right and in the land are similar both in quantum and in quality.[1] Thus a profit appurtenant is extinguished if one person becomes seised in fee both of the dominant and of the servient tenement, but if the owner of the profit takes a lease of the servient tenement, the result of this unity of possession, as distinguished from unity of seisin in the former case, is that the profit is only suspended and will revive again upon the expiration of the lease.[2]

(2) **Release.** A release of a profit in favour of the servient owner extinguishes the right in the sense that it ceases to exist as a right *in alieno solo*, since a man cannot have a profit or common in his own land.

(3) **Alteration of dominant tenement.** Although it has been said that

> "Common is obtained by long sufferance and also it may be "lost by long negligence."[3]

it is not true that mere non-user of a profit will by itself produce an extinguishment of the right,[4] but if the character of the dominant tenement is so altered as to make any further appurtenancy impossible, a presumption is raised in favour of extinguishment. If, for instance, land to which a common of pasture was appurtenant entirely loses its agricultural character by conversion into a building estate, the common is destroyed, but if the conversion is not irrevocable, as where arable land is turned into an orchard, the profit is merely suspended and is capable of being resumed on the restoration of the land to its original state.[5]

Approvement.

(4) **Approvement and inclosure of commons.** Rights of common may be partially extinguished by the process known as approvement or wholly extinguished by inclosure.

(*a*) Even at common law it appears that the lord of a manor was entitled to *approve* the manorial waste upon which the freehold tenants had the right of pasturing their cattle, by appropriating part thereof to himself and holding it in separate ownership.[6] This practice was

---

[1] *Tyrringham's Case* (1584), 4 Co. Rep. 36*b*; Hall, *Law of Profits à Prendre and Rights of Common*, p. 335.
[2] Co. Litt. 313*a*, 114*b*.
[3] *Gateward's Case* (1607), 3 Leonard 202.
[4] *Seaman* v. *Vawdrey* (1810), 16 Ves. 390.
[5] *Carr* v. *Lambert* (1866), L. R. 1 Exch. 168 ; *Tyrringham's Case* (1584), 4 Co. Rep. 36*b*.
[6] See authorities collected—Hall, *Law of Profits à Prendre and Rights of Common*, pp. 345 *et seq.*

justified by the lords on the ground that the multiplicity of commoners rendered the manor unprofitable, but as it not unnaturally caused dissension it was ultimately regulated by two statutes—the Statute of Merton, 1235, Chapter 4, and the Statute of Westminster the Second, 1285, Chapter 46.[1] These expressly permitted the lord of a manor to appropriate or approve the manorial waste, subject to the condition that he left sufficient pasturage for the commoners. The onus of proving such sufficiency lay upon him, and the statutory right did not justify the extinction of profits in gross, but only of those that were appendant or appurtenant to land.

(b) The other method of deliberate extinguishment is inclosure under the various Inclosure Acts. Inclosure differs in three respects from approvement :— Inclosure.

(i) it applies to all kinds of commonable rights, such as common of turbary and estovers, and is not restricted to pasture ;

(ii) it involves the discharge of the whole of the lands from the rights of common ; and finally

(iii) it does not depend upon the discretion of any one man, but requires for its validity the sanction of an Act of Parliament.

Inclosures. " Inclosure " is the process whereby a commoner, in place of the rights over the manorial waste which he formerly enjoyed, is granted a definite piece of land to be held in fee simple. It is now virtually a dead letter, but in the comparatively short period of a hundred years, from about 1760 to 1860, it led to the almost entire disappearance of those rights of common which from the earliest days had been such a striking feature of English landholding. To understand this sudden and rapid extinction of ancient rights, it is necessary to realize that even as late as the eighteenth century the greater part of the cultivated land of England was still farmed on what may be called the village community system. That system, which has been described above,[2] had outlived its *raison d'être* and had become by the eighteenth century nothing but a hindrance to proper cultivation. Inclosures.

" Village farmers farmed as they farmed centuries before. They were bound by the same rigid rules of cropping, followed the same unvaried rotation of corn and triennial fallow, used the same implements, kept the same class of live-stock. They raised enough food for themselves, they produced little, if anything, for sale. Necessity for inclosures in 18th century.

---

[1] The Statute Law Revision Act, 1948, renamed these two statutes as the Commons Act, 1236, and the Commons Act, 1285. The former was repealed *in toto* by the Statute Law Revision Act, 1953.

[2] *Supra*, pp. 514–5.

"They formed isolated, self-supporting communities. In those
"easy-going days it did not matter. Before the middle of the
"eighteenth century no demand for change arose, either from an
"improved agriculture or from a growing population. But from
"1760 onwards pressure was increasingly felt from both directions.
"The resources of agriculture were multiplied by the use of such
"new crops as roots and artificial grasses, and by improvements in
"the science and art of stock-breeding. The means were known by
"which the production of food could be doubled. But so long as
"village farmers turned their cattle and sheep on to the common
"arable fields from harvest to seed-time, it was impossible to grow
"either turnips or clover, and so long as their stunted live-stock
"were promiscuously herded on the worn-out common pasture, it
"was idle to think of improving the breeds. If an urgent demand
"for food arose, it could not be met from land occupied by village
"farmers. After 1760 that demand came with rapidly increasing
"insistence. With the invention of machinery manufactures
"developed, domestic handicrafts were swept into factories;
"population leaped upwards, it gathered in great industrial centres;
"it shifted from the South to the North. New manufacturing
"districts cried out for ' Bread and Meat,' and, as the century drew
"to its close, the cry was swollen by the panic-stricken clamour of a
"nation engaged in war and haunted by the spectre of famine. In
"this difficult crisis village farms seemed to prevent land from being
"put to its most productive use, to be a menace to the national supply
"of food, and an obstacle to the manufacturing expansion of
"England." [1]

Private Inclosure Acts.   At first inclosures were carried out by private Acts of Parliament by which allotments of land to be held in separate ownership and discharged from commonage were awarded to the lord and the commoners. The expense of these private Acts was very great, and in 1801 the procedure was simplified by the passing of the Inclosure (Consolidation) Act, which set out a number of general provisions capable of being incorporated into private Acts. Where a petition for inclosure was presented, Commissioners visited the locality, publicly took evidence from those who desired and those who opposed inclosure, and made a final award by which they granted to each person a self-contained freehold estate in lieu both of the scattered strips and of the rights of common that he formerly possessed.

Report of Select Committee.   As time went on the number of inclosures decreased, and in 1844 a Select Committee, which had been set up to inquire how the process might be encouraged, recommended that all petitions for inclosures should be submitted to some central body, but that the awards of this body should have no legal effect until they had been sanctioned by Parliament. The outcome of this recommendation was the passing of the Inclosure Act, 1845, which established the central body in the shape of the Inclosures Commissioners for England and Wales, whose duties are now carried out by the Ministry of Agriculture, Fisheries and Food.

The result of this Act, which was described in its title as

---

[1] *The Times*, December 16, 1924.

"An Act to facilitate the Inclosure and Improvement of Commons **
"and lands held in common, the Exchange of lands, and the Division
"of intermixed lands,"

was that, between 1485 and 1875, 590,000 acres were inclosed
and divided among 25,930 persons. But during the last decade
of this period it became practically impossible to obtain parliamentary sanction for inclosure awards, since, under the influence
of the Commons Preservation Society, the nation became con-
vinced that one of the most urgent national needs was the provision
of open spaces. From 1760 to 1860 inclosures were favoured
because it was thought desirable to bring as much land as possible
under cultivation, but by the latter date the introduction of free
trade had lessened the importance of this consideration, while the
growth of large towns had rendered it imperative that places should
be set aside for the recreation of the people. The new policy was **
not to parcel out common lands among private owners, but to
throw them open to the public and provide for their management
and regulation by public bodies. Effect was given to this by the
Commons Act, 1876, which, after reciting that

"inclosures in severalty as opposed to regulation of commons
"should not be hereafter made unless it can be proved to the
"satisfaction of the said Inclosure Commissioners and of Parliament
"that such inclosure will be of benefit to the neighbourhood as well
"as to private interests,"

contained provisions designed to protect the public and to give
local authorities an opportunity of acquiring land for the public.
Thus the Ministry of Agriculture, Fisheries and Food when making **
its provisional award for submission to Parliament must now
insert provisions, where applicable, for securing free access to any
particular prospect, the preservation of objects of historical
interest, the reservation of the right of playing games where a
recreation ground has not been set out, and so on.[1] This
concern for the interests of the public has been carried further
by the Law of Property Act, 1925, one section of which enacts [2]
that members of the public shall have *rights of access for air and
exercise* to any land which is

(a) a metropolitan common ; or

(b) a manorial waste or a common wholly or partially situate
within a borough or urban district ; or

(c) an area subject to rights of common and to which the
provisions of the section are applied.

These rights of the public are subject to any Act passed for
the regulation of the land, or to any limitations on the exercise of
the rights made by the Minister of Agriculture, Fisheries and Food

---

[1] S. 7.   [2] S. 193.

with a view to *preventing any estate, right or interest of a profit-able or beneficial nature* over the land from being injuriously affected. This enables regulations to be made for the purpose of protecting golf courses and other similar places from improper interference by the persons to whom a right of access is given.

Further protection to the public is provided by another section [1] which makes it unlawful to erect any building, fence or other work whereby access to common land is prevented or impeded, and authority is given to a County Court judge to order the removal of any such erection.

Distinction between inclosure and regulation as a public common. Thus, land which has hitherto been subject to rights of common may either be inclosed in the proper sense of the term or be regulated as a common and thrown open to the public. It is when land is dealt with in this latter way that it becomes a *common* in the popular sense, but of course it is quite different from a right of common such as that described in this chapter.

How inclosure is effected. The stages in an inclosure at the present day are as follows :

(i) An application supported by persons representing at least one-third of the value of the lands must first be made to the Minister of Agriculture, Fisheries and Food.

(ii) The application must explain why inclosure is preferable to the regulation of the land as a public common.

(iii) If the Ministry is of opinion that a *primâ facie* case has been made out, it orders a local inquiry to be made by an Assistant Commissioner.

(iv) The Assistant Commissioner inspects the locality, holds a public meeting at which he hears the views of all persons who wish to be heard and makes a report to the Ministry.

(v) The Ministry, if it is satisfied that the matter ought to go further, prepares a draft provisional order which is ultimately submitted to Parliament.

Inclosure now rare. So then at the present day inclosures are still possible, but owing to the very strong case which must be made out by the petitioners, and also to the important part played by local authorities, who are afforded facilities for making a portion of the land common to the public, it is unlikely that they will be continued. But it must be remembered that the Acts of 1845 and 1876 do not affect the power of the lord of a manor to approve the waste under the Statute of Westminster the Second, now called the Commons Act, 1285,[2] by inclosing so much of the land as is not **Approvement still possible, but unlikely.** required to satisfy the needs of the commoners. Indeed, towards the end of the last century attempts were made by the London landowners to defeat the new ebullition of public feeling by claim-

---

[1] S. 194.   [2] See note 1, *supra*, p. 523.

ing to approve commons under those old statutes, but in the proceedings that ensued the public was successful—mainly because it was decided in *Robertson* v. *Hartopp*[1] in 1888 that the question whether a sufficiency of common was being left must be determined, not according to the number of animals which the commoners had for a great number of years been in the habit of turning out, but according to the aggregate number which they were entitled to turn out. Moreover, landowners are no longer able to circumvent the new policy by stealth, for secret approvements have been prevented by the Commons Act, 1876. This requires a person seeking to approve a common to publish his intention in the local press on three successive occasions,[2] and the Law of Commons (Amendment) Act, 1893, further provides that an approvement of any part of a common purporting to be made under the Commons Acts of 1236 and 1285 shall not be valid unless it is made with the consent of the Board of Agriculture and Fisheries (now the Ministry of Agriculture, Fisheries and Food). Also the Minister is directed, in deciding whether consent shall be given or withheld, to have regard to the same considerations and to hold the same inquiries as in the case of an application for inclosure under the Inclosure Acts.

SECTION IV. RIGHTS IN THE NATURE OF EASEMENTS AND PROFITS ACQUIRED BY FLUCTUATING AND UNDEFINED CLASSES OF PERSONS.

There is no doubt that indefinite and fluctuating classes of persons, such as the inhabitants of a village, may acquire rights, analogous in nature to easements, over the land of another.[3] For example, they have succeeded in establishing rights to enter another's close and take water from a spring,[4] to dry their fishing nets on the land of a private person,[5] to hold horse races[6] or a fair[7] on such land, and to pass to church[8] or market over a man's private property.

Fluctuating classes may acquire rights in the nature of easements.

Such rights are not easements capable of acquisition by prescription, for all forms of prescription pre-suppose the possibility of a grant, and no grant can be made to an indefinite body of persons. Nevertheless, the law, in its anxiety to protect the long sustained enjoyment of a privilege, has surmounted the technical

Method of acquisition is custom.

---

[1] (1888), 43 Ch. D. 484. [2] S. 31.
[3] *Gateward's Case* (1607), 6 Co. Rep. 59*b* ; *Race* v. *Ward* (1855), 4 E. & B. 702.
[4] *Weekly* v. *Wildman* (1698), 1 Ld. Raym. 405 ; *Race* v. *Ward, supra.*
[5] *Mercer* v. *Denne*, [1905] 2 Ch. 538.
[6] *Mouncey* v. *Ismay* (1865), 3 H. & C. 486.
[7] *Tyson* v. *Smith* (1838), 9 A. & E. 406.
[8] *Brocklebank* v. *Thompson*, [1903] 2 Ch. 344.

difficulty incident to prescription by allowing rights of this nature to be established by *custom*. Hence the name *customary* rights. Custom is an unwritten rule of law which has applied from time immemorial in a particular locality and which displaces the common law in so far as that particular locality is concerned.[1]   To quote the words of TINDAL, C.J. :

Lockwood v. *Wood* (1844), 6 Q. B. 50 at p. 64.

" A custom which has existed from time immemorial without inter-
" ruption within a certain place, and which is certain and reasonable
" in itself, obtains the force of a law, and is in effect the common law
" within that place to which it extends, though contrary to the
" common law of the realm."

Requisites for valid custom.

It has been said[2] that a custom must be

(1) certain,[3]
(2) not unreasonable,[4]
(3) commencing from time immemorial,
(4) continued without interruption, and
(5) applicable to a particular district.

The two outstanding requirements are existence for time immemorial[5] and restriction to a definite locality.[6]

Length of enjoyment.

Strictly speaking the first of these requirements means that the custom must have existed since 1189, but although the nature of the right precludes the court from presuming a lost modern grant if enjoyment cannot be proved for so long, yet the practice is to presume that the right originated at the proper time if it is obviously of respectable antiquity.[7]   It is generally enough to show continuous enjoyment going as far back as living testimony can go.

To quote TINDAL, C.J., again :

" As to the proof of the custom, you cannot indeed expect to have
" it proved before you that such a custom did in fact exist before
" time of legal memory, that is before the first year of the reign of
" Richard I, for if you did, it would in effect destroy the validity of
" almost all customs ; but you are to require proof, as far back as
" living memory goes, of a continuous, reasonable and uninter-
" rupted user of the custom."[8]

---

[1] See *Termes de la Ley, sub voce* " Custom " ; *Tanistry Case* (1608), Dav. Ir. 29, Litt. s. 169 ; *Hammerton* v. *Honey* (1876), 24 W. R. 603.

[2] *Mercer* v. *Denne*, [1905] 2 Ch. 538.

[3] *I.e.* the persons entitled to the right must be certain and not, *e.g.*, " poor householders " ; *Selby* v. *Robinson* (1788), 2 Term Rep. 758.

[4] *E.g.* a custom to do something which would exhaust the subject-matter, is void, as for inhabitants of a parish to fish in a river—*Bland* v. *Lipscombe* (1854), 4 E. & B. 713 *n.*

[5] Blackstone, vol. i. p. 76 ; *Chapman* v. *Smith* (1754), 2 Ves. Sen. 505.

[6] *R.* v. *Rollett* (1875), L. R. 10 Q. B. 469, 480.

[7] *Mercer* v. *Denne, supra,* at p. 556 ; *Wolstanton, Ltd. and A.-G. of Duchy of Lancaster* v. *Newcastle-under-Lyme Borough Council,* [1940] A. C. 860, at p. 876 ; [1940] 3 All E. R. 101, at p. 109.

[8] *Bastard* v. *Smith* (1837), 2 Mood. & R. 129, 136.

Although the presumption in favour of enjoyment from time immemorial will readily be raised, it can undoubtedly be rebutted by positive evidence showing that it actually began at some later date.[1] The courts, however, are slow to rebut the presumption. In *Mercer* v. *Denne*

> it was proved by witnesses that for as long as they could remember— a matter of 70 years—the fishing inhabitants of Walmer had used part of the defendant's beach for the purpose of drying their nets. The defendant, having proved that in 1844 a considerable portion of this part of the beach was under water, argued that the custom of using that particular portion must be disallowed as obviously having arisen since 1189.

In rejecting this plea FARWELL, J., said [2] :—

> " A defendant may no doubt defeat a custom by showing that it
> " could not have existed in the time of Richard I, but he must
> " demonstrate its impossibility and the onus is on him to do so if the
> " existence of the custom has been proved for a long period ; this was
> " done for instance in *Simpson* v. *Wells*,[3] where a claim to a custom to
> " set up stalls at the Statute Sessions for the hiring of servants was
> " defeated by showing that such sessions were introduced by the
> " Statutes of Labourers, the first of which was in the reign of
> " Edward III. But no such impossibility is shown in the present
> " case. If the beach was of its present extent in 1795, why am I
> " bound to infer that it cannot have been the same in 1189, from
> " the mere fact that between 1795 and 1844 the extent diminished
> " and has since again increased ? The mere non-user during the
> " period that the sea flowed over the spot is immaterial, for it was
> " no interruption of the right but only of possession, and an ' inter-
> " 'ruption of the possession only for 10 or 20 years will not destroy
> " 'the custom.' "

A customary right, once acquired, cannot be lost by mere non-user or by waiver.[4]

Custom and prescription. Enough has been said to show that custom bears a close and striking resemblance to prescription. Both methods depend on continuous and uninterrupted enjoyment which has lasted for the time whereof the memory of man runneth not to the contrary, and both are liable to be defeated in the same manner. COKE, C.J., emphasized the resemblance in quaint language :— *[Distinction between custom and prescription.]*

> " Prescription and custom are brothers and ought to have the
> " same age, and reason ought to be the father and congruence the
> " mother, and use the nurse, and time out of memory to fortify
> " them both." [5]

But for all that there is an important difference between the two methods, for while prescription always connects the right with a definite person, custom connects it with some particular

---

[1] *Hammerton* v. *Honey* (1876), 24 W. R. 603, *per* JESSEL, M.R., at p. 604.
[2] [1904] 2 Ch. 534, at p. 555.   [3] (1872), 7 Q. B. 214.
[4] *Wyld* v. *Silver*, [1963] Ch. 243 ; [1962] 3 All E. R. 309.
[5] *Rowles* v. *Mason* (1612), 2 Brownl. 192.

locality. Prescription is personal, custom is local. A right is always prescribed for in the name of a certain person and his ancestors, or of those whose estate he owns, or in the name of corporations and their predecessors.[1] But a right claimed by custom is not alleged to be vested in any definite person or body of persons, but is claimed on the ground that it is vested in the shifting class of persons connected from time to time with the definite locality to which the right is attached.[2] In custom you first prove the attachment of the right to a locality and then prove your connection with that locality; while in prescription you show the existence of the right in some person from whom your title is derived, or else you prove yourself to be the owner of a tenement to which the right is attached.

The importance of the distinction lies in the fact that persons who are quite unable to establish their claim to an easement by means of prescription, because prescription pre-supposes a grant to some definite person, may very well succeed under the cover of custom. A customary right is part of the general law applicable to a particular locality; and persons resident there, whether capable grantees or not, are entitled to enjoy the benefit of the law which runs throughout the locality.

Profits à prendre. So far our account has been restricted to the capacity of a fluctuating and ever-changing class of persons to establish a claim to quasi-easements, and it remains to be considered whether such persons can sustain a claim to *profits à prendre*. It has been the law at least since 1607 [3] that indefinite persons cannot acquire a profit by custom.[4] JAMES, L.J., in one case, said :—

Profits cannot be claimed by custom.

> " Of course it is settled and clear law that you cannot have any
> " right to a *profit à prendre in alieno solo* in a shifting body like the
> " inhabitants of a town or the residents of a particular district." [5]

Distinction between custom and prescription.

Were the rule otherwise the result would be to exhaust and destroy the subject-matter of the custom. Thus claims by inhabitants or classes of persons equally indefinite have been disallowed where the customs alleged were to enjoy common of pasture,[6] to collect dead wood for fuel,[7] to carry away sand that has drifted from the sea shore,[8] or to take minerals from the soil.[9]

---

[1] *Per* Sir Edward Coke, 4 Co. Rep. 32a.
[2] Co. Litt. 113b ; Blackstone, vol. ii. p. 263 ; *Foiston* v. *Crachroode* (1587), 4 Co. Rep. 32a ; *Gateward's Case* (1607), 6 Co. Rep. 59b.
[3] *Gateward's Case, supra.*
[4] *Ibid. Race* v. *Ward* (1855), 4 E. & B. 702 ; *Chilton* v. *London Corpn.* (1878), 7 Ch. D. 735 ; *Constable* v. *Nicholson* (1863), 14 C. B. (N. S.) 230.
[5] *Commissioners of Sewers of the City of London* v. *Glasse* (1872). 7 Ch. App. 456, 465.
[6] *Grinstead* v. *Marlowe* (1792), 4 Term Rep. 717.
[7] *Selby* v. *Robinson* (1788), 2 T. R. 758.
[8] *Blewett* v. *Tregonning* (1835), 3 A. & E. 554.
[9] *A.-G.* v. *Mathias* (1858), 4 K. & J. 579.

But in all cases where ancient claims are in question we have to reckon with the tendency of the courts to presume everything reasonably possible in order to uphold a right of which there has been long enjoyment, and it is in furtherance of this general principle that two methods have been evolved whereby fluctuating classes can in certain circumstances maintain a claim even to profits *in alieno solo.* These may be termed (1) the " presumed Crown grant " method and (2) the " presumed charitable trust " method.

1. To take the Crown grant first, we start with this, that although a private person cannot make a grant to indefinite classes of persons, yet the Crown may do so. Lord ROMILLY said [1] :

Can be claimed under presumed Crown grant.

> " The distinction between a grant by a private individual
> " and a grant by the Crown is this, that as the Crown has the
> " power to create corporations, so, if it is necessary for the
> " purpose of establishing the validity of a grant, the grantees
> " will be treated as a corporation *quoad* the grant, which is not
> " the case with a grant by a private individual, because a
> " private individual has no power of creating a corporation."

The Crown by virtue of this power may make a grant to the inhabitants of a town, with the result that they become by implication a corporation for the purposes of the grant and, as such, capable of enjoying a profit in the land of another. So in *Willingale* v. *Maitland*,

> where an actual Crown grant had been made in the time of
> Elizabeth to the inhabitants of a parish allowing a certain
> section of the parishioners to lop the branches of trees growing
> in the waste of a manor, it was held on demurrer that the grant
> was legal.[2]

Cases where an actual grant can be found must be rare, and the real question is whether the court will presume a grant so as to incorporate the inhabitants and thus render them eligible to take profits. All that can be said is that such a presumption will be raised only where the circumstances that have accompanied the enjoyment go to show that the claimants have always regarded themselves as a corporation and have acted as such. Such a grant was presumed in the *Faversham Fishery Case* [3]; but in *Lord Rivers* v. *Adams*,[4] where it appeared that the enjoyment of an alleged right of inhabitants to carry away wood from a manorial waste was inconsistent with the fact that the tenants of the manor had openly asserted and exercised control over the wood, the court refused to raise the presumption.

---

[1] *Willingale* v. *Maitland* (1866), L. R. 3 Eq. 103, 109.
[2] *Ibid.*
[3] *Re Free Fishermen of Faversham* (1887), 36 Ch. D. 329 ; see especially *per* BOWEN, L.J., at p. 343.
[4] (1878), L. R. 3 Ex. D. 361.

KELLY, C.B., in this case said :—

> " If the inhabitants had held meetings in reference to this
> " right, or appointed any officer to look to the right, or done any
> " act collectively of that description, the case would be different.
> " We should then have the inhabitants acting in a corporate
> " capacity in reference to this right, and from their doing so,
> " and from their existence *de facto* as a corporation, we might
> " according to the ordinary rule find a legal origin by a grant
> " from the Crown." [1]

Can be
claimed
under
presumed
charitable
trust.

2. The second method, whereby uncertain bodies may establish
a claim to profits, namely, that of a presumed charitable
trust, is very similar to the one just described. It depends
upon the decision of the House of Lords in *Goodman* v.
Mayor of Saltash,[2] where the following principle was in
effect established.

> Where it appears that a definite body capable of taking by grant,
> such as the corporation of a borough, has enjoyed a profit *in
> alieno solo* for a great number of years, and where it also appears
> that an indefinite body has shared in this enjoyment, then the
> court presumes a lost grant in favour of the corporation, but
> declares that the corporation must hold the profit in trust for
> the indefinite body

In *Goodman* v. *Mayor of Saltash* :—

> Two facts were clearly proved : first, that the Corporation of
> Saltash had from time immemorial exercised the right of
> dredging for oysters in the river Tamar ; secondly, that the
> free inhabitants of ancient tenements in the borough had from
> Candlemas to Easter exercised a similar right for the previous
> 200 years. An action was brought by the corporation against
> two free inhabitants of ancient tenements for trespass committed
> in the Tamar and for converting to their own use quantities of
> oysters.

After holding that the free inhabitants could not be
presumed to be separately incorporated, the House addressed
itself to the task of discovering a legal origin for the right
which undoubtedly had been enjoyed for a very considerable
time. The majority of the House (Lord BLACKBURN dissenting) held that the fishery must have originally been granted to
the corporation subject to a condition that the free inhabitants were to be allowed to fish for a certain period each year.
Lord CAIRNS said :—

> " It appears to me that there is no difficulty at all in sup-
> " posing such a grant, a grant to the corporation before the time
> " of legal memory of a several fishery, a grant by the Crown,
> " with a condition in that grant in some terms which are not
> " before us, but which we can easily imagine—a condition that

---

[1] *Rivers (Lord)* v. *Adams* (1878), L. R. 3 Ex. D. 361, 366–7. This is a
most instructive case on the whole subject of claims to profits by fluctuating
bodies.   [2] (1882), 7 App. Cas. 623.

" the free inhabitants of ancient tenements in the borough should
" enjoy the right, which as a matter of fact the case tells us they
" have enjoyed from time immemorial. . . . Such a condition
" would create that which in the very wide language of our courts
" is called a charitable, that is to say a public trust or interest,
" for the benefit of the free inhabitants of ancient tenements." [1]

But for this principle to apply, it must be established
that the enjoyment of the profit was regarded by the indefinite body of persons as a right to which they were intitled
without anybody's permission, not as a privilege of little
significance that was tolerated by the indulgence or good
nature of the servient owner.[2]

Claim must be as of right.

In conclusion, then, we may say that before a fluctuating
class can sustain a claim to a profit, they must show either that
a grant was probably made in such a way as to incorporate
them, or that there is some definite corporation which is
capable of taking a grant and of holding the right granted
in trust for them. These points were brought out in
Constable v. *Nicholson*,[3] where, in an action of trespass for
taking gravel from the plaintiff's land, the defendant pleaded,

first, that he was one of the inhabitants of a town who
from time immemorial had been accustomed to
take gravel ; and

secondly, that the inhabitants and the overseers of the
highways in the said town had the same prescriptive
right.

Both pleas failed, the first because an uncertain body
could not prescribe for a profit, and the second because
inhabitants and overseers did not constitute a corporation
capable of taking a grant.

---

[1] At p. 650.
[2] *Beckett (Alfred F.) Ltd.* v. *Lyons*, [1967] 2 W. L. R. 421.
[3] (1863), 14 C. B. (N. S.) 230.

" the free inhabitants of an cient tenements in the borough should
" enjoy the right, which as a matter of fact the case tells us they
" have enjoyed from time immemorial. . . . Such a condition
" would create that which in the very wide language of our courts
" is called a charitable, that is to say a public trust or interest,
" for the benefit of the free inhabitants of ancient tenements."

But for this principle to apply, it must be established
that the enjoyment of the profit was regarded by the indefinite body of persons as a right to which they were intitled
significance that was tolerated by the indulgence or good

CHAPTER III.

RESTRICTIVE COVENANTS.

Does a covenant relating to land affect only the contracting parties?

It sometimes happens that a landowner desires to impose a positive or a negative duty upon the owner of neighbouring land with the object of preserving the saleable value or the residential amenities of his own property. X., the owner of Whiteacre, for instance, may be persuaded to covenant with Y., the owner of the adjoining Blackacre, that he will not build shops on Whiteacre or that he will construct and maintain a road across it for the benefit of Y. and his successors in title. Such a covenant remains binding *qua* contract between X. and Y. personally, but does its benefit run with Blackacre and its burden with Whiteacre in the sense that it is enforceable by the successors in title of the former against the successors in title of the latter?

If the privilege granted by the covenant constitutes an easement known to the law, there is no difficulty. It permanently binds the servient Whiteacre and permanently enures for the benefit of the dominant Blackacre. If the covenant is contained in a lease, again there is no difficulty, for it will normally run both with the land and with the reversion.[1] Otherwise there is the fundamental objection that a stranger to a contract can neither enforce nor be bound by its terms.[2]

We must now consider the extent to which in this context the doctrine of privity of contract has been relaxed, first by the common law, secondly by equity.

(1) THE EXTENT TO WHICH COVENANTS MADE ON THE OCCASION OF A SALE IN FEE SIMPLE RUN AT COMMON LAW.

Common Law rule ; benefit may run.

Benefit may run at Common Law. The rule at law for several centuries has been that the *benefit* of covenants, whether positive or negative, which are made with a covenantee,

---

[1] *Supra,* p. 404 *et seq.*
[2] But see now *Beswick* v. *Beswick,* [1966] Ch. 538; [1966] 3 All E. R. 1, 396.

having an interest in the land to which they relate, passes to his successors in title.[1] Thus in *Sharp* v. *Waterhouse*[2] it was admitted that—

A covenant by the owner of a mill that he " his heirs executors and administrators " would supply pure water to the adjacent land of X., ran with that land and could be put in suit by X.'s devisee.

The covenantor is liable to the successors in title merely because of the covenant that he has made, not because of his relationship to any servient tenement.[3] He is liable even though he himself owns no land.[4]

Three things, however, are essential to bring this rule into operation at common law:—

(i) The covenant must touch and concern the land of the covenantee.[5]

(ii) The covenantee, at the time of making the covenant, must have the legal estate in the land which is to be benefited.[6]

(iii) An assignee who seeks to enforce the covenant must have the same estate in the land as the original covenantee, for the covenant is incident to that estate.[7]

Thus, at common law a covenant taken by an owner in fee simple does not avail his lessee. This rule, however, has been abrogated for covenants made after 1925 by the statutory provision that:—

" A covenant relating to any land of the covenantee shall be deemed " to be made with the covenantee and his successors in title and the " persons deriving title under him or them, and shall have effect as " if such successors and other persons were expressed."[8]

In the present context, of course, this provision will avail a successor in title, such as a lessee, only where the covenant is one that touches and concerns the land that he holds.

Burden does not run at Common Law.—In *Auster-berry* v. *The Corporation of Oldham*,[9] some eighty years ago, the view was expressed by two Lords Justices that the burden of a

Burden does not run.

---

[1] *The Prior's Case* (1369), Y. B. 42 Ed. III., pl. 14, fol. 3 A.; Co. Litt. 384a; *Shayler* v. *Woolf*, [1946] Ch. 320; [1946] 2 All E. R. 54 (express assignment by covenantee of the benefit of the covenant); *Smith and Snipes Hall Farm, Ltd.* v. *River Douglas Catchment Board*, [1949] 2 K. B. 500; [1949] 2 All E. R. 179; 1 Smith's *Leading Cases* (13th Edn.), pp. 51, 65, 73.

[2] (1857), 7 E. & B. 816.

[3] *Smith and Snipes Hall Farm, Ltd.* v. *River Douglas Catchment Board, supra.*

[4] *Ibid.*   [5] *Rogers* v. *Hosegood*, [1900] 2 Ch. 388, 395.

[6] *Webb* v. *Russell* (1789), 3 Term Rep. 393.

[7] *Smith and Snipes Hall Farm, Ltd.* v. *River Douglas Catchment Board*, [1949] 2 K. B. 500, at p. 516.

[8] Law of Property Act, 1925, s. 78 (1); *Smith and Snipes Hall Farm, Ltd.* v. *River Douglas Catchment Board, supra.*

[9] (1885), 29 Ch. D. 750.

positive covenant made between a vendor and a purchaser does not run with the fee simple at common law.

In that case

> A. conveyed part of his land to trustees with a view to their forming it into a road, which was to pass across the land of A. and other adjacent owners. The trustees for themselves, their heirs and assigns covenanted with A., his heirs and assigns that they would form this strip of land into a road and would ever afterwards keep it in repair. The road was duly made, and later A. sold to the plaintiff the part of his land which ran along both sides of the road. The Corporation of Oldham then took the road over from the trustees and sought to make the plaintiff bear a share of the cost of its maintenance, but he resisted this claim on the ground that the benefit of the original covenant had passed from A. to himself, and the burden of it from the trustees to the Corporation.

It will be noticed that the plaintiff was obliged to prove two things, namely, that the benefit of the covenant had passed to him and that the burden had passed to the Corporation. In neither case did he succeed. As regards his right to take the benefit, it was held that no such right was acquired by him, because the covenant, since it did not pointedly refer to the covenantee's land, but was meant to confer the boon of a road on the public, lacked the primary essential of being one which touched and concerned the land. Then LINDLEY and FRY, L.JJ., expressed their strong opinion that, apart from the case of landlord and tenant, the burden of a covenant can never run with the land of the covenantor at law.

A decision in accordance with these opinions was ultimately given in the case of *E. & G. C., Ltd.* v. *Bate*[1] where the point arose in a neat form.

> In 1909 A. conveyed a strip of land to X. and covenanted to construct a road upon part of it when required to do so. Both parties owned land abutting on the proposed road.

It was held in 1935 that an assignee of the covenantee, X., was not entitled to recover damages for breach of covenant from the defendant, who was the devisee of A.'s land.

Proposed amendment of the law.

Thus, the burden of a covenant, whether positive or negative, does not run at common law with the servient land upon which it is imposed. As we are about to see, this rule has been radically relaxed by equity in the case of a negative covenant which merely restricts an owner from making certain defined uses of his land, but it still governs a positive covenant, such as one to maintain a fence for the benefit of a neighbouring owner or to contribute towards the cost of constructing and maintaining a private road. That such a covenant should be unenforceable against the successors in title of the covenantor is in many cases unreasonable, as, for instance, where the purchaser of a flat has entered into positive covenants

---

[1] (1935), L. J. Newspaper, p. 203.

that are essential to the comfort of his neighbours in the same building. However, an expert committee, appointed to consider whether the law on this matter should be amended, has now recommended that:—

"the assignability and enforcement of positive covenants should, as "far as possible, be assimilated to that of negative covenants."[1]

(2) THE EXTENT TO WHICH RESTRICTIVE COVENANTS, WHETHER MADE BETWEEN LESSOR AND LESSEE, OR BETWEEN THE VENDOR AND THE PURCHASER OF A FEE SIMPLE, RUN WITH THE LAND IN EQUITY.

(A) GENERAL NATURE OF THE EQUITABLE DOCTRINE.

In the historic case of *Tulk* v. *Moxhay*,[2] the common law rule, that the burden of a covenant does not run with the land of the covenantor except in the case of a lease, was radically modified by equity so far as negative covenants are concerned. The general effect of the doctrine established by this case is that, subject to certain conditions to be discussed at length later, a covenant *negative in substance* entered into by the owner of Blackacre with the neighbouring owner of Whiteacre, imposes an equitable burden upon Blackacre that is enforceable to the same extent as any other equitable interest such as a trust. The right to obtain an injunction against a breach of the negative undertaking will pass to the subsequent owners of Whiteacre, and the liability to observe it will pass to all persons who take the burdened Blackacre, except a purchaser for value of the legal estate therein without notice, actual or constructive, of the covenant. The facts of *Tulk* v. *Moxhay*[3] were as follows :— *The doctrine of* Tulk v. Moxhay.

In 1808 the plaintiff, being then the owner in fee of the vacant piece of ground in the middle of Leicester Square, London, sold the ground to one Elms in fee, Elms covenanting for himself, his heirs and assigns that he would

"keep and maintain the said piece of ground and Square "Garden, and the iron railing round the same, in its then form, "and in sufficient and proper repair as a Square Garden and "Pleasure Ground, in an open state, uncovered with any "buildings . . . etc."

The piece of ground passed by divers conveyances into the hands of the defendant Moxhay, who, although he had made no similar covenant with his immediate vendor, admitted that he took the land with notice of the original covenant. The defendant then openly proposed to erect buildings upon the square, but the plaintiff,

---

[1] Report of the Committee on Positive Covenants affecting Land, Cmnd. 2719 (1965) p. 7.
[2] (1848), 2 Ph. 774.
[3] *Tulk* v. *Moxhay* (1848), 2 Ph. 774.

who still remained the owner of several adjacent houses, succeeded in obtaining an injunction to stop the breach of covenant.

Doctrine
originally
based on
notice.

This doctrine has been the subject of an exceedingly rapid development, in the course of which the nature of the right and obligation arising from a restrictive covenant has undergone a radical change.[1] The earlier decisions, culminating in *Luker* v. *Dennis*,[2] in 1877, proceeded solely upon the fact of notice,[3] since this was the element that Lord COTTENHAM stressed in *Tulk* v. *Moxhay* in the following words :—

" It is said that the covenant being one which does not run with the " land, this court cannot enforce it ; but the question is not whether " the covenant runs with the land, but whether a party shall be " permitted to use the land in a manner inconsistent with the con- " tract entered into by his vendor and with notice of which he " purchased."[4]

To rest the enforcement of a contract against a third party on this basis is not without its dangers.

First, if the emphasis is laid upon whether the conscience of the third party acquiring the land of the covenantor is affected, instead of upon whether the land itself is affected, there will be certain persons, such as a squatter obtaining a title by twelve years' adverse possession,[5] who will enjoy an immunity that they do not deserve.

Secondly, if notice alone justifies the issue of an injunction, the remedy can scarcely be withheld in principle even though the contract is collateral in the sense that its purpose is not to protect the covenantee's land against an undesirable use of the covenantor's land, but to confer some personal privilege upon the covenantee. The doctrine of *Tulk* v. *Moxhay* was indeed carried to these lengths in *Luker* v. *Dennis*.[6]

A publican, who already held a lease from X. of a public house called the " Milton Arms," took a lease of a second house, the " Sutton Arms," from a different landlord who was a brewer.

In this second lease he covenanted for himself and his assigns that he would buy from the brewer all the beer which he sold not only at the " Sutton Arms," but also at the " Milton Arms." Later the publican assigned the " Milton Arms " lease to the defendant, who took with notice that the public house was " tied " by the covenant to the brewer—that is to say, to a person who, apart from the covenant, was an absolute stranger to the property.

It was held that the defendant was bound by the covenant, since he had notice of it at the time when he took the assignment. It was regarded as immaterial that no proprietary relation in respect of the " Milton Arms " such as that of vendor and vendee, or lessor and lessee, existed between the original covenanting parties.

---

[1] See especially Behan, *Covenants affecting Land*, pp. 27 *et seq*.
[2] (1877), 7 Ch. D. 227.
[3] *London County Council* v. *Allen*, [1914] 3 K. B. 642, 658–9, 664–6.
[4] *Tulk* v. *Moxhay*, *supra*, at p. 777.
[5] *Infra*, pp. 551–2.
[6] (1877), 7 Ch. D. 227.

This was an indefensible extension of a contractual liability to a non-contracting party, but it was the last case in which *Tulk v. Moxhay* was based on the doctrine of notice pure and simple. Since the 'eighties the judicial approach to the matter has altered. The courts, choosing as the appropriate analogy either the negative easement, such as the right to light, or the tenant's covenant that is annexed to the land by virtue of Spencer's case,[1] have required a restrictive covenant to possess what may be called a real, as distinct from a personal, flavour, before it becomes available to and enforceable against third parties. It must, as VAUGHAN WILLIAMS, L.J., said, "arise from the relation of two estates, the one to the other," [2] or, to use more familiar language, it must touch and concern the dominant tenement of the covenantee and must be intended to protect that land against certain uses of the quasi-servient tenement. But once it satisfies this requirement it creates an equitable right that will run with the quasi-dominant tenement and a corresponding equitable obligation binding on the quasi-servient tenement. Being an equitable burden, it affects every person in the world who comes to the quasi-servient tenement, except one who acquires the legal estate therein without notice, actual or constructive, of the covenant. The position cannot be better described than in the words of COLLINS, L.J. :—

> "When the benefit has once been clearly annexed to one piece of
> "land, it passes by assignment of that land and may be said to run
> "with it . . . without proof of special bargain or representation on
> "the assignment. In such a case it runs not because the conscience
> "of either party is affected, but because the purchaser has bought
> "something which adhered in, or was annexed to, the land bought.
> "That is the reason why in dealing with the burden the purchaser's
> "conscience is not affected by notice of covenants which were part
> "of the original bargain on the first sale, but were merely collateral,
> "while it is affected by notice of those which touch and concern the
> "land. The covenant must be one that is capable of running with
> "the land before the question of the purchaser's conscience and the
> "equity affecting it can come into discussion." [3]

As the law now stands, certain essentials must be satisfied before the benefit of a covenant can be exploited by an assignee of the dominant tenement or before its burden can be laid upon an assignee of the servient tenement. These will now be stated.

(B) CONDITIONS PRECEDENT TO THE ENFORCEMENT OF A RESTRICTIVE COVENANT BY ASSIGNEES OF THE COVENANTEE.

(i) **The Covenant must be Negative in Nature.** It is essential that the covenant should be negative in substance,

Marginal notes:
Doctrine now rests on general equitable principles.

Notice alone insufficient to impose liability.

Doctrine does not apply to positive covenants.

---

[1] *L. and S. W. Rly.* v. *Gomm* (1882), 20 Ch. D. 562, 583.

[2] *Formby* v. *Barker*, [1903] 2 Ch. 539, 553. No such relation existed, for instance, in *Tophams, Ltd.,* v. *Sefton (Earl)* [1966] 1 All E. R. 1039; [1966] 2 W. L. R. 814.

[3] *Rogers* v. *Hosegood*, [1900] 2 Ch. 388, 407.

not a positive one requiring the expenditure of money for its performance.[1] This condition is satisfied if the owner of the land undertakes to use the premises for private residence only, or to keep certain windows obscured, or not to build, not to open a public house, not to carry on a business, and so on. But in every case it is the substance and not the form of the contract that must be regarded, for if an undertaking, though couched in affirmative terms, clearly implies a negative, it will be caught by the doctrine of *Tulk* v. *Moxhay*. Indeed, in that case itself, the covenant was not in terms restrictive, but its provision that the piece of ground was to be used only as an ornamental garden implied a prohibition against building.[2] Again, a covenant to give the first refusal of land is regarded as negative in substance, since in effect it is a promise not to sell without giving the covenantee an option to buy.[3]

Intention must be to annex benefit of covenant to dominant land. (ii) **It must be the common intention of the parties that the covenant shall enure for the benefit of land retained by the covenantee.** A restrictive covenant taken from the purchaser of a freehold estate is a mere covenant in gross personal to the contracting parties, unless it is their common intention that it shall impose an equitable burden upon the covenantor's land for the benefit of land owned by the covenantee. Equity, acting on the analogy of a negative easement will not regard a restrictive covenant as other than personal, unless there is the relation of dominancy and serviency between the respective properties.

Effect of covenant if no dominant land. It follows, therefore, that if the covenantee retains no adjacent land or owns no land capable of deriving profit from the covenant its benefit cannot avail other persons.[4]

Thus in *Formby* v. *Barker*,[5]

where a man, on selling the whole of his property in the neighbourhood, took a covenant from the purchaser whereby the latter agreed not to put the land to certain uses, it was held that the vendor's widow as administratrix was not entitled to an injunction forbidding a breach of the covenant by an assignee of the purchaser.

ROMER, L.J., in the course of his judgment said:

"I also agree in thinking that in this case . . . the administratrix of the "covenantee is not entitled to an injunction. If restrictive covenants "are entered into with a covenantee not in respect of or concerning "any ascertainable property belonging to him or in which he is "interested, then the covenant must be regarded, as far as he is con- "cerned, as a personal covenant—that is, as one obtained by him

---

[1] *Haywood* v. *Brunswick Building Society* (1881), 8 Q. D. B. 403.
[2] *Clegg* v. *Hands* (1890), 44 Ch. D. 503, 519.
[3] *Manchester Ship Canal Co.* v. *Manchester Racecourse Co.*, [1902] 2 Ch. 37.
[4] But a lessor's interest in the reversion suffices to make a covenant touching and concerning the land enforceable against a sub-lessee; *Regent Oil Co.* v. *J. A. Gregory (Hatch End), Ltd.*, [1966] Ch. 402, 432-3; [1965] All E. R. 673.
[5] [1903] 2 Ch. 539.

"for some personal purpose or object. It appears to me that it is
"not legally permissible for him to assign the benefit of such a
"covenant to any person or persons he may choose, so as to place the
"assign or assigns in his position, with power again for them to
"assign, and so on indefinitely."[1]

Again, once a covenantee has assigned the dominant land, he
cannot enforce the covenant against the servient owner. His one
remedy is to sue the covenantor personally on the contract, but
even so he is entitled only to nominal damages, not to an injunction. This remains true even though, as may well happen,[2] the
benefit of the covenant has not passed to the new dominant owner.
The principle of *Formby* v. *Barker* and of the later case of *L.C.C.*
v. *Allen*[3] is, in fact, that the equitable doctrine ought to be applied
with the sole object of protecting the enjoyment of the land which
the covenant was intended to protect. If it were possible for a
covenantee to enforce a covenant, despite the fact that he never
retained any land at all or that he later disposed of the land which
he had retained, the result would be to place an unwarranted and
useless burden upon subsequent purchasers from the covenantor.[4]

Although it may be clear beyond doubt that a covenant is taken
for the benefit of land owned by the covenantee, it will not confer
upon him an equitable interest that runs with the land unless two
further conditions are satisfied.

First the exact land to which the parties intend to annex the
benefit of the covenant must be ascertainable.[5] Whether this is so
depends primarily upon the construction of the deed of conveyance.
A competent draftsman will describe the land in precise terms, as
for instance by declaring that the covenant is taken for the benefit
of "the property known as Blackacre"; or for the "land marked
red on the plan drawn on these presents." If the description is
more vague, as for instance "the land adjoining" the servient land,
extrinsic evidence is admissible to identify the particular land that
the parties had in mind.[6] Also, if no dominant land is mentioned
in the conveyance, as where the purchaser covenants with the
vendor "and his successors in title", the court may infer from the
surrounding circumstances that the common intention was to
benefit the particular land retained by the vendor.[7]

[margin note:] Dominant land must be ascertainable.

---

[1] Exceptionally, a statute may provide, as the National Trust Act, 1937,
s. 8 does, that a covenantee shall be regarded as owning land adjacent to the
servient land, though in fact he does not; see *Gee* v. *National Trust for Places
of Historic Interest and Natural Beauty*, [1966] 1 All E. R. 954; [1966] 1 W. L.
R. 170. See also the Housing Act, 1957, s. 151.

[2] *Infra,* p. 543 *et seq.*

[3] *L.C.C.* v. *Allen*, [1914] 3 K. B. 642; *Kelly* v. *Barrett*, [1924] 2 Ch. 379.

[4] *Chambers* v. *Randall*, [1923] 1 Ch. 149, at p. 157; *Re Union of London
and Smith's Bank, Ltd.'s Conveyance, Miles* v. *Easter*, [1933] Ch. 611, at p. 632

[5] *Renals* v. *Cowlishaw* (1878), 9 Ch. D. 125; *Rogers* v. *Hosegood*, [1900] 2
Ch. 388; *Re Union of London and Smith's Bank, Ltd.'s Conveyance, Miles* v.
Easter, [1933] Ch. 611, at p. 631.

[6] *Marten* v. *Flight Refuelling, Ltd.*, [1962] Ch. 115, at pp. 130–5; [1961] 2
All E. R. 696, at pp. 702–5.

[7] *Marten* v. *Flight Refuelling, Ltd.*, [1962] Ch. 115; [1961] 2 All E. R. 696.

The
covenant
must touch
and concern
the
dominant
land.

Secondly, the covenant must be capable of benefiting the dominant land in the sense that it must be one which touches and concerns that land.[1] To satisfy this condition in the case where a freehold estate is conveyed,

> "the covenant must either affect the land as regards mode of occupa-
> "tion, or it must be such as *per se*, and not merely from collateral
> "circumstances, affects the value of the land."[2]

This question seldom causes difficulty, for if a vendor imposes a restriction upon the user of the servient land for the purpose of protecting the amenities or the selling value of the dominant land, the court will generally assume that it is capable of doing so.[3] But if the covenant is imposed for a personal reason, as for instance to indulge some fanciful prejudice, it is not enforceable by subsequent owners of the dominant land. A restrictive covenant, no less than a negative easement, must have some natural connection with the dominant tenement if it is to run with the land.

Effect
where the
covenant
affects part
only of
the land.

If a covenant is capable of affecting only part of the vendor's land, the legal position varies according as the conveyance annexes it to the whole, or to the whole and each and every part, of the land.[4]

If the annexation is expressly or by implication to the whole, the covenant is unenforceable by assignees of the dominant land unless it touches and concerns the whole of that land as a whole. This was the position in *Re Ballard's Conveyance*[5].

> In that case, the benefit of the covenant was annexed by the con-
> veyance to "the Childwickbury Estate." The area of this estate
> was about 1700 acres, far the largest part of which could not pos-
> sibly be directly affected by a breach of the covenant.

Although it would seem that an injury to a part of any unity is inevitably an injury to the whole, Clauson, J. held that the covenant was not enforceable by assignees of the whole of the dominant land. Moreover, he refused to sever the covenant and thus to regard it as annexed to the part of the land that was in fact touched and concerned. The decision seems to amount to this: that if a convenantee over-estimates to a moderate degree the area of the dominant land capable of deriving advantage from a restrictive covenant, his attempt to preserve the amenities of the neighbour-hood and to maintain the selling value of what he retains will utterly fail.[6] Why the well-known doctrine of severance should be excluded from this type of contract is difficult to appreciate.[7]

---

[1] *Rogers* v. *Hosegood*, [1900] 2 Ch. 388, at p. 395; *Kelly* v. *Barrett*, [1924] 2 Ch. 379, at p. 395; *Marquess of Zetland* v. *Driver*, [1939] Ch. 1, at p. 8; [1938] 2 All E. R. 158, at p. 161.
[2] *Congleton Corpn.* v. *Pattison* (1808), 10 East, 130; adopted *Rogers* v. *Hosegood, supra,* at p. 395, *per* Farwell, J.
[3] *Marten* v. *Flight Refuelling, Ltd.*, [1962] Ch. 115, at p. 136, *per* Wilber-force, J.
[4] Preston and Newsom, *Restrictive Covenants*, pp. 15–18; 20–23.
[5] [1937] Ch. 473; [1937] 2 All E. R. 691.
[6] 57 *L. Q. R.* pp. 210–11 (G. R. Y. Radcliffe).
[7] See Elphinstone, *Covenants Affecting Land*, p. 60, note 10.

On the other hand, a covenant which is annexed expressly or by implication to the whole and each and every part of the dominant land is enforceable by an assignee of the land, but only by one who takes a part that is in fact affected. In *Marquess of Zetland* v. *Driver*,[1] for instance:

> The covenant was expressed to be for the benefit and protection of "such part or parts of the [dominant land] (a) as shall for the time being remain unsold or (b) as shall be sold by the vendor or his successors in title with the express benefit of this covenant." Certain parts of the unsold land were contiguous to the land of the covenantor, but other parts were more than a mile distant. The covenant, therefore, did not touch and concern the whole of the dominant land.

It was held that the person who succeeded to the dominant land could enforce the covenant against a purchaser of the servient land. The Court of Appeal, without expressing approbation of *Re Ballard's Conveyance*, distinguished it on the ground that:—

> "in that case the covenant was expressed to run with the whole "estate, whereas in the present case . . . the covenant is expressed "to be for the benefit of the whole or any part or parts of the unsold "settled property."[2]

Extrinsic evidence is admissible in a doubtful case to show whether a covenant is capable of operating to the advantage of the dominant land.[3] *Extrinsic evidence.*

To summarize what has been said in this part of the discussion—if a restrictive covenant is intended by the parties to operate to the advantage of adjacent and ascertainable land retained by the covenantee and capable of yielding that advantage, its benefit, in the technical language of the law, is said to be *annexed to* that land. *"Benefit of covenant annexed to land."*

(iii) An Assignee of the Dominant Land must prove that the Benefit of the Covenant has passed to him.

Suppose that on the sale of Whiteacre to X. a restrictive covenant has been taken from him for the protection of Blackacre still retained by the vendor, A. ; and suppose further that A. has subsequently sold Blackacre, the dominant land, to the plaintiff. Can the plaintiff enforce the covenant against X. or against an assignee of X.'s land ? The answer is that enforcement is not a certainty merely because the dominant land has come into the hands of the plaintiff. The plaintiff must go further. He must prove, not only that he has acquired the land, but also that he has acquired the benefit of *Acquisition of dominant land does not necessarily carry with it benefit of covenant.*

---

[1] [1939] Ch. 1; [1938] 2 All E. R. 158.
[2] *Ibid.*, at p. 10. In *Russell* v. *Archdale*, [1964] Ch. 68, [1962] 2 All E. R. 305, Buckley, J., after holding that the covenant was annexed to the whole of the land as a whole, ultimately held that it was nevertheless enforceable against the original covenantor by an assignee of part only of the dominant land, on the ground that the benefit of the covenant had been expressly assigned to him.
[3] *Newton Abbot Co-operative Society, Ltd.* v. *Williamson and Treadgold*, [1952] Ch. 286; [1952] 1 All E. R. 279; *Marten* v. *Flight Refuelling, Ltd.*, [1962] Ch. 115; [1961] 2 All E. R. 696.

the covenant itself. There are only three ways in which he can do this,[1] namely by proving:

(*a*) that the benefit of the covenant has been effectively annexed to the dominant land, and that he has acquired the whole of that land, or the part of it to which the covenant was annexed; or,

(*b*) that the benefit of the covenant was separately and expressly assigned to him at the time of the sale ; or,

(*c*) that both the dominant and servient lands are subject to a building scheme.

Let us take these methods separately.

(*a*) *Annexation of Covenant to Dominant Land.*

The benefit of a restrictive covenant, once it has been annexed to the dominant land in the sense described above,[2] runs automatically with that land and is enforceable by the successors in title of the covenantee, even though they do not learn of its existence until after execution of the conveyance.[3] If a successor in title acquires the whole of the land, the benefit passes to him without question; but if he acquires only part he must show that the benefit was annexed to that particular part alone or to each portion of the whole.[4]

For instance, A., the owner of a large property, sells part of it to Y. and takes a covenant that no public house shall be opened on it. This covenant is annexed to A's land. Later A. sells part of the dominant land to B. If B. seeks to enforce the covenant by virtue of its annexation to A's land, he must prove that its benefit was annexed to each and every part of those lands or to the very part bought by him.

The Law of Property Act, 1925, defines the term "successors in title" in the present context as follows:

A covenant relating to the land of any covenantee shall be deemed to be made with the covenantee and his successors in title under him or them, and shall have effect as if such successors and other persons were expressed.

For the purposes of this subsection in connexion with covenants restrictive of the user of land "successors in title" shall be deemed to include the owners and occupiers for the time being of the land of the covenantee intended to be benefited.[5]

---

[1] *In re Pinewood Estate, Farnborough,* [1958] Ch. 280; [1957] 2 All E. R. 517.
[2] *Supra,* p. 543.
[3] *Rogers* v. *Hosegood,* [1900] 2 Ch. 388.
[4] *Rogers* v. *Hosegood, supra; Reid* v. *Bickerstaff,* [1909] 2 Ch. 305; *Re Union of London and Smith's Bank, Ltd.'s Conveyance, Miles* v. *Easter,* [1933] Ch. 611, at p. 628; *Re Jeff's Transfer (No. 2), Rogers* v. *Astley,* [1966] 1 All E. R. 937.
[5] Law of Property Act, 1925, s. 78 (1).

But it is important to observe that for a restrictive covenant to avail successors by virtue of this subsection it must satisfy the conditions of annexation already explained.

A purchaser or lessee may covenant in the deed of conveyance that a restrictive covenant, therein imposed upon him, shall enure for the benefit of a third person such as the owner of adjoining land, although the latter is not a party to the deed. *Benefit of covenant may be made available to other land-owners.*

Such a covenant was wholly nugatory at common law owing to the technical rule that only a party to a deed could enforce its provisions. This rule, however, was abrogated by the Real Property Act, 1845,[1] in a section that was reproduced and extended as follows by the Law of Property Act, 1925.

> A person may take an immediate or other interest in land or other property, or the benefit of any condition, right of entry, covenant or agreement over or respecting land or other property, although he may not be named as a party to the conveyance or other instrument.[2]

The effect of this enactment may be illustrated by *In Re Ecclesiastical Commissioners for England's Conveyance*,[3] where the facts were these:

> In 1887, the purchaser of Blackacre entered into restrictive covenants in favour of the Ecclesiastical Commissioners, the vendors. A separate covenant was also included in the conveyance declaring that the covenants providing that the benefit of the covenants should avail the vendors' "assigns, owners for the time being of the land adjoining or adjacent to" Blackacre. Prior to 1887, the commissioners had sold various freehold plots, situated near Blackacre, to different purchasers and these had passed into other hands by the time of the action.

It was held that the successors in title of the adjacent owners were entitled to enforce the covenants although their respective predecessors in title had not joined in the conveyance of 1887.

This statutory right is confined to a covenant that runs with the land of the person for whose benefit it was taken,[4] and it will not avail him unless he might have been a party to the deed in question. If he is an ascertainable person at the time of the execution of the deed which purports to grant him an interest in property[5] or to make a covenant available to him, he and his successors in title are in as good a position as if he had been one of the original parties. On the other hand, a deed is inoperative in so far as it purports to extend the advantage of a covenant to an unascertainable person, such as the future owner of specified land.[6]

---

[1] Real Property Act, 1845, s. 5.
[2] Law of Property Act, 1925, s. 56 (1).
[3] [1936] Ch. 430. See also *Forster* v. *Elvet Colliery Co., Ltd.,* [1908] 1 K. B. 629; *affirmed sub. nom. Dyson* v. *Forster,* [1909] A. C. 98.
[4] *Grant* v. *Edmondson,* [1930] 2 Ch. 245, at p. 258.
[5] *Stromdale and Ball, Ltd.* v. *Burden,* [1952] 2 Ch. 223; [1952] 1 All E. R. 59; *Drive Yourself Hire Co. (London), Ltd.* v. *Strutt,* [1954] 1 Q. B. 250; [1953] 2 All E. R. 1475.
[6] *Kelsey* v. *Dodd,* (1881) 52 L. J. Ch. 24, at p. 39; *White* v. *Bijou Mansions, Ltd.,* [1937] Ch. 610, at p. 625; [1937] 3 All E. R. 269, 277; affirmed [1938] Ch. 351, at p. 365; 1 All E. R. 546, at p. 554.

(b) Express Assignment of Covenant.

Limits within which assignment of covenant allowed.

Failure to establish the annexation described above is not necessarily fatal to an assignee of the covenantee's land, for he will succeed in an action for an infringement of the restriction if he shows that he is not only an assignee of the land, but also the express assignee of the *covenant* itself.[1] A restrictive covenant, *if capable of running according to the rules already given*, can be expressly assigned, and, what is more, can be assigned from time to time to one person after another.[2] It is also capable of assignment by operation of law. Thus, on the death of the covenantee it passes to his executors and is held by them as bare trustees for the devisee of the dominant land and becomes assignable by him.[3] As SARGANT, J., observed in one case[4]:

" *Renals* v. *Cowlishaw*[5] clearly recognizes that, where a vendor takes " a restrictive covenant from a purchaser in order to enable the " vendor to deal more advantageously with his other property, the " benefit of such a covenant may be expressly assigned together " with the whole or part of such property. Indeed it is precisely " by being able to assign such a covenant that the vendor secures " the advantageous realization of such other property."

Dominant land must be ascertainable with reasonable certainty.

Express assignment is not permissible, however, unless the covenant has been taken for the benefit of the land of the covenantee and unless that land is indicated with reasonable certainty.[6] This indication need not appear in the conveyance creating the covenant. It is sufficient if in the light of the attendant circumstances the identity of the dominant land is in some other way ascertainable with reasonable certainty.

Whether these two requirements were satisfied was neatly raised in *Newton Abbot Co-operative Society* v. *Williamson and Treadgold, Ltd.*[7] on the following facts:

The owner of Devonia, in which she carried on the business of an ironmonger, sold a shop on the opposite side of the street to a purchaser who traded there as a grocer. The purchaser covenanted not to trade as an ironmonger at the premises. The conveyance did not define any dominant land for the benefit of which the covenant was taken, but simply described the vendor as 'of Devonia'.

UPJOHN, J. held in the first place that the covenant was not a mere covenant in gross. Its objects were not only to protect the vendor

---

[1] *Reid* v. *Bickerstaff*, [1909] 2 Ch. 305, at p. 320; *Re Union of London and Smith's Bank, Ltd.'s Conveyance, Miles* v. *Easter*, [1933] Ch. 611.

[2] *Re Union of London and Smith's Bank, Ltd.'s Conveyance, Miles* v. *Easter, supra*, at p. 630.

[3] *Newton Abbot Co-operative Society, Ltd.* v. *Williamson and Treadgold, Ltd.*, [1952] Ch. 286; [1952] 1 All E. R. 279.

[4] *Ives* v. *Brown*, [1919] 2 Ch. 314, at p. 323.

[5] (1878), 9 Ch. D. 125; affirmed (1879), 11 Ch. D. 866.

[6] *Re Union of London and Smith's Bank, Ltd.'s Conveyance, Miles* v. *Easter*, [1933] Ch. 611.

[7] [1952] Ch. 286; [1952] 1 All E. R. 279, approved by WILBERFORCE, J. in *Marten* v. *Flight Refuelling, Ltd.*, [1962] Ch. 115, at p. 133,; [1961] 2 All E. R. 696.

personally against competition, but also to enhance the selling value of Devonia if sold to someone intending to trade there as an ironmonger. The learned judge further held that the identity of the dominant land was sufficiently clear. The only reasonable inference to draw from the surrounding circumstances, especially from the propinquity of the two shops, was that the covenant was taken for the benefit not only of the vendor's business, but also of the land that she retained.

Nevertheless, in order to appreciate the limits within which assignment is permissible it is essential to stress that the reason why equity allows a restrictive covenant to be enforced against third parties is that the land of the covenantee may be protected, and in particular, that its sale value shall not be diminished.[1] Such a covenant is not an independent entity having its own intrinsic value. It has no *raison d'être* apart from the land for whose protection it was taken. Therefore, as we have already seen, even the covenantee himself cannot enforce the covenant against an assignee of the covenantor after he has disposed of the whole of his dominant land, for it is obvious that he no longer requires protection.[2] This theory, that the maintenance of the value of the covenantee's land is the sole justification for allowing restrictive covenants to run in favour of his successors in title, leads to this result, that the express assignment of the benefit of a covenant is ineffective unless it is contemporaneous with the assignment of the land affected. The covenant has spent its force if the covenantee has not required its aid in disposing of the dominant land.[3] *Assignment and conveyance must be contemporaneous.*

" But if he has been able to sell any particular part of his property
" without assigning to the purchaser the benefit of the covenant,
" there seems no reason why he should at a later date and as an
" independent transaction be at liberty to confer upon the purchaser
" such benefit. To hold that he could do so would be to treat the
" covenant as having been obtained not only to enable the covenantee
" to dispose of his land to the best advantage, but also for the purpose
" of enabling him to dispose of the benefit of the covenant to the
" best advantage." [4]

Subject to these limitations, however, an express assignment of a covenant to a purchaser of the whole or part of the dominant land made at the time of the purchase is effective.

(c) Building Scheme.

The third case in which a restrictive covenant is enforceable *Meaning of " building scheme."*

---

[1] *Chambers* v. *Randall*, [1923] 1 Ch. 149 ; *Re Union of London and Smith's Bank, Ltd.'s Conveyance, Miles* v. *Easter*, [1933] Ch. 611, at p. 632.
[2] See last note.
[3] *Chambers* v. *Randall*, *supra* ; *Re Union of London and Smith's Bank, Ltd.'s Conveyance, Miles* v. *Easter*, *supra* ; *Re Rutherford's Conveyance*, [1938] 1 Ch. 396 ; [1938] 1 All E. R. 495.
[4] *Re Union of London and Smith's Bank, Ltd.'s Conveyance, Miles* v. *Easter*, [1933] Ch. 611 ; at p. 632, *per* ROMER, L.J.

by and against persons other than the original covenanting parties is when lands are held by their respective owners under a building scheme.

A building scheme comes into existence where land is laid out in plots and sold to different purchasers or leased to different lessees, each of whom enters into a restrictive covenant with the common vendor or lessor agreeing that his particular plot shall not be used for certain purposes. In such a case these restrictive covenants are taken because the whole estate is being developed on a definite plan, and it is vital, if the value of each plot is not to be depreciated, that the purchasers or lessees should be prevented from dealing with their land so as to lower the tone of the neighbourhood. When the existence of a building scheme has been established, the rule is that each purchaser and his assignees can sue or be sued by every other purchaser and his assignees for a breach of the restrictive covenants.[1] In such an action for breach it is immaterial whether the defendant acquired his title before or after the date on which the plaintiff purchased his plot. In other words, the restrictive covenants constitute a special local law for the area over which the scheme extends, and not only the plot-owners, but even the vendor himself, become subject to that law,[2] provided that the area and the obligations to be imposed therein are defined. Where an owner sells his land in plots on the footing that the use of each plot shall be restricted for the benefit of himself and other purchasers, then a court of equity will give effect to this common intention even though the various parties have not entered into express mutual covenants, for it is well established that the intention that there shall be mutual obligations may be implied.[3] The subject-matter of a scheme generally consists of freehold land which is to be sold in plots to persons who desire to erect houses, but it may equally well comprise leasehold houses or flats that have already been built.[4]

But a building scheme does not come into being merely because the owner of an estate sells it off in plots taking restrictive covenants from each purchaser. Pre-eminent among the essentials is proof of a common intention that the restrictive

---

[1] *Spicer* v. *Martin* (1888), 14 App. Cas. 12 ; *Renals* v. *Cowlishaw* (1878), 9 Ch. D. 125 ; affirmed (1879), 11 Ch. D. 866 ; *Hudson* v. *Cripps*, [1896] 1 Ch. 265 (lease).

[2] *Reid* v. *Bickerstaff*, [1909] 2 Ch. 305 at p. 319. Of course the scheme may expressly entitle the vendor to dispose of plots free from its restrictions; *Mayner* v. *Payne*, [1914] 2 Ch. 555.

[3] *Renals* v. *Cowlishaw, supra* ; *Torbay Hotel, Ltd.* v. *Jenkins*, [1927] 2 Ch. 225, 240.

[4] *Spicer* v. *Martin* (1888), 14 App. Cas. 12 ; *Hudson* v. *Cripps*, [1896] 1 Ch. 265.

covenants have been taken for the mutual benefit of the respective purchasers, not for the sole protection of the vendor in respect of the land still unsold and retained by him.[1] Whether such an intention exists is a question of fact that depends upon a variety of circumstances. If, for instance, the vendor is left with no land, as the result perhaps of a successful auction sale, an intention that the covenants are designed for the mutual benefit of all the purchasers is readily inferred. If, on the other hand, at the time of the respective sales the purchasers are ignorant that similar covenants have been taken from others, the inference is almost irresistible that the object is to benefit the vendor.[2] It has been laid down by PARKER, J. that before the benefit and the burden of such covenants can pass to the various purchasers and their assignees, the following conditions must exist [3] :—

(a) Both the plaintiff and the defendant to the action for breach of the restrictive covenant must have derived their titles to the land from a common vendor.

(b) Before the sale of the plots to the plaintiff and the defendant, the vendor must have laid out his estate for sale in lots subject to restrictions which it was intended to impose on all the lots, and which were only consistent with some general scheme of development.[4] The failure to do this, however, is irrelevant if there is a clear and common intention that the covenants shall be binding between all the purchasers or lessees.[5]

(c) The vendor must have intended that the benefit of the restrictions should pass to each purchaser. This intention is gathered from all the circumstances of the case, but if the restrictions are obviously calculated to enhance the value of each lot, the intention is readily inferred.

To a certain extent these three conditions overlap, but the basic requirement is the existence of common regulations obviously intended to govern the area that is to be developed.

" The material thing I think is that every purchaser . . . must
" know when he buys what are the regulations to which he is sub-
" jecting himself and what are the regulations to which other
" purchasers on the estate will be called upon to subject themselves.
" Unless you know that, it is quite impossible in my judgment to
" draw the necessary inference, whether you refer to it as an agree-
" ment or as a community of interest importing reciprocity of
" obligation." [6]

(d) The original purchasers must have bought their lots on the

---

[1] *Nottingham Patent Brick & Tile Co.* v. *Butler* (1886), 15 Q. B. D. 261, at p. 268, *per* WILLS, J. ; approved *White* v. *Bijou Mansions, Ltd.*, [1938] Ch. 351, at p. 361 ; [1938] 1 All E. R. 546, at p. 552.
[2] *Osborne* v. *Bradley*, [1903] 2 Ch. 446, 454.
[3] *Elliston* v. *Reacher*, [1908] 2 Ch. 374, 385
[4] *Willé* v. *St. John*, [1910] 1 Ch. 84 ; affd., [1910] 1 Ch. 325.
[5] *Baxter* v. *Four Oaks Properties, Ltd.*, [1965] Ch. 816; [1965] 1 All E. R. 906.
[6] *White* v. *Bijou Mansions*, [1938] Ch. 351, at p. 362 ; [1938] 1 All E. R. 546, at p. 552, *per* GREENE, M.R.

understanding that the restrictions were to enure for the benefit of the other lots.

(e) The geographical area to which the scheme extends must be ascertainable with reasonably clear definitiveness.[1] There must, in fact, be clear evidence of an original layout in building plots.[2]

(C) PERSONS AGAINST WHOM A RESTRICTIVE COVENANT IS ENFORCEABLE

Restrictive covenants as equitable interests.

The doctrine of *Tulk* v. *Moxhay* stands on quite a different footing from the rules which regulate the running of covenants at law, and being of a far more elastic nature it affects a more extensive class of persons and embraces a more extensive class of covenants.   The essence of the matter is that when once the above conditions are satisfied a restrictive covenant becomes an equitable interest, and as such is enforceable on general principles against all persons who acquire the burdened land, with the one exception of the purchaser for valuable consideration of the legal estate therein without notice of the covenant.   Moreover, the occupier of the burdened land is liable irrespectively of the character of his occupation.   This is in sharp contrast with the common law and statutory rules that govern covenants contained in a lease.   Under these rules, as we have seen,[3] the burden of a covenant, whether positive or negative, that touches and concerns the land passes to an assignee of the tenant, and it is immaterial that the landlord retains no dominant land.[4]   But no one is an "assignee' for this purpose unless there is privity of estate between him and the reversioner.   Thus, though the burden is traditionally said to run with the land, what in fact it runs with is the estate created by the lease.   Under the developed doctrine of *Tulk* v. *Moxhay*, on the other hand, it runs with the servient land as such, and there is no question of privity of estate.   A restrictive covenant is enforceable against the successors in title of the original covenantor, including a mere occupant of the land, provided that the requisites for the annexation of its benefit to the dominant land have been satisfied.[5]

The effect of this distinction between running with the land and running with the estate may be illustrated by a reference to three classes of persons who are all caught by the doctrine of *Tulk* v. *Moxhay*, but none of whom is liable at common law under the rules derived from *Spencer's* case.

---

[1] *Osborne* v. *Bradley*, [1903] 2 Ch. 446; *Torbay Hotel, Ltd.* v. *Jenkins*, [1927] 2 Ch. 225.

[2] *Lawrence* v. *South County Freeholds, Ltd.*, [1939] Ch. 656 ; [1939] 2 All E. R. 503.

[3] *Supra*, p. 414, note 4.

[4] *Regent Oil Co., Ltd.* v. *J. A. Gregory (Hatch End), Ltd.*, [1966] Ch. 402; [1965] 3 All E. R. 673.

[5] Law of Property Act, 1925, s. 79 (2).

A restrictive covenant imposed upon a lessee binds an under-lessee, despite the absence of privity of estate between him and the lessor.[1]

A person who is merely occupying land without having any definite estate or interest therein is bound by restrictive covenants. Thus in *Mander* v. *Falcke*,[2]

> a lessee who had covenanted not to use the demised premises for purposes which would cause annoyance or inconvenience to adjoining property owned by the lessor granted an under-lease of the premises. The reversion was ultimately assigned to the plaintiff and the under-lease became vested in X. Apparently X. did not occupy the premises himself, but allowed his father to have possession, and the evidence clearly showed that the latter, while purporting to keep an oyster bar, was in fact using the place as a brothel to the great scandal of the neighbourhood.

In an injunction to restrain a breach of the covenant it was argued that such relief could not be granted against the father, as he had no interest whatever, either legal or equitable, in the land. This argument failed, and an injunction was granted against the father, LINDLEY, L.J., saying :

" I treat him simply as an occupier managing the business. He " may be neither an assignee nor purchaser, but he is in occupation " and that is enough to affect him, he having notice of the covenants " in the lease." [3]

A person who acquires a title to land by lapse of time under the Limitation Act is bound by any restrictive covenants which are annexed to the land. We have seen that a covenant entered into between landlord and tenant does not at law bind a person who by long-continued possession of the premises acquires a superior right to the tenant, because the effect of the Limitation Act is merely to extinguish the right of the tenant and not to transfer his identical interest to the adverse possessor.[4] There is no privity of estate between the disseisor and the lessor. This lack of privity, however, will not free a disseisor of the servient land from a restrictive covenant unless he can prove that he is a purchaser for value of the legal estate without notice. The case of *In re Nisbet and Potts' Contract*[5] affords an illustration.

> Lands were sold in 1867 by A. to W., a covenant being entered into by the latter that he would not build on the purchased property within 30 feet of a certain road. This covenant was for the benefit of other property owned by A. In 1872 W. re-sold the land to X. with a similar covenant. Somewhere about 1878 Y. wrongfully seized the land and remained in occupation for over 12 years, after

---

[1] *Clements* v. *Welles* (1863), L. R. 1 Eq. 200 ; *Hall* v. *Ewin* (1887), 37 Ch. D. 74 ; *John* v. *Holmes*, [1900] 1 Ch. 188.
[2] [1891] 2 Ch. 554.
[3] At p. 557.
[4] *Supra*, pp. 415-6.
[5] [1905] 1 Ch. 391 ; [1906] 1 Ch. 386.

which he automatically acquired what is called a possessory title, and became entitled to keep the land as against X. In 1890 Y.'s son, who had succeeded his father, sold the land to Z., who agreed that instead of requiring the title to be proved for the last 40 years he would be content with proof that Y. had been in possession since before 1878. Later still the land was sold to Nisbet, and he agreed in 1903 to sell it to Potts. The question was whether Potts, if he took a conveyance of the land, would be subject to the restrictive covenant imposed by the original deed of 1867.

It was argued that the covenant no longer bound assignees of the servient land, for Y., who had seized the land in 1878, acquired a title quite independent of any prior holder's title, and that, even if it made any difference, which was denied, neither Z. nor Nisbet had notice of the covenant and therefore could not be bound thereby. But it was held that the equitable interest created by the covenant remained enforceable against Z. and Nisbet, unless they could satisfy the Court that they had acquired the legal estate for valuable consideration without notice.

They certainly had acquired the legal estate for value without actual notice, but nevertheless they were affected by constructive notice, for if they had insisted, as they might have done, upon proof of a good root of title at least 40 years old, they would have been led back through the squatter Y. to the original covenantor W. If they chose to accept less than they might have done, they were bound to take the consequences.

Further, it was clear that the lapse of time and the changes of title that had occurred since 1867 did not bar the remedy of the person in whom the benefit of the covenant was now vested. Time under the Limitation Act does not begin to run against a person until his right of action accrues. In the instant case no right of action would accrue until the covenant was broken, and there had been no question of this until 1903.

Binding effect of restrictive covenants. A final word is now required as to the binding effect of restrictive covenants under the modern law.

Since 1925 restrictive covenants have been divided into two classes :—

1. those created before January 1st, 1926, when the Law of Property Act, 1925, came into force ;
2. those created after 1925.

1. The rule which governs covenants created before January 1st, 1926, is that laid down above, viz. that they bind all persons who acquire the burdened land, with the exception of a purchaser for value of the legal estate therein without notice, actual or constructive, of the covenants. Such a purchaser can, however, pass a title free from the restriction to a pur-

chaser from him, even though the latter has actual notice of the covenant.[1]

2. Covenants created after 1925, except those made between lessor and lessee, are void against a purchaser (including a mortgagee and lessee) of the *legal estate* in the burdened land *for money or money's worth*, unless they are registered as land charges in the appropriate register.[2] If not registered they are void against the purchaser for value of the legal estate even though he had express notice of them. Thus non-registration does not avail an assignee of a mere equitable interest in the burdened land, or an assignee of the legal estate who does not give money or money's worth. The reason why a restrictive covenant between a lessor and lessee cannot be registered, is that it is a simple and normal step for an assignee to inspect the lease which contains the terms of the tenancy.

(D) EXTINCTION OF RESTRICTIVE COVENANTS.

The Law of Property Act provides for the total extinction of restrictive covenants. Under the law apart from the Act a covenantee (including his assignees) is deprived of his right to enforce the covenant if he has submitted to a long course of usage wholly inconsistent with its continuance, as where he remains inactive for a considerable time while open breaches of the covenant are taking place;[3] if he disregards breaches in such a way as to justify a reasonable person in believing that future breaches will be disregarded;[4] or if the character of the neighbourhood in which the protected property lies is so entirely altered that it would be inequitable and senseless to insist upon the rigorous observance of a covenant that is no longer of any value.[5] *Mode of discharging obsolete covenants.*

The Law of Property Act, 1925, develops this last ground of extinction, and sets up a new method whereby restrictions may be discharged or modified.[6] *Statutory power to discharge or modify covenants.*

The first point to notice is that the Act mainly applies to restrictions imposed on freehold estates. It has no application to

---

[1] *Wilkes* v. *Spooner*, [1911] 2 K. B. 473.

[2] Land Charges Act, 1925, ss. 10 (1); 13 (2); s. 20 (8), *infra*, p. 670.

[3] *Gibson* v. *Doeg* (1857), 2 H. & N. 615; *Hepworth* v. *Pickles*, [1900] 1 Ch. 108; *In re Summerson*, [1900] 1 Ch. 112 n.; discussed in *Lloyds Bank, Ltd.* v. *Jones*, [1955] 2 Q. B. 298, 320–2.

[4] *Chatsworth Estates Co.* v. *Fewell*, [1931] 1 Ch. 224.

[5] *Chatsworth Estates Co.* v. *Fewell*, *supra*; see generally, Behan, *Covenants affecting Land*, pp. 148 *et seq.*; Elphinstone, *Covenants affecting Land*, pp. 110 *et seq.*; *Westripp* v. *Baldock*, [1938] 2 All E. R. 779; affirmed, [1939] 1 All E. R. 279. *Melbourne University Law Review*, pp. 209–14 (D. Mendes da Costa).

[6] S. 84 (1); see *Richardson* v. *Jackson*, [1954] 1 All E. R. 437; [1954] 1 W. L. R. 447. The section does not apply to a forestry dedication covenant; Forestry Act, 1947, s. 1 (3). A list of the applications made under s. 84 (1) and of their results is given in each issue of *Current Law* under the heading "Real Property and Conveyancing."

T*

leaseholds which are subject to restrictive covenants, except where
the lease was originally made for more than 40 years, and 25 years
of this term have expired when the question of extinction arises.[1]

It is then provided that any person interested in any such freehold or leasehold land, or affected by the restrictive covenant, may
apply to the Lands Tribunal [2] to have the restriction either wholly
or partially discharged, or modified, whether with or without
payment of compensation. The tribunal should be more reluctant
to interfere with leasehold than with freehold covenants.[3]

Before making any order the tribunal must be satisfied :

" (*a*) that by reason of changes in the character of the property or
" the neighbourhood or other circumstances of the case which the
" [tribunal] may deem material, the restriction ought to be deemed
" obsolete, or that the continued existence thereof would impede the
" reasonable user of the land for public or private purposes without
" securing practical benefits to other persons, or, as the case may be,
" would unless modified so impede such user ; or

" (*b*) that the persons of full age and capacity for the time being or
" from time to time entitled to the benefit of the restriction, whether
" in respect of estates in fee simple or any lesser estates or interests
" in the property to which the benefit of the restriction is annexed,
" have agreed, either expressly or by implication, by their acts or
" omissions, to the same being discharged or modified; or

" (*c*) that the proposed discharge or modification will not injure the
" persons entitled to the benefit of the restriction."

The statutory provisions apply to restrictive covenants
entered into either before or after the commencement of the
Act, but do not apply where the restriction was imposed on the
occasion of a disposition made gratuitously, or for a nominal
consideration, for public purposes. Any person aggrieved by the
decision of the tribunal on the ground that it is erroneous in point
of law may require that a case be stated for the decision of the
Court of Appeal.[4]

**Limits
to the
statutory
power.**
The limits to this statutory power should be realized. It
was not the intention of the Legislature that a person, by the
payment of compensation, should be free to expropriate the
private rights of another purely for his own advantage. There
are, for instance, many cases in these less spacious days where the
greatest benefit would accrue to the owner of a house if he could
ignore a covenant, imposed perhaps many years ago, restraining
him from building upon the adjacent land. Nevertheless, if the
object of the restriction was to preserve the tone of the neigh-

---

[1] S. 84 (12), as amended by Landlord and Tenant Act, 1954, s. 52. The
25 years is reckoned from the date of the lease, and not from any earlier date
at which the term is expressed in the lease to begin ; *Cadogan (Earl)* v.
Guinness, [1936] Ch. 515 ; [1936] 2 All E. R. 29.
[2] Lands Tribunal Act. 1949, s. 1 (4) (a).
[3] *Ridley* v. *Taylor*, [1965] 2 All E. R. 51; [1965] 1 W. L. R. 611.
[4] *Ibid.*, s. 3 (4), proviso.

bourhood, and if the district is still of a high-class residential character, there is no justification for the application of the Act.

> " If a case is to be made out under this section," said FARWELL, J.,
> " there must be some proper evidence that the restriction is no longer
> " necessary for any reasonable purpose of the person who is enjoying
> " the benefit of it, or that by reason of a change in the character of
> " the property or the neighbourhood, the restriction is one which
> " is no longer to be enforceable or has become of no value." [1]

Thus the courts have taken the view that a covenant is not " obsolete " within the meaning of the section unless " its original object can no longer be achieved," and that this cannot be the case if its discharge would severely injure persons for whose benefit it exists.[2]

In order to meet the case where it may be doubtful whether an effectual restrictive covenant has been imposed on land and if so what persons it now affects, the Act confers jurisdiction upon the court, **Statutory power to declare whether restriction binding.**

(*a*) to declare whether or not in any particular case any freehold land is affected by a restriction imposed by any instrument ; or

(*b*) to declare what is the true nature and extent of the restriction thereby imposed and whether the same is enforceable and if so by whom.[3]

If it is proved that a house cannot readily be let as a single tenement but can readily be let if converted into two or more tenements, the Housing Act, 1957, empowers the County Court to vary any provisions in a lease or any restrictive covenant affecting the lease if these impede the proposed conversion.[4] Such a variation is not permissible unless the converted tenements will be wholly contained within one house.[5] **Housing Act, 1957.**

The Town and Country Planning Act, 1962,[6] authorizes a local planning authority, subject to the payment of compensation, to carry out a scheme of development, notwithstanding that it interferes with an easement or infringes a restrictive covenant. **Town and Country Planning Act.**

---

[1] *Re Henderson's Conveyance*, [1940] Ch. 835, at p. 846 ; [1940] 4 All E. R. 1, at p. 7. *In re Ghey and Galton's Application*, [1957] 2 Q. B. 650 ; [1957] 3 All E. R. 164.

[2] *In re Truman, Hanbury, Buxton & Co., Ltd.'s Application*, [1956] 1 Q. B. 261 ; [1955] 3 All E. R. 559 ; *Driscoll* v. *Church Commissioners for England*, [1957] 1 Q. B. 330 ; [1956] 3 All E. R. 802.

[3] Law of Property Act, 1925, s. 84 (2) ; *Re Sunnyfield*, [1932] 1 Ch. 79; *In re Freeman-Thomas Indenture*, [1957] 1 All E. R. 532. A declaration as to what will be the effect of a future breach of covenant may be made under the general jurisdiction of the court, but not under this sub-section of the Act; *Re Gadd's Land Transfer, Cornmill Developments, Ltd.*, [1966] Ch. 56; [1965] 2 All E. R. 800.

[4] S. 165.

[5] *Josephine Trust, Ltd.* v. *Champagne*, [1962] 2 Q. B. 160; [1962] 3 All E. R. 136.

[6] S. 81.

CHAPTER IV.

RENTCHARGES.

SUMMARY.

SECTION I.   NATURE OF A RENTCHARGE.

Distinction between rentcharge and rent-service.

Origin and History. We have already seen that a rent payable by a tenant to a landlord is called rent-service because of the tenure which exists between the parties, but that it is called a rentcharge if there is no tenure between the creditor and the debtor from whose land it issues.[1]   In former days this lack of

---

[1] *Supra*, pp. 385–6.

tenurial interest between the parties meant that the rent owner
had no automatic right at law to distrain upon the land of the
debtor for the recovery of arrears, and generally speaking,
rentcharges, though of considerable antiquity, were regarded as
contrary to the policy of the common law, since the debtor was
rendered less able to perform the military service due to his overlord, while the rent owner himself was free from all feudal obligations in respect of the land.[1] It became usual, therefore, for the
parties to enter into an express agreement that the creditor
should have a power of distress over the debtor's land. A rent
supported in this way by a specially reserved power of distress,
as distinct from a rent-service where such power existed of
common right, was called a rentcharge, since the land liable for
payment was charged with a distress.[2] We have seen that there
is no longer any necessity to charge the land expressly, for the
Law of Property Act, 1925, re-enacting the Landlord and Tenant
Act, 1730, and the Conveyancing Act, 1881, confers the right of
distress upon all rentcharge owners.[3]

A rentcharge may therefore be defined as an annual sum of
money issuing and payable out of land, the due payment of which
is secured by a right of distress that is not the result of tenure
between the parties but is either expressly reserved or allowed
by statute.[4]

Definition of rent-charge.

Creation. There are three distinct transactions that may
lead to the creation of such a rent :—

first, the owner of an estate may grant the whole of his
estate to A., leaving no reversion in himself, but reserving
a rent to be paid to him out of the land ;

secondly, he may retain the whole of his estate, but grant a
rent to another payable out of the land ; and

thirdly, the owner of a reversion to which a rent-service is
attached may sever the rent from the reversion, either by
granting the reversion to a stranger and keeping the rent,
or by granting the rent to a stranger and keeping the
reversion.[5]

In each of these cases it will be seen that, since no tenure exists
between the debtor and creditor, the rent lacks the characteristic
of a rent-service.

---

[1] Cruise, Tit. xxviii. c. i. ss. 1, 7.
[2] Co. Litt., 144a.
[3] Law of Property Act, 1925, s. 121.; *supra*, p. 386.
[4] See Co. Litt., 143b, 147b.
[5] Leake, *Uses and Profits of Land*, 373, 385.

Rentcharge is real property.

Incidents. A rentcharge is an incorporeal interest that may be limited for all the estates recognized at common law.[1]

Thus it may be limited to a person in perpetuity for an estate in fee simple, in tail, for life, for years or in remainder, but under the Law of Property Act, 1925, the interest conferred on the rent owner is a legal interest only where it is limited to him in possession in perpetuity or for a term of years absolute.[2] Thus, an annual sum of money granted to a widow for life and charged upon the settled lands by a marriage settlement confers a mere equitable interest.

No rent-charge on a rentcharge at common law.

As the essence of a rentcharge lies in the power of the owner to distrain upon lands, it follows that, strictly speaking, it can issue only out of corporeal hereditaments. A dominant owner, for instance, cannot charge a right of way to which he is entitled, since there is nothing on which the rent owner can distrain, though of course the debtor will be liable in debt for the amount he has agreed to pay.[3] For the same reason at common law a rent cannot be reserved out of a rent,[4] and therefore if A., who is entitled to a rentcharge of £50, grants it to B., but reserves to himself thereout a rentcharge of £25, the reservation is void in the sense that the £25 does not constitute a rentcharge properly so called.

Rule altered by statute.

But this rule of the common law has in part been abrogated by the Law of Property Act, which enacts that a rentcharge or annual sum of money (not being a rent-service) may be reserved out of or charged on another rentcharge in the same manner as it could have been charged on land.[5] In such a case the ordinary remedies of distress and entry upon the lands are impossible, and therefore it is provided that where the rent is in arrears for twenty-one days, the owner of the second rent (£25) shall have power to appoint a receiver of the rent (£50) on which it is charged. The receiver is then entitled to acquire the £50 by action, distress or otherwise, and out of this to pay arrears, expenses and his own remuneration.

SECTION II. CREATION OF A RENTCHARGE.

A rentcharge may be created by instrument *inter vivos*, by will, or by statute.

Creation by deed of grant.

(1) **By Instrument** *inter vivos.* At common law a rentcharge, if created *inter vivos*, must be granted by deed.[6] But the

[1] Cruise, Tit. xxviii. c. ii. s. 1.

[2] A rentcharge, provided that it is not limited to take effect upon the determination of some other interest, is "in possession" notwithstanding that its payment is to commence at some time subsequently to its creation. Law of Property (Entailed Interests) Act, 1932, s. 2.

[3] Co. Litt., 47*a*.

[4] *Stafford* v. *Buckley* (1750), 2 Ves. Sen. 170, 177.

[5] Law of Property Act, 1925, s. 122.

[6] Co. Litt., 169*a* ; *Hewlins* v. *Shippam* (1826), 5 B. & C. 221, 229.

equitable principle underlying the doctrine of *Walsh v. Lonsdale* applies here just as it does in the case of an agreement to grant a term of years[1] or an easement, so that, where one person has agreed in a signed memorandum to grant a rentcharge to another, the grantee is entitled to institute a suit for specific performance in order to compel the grantor to execute a formal deed.[2]

The quantum of the interest in a rentcharge depends upon the words of limitation which are inserted in the deed of grant, and the rule is that such words are construed in exactly the same way as in a grant of corporeal hereditaments. Thus before January 1st, 1926, in order to pass a rent in perpetuity it was necessary to convey the rent to the grantee *and his heirs*, or to the grantee *in fee simple*, but the changes which have been effected by the Law of Property Act in regard to words of limitation sufficient to pass a fee simple estate in land[3] apply to rentcharges, and at the present day the effect of a grant which contains no technical words of limitation is to give the grantee a rent in perpetuity, or if that is impossible owing to the grantor only having a smaller estate, then to give him a rent for the whole interest—whatever that may be—possessed by the grantor. This rule is, however, displaced if a contrary intention is shown in the conveyance, and in such a case the size of the grantee's interest will depend upon the intention of the parties.[4]

Words of limitation.

Perhaps the most usual example of the grant of a rent in perpetuity occurs where a vendor on the sale of a fee simple, instead of receiving the purchase money in the form of a lump sum, reserves to himself a rent—generally known as a *fee farm rent* or a *chief rent*—which is payable to him and his heirs in perpetuity.[5] Several statutes have sanctioned this practice.[6] One drawback is that a positive covenant by the purchaser, such as to build and repair buildings, does not run with the land and bind his successors in title, though they remain liable for the rent.[7] Moreover, the benefit of a covenant to pay a rentcharge does not run with the rentcharge so as to entitle an assignee thereof to maintain an action *on the covenant* against the covenantor or his assignee.[8] Thus,

Fee farm rents.

A covenant to pay a rentcharge is only in gross.

where A. granted a fee simple to B. on the terms that A. his heirs and assigns should be entitled to a rent issuing out of the land, and the conveyance contained a covenant by B. to pay the rent to A. his heirs and assigns, it was held that X.,

---

[1] *Supra*, pp. 356 *et seq.*
[2] *Jackson v. Lever* (1792), 3 Bro. C.C. 605.
[3] *Supra*, p. 115. Law of Property Act, 1925, s. 60.
[4] Section 60 (1).
[5] *Supra*, pp. 112–3.
[6] *E.g.* Lands Clauses Consolidation Act, 1845, s. 10.
[7] *Haywood v. Brunswick Building Soc.* (1881), 8 Q. B. D. 403.
[8] *Grant v. Edmondson*, [1931] 1 Ch. 1. But see *infra*, p. 563, as to liability of the *terre tenant* in debt.

to whom A. had demised the rent for 1000 years, could not sue B. on the covenant.[1]

The technical nature of this rule was demonstrated by P. O. LAWRENCE, L.J. :—

" Whatever may be the foundation of the rule, and whether it rests " on the broader principle that (except as between lessor and lessee) " no covenant can run with an incorporeal hereditament, or whether " it rests on the narrower principle that a covenant to pay a rent- " charge is a collateral covenant or a covenant in gross which does " not touch and concern the rentcharge, or whether it rests on no " principle and is merely arbitrary, I am of opinion that it is too " firmly established to be disturbed by this court " [2]

Creation by will.

(2) **By Will.** Despite the general requirement of a deed a rentcharge may even at common law be validly created by will, and whether it is so or not depends upon the intention of the testator. If he directs that an annual sum shall be paid to a donee and uses words which show that the money is to be a charge upon the land and not upon his personal property, it is a rentcharge as distinct from an annuity, as for instance where he devises land to A.

" subject to and charged and chargeable with the payment of £100 a " year to B. for 25 years." [3]

Creation by statute.

(3) **By Statute.** There are two distinct series of enactments under which an owner of land may carry out certain improvements and arrange that the cost shall be charged upon the land and reimbursed in full, together with interest, by a definite number of annual payments. The chief statute of the first class is the Improvement of Land Act, 1864, which allows " landowners " (*i.e.* anyone except a lessee at a rack rent[4] who is in actual possession of the rents and profits) to borrow money for improvements from certain private land improvement companies.

Improvement of Land Act, 1864.

Money may not be borrowed in this way for every improvement, but only for those specified in the Settled Land Act, 1925.[5] No rentcharge can be imposed upon the land until the Ministry of Food, Agriculture and Fisheries has, on the application of the land owner, satisfied itself that the suggested improvement will permanently increase the yearly value of the land to an extent greater than the annual rentcharge which is contemplated.[6]

---

[1] *Milnes* v. *Branch* (1816), 5 M. & S. 411.
[2] *Grant* v. *Edmondson*, [1931] 1 Ch. 1, at p. 26.
[3] *Ramsay* v. *Thorngate* (1849), 16 Sim. 575.
[4] *I.e.* the full yearly value of the land.
[5] *Supra*, p. 135. The improvements specified in the 1864 Act are all covered by those set out in the Settled Land Act, and the latter are expressly brought within the operation of the earlier Act.
[6] There are certain improvements which may be allowed although they will not permanently increase the yearly value of the land, *i.e.* construction of waterworks for use of residents on the estate (40 & 41 Vict. c. 31, s. 5) ;

If satisfied on this point the Ministry issues a provisional Order which specifies the sum to be charged upon the land, the rate of interest and the number of years within which it must be paid off. The rate of interest is now left to the discretion of the Minister,[1] but the period for payments must not exceed forty years.[2] After the improvements are completed the Ministry issues an absolute Order imposing the annual sum as a rentcharge upon the fee simple, and this has priority over all existing and future incumbrances affecting the land with certain specified exceptions.[3] The remedies for its recovery are the same as in the case of other rentcharges,[4] except that the landowner is not personally liable.

The second class of statute is represented by the Settled Land Act, 1925, which allows a limited owner to raise money for the purpose of carrying out permanent improvements on the settled land. Prior to January 1st, 1926, there was an important difference between the operation of the Improvement of Land Acts and that of the Settled Land Acts in this matter, for, while under the former a tenant for life could raise new money for the purpose, all that the Settled Land Acts did was to authorize the expenditure upon improvements of capital money which happened to be in the hands of the trustees. A tenant for life could not raise new money by mortgage under the Settled Land Acts for carrying out improvements, but this power, as we have seen, has now been expressly conferred upon him by the Settled Land Act, 1925.[5]

(marginal note) Settled Land Act, 1925.

SECTION III. REMEDIES FOR THE RECOVERY OF A RENTCHARGE.

The following remedies are available to a rentcharge owner :

(1) **Distress.** A power to distrain upon the land out of which the rent issues is, as we have seen, an implicit incident of a rentcharge, though formerly it had to be specially reserved. Even when the Landlord and Tenant Act, 1730, had conferred the power of distraint on rent owners, it was the usual practice to insert an express provision to the same effect in all instruments creating rentcharges, but this has ceased to be the practice in the case of instruments coming into effect after December 31st, 1881. The Con-

(marginal note) Distress when 21 days' rent due.

---

erection of mansion house under Limited Owners Residence Acts, 1870, 1871 ; planting, Improvement of Land Act, 1864, s. 15 ; erection or improvement of farmhouse or cottage for use of workers on the land, Agricultural Credits Act, 1923, s. 3 (3).

[1] Agricultural Credits Act, 1923, s. 3 (1).
[2] Improvement of Land Act, 1899, s. 1 (1).
[3] Settled Land Act, 1925, s. 59.
[4] *Infra.*
[5] Settled Land Act, 1925, s. 71 (1) (ii) ; *supra,* p. 135.

veyancing Act of that year provides that where any rent (not incident to the relationship of landlord and tenant) is in arrears for 21 days, the person entitled to receive it may enter into and distrain upon the land charged or any part thereof, and dispose of any distrainable objects according to the general law.[1] This remedy is now re-enacted by the Law of Property Act, 1925.[2]

Entry when 40 days' rent due.

(2) **Entry upon the land charged.** The Law of Property Act, 1925, provides that, when a rentcharge is in arrears for 40 days, even though no legal demand has been made for payment, the owner may enter into possession of and hold the land charged or any part thereof and take the income thereof until all arrears and costs and expenses occasioned by the non-payment of the rent are satisfied.[3] The Act, it will be noticed, does not give the owner of the rent a power of entry that will cause a forfeiture of the debtor's interest in the land, as is usual between landlord and tenant, but such a power may be, and generally is, reserved in the instrument of creation.

As we have seen, neither type of power, whether to hold the land until payment or to determine the debtor's interest, is subject to the rule against perpetuities.[4]

Appointment of trustees when 40 days' rent due.

(3) **Lease to trustees.** When a rentcharge is in arrears for 40 days, the person entitled to payment, whether taking possession or not, may by deed lease the whole or part of the land to a trustee for a term of years, with or without impeachment of waste, on trust to raise and pay the rent together with all arrears, costs and expenses.[5] The trustee may adopt any *reasonable means*[6] to raise the money, as for instance by the mortgage, assignment or sub-lease of the term vested in him, or by appropriating the income of the land, but he cannot create a *legal* mortgage unless the rentcharge itself is held for a legal estate.

The above three remedies are not enforceable if a contrary intention is expressed in the instrument under which the annual sum arises,[7] and they are subject to the provisions of such instrument. Moreover, when a rentcharge is charged on another rentcharge, the above remedies are excluded and replaced by a right in the rent owner to appoint a receiver of the annual sum charged whenever payment is in arrears for 21 days.[8]

---

[1] *Supra*, p. 386.
[2] Section 121 (2).
[3] Section 121 (3).
[4] Law of Property Act, 1925, s. 121 (6), *supra*, p. 260 (right to enter for purpose of distraint or leasing); Perpetuities and Accumulations Act, 1964, s. 11 (1), *supra*, p. 276 (right to effect forfeiture).
[5] Law of Property Act, 1925, s. 121 (4).
[6] *Ibid.*
[7] *Ibid.*, s. 121 (5).
[8] *Ibid.*, s. 122, *supra*, p. 558.

(4) **Action of debt.** It is well settled that an action of debt *Action of* for the recovery of arrears lies against the *terre tenant* for the *debt.* time being of the whole or part only of the land charged,[1] provided that he holds a freehold as distinct from a leasehold interest.[2] It is no defence that the profits of the land do not equal in amount the value of the rentcharge.[3] Thus in one case:

> Lands were charged with the payment of a rentcharge of £80 a *Pertwee v.* year. A certain portion of these lands was acquired by the *Townsend,* defendant's predecessor in title, who released the rest of the *[1896] 2 Q.B.* land from the burden of the charge and imposed it upon the *129.* portion so acquired. At the time of the action for the recovery of £80, being one year's arrears, the defendant was able to show that the annual profits of the portion charged, of which he was tenant for life, amounted only to £7 5s., but nevertheless he was held personally liable for the whole £80.

COLLINS, J., said [4] :—

> " The defendant holds the land subject to a charge and he " cannot keep the land and refuse to pay the charge. If he does " refuse, the remedy against him is personal for the amount of " the charge itself."

Where land which is subject to a rentcharge is split up as the *Equitable* result of some conveyance, and the charge is either made payable *apportion-* out of one of the portions or apportioned between them, the *ment of rent-charges,* parties possess certain statutory rights whose object it is to give effect to any such arrangement that may have been made. This kind of apportionment is called equitable as distinct from legal apportionment, since it is made without the consent of the owner of the rent. The Law of Property Act, 1925,[5] provides that where in such a case the rentcharge, without the consent of the owner, is

(*a*) charged exclusively on the land conveyed in exoneration of the land retained, or

(*b*) charged exclusively on the land retained in exoneration of the land conveyed, or

(*c*) apportioned between the land conveyed and the land retained,

then the agreement, without prejudice to the rights of the rent owner, shall be binding between the grantor and the grantee under the conveyance and their respective successors in title. If the owner of part of the land fails to pay the rentcharge in accordance with the agreement or fails to perform some covenant, and the owner of the other part is in consequence obliged to pay the

---

[1] *Thomas* v. *Sylvester* (1873), L. R. 8 Q. B. 368. A *terre tenant* is the person who has the actual possession or occupation of land.
[2] *Re Herbage Rents*, [1896] 2 Ch. 811. Distress, however, may be levied on the premises.
[3] *Pertwee* v. *Townsend*, [1896] 2 Q. B. 129. [4] At p. 134. [5] S. 190.

charge or damages, the latter may distrain upon the land of the former and may also take the income thereof until he has been satisfied.[1]

SECTION IV. EXTINCTION OF A RENTCHARGE.

There are several ways in which a rentcharge may be extinguished and the land freed from liability.

Release of whole land.

(1) **Release.** If the rent owner releases the whole of the land charged from any further liability to pay, the rent is extinguished. Indeed, on the somewhat questionable ground that a rent, being entire and issuing out of every part of the land, cannot be thrown upon one particular part nor apportioned between several parts, the old rule was that a release of *part* of the land discharged the whole land and produced a total extinguishment of the rent.[2] But the Law of Property Act, 1925,[3] re-enacting the Law of Property Amendment Act, 1859, provides that the release from a rentcharge of part of the lands charged shall not extinguish the whole rentcharge, but shall only render it unenforceable against the part released. This provision, however, is not to prejudice the rights of the persons who are interested in the unreleased part of the lands unless they concur in or confirm the release. The effect of this enactment is that where the owner of land which is subject to a rentcharge sells the land in separate portions to different persons, and only one portion is released from the charge by the rent owner, the purchasers of the unreleased portions will be liable for the whole rent if they concur in the release, but will be liable only for an apportioned part if they do not concur.[4]

Release of part of land.

Merger at common law.

(2) **Merger.** A rentcharge may also be extinguished by merger.[5] The rigid rule of common law is that, whenever a lesser and a greater estate in the same lands become united in one person in his own right, the lesser estate is merged in the greater and extinguished without regard to the intention of the parties. As we shall see later, however, the equitable view that no merger occurs if it is contrary to the intention of the party in whom the two estates vest now obtains in all courts,[6] and it will suffice to say here that this principle applies to the merger of a rentcharge. Thus :

---

[1] S. 190 (2) ; *Whitham* v. *Bullock*, [1939] 2 K. B. 81 ; [1939] 2 All E. R. 310.
[2] Co. Litt., 147*b*.   [3] S. 70.
[4] *Booth* v. *Smith* (1884), 14 Q. B. D. 318.
[5] As to merger generally, see *Forbes* v. *Moffatt* (1811), Tudor, *Leading Cases in Real Property*, p. 244. *Infra*, pp. 831 *et seq.*
[6] *Infra*, pp. 831-3.

if the absolute owner of a rentcharge also becomes absolute owner in his own right of the land charged, either by grant or by devise, there is *primâ facie* a merger of the rent in the estate because there is no obvious advantage in keeping both the interests alive.[1]

But on the other hand :

if the person who is responsible for the rent mortgages the land charged to the rent owner, there is no merger, since the two interests do not unite in one person in the same right.

(3) Statute. Lastly, means have been devised by statute [2] whereby the owner of the land charged, or any person interested therein, may redeem a rentcharge by payment to the rent owner of a capital sum of money certified by the Minister of Agriculture, Fisheries and Food as being a fair equivalent for the rent. An estate owner who desires to free his land by this method must request the Minister to certify the amount payable, and when this has been done he is entitled, after serving a month's notice, to pay the amount to the rent owner provided that the latter is entitled to give a good discharge for the capital value of the rent.[3] But if the rent owner cannot be found or ascertained, or if he is unable or unwilling to prove his right to give a discharge, or if the redemption is held up owing to complications of title, the Minister may authorize the owner of the land charged to pay the redemption money into court. When the certified capital sum has been paid to the rent owner or into court, the Minister issues a certificate to the effect that the land is discharged from the rent.[4]

Redemption of rent-charge.

This statutory mode of redemption does not apply to a rent reserved on a lease or tenancy, but it does include a rent reserved on a sale of land, or made payable under a grant for building purposes, and a rent may be redeemed even though it is not perpetual.[5] If an estate owner desires to discharge part of his land from a rentcharge, the Minister may apportion the rent between the parts of the land indicated by the owner, and then any such apportioned part may be redeemed.[6]

---

[1] *Freeman* v. *Edwards* (1848), 2 Ex. 732.
[2] Law of Property Act, 1925, s. 191.
[3] *Ibid.*
[4] *Ibid.*   [5] *Ibid.*, s. 191 (1).
[6] *Ibid.*, s. 191 (7). These provisions for redemption follow, in the main, similar provisions contained in s. 45 of the Conveyancing Act, 1881.

CHAPTER V

MORTGAGES.

SUMMARY.

SECTION I. HISTORY OF THE METHODS WHEREBY MORTGAGES HAVE BEEN EFFECTED.

Definition and Terminology. A mortgage is a conveyance or other disposition of land designed to secure the payment of money or the discharge of some other obligation. The party who conveys the property by way of security is called the mortgagor, the lender or obligee who obtains an interest in the property is called the mortgagee, and the debt for which the security is created is termed the mortgage debt. The mortgagee, since he is the grantee of a proprietary interest acquires a real, not merely a personal, security that prevails against the general body of creditors in the event of the mortgagor's bankruptcy.

Terminology.

History of Mortgages.[1] If we are to understand the radical alterations that were made by the legislation of 1925 in the methods of creating mortgages, it is necessary to appreciate the principles and to master the details of the old law.

History.

The developed law of mortgages is the joint product of common law, equity and statute. In the earliest days of the common law a mortgage was a mere pledge, which took one of two forms. It might be agreed that the lender should enter into possession of the land, and should take the rents and profits in discharge of both the principal and the interest of the loan. This was called a *vivum vadium,* or living pledge, since it automatically and by its own force discharged the entire debt. But, on the other hand, the arrangement might be that the lender should take the rents and profits of the land in discharge of the interest only, in which case the transaction was called a *mortuum vadium,* a dead pledge, since it did not effect the gradual extinction of the debt.

Earliest position.

By the time of Littleton (1402-1481), however, a mortgage had become a species of estate upon condition created by a feoffment defeasible upon condition subsequent.

Position in time of Littleton.

The land was conveyed in fee simple to the mortgagee on condition that if the loan was repaid upon the day which had been fixed by agreement, the conveyance should be defeated, and the mortgagor be free to re-enter. If repayment was not made on the exact date fixed, then the estate of the mortgagee became absolute, and the mortgagor's interest in the land was extinguished. In the words of Littleton:

" If a feoffment be made upon such condition that if the feoffor pay
" to the feoffee at a certain day etc. 40 pounds of money, that then
" the feoffor may re-enter, etc., in this case the feoffee is called
" tenant in morgage, which is as much to say in French as mortgage,
" and in Latin *mortuum vadium.* And it seemeth that the cause why
" it is called mortgage is, for that it is doubtful whether the feoffor

---

[1] Holdsworth, *History of English Law,* vol. iii. p. 128 ; Plucknett, *A Concise History of the Common Law* (5th Edn.), pp. 603–9.

" will pay at the day limited such sum or not, and if he doth not pay,
" then the land which is put in pledge upon condition for the pay-
" ment of the money is taken from him for ever, and so dead to him
" upon condition etc. And if he doth pay the money then the pledge
" is dead as to the tenant." [1]

That a feoffor should be bound to repay the loan on the exact day fixed or be precluded for ever from redeeming his property was a hard rule,

" and what made the hardship on the debtor a glaring one was that
" the debt still remained unpaid and could be recovered from the
" feoffor notwithstanding that he had actually forfeited his land to
" the mortgagee." [2]

Alteration by equity.

But by the time of Charles I, equity had so fundamentally altered this strict legal view that the law of mortgages was transformed.[3] The form as indicated by Littleton remained, but equity interfered on the general principle that relief should be granted against forfeiture for breach of a penal condition.[3] No longer was redemption to depend upon a strict compliance with the contract. In the view of equity the essential object of a mortgage is to afford security to the lender, and as long as the security remains intact there is no justification for expropriating the property of the mortgagor merely because of his failure to make prompt payment. In the words of Lord NOTTINGHAM :—

" In natural justice and equity the principal right of the mortgagee
" is to the money, and his right to the land is only as a security for
" the money." [4]

Hence the rule ultimately established by courts of equity was that a mortgagor must be allowed to redeem his fee simple despite his failure to make repayment on the appointed day. Time was not to be of the essence of the transaction. This is still the rule, although a mortgage is no longer created by the conveyance of a fee simple estate. The position, then, is this :—

Equity of redemption.

Upon the date fixed for repayment, the mortgagor has a contractual right of redemption.

If this date passes without repayment, he obtains an equity of redemption, *i.e.* a right in equity to redeem his property.[5]

The equity of redemption is not personal to the mortgagor, but may be conveyed, devised or entailed, and it may descend on intestacy or pass as *bona vacantia* to the Crown.[6] It is destructible

---

[1] Litt. s. 332.
[2] *Kreglinger* v. *New Patagonia Meat and Cold Storage Co., Ltd.,* [1914] A. C. 25, at p. 35, *per* Lord HALDANE.
[3] Holdsworth, *History of English Law,* vol. v. p. 330.
[4] *Thornborough* v. *Baker* (1675), 3 Swans. 628, 630.
[5] *Kreglinger* v. *New Patagonia Meat and Cold Storage Co., Ltd.,* [1914] A. C. 25, 48, *per* Lord PARKER.
[6] *Casborne* v. *Scarfe* (1738), 1 Atk. 603 ; *Re Wells, Swinburne-Hanham* v. *Howard,* [1933] 1 Ch. 29 ; White and Tudor, *Leading Cases in Equity,* vol. ii. p. 24 ; Waldock, *op. cit.,* pp. 202 *et seq.*

only by four events, namely, its release by the mortgagor, the lapse of time under the Limitation Act,[1] the exercise by the mortgagee of his statutory power of sale,[2] and a foreclosure decree, *i.e.* a judicial decree that the subject-matter of the mortgage shall be vested absolutely in the mortgagee free from any right of redemption.[3]

Position immediately prior to 1926. Up to January 1st, 1926, the normal method by which a mortgage of the fee simple was created was for the mortgagor to convey the legal fee simple to the mortgagee together with a covenant to repay the loan in, say, six months' time, with a proviso, however, that if the loan were repaid at such date, the mortgagee would reconvey the legal estate. Outwardly it still seemed as if the mortgagee became absolute owner failing repayment within six months, but essentially, owing to the doctrine of the equity of redemption, the mortgagor was the true owner. Technically he was a mere equitable owner, but in the eyes of equity he was the real owner since he could reacquire his legal title by payment of principal and interest after giving six months' notice of his intention to repay.

A still older method of creating a mortgage, used between the thirteenth and fifteenth centuries and worthy of notice because of its revival by the 1925 legislation, was for the mortgagor to lease his land to the mortgagee for a short term of years. If the debt was not repaid at the end of the lease, the right of the mortgagor was extinguished, and the term was automatically enlarged into a fee simple which vested absolutely in the mortgagee.[4] This method, however, fell into desuetude, mainly because the law in its growing strictness could not countenance this facile mode of enlarging a term of years into a fee. An attempt to resuscitate it was made about the beginning of the nineteenth century, but owing to certain disadvantages, such as the doubt whether the mortgagee was entitled to possession of the title deeds, it failed, and the term of years was used only in family settlements where it was desired to secure money lent for the payment of portions.[5]

Mortgage of a term of years. If the security offered by the borrower was a leasehold interest, not the fee simple, there were two methods before 1926 by which the mortgage might be created. Usually the mortgagor subleased his term of years to the mortgagee for a period slightly shorter than the remainder of the term. This was the most desirable method, since the sublease did not involve privity of estate between the mortgagee and the superior landlord, and therefore the mortgagee was immune from liability on the

Marginal notes: Summary of old law. — Alternative form of mortgage under old law. — Mode of mortgaging leaseholds.

---

[1] *Infra,* p. 591.
[2] *Infra,* p. 600.
[3] *Infra,* p. 605
[4] Holdsworth, *History of English Law,* vol. iii. p. 129.
[5] See an article by J. M. Lightwood in *The Law Journal,* 1925, p. 46.

covenants contained in the original lease, unless indeed there were negative covenants enforceable under the doctrine of *Tulk* v. *Moxhay*.[1] The alternative method was for the mortgagee to take an assignment of the whole remainder of the term, but in this case he became liable to covenants and conditions under the doctrine of *Spencer's Case*.[2]

Equitable Mortgages. In addition to the conveyance of a legal estate, whether a fee simple or a term of years, by way of security, it has long been possible, of course, to create an equitable mortgage by the grant of an equitable interest. This is necessarily the method where the borrower himself is a mere equitable owner, but it may also be adopted by the owner of a legal estate. Thus, for instance, an agreement by him to create a legal mortgage entitles the lender in equity to enforce specific performance of the promise. Indeed, without the grant even of an equitable interest, an owner may charge his land with the repayment of a loan and so entitle the lender in equity to enforce a judicial sale of the property. These equitable mortgages are considered in more detail later.[3]

Equitable mortgages under old law.

Alterations made by the legislation of 1925. The prevailing practice, by which the legal fee simple was conveyed to a mortgagee, presented a difficult problem to the draftsmen of the 1925 legislation. How were they to bring it into line with the principles that they intended to introduce ?

The corner-stone of their policy was that the legal fee simple should always be vested in its true owner and that he should be able to convey it free from equitable interests. In the eyes of the law the true owner is the mortgagor. Yet, all that he held before 1926 was an equitable interest, and unless some alteration were made there could be no question of his ability to convey any kind of legal estate during the continuance of the mortgage.

On the other hand it was important to protect the mortgagee in the enjoyment of certain valuable advantages that he derived from his legal ownership. Pre-eminent among these was the priority which, by virtue of the legal fee simple, he obtained over other mortgages created in the same land, for these were necessarily equitable in nature. Moreover, his possession of the title deeds enabled him to control the actions of the mortgagor in his dealings with the land. He also enjoyed the right to take actual possession of the land, and therefore to grant leases ; and lastly, when he exercised his power of sale on failure by the mortgagor to repay the loan, he was able to vest the legal estate in the purchaser.[4]

---

[1] *Supra*, pp. 537 *et seq.*
[2] *Supra*, pp. 404 *et seq.*
[3] *Infra*, p. 580–3; 611–4.
[4] See an article by J. M. Lightwood, *The Law Journal*, 1925, p. 91.

The solution contained in the Law of Property Act, 1925, is to revert to the old fifteenth-century method of effecting mortgages by means of a lease for a term of years.

Mortgages by which the legal fee simple is vested in the mortgagee are prohibited, and a mortgagee who requires a legal estate instead of a mere equitable interest is compelled to take either a long term of years or a newly invented interest called a *charge by way of legal mortgage.* Thus in the first case both parties have legal estates :

> the mortgagee has a legal term of years absolute, and
> the mortgagor has a reversionary and legal fee simple, subject
>   to the mortgagee's term ;

while in the case of a charge by way of legal mortgage the mortgagee has the same protection and remedies as if he had taken a legal term of years.

In this way the principle that the legal fee simple should always remain vested in the true owner has been maintained. Nevertheless, it is doubtful whether this is more than lip-service to the principle, for it can scarcely be said that the mortgagor's ownership of his estate is fully effective. Thus we shall see that he is not allowed to retain the title deeds, and that if he defaults in his obligations the power to sell and convey the fee simple resides in the mortgagee.

Law of mortgages now re-cast.

SECTION II. METHODS OF CREATING MORT-GAGES UNDER THE MODERN LAW.

SUMMARY.

(1) LEGAL MORTGAGES.

(A) BY LEASE.

A *legal* mortgage of an estate *in fee simple* must be effected by either—

1. a demise for a term of years absolute, subject to a provision (called a provision for cesser) that the term shall cease if repayment is made on a fixed day ;
2. a legal charge *by deed.*[1]

Legal mortgages to be effected by lease or legal charge.

---

[1] Law of Property Act, 1925, s.85 (1).

Length of
lease.

To confine our attention for the moment to the former method, the Act does not state for what period the lease must be made, but it enacts that if any person in future attempts to create a mortgage by the old method of a transfer of the fee simple, the conveyance shall operate as a lease of the land for 3000 years, without impeachment for waste, but subject to cesser on redemption.[1]   There is, of course, no obligation for a mortgage term to be granted for so long a period as this.

Subsequent
mortgages.

If it is desired to create further *legal* mortgages in the same land, the mortgagor may lease the land to each mortgagee after the first for a term which is usually at least one day longer than the term limited to the immediately preceding mortgagee.[2]   If, for instance, the mortgagor raises money first from A., then from B. and then from C. on the security of Blackacre, there may be

a lease to A. for 3000 years,

a lease to B. for 3000 years and one day (subject to A.'s term), and

a lease to C. for 3000 years and two days (subject to the terms of A. and B.).

Subsequent
mortgages
now legal.

The effect in such a case is that the second and all subsequent mortgagees now take legal interests in the land instead of mere equitable interests as formerly.   This is a radical change in the law. Before 1926, if the legal fee simple were vested in the first mortgagee, all subsequent mortgages were necessarily equitable, for there can be only one legal fee simple in the same land.   But under the new system as illustrated above, since a term of years absolute may be subject to another legal estate, the lease to B. for 3000 years and one day is a legal estate notwithstanding that it cannot take effect in possession until after the determination of the preceding term.

At first sight the possession by B. of a term of 3000 years and one day, subject to a prior term of 3000 years, does not seem of much value, but when the first term ceases on redemption, B. acquires the first right to the land for the residue of the term; and moreover he always has the right, after giving adequate notice, to pay to A. what A. lent to the mortgagor, and thus to succeed to A.'s position.   In such a case B. remains entitled to hold the land under the lease until the advances made both by A. and by himself have been paid.

The following is a precedent of a modern mortgage deed [3] :—

THIS MORTGAGE is made the first day of
January 1967 between A. B. of etc. (herein-

---

[1] Law of Property Act, 1925, s. 85 (2).
[2] *Ibid.*, s. 85 (2) (b).
[3] Adapted from Form No. 86, *Encyclopædia of Forms and Precedents* (3rd Edn.), vol. x. p. 150.

Parties. after called the borrower) of the one part and X. Y. of etc. (hereinafter called the lender) of the other part.

Recital of title of borrower. Whereas the borrower is seised in fee simple free from incumbrances of the property described in the Schedule hereto.

Recital of agreement to lend. And whereas the lender has agreed to lend to the borrower the sum of £2000 upon having the repayment thereof together with interest thereon secured in manner hereinafer appearing.

NOW THIS DEED WITNESSETH as follows:

Covenant for payment of principal and interest. 1. In consideration of the sum of £2000 now paid by the lender to the borrower (the receipt of which sum the borrower hereby acknowledges) the borrower hereby covenants with the lender that he will pay to the lender on the first day of July next the sum of £2000 with interest thereon from the date hereof at the rate of £5 per cent. per annum and if the said sum or any part thereof shall not be paid on the said date will pay to the lender (as well after as before any judgment) interest on so much of the said sum as shall for the time being be unpaid at the rate aforesaid by equal half yearly payments on the first of July and first of January in each year.

Demise of mortgaged property. 2. For the consideration aforesaid the borrower as beneficial owner hereby demises to the lender ALL the property specified in the schedule hereto TO HOLD the same unto the lender for the term of 3000 years from the date hereof without impeachment of waste subject to the provision of cesser hereinafter contained.

Proviso for cesser. 3. Provided that if the borrower shall on the first day of July next pay to the lender the said sum of £2000 with interest thereon from the date hereof at the rate of £5 per cent. per annum the term hereby created shall cease.

Covenants by borrower. 4. The borrower hereby further covenants with the lender
[Here follow covenants by the borrower to insure and repair buildings etc.]

IN WITNESS ETC.

THE SCHEDULE ABOVE REFERRED TO.

Position of
the parties
to a legal
mortgage
of the fee
simple.

The obvious effect of such a deed is that the mortgagor remains seised in fee simple, while the mortgagee acquires a legal term of years that entitles him, if he so desires, to take possession of the land.   Outwardly, indeed, he appears to acquire a term that will necessarily last for 3000 years unless the capital sum is paid on July 1st, 1967.   Such, of course, is not the true position, for the equity of redemption that arises after that date entitles the mortgagor to procure the cessation of the term by the repayment in full of all that is due by way of capital and interest.

Where the mortgagor has a term of years only.   The next question to examine is how a mortgage is made when the mortgagor holds, not the fee simple, but a term of years.   Again, the only possible methods of creating a legal mortgage are by a lease (in this case a sub-lease) for a term of years absolute, or by a legal charge.[1]

Confining ourselves for the moment to a sub-lease, let us suppose that

A., the owner in fee simple, has leased his land to T. for 99 years, and T. wishes to mortgage his tenancy, which has still 70 years to run, to L^1 as security for an advance.   The Act provides that T. may sublet the premises to L^1 for a period which must be less by at least one day than the term he himself holds.[2]   He will therefore grant a sub-lease for, say, 69 years and 355 days, subject to a proviso that the title of L^1 shall cease on the repayment of the loan by T.

If T. later wishes to borrow more money from L^2 on the same premises, he must grant him another sub-lease for a period longer by one day than that of L^1; in fact, however many later mortgagees there may be, they will each take a term one day longer than the immediately preceding term.[3]

The case, then, works out as follows :

A. is entitled to the reversion in fee simple ;

L^1 is sub-tenant for 69 years and 355 days;

L^2, subject to the tenancy of L^1, is sub-tenant for 69 years and 356 days ;

T. (the mortgagor), subject to the two sub-tenancies, is tenant for 70 years.

If L^1 chooses to take possession, he can do so, and can remain in possession until paid off either by T. (the mortgagor) or by L^2.   If L^1 is paid off by T., then L^2 possesses the same rights until he is paid off by T.   If L^1 is paid off by L^2 the latter can take possession and hold it until the advances made both by L^1 and by himself have been paid.

---

[1] Law of Property Act, 1925, s. 86 (1).
[2] *Ibid.*   [3] *Ibid.*, s. 86 (2).

If L[1] sells, as he has a statutory right to do,[1] his conveyance to the purchaser will pass not only his mortgage term of 69 years and 355 days, but also the whole term of 70 years held by the mortgagor, and it will thus extinguish the mortgage terms held by L[2] and any later lender.[2]

Thus, the interest of a subsequent mortgagee, although it amounts to a legal estate, is a somewhat precarious security, since it will be destroyed if a prior mortgagee exercises his statutory power of sale or obtains a foreclosure decree.[3] The only remedy then left is to sue the mortgagor upon the personal covenant.

The alternative method under the old law of creating a mortgage by an assignment of the entire residue of the term to the mortgagee is prohibited, and any purported assignment intended to be by way of mortgage necessarily operates as a sub-lease for a term of years absolute, subject to cesser on redemption.[4]

Abolition of mortgage by assignment of term.

Sub-Mortgages. A mortgage term, whether created by lease or sub-lease, is available as a security to the mortgagee if he himself wishes to raise a loan.

Meaning of sub-mortgage.

For example, the mortgagee, B., has lent £10,000 to A. and has taken a lease of A's fee simple as security. If he now requires £1,000 for his immediate use, it may be inconvenient to enforce his rights against A. and to demand repayment in full of £10,000, for perhaps at the moment there is no suitable investment for £9000. Again, the danger of calling upon A. for £1000 is that he, not having the funds, may be compelled to borrow £10,000 from a third party, X., and to transfer the mortgage to the latter.[5] B., however, may sub-mortgage his own security to C. in return for a loan of £1000. This is effected by an assignment to C. of the mortgage debt (*i.e.* the right to receive £10,000) and by the grant to him of a sub-lease for a period shorter than his own mortgage term, but subject to a right of redemption in B. on payment of £1000.[6] Since a mortgage debt is a chose in action, C. should protect himself by giving written notice to A. of its assignment.[7]

The effect of this transaction is to put C. in the position of B.[8]

Thus, the statutory power of sale is not exercisable by B.

---

[1] *Infra*, p. 600
[2] Law of Property Act, 1925, s. 89 (1), *infra*, p. 601.
[3] *Ibid.*, s. 89 (2).
[4] *Ibid.*, s. 86 (2); *Grangeside Properties, Ltd.* v. *Collingwood's Securities, Ltd.*, [1964] 1 All E. R. 143; [1964] 1. W. L. R. 139.
[5] See Elphinstone, *Introduction to Conveyancing*, p. 290.
[6] Law of Property Act, 1925, s. 86 (3) ; 1st Sched., Part VII, para. 4.
[7] *Ibid.*, s. 136 ; *infra*, pp. 622–5   [8] *Ibid.*, s. 88 (5).

during the existence of the sub-mortgage,[1] and, therefore, if A. defaults in the repayment of the £10,000, C. may sell the land by virtue of the original mortgage and transfer a title to the purchaser free from the mortgage and sub-mortgage. Out of the purchase money, he will retain £1000, pay £9000 to B. and give any surplus to A.

Alternatively, if B. defaults in the repayment of £1000, C. may exercise the statutory power of sale incidental to the sub-mortgage. In this case he transfers to the purchaser the mortgage debt together with the original mortgage term, but of course leaves A.'s equity of redemption intact. After retaining £1000, he will pay any surplus to B.

The following is a precedent of a sub-mortgage [2] :—

Parties.	THIS SUB-MORTGAGE is made the first day of July 1967 between A. B. of etc. (hereinafter called the borrower) of the one part and X. Y. of etc. (hereinafter called the lender) of the other part.
Recital of mortgage.	Whereas by a mortgage (hereinafter called the mortgage) dated the first of January 1967 and made between M. N. of the one part and the borrower of the other part the freehold property described in the schedule hereto was demised to the borrower for the term of 3000 years from the date thereof without impeachment of waste by way of mortgage to secure the repayment to the borrower of the principal sum of £10,000 with interest thereon at the rate of £5 per cent. per annum.
Recital of state of debt.	AND WHEREAS the said sum of £10,000 is still owing on the security of the said mortgage together with the current interest thereon.
Recital of agreement for loan.	AND WHEREAS the lender has agreed to advance to the borrower the sum of £1000 upon having the repayment thereof with interest secured in manner hereinafter appearing.
	NOW THIS DEED WITNESSETH as follows:—
	1. In consideration of the sum of £1000 now paid by the lender to the borrower (the receipt whereof the borrower hereby acknowledges) the borrower hereby covenants with the lender that the borrower

---

[1] Said to be doubtful in *Cruse* v. *Nowell* (1856), 25 L. J. Ch. 709.
[2] See *Encyclopædia of Forms and Precedents* (3rd Edn.), No. 329, vol. x., p. 714.

Covenant for payment of principal and interest.

will on the first day of January next pay to the lender the said sum of £1000 with interest thereon from the date hereof at the rate of £5 per cent. per annum and if the said sum shall not be paid on that day then so long as any part thereof shall remain owing will pay to the lender interest at the rate aforesaid on the principal money for the time being so remaining owing by equal half-yearly payments on the first of July and the first of January in each year.

Transfer of mortgage debt.

2. For the consideration aforesaid the borrower as beneficial owner hereby assigns unto the lender ALL THAT the principal sum of £10,000 owing on the security of the said mortgage and all interest now due or to become due thereon and the benefit of all securities for the same (including the powers expressly or impliedly conferred by the said mortgage) TO HOLD unto the lender absolutely subject to the proviso for redemption hereinafter contained.

Sub-demise.

3. For the consideration aforesaid the borrower as beneficial owner hereby demises unto the lender ALL the property comprised in the said mortgage TO HOLD unto the lender for the residue of the said term of 3000 years less the last day thereof without impeachment of waste subject to the proviso for cesser hereinafter contained.

Redemption and cesser.

4. Provided that if the borrower shall on the first day of January next pay to the lender the principal sum of £1000 with interest thereon from the date hereof at the rate of £5 per cent. per annum the lender will at any time thereafter at the request and cost of the borrower reassign the mortgage debt hereby assigned and the sub-term hereby created in the mortgaged premises shall cease.

(B) BY A LEGAL CHARGE.

The Law of Property Act provides that a legal mortgage may also be created by

" a charge by deed expressed to be by way of legal mortgage." [1]

Charges have been utilized for a long time as a means of

---

[1] Law of Property Act, 1925, s. 85.

affording security to lenders, but hitherto they have for the most part been less efficacious than legal mortgages. If, for instance, a borrower agrees in writing that his land shall stand charged with the payment of £500, the lender, or chargee, obtains a mere equitable interest which does not entitle him either to recover possession or to grant leases, and which before 1926 also exposed him to the risk of being postponed to a later lender who acquired a legal mortgage in the land.

But, presumably in the pursuit of simplicity, the legislature in 1925 invented a new species of charge which operates to pass a legal interest to the chargee, though it does not convey to him a legal term of years. A short precedent of such a charge, which in practice is expanded so as to contain further appropriate covenants by the borrower,[1] is furnished by the Law of Property Act, 1925.[2]

Form of charge.

THIS LEGAL CHARGE is made the First day of January, 1967, between A. of the one part and B. of the other part.

WHEREAS A. is seised of the hereditaments hereby charged and described in the schedule hereto for an estate in fee simple in possession free from incumbrances ;

NOW IN CONSIDERATION of the sum of £1000 now paid by B. to A. (the receipt whereof A. doth hereby acknowledge) this Deed witnesseth as follows :

    i. A. hereby covenants with B. to pay on the first day of July next the sum of £1000 with interest thereon at the rate of £5 per cent. per annum.

    ii. A. as beneficial owner hereby charges by way of legal mortgage All and Singular the property mentioned in the Schedule hereto with the payment to B. of the principal money, interest and other money hereby covenanted to be paid by A.

Effect of charge.

The Act does not vest a term of years in the mortgagee,[3] but it provides that he shall have "the same privileges, powers and remedies" as if he had taken a lease of a fee simple or a sub-lease of demised premises.[4] In other words, he is in exactly the same position as if the relationship of landlord and tenant existed between him and the mortgagor.[5]

If, for instance, A. has charged his term of years in favour of B. and later commits a breach of a covenant contained in the lease by reason of which his landlord starts proceedings

---

[1] For fuller precedents, see Burnett, *Elements of Conveyancing* (6th Edn.), p. 415 ; *Encyclopædia of Forms and Precedents* (3rd Edn.), vol. x. Forms Nos. 87, 88, 167, pp. 155, 159, 346.

[2] 5th Schedule, Form No. 1.

[3] *Weg Motors, Ltd.* v. *Hales*, [1962] Ch. 49; [1961] 3 All E. R. 181; *Cumberland Court (Brighton), Ltd.* v. *Taylor*, [1964] Ch. 29; [1963] 2 All E. R. 536.

[4] Law of Property Act, 1925, s. 87 (1).

[5] *Regent Oil Co., Ltd.* v. *J. A. Gregory (Hatch End), Ltd.*, [1966] Ch. 402, at p. 431; [1965] 3 All E. R. 673, at p. 681.

for the enforcement of his right of re-entry under a forfeiture clause, B. is entitled to claim relief under section 146 of the Law of Property Act, 1925.[1]

This method of creating a mortgage has steadily gained popularity since its introduction, and at the present day is adopted by most, though not all,[2] practitioners in preference to the long lease. Its defect is that it does not contain the proviso for cesser that always figures in the mortgage by demise. This proviso corresponds to the old proviso for redemption, the importance of which lay in fixing the date at which the mortgagor's right to redeem and the mortgagee's right to foreclose came into being. In the mortgage given above on page 572, for instance, the property can neither be redeemed by the mortgagor nor foreclosed by the mortgagee before July 1st, 1967,[3] and although the right of a legal *chargee* to foreclose probably arises by implication at the date fixed in the covenant for repayment, provided that the mortgagor makes default, yet the matter cannot be regarded as settled until it has been judicially decided. It is safer, therefore, to amplify the statutory form by the insertion of a proviso for redemption or discharge in addition to the covenant for repayment.

There are, however, two advantages that may justly be claimed for the charge as compared with the demise.

First, the charge is as appropriate for leaseholds as it is for freeholds, and therefore it provides a simple method of executing a compound mortgage which relates to both these different interests.

Secondly, a mortgagor with a leasehold interest who holds his term on condition that he will not sub-lease without the consent of his landlord, must clearly obtain this consent if his mortgage takes the form of a sub-demise,[4] but a charge, since it does not create an actual legal estate, is presumably not a breach of a covenant against underletting.[5]

If the legal chargee desires to create a sub-mortgage, he cannot do so by means of a sub-lease, since he himself holds no term of years. He must, therefore, assign the mortgage debt to the submortgagee subject to a right of redemption.

Sub-mortgage.

---

[1] *Grand Junction Co., Ltd.* v. *Bates*, [1954] 2 Q. B. 160; [1954] 2 All E. R. 358; *Church Commissioners for England* v. *Ve-Ri-Best Manufacturing Co. Ltd.*, [1957] 1 Q. B. 238; [1956] 3 All E. R. 777. See also p. 399, *supra*.

[2] See the remarks in *Prideaux's Forms and Precedents in Conveyancing* (24th Edn.) Vol. 2, pp. 337, 8, and compare them with *ibid.*, 25th Edn., Vol. 2, p. 342.

[3] *Williams* v. *Morgan*, [1906] 1 Ch. 804; *Kreglinger* v. *New Patagonia Meat and Cold Storage Co., Ltd.*, [1914] A. C. 25, 48.

[4] *Matthews* v. *Smallwood*, [1910] 1 Ch. 777.

[5] *Grand Junction Co., Ltd.* v. *Bates*, [1954] 2 Q. B. 160, at p. 168; [1954] 2 All E. R. 385, at p. 388, *per* UPJOHN, J.

Mortgages to tenants in common.

Mortgages to several persons. If land is mortgaged to two or more persons the mortgage term vests in the mortgagees, or the first four of them, as joint tenants, and, failing a contrary intention expressed in the deed, they hold it in the same way as if the money belonged to them on a joint account.[1] This, as we have seen,[2] enables the surviving mortgagees to give a good discharge for the money, but the conversion into a joint tenancy is not allowed to prejudice the beneficial interests of the mortgagees in the principal and interest. Thus they are entitled to dispose of their shares in the money, and to hold the trustees liable to account for the income.[3]

(2) EQUITABLE MORTGAGES.

Equitable mortgages still permissible.

The statutory provisions that have been noticed so far apply only to a case in which it is desired to create a legal mortgage, and do not affect equitable mortgages and charges.[4] It always has been, and still is, possible to confer upon a lender a mere equitable right over the land by way of security, instead of passing a legal estate to him.

The commonest examples of equitable mortgages prior to the Act were those which followed a legal mortgage in the same land, but, as we have seen, second and subsequent mortgages may now be created by a long lease or by a charge so as to give each lender a legal estate or interest. The following forms of equitable mortgages, however, still remain:—

(A) AGREEMENT TO CREATE A LEGAL MORTGAGE.

Effect of agreement to give a mortgage.

Equity regards that as done which ought to be done, and therefore if A. agrees that, in consideration of money advanced, he will execute a legal mortgage in favour of B., an equitable mortgage is created in favour of B., and he can enforce the execution of a legal mortgage by suing in equity for specific performance.[5] But such an agreement does not have this effect unless the money has been actually advanced, for a contract to make a loan, whether under seal or not, can never be specifically enforced by either party.[6] The only remedy is the recovery of damages. As a mortgage of land is an interest in land within the meaning of section 40 of the Law of Property Act, 1925, the agreement is not specifically enforceable unless it is evidenced by a sufficient memorandum or supported by an act of part performance.[7]

---

[1] Law of Property Act, 1925, s. 34 (2), proviso.   [2] *Supra,* p. 301.
[3] Law of Property Act, 1925, s. 102.   [4] *Ibid.,* s. 117 (1).
[5] *Tebb* v. *Hodge* (1869), L. R. 5 C. P. 73.
[6] *Sichel* v. *Mosenthal* (1862), 30 Beav. 371.
[7] *Ex parte Leathes* (1833), 3 Deac. & C. 112. As to what constitutes an act of performance, see *supra,* pp. 349 *et seq.*

The result of a successful suit is that B. obtains a legal term for 3000 years, and can then pursue all the statutory remedies open to a legal mortgagee.[1]

(B) Deposit of Title Deeds.

Although a mortgage is an interest in land, and therefore not enforceable in the absence of a written memorandum or an act of part performance, it has been held, since the case of *Russel* v. *Russel*[2] in 1783, that an equitable mortgage is created by the delivery to the lender of the title deeds relating to the borrower's land, provided that it is intended to treat the land as security.

In this particular case there need be no memorandum, since the deposit ranks as an act of part performance,[3] and the deposit alone is treated as constituting an agreement to execute a legal mortgage.[4] An actual deposit, though essential, is not in itself sufficient. The depositee must go further, and prove by parol or by written evidence that the deposit was intended to be by way of security,[5] for the mere deposit by a customer of his deeds with a bank will not, for instance, constitute the bank an equitable mortgagee in respect of an overdraft.

In practice, however, the borrower usually signs a memorandum under seal contemporaneously with the delivery of the deeds, for a memorandum under seal makes the transaction a mortgage by deed within the meaning of the Law of Property Act, 1925, and entitles the equitable mortgagee to exercise all the powers, including the power of sale, given by the Act.[6] But since an equitable mortgagee cannot convey the legal estate to a purchaser, it is usual to insert a power of attorney or a declaration of trust, or both, in the memorandum, so as to enable the mortgagee to deal with the legal estate.[7]

Effect of deposit of deeds.

(C) Mortgage of an Equitable Interest.

A mortgage of an equitable interest, such as an entailed or a life interest arising under a settlement, or an agreement for a lease,[8] is itself necessarily equitable. The method of creation corresponds to that employed before 1926 in the case of a legal mortgage of the fee simple, namely, the entire equitable interest is assigned to the mortgagee, subject to a proviso for redemption.[9]

---

[1] *Infra*, pp. 599 *et seq.*   [2] (1783), 1 Bro. C. C. 269.
[3] *Bank of N.S.W.* v. *O'Connor* (1889), 14 App. Cas. 273, 282.
[4] *Carter* v. *Wake* (1877), 4 Ch. D. 605, 606 ; Jessel, M.R.
[5] *Dixon* v. *Muckleston* (1872), L. R. 8 Ch. 155.
[6] *Infra*, pp. 599 *et seq.*
[7] *Encyclopædia of Forms and Precedents* (3rd Edn.), vol. x, p. 504.
[8] *Rust* v. *Goodale*, [1957] Ch. 33 ; [1956] 3 All E. R. 373.
[9] Waldock, *The Law of Mortgages* (2nd Edn.), p. 137.

The assignment, if not made by will, must be in writing signed by the mortgagor or by his agent thereunto lawfully authorized,[1] and the mortgagee should protect himself by giving written notice of it to the owner of the legal estate.[2]

(D) EQUITABLE CHARGES.

Description of a charge.

Another form of equitable security, differing in respect of the remedies it confers from the three forms already described, is the equitable charge. This arises where, without any transfer of, or agreement to transfer, ownership or possession, property is appropriated to the discharge of a debt or some other burden.[3]

In one case[4] KINDERSLEY, V.-C., said :—

" With regard to what are called equitable mortgages, my notion
" is this. Suppose a man signed a written contract, by which he
" simply agreed that he thereby charged his real estate with £500 to
" A., what would be the effect of it ?
   " It would be no agreement to give a legal mortgage, but a security
" by which he equitably charged his land with payment of a sum of
" money, and the mode of enforcing it would be by coming into a
" court of equity to have the money raised by sale or mortgage ;
" that would be the effect of such a simple charge. It is the same
" thing as if a testator devised an estate to A. charged with the pay-
" ment of a sum of money to B. B.'s right is not to foreclose A., but
" to have his charge raised by sale or mortgage of the lands. . . .
" But the thing would be distinctly an equitable charge, and not a
" mortgage nor an agreement to give one. On the other hand the
" party might agree that, having borrowed a sum of money, he
" would give a legal mortgage whenever called upon. That agree-
" ment might be enforced according to its terms, and the court
" would decree a legal mortgage to be given, and would also foreclose
" the mortgage unless the money was paid."

The remedies of an equitable chargee will be considered later.[5]

Summary of forms of mortgages

If we now glance back at the different kinds of mortgages, we shall find that they may be either legal or equitable, and that the same land may be subjected both to several legal and to several equitable mortgages. For instance the tenant in fee simple of Blackacre may have created the following mortgages upon his land in the subjoined order :

A lease of 500 years to A.
A lease of 500 years and one day to B.
A written agreement charging the land in favour of C.
A lease of 500 years and two days to D.

The first mortgagee, A., may demand the title deeds relating to the property, and, as we shall see later, failure to enforce this right may entail serious consequences.[6] If A. does obtain the deeds,

---

[1] Law of Property Act, 1925, s. 53 (1) (c).
[2] *Ibid.*, s. 137 (1).
[3] *London County and Westminster Bank* v. *Tompkins*, [1918] 1 K. B. 515, 528.
[4] *Matthews* v. *Goodday* (1861), 31 L. J. Ch. 282, at pp. 282–3.
[5] *Infra*, p. 613.   [6] *Infra*, pp. 615 *et seq.*

then B. and D. are called *puisne mortgagees,* since they have acquired legal estates, but have not obtained possession of the deeds.[1] On the other hand, C. is called a *general equitable chargee.* A general equitable charge is statutorily defined as any equitable charge (with a few exceptions)

"which is not secured by a deposit of documents relating to the "legal estate affected and does not arise or affect an interest arising "under a trust for sale or a settlement."[2]

These terms become of importance when we consider the question of the priorities of mortgages.[3]

SECTION III. POSITION AND RIGHTS OF THE MORTGAGOR.

SUMMARY.

(1) THE EQUITY OF REDEMPTION.

(A) ITS NATURE.

Introductory Note. The equity of redemption that has already been described[4] is the fundamental characteristic of a mortgage. It arises in the case of every conveyance or other transaction relating to property, whether styled a mortgage or not, in which the true intention of the parties is that the subject-matter shall be security for a debt or other obligation. Outwardly a transaction may wear the appearance of an absolute conveyance, it may even be deliberately couched in language calculated to give that appearance, yet evidence is admissible to disclose the true intention of the parties.[5] A transaction, for instance, which takes the form of a sale by A. to B., with a right in B. of re-purchase upon payment of a given sum on a day certain may or may not be a mortgage. It is a matter of intention.

Test that determines redeemability.

---

[1] Land Charges Act, 1925, s. 10 (1), Class C (i).
[2] *Ibid.*, s. 10 (1), Class C (iii). [3] *Infra,* pp. 614 *et seq.*
[4] *Supra,* pp. 568–9.
[5] "No mortgage by any artificial words can be altered, unless by subsequent agreement," *Jason* v. *Eyres* (1681), 2 Cas. in Ch. 33, cited Ashburner, *Principles of Equity* (2nd Edn.), p. 204.

" The question always is—was the original transaction a *bona fide*
" sale with a contract for repurchase, or was it a mortgage, under
" the form of a sale." [1]

If it was the former, there is no right in B. to redeem the
property after the contract date.

Right of redemption must not be fettered. What particularly concerns us here, however, is to notice that
equity, in order to ensure that a transaction intended to be by way
of mortgage shall afford nothing more than security to the lender,
has laid down two important rules concerning, first, the inviolability
of the right of redemption; and secondly, the limits within which
collateral advantages may be reserved to a mortgagee.

Let us consider these rules separately.

Any clog on equity of redemption is void. (i) **The right of redemption is inviolable.** Since the
object of a mortgage is merely to secure the mortgagee, any pro-
vision which directly or indirectly prevents the recovery by the
mortgagor of his property upon performance of the obligation for
which the security was created, is repugnant to the very nature
of the transaction and therefore void, for when performance is
completed there is no longer any need or justification for the
retention of the security.

" Now," said ROMER, J., " there is a principle which I will
" accept without any qualification, . . that on a mortgage you
" cannot by contract between the mortgagor and mortgagee clog,
" as it is termed, the equity of redemption so as to prevent the
" mortgagor from redeeming on payment of principal, interest and
" costs." [2]

Once a mortgage always a mortgage. This principle is generally expressed in the aphorism, *once a
mortgage always a mortgage,* [3] and the most obvious example of
its infringement is a provision which leaves the mortgagor with
nothing more than an illusory right of redemption. In *Fairclough
v. Swan Brewery Co., Ltd.,* [4] for instance :

A mortgage of a term of twenty years contained a clause postponing
the contractual right of redemption for nineteen years and forty-six
weeks.

This provision for redemption rendered the property substantially irredeemable, and it was held that the mortgagor was
entitled to redeem at an earlier date. [5]

---

[1] *Williams v. Owen* (1840), 5 My. & Cr. 303, 306, *per* Lord COTTENHAM.
[2] *Biggs v. Hoddinott,* [1898] 2 Ch. 307.
[3] *Samuel v. Jarrah Timber Corporation,* [1904] A. C. 323, 329.
[4] [1912] A. C. 565.
[5] This decision of the P.C., is in conflict with the decision of the Court of
Appeal in *Santley v. Wilde,* [1899] 2 Ch. 474. A term of years in a theatre was
mortgaged by the tenant and the deed provided that the mortgagee should
receive *during the whole of the remainder of the term* a third of the net profits
derived from sub-leases made by the mortgagor. This provision was held to
be binding upon the mortgagor, even though he was ready and willing to pay
principal, interest and costs in full. Yet, in effect, it made the mortgage
irredeemable. It meant that the mortgagor, despite payment of principal, in-

Further, the courts refuse to countenance any provision which unduly restricts, though it does not altogether prevent, the right of redemption. Each of the following cases exemplifies an agreement that was held void as being inconsistent with or repugnant to the true nature of a mortgage transaction.

An agreement that redemption should be available to the mortgagor and *the heirs of his body,* and not to anyone else.[1]

An agreement which renders part of the mortgaged property absolutely irredeemable.[2]

A covenant by the mortgagor that the mortgagee, if he so desired, should be entitled to a conveyance of so much of the mortgaged estate as should equal the value of the loan at twenty years purchase.[3]

A covenant that if the borrower died before his father the subject-matter of the mortgage should belong absolutely to the mortgagee.[4]

An option to purchase the mortgaged property given to the lender upon the creation[5] or the assignment[6] of the mortgage. Such an option, however, is valid if it is given by a subsequent and independent transaction, even though the only consideration is the release of the mortgagor from his obligation to pay the original loan.[7]

An important question is whether the postponement for a considerable period of the contractual right to redeem is objectionable as being an unreasonable interference with the rights of the mortgagor. If a mortgage is in essence a mere security, it is arguable that a clause which prolongs the security after the mortgagor is ready and willing to pay all that is due, is one that ought not to be upheld, even though it was accepted by him without objection at the time of the loan. The question was much canvassed by the Court of Appeal in *Knightsbridge Estates Trust, Ltd.* v. *Byrne,*[8] where the facts were as follows :—

Right to redeem may be postponed.

---

terest and costs, could never recover the term in its former condition, since it would remain charged with the payment to the mortgagee of the profits. See the opinions to this effect of Lord MACNAGHTEN and Lord DAVEY in *Noakes & Co., Ltd.* v. *Rice,* [1902] A. C. 24, 31–2, 34. In *Knightsbridge Estates Trust, Ltd.* v. *Byrne,* [1939] 1 Ch. 441, 456–7, the C.A. cited *Fairclough* v. *Swan Brewery Co., Ltd.,* in support of the above rule, and ignored *Santley* v. *Wilde, supra.*

 [1] *Howard* v. *Harris* (1681), 1 Vern. 33 ; *Salt* v. *Northampton (Marquis),* [1892] A. C. 1.

 [2] *Davis* v. *Symons,* [1934] 1 Ch. 442.

 [3] *Jennings* v. *Ward* (1705), 2 Vern. 520, as explained in *Biggs* v. *Hoddinott,* [1898] 2 Ch. 307, 315, 323.

 [4] *Salt* v. *Northampton (Marquis),* [1892] A. C. 1.

 [5] *Samuel* v. *Jarrah Timber Corporation,* [1904] A. C. 323. For a searching criticism of this scholastic attitude, see 60 *L. Q. R.,* p. 191.

 [6] *Lewis* v. *Frank Love, Ltd.,* [1961] 1 All E. R. 446; [1961] 1 W. L. R. 261

 [7] *Reeve* v. *Lisle,* [1902] A. C. 461; affirming *Lisle* v. *Reeve,* [1902] 1 Ch. 53.

 [8] [1939] Ch. 441 ; [1938] 4 All E. R. 618.

U*

The Knightsbridge Company had mortgaged their property, consisting of 75 houses, eight shops and a block of flats, to the Prudential Assurance Company in return for a loan of £300,000 at 6½ *per cent.* The loan was liable to be called in at any time, and the mortgagors, desiring to obtain a reduction in the rate of interest and also to spread the repayment of the principal sum over a long term of years, transferred the mortgage to the Royal Liver Friendly Society. This mortgage was for £310,000 at 5¼ *per cent.*, and at the suggestion of the mortgagors it was agreed that the loan should be repaid in forty years by half-yearly instalments. The mortgagees agreed not to call the money in before the end of this period, provided that the instalments were punctually paid. A few years later the mortgagors sued for a declaration that they were entitled, on giving the usual six months' notice, to redeem the mortgage upon payment of principal, interest and costs.

It was argued for the mortgagors that this suspension for forty years of the contractual right to redeem their property was unreasonable and therefore void. The Court of Appeal, however, upheld the suspension and denied that reasonableness, whether in respect of time or in other respects, is the true criterion of validity in such a case. A contract freely entered into after due deliberation by parties dealing with each other at arms' length is not lightly to be interfered with. A court of equity, indeed, is vigilant in its support of the principle that " redemption is of the very nature and essence of a mortgage," [1] but none the less it does not attempt to reform mortgage transactions. The rule, in short, is that a provision postponing the contractual date for redemption is not void unless

> it renders redemption illusory, as in *Fairclough* v. *Swan Brewery Co., Ltd.*,[2] or
>
> it is a device to fetter the right of redemption as in *Davis* v. *Symons*,[3] or
>
> it is in fact oppressive or unconscionable.[4]

Doctrine of restraint of trade applicable to mortgages.

A mortgage, however, is subject to the common law doctrine that invalidates any contract in restraint of trade which places an unreasonable restriction upon the freedom of a man to pursue his

---

[1] *Noakes* v. *Rice*, [1902] A. C. 24, at p. 30, *per* Lord MACNAGHTEN.

[2] [1912] A. C. 565; *supra*, p. 584.

[3] [1934] Ch. 442, as explained in the *Knightsbridge Case*, [1939] Ch. 441, at p. 462; [1938] 4 All E. R. 618, at p. 629.

[4] *Knightsbridge Estates Trust, Ltd.* v. *Byrne*, [1939] Ch. 441, at p. 457; [1938] 4 All E. R. 618, at p. 626; on appeal, [1940] A. C. 613; [1940] 2 All E. R. 401, the House of Lords decided the case on an entirely different ground, namely that the mortgage was a valid debenture under the Companies Act, and expressed no opinion upon whether the Court of Appeal had laid down the correct rule as to the validity of a suspension of the contractual date for redemption. There is no tendency in the profession to doubt its correctness, though earlier cases had more than suggested that the appropriate test was reasonableness; see for example, *Talbot* v. *Braddill* (1683), 1 Vern. 183; *Teevan* v. *Smith* (1882), 20 Ch. D. 724, 729; *Morgan* v. *Jeffreys*, [1910] 1 Ch. 620.

trade or profession.[1] It may happen, therefore, that a postponement of the right of redemption which is not *per se* oppressive may
nevertheless become so if it is accompanied by an excessive restraint upon the mortgagor's business activities. This was the
position, for instance, where a garage was mortgaged to suppliers
of motor fuels, and the mortgagors covenanted that they would not
exercise their right of redemption for twenty-one years and, during
the same period, would not buy or sell any fuel other than that
supplied by the mortgagees.[2]

(ii) Equitable rules concerning collateral advantages.
A collateral advantage means something that is granted to the
mortgagee in addition to the return of his loan with interest, as
for instance where a publican mortgagor agrees that for a given
number of years he will sell no beer on the premises except that
which is brewed by the mortgagee.

The question whether the reservation of such an advantage is
valid is rendered difficult by a number of apparently irreconcilable
decisions stretching back for more than a century. Indeed, the
case law will be unintelligible unless it is realized that the attitude
of the courts towards the matter has changed materially in the
course of the last hundred years, and that reliance can no longer
be placed upon many of the older decisions. Lord HALDANE, in
a reference to one of the more modern cases,[3] said :

*Modern
tendency
to uphold
collateral
advantages.*

> " In the 17th and 18th centuries a Court of equity could hardly
> " have so decided, and the judgments illustrate the elastic character
> " of equity jurisdiction and the power of equity judges to mould
> " the rules which they apply in accordance with the exigencies of
> " the time."[4]

In early days the judges frowned upon any attempt by a
mortgagee to reap some additional advantage, as is shown by a
remark of the Master of the Rolls in 1705 that " a man shall not
have interest and a collateral advantage besides." [5] In modern
times a more realistic and favourable note has been struck, and
for this change of heart probably the most significant reason
is that at the present day a mortgagor can scarcely be regarded
as in need of special protection. In the eye of the novelist, no
doubt, he is an impoverished debtor on the brink of ruin, unable to
resist the demands of the rapacious lender, and it is perhaps true
that the Court of Chancery in its more paternal days tended to take
a somewhat similar view of his predicament. In fact, however,
the parties to a modern mortgage are generally hard-headed

*Reasons for
changed
attitude.*

---

[1] *Esso Petroleum Co., Ltd.* v. *Harper's Garage (Stourport), Ltd.,* [1966] 1 All
E. R. 725; [1966] 2 W. L. R. 1043.
[2] *Ibid.*
[3] *Biggs* v. *Hoddinott, Hoddinott* v. *Biggs,* [1898] 2 Ch. 307.
[4] *Kreglinger* v. *New Patagonia Meat and Cold Storage Co., Ltd.,* [1914]
A. C. 25, at p. 38.
[5] *Jennings* v. *Ward* (1705). 2 Vern. 520.

business men well able to protect their own interests, and in these days, when so much stress is laid upon the sanctity of contracts, it is difficult to appreciate why one of them should be allowed to disregard a bargain freely made, simply because he happens to be a mortgagor. Such maxims as " Once a mortgage, always a mortgage " and " A mortgage cannot be made irredeemable," undoubtedly express an important principle, but to apply them in an unbending and inflexible fashion so as to upset an ordinary commercial transaction would be out of keeping with the times.

Modern rule stated.　Despite the judicial uncertainties of the past, the modern law on the subject is perfectly clear, though its application to particular cases may be a difficult matter and may cause a sharp divergence of opinion among the learned. It can be summarized quite shortly.

> A contract that grants a collateral advantage to a mortgagee is valid and enforceable unless it is oppressive and unconscionable or unless it is calculated to prevent or unduly to hamper redemption.[1]

Oppressive contracts void.　First, if a contract is oppressive or unconscionable, which is a pure question of fact, it is void not so much because of its association with a mortgage, but because of the general principle of public policy that a contract shall not be used as an engine of oppression. It has repeatedly been affirmed that the courts will set aside " any oppressive bargain, or any advantage exacted from a man under grievous necessity and want of money,"[2] and instances are not wanting of where this principle has been applied to a mortgage transaction.[3] In fact, if the mortgagee stands in a fiduciary relationship to the mortgagor, as for instance where he is his trustee, solicitor or spiritual adviser, the burden is on him to prove the fairness of the transaction if it is challenged on the ground of undue influence or unconscionable conduct.[4]

Contract which hampers redemption is void.　Secondly, a provision is void if its effect is to render either the contractual or the equitable right of redemption virtually inoperative. If it prejudices the contractual right of redemption it is inconsistent with the intention of the parties. If it prejudices the right of the mortgagor to recover his property after the contractual date has passed, it is void as being a clog on the equity of redemption, for anything is stigmatized as a clog which " prevents the mortgagor from getting back his property free from any fetter when it is redeemed." [5] Such will be the position if the

---

[1] *Biggs* v. *Hoddinott, Hoddinott* v. *Biggs,* [1898] 2 Ch. 307.
[2] *Barrett* v. *Hartley* (1866), L. R. 2 Eq. 789, at p. 795, *per* STUART, V.-C.
[3] *James (E. G.)* v. *Kerr* (1889), 40 Ch. D. 448. *Cf. Horwood* v. *Millar's Timber and Trading Co.,* [1917] 1 K. B. 305.
[4] Waldock, *The Law of Mortgages* (2nd Edn.), chapter viii, and cases there cited.
[5] *Knightsbridge Estates Trust, Ltd.* v. *Byrne,* [1939] Ch. 441, at p. 448; [1938] 4 All E. R. 618, at p. 623, *per* GREENE, M.R. In the view of LINDLEY, L.J., the application of the rule depends upon whether the mortgage deed provides

obligation imposed upon him by the provision renders the recovery of his property unprofitable, hazardous or economically and substantially less valuable. This was the position in *Noakes v. Rice.*[1]

Noakes v. Rice.

> The tenant of a public-house, under a lease which had 26 years to run, mortgaged the premises as security for a loan and covenanted that *during the remainder of the term* he would not sell any malt liquors except those provided by the mortgagees. Three years later he claimed a declaration that he should be released from the covenant upon payment of all moneys due under the security.

It was held by the House of Lords, affirming the decisions of the two lower courts, that he was entitled to the release he claimed. It was clear that the benefit of redemption would be to a great extent nullified if the mortgagor were to remain bound by the covenant. His right of redemption was hampered in the sense that after attainment of the object for which the security was created he would not be master in his own house—he would not recover his property as it was before the mortgage. " The public-house, which was free when mortgaged, would have been tied to the mortgagee when redeemed." [2] The covenant was in fact inconsistent with the express proviso for redemption, and was also a clog upon the equity.

Biggs v. Hoddinott,[3] however, serves as a reminder that the application of the general rule must depend upon the view that the court takes of the facts. In that case :

Biggs v. Hoddinott.

> A. mortgaged his hotel to B., a brewer, in return for an advance of £7654, and agreed that during the continuance of the mortgage he would sell no other beer than that supplied by B. It was mutually agreed that the mortgage should not be redeemable, nor should the loan be repayable, for five years.

The claim of A., made two years later, that he was entitled to procure beer elsewhere upon repayment of the loan, was dis-

---

that there shall be no redemption until the collateral advantage has been fully implemented, or whether it first allows redemption upon payment of principal, interest and costs, and then expresses the collateral advantage in a superadded clause. In the first case he insists that the mortgagor cannot redeem until he has satisfied his own contractual obligations, including his obligation to allow the collateral advantage to operate. " When you get a security for a debt or obligation, that security can be redeemed the moment the debt or obligation is paid or performed, *but on no other terms* "; *Santley* v. *Wilde,* [1899] 2 Ch. 474, at p. 475. It is doubtful, however, whether the distinction is helpful in the present connection, for, if it is to be adopted, the validity of a collateral advantage will apparently depend upon the drafting of the mortgage deed, not upon the substantial merits of the case. As against this, however, it may be argued that if the advantage is deliberately and consciously made part of the security, then this is a business transaction that ought to be upheld.

[1] [1902] A. C. 24. See also *Morgan* v. *Jeffreys,* [1910] 1 Ch. 620. The discussions in these two cases could now be justified on the ground that the tie imposed upon the publican was void as being in restraint of trade; see *Esso Petroleum Co., Ltd.* v. *Harpers' Garage (Stourport), Ltd., supra,* p. 587.

[2] *Bradley* v. *Carritt,* [1903] A. C. 253, at pp. 277–8, *per* Lord LINDLEY.

[3] [1898] 2 Ch. 307 ; approved by the House of Lords in *Noakes v. Rice, supra.*

missed. It was held that the bargain, which was to cease with redemption, was advantageous to both parties and must remain in force. It in no way hampered the right of redemption.

Bradley v. Carritt.

The position is further illustrated by *Bradley v. Carritt.*[1]

> In that case the defendant, a shareholder in a tea company, mortgaged his shares to the plaintiff, and in further consideration for the loan entered into the following contract :
>
> " I further agree . . . to use my best endeavours to secure that " you or any firm of brokers of which you for the time being " shall be a partner shall *always hereafter* have the sale of the " company's teas as broker, and in the event of the company's " teas being sold otherwise than through you or your firm, I " personally agree to pay you or your firm the amount of " commission which you or your firm would have earned if " the tea had been sold through you or your firm."
>
> The plaintiff was appointed broker; but the defendant repaid the loan, redeemed his shares and transferred them to another mortgagee, X., who succeeded in ousting the plaintiff from his appointment.

The House of Lords, reversing the court of first instance and the Court of Appeal, held that the defendant was not liable for breach of the agreement set out above. Lord LINDLEY and Lord SHAND, however, dissented. What weighed with the majority, was that if the defendant were to remain liable for payment of commission the shares would have far less value after redemption than they had before the mortgage. The only likely purchasers of shares of that particular kind were tea brokers, whose sole object in buying would be to acquire the privilege of selling the company's tea. After redemption, therefore, the shares would be more or less frozen assets in the hands of the mortgagor, since, unless he showed great vigilance, their sale would almost certainly result in his being liable to the plaintiff for loss of brokerage. The agreement was, therefore, said to be repugnant both to the contractual right of redemption and to the equity.

Kreglinger v. New Patagonia Meat Co.

The House of Lords came to a different conclusion in *Kreglinger v. New Patagonia Meat and Cold Storage Co., Ltd.,*[2] where the facts were as follows :

> A firm of woolbrokers lent £10,000 to a company which carried on business as meat preservers, the agreement being that the company might pay off the loan at any time by giving a month's notice. The loan was secured, not by an ordinary mortgage, but by an analogous security called a floating charge. [This, though a charge upon the assets for the time being, does not prevent a company from dealing with its property in the ordinary course of business, but it does so when the chargee takes steps, such as by the appointment of a receiver, to crystallize the security.] It was agreed that for five years from the date of the loan the company should not sell sheepskins to any person other than the lenders, so long as the latter were willing to pay the full market price. It was also agreed

---

[1] [1903] A. C. 253.   [2] [1914] A. C. 25.

that the lenders would not demand repayment before five years had elapsed. The loan was repaid within two and a half years. The point that fell to be decided was whether the option on the sheepskins was enforceable by the lenders after repayment of the loan.

The House held unanimously that the lenders were entitled to an injunction restraining the company from selling skins to third parties during the remainder of the five years. While it was true that the company would not be as free in the conduct of their business after repayment of the loan as they were before the grant of the charge, the House of Lords was of opinion that the agreement was a reasonable one that ought to be upheld.

Bradley v. *Carritt* represents the high-water mark of the conception of a mortgage as an onerous obligation imposed upon a necessitous borrower, in whose favour the court should therefore intervene.[1] The *Kreglinger Case*, on the other hand, reveals a judicial appreciation of a mortgage as a transaction freely concluded by business men without colour of oppression, which should therefore form no exception to the maxim *pacta sunt servanda*. It is submitted that this is a more realistic and reasonable approach, and one more compatible with the business conditions of the twentieth century.

(B) Enforcement of the Equity of Redemption.

The right of redemption is lost if any one of the following events occurs :—

The release of the right by the mortgagor to the mortgagee ; the lapse of time under the Limitation Act, 1939; the sale of the land by the mortgagee under his statutory power; or a foreclosure decree obtained by the mortgagee.

The last two methods are discussed later.[2]

Although a provision in the mortgage deed itself giving the mortgagee an option to purchase the land is void as being a clog on the equity,[3] there is nothing to prevent the mortgagor from getting rid of the debt by releasing the equity of redemption to him, provided that it is the result of an independent bargain made subsequently to the mortgage deed. Release of equity of redemption.

As regards lapse of time it is enacted that :—

" When a mortgagee of land has been in possession of any of the " mortgaged land for a period of twelve years, no action to redeem " the land of which the mortgagee has been so in possession shall " thereafter be brought by the mortgagor or any person claiming " through him."[4] Limitation Act, 1939.

---

[1] Waldock, *The Law of Mortgages* (2nd Edn.), chapter viii.
[2] *Infra*, p. 600 (sale); p. 605 (foreclosure).   [3] *Supra*, p. 585.
[4] Limitation Act, 1939, s. 12, replacing Real Property Limitation Act, 1874, s. 7.

If, however, the mortgagee in possession either receives any sum in respect of principal or interest or signs an acknowledgment of the mortgagor's title, an action to redeem the land may be brought at any time before the expiration of twelve years after the last payment or acknowledgment.[1]   An acknowledgment given after the mortgagee has been in possession for twelve years, without receiving a payment in respect of principal or interest, is ineffective.[2]

When, as in the ordinary case, a mortgagee does not take possession of the land, the mortgagor can redeem regardless of the lapse of time.

Enlargement of the term into a fee simple.   When a mortgagee has obtained a title to the land free from the mortgage by remaining in possession for twelve years he may by deed enlarge the term of years into a fee simple under the Law of Property Act, 1925.[3]   Before the enlargement, which is equivalent to a foreclosure decree, can be effected, however, the following conditions must exist:

(i) The term must originally have been created for not less than 300 years, and at the time of the proposed enlargement there must be at least 200 more years to run.

(ii) There must be no trust or right of redemption still existing in favour of the reversioner.

(iii) The term must not be one which is liable to be determined by re-entry for condition broken.

Notice to mortgagee.   Presuming that the mortgagor has not lost his right to redeem the security, he is entitled, under the contract contained in the mortgage deed, to tender the exact amount due, and to claim redemption on the date fixed for repayment. This date is not usually, however, meant to be taken seriously, and if it has elapsed, the mortgagor must give either six months' notice or six months' interest before he can redeem.[4] If a notice so given is not followed by repayment upon the date notified, he must give a fresh notice of a reasonable length.[5]

Reconveyance by endorsed receipt.   Before January 1st, 1926, a reconveyance by the mortgagee was necessary to revest the legal estate in the mortgagor upon redemption, but now, when redemption has been effected, there is no need for the mortgagee to execute a deed surrendering the term. A receipt written at the foot of the mortgage deed will be sufficient to extinguish the mortgage, provided that it states the name of the person who pays the money and is executed by the person in whom the mortgage is vested. In the ordinary case of a mortgage by demise this receipt effects a surrender of the term

---

[1] Limitation Act, 1939 ss. 23 (3), 24 (1).   [2] *Ibid.*, s. 16.
[3] Law of Property Act, 1925, ss. 88 (3); 153.
[4] *Cromwell Property Investment Co.* v. *Western and Toovey*, [1934] Ch. 322.
[5] *Ibid.*

and merges it in the reversion held by the mortgagor.[1] If a person, such as a second mortgagee, to whom the immediate equity of redemption does not belong pays the money that is due, the benefit of the mortgage passes to him by virtue of the receipt,[2] and thus his incumbrance is kept alive. But of course where there are two mortgages of the same land and the mortgagor pays off the first, the receipt does not transfer the first mortgage term to him so as to enable him to keep it alive against the second mortgagee.[3] Moreover, it is enacted that a mortgage term shall, after repayment of the money, become a satisfied term, and shall cease.[4]

It is the duty of a mortgagee, upon receiving repayment of the loan, to deliver the title deeds to the person who has the best right to them, *i.e.* the mortgagor if there is only one incumbrance, or the next mortgagee if the land has been subjected to more incumbrances than one.[5] A mortgagee will not, however, incur liability to a later mortgagee for delivering the deeds to the mortgagor, unless he has actual notice of the later mortgage.[6] Mere registration of a mortgage as a land charge[7] does not in this case constitute notice, but nevertheless he is for several reasons well advised to search at the Registry before handing over the deeds to the mortgagor.[8] Disposal of deeds by mortgagor.

The mortgagor may commence proceedings to enforce redemption, and if he is successful, an order will be made directing the mortgagee to surrender the lease upon receiving payment within six months. But where such proceedings are taken, the mortgagor may have a judgment for sale instead of for redemption, and the court may, on the request either of the mortgagor or of the mortgagee, and despite the dissent of the other party, direct a sale on such terms as it thinks fit.[9] Sale in lieu of redemption.

Finally, upon payment of the amount due, a mortgagor is entitled to require the mortgagee to transfer the debt and the property to a third person, and the mortgagee unless he is or has been in possession, is bound to comply.[10] This is the procedure adopted where a third person pays the amount of the loan to the mortgagee, and then himself assumes the position of mortgagee. Transfer of mortgage.

---

[1] Law of Property Act, 1925, s. 115 (1).

[2] *Ibid.*, s. 115; (2) *Cumberland Court (Brighton), Ltd.* v. *Taylor,* [1964] Ch. 29; [1963] 2 All E. R. 536.

[3] *Ibid.*, s. 115 (2). [4] *Ibid.*, s. 116.

[5] *Re Magneta Time Co., Ltd., Molden* v. *Magneta Time Ltd.* (1915), 84 L. J. Ch. 814.

[6] Law of Property Act, 1925, s. 96 (2), as amended by Law of Property (Amendment) Act, 1926, Schedule.

[7] *Infra,* p. 668.

[8] See four articles by Cyprian Williams, *The Law Journal,* 1926, May 22, 29, June 5 and 12.

[9] Law of Property Act, 1925, s. 91.

[10] Law of Property Act, 1925, s. 95. The reason for the exception is that a mortgagee, having once been in possession, remains liable to account for the profits that the transferee has, or ought to have, received after the transfer. He should, therefore, never transfer the security without an order of the court; *Hall* v. *Heward* (1886), 32 Ch. D. 430, 435.

(C) EFFECT OF DEATH OF MORTGAGOR.

Land
remains
liable to
debt.

On the death of a mortgagor the equity of redemption goes through his personal representatives to the persons entitled on intestacy if he dies without leaving a will, and to his devisee if he leaves a will. Under the law as it existed prior to 1854, such an heir or devisee was entitled to have the mortgage debt paid out of the personal estate of the deceased, and to take the property free from the mortgage burden, but, in accordance with the general principle that he who has the benefit ought to have the burden, this rule was reversed by the Real Estate Charges Acts of 1854, 1867 and 1877. These statutes have now been repealed, although their general tenour is retained, and it is enacted that property, whether land or not, which at the time of the owner's death is charged with the payment of money, whether by way of legal mortgage, equitable charge or otherwise, shall, as between the different persons claiming through the deceased, be primarily liable for the payment of the charge.[1] This rule is not to apply, however, if the deceased has expressed a contrary intention by deed or will, but such intention must be clear and unambiguous, and is not to be implied merely because the deceased has directed that his debts are to be paid out of his personal estate or his residuary estate.[2]

(2) RIGHTS OF A MORTGAGOR WHO REMAINS IN POSSESSION.

Mortgagor
usually
retains
possession.

In the eyes of equity the mortgagor remains the true beneficial owner of the property notwithstanding his grant of a term of years absolute to the mortgagee, and as long as he remains in possession he is entitled to appropriate the rents and profits to his own use without any liability to account for them, even though he may be in default in the payment of interest. The mortgagee may, indeed, take possession of the land at any moment and may retain the rents and profits in satisfaction of interest due to him after paying current outgoings such as rates and taxes.[3] Such a step is, however, not in accordance with the spirit of the transaction, and it is not usual for a mortgagee, despite his legal right, to enter into actual possession unless the interest has fallen into arrears, and it has become desirable to prevent the rents and profits from reaching the mortgagor. One formidable deterrent

---

[1] Administration of Estates Act, 1925, s. 35 (1).
[2] *Ibid*, s. 35 (1), (2). *In re Neeld, Carpenter v. Inigo-Jones*, [1962] Ch. 643; [1962] 2 All E. R. 335.
[3] *Four-Maids, Ltd. v. Dudley Marshall (Properties), Ltd.*, [1957] Ch. 317; [1957] 2 All E. R. 35. He may apply to the court by an originating summons, R.S.C. Order LV, r. 5c (but see now R.S.C. Order 88, r.1); see *Birmingham Citizens Permanent Building Society v. Caunt*, [1962] Ch. 883; [1962] 1 All E. R. 163.

to this course is the strict supervision which Equity exercises over a mortgagee in possession. The rule is that he must get no advantage out of the mortgage beyond the payment of principal, interest and costs, and he is made to account not only for what he has actually received, but also for what he might have received but for his own wilful default or neglect.[1] Thus he is liable for voluntary waste, and again if he allows property to remain vacant which might have been let, he is personally liable to pay an occupation rent.[2] In one case, for instance :

> Mortgagees, who happened to be brewers, took possession of the mortgaged premises and leased them to a tenant, subject to a restriction that he should take his supply of beer entirely from them. It was held that they must account for the additional rent that they would have received had they let the premises as a " free," instead of a " tied," house.

White v. City of London Brewery Co. (1889), 42 Ch. D. 237.

So in the normal case the mortgagor remains in possession free from the liability to pay rent, and entitled to appropriate the rents and profits to his own use. Until the mortgagee has given notice of his intention to take possession or to receive the rents, the mortgagor may sue third parties in his own name for the recovery of possession or rents, or for damages in respect of any trespass or other wrong done to the land.[3]

Where a mortgagor retained possession, it was formerly a common practice to include in the mortgage deed a clause by which he *attorned* to the mortgagee, i.e. acknowledged that he held the land as a tenant at will at a yearly rent equivalent to a year's mortgage interest. The chief advantages were that it enabled the mortgagee to pursue the remedies available to a landlord for the recovery of arrears of rent, and also to obtain a summary judgment for possession if the need arose.

Attornment.

These two advantages, however, no longer exist, for the mortgagee cannot distrain upon the premises for arrears unless the attornment clause has been registered as a bill of sale;[4] and a summary judgment is available to him independently of attornment.[5] Nevertheless, an attornment clause is not altogether superfluous, for it enables a covenant by a mortgagor which touches and concerns the land to be enforced against his successors in title.[6]

---

[1] *Chaplin* v. *Young* (1864), 33 Beav. 330 ; *White* v. *City of London Brewery Co.* (1889), 42 Ch. D. 237, 243.

[2] *Gaskell* v. *Gosling* (1896), 1 Q. B. 669, 691.

[3] Law of Property Act, 1925, s. 98.

[4] *Re Willis, ex parte Kennedy* (1888), 21 Q. B. D. 384.

[5] Ord. 55, R. 5c.

[6] *Regent Oil Co., Ltd.* v. *J. A. Gregory (Hatch End), Ltd.*, [1966] Ch. 403; [1965] 3 All E. R. 673, where the charge was included in a charge by way of legal mortgage. But since the relationship between the parties is in effect that of landlord and tenant, would not the covenant run even in the absence of attornment?; see 82 *L. Q. R.*, p. 22 (P.V.B.).

A mortgagor, *while in actual possession* is given the following statutory powers:—

(A) RIGHT TO GRANT VALID LEASES.

Leasing power at common law.

At common law a mortgagor is entitled to grant a lease binding between him and the lessee, and his power in this respect has not been affected by statute.[1] But if granted without the concurrence of the mortgagee[2] it confers only a precarious title upon the lessee, since the paramount title of the mortgagee may be asserted against both him and the mortgagor.[3]

Statutory leasing powers.

The Conveyancing Act, 1881, expanded the power of the mortgagor in this particular by allowing him to grant leases for limited periods which would be binding upon the mortgagee. The present position is governed by the Law of Property Act, 1925, which confers upon a mortgagor *in possession* a statutory right to grant the following leases that will be binding upon all incumbrancers:—

1. Agricultural or occupation leases for any term not exceeding 21 years, or, if the mortgage was made on or after January 1st, 1926, for any term not exceeding 50 years.
2. Building leases, either for 99 or for 999 years, according as the mortgage was made before or after January 1st, 1926.[4]

Essentials of lease.

Such a lease must be made to take effect in possession not later than twelve months after its execution; it must reserve the best rent that can reasonably be obtained, and no fine must be taken[5]; it must contain a condition of re-entry in the event of rent being in arrears for 30 days,[6] and the mortgagor is bound to deliver to the mortgagee within one month a counterpart of the lease executed by the lessee.[7]

Thus,

> when a mortgagor makes a lease to A. for 50 years, the effect is that the mortgagee, though he holds a long term of years, is not entitled to actual possession during the continuance of A.'s term; but if he is driven to pursue his remedies, he is entitled to receipt of the rent paid by A.

---

[1] *Iron Trades Employers' Insurance Association* v. *Union Land and House Investors, Ltd.,* [1937] Ch. 313; [1937] 1 All E. R. 481.

[2] The mortgage deed itself may confer leasing powers within defined limits upon the mortgagor; Law of Property Act, 1925, s. 99 (14).

[3] *Corbett* v. *Plowden* (1884), 25 Ch. D. 678, at p. 681, *per* Lord SELBORNE, L.C.

[4] Law of Property Act, 1925, s. 99 (1), (3).

[5] *Ibid.,* s. 99, (5), (6). See, for example, *Rust* v. *Goodale,* [1957] Ch. 33, 39; [1956] 3 All E. R. 373, 376, where the consideration for a sub-lease was an immediate payment of £2,260 and a rent of £5.

[6] Law of Property Act, 1925, s. 99 (7). It is doubtful whether this requirement must be satisfied in the case of an oral tenancy; *Pawson* v. *Revell,* [1958] 2 Q. B. 360; [1958] 3 All E. R. 233.

[7] Law of Property Act, s. 99 (11). A lease which fails to comply with one or more of these requirements may be validated under s. 152, *supra,* p. 200. See, *e.g., Pawson* v. *Revell, supra.*

These statutory powers of leasing may be, and in practice frequently are, excluded by the mortgage deed,[1] but no such exclusion is allowed in the case of a mortgage of agricultural land made after March 1st, 1948.[2]

If the statutory powers are excluded, a lease granted by a mortgagor is void as between the lessee and the mortgagee and his successors in title.[3] The mortgagee has an option. He may either treat the lessee as a trespasser or accept him as his own tenant. If, for instance, he demands that the rent be paid direct to him instead of to the mortgagor, the original tenancy is destroyed and replaced by a yearly tenancy between the mortgagee and the lessee.[4] Moreover, the acceptance of rent without any such demand raises the implication of a yearly tenancy. This implication, however, does not arise merely because the mortgagee, being aware of the lease, allows the tenant to remain in possession.[5]

Effect of unauthorised lease.

If a mortgagee refuses to recognize an unauthorized lease, the tenant may redeem the mortgage and thus secure himself against eviction.[6]

A lease made before the creation of a mortgage is, of course, binding upon the mortgagee, but whether it enjoys this priority in point of time may be affected by the doctrine of estoppel. The relevant rule of that doctrine is that if a person purports to grant a lease of land in which he has no legal estate, he is estopped from repudiating the tenancy and the tenant is estopped from denying its existence. There thus arises what is called a *tenancy by estoppel* which, as between the parties estopped, possesses the attributes of a true tenancy.

Tenancy by estoppel.

"It is true that a title by estoppel is only good against the person "estopped and imports from its very existence the idea of no real "title at all, yet as against the person estopped it has all the elements "of a real title."[7]

Thus, the covenants contained in the lease are enforceable by the lessor against the tenant, and the successors in title to either party are themselves equally estopped.[8]

A tenancy by estoppel, however, may be transformed into an effective tenancy. The rule is that if the lessor later acquires the legal estate in the land, the effect is to "feed the estoppel" and to clothe the tenant also with a legal estate. The lease then takes

Effect on later mortgage if estoppel is fed.

---

[1] Law of Property Act, 1925, s. 99 (13).
[2] Agricultural Holdings Act, 1948, 7th Sched., para. 2 (1).
[3] *Rust* v. *Goodall*, [1957] Ch. 33; [1956] 3 All E. R. 373.
[4] *Taylor* v. *Ellis*, [1960] Ch. 368, at pp. 375–6,; [1960] 1 All E. R. 549.
[5] *Ibid.*
[6] *Tarn* v. *Turner* (1888), 39 Ch. D. 4465.
[7] *Bank of England* v. *Cutler*, [1908] 2 K. B. 208, at p. 234, *per* FARWELL, L.J.
[8] *Cuthbertson* v. *Irving* (1859), 4 H. & N. 742. If the lessor has any legal estate in the land, though one less in extent than that which he purports to lease, there is no estoppel. The tenant acquires the interest, whatever it may be, that the lessor holds; *Hill* v. *Saunders* (1825), 4 B. & C. 529.

effect in interest, not merely by way of estoppel. The tenancy commenced by estoppel, but for all purposes it has now become an estate or interest,[1] and it prevails against a later mortgage of the same land however short the interval of time may be between the feeding of the estoppel and the creation of the mortgage.[2] For instance:

> P. agrees to purchase a house from V. and is let into possession before completion. Though at present entitled only to an equitable interest, he purports to lease the premises to T., whereupon a tenancy by estoppel arises between these two parties. The conveyance of the legal estate to P. is completed some weeks later and this is followed immediately by a mortgage of the premises to M. who has agreed to advance the purchase money and who pays it direct to V.

In a sense, the conveyance to P. (which feeds the estoppel and gives T. a legal tenancy), and the mortgage to M. constitute one indivisible transaction, but such is not the effect in law of what has been done. There is a *scintilla temporis* between the conveyance and the mortgage, with the result that the legal tenancy acquired by T. precedes and takes priority over M's mortgage.[3] Normally, M. may no doubt determine the tenancy by serving a notice to quit, but he cannot do so if the premises are controlled by the Rent Restriction Acts.

(B) RIGHT TO ACCEPT SURRENDERS OF LEASES.

Statutory power to accept surrenders of leases.

Although the statutory powers just mentioned enable a mortgagor to grant a lease out of the mortgagee's term, yet the effect of such a lease is to vest the reversion thereon in the mortgagee, and without the latter's concurrence it would normally be impossible for a mortgagor to accept a surrender of an existing lease with a view to the grant of a new one.[4] The Law of Property Act, therefore (re-enacting the Conveyancing Act, 1911), authorizes a mortgagor to accept a surrender of any lease, if, and only if, his object in doing so is to grant a new lease that falls within his statutory powers.[5] Such a surrender, however, is not valid unless a new lease is granted within one month, for a period no shorter than the unexpired term of the surrendered lease, and at a rent not less than the old rent.[6]

A subsequent mortgagee who exercises the statutory powers of leasing and of accepting surrenders exercises them in his capacity

---

[1] *Webb* v. *Austin* (1844), 7 Man. & G. 701, at p. 724, *per* TINDAL, C.J., citing Preston, *Treatise on Abstracts.*
[2] For a full discussion, see 80 *L. Q. R.* pp. 370–398 (A. M. Prichard).
[3] *Church of England Building Society* v. *Piskor*, [1954] Ch. 553; [1954] 2 All E. R. 85, overruling in this respect *Coventry Permanent Economic Building Society* v. *Jones*, [1951] 1 All E. R. 901.
[4] *Robbins* v. *Whyte*, [1906] 1 K. B. 125.
[5] Law of Property Act, 1925, s. 100 (1).   [6] *Ibid.*, s. 100 (5).

as mortgagee and not because he derives his title from the mortgagor.[1] There is therefore, for instance, no obligation on him to deliver a counterpart of the lease to the mortgagor.[2]

SECTION IV. POWERS AND REMEDIES OF THE MORTGAGEE.

(A) *POWERS AND REMEDIES OF LEGAL MORTGAGEES.*

SUMMARY

(1) POWER OF MORTGAGEE IN POSSESSION TO GRANT LEASES.

If a mortgagee takes possession of the land with a view to utilizing the profits in satisfaction of the money due to him, he is authorized by statute to grant leases, and to accept surrenders of leases, within the limits made applicable to a mortgagor who is in actual possession.[3] He is also permitted, where the mortgage is made by deed, to cut and sell timber and other trees if they are ripe for cutting and are not planted for shelter or ornament.[4]

Leasing and timber powers.

(2) POWER TO INSURE THE MORTGAGED PROPERTY:

Where a mortgage is made by deed, the mortgagee has statutory authority to insure the property against loss or damage by fire, and to charge the premiums on the mortgaged property.[5] But the amount of the insurance must not exceed the amount specified in the mortgage deed, or, if no amount is specified, must not exceed two-thirds of the sum it would take to restore the premises in the event of their total destruction. Moreover, the mortgagee does not possess this statutory right where the mortgage deed contains a declaration that no insurance is required, or where an insurance is kept up by the mortgagor according to the mortgage deed, or where that deed contains no provision and the mortgagor

When mortgagee may insure.

---

[1] Law of Property Act, 1925, ss. 99 (18), 100 (12).
[2] *Cf. Robbins* v. *Whyte, supra.*
[3] Law of Property Act, 1925, ss. 99 (2), 100 (2) ; *supra*, p. 596.
[4] *Ibid.*, s. 101 (1) (iv).   [5] *Ibid.*, s. 101 (1) (ii).

himself insures up to the statutory amount.[1] Insurance money, when received, may be applied at the instance of the mortgagee in the discharge of the mortgage debt.[2]

Comprehensive nature of remedies.

We now come to the remedies of a mortgagee properly so called. These are numerous and varied, and they serve to explain the attraction that a mortgage of land has for investors. Further, all the remedies may be pursued concurrently as soon as the mortgagor is in default, so that for instance, the mortgagee at one and the same time may sue upon the personal covenant and begin foreclosure proceedings.

(3) RIGHT TO SUE ON THE PERSONAL COVENANT.

Personal remedy.

A mortgage deed not only grants a long term of years to the mortgagee, but also contains an express covenant whereby the mortgagor covenants to repay the principal sum on a definite date, and meanwhile to pay interest at a certain rate per cent. The moment that date has passed, the mortgagee can sue on this personal covenant for the recovery of the principal sum and any interest that may be in arrear, and can have the judgment satisfied out of any property belonging to the mortgagor, though it is not comprised in the mortgage.

Effect of Limitation Act.

An action to recover the principal sum is barred unless it is brought within twelve years from the date when the right to receive the money accrued.[3] This date is that which is fixed by the mortgage deed for repayment, but on each occasion that some part of the principal or interest is paid or a written acknowledgment of his liability to pay is given by the mortgagor, the period of twelve years begins to run afresh.[4] In the case of interest, only six years' arrears are recoverable.[5] Once the mortgagee's right to recover the principal sum is statute barred, he loses his status as a mortgagee. He can no longer sue for possession or for foreclosure, nor can he redeem a prior mortgage.[6]

(4) POWER OF SALE.

When statutory power of sale arises.

As soon as the mortgage money has become due, that is, as soon as the date fixed for repayment has passed, the mortgagee or legal chargee has a statutory power, which may be varied or extended by the parties or excluded altogether,[7] to sell the mortgaged property or any part thereof, either by public auction or by private contract, *provided that the mortgage has been made by deed.*[8] If the money secured by the mortgage is payable by instal-

---

[1] Law of Property Act, 1925, s. 108 (1), (2).   [2] *Ibid.,* s. 108 (4).
[3] Limitation Act, 1939, s. 18 (1).   [4] *Ibid.,* s. 23 (3) ; 24 (1).
[5] *Ibid.,* s. 18 (5).
[6] *Cotterell* v. *Price,* [1960] 3 All E. R. 315; [1960] 1 W. L. R. 1097.
[7] *Alliance Building Society* v. *Shave,* [1952] Ch. 581 ; [1952] 1 All E. R. 1033.
[8] Law of Property Act, 1925, s. 101 (1) (i).

ments, his power of sale is not postponed until the whole sum falls due, but becomes exercisable as soon as an instalment is due and unpaid.[1] He may sell the land either with or apart from the minerals, and may impose either on the sold or on the unsold part of the mortgaged land such conditions or restrictive covenants as seem desirable.[2]

Although the power of sale arises as soon as the mortgage money becomes due, it nevertheless does not become exercisable until *one* of the following things has occurred :— *When exercisable.*

1. Until notice requiring payment of the mortgage money has been served on the mortgagor, and default has been made in payment of the money, or part thereof, for three months after such service.[3]

> This notice, which must be in writing,[4] may demand payment either immediately or at the end of three months, and if it is drafted in the latter form, the mortgagee need not wait for a further three months before selling, but can exercise his power after the lapse of three months from the service of notice.[5]

If there are more mortgages than one, the notice should also be served upon the later mortgagees.

2. Until some interest is in arrear and remains unpaid for two months after becoming due.[6]

3. Until there has been a breach of some provision (other than the covenant to pay the loan and interest) which is contained either in the mortgage deed or in the Law of Property Act 1925, and which imposes an obligation upon the mortgagor.[7]

> For instance, if the mortgagor has broken a covenant to keep the premises in repair, the mortgagee can exercise his power of sale immediately, despite the fact that no interest is in arrear and that he has not demanded repayment of the loan.

Effect of sale. If a mortgagee realizes his security by exercising the statutory power of sale or by successfully bringing a foreclosure action,[8] the effect is to extinguish the mortgagor's equity of redemption. The Law of Property Act, 1925, contains minute provisions dealing with the particular case of sale. *Equity of redemption extinguished*

A mortgagee, although he holds only a term of years or a charge by way of legal mortgage, is given express statutory power to vest the fee simple in the purchaser. The conveyance may be *Fee simple passes to purchaser.*

---

[1] *Payne* v. *Cardiff R.D.C.*, [1932] 1 K. B. 241.
[2] Law of Property Act, 1925, s. 101 (2). This section, however, only applies to mortgage deeds executed after December 31st, 1911.
[3] *Ibid.*, s. 103 (i).   [4] *Ibid.*, s. 196.
[5] *Barker* v. *Illingworth*, [1908] 2 Ch. 20.
[6] Law of Property Act, 1925, s. 103 (ii).
[7] *Ibid.*, s. 103 (iii).
[8] *Infra*, p. 605.

made in the name of the mortgagor as estate owner, and it operates to pass his legal fee simple to the purchaser and to extinguish the mortgage terms vested both in the selling mortgagee and in any subsequent mortgagees.[1]   If the person exercising the power of sale is not the first mortgagee, then the purchaser takes the fee simple subject to prior mortgages.

Realization of leasehold mortgages.

Where a term of years has been mortgaged by a sub-lease, the effect of a sale by the mortgagee is to convey to the purchaser both the mortgage sub-term and the residue of the term vested in the mortgagor.[2]   The sub-term is extinguished, since it merges in the mortgagor's reversion that thus passes to the purchaser.   The conveyance, however, does not have this effect if the mortgage term does not comprise the whole of the land included in the mortgagor's term, unless the rent and the covenants have been apportioned, or unless the land excluded from the mortgage term bears a rent of no money value.[3]   The acquisition of the reversion by the purchaser results in his becoming liable, in his capacity as assignee, upon the covenants contained in the lease from the lessor to the mortgagor. The Act, therefore, provides that if the leave of the court is obtained the sub-term alone may be conveyed to the purchaser to the exclusion of the mortgagor's reversion.[4]

The above provisions also apply where the owner of a charge by way of legal mortgage exercises his power of sale.

Position of purchaser from a mortgagee.

It is clear, therefore, that there is no difficulty in transferring to a purchaser a valid legal title to the whole interest vested in the mortgagor.   Such a purchaser takes the estate freed from all estates, interests and rights to which the mortgage has priority;[5] but if he buys from a second mortgagee he will take the fee simple subject to the term vested in the first mortgagee, and he will himself be deprived of the fee simple if such a first mortgagee exercises his powers of sale or foreclosure. A sale which is made in the professed exercise of the statutory power of sale (and after December 31st, 1925, every sale made by a mortgagee is deemed so to have been made unless a contrary intention appears) cannot be impeached on the ground that no case has arisen to authorize the sale, or that the power has been improperly exercised. If either of these facts is proved, then the injured person has his remedy against the mortgagee who exercised the power, not against the purchaser.[6]

Application of purchase money.

The money received from a purchaser is held by the mortgagee, after any prior mortgages have been paid off, on trust :—

First, to pay all expenses incidental to the sale,

---

[1] Law of Property Act, 1925, s. 88 (1) ; 113.   [2] *Ibid.*, s. 89 (1).
[3] *Ibid.*, s. 89 (6).   " Apportionment " includes an equitable apportionment, *i.e.* one made without the consent of the lessor ; Law of Property (Amendment) Act, 1926, Schedule, amending s. 89 of the principal Act.
[4] Law of Property Act, 1925, s. 89 (1) (a).   [5] *Ibid.*, s. 104 (1).
[6] *Ibid.*, s. 104 (2), (3).

Secondly, to pay to himself the principal, interest and costs due under the mortgage, and

Thirdly, to pay the surplus, if any, to the person entitled to the mortgaged property.[1]   The words " person entitled to the mortgaged property " include subsequent mortgagees, and the rule is that where there are several mortgagees interested in the same land, a prior mortgagee holds any surplus proceeds on trust for those later mortgagees of whose incumbrances he has notice.[2]   Registration now constitutes notice, and therefore if he pays the surplus to the mortgagor he is liable to that extent to the next mortgagee whose charge has been registered.[3]   In case of doubt he may pay the money into court.[4]

If, however, the right of redemption of a mortgagor and of persons claiming through him has been extinguished under the Limitation Act, 1939 (by reason of the mortgagee having been in possession for 12 years without receiving any sum in respect of principal or interest and without acknowledging the title of the mortgagor), a subsequent mortgagee is not a " person entitled to the mortgaged property."   Since the title which he claims through the mortgagor is extinguished, his interest has ceased.   Therefore, if the mortgagee sells under his statutory power, he is entitled to retain the whole proceeds, although they may exceed the amount due to him for principal and interest.[5]

Protection of mortgagee exercising power of sale.   A mortgagee who exercises his power of sale is not in other respects a trustee for the mortgagor,[6] and in the absence of fraud, provided that he acts prudently and obtains a fair price and, above all, sells only after the statutory essentials have been satisfied, the sale will not be impeached by the court on the ground that his motive was dishonest.   JESSEL, M.R., in *Nash* v. *Eads* [7] said :—

Selling mortgagee not a trustee.

---

[1] Law of Property Act, 1925, s. 105 ; replacing Conveyancing Act, 1881, s. 21 (3). *Weld-Blundell* v. *Synott*, [1940] 2 K. B. 107 ; [1940] 2 All E. R. 580.
[2] *Thorne* v. *Heard and Marsh*, [1895] A. C. 495.
[3] *West London Commercial Bank* v. *Reliance Building Society* (1884), 27 Ch. D. 187, 29 Ch. D. 954. *In re Thomson's Mortgage Trusts*, [1920] 1 Ch. 508.   Distinguish the mortgagee's duty with regard to delivery of the title deeds after redemption, for which purpose registration of a later mortgage does not constitute notice ; *supra*, p. 593.
[4] Trustee Act, 1925, s. 63.
[5] *Young* v. *Clarey*, [1948] Ch. 191 ; [1948] 1 All E. R. 197.
[6] *Warner* v. *Jacob* (1882), 20 Ch. D. 220 ; *Waring* v. *London & Manchester Assurance Co.*, [1935] Ch. 310.   In the case, however, of a building society mortgage, a mortgagee vendor occupies a fiduciary position, Building Societies Act, 1962, s. 36; replacing the Act of 1939; see *Reliance Permanent Building Society* v. *Harwood-Stamper*, [1944] Ch. 362 ; [1944] 2 All E. R. 75.
[7] (1880), 25 Sol. Jo. 95.   A higher duty rests upon a building society which sells mortgaged property, *Reliance Permanent Building Society* v. *Harwood-Stamper*, [1944] Ch. 362 ; [1944] 2 All E. R. 75.

" The mortgagee was not a trustee of the power of sale for the mort-
" gagor, and if he was entitled to exercise the power the court could
" not look into his motives for so doing. If he had the right to sell on
" June 1st and he then said, ' the mortgagor is a member of an old
" ' county family, and I don't wish to turn him out of his property, and
" ' will not sell it at present,' and then on July 1 he said, ' I have had
" ' a quarrel with the mortgagor and he has insulted me ; I will show
" ' him no more mercy but will sell him up at once . . . ,' if all this was
" proved, the court could not restrain the mortgagee from exercising
" his power of sale, except on the terms of payment of the mortgage
" money. . . . Of course there were some limits to the powers of the
" mortgagee. He, like a pledgee, must conduct the sale properly, and
" must sell at a fair value, and he could not sell to himself. But he
" was not bound to abstain from selling because he was not in urgent
" want of his money, or because he had a spite against the mortgagor."

Thus the mortgagee can allow the whole of the money due from the purchaser to remain on loan secured on the very property sold,[1] but he cannot sell to himself either alone or with others, nor to a trustee for himself, nor to anyone employed by him to conduct the sale. Such a sale is no sale at all, even though the price fixed is the full value of the property.[2]

(5) POWER TO APPOINT A RECEIVER.

Object of appointing receiver.

We have seen that, owing to the strict supervision that the court exercises over a mortgagee, it is undesirable for him to take possession of the land, but, on the other hand, there are cases where it is essential that he should be able to intercept the rents and the profits, and employ them in keeping down the interest. The mortgaged property may have been leased by the mortgagor to third parties under his statutory powers or the property may consist not of land but of a rent-charge, so that there is an annual sum which can be prevented from reaching the mortgagor and can be set against interest. In such cases the most effective procedure is to appoint a receiver of the income of the property.

Statutory power to appoint receiver.

The mortgage deed may contain special provisions with regard to this matter, and in some cases, as for instance where the property is already let to tenants, it is not uncommon to appoint a receiver from the moment when the mortgage is created. But apart from this a mortgagee has a statutory power of appointing a receiver in the case of every mortgage created by deed,[3] even though he has already gone into possession before the appointment.[4]

When exercisable.

Although this statutory power arises as soon as the mortgage money has become due, it cannot be exercised until one of those

---

[1] *Belton* v. *Bass, Ratcliff and Gretton, Ltd.*, [1922] 2 Ch. 449.
[2] *Farrar* v. *Farrars, Ltd.* (1888), 40 Ch. D. 395, 409, and authorities cited by LINDLEY, L.J.
[3] Law of Property Act, 1925, s. 101 (1) (iii).
[4] *Refuge Assurance Co., Ltd.* v. *Pearlberg*, [1938] Ch. 687 ; [1938] 3 All E. R. 231.

three events that qualify a mortgagee to exercise his power of sale has occurred.[1]

The advantage of such an appointment from the mortgagee's point of view is that the receiver is deemed to be the agent of the mortgagor, and that the sole responsibility for his acts and defaults falls on the latter.[2] The receiver is not entitled to grant leases without the sanction of the court,[3] but he has power to recover the income of the property by action or distress or otherwise,[4] and to give effectual receipts, and he is bound to apply any money received by him in the following order [5] :—

1. In discharge of rents, taxes, rates and outgoings.
2. In keeping down payments that rank before the mortgage.
3. In paying his own commission, fire and other insurances, and the cost of repairs.
4. In payment of the mortgage interest.
5. In discharging the principal sum if so directed by the mortgagee. A breach of this direction renders him liable to an action for an account.[6]

Any residue that remains must be paid to the mortgagor.

(6) RIGHT TO FORECLOSE THE MORTGAGE.

Method and Procedure. Foreclosure is the method by which the mortgagee acquires the land for himself freed from the mortgagor's equity of redemption. We have seen that Equity regards the mortgagor's right to redeem the property as inviolable, and that despite the lapse of the contractual right to redeem, it forbids the mortgagee to appropriate the legal fee simple without making an application to the court. Until the time fixed in the deed for repayment of the loan has arrived, no question of foreclosure can arise, but as soon as that date has passed and the contractual right to redeem has been converted into the equitable right, the mortgagee can bring an action in the Chancery Division praying that the mortgagor shall either pay what is due or be foreclosed, that is, deprived altogether of his right to redeem. *(margin: Foreclosure action.)*

If the mortgagor does not pay, the court issues what is called an order for *foreclosure nisi*, the effect of which is that the mortgagor loses his property unless he pays upon a certain date (generally six months later) specified by the Master's certificate. The judgment orders that an account shall be taken of what is due to the plaintiff for principal, interest and costs, and directs *(margin: Order nisi.)*

---

[1] Law of Property Act, 1925, s. 109 (1), *supra*, p. 601.
[2] *Ibid.*, s. 109 (2).   [3] *Re Cripps*, [1946] Ch. 265.
[4] Law of Property Act, 1925, s. 109 (3).   [5] *Ibid.*, s. 109 (8).
[6] *Leicester Permanent Building Society* v. *Butt*, [1943] Ch. 308 ; [1943] 2 All E. R. 523.

that if this amount is paid within six months, the mortgage term shall be surrendered to the defendant, but that if default in payment is made, the defendant shall stand absolutely debarred and foreclosed of and from all right, title, interest and equity of redemption in and to the mortgaged premises. The mortgagee then proves in Chambers what is due to him for principal, interest and costs, and the Master draws up a certificate of what is due and fixes a day and an hour for repayment. On that day the mortgagee attends, and waits for the mortgagor, and if the latter does not appear, an affidavit is sworn in proof of non-payment either prior to or at the appointed time, and a motion is made for *foreclosure absolute.*

Order absolute.

Effect of Foreclosure Order. The effect of the order absolute is to vest the fee simple absolute (or other the whole estate of the mortgagor) in the mortgagee, and to extinguish his mortgage term and all subsequent mortgage terms.[1]

" Redeem up, foreclose down."

It cannot, however, affect the rights of prior mortgagees, since the maxim of the law is " redeem up, foreclose down."

This means that if there are more mortgagees than one interested in the same land, an order absolute obtained by the first mortgagee forecloses all subsequent incumbrancers, while if (say) the second mortgagee obtains such an order, its effect is to foreclose the third and later mortgagees, but to leave untouched the rights of the first mortgagee. If the second mortgagee desires to realize his security and to acquire the fee simple as absolute owner, he must redeem up, that is, must pay off the first mortgagee ; if the third mortgagee has the same desire, he must pay off both the first and the second incumbrancers.

Where there are in this way several mortgagees and the first brings an action for foreclosure, not only the mortgagor, but also each of the subsequent mortgagees must be given an opportunity to redeem, and the ordinary practice is to direct in the order *nisi* that any of the subsequent incumbrancers may repay the amount due to the first man on the date appointed.[2] If subsequent mortgagees are not made parties they are not foreclosed.

Right of foreclosure barred by lapse of time.

An action for foreclosure is an action to recover land,[3] and must therefore be brought within twelve years from the date upon which the right of recovery accrues.[4] The right accrues at the date fixed for payment of the principal,[5] but there is a fresh accrual, and the twelve years begin to run again, from any

---

[1] Law of Property Act, 1925, s. 88 (2).
[2] If subsequent mortgagees request that they may be granted successive periods for repayment, an order to that effect is generally issued ; *Platt* v. *Mendel* (1884), 27 Ch. D. 246.
[3] Limitation Act, 1939, s. 18 (4).   [4] *Ibid.*, s. 4 (3).
[5] *Purnell* v. *Roche*, [1927] 2 Ch. 142 ; *Lewis* v. *Plunkett*, [1937] Ch. 306 ; [1937] 1 All E. R. 530.

payment of principal or interest by the mortgagor or from a written acknowledgment by him of the mortgagee's title.[1]

Revival of Equity of Redemption. But it must not be thought that a foreclosure absolute irrevocably passes the mortgagor's interest to the mortgagee, although it appears on the surface to do so, for there are certain circumstances in which the foreclosure may be re-opened and the equity of redemption revived. This re-opening takes place if the mortgagee, after obtaining an order absolute, proceeds to sue on the personal covenant; [2] but in addition to this case the court has a discretion to re-open a foreclosure if such relief appears in the special circumstances of the case to be due to the mortgagor. Moreover, the foreclosure may be re-opened against one who has purchased the estate from the mortgagee. It is impossible to lay down a general rule as to when the relief will be granted, for everything turns upon the particular circumstances of each case.[3] *(margin: Foreclosure may be re-opened.)*

The court has statutory jurisdiction in a foreclosure action to order a sale instead of a foreclosure on the request of the mortgagee or mortgagor, or of any person interested in the mortgage money or the equity of redemption, notwithstanding the dissent of any other person.[4] *(margin: Sale in lieu of foreclosure.)*

(7) RIGHT TO POSSESSION OF TITLE DEEDS.

A legal mortgagee takes a lease or, if he is a chargee, is in the same position as if he had done so, and the ordinary rule is that a leaseholder is not entitled to hold title deeds appertaining to the fee simple of the lessor. But, since the continued possession of the deeds by the mortgagor involves considerable risk to one who has advanced money on the security of the land, it is enacted that a first mortgagee shall have the same right to possession of documents as if his security included the fee simple.[5]

(8) RIGHT TO TACK FURTHER ADVANCES.

We shall see later that a mortgagee who makes a further loan to the mortgagor is allowed, in certain circumstances, to demand that both loans shall be paid out of the land in priority to loans made by other mortgagees, although the latter may have taken their securities before the date of such further loan.[6]

---

[1] Limitation Act, 1939, s. 23 ; *Harlock* v. *Ashberry* (1882), 19 Ch. D. 539.
[2] *Perry* v. *Barker* (1806), 13 Ves. 198.
[3] *Campbell* v. *Holyland* (1877), 7 Ch. D. 166, 172–4.
[4] Law of Property Act, 1925, s. 91 (2) ; *Silsby* v. *Holliman,* [1955] Ch. 552 ; [1955] 2 All E. R. 373.
[5] Law of Property Act, 1925, s. 85 (1).
[6] *Infra,* pp. 620; 634.

(9) RIGHT OF CONSOLIDATION.

Description of right. Consolidation is the right of a person who holds two or more mortgages granted by the same mortgagor on different properties to refuse in certain circumstances to be redeemed as to one, unless he is also redeemed as to the other or others.[1]

The mortgages in actual fact are quite separate, having been given on different properties and perhaps at different times, but none the less the mortgagee is allowed in certain cases to consolidate them and treat them as one. The right is based upon the doctrine that *he who comes to equity must do equity*; for a mortgagor who is seeking to redeem is in truth asking a favour in the sense that he is petitioning equity for the restoration of his property after the date fixed by the mortgage deed for redemption has passed, and this being so, he must himself be prepared to act equitably.

Suppose, for instance,

that A. has mortgaged Blackacre to B. for £5000 and White-acre to B. for £5000. If Blackacre diminishes, while White-acre appreciates, in value, it is obviously wrong that A. should be allowed to redeem the latter unless he is also prepared to repay the loan of £5000 on Blackacre. In such a case B. can insist that both properties shall be treated as one and redeemed together.

Extension of right to consolidate. This example illustrates the primary meaning and the simplest application of consolidation, but the doctrine has been developed further and extended to cases where the mortgages were originally made *to* different mortgagees. In such a case if the mortgages ultimately become vested in one person, that is, in one mortgagee, he possesses the right of consolidation.[2] Thus, if—

A. mortgages W. to B.,
A. mortgages X. and Y. to C.,
B. and C. transfer their mortgages to D.,

A. cannot redeem any one of the properties W., X., Y., unless, if called upon, he pays the amount due on the other two.

But consolidation extends even further than this, and applies to a case where the person who is entitled to redeem is not the original mortgagor, but a transferee of one or more of the equities. There are two different cases to be considered, since the law differs according as the equities of redemption have all become united in one person, or have become separated so

---

[1] *Jennings* v. *Jordan* (1881), 6 App. Cas. 698, 700 ; White and Tudor, *Leading Cases in Equity*, vol. ii. p. 129.
[2] *Vint* v. *Padgett* (1858), 2 De G. & J. 611 ; *Pledge* v. *White*, [1896] A. C. 187.

that the person claiming to redeem, that is, the person against whom the doctrine of consolidation is invoked, is not the owner of all the equities.

1. If a person acquires the equities upon all the properties, whether as heir, trustee in bankruptcy, purchaser or second mortgagee, the mortgages can in all cases be consolidated against him, even though the mortgage terms did not become vested in one mortgagee until after the person seeking to redeem had obtained the equities.

Application of doctrine where all equities transferred to one person.

An illustration may elucidate this statement [1] :

> 1960 A. mortgages U. and V. to B.
> 1962 A. mortgages W. to C.
> 1963 A. mortgages X., Y., and Z. to D.
> 1965 A. sells the *equities* on U., V., W., X., Y., and Z. to F.
> 1967 E. acquires all the mortgages from B., C., and D.

> Here all the mortgages are vested in one person, E. and, although he knew, when he bought out B., C., and D., that the equities were not vested in the original mortgagor, he can require F. to redeem all the properties or none.

As Lord DAVEY said in *Pledge* v. *White* [2] :—

> " It appears to me, my Lords, that an assignee of two or more
> " equities of redemption from one mortgagor stands in a widely
> " different position from the assignee of one equity only.   He
> " knows, or has the opportunity of knowing, what are the mort-
> " gages subject to which he has purchased the property and he
> " knows they may become united by transfer in one hand.   If
> " the doctrine of consolidation be once admitted, it appears to
> " me not unreasonable to hold that a person in such a position
> " occupies the place of the mortgagor towards the holders of
> " the mortgages, subject to which he has purchased. . . ."

2. Turning now to the case where the equities are separated and do not all pass to one person, it will be as well, before stating the general principle, to present an illustration showing how the purchaser of a single equity of redemption may find himself saddled with the burden of redeeming other mortgages of whose very existence he was unaware.

Application of doctrine when equities separated.

Thus :

> If at different times A. mortgages X., Y., and Z. to B., and then later transfers the fee simple of X. to C., who gives full value and knows nothing of the other two properties

---

[1] *Pledge* v. *White*, [1896] A. C. 187.
[2] [1896] A. C. 187, at p. 198.

which have been mortgaged, C., on tendering the amount of the loan due on X., may be unable under the doctrine of consolidation to redeem X. unless he also pays what is due on Y. and Z.

Where the mortgage transactions entered into by the original mortgagor are many, and where dealings have taken place both in the equities and in the mortgages, the question whether in any particular case consolidation is enforceable appears at first sight to be both difficult and complicated. But all difficulty disappears if attention is paid to the cardinal rule. This rule covers all cases of separation of equities, and clearly defines the limits within which consolidation is applicable. It may be stated in this way :

Test for
application
of doctrine.

> Consolidation is allowed only if, at the date when redemption is sought, all the mortgages, having originally been made by one mortgagor, are vested in one mortgagee and all the equities are vested in one person, or if, *after these two things have once happened, the equities of redemption have become separated.*[1]

If all the mortgages are in one hand and all the equities in another, it is clear that the right of consolidation exists against the mortgagor. It is equally clear that, *once this right has been established in respect of all the properties*, a transferee of one or more of the equities cannot stand in a better position than the mortgagor from whom he took the transfer. The principle of law involved here is that a person who buys an equity of redemption from a mortgagor takes it subject to all liabilities to which it was subject at the time of the sale ; one of these is the liability to have certain other mortgages consolidated with it, provided, however, that the consolidation was enforceable against that particular equity *at the time of the purchase.*[2] In the words of Lord SELBORNE :—

> " The purchaser of an equity of redemption must take it as it stood
> " at the time of his purchase, subject to all other equities which then
> " affected it in the hands of his vendor, of which the right of the
> " mortgagee to consolidate his charge on that particular property
> " with other charges *then* held by him on other property at the
> " same time redeemable under the same mortgagor was one."[3]

But on no principle of law would it be justifiable to hold the purchaser of an interest bound by equities which were not enforceable against that interest at the time of its sale. It follows from this that the assignee of an equity does not become subject to consolidation in respect of mortgages created *after* the

---

[1] *Pledge* v. *White*, [1896] A. C. 187, 198, *per* Lord DAVEY.
[2] *Cummins* v. *Fletcher* (1880), 14 Ch. D. 699, 712.
[3] *Jennings* v. *Jordan* (1881), 6 App. Cas. 698, 700.

sale to him, nor in respect of mortgages which, though created before that date, became united in one mortgagee afterwards.[1] Suppose, for instance, that the following transactions successively occur:

A. mortgages X. to B.,
A. mortgages Y. to B.,
A. sells the equity of redemption in Y. to C.,
A. mortgages Z. to B.[2]

When C. seeks to redeem his own property Y., he can be compelled by B. to redeem X., because, at the time when he bought his equity, the equities on X. and Y. were vested in one person, and the mortgages were vested in one person. But he cannot be compelled to redeem Z., for the mortgage on it was created only after the sale of the equity on Y. to C., so that the right to have Z. consolidated with X. and Y. obviously did not exist at that time.

The holder of an equity of redemption who is compelled under the doctrine of consolidation to redeem some other mortgage steps into the shoes of the mortgagee, and can demand payment from the mortgagor in respect of the mortgage he has had to redeem.

No right to consolidation arises if the mortgages were originally made *by* different mortgagors, even though the equities subsequently become united in one hand.[3]

Mortgages must be *by* same person.

The right of consolidation does not exist as a matter of course, but only where it is expressly reserved in the various deeds *or in one of them.* When the right is not so reserved, it is enacted that [4]:—

Consolidation under modern law.

" A mortgagor seeking to redeem any one mortgage is entitled to " do so without paying any money due under any separate mortgage " made by him or by any person through whom he claims, solely on " property other than that which he seeks to redeem."

This is a re-enactment of the Conveyancing Act, 1881, and it does not apply where all the mortgages were made before January 1st, 1882. In mortgages made before that date the right of consolidation existed as a matter of course.

(B) *POWERS AND REMEDIES OF EQUITABLE MORTGAGEES.*

The remedies of an equitable mortgagee vary according as the security is a mortgage in the strict sense, namely,

Twofold division of equitable mortgages.

---

[1] *Harter* v. *Colman* (1882), 19 Ch. D. 630.
[2] *Hughes* v. *Britannia Building Society,* [1906] 2 Ch. 607.
[3] *Sharp* v. *Rickards,* [1909] 1 Ch. 109.
[4] Law of Property Act, 1925, s. 93.

an agreement to create a legal mortgage,
a deposit of title deeds,
a mortgage of an equitable interest,[1]

or is a mere charge upon property.[2] We will take these two classes separately.

If the mortgage falls within the first class the general principle is that the remedies available to the lender correspond as nearly as possible with those available to a legal mortgagee.

Foreclosure.

Thus the primary remedy of foreclosure applies where a deposit of title deeds with the lender has been accompanied by an agreement by the borrower to give a legal mortgage if required to do so [3] ; and the same is true where there has been a deposit without any memorandum, since the law considers that the deposit is evidence of an agreement to create a legal mortgage.[4] When such an equitable mortgagee takes foreclosure proceedings to enforce his security the decree of the court declares that the deposit operated as a mortgage, that in default of payment the mortgagor is trustee of the legal estate for the mortgagee and that he must convey that estate to him.[5]

Sale.

The general rule is that foreclosure and not sale is the proper remedy for an equitable mortgagee.[6] But if the mortgage is made in a form which entitles him to require the execution of a mortgage containing a power of sale, he can exercise the statutory power of sale which is given by the Law of Property Act, 1925.[7] This statutory power, however, is exercisable only when the mortgage is made by deed, and therefore the proper course is for an equitable mortgagee not to be content with a mere deposit or with a deposit supported by a written memorandum, but to take a memorandum under seal. If this is done he can sell the property subject to the conditions specified by the Act. The memorandum should also give the mortgagee a power of attorney authorizing him, upon exercising the power of sale to convey the mortgaged property in the name of the mortgagor to the purchaser. This enables the mortgagee, though only an equitable incumbrancer, to convey the legal estate in the profits to the purchaser.[8]

Again, the statutory power of the court to order a sale instead of foreclosure, which we have already noticed, is exercisable in favour of an equitable mortgagee even though he has taken a mere deposit of deeds without a memorandum.[9]

---

[1] *Supra*, pp. 580–2.   [2] *Supra*, pp. 582–3.
[3] *York Union Banking Co.* v. *Artley* (1879), 11 Ch. D. 205.
[4] *Backhouse* v. *Charlton* (1878), 8 Ch. D. 444; *Carter* v. *Wake* (1877), 4 Ch. D. 605.
[5] *Marshall* v. *Shrewsbury* (1875), 10 Ch. App. 250, 254.
[6] *James* v. *James* (1873), L. R. 16 Eq. 153.
[7] S. 101 (1) (i), *supra*, p. 600.
[8] *Re White Rose Cottages*, [1965] Ch. 940; [1965] 1 All E. R. 11.
[9] Law of Property Act, 1925, s. 91.

If an equitable mortgage is created by deed, the statutory power of appointing a receiver is available to the mortgagee,[1] but in the absence of a deed the appointment must be made by the court.[2]

Appointment of receiver.

An equitable mortgagee is not entitled to take possession of the land unless the right to do so has been expressly reserved [3] or unless the court makes an order to that effect. Though this is the prevalent view, it has been argued with considerable force that it is justified neither on principle nor on the authorities.[4]

Possession.

An equitable mortgagee can sue the mortgagor personally for recovery of the money lent.

The second class of equitable security is the charge, which involves no transfer of a legal or equitable interest to the lender, but entitles him to have the debt discharged out of the land. His sole remedies in this respect are to have the charge satisfied by the sale of the land or by the appointment of a receiver under the direction of the court. He has no right to take possession of the land. In the words of Lord HATHERLEY :—

Equitable charge.

> " Although some of the authorities appear to conflict with each
> " other, it seems on the whole to be settled that if there is a charge
> " *simpliciter*, and not a mortgage or an agreement for a mortgage,
> " then the right of the parties having such a charge is a sale and not
> " foreclosure".[5]

From a mere equitable charge, must be distinguished the charge by way of legal mortgage introduced by the legislation of 1925, for as we have seen such a chargee has the same remedies as if he held a term of years absolute.[6]

SECTION V. PRIORITY OF MORTGAGES.[7]

Introductory Note. If two or more mortgagees have advanced money on the security of the same land and if the land is of insufficient value when realized to satisfy the claims of all, it is vital to know in what order they are entitled to be paid out of the land. The mortgagor has, let us say, granted separate and successive mortgages on Blackacre to A., B., C. and D. Owing to unforeseen circumstances Blackacre has depreciated in value and its sale will produce sufficient money to repay only one or

Rules for order of payment to mortgagees.

---

[1] Law of Property Act, 1925, s. 101 (1) (iii) ; *supra*, p. 604.
[2] *Meaden* v. *Sealey* (1849), 6 Hare, 620.
[3] *Finck* v. *Tranter*, [1905] 1 K. B. 427, 429 ; *Barclays Bank, Ltd.* v. *Bird*, [1954] Ch. 284, at p. 280 ; [1954] 1 All E. R. 449, at p. 452.
[4] 71 *L. Q. R.*, pp. 204–22 (H. W. R. Wade).
[5] *Tennant* v. *Trenchard* (1869), L. R. 4 Ch. 537, 542 ; *Re Owen*, [1894] 3 Ch. 220.
[6] *Supra*, p. 578.
[7] For a closely reasoned study of this important topic see an article by R. E. Megarry, *Cambridge Law Journal*, 1940, pp. 243–260.

perhaps two of the mortgagees the amount of their advances. This does not mean that mortgagees who fail to get satisfaction out of the land are remediless, for they can of course sue the mortgagor on his personal covenant, but since his other property may be of little value it will be their object to proceed against the land if the law allows them to do so. A knowledge of the former rules that governed this matter, although they were substantially affected by the legislation of 1925, is still essential to an understanding of the modern law on this subject.

(A) PRIORITY OF MORTGAGES UNDER THE OLD LAW.

(1) The Priority of the Legal Mortgagee of Land.

Where equities are equal the law prevails.

To understand the order in which mortgages ranked for repayment out of the land before 1926 we must recall that under the practice then prevailing it was usual in the case of a mortgage of the fee simple to convey the legal estate in fee simple to the mortgagee. There might be several mortgages of Blackacre, but there could be only one *legal* mortgage, and all the others, whether created before or after the legal mortgage, were necessarily equitable in nature.

The fundamental rule before 1926, based upon the maxim " where the equities are equal the law prevails," was that the mortgagee who held the legal estate ranked, for the purpose of obtaining satisfaction out of the land, before all other mortgagees of whose securities he had no notice at the time when he made his advance.[1] Equity respected the legal title, and it was a rule without exception that a court of equity took away from a purchaser for value without notice nothing that he had honestly acquired.[2] Lord Hardwicke said :—

> " As courts of equity break in upon the common law where " necessity and conscience require it, still they allow superior force " and strength to a legal title to estates ; and therefore where there " is a legal title and equity on one side, this court never thought fit " that by reason of a prior equity against a man who had a legal title " that man should be hurt, and this by reason of that force this " court necessarily and rightly allows to the common law and to " legal titles."[3]

If therefore a mortgagor granted an equitable mortgage to A and later conveyed the legal estate to B by way of mortgage, the latter had the best right to the land provided that, when he made his own advance, he had no notice of the earlier mortgage to A.

---

[1] *Plumb* v. *Fluitt* (1791), 2 Anst. 432.
[2] *Heath* v. *Crealock* (1874), 10 Ch. App. 22, 33.
[3] *Wortley* v. *Birkhead* (1754), 2 Ves. Sen. 571, 573.

The onus lay on him to prove this affirmatively.[1] B had an even
stronger case against mortgagees who obtained their securities
at a date *later* than his own, for not only did he alone hold the
legal title, but having acquired it first in order of time he could
invoke the maxim *qui prior est tempore potior est jure.*

This principle, however, applied only where the equities were
equal, *i.e.* where the legal mortgagee had as good a moral right as
the equitable mortgagees, and in the following cases he was displaced in favour of equitable mortgagees :—

(*a*) **Where the Legal Mortgagee had notice of an**
Earlier Mortgage. If, at the time when he advanced his
money, the legal mortgagee had actual or constructive notice
of an earlier incumbrance, he was postponed to the earlier
incumbrancer. A legal mortgagee who failed to investigate
his mortgagor's title according to the usual practice or who
abstained from investigation altogether, was affected with
notice of, and therefore postponed to, any earlier mortgage
that he would have discovered had he followed the customary
practice.[2]

Cases where equities not equal.

(*b*) **Where the Legal Mortgagee was negligent with**
regard to the Title Deeds. The obvious duty of a person
who acquires a legal estate is to obtain and to keep possession
of the title deeds, or, if for some reason this is impossible, to
make inquiries for them. Title deeds are the symbol of
ownership, and if they are not produced by a mortgagor the
suspicion naturally arises that they have been utilized by him
in order to vest some right in a third person, and that he is
deliberately concealing this transaction from the mortgagee.

There are two indiscretions in this connection that a
mortgagee may commit, namely, failure to obtain the deeds
at the time of the transaction, and failure to retain deeds of
which he has once had possession.

It was well established before 1926 that a legal mortgagee
who made no inquiries whatever for the deeds must be
postponed to a prior equitable incumbrancer who had
already secured them, and even to a later innocent incumbrancer who was more diligent in getting them into his
custody.[3] On the other hand, if he made inquiry and yet
failed to obtain them, it depended upon the circumstances
whether he was postponed to an earlier equitable incumbrancer
in whose possession they were. Postponement was not an
automatic result of failure to obtain possession, for it was
always held that in addition there must have been some

(i) Postpone-
ment owing
to failure to
obtain
deeds.

---

[1] *A.-G.* v. *Biphosphated Guano Co.* (1879), 11 Ch. D. 327.
[2] *Berwick & Co.* v. *Price,* [1905] 1 Ch. 632.
[3] *Walker* v. *Linom,* [1907] 2 Ch. 104.

degree of negligence. The cases show a growing severity against the legal mortgagee. At first it was laid down that he must not be postponed unless he had been guilty of fraud in the transaction under which he acquired the legal estate, or unless he had shown such wilful negligence as to indicate complicity in the fraud.[1] But a new rule more favourable to an earlier equitable mortgagee was pronounced by the Court of Appeal in 1899 in the case of *Oliver v. Hinton.*[2] This may be stated in the words of LINDLEY, L.J. :

Degree of negligence necessary to postpone.

> " To deprive a purchaser for value [3] without notice of a " prior incumbrance of the protection of the legal estate it is " not, in my opinion, essential that he should have been guilty " of fraud ; it is sufficient that he has been guilty of such gross " negligence as would render it unjust to deprive the prior " incumbrancer of his priority."

The case related to a purchaser of a legal estate, but the result would have been the same had the person who acquired the legal estate been a mortgagee. The facts were as follows :

> A., the owner of the legal estate, deposited the title deeds with X. as security for advances to the value of £400 made by the latter. Some two years later A. conveyed the legal estate to the purchaser, P., in consideration of £320. P. inquired about the deeds, but was told that they could not be delivered as they related also to some other property. This answer was accepted, and A. was not even asked to produce the deeds for inspection. It was held that P., though entirely innocent of fraud or of any complicity in fraud, must be postponed to X.

Epithets such as " gross " are unreliable guides, and the rule as stated by the Court of Appeal left open in each case the question whether the requisite degree of negligence had been shown, but the expression " gross negligence " was described in a later case as meaning something more than mere carelessness. EVE, J., said [4] :—

> " It must at least be carelessness of so aggravated a nature " as to amount to the neglect of precautions which the ordinary " reasonable man would have observed, and to indicate an " attitude of mental indifference to obvious risks."

Postponement to earlier incumbrancers.

If, therefore, a mortgagee had inquired for the title deeds and had been given a reasonable excuse for their non-delivery,

---

[1] *Hunt v. Elmes* (1860), 2 De F. & J. 578 ; *Ratcliffe v. Barnard* (1870), L. R. 6 Ch. 652 ; (1871), 6 Ch. App. 652 ; see *Hudston v. Viney*, [1921] 1 Ch. 98, 103–4 ; *Northern Counties of England Fire Insurance Co. v. Whipp* (1884), 26 Ch. D. 482.
[2] [1899] 2 Ch. 264.
[3] This includes a mortgagee.
[4] *Hudston v. Viney*, [1921] 1 Ch. 98, 104.

he would not be postponed to an earlier equitable mortgagee. An extreme case is, perhaps, *Hewitt* v. *Loosemore*,[1] where the defendant, who had taken a legal mortgage of a leasehold interest from a solicitor by way of assignment, failed to obtain possession of the lease, which, as a matter of fact, had already been deposited with the plaintiff. Part of the answer made by the defendant to the bill which the plaintiff brought against him was as follows :—

> " The defendant . . . was a farmer and unacquainted with
> " legal forms ; but upon the said indenture of assignment
> " being handed to him as aforesaid, he inquired of (the mort-
> " gagor) whether the lease of the premises ought not to be
> " delivered to him as well ; when (the mortgagor) replied that
> " it should, but that, as he was rather busy then, he would look
> " for it and give it to the defendant when he next came to
> " market."

It was held that in the circumstances the plaintiff had failed to make out a sufficient case for postponing the defendant.

Likewise failure to obtain the deeds might entail post- **Postpone-** ponement of a legal mortgagee to a *later* equitable incum- **ment to later** brancer. Again, however, nothing short of gross negligence **incum-** was sufficient to produce this result. Thus in *Grierson* v. **brancers.** *National Provincial Bank of England Ltd.*[2] :

> A mortgagor, having already deposited the deeds with a
> bank as security for a loan, executed a legal mortgage in favour
> of the plaintiff. The plaintiff had actual notice of this earlier
> equitable mortgage, but he neither informed the bank of his
> legal mortgage, nor instructed them to deliver the deeds
> to him should the mortgagor repay their loan. The mort-
> gagor later paid off the bank, obtained the deeds and deposited
> them with the defendant as security for an advance. The
> defendant was ignorant of the plaintiff's legal mortgage.

It was held that the plaintiff had not been sufficiently **(ii) Post-** negligent to justify his postponement to the defendant. **ponement**

It was also the case under the old law that the conduct of **due to** the legal mortgagee in dealing with the title deeds *after* he had **subsequent** obtained them might be such as to justify his postponement **negligence.** to subsequent equitable mortgagees.

In the first place the principle of *Oliver* v. *Hinton* applied, and any conduct on the part of the legal mortgagee in relation to the deeds which would have made it inequitable for him to claim priority over an earlier equitable mortgagee was sufficient to postpone him to a subsequent mortgage the creation of which was due entirely to his own conduct.[3]

---

[1] (1851), 9 Hare, 449. See also *Agra Bank* v. *Barry* (1874), L. R. 7 H. L. 135.

[2] [1913] 2 Ch. 18.

[3] *Walker* v. *Linom*, [1907] 2 Ch. 104, 114 ; *Northern Counties of England Fire Insurance Co.* v. *Whipp* (1884), 26 Ch. D. 482. *Cf. In Re King's Settlement*, [1931] 2 Ch. 294.

x*

There need not have been fraudulent conduct, but there must have been gross negligence. Thus in a leading case [1] the priority of the legal mortgagee was not displaced where :

> A company took a legal mortgage from its manager, and the manager, having stolen the deeds from a safe to which he had access, used them to create another mortgage in favour of an innocent person.

The following remarks were passed by the court upon the arguments that had been advanced in favour of postponement :

> " The case was argued as if the legal owner of land owed a
> " duty to all other of Her Majesty's subjects to keep his title
> " deeds secure ; as if title deeds were in the eye of the law
> " analogous to fierce dogs or destructive elements, where
> " from the nature of things the courts have implied a general
> " duty of safe custody." [2]

In the second place a legal mortgagee was postponed if he constituted the mortgagor his agent with authority to raise more money on the security of the land. This postponement occurred for instance where the mortgagor, having been entrusted with the deeds for the purpose of obtaining a further loan of a given amount, procured one of a greater amount without disclosing to the lender the existence of the first mortgage. In such a case the legal mortgagee was postponed on the ground that, having enabled the mortgagor to represent himself as unincumbered owner, he was estopped from asserting that the actual authority had been exceeded. [3]

(2) PRIORITY AS BETWEEN EQUITABLE MORTGAGEES OF LAND.

Qui prior est tempore potior est jure.

Where the legal estate was outstanding and a conflict arose between incumbrancers who all held equitable mortgages, the rule was that the several mortgagees must be paid according to their priority of time, *qui prior est tempore potior est jure.* [4]

If, therefore, a mortgagor subjected his land to equitable charges first in favour of A. and then in favour of B., or if, after granting a legal mortgage to X., he made subsequent mortgages first to A. and then to B., A. had the prior right as against B. to receive payment out of the land. He had a better and superior equity because it was an earlier equity. This rule was based upon the principle that :

---

[1] *Northern Counties, etc.* v. *Whipp, supra.*
[2] *Ibid.*, at p. 493.
[3] *Perry Herrick* v. *Attwood* (1857), 2 De G. & J. 21 ; *Northern Counties of England Fire Insurance Co.* v. *Whipp* (1884), 26 Ch. D. 482, 493 ; *Brocklesby* v. *Temperance, etc., Society,* [1895] A. C. 173.
[4] *Brace* v. *Duchess of Marlborough* (1728), 2 P. Wms. 491, 495 ; *Willoughby* v. *Willoughby* (1756), 1 Term Rep. 773.

"An owner of property dealing honestly with it cannot confer upon
"another a greater interest in that property than he himself has."[1]

All that the mortgagor had to dispose of when he had once
made a legal mortgage was the equitable interest, and it had long
been the rule that:

> "Every conveyance of an equitable interest is an innocent con-
> "veyance, that is to say, the grant of a person entitled merely in
> "equity passes only that which he is justly entitled to, and no
> "more."[2]

The rule that priority of time gave the better right to payment
might, however, be excluded in two cases:

First, where the equities were in other respects not equal.

Secondly, where the doctrine of tacking operated.

Priority of time not always decisive.

Equities not equal. In a contest between equitable claimants, the court had to be satisfied that the party with the earlier
equity had acted in such a way as to justify his retention of priority
over the later incumbrancer.[3] Thus, he lost the protection that
was normally due to him if his negligent failure to obtain or to retain the title deeds had misled the later mortgagee into believing
that no earlier equity existed. The question as to what degree of
negligence sufficed to produce this result scarcely admits of a dog-
matic answer, for the judges expressed varying opinions, and one
view was that the priority of an equitable mortgage was more easily
displaced than that of a legal mortgage.[4] No decision has been
found, however, in which the negligence held sufficient to postpone
an equitable mortgagee would not also have defeated a legal mortgagee.[5] In the case before 1926 of a legal mortgage to A., followed
by equitable mortgages to B. and C., the question could arise only
exceptionally, since A. would normally hold the deeds, but it would
arise in an acute form if the only transactions effected by the
mortgagor were of an equitable nature. In this connection two
rules at least were definitely established:

*Postpone-
ment due to
negligence.*

First, if an incumbrancer was entitled to have the deeds as
part of his security but did not insist upon his right, he
was postponed to a later equitable incumbrancer who
obtained them without notice of the earlier equity.
This occurred in *Farrand* v. *Yorkshire Banking Co.*,[6]
where the facts were these:

*Failure to
obtain deeds.*

> The mortgagor agreed to deposit the deeds relating to the
> mortgaged property with A., but the deposit was never made.

---

[1] *West* v. *Williams*, [1899] 1 Ch. 132, at 143; LINDLEY, M.R.

[2] *Cory* v. *Eyre* (1863), 1 De G. J. & Sm. 149, 167, *per* TURNER, L.J.

[3] *National Provincial Bank of England* v. *Jackson* (1886), 33 Ch. D. 1,
at p. 13, *per* COTTON, L.J.

[4] *Taylor* v. *Russell*, [1891] 1 Ch. 1, at p. 17; s.c., [1892] A. C. 244, at
p. 262.

[5] See the discussion in Waldock, *The Law of Mortgages* (2nd Edn.), pp. 397–8.

[6] (1888), 40 Ch. D. 182.

A year later he handed the deeds to a bank with which he had made a similar agreement.

It was held that A. must be postponed, for it was entirely due to his inactivity that the bank had been defrauded into advancing a second loan.

Failure to retain deeds.

Secondly, if an equitable incumbrancer obtained the deeds but later delivered them to the mortgagor, he was postponed to a later lender to whom they had been delivered as security.[1]

> " It is an elementary principle," said KINDERSLEY, V.-C.,
> " that a party coming into equity in such a case is bound to
> " show that he has not been guilty of such a degree of
> " neglect as to enable another party so to deal with that
> " which was the plaintiff's right, as to induce an innocent
> " party to assume that he was dealing with his own." [2]

Doctrine of tacking.

Tacking. The general rule that equitable mortgagees ranked for payment according to the dates at which they took their mortgages was also liable to be displaced by the operation of the doctrine of tacking, or " the creditor's *tabula in naufragio*," as it has been called.[3] This doctrine, which is founded on technical and justly suspected reasoning, is an example of the superiority attached by courts of law and of equity to the legal estate. Equitable owners who were equally meritorious in regard to honesty of dealing might compete for the legal estate, and the one who succeeded in obtaining it won the right to rank before an earlier equitable mortgagee despite the maxim *qui prior est tempore potior est jure.* The reason was that, having obtained the legal estate, he could take advantage of that other and more potent maxim " where the equities are equal the law prevails." [4]

There were two distinct branches of tacking under the old law, and we must consider these separately.

(i) Where equitable mortgagee acquired the legal estate.

1. The first form consisted of joining an equitable mortgage to the legal mortgage in order to squeeze out and gain priority over an intermediate mortgage. If a legal mortgage to A. was followed by equitable mortgages first to B. and secondly to C., then C. would gain priority of payment over B. if he paid off A. and took a conveyance of his legal estate. C. now had the prior right to recover from the land not only the amount which A. had advanced on the first mortgage, but also the amount which C. himself had advanced to the mortgagor. But he could not tack his own advance to the legal estate and squeeze out B. unless he had an equal equity with B.; and the equities were not equal unless, *at the time when*

---

[1] *Waldron* v. *Sloper* (1852), 1 Drew. 193.   [2] *Ibid.,* at p. 200.
[3] *Brace* v. *Duchess of Marlborough* (1728), 2 P. Wms. 491.
[4] *Bailey* v. *Barnes,* [1894] 1 Ch. 25, 36.

he made his advance, he was without notice that B. had made an earlier advance.

2. The second form of tacking was available only to a legal mortgagee who had made a further advance. It was not available to equitable mortgagees before 1926. If a legal mortgagee, subsequently to his original loan, made a further advance to the mortgagor without *at that time* having notice of equitable mortgages created after the legal mortgage, he could, by virtue of his ownership of the legal estate, tack the second to the first advance and recover the whole amount due to him in priority to all other incumbrancers.[1]

(ii) Where the legal mortgagee made a further advance.

If, for instance :

> The mortgagor made a legal mortgage to A. for £2000, a second mortgage to B., a third mortgage to C., and then borrowed a further £500 from A., A. was entitled to be paid £2500 out of the land before B. and C. received anything.

But this right did not avail the legal mortgagee if, at the time when he made his further advance, he knew that other persons had already lent money on the security of the land. Thus in *Freeman* v. *Laing* [2] :

Notice excluded tacking.

> Three trustees advanced money jointly on a legal mortgage of land and subsequently made a further advance. At the time of this second advance one alone of the trustees had notice of an intermediate mortgage. It was held that the successors in title of the trustees could not tack the second loan to the first, for since each of them was individually entitled to the entire security, notice to one was notice to all.

An important application of this rule, that notice excluded the right to tack, occurred where land was mortgaged by way of security not only for the original loan, but also for such future advances as might be made. A mortgagee likes to know that he can have recourse to the land in respect of any money he may advance later, and when such further loans are contemplated it has always been customary to provide expressly in the deed that they, equally with the original loan, shall be secured by the land. But it was laid down in *Hopkinson* v. *Rolt* [3] that notwithstanding such an express provision the right to tack was excluded by notice of other incumbrances. This principle was carried further by the case of *West* v. *Williams* [4] and made applicable where the legal mortgagee had not (as in *Hopkinson* v. *Rolt*) taken security merely for such further advances as he might *voluntarily* make, but had entered into a binding

---

[1] *Brace* v. *Duchess of Marlborough* (1728), 2 P. Wms. 491.
[2] [1899] 2 Ch. 355.   [3] (1861), 9 H. L. C. 514.
[4] [1899] 1 Ch. 132.

covenant to make further advances upon the security of the land, if called upon to do so. The fact that he was under a contractual obligation to increase his original loan did not entitle him to priority in respect of a further advance made with notice of a later incumbrance.

The doctrine of tacking was abolished in 1874 by the Vendor and Purchaser Act, but as this prejudiced the ability of mortgagors to obtain further advances from first mortgagees, it was restored by the Land Transfer Act of 1875.

(3) PRIORITY BETWEEN ASSIGNEES AND MORTGAGEES OF AN EQUITABLE INTEREST IN PURE PERSONALTY.

The Rule in *Dearle* v. *Hall.*

Priority between mortgagees of pure personalty has been governed since 1823 by the rule in *Dearle* v. *Hall.*[1] This rule, which is of greater importance now than formerly because of its extension by the Law of Property Act, 1925, applied whenever successive mortgages or assignments were made of an equitable interest in pure personalty, as distinct from an interest, whether legal or equitable, in freeholds or leaseholds. To make the rule applicable, the mortgagor or assignor must have had an equitable interest in a debt or fund and he must have made two or more successive assignments of that subject matter in favour of different persons.[2] It is chiefly remarkable as being a departure from the fundamental principle that equities are entitled to rank according to the order of time in which they have been created.

The rule was (and is) that a mortgagee or assignee of an equitable interest in personalty, who at the time of his advance or purchase has no notice of an earlier mortgage or assignment, and who *gives notice* of the transaction to the legal owner of the personalty (*i.e.* in most cases to the trustees), gains priority over an earlier mortgagee or assignee who has failed to give earlier notice. The head-note to the report of *Dearle* v. *Hall* makes the position clear :

> " A person having a beneficial interest in a sum of money
> " invested in the names of trustees, assigns it for valuable con-
> " sideration to A., but no notice of the assignment is given to the
> " trustees ; afterwards the same person proposes to sell his interest
> " to B., and B., having made inquiry of the trustees as to the nature
> " of the vendor's title and the amount of his interest, and receiving
> " no intimation of the existence of any prior incumbrance, completes
> " the purchase and gives the trustees notice : B. has a better equity
> " than A. to the possession of the fund, and the assignment to B.,
> " though posterior in date, is to be preferred to the assignment to A."

Thus in equitable mortgages of personalty notice to the trustees supplants order of time as the determining factor in the question of priorities.

---

[1] (1823), 3 Russ. 1.
[2] *Lyle (B.S.) Ltd.* v. *Rosher*, [1958] 3 All E. R. 597 at pp. 603, 605; [1959] 1 W. L. R. 8, at pp. 16, 19.

Although the principle upon which *Dearle* v. *Hall* was decided Principle
of the rule. has been obscured by later cases, it would appear to be simply this, that in order to perfect his title a mortgagee of equitable personalty must do that which in equity is the nearest approach to the delivery of a personal chattel.[1] PLUMER, M.R., explained this as follows:—

> "They say that they were not bound to give notice to the
> "trustees, for the notice does not form part of the necessary con-
> "veyance of an equitable interest. I admit that if you mean to rely
> "on a contract with an individual, you do not need to give notice ;
> "from the moment of the contract, he with whom you are dealing is
> "personally bound. But if you mean to go further and to make
> "your right attach upon the thing which is the subject of the con-
> "tract, it is necessary to give notice ; and unless notice is given you
> "do not do that which is essential in all cases of transfer of personal
> "property. The Law of England has always been that personal
> "property passes by delivery of possession ; and it is possession
> "which determines the apparent ownership. If therefore an
> "individual who, in the way of purchase or mortgage, contracts
> "with another for the transfer of his interest, does not divest the
> "vendor or mortgagor of his possession, but permits him to remain
> "the ostensible owner as before, he must take the consequences
> "which may ensue from such a mode of dealing."

It is in fact the duty of an assignee or mortgagee to affect the Rule ex-
tended by
judicial in-
terpretation. conscience of the trustees, for by doing so he acquires a better equity than a prior mortgagee who has failed to act likewise, and where one of two innocent parties must suffer through the fraud of the mortgagor, it certainly should not be the one who has done all in his power to prevent any fraudulent dealing. But this consideration was lost sight of in later years, and instead of the principle being that priority should depend upon the diligence of the claimants in perfecting their title, it was gradually made dependent upon the bare fact of notice, it being held that it was immaterial whether notice was given with the deliberate intention of completing the title or whether it was purely informal or even accidental.[2] The following will serve to illustrate this fact and, at the same time, to state the main rules that have grown up in the application of *Dearle* v. *Hall.*

(*a*) **The Notice may be informal.** It is not neces- Nature of
the notice. sary, in order to gain priority, that a mortgagee should give express notice to the trustees with the intention of doing all that is possible to perfect his title. In fact it is not necessary that *he* should give notice at all, provided that the trustees have notice. It is enough if he can prove that the mind of the trustee has in some way been brought to an intelligent appre- hension of the existence of the incumbrance, so that a reason-

---

[1] *Meux* v. *Bell* (1841), Hare, 73, 85 ; *Foster* v. *Cockerell* (1835), 3 Cl. & Fin. 456, 476 ; but see Lord MACNAGHTEN, *Ward* v. *Duncombe*, [1893] A. C. 369. 392-3.
[2] See an article in 11 *L. Q. R.* (1895), p. 337.

able man or an ordinary man of business would regulate his conduct by that knowledge in the execution of the trust.[1] Thus, notice which a trustee obtained from reading a newspaper has been held to be sufficient,[2] and in a later case it was held that where a trustee *before* his appointment acquired knowledge of an incumbrance on the trust estate in such a way that when appointed he would normally act on the information, the priority thereby attached to the incumbrance was not displaced by an express formal notice given after his appointment by another incumbrancer.[3]

(b) Effect of notice not given to *all* the Trustees. The course which a diligent mortgagee should pursue is to give notice to each trustee, for a failure to do so may cause his postponement to a later mortgagee who has been more careful. The two principles relevant to the situation are, first, that a notice given to one alone of several trustees is effective against later mortgages created while that one trustee remains in office, but is ineffective against mortgages created after he vacates office [4] ; secondly, that a notice to all existing trustees remains effective even after they have vacated office. The result may be appreciated from three examples.

1. A., B. and C. are the trustees. Mortgagee, X., notifies A. only. A later mortgagee, Y. notifies A., B. and C. A. dies. X. ranks before Y., for when Y. took his mortgage X.'s notice to A. was still effective.[5]
2. A., B. and C. are the trustees. Mortgagee X. notifies A. only. A. dies. A later mortgagee, Y., notifies B. and C. Y. ranks before X., since the effectiveness of X.'s notice ceased with the death of the one person to whom he gave it.[6]
3. A., B. and C. are the trustees. Mortgagee, X., notifies A., B. and C. A., B. and C. retire in favour of D., E. and F., who are not informed of X.'s mortgage. A later mortgagee, Y., notifies D., E. and F. X. ranks before Y.[7]

Limits of rule in *Dearle* v. *Hall.*

We must finally observe that before 1926 the rule in *Dearle* v. *Hall* was restricted to the assignment of choses in action, of which an equitable interest in pure personalty is an example, and to assignments of such interests in real estate as could reach the hands of the assignor only in the shape of money, as for instance a beneficial interest given to him by a trust for sale.[8] The rule did not apply to mortgages or assignments of equitable

---

[1] *Lloyd* v. *Banks* (1868), L. R. 3 Ch. 488, 490 ; Lord CAIRNS.
[2] *Lloyd* v. *Banks, supra.*
[3] *Ipswich Permanent Money Club, Ltd.* v. *Arthy*, [1920] 2 Ch. 257.
[4] *Smith* v. *Smith* (1833), 2 Cr. & M. 231.
[5] *Ward* v. *Duncombe*, [1893] A. C. 369.
[6] *Timson* v. *Ramsbottom* (1837), 2 Keen, 35 ; *Re Phillip's Trusts*, [1903] 1 Ch. 183.
[7] *Re Wasdale, Britten* v. *Partridge*, [1899] 1 Ch. 163.
[8] *Re Wasdale, Britten* v. *Partridge, supra* ; *Ward* v. *Duncombe, supra.*

interests in *land*, whether freehold or leasehold. Thus in a case where

> a testator, having bequeathed a leasehold interest to trustees, charged it with the payment of an annuity of £45 to his daughter, and the daughter mortgaged the annuity first to A. and then to B., it was held that A. had the prior claim against the land, although B. alone had given notice to the trustees.[1]

Having thus reviewed the rules which obtained before the legislation of 1925, we are in a position to examine the existing law governing the priorities between mortgages in general.

(B) PRIORITY OF MORTGAGES UNDER THE MODERN LAW.

Introductory Note. The Law of Property Act, 1925, and the Land Charges Act of the same year introduced a new system for the determination of priorities. The apparent design of this is to fix the priority of a mortgage according to the time of its creation, provided that the mortgagee has taken steps to render the completion of the transaction easily ascertainable by persons who later have dealings with the mortgagor.[2] There are three ways of doing this which vary with the circumstances.

(margin: General design of the 1925 legislation concerning priority.)

First, by obtaining possession of the title deeds. This will put a later mortgagee upon enquiry and will normally affect him with notice of the earlier encumbrance.

Secondly, if possession of the deeds is unobtainable and if the property given as security is a *legal* estate, by recording the mortgage, whether legal or equitable, in a public register.

Thirdly, if the property given as security is an *equitable* interest in land or pure personalty by notifying the mortgage to the owner of the legal interest, thereby putting it on record.

Such is the design in outline, but it is not fully worked out by the Acts and we shall see that certain doubts and complexities remain.

The modern rules vary not with the nature of the mortgage as under the old law, but with the nature of the mortgaged property, and we must therefore consider

(margin: Scheme of present account.)

first, legal and equitable mortgages of a *legal estate* ; and

secondly, mortgages of an *equitable interest*, whether in land or in personalty.

---

[1] *Wiltshire* v. *Rabbits* (1844), 14 Sim. 76.
[2] Waldock, *op. cit.*, pp. 409–10.

(1) PRIORITY AS BETWEEN LEGAL AND EQUITABLE MORTGAGEES OF A LEGAL ESTATE.

Why the law was changed by legislation.

We have seen that under the old law a legal mortgagee who had not been guilty of gross negligence in respect of the title deeds enjoyed priority over the other mortgagees (necessarily equitable) of the same land of which he had no notice. It is obvious that the introduction of the new method of creating mortgages, under which there may be several *legal* mortgages and not one only as before 1926, precluded the retention of the old rule that the legal estate as such gave priority. Some substitute had to be found. The other rule of the old law, that equitable mortgages ranked according to the order of their creation, could scarcely be made universally applicable, since it would render it difficult for a mortgagee to ascertain by inquiry the true state of the mortgagor's commitments. The Acts of 1925, therefore, attempted to introduce a new scheme, the *motif* of which apparently was that priorities should depend upon the order of registration, though whether in the actual result registration is as important as it was intended to be is, perhaps, a little doubtful.

Relevant statutory provisions.

It is necessary to set out the relevant statutory provisions in order that the matter may be viewed in the right perspective.

The Law of Property Act, 1925, in section 97, provides as follows :

> " Every mortgage affecting a legal estate in land made after the
> " commencement of this Act, whether legal or equitable (not being
> " a mortgage protected by the deposit of documents relating to the
> " legal estate affected) shall rank according to its date of registration
> " as a land charge pursuant to the Land Charges Act, 1925."

Registration of mortgages constitutes notice.

The same statute, in section 198 (1), provides that registration shall constitute notice :

> " The registration of any instrument or matter under the pro-
> " visions of the Land Charges Act, 1925, in any register kept at the
> " Land Registry or elsewhere, shall be deemed to constitute actual
> " notice of such instrument or matter and of the fact of such
> " registration, to all persons and for all purposes connected with
> " the land affected, as from the date of registration or other pre-
> " scribed date and so long as the registration continues in force."

What mortgages are registrable.

The Land Charges Act contains two relevant sections. Section 10 [1] specifies the two kinds of mortgages that may be registered, namely :

(a) Puisne mortgage.

> (a) " Puisne mortgages," *i.e.* any *legal* mortgage except one that is
> protected by a deposit of documents relating to the legal estate
> affected.

(b) General equitable charge.

> (b) " General equitable charges," *i.e.* any charge in the nature of a
> mortgage which is not secured by a deposit of documents

---

[1] S. 10 (1), Class C (i), (iii).

relating to the legal estate affected, and does not arise, or affect an interest arising, under a trust for sale or a settlement.

The Act finally states what the effect shall be of a failure to register.   Section 13 enacts that :

Effect of non-regis-tration.

> A puisne mortgage or a general equitable charge arising or created after 1925 shall be void against a purchaser of the land charged therewith, or of any interest in such land, unless it is registered before the *completion* of the purchase.
> " Purchaser " includes a mortgagee.

A mortgagee, X., does not pay the amount of the loan until the transaction has been completed by the execution of the deed. There is, therefore, a danger that after he has searched the register another mortgage of the same land may have been registered in favour of Y., the effect of which will be to render X.'s mortgage at the moment of its completion void against Y.   X. is, therefore, allowed to protect himself by registering a *priority notice*, giving notice of his contemplated mortgage.[1]

Priority notice.

One outstanding feature, then, of this legislation is that no mortgage, legal or equitable, under which the mortgagee obtains the title deeds, is capable of registration.   The principal reason for this exclusion is to avoid the inconvenience that would arise if the efficacy of temporary advances that are so frequently made against a deposit of deeds were to be affected by a failure to register.   Section 10, however, provides in the next sub-section that an estate contract shall be registrable.   An estate contract is a contract by an estate owner to create a legal estate.   The normal example is a contract for the sale of a legal fee simple or for the grant of a term of years absolute, but it also includes an agreement to create a legal mortgage, *i.e.* to grant a mortgage term.   Further, it would seem to include the equitable mortgage that arises from a deposit of title deeds, for as we have already seen the deposit constitutes an implicit agreement to create a legal mortgage. It has therefore been suggested that an express agreement, accompanied by the title deeds, to create a legal mortgage, and a deposit of title deeds by way of security, are registrable as estate contracts, in spite of the fact that because accompanied by the deeds they are excluded from registration by the sub-section which deals specifically with mortgages.[2]   It is submitted, how-ever, that the correctness of this view is at least doubtful.   If the sub-section which explicitly defines what mortgages shall be registrable deliberately excludes those that are accompanied by a deposit of documents, it seems inconsistent to permit their registration in their other capacity as estate contracts.   The

A mortgage accompanied by the deeds is not registrable.

[1] Law of Property (Amendment) Act, 1926, s. 4 ; for details, see *infra*, p. 671.
[2] *Cambridge Law Journal*, 1940, pp. 250–1 ; Williams, *Contract of Sale of Land*, p. 247 ; Wolstenholme and Cherry's *Conveyancing Statutes*, vol. ii. p. 840.

result of doing so would be to render void against a subsequent incumbrancer an unregistered mortgage to which the sub-section concerned with mortgages denies the possibility of registration. Moreover, to put this construction upon the statute would prejudice the commercial practice by which deeds are deposited with bankers to secure a temporary loan, for the result of invalidating against later lenders an arrangement that is often only transient would be to discourage a convenient business transaction. The question can scarcely be answered with assurance until it has come before the courts, and meanwhile the following account is based on the assumption that a mortgage accompanied by a deposit of the deeds is not registrable.

Priorities where no mortgagee obtains the deed. The question of priorities seems comparatively simple to determine against the legislative background if we confine ourselves to a series of mortgage transactions *none of which is accompanied by a delivery of the title deeds*. It depends upon a combination of section 97 of the Law of Property Act and section 13 of the Land Charges Act, but it would appear that the latter is the dominating enactment. The decisive factor, in other words, is that a registrable mortgage is void against a later mortgage unless it is registered before completion of the latter transaction.[1] Suppose that:

> A. takes a mortgage without the title deeds on May 1st.
> B. takes a mortgage without the title deeds on May 10th.
> A. registers on May 11th.
> B. registers on May 20th.
> C. takes a mortgage without the deeds on May 30th and registers.

The order in which the parties rank, whether their mortgages are legal or equitable, is B.–A.–C., for A.'s mortgage, though created before B.'s was created and registered before B.'s was registered, was nevertheless not registered upon completion of the second mortgage. It is therefore void under section 13 as against B. It is not of course void as against C., since its registration was effected before completion of C.'s mortgage on May 30th. Moreover, by virtue of section 198 (1) of the Law of Property Act, C. has, but B. has not, statutory notice of A.'s mortgage.

Priority of registration not in itself sufficient. It is arguable that in accordance with section 97 of the Law of Property Act A. should rank before B. since he was the first to register, but it is difficult to agree that a void charge can be revivified and given precedence over the very charge in relation to which its invalidity has been declared by statute. There can be no renascence of what is void. One of the main objects of registration is to enable a mortgagee to discover the state of the mortgagor's title, but if he is to be displaced by a registration effected

---

[1] But for another view, see 13 *M. L. R.* pp. 534–5 (A. D. Hargreaves).

after it has been certified to him by the Registrar that no prior charge stands in his way, the object will certainly be frustrated.[1] The truth appears to be that there was a lack of co-ordination in the drafting of this section 97 and section 13 of the Land Charges Act.

In the example given above priority is not difficult to determine, but this is by no means always true. Suppose, for instance, that, after a mortgage with possession of the title deeds has been granted to X., further mortgages of the same land are given in the sub-joined order : Subrogation sometimes necessary to determine priorities.

A puisne mortgage to A. on May 1st to secure £1000.
A general equitable charge to B. on May 10th to secure £1000.
A puisne mortgage to C. on May 20th to secure £2000.

> A. registers on May 11th.
> C. registers on May 20th.
> B.'s charge is not registered.

We know that A.'s mortgage is statutorily void against B., and that B.'s mortgage is void against C., but at first sight it seems impossible to arrange all three claimants in order of priority. An objection can be raised to every possible permutation. For instance, the order is not A.–B.–C., for though A. ranks before C. he must be postponed to B. ; neither is it B.–A.–C., for C. is to be preferred to B. though not to A. ; neither is it A.–C.–B., since A. must rank after B. If such a case were to arise the court would presumably be driven to base its decision upon the doctrine of subrogation.[2] Subrogation is the process by which one creditor is substituted for another creditor when both have claims against the same debtor.[3] The relevant factors in its application to the present example are that:

> B. ranks before A.,
> A. ranks before C., and
> C. ranks before B.,

so that any starting point is as arbitrary as any other in this *circulus inextricabilis.* But a solution may be found by transferring to C. the right of B. to be paid £1000 before A. C. is subrogated to B., *but only to the extent to which B. has priority over A.* The actual order of payment will therefore be as follows :

(i) C. is entitled to a first payment of £1000.

This is the £1000 that is due to B. in priority to A.

---

[1] For a discussion of the question, see *Cambridge Law Journal,* 1940, pp. 255–6. (R. E. Megarry).

[2] *Benham* v. *Keane* (1861), 1 John. & H. 685, 710–12 ; *In re Wyatt, White* v. *Ellis,* [1892] 1 Ch. 188, 208–9 ; *cf. In re Weniger's Policy,* [1910] 2 Ch. 291.

[3] White and Tudor's *Leading Cases in Equity,* vol. i, pp. 147 *et seq.*

(ii) A. is entitled to the next payment of £1000.

Theoretically, at any rate, A. suffers no injury. His claim
is not sustainable until £1000 has been paid out of the land, and
it is no concern of his whether that sum is paid to B. or to C.

(iii) C. is entitled to the next payment of £1000.

This represents the remainder of C's. advance, the whole of
which is payable before that of B.

(iv) B. is entitled to £1000 if the proceeds arising from
the sale of the land are sufficient.

If the sums advanced were £1000 by A., £1000 by B. and
£600 by C., the order would be this :

    (i) C. : £600.
    (ii) B. : £400.
    (iii) A. : £1000.
    (iv) B. : £600.[1]

Subrogation scarcely provides a satisfactory solution. However, it cannot be said that the doctrine of subrogation
provides more than a rough and ready method of solving the
difficulty. It cannot escape the criticism of being arbitrary, for
it is not obvious why the subrogation should begin with one
claimant rather than with another. In the example just given the
process might equally well start with B. rather than with C.
Neither is the justice of the solution obvious. In the first example, B. gets nothing until £2000 has been paid to C. and £1000
to A., and yet he has a prior right to A.

Where the value of the land is insufficient to satisfy all the
mortgages in full, it might be more just to admit the inextricable
circle and to decree a payment *pari passu*, *i.e.*, a division of
the proceeds among the various claimants in proportion to
the respective amounts of their advances.

Priorities where one mortgage protected by the deeds. We must now consider the question of priorities where one of
the competing mortgages is accompanied by the title deeds, which
is, of course, the usual case. The chief problem here is : What
is the significance of excluding such a mortgage from the list of

---

[1] A similar problem may arise under *Dearle* v. *Hall* (*supra*, p. 622). See,
for instance, the illustration given by FRY, L.J., in *In re Wyatt, White* v.
Ellis, [1892] 1 Ch. at pp. 208–9. There are two trustees of a fund, X. and Y.
The first incumbrancer, A., notifies X. only ; the second incumbrancer, B.,
notifies X. and Y. ; X. then dies and the third incumbrancer, C., notifies the
surviving trustee, Y. Here A. ranks before B. (*Ward* v. *Duncombe, supra*,
p. 624) ; B. before C. (*ibid.*) ; C. before A., for A.'s notice is nullified as against
incumbrances created after X.'s death (*Timson* v. *Ramsbottom, supra*, p. 624).
Therefore, says FRY, L.J. : " The fund would be distributed as follows :
First, to the third incumbrancer to the extent of the claim of the first.
Secondly, to the second incumbrancer. Thirdly, to the third incumbrancer to
the extent to which he might remain unpaid after the money he had received
whilst standing in the shoes of the first incumbrancer ; see *Benham* v. *Keane*
(1861), 1 John. & H. 710, where a similar problem was similarly solved."

registrable incumbrances ? Is the implication that in all cases a person who obtains possession of the deeds ranks first ? Presumably not, for it must never be forgotten that the governing principles which obtained under the old law were not expressly altered by the legislation of 1925. These principles were that:

> A legal was preferred to an equitable mortgage ; mortgages ranked in the order of their creation, subject to the preference given to the legal mortgage ; but either of these principles might be displaced by negligent conduct with reference to the deeds.

The old law, therefore, cannot be ignored altogether, though obviously its application is materially affected by the introduction of the system of registration. Another difficulty is the uncertainty of the statutory expression " protected by a deposit of documents," for a mortgagee may be entitled to this protection if he receives only some of the deeds relating to the legal estate, honestly and reasonably believing that he has received all.[1] Thus a contest may arise between two mortgagees, both of whom are protected by a deposit of documents and neither of whom, because of the deposit, has registered his incumbrance.[2] The following account of the general question is based upon two hypothetical cases, first, that the mortgage with the deposit of deeds comes first in order of date, secondly that it comes later.[3]

(*a*) First mortgagee acquires the deeds.

Example of
a mortgage
by deposit
followed by
second
mortgage.

Let us suppose that :

A. takes a mortgage protected by the title deeds ;
B. takes a later mortgage, necessarily without the deeds.

We require to ascertain whether the order is A.–B., but to do this it is necessary, having regard to the principles of the old law which are still to a large extent relevant, to consider the problem according as the parties obtain legal or equitable mortgages.

(i) *A.'s mortgage is legal, B.'s is equitable.*

Under the pre-1926 law, as we have seen,[4] the rule in such a case as this was that, by force of the legal estate and also by virtue of the maxim *qui prior est tempore potior est jure,* A. ranked first, unless his subsequent negligence with regard to the deeds, as for instance by handing them back to the mortgagor, justified his postponement to B. These rules of the old law, which specify

First mort-
gage legal,
second
equitable.

---

[1] *Ratcliffe* v. *Barnard* (1871), 6 Ch. App. 652 ; *Dixon* v. *Muckleston* (1872), 8 Ch. App. 155.
[2] For a discussion of this particular case, see *Cambridge Law Journal,* 1940, pp. 249–253.
[3] I am greatly indebted for what follows to the able series of articles written by Mr. R. L. Bignell and Mr. C. H. H. Wilss in 1933, and published in the 76 *Law Journal,* pp. 83–4, 95, 106–7, 122–3, 131–3.
[4] *Supra,* pp. 618 *et seq*

the limits within which conduct with regard to deeds causes loss of priority, still hold good, for section 13 of the Law of Property Act, 1925, provides that :

> " This Act shall not prejudicially affect the right or interest of
> " any person arising out of or consequent on the possession by him
> " of any documents relating to a legal estate in land, nor affect any
> " question arising out of or consequent upon any omission to obtain
> " or any other absence of possession by any person of any documents
> " relating to a legal estate in land."

Presuming that this section is linked to the Land Charges Act by section 97 quoted above,[1] it seems clear that the ranking of A. and B. still depends upon precisely the same considerations as before 1926. A will rank first unless his subsequent negligence justifies his postponement.

(ii) *The mortgages both of A and of B are legal.*

Both mortgages legal.

The position could not arise before 1926, when only one legal mortgage of the fee simple was possible. There seems no doubt, however, that A. ranks first, since he has the earlier legal estate and also possession of the deeds, though of course if he negligently parts with the deeds and thereby causes the deception of B., he may as in the last case lose his priority.

(iii) *A.'s mortgage is equitable, B.'s is legal.*

First mortgage equitable, second legal.

This position arises, for instance, where a mortgage by deposit of deeds is made to A., and later a term of 500 years is granted to B. Under the old law, B., as the holder of the legal estate, ranked first, unless he had failed to inquire for the deeds or had rested content with an unreasonable excuse for their non-production, or unless he had notice of A.'s equitable mortgage at the time when he took his own. The question now arises—what constitutes notice of A.'s mortgage? Certainly not registration, for a mortgagee with the deeds cannot register. The answer is contained in section 199 (1) (ii) of the Law of Property Act, 1925, which here re-enacts the Conveyancing Act, 1881. It provides that a purchaser, including a mortgagee, shall not be prejudicially affected by notice of any instrument or matter which is incapable of registration under the Land Charges Act unless :

What constitutes notice of non-registrable mortgage.

> " (*a*) it is within his own knowledge, or would have come to
> " his knowledge if such inquiries and inspections had been
> " made as ought reasonably to have been made by him ; or
> " (*b*) in the same transaction in respect to which a question of
> " notice to the purchaser arises, it has come to the know-
> " ledge of his counsel, as such, or of his solicitor or other
> " agent, as such, or would have come to the knowledge of
> " his solicitor or other agent, as such, if such inquiries and

---

[1] *Supra,* p. 626, *sed quaere.*

" inspections had been made as ought reasonably to have
" been made by the solicitor or other agent."

In other words, the old doctrine of actual or constructive notice
is still in force with regard to mortgages that are incapable of
registration. Again, there is nothing in the legislation of 1925
which deprives the owner of the legal estate of that pre-eminent
position which he has always enjoyed.

It would seem, therefore, that in the majority of circumstances
B. will rank second, for he will have actual notice of A.'s mortgage
if he inquires for the deeds, and constructive notice if he makes no
inquiry. Presumably, however, a case like *Hewitt* v. *Loosemore* [1]
would still be decided as it was before 1926.

(iv) *The mortgages both of A. and of B. are equitable.*

In this case there has been a deposit of the deeds with A. fol- Both
lowed by a general equitable charge in favour of B. When there mortgages
equitable.
was a contest under the pre-1926 law between equitable incum-
brancers, it was the maxim *qui prior est tempore potior est jure* that
prevailed. In the circumstances that we are now considering
A. would have ranked first, unless, by a voluntary redelivery of
the deeds to the mortgagor, he had negligently allowed a fraud
to be perpetrated on B. [2] There is nothing in the modern legislation to upset the old law, and there is little doubt that the maxim
qui prior est tempore potior est jure is still applicable. [3]

(b) First mortgagee does not acquire the deeds.

Let us suppose that the following transactions occur :

A. takes a puisne mortgage.
B. takes a later mortgage, either legal or equitable, and also obtains
possession of the deeds.

It is perfectly clear that if A. has registered his mortgage before
the completion of B.'s, he will rank first, since section 97 of the
Law of Property Act provides that his mortgage shall rank
according to its date of registration, and furthermore section 198
provides that registration under the Land Charges Act shall
constitute notice to all persons and for all purposes connected
with the land affected. If, however, it was due to A.'s gross
negligence that he failed to obtain the deeds, it is conceivable, but
scarcely probable, that despite registration he might, by virtue of
section 13 of the Law of Property Act, 1925, [4] be postponed to B.
in accordance with the principles of the old law. [5]

It seems equally clear that if A. has failed to register his mort-

Example of
mortgage
without
deeds
followed by
mortgage
with deeds.

Where the
first mort-
gage is legal

---

[1] *Supra*, p. 617.   [2] *Supra*, p. 620.
[3] *Cf. Beddoes* v. *Shaw*, [1937] 1 Ch. 81 ; [1936] 2 All E. R. 1108.
[4] *Supra*, p. 627.
[5] *Cambridge Law Journal*, 1940, p. 259.

gage before the transaction with B. is completed, he will in all circumstances be postponed to B.   This follows from the enactment that a registrable mortgage shall be void against a purchaser of the land charged, unless it is registered before completion of the purchase.[1]   It may be argued, however, that, if A. inquired for the deeds in the first place and received a reasonable excuse for their non-delivery, his legal estate, as under the old law, will still give him priority by virtue of section 13 of the Law of Property Act.[2]

This seems doubtful.   Not only is the mortgage rendered absolutely void against B., but it may also be said that A. has been negligent in not taking advantage of the protection that registration would have afforded him.

Where the first mortgage is equitable.

If the facts are altered slightly and we suppose that

A. takes a general equitable charge, and
B. takes a mortgage, either legal or equitable, also obtaining possession of the deeds,

it would seem that the same result ensues.   If the charge is registered, A. ranks first, otherwise B. will be preferred.

Partial abolition of tacking.

Tacking. The doctrine of tacking has been materially affected by the Law of Property Act, 1925.[3]   One branch of that doctrine has been abolished, the other has been retained.   The first branch, which under the old law [4] comprised the right of a later mortgagee to buy in the legal estate from the first incumbrancer and to squeeze out an intermediate mortgage, has been abolished.[5]   The second branch has been retained, for it is important that a mortgagee should be at liberty to tack further advances to his first loan.   In fact, the preservation of this right is essential where a bank takes a mortgage from a client as security for his current account, since a further advance is made whenever his cheque is honoured.   It is therefore enacted that in certain cases, which will be given in a moment,

Further advances may be tacked.

" a prior mortgagee shall have a right to make further advances
" to rank in priority to subsequent mortgages (whether legal or
" equitable)." [6]

Circumstances in which further advances may be tacked.

It will be noticed that this enactment does not confine the right to the first mortgagee or to a legal mortgagee, but grants it to any " prior " mortgagee, legal or equitable, against every later

---

[1] Land Charges Act, 1925, s. 13.
[2] *Supra*, pp. 615-6.   61 *Law Journal*, p. 398 (article by J. M. Lightwood). cited and considered, 71 *Law Journal*, p. 132.
[3] S. 94.
[4] *Supra*, p. 620.
[5] Law of Property Act, 1925, s. 94 (3).
[6] *Ibid*. s. 94 (1).

mortgagee. But it is only in the three following cases that the right may be exercised :

(a) **When Later Mortgagees agree.**[1] This is an obvious and not an unusual case. After mortgages of Blackacre have been granted to A., B. and C., the mortgagor may seek a further advance from B. on the same security. B. will rank for payment of both his loans before C. if he makes an arrangement to that effect with C. before advancing further money. C. is not likely to agree unless the land is sufficient cover for all the money with which it is charged.

(b) **When there is no Notice of Later Mortgages.**[2] A mortgagee who has no notice of subsequent mortgages at the time when he makes his further advances may claim priority for both his loans over subsequent mortgagees. This is the same rule as applied under the old law,[3] with this important difference, however, that registration of a later mortgage as a land charge is deemed to constitute *actual* notice of that mortgage.[4] A mortgagee therefore who contemplates a further advance should not make it until he has ascertained by a search at the Land Registry that no later mortgages have been made.

There is, however, an important exception to this rule that the mere registration of a mortgage will prevent a prior mortgagee from tacking later advances. It is enacted that in the case of a mortgage made expressly for securing,

> Two cases in which registration is not notice.

    (a) a current account, or
    (b) other further advances,

the mere registration of a subsequent mortgage shall not constitute notice sufficient to deprive the earlier mortgagee of his right to tack. In those two cases the rule is that :

" A mortgagee shall not be deemed to have notice of a mortgage
" merely by reason that it was registered as a land charge or in
" a local deeds registry, if it was not so registered at the time
" when the original mortgage was created or when the last
" search (if any) by or on behalf of the mortgagee was made,
" whichever last happened." [5]

Thus registration of a subsequent mortgage constitutes actual notice of that mortgage to a prior incumbrancer and necessarily displaces his right to tack, except where the prior mortgage was taken not merely as security for the original loan, but as security either for the original loan and further

---

[1] Law of Property Act, 1925, s. 94 (1) (a).
[2] *Ibid.*, s. 94 (1) (b).   [3] *Supra*, p. 621.
[4] Law of Property Act, 1925, s. 198 (1).
[5] Law of Property Act, 1925, s. 94 (2), as amended by Law of Property (Amendment) Act, 1926, Schedule.

advances or for a current account. In either of these cases registration will be notice only if it was in being when the prior mortgage was created (which might of course be before any money was actually advanced by the prior mortgagee, as often happens where a current account is secured), or when the prior mortgagee last made a search at the Land Registry. Failing registration at one of these dates a prior mortgagee will not be deprived of the right to tack unless, at the time of the further advance, he had notice, in the old sense of actual or constructive notice, of the later mortgage.

Reason why
registration
is not notice.

This exception to the rule that registration is equivalent to actual notice has been made in the interest of bankers, for were the rule unqualified it would be impracticable to take a mortgage as security for a current account. An illustration will make this clear.

If A. mortgages his land to a bank in order to secure an overdraft which at the time of the mortgage is £3000, and if he subsequently grants a mortgage of the same land to B., notice of which is given to the bank, the rule as laid down in *Hopkinson* v. *Rolt* [1] is that the bank obtains priority only for the amount due from the mortgagor at the time when the second mortgage to B. was made. If the overdraft at that moment is £4000, then £4000 is the amount with which the land is charged in favour of the bank. When, moreover, A. from time to time pays sums into his account, and the overdraft is thus reduced below £4000, only the reduced amount is recoverable under the mortgage;[2] and although, after notice of the second mortgage, the actual overdraft may be increased as a result of drawings out, the payments or further advances by the bank in respect of these drawings cannot be tacked to the loan as it stood at the time when notice of the second mortgage was received.[3] To fix the mortgage at £4000 is equitable if the bank has actual notice of the second mortgage, but it would make this side of banking business impossible if mere registration constituted notice, for it would be unsafe to honour the customer's cheques unless on each occasion a search were made at the Land Registry.

Two practical results emerge from this legislation. First, a mortgage will generally provide expressly that the land shall be security for further advances, since this will enable a further advance to be made without a search at the Land Registry; secondly, a mortgagee who searches and discovers the existence of a prior mortgage expressly made to secure a current account or further advances will be careful to notify his mortgage to the prior mortgagee.

(c) When the Mortgage imposes an *Obligation* on the Mortgagee to make Further Advances.   When the

---

[1] (1861), 9 H. L. C. 514 ; *supra*, p. 621.
[2] *Clayton's Case* (1816), 1 Mer. 572.
[3] *Deeley* v. *Lloyds Bank*, [1910] 1 Ch. 648 ; [1912] A. C. 756.

provision in the prior mortgage is not that the land shall be security for any further advances which *may* be made, as in the case (*b*) just considered, but that the mortgagee shall be bound to make further advances if called upon to do so, the new rule is [1] that the doctrine of tacking shall apply to such advances notwithstanding the fact that at the time of making them the prior mortgagee had notice of a later mortgage. The law as laid down in *West* v. *Williams* [2] is therefore reversed.

(2) PRIORITY AS BETWEEN MORTGAGEES OF AN EQUITABLE INTEREST IN LAND OR PERSONALTY.

We have already seen that under the old law the priority as between mortgagees of an equitable interest in pure personalty depended, in accordance with the rule in *Dearle* v. *Hall*, upon the order in which the mortgagees had given notice to the trustees, but that this principle did not apply to mortgages of freeholds or of leaseholds. [3] The innovation made by the 1925 legislation is the extension of the rule in *Dearle* v. *Hall* to mortgages of *all* equitable interests, realty being put on the same footing as personalty. This assimilation is accomplished by the following enactment [4] :

Statutory extension of Dearle v. Hall.

" The law applicable to dealings with equitable things in action " which regulates the priority of competing interests therein shall, as " respects dealings with equitable interests in land, capital money and " securities representing capital money effected after the commence- " ment of this Act, apply to and regulate the priority of competing " interests therein."

This extension of the rule to all mortgages and assignments of equitable interests in freeholds and leaseholds is of especial importance owing to the increased number of interests that under the modern law are necessarily equitable. Thus, the purchaser or mortgagee of an interest arising under a strict settlement, such as an entailed interest, a life interest or any species of future interest, must protect himself by giving the necessary notice.

The rules that existed under the old law with regard to the nature of the notice still hold good, [5] subject to one exception. This is that a notice given otherwise than in writing in respect of any dealing with an equitable interest in real or personal property shall not affect the priority of competing claims of purchasers or mortgagees. [6]

New rules regarding notice.

The Act contains the following rules with regard to the persons upon whom the written notice must be served :

Persons to whom notice must be given.

---

[1] Law of Property Act, 1925, s. 94 (1) (*c*).
[2] [1899] 1 Ch. 132 ; *supra*, p. 621.
[3] *Supra*, pp. 622; 624-5.   [4] Law of Property Act, 1925, s. 137 (1).
[5] *Supra*, pp. 623-4.   [6] Law of Property Act, 1925, s. 137 (3).

(1) Where the equitable interest is in settled land or capital money.[1]

Where dealings take place with such an interest, notice must be given to the *trustees of the settlement*. If the interest in question has been created by a derivative settlement (*i.e.* one by which an interest already settled is re-settled), then notice must be given to the trustees of the derivative settlement.

(2) Where the equitable interest is in land held on trust for sale.

In this case notice must be given to the *trustees*.[2]

(3) Where the equitable interest is neither (1) nor (2).[3]

If, for instance, the subject of the transaction is a life annuity charged on land by a tenant in fee simple, it is provided that notice shall be given to the *estate owner*.

It will be remembered that certain complexities had arisen under the old law with regard to a notice served on a single trustee.[4] The proper course, which, however, is not always adopted, is to serve the notice on each of the trustees and to take a receipt from each, and it is perhaps regrettable that the Act has not made this practice compulsory. No statutory direction has, however, been given, and it therefore appears that in this regard the old decisions continue to represent the law.[5]

Notice by way of endorsed memorandum.

To meet any difficulty that may arise in identifying the appropriate person to receive notice, the Act provides that where

(*a*) the trustees are not persons to whom a valid notice can be given ; or

(*b*) there are no trustees ; or

(*c*) for any other reason a valid notice cannot be served, or cannot be served without unreasonable delay or cost,

the assignee may require that a memorandum of the transaction be endorsed on the instrument which creates the equitable interest.[6] Such a memorandum, as respects priorities, operates in like manner as if a written notice had been given to trustees. Thus if the land in which the equitable interest exists is subject to a strict settlement, the memorandum will be annexed to the trust instrument ; if it is land belonging to an owner who has died intestate, the memorandum will be annexed to the letters of administration. The objection to a memorandum of this nature is that trust instruments may become overladen with endorsements of charges and assignments. Therefore an alternative method of registering a notice has been furnished.[7] It is provided that a settlor when drafting a settlement, or the court

Notice to nominated trust corporation.

---

[1] Law of Property Act, 1925, s. 137 (2) (i).   [2] *Ibid.*, s. 137 (2) (ii).
[3] *Ibid.*, s. 137 (2) (iii).   [4] *Supra*, p. 624.
[5] See *Law Journal Newspaper*, March 21st, 1925 ; Wolstenholme and Cherry's *Conveyancing Statutes*, vol. i. p. 361.
[6] Law of Property Act, 1925, s. 137 (4).
[7] *Ibid.*, s. 138.

at a later date, may nominate a trust corporation to whom notice of dealings affecting real or personal property may be given. Where such a nomination has been made, notice of any dealings with the equitable interest must be given to the trust corporation, and if given to the trustees must be transmitted by them to the corporation. A notice which is not received by the corporation has no effect on priorities.

The object of the rule in *Dearle* v. *Hall* is to enable a person to discover by inquiries addressed to the trustees whether the owner of an equitable interest has created any earlier incumbrances. But this object was not always attained under the old law, for since, in the language of LINDLEY, L.J., " it is no part of the duty of a trustee to assist his *cestui que trust* in selling or mortgaging his beneficial interest and in squandering or anticipating his fortune," [1] it was held that a trustee owed no greater duty to a person who was proposing to deal with a *cestui que trust*.[2]

Thus a trustee might refuse to answer inquiries, and even if he gave an answer that contained wrong information, he was not liable for the consequences unless he had been guilty of fraud or had made such a clear and categorical statement that he was estopped from denying its truth.[3] A prospective assignee, however, is given at least this advantage by the Act, that he may demand production of any written notice that has been served on the trustees.[4]

Right to production of notice.

---

[1] *Low* v. *Bouverie*, [1891] 3 Ch. 82, 99.
[2] *Burrows* v. *Lock* (1805), 10 Ves. 470.   [3] *Ibid,*
[4] Law of Property Act, 1925, s. 137 (8).

BOOK III.

THE TRANSFER AND EXTINCTION OF ESTATES AND INTERESTS.

SUMMARY.

PART I.

INTRODUCTORY NOTE.

Law in motion. It may be said that what we have described so far is the law at rest. Our attention has been directed to the actual rights that can be enjoyed in land. We have taken each estate and interest that is capable of subsisting, either at law or in equity, and have explained by what methods it may be brought into existence and what incidents are applicable to it when it exists. It now remains to treat of the law in motion, that is, to show how estates and interests, once validly created, may be transferred and dealt with generally, and how they may be extinguished.

Conveyancing. The principal function of conveyancers as regards real property is to draft appropriate instruments for creating or transferring the landed interests already described, and in connection with this task, to ensure that the person who makes the transfer has an estate or interest that is sufficient to justify the transaction contemplated. Thus, in the case of a conveyance by way of sale of the fee simple, it is essential to see that the vendor has, as the result of conveyances and acts in the law extending over a number of years, acquired a fee simple estate and is therefore in a position to pass that estate to the purchaser. This preliminary inquiry is known as investigation of title. Again, where the task in question is to draft a will, it is essential to remember, for example, that whatever the testator may desire, it is useless to frame a limitation that offends the rule against perpetuities.

Some of the instruments by which estates and interests may be dealt with have already been described and need little further mention, but it is well to notice that though it is usual to regard conveyancing as the transfer of rights in property from one person to another, yet frequently an instrument creates rather than transfers a right, as for instance, in the case of the creation of a trust or the grant of a mortgage or a lease. Furthermore, all transfers are not necessarily effected by an instrument, but may operate independently of the person whose interest is primarily affected, as for instance, where land passes to a trustee in bankruptcy on the adjudication of its owner as bankrupt.

642

Transfer. The first point that requires discussion is transfer, which falls naturally into transfer *inter vivos* and transfer upon death.

Transfer *inter vivos* may be either (A) by act of parties, or (B) by act in the law, *i.e.* either due to the deliberate intention of the estate owner or in spite of his intention.

(A) The principal occasions of voluntary transfer by act of parties arise when the land is sold or settled, and also where an entailed interest is converted into a fee simple absolute by a disentailing assurance.

The main object of the next three chapters, which deal with transfer by act of parties, is to discuss the conveyance of a legal fee simple by way of sale. The general scheme is to show, first, the practice that conveyancers adopt in effecting a conveyance of the legal estate; secondly, the effect of the conveyance upon the third party rights.

In the second respect we encounter a difficulty, since not only the details of the conveyance, but more especially its effect upon third party rights, vary with the status of the vendor. We must recall that the legal estate in the entirety of every piece of land is necessarily vested in an *estate owner.* An estate owner is the owner of a legal estate. Every legal estate must have an estate owner. Blackacre may have been subjected to a trust, a settlement or a mortgage ; it may have been devised to a number of beneficiaries, either in succession or in common ; it may have been charged with a variety of incumbrances ; but in each case the fee simple absolute in possession is necessarily vested in one person or in a number of persons jointly. Further, every conveyance of the legal estate must be made by the estate owner except where a mortgagee under his power of sale conveys the legal fee simple that is vested in the mortgagor, and even in this case the conveyance may be made in the name of the mortgagor. The possible estate owners are the following :—

Beneficial owners.
Personal representatives.
Trustees for sale.
Tenants for life and statutory owners.
Mortgagors and mortgagees.
Bare trustees.[1]

The plan adopted in the following three chapters, therefore, is to begin with a description of a sale by a beneficial owner, *i.e.* a person entitled to the whole

---

[1] For definition of bare trustee, see *supra*, p. 99, note 2.

ownership for his own benefit, and then to notice any variation from the law applicable to this transaction that is peculiar to the other estate owners. The main chapter is the first which deals with the beneficial owner, since it contains a general account of the proof and investigation of title that under the system of private conveyancing is necessary in all cases irrespective of the character of the vendor. The different method that must be adopted where the title to the land is registered under the Land Registration Act, 1925, is explained later in Part VI. The first chapter is followed by a short one treating of personal representatives, for their position raises matters that have not been discussed in the preceding pages. The remaining estate owners—tenants for life, statutory owners, trustees for sale and mortgagors—are grouped together in the third chapter, for to deal with them *in extenso* would involve a considerable repetition. Nevertheless, this chapter inevitably runs to some length, since it contains the conveyancing details affecting the transfer of settled land and land held on trust for sale that in the interests of simplicity have been omitted from the account of settlements and trusts for sale given in Part II of Book II.

Involuntary transfer. (B) Involuntary transfer by operation of law arises where the owner of an estate or interest is either

    (i) sued to judgment for non-payment of a debt,

    (ii) made bankrupt, or

    (iii) dies insolvent,

in each of which cases his land is liable to be seized in satisfaction of the debts.

Transfer on death. Turning to transfer on death, testacy and intestacy are dealt with in Part IV.

Extinction of estates and interests. The next subject of discussion in Part V is the extinguishment of estates and interests. Under the modern law a right to land may be extinguished by

    1. forfeiture,

    2. lapse of time, or

    3. merger.

    1. Forfeiture may operate where, for instance, land is leased to a tenant with a condition for forfeiture on non-payment of rent, or where an interest is subjected to a condition subsequent, but, these cases having already been considered, the subject of forfeiture will be omitted from the following pages.

    2. Lapse of time causes the extinguishment of an interest whose owner remains out of possession, either of the land or of its

profits, for the appropriate period designated by the Limitation Act, 1939.

3. Where a smaller interest and a larger interest in the same land become united in one person, the doctrine of merger, subject to certain conditions, operates to extinguish the smaller interest.

The discussion of extinction, therefore, is confined to lapse of time and merger.

Finally, after the system of registered conveyancing has been explained in outline, attention is given to those special persons, such as infants and mental patients for whom the law has prescribed special rules with respect both to the holding and to the transfer of interests in land.

BOOK III.

THE TRANSFER AND EXTINCTION OF ESTATES AND INTERESTS.

PART II.

TRANSFER *INTER VIVOS* BY ESTATE OWNERS.

SUMMARY.

CHAPTER I.

BENEFICIAL OWNERS: THE SALE OF LAND.

SUMMARY.

SECTION I. THE CONTRACT OF SALE.

(1) EFFECT OF A VALID CONTRACT FOR SALE

Law of
Property
Act, 1925.

A contract for the sale of land must comply with section 40 of the Law of Property Act, 1925, which renders it unenforceable by action unless it is evidenced by a written memorandum signed by the defendant or by his lawfully authorized agent. The only addition that need be made to the account of this enactment

648

already given in the context of an agreement for a lease,[1] is that in the particular case of a sale by auction, the auctioneer becomes the agent of both parties upon the fall of the hammer. He derives his authority to act for the vendor from his instructions to sell, while his authority to sign on behalf of the purchaser is implied from the bid.[2] If, therefore, he signs a memorandum, either at the time of the sale or so soon afterwards that his signature can reasonably be regarded as part of the transaction of sale, the memorandum is binding upon both parties.[3]

If, as the result of a mistake common to both parties, the written evidence omits some material term and therefore does not express the true bargain between the parties, the court has jurisdiction to rectify the contract.[4] In such a case it first rectifies the written contract by adding the oral omission or variation, and then decrees specific performance of the contract as rectified. At one and the same time it reforms and enforces the contract.[5] This remedy will be granted even where the mistake is embodied in the final deed of conveyance.[6]

Oral terms excluded from writing by mistake.

What constitutes a final contract. If a contract for sale specifies merely the names of the parties, a description of the property and a statement of the price, it is called an *open contract.* When this form of contract is made, the parties are bound by certain obligations implied by the law. These implied obligations, as we shall see, impose a burdensome duty of proof of title upon the vendor, and in the majority of cases the vendor is anxious to procure the insertion in the written agreement of special stipulations, in order that his strict legal liability may be modified.[7] Such stipulations, of course, become binding if they are contained in the written agreement, but if there once comes into existence a complete and properly evidenced contract without their inclusion, they cannot avail the vendor. It thus becomes of importance to distinguish between negotiations which constitute a completed contract, and those which no not. If an offer is made by the purchaser and unconditionally accepted by the vendor, any special stipulations intended by either party are excluded, and their place is taken by the implied obligations. But if the accept-

Open contract

Contract to enter into a contract not binding.

---

[1] *Supra,* pp. 344 *et seq.*
[2] *Emmerson* v. *Heelis* (1808), 2 Taunt 38.
[3] *Bell* v. *Balls,* [1897] 1 Ch. 663; *Chaney* v. *Maclow,* [1929] 1 Ch. 461; *Phillips* v. *Butler,* [1945] Ch. 358; [1945] 2 All E. R. 258.
[4] *United States* v. *Motor Trucks, Ltd.,* [1924] A. C. 196.
[5] *Ibid.,* p. 201 ; *per* Lord Birkenhead.
[6] *Craddock Bros.* v. *Hunt,* [1923] 2 Ch. 136. On the subject generally see Cheshire and Fifoot, *The Law of Contract* (6th Edn.), pp. 200–2.

[7] If, however, an open contract is made by correspondence, the conditions to which it is subject are " The Statutory Form of Conditions of Sale, 1925," which were prescribed by the Lord Chancellor acting under the powers given to him by the Law of Property Act, 1925, s. 46. These differ considerably from the conditions, set out below at pp. 659 *et seq.,* which apply to open contracts generally.

Y*

ance is not final, as for instance where it is made subject to a formal contract being drawn up, there is no binding agreement until the copies of the formal contract have been exchanged,[1] and either party can recede without liability, while any special stipulations subsequently proposed by either party will amount to a new offer requiring acceptance. This matter has already been considered in the analogous case of an agreement to grant a lease, to which reference may be made.[2]

Vendor in a fiduciary position. The immediate effect of a binding contract for sale is to pass the equitable interest in the land to the purchaser. The legal estate remains in the vendor until the conveyance has been executed, but meanwhile equity regards the vendor as a trustee for the purchaser, and is prepared to decree specific performance at the instance of the latter,[3] even though, in the interval between the contract and its completion, a compulsory purchase order affecting the land may have been made by a local authority.[4] In the words of JESSEL, M.R.[5]:

> " The moment you have a valid contract for sale the vendor " becomes in equity a trustee for the purchaser of the estate sold, " and the beneficial ownership passes to the purchaser, the vendor " having a right to the purchase money, a charge or lien on the estate " for the security of that purchase money, and a right to retain " possession of the estate until the purchase money is paid, in the " absence of express contract as to the time of delivering possession."

Thus, for instance, pending completion of the contract,

the purchaser is at liberty to dispose of the property by sale or otherwise ; he becomes owner of the rents and profits which fall due after the time fixed for completion ; and he can demand an occupation rent if the vendor remains in possession after that time.

On the other hand, as from the date of the contract, the purchaser must bear the risk of any loss or damage suffered by the property, as, for instance, from an accidental fire or from a fall in prices ; and from the date fixed for completion he must meet the cost of all necessary outgoings.

Vendor's rights. Pending the completion of the sale, the vendor occupies a fiduciary position, and therefore he must manage and preserve the property with the same care as a trustee must show with regard to trust property. He must, for instance, relet the premises if an existing lease runs out, but before doing so he must consult the purchaser.[6] Nevertheless, the vendor is not an absolute or

---

[1] *Eccles* v. *Bryant and Pollock,* [1948] Ch. 93 ; [1947] 2 All E. R. 865.
[2] *Supra,* pp. 342–4.
[3] *Shaw* v. *Foster* (1872), L. R. 5 H. L. 321, 333, 338 ; *Howard* v. *Miller,* [1915] A. C. 318, 326.
[4] *Hillingdon Estates Co.* v. *Stonefield Estates, Ltd.,* [1952] Ch. 627 ; [1952] 1 All E. R. 85.
[5] *Lysaght* v. *Edwards* (1876), 2 Ch. D. 499, 506.
[6] *Egmont (Earl of)* v. *Smith* (1877), 6 Ch. D. 469; *Abdulla* v. *Shah,* [1959] A.C. 124.

passive trustee in the usual meaning of that expression, since he possesses certain personal rights of a valuable nature in the land, which he is entitled to protect on his own behalf. Thus :

1. he has a right to remain in possession until the purchase money is paid, and to protect that possession, if necessary, by the maintenance of an action, though while in possession he is under a duty to maintain the property in a reasonable state of preservation and so far as may be in the state in which it was when the contract was made[1] ;

2. he is entitled to take the rents and profits until the time fixed for completion ; and

3. he possesses an equitable lien on the property for the amount of the purchase money. An equitable lien is not a mere right of retention dependent upon continued possession of the subject-matter, as is the common law lien of an unpaid seller of goods, but is an equitable right in the property of another which may exist independently of possession, and which entitles the person in whom it resides to apply to the court for a sale of the property in satisfaction of his claim.[2]

Although the equitable ownership has passed to the purchaser, the vendor retains a substantial interest in the land, and for that reason is generally called a qualified trustee. Lord CAIRNS, dealing with a case where a valid contract had been made for the sale of a London theatre, said[3] :— **Vendor a qualified trustee.**

> " There cannot be the slightest doubt of the relation subsisting
> " in the eye of a Court of Equity between the vendor and the pur-
> " chaser. The vendor was a trustee of the property for the pur-
> " chaser ; the purchaser was the real beneficial owner in the eye of
> " a Court of Equity of the property, subject only to this observation,
> " that the vendor, whom I have called the trustee, was not a mere
> " dormant trustee, he was a trustee having a personal and substantial
> " interest in the property, a right to protect that interest, and an
> " active right to assert that interest if anything should be done in
> " derogation of it. The relation, therefore, of trustee and *cestui que*
> " *trust* subsisted, but subsisted subject to the paramount right of the
> " vendor and trustee to protect his own interest as vendor of the
> " property."

Thus, the trusteeship relates only to the property sold, which, failing express agreement, is confined to vacant possession of the land together with any physical accretions thereto. Therefore the vendor is entitled to retain compensation money payable in respect of the requisitioning of the property and falling due between the date of the contract and the date of the conveyance.[4]

---

[1] *Clarke* v. *Ramuz*, [1891] 2 Q. B. 456 ; *Phillips* v. *Lamdin*, [1949] 2 K. B. 33 ; [1949] 1 All E. R. 770.
[2] White and Tudor, *Leading Cases in Equity*, vol. ii., p. 857.
[3] *Shaw* v. *Foster* (1872), L. R. 5 H. L. 221, 338.
[4] *In re Hamilton–Snowball's Conveyance*, [1959] Ch. 308 ; [1958] 2 All E. R. 319.

Likewise, if between these dates the premises are damaged by fire, the former rule was that the money paid by the insurance company in respect of the loss belonged to the vendor, not to the purchaser, for the policy of insurance was no part of the property sold.[1] This particular aspect of the principle, however, has been reversed by the Law of Property Act, 1925, which provides [2] that where, after the date of any contract for sale or exchange of land, money becomes payable under any policy maintained by the vendor in respect of any damage to, or destruction of, property included in the contract, the money shall on completion of the contract be paid by the vendor to the purchaser. This obligation may be varied by the contract, it is subject to the liability of the purchaser to pay the premiums falling due after the date of the contract, and is also subject to any requisite consents of the insurers.[3]

The contract may be registered.

A binding agreement for the sale of land is registrable as an *estate contract* under the Land Charges Act, 1925.[4] If not registered it is void against later purchasers for money or money's worth of the legal estate in the land.[5]

(2) REMEDIES OF THE PARTIES.

The remedies which are available to either party in the event of a breach of a contract for sale are :

1. an action for damages, or
2. an action for specific performance, or
3. an action for rescission, or
4. a vendor and purchaser summons under section 49 of the Law of Property Act, 1925.

Remoteness of damage.

1. **Action for Damages.** In the event of a breach of any contract the rule of law that governs remoteness of damage limits the liability of the defendant to the actual loss caused, provided that having regard to the knowledge, actual or constructive, possessed by him at the time of the contract he ought reasonably to have foreseen that such loss was likely to

---

[1] *Rayner* v. *Preston* (1881), 18 Ch. D. 1. See also *Re Watford Corpn. and Ware's Contract*, [1943] 1 Ch. 82; [1943] 1 All E. R. 54.

[2] Law of Property Act, 1925, s. 47.

[3] This would appear to put the purchaser in a doubtful position. If the house which is the subject of the sale is burnt down, the purchaser is nevertheless obliged to pay the purchase money, and if the insurance company refuses to give the requisite consent to the transfer of the insurance money, he will be unable to obtain payment of that money under the section. On the other hand, having regard to the nature of fire insurance, it seems clear that the vendor is not entitled both to the insurance money and to the purchase money. A purchaser is well advised to insure the property himself immediately after the contract and not to rely on this section.

[4] S. 10 (1), C. (iv).

[5] *Ibid.*, s. 13 (2), proviso ; *infra*, pp. 670–1.

occur.[1] The only duty cast upon a party in this respect is to foresee the loss that will occur in the usual course of things, unless he knows of exceptional circumstances by which it may be increased.[2]

In the case of a contract for the sale of land this rule applies when it is the vendor who brings the action. The loss caused to the vendor in the usual course of things by the failure of the purchaser to complete is the deprivation of the purchase price diminished by the value of the land that he still holds, and he is therefore entitled to recover by way of damages the difference, if any, between the value of the land which remains in his possession and the price he would have got had the contract been completed.[3] Thus, if he re-sells, he is entitled to recover both the difference in price and the expenses attending the re-sale.[4] *{Damages recoverable by vendor.}*

When it is the purchaser who sues for breach, the measure of damages depends upon whether the breach was due *{Damages recoverable by purchaser.}*

(i) merely to the vendor's inability to make a good title, or

(ii) to his failure to do all that he could to complete the conveyance.

(i) Where the vendor is unable to complete the conveyance owing to a defect in his title, and is not personally at fault, the general rule is excluded ; the purchaser cannot recover damages for the loss of his bargain, but is limited to the recovery of his deposit, if any, and of the expenses incurred by him in investigating the title.[5] The justification for this anomalous departure from the general rule is said to be the extreme difficulty that attends the making of a good title to English land.[6] Thus if the owner of leaseholds agrees to sell them without stating that his lessor's licence is necessary, and if the licence is refused, the purchaser will not be entitled to recover general damages.[7]

(ii) But a vendor who fails or refuses to take the steps which are necessary to complete the title and which are within

---

[1] *Hadley* v. *Baxendale* (1854), 9 Ex. 341 ; *Victoria Laundry (Windsor). Ltd.* v. *Newman Industries, Ltd.*, [1949] 2 K. B. 528; [1949] 1 All E. R. 997.

[2] *Cottrill* v. *Steyning and Littlehampton Building Society*, [1966] 2 All E. R. 295; [1966] 1 W. L. R. 753; dist. *Diamond* v. *Campbell-Jones*, [1961] Ch. 22; [1960] 1 All E. R. 583.

[3] *Laird* v. *Pim* (1841), 7 M. & W. 474 ; *Harold Wood Brick Co., Ltd.* v. *Ferris*, [1935] 1 K. B. 613 ; affirmed, [1935] 2 K. B. 198.

[4] *Noble* v. *Edwardes* (1877), 5 Ch. D. 378 ; *Keck* v. *Faber* (1916), 60 Sol. Jo. 253.

[5] *Flureau* v. *Thornhill* (1776), 2 Wm. Bl. 1078.

[6] *Bain* v. *Fothergill* (1874), L. R. 7 H. L. 158 ; *Barnes* v. *Cadogan Developments, Ltd.*, [1930] 1 Ch. 479, 488 ; *J. W. Café's, Ltd.* v. *Brownlow Trust*, [1950] 1 All E. R. 894.

[7] *Day* v. *Singleton*, [1899] 2 Ch. 320.

his power is liable in damages.[1]   So if he has not acted honestly, or has refused or neglected to make a good title,[2] as for instance where a vendor of leaseholds induces his lessor to withhold the necessary licence,[3] or declines to carry out the contract, or fails to clear the land of a mortgage,[4] or if his agreement to sell is unlawful,[5] he is liable to pay substantial damages.   If the value of the property is greater than the purchase price, the plaintiff recovers the difference, though in this case he cannot recover his conveyancing costs.[6]   If the value of the property is less than the purchase price, he is entitled to a return of the deposit with interest and also to damages in respect of the cost of investigating the title.[7]

Specific performance where damages not adequate remedy.

2. **Action for Specific Performance.** The most effective remedy available to either party is to sue for specific performance, *i.e.* to demand that the contract be completed according to its terms.   One of the general principles established by equity is that this relief should be given only where damages do not afford an adequate remedy.   It is clear that damages do not adequately compensate a purchaser, since in most cases he desires the land itself, and although it is equally clear that a vendor is adequately recompensed by a money payment, yet, in pursuance of the doctrine that remedies should be mutual, equity grants specific performance to a vendor as well as to a purchaser.[8]

An adequate discussion of specific performance is outside the scope of this book, but it may be noticed that the remedy is discretionary, though the discretion is not exercised in an arbitrary or capricious manner, but according to the rules that have been established by the judges.   If the defendant can show any circumstances independent of the written contract which make it inequitable to decree specific performance, as for instance where the terms are ambiguous, and are understood by the parties in different senses, or where the vendor or the purchaser has not acted fairly, or where the

[1] *Williams* v. *Glenton* (1866), L. R. 1 Ch. 200, 209 ; *Phillips* v. *Lamdin*, [1949] 2 K. B. 33 ; [1949] 1 All E. R. 770.
[2] *Wallington* v. *Townsend*, [1939] Ch. 588 ; [1939] 2 All E. R. 225.
[3] *Day* v. *Singleton*, [1899] 2 Ch. 320.
[4] *Thomas* v. *Kensington*, [1942] 2 K. B. 181.
[5] *Milner* v. *Staffordshire Congregational Union (Incorporated)*, [1956] Ch. 275 ; [1956] 1 All E. R. 494.
[6] *Re Daniel, Daniel* v. *Vassall*, [1917] 2 Ch. 405. The loss for which compensation is recoverable is the difference between the purchase price and the value of the property if it had been conveyed in accordance with the contract. But if the property had in fact been so conveyed, the conveyancing costs would have fallen on the purchaser, and therefore he cannot recover both the difference and the costs ; *ibid.*, at p. 412, *per* SARGANT, J.
[7] *Wallington* v. *Townsend, supra.*
[8] *Kenney* v. *Wexham* (1822), Madd. & G. 355, 357 ; LEACH, V.-C.

completion of the contract would cause hardship to an innocent vendor or purchaser, the court will not grant the remedy.[1]

In certain circumstances the court will decree specific performance in favour of the plaintiff subject to the condition that he pays compensation in respect of some term of the contract which he has not literally fulfilled.

Specific performance with compensation.

" Where for instance, some steps towards the completion of the " contract have not been taken or . . . the contract itself has not " been completed at the time agreed upon between the parties, " or where the vendor has not the same interest in the estate as " that which he had contracted to sell, or there was some " deficiency in the quality or quantity of it, the party not able " strictly to perform the contract on his part formerly, at law, " had no remedy by way of damages against the other ; but, in " equity, in many cases he would be able to obtain specific " performance if adequate compensation could be made for the " non-literal performance of the contract." [2]

The most important case in which equity grants specific performance with compensation is where a contract for the sale of land is not completed upon the date fixed in the contract. *At law* time was always considered to be of the essence of the contract, and a party who failed to complete upon the agreed date was remediless. Thus, if the vendor failed to complete, the purchaser could repudiate the contract and recover the deposit and the costs of investigating the title. Equity, however, taking a different view that now prevails in all courts,[3] has always been prepared to decree specific performance notwithstanding failure to observe the exact date fixed for completion, *provided that this will not cause injustice to either party*. Equity looks

Specific performance when completion delayed.

"not at the letter but at the substance of the agreement, to ascer-"tain whether the parties, notwithstanding that they named a "specific time within which completion was to take place, "really and in substance intended no more than that it should "take place within a reasonable time."[4]

Thus specific performance will not be decreed if the parties have expressly stipulated that time shall be essential, or if there is something in the nature of the property or in the surrounding circumstances which renders it inequitable to treat the appointed date as non-essential.[5]

So, if the nature of the property is such as to make its

---

[1] See generally White and Tudor, *Leading Cases in Equity*, vol. ii. pp. 372 *et seq.*

[2] *Ibid.*, p. 434.

[3] Law of Property Act, 1925, s. 41, re-enacting the Judicature Act, 1873.

[4] *Jamshed Khodaram Irani* v. *Burjorji Dhunjibhai* (1915), 32 T. L. R. 156, at p. 157, *per* Lord HALDANE.

[5] *Stickney* v. *Keeble*, [1915] A. C. 386, 415–16 ; *per* Lord PARKER.

conveyance at the agreed date imperative, *e.g.* when the contract is for the sale of licensed premises,[1] or of a shop as a going concern, specific performance, even with compensation, will not be decreed ; but if there is nothing special in the nature of the property or in the purposes for which it is required and if there has been no unreasonable or negligent conduct, the court will decree specific performance, subject to the condition that the defaulting party gives compensation for the delay.

A new contract cannot be made at the will of one of the parties and therefore, where time is not initially essential, one party cannot make it so of his own volition.[2] Nevertheless, there must be some limit to delaying tactics, and it is established that after the date fixed for completion has passed one party may serve a notice on the other requiring completion within a specified time.[3] The notice will be valueless unless the time allowed is reasonable,[4] but if satisfactory in this respect it will bind both parties.[5]

Discharge of contract.

3. Rescission. A breach of contract in every case gives the innocent party a right to sue for damages, but if it is a breach of some term which is a condition precedent to his liability (*e.g.* failure of the vendor to show a good title or to deliver the actual land or interest described in the contract), he may treat the contract as discharged, and elect either to rescind the contract altogether, or to hold the defaulting party to it and recover damages.

Rescission.

If the vendor elects to rescind, he may re-sell the property as owner, but he cannot recover damages in addition, for if this were allowed he would enjoy a double remedy.[6] He is entitled, however, to retain any deposit that the purchaser may have paid. Thus in *Howe* v. *Smith*,[7]

Forfeiture of deposit.

Howe v. *Smith.*

£500 was paid as deposit and part payment of the purchase money. The purchaser, who was in default in completing the contract, sued to recover the £500, but it was held that, since it was the intention of the parties that this sum should be deposited as a guarantee for the due performance of his obligations, it must be forfeited to the vendor.

But whether this rule applies or not is in each case a matter of construction, and if the terms show that the money has not been paid as a guarantee of performance, but solely by way of

---

[1] *Lock* v. *Bell*, [1931] 1 Ch. 35.
[2] *Green* v. *Sevin* (1879), 13 Ch. D. 589, 599.
[3] *Finkielkraut* v. *Monohan*, [1949] 2 All E. R. 234.
[4] *Smith* v. *Hamilton, supra ; In re Barr's Contract*, [1956] Ch. 551 ; [1956] 2 All E. R. 853; *Ajit* v. *Sammy*, [1966] 3 W.L.R. 983.
[5] *Finkielkraut* v. *Monohan, supra.*
[6] *Barber* v. *Wolfe*, [1945] Ch. 187 ; [1945] 1 All E. R. 399.
[7] (1884), 27 Ch. D. 89.

part payment, it is recoverable by the purchaser even though the contract is rescinded owing to his own default.[1]

It was held under the old law in the case of *Re Scott and Alvarez's Contract* [2] that, although the court might refuse specific performance because of the inequitable conduct of the vendor, it nevertheless had no jurisdiction to order the return of the deposit unless there had been a breach of contract. In that case

> the vendor had committed no breach at law, because he had taken an express stipulation from the purchaser that a certain transaction should not be investigated. From outside sources the purchaser discovered that the transaction in question vitiated the title, but, although the court refused to force the title upon him, it held that it could not interfere with the common law rule that the deposit belonged to the vendor.

This decision, however, no longer represents the law, since it is enacted that [3] :

> " Where the court refuses to grant specific performance of a "contract, or in any action for the return of a deposit, the "court may, if it thinks fit, order the repayment of any deposit."

4. **Vendor and Purchaser Summons.** The Vendor and Purchaser Act, 1874, introduced a new method whereby parties to a contract of sale, whose disagreement upon some matter prevents the completion of the contract, may apply in a summary way to a judge in Chambers, and obtain such an order as may appear just. This summary proceeding is termed a vendor and purchaser summons, and is now governed by the Law of Property Act, 1925.[4] Typical questions which lead to a summons are the sufficiency of the title shown by the vendor, the sufficiency of an answer made to a requisition, the construction of the contract, and the question whether a vendor is entitled to rescind.

The Act expressly excludes the possibility of raising any question that affects the existence or the validity of the contract in its inception, as for instance, the question whether there is a sufficient memorandum.

Not only may the court decide the question submitted to it, but it may also grant consequential relief, that is, may order such things to be done as are the natural consequence of the decision. For instance, it may order rescission in favour of a purchaser, together with the return of his deposit.

Return of deposit.

Object and scope of summons.

---

[1] *Mayson* v. *Clouet*, [1924] A. C. 980.   [2] [1895] 2 Ch. 603.
[3] Law of Property Act, 1925, s. 49 (2). See *Charles Hunt, Ltd.* v. *Palmer*, [1931] 2 Ch. 287.
[4] *Ibid.*, s. 49 (1).

Delivery of abstract.

Duties of Parties to a Contract of Sale. Once a binding contract has been made, and provided that the title to the land is not registered,[1] the following are the successive duties that devolve upon the parties:—

1. The vendor is bound to show a good title to the interest that he has contracted to sell, and to this end and with a view to simplifying the purchaser's task, he must at his own expense deliver to the purchaser an abstract of title, that is, a summary of all the documents, such as wills and deeds of conveyance, that have dealt with the interest during the period for which his ownership has to be proved, and of all the events, such as deaths, that have affected the devolution of the ownership during that period. The period is either the 30 years fixed by statute, or that which is prescribed by a special stipulation in the contract of sale, though, as we shall see, the period will be longer than the statutory 30 years if a good root of title cannot otherwise be shown.

Perusal of abstract.

2. The vendor then verifies the abstract by producing evidence of the accuracy of the statements that he has made in the course of setting out his title. After this the purchaser's solicitor, at the expense of the purchaser, peruses the abstract, requisitions (*i.e.* addresses inquiries to) the vendor about any defects he may observe, satisfies himself that the property described in the contract is identical with that which has been dealt with in the documents abstracted, calls for evidence (such as death certificates) of events material to the title, and finally advises the purchaser whether he must or can with safety accept the title offered.

Conveyance.

3. The vendor is then obliged to convey the property free from incumbrances, to execute a deed of conveyance and to hand over to the purchaser all the title deeds relating to the property. The expense of preparing the deed of conveyance falls upon the purchaser.

The exact obligations of a vendor may, as we have said, be either specified or unspecified. If they are unspecified, and so left to be implied by law, the vendor is said to sell under an *open contract.* We will now proceed to state the rights and obligations of the parties, first where the contract is open, secondly where it contains the special stipulations generally found in practice.

---

[1] For registered conveyancing, see *infra*, pp. 837 *et seq.*

SECTION II.   INVESTIGATION OF TITLE UNDER THE SYSTEM OF PRIVATE CONVEYANCING.[1]

SUMMARY.

(1) UNDER AN OPEN CONTRACT.

The rights and the duties of the parties under an open contract are as follows :—

(A) Duty of Vendor to show Title for 30 Years.

Since the obligation of the vendor is to convey to the purchaser the interest that he has agreed to sell, free from incumbrances and competing interests, it follows that he must disclose and verify the state of his title to the land.   Save in the rare case where he has been invested with an absolute title by Act of Parliament, he can scarcely show that he is entitled to an interest good against the whole world, for, however long he and his predecessors may have possessed and administered the land, the existence of some adverse claimant, such as a remainderman or reversioner, is always a possibility.   But possession is *primâ facie* evidence of seisin in fee and if he shows that he and his predecessors have been in possession for a considerable time, the existence of an earlier and therefore better title is at least improbable.   On this assumption, the practical rule was ultimately evolved that proof of the exercise of acts of ownership over the land by the vendor and his predecessors for a period of not less than sixty years was *primâ facie* evidence of his right to convey what he had agreed to sell. " It is a technical rule among conveyancers to approve a possession

Possession is evidence of title.

---

[1] For registered conveyancing, see *infra*, pp. 837 *et seq.*

of sixty years as a good title to a fee simple."[1]   This period was statutorily reduced to forty years in 1874[2] and to thirty years in 1925.[3]

Necessity to explain origin of possession.

Enjoyment for this period, however, is not conclusive evidence of a good title, and if it appears from the information supplied by the vendor or if it can be shown *ab extra* that the title falls short of what is required by the contract, the purchaser is not bound to complete.   Possession by the vendor is no doubt evidence of seisin in fee, but nevertheless he must show its origin, for though it is probably attributable to his position as tenant in fee, there is always the possibility that he is a mere tenant for life or years. As Lord Erskine once said : " No man in his senses would take an offer of a purchase from a man merely because he stood on the ground."[4]   Even the rule under the Limitation Act, that a person's title to land is extinguished after twelve years' adverse possession by a disseisor,[5] does not in itself enable a disseisor to show a good title by proving possession in himself for even thirty years, since possession for the statutory period does not bar the rights of remaindermen and reversioners entitled to the land upon the determination of the disseisee's interest.   He must go further and show what persons were entitled to the land when he took possession and prove that their claims have been barred by his continuance in possession.[5]

Evidence of title usually documentary.

The usual way, therefore, in which the vendor proves his title is to produce the deeds or other documents by which the land has been disposed of in the past in order to show that the interest which he has agreed to sell has devolved upon him.   Thus, in the normal case the evidence of his title is documentary and is set out in the abstract of title that he delivers to the purchaser.   This abstract must start with what is called a *good root of title, i.e.* a document which deals with the legal estate in the land, which is valid without requiring a reference to any earlier document, which adequately identifies the *res vendita*, and which contains nothing to cast doubts on the title of the disposing party.

Thus a conveyance by way of sale or of mortgage effected at least 30 years ago is a perfect root of title, since it may be presumed that the alienee was satisfied at that time with the state of the alienor's title, and if the intervening dispositions have been satisfactory, the present purchaser will obviously acquire a good title. A *general*, as distinct from a *specific*, devise of land is not a good root of title, since it does not identify the property and therefore does not show that the will passed the ownership of the same land as the vendor has now agreed to sell.   A disentailing assurance

---

[1] *Barnwell* v. *Harris* (1809), 1 Taunt. 430, 432, *per* Heath, J.
[2] Vendor and Purchaser Act, 1874, s. 1.
[3] Law of Property Act, 1925, s. 44 (1).
[4] *Hiern* v. *Mill* (1806), 13 Ves. 114, 122.
[5] *Games* v. *Bonnor* (1884), 54 L. J. 517 ; *Scott* v. *Nixon* (1843), 3 Dr. and War. 388 (Ireland).

executed after December 31, 1925, is not a good root of title unless in addition to the disentailment it contains a disposition of the resultant legal estate, for otherwise it is a document that affects only the equitable interest.

The obligation to begin the abstract with a good root of title may, of course, necessitate going back to some document more than thirty years old. NORTH, J., in one case said :—

> " And when I say a [30] years' title, I mean a title deduced for [30]
> " years and for so much longer as it is necessary to go back in order
> " to arrive at a point at which the title can properly commence.
> " The title cannot commence *in nubibus* at the exact point of time
> " which is represented by 365 days multiplied by [30]. It must
> " commence at or before the [30] years with something which is
> " in itself . . . a proper root of title." [1]

There are a few cases in which the period for which title must be shown is longer than thirty years. Thus,

(i) where an advowson is sold, title must be shown for 100 years ;

(ii) upon the sale of a leasehold, the lease, however old, must be produced, but the purchaser is not entitled to call for the title to the reversion [2] ;

(iii) if the subject-matter of the sale is a reversionary interest, the title must be carried back to the instrument which created the interest.

(B) DUTY OF VENDOR TO ABSTRACT AND PRODUCE DOCUMENTS.

The vendor must at his own expense abstract and, if under his own control, produce the document which forms the root of his title, and all subsequent documents that affect the legal estate. In addition he must state and prove all facts that have affected the legal estate in the last 30 years.

But there are certain things that must not be abstracted, and certain titles and documents that cannot be called for.

(i) **Certain equitable interests not to be abstracted.** Overreached equities not to be abstracted. Under the old law a purchaser who took a conveyance of the legal estate was bound by any equitable interests affecting that estate of which he had notice. If, for instance,

> the abstract showed that the legal estate was held by the vendor as trustee, then, provided that he was not an express trustee for sale, the equitable interests were *ipso facto* notified to the purchaser. It was necessary for the vendor to abstract the title to the equitable interests, and to obtain the concurrence of the beneficiaries in the conveyance.

---

[1] *In re Cox and Neve's Contract,* [1891] 2 Ch. 109, 118.
[2] Law of Property Act, 1925, s. 44 (2), (3), (4).

But, as we have seen, one of the chief objects of the legislation of 1925 was to enable a purchaser to acquire the legal estate from the estate owner without being required to concern himself with equitable interests enforceable against the land. In general pursuance of this idea the Law of Property Act, 1925, provides that in certain cases it shall not be proper to mention equitable interests in the abstract. It does not exclude all such interests, but only those that are overreached by the conveyance. What these are will be stated below.[1] The section in question is as follows [2]:—

> " Where title is shown to a legal estate in land, it shall be
> " deemed not necessary or proper to include in the abstract of
> " title an instrument relating only to interests or powers which
> " will be overreached by the conveyance of the estate to which
> " title is being shown ; but nothing in this part of this Act
> " affects the liability of any person to disclose an equitable
> " interest or power which will not be so overreached, or to
> " furnish an abstract of any instrument creating or affecting
> " the same."

Thus, to take a simple illustration, a mortgagee who has contracted to sell the fee simple absolute by virtue of his statutory power of sale, is not required to abstract mortgages which are subsequent to his own.[3]

Contents of abstract when leasehold assigned.

(ii) **Freehold title not to be abstracted on sale of lease-hold.** If the subject-matter of the sale is a term of years, the vendor is bound, as we have seen, to abstract and produce the lease under which he holds the land ; but it is enacted that in an open contract he shall not be required to prove the title to the freehold.[4] This latter rule applies where a fee simple owner agrees to *grant* a lease.

Thus :

> If A. is fee simple owner of the land, and if he agrees to grant a lease to B. for 99 years, B. is not entitled to call for proof of A.'s title to the fee simple, unless he has inserted an express stipulation to that effect in the contract. Again, if B. agrees later to sell his estate to C., the latter is precluded from calling for the title of A.

Similar rules apply to an agreement to sell a leasehold interest that is derived out of a leasehold interest, or to an agreement to grant such a lease.[5] If, for example :

> A. leases to B. and B. underleases to C., and C. agrees to sell his interest to D., then D. is entitled to production of the underlease,[6] but he cannot call for the lease to B.

---

[1] *Infra*, pp. 691-2; 696.
[2] Law of Property Act, 1925, s. 10.
[3] *Supra*, pp. 601-2.
[4] Law of Property Act, 1925, s. 44 (2).
[5] *Ibid.*, s. 44 (3), (4).
[6] *Gosling* v. *Woolf*, [1893] 1 Q. B. 39.

These rules were formerly contained in the Vendor and Purchaser Act, 1874, and the Conveyancing Act, 1881, and it was held under those statutes that, failing their express exclusion by the contract, a lessee or a purchaser of a term of years was bound by equities affecting the legal estate that would have come to his notice had he expressly required the freehold title to be disclosed. This was decided in *Patman* v. *Harland*.[1]

Liability of assignee to equities.

> In that case plaintiff sold land to A. subject to a restrictive covenant. A. sold to B., and B. leased part of the land to the defendant, who committed a breach of the covenant. Defendant had no knowledge of the existence of the restrictive covenant, and, in an action brought against her for an injunction, it was argued that, as in an open contract she was debarred by the statute from inquiring into the title to the freehold out of which her lease was derived, she had no notice, actual or constructive, of the restrictive covenant, and therefore was not liable for its breach.

Patman v. *Harland.*

This argument was rejected by the Court of Appeal.

It is now, however, provided that a person who, under the above rules, is not entitled to call for the title to the freehold or the leasehold reversion shall not be deemed to be affected with notice of any matter or thing of which, if he had contracted that such title should be furnished, he might have had notice.[2] The doctrine of *Patman* v. *Harland* is therefore abolished in cases where a purchaser of a lease-hold interest has no right to call for the freehold title, though, in the case of registered land, it still applies to incumbrances which are entered in the register.[3] This statutory alteration operates, therefore, to the detriment of the owner of the equity, but the alteration is subject to the qualification that the lessee remains bound by any equities that have been registered under the land Charges Act, 1925.[4]

Abolition of rule in Patman v. *Harland.*

There is also a more general enactment to the effect that a purchaser shall not be deemed to have notice of any matter or thing of which, if he had investigated the title prior to the beginning of the 30 years' period, he might have had notice, unless he actually makes the investigation.[5]

Purchaser in this connexion means one who acquires an interest for money or money's worth, and includes a lessee and a mortgagee.[6] The expression *money's worth* excludes the consideration of marriage.

---

[1] (1881), 17 Ch. D. 353 See 56 *L. Q. R.* 361.
[2] Law of Property Act, 1925, s. 44 (5).
[3] *White* v. *Bijou Mansions, Ltd.,* [1937] Ch. 610.
[4] *Ibid.,* at p. 619. As to what equities are registrable, see *infra,* pp. 669–70.
[5] Law of Property Act, 1925, s. 44 (8).
[6] *Ibid.,* s. 205 (1) (xxi).

(C) OBLIGATION OF PURCHASER TO BEAR THE COST OF PRODUCING CERTAIN DOCUMENTS.

In general vendor bears cost.   We have seen that one of the duties of a vendor is to produce a perfect abstract of title ; it is incidental to this that he must produce at his own expense the documents which go to prove the title. If these are not in his possession, he must arrange for the production of those dated after the period of 30 years began in so far as they are material.[1] But as regards the expense of producing documents, the rule varies according as they are in the possession of the vendor or not.

Where purchaser bears cost.   At common law a vendor was bound to bear the cost of producing documents whether in his own possession or not, but the Conveyancing Act, 1881, provided that the expenses of the production and of the inspection of documents *not in the vendor's possession*, the expenses of all journeys incidental thereto, and the expenses of procuring all evidences and information not in the vendor's possession should be borne by the purchaser.[2]

It was held under this section that where the vendor had mortgaged his property, the purchaser must pay the mortgagee's solicitor a fee for producing the deeds relating to the property.[3] This was a harsh application of the rule, and therefore the Law of Property Act, 1925, while re-enacting the provisions of the Conveyancing Act, expressly provides that the expense of producing deeds which are in the possession of the vendor's *mortgagee or trustee* shall fall upon the vendor.[4] If, however, the mortgagee retains possession of a document, the purchaser must pay for any copy which he desires to have.

(D) OBLIGATION OF PURCHASER TO EXAMINE THE ABSTRACT AT HIS OWN EXPENSE.

Perusal of abstract.   The perusal of the abstract is carried out by the purchaser's solicitor, whose duty it is to advise whether the vendor has shown a good title to the exact interest that he has agreed to sell. He must satisfy himself that the abstract exhibits an ordered sequence of all the documents and events which have disposed of or affected the interest during the last 30 years, and if he observes defects or omissions, he must requisition the vendor on the matter. He must compare the abstract with the original deeds which are produced by the vendor's solicitor, and put in requisitions on points of discrepancy.

The solicitor must, for instance, require proper evidence of facts which affect the interest, ascertain that the abstracted docu-

---

[1] *Re Stamford, etc., and Knight's Contract*, [1900] 1 Ch. 287.
[2] S. 3 (6).
[3] *Re Willett and Argenti* (1889), 60 L. T. 735.
[4] Law of Property Act, 1925, s. 45 (4).

ments bear stamps of the proper value, and inquire concerning the existence of tenancies and easements.

Investigation of title and registration. One of the first essentials in the investigation of an abstract of title is that a purchaser should search for incumbrances and equitable interests which affect the land to be sold, and which may have been registered by their owners in a public register. This will be seen to be of great importance when we come to examine whether the purchaser of a legal estate takes the estate free from equitable interests charged thereon. There are two registries to be noticed, namely,

(margin: Registration of charges, etc.)

1. the Land Registry in London, and
2. the Local Registry which is kept by the proper officers of the various local authorities.[1]

The Registrar of the Land Registry keeps five separate Registers, namely,

(1) a register of pending actions ;
(2) a register of annuities ;
(3) a register of writs and orders affecting land ;
(4) a register of deeds of arrangements affecting land ; and
(5) a register of land charges.[2]

We will take these registers separately, and notice what kind of right or interest in land may be registered in each.

(i) Register of pending actions. It is obviously impossible to bring an action relating to land to a successful termination if alienation *pendente lite* is permissible, and therefore, in order that a plaintiff may not lose the fruits of his action, the law provides him with the means of protecting himself. This is afforded by the right to register any action, information or proceeding which is pending in court, and which relates to land or to any interest in, or charge on, land.[3]

(margin: Actions relating to land.)

Again, if a creditor wishes to make his debtor's property available for distribution among creditors generally, he may register in the same register the petition in bankruptcy which is the first step in setting bankruptcy proceedings in motion.[4]

(margin: Petition in bankruptcy.)

If a pending action (*i.e.* either an action relating to land or a petition in bankruptcy) is registered, the registration remains effective for five years, but it may be renewed from time to time.[5] A purchaser (which word includes a mortgagee and lessee) of any interest in the land takes free from an *unregistered* pending action unless he has express, as distinct from constructive, notice of it. In the case of an

(margin: Effect of failure to register.)

---

[1] Land Charges Act, 1925, s. 15. [2] *Ibid.*, s. 1 (1).
[3] *Ibid.*, s. 2 (1). [4] *Ibid.*
[5] Land Charges Act, 1925, s. 2 (8).

unregistered bankruptcy petition, however, this protection avails him only if he is a purchaser of the *legal* estate in good faith for money or money's worth.[1]

Annuities.   **(ii) Register of annuities.** Under the old law annuities or rentcharges did not affect purchasers of the land upon which they were charged unless they were registered in the Register of Annuities. This Register has now, however, been abolished for the future, and it will be closed as soon as the annuities registered before January 1, 1926, have been worked off.[2]

Annuities, being interests for life merely, are necessarily equitable in nature under the modern law of property, and they may now be registered as *general equitable charges* in the Register of Land Charges.[3]

Writs and Orders.   **(iii) Register of writs and orders affecting land.** Any writ or order affecting land issued by a court for the purpose of enforcing a judgment,[4] any order which appoints a receiver of land, and any receiving order in bankruptcy, whether it is known to affect land or not, is void against a purchaser of the land unless it is registered.[5]

Receiving Order.   A receiving order is an order of the Bankruptcy Court placing the debtor's property under the control of the court through its officer, the official receiver, and it is practically equivalent to a decision that the debtor is to be adjudged bankrupt. It is enacted that an unregistered receiving order is to be void only against a purchaser of a legal estate in good faith, for money or money's worth and without notice of an available act of bankruptcy.[6]

Arrangements with creditors.   **(iv) Register of deeds of arrangement affecting land.** An insolvent debtor sometimes comes to an arrangement with the general body of his creditors whereby, although he does not pay his debts in full, he obtains a release from the claims of the creditors. As a rule the debtor either compounds with his creditors, or assigns his property to a trustee for distribution among the creditors.

If such an arrangement is reduced to writing, it is called a deed of arrangement whether it is made under seal or not.[7] It is enacted that such an arrangement shall be void against a purchaser of the debtor's land unless it is registered in the

---

[1] Land Charges Act, 1925, s. 3 (1).
[2] *Ibid.*, s. 4.   [3] *Infra*, p. 668.
[4] *Infra*, pp. 726–8.
[5] Land Charges Act, 1925, ss. 6, 7 (1).
[6] *Ibid.*, s. 7 (1) proviso. For receiving order, see *infra*, p. 729.
[7] Deeds of Arrangement Act, 1914, s. 1.

above Register.   Registration ceases to have any effect after five years unless it is renewed.[1]

(v) **Register of land charges.**   The term *land charge* is comprehensive ; it includes a number of different rights and interests affecting land.   The Land Charges Act, 1925, which made considerable additions to this part of the law, divides all land charges into four classes, denominated A, B, C, and D, and provides that they may be registered in the above Register.[2]

Land charges.

Class A.[3]

This comprises a rent or a sum of money which is charged upon land, *pursuant to the application of some person*, under the provisions of any Act of Parliament, and with the object of securing money which has been spent on the land under the provisions of such Act.   It also comprises a rent or a sum of money charged upon land in accordance with certain sections in :

Voluntary statutory charges.

the Land Drainage Act, 1930,[4]
the Agricultural Holdings Act, 1948,[5]
the Tithe Annuities Apportionment Acts, 1921[6] and
  the Tithe Act, 1951,[7]
the Landlord and Tenant Act, 1927,[8] and
the Town and Country Planning Act, 1962.[9]

Thus, if an estate owner borrows money for the improvement of the property under the Improvement of Land Acts, the charge which is created in favour of the lender may be registered, or, if a tenant for life is compelled to pay compensation to an outgoing agricultural tenant, he may obtain an order charging the holding with the repayment of the amount, and may have the charge registered.   A land charge of this class is void against a purchaser unless it is registered before the completion of the purchase.[10]

Class B.[11]

This comprises a charge on land (not being a local land charge) of any of the kinds described in Class A, provided

Statutory charges in invitum.

---

[1] Land Charges Act, 1925, ss. 8, 9.
[2] There is a fifth class, E, which comprises annuities created before 1926 and not registered in the Register of Annuities.   This register, as we have seen, was closed to new entries as from January 1, 1926, but annuitants who omitted to register before that date may now take advantage of the new register, Class E.
[3] Land Charges Act, 1925, s. 10 (1), Class A.
[4] S. 9.   [5] Ss. 72, 73, 74, 82.   [6] S. 1.   [7] S. 10 (4).
[8] First Schedule, as amended by Landlord and Tenant Act, 1954, s. 45 and 7th Schedule, Pt. I.
[9] 10th Schedule, para. 8 (charge in respect of unauthorised development).
[10] Land Charges Act, 1925, s. 13 (1).
[11] *Ibid.*, s. 10 (1), Class B.

that it has not been created " pursuant to the application of any person."

This class has been added by the Act of 1925 in order to reverse the decision in *R. v. Land Registry*,[1] where it was held

> that charges created upon property independently of the wish of the owner could not be registered under Class A.

Charges of this class, consisting, as we see, of those which are created in land independently of the wishes of the owner, are not important as regards searches in the Land Registry, because they mostly arise under the Public Health Act, 1936, and being in the majority of cases of a local nature (as, for instance, those arising in respect of paving expenses) they are *local land charges* and must therefore be registered locally.[2] However, failure to register such a charge (not being a local charge) at the Land Registry renders it void as against a purchaser for valuable consideration of the land or of any interest therein

(i) if it arises after December 31, 1925, and has not been registered ;

(ii) if it arose before that date and has not been registered within a year from the first conveyance of the charge made after December 31, 1925.[3]

Class C.[4]

This class is mainly important in that it extends the system of registration of mortgages. It comprises four different charges, namely :—

(a) **Puisne mortgages.** Any *legal* mortgagee, whether a first or a later mortgagee, who does not get possession of the title deeds, is said to have a puisne mortgage.

(b) **A limited owner's charge.** This is a charge which arises under the Finance Act, 1894, in favour of a tenant for life who pays estate duty in respect of the estate out of which his life interest is carved.

(c) **A general equitable charge.** This is a comprehensive expression that includes all equitable charges that are not assigned to a class of their own (such as estate contracts), and which do not arise or affect an interest arising under a settlement or a trust for sale. In particular it includes an equitable mortgage of a legal estate which is not secured by a deposit of the title deeds, but it also comprises a rentcharge for life and a vendor's or

---

[1] *R. v. Land Registry* (1889), 24 Q. B. D. 178.
[2] *Infra*, p. 671.
[3] Land Charges Act, 1925, ss. 13 (2), 14 (2).
[4] *Ibid.*, s. 10 (1), Class C.

a purchaser's lien. To be registrable, the charge must be on land, and not for instance upon the purchase money that will arise from the sale of land.[1]

(*d*) **An estate contract.** This is the only item included within Class C which is not in the nature of a mortgage. It is defined as being " any contract by an estate owner, or by a person entitled at the date of the contract to have a legal estate conveyed to him, to convey or create a legal estate, including a contract conferring either expressly or by statutory implication a valid option of purchase, a right of pre-emption or any other like right." [2] This in practice means a contract for the sale of a legal fee simple, an agreement for the grant of a term of years absolute,[3] or an option to acquire either of these interests.[4] We have already seen that the effect of such a contract is to confer an equitable interest upon the intending purchaser or tenant. The effect of the Land Charges Act is to make it capable of registration whether it is written or oral.[5]

Class D.[6]

This comprises the three following different charges :—

(*a*) **Charges for death duties.** The Law of Property Act, 1925, provides in general that the liability to pay death duties in respect of land shall fall upon the personal representatives of the deceased,[7] but it departs from the former practice by enacting that where a charge in respect of such duties is not registered as a land charge, a purchaser of the legal estate shall take free from all liability in connection with them.[8] The Land Charges Act therefore provides in Class D that the

---

[1] *Georgiades* v. *Edward Wolfe & Co., Ltd.*, [1965] Ch. 487; [1964] 3 All E. R. 433.

[2] Land Charges Act, 1925, s. 10 (1), Class C. (iv).

[3] *Sharp* v. *Coates*, [1949] 1 K. B. 285; [1948] 3 All E. R. 871. Contract by estate owner to convey an estate greater than he was entitled to at the time of the contract. It also includes a contract by which A. agrees with B. to create a legal estate in favour of such third person as B. may nominate, *Turley* v. *Mackay* [1944] Ch. 37; [1943] 3 All E. R. 1.

[4] *Beesly* v. *Hallwood Estates Ltd.*, [1960] 2 All E. R. 314; [1960] 1 W. L .R. 549. BUCKLEY, J., was able to reach this decision despite the difficulty that the statutory definition pre-supposes a contract, and yet an option is not a contract but a standing offer which the offeree may or may not convert into a contract. The decision was affirmed on another point, [1961] Ch. 105; [1961] 1 All E. R. 90. A notice to treat served under a compulsory purchase order is not a contract, though it may lead to one, and therefore is not registrable; *Capital Investments, Ltd.* v. *Wednesfield U.D.C.*, [1965] Ch. 774; [1964] 1 All E. R. 655.

[5] *Universal Permanent Building Society* v. *Cooke*, [1952] Ch. 95, 104; [1951] 2 All E. R. 893, 898.

[6] Land Charges Act, 1925, s. 10 (1), Class D.

[7] Law of Property Act, 1925, s. 16.　　　　　[8] *Ibid.*, s. 17 (1).

Commissioners of Inland Revenue may register such a charge as soon as it arises, that is, upon the death of the person whose interest is liable for duty.

(*b*) **A restrictive covenant.** This has already been des- cribed,[1] and the only remark needed here is that restrictive covenants made between a lessor and a lessee are ex- pressly excluded, and are not capable of registration.

(*c*) **An equitable easement.** This is defined as [2] " any easement, right or privilege over or affecting land arising after the commencement of this Act and being merely an equitable interest." Thus, an easement held for some smaller interest than a fee simple absolute in possession or for a term of years absolute, or an ease- ment that has been informally created, satisfies this definition and is therefore registrable.

The three charges in this Class D are not registrable unless they have arisen after 1925.

The effect of a failure to register the charges comprised in Classes C and D is as follows :

> Puisne mortgages,
> Limited owners' charges,
> General equitable charges

are void against

> any purchaser for valuable consideration of the land charged therewith or of *any interest therein*, unless registered before completion of the purchase.[3] " Purchaser " means any person, including a mortgagee or lessee, who takes any interest in land for valuable consideration.[4] " Valuable consideration " includes marriage, but does not include a nominal consideration in money.[5]

It will be seen from the words italicized that a purchaser even of an equitable interest in the land affected takes free from these charges if unregistered, irrespectively of whether he has actual notice or not.

> Estate contracts,
> Charges for death duties,
> Restrictive covenants,
> Equitable easements

are void against

Marginal notes: Effect of non-regis- tration. Effect of failure to register.

---

[1] *Supra*, pp. 537 *et seq.*
[2] The words " right or privilege " must be construed *ejusdem generis* with " easement " ; *Lewisham Borough Council* v. *Maloney*, [1948] 1 K. B. 50 ; [1947] 2 All E. R. 36.
[3] Land Charges Act, 1925, s. 13 (2).
[4] *Ibid.*, s. 20 (8).
[5] *Cf.* Law of Property Act, 1925, s. 205 (1) (xxi).

a purchaser of the *legal estate* in the land for *money or money's worth* unless registered before completion of the purchase.[1]

It therefore follows that these four charges, even if unregistered, bind a purchaser of an equitable interest whether he has notice or not. Again, a purchaser even of a legal estate, whose title is supported only by a marriage consideration, cannot rely upon the omission to register.

In addition to the Registers kept at the Land Registry, local registers are maintained by the various district and borough councils and county councils in which charges over land acquired by these bodies may be registered.[2] Such charges, as, for instance, one arising in respect of paving expenses, are called local land charges.[3]

Local land charges.

The fact that a charge cannot be registered until it has actually been created occasioned some difficulty after the Land Charges Act, 1925, came into operation. The provision of the Act that a charge on land, such as a restrictive covenant, shall be void against a subsequent purchaser of the legal estate for money or money's worth unless it is registered before *completion* of that purchase, produces an *impasse* in certain cases, for it is sometimes impossible to effect registration before completion. A common example of this arises where

Priority notices.

> X. agrees to sell Blackacre to Y. and takes a restrictive covenant from Y. Y., being unable to find the whole of the purchase money, arranges to mortgage Blackacre to Z. The conveyance from X. to Y. which creates the restrictive covenant and the mortgage from Y. to Z. are in practice completed at the same time, so that it is practically impossible for X. to register his restrictive covenant before it is rendered void under the Act by the completion of the purchase in favour of Z.

The Law of Property (Amendment) Act, 1926,[4] has removed this difficulty by providing that any person *intending* to apply for the registration of any *contemplated* charge may register notice of his intention at the Land Registry. This notice, which is called a *priority notice*, must be given at least fourteen days before the registration is to take effect.[5] When the contemplated charge is actually created and later registered, then, provided that it is registered within twenty-eight days after the priority notice, it

---

[1] Land Charges Act, 1925, s. 13 (2).
[2] *Ibid.*, s. 15. The number of local land charges has been vastly increased by successive statutes; see e.g. 38 Halsbury's Laws of England (3rd Edn.), pp. 79–80 and the Annual Supplement.
[3] Certain land charges affecting land in Yorkshire are not registrable at the Land Registry but in the Registers kept at Northallerton, Beverley and Wakefield under the Yorkshire Registries Act, 1884; Law of Property (Amendment) Act, 1926, Schedule, amending Land Charges Act, 1925, s. 10 (6).
[4] S. 4 (1).
[5] S. R. & O., 1940, No. 1998/L. 37.

takes effect as if registration had been secured at the very moment of its creation.[1]

Official searches.

A purchaser, instead of searching in a register himself, may, on payment of the prescribed fee, demand an official search. Upon receipt of such a requisition (as it is called) the registrar, after making the search, issues an official certificate, which is conclusive in favour of the purchaser.[2] If another charge is registered by a third person between the time when the certificate is issued and the time when the purchase is completed by the certificate holder, the registration does not affect the latter, provided that he completes his purchase within fourteen days of the issue of the certificate.[3]

Summary of position as regards registration.

Lest we should fail to see the wood for the trees, we may conclude this section with the remark that none of the adverse claims, legal interests and charges detailed in the preceding pages *need* be registered.   The Land Charges Act does two things :

first, it establishes a certain number of registers, and provides that the interests described above *may* be registered ;

secondly, it provides that the interests shall not be enforceable against a purchaser of the land unless they are registered.

A purchaser knows that the land he intends to buy may be subject to estates, interests, charges and claims vested in third parties.   It is his duty to discover whether any of these exist. A great many of these third party rights will emerge if the purchaser makes a proper perusal of the abstract of title, and if he inspects the actual land to be sold and interrogates any occupier in whose possession it may be.   He will, for instance, acquire knowledge of a legal mortgage because his vendor will be unable to produce the title deeds ; he can discover the existence of a lease by inquiring of the occupier ; and the existence of a right of way will probably become apparent from a careful inspection of the premises.   But as long as we have a system of conveyancing under which title to land is proved by production of deeds kept in private custody, it is clear that there must be a number of third party rights, such as pending actions, deeds of arrangement and so on, which will be revealed neither by an examination of title deeds nor by inspection of the ground.   Nevertheless such rights may lead to a purchaser being deprived of the land he has paid for.   Therefore the principle of the Land Charges Act is to provide a State Registry in which all those charges and liabilities that will not be revealed under our system of private conveyancing may be registered.   All that a purchaser need do is to examine the registers.   If he finds nothing registered against the vendor and

---

[1] S. R. & O. 1940, No. 2195/L. 42.
[2] Land Charges Act, 1925, s. 17.
[3] Land Charges (No. 1) Rules, 1940, R. 1 (2).

other persons previously entitled to the land, he takes free from claims which might have been, but have not been entered.[1]   The registrable items are *primâ facie* unrelated, but actually they consist of all instruments and facts which would otherwise not be discoverable.[2]

(E) Duty of Vendor to Convey the Identical Property that he has agreed to Sell.

The vendor must prove that the property which he is able to convey is substantially the same in nature, situation and quantity as that which he has agreed to sell, and it is advisable, when a contract for the sale of land is drafted, to obtain a description of the land from the " parcels " clause of the last conveyance.[3]

Distinction between trifling and material variation.

If, in the case of an open contract, the property is not identical in quantity or quality with that agreed to be sold, the vendor cannot compel enforcement of the contract subject to compensation, unless the difference is insignificant and his conduct has been honest.[4]

> " If a vendor sues and is in a position to convey substantially what
> " the purchaser has contracted to get, the court will decree specific
> " performance with compensation for any small and immaterial
> " deficiency, provided that the vendor has not, by misrepresentation
> " or otherwise, disentitled himself to his remedy."[5]

Thus, if an agreement for sale is made, and investigation of the title shows that the property is subject to restrictive covenants, the vendor cannot force the title on the purchaser subject to compensation,[6] but he can do so, for example, if the sole mistake is that a right of common attached to the land extends only to sheep instead of being, as represented, unlimited.[7]

A purchaser, on the other hand, is in a more favourable position, for as a general rule he is allowed to take all that he can get, and to subject the vendor to a proportionate diminution of the purchase-money.   But specific performance will not be decreed at the suit of the purchaser if the property which the vendor is in a position to convey is entirely different from that

---

[1] The weakness of the system is that the registration is not against the land but against the estate owner or other person whose interest in the land is affected.

[2] 41 *L. Q. R.*, p. 176, " The Land Charges Act in Jurisprudence."

[3] Williams, *Vendor and Purchaser* (4th Edn.), p. 36; for the " parcels " clause," see *infra*, pp. 683 ; 686.

[4] *Cox* v. *Coventon* (1862), 31 Beav. 378 ; *Re Arnold* (1880), 14 Ch. D. 270, 279 ; *supra*, p. 655.

[5] *Rutherford* v. *Acton-Adams*, [1915] A. C. 866, 869-70.

[6] *Cf. Rudd* v. *Lascelles*, [1900] 1 Ch. 815.

[7] *Howland* v. *Norris* (1784), 1 Cox, Eq. Cas. 59.

which he agreed to sell, or if the difference is one for which it is impossible to fix pecuniary compensation, or if the effect of decreeing specific performance would be to cause injustice to third parties.[1]

(F) Duty of the Purchaser to Complete the Contract.

Completion.   After the purchaser has investigated the abstract, it is his duty either to accept or to reject the title offered to him. If he takes the latter course, the parties are left to their remedies as specified above.[2] If, however, the purchaser is satisfied with the title, then the contract must be completed at once. Completion of a contract means that the purchaser must at his own expense prepare a proper deed of conveyance which is effectual to pass the interest to be sold and which contains the usual covenants for title by the vendor. He must also tender the price that he has agreed to pay. On the vendor's side completion involves the execution of the conveyance and the delivery of possession of the land to the purchaser.[3]

But such acceptance of the title does not prevent a purchaser from objecting to some defect which has emerged subsequently, and which has been discovered from information other than that supplied by the vendor. If, for instance, in making the usual searches, he discovers some charge that will be binding upon him, he may reject the title.

(G) Duty of Vendor to Deliver the Title Deeds.[4]

The vendor must deliver to the purchaser all title deeds which relate solely to the property sold, though he may retain such documents where he retains any part of the land to which they relate, or where the document consists of a trust instrument creating a trust that is still subsisting.[5] Where the documents which are necessary to show a good title remain in the vendor's possession, or where their custody belongs to some person other than the vendor, it is the vendor's duty to give a written acknowledgment of the purchaser's right to their production and to delivery of copies and a written undertaking for their safe custody. The effect of such an acknowledgment is that the purchaser, or persons claiming under him, can, at their own expense, demand to see the documents, or claim to be furnished with copies.[6]

---

[1] *Willmott* v. *Barber* (1880), 15 Ch. D. 96.
[2] *Supra,* pp. 652 *et seq.*
[3] Williams, *Vendor and Purchaser* (4th Edn.), p. 37.
[4] As to the right to possession of title deeds, see *Clayton* v. *Clayton,* [1930] 2 Ch. 12.
[5] Law of Property Act, 1925, s. 45 (9).   [6] *Ibid.,* s. 64.

(H) Duty to Deliver Vacant Possession.

Lastly, it is an implicit term of a contract of sale that vacant possession shall be given to the purchaser on completion.[1] Therefore a refusal by the purchaser to complete is justified if the land is subject to an unexpired tenancy, or if it has been lawfully requisitioned by a public authority.[2]

(2) CONDITIONS OF SALE UNDER CONTRACTS CONTAINING SPECIAL STIPULATIONS.

We have now described in bare outline the nature of the parties' obligations under an open contract. Land, however, is not usually sold in this manner, for the vendor, with a view of mitigating some of the obligations that are imposed upon him under such a transaction, generally limits his obligations by the insertion of special conditions in the contract of sale. These conditions naturally vary in each case and an account of them falls within the province of a book on conveyancing, so that we must here be content to mention a few examples.

Perhaps the most important example is the length of title which the vendor must show. There is nothing to prevent a stipulation that the purchaser shall accept proof of title for a period less than the period of 30 years required by law in the case of an open contract, and it is common to find a condition providing that the title shall begin with, say, a mortgage deed executed 20 years ago. A contract containing such a condition, though readily accepted in practice, should be made with caution by the purchaser's solicitor, for under the doctrine of constructive notice the rule is that a purchaser is bound by any interest charged upon the land that he would have discovered had he investigated the title for the statutory period of 30 years.[3]

Condition as to length of title.

In addition there are several other obligations and rules that a vendor may wish to vary. For instance he may

> reserve the right to rescind the contract upon return of the deposit if too onerous a requisition is made ;[4]

---

[1] *Cook* v. *Taylor*, [1942] Ch. 349 ; [1942] 2 All E. R. 85.

[2] *Cook* v. *Taylor, supra* ; dist. *Re Winslow Hall Estates Co. and United Glass Bottle Manufacturers, Ltd.'s Contract,* [1941] Ch. 503 ; [1941] 3 All E. R. 124.

[3] *Re Cox and Neve's Contract,* [1891] 2 Ch. 109 ; *Re Nisbet and Potts' Contract,* [1905] 1 Ch. 391 ; affirmed, [1906] 1 Ch. 386. This rule has not been altered by the Law of Property Act, 1925. s. 44 (8) ; *supra,* p. 663.

[4] The court will restrain the exercise of the right if the vendor seeks to enforce it capriciously or arbitrarily; or if he has recklessly offered a title that he cannot reasonably expect to deliver; *Selkirk* v. *Romar Investments, Ltd.,* [1963] 3 All E. R. 994; [1963] 1 W. L. R. 1415.

provide that the purchaser shall be deemed to have accepted the title unless requisitions are made within a limited time ;

provide that the sale shall not be invalidated by reason only that there is some error in the description of the property as contained in the contract ;

provide that the purchaser shall pay interest if *from any cause whatever* other than the wilful default of the vendor the transaction is not completed on the agreed date.

SECTION III. THE CONVEYANCE.

SUMMARY.

(1) NECESSITY FOR A DEED.

Deed of grant not universal till 1845.

Forms of Alienation. The appropriate form at the present day for the conveyance of any interest in land is a deed of grant, but this form, though always required for the transfer of incorporeal hereditaments, was not extended to freehold estates in possession until 1845. Before that date the distinction drawn by the law was that freehold estates in possession *lay in livery, i.e.* were transferable by delivery of possession, and that incorporeal interests *lay in grant, i.e.* must be conveyed by deed of grant.[1] The Real Property Act of 1845, however, provided that all corporeal hereditaments should, as regards the conveyance of the immediate freehold thereof, be deemed to lie in grant as well as in livery. This Act did not, however, abolish the old forms of conveyance, and although it led to the general use of a deed of grant as a means of transferring all kinds of landed interests, there were still occasions upon which such forms as the feoffment and the bargain and sale were used.

Real Property Act, 1845.

Modern law requires deed.

The Law of Property Act, 1925, simplified practice by providing that [2] :

" All lands and all interests therein lie in grant and are incapable of "being conveyed by livery or livery and seisin, or by feoffment, or by "bargain and sale ; and a conveyance of an interest in land may "operate to pass the possession or right to possession thereof, without "actual entry, but subject to all prior rights thereto."

This section, which shows that a grant is the usual method of conveying any interest in land, is followed by another which provides that all conveyances of land, or of any interest therein, are

---

[1] For the history of the forms of alienation, see Holdsworth, *History of English Law*, vol. iii. pp. 217–46 ; vol. vii. pp. 357–62. See *supra*, p. 49, n. 1.

[2] Law of Property Act, 1925, s. 51 (1).

void for the purpose of transferring or creating a legal estate unless they are made by deed.[1] This enactment, if unqualified, would cause inconvenience in certain cases, and it is therefore subject to a few exceptions. These are as follows [2] :— Cases where deed not necessary.

1. **Assents by personal representatives.** The land of a Assents. deceased person vests in his personal representatives for the purposes of administration, and any devises he may have made are suspended until the administration is completed.[3] Upon such completion the land does not pass automatically to a devisee, but only when the assent of the personal representatives has been given. It is enacted that an assent to the vesting of a legal estate shall be *in writing*, signed by the personal representatives, and shall specify the person in whose name it is given and shall operate to vest in that person the legal estate to which it relates. An assent not in writing or not in favour of a named person is ineffectual to pass a legal estate.[4] An implied assent, *i.e.* one inferred from conduct, may be effective to pass a title to equitable interests or to *choses in action* and personal chattels.[5]

2. **Disclaimers by a trustee in bankruptcy.** When any Disclaimer. part of the estate of a bankrupt consists of land which is burdened with onerous covenants and is therefore unsaleable, the trustee in bankruptcy may, by writing, disclaim the property. Such a disclaimer operates to determine the rights and the liabilities of the bankrupt in respect of the property, but it does not affect the rights of third parties. The court may, on the application of any person who is interested in the disclaimed property, make an order vesting the property in him, and the effect of such an order is that the property vests in that person without any conveyance.[6]

3. **Leases for a term not exceeding three years.**[7] Parol leases.

4. **Vesting orders.** A vesting order is an order made by the Vesting order. court which may operate to convey a legal estate in the same way as if a conveyance had been executed by the estate owner.[8] If, for instance,

> an equitable chargee applies for a sale of the land, the court may make an order vesting the land for a legal estate in the purchaser.[9]

---

[1] Law of Property Act, 1925, s. 52 (1).
[2] *Ibid.*, s. 52 (2).   [3] *Infra*, pp. 691 *et seq.*
[4] Administration of Estates Act, 1925, s. 36 (1), (4).
[5] *Re Hodge, Hodge* v. *Griffiths*, [1940] Ch. 260.
[6] Bankruptcy Act, 1914, s. 54, *infra*, pp. 710–1.   [7] *Supra*, p. 352.
[8] Law of Property Act, 1925, s. 9.   [9] *Ibid.*, s. 90.

5. Surrenders by operation of law. *Surrender* is not an instrument, but means that the owner of a smaller estate yields up that estate to the person who is entitled in reversion or remainder to the larger estate in the same lands, as for instance, where the tenant for life of Blackacre surrenders his life interest to the person who is entitled to the fee simple in the land. In such a case the life interest is merged in the fee simple.

(margin) Express surrender requires deed.

Surrenders are either express or implied and when implied they are said to arise by operation of law.

An express surrender is void at law unless it is made by deed, but an implied surrender is effectual without any formality.[1]

(margin) No deed in implied surrender.

6. Conveyances taking effect by operation of law.[2] Examples of these are grants of probate or of letters of administration and adjudications in bankruptcy.

7. Receipts not required to be under seal. We have already seen that the legal estate of a mortgagee is re-vested in the mortgagor upon redemption not by a reconveyance under seal, but by an endorsed receipt.[3]

As regards equitable interests, the statutory rule is that " a disposition of an equitable interest or trust subsisting at the time of the disposition must be in writing signed by the person disposing of the same or by his agent thereunto lawfully authorized, or by will."[4] In this context the word " disposition " must be given the wide meaning that it bears in normal usage, and therefore, for instance, an oral direction to trustees to hold an equitable interest upon new trusts is a disposition that is ineffective for want of writing.[5]

(margin) Transfer of equitable interests.

(2) THE GENERAL NATURE OF A DEED.

Signing, sealing, and delivery. It is difficult to give an exact definition of a deed. In general, however, a deed of grant is a written instrument, which is signed, sealed and delivered by the grantor as his act, and in which he expresses an intention to pass an interest to the grantee. Before 1926 it was a moot question whether it was necessary for a deed to be signed, though in practice it has always been customary for all parties to append their signatures. But signing is now essential in the case of an

(margin) Form of deed.

(margin) Signature essential.

---

[1] *Supra*, p. 416.
[2] Law of Property Act, 1925, s. 52 (2) (*g*).   [3] *Supra*, p. 592.
[4] Law of Property Act, 1925, s. 53 (1) (*c*).
[5] *Grey* v. *I. R. Comrs*, [1960] A.C. 1; [1959] 3 All E. R. 603; contrast *Vandervell* v. *I. R. Comrs.*, [1966] Ch. 261; affirmed, [1967] 1 All E. R. 1, H. L.

individual,[1] for it is enacted that where an *individual* executes a deed after December 31, 1925, he shall either sign or place his mark against the same, and sealing alone shall not be sufficient.[2] To satisfy the requirement of sealing, it is sufficient if a party signs the document with the intention of executing it as a deed, provided that it bears wax, or a wafer or some other indication of a seal.[3]

Signing and sealing a deed are ineffectual to pass the interest to the grantee without delivery. This does not mean a mere physical delivery, but a delivery accompanied by words or conduct signifying the grantor's intention to be bound by the provisions in the deed. The most apt and expressive mode of acknowledging this liability is for the grantor to hand the deed over, saying, " I deliver this as my deed," but any other words or acts that show an undoubted acknowledgment of immediate liability will suffice.[4] A physical delivery, however, unaccompanied by this express or implied acknowledgment, is insufficient, so that if, for instance,

> the grantor signs and seals the deed and then delivers it to his solicitor to be dealt with according to instructions to be given later, it does not operate as an immediate grant of the interest.

Escrow. There are, therefore, two kinds of delivery recognized by the law in this connection, one absolute and the other conditional.[5] If a document is delivered, either to a party to it or to a stranger,[6] with an intimation, express or implied, that it is not to become effective until some condition has been performed, it is called an escrow. In such a case the deed is inoperative until the condition is performed, but upon performance it takes effect as a deed without further delivery, and relates back to the time when it was delivered as an escrow. A delivery of a deed as an escrow is a final delivery in the sense that it cannot be withdrawn by the grantor before the grantee has had an opportunity to decide whether to fulfil the condition or not. A deed delivered subject to a condition and subject to such a right of withdrawal is not an

[margin note:] Delivery.

[margin note:] Conditional delivery.

---

[1] Deeds executed by a corporation must be executed according to the special regulations, if any, prescribed by its constitution. A company incorporated under the Companies Act, 1948, is in this particular governed by the articles of association. But in order to relieve a purchaser from the obligation of ascertaining whether such regulations have been observed, the Law of Property Act, 1925, s. 74 (1), provides that a deed executed after 1925 shall be deemed to have been duly executed by a corporation aggregate if the seal is affixed thereto in the presence of and attested by its clerk, secretary, or other permanent officer, or his deputy, and a member of the directorate, council or other governing body of the corporation.

[2] Law of Property Act, 1925, s. 73.

[3] *Stromdale and Ball, Ltd.* v. *Burden*, [1952] Ch. 223; [1952] 1 All E. R. 59.

[4] *Xenos* v. *Wickham* (1866), L. R. 2 H. L. 296, 312.

[5] *Foundling Hospital* v. *Crane*, [1911] 2 K. B. 367, 377.

[6] *London Freehold and Leasehold Property Co.* v. *Baron Suffield*, [1897] 2 Ch. 608, 621–2.

escrow, but merely an undelivered deed.[1] A common example of delivery as an escrow occurs where a vendor executes a deed of conveyance and gives it to his solicitor for transference to the purchaser upon payment by the latter of the purchase money. Were the rule otherwise the purchaser might keep the legal estate passed to him under the fully executed deed and raise difficulties by refusing to pay the money.

Witness not essential.

Attestation. Signing, sealing and due delivery are, then, essential to constitute a valid deed. Strictly speaking, attestation is not necessary, but it is the invariable practice for parties to execute deeds in the presence of a witness, and to add a statement that the deed has been signed, sealed and delivered in the presence of the witness, who himself signs.

Indentures.

Deeds poll and indentures. Deeds are either deeds poll or indentures. A deed poll is one which is executed by a party of one part, an indenture is a deed (such as a conveyance by way of sale) to which there are parties of two or more parts.

In ancient days, when deeds were more concise than they are at present, it was usual, when they were made between two parties, to write two copies on the same parchment with some words written in the middle through which the parchment was cut in acute angles or indentations.[2] These two parts were called "counterparts," and, when put together so that the indentations fitted into each other, constituted the complete deed. Hence the name "indenture." (Counterparts are not nowadays written on the same parchment, but that which is executed by the grantor of an interest is called the *original*, while that which is executed by the party to whom the interest passes—for example, a lessee— is called the *counterpart*.[3]) The custom of indenting deeds gradually died out, and all that the term "indenture" now indicates is that the deed in question involves parties of more than one part. Despite the provision of the Real Property Act, 1845, that a deed should have the effect of an indenture although not actually indented, it remained customary to introduce every deed which involved more than one party by the expression *This Indenture*. But even this survival has now gone, for it is enacted [4] that any deed may be described according to the nature of the transaction to be effected, so that now the introductory words are

" This Trust Deed,"
" This Legal Charge,"

---

[1] *Beesly* v. *Hallwood Estates, Ltd.*, [1961] Ch. 105; [1960] 1 All E. R. 90; *Windsor Refrigerator Co., Ltd.* v. *Branch Nominees Ltd.*, [1961] Ch. 88; [1960] 2 All E. R. 568; reversed on a different point, [1961] Ch. 375; [1961] 1 All E. R. 277.
[2] Blackstone, vol. ii. p. 295.
[3] Elphinstone, *Introduction to Conveyancing*, p. 60.
[4] Law of Property Act, 1925, s. 57

" This Conveyance,"
" This Lease,"

or a similar appropriate expression.

A deed poll is so called because, unlike an indenture, it was formerly polled (or cut even) at the top.

Conveyance by a person to himself. It is sometimes necessary that an interest shall be conveyed by the grantor to himself jointly with another person, as for instance where a surviving trustee desires to vest the legal estate in himself and a new trustee. At common law this could not be done by one deed, for the effect of a grant by A. to A. and B. was to vest the whole estate in B. The only solution was that A. should convey to X., who would then convey to A. and B., though an alternative method became available, and in fact general, under the doctrine of uses, for if A. conveyed to X. *to the use* of himself and B., the effect of the Statute of Uses was to vest an immediate legal estate in A. and B. jointly. It has been possible, however, since August 1859 in the case of leaseholds, and since 1881 in the case of freeholds, for a person to convey land to himself jointly with another person by a direct deed of grant, and as the Statute of Uses has been repealed, this is now the only method.[1]

There are also occasions when it is necessary that a person should convey land to himself (as, for example, where personal representatives assent to the land vesting in themselves as trustees for sale). Although, in the example given, the design could be effected in a direct manner under statutory provisions, it remained generally true, prior to 1926, that a conveyance by a person to himself required a grant to uses. It is now provided, however, that

" a person may convey land to or vest land in himself." [2]

This, however, does not enable an owner to grant a tenancy to himself, for a lease, though it falls within the statutory definition of a "conveyance" and no doubt vests a legal estate in the lessee, is essentially a contractual transaction. At the lowest it creates a number of implied obligations and liabilities, a situation that is impossible where only one person is involved. A man cannot contract with himself.[3]

Two or more persons (whether trustees or personal representatives or not) may convey any property vested in themselves to any one or more of themselves, though if the conveyance amounts to a breach of trust, it is liable to be set aside.[4]

Marginal notes:
Conveyance to oneself and to another.
Conveyance to oneself.
Grant by two persons to one of themselves

---

[1] Law of Property Act, 1925, s. 72 (1), (2) ; replacing Law of Property (Amendment) Act, 1859, s. 21, and Conveyancing Act, 1881, s. 50.

[2] *Ibid.*, s. 72 (3).

[3] *Rye* v. *Rye*, [1962] A. C. 496; [1962] 1 All E. R. 146.

[4] Law of Property Act, 1925, s. 72 (4).

z*

(3) THE MODERN FORM OF A DEED OF CONVEYANCE ON SALE.

It will perhaps elucidate the subject if we now set out a simple deed of conveyance, and state and explain the effect of each of its parts. The following is a precedent of a conveyance executed by the owner in severalty of a fee simple absolute. The words which form part of the deed are put in heavier type in order to distinguish them from what is added by way of comment or explanation.

Parties. **THIS CONVEYANCE is made the 1st day of January 1967 BETWEEN ADAM SMITH of Balliol College, Oxford, Gentleman (hereinafter called the vendor) of the one part, AND WILLIAM BLACKSTONE of All Souls College, Oxford, Knight (hereinafter called the purchaser) of the other part.**

All parties whose intentions are expressed later in the deed must be mentioned, and there are said to be parties of as many " parts " as there are different intentions expressed. Smith intends to transfer the land and receive the purchase money, Blackstone intends to transfer the money and receive the land, and therefore they are parties of different parts. If Smith and Robinson were selling as trustees for sale, they would be parties of one part.[1]

Recitals. **WHEREAS the vendor is seised of the hereditaments intended to be hereby conveyed for an estate in fee simple absolute in possession free from incumbrances and has agreed to sell the same to the purchaser for the sum of £5000 ;**

Recitals. Recitals are not a necessary part of a deed, but they are generally inserted in order to indicate the purpose of the deed in which they are contained, and to state the past history of the property conveyed.

Narrative recitals. *Narrative recitals* are those which show the nature of the interest that is being transferred, and if the vendor is seised in fee simple (as in our example), they merely state that fact. On the other hand, where a mortgagee sells under his statutory power, the recitals must state that the mortgage was made, and that the mortgage loan remains owing. Again, if it is not obvious

---

[1] Elphinstone, *Introduction to Conveyancing*, pp. 61-2.

why certain persons are parties to the deed, the explanation will be given in the recitals. Thus a conveyance by personal representatives will recite the will, the appointment of the vendors as executors, the death of the testator and the grant of probate.

Introductory recitals are inserted in order to explain the object of the deed—that is, in our example, the transfer from Smith to Blackstone of a fee simple absolute.

Introductory recitals.

Owing to the doctrine of estoppel, great care is necessary in the framing of recitals. Any recital which is precise and unambiguous, and which is clearly intended to bind the person by whom it is made, estops him and all persons claiming through him from denying the truth of the statement. A recital that the vendor is seised in fee simple raises an estoppel, and if this statement is untrue, but the vendor at a later date actually acquires the fee simple from the true owner, he is estopped from denying that he was owner at the time of the sale.

The recitals are followed by what is called the *testatum*, which comprises the *operative part* of the deed, *i.e.* the part by which the object is actually effected.

Testa-tum.	**NOW THIS DEED WITNESSETH** that in consideration of the sum of £5000 paid to the vendor by the purchaser (the receipt of which sum the vendor hereby acknowledges) the **VENDOR AS BENEFICIAL OWNER**
Opera-tive words.	**HEREBY CONVEYS unto the purchaser**
Parcels.	**ALL and singular the hereditaments known as Blackacre and situate at Kidlington in the County of Oxford and containing 24 acres 2 roods or thereabouts.**

A deed is not void for want of consideration, but it is the invariable practice to state the amount of the purchase money and the fact of its receipt, because the amount of stamp duty payable thereby becomes ascertainable, while a receipt so inserted in the body of a deed is a sufficient discharge to the purchaser without any further receipt being indorsed on the deed.[1] (Originally a further receipt indorsed on the deed was necessary to discharge the purchaser.) Again, such a receipt is sufficient evidence to a subsequent purchaser of the payment, provided that he has no notice that the money was not actually paid.[2]

Statement of consideration.

The words " Beneficial Owner." The effect of using the expression " beneficial owner " requires explanation. In former

Object of conveying as " beneficial owner."

---

[1] Law of Property Act, 1925, s. 67   [2] *Ibid.,* s. 68.

days a deed of conveyance ran to considerable length since it usually contained elaborate covenants for title, the object of which was to render the vendor liable in covenant if a flaw were later discovered in his title. Although titles were traditionally investigated with such care that a purchaser would seldom need to enforce this contractual liability, it was usual before 1882 to set out the appropriate undertakings at length, a practice which, while it militated against simplicity and brevity, increased the profits of solicitors, whose remuneration in those days depended upon the length of the documents they prepared. Since 1881, however, covenants for title need not be expressly stated. If the appropriate words designated by statute [1] are used (and the appropriate words vary according as the grantor conveys freeholds or assigns leaseholds for valuable consideration, or by way of settlement, or as trustee and so on), the effect is that certain covenants for title, also designated by the Act,[2] are implied.

Implied covenants.

The appropriate words for raising these covenants upon sale of land are " beneficial owner." If the conveyance is for valuable consideration, and if the vendor " conveys and is expressed to convey as beneficial owner," and if in fact he possesses that status,[3] the effect is that the four following covenants are implied:—

1. **Covenant that vendor has a good right to convey.** This means that the vendor is entitled to convey the interest which he has agreed to sell. Hence, if he has agreed to sell 84 acres, and it happens that 150 feet of this area have been acquired by strangers under the Limitation Act,[4] he will be liable under the implied covenant to lose the difference between the value of the property he agreed to sell and that of the property which he is entitled to convey.

2. **Covenant that purchaser shall have quiet possession.** A physical interference with the enjoyment of the land, as, for instance, the exercise of a right of way lawfully acquired by a stranger from the vendor prior to the sale, constitutes a breach of the covenant, though of course in such a case the existence of the easement also constitutes a breach of the covenant that the vendor has a right to convey.

   The object of implying this covenant in addition to the covenant that the vendor has a good right to convey is that the Limitation Act begins to run from the date of the deed in the latter case, since that is the time at which the breach occurs,

---

[1] Law of Property Act, 1925, s. 76.
[2] *Ibid.*, 2nd Schedule.
[3] *Fay* v. *Miller, Wilkins & Co.*, [1941] Ch. 360 at p. 362; [1941] 2 All E. R. 18 at p. 23; *Pilkington* v. *Wood*, [1953] Ch. 770 at p. 777; [1953] 2 All E. R. 810 at p. 813.
[4] *Eastwood* v. *Ashton*, [1915] A. C. 900.

but from the date of the interference in the case of a covenant for quiet possession.

3. **Covenant that the property is free from incumbrances.** This means that the property is free from all estates, incumbrances, claims and demands other than those to which the conveyance is expressly made subject.

4. **Covenant for further assurance.** This obliges the vendor, where the title conveyed is defective as compared with that which he has agreed to sell, to do everything that is right and possible in order to perfect the title. Thus he may be compelled to pay off an incumbrance.

It should be noted that the undertakings which have been set out are not four independent and separate covenants, but parts of one entire contract. They are not absolute, but qualified, since they extend only to the acts of the vendor and those claiming through him and to the acts of persons through whom he claims, except those from whom he has taken the property for a money consideration. Thus, a vendor who himself purchased the land for value from X. on a previous occasion is not liable under the covenant for quiet possession if X. disturbs the possession of the ultimate purchaser.[1]

Qualified nature of implied covenants.

The covenants implied by the Act may be varied or extended. The different covenants that are implied when the conveyance is by a mortgagor, settlor, trustee, mortgagee and so on, are set out in the second schedule to the Law of Property Act, 1925.

We will now turn to the *operative words* of the conveyance. In old deeds, instead of using the single word *convey*, it was customary *per majorem cautelam* to employ a much more extensive series of words, such as *grant, bargain, sell, aliene, convey, release and confirm*. Since the Real Property Act, 1845, however, which enacted that all corporeal hereditaments should lie in grant, the word *grant* alone has been sufficient to transfer both corporeal and incorporeal interests. This is, however, not essential,[2] and *convey* is the word adopted in the various forms of instrument given in the Law of Property Act, 1925.

Operative words.

It sometimes happens that the recitals are inconsistent with the operative words. In this case the law has been judicially stated as follows [3]:

Discrepancy between recitals and operative words.

" If the recitals are clear and the operative part is ambiguous, the
" recitals govern the construction. If the recitals are ambiguous, and
" the operative part is clear, the operative part must prevail. If both

---

[1] *David* v. *Sabin*, [1893] 1 Ch. 523; *Stoney* v. *Eastbourne R.D.C.*, [1927] 1 Ch. 367. " Purchase for value " in this context does not include a conveyance in consideration of marriage; Law of Property Act, 1925, Sch. 2, Part I.

[2] Law of Property Act, 1925, s. 51 (2).

[3] *Ex parte Dawes* (1886), 17 Q. B. D. 275, 286, *per* Lord ESHER; *Re Sassoon*, [1933] Ch. 858; affirmed, [1935] A. C. 96.

" the recitals and the operative part are clear, but they are inconsistent
" with each other, the operative part is to be preferred."

" General words " now implied.

The Parcels Clause. The operative words are followed by the *parcels clause*, the object of which is to give a physical description of the property sold. The maxim of the law is *cuicunque aliquid conceditur, conceditur et id sine quo res ipsa non esse potuit*, and therefore a grant operates to pass the rights incidental to the land, such as easements and profits which have become attached thereto. But since rights such as *quasi*-easements which have not become legally appurtenant to the land would not pass without special mention, it was usual, prior to 1882, to insert *general words*, which were framed widely enough to include all rights actually enjoyed by the vendor in respect of the land. Since 1881, however, unless a contrary intention is expressed, such *general words* are implied in every conveyance.[1] Thus a conveyance of land now operates, by virtue of the Law of Property Act, 1925, to convey all buildings, erections, fixtures, commons, hedges, ditches, fences, ways, waters, liberties, privileges, easements, rights and advantages whatsoever, appertaining or reputed to appertain to the land or any part thereof. An equally wide implication is raised with regard to rights appertaining to buildings.[2]

Grantor's whole interest passes.

" All Estate Clause." It was also usual before 1882 to add what was called an *all estate clause* with the object of ensuring that the entire interest of the grantor should be transferred. This was as a matter of fact quite ineffective to transfer anything that would not pass automatically, and it is now omitted in reliance on the enactment that, unless a contrary intention is expressed, every conveyance is effectual to pass all the estate, right, title, interest, claim, and demand which the conveying parties respectively have in, to, or on the property.[3]

Proceeding now with the precedent, we next arrive at the *habendum clause*.

**Haben-
dum.**   **To hold unto the purchaser in fee
           simple.[4]**

The object of this is to define the extent of the interest taken by the purchaser.

Finally comes the *testimonium*, which states that the parties have signed and sealed the deed in witness of what it contains.

**Testi-
monium.**   **In witness whereof the said parties
           hereto have hereunto set their re-
           spective hands and seals the day and
           year first above written.**

---

[1] Law of Property Act, 1925, s. 62.
[2] *Ibid.*, s. 62 (2) ; *supra*, pp. 485–7.   [3] *Ibid.*, s. 63.
[4] It is no longer necessary to adopt the expression " unto and to the use of," see *supra*, p. 116.

The whole precedent, then, stands as follows :—

Parties.	THIS CONVEYANCE is made the 1st day of January 1967 BETWEEN ADAM SMITH of Balliol College, Oxford, Gentleman, (hereinafter called the vendor) of the one part, AND WILLIAM BLACKSTONE of All Souls College, Oxford, Knight (hereinafter called the purchaser) of the other part.
Recitals.	WHEREAS the vendor is seised of the hereditaments intended to be hereby conveyed for an estate in fee simple absolute in possession free from incumbrances and has agreed to sell the same to the purchaser for the sum of £5000 ;
Testa-tum.	NOW THIS DEED WITNESSETH that in consideration of the sum of £5000 paid to the vendor by the purchaser (the receipt of which sum the vendor hereby acknowledges) the VENDOR AS BENEFICIAL OWNER
Opera-tive words.	HEREBY CONVEYS unto the pur-chaser
Parcels.	ALL and singular the hereditaments known as Blackacre and situate at Kidlington in the County of Oxford and containing 24 acres 2 roods or thereabouts,
Haben-dum.	To hold unto the purchaser in fee simple.
Testi-monium.	In witness whereof the said parties hereto have hereunto set their re-spective hands and seals the day and year first above written.

SECTION IV. THE EFFECT OF THE CONVEYANCE UPON THE INTERESTS OF THIRD PARTIES.[1]

The effect of the conveyance upon interests in the land held by third parties varies according as those interests are legal or equit-able.

Legal interests bind pur-chaser.

---

[1] We are not concerned here with the over-reaching effect of a conveyance by a tenant for life of settled land (*infra*, pp.713–4), or by trustees for sale (*infra*, pp. 718–21).

The purchaser of a legal estate is subject to all *legal* estates and interests which were enforceable against the land while it was in the hands of the vendor. It is immaterial whether the purchaser has notice of such interests or not. To take a simple illustration :

> An easement in perpetuity or for a term of years absolute, is a legal interest which constitutes a right *in rem* and which is enforceable against all who take the servient tenement. If therefore a purchaser takes a conveyance of that tenement, he continues to be bound by all legal easements, no matter whether they were brought to his notice or not and no matter whether one of the overreaching forms of conveyance (to be mentioned later) has been adopted or not.

The same is true of all other legal interests, such as terms of years absolute and legal rentcharges, which may affect the land conveyed.

Some legal interests require registration. But the liability of a purchaser to take the land subject to legal interests has been mitigated by the Land Charges Act, 1925, which provides that puisne mortgages shall be void against all purchasers unless they have been registered at the Land Registry.[1] A puisne mortgage is, as we have seen, a legal mortgage under which the mortgagee does not acquire the title deeds. Again, a purchaser of a legal estate, whether with or without actual notice, takes free from certain statutory charges (namely, death duty charges and land charges of classes A and B),[2] and also from certain adverse claims (namely, pending actions, writs, and orders affecting land, and deeds of arrangement),[3] unless they are registered.

Purchaser and equitable interests. As regards equitable interests, the rule is that a purchaser who takes the legal estate is liable to all equitable interests of which he has actual or constructive notice. But here we must notice two important facts :

Some equitable interests require registration. (*a*) In the first place, there are certain equitable interests which are void against purchasers unless they are registered under the Land Charges Act, 1925. An unregistered general equitable charge is void against all purchasers ; and unregistered estate contracts, restrictive covenants and equitable easements are void against a purchaser of the legal estate for money or money's worth.[4]

Modification of a constructive notice. (*b*) In the second place, the original doctrine of constructive notice has undergone modification in the following four respects :

(i) It is provided [5] (re-enacting section 3 of the Conveyancing Act, 1882) that a purchaser shall not be prejudicially affected by any instrument, matter, fact, or

---

[1] *Supra*, p. 668.   [2] *Supra*, pp. 667–8; 669.
[3] *Supra*, pp. 665–6.   [4] *Supra*, p. 670.
[5] Law of Property Act, 1925, s. 199 (1) (ii).

thing unless it is within his own knowledge, or would have come to his knowledge if such inquiries and inspections had been made as ought reasonably to have been made by him. Thus, as we have seen in the discussion of mortgages, if a purchaser through fraud or gross negligence omits to inquire for the deeds and they are found to be in the hands of an equitable incumbrancer, he is bound by the incumbrance[1]; again, if he omits to investigate tenancies, he takes subject to the rights of the tenants[2]; or if he accepts less than a thirty years' title, he is affected with notice of what he would have discovered had he insisted upon proof of title for the full period.[3]

(ii) It is also provided by the same section that a purchaser is not affected by notice of anything known to his solicitor or agent unless it came to the knowledge of the agent as such in the same transaction, or would have so come to his knowledge if such inquiries and inspections had been made as ought reasonably to have been made. It has been held that notice is not to be imputed under this section to a purchaser of facts which came to the knowledge of his solicitor during a previous transaction concerning the same property.[4]

(iii) We have seen that the period for which a vendor must show title has been reduced from forty to thirty years, and that a purchaser is not affected with notice of any matter or thing of which he would have had notice had he carried his investigation back to some time prior to the commencement of the thirty years' period, unless he has actually investigated the title.[5] It follows that the liability of a purchaser under the doctrine of notice is diminished, since his inquiries need not date back so far as was necessary before 1926.

(iv) Registration of an equitable interest, so long as it continues in force, constitutes *per se* actual notice to a purchaser,[6] but it is expressly enacted that equitable interests which are capable of being registered but which in fact have not been registered shall not prejudicially affect a purchaser [7] even though in actual fact he is aware

---

[1] *Oliver* v. *Hinton.* [1899] 2 Ch. 264 ; *supra*, pp. 615–6.

[2] *Hunt* v. *Luck*, [1902] 1 Ch. 428. If he does not examine the tenancy agreement he is bound by its provisions, but he is entitled to take it at its face value ; *Smith* v. *Jones*, [1954] 2 All E. R. 823; [1954] 1 W. L. R. 1089.

[3] *Re Cox and Neve's Contract*, [1891] 2 Ch. 109, 117–8 ; *Re Nisbet and Potts' Contract*, [1906] 1 Ch. 386 ; *supra*, p. 675.

[4] *Re Cousins* (1886), 31 Ch. D. 671.

[5] Law of Property Act, 1925, s. 44 (8).   [6] *Ibid.*, s. 198.

[7] *Ibid.*, s. 199 (1) (i). An unregistered interest is not always void and unenforceable owing to lack of registration (*e.g.* a pending action, Land Charges Act, 1925, s. 3) and in such a case a purchaser with express notice is bound.

of their existence. In the case, however, of restrictive covenants, estate contracts, death duty charges and equitable easements, the immunity is enjoyed only by a purchaser of the legal estate for money or money's worth.[1]

Special over-reaching con-veyance.

It must finally be observed that a vendor may clear certain equitable interests off the title and convey an unincumbered legal estate to the purchaser by adopting the device of an *ad hoc* trust for sale or an *ad hoc* settlement.[2]

---

[1] Land Charges Act, 1925, s. 13 (2).   [2] *Infra*, pp. 719-21.

CHAPTER II.

PERSONAL REPRESENTATIVES.

The next class of estate owner consists of personal representatives, *i.e.* the persons, whether executors or administrators, to whom the property of a deceased owner passes. The functions and powers of those persons are described later,[1] but certain matters must be anticipated. Broadly speaking, all the property of a deceased person, real as well as personal, with the exception of life interests, joint tenancies and entailed interests not disposed of, becomes vested in his personal representatives. Their duties are to pay the debts of the deceased and all expenses and dues arising on his death out of the property, and then to distribute the residue among the beneficiaries under the will or among those entitled in the case of intestacy. Both at common law and by statute they have exceedingly wide powers of disposition over the property.[2]

Thus a conveyance by personal representatives of the legal estate may become necessary in two types of cases ; first where, in order to raise money for the payment of debts, they convey to a purchaser in the ordinary course of administration ; secondly, where they transfer the land to a beneficiary. Amongst the powers of disposal conferred upon them are included :

> " All the powers, discretions and duties conferred or imposed by
> " law on trustees holding land upon an effectual trust for sale
> " (including power to overreach equitable interests and powers as
> " if the same affected the proceeds of sale)." [3]

The transfer of land to a beneficiary is effected in practice, not by a conveyance, but by an *assent, i.e.* an acknowledgment in writing that the interest is vested in the person entitled.[4] Prior to 1926 an assent was valid if it was oral or even if it could be inferred from conduct,[5] but, as we have already seen, this is no longer true where the interest to be transferred is a *legal estate*.[6]

Functions of personal representatives.

They have the powers of trustees for sale.

Transfer to beneficiary effected by assent.

---

[1] *Infra*, pp. 768 *et seq.*   [2] *Infra*, p. 768.
[3] Administration of Estates Act, 1925, s. 39 (1) (ii).
[4] *Ibid.*, s. 36 (1).
[5] *E.g.*, *Wise* v. *Whitburn*, [1924] 1 Ch. 460.   [6] *Supra*, p. 677

Notice of
assent should
be indorsed
on the
probate.

The beneficiary, in order to protect himself against a later conveyance of the same land by the personal representative, usually requires that notice of the assent be indorsed on the probate copy of the will or letters of administration, *i.e.* on the official documents which certify that the representative is entitled to act as such.[1] Even so, a beneficiary in whose favour an assent has been made is not secure, for an unpaid creditor of the deceased may enforce payment by following the property into the hands of a devisee, except one who takes in consideration of money or marriage.[2] When this course is taken, the court, notwithstanding the assent, may declare a beneficiary to be a trustee of the land for a creditor, or may order a sale or other transaction to be carried out in order to satisfy the rights of the persons interested, or may make a vesting order with a view to the execution of a conveyance.[3]

Right of
creditors to
follow
property.

Overreach-
ing powers
of personal
repre-
sentatives.

The statutory provision that personal representatives shall have the overreaching powers of trustees holding land " upon an effectual trust for sale," [4] shows that the overreaching effect of their conveyance is normally that of a conveyance made by ordinary trustees for sale,[5] and also, if the occasion arises, that of a conveyance made by approved trustees under an *ad hoc* trust for sale.[6] Thus, even equities charged on the land prior to the death of the deceased may be overreached. No approval by the court is necessary; neither is it necessary, as it is in the case of trustees for sale, that there should be at least two personal representatives.[7]

Conveyance
by bene-
ficiary in
whose
favour an
assent has
been made.

The assent plays an important part when the beneficiary in whose favour it has been made conveys the legal estate to a purchaser, since it acts as a "curtain" to keep the equities off the title. The Administration of Estates Act, 1925,[8] provides that the assent shall, in favour of a purchaser for money or money's worth, be sufficient evidence that the beneficiary is entitled to have the estate conveyed to him, unless notice of a previous conveyance or assent has been indorsed on the probate copy or letters of administration. It has been held, however, that an assent will not avail a purchaser if his investigation of title discloses that the person in whose favour it was given was not entitled to the legal estate.[9] The first duty, then, of the purchaser is to inspect the probate copy, for in the normal case he will find there an indorsement of an assent in favour of the beneficiary. Thus, the last two links in the title made by a beneficiary are the probate copy or letters of administration and the assent. The assent operates as a " curtain " in the sense that the purchaser need not investigate the will (which

---

[1] Administration of Estates Act, 1925, s. 36 (5).
[2] *Ibid.*, s. 38 (1); *Salih* v. *Atchi*, [1961] A. C. 778.
[3] Administration of Estates Act, 1925, s. 38 (2).
[4] *Ibid.*, s. 39 (1) (i) (ii).   [5] *Infra*, pp. 718–9.
[6] *Infra*, pp. 719–21.
[7] Law of Property Act, 1925, s. 27 (2).   [8] S. 36 (7).
[9] *Re Duce and Boots Cash Chemists Contract*, [1937] Ch. 642.

operates only in equity) in order to ascertain whether the assent has been given in favour of the proper beneficiary. The beneficial interests under a will, like those arising under a settlement or a trust for sale, are thus kept off the title to land, the legal estate in which has passed to a beneficiary by virtue of an assent.

Another section of the Act comes into play when the personal representatives themselves convey to a purchaser. The danger here is that the legal estate may already have been passed to a beneficiary under the will, but it is provided that : *[Conveyance by personal representatives to a purchaser.]*

" A written statement by a personal representative that he has not " given an assent or made a conveyance in respect of a legal estate, " shall, in favour of a purchaser for money or money's worth, be " sufficient evidence that no previous assent or conveyance has been " given, unless notice of such has been endorsed on the probate or " administration." [1]

A purchaser who obtains this written statement acquires a good title to the legal estate, subject, however, to one exception, for it is provided that the statement shall not be conclusive against an earlier purchaser for money or money's worth who has taken a conveyance either from the personal representative or from a beneficiary in whose favour an assent has been given. If, therefore, A. takes a conveyance for value of a legal estate from a personal representative without having the fact indorsed on the probate, and B. later takes a conveyance from the personal representative of the same estate, relying upon the written but untrue statement that no previous conveyance has been made, it would seem that B. obtains no protection from the statute.

The revocation of the probate or administration after a conveyance has been made by a personal representative does not affect the title of the purchaser.[2] If, for instance, probate of a will dated 1960 is granted to an executor, A., and subsequently a different will dated 1961 is discovered, the grant of probate to A. will be revoked and a new one made to the executor appointed by the 1961 will. All conveyances, however, of any interest in real or personal estate made by A. *virtute officii* in favour of a purchaser remain valid. *[Validity of conveyance not affected by revocation of probate.]*

As we shall see, general personal representatives give way to special personal representatives in respect of property which the deceased held as tenant for life under a settlement.[3] In such a case, after paying death duties the special executors or administrators execute a vesting assent by which they transfer the legal estate to the next tenant for life. The vesting assent and the special probate or letters of administration, since they are docu- *[Special grants of probate in respect of settled land.]*

---

[1] Administration of Estates Act, 1925, s. 36 (6).
[2] *Ibid.*, s. 37; confirming *Hewson* v. *Shelley*, [1914] 2 Ch. 13. " Purchaser " means a lessee, mortgagee or other person who in good faith acquires an interest in property for valuable consideration, s. 55 (1) (xviii).
[3] *Infra*, p. 710.

ments passing the legal estate, will appear on the title if the tenant for life subsequently exercises his power of sale.

It has been held, however, in *Re Bridgett and Hayes' Contract,*[1] that if the settlement ceases on the death of the tenant for life there is no necessity for a special grant of probate or administration. The facts of the case are simple and they represent what is perhaps the most usual kind of settlement found in practice.

> By a will which took effect before 1926 land was devised to A. for life, and if (as happened) she should die without leaving children, to trustees upon trust for sale.
>
> A. died in 1926 and a general grant of probate of her will was made to the executor, X. X. made a contract to sell the land.

It was held that a special grant of probate to the trustees was unnecessary, and that X. could make a good title to the land under his general grant.

The statute requires a special grant of probate in the case of " settled land." " Settled land," however, means land which continues to be settled after the death of the testator. In the instant case the land ceased to be settled on the death of A. and became subject to a trust for sale. The provisions relating to special grants do not apply to trusts for sale. Therefore, the land was vested in X., to whom a general grant of A.'s property had been made, and X., by virtue of his executorship under the grant, could make title.

---

[1] [1928] Ch. 163 ; followed in : *In the Estate of Bordass,* [1929] P. 107; *In the Estate of Birch,* [1929] P. 164.

CHAPTER III.

TENANTS FOR LIFE AND
STATUTORY OWNERS, TRUSTEES
FOR SALE, MORTGAGORS.

SUMMARY.

SECTION I. TENANTS FOR LIFE AND
STATUTORY OWNERS.

What has emerged from the account of the strict settlement already given in the earlier part of this book may be summarized as follows :— *Effect of a settlement summarized.*

> The object of a strict settlement is to tie up the land in the family to this extent, that, after provision has been made for the settlor's surviving spouse and younger children, the eldest son is to have an entailed interest capable of descending *ad infinitum* to his issue.
>
> This retention of the land in the family, however, is unlikely to happen unless there is a continuous process of re-settlement,[1] for any tenant in tail in possession may destroy the possibility of descent by barring the entail in his lifetime,[2] by including it in his will [3] or by exercising his power of sale under the Settled Land Act.[4]

---

[1] *Supra*, pp. 70; 127–30.   [2] *Supra*, pp. 175–7.
[3] *Supra*, p. 181.   [4] *Infra*, p. 700.

695

During the continuance of the settlement, the tenant for life for the time being occupies a dual position, since by virtue of the vesting deed he is invested with the legal estate in the land affected, while by virtue of the trust instrument he is beneficially entitled merely to the income derived from the land.[1]

In his capacity as estate owner, he is competent to perform two main functions : first, to exercise any of the powers of disposition and management permitted by the Act[2]; secondly, in the event of a disposition such as a sale or lease of the fee simple, to convey the land free from the limitations of the settlement.[3]

Such, then, is the general picture.   On the conveyancing side, however, the following topics now require consideration in rather more detail :—

The statutory definition of a settlement.
The persons regarded by the Act as tenants for life or competent to exercise the powers of a tenant for life.
The persons who are trustees within the meaning of the Act.
The form in which a settlement must be made.
The manner in which this form simplifies a conveyance of the settled land.

Extended meaning of settlement.

The definition of a settlement.   The word *settlement* properly so called connotes succession.   Its normal meaning is any instrument or series of instruments by which successive interests are carved out of realty or personalty and under which, in the case of land, there will usually be at any given time some person entitled in possession to a beneficial interest for life.   The strict settlement represents a settlement in this true sense of the term, and exemplifies the normal situation where the statutory powers are exercisable by the tenant for life.   But the Act has a far more ambitious aim than merely to confer these powers upon the normal tenant for life. It is not content to stop short at cases where there is a succession properly so called.   Its further aim is to facilitate dealings wherever the disposition of the land is retarded or obstructed by some impediment affecting its title.   Infancy affords a simple illustration.

If a favourable offer has been made for the purchase of land to which an infant is entitled in fee simple, the rule that no person under 21 years of age can execute a valid conveyance will cause the loss of a profitable bargain, unless some way out of the impasse can be contrived.   But all difficulty disappears if the will is regarded as a " settlement " and if some person of full age is designated to exercise the statutory power of sale.

---

[1] *Supra*, pp. 96–7.   [2] *Supra*, pp. 131 *et seq.*
[3] *Supra*, p. 97; *infra*, pp. 712–13.

In a case of this nature there is, of course, no settlement and no life tenant as usually understood, but any device which renders the statutory powers exercisable in respect of the infant's land is an undoubted advantage to all concerned. What the Act does, therefore, with the laudable object of rendering an absolute title easily transferable despite the existence of what would normally be inhibitory factors, is to define " settlement " in broad terms so as to include a number of cases where there is no succession in the ordinary sense, and also, where necessary, to grant the statutory powers to a person who according to ordinary language is not a tenant for life. In fact, not only is the statutory definition of a " settlement " very wide, but wherever there is a settlement within the meaning of the Act and no life tenant properly so called, and therefore no person normally competent to exercise the statutory powers, one of two things will occur, namely, either

some person will be designated by the Act as entitled to exercise the powers ; or

the powers will be exercisable by trustees, who in this context are called " statutory owners."[1]

A settlement for the purposes of the Act exists in each of the following cases [2] :

Definition of a " settlement."

(i) Where land is limited in trust for any persons *by way of succession.*

This refers to the normal case where land is limited to a series of persons by way of succession, as for instance by the limitations contained in a strict settlement.

We now come to the cases where instruments are deemed to be settlements.

(ii) Where land is limited in trust for any person *in possession*—

(*a*) for an entailed interest whether barrable or not ;

(*b*) for a fee simple or term of years absolute subject to a gift over on failure of issue or in any other event ;

(*c*) for a base or determinable fee ;

(*d*) for an estate in fee simple or a term of years absolute in favour of an infant.

We have here several examples of the extended meaning given to the term " settlement." Thus :

where the possessor is a tenant in tail or tenant of a base fee, the instrument of creation is a settlement, and the tenant is deemed to hold the land under a settlement.

Entailed interests.

---

[1] *Infra* p. 701.
[2] Settled Land Act, 1925, s. 1.

Limitation subject to gift over.

The same position arises where property is vested in a possessor, subject, however, to a gift over to somebody else on the happening of a certain event, as for instance:

> where a house is devised to A. in fee simple subject to a condition that he resides and provides a home for X. there, and if he breaks this condition, then devise over to B. in fee simple.

In such a case the will is a settlement and A. is tenant for life within the meaning of the Act.[1]   Lastly,

Infant as beneficial owner.

a conveyance which purports to grant a fee simple absolute to an infant cannot take effect according to its terms, for an infant is incapable of holding a legal estate. Instead, the conveyance operates as an agreement by the grantor to execute a settlement by means of a vesting deed in favour of trustees (statutory owners),[2] and a trust instrument in favour of the infant.

Springing Interest.

(iii) Where land is limited in trust for any person to take effect as a fee simple or term of years absolute on the happening of some event.

If, for instance, a fee simple estate is limited in trust for the two sons of X. who attain the age of twenty-one years, the first son to reach that age becomes absolutely entitled to a half share, but also entitled to the fee simple in the entirety of the land contingent on the death of his brother during infancy.[3] This is one of the cases where, pending the occurrence of the contingency, the powers are exercisable by the statutory owners.[4]

Land subject to family charges.

(iv) Where land is charged *voluntarily*,[5] *or in consideration of marriage or by way of family arrangement*[6] with the payment of any rentcharge or capital sums for the portions, advancement, maintenance or other benefit of any persons.[7]

If, for example, A. charges his fee simple absolute with an annuity for his wife and capital sums for his children, the instrument which creates the charge is a " settlement," and,

---

[1] *Re Richardson*, [1904] 2 Ch. 777.
[2] Settled Land Act, 1925, s. 27 (1) ; *infra*, p. 701.
[3] *In re Bird*, [1927] 1 Ch. 210.
[4] Settled Land Act, 1925, s. 23.
[5] *I.e.*, not for valuable consideration.
[6] Presumably " family arrangement " in this context includes an arrangement made not voluntarily, but for valuable consideration, cf *Williams* v. *Williams* (1867), 2 Ch. App. 294 at p. 301.
[7] Settled Land Act, 1925, s. 1 (1) (v), which contained a fifth case relating to land held by a married woman subject to a restraint on anticipation. All such restraints, however, were later abolished by the Married Women (Restraint Upon Anticipation) Act, 1949.

although the rentchargor, A., is not a tenant for life, yet by s. 20 (1) (ix) of the Act he is given the powers of a tenant for life. Strictly speaking, therefore, he should execute a vesting deed and appoint trustees. If he does so, he may sell the fee simple under the Act, and overreach the rentcharges so as to make them recoverable from the trustees to whom payment will have been made. If, however, the purchaser is willing to buy subject to the charges, A. is permitted by a later statute to sell as absolute owner without the necessity of executing a vesting deed. This statute provides as follows :—

> Nothing in the Settled Land Act, 1925, shall prevent a person on whom the powers of a tenant for life are conferred by s. 20 (1) (ix) from conveying a legal estate subject to a prior interest as if the land had not been settled land.[1]

What emerges from the account given above is that a settlement may consist of a number of instruments. This will occur, for instance :

Compound settlement.

> where lands, which in the first place have been settled on A. for life with remainder in tail to his eldest son, are resettled on A. for life, remainder (subject to the charges created by the original settlement) to the eldest son for life, with remainder over.

In this case the two settlements may be read as one, being together called a *compound settlement*, and the Act provides that the word *settlement* shall be construed as referring to such compound settlement where it exists.[2]

The Person entitled to exercise the Statutory Powers.
The general principle of the Settled Land Act is that the statutory powers of disposition shall be exercisable by the tenant for life, a person who is defined as follows in s. 19 (1) :—

Definition of tenant for life.

> "The person of full age who is for the time being beneficially "entitled under a settlement to possession of settled land for his "life is for the purposes of this Act the tenant for life of that land "and the tenant for life under that settlement."

He continues to occupy this position for the purpose of exercising the statutory powers, notwithstanding that the land or his estate therein is charged with the payment of incumbrances.[3] If two or more persons are jointly entitled to possession, they together constitute the tenant for life.[4]

---

[1] Law of Property (Amendment) Act, 1926, s. 1 (1).
[2] Settled Land Act, 1925, s. 1 (1) (i), proviso.
[3] *Ibid.*, s. 19 (4).   [4] *Ibid.*, s. 19 (2).

Persons with the Powers of a Tenant for Life.
Obviously however there are several cases where land is settled
in the sense that it is subject to a " settlement " within the
statutory meaning of that word,[1] and yet where there is no tenant
for life as defined in s. 19. A tenant in tail in possession is
a simple example of the situation.[2] The Act, therefore, takes care
to ensure that wherever there is a " settlement " there shall always
be some person competent to exercise the statutory powers. In
the first place it provides that the following persons shall have the
powers of a tenant for life [3] and shall be included in the expression
" tenant for life." [4]

(i) A tenant in tail, including both a tenant after possibility [5]
and one who is by statute restrained from barring
his estate tail, but excluding a tenant in tail whose
land has been bought with money provided by
Parliament in consideration of public services.

(ii) A person entitled to a legal estate subject to a gift over
on failure of issue or in any other event.[6]

(iii) A person entitled to a base [7] or a determinable fee [8] or a
similar interest in leaseholds.

(iv) A tenant for years determinable on life not holding
merely under a lease at a rent.

> We have seen that leases *at a rent* for a term of years
> determinable at the death of the tenant are now con-
> verted into terms for 90 years,[9] and that such a person
> cannot have the powers of a tenant for life,[10] but this
> conversion does not operate where such a term takes
> effect under a settlement. For instance, a devisee to
> whom lands are given for 30 years if he should so long
> live has the powers of a tenant for life.

(v) A tenant *pur autre vie* not holding merely under a lease
at a rent.[11]

(vi) A tenant for his own life or the life of another, or for
years determinable on life, whose interest is liable to
cease in any event during that life, or is subject to a
trust for accumulation of income.

> For instance, a devise to A. so long as he shall live on
> the estate for at least three months in each year, with a
> gift over to B. upon failure to observe this condition,
> makes A. tenant for life within the present section.[12]

---

[1] *Supra*, pp. 696-9.   [2] *Supra*, p. 697.
[3] Settled Land Act, 1925, s. 20.
[4] *Ibid.*, s. 117 (1) (xxviii).   [5] *Supra*, pp. 163-4.
[6] But a gift over on failure of issue becomes incapable of taking effect
as soon as there is any issue who attains 21 ; Law of Property Act, 1925,
s. 134 (1) ; *infra*, pp. 776-7.
[7] *Supra*, pp. 178-9.   [8] *Supra*, pp. 282 *et seq.*
[9] *Supra*, p. 338.   [10] *Re Catling*, [1931] 2 Ch. 359.
[11] *Re Johnson*, [1914] 2 Ch. 194.   [12] *Re Paget* (1885), 30 Ch. D. 161.

(vii) A tenant by the curtesy.[1]

(viii) A person entitled to the *income* of land under a trust for payment thereof to him during his own or any other life,[2] or until sale of the land, or until some event (*e.g.* bankruptcy) terminates his interest. But if the land is subject to an immediate trust for sale, the person so entitled is not to be deemed tenant for life.

(ix) A person beneficially entitled to land for an estate in fee simple or for a term of years absolute subject to any estate, interests, charges or powers of charging, subsisting or capable of being exercised under a settlement.

> If, for instance, lands are settled on A. for life with remainder in fee simple to his eldest son B., with powers for A. to charge the land with portions for his younger children, B., on the death of A., will hold the fee simple subject to any such charges that may have been created. He is tenant for life under the above clause and as such can deal with the estate, notwithstanding the charge to which it is subject.[3]

Comprehensive though this list is, it still fails to provide for the exercise of the statutory powers in the case of every settlement. For instance, a settlement within the meaning of the Act exists if land is limited in trust for any person in fee simple contingently upon the happening of some event,[4] or again if land is devised in fee simple to an infant,[5] but in neither case is the beneficiary a tenant for life or a person to whom the powers of a tenant for life are expressly given. The Act, therefore, provides that where such a situation arises the statutory powers shall be exercisable by

Position where there is no person having powers of tenant for life.

(a) any person of full age upon whom they are conferred ; and

(b) in any other case by the trustees of the settlement.[6]

Persons to whom the powers are thus given are called *statutory owners.*[7]

Trustees for the purposes of the Settled Land Act. There can be no valid exercise of the statutory powers over settled land, unless there are persons statutorily qualified to act as trustees. The statute gives a list of five different classes of

Who are trustees.

---

[1] *Supra*, pp. 161–2.
[2] *Re Llanover Settled Estates*, [1926] Ch. 626.
[3] He also has the option under the Law of Property (Amendment) Act, 1926, s. 1 (1), *supra*, p. 699, of conveying the legal estate to a purchaser subject to the charge, provided that the purchaser is agreeable.
[4] *Supra*, p. 698.   [5] *Supra*, p. 698.
[6] Settled Land Act, 1925, s. 23.
[7] *Ibid.*, s. 117 (1) (xxvi); *infra*, p. 715.

persons competent to act in this capacity and arranges them in a binding order of priority as follows [1] :—

(i) The persons, if any, who under the settlement are trustees with power of sale of the settled land.

A power given to trustees to sell settled land is in fact abortive, since the Act provides that it shall be exercisable not by them, but by the tenant for life.[2] The only effect is to make the persons to whom it is given trustees *ex necessitate* of the settlement.

(ii) The persons who are declared by the settlement to be trustees for the purpose of the Settled Land Act.

These persons will normally constitute the trustees, for an express reservation of the power of sale contemplated by the first paragraph will rarely occur in practice.

(iii) The persons, if any, who are trustees with power of sale of any other land comprised in the settlement which is subject to the same limitations as the land that is being dealt with.

(iv) The persons, if any, who under the settlement have a future power of sale.

If, for example, a testator devises his land to his wife for life and after her death to X. and Y. upon trust to sell the fee simple, then, failing persons qualified under the first three paragraphs, X. and Y. will be the trustees of the settlement during the wife's life.

(v) The persons appointed by the beneficiaries, provided that the beneficiaries are of full capacity and entitled to dispose of the whole settled estate.

Where a settlement is created by will, or has arisen by reason of an intestacy, and there are no trustees, the personal representatives of the deceased are trustees of the settlement until others are appointed ; but if there is only one personal representative, not being a trust corporation, he must appoint an additional trustee to act with him.[3]

If at any time there are no trustees as defined above, or if for any reason it is expedient that new trustees should be appointed, the court may appoint fit persons to hold the office.[4]

Compound settlement.

Compound Trustees. Where land is settled by a series of separate deeds, the deeds together form one settlement which is called a *compound settlement*.[5] The commonest example of this occurs in the case of a re-settlement, which, as we have seen,

---

[1] Settled Land Act, 1925, s. 30 (1) (i)–(v).   [2] *Ibid.*, s. 108 (2).
[3] *Ibid.*, s. 30 (3).   [4] *Ibid.*, s. 34.
[5] *Re Ogle's Settled Estates*, [1927] I Ch. 229, 233–4, *per* ROMER, J.

involves three deeds.[1] The principle that the several instruments may be regarded as constituting one settlement becomes important when the tenant for life, in exercise of his statutory power of sale, desires to convey the fee simple to the purchaser free from the limitations of the various instruments.

If, after a re-settlement, the sale has been effected by the father as first tenant for life he can execute the conveyance in any one of three capacities : {.margin} Conveyance of settled land.

(a) He may convey as life tenant under the original settlement.

> The merit of this is that his conveyance overrides the limitations of both settlements, and if the purchase money is paid to the trustees of the old settlement the purchaser acquires a title free from the rights of the beneficiaries. The disadvantage is that the tenant for life, since he is acting under the original settlement, cannot avail himself of any additional powers which may have been reserved by the deed of re-settlement.

(b) He may convey as life tenant under the re-settlement.

> The position here is reversed, for although he can exercise any additional powers, he cannot convey a title free from the portions, etc., that have been created by the original settlement. Conveyancers sought before 1926 to overcome this difficulty by reciting in the re-settlement that the life interest re-settled upon the father was " in restoration and by way of confirmation of " his life interest under the original settlement, but it was only on the eve of a statutory amendment of the law[2] that this device was held to be effective.[3] It had previously been held that " when once conveyancers have in fact " transmuted the old body into a new body, they can- " not claim to have retained the old body, whatever " incantations they may use in the process." [4]

(c) He may convey as life tenant under the compound settlement.

> This plan combines the advantages of the two preceding methods, since the tenant for life can exercise additional powers given by the re-settlement and can override, within the statutory limits,[5] the limitations of both settlements. Under the old law, however, this method was often open to a fatal objection, for its efficacy depends upon the existence of compound trustees, and before the legislation of 1925, it frequently happened that there were no such trustees. If compound

---

[1] *Supra*, pp. 128–30.   [2] *Infra*, p. 704.
[3] *Parr* v. *A.-G.*, [1926] A. C. 239 (December 18, 1925).
[4] *A.-G.* v. *Parr*, [1924] 1 K. B. 916, 931 (ATKIN, L.J.) ; *Re Constable's Settled Estates*, [1919] 1 Ch. 178.   [5] *Infra*, pp. 713–4.

trustees had not been appointed in the original settlement it was impossible to rectify the omission in the re-
settlement, and unless all the beneficiaries were of full
age (an improbable event), it was necessary to incur the
expense of making an application to the court.

The position is much the same where, upon the death of the
father, the eldest son as new tenant for life desires to execute a
conveyance in favour of a purchaser. He cannot, of course,
convey as life tenant under the original settlement, but he can
convey either under the re-settlement subject to the limitations of
the original settlement, or under the compound settlement if
compound trustees have been appointed.

Compound trustees.　The difficulty that there may be no compound trustees has
been avoided by the legislation of 1925 which is retrospective and
is as follows :—

> (i) trustees under an instrument which is a settlement are
> trustees also of a settlement constituted by that instru-
> ment and any subsequent instruments, *i.e.* the original
> trustees are trustees of any compound settlement
> which later comes into being ; [1]
>
> (ii) trustees under a re-settlement, where there are no
> trustees under the original settlement, are trustees of
> the compound settlement ; [2]
>
> (iii) where a re-settlement states that a life interest limited to
> a life tenant is *in restoration or confirmation* of his
> interest under the original settlement, he is entitled as
> of his former interest, and can exercise the statutory
> powers both under the original settlement and under
> the re-settlement. [3]

Protection of trustees.　**Protection of Trustees.**　It is not the policy of the legislature to subject the trustees of the settlement to a strict liability
for the acts of the estate owner. Provisions are therefore inserted
in the Settled Land Act designed to protect them in certain circumstances, and they now enjoy a greater measure of immunity
than under the Act of 1882. Thus they are not liable for giving
any consent or for not bringing any action which they might have
brought, and, in the case of a purchase of land with capital money
or in the case of a lease of the settled land by the tenant for life,
they are not bound to investigate the propriety of the disposition. [4]
Again, where the tenant for life directs capital money to be invested in any authorized security, the trustees are not liable for
the acts of an agent employed by him or for failing to obtain a

---

[1] Settled Land Act, 1925, s. 31.
[2] Law of Property (Amendment) Act, 1926, Schedule.
[3] Settled Land Act, 1925, s. 22 (2) ; *Re Cradock's Settled Estates*, [1926]
Ch. 944.　　　　　　　　　　　　[4] Settled Land Act, 1925, s. 97.

valuation of the proposed security[1]; neither are they liable for having delivered documents of title to the tenant for life, though they are responsible for securities representing capital money.[2] Each trustee is answerable only for what he actually receives, notwithstanding his signing any receipt for conformity, and he is not answerable for the acts and defaults of his co-trustees or for any loss not due to his own wilful default.[3] In short, the rôle of the trustees is to manage and protect the money that is paid to them.

The mode of creating a settlement. We have already seen that in order to emphasize the separation of the legal estate from the equitable interests of the beneficiaries and also to facilitate a conveyance of the former, the Settled Land Act, 1925, introduced a new method for the creation of a settlement by enacting as follows :—

> " Every settlement of a legal estate in land *inter vivos* shall, save " as in this Act otherwise provided, be effected by two deeds, " namely a *vesting deed* and a *trust instrument*, and if effected in " any other way shall not operate to transfer or create a legal estate."[4]

This method must now be examined in more detail.

1. **The Vesting Deed.** The function of the vesting deed is to vest the legal fee simple in the person who for the time being is to have the actual enjoyment of the land, or, if he is an infant or otherwise legally incapable, then to vest it in some other person who is denominated a *statutory owner*.[5] The virtue of thus passing the legal fee simple to a person who is beneficially entitled to some lesser interest is that, should he later desire, in the interests of the beneficiaries generally, to dispose of the fee simple by way of sale, lease or otherwise under one of the powers conferred upon him by the Settled Land Act, he can produce a document which not only shows that the legal estate is vested in him, but also certifies the facts essential to a valid exercise of the statutory power.

This vesting deed, then,—called the *principal vesting deed*—conveys to the tenant for life or the statutory owner the whole legal estate which is being split up by way of equitable interests among a succession of persons.[6] It is a

Creation of settlement requires two deeds.

Function of vesting deed.

Contents of vesting deed.

---

[1] Settled Land Act, 1925, s. 98 (1), altering the effect of *Re Hotham, Hotham* v. *Doughty,* [1902] 2 Ch. 575.
[2] Settled Land Act, 1925, s. 98 (3).
[3] *Ibid.,* s. 96. This is a rule applicable to trustees generally ; Trustee Act, 1925, s. 30 (1).
[4] Settled Land Act, 1925, s. 4 (1).
[5] *Ibid.,* ss. 23, 26, 117 (1) (xxvi.).
[6] *Ibid.,* s. 4 (2).

short document and must contain the following statements and particulars [1] :

(*a*) a description of the settled land ;

(*b*) a statement that the fee simple is vested in the life tenant upon the trusts of the settlement ;

(*c*) the names of the settlement trustees ;

(*d*) a statement of any powers, over and above those conferred upon every life tenant by the Act, which it is desired to give to life tenants under the settlement ;

(*e*) the name of the person entitled to appoint new trustees.

Subsidiary vesting deed.   If after the execution of a principal vesting deed more land is acquired which is to become subject to the settlement, it is conveyed to the life tenant by what is called a *subsidiary vesting deed.*[2]

Precedent of vesting deed.   The following is a precedent of a principal vesting deed :—

THIS VESTING DEED made (&c.) between JOHN H. of (&c.) of the first part, JANE W. of (&c.) of the second part and X. of (&c.), Y. of (&c.), and Z. of (&c.) (hereinafter called the trustees) of the third part.

WITNESSETH and it is hereby declared as follows :—

1. In consideration of the intended marriage between John H. and Jane W. the said John H. as Settlor hereby declares that :

ALL THAT (*setting out the parcels by reference to a schedule or otherwise*) are vested in John H. in fee simple (*or in the case of leaseholds refer to the terms*).

UPON THE TRUSTS declared concerning the same by a Trust Instrument bearing even date with but intended to be executed contemporaneously with these presents and made between the same parties and in the same order as these presents or upon such other trusts as the same ought to be held from time to time.

2. The trustees are the trustees of the settlement for all the purposes of the Settled Land Act, 1925.

3. The following additional or larger powers are conferred by the said trust instrument in relation to the settled land and by virtue of the Settled Land Act, 1925, operate and are exercisable as if conferred by that Act on a tenant for life. (*Here insert the additional powers.*)

4. The power of appointing a new trustee or new trustees of the settlement is vested in the said John H. during his life.

IN WITNESS (&c.) [3]

Function of trust instrument.   **2. The Trust Instrument.** At the same time another deed, called the trust instrument, is executed which sets out the trusts upon which the person who for the time being is entitled to the actual enjoyment of the land (namely, the

---

[1] Settled Land Act, 1925, s. 5 (1).   [2] *Ibid.*, s. 10.
[3] *Ibid.*, 1st Schedule, Form No. 2.

husband in the case of a settlement made in contemplation of marriage) must hold the fee simple that has been transferred to him by the vesting deed. If we look at the vesting deed alone, H. seems to be fully entitled to sell the fee simple. So he is. An intending purchaser need not look beyond the deed, but at the same time such a person cannot help seeing that there is a trust instrument somewhere and that there are trustees, and this knowledge throws upon him the obligation to pay the purchase money, not to H., but to the trustees. If he does this, his obligations are at an end, and it is no concern of his what is done with the money. But what we need to look at for the moment is the trust instrument, since it records the equitable interests which it is the object of the settlement to confer upon H. and W. and the children of the marriage. The property comprised in the settlement, whether it remains in the form of land or is sold and converted into money, is actually enjoyed by the persons who are described in, and upon the conditions which are prescribed by, the trust instrument. We must not be misled by the vesting deed into thinking that H., who is thereby declared to be the fee simple owner, can sell the whole estate and pocket the proceeds.

The surest guide to the nature of the equitable interests created by a strict settlement is to quote the material part of a normal trust instrument.[1]

Precedent of trust instrument.

Whereas this deed is supplemental to a Vesting Deed (hereinafter referred to as the vesting deed) bearing even date with but executed immediately before this deed and made between the same parties and in the same order as this deed the freehold and leasehold properties therein described were vested in the settlor upon the trusts declared concerning the same by a trust instrument of even date therewith therein referred to being this deed and it was declared that the trustees were trustees thereof for the purposes of the Settled Land Act, 1925.

Recital of vesting deed.

Now in consideration of the marriage which is intended to take place between the settlor and the wife THIS DEED WITNESSETH as follows :—

1. The settlor hereby declares that he will hold the said freehold and leasehold properties (hereinafter collectively referred to as the settled land) in trust for himself until the solemnization of the said marriage (A) and thereafter upon the trusts following that is to say:

Trust until marriage.

Trusts after marriage.

   (1) Upon trust for the settlor during his life without impeachment of waste (B) with remainder

Husband's life interest.

   (2) Upon trust that if the wife survives the settlor the trustees shall during the remainder of her life receive a jointure rentcharge of £—— per annum payable

Jointure for wife on protective trusts.

[1] *Encyclopædia of Forms and Precedents* (3rd Edn.), vol. xvi. pp. 395-7; Precedent 242.

by equal quarterly payments commencing at the end of three months from the death of the settlor and shall hold such rentcharge upon protective trusts for the benefit of the wife (C) and subject thereto

Portions.

(3) Upon trust after the death of the settlor or with his consent in writing during his lifetime to raise and pay to the trustees the sum of £—— for the portions of the younger children of the marriage as hereinafter stated (D) and subject thereto

Sons in tail male.

(4) Upon trust for the first and every other son of the said marriage successively according to seniority in tail male (E) with remainder

Sons in tail general.

(5) Upon trust for the first and every other son of the said marriage successively according to seniority in tail general (F) with remainder

Daughters.

(6) Upon trust for all the daughters of the said marriage as tenants in common in tail with cross remainders between them as to both their original and accruing shares and if there shall only be one daughter in trust for her in tail with remainder (G)

Ultimate trust.

(7) Upon trust for the settlor in fee simple or absolutely.

Portions.

2. (1) The trustees shall hold the said sum of £—— for portions upon trust for such one or more exclusively of the others or other of the younger children of the marriage and the issue of such younger children as the settlor shall by deed revocable or irrevocable or by will or codicil appoint and in default of and subject to any such appointment in trust for all such younger children if more than one equally Provided always that none of such younger children to whom or to whose issue any part of the said sum of £—— shall have been appointed shall unless the appointment otherwise directs be entitled to share in any unappointed part of the said sum without bringing into hotchpot the part appointed to such younger child or his or her issue and accounting for the same accordingly.

(2) For the purposes of this settlement the expressions younger child and younger children mean any child or children of the said marriage who attain the age of twenty-one years other than any child or children who becomes or would if of full age become indefeasibly entitled (subject to any charges on the settled land or any share therein) in possession or remainder immediately expectant on the life interest of the father.

Settled Land Act trustees.

3. The trustees are trustees hereof for the purposes of the Settled Land Act, 1925.

New trustees.

4. The power of appointing new trustees hereof is vested in the settlor during his life.

Clauses of strict settlement.

In this example of a strict settlement there are eight several clauses which require explanation and which have been distinguished by the insertion of capitals.

(A) conveys to the settlor H. a fee simple that will come to an end when the marriage actually takes place. It is a determinable and not an absolute fee simple [1] and, like all the remaining estates created by the trust deed, is purely equitable.

Determinable fee simple.

(B) confers a life interest upon H. Its effect is to cut down H.'s former fee simple to an interest which entitles him to the enjoyment of the use and profits of the land for the rest of his life. While he lives he is the manager and administrator of the property, and he can exercise the wide powers conferred by the Settled Land Act.

Life interest.

(C) affords a competence in the shape of a yearly rentcharge to W. in case she survives her husband. It becomes a first charge upon the settled property after H.'s death.

Widow's rentcharge.

(D) in conjunction with (H) sets up a trust under which portions may be paid to the younger children. The creation of the trust is effected at this particular place in the settlement in order that it may rank before the subsequent limitations, but the details connected with the raising and the allocation of the money are specified in the later clause (H). If the eldest son, upon becoming tenant in tail in possession, is unable to defray the portions out of his own pocket, he may be required to raise the money by the creation of a legal mortgage.[2]

Trust for portions.

(E) creates an interest in tail male, but, in order to provide for a possible failure of the male line, clause

Entailed interests.

(F) is inserted setting up an interest in tail general.

(G), which meets the case where the tenant for life leaves no male heirs, has already been explained.[3]

The effect of a strict settlement, then, is that the eldest son becomes tenant in tail in possession upon the death of his father, subject, however, to his liability to provide a jointure for his mother and portions for his brothers and sisters. Unless he can find the money to satisfy these purposes out of his own resources, his interest will remain incumbered by such charges and mortgages as he may have been obliged to create.

---

[1] *Supra*, p. 282.

[2] Settled Land Act, 1925, s. 16 (1) (iii) ; Law of Property Act, 1925, s. 3 (1) (a). The former practice was to grant to trustees a long term of years, called a *portions term*, out of which they themselves could create a mortgage by sub-lease, but if such a term were created by the modern trust instrument it would be merely equitable.

[3] *Supra*, pp. 308–9.

Settlement by will.   The rule that an *inter vivos* settlement must be created by two contemporaneous deeds called the principal vesting deed and the trust instrument, applies differently to a settlement by will. In this case the legal estate devolves upon the personal representatives of the settlor, who hold it upon trust to convey it to the person entitled to the life tenancy under the will.[1] This conveyance may be made by a *vesting assent, i.e.* by an assent in writing but not under seal.[2] The position then is, that the vesting assent corresponds to the vesting deed that forms part of a settlement *inter vivos*, and the will itself is deemed to be the trust instrument.

Procedure on cessation of life interest.   The scheme of the Act, as we have already noticed, is that the legal estate shall be vested from time to time in each new tenant for life as and when he becomes entitled to possession. Let us take the different circumstances that may arise and observe how this procedure operates.[3]

(*a*) Death of tenant for life.

Let us suppose that under a settlement and a later re-settlement lands stand limited to H. for life and then, after certain interests in favour of the other members of H.'s family, to his son, S., for life. When H. dies the legal estate devolves upon his special personal representatives, *i.e.* the trustees of the settlement, and not upon his general personal representatives whose task it is to administer his non-settled property.[4] Upon the death of H. the special representatives come under an obligation to convey the legal estate to S., either by a vesting deed or by a vesting assent, which contains the particulars set out above at page 706.[5]

(*b*) Infant life tenant reaches full age.

An infant cannot be an estate owner,[6] and if he becomes entitled to a life tenancy under a settlement the statutory powers are exercisable by the trustees, to whom, in their capacity as *statutory owners*,[7] the legal estate must be conveyed. It is their duty, however, upon the attainment by the infant of his majority, to convey the legal estate to him by a vesting deed or a vesting assent.[8]

(*c*) Tenant for life deprived of his statutory powers.

Where for example there is a limitation to A. for life with a limitation over to X. and Y. on *discretionary trusts* (*i.e.* trusts which give certain powers to X. and Y. if A. becomes bankrupt or

---

[1] Settled Land Act, 1925, s. 6.   [2] *Ibid.*, s. 8 (1).
[3] *Ibid.*, s. 7. See Burnett, *Elements of Conveyancing* (8th Edn.), pp. 279 *et seq.* The whole of this learned author's Chapter 14 should be studied.
[4] Administration of Estates Act, s. 22 (1) ; *infra*, pp. 740 ; 767 *et seq.*
[5] Settled Land Act, 1925, s. 7 (1), 1st Schedule, Form No. 5.
[6] *Infra*, p. 858.
[7] *Supra*, p. 701. Wide powers of management are conferred by s. 102 upon the trustees during a minority, see *infra*, pp. 863–4.
[8] Settled Land Act, 1925, s. 7 (2), (3) ; s. 19 (3).

attempts to part with his life interest in favour of his creditors),[1]
A. is bound to convey the legal estate to X. and Y. as statutory
owners upon the occurrence of an event bringing the trusts into
operation.[2]

(*d*) Person of full age becoming absolutely entitled.

If a person of full age becomes absolutely entitled to the land,
e.g. where there is a limitation to A. for life with remainder to
X. in fee simple and A. dies, the settlement comes to an end
and the land is no longer settled. There is, therefore, no
room for *special* personal representatives and the legal estate
must be conveyed by A.'s general personal representatives to
X., the absolute owner.[3]

The evasion of the statutory requirement of a vesting deed
is prevented by another section of the Act.[4] This provides that
where a tenant for life has become entitled to have a vesting deed
or assent executed in his favour, then, until such an instrument
has in fact been executed, no disposition of the land made *inter
vivos* by any person shall operate to pass a legal estate, unless it is
made in favour of a purchaser having no notice that the tenant for
life has become so entitled. Such a purported disposition operates as a contract to convey the legal estate as soon as the vesting
deed has been executed, and it is a contract that requires
registration as a land charge.[5]

Evasion
of Act
prevented.

There is an exception, however, in favour of personal representatives, for they are allowed to sell settled land in the ordinary
course of administration even though no vesting deed has been
executed when their title accrues.

Moreover, there are three cases in which there is no necessity
for a vesting deed :—

Cases where
vesting deed
not
necessary.

    (i) Where the land ceases to be settled.

        If, for instance, a tenant in tail in possession, who is
        not bound by prior interests, bars the entail, the settle-
        ment ceases and he can make title as absolute owner.[6]

---

[1] *Supra*, p. 148.   [2] Settled Land Act, 1925, s. 7 (4).
[3] *Ibid.*, s. 7 (5). *Re Bridgett and Hayes' Contract,* [1928] Ch. 163, *supra*,
p. 694; *In the Estate of Bordass*, [1929] P. 107.
[4] Settled Land Act, 1925, s. 13, as amended by Law of Property (Amendment) Act, 1926, Schedule.
[5] See *supra*, p. 669.
[6] *Re Alefounder's Will Trusts, Adnams* v. *Alefounder*, [1927] 1 Ch. 360 ;
Alefounder became entitled on December 16, 1925, to settled estates as legal
tenant in tail in possession with remainders over, but without any overriding
trusts or incumbrances. The effect of the Property Acts was that on January
1, 1926, he automatically became entitled to the legal fee simple, while his
legal estate tail became an equitable entailed interest, which, so long as it
remained unbarred, kept the settlement alive. He was held entitled to bar
the entail and then to make a valid disposition of the land without first
obtaining a vesting deed. He was entitled to the legal fee simple in trust for
himself as equitable tenant in tail, so that on disentailment he would acquire
the fee simple both at law and in equity. The sale that he contemplated,
therefore, was not a disposition under the Settled Land Act.

(ii) Where the beneficiaries terminate the settlement.

Beneficiaries, if of full age, may terminate the settlement and so avoid the necessity for a vesting deed. If, for instance, an owner devises his residence to his wife for life with remainder to his children in fee simple, the widow becomes tenant for life on his death and as such is entitled to a vesting deed. Instead, however, she may surrender her life interest to the remaindermen in fee, and then all the parties can create a trust for sale, with themselves as trustees, the income until sale and the ultimate proceeds to be held on trusts corresponding to those of the settlement.

(iii) If the land has become settled merely because it has been voluntarily subjected to family charges,[1] the tenant for life, as we have seen, is allowed by the Law of Property (Amendment) Act, 1926, to convey a legal estate subject to the charges without being required to procure the execution of a vesting deed.[2]

Position of purchaser from life tenant.

Simplification of Conveyancing. Taking the normal case, and presuming that the legal estate has been vested in the tenant for life by virtue of a vesting deed, it is worth our while to notice how the sale of the settled land to a purchaser is expedited and simplified, as compared with the practice prevailing before 1926. The main object of reducing the rights of the various beneficiaries to the status of equitable interests is to keep those rights off the title to the legal estate and to relieve a purchaser from the responsibility of seeing that they are not prejudiced by the sale. The fate of the equitable interests is to be no concern of the purchaser. His one concern is that the title to the *legal* estate shall be proved. He must, therefore, investigate the title down to the first vesting deed, *i.e.* he must require the vendor to prove that the person who purported to vest the legal estate in the estate owner by the principal vesting deed was entitled to do so, though of course if land remains settled for a generation or two the time will come when title is made by the production of a series of vesting deeds or assents. But the former practice of abstracting the beneficial limitations is forbidden. The trust instrument is not disclosed; it is not allowed to appear on the title; and with a few exceptions [3] the purchaser is not entitled to call for it or to make it the subject of interrogatories. Moreover, once satisfied that the vesting deed was executed by a party competent to execute it, he must take it at its face value and make the following assumptions :—

---

[1] Settled Land Act, 1925, s. 20 (1) (ix) ; *supra*, pp. 698–9.
[2] *Supra*, p. 699.
[3] Settled Land Act, 1925, s. 110 (2) (a), (b), (c), (d). For example, where the settlement has not been created by the proper method or where it existed before 1926. For a full account, see Burnett, *The Elements of Conveyancing* (8th Edn.), pp. 308–9.

That the estate owner named in the vesting deed is the life tenant and entitled to exercise the statutory powers.

That the trustees named in the deed are the properly constituted trustees.

That the statements contained in the deed in accordance with the requirements of the Act are correct.

That a later deed appointing new trustees is correct.[1]

This is a distinct simplification of the practice that obtained before 1926. Before that date, as we have seen,[2] a purchaser was compelled to investigate the whole settlement, including resettlements, so as to satisfy himself that the land was settled land within the meaning of the Act, that the vendor was tenant for life within the same meaning, and that there were proper trustees of the settlement. But all these facts are now certified by the vesting deed, for this short document guarantees the fundamentals concerning which enquiries had formerly to be made. Moreover any dispositions that the beneficiaries may have made of their equitable interests no longer affect the purchaser. He is secure in taking a conveyance of the legal estate from the person by whom the vesting deed asserts that this estate is held ; he can presume, in reliance on the same deed, that the Settled Land Act powers apply to the property ; and, provided that he pays the purchase money to the certified trustees, he can ignore the equitable rights of the beneficiaries.

In other words, the conveyance by the tenant for life overreaches the equitable interests of the beneficiaries and also certain other interests, *i.e.*, makes them enforceable against the money in the hands of the trustees, and no longer against the land. More precisely, the position in this respect is as follows :— *Interests that are overreached by conveyance of settled land.*

The conveyance by the tenant for life passes to the purchaser a title to the legal estate discharged from the following :—

    (i) All legal or equitable estates, interests and charges arising *under* the settlement.[3]

    (ii) Limited owner's charges,[4] general equitable charges[5] and certain annuities.[6]

        These three interests are overreached even though they have been registered as land charges and even

---

[1] Settled Land Act, 1925, s. 110 (2) ; but the proviso to the section contains exceptions.

[2] *Supra*, pp. 78-9.

[3] Settled Land Act, 1925, s. 72 (2).

[4] Described, *supra*, p. 668.

[5] Described, *supra*, pp. 668-9.

[6] *I.e.*, under the Land Charges Act, 1925, Part II. " Annuity " is here limited to annuities for one or more life or lives created after April 25th, 1855, and before January 1st, 1926. The register in which they might formerly have been entered was closed as from January 1st, 1926. All annuities created after 1925 are registrable as general equitable charges.

2A*

though they were created prior to the settlement.[1]   The reason is that they lose nothing in value or protection by their conversion into claims against the purchase money.

Interests
that are not
overreached.

On the other hand the conveyance by the tenant for life does not overreach the following :—

(i) Legal estates and legal charges having priority to the settlement.[2]

(ii) Legal estates and legal charges to secure money which has been actually raised before the date of the conveyance.[3]

An example is a mortgage created before the conveyance by which money has been raised for the payment of portions.

(iii) Terms of years, easements and profits granted for money or money's worth under the settlement.[4]

(iv) Estate contracts, restrictive covenants and equitable easements created after 1925,[5] if registered as land charges.[6]

(v) Restrictive covenants and equitable easements created before 1926, but only if the purchaser has actual or constructive notice of them.[7]

(vi) Estate contracts created before 1926 if the purchaser has actual or constructive notice of them, or if they are capable of registration and have been registered.   Such a contract becomes capable of registration upon its assignment after 1925.[8]

Position of
beneficiaries
under
settlement.

Obligations of Estate Owners. So far we have concentrated our attention upon the fact that in all settlements the actual tenant for life in possession acquires the legal estate in the settled lands, whether it be the fee simple or a term of years, in order that its transfer may be facilitated, but it is now necessary to look at the other side of the picture and inquire how the rights of the various beneficiaries are preserved and protected. The general principle is that all equitable interests in or over the settled land are enforceable against the *estate owner*,[9] that is to say, the person in whom the legal estate in the settled land is vested.[10]

---

[1] Settled Land Act, 1925, s. 72 (3) ; see *Law Journal*, 1934, January 6th, 13th, 20th and 27th.

[2] *Ibid.*, s. 72 (2) (i).

[3] *Ibid.*, s. 72 (2) (ii).

[4] Settled Land Act, 1925, s. 72 (2) (iii) (a).

[5] Described, *supra*, pp. 669; 670.

[6] Settled Land Act, 1925, s. 72 (2) (iii) (a), (b).

[7] See *supra*, p. 670.

[8] Land Charges Act, 1925, s. 14 (2).

[9] Settled Land Act, 1925, s. 16 (1).

[10] Law of Property Act, 1925, ss. 1 (4), 205 (1) (v).

There are two classes of estate owners whom we must keep in mind in connection with strict settlements :

(a) The tenant for life entitled in possession or the person who, by section 20,[1] is expressly given the powers of a tenant for life.

(b) The trustees of the settlement in their capacity as *statutory owners.* Statutory owners function when there is no tenant for life [2] or no person with the powers of a tenant for life, or when the person entitled to the life interest in possession is an infant.[3] In a few exceptional cases there may be no person having the powers of a tenant for life, as for example where the person entitled in possession is entitled only to a *part* of the income of the land,[4] or where a person is entitled to the settled land contingently upon the happening of some event,[5] or where land is held by the trustees during a life upon discretionary trusts, as in the case of a protected life interest.[6] In all these cases, whether of infancy or of the absence of a tenant for life, the trustees of the settlement, *qua* estate owners, take the legal fee simple and become entitled to exercise the statutory powers.[7]

Such an estate owner is bound to hold the land and its income upon such trusts as are necessary for giving effect to the equitable interests in the settled land of which he has notice and according to their respective priorities,[8] and any disposition of the land that he may make, other than one authorized by the Act or by the settlement, is void.[9]

If, for example, a tenant for life, X., suppresses the settlement and purports to grant a legal mortgage to Y. as security for advances made to him personally, professing to be absolute and beneficial owner of the fee simple, the mortgage is void as against the beneficiaries.[10]

A purchaser or mortgagee, such as Y. in this example, is indeed statutorily protected if he deals in good faith with a tenant for life,[11] but this protection is available to him only where he knows X. to be a limited owner and deals with him on that footing.[12]

In certain cases a tenant for life may be compelled to create a

---

[1] *Supra*, pp. 700-1.
[2] Settled Land Act, 1925, s. 23.
[3] *Ibid.*, s. 26.
[4] *Re Frewen*, [1926] Ch. 580.
[5] *Re Bird*, [1927] 1 Ch. 210.
[6] *Supra*, p. 148.
[7] Settled Land Act, 1925, s. 117 (1) (xxvi).
[8] *Ibid*, s. 16 (1).
[9] *Ibid.*, s. 18 (1).
[10] *Weston* v. *Henshaw*, [1950] Ch. 510. This is apparently the sole exception to the immunity of the purchaser for value of the legal estate without notice of equitable interests.
[11] Settled Land Act, 1925, s. 110 (1).
[12] *Weston* v. *Henshaw, supra.*

legal estate in order to give effect to an equitable interest. If, for instance,

> a sum of money has to be raised on the security of the settled land by virtue of a trust or in the exercise of a power of appointment, the estate owner is entitled to create a legal mortgage for the purpose.[1] Thus if there is a provision that portions shall be paid to the younger children, he must, on request, create a legal mortgage as security for their payment.

Purchase money paid to trustees, not to life tenant. The most effective safeguard of the equitable owners is that upon a sale of the land by the tenant for life or the statutory owner, the conveyance to the purchaser only takes effect under the Act if the purchase money is paid either to the trustees or into court[2]; moreover, except where the trusteeship is held by a trust corporation,[3] there must be at least two trustees to whom this payment is made.[4]

Termination of settlement. A settlement comes to an end if all equitable interests have ceased and if there can be no further occasion to exercise the statutory powers, provided that the person entitled to the legal estate is of full age.[5] When this occurs it is essential that the person beneficially entitled should be fortified by a document showing his right to deal freely with the land, and it is therefore provided that he may require the trustees to execute a *deed of discharge* declaring that the land is free from the trusts.[6] The termination of a settlement, however, most frequently occurs on the death of a tenant for life, as for example when he dies leaving no widow, but an only son who bars the entail limited to him by the settlement. In this case there is no need for a deed of discharge. It is sufficient if the personal representatives of the life tenant vest the legal estate in the son by an absolute vesting assent, *i.e.* one which does not nominate trustees.[7]

SECTION II. TRUSTEES FOR SALE.

Proof of title and overreaching. The nature of a trust for sale, the beneficial limitations that it usually contains and the powers of the trustees pending sale have already been discussed.[8] It remains to consider the investigation of title when the land is sold and the overreaching effect of the conveyance to the purchaser. There is, in fact, little that need be said about either matter.

---

[1] Settled Land Act, 1925, s. 16 (1) (iii); *Re Egerton's Settled Estates*, [1926] Ch. 574.
[2] Settled Land Act, 1925, s. 18 (1) (b).
[3] For definition, see *infra*, p. 718, note 3.
[4] Settled Land Act, 1925, s. 18 (1) (c).
[5] *Ibid.*, s. 3; Law of Property (Amendment) Act, 1926; Schedule.
[6] Settled Land Act, 1925, s. 17 (1).
[7] *Ibid.*, s. 110 (5).   [8] *Supra*, pp. 148–53.

Proof of title. What has been said above about the proof and investigation of title in the case of a sale by a person beneficially entitled in his own right to a fee simple estate applies equally to trustees for sale.[1] Failing a special stipulation, they must show by reference to a good root of title at least thirty years old that the creator of the trust was entitled to vest the legal estate in them. There are, however, certain statutory provisions designed to protect the purchaser and to facilitate dealings with the land, that must be noticed.

Statutory protection of purchasers.

Complete power to postpone a sale is implied in every case, unless a contrary intention appears, and the trustees are not liable for an indefinite postponement in the absence of an express direction to the contrary.[2] A disregard of such an express direction, however, does not prejudice a purchaser, for it is enacted that he shall not be concerned with directions that relate to postponement.[3]

Provisions affecting postponement of sale.

If the consent of not more than two persons is required before a sale is effected, a purchaser is required to ascertain that the requirement has been satisfied. If, however, the consent of more than two persons is required, his obligation is satisfied if any two of the persons specified give their consent.[4] If the person whose consent is required is under a disability, the purchaser is under no obligation with regard to him.[5] If a person refuses to give his consent or if the trustees refuse to sell, the court in its discretion may direct the trustees to carry out the sale upon an application being made by any person interested in some proprietary right under the trust.[6]

Provisions affecting consents.

If the beneficiaries are all of full age and have become absolutely entitled under the limitations of the settlement, they may terminate the trust and direct the trustees not to sell the land. Theoretically, this confronts a purchaser with a difficulty, for how does he know that such a direction has not been given to the trustees ? It is, therefore, enacted that, so far as regards the safety and protection of the purchaser, the trust is to be deemed to be subsisting until the land has been conveyed to, or under the directions of, the persons interested in the proceeds of sale.[7] In other words, the purchaser is safe in taking a conveyance from the trustees until the beneficiaries, being absolutely entitled and of full age, have terminated the trust by taking a conveyance to themselves.

Duration of trust for sale.

---

[1] *Supra*, pp. 659 *et seq.*

[2] Law of Property Act, 1925, s. 25 (1) (2) ; *Re Rooke's Will Trusts*, [1953] Ch. 716 ; [1953] 2 All E. R. 110.

[3] Law of Property Act, 1925, s. 25 (2).

[4] *Ibid.*, s. 26 (1). [5] *Ibid.*, s. 26 (2).

[6] *Ibid.*, s. 30 ; Trustee Act, 1925, s. 57 ; *In re Beale's Settlement Trusts, Huggins* v. *Beale*, [1932] 2 Ch. 15 ; *Stevens* v. *Hutchinson*, [1953] Ch. 299 ; [1953] 1 All E. R. 699.

[7] Law of Property Act, 1925, s. 23 ; re-enacting Conveyancing Act, 1911, s. 10. For the manner in which this difficulty was formerly overcome, see Burnett, *Elements of Conveyancing* (8th Edn.), p. 352.

Equities
arising under
the trust
over-
reached.

Overreaching. As we have already seen, a virtue long possessed by the trust for sale is that upon the sale of the land the equitable interests of the beneficiaries are kept off the title to the legal estate and are not disclosed to the purchaser.[1] The conveyance by the trustees overreaches the beneficial interests that arise *under* the trust for sale. To be more precise, the purchaser acquires a title to the legal estate, unaffected by the trusts that have been declared of the proceeds of sale and of the rents and profits until sale, even though the trusts have been declared by the same instrument as that which creates the trust for sale.[2] He does not enjoy this immunity, however, unless he pays the purchase money to at least two trustees or to a trust corporation, if one has been appointed.[3]

Third party
rights not
arising
under the
trust.

The liability of the purchaser to third party rights not arising under the trust, such as restrictive covenants and equitable easements, is the same as that which exists in the case of a conveyance by a beneficial owner.[4]

Statutory
trusts for
sale.

What has been said above applies not only to a trust for sale expressly created by act of parties, but also to those imposed by statute. The following is a summary of the circumstances in which such a statutory trust for sale arises :—

(*a*) Where an estate owner dies intestate.[5]

(*b*) Where property vested in trustees by way of security becomes discharged from the debtor's right of redemption.[6]

If, for example, trust money has been invested in a mortgage of a legal estate and the right of the mortgagor to redeem the land has been extinguished under the Limitation Act, 1939,[7] or by a foreclosure order,[8] the land, being thus subjected to a trust for sale, is regarded as converted into money and it will pass as such under a beneficiary's will.

In the following cases an express trust for sale is usually created, but if not a statutory trust arises automatically.

(*c*) Where land is devised or conveyed to two or more persons as tenants in common.[9]

---

[1] *Supra*, pp. 78–80.

[2] Law of Property Act, 1925, s. 27 (1) ; Trustee Act, 1925, s. 14 (1) ; *supra*, p. 80. Although it is better to execute two deeds on the creation of a trust for sale, there is no necessity for this.

[3] Law of Property Act, 1925, s. 27 (2). " Trust corporation " means, " The Public Trustee or a corporation either appointed by the court in any particular case to be a trustee or entitled by rules made under sub-s. (3) of s. 4 of the Public Trustee Act, 1906, to act as custodian trustee " ; Law of Property Act, 1925, s. 205 (xxviii). This definition is extended by the Law of Property (Amendment) Act, 1926, s. 3, to include *inter alios* a trustee in bankruptcy, the Treasury Solicitor and the Official Solicitor.

[4] *Supra*, pp. 687 *et seq.*

[5] Administration of Estates Act, 1925, s. 33 (1) ; *infra*, pp. 786; 793.

[6] Law of Property Act, 1925, s. 31 (1).

[7] *Supra*, p. 591–2.   [8] *Supra*, p. 605.

[9] Law of Property Act, 1925, s. 34 (2), (3) ; *supra*, pp. 312–4.

(*d*) Where land is devised or conveyed beneficially to two or more persons as joint tenants.[1]

(*e*) Where a legal estate is conveyed to an infant jointly with one or more persons of full age other than trustees or mortgagees.[2]

(*f*) Where the trustees of a *personalty* settlement purchase land in virtue of a power contained in the settlement.[3]

The effect of this, having regard to the doctrine of conversion, is that the land remains money in the eyes of equity and thus the original character of the settlement is preserved.

SECTION III. APPROVED TRUSTEES.

The overreaching effect of a conveyance either by trustees for sale or by a tenant for life under a settlement is limited in the sense that it obviously cannot extend to equitable interests that were in existence before the creation of the trust or settlement.

Ad hoc trust for sale.

> If, for instance, a fee simple owner charges his land with the payment of a sum of money, and later subjects it to a trust for sale, the normal rule is that a purchaser from the trustees takes the legal estate burdened by the equitable charge.

The Law of Property Act, 1925, however, introduced what is variously called an *ad hoc*, or a *special* or an *approved* trust for sale which enables the trustees to overreach even prior interests.[4] Whether it is of this special nature depends entirely upon the character of the trustees. They must be either,

" (*a*) two or more individuals approved or appointed by the court
" or the successors in office of the individuals so approved or
" appointed ; or
" (*b*) a trust corporation." [5]

An alternative open to an estate owner whose land is already subject to an equity is to create an *ad hoc* settlement under the Settled Land Act. If he executes a vesting deed, declaring the legal estate to be vested in him upon trust to give effect to equitable interests to which it is subject, and if at the same time he names as trustees either a trust corporation or two persons appointed or approved by the court,[6] the result is that he acquires the statutory powers of a tenant for life, including the power of sale.[7]

Ad hoc settlement.

The *ad hoc* trust for sale and the *ad hoc* settlement are similar in their effects. The land will be conveyed by the estate owner— by the trustees in the one case, by the notional tenant for life in

Operation of ad hoc assurances.

---

[1] Law of Property Act, 1925, s. 36 (1) ; *supra*, pp. 316–7.
[2] *Ibid.*, s. 19 (2) ; *infra*, p. 858.   [3] *Ibid.*, s. 32 (1).
[4] *Ibid.*, s. 2 (2).   [5] Defined *supra*, p. 718, note 3.
[6] Settled Land Act, 1925, s. 21.   [7] *Ibid.*, s. 21 (1) (a).

the other—and, though the equitable charge will be overreached by the conveyance to the purchaser, it will be the duty of the trustees to see that it is paid out of the proceeds of sale to which it has now become attached.

Over-
reaching
effect of
conveyance
under *ad hoc*
trust or
settlement.

Neither device, however, is of great practical use, for the number of equitable interests capable of being overreached is severely limited. It is enacted that a conveyance, whether under the trust for sale or under the settlement, shall not affect the following interests.[1]

(i) Equitable interests protected by a deposit of documents, *e.g.*, where title deeds are deposited with a bank to secure an overdraft.

(ii) Certain equitable interests that cannot be represented in terms of money, namely,

(*a*) restrictive covenants ;

(*b*) equitable easements ;

(*c*) estate contracts.[2]

These three interests, however, if created after 1925, will be void as against a purchaser of the legal estate for money or money's worth, unless they are registered under the Land Charges Act. If they were created before 1926, they do not bind a purchaser unless he has actual or constructive notice of them.[3]

(iii) Any equitable interest that has been registered in accordance with the Land Charges Act,[4] *except*

(*a*) certain annuities ; [5]

(*b*) a limited owner's charge ; [6] and

(*c*) a general equitable charge.[7]

Registration of these three interests does not prevent them from being overreached, since they are adequately protected if enforceable against the money instead of against the land.

Methods by
which legal
estate may
be cleared
of equities.

Thus, if land held by a beneficial owner in his own right, *i.e.*, land that is subject neither to a trust for sale nor a settlement, is burdened with the payment of, for instance, a general equitable charge which impedes the transfer of an absolute title to a purchaser, there are four possible methods of clearing off the incumbrance, namely :

[1] Law of Property Act, 1925, s. 2 (3) ; Settled Land Act, 1925, s. 21 (2).
[2] *Supra*, pp. 669-70.
[3] Law of Property Act, 1925, s. 2 (5).
[4] *Supra*, p. 668.
[5] *I.e.*, annuities created before 1926 and registered under the previous legislation ; *supra* p. 666.
[6] *Supra*, p. 668.
[7] *Supra*, pp. 668-9.

(*a*) The creation of an *ad hoc* trust for sale.

(*b*) The creation of an *ad hoc* settlement.

(*c*) A conveyance of the land to the purchaser by the beneficial owner with the concurrence of the incumbrancer.

(*d*) An application for leave to pay into Court a sum of money in discharge of the incumbrance.[1]

SECTION IV. MORTGAGORS AND MORTGAGEES.

It will be recalled that both parties to a legal mortgage become estate owners. The mortgagor holds the fee simple absolute in possession, the mortgagee holds the term of years absolute. *Mortgagors and mortgagees.*

The mortgagor, however, is scarcely the effective owner of the legal fee simple, since it is overreached upon the exercise by the mortgagee of his power of sale.[2]

The rules concerning proof of title by a beneficial owner apply to a sale by a mortgagee. He must satisfy the purchaser in the usual manner that the legal estate is vested in the mortgagor. The purchaser, however, although he must investigate the title to the legal estate, is not concerned to inquire whether a case has arisen to authorize the sale or whether notice has been given by the mortgagee to the mortgagor.[3] *Proof of title.*

---

[1] Law of Property Act, 1925, s. 50.
[2] *Supra*, pp. 601–2.　　　　[3] *Supra*, p. 602.

BOOK III.

THE TRANSFER AND EXTINCTION OF ESTATES AND INTERESTS.

PART III.

TRANSFER BY OPERATION OF LAW

SUMMARY.

Note. The land of a debtor, equally with his personal property, is liable to be seized at the instance of a creditor in satisfaction of unpaid debts. If we omit the case in which land has been expressly mortgaged by way of security for a loan, there are three different situations in which land may be taken from an owner for the benefit of his creditor or creditors : (*a*) where he is sued to judgment in respect of a debt, and thus becomes a judgment debtor ; (*b*) where he is made bankrupt ; and (*c*) where he dies and his property passes to his personal representatives for the purposes of administration. We will take these cases separately.

CHAPTER 1.

TRANSFER AS A RESULT OF EXECUTION AGAINST LAND BELONGING TO A JUDGMENT DEBTOR.

History. At common law, in all actions where judgment for money alone was obtained, the creditor was entitled to seize the goods and chattels of the debtor (including chattels real) and the growing profits of the land, but not the land itself ; for just as the original feudal law forbade the alienation of feuds, so also did it forbid them to be incumbered with debts. The writ under which the goods and chattels and growing profits were seized was, and still is, called the writ of *fieri facias*, " from the words in it where the sheriff is commanded, *quod fieri facias de bonis*, that he cause to be made of the goods of the debtor the sum or debt recovered." [1] When the power of alienation became available to feudal landowners, the rule that feuds could not be incumbered with debts still remained, with the result that a creditor could seize only the rents and profits of the land, and he lost even this right if the debtor conveyed his land to a stranger.

Origin of elegit.

To remedy this it was enacted in 1285 by the Statute Westminster II that a judgment creditor should be allowed to choose between two courses. He might either have execution upon the goods of the debtor by the writ of *fieri facias*, or have a writ of *elegit* by virtue of which *half* the land of the debtor and all his chattels with the exception of his oxen and the beasts of the plough, were seized and held till the debt was paid. [2] In pursuance of this statute a new writ was invented called a writ of *elegit* because, when a creditor chose this method, the entry on the roll was *quod elegit sibi executionem fieri de omnibus catallis et medietate terrae*. The effect of the statute was that a judgment recovered

Originally no remedy against freehold.

Available for half of land.

---

[1] Blackstone, vol. iii. p. 417

[2] 13 Edw. I, c. 18. Holdsworth, *History of English Law*, vol. iii. p. 131. This was an extension of an earlier rule obtaining under the laws of the Jewry by which a Jewish creditor was entitled to take his debt from the chattels or from the lands of his debtor : Lincoln, *The Legal Background to the Starrs*, p. 54.

in a court of record became a charge upon the debtor's freehold estates, since it enabled a creditor to seize one-half of the debtor's lands and tenements.[1] Such a judgment, when followed by the issue of the writ, operated to transfer a definite interest in the land, called a tenancy by *elegit*, to the judgment creditor, who moreover could pursue his remedy against the land even though it had meanwhile come into the hands of a purchaser or of the heir of the debtor.

In 1838, however, it was provided by the Judgments Act that it should be lawful for the sheriff to whom any writ of *elegit* was directed to take *all* the lands, tenements and hereditaments of the debtor.[2] The operation of the writ was thereafter confined to land, so that a creditor who chose to proceed against chattels sued out a *fi. fa.*, while if he chose to seize freeholds, he sued out an *elegit*.[3] Leaseholds might be seized and sold under a *fi. fa.* or under an *elegit*, but it was usual to proceed under a *fi. fa.*, not under an *elegit*, for when once the latter had been executed, it was not possible to obtain another writ of execution : {.margin-note}*Available for whole land.*

" And though he takes but an acre of land in execution, yet it is held " a satisfaction of the debt, because it may in time come out of it."[4]

The Modern Law. The writ of *elegit* was abolished by the Administration of Justice Act, 1956, as from January 1, 1957,[5] and a judgment creditor may now apply to the court either for a charging order under the Act or for the appointment of a receiver by way of equitable execution, though he may indeed pursue both these remedies. {.margin-note}*Remedies now available.*

The High Court or a County Court, having given judgment for the payment of money to a person, is empowered by the Act to impose a charge on the land of the debtor or upon any interest that he may hold in land for the purpose of securing payment of the amount adjudged to be due.[6] Such a charge has the same effect and is enforceable in the same manner as an equitable charge created by the debtor himself,[7] *i.e.* it entitles the creditor to apply for the sale of the land or for the appointment of a receiver.[8] {.margin-note}(1) *Charging order.*

The order is registrable as an order affecting land within the meaning of the Land Charges Act, 1925,[9] and if not registered is void against a purchaser of the land for valuable consideration.[10] If the order is so registered, a later order appointing a receiver, whether made in proceedings to enforce the charge or by way of equitable execution, will bind a purchaser even though not itself registered.[11] {.margin-note}*Registration of the order.*

---

[1] Cruise, Digest, Tit. xiv. s. 1, 17–19.   [2] S. 11.
[3] The seizure of goods under a writ of *elegit* was prohibited by the Bankruptcy Act, 1883, s. 146 (1).   [4] Bac. Abr. " Execution."
[5] S. 34 (1) ; S. I. 1956, No. 1979.   [6] *Ibid.*, s. 35 (1).
[7] *Ibid.*, s. 35 (3).   [8] *Supra.*, p. 613.
[9] Land Charges Act, 1925, s. 6 (1).   [10] *Ibid.*, ss. 7 (1) ; 20 (8).
[11] Administration of Justice Act, 1956, s. 36 (3).

(2) Appoint-
ment of
receiver by
way of
equitable
execution.

Courts of Equity from an early period were prepared to aid a creditor who was unable to reach the land of his debtor under the common law writ of *elegit*, as for instance where the debtor was entitled to an equity of redemption or to an interest limited by a trust under which he was not the sole beneficiary. Despite the abolition of the writ of *elegit*, this equitable jurisdiction continues in full force and it is made effective, as it always has been, by the appointment of a receiver with a direction to him to realize the interest of the judgment debtor in the land and to apply the proceeds in satisfaction of the debt.[1]

The Administration of Justice Act, 1956, however, has enlarged the jurisdiction by providing that the power of the High Court or of a County Court to appoint a receiver by way of equitable jurisdiction shall extend to all legal estates and interests.[2]   This power of the court is additional to its power to appoint a receiver in proceedings to enforce a charging order and is exercisable whether or not such an order has been made.[3]   The order by which the appointment is made is registrable under the Land Charges Act, 1925.[4]

---

[1] Ashburner, *Principles of Equity* (2nd Edn.), p. 354.
[2] S. 36 (1).   [3] *Ibid.*, s. 36 (3).
[4] Land Charges Act, 1925, s. 6 (1) (b).

CHAPTER II.

TRANSFER OF LAND BELONGING TO A BANKRUPT DEBTOR.

Bankruptcy procedure. After a debtor has committed an act of bankruptcy as defined by the Bankruptcy Act, 1914,[1] either he or his creditors may present a bankruptcy petition to the court requesting that a *receiving order* be made for the protection of his estate. The effect of such an order is not to make him bankrupt, but to place his property under the control of the official receiver. If no arrangement for the discharge of his liabilities is accepted by the creditors, an *adjudication order* is made by the court, whereupon the debtor is rendered bankrupt, and his property vests in the trustee in bankruptcy appointed by the creditors. Receiving order followed by adjudication order.

The certificate of the Board of Trade confirming the trustee's appointment is deemed to be a conveyance from the debtor to the trustee, and the general rule is that all the property which was formerly vested in the debtor as beneficial owner is transferred to the trustee in bankruptcy for distribution among the creditors. But we must observe, and this is the important fact, that it is not merely the property which was owned by the debtor at the date of the adjudication, or even at the date of the receiving order, that is transferred to the trustee, but also the property which he had at the *commencement of the bankruptcy*. This commencement is earlier than either the receiving order or the adjudication. The bankruptcy is deemed by statute to relate back to, and to commence at, the time when the act of bankruptcy was committed upon which the receiving order has been made. If more than one act has been committed, the bankruptcy commences at the *first* act, provided that it occurred not more than three months before the presentation of the bankruptcy petition.[2] An act of bankruptcy ceases to be available after three months. Commencement of bankruptcy.

Property of debtor at commencement of bankruptcy. Having thus fixed the moment at which the bankruptcy is deemed Property that passes to trustee.

---

[1] There are eight available acts of bankruptcy, *e.g.* a notice by a debtor that he has suspended payment of his debts.
[2] Bankruptcy Act, 1914, s. 37 (1).

to begin, the Act provides that with certain exceptions[1] there shall pass to the trustee,

> (*a*) all such property as may belong to or be vested in the bankrupt *at the commencement of the bankruptcy*, or may be acquired by or devolve on him before his discharge ; and
>
> (*b*) the capacity to exercise all such powers in or over or in respect of property as might have been exercised by the bankrupt for his own benefit at the commencement of his bankruptcy or before his discharge, except the right of nomination to a vacant ecclesiastical benefice.[2]

Examples of interests in land which pass.

The following illustrations show the comprehensive nature of these statutory provisions.

General power.

1. A general power of appointment is property within the meaning of the Act, and if such power is exercisable by deed as distinct from will, it can be exercised by the trustee in bankruptcy during the lifetime of the debtor for the benefit of the creditors.[3]

Entailed interest.

2. If the bankrupt is entitled to an entailed interest, the trustee in bankruptcy may bar the entail, and dispose of the land for the benefit of the creditors.[4]

Future interest.

3. Again, if property is settled upon a tenant for life, and then upon such of his children as may be living at his death, the future interest of a child who becomes bankrupt before the life tenant's death passes to the trustee in bankruptcy.[5]

On the other hand, an interest in land determinable upon the debtor's bankruptcy does not pass to the trustee. We have already seen [6] that although a person may not settle his own property upon himself *until he becomes bankrupt*, yet he may so settle it upon another person. In the same way a lease may provide that the tenancy shall be forfeited if the tenant becomes bankrupt, and the effect of this is that, subject to the provisions of the Law of Property Act, 1925,[7] the term does not pass to the trustee upon the bankruptcy of the tenant.

Position of trustee as regards the land.

The trustee in bankruptcy stands with regard to the property which passes to him in the same position in which the debtor

---

[1] (i) personal earnings so far as they are necessary for the support of the bankrupt and his family ; (ii) interests limited by third parties and made defeasible upon bankruptcy (*supra*, pp. 291–2) ; (iii) rights of action in respect of bodily or personal injury ; (iv) rights under contracts of insurance (Third Parties (Rights and Insurers) Act, 1930) ; (v) property held by the bankrupt on trust for any other person ; (vi) the tools of his trade and the necessary wearing apparel and bedding of himself and his family up to the value of £20.
[2] Bankruptcy Act, 1914, s. 38.
[3] *Nichols* v. *Nixey* (1885), 29 Ch. D. 1005.
[4] Bankruptcy Act, 1914, s. 55 (5).
[5] *Higden* v. *Williamson* (1731), 3 P. Wms. 132.
[6] *Supra*, pp. 291–2.   [7] *Supra*, pp. 402–3.

would have stood had he not become bankrupt. The broad general principle is that the trustee takes all the property, but takes it subject to all the liabilities which affected it while it was in the debtor's hands,[1] so that if, for instance, the property is mortgaged, the trustee takes only the equity of redemption, and if the property consists of a term of years, he is liable to pay rent and to observe the covenants contained in the lease.

He may, however, disclaim a lease within twelve months of his appointment if in his opinion it is burdened with onerous covenants.[2] Normally, this presents no difficulty and inflicts no hardship, for the term is surrendered to the landlord by operation of law. But the case is different if there has been a sub-lease. At common law, if the lease disappears, the sub-lease disappears also, the branch falls with the tree,[3] but as the intention of the legislature is to allow disclaimer with the least possible injury to third parties, the Act contains a provision designed to protect the rights of third parties and particularly of sub-tenants.[4] It allows the court to vest a disclaimed leasehold interest in any person who is interested therein, as, for instance, a mortgagee or a sub-tenant, but it can do so only upon the terms of making that person

Disclaimer of lease.

(1) subject to the same liabilities and obligations as affected the bankrupt at the date when the bankruptcy petition was filed ; or

(2) if the court thinks fit, subject only to the same liabilities and obligations as would have existed if the lease had been assigned to the mortgagee or the sub-tenant at that date.[5]

The advantages of the second clause are that the person in whom the interest is vested becomes liable only for breaches of covenant which occur after the date of the bankruptcy petition, and he may also escape from liability for future breaches by assigning the lease to a third party. It has been said that the court should exercise its discretion in favour of imposing condition (2) if the result will be to place the sub-lessee in no better position and the lessor in no worse position than if there had been no disclaimer.[6]

After acquired Property. There is an important distinction between property belonging to the bankrupt at the commencement of the bankruptcy and property acquired by him afterwards.

Rule in *Cohen* v. *Mitchell.*

---

[1] *Ex parte Newitt* (1881), 16 Ch. D. 522, 531 ; JAMES, L.J. ; *Bendall* v. *McWhirter*, [1952] 2 Q. B. 466 ; [1952] 1 All E. R. 1307.

[2] *Supra*, p. 731 ; Bankruptcy Act, 1914, s. 54 (1). A similar power is exercisable by the liquidator of a company (Companies Act, 1948, s. 323). In certain cases the leave of the court must first be obtained ; Bankruptcy Rules, 1952, r. 278, made under Bankrupty Act, 1914, s. 54 (3).

[3] *Re Carter and Ellis*, [1905] 1 K. B. 735, 743, VAUGHAN WILLIAMS, L.J.

[4] *Re Holmes*, [1908] 2 K. B. 812, 815 ; JELF, J.

[5] Bankruptcy Act, 1914, s. 54 (6).

[6] *Re Carter and Ellis*, [1905] 1 K. B. 735, 747.

Over the former he has no right of disposition whatsoever, but, by the rule in *Cohen* v. *Mitchell*,[1] if he completes a disposition of the after-acquired property in favour of a person dealing with him *bonâ fide* and for value before the trustee intervenes, the disposition is unimpeachable.

It should be noticed that the property as soon as acquired belongs to the trustee, not to the bankrupt. All that the rule means is that the ownership of the trustee is liable to be defeated if he fails to intervene before its disposition by the bankrupt is completed.[2]

This rule, which originally applied only to personalty was extended to realty by the Bankruptcy Act, 1914.[3]

The fact that the alienee has notice of the bankruptcy does not constitute lack of *bona fides*, since, so far as he knows, the trustee may have authorized the transaction.

Dispositions after act of bankruptcy void against trustee.

Position of Third Parties.—The rule that the title of the trustee relates back to the commencement of the bankruptcy seriously affects transactions occurring in the interval between an available act of bankruptcy and the order of adjudication. If the trustee is entitled to all that was in the apparent ownership of the bankrupt during this interval, is a conveyance of land made in favour of a third party after the commission of an act of bankruptcy to be upset ? The general principle is clear and has been stated in these words :

> " Nothing is more firmly established than that a man who has
> " committed an act of bankruptcy is not entitled to deal with his
> " estate."[4]

It follows from this that every disposition of property made by a man after the commission of an act of bankruptcy is void against the trustee, and the property is recoverable by him from the person to whom it has been conveyed.[5] This principle, however, is subject to the following statutory modifications.

Exceptions.

(i) Conveyances for value.

Conveyances before date of receiving order.

Any conveyance or assignment made by the bankrupt for valuable consideration is valid, provided that it takes place before the date of the receiving order, and that the alienee has no notice at the time of the conveyance of an available act of bankruptcy.[6] The Land Charges Act, 1925, affects the question of notice.

---

[1] (1890), 25 Q. B. D. 262.
[2] *Re Pascoe*, [1944] Ch. 219 ; [1944] 1 All E. R. 281.
[3] S. 47.
[4] *Ponsford, Baker & Co.* v. *Union of London and Smith's Bank, Ltd.*, [1906]
2 Ch. 444, at p. 52, *per* FLETCHER MOULTON, L.J.
[5] *Ibid.*
[6] Bankruptcy Act, 1914, s. 45.

If a bankruptcy petition or a receiving order is registered, the title of the purchaser is void against the trustee, since registration constitutes notice. If neither is registered, then a purchaser for money or money's worth is protected unless he had notice at the time of conveyance of an available act of bankruptcy.[1]

(ii) Executions completed by judgment creditors.

A judgment creditor who issues execution against the land of a debtor, is entitled to the *benefit of the execution, i.e.* to a prior right to be paid in full out of the land,[2] provided that he *completes the execution*, as for example by procuring the appointment of a receiver, before the date of the receiving order *and* before notice of the presentation of any bankruptcy petition or of the commission of an act of bankruptcy by the debtor.[3] Hence, if a receiving order is made or if a petition or act of bankruptcy becomes known to the judgment creditor before completion of the execution, he loses the fruits of his diligence and the land becomes divisible among the general body of creditors.

Completed executions.

(iii) Distress levied by a landlord.

A landlord may distrain for rent due from a bankrupt tenant, but if he levies the distress after the commencement of the bankruptcy he can recover only six months' rent accrued due prior to the date of the adjudication order.[4] There is no limit in the case of rent accruing due *after* adjudication, so that if the trustee takes possession and does not disclaim the lease, the remedy of distress is available to the landlord for rent actually due.[5]

Distress for six months' rent.

Transactions voidable by the Trustee. A trustee is permitted to set aside certain transactions that have taken place even before the commencement of a bankruptcy. These are as follows :

(i) Voluntary Settlements.

In order to prevent a debtor from transferring property to relatives to the detriment of his creditors, section 42 of the Bankruptcy Act provides that a voluntary settlement shall be "void" against the trustee.

(*a*) if the settlor becomes bankrupt within two years after the date of the settlement ; or

---

[1] Land Charges Act, 1925, ss. 2, 3, 6, 7.
[2] *Re Andrew, Ex parte Official Receiver (Trustee)* (No. 2), [1937] Ch. 122; [1936] 3 All E. R. 450.
[3] Bankruptcy Act, 1914, s. 40 (1).
[4] *Ibid.*, s. 35 (1).
[5] *Ibid.*, s. 35 (2). Distress cannot be levied for rent payable in advance.

(*b*) if the settlor becomes bankrupt within ten years after the date of the settlement, unless the beneficiaries can prove that the settlor at the date of the settlement was able to pay all his debts without the aid of the settled property, and also that his interest passed to the trustees of the settlement on its execution.[1]

A settlement is said to be " voluntary " if it is not made for money or for money's worth, or in consideration of a *future* marriage. Normally, if a man settles property acquired by him *after* his marriage in right of his wife he is deemed to make a voluntary settlement, but for the purposes of the present rule this particular form of settlement is expressly regarded as having been made for valuable consideration. In the result, therefore, the following transactions are unaffected by section 42:

Meaning of "voluntary" settlement.

First, a transfer to a purchaser or incumbrancer in good faith and for valuable consideration. "Purchaser" in this context means a purchaser in the commercial sense, *i.e.*, one who furnishes the debtor with consideration in replacement of the property extracted from his creditors.[2]

Secondly, a settlement made before and in consideration of marriage, unless the intention of the parties is to defeat creditors.[3]

Thirdly, a settlement made in favour of the wife or children if the property has accrued to the settlor after the marriage in right of the wife, as for example where he acquires property under his wife's intestacy.[4]

The Act provides that a settlement falling within the above provisions shall be *void* " against the trustee in bankruptcy." These words mean, not that the settlement is void generally, but that it becomes voidable at the instance of the trustee *if bankruptcy supervenes*.[5] It follows from this that if the beneficiary under the settlement transfers the settled property for value before the commencement of the bankruptcy, the title of the transferee cannot be avoided.[6] Moreover, a disposition made after the commencement of bankruptcy but before intervention by the trustee is unassailable if the transferee for value had no notice of an available act of bankruptcy.[7]

The settlement is voidable, not void.

---

[1] Bankruptcy Act, 1914, s. 42 (1). For the purposes of this section, "settlement" includes any conveyance or transfer of property, s. 42 (4).
[2] *Re A. Debtor, ex parte Official Receiver, Trustee [Of Property of Debtor* v. *Morrison,* [1965] 3 All E. R. 453; [1965] 1 W. L. R. 1498.
[3] *Columbine* v. *Penhall* (1853), 1 Sm. & G. 228.
[4] Bankruptcy Act, 1914, s. 42 (1) ; *Re Bower Williams,* [1927] 1 Ch. 441.
[5] *Re Carter and Kenderdine's Contract,* [1897] 1 Ch. 776.
[6] *Re Carter and Kenderdine's Contract, supra* ; *Re Vansittart,* [1893] 2 Q. B. 377.
[7] *Re Hart,* [1912] 3 K. B. 6.

Section 42 operates where the settlor becomes bankrupt, and therefore it does not apply where he dies insolvent and the court orders that his estate shall be administered according to the law of bankruptcy. In such a case he has never been adjudicated bankrupt.[1]

Re Gould.

(ii) Conveyances in Fraud of Creditors.

It was provided in 1571 by the Statute 13 Eliz. c. 5 (and this is a statute which applied generally and not merely to a case of supervening bankruptcy) that any alienation of real or personal property made with the intention of delaying, hindering or defrauding creditors should be void as against such creditors. The statute, however, contained an exception in favour of purchasers for valuable consideration who had no notice that the grantor was actuated by a fraudulent intention.

Conveyances in fraud of creditors voidable.

The Statute of Elizabeth has now been re-enacted in a modern form by the Law of Property Act, 1925, as follows[2] :

> " Save as provided in this section, every conveyance of property,
> " made whether before or after the commencement of this Act,
> " with intent to defraud creditors, shall be voidable at the instance
> " of any person thereby prejudiced. . . . This section does not
> " extend to any estate or interest in property conveyed for valuable
> " consideration and in good faith, or upon good consideration and
> " in good faith to any person not having, at the time of the conveyance,
> " notice of the intent to defraud creditors."

It will be noticed that a person who takes an estate or interest in good faith will be protected if the conveyance to him was supported either by valuable or by good consideration. Good consideration arises where a person conveys land to someone to whom he is supposed to bear natural love and affection, as for instance to his children, brothers, sisters, nephews and nieces. The rule under 13 Eliz. c. 5 was that a conveyance which was supported by good, as distinguished from valuable, consideration could be set aside in favour of creditors, notwithstanding that the grantee took in good faith,[3] but the intention of the legislature in the Act of 1925 apparently is to reverse this rule.[4]

This enactment must be distinguished from section 42 of the Bankruptcy Act, for since it is of general application and in no way dependent upon the bankruptcy of the alienor it may be invoked if an order for the administration of his estate in bankruptcy is made after his death.[5]

---

[1] *Re Gould, Ex parte Official Receiver* (1887), 19 Q. B. D. 92.

[2] Law of Property Act, 1925, s. 172.

[3] *Twyne's Case* (1602), Smith's *Leading Cases*, vol. i. p. 1.

[4] HARMAN, J., however, in *Re Eichholz, Eichholz's Trustee* v. *Eichholz*, [1959] Ch. 708, at pp. 725–6; [1959] 1 All E. R. 166, took the view that the Act of 1925 is a consolidating statute that *prima facie* is not to be construed as making any substantial alteration in the pre-existing law. But see 75 *L.Q.R.*, pp. 307–10 (R.E.M.).

[5] *In re Eichholz*, [1959] Ch. 708; [1959] 1 All E. R. 166. See 22 *Modern Law Review*, pp. 423–6 (P. M. Bromley).

What must be proved in order to set aside an alienation under the statute varies according as the alienee is a voluntary alienee or a purchaser for good or valuable consideration. A voluntary conveyance is voidable if its necessary effect is to defeat creditors, although a fraudulent intention cannot actually be proved.[1] Thus a voluntary conveyance made by a man upon the eve of starting a hazardous business, which is likely to embarrass him financially, is voidable upon his subsequent insolvency, even though he could have paid his debts in full at the time of the conveyance.[2] In such cases the onus of disproving a fraudulent intent lies upon the alienee.

On the other hand, a conveyance made for valuable or good consideration is not voidable unless it is proved,

> first, that the grantor was actuated by a fraudulent intention,
> and, secondly, that the grantee was aware of that fraudulent
>   intention, not necessarily that he actively participated in
>   the fraud.[3]

With regard to the first matter, the court, in each particular case, must determine what was the true object of the conveyance. If, for instance, a trader, sorely pressed by creditors, forms a company and sells the whole of his property to it, receiving in return all or nearly all the shares, the almost irresistible inference is that he intends to delay and hinder his creditors.[4]

Nevertheless, it is not the intent of the statute to prevent honest dealings between one person and another, even though the result may be to hinder creditors. Thus in one case[5]:

> J. assigned a farmhouse in trust for her daughters, in consideration
> of which they covenanted to pay the debts
>
> " incurred by J. up to the date of the deed in connection with
> " the working and management of the farm."
>
> J. had no other property, and the result of the conveyance was that
> the plaintiff, to whom J. owed a debt having no connection with the
> farm, was defeated.

It was held that this conveyance could not be set aside, because it represented a perfectly honest family arrangement, whereby the daughters undertook to pay part of their mother's debts, in consideration of which they were to take immediately property which in all probability they would have received on her death.

In this case it will be noticed that the conveyance was founded

---

[1] *Freeman* v. *Pope* (1870), 5 Ch. App. 538; *In re Eicholz*, [1959] Ch. 708; [1959] 1 All E. R. 166.
[2] *Mackay* v. *Douglas* (1872), L. R. 14 Eq. 106 ; *Re Butterworth, Ex parte Russell* (1882), 19 Ch. D. 588.
[3] *In re Fasey*, [1923] 2 Ch. 1.
[4] *In re Fasey, supra.*   [5] *Re Johnson* (1881), 20 Ch. D. 389.

partly upon good consideration and partly upon valuable consideration. The former consisted of the relationship of the grantees to the grantor, and the latter of the agreement to pay the mother's debts. In the then state of the law the relationship alone (*i.e.* good consideration) would not have sufficed to protect the interest granted to the daughters, but presumably, in view of the alteration introduced by the Act of 1925 which has already been mentioned, that interest could not now be defeated under the statute even though there were no promise to pay debts.[1]

It is provided that the enactment shall not affect the operation of a disentailing assurance.[2] Thus a resettlement of property which has been preceded by a disentailment is not voidable.

Resettlement not voidable.

Statute 27 Eliz. c. 4. There was another statute passed in the reign of Elizabeth which, though it was aimed against conveyances made in fraud of subsequent *purchasers*, is *in pari materiâ* with 13 Eliz. c. 5, and may be discussed here. This was the Statute 27 Eliz. c. 4. It enacted that every conveyance, grant, charge and lease of any lands, made with the intent and purpose of defrauding such persons as should *subsequently* purchase the same lands for money or other good consideration, should be *utterly void*.[3] There was a proviso that the enactment should not invalidate any conveyance which was made *bonâ fide* and for good consideration to any person or persons.

Conveyances in fraud of purchasers, void under 27 Eliz. c. 4.

This statute was required because at common law a purchaser was without a remedy if he was prevented by a pre-existing fraud from obtaining the interest that he had contracted to buy.[4] If, for instance,

A., the owner of lands, fraudulently made a voluntary conveyance purporting to pass the legal estate to B., and then, being still in possession, agreed to sell the same land to C. for valuable consideration, C. under the statute could set aside the conveyance to B. The conveyance from A. to B. was clearly made with the express intention of defrauding C., and it was against this form of fraud that the statute was directed. The voluntary conveyance was binding between A. and B., but voidable at the instance of C.

But when the courts were called upon to construe the statute, they held that all *voluntary* conveyances were void against subsequent purchasers, even though no expressly fraudulent intention could be shown. It was said that the mere fact that a later conveyance was made was sufficient to prove a fraudulent intent in the first conveyance.[5]

How statute interpreted.

---

[1] But see *supra*, p. 735, note 4.
[2] Law of Property Act, 1925, s. 172 (2). [3] *I.e.*, in effect, voidable.
[4] Cro. Eliz. 445, cited Cruise, Tit. xxxii, cxxvii.
[5] *Doe d. Otley* v. *Manning* (1807), 9 East, 59.

Thus :

> If the owner of Blackacre settled it upon his wife or children
> after marriage, unsupported by any other consideration than
> that of natural love and affection, or if he conveyed it to his
> son or to any other person without receiving valuable con-
> sideration, the settlement in the one case and the conveyance
> in the other could be invalidated at the suit of a subsequent
> purchaser for value of Blackacre.[1]   The effect was the same
> even though the subsequent purchaser had notice of the
> voluntary conveyance at the time when he made his purchase.

The result of this somewhat strained interpretation was that
a voluntary alienee of lands, however honestly he might have
acted, never possessed a secure title, since he remained liable
to lose his interest should the alienor make a later sale of the same
land to a purchaser for value.

Voluntary
Conveyances
Act, 1893.

To remedy this particular interpretation it was provided by
the Voluntary Conveyances Act, 1893, that a purchaser for value
whose title was acquired after 28th June, 1893, should not defeat
a prior voluntary conveyance of the same land if in fact the
voluntary conveyance had been made without any fraudulent
intention.[2]

The Act of 1893 did not repeal or affect the Statute of Elizabeth.
All that it did was to reverse the judicial interpretation which had
been put upon the earlier statute.

With respect to persons who were deemed to be subsequent
purchasers within the Statute of Elizabeth, it was held in *Twyne's
Case*[3] that no purchaser should avoid a preceding conveyance
except one who gave money or other *valuable consideration*.
But the word *purchaser* has been held (if valuable consideration
is given) to include a lessee,[4] a mortgagee,[5] and a beneficiary
under a settlement which has been made in view of an intended
marriage.[6]

The modern
statutory
law.

The Statute of Elizabeth and the Voluntary Conveyances
Act, 1893, have been repealed by the Law of Property Act, 1925,
and replaced by a short section which runs as follows [7] :—

> " Every voluntary disposition of land made with intent to defraud
> " a subsequent purchaser is voidable at the instance of that purchaser.
> " For the purposes of this section no voluntary disposition, when-
> " ever made, shall be deemed to have been made with intent to

---

[1] *Woodie's Case cited Colvile* v. *Parker* (1607), Cro. Ja. 158.
[2] S. 2.   [3] (1602), Smith's *Leading Cases*, vol. i. p. 1.
[4] *Goodright* v. *Moses* (1775), 2 W. Bl. 1019.
[5] *Chapman* v. *Emery* (1775), 1 Cowp. 278.
[6] *Doe d. Watson* v. *Routledge* (1777), 2 Cowp. 705.
[7] Law of Property Act, 1925, s. 173.

" defraud by reason only that a subsequent conveyance for valuable
" consideration was made, if such subsequent conveyance was made
" after the 28th day of June, 1893."

" Purchaser " means a purchaser in good faith for valuable consideration and includes a lessee, mortgagee or other person who for valuable consideration acquires an interest in property; and " valuable consideration " includes marriage but does not include a nominal consideration in money.[1]

---

[1] Law of Property Act, 1925, s. 205 (1), (XXI).

CHAPTER III.

TRANSFER OF THE LAND OF A DECEASED DEBTOR.

Assets.

Introductory Note. Property which belongs to a person for an interest not ceasing with his life is transferred upon his death to his personal representatives,[1] and it becomes liable for the payment of his debts. Property which thus becomes available for creditors is called assets, and the phrase *administration of assets* is employed to indicate the obligation of the personal representatives to pay the funeral and testamentary expenses and the debts of the deceased out of the property, before distributing the residue among those who are beneficially entitled.

Personalty as assets in case of a will.

History—Personalty. Originally, whether property was assets varied according as it was personalty or realty.

In the earliest days of English Law a man's personal property was apparently divided into three parts, one of which went to his heirs, another to his wife, while the third was at his own disposal, but by imperceptible degrees the rights of the wife and the children disappeared, and a man became entitled to bequeath his personal property as he liked.[2]

Bequeathed personalty did not pass directly to the donees under the will, but vested first in the executors and became in their hands assets for the payment of debts.

Personalty as assets in case of intestacy.

If a man neglected to make a will, his property could in the earliest times be seized by the king, but as it was thought that the clergy, being supposedly of better conscience than laymen, were more fitted to make a disposition that would bring repose to the soul of the deceased, the king allowed the bishop of a diocese to seize the personalty of one who had died intestate. The bishop was expected to use the property for pious purposes, his only liability being to God, but as the result of this freedom from control was that the clergy arrogated to themselves one-third of the property

---

[1] *Infra*, pp. 744 *et seq.*   [2] Blackstone, vol. ii. pp. 492-3.

and generally omitted to pay the debts of the deceased, it was enacted by the Statute Westminster II that the bishop should be bound to pay those debts so far as the goods extended, just as executors were bound where the deceased had left a will. But as the clergy were still enabled to appropriate anything that was left after payment of debts, it was finally provided that in case of intestacy the bishop should depute the nearest and most lawful friends of the deceased to administer his goods, and that such administrators should be on the same footing as executors appointed by will.[1] So it is true to say that from an early date the personal property of a deceased person, including both chattels personal and chattels real, passed to his personal representatives and became in their hands answerable for his debts.

History—Realty. The case stood differently, however, with realty. At common law, before the Statute of Wills, the fee simple estate of a deceased person passed directly to his heir, and after a will of lands was permitted, passed directly to his devisee if he had exercised his testamentary power. Whether he died testate or intestate, his land did not go to his personal representatives, and whether it went to the heir-at-law or to a devisee, it did not constitute assets for the payment of debts.

Land originally not assets.

There were, however, three cases in which a fee simple estate was liable to the creditors of the deceased. Debts due to the Crown and debts due to *judgment* creditors were enforceable against the land notwithstanding the death of the owner, and thirdly, if the fee simple tenant had in his lifetime covenanted by deed for himself and his heirs to pay a sum of money, the creditor (called a *specialty creditor*) could make the heir liable for the debt to the extent of the land which had descended to him. But this privilege of the specialty creditor was not at first enforceable against an equitable fee simple, and it was strictly limited to a right of action against the *heir* of the deceased, so that the creditor was defrauded of his money if the deceased devised his land to a stranger. These two defects were later remedied, for the Statute of Frauds in 1677 made equitable fees simple liable equally with legal estates, and in 1691 the Statute of Fraudulent Devises[2] provided that a devisee should be liable in the same way as an heir for the specialty debts of his testator. Real estate which in this manner became liable in the hands of an heir or devisee for specialty debts was called " assets by descent."

Exceptions.

The result of the common law treatment as thus modified by statute was, then, that specialty creditors had a remedy against the fee simple estates of a deceased owner, while simple contract creditors had not.

---

[1] Blackstone, vol. ii. pp. 295–6 ; *Hewson* v. *Shelley*, [1914] 2 Ch. 13, 38–9.
[2] 3 Will. & Mar. c. 14.

An estate tail was not liable for payment of debts, for unless it was barred by the tenant during his life it descended to the appropriate heir freed from the obligations of the deceased.

Estates *pur autre vie* were not liable for the debts of a deceased owner, whether they passed to a general or to a special occupant.[1] The Statute of Frauds, however, which allowed a tenant *pur autre vie* to devise his interest, enacted that if there was no devise, the interest should be assets by descent in the hands of the heir to the same extent as if it were a fee simple; and if there was a devise, it should go to the personal representatives and be assets in their hands.

Intervention of equity.

Such were the rules at common law, but in certain cases equity stepped in and afforded simple contract creditors a remedy against the land. We have seen that personal representatives had no power over real estate, since it passed directly to the heir or the devisee, but if a testator gave his executors a power of sale over his land for the purpose of paying his debts, equity treated the land to which the power related as being

Equitable assets.

equitable assets. Land became available in this way for payment of debts if a testator gave his executors an express power of sale for that purpose, or if he gave them merely an implied power of sale (as for instance by the creation of a general charge of debts upon his real estate), or if he devised his land to the executors upon trust to sell and pay debts out of the proceeds.

Again, acting on the view that assets must be confined to property actually owned by the deceased, common law refused to include in this category property over which he had a power of appointment.[2] In the case of a general power, however, equity permitted proceedings in Chancery to be taken in order to make the appointed property available for payment of debts. The appointee became a trustee for creditors.[3]

Administration of Estates Act, 1833.

Such was the position with regard to assets when the Administration of Estates Act, 1833, was passed, except that an Act passed in 1807 had already provided that the land of a deceased *trader* should be liable in equity for the payment of his debts, whether specialty or simple contract. The Act of 1833 provided that any estate or interest in lands which the deceased owner had not charged with, or devised subject to, the payment of debts should be assets to be administered in courts of equity for the payment both of specialty and of simple contract debts. Simple contract creditors thus obtained a remedy against land, even where a testator had omitted to make express provision for the payment of their debts, but the Act of 1833 still favoured specialty creditors to

---

[1] *Supra*, p. 185, note 1.

[2] *Lord Townshend* v. *Windham* (1750), 2 Ves. Sen. 1 (10) (ii); *O'Grady* v. *Wilmot*, [1916] 2 A. C. 231.

[3] *O'Grady* v. *Wilmot*, at pp. 246–8 ; Lord BUCKMASTER.

the extent of allowing them, if the heirs of the debtor were bound, to be paid the full amount of the debts due to them before any creditors by simple contract, or creditors by specialty in which the heirs were not bound, received satisfaction for any part of their demands. This priority was, however, removed by Hinde Palmer's Act, 1869,[1] which provided that all creditors, as well specialty as simple contract creditors, should be treated as standing in equal degree.

The distinction that existed between legal and equitable assets did not depend upon whether the property was legal or equitable in nature (for instance, an equitable fee simple was legal assets for specialty debts), but upon whether the remedy lay at law or at equity. If a creditor could make property available for the payment of debts by suing at common law, the property was legal assets, but if he was compelled to take proceedings in equity, the property was equitable assets.[2]

Distinction between legal and equitable assets.

Thus equitable assets included land charged or devised for payment of debts, land which was made available under the Administration of Estates Act, 1833, and personal estate in respect to which the testator had exercised a general power of appointment. Legal assets were themselves divided into *real* assets and *personal* assets. Real assets consisted of property which was held by an heir or a devisee, and for the recovery of which a creditor could maintain an action : personal assets consisted of the personal property which devolved upon the executor or the administrator *virtute officii*.

Land Transfer Act, 1897. The Land Transfer Act, 1897, placed the law upon an entirely new basis and abolished most of the old distinctions.

Establishment of real representation.

We have seen that under the old law, while personal property passed to the personal representatives and became in their hands liable to the payment of debts, real property went straight to the heir or the devisee. Personal property constituted legal assets ; real property constituted legal assets if it had been made subject to a specialty in which heirs were bound, but equitable assets if it was made available by proceedings in Chancery under the Administration of Estates Act, 1833. The object of the first part of the Land Transfer Act, 1897, was to simplify and improve the machinery for the administration of *real* assets without disturbing the ultimate rights of the beneficiaries. It effected this by providing that those persons who already had control over the personal property should also have control over the real estate.[3] The Act, in other words, established a *real* representative,

---

[1] Administration of Estates Act, 1869.
[2] *Cook* v. *Gregson* (1856), 3 Drew, 547.
[3] *Re Williams*, [1904] 1 Ch. 52 ; *Re Vickerstaff*, [1906] 1 Ch. 762.

who was always the same person as the personal representative.
It enacted that the real estate of persons dying after 1897 should,
notwithstanding any testamentary disposition, devolve to and
become vested in the personal representatives as if it were a
chattel real. The personal representatives were given the same
powers and duties with respect to the realty as if it had been
personalty; and, as regards administration of assets, it was enacted
that the real estate should be administered in the same manner
and should be subject to the same liabilities for debts as if it were
personal estate.

Before this Act was passed, if a deceased person had charged
his debts on his real estate, the executors had power to raise the
necessary money by a sale of the land; where the deceased
either died intestate or made no provision in his will for the
payment of debts, the creditors, in order to make his land available, were obliged to bring an administration action in the
Chancery Division to which the heir or the devisee, as well as
the executors, had to be made parties. But after the Act was
passed (*i.e.* in the case of any person dying after December 31,
1897), the land of a deceased person could in all cases be made
available for the payment of debts without the necessity for any
proceedings.

The following interests, however, were excepted from the
operation of the Act:

1. real estate which some other person had a right to take by
   survivorship (joint tenancy);

2. land of copyhold tenure or customary freehold;

3. estates tail.

Administration of Estates Act, 1925. The first part of
the Land Transfer Act, 1897, was re-enacted, with a number of
amendments, by the Administration of Estates Act, 1925.

The first section provides that real estate to which a deceased
person was entitled for an interest not ceasing on his death is
to devolve, like a chattel real, on his personal representative, *i.e.*
on the executor in the case of a will, and on the administrator
when the deceased dies intestate.[1] The expression *real estate*
includes a variety of interests. Thus land with respect to which
the deceased has by his will exercised a general power of appointment is to pass to the personal representatives as if it had belonged
to the testator.[2] Again, and this is a striking innovation, an
entailed interest of which a testator has disposed of by will is to
vest in the personal representatives.[3] If, however, he dies

---

[1] Administration of Estates Act, 1925, s. 1 (1).
[2] *Ibid.*, s. 3 (2).   [3] *Ibid.*, s. 3 (3).

without making any such disposition, and without having barred the entail, his interest ceases on his death, and therefore does not pass to the personal representatives.[2] *Real estate* includes chattels real, land in possession, remainder or reversion, and every interest in or over land to which a deceased person was entitled at the time of his death ; also real estate held on trust (including settled land) or held by way of mortgage or security.[1] It does not include an interest under a joint tenancy where another person survives the deceased,[2] nor the interest of a corporator sole in the corporation property.[3]

As regards administration of assets, the Act, in the following section, declares what property shall be available for the payment of debts [4] :— *(Administration of assets.)*

" The real and personal estate, whether legal or equitable, of a " deceased person, to the extent of his beneficial interest therein, and " the real and personal estate of which a deceased person in pur- " suance of any general power (including the statutory power to dis- " pose of entailed interests) disposes by his will, are assets for payment " of his debts and liabilities, whether by specialty or simple contract, " and any disposition by will inconsistent with this enactment is void " as against the creditors, and the court shall, if necessary, administer " the property for the purpose of the payment of the debts and " liabilities.

" If any person to whom such beneficial interest devolves or is " given or in whom any such interest vests, disposes thereof in good " faith before an action is brought or process is sued out against him, " he shall be personally liable for the value of the interest so dis- " posed of by him, but that interest shall not be liable to be taken in " execution in the action or under the process."

Thus broadly speaking, all the property of a deceased person is now available in the hands of the personal representatives for the payment of debts, and the distinction between legal and equitable assets is obsolete.

Procedure. There are three methods by which an estate may be administered.

(i) **Administration by the personal representatives out of court.** If this method is adopted, as is usually the case, *(Modes of administration.)* the personal representatives themselves undertake the task of satisfying the debts of the deceased out of the assets.

(ii) **Administration in court.** The Chancery Division of the High Court has jurisdiction, upon an action for admini- stration being brought by the personal representatives or by a creditor or a beneficiary, to order that the estate shall be admini- stered in court. This is the method that is adopted where some

---

[1] Administration of Estates Act, 1925, s. 3 (1).   [2] *Ibid.*, s. 3 (4).
[3] *Ibid.*, s. 3 (5).   [4] *Ibid.*, s. 32.

2B*

dispute has arisen between the interested parties or where a point of law requires decision, as, for instance, if the conduct of the executors is contested by the creditors or beneficiaries, or if a claimant's right to a legacy is questioned.

(iii) **Administration of an insolvent estate in court.** An estate is insolvent if it is not sufficient to satisfy all personal and testamentary expenses and debts. In such a case a petition, praying for an order that the estate be administered according to the law of bankruptcy, may be presented either by the personal representatives or by any creditor who would have been entitled to present the petition had the deceased been still alive.[1] The order, if made, is equivalent to an adjudication order.[2]

Ranking of creditors and beneficiaries.

Two important matters, which may conveniently be called *priority of creditors* and *priority of beneficiaries*, arise in connection with the administration of assets. If an estate is solvent the question of priority of creditors obviously does not arise, for all will be paid in full; but in the case of insolvency it is essential to know whether all creditors rank *pari passu* or whether some have a prior right of payment to others. The question of priority of beneficiaries may arise when the estate is solvent, *i.e.* if it is sufficient to satisfy all the creditors but not all the legatees and devisees. Here, since some of the beneficiaries must suffer in the sense that some of them must surrender their beneficial interests to satisfy the creditors, it is essential to have fixed rules that determine which of the beneficial interests must be taken first. In other words, there must be an *order of application of assets.*

Rules as to payment of debts where estate insolvent.

Priority of Creditors. The law before 1926 with regard to the order in which creditors were paid out of an insolvent estate was unnecessarily difficult, for it varied according as administration was effected in or out of court, and according to the nature of the assets, whether legal or equitable. These old rules, however, may happily be allowed to fall into oblivion, for it was enacted by the Administration of Estates Act, 1925,[3]

Bankruptcy rules prevail.

that no matter what may be the mode of administration the bankruptcy rules that regulate the order of payment of creditors shall prevail.

The bankruptcy order is as follows :

Subject to the payment of funeral and testamentary expenses the following debts have priority [4] :

(i) Property belonging to a friendly society which was in the possession of the deceased as an officer of the society.

---

[1] Bankruptcy Act, 1914, s. 130.
[2] *Supra*, p. 729   [3] S. 34 (1) ; 1st Schedule, Part I.
[4] Bankruptcy Act, 1914, s. 33 (9).

(ii) Property belonging to a trustee savings bank which was in the possession of the deceased as an officer of the bank.

Subject to the above, the following classes of debts are entitled to preferential payment :

(a) Local rates.[1]

(b) Income tax assessed on the deceased up to the 5th of April next before his death, but not exceeding one year's assessment.

(c) Wages not exceeding £200 of any clerk or servant in respect of services rendered during four months before the death of the deceased.[2]

(d) Wages not exceeding £200 of any labourer or workman in respect of services rendered during four months before the death of the deceased.[3]

(e) Contributions due from the deceased under the National Insurance (Industrial Injuries) Act, 1946, or the National Insurance Acts, 1946 and 1959.[4]

(f) Holiday remuneration payable to an employee on the termination of his employment with the deceased.[5]

(g) Purchase tax that became due from the deceased within the twelve months preceding his death.[6]

(h) Service compensation not exceeding £50, *i.e.* compensation due to an employee who has not been reinstated after performance of national service.[7]

These eight preferential debts rank equally between themselves.

Subject to the above all debts are paid *pari passu* except that the following three classes are deferred and rank last for payment :

(i) Money lent by the husband of the deceased for the purposes of her business.[8]

(ii) Money lent by the wife of the deceased for the purposes of his business.[9]

(iii) A loan bearing interest which was to vary with the profits made by the deceased in his business [10]

A secured creditor, *i.e.* one who holds a mortgage, charge or lien upon the property of the deceased, occupies a stronger position than unsecured creditors, for since he holds a definite interest in the property he is unaffected by the amount of assets or the number or class of other creditors. He may either[11]

Rights of secured creditors.

---

[1] *Ibid.*, s. 33 (1) (a), (5).

[2] *Ibid.*, s. 33 (1) (b), (5) ; Companies Act, 1947, ss. 91 (1), (4), (6) (b), 115 (1) ; Companies Act, 1948, Schs. 16, 17.

[3] Bankruptcy Act, 1914, s. 33 (1) (c), (5) ; Companies Act, 1947, ss. 91 (1), (2), (4), (6) (b), 115 (1) ; Companies Act, 1948, Schs. 16, 17.

[4] Bankruptcy Act, 1914, s. 33 (1) (f), (5) ; National Insurance (Industrial Injuries) Act, 1946, s. 71 (2); National Insurance Act, 1946, s. 55 (2); National Insurance Act, 1959, s. 11.

[5] Companies Act, 1947, ss. 91 (5), 6 (a), 115 (1) ; Companies Act, 1948, Schs. 16, 17.

[6] Finance Act, 1942, s. 20 (1).

[7] National Service Act, 1948, ss. 48, 51 (4).

[8] Bankruptcy Act, 1914, s. 36 (1).

[9] *Ibid.*, s. 36 (2). [10] *Ibid.*, s. 33 (9).

[11] Bankruptcy Act, 1914, Sch. 2, paras. 10–12, 17.

realize his security and prove in the bankruptcy for the balance of the principal and interest ; or

surrender the security and prove for the whole debt ; or

without realization or surrender, put a valuation upon his security and prove for the balance after deducting the assessed value.

Right of preference.

There are two rights possessed by a personal representative. namely his right of preference and his right of retainer, which if exercised disturb the normal order of payment of debts.

The right of preference entitles a personal representative to pay one creditor before he pays another of equal degree. He can make such a preferential payment even though an action has been started against him by another creditor, but he cannot do so after an order has been made for administration of the estate by the court.[1]

Right of retainer.

A personal representative cannot sue himself, and it has therefore long been the rule that, as against creditors of equal degree, he may take sufficient assets to satisfy a debt that is due to him from the deceased. He is entitled, in other words, to prefer himself. This privilege has now been recognized by the Administration of Estates Act, 1925, which provides that it may be exercised in respect of all assets of the deceased, but only in respect of debts owing to the personal representative in his own right whether solely or jointly with another person.[2] This enactment has altered the law in two respects :

(a) Before 1926 the right was strictly confined to legal assets, *i.e.* to property which a creditor could make available for the payment of his debt by bringing an action at common law. The distinction between the two classes of assets is now obsolete, and all property that vests in the representative is subject to the right of retainer.

(b) Before 1926 a personal representative could retain a debt even though it was not due to him personally, as for instance if it was due to him as trustee for a third person.[3] Now, however, he must be beneficially entitled in his own right.[4]

No retainer against creditor of higher degree.

Retainer is possible only against creditors of equal degree.[5] Thus, if the personal representative is administering an insolvent estate, he cannot retain a simple contract debt against a claim by the Crown for income tax not exceeding one year's assessment,[6] but, since the Crown is bound by the Administration of Estates Act,

---

[1] *George* v. *George* (No. 1) (1865), 35 Beav. 350.

[2] S. 34 (2).   [3] *Re Hubback* (1885), 29 Ch. D. 935.

[4] *Re Rudd, Royal Exchange Assurance* v. *Ballantine*, [1942] Ch. 421 ; [1942] 2 All E. R. 206.

[5] *Re S. P.*, [1936] Ch. 735. It prevails against the right of a creditor to recover his costs in an administration action : *Re Wester Wemyss, Tilley* v. *Wester Wemyss*, [1940] Ch. 1 ; [1939] 3 All E. R. 746.

[6] See *supra*, p. 747.

any excess of tax over one year's assessment is of the same quality as a simple contract debt and to that extent may be retained.[1]

Priority of beneficiaries. As we have seen, if an estate, though sufficient to pay the debts in full, is insufficient to pay all the legatees and other beneficiaries, some of the beneficiaries must suffer, and it thus becomes imperative to have definite rules prescribing which of them must forfeit their gifts in order that the creditors may be paid. If, for example, the residuary personalty is taken first, the result is to benefit the specific legatees and the devisees, including the residuary devisee, at the expense of the residuary legatee. The outstanding feature of the order prevailing before 1926 was that residuary personalty had to be taken first. Property comprised in a residuary devise came sixth on the list. The old rules, however, have been abolished, and the following new order of the application of assets in the case of a solvent estate was introduced by the Administration of Estates Act, 1925.[2]

Order of application of assets where estate is solvent.

(1) Property undisposed of by will, subject to retention thereout of a fund sufficient to meet pecuniary legacies.

Property is "undisposed of by will" not only in the rare case where the testator fails to dispose of some specific part of the estate, but also where a gift lapses owing to the death of the donee before the testator or for some other reason, such as the attestation of the will by the beneficiary. Thus in effect the primary fund for the payment of debts is no longer the residuary personalty, but property, real or personal, that has lapsed. It may be a devise of land,[3] or a share of income[4] or of residue.[5]

We may perhaps venture upon an example in order to illustrate the difference between the old order of application and the new. Suppose, for instance, that a testator, who at the time of his death owes debts to the amount of £2000, leaves a will containing the following gifts :

The new order illustrated.

(a) Pecuniary legacies to the amount of £3000.
(b) A specific devise.
(c) Several specific bequests.
(d) A residuary bequest to X., and a residuary devise to Y.

Let us further suppose that Y. predeceases the testator, and that therefore his share of the residue lapses.

---

[1] *A.-G. v. Jackson*, [1932] A. C. 365.
[2] S. 34 (3) ; 1st Schedule, Part II.
[3] *Re Atkinson*, [1930] 1 Ch. 47 ; *In re Martin*, [1955] Ch. 698 ; [1955] 1 All E. R. 865.
[4] *Re Tong*, [1931] 1 Ch. 202.
[5] *Re Lamb*, [1929] 1 Ch. 722 ; *Re Worthington*, [1933] Ch. 771 ; *Re Sanger, Taylor v. North*, [1939] Ch. 238 ; [1938] 4 All E. R. 417 ; *Re Harland-Peck, Hercy v. Mayglothing*, [1941] Ch. 182 ; [1940] 4 All E. R. 347 ; *In re Midgley*, [1955] Ch. 576 ; [1955] 2 All E. R. 625.

On these facts, under the law as it stood before 1926, the general rule that the primary fund for the payment of debts was the residuary personalty would have operated to reduce by £2000 X.'s share of the estate.   Under the new rule, however, the land comprised in the residuary devise to Y., as being property undisposed of by the will, constitutes the primary fund. This is held by the executors upon trust for sale and out of the proceeds, first to set aside £3000 to meet the pecuniary legacies,[1] then to pay the debts, and finally to distribute the balance among the persons entitled under the rules that govern distribution upon intestacy.   Thus X. occupies a better position than he would have done before 1926.

    (2) Property not specifically devised or bequeathed but included in a residuary gift, subject to the retention thereout of a fund sufficient to meet pecuniary legacies, so far as not provided for as aforesaid.[2]

Thus property, whether realty or personalty, comprised in a residuary gift, is taken after undisposed of property.   Before 1926, as we have seen, residuary personalty came first, but a residuary devise was treated as a specific devise and came sixth in the list, ranking with specific bequests.   So, under this new rule, if there had been no lapse in the example given above, the pecuniary legacies and the debts would have been satisfied at the expense of X. and Y. equally.[3]

    (3) Property specifically appropriated or devised or bequeathed for the payment of debts.

It seems a little curious that property which has deliberately been earmarked as a fund for the payment of debts should not be used first.   The same principle, however, obtained before 1926, when realty devised in trust for the payment of debts ranked second in the list after residuary personalty, and it was generally justified by the observation that since a man does not normally realize property for the payment of debts if he has sufficient cash in his possession, it is only consistent to adopt the same course after his death.

    (4) Property charged with, or devised or bequeathed subject to a charge for, the payment of debts.

    (5) The fund, if any, retained to meet pecuniary legacies.

    (6) Property specifically devised or bequeathed, rateably according to value.

---

[1] *Re Anstead*, [1943] 1 Ch. 161 ; [1943] 1 All E. R. 522.
[2] *Re Wilson, Wilson* v. *Mackay*, [1966] 2 All E. R. 867.
[3] This would seem to be so despite *Re Thompson, Public Trustee* v. *Husband*, [1936] Ch. 676 ; [1936] 2 All E. R. 141 ; *Re Rowe, Bennetts* v. *Eddy*, [1941] Ch. 343 ; [1941] 2 All E. R. 330 ; *Re Anstead, supra.*

If, for instance, there is a devise of Blackacre to X., of White-acre to Y. and a bequest of a diamond ring to Z., and debts to the amount of £900 are still due after exhaustion of the properties enumerated (1) to (5) above, the rule is that X., Y. and Z. must contribute *pro rata* and *pari passu*. To ascertain the amount of the contributions it is necessary to value each property. Thus if the value of Blackacre is £1500, of Whiteacre £1200 and of the ring £300, each of the donees must contribute 3–10ths, *i.e.* X., £450 ; Y., £360 ; and Z., £90.

(7) Property appointed by will under a general power, including the statutory power to dispose of entailed
interests.

This rule, which obtained also under the old law, is confined to property subject to a *general* power, and does not apply unless the power has been actually exercised.

The final observation to make is that the order set out above *Statutory* may be varied by the will of the deceased.[1] If the testator *order may* indicates with sufficient clearness that some particular property *be varied* shall constitute the primary fund for payment, as for instance *by testator.* where he creates a mixed fund for the purpose, his intention must be followed.[2] Thus in one case :

> The testator devised and bequeathed his real and personal estate upon trust for sale and conversion, and after directing that debts should be paid out of the mixed fund, he gave half of it to his wife and half to two daughters. His wife predeceased him.

It will be seen that the lapsed share of the wife constituted the primary fund for payment under the statutory order, but it was held that since the debts had clearly been thrown rateably on the mixed fund they must be paid out of it and not primarily out of the lapsed half.[3] The same result ensues if the will provides that " subject to the payment of funeral and testamentary expenses, debts and legacies " the residue shall pass to two persons, one of whom predeceases the testator.[4]

---

[1] Administration of Estates Act, 1925, 1st Schedule, Part II, para. 8.

[2] *Re Petty,* [1929] 1 Ch. 726 ; *Re Kempthorne,* [1930] 1 Ch. 268 ; *Re Atkinson,* [1930] 1 Ch. 47 ; *Re Littlewood,* [1931] 1 Ch. 443 ; *In re Ridley, Nicholson* v. *Nicholson,* [1950] Ch. 415 ; [1950] 2 All E. R. 1 ; *In re Meldrum's Will Trusts, Swinson* v. *Meldrum,* [1952] Ch. 208; [1952] 1 All E. R. 274; *In re Berrey's Will Trusts, Greening* v. *Warner,* [1959] 1 All E. R. 15; [1959] 1 W. L. R. 30.

[3] *Re Petty, supra.*

[4] *Re Harland-Peck, Hercy* v. *Mayglothing,* [1941] Ch. 182 ; [1940] 4 All E. R. 347 ; and see *Re James, Lloyds Bank, Ltd.* v. *Atkins,* [1947] Ch. 256 ; [1947] 1 All E. R. 402.

If, for instance, there is a devise of Blackacre to X., of Whiteacre to Y., and a bequest of a diamond ring to X., and debts to the amount of £900 are still due after exhaustion of the properties enumerated (1) to (5) above, the rule is that X., Y., and Z. must contribute pro rata and pari passu. To ascertain the amount of the contributions it is necessary to value each property. Thus if the value of Blackacre is £500, of Whiteacre £300 and of the ring £200, each of the donees must contribute; net is X. £450, Y. £270 and Z. £180.

(2) Property appointed by will under a general power, including the statutory power to dispose of entailed interests.

This rule, which obtained also under the old law, is confined to property subject to a general power, and does not apply unless the power has been actually exercised.

The final observation to make is that the order set out above may be varied by the will of the deceased. If the testator indicates with sufficient clearness that some particular property shall constitute the primary fund for payment, as for instance where he creates a mixed fund for the purpose, his intention must be followed. Thus in one case:

The testator devised and bequeathed his real and personal estate upon trust for sale and conversion, and after discharge of his debts should he read of out the mixed fund, he gave half of residue to his wife and half to two grandsons. His wife predeceased him.

It will be seen that the lapsed share of the wife constituted the primary fund for payment under the statutory order; but it was held that since the debts had clearly been thrown rateably on the mixed fund they must be paid out of it and not primarily out of the lapsed half. The same result ensues if the will provides that "subject to the payment of funeral and testamentary expenses, debts and legacies" the residue shall pass to two persons, one of whom predeceases the testator.

BOOK III.

THE TRANSFER AND EXTINCTION OF ESTATES AND INTERESTS.

PART IV.

TRANSFER ON DEATH.

SUMMARY.

CHAPTER I.

TESTACY.

SUMMARY.

SECTION I. GENERAL NATURE OF A WILL.

Will of Lands. A will is a declaration made by a testator, Nature of
in the form required by law, of what he desires to be done after his a will.
death. It may define his desires with regard to several matters,
such as the manner in which his funeral shall be conducted, the
appointment of guardians for his children and the like, but we are
concerned to examine a will only in so far as it operates as a disposition of property. There is a palpable distinction between a
will and a deed. As BACON, V.-C., said [1] :—

> " A deed is a contract by which the owner of property gives a
> " certain destination to it then and thenceforth for ever, and he parts

---

[1] *Olivant* v. *Wright* (1878), 9 Ch. D. 646, 650.

" with all his power over it.   A will is an instrument which is not to
" take effect till the death of the testator."

Distin-
guished
from
settlement.

A settlement, for instance, expresses the intentions of the
settlor with regard, *inter alia*, to the manner in which his property
shall be enjoyed after his death, but while a settlement may
be irrevocable, a will is always revocable notwithstanding the
strongest expressions to the contrary that it may contain.

> Thus, if a person makes a disposition by will in fulfilment of
> an agreement to leave certain property to another, the power
> of revocation remains open to him, though if the contract
> is made for consideration and is, in the case of land,
> evidenced by a memorandum in writing under section 40
> of the Law of Property Act, 1925, he or his executors will be
> liable for breach of contract.   If he puts such testamentary
> disposition out of his power by conveying the property in
> his lifetime to a third person, he is, personally and at once,
> liable in damages ; if he dies possessed of the property, but
> without having made the disposition he agreed to make, the
> court, although it does not set the will aside, may order the
> property to be conveyed to the promisee.[1]

A will is
ambulatory.

So a will has no effect, either upon the testator's property or
in any other regard, until death, but when that event occurs the
will takes effect as a disposition of property.   Its essential characteristic is that it is ambulatory, a fact which is clear if we again
contrast the case of a settlement.   The effect upon the usu-
fructuary enjoyment is exactly the same where A. devises Blackacre
to B. in fee as where he settles it upon himself for life with remainder to B. in fee, but in the former case B. is entitled to nothing
until the death of A., while in the latter he immediately becomes
entitled to a vested interest.[2]

Before 1837
will of
realty
did not
speak from
testator's
death.

A devise of land before the Wills Act, 1837, was treated very
differently from a bequest of personalty.   It was regarded as a
species of posthumous conveyance, and therefore acquired several
attributes of a conveyance.   Thus, since it is impossible for a man
to convey what he has not got, every devise was necessarily specific,
i.e., it was capable of passing only specific property owned by the
testator at the time of the will.   It did not pass land that he
acquired later, or land that he disposed of after the will, notwithstanding that he later re-acquired it.   Even a residuary devise was
specific.

> Hence, if T., seised of Blackacre and Whiteacre, devised Blackacre
> to A. and the residue of his land to B., and the gift of Blackacre
> failed owing to the death of A. before T., Blackacre did not pass to B.,

---

[1] *Synge* v. *Synge,* [1894] 1 Q. B. 466.
[2] Jarman on Wills (7th Edn.), p. 29.

for the gift to him of the residue was nothing more than a gift of the specific Whiteacre under the denomination " residue." [1]

On the other hand, it was well established that a bequest of personalty included all the personalty belonging to the testator at the time of his death. It spoke from his death, not from its execution.

Real estate, however, was put on the same footing as personalty in this respect by the following section of the Wills Act, 1837.

Alteration by Wills Act 1837.

" Every will shall be construed, with reference to the real estate and " personal estate comprised in it, to speak and take effect as if it had " been executed immediately before the death of the testator, unless a " contrary intention shall appear by the will.[2] "

A further section provides that a residuary devise shall include devises that have lapsed or become void.[3]

Consequently, if the subject-matter of a devise is described generically, it may be increased or diminished after the will is made, and whether the testator has parted with land that he owned at the time of the will or has acquired more land subsequently, his devise will pass what he actually owns at his death. Thus a will is ambulatory in the sense that it may pass property coming to the testator after its execution.

Although, strictly speaking, a will consists of all the properly executed writings in which a person has expressed his intentions, it is usual to contrast it with a codicil. A codicil is part of a person's will, and must be executed in precisely the same manner, but whereas the will is the principal, the codicil is the accessory instrument. It is in effect a supplementary instrument by which a testator alters or adds to his will.

Codicil.

Maintenance of dependants.—In most European countries testamentary freedom has been restricted by the rule that the members of a testator's family are entitled to a definite proportion of his estate. A similar rule obtained in England in early days with regard to wills of personalty, but it has long disappeared and for many years an English testator has been free to confer a princely endowment upon a prostitute or a charity and to leave his family penniless.[4] This, indeed, is still the case, but in 1938, the Inheritance (Family Provision) Act introduced a new principle by empowering the court to vary a will at the instance of the testator's dependants.

Inheritance (Family Provision) Act, 1938.

This Act applied only when the deceased left a will, but it was extended to cases of total intestacy and was amended in other

---

[1] Hayes, *Introduction to Conveyancing*, pp. 343–4 ; on the subject generally see Digby, *History of Real Property* (5th Edn.), p. 385.
[2] S. 24.   [3] S. 25.
[4] In the case of the fee simple and the estate tail, a widow might be fortunate enough to obtain her third by way of dower, but in practice she was generally deprived of this by the device of uses to bar dower and since 1833 she has in this respect been entirely in her husband's power, *infra*, pp. 792.

respects by the Intestates' Estates Act, 1952 and by the Family
Provision Act 1966.[1] The present law is now set out in the fourth
schedule of the latter Act and it applies only to persons dying
domiciled in England.[2]

Meaning of "dependants."

The main feature of the Act is that it enables the court to
vary either a will or the rules of distribution applicable to a case
of intestacy, if it considers that a *dependant* is not reasonably
provided for. The class of dependants is restricted to the following persons :—

    (*a*) A wife or husband ;

    (*b*) a daughter who has not been married, or who is, by
           reason of some mental or physical disability, incapable
           of maintaining herself ;

    (*c*) an infant son, or

    (*d*) a son who is, by reason of some mental or physical dis-
           ability, incapable of maintaining himself.[3]

Thus, grandchildren and illegitimate children [4] are excluded, and
in the case of a husband the courts have shown a reluctance,
though not a refusal, to exercise their discretion in his favour.[5]
The court, moreover, is disinclined to vary a will or the rules of
intestacy if it considers that in the circumstances the deceased was
no longer under a moral obligation to provide for the applicant.[6]

Court may
provide for
maintenance
of
dependants.

If the court is of opinion, on an application being made to it,
that the will of the deceased or the law relating to intestacy, or the
combination of the will and that law, does not make reasonable
provision for the maintenance of the dependant, it may order that
such reasonable provision as it thinks fit shall be made out of the
net estate, subject to such conditions or restrictions as may seem
appropriate.[7] The enactment by the Act of 1938, that no applicant
was eligible for provision if the surviving spouse was entitled
under the will or intestacy to not less than two-thirds of the income of the net estate, has now been repealed.[8]

---

[1] For the subject generally, see Albery, *Inheritance (Family Provision)
Act, 1938,* which was published, however, before 1952.

[2] As to the unfortunate effect this limitation may have, see 62 *L. Q. R.*
178–9. The onus is on the applicant to prove that the deceased was domiciled
in England at the time of death ; *Mastaka* v. *Midland Bank Executor & Trustee
Co., Ltd.,* [1941] Ch. 192 ; [1941] 1 All E. R. 236.

[3] Inheritance (Family Provision) Act, 1938, s. 1 (1) as amended by the
Intestate Estates Act, 1952.

[4] *In re Makein,* [1955] Ch. 194 ; [1955] 1 All E. R. 57.

[5] *Re Sylvester, Sylvester* v. *Public Trustee,* [1941] Ch. 87 ; *Re Lawes* (1946),
62 T. L. R. 231 ; *Re Pointer, Pointer & Shonfeld* v. *Edwards,* [1941] Ch. 60 ;
Re Styler, Styler v. *Griffith,* [1942] Ch. 387; [1942] 2 All E. R. 201; *Re Clayton,
Clayton* v. *Howell,* [1966] 2 All E. R. 370; [1966] 1 W. L. R. 969.

[6] *In re Andrews,* [1955] 3 All E. R. 248; [1955] 1 W. L. R. 1105; where the
applicant, the testator's daughter, had lived for forty-two years with a married
man as his wife.

[7] Inheritance (Family Provision) Act, 1938, s. 1 (1) as amended by the
Intestates' Estates Act, 1952.

[8] Family Provision Act, 1966, s. 2, repealing the proviso to s. 1 (1) of the
Act of 1938.

Whatever may be the value of the estate, the court may order Form of
that maintenance shall be provided by way either of a lump sum the order.
payment[1] or of periodical payments.[2] These latter may be of a
specific amount, or equal to the whole or part of the income of the
net estate or may be determined in any other way that the court
thinks fit.[3]

Periodical payments must terminate not later than the follow- Events upon
ing events : which
payments
cease.

    (i) The re-marriage of a wife or husband.

    (ii) In the case of a daughter, her marriage or cessation of
         disability, whichever is the later.[4]

    (iii) The attainment of majority by an infant son.

    (iv) The cessation of disability in the case of a disabled son,

and in any case, his or her earlier death.[5]

If it appears that the applicant is in immediate need of assist- Interim
ance but that it is not yet possible to determine what order should order.
be made, and if there is available property to meet the need of the
applicant, the court may make an interim order for the payment
to him of such sums and at such intervals as appear reasonable.[6]

In estimating what is a reasonable provision, the judge, in the Mode in
exercise of his judicial discretion, must as far as possible regard which the
court's
the matter impersonally in the light of the facts brought to his discretion
attention, and mainly in the light of the circumstances present to is
the mind of the testator up to the time of his death.[7] A judge, for exercised.
instance, is not justified in ordering the provision made by the will
to be increased, merely because he himself would have been inclined to be more generous.[8] If the application is made in respect
of a testate estate the first task is to ascertain whether it was
unreasonable of the testator to make no provision or unreasonable
not to make a larger provision.[9] Unless this question is answered
affirmatively, that is the end of the case.

    Thus, where an annuity of £2,550 out of an estate valued
    at £85,000 had been left to a widow, the argument that this

---

[1] Family Provision Act, 1966, s. 4.

[2] Inheritance (Family Provision) Act, 1938, s. 1 (2).

[3] Family Provision Act, 1966, s. 3 (1) (2); reversing to this extent *In the
Estate of Gale, Gale* v. *Gale,* [1966] Ch. 236; [1966] 1 All E. R. 945. Orders
valied under this section made before the Act came into force, but after 1952,
remain valid; s. 3 (3).

[4] As to the difficulty of interpreting these words, see *Re Pointer, Pointer
and Shonfeld* v. *Edwards,* [1941] Ch. 60, 68.

[5] Inheritance (Family Provision) Act, 1938, s. 1 (2) as amended by the
Intestates' Estates Act.

[6] Family Provision Act, 1966, s. 6 and Sched. 1. This was not possible
before 1966; see for example *Re Ferrar, Ferrar* v. *Roberts,* [1966] 3 All E. R. 78.

[7] *Re Catmull, Catmull* v. *Watts,* [1943] Ch. 262, 268 ; [1943] 2 All E. R.
115. On the whole question see especially Albery, *op. cit.,* pp. 8–10 ; 20–31.
In re Howell, [1953] 1 W. L. R. 1034.

[8] *Re Styler, Styler* v. *Griffith,* [1942] Ch. 387, 389 ; [1942] 2 All E. R. 201 ;
Re Pugh, Pugh v. *Pugh,* [1943] Ch. 387, 395 ; 2 All E. R. 361.

[9] *Re Pugh, supra : Re Franks, Franks* v. *Franks,* [1948] Ch. 62, 64–5.

did not enable her to occupy and maintain the mansion house according to the wishes of the testator and that therefore it was unreasonably small did not prevail.[1]

But once it has been found that no reasonable provision has been made, or that a reasonable provision has been subjected to an unreasonable condition,[2] the court has considerable latitude. In another case, for instance, a bequest to a widow of an annuity of £250 out of an estate of £130,000 was increased to £1,000.[3] No doubt the object of the Act is that a dependant shall be provided with maintenance, but as HARMAN, J., said:—

" Maintenance does not only mean the food she puts in her mouth,
" it means the clothes on her back, the house in which she lives and
" the money which she has to have in her pocket, all of which vary
" according to the means of the man who leaves a wife behind him.
" I think that must be so. Maintenance cannot mean only mere
" subsistence." [4]

Factors to be considered by the court. Some of the factors that must be considered by the court in reaching a conclusion are indicated by the Act itself. Regard must be had to any capital or income from any source that the dependant will become entitled to ; to the conduct of the dependant in relation to the deceased ; " and to any other matter or thing which in the circumstances of the case the court may consider relevant or material in relation to that dependant, to persons interested in the estate of the deceased, or otherwise." [5] Further, the court must have regard to the reasons that impelled the deceased to die intestate or, if he died testate, to make no provision or no greater provision for the dependant, and the court may accept such evidence of these reasons as it considers sufficient, including any written statement signed by the deceased and dated, though in estimating the weight to be attached to such a statement it must have regard to all the circumstances from which any inference can be drawn as to its accuracy.[6] It has been held, perhaps somewhat doubtfully, that unwritten or unsigned statements by the deceased of facts from which his reasons may be inferred are not rendered inadmissible in evidence by this enactment.[7]

Limit of time for application. An application by a dependant for an order under the Act must be made within six months from the date on which repre-

---

[1] *Re Inns, Inns* v. *Wallace*, [1947] Ch. 576 ; [1947] 2 All E. R. 308.

[2] *In re Doring*, [1955] 3 All E. R. 389; [1955] 1 W. L. R. 1217; *Re E. E. V. E.*, [1966] 2 All E. R. 44; [1966] 1 W. L. R. 709.

[3] *Re Borthwick, Borthwick* v. *Beauvais*, [1949] Ch. 395 ; [1949] 1 All E. R. 472. See also *Re Jackson, Jackson* v. *Nottidge*, [1952] 2 T. L. R. 90.

[4] *Re Borthwick, Borthwick* v. *Beauvais*, [1949] Ch. 395, at p. 401 ; [1949] 1 All E. R. 472 at p. 475.

[5] Inheritance (Family Provision) Act, 1938, s. 1 (6), as amended by the Intestates Estates Act, 1952 ; *Re Searle, Searle* v. *Siems*, [1949] Ch. 73 ; [1948] 2 All E. R. 426.   [6] *Ibid.*, s. 1 (7).

[7] *Re Smallwood, Smallwood* v. *Martins Bank, Ltd.*, [1951] Ch. 369 ; [1951] 1 All E. R. 372.

sentation is first taken out,[1] but the court may extend this period if satisfied that it will operate unfairly owing to the fact that after representation has been taken out:

(*a*) a later will has been found; or

(*b*) some question concerning the right of a person to a beneficial interest has been determined; or

(*c*) some other circumstances have occurred that affect the administration or distribution of the estate.[2]

An order may be later varied by the court if it appears that some material fact was not disclosed in the original proceedings; if any substantial change has occurred in the circumstances of a dependant[3] or of a beneficiary under the will; or if maintenance is desirable for an additional dependant.[4] *Variation of order.*

The policy of these statutes has been extended to the case where, after a marriage has been dissolved or annulled by an English court, one of the parties dies domiciled in England. In this event the survivor, if not remarried, may apply to the court for a maintenance order. It must be shown (a) that it would have been reasonable for the deceased to make provision for the survivor's maintenance, and (b) that no provision or no reasonable provision has been made.[5] The first of these conditions is not imposed by the Act of 1938. *Maintenance from estate of deceased former spouse.*

Normally, provision will be ordered by way of periodical payments, but the court, if it thinks fit, may in every case require the payment of a lump sum.[6]

In reaching its decision, the court must have regard, *inter alia*, to the survivor's conduct in relation to the deceased and to any application for maintenance made by the survivor during the lifetime of the deceased.[7] No order must be made that would require an improvident realization of property having regard to the interests of the dependants of the deceased and of the persons otherwise entitled to that property.[8]

An order may be discharged or varied by the court at the instance of any of the following persons — the original applicant,

---

[1] Inheritance (Family Provision) Act, 1938, s. 2 (1), as amended by the Intestates' Estates Act, 1952, s. 2 (1) and by the Family Provision Act, 1966, s. 5.

[2] *Ibid.*, s. 2 (1A); *In re Trott, Trott* v. *Miles*, [1958] 2 All E. R. 296. As to (c), see *Re Bluston, Bluston* v. *Davis*, [1966] 3 All E. R. 220, overruling *Re McNare, McNare* v. *McNare*, [1964] 3 All E. R. 373; [1964] 1 W. L. R. 1255.

[3] See, for example, *In the Estate of Gale, Gale* v. *Gale*, [1966] Ch. 236; [1966] 1 All E. R. 945.

[4] Inheritance (Family Provision) Act, 1938, as amended by the Intestates' Estates Act, 1952, s. 4.

[5] Matrimonial Causes Act, 1965, s. 26 (1) (2); replacing equivalent provisions in the Matrimonial Causes (Property and Maintenance)Act, ss. 1–6; as amended by Family Provision Act, 1966.

[6] Matrimonial Causes Act, 1965, s. 26 (4).

[7] Matrimonial Causes Act, 1965, s. 26 (3), as amended by Family Provision Act, 1966, s. 4.

[8] *Ibid.*, ss. 26 (5) and 6 (2) respectively.

a dependant, some other former wife or husband of the deceased, the trustees of any relevant property and any person who is beneficially interested under the will or the intestacy of the deceased in property affected by the order.[1]

SECTION II. IN WHAT FORM A WILL MUST BE MADE.

Essentials for validity of will.

The formalities essential to the creation of a valid will are prescribed by the Wills Act, 1837, in the following words :—

" No will shall be valid unless it shall be in writing and executed in the manner hereinafter mentioned; (that is to say) it shall be signed at the foot or end thereof by the testator or by some other person in his presence and by his direction ; and such signature shall be made or acknowledged by the testator in the presence of two or more witnesses present at the same time ; and such witnesses shall attest and shall subscribe the will in the presence of the testator, but no form of attestation shall be necessary."

The essentials, then, are these :

1. writing,
2. signature of the testator, either made or acknowledged in the presence of the witnesses, and
3. attestation by the witnesses.

Nature of signature.

Signature. The testator must sign the will either by writing his name at its end in the normal fashion or by adding some mark or phrase intended to represent his name. Thus, the signature may be represented, for instance, by a rubber stamp or by the impress of an ink-smudged thumb,[2] or by some such phrase as " your loving mother."[3] Alternatively he may procure some person to sign on his behalf in his presence and under his direction.

The Act of 1837 required that the signature should be *at the foot or end* of the will, but as the courts construed this strictly and refused to admit a signature unless it was so placed that nothing could be written between it and the last words of the will, the law was altered by the Wills Act Amendment Act, 1852. This provides that a signature shall be valid if it is

" so placed at or after, or following, or under, or beside or opposite
" to the end of the will, that it shall be apparent on the face of the
" will that the testator intended to give effect by such his signature
" to the writing signed as his will."[4]

---

[1] Matrimonial Causes Act, 1965, s. 27 (1) (2). For cases under the Acts. see *Askew* v. *Askew*, [1961] 2 All E. R. 60; [1961] 1 W. L. R. 725; *Talbot* v, *Talbot*, [1962] 2 All E. R. 174; [1962] 1 W. L. R. 1113; *Re Bellman*, [1963] P. 239; [1963] 1 All E. R. 513; *Roberts* v. *Roberts*, [1965] 3 All E. R. 503; [1965] 1 W. L. R. 560.

[2] *In the estate of Finn* (1936), 53 T.L.R. 153.

[3] *In the Estate of Cook, Murison* v. *Cook*, [1960] 1 All E. R. 689; [1960] 1 W. L. R. 353.

[4] S. 1 *Re Little, Foster* v. *Cooper*, [1960] 1 All E. R. 387; [1960] 1 W. L. R. 495.

On the other hand, the Act provides that no disposition underneath or following the signature shall be valid. The courts have put a liberal construction upon this enactment. They admit a signature, even though written in the margin, if they are satisfied that the whole document was written before signature, and that the dispositive part of the document may fairly be read as preceding and leading up to the part containing the signature.[1] But they refuse to regard a document as part of a will, unless it was attached to the signed portion of the will at the time of signature. Thus, two separate papers, one of which is signed by the testator, the other by the witnesses, will not be admitted to probate,[2] though the reverse is the case if they are both fastened together.[3] Again, merely to sign the envelope in which the will is contained is not sufficient.[4]

Attestation. The testator must sign, or acknowledge his signature, in the simultaneous presence of the witnesses, *i.e.* both the witnesses must be present at the moment of signature or acknowledgment, and finally they must attest and subscribe the will in the presence of the testator. If the testator has signed his name in more places than one, the attestation will not be effective unless the witnesses attest the operative signature, *i.e.* the one that comes at the foot or end of the will.[5] Although not specifically required by the statute, the usual practice is for the witnesses to attest in the presence of each other and to record the fact in the following attestation clause, which records that all the statutory requirements have been observed :— *No form of attestation necessary.*

" Signed by the said testator as his last will in the presence of us, *Usual form.*
" present at the same time, who in his presence and at his request
" and in the presence of each other have hereunto subscribed our
" names as witnesses."

If this clause is omitted, probate will not be granted unless it is proved by an affidavit of one of the witnesses or by some other satisfactory evidence that the statutory requirements have been observed.[6] Such evidence, however, is not conclusive.[7]

---

[1] *In the Estate of Mabel Amy Long*, [1936] P. 166 ; [1936] 1 All E. R. 435 ; *Re Stalman* (1931), 145 L. T. 339 ; contrast *In the Goods of Mary Moorhouse Smith*, [1931] P. 225 ; *In the Estate of Roberts*, [1934] P. 102 ; *In the Goods of Hornby*, [1946] P. 171 ; [1946] 2 All E. R. 150 ; dist. *Re Harris, Murray* v. *Everard*, [1952] P. 319 ; [1952] 2 All E. R. 409.

[2] *In the Goods of J. Hatton* (1881), 6 P. D. 204. In a later case LANGTON, J., departed from the rule where a holograph will signed by the witnesses only was placed in an envelope signed by the testator ; *In the Goods of Mann*, [1942] P. 146 ; [1942] 2 All E. R. 193. See the Senior Registrar's *Practice Direction*, [1953] 1 W. L. R. 689, dealing with the case where a will, extending to two pages, is signed only at the foot of the first page.

[3] *In the Goods of Horsford* (1874), L. R. 3 P. & D. 211.

[4] *In the Estate of Bean*, [1944] P. 83 ; [1944] 2 All E. R. 348.

[5] *In the Estate of Bercovitz, Canning* v. *Enever*, [1961] 2 All E. R. 481; [1961] 1 W. L. R. 892.

[6] Non-Contentious Probate Rules, 1954 r. 10 ; *Re Selby-Bigge*, [1950] 1 All E. R. 1009. A blind person is incapable of witnessing a will, *In the Estate of Charles Gibson*, [1949] P. 434 ; [1949] 2 All E. R. 90.

[7] *Vere-Wardale, Vere-Wardale* v. *Johnson*, [1949] P. 395 ; [1949] 2 All E. R. 250.

Effect of
gift to a
witness.

The Wills Act also provides that if any beneficial interest is given to a witness or to the spouse of a witness who is married at the time of the attestation, the attestation is valid and effective, but the gift is void.[1] An attesting witness is not excluded as a beneficiary under this enactment unless he is interested under the will at the time of attestation. He may retain any benefit that accrues to him later.[2] Again, the gift to him is void only if it is contained in the very document that he has attested, not, for instance, where he is a beneficiary under a secret trust,[3] nor where his attestation is confined to a codicil that merely confirms the will under which he claims.[4]

Statute of Frauds.

Privileged Wills of Soldiers, Sailors and Airmen.— At common law no particular form was required for wills, which in the case of pure personalty might even be nuncupative. This was altered by the Statute of Frauds, which, besides placing such restrictions upon the nuncupative will that it fell into disuse, required a will of *land* to be in writing and attested by three or four credible witnesses. It provided, however, in section 22 that soldiers' wills with regard to their " movables, wages and personal estates " might still be made in the informal manner hitherto recognized as sufficient.

Wills Act, 1837.

This indulgence was continued by section eleven of the Wills Act, 1837, which provided that

" Any soldier being in actual military service or any mariner or sea-
" man being at sea,"

might dispose of his *personal estate* (an expression which has been held to include personal property over which there is a general or special power of appointment),[5] as he might have done before the passing of the Act. Such a will is privileged in the sense that the usual statutory formalities are not essential for its making or its revocation,[6] and it is valid even though made by an infant.[7] But for spoken words to constitute a nuncupative will, they must have been intended by the deceased to operate as a disposition of his property. They must not merely inform his hearers of what

---

[1] S. 15. Under the previous law the effect of such a gift was to invalidate the will, unless there were sufficient other witnesses who were not beneficiaries. S. 15 does not apply to the privileged will described in the following paragraph, *Re Limond, Limond* v. *Cunliffe*, [1915] 2 Ch. 240.
[2] *In Re Royce's Will Trusts, Tildesley* v. *Tildesley* [1959] Ch. 626; [1959] 3 All E. R. 278.
[3] *Re Young, Young* v. *Young*, [1951] Ch. 344; [1950] 2 All E. R. 1040. As to secret trust, see *supra*, p. 325–6.
[4] *Re Trotter, Trotter* v. *Trotter*, [1899] 1 Ch. 764.
[5] *Re Chichester's (Earl) Will Trusts, Pelham* v. *Chichester (Countess)*, [1946] Ch. 289; [1946] 1 All E. R. 722.
[6] *In the Estate of Gossage, Wood* v. *Gossage*, [1921] P. 194.
[7] **Wills (Soldiers & Sailors) Act,** 1918, s. 1, confirming *Re Wernher, Wernher* v. *Beit*, [1918] 2 Ch. 82.

he proposes to do,[1] but must be intended to guide them in carrying out his wishes.[2]

The Wills (Soldiers and Sailors) Act, 1918, extended the privilege by providing that it should apply to wills of realty in England or Ireland[3] and that the expression " soldier " should include a member of the Air Force.[4] In the result there are two classes of privileged testators :— Two classes of privileged testators.

> First, any soldier or airman who is *in actual military service* at the time of making his will, or any member of the naval or marine forces of the Crown who at that time " is so circumstanced that if he were a soldier he would be *in actual military service* within the meaning of " the Wills Act, 1837, s. 11.[5]
>
> Secondly, any member of the naval or marine forces of the Crown or any member of the merchant marine who is *at sea* at the time of making his will.

The difficulty experienced by the courts has been to determine the meaning of the two expressions *in actual military service*[6] and *at sea.*

The statutory privilege has existed for over 250 years and it is not surprising that with the gradual change in the nature of war the courts, in construing the expression " in actual military service," have at different times laid the emphasis upon different factors. Until comparatively recent times, the instinct of the courts was to construe the expression in the light of Roman law from which the rule in the Statute of Frauds had admittedly been copied.[7] An English soldier was not to be privileged unless a Roman legionary, placed in like circumstances, would have been regarded as *in expeditione.* According to this test, which has now, however, been discarded,[8] the will of a soldier made while he was quartered in barracks even in time of war would not be privileged.[9] In the first half of the nineteenth century, the Ecclesiastical Courts, which had exclusive jurisdiction in probate until 1857, further insisted that the testator should be *inops consilii* at the time of making the will, and on this ground it was held in one case that the privilege did not apply to an officer stationed in Bombay, whose unit had been ordered to proceed to attack the citadel of Joadhpore and who made his will two days before setting out.[10]

Meaning of in actual military service.

---

[1] *In the Estate of Knibbs, Flay* v. *Trueman,* [1962] 2 All E. R. 829; [1962] 1 W. L. R. 852.

[2] *In the Goods of Spicer, Spicer* v. *Richardson,* [1949] P. 441; [1949] 2 All E. R. 659.

[3] S. 3.   [4] S. 5 (2).   [5] *Ibid.*, s. 2.

[6] See 12 *M.L.R.* pp. 183 *et seq.*

[7] The eminent civilian, Sir Leoline Jenkins, was responsible for it.

[8] *Re Booth, Booth* v. *Booth,* [1926] P. 118, 135 ; *Re Wingham, Andrews* v. *Wingham,* [1949] P. 187 ; [1948] 2 All E. R. 908.

[9] *Drummond* v. *Parish* (1843), 3 Curt. 522.

[10] *Bowles* v. *Jackson* (1854), 1 Spinks 294.

In the course of the Boer War and of the First World War the conception of actual military service was broadened in the sense that emphasis was now laid upon whether the testator had taken some active step towards engaging in hostilities, as for example by going into barracks preparatory to being drafted to the seat of war.[1] The decisions during the Second World War went further in the same direction and showed so marked a tendency to extend the class of privileged testators as to evoke the criticism that the mere wearing of uniform in time of war is equivalent to being in actual military service.[2] The authorities, indeed, seem to justify the statement that

> not only the fighting troops, but also men and women, such as doctors, nurses and chaplains, who are " actually serving with the armed forces in connection with military operations which are or have been taking place or are believed to be imminent " are in actual military service within the meaning of the Wills Act.[3]

The statute is satisfied in that respect, for instance, if at the time of making the will and while war is impending or in progress, the testator or testatrix is an airman undergoing training in Saskatchewan,[4] an artillery officer under orders to rejoin his battery just before the outbreak of war,[5] a soldier quartered at a camp in England though not under orders to proceed to the scene of fighting,[6] a member of the W.A.A.F. in charge of a depot in Gloucestershire,[7] a person on duty as a member of the Home Guard,[8] or an infant member of the British Army of the Rhine stationed in Germany nine years after the cessation of hostilities.[9]

Meaning
of
at sea.

A mariner in the Royal Navy or in the merchant service, though not in actual military service, is entitled to the statutory privilege even in time of peace, subject to the condition that he is *at sea* at the time of making his will. The expression " *at sea* " has been liberally construed and is considerably wider than " on the sea."[10]   Thus the condition was held to be satisfied where at the critical moment the testator was the mate of a gunnery vessel permanently moored in Portsmouth Harbour,[11] a woman living in lodgings until the next sailing of the *Lusitania* on which she was

---

[1] *In the Goods of Hiscock*, [1901] P. 78.
[2] 12 *M.L.R.* p. 188.
[3] *Re Wingham, Andrews* v. *Wingham*, [1949] P. 187; [1948] 2 All E. R. 912, at pp. 196, 913 respectively, *per* Denning, L.J.
[4] *Re Wingham, Andrews* v. *Wingham, supra.*
[5] *In the Estate of Rippon*, [1943] P. 61; [1943] 1 All E. R. 676.
[6] *In the Estate of Spark*, [1941] P. 115; [1941] 2 All E. R. 782.
[7] *In the Estate of Rowson*, [1944] 2 All E. R. 36.
[8] *Blyth* v. *Lord Advocate*, [1945] A. C. 32; [1944] 2 All E. R. 375.
[9] *In the Estate of Colman*, [1958] 2 All E. R. 35; [1958] 1 W. L. R. 457.
[10] The authorities are fully discussed in *In the Estate of Newland*, [1952] P. 71; [1952] 1 All E. R. 841.
[11] *In the Goods of M'Murdo* (1868), L. R. 1 P. & D. 540.

employed as a typist,[1] an officer of a tanker under orders to rejoin his ship at Sunderland within the next three days.[2]

Lost Will. The contents of a private document must, if possible, be proved by primary evidence, that is, by production of the document itself, but they may be proved by secondary evidence, as for instance by oral testimony, when the document has been lost. Such extrinsic evidence is admissible in the case of a will that has been lost or destroyed *sine animo revocandi.*[3]

" Declarations, written or oral, made by a testator, both before and
" after the execution of his will, are, in the event of its loss, admissible
" as secondary evidence of its contents. The contents of a lost will
" may be proved by the evidence of a single witness, though
" interested, whose veracity and competency are unimpeached.
" When the contents of a lost will are not completely proved,
" probate will be granted to the extent to which they are proved." [4]

If, however, only parol evidence is adduced, it should be sufficiently cogent to remove all reasonable doubts as to the dispositions made by the testator.[5]

SECTION III. PERSONAL REPRESENTATIVES AND THEIR DUTIES AND POWERS.

(1) APPOINTMENT OF EXECUTORS.

We have already seen that the property of a testator does not go directly to the beneficiaries under the will, but devolves upon his personal representatives for the purposes of administration. Personal representatives are either executors or administrators. An executor is a person who is appointed by the testator for the purpose of carrying the provisions of his will into effect. If no such appointment is made, or if the appointment fails, for instance, by the death, renunciation, infancy or lunacy of the executor, the court grants the right of administration to the person who has the greatest interest in the property. This is called the grant of administration *cum testamento annexo.*[6]

If a last surviving executor proves the will of X., and dies testate without having completed his office, then *his* executor steps into his place and becomes the executor of X.

---

[1] *In the Goods of Sarah Hale,* [1915] 2 I. R. 362.
[2] *In the Estate of Wilson, Wilson* v. *Coleclough,* [1952] P. 92 ; [1952] 1 All E. R. 852 ; *In the Estate of Newland,* [1952] P. 71 ; [1952] 1 All E. R. 841.
[3] *Re Webb, Smith* v. *Johnston,* [1964] 2 All E. R. 91; [1964] 1 W. L. R. 509.
[4] Taken verbatim from the headnote to *Sugden* v. *St. Leonards (Lord)* (1876), L. R. 1 P. D. 154. The question whether in that case the Court of Appeal was correct in admitting evidence of declarations made *after* the execution of the will was left open by the House of Lords in *Woodward* v. *Goulstone* (1886), 11 A. C. 469, but as the law stands at present such evidence is admissible, *In the Estate of Macgillivray,* [1946] 2 All E. R. 301.
[5] *Woodward* v. *Goulstone, supra,* at p. 475 ; *In the Estate of Macgillivray, supra.* This last decision does not seem to have been brought to the attention of the Court in *In the Estate of Wipperman, Wissler* v. *Wipperman,* [1953] 1 All E. R. 764.
[6] Supreme Court of Judicature (Consolidation) Act, 1925, s. 166.

" An executor of a sole or last surviving executor of a testator is the " executor of that testator."[1]

But if such last surviving executor dies intestate, his administrator does not become the executor of the will of X.,[2] and in such a case it is necessary for the court to appoint another person to administer such property as is still unadministered. This is called administration *de bonis non*.

While any legal proceeding that concerns the validity of a will is pending, the court may appoint an administrator *pendente lite*, who has all the powers of a general administrator except that he cannot distribute the residue among those entitled.[3]

(2) THEIR DUTY TO OBTAIN PROBATE.

Jurisdiction to grant probate.

The first duty of an executor is to prove the will in court. The jurisdiction to grant and revoke probates, which was formerly vested in the ecclesiastical courts, was transferred in 1858 to the Court of Probate.[4] When the Supreme Court of Judicature was set up under the Judicature Act, 1873, the jurisdiction was vested in the Probate, Divorce and Admiralty Division of the High Court of Justice. The business of this court is divided into common form business and contentious business, and grants of probate afford a frequent example of the former class.

The proof of a will may be either in common or in solemn form.

Probate in common form.

1. Probate in common form is granted, not by the court itself, but by the principal probate registry in London or by a district registry, and such a grant has effect over the estate of the deceased in all parts of England.[5] The executor must swear an oath before a Commissioner of Oaths, in which he states his belief that the instrument he submits for probate is the true and last will of the testator, and in which he declares the gross value of the real and personal estate. If the will is correct in form and contains the attestation clause which has been given above, probate is granted on the oath of the executor alone.[6]

Will altered after execution.

Any obliteration, interlineation or other alteration made *after* the execution of a will is not admitted to probate unless it

---

[1] Administration of Estates Act, 1925, s. 7 (1).
[2] *Ibid.*, s. 7 (3).
[3] Supreme Court of Judicature (Consolidation) Act, 1925, s. 163.
[4] Court of Probate Act, 1857.
[5] Supreme Court of Judicature (Consolidation) Act, 1925, s. 151 (1). In the case of small estates, where the value of the net estate is less than £1,000 and that of the gross estate less than £3,000 an application for grant of administration may be made through an authorized officer of customs and excise; Small Estates (Representation) Act, 1961, s. 1 (1).
[6] *Supra*, p. 763.

has been signed by the testator and duly attested.[1] Moreover, the onus is on those who will benefit by the alteration to prove that it was made before execution.[2] If there has been no signature and attestation, probate is granted of the will as it stood before the alteration, provided that the original words are still *apparent*.[3] In this event the original words remain in force contrary to the obvious intention of the testator. If, however, they are not apparent, probate is granted with the altered part of the will left blank.

Words are " apparent " if they can be read by looking at the will itself, however elaborate may be the devices used and however skilful the eye of the reader.[4] But they are not apparent if their elucidation requires the creation of a new document, as for example, by taking an infra-red photograph.[5]

2. Proof in solemn form, which is an action before the court, is necessary where the validity of the will is doubtful, or where there is a likelihood that it may be opposed. The action may be brought by the executor, a person who contests the will, or a " person interested," *i.e.*, a widow or widower, a legatee or devisee and the persons who would be entitled to take on intestacy. A creditor is not a " person interested."

Probate in solemn form.

A will, after it has been proved, is kept in the Registry of the court, and a copy, together with a certificate that the will has been proved, is given to the executor. The copy and the certificate are called the probate of the will, and they are conclusive as to the validity both of the testamentary dispositions and of the right of the executor to perform his duties. But an executor derives his title from the will and not from the grant of probate, and therefore the general rule is that he may do all such things and perform all such duties upon the death of the deceased as fall within the province of an executor.

Title of executor.

If a person without obtaining a grant of probate takes upon himself to meddle with the property of a deceased person in such a way as to indicate that he assumes the rights of an executor, he is said to be an executor *de son tort*. The statutory rule is that if any person, to the defrauding of creditors or without full and valuable consideration, obtains, receives or holds any real and personal estate of a deceased person or releases any debt due to the estate, he shall be liable as an executor *de son tort* to the extent of the estate in his hands or of the debt released, after deducting

Executor de son tort.

---

[1] Wills Act, 1837, s. 21.
[2] *In the Estate of Oates, Callow* v. *Sutton*, [1946] 2 All E. R. 735.
[3] Wills Act, 1837, s. 21.
[4] *Ffinch* v. *Combe*, [1894] P. 191.
[5] *In the Goods of Itter, Dedman* v. *Godfrey*, [1950] P. 130 ; [1950] 1 All E. R. 68.

1. any debt for valuable consideration and without fraud due to him from the deceased, and

2. any payment made by him which might properly be made by a personal representative.[1]

(3) THEIR DUTY TO ADMINISTER THE ESTATE

Inventory.

It is not within the scope of this book to give an exhaustive account of an executor's duties, and only a *résumé* will be attempted.

An executor should make an inventory of all the goods and chattels of the deceased, and he may be compelled, upon an application to the court by a person interested in the estate of the testator, to exhibit the inventory on oath.[2]

Realization of estate.

His next duty is to collect all the goods and chattels, to realize investments which it is undesirable to keep, to recover loans which are protected merely by personal security, to call in money lent on mortgage if it is required for some testamentary purpose, and to get in the testator's estate generally. For these purposes all causes of action vested in the deceased survive to the personal representative, except in the cases of seduction, defamation, the enticement of a spouse and claims to recover damages for adultery.[3]

Power to dispose of estate in order to pay debts.

Having collected and obtained control over the assets, the executor must next pay the debts of the deceased. We have already seen what his duty is in this respect. In order that this may be effectually performed, the Administration of Estates Act, 1925, after providing that the real as well as the personal estate of the deceased shall vest in the personal representatives, enacts that they shall have the same power to dispose of and deal with the land as they formerly possessed in respect of personal property.[4] Personal representatives always had complete power of alienation over personal property, and since the Land Transfer Act, 1897, they have been in the same position as regards land.

Thus they can sell, mortgage or partition the land,[5] and they are now empowered by statute to grant a lease for a term of years absolute (with or without impeachment of waste) to trustees upon trust for raising any sum of money for which the land is liable, and also to grant a rentcharge for giving effect to any annual sum for which the land is liable.

Disposition of land.

But a sale of land by executors differs, in its method, from a sale of personalty. One executor may sell pure personalty without the concurrence of his co-executors, but it is enacted that a conveyance of land shall not be made without the concurrence

---

[1] Administration of Estates Act, 1925, s. 28.   [2] *Ibid.*, s. 25.
[3] Law Reform (Miscellaneous Provisions) Act, 1934, s. 1.
[4] S. 2.   [5] *Re Kemnal and Still's Contract*, [1923] 1 Ch. 293.

of all the proving executors, unless an order of the court is obtained.[1]

In order that personal representatives may have full powers of management while they are dealing with the property of the deceased, it is provided that in addition to having power to raise money by mortgage they shall be in the position of trustees for sale as regards both the ability to overreach equitable interests and the right to exercise the powers conferred by statute upon trustees for sale.[2]　These powers are those which are conferred upon a tenant for life under the Settled Land Act, in addition to the powers given by the Trustee Act, 1925, and the Law of Property Act, 1925.[3]

Representatives are trustees for sale.

After the debts have been paid, the duty of the executor is to distribute the residue among those persons who are beneficially entitled under the will.　Before he does this, however, he should protect himself against claims of which he may not be aware by publishing advertisements in accordance with the directions of the Trustee Act, 1925.[4]　This provides that with a view to the conveyance of real or personal property to beneficiaries either trustees or personal representatives may give notice by advertisement in the *Gazette* and in a newspaper circulating in the district where the land is situated, requiring persons to give particulars of any claim they may have against the estate of the deceased.　At the expiration of the time fixed by the notice (which must not be less than two months) the personal representatives may convey the property to the beneficiaries, and they are not liable to any person of whose claim they had no notice at the time of the conveyance.

Distribution of estate.

Protection by means of advertisement.

But the creditors may follow the property even after it has been conveyed to beneficiaries.　Notwithstanding such a conveyance, a creditor or other person interested in the property may apply to the court, and the court may declare a beneficiary to be a trustee of the land for the creditor, or may order a different conveyance to be made or may make a vesting order.[5]　This power to follow the property does not, however, exist where the conveyance is made not to a beneficiary, but to a purchaser in the ordinary way of administration.[6]　In such a case the purchaser receives ample protection.[7]　Thus all conveyances of *any interest* in real or personal property made to a purchaser, either by an executor who has proved the will or by the administrator of a

Right to follow property.

---

[1] Administration of Estates Act, 1925, s. 2 (2).
[2] *Ibid.*, s. 39.
[3] Law of Property Act, 1925, s. 28.
[4] Trustee Act, 1925, s. 27 ; as amended by the Law of Property (Amendment) Act, 1926, Sch.
[5] Administration of Estates Act, 1925, s. 38.
[6] *Ibid.*, s. 38.
[7] *Ibid.*, s. 36 (6), (7), (8).

person who has died intestate, are valid notwithstanding a subsequent revocation of the probate or administration.[1]

SECTION IV. PARTICULAR RULES.

SUMMARY.

(1) FAILURE OF GIFTS BY LAPSE.

Commori-
entes.

A lapse occurs where the donee predeceases the testator, and a preliminary point to notice is that it may be difficult to decide whether this has been the sequence of events if both have been the victims of a common calamity, as for instance where they have both been killed by the same bomb.   The common law rule in such a case is that the representatives of the donee who claims under the will must prove that in fact he survived the testator.   Otherwise the claim fails.[2]   This rule was altered by the following section of the Law of Property Act, 1925.[3]

" In all cases where, after the commencement of this Act, two or more
" persons have died in circumstances rendering it uncertain which of
" them survived the other or others, such deaths shall (subject to any
" order of the court), for all purposes affecting the title to property,
" be presumed to have occurred in order of seniority, and accordingly
" the younger shall be deemed to have survived the elder.

Hickman
v. Peacey.

It was thought that this section had finally solved the question, but in *Hickman* v. *Peacey*,[4] where four persons had been killed by the explosion of a bomb, it was contended that the common law rule still prevailed if the deaths were simultaneous.   If, it was argued, two persons have died simultaneously, it is not " uncertain which of them survived the other."   For the section to apply the deaths must have been consecutive.   This argument, which *inter alia* ignores the virtual impossibility of two human beings ceasing to breathe at exactly the same moment of time, was rejected by a bare majority of the House of Lords, and the simple rule laid down that

unless it is possible to say for certain which of the persons died first, the younger is presumed to have survived.

In other words, the section is not excluded unless there is clear evidence that one person survived the other.[5]   In one case, for

---

[1] Administration of Estates Act, 1925, s. 37, extending *Hewson* v. *Shelley*, [1914] 2 Ch. 13.
[2] *Wing* v. *Angrave* (1860) 8 H. L. Cas. 183.
[3] S. 184.
[4] [1945] A. C. 304 ; [1945] 2 All E. R. 215.
[5] *Re Bate, Chillingworth* v. *Bate*, [1947] 2 All E. R. 418.

instance, a man aged twenty-nine, left all his property to his wife, aged twenty-six, with a gift over to his nephew in the event of her death "preceding or coinciding" with his own. A month later the husband and wife set sail on a ship which sunk with all on board, only one body being found. It was held that the words "coinciding with" were not intended to denote two deaths occurring on the same occasion from the same cause, but two deaths coincident in point of time, *i.e.* so close to each other that the normal man would describe them as simultaneous. There was no evidence as to the order of their occurrence, and therefore the wife was presumed to have survived her husband.[1]

Once it is proved that the donee under a will died before the testator, the rule is that the gift lapses and ceases to take effect.[2] This is so despite the addition to the gift of words of limitation such as to the donee and his heirs or to him and his executors.[3] It is usual to provide against the event, but to render this effective something more is required than a mere declaration that the gift shall not lapse. There must be a further gift limited to take effect upon the premature death of the first donee, as for example by a provision that

Meaning of lapse.

> " the devise to A. shall not lapse if he predeceases the testator but
> " shall take effect in favour of his eldest surviving son." [4]

The Wills Act, 1837, provides that no lapse shall occur in the following two cases, unless there is a contrary intention :

Two cases where no lapse.

1. **Gift of Entailed Interest.** Where a person, to whom realty or personalty has been left by will in tail, dies in the lifetime of the testator leaving issue capable of inheriting under the entail, and any such issue shall be living at the death of the testator, the gift does not lapse, but takes effect *as if the death of such person had happened immediately after the testator's death.*[5]

2. **Gift to Testator's Issue.** A devise or bequest to the child or other issue of the testator for an interest not determinable at or before the death of the donee does not lapse if the donee predeceases the testator *leaving issue alive at the testator's death*, but takes effect *as if the death of the donee had happened immediately after the testator's death.*[6]

The second exception does not apply where the gift to the issue of the testator is a class gift, for the essence of such a gift is that it

Class gifts.

---

[1] *In re Rowland, Smith* v. *Russell,* [1963] Ch. 1; [1962] 2 All E. R. 837 (Lord DENNING, M.R., dissenting); fully discussed 26 *M.L.R.,* pp. 353–66 (Michael Albery).

[2] For the explanation, see *Re Harvey's Estate, Harvey* v. *Gillow,* [1893] 1 Ch. 567, 570.

[3] *Elliott* v. *Davenport* (1705), 1 P. Wms. 83 ; *Browne* v. *Hope* (1872), L. R. 14 Eq. 343.

[4] *Re Ladd, Henderson* v. *Porter,* [1932] 2 Ch. 219.

[5] Wills Act, 1837, s. 32 ; Law of Property Act, 1925, s. 130 (1).

[6] Wills Act, 1837, s. 33.

is made to a fluctuating class of objects who are to be ascertained at the death of the testator.[1] Hence, if there is a devise to the children of A., or to the children of A. equally, the entire property vests in those children who survive the testator irrespective of prior deaths.[2]

Operation of the statutory exceptions.

The Act, it will be noticed, fictitiously prolongs the life of the donee until immediately after the death of the testator. The sole purpose of this, however, is to amplify the preceding words and to leave no manner of doubt that the gift is to be effective despite the premature death in fact of the donee. His life is not deemed to have been prolonged for any other purpose. The estate that he himself may have left is, indeed, posthumously increased by virtue of his ancestor's will, but this increase falls to be administered with the rest of his estate according to the circumstances as they existed at the time of his actual death.[3] The significance of this may be seen from a hypothetical case :

> The testator, T., devises Blackacre to his son, X., in fee simple. X. predeceases T. but is survived by his own son Y.

In this case, if X. died intestate, the ascertainment of the persons entitled to the additional property, Blackacre, will depend upon the circumstances existing at the time of his death, not at the moment immediately after T.'s death. If he left a will disposing of his residuary estate to Z., Blackacre will fall into the residue,[4] for, although the survival of Y. prevents the lapse of the gift, there is no provision that what has been given to X. shall pass beneficially to Y. Again, since Blackacre is deemed to have belonged to X. at his death, it follows that it will vest in his trustee in bankruptcy if he died a bankrupt,[5] and that estate duty is payable in respect not only of T.'s death, but also of X.'s death.[6]

Destination of lapsed property.

Where neither of the exceptions applies, the destination of lapsed property depends upon whether the will contains a residuary gift. If so, the property passes to the residuary devisee or legatee according as it is realty or personalty[7]; otherwise it enures for the benefit of those persons entitled on intestacy.

(2) EFFECT OF A GENERAL DEVISE OF LAND.

A devise of land is either specific or general.

General devise includes leaseholds.

A specific devise is a gift by will of a particular part of the testator's real estate, as for instance a gift of " my farm Blackacre " or of " all my lands in the parish of X."

---

[1] *Supra*, pp. 244–5.
[2] *Olney* v. *Bates* (1855), 3 Drew, 319 ; *Re Harvey's Estate, Harvey* v. *Gillow*, [1893] 1 Ch. 567.
[3] *Re Basioli, Re Depaoli, McGahey* v. *Depaoli*, [1953] Ch. 367 ; [1953] 1 All E. R. 301 ; where all the authorities are collected.
[4] *Johnson* v. *Johnson* (1843), 3 Hare, 157.
[5] *Re Pearson, Smith* v. *Pearson*, [1920] 1 Ch. 247.
[6] *Re Scott*, [1901] 1 K. B. 228.   [7] Wills Act, 1837, s. 25.

A general devise is a gift of land which does not specify any particular part, but is couched in generic terms, as for instance a gift of " all my freehold lands."

The rule before the Wills Act, 1837, was that if a testator had both freeholds and leaseholds and made a devise of all his " land," the devise operated to pass only the freeholds.[1]   If, however, he had leaseholds only, then they passed under the general gift.   This rule was altered by that Act, which provides that a devise of land described in a general manner shall be construed to include the leasehold as well as the freehold interests unless a contrary intention appears in the will.[2]   This enactment does not apply to entailed interests, which, despite the new power of testamentary disposition given by the Law of Property Act, 1925, to a tenant in tail, are not caught by a general devise.[3]

Power of Appointment. Similarly, the rule before the Wills Act, 1837, was that a general devise of land did not operate to pass land over which the testator had a power of appointment, unless he had no land other than that which was subject to the power.[4]   This rule was altered by section 27, which provides that a general devise of land shall include estates over which a testator has " power to appoint in any manner he may think proper," and shall operate as an execution of such power, unless a contrary intention shall appear by the will.[5]   A similar rule is prescribed for a general bequest of personalty.   The Act, it will be noticed, does not refer to a general as distinct from a special power, but to one which the donee may exercise without restriction.   The power vested in the testator may not be " special " in the sense that it is exercisable in favour only of defined objects,[6] yet, if it in any manner limits his choice, as where it is exercisable in favour of any person in the world except himself[7] or his wife,[8] he cannot be described as entitled to appoint " in any manner he may think proper," and therefore section 27 is inapplicable.

General devise includes land subject to general power.

There are few more difficult questions in practice than to decide whether a general gift operates as an exercise of a special power of appointment, and indeed the relevant authorities defy reconciliation.   It is no doubt true

Special powers on different footing.

> " that in order to exercise a special power there must be a sufficient
> " expression or indication of intention in the will or other instrument
> " alleged to exercise it ; and that either a reference to the power

---

[1] Carson, *Real Property Statutes*, p. 466.   [2] Wills Act, 1837, s. 26.
[3] *Supra*, p. 181.   [4] Hawkins on Wills, pp. 22 *et seq.*
[5] Wills Act, 1837, s. 27; *In re Thirlwell*, [1958] Ch. 146; [1957] 3 All E. R. 465.   [6] *Supra*, pp. 194–5.
[7] *Re Park, Public Trustee* v. *Armstrong*, [1932] 1 Ch. 580 ; *Re Jones, Public Trustee* v. *Jones*, [1945] Ch. 105.
[8] *Re Byron's Settlement, Williams* v. *Mitchell*, [1891] 3 Ch. 474 ; dist. *Re Harvey, Banister* v. *Thirtle*, [1950] 1 All E. R. 491 ; where the excepted appointee did not and could not exist.

" or a reference to the property subject to the power constitutes
" in general a sufficient indication for the purpose "[1];

but the embarrassing problem is to determine whether the
testator's language is sufficiently precise where he has referred
neither to the power nor to its subject-matter.[2]

(3) EFFECT OF A GIFT OVER ON FAILURE OF ISSUE.

The natural meaning of a devise of realty

" to A., but if he shall die without issue, then to B.,"

Former
construction
of such gifts.
is that A. is to take a fee simple, which, if he has no children or
other issue *at the time of his death*, is to go over to B.   Before 1837,
however, the courts construed such expressions as

" die without issue," or
" die without leaving issue,"

as meaning an indefinite failure of issue, *i.e.*, that the estate given
to A. was to endure until his issue failed, no matter how long it
might be before the failure occurred.   The effect of this construction was that A. took an estate tail by implication, with remainder
to B. and his heirs.[3]   A. could, therefore, bar the entail and so
defeat both his issue and the remaindermen.

Alteration
by Wills
Act, 1837.
In order, therefore, to assimilate the legal and the natural
meaning of the expression it was provided by the Wills Act that
the words " die without issue " or " die without leaving issue,"
or any other words which import a failure of the issue of a person
either at his death or at some indefinite time, shall be construed
to mean a want or failure in his lifetime, and not an indefinite
failure.[4]

The effect of this enactment, which applies to gifts both of
realty and personalty, if taken alone, is that in the example given
above B. becomes entitled to take the fee simple if A. dies leaving
no issue.   But as this would mean that A. could never know during
his lifetime whether the fee simple given to him by the will was
absolute or not, because of the possibility that his existing children
might predecease him and so entitle B. to take, further statutory
alterations have been made.

Alteration
by Law of
Property
Act, 1925.
The Conveyancing Act, 1882,[5] enacted in the case of instruments coming into operation after December 31, 1882, that
where there is a person entitled to land for an estate in fee, or for
a term of years absolute, or for term of life *with an executory
limitation over on failure of his issue* whether within a specified

---

[1] *In re Ackerley*, [1913] 1 Ch. 510, at p. 515, *per* SARGANT, J., adapting
similar language used by BUCKLEY, J., in *In re Weston's Settlement*, [1906]
2 Ch. 620, 624.

[2] See *In re Knight decd.*, [1957] Ch. 441 ; [1957] 2 All E. R. 252, and cases
there cited.

[3] A similar gift of personalty was construed to give A. the absolute ownership, since personalty was not entailable before 1926.

[4] Wills Act, 1837, s. 29.   [5] S. 10.

time or not, such executory limitation shall be void and become incapable of taking effect as soon as there is living any issue who has attained the age of 21 years. It will be noticed that this enactment applies only to land and that its operation is restricted to the interests specifically mentioned. It is still the governing enactment with regard to instruments coming into operation between December 31, 1882, and December 31, 1925. But in furtherance of the general principle of assimilation it is now enacted for instruments coming into operation after December 31, 1925, that where there is a person entitled to

"(*a*) an equitable interest in land for an estate in fee simple or for any less interest not being an entailed interest, or

(*b*) any interest in *other property*, not being an entailed interest,"

a gift over on failure of issue shall be void as soon as there is living any issue who has attained the age of 21 years.[1] This rule applies to deeds as well as to wills, and to all interests in property, whether real or personal, with the exception of entailed interests. The reason for excepting an entailed interest is that the gift over can, in any event, be defeated by disentailment. The reason for confining the rule to an *equitable* fee simple is that, under the modern law, a fee simple subject to a gift over cannot subsist as a legal estate, but is necessarily equitable.

SECTION V. CONSTRUCTION OF WILLS.

The duty of a court which is called upon to construe a will is first to discover what was the intention of the testator as expressed by his will, and then to give effect to that intention. The fundamental rule to which all others must bend is that the intention of a testator must be obeyed, however informal the language may be by which it has been expressed [2]; but, though this principle has been asserted with vehemence from the earliest times, and has on various occasions been referred to as *the pole star, the sovereign guide*, and *the cardinal rule*, it is important to remember that in ascertaining intention the court considers the writing alone. It does not indulge in conjecture. It attributes to the written words their ordinary grammatical meaning, it gives to technical words, such as " heir," their technical meaning, and does not allow itself to be influenced by the probability that such could not have been the meaning intended by the testator.[3] For one thing, the facts known to the testator may not be before the court [4]; for another, it would be futile to require a will to be in

Effect must be given to testator's intention.

---

[1] Law of Property Act, 1925, s. 134.
[2] A statutory exception to this rule has been made by the Law of Property Act, 1925, s. 130, which provides that an entailed interest can be created only by formal words of limitation ; *supra*, pp. 166–7.
[3] *Boyes* v. *Cook* (1880), 14 Ch. D. 53.
[4] *Ralph* v. *Carrick* (1879), 11 Ch. D. 873, 878.

2C*

writing if the clearly written wishes of the testator were to be open to revision after his death.

Consequently, parol evidence is in general inadmissible to contradict, add to or vary what he meant to write.[1]   There are, however, exceptions to this principle.

Exceptionally court will add words.

Thus, if it is clear on the face of the will that he has not accurately or completely expressed his intention, the court will add the words that he has omitted, provided that no person applying common sense can have any doubt what in fact he intended.[2]

Parol evidence sometimes admissible.

Again, the words used by a testator refer to facts and circumstances within his knowledge concerning his property and the persons mentioned in his will, and therefore it would often be impossible to fulfil his intention unless parol evidence were admissible.   " You may place yourself, so to speak, in the testator's armchair, and consider the circumstances by which he was surrounded when he made his will to assist you in arriving at his intention."[3] As has been said: "When seated there, however, the court is not entitled to make a fresh will for the testator merely because it strongly suspects that he did not mean what he has plainly said."[4] In other words, "the function of a court of construction is not to declare the actual subjective intention of the testator, but the objective intention as expressed in his language."[5]

" Thus if a testator devises the house he lives in, or his farm called " Blackacre, or the lands which he purchased of A., parol evidence " must be adduced to show what house was occupied by the testator, " what farm is called Blackacre or what lands were purchased of A., " such evidence being essential for the purpose of ascertaining the " actual subject of disposition.   The distinction obviously is that, " though evidence *dehors* the will is not admissible to show that the " testator used his terms of description in any peculiar or extra- " ordinary sense, yet it may be adduced to ascertain what the " description properly comprehends."[6]

Other cases where parol evidence is admitted for the same reason occur where a testator uses nicknames in the will, or expressions which, though bearing a definite meaning in ordinary language, are used in a peculiar sense by persons of the class to which the testator belonged or in the locality where he dwelt.[7]

Equivocation.

Further, parol evidence is admissible to explain an equivo-

---

[1] *Earl of Newburgh* v. *Countess of Newburgh* (1820), 5 Madd. 364.

[2] *In re Whitrick*, [1957] 2 All E.R. 467; [1957] 1 W.L.R. 884, and authorities there cited.

[3] *Boyes* v. *Cook* (1880), 14 Ch. D. 53, at p. 56, *per* James, L.J.

[4] *Perrin* v. *Morgan*, [1943] A. C. 399, at p. 420; *per* Lord Romer; [1943] 1 All E. R. 187.

[5] 26 *M.L.R.*, p. 357 (Michael Albery).

[6] Jarman (7th Edn.), pp. 484–5.   [7] *Ibid.*, p. 477.

cation. The word *equivocation* in this connection means that although the devise is on the face of it perfect and intelligible, yet an ambiguity arises making it hard to determine which of two persons or things the testator meant to denote, since the words of the will point equally well to either. An early instance of such a latent ambiguity was where,[1]

> a testator devised one house to George Gord the son of George Gord, a second to George Gord the son of John Gord, and a third to "George the son of Gord." It was held that evidence of the testator's declarations were admissible to show that he intended by this last description to indicate George Gord the son of George Gord.

But although extrinsic evidence is admissible in such cases, it is never admitted to prove that words which are perfectly clear in themselves were intended by the testator to bear some different meaning. If a will bears a definite construction it cannot have another and a different construction imposed upon it by extrinsic evidence, for there is a fundamental distinction between evidence which is simply explanatory of the words of a will and evidence which is designed to prove intention itself as an independent fact.[2] This was explained by Lord CAVE in the following manner [3] :— {*Limits to admissibility of extrinsic evidence.*}

> "No doubt a court, called upon to construe a will, is entitled to "know the facts which the testator knew, and to use that knowledge "for the purpose of resolving doubts as to the identity of persons or "things mentioned in the will, or of assigning a meaning to ex-"pressions which otherwise would have no adequate or intelligible "sense. . . .
>   "But it is quite another thing to say that when a testator has used "an unambiguous expression such as '*my brothers and sisters*,' ex-"trinsic evidence can be adduced to show that he must have intended "the expression to refer to brothers and sisters already born. That "would be to use the facts, not as evidence of identity, but as evidence "of intention ; and such a use of them would be contrary to settled "principles of construction."

SECTION VI. REVOCATION OF WILLS.

A will is revoked in any of the following ways :—

(1) **Subsequent Marriage of a Testator.** Marriage, since it raises a moral obligation to provide for the new family, requires a reconsideration of any testamentary gifts that may have already been made by either party. At common law, subsequent marriage revoked the will of a woman, but not that of a man, since in any event his wife was adequately provided for under the law of dower. {*Marriage now revokes will.*}

---

[1] *Doe d. Gord* v. *Needs* (1836), 2 M. & W. 129 ; *Re Jackson, Beattie* v. *Murphy*, [1933] Ch. 237. But see *Re Mayo*, [1901] 1 Ch. 404.
[2] *Re Grainger, Dawson* v. *Higgins*, [1900] 2 Ch. 756, 763–4 ; RIGBY, L.J. ; reversed *sub nom. Higgins* v. *Dawson*, [1902] A. C. 1, 10.
[3] *Ward* v. *Van der Loeff*, [1924] A. C. 653, 663–4.

Exceptions.   It is enacted, however, by the Wills Act that a will made by a man or a woman shall be revoked by his or her marriage.[1] There are two exceptions to this rule.

The first derives from the postulate that it is useless to invalidate a prior will if in the result no benefit will accrue to the testator's family. The Act, therefore, provides that the testamentary exercise of a power of appointment shall not be revoked by the testator's subsequent marriage unless the property if unappointed would go to his heir, executor, administrator or the persons entitled as his next-of-kin under the Statutes of Distribution.[2]

Secondly, the Law of Property Act, 1925, provides[3] that a will expressed to be made *in contemplation of marriage* shall not be revoked by the solemnization of the marriage contemplated.[4] To escape revocation, however, the will must expressly state that it is made in contemplation of marriage to a particular person, and moreover it must be followed by the solemnization of that marriage.[5]

(2) Later Will or Codicil.

A will may be revoked by a later will or codicil, provided that the later instrument observes the formalities required by law for the execution of a valid will.[6]

Express revocation.   A will or a codicil may revoke a prior will either by an express clause of revocation or by disposing of property in a manner inconsistent with a previous devise. The first method requires no comment, except that there is no technical rule as to the words necessary to operate as a revocation or as to the extent of the revocation, the question being simply one of intention.[7] The usual practice is, however, for a testator to use the simple formula :—

" I hereby revoke all former wills, codicils and testamentary in-
" struments made by me, and declare this to be my last will."

Implied revocation.   As regards a later disposition of property inconsistent with one made in a prior will, we must note that the mere use of the words " last will " does not necessarily revoke a former will. A will may consist of several independent instruments executed at different times, and where a testator expresses his intention in several instruments without having executed an express clause of revocation, the earlier instruments are revoked by implication in so far, but only in so far, as they are inconsistent with the later ones.

---

[1] Wills Act, 1837, s. 18.
[2] S. 18 ; *In the Goods of Gilligan*, [1950] P. 32.
[3] S. 177 (1).
[4] *Pilot* v. *Gainfort*, [1931] P. 103.
[5] *Sallis* v. *Jones*, [1936] P. 43 ; *In the Estate of Langston*, [1953] P. 100 ; [1953] 1 All E. R. 928.
[6] Wills Act, 1837, s. 20.
[7] *Cotterell* v. *Cotterell* (1872), 2 P. & D. 397, 399. *Lowthorpe-Lutwidge* v. *Lowthorpe-Lutwidge*, [1935] P. 151.

" The mere fact of making a subsequent testamentary paper does
" not work a total revocation of a prior one, unless the latter, ex-
" pressly or in effect, revoke the former, or the two be incapable of
" standing together; for though it be a maxim . . . that no man can
" die with two testaments, yet any number of instruments, whatever
" be their relative date or in whatever form they may be (so as they
" be all clearly testamentary), may be admitted to probate, as to-
" gether containing the last will of the deceased." [1]

If, for instance,

a testator, having devised Blackacre to A. in fee, by a subsequent will devises it to B. in fee, the former devise is obviously
revoked ; but if he devises Blackacre to C. in fee and then, by
codicil, devises it to the first son of D. who shall attain the
age of 21 years, the first devise is revoked only to the extent
necessary to give effect to the springing future interest, so that
C. will take the fee simple until the son of D. attains the
required age. [2]

But if a subsequent and inconsistent gift, which, if valid, *Doctrine of*
would override a prior gift, fails by reason of the rule against *dependent*
perpetuities or for any other reason, it does not operate as a revo- *relative*
cation unless an independent and clear intention to revoke is *revocation.*
expressed. [3]   This is known as the doctrine of dependent relative
revocation.   " The revocation is relative to the new gift, and if the
gift fails the revocation fails also, unless the testator clearly shows
in the later instrument that he intends in any event to revoke the
earlier will." [4]   In other words, the revocation of the prior gift is
conditional on the effectiveness of its substitute.   This doctrine
applies even where there is an express clause of revocation in the
later instrument, for at bottom the question is always one of
intention, but in this case a heavy burden lies upon those who
allege that what was expressly prescribed was intended to be
conditional upon the validity of the substituted gift. [5]

If the court is satisfied that such was the testator's intention,
it may in certain circumstances spell one composite will out of the
two that he has executed.   This solution was reached on the
following facts :

By the earlier will the testatrix appointed X. executor, made
certain bequests and left the residue of her estate to X.

---

[1] Williams on Executors (12th Edn.), vol. i. p. 100, adopted *Lemage* v.
Goodban (1865), 1 P. & D. 57, 62, and other cases ; *Re Plant, Johnson* v.
Hardwicke, [1952] Ch. 298 ; [1952] 1 All E. R. 78. n.
[2] *Duffield* v. *Duffield* (1829), 1 Dow and Cl. 268.   *Cf. Re Baker*, [1929] 1
Ch. 668.   *Re Pearson, Rowling* v. *Crowther*, [1963] 3 All E. R. 763; [1963].
[3] *Ward* v. *Van der Loeff*, [1924] A. C. 653.   *Re Robinson*, [1930] 2 Ch. 332;
Re Hawksley's Settlement, [1934] Ch. 384, 400-1.   *In the Estate of Brown*,
[1942] P. 136 ; [1942] 2 All E. R. 176.
[4] *Ward* v. *Van der Loeff*, [1924] A. C. at p. 656, in argument. See 71 *L.Q.R.*
pp. 374-87 (F. H. Newark).
[5] *In re Murray*, [1956] 2 All E. R. 353.

absolutely.   By the later will, she revoked all previous wills, appointed X. executor, made certain bequests which were entirely inconsistent with those contained in the earlier will, and then left the residuary clause incomplete so that in fact the residue was undisposed of.

It was held that she had inserted the revocation clause in the mistaken belief that she had disposed of the whole of her estate, and that therefore the later will, omitting the revocation clause, and the earlier will, omitting the bequests, must both be admitted to probate as together constituting the true last will of the testatrix.[1]

The Wills Act provides that revocation may be effected not only by a later will or codicil duly executed, but also by " *some writing* declaring an intention to revoke " a will.   A writing, however, is ineffectual to cause revocation unless it is executed in accordance with the formalities prescribed by the Act.[2]

Two elements necessary.

(3) **Destruction** *animo revocandi.*   The Wills Act, 1837, provides that a will may be revoked [3]

> " by the burning, tearing or otherwise destroying the same by the
> " testator or by some person in his presence and by his direction,
> " with the intention of revoking the same."

Physical destruction.

It will be seen that two distinct things must occur if a will is to be revoked by destruction.   There must be the physical act of destruction and the mental act of the intention to revoke.

> " All the destroying in the world without intention will not revoke
> " a will nor all the intention in the world without destroying :   there
> " must be the two." [4]

Again, the act of destruction, if not carried out by the testator, must be carried out in his presence by some person acting under his direction.[5]   Destruction without intention, intention without destruction, destruction with intention but carried out in the absence of the testator, none of these is operative to produce revocation.

Thus in one case, a testator drew his pen through parts of his will, wrote on the back of it " this will is revoked " and threw it into the waste-paper basket.   A servant later rescued it and placed it on the table where it was found seven years later at the testator's death.   The will was admitted to probate.   It had not been revoked by a signed and attested writing, neither had it been physically destroyed.   Indeed, had the servant burnt the contents of the basket, there would have been no destruction within the meaning of the Act.[6]

---

[1] *In the Estate of Cocke,* [1960] 2 All E. R. 289; [1960] 1 W. L. R. 491.
[2] Wills Act, 1837, s. 20.   [3] *Ibid.*
[4] *Cheese* v. *Lovejoy* (1877), 2 P. D. 251, 253.
[5] *In the Goods of Dadds* (1857), Dea. and Sw. 290.
[6] *Cheese* v. *Lovejoy, supra.*

The physical act of destruction is in itself inconclusive, and it may be necessary to show whether it was accompanied by the *animus revocandi* or not. For this purpose extrinsic evidence is admissible. Thus, if a testator has destroyed a will in a fit of drunkenness[1] or of insanity[2] or under the mistaken impression that it is useless,[3] parol evidence of his declarations, his capacity or his conduct may be adduced in order to show that the necessary intention to revoke was wanting.

Intention to revoke.

The doctrine of dependent relative revocation operates where the act of destruction is conditional upon an assumption that is in fact false,[4] as for example that a new will is valid;[5] that the effect is to revive a former will;[6] or that the beneficiary under the destroyed will is entitled to equal benefits if the testator dies intestate.[7]

Doctrine of dependent relative revocation.

" If the truth of a particular fact is a condition of the destruction, and
" the fact turns out not to be true, there is no revocation."

These strict rules concerning revocation do not apply to the privileged will of the soldier, sailor or airman. For instance, a soldier before proceeding to South Africa on active service left his will with his fiancée, but in consequence of certain statements made as to her conduct wrote from that country instructing her to hand the will to his sister, which she did. Later, in accordance with his written request, the sister burnt the will and it was held that this was a sufficient revocation notwithstanding that the destruction did not take place in the testator's presence.[8]

Revocation by soldiers, sailors and airmen.

Revival of Will. It is provided by the Wills Act, 1837, that a will which has been revoked cannot be revived unless the testator re-executes it with the proper formalities, or unless he executes a codicil showing an intention to revive the will.[9] The object of this enactment was to abolish implied revivals, for under the law prior to 1837 a revoked will was presumed to be revived if the will which effected the revocation was itself later revoked. Now, however, the intention to revive the revoked will must appear on the face of the later instrument, either by express words referring to a will as revoked and importing an intention to revive the same, or by some expression conveying to the mind of the court with reasonable certainty the existence of the intention.[10]

Intention to revive.

---

[1] *In the Goods of Brassington,* [1901] P. 1.
[2] *In the Goods of Hine,* [1893] P. 282.
[3] *Beardsley* v. *Lacey* (1897), 78 L. T. 25 ; *In the Estate of Southerden, Adams* v. *Southerden,* [1925] P. 177.
[4] *Re Feis, Guillioume* v. *Ritz-Remorf,* [1964] Ch. 106; [1963] 3 All E. R. 303.
[5] *Onions* v. *Tyrer* (1716), 1 P. Wms. 343, 345.
[6] *Powell* v. *Powell* (1866), L. R. 1 P. & D. 209; *In the Estate of Bridge-water,* [1965] 1 All E. R. 717; [1965] 1 W. L. R. 416.
[7] *In the Estate of Southerden, Adams* v. *Southerden,* [1925] P. 177.
[8] *In the Estate of Gossage, Wood* v. *Gossage* [1921] P. 194; [1921] All E. R. Rep. 107.   [9] Wills Act, 1837 s. 22.
[10] *In the Goods of Steele* (1868), L. R. 1 P. & D. 575 ; *Goldie* v. *Adam,* [1938] P. 85 ; [1938] 1 All E. R. 586.

CHAPTER II.

INTESTACY.

SUMMARY.

SECTION I. APPOINTMENT OF THE ADMINISTRATOR AND HIS GENERAL POWERS.

Grant of administration. The administration of the estate of an intestate and of that of a person who has died testate is the same up to the moment when the division of the property among the beneficiaries is reached, the only material difference being that, as there is no will under which executors have been appointed, the court is itself obliged to appoint personal representatives for the purposes of administration. When it does this, it is said to grant administration, or more fully, to grant letters of administration, and the personal representative to whom the grant is made is called an administrator.

The property of the deceased, both real and personal, passes to an administrator upon his appointment by the court to the same extent as it passes to an executor, but in the interval between the death of the deceased and the appointment of an administrator both the real and personal estate of the deceased vests in the Probate Judge until administration is granted.[1]

To whom grant made. **Who may be appointed Administrators.** The first question that requires consideration is this : To what persons will

---

[1] Administration of Estates Act, 1925, s. 9.

the court grant letters of administration? The matter lies within its discretion, but the Judicature Act, 1925,[1] as amended by the Administration of Justice Act, 1928,[2] contains somewhat detailed provisions for the guidance of the court in the exercise of its discretion.

Position after 1925.

After prescribing in general that the court shall have regard to the rights of all persons interested in the real and personal estate or the proceeds of sale thereof, the Act provides that where the deceased died wholly intestate as to his real and personal estate,

> " administration shall, unless by reason of the insolvency of the
> " estate or other special circumstances the court thinks it expedient
> " to grant administration to some other person, be granted to some
> " one or more of the persons interested in the residuary estate of the
> " deceased, if they make an application for the purpose." [3]

Where land has been settled by the intestate in his lifetime, administration thereof must be granted to the trustees of the settlement if they are willing to act.[4] Representation is not to be granted to more than four persons in regard to the same property, and if any beneficiary is an infant, administration must be granted either to a trust corporation (with or without an individual) or to not less than two individuals.[5]

The court may limit its grant in any way it considers to be proper. For instance, it may grant representation in respect of the realty separately from the personalty, or in respect of a trust estate alone, or in respect of the realty alone if there is no personal estate.[6]

Administrator's Bond. A person to whom letters of administration are granted is obliged to give a bond, called an *administrator's bond*, to the principal probate registrar.[7] A bond is a deed which binds the obligor to pay a certain sum of money, provided however that the obligation shall be void if certain conditions are fulfilled by him. The condition contained in a bond given by an administrator is that he shall

Administrator's bond.

    1. when lawfully called upon, make an inventory of the estate
        which passes to him ;

---

[1] S. 162.   [2] S. 9.

[3] It is now provided by the Non-Contentious Probate Rules, 1954, r. 21, that the order in priority of rights to a grant of administration shall be as follows :—(1) Husband or wife ; (2) children, or other issue of deceased taking *per stirpes* ; (3) father or mother ; (4) brothers and sisters of the whole blood, or the issue of deceased brothers and sisters of the whole blood taking *per stirpes* ; (5) brothers and sisters of the half blood, or the issue of deceased brothers and sisters of the half blood taking *per stirpes* ; (6) grand-parents ; (7) uncles and aunts of the whole blood, or the issue of deceased uncles and aunts of the whole blood taking *per stirpes* ; (8) uncles and aunts of the half blood, or the issue of deceased uncles and aunts of the half blood taking *per stirpes* ; (9) the Crown ; (10) creditors. As to the discretion of the Court to grant administration to some other person, see *In the Goods of Edwards-Taylor*, [1951] P. 24.

[4] Supreme Court of Judicature (Consolidation) Act, 1925, s. 162 (1) (b).

[5] *Ibid.*, s. 160.   [6] *Ibid.*, s. 155.   [7] *Ibid.*, s. 167 (1).

2. well and truly administer the estate ;

3. render a just account of the administration whenever required by law to do so ; and

4. deliver up the letters of administration if a will is produced for probate.

It is essential under the Act of 1925 that there should be sureties to the bond, but probate rules have been made for dispensing with them when administration is granted to a trust corporation and in certain other cases.[1]

Title of an Administrator. An administrator, unlike an executor, derives his title solely from the grant of letters, and until he receives the grant he is not entitled to deal with the estate of the deceased. But in order that no wrong may go without a remedy, it has been the rule from the earliest times that the administrator's title upon his appointment relates back to the death of the intestate, so that he may maintain trespass or trover against a wrongdoer who has interfered with the estate of the deceased between the death and the grant of administration.[2] Although this rule is more often of importance in the case of goods, it applies equally to wrongs committed against land.[3]

The death of an administrator before the administration has begun or been completed necessitates the appointment of another person, for the office does not devolve on death as does that of an executor.[4]

Relation back of administrator's title.

Powers of an Administrator. An administrator, as we have said, has the same powers with regard to the administration of the estate as are possessed by executors, but a new departure was made by the Administration of Estates Act, 1925, by vesting in him a statutory trust for sale. This is required because the property of the intestate is usually distributable in shares among the beneficial successors, and it has the added advantage of enabling the administrator to make an overriding conveyance of land. It is expressly enacted that upon the death of a person intestate his real and personal estate shall be held by his personal representatives

Administrator holds on trust for sale.

" (*a*) as to the real estate upon trust to sell the same ; and
" (*b*) as to the personal estate upon trust to call in, sell and convert
"into money such part thereof as may not consist of
"money." [5]

The administrator, however, has full power to postpone the sale for such period as he may think proper. He is not to sell any reversionary interest until it falls into possession unless there is

---

[1] Supreme Court of Judicature (Consolidation) Act, 1925, s. 167 ; Non-Contentious Probate Rules, 1954, r. 38 (3).
[2] *Tharpe* v. *Stallwood* (1843), 12 L. J. (N.S.) C. P. 241.
[3] *In the Goods of Pryse*, [1904] P. 301.　　　[4] *Supra*, pp. 767-8.
[5] Administration of Estates Act, 1925, 31 (1).

some special reason to justify the sale, neither is he to sell personal chattels unless they are required for purposes of administration owing to a deficiency of other assets, or unless there is some other special reason for the sale.[1]

Personal chattels means carriages, horses,[2] stable furniture and effects (not used for business purposes),[3] garden effects, domestic animals, plate, linen, china, glass, books, pictures, prints, furniture, jewellery,[4] articles of household or personal use or ornament, wines, liquors and consumable stores ; but the term does not include any chattels used at the death of the intestate for business purposes, nor money or securities for money.[5]

The administrator must use the money arising from the sale, and also any ready money that the intestate may have left, in discharging the funeral, testamentary and administration expenses, and the debts due from the estate.[6] During the minority of any person beneficially entitled and pending the final distribution of the estate the administrator may invest in trustee securities so much of the money as is not required for the payment of debts.[7]

Residuary
estate of
intestate.

After all the debts have been paid, the residue of the money arising from sale and any investments which may have been made, and any property which may have been retained unsold, are together called *the residuary estate of the intestate*.[8] It is this estate that is distributed among the persons who are entitled to succeed to the property of the intestate.

SECTION II. DISTRIBUTION OF THE RESIDUARY ESTATE OF THE INTESTATE.

SUMMARY

(1) INTRODUCTORY NOTE.

Assimilation of Real to Personal Property. A far-reaching reform of the law governing the beneficial distribution of the property of an intestate dying after 1925 was effected by the Administration of Estates Act, 1925. Before 1926 the destination

Rules of
descent now
changed.

---

[1] Administration of Estates Act, 1925, s. 33 (1).
[2] *In re Hutchinson*, [1955] Ch. 255 ; [1955] 1 All E. R. 689.
[3] For meaning of " business " see *Re Ogilby*, [1943] Ch. 288 ; [1942] 1 All E. R. 524.
[4] *Re Whitby, Public Trustee* v. *Whitby*, [1944] Ch. 210 ; [1944] 1 All E. R. 299.
[5] Administration of Estates Act, 1925, s. 55 (1) (x).
[6] *Ibid.*, s. 33 (2).   [7] *Ibid.* s. 33 (3).
[8] Administration of Estates Act, 1925, s. 33 (4).

of the property varied according as it consisted of freehold estates of inheritance or of leaseholds and chattels personal. The rules of descent relating to the fee simple and the fee tail depended partly upon the common law and partly upon statute ; the rules by which leaseholds and chattels personal were distributed depended entirely upon statutes, the chief of which were the Statutes of Distribution of 1670 and 1685. The Administration of Estates Act, 1925, however, abolished the law of descent so far as it related to the fee simple, and introduced a new scheme of distribution which applies both to realty and to personalty. This scheme is not the same as that laid down for chattels by the Statutes of Distribution. Those statutes have been swept away, and a fresh start has been made. Unfortunately, however, there are four reasons why conveyancers must still acquaint themselves with the canons of descent in respect of the fee simple that prevailed before 1926.

Four reasons why knowledge of old rules still essential.

Old titles.

The investigation of title upon the sale of land may disclose the intestacy of a former owner. The vendor or some predecessor in title may have claimed the estate as heir of that intestate, and it will therefore be necessary for the purchaser to ascertain who was entitled under the old rules to succeed to the estate, and to satisfy himself that the right person did succeed.

Entailed interests.

Secondly, the persons who are entitled to succeed to an entailed interest which has neither been barred nor devised by its owner must be ascertained according to the old rules of descent.[1]

Heirs taking by purchase.

Thirdly, the Law of Property Act, 1925, provides as follows [2] :—

A limitation of real or personal property in favour of the heir, either general or special, of a deceased person which, if limited in respect of freehold land before the commencement of this Act, would have conferred on the heir an estate in the land by purchase, shall operate to confer a corresponding *equitable* interest in the property on the person who would, *if the general law in force immediately before such commencement had remained unaffected*, have answered the description of the heir, either general or special, of the deceased in respect of his freehold land, either at the death of the deceased or at the time named in the limitation, as the case may require.

The object of this provision is clear. A testator who has no wish to die intestate, yet who desires that his land shall go to the person who will be his heir-at-law, may make a will devising his land to his heir. The effect of this is that the heir, when ascertained according to the rules of intestate

---

[1] *Supra*, p. 160–1.
[2] Law of Property Act, 1925, s. 132.

succession, takes the land as devisee, *i.e.* as a purchaser and not by title of descent.[1] A will in these terms before 1926 was convenient and reasonable, for in every case but one the heir was a single person. The legislation of 1925, however, abolished heirship except for entailed interests, and introduced a system under which the fee simple is sold and the proceeds distributed among near relatives. The effect of the present enactment is, therefore, that a testator who is so minded may still devise land to his heir, and that if he does so the devisee shall be ascertained according to the old law of descent. When ascertained he takes the fee simple in the case of inheritable freeholds, and the absolute ownership of personalty.

Fourthly, it is provided that in certain cases the property of a person suffering from mental disorder within the meaning of the Mental Health Act, 1959, who dies intestate shall descend according to the old rules.[2] Mental patient's property

(2) THE DESCENT OF THE FEE SIMPLE BEFORE 1926.

Rule 1. Descent must be traced from the last purchaser.[3] We have seen in dealing with entailed interests[4] that this rule obliges us to look for the heir of the person who last took the land otherwise than by descent, escheat, partition or enclosure; in other words, by act of parties, not by operation of law. This rule persisted till 1926, save only for a modification in 1859 by Lord St. Leonards Act, which provided that if there are no heirs of the last purchaser, the descent shall be traced from the person who was last *entitled* to the land, although he may not have been a *purchaser*. If, for instance, Meaning of " purchaser."

> a purchaser dies intestate leaving a widow and one son, but no other relative, the son becomes *entitled* by descent to take the land. If the son dies intestate and a bachelor, the land would, apart from this statutory rule, escheat to the Crown. But since the statute permits the heir of the person last entitled (that is, the son) to take, the land may go to the son's mother, because, although she is not of the blood of her husband, the last purchaser, she *is* of the blood of the son.[5]

Rule 2. Males have a prior right to females. The fee simple passes in the first place to the lineal descendants of the purchaser, and the male are preferred to the female descendants. Priority of males.

---

[1] Inheritance Act, 1833, ss. 3, 4.
[2] Administration of Estates Act, 1925, s. 51 (2), as amended by the Mental Health Act, 1959, Sch. 8.
[3] Inheritance Act, 1833, ss. 1, 2.   [4] *Supra*, p. 160.
[5] And see *Bradley* v. *McAtamney*, [1936] N. I. 74.

Primogeni-
ture and
coparcenary.

Rule 3. Primogeniture. If there are several males and females in equal degree, the eldest male takes to the exclusion of all other persons. If, for instance, the intestate dies leaving two sons and two daughters, the eldest son takes the whole of the land. If, however, there are no male descendants, then the female descendants who are in equal degree share the land equally as coparceners.

Representa-
tion.

Rule 4. Representation. Succession is *per stirpes*, so that the lineal descendants of a deceased child who, had he lived, would have been heir, stand in the place of that child. If, for instance, the purchaser has two sons and dies leaving his younger son alone alive, the estate will pass to the eldest son of his deceased elder son and not to his living younger son.

Ancestral
line.

Rule 5. Lineal ancestors take after lineal descend-ants.[1] The rule prior to the Inheritance Act, 1833, was that a fief could not ascend, but that Act provides that if there are no lineal descendants of the purchaser, or if they have all failed, the estate shall go to the nearest lineal ancestor.

Male
paternal
ancestors.

Rule 6. The paternal ancestors are preferred to the maternal.[2] The effect of this rule and the preceding one is that if there are no lineal descendants of the purchaser, the land will go to the nearest male ancestor or, if he is dead leaving issue, then to the issue representing the ancestor under rule 4. Thus the nearest lineal ancestor is the father of the intestate, or, if the father is dead, the eldest son of the father. A father therefore is a nearer heir than a brother. But in searching for the heir among the paternal ancestors and their issue, the rule is that preference must be given to the whole blood as against the half blood.[3]

Half blood
on male side.

Before the Inheritance Act, 1833, the half blood were excluded altogether, but that Act provided that where the common ancestor is a male (*i.e.* where a man has married two wives), a relative by half blood ranks next after a relative in the same degree of the whole blood and his or her issue. If, for instance,

> the father of a purchaser who dies without descendants married Emma and had by her the purchaser and a sister Julia, and then married Arabella, by whom he had John, the effect of the statutory rule is that, while Julia and her issue take first, the estate passes to John if they fail.

If the purchaser's father is dead and the father's issue non-existent or extinct, recourse is next had to the father's father and his issue, and so on up through the male *paternal* ancestors ; and when the males in this class are exhausted they are followed by the females.

---

[1] Inheritance Act, 1833, s. 6.   [2] *Ibid.*, ss. 7, 8.
[3] *Ibid.*, s. 9.

If there is no reasonable likelihood of ascertaining that there Female
paternal
ancestors. are descendants from the male paternal ancestors still alive,[1] then the next persons who are entitled, and who must be sought for, are the female paternal ancestors and their descendants.[2]   But the search for the heir within this class is not the same as in the case of the male paternal ancestors.   We have seen that after the purchaser's descendants are exhausted, we go to the male paternal ancestors, and that we start with the father and work upwards. In other words, we go from the father to the grandfather and then to the great-grandfather and so on.   But the Inheritance Act provides that in dealing with the female paternal ancestors we start with the mother of the remotest male *paternal* ancestor known and her descendants.

Suppose, for instance, that the purchaser's father, grand-father and great-grandfather are dead, and their descendants extinct.   The next person whose descendants are entitled is the great-great-grandfather.   If, however, he is not known, then we take the last paternal ancestor who *is* known, *i.e.* the great-grandfather, and look for the descendants of his mother.

That is the meaning of the enactment that [3]

" Where there shall be a failure of male paternal ancestors of the
" person from whom the descendant is to be traced and their de-
" scendants, the mother of his more remote male paternal ancestor,
" or her descendants, shall be the heir or heirs of such person, in
" preference to the mother of a less remote male paternal ancestor,
" or her descendants."

If there are no descendants of the great-grandfather's mother, the next persons entitled are the descendants of the grandfather's mother, then the grandmother and her descendants, and lastly the mother and her descendants.

Having exhausted the male and female paternal ancestors, the Male and
female
maternal
ancestors. next step is to start with the mother and work up the male and down the female line, as in the case of the father.

When the person entitled to succeed is a female ancestor who is dead, the estate will descend to her issue as representing her.

If, for instance,

the only ancestor with issue is the purchaser's mother, and she is dead having left a child by another husband than the father of the purchaser, that child will be entitled to take.   The child, of course, is a relative of the half blood to the purchaser.

---

[1] *Greaves* v. *Greenwood* (1877), 2 Ex. D. 289.
[2] Inheritance Act, 1833, s. 7.
[3] *Ibid.*, s. 8. For this curious rule, said to be justified by feudal principles, but which has given rise to no decision, see Blackstone, vol. ii. p. 238.

We have seen that where the common ancestor is a male, the relatives of the half blood take after the relatives of the same degree of the whole blood. Where, however, as in the present case, the common ancestor is a female, *i.e.* where the purchaser's *mother* has married twice, it is enacted that the relatives of the half blood shall take next after the female ancestor.[1]

Curtesy.

Curtesy and Dower. It must be remembered that the above rules of descent were subject, under the old law, to the respective rights of a surviving husband and a surviving wife. If a wife died intestate, the husband was entitled, in certain circumstances, to an estate by the curtesy in her freeholds of inheritance. This species of estate has already been discussed.[2]

Dower.

Similarly, when a husband died having at some time been solely seised of a fee simple or an estate tail, his surviving wife became entitled by way of dower to a life estate in one-third of the land. In order to establish this right, however, she must have been able to show

1. that issue capable of inheriting the land *might* have been born, and

2. that she had not been expressly deprived of the right to her third.

1. As regards the first point, she must have shown that she herself might have had a child capable of inheriting the land out of which she claimed dower. Thus :

   if land was settled on a husband and his heirs begotten on the body of X., X. was dowable even though the husband died childless ; but if X. died and the husband married Y., the latter had no claim to dower, for she could never have had children capable of inheriting the land in accordance with the terms of the original limitation.

2. As to the second point, the rule after the Dower Act, 1833, was that a husband could deprive his wife either expressly or by implication of her right to dower, and the law was that no such right existed if the husband had disposed of the estate by deed or will ;[3] if he expressly stated in a deed or will that she was not to have dower ;[4] if he devised to her other land out of which she was not dowable ;[5] or if, as for instance under a settlement, she accepted a jointure. Thus in effect it was only where a husband died intestate actually seised of an unbarred interest in tail or of a fee simple estate that a question of dower arose.

---

[1] Inheritance Act, 1833, s. 9.   [2] *Supra*, p. 161.
[3] Dower Act, 1833, s. 4
[4] *Ibid.*, s. 6.   [5] *Ibid.*, s. 7.

(3) THE MODERN RULES OF DISTRIBUTION.

The Administration of Estates Act, 1925, prepared the way for new rules of distribution by abolishing with regard to the real and personal estate of persons dying on or after January 1, 1926, all the former rules of descent and distribution. Moreover, it abolished the husband's curtesy, the widow's dower, and all customary modes of descent, such as gavelkind and borough-English, that formerly obtained in any part of the country. Escheat, whether to the Crown or to a mesne lord, was also abolished and replaced by the right of Crown to take all undistributed property as *bona vacantia*.[1]

Abolition of old rules.

On the death of a person intestate, his estate, as we have seen, is held by his personal representatives upon trust

    (*a*) to sell the real estate, and

    (*b*) to sell such part of the personal estate as does not consist of money,

with power to postpone the sale for so long as may seem fit.[2]

The Act then provided that the residuary estate (*i.e.* the residue after payment of debts of the proceeds of sale and any investments by which they are represented, including any part of the estate still unsold)[3] should be distributed according to certain rules which varied according as the intestate left or did not leave a surviving spouse. Where a surviving spouse is left, however, these rules have been radically altered by the Intestates' Estates Act, 1952, and the present position is as follows.

1. Where the Intestate leaves a Surviving Spouse.—If it is uncertain which spouse survived the other the statutory rule that the younger survived does not apply. The estate of each is distributed separately.[4] If a wife dies intestate after a decree of judicial separation and whilst the separation is still continuing, any property acquired by her after the decree devolves as if her husband were dead.[5]

Intestate leaves issue.

(1) *If the intestate also leaves issue*, the surviving spouse takes

    (*a*) all the personal chattels absolutely,[6]

    (*b*) a fixed net sum of £8,750 (or such larger sum as may from time to time be fixed by the Lord Chancellor), free of

---

[1] Administration of Estates Act, 1925, s. 45. Certain of the old rules, of course, still apply to the entailed interest, *supra*, p. 161. Curtesy is still possible in the case of an entailed interest not disposed of by will.

[2] Administration of Estates Act, 1925, s. 33 (1); *supra*, p. 786.

[3] *Ibid.*, s. 33 (4).

[4] Intestates' Estates Act, 1952, s. 1 (4).

[5] Matrimonial Causes Act, 1950, s. 21 (*a*).

[6] For definition, see *supra*, p. 787.

death duties with interest thereon at the rate of 4 per cent. from the date of death;[1]

(*c*) a life interest in half the residue of the estate.

The other half of the residue and the reversion on the life interest is held upon the statutory trusts for the issue.[2]

The evidence given to the Morton Committee shows that 87 per cent. of the estates of all persons, whether dying testate or intestate, are under £5,000 in value, and the proportion is no doubt even higher in the case of intestacies. In practically all cases, therefore, the whole estate will pass to the widow or widower and the rights of the issue will seldom mature.

No issue, but a parent or brother or sister.

(2) *If the intestate leaves no issue*, but leaves one or more of the following, namely, a parent, a brother or sister of the whole blood or issue of such brother or sister, the surviving spouse takes :—

(*a*) the personal chattels absolutely ;

(*b*) £30,000 (or such larger sum as may from time to time be fixed by the Lord Chancellor), free of death duties with an interest at 4 per cent. from the date of death;

(*c*) one-half of the residue absolutely.

The other half of the residue goes to the parents absolutely or, if there is no surviving parent, to the brothers and sisters or their issue upon the statutory trusts.[3]

It must be observed that where, after the making of an adoption order, the adopter or the adopted person or any other person dies intestate, his or her real or personal property (other than an entailed interest) devolves as if the adopted person were the child of the adopter born in lawful wedlock.[4]

No issue, parents or brothers and sisters.

(3) If the intestate leaves *no issue, no parents, and no brothers or sisters of the whole blood or their issue*, the surviving spouse takes the whole estate absolutely to the exclusion of all other relatives.[5] Thus where there is a surviving spouse, the brothers and sisters of the half-blood are entirely excluded.

Redemption of life interest.

We have seen that where the intestate leaves issue, the surviving spouse takes a life interest in one-half of what is left of the estate after deduction of the personal chattels and £7,500. The existence of this life interest precludes a final distribution of the estate, and in most cases the survivor prefers to receive a lump sum. The Act, therefore, provides that if the surviving spouse so elects the personal representatives must redeem the life interest by paying

---

[1] Administration of Estates Act, 1925, s. 46 (1), as amended by Intestates' Estates Act, 1952, s. 1 and by Family Provision Act, 1966, s. 1 (1) (a).
[2] Intestates' Estates Act, 1952, s. 1 (2), as amended by Family Provision Act, 1966, s. 1. For the rights of the issue, see *infra*, pp. 798–9.
[3] *Ibid.*, s. 1 (2) as amended by Family Provision Act, 1966, s. 1 (1) (b).
[4] Adoption Act, 1958, ss. 16 (1), 17 (1).
[5] Intestates' Estates Act, 1952, s. 1 (2).

its capital value to the tenant for life.[1] Thus the initiative lies with the surviving spouse, but the election must be made within twelve months from the date on which representation is first taken out, unless the court extends the period on the ground that it will operate unfairly.[2] Once made, it cannot be revoked without the consent of the personal representatives.[3] Owing to the difficulty of valuing reversionary interests, it is provided that a demand for redemption can be made only in respect of property to which the intestate was entitled in possession.[4]

The Administration of Estates Act, 1925, empowers a personal representative to appropriate any part of the estate of the deceased in its actual condition or state of investment in or towards satisfaction of any share or interest in the estate to which a beneficiary may be entitled.[5] Thus, for example, an investment held by the intestate at the time of his death may be allocated to his widow in part satisfaction of her right to £7,500. The consent of any beneficiary who is absolutely and beneficially entitled in possession must first be obtained.[6]

Rights of surviving spouse as respects the matrimonial home.

This power of appropriation has been extended to include the matrimonial home. The Intestate Estates Act, 1952, provides that

> where the residuary estate comprises an interest in a dwelling-house in which the *surviving* husband or wife was resident at the time of the intestate's death, the surviving spouse may *require* the personal representative to appropriate the house in or towards satisfaction of any *absolute* interest of the survivor in the estate.[7]

This right is personal to the survivor and is not exercisable after his or her death.[8] If the house is worth more than the interest to which the survivor is entitled, it may be appropriated upon payment in cash of the balance.[9]

The expression " dwelling-house " includes part of a building that at the time of the intestate's death was used as a separate dwelling.[10] In the following four cases, however, the right of the survivor is not enforceable unless an application is made to the court and the court is satisfied that the appropriation is not likely to diminish the value of assets in the residuary estate (other than the interest in the dwelling-house) or to make them more difficult to dispose of, namely where—

Meaning of " dwelling-house."

(a) the dwelling-house is part of a building the whole of which is comprised in the residuary estate ; or

---

[1] Administration of Estates Act, 1925, s. 47A (this section was added by Intestates' Estates Act, 1952, Sched. 1). For rules upon which the capital value must be calculated, see s. 47 A (2).

[2] *Ibid.*, s. 47 A (5). [3] *Ibid.*, s. 47 A (6).

[4] *Ibid.*, s. 47 A (3).

[5] Administration of Estates Act, 1925. s. 41. [6] *Ibid.*, s. 41 (1) (ii) (a).

[7] Intestates' Estates Act, 1952, 2nd Sched., para. 1 (1). Although this power of appropriation is exercisable only in satisfaction of an " absolute interest," the latter expression includes a life interest which the survivor has elected to have redeemed, *ibid.*, para. 1 (4).

[8] *Ibid.*, s. 3 (1) (b). [9] *Ibid.*, s. 5 (2). [10] *Ibid.*, para. 1 (5).

(*b*) the dwelling-house is held with agricultural land, an interest in which is comprised in the residuary estate ; or

(*c*) the whole or part of the dwelling-house was used as a hotel or lodging-house at the time of intestate's death ; or

(*d*) part of it was at the time used for purposes other than domestic purposes.[1]

There is no right to the appropriation if the house was held by the intestate on a lease due to end within two years of his or her death or on a lease, such as one from year to year, that the landlord can determine by a notice given within two years after the death.[2]

Time within which claim must be made.

The right must be claimed within twelve months after representation has first been taken out[3] and it must be exercised by a written notification to the personal representatives, or, where there are two or more representatives of whom one is the claimant, to all of them.[4] During this period of twelve months the house may not be sold without the written consent of the surviving spouse, unless there is an insufficiency of assets for the payment of debts.[5] If a sale is effected in violation of this prohibition, however, no right against the purchaser is conferred upon the surviving spouse.[6]

The requirement of a written notice to the representative is expressly excluded where the surviving spouse is the sole personal representative, for a person can scarcely demand of himself that he shall effect a certain transaction for his own benefit.[7] Unfortunately, however, it is not clear whether a surviving spouse who is also the sole personal representative can exercise this right of appropriation under the Act of 1952. It may be that his only course is to proceed under section 41 of the Administration of Estates Act, 1925.[8]

2. Where the intestate leaves no surviving spouse. The rules for the distribution of the residuary estate in this event are laid down by the Administration of Estates Act, 1925, and are unaffected by the Act of 1952.

They prescribe that the estate shall be distributed among the relatives of the deceased according to the following scheme :—

(1) If the intestate leaves issue the residuary estate is held on the *statutory trusts* for the issue.[9]

---

[1] Intestates' Estates Act, 1952, 2nd Sched. para. 2.
[2] *Ibid.*, 2nd Sched. para. 1 (2).   [3] *Ibid.*, para. 3. (1) (*a*).
[4] *Ibid.*, para. 3 (1) (*c*).   [5] *Ibid.*, para. 4 (1).
[6] *Ibid.*, para. 4 (5).   [7] *Ibid.*, para. 3 (1) (*c*).
[8] *Supra*, p. 795; see 16 *The Conveyancer*, pp. 417–19.
[9] Administration of Estates Act, 1925, s. 46 (1) (ii).

The word " issue " means the legitimate or legitimated lineal descendants of the intestate. It does not include illegitimate children. There is, however, one exception to this, for if the mother of an illegitimate child dies intestate without leaving any legitimate issue, the child or, if he is dead, his issue, is entitled to take any interest in her real or personal property (except an entailed interest), to which he would have been entitled had he been born legitimate.[1]

Meaning of " issue."

Under this first rule, then, the beneficiaries are the surviving children and the descendants of children who predeceased the intestate. Such descendants represent the deceased child and take among themselves the exact share that the child would have taken had he survived the intestate. This taking by representation is called taking *per stirpes*—according to the roots.

Doctrine of representation.

"All the branches inherit the same share that their root, whom " they represent, would have done." [2]

If, for instance, the intestate is survived by two children and by four grandchildren, the offspring of a daughter who predeceased him, the children each take one-third of the estate and the remaining third is divisible equally between the four grandchildren.

(2) If the deceased leaves no issue but is survived by a parent or parents, his father and mother take the whole estate absolutely in equal shares.[3] If only one parent survives, the whole estate is held in trust for that parent absolutely.[4]

In the case of an illegitimate intestate the common law rule is that his only heirs are his lineal descendants, for an illegitimate having no legal ancestor, can have no collateral relatives.[5] This rule has, however, been modified by statute and now the surviving mother is entitled to take any interest in the realty or personalty of the intestate to which she would have been entitled if the intestate had been born legitimate and she had been the only surviving relative.[6] Thus, the mother takes absolutely the residuary estate of a bastard who dies without issue, subject, of course, to the rights of his spouse. If he is survived neither by his spouse nor by his mother, the estate passes to the Crown as *bona vacantia*.

Illegitimate intestate.

(3) If the intestate leaves no issue or parent, the following persons " living at the death of the intestate " are entitled in the following order :— [7]

---

[1] Legitimacy Act, 1926, ss. 4 ; 9 (3).   [2] Blackstone, vol. ii. p. 217.
[3] Administration of Estates Act, 1925, s. 46 (1) (iii).
[4] *Ibid.*, s. 46 (1) (iv).
[5] Blackstone, vol. ii. p. 249. But where he is a mental patient see *Re. T. B.*, [1966] 3 All E. R. 509; [1967] 2 W. L. R. 15.
[6] Legitimacy Act, 1926, s. 9 (2).
[7] Administration of Estates Act, 1925, s. 46 (1) (v).

(a) His brothers and sisters of the whole blood, subject to the statutory trusts ; failing these

(b) his brothers and sisters of the half-blood, subject to the statutory trusts ; failing these

(c) his grandparents ; failing these

(d) his uncles and aunts of the whole blood, subject to the statutory trusts ; failing these

(e) his uncles and aunts of the half-blood, subject to the statutory trusts.

If the deceased leaves none of the relatives just enumerated and no issue or surviving spouse, his estate belongs to the Crown or to the Duchy of Lancaster or Cornwall, as the case may be, as *bona vacantia* and in lieu of any right to escheat.

Representation.
The words " living at the death of the intestate " in the opening statement of the enumeration do not exclude the issue of a brother, sister, uncle or aunt who predeceased him, for under the doctrine of representation they take the share that their parent would have taken had he survived the intestate.[1]

Distant relatives excluded.
The list of beneficiaries, it will be noticed, does not include distant relatives. Since the oldest ancestor entitled is the grandparent, the claimant must at least have descended from him or her, and it follows that the most remote relative entitled to a share is a first cousin and his issue, *i.e.* first cousins once, twice or further removed. Thus, second cousins are excluded.

The statutory trusts.
The statutory trusts. Whenever the property is distributable among a class of persons the members of which may be indefinite in number and some of them under age, the Act provides that it shall be held for them on the *statutory trusts*.[2] This is so in the case of issue, brothers, sisters, uncles and aunts, but not in the case of parents or grandparents.

Statutory trusts for the issue.
The statutory trusts for the issue mean that the property is held in trust in equal shares for the children of the intestate alive at his death who attain the age of twenty-one years or who, whether male or female, marry under that age. Thus the children take *per capita*. But if a child predeceases the intestate leaving issue alive at the death of the intestate, such issue as attain twenty-one or marry represent their parent and take his share *per stirpes*.[3]

Position during infancy of a beneficiary.
The result is that an infant, whether a child or more remote issue, takes only a contingent share that will not vest until marriage or the attainment of majority. In the meantime, however, the personal representatives may, at their sole discretion, apply the

---

[1] Administration of Estates Act, 1925, ss. 47 (1) (i) ; 47 (3).
[2] Unfortunately the same expression in used by the Law of Property Act, 1925, in the entirely different context of tenancies in common and joint tenancies, see *supra*, p. 313.
[3] Administration of Estates Act, 1925, s. 47 (1).

whole or part of the income of the property to which the infant is contingently entitled for or towards his maintenance, education or benefit.[1] They may also apply the capital for his advancement to an amount not exceeding one-half of his presumptive share, but this must be brought into account when he becomes entitled to a vested interest at his majority or marriage.[2] Subject to the exercise of these powers, the personal representatives must accumulate the income at compound interest and hold the accumulation in trust for the infant.[3] The personal representatives may also permit any infant contingently entitled to have the use and enjoyment of any personal chattels in such manner and subject to such conditions (if any) as they may consider reasonable, and without being liable to account for any consequential loss.[4]

The operation of the statutory trusts may be elucidated by a simple illustration. Suppose the following facts :—

The intestate had four sons, A. to D. At his death,

A. and B. are alive.

C. is dead, but he is survived by two children, C.ᵃ and C.ᵇ both over 21 years of age.

D. and his son D.ᵃ are dead, but D.ᵃ left two daughters D.ᵇ and D.ᶜ who are alive at the intestate's death, but are still infants and unmarried.

The residuary estate, therefore, is divided into fourths. A. and B. each take one-fourth ; C.ᵃ and C.ᵇ represent their father, C., and share equally the fourth that would have accrued to him had he lived ; the infants, D.ᵇ and D.ᶜ, being issue of D., are equally, but contingently, entitled to the remaining fourth part. If one of them dies in infancy and still unmarried, her share passes to her sister. While their shares remain contingent, the income may be spent on their maintenance or education and up to one-half of the capital may be employed for their advancement.

Hotchpot.—The distribution of the property among the issue, however, is subject to what is called the *hotchpot rule*, which is designed to ensure equality of distribution. The rule, failing a contrary intention, is that any money or property which the intestate in his lifetime has paid to, or settled or covenanted to settle on, a child, either by way of advancement or in view of marriage, shall be brought into account and deducted from the share which is payable to that child or to that child's issue under the intestacy.[5] If the advance was made directly to a grandchild (or remoter issue) it is not taken into account if that grandchild

---

[1] Administration of Estates Act, 1925, s. 47 (1) (ii); Trustee Act, 1925, s. 31 (1).

[2] Trustee Act, 1925, s. 32 (1).

[3] *Ibid.*, s. 31 (2).

[4] Administration of Estates Act, 1925, s. 47 (1) (iv), as added by Intestates' Estates Act, 1952, s. 4 and 1st Sched.

[5] *Ibid.*, s. 47 (1) (iii).

becomes entitled to share in the intestacy as representing his
deceased parent.

Meaning of
advance-
ment.
No absolute test can be laid down as to what constitutes an
advancement for the purposes of the rule, but its broad meaning
is a gift intended to make a permanent provision for the child—an
intention that is more readily inferred if the sum is substantial and
if it has been paid at an early stage in the life of the child.[1]   It does
not include casual payments or money given to relieve a child from
some temporary embarrassment.   JESSEL, M.R., dealt with the
matter in these words :—

" I have always understood that an advancement by way of
" portion is something given by the parent to establish the child
" in life, or to make what is called a provision for him. . . . You
" may make the provision by way of marriage portion on the
" marriage of the child.   You may make it on putting him into
" a profession or business in a variety of ways.   You may pay for
" a commission, you may buy him the goodwill of a business
" and give him stock in trade ; all these things I understand to
" be portions or provisions.   Again, if in the absence of evidence
" you find a father giving a large sum to a child in one payment,
" there is a presumption that that is intended to start him in life
" or make a provision for him ; but if a small sum is so given you
" may require evidence to show the purpose." [2]

In the case from which these words are quoted it was
held that the payment of the admission fee to an Inn of Court
was an advancement, but that the price of an outfit and the
passage money of a military officer who was going with his
regiment to India, the payment of debts incurred by an
officer in the army, and sums given to a clergyman towards
his housekeeping expenses were not advancements.

Statutory
trusts for
classes
other than
issue.
The statutory trusts for brothers, sisters, uncles and aunts are
the same as those applicable to issue, except that the hotchpot rule
is excluded.[3]

If, for instance, the intestate dies unmarried leaving no
parents, but survived by a brother and a nephew, the son of
a deceased brother, his estate will be divided equally between
these two survivors, and any advancement that he may have
made in his lifetime to his deceased brother will not be
deducted from the nephew's share.

Application
of hotchpot
rule to
partial
intestacy.
Partial Intestacy.—The above rules apply to a case of
partial intestacy, which occurs where a person leaves a will disposing only of part of his property.   In these circumstances the
property that is undisposed of is distributed among the persons
in the manner and order applicable to a case of total intestacy.

---

[1] *In re Hayward, decd.*, [1957] Ch. 528; [1957] 2 All E. R. 474.
[2] *Taylor* v. *Taylor* (1875), L. R. 20 Eq. 155, 157.
[3] Administration of Estates Act, 1925, s. 47 (3); added by Intestates'
Estates Act, 1952, Sch. I.   For the interpretation of s. 47 (5), see *In re Lockwood, Atherton* v. *Brooke*, [1958] Ch. 231; [1957] 3 All E. R. 520.

There is a distinction, however, between a total and partial intestacy with regard to the hotchpot rule. The position is this :—

First, the value of any beneficial interest, other than a bequest of chattels, left by the will to the surviving spouse must be set off against the sum of £8,750 or £30,000 (as the case may be)[1] payable to that spouse under the partial intestacy.[2]

Secondly, children must account for beneficial interests given to them by the will as well as for advancements made to them in the lifetime of the deceased.[3]

Thirdly, remoter issue must account for beneficial interests left to them by the will and for advancements made to children through whom they claim, but not for advancements made to them personally by the deceased in his lifetime.[4]

The term "beneficial interest" includes a life or a lesser interest[5] and also an interest given by the testamentary exercise of a general power of appointment, but not of a special power.[6]

---

[1] *Supra,* pp. pp. 793–4.
[2] Administration of Estates Act, 1925, s. 49 (1) (*aa*) added by Intestates' Estates Act, 1952.   [3] *Ibid.,* s. 49 (1) (*a*).
[4] *Ibid.,* s. 47 (1) (iii) ; 49 (1) (*a*). For a clear table setting out the rules in respect of advancements, see 16 *The Conveyancer,* pp. 408–9.
[5] *In re Morton,* [1956] Ch. 644 ; [1956] 2 All E. R. 259.
[6] Intestates' Estates Act, 1952, s. 3 (3), amending Administration of Estates Act, 1925, s. 49.

BOOK III.

THE TRANSFER AND EXTINCTION OF ESTATES AND INTERESTS.

PART V.

EXTINCTION OF ESTATES AND INTERESTS.

SUMMARY.

CHAPTER I.

EXTINCTION UNDER THE STATUTES OF LIMITATIONS.

SUMMARY.

SECTION I. INTRODUCTORY NOTE.

Most systems of law have realized the necessity of fixing some definite period of time within which persons who have been unlawfully dispossessed of their land must prosecute their claims. It is, no doubt, an injustice that after this period has elapsed the wrongdoer should be allowed to retain the land against the person whom he has ousted, but it would be an even greater injustice to the world at large if the latter were allowed after any interval of time, however, long to commence proceedings for recovery of

Necessity for Statutes of Limitations.

possession. If A., having ejected B., is allowed to remain in long and undisturbed possession of the land, the impression will grow that his title is superior to B.'s, and the public should be allowed to deal safely with him on that footing. As Lord St. Leonards remarked[1]:

> " All statutes of limitation have for their object the prevention of
> " the rearing up of claims at great distances of time when evidences
> " are lost ; and in all well regulated countries the quieting of
> " possession is held an important point of policy."

Operation of English statutes is negative.

The effect of a person remaining in possession of the land of another for the period of time fixed by law varies in different countries and in different ages. Thus the effect of *usucapio* in Roman Law was to confer a positive title to the land upon a person who had remained in possession for a certain time. Under the Statutes of Limitation which were in force in England prior to 1833 the effect of remaining in possession for the prescribed period was to bar only the remedy of the person dispossessed, not his right. His *title* remained intact, and if he came lawfully into possession of the land again, his title might prevail against the possessor.[2] Under the statutes that have been in force since 1833[3] the effect of remaining in possession for the statutory period of twelve years is still merely negative, but now in the sense that the right as well as the remedy of the person dispossessed is extinguished. The *usucapio* of Roman Law exemplified what is sometimes called acquisitive prescription in the sense that possession of another's land for a given period conferred a positive title upon the occupier, or squatter as he is familiarly described, but English law has never adopted this theory in its treatment of corporeal hereditaments and chattels, though it has done so in the case of easements and profits.

The modern Acts.

The English law relating to the period within which an action for the recovery of land must be brought was recast and simplified by the Real Property Limitation Act of 1833, and was finally consolidated and amended by the Limitation Act, 1939. Originally the period was fixed at the discretion of individual judges. Later, certain dates (such as the first coronation of Henry II) were chosen from time to time by the legislature. Then in 1623 the Statute 21 James I introduced the modern principle that actions must be brought within a fixed number of years. But even so the state of the law was unsatisfactory owing to the variety of remedies that lay for the recovery of land, and to the fact that the period of limitation varied according to the nature of the remedy adopted. An account of the old law must, however,

---

[1] *Dundee Harbour Trustees* v. *Dougall* (1852), 1 Macq. 317.
[2] Lightwood, *Possession of Land*, p. 153.
[3] Real Property Limitation Act, 1833 ; Real Property Limitation Act, 1874 ; Limitation Act, 1939.

be sought in works on legal history.[1] We will confine ourselves to describing the law as it has been established by the Limitation Act, 1939.

SECTION II. PERIOD OF LIMITATION FOR ACTIONS TO RECOVER LAND.

The Act has retained the old law by enacting that no action shall be brought to recover any land after the expiration of twelve years from the date on which the *right of action accrued* to the plaintiff, or to the person through whom he claims,[2] This limitation applies to a foreclosure action.[3]

Normal period : twelve years.

" Land " is defined in wide terms.   It includes [4]:

" corporeal hereditaments, tithes [5] (except those belonging to a " spiritual or eleemosynary corporation sole), and rentcharges, and " any legal or equitable estate or interest therein, including an " interest in the proceeds of the sale of land held upon trust for " sale, but save as aforesaid does not include any incorporeal here- " ditament."

It will be observed that although land held upon trust for sale is deemed to be money under the doctrine of conversion,[6] yet the interests of the beneficiaries in the proceeds of sale are regarded as interests in land for the purposes of limitation.

There are certain exceptional cases in which the ordinary period of twelve years is increased.

Exceptions.

Actions by the Crown.—The Crown Suits Act, 1769, generally called the *Nullum Tempus Act*, altered the ancient rule that Statutes of Limitations do not bind the Crown and pre- scribed a period of sixty years in the case of an action to recover land. This period is now reduced to thirty years,[7] and there is a general provision that the " Act shall apply to proceedings by or " against the Crown in like manner as it applies to proceedings " between subjects." [8] An action to recover land brought *against* the Crown, however, is subject to the twelve years' period.

Actions by Crown : thirty years.

Action by Corporation Sole. An action to recover land by a spiritual or an eleemosynary corporation sole, such as a bishop, dean or master of a hospital, must be brought within

Actions by corporation sole : thirty years.

---

[1] See especially Hayes, *Introduction to Conveyancing*, pp. 222 *et seq.* ; Holdsworth, *History of English Law*, vol. iv. p. 484 ; vol. vii. pp. 29 *et seq.*
[2] Limitation Act, 1939, s. 4 (3). An appointee under a special power is not deemed to claim through the appointor, s. 31 (4).
[3] *Ibid.*, s. 18 (4).   [4] *Ibid.*, 1939, s. 31 (1).
[5] This means uncommuted tithes, not tithe rentcharge. These, though rare, are occasionally found.
[6] *Supra*, p. 79.   [7] Limitation Act, 1939, s. 4 (1).
[8] *Ibid.*, s. 30 (1). This applies to proceedings by or against the Duke of Cornwall or the Duchy of Lancaster.

thirty years after the date on which the right of action accrued to the corporation or to the person through whom the corporation claims.[1]   The ordinary period of twelve years applies in the case of a corporation aggregate, such as one of the colleges of Oxford or Cambridge.

Meaning of "claiming through a person".   In the case of the Crown or a spiritual or eleemosynary corporation the position with regard to *claiming through a person* may be illustrated by examples :

> The Crown purchases from X. in 1960 land which is in the wrongful possession of a third party.

If a right of action to recover the land from the wrongful possessor accrued to X. more than twelve years before 1960, X.'s title is extinguished and the Crown acquires nothing.   If, however, X.'s right of action accrued less than twelve years before 1960, say in 1955, then the Crown can sue the wrongdoer at any time within thirty years after 1955.[2]

The reverse case arises where a person claims through the Crown or a corporation sole after a cause of action has already accrued, as for example where,

> in 1960 the Crown conveys to X. land which has been in the wrongful possession of W. P. since 1940.

The statutory rule here is that X.'s remedy against W. P. is barred either thirty years after 1940, when the cause of action accrued to the Crown, or twelve years after the cause of action accrued to himself, *whichever period expires first*.[3]   The cause of action accrued to X. by virtue of the conveyance of 1960, but nevertheless his remedy is barred in 1970.

SECTION III.   THE DATE FROM WHICH TIME BEGINS TO RUN.

SUMMARY.

Time runs from accrual of right of action.   Time begins to run against a plaintiff only from the date on which the right of action accrued to him or to the person through whom he claims.   In the case of land, as distinct from other cases

---

[1] Limitation Act, 1939, s. 4 (2).   The former period was two successive incumbencies plus six years after a third incumbent had been appointed, *or* sixty years, whichever was the longer period ;   Real Property Limitation Act, 1833, s. 29.

[2] Limitation Act, 1939, s. 4 (1), (2).   [3] *Ibid.*, s. 4 (3) proviso.

such as contract or tort, the Act lays down specific rules fixing the date at which in varying circumstances this accrual occurs. It deals separately with present interests, future interests, settled land, land held on trust for sale, tenancies and forfeiture for breach of condition.

Before dealing with these different cases, however, it is necessary to notice an overriding provision of the greatest importance. This is that time does not begin to run from the specified dates unless there is some person in adverse possession of the land. It does not run merely because the land is vacant.[1] There must be both absence of possession by the plaintiff and actual possession by the defendant.

This rule, founded on the obvious reason that a right of action cannot accrue unless there is somebody against whom it is enforceable, was well established after the Real Property Limitation Act, 1833, in the case where an *actual possessor* left possession vacant, though there was some doubt whether it applied where the land of a deceased owner remained vacant owing to the failure of the person entitled thereto to take possession. All doubts are now dispelled, for each statutory rule fixing the date at which the right of action accrues is subject to the overriding condition that there must be some person in possession of the land in whose favour time can run. This condition is enacted in the following words [2]:

> "No right of action to recover land shall be deemed to accrue
> "unless the land is in the possession of some person in whose favour
> "the period of limitation can run (hereafter in this section referred

---

[1] *M'Donnell* v. *M'Kinty* (1847), 10 I. L. R. 514 ; *Smith* v. *Lloyd* (1854), 9 Exch. 562.

[2] Limitation Act, 1939, s. 10 (1). "Adverse possession" bore a technical meaning before the Real Property Limitation Act, 1833. Before that date wrongful possession did not ripen into a claim to bar the owner's remedy unless there had been ouster of the seisin in one of five ways (for which see Carson, *Real Property Statutes*, notes to R.P.L.A., 1833, s. 2). Moreover, possession where possible was referred to a lawful title, and there were several cases where possession obviously held without title was held not to be "adverse." For instance, possession of a younger brother was possession of the heir ; possession of one co-parcener, joint tenant or tenant in common was the possession of all, unless an intention to claim the whole was expressed ; tenant for years continued to hold for lessor after the lease ended ; if a squatter was entitled to an interest in the land less in extent than that which he claimed under the statute, his possession was referred to his lawful title ; see Lightwood on Possession, pp. 159 *et seq.* Lord St. Leonards described the effect of the 1833 Act in these words : " It is perfectly settled that adverse possession is no longer necessary in the sense in which it was formerly used, but that mere possession may be and is sufficient under many circumstances to give a title adversely " : *Ely (Dean)* v. *Bliss* (1852), 2 De G. M. & G. at pp. 476–7. The effect of the Act was " to substitute for a period of adverse possession in the old sense a simple period of time calculated from the accrual of the right of action " : Preston and Newsom, *Limitation of Actions* (2nd Edn.), p. 69. So "adverse possession" is now a useful expression to describe the possession of those against whom a right of action has accrued to the owner. See generally, Smith's *Leading Cases*, vol. ii, notes to *Nepean* v. *Doe*; Lightwood on Possession, pp. 159 *et seq.*, pp. 180–1 ; Holdsworth, *History of English Law*, vol. vii. pp. 69–72, 78–9.

2D*

" to as *adverse possession*), and where . . . any such right of action
" is deemed to accrue on a certain date and no person is in adverse
" possession on that date, the right of action shall not be deemed to
" accrue unless and until adverse possession is taken of the land." [1]

Successive adverse possessors.

This general principle may be illustrated by the case where the adverse possessor (let us call him X.) fails for one reason or another to occupy for the full period of twelve years. In this connection there are four possible situations which must be considered separately.

(a) Successor of deceased adverse possessor.

(*a*) X. dies or transfers his interest to another person before the lapse of twelve years.

The principle obtaining here is that since possession is *prima facie* evidence of seisin in fee, X. holds a transmissible interest in the land. The time during which he has possessed is available to his successor in title, and therefore a purchaser or devisee who immediately follows him into possession and holds for the remainder of the twelve years acquires as good a right to the land as if he himself had been in possession for the whole period.[2]

(b) Adverse possessor leaves land vacant.

(*b*) Possession is abandoned by X. and is not retaken by another person.

After this abandonment the dispossessed person is in the same position as if he had never been deprived of possession by X. There is no one whom he can now sue. There is no need for him to perform some act or ceremony in order to rehabilitate himself. The former possession of X., as Lord MACNAGHTEN said, is not available to "some casual interloper or lucky vagrant."[3] This rule is now confirmed by the following new enactment.

" Where a right of action to recover land has accrued and there-
" after, before the right is barred, the land ceases to be in adverse
" possession, the right of action shall no longer be deemed to have
" accrued, and no fresh right of action shall be deemed to accrue
" unless and until the land is again taken into adverse possession." [4]

(c) Land left vacant by one adverse possessor is taken by another.

(*c*) Possession is abandoned by X. and *after an interval of time* is taken by Y.

It follows from what was said by Lord MACNAGHTEN and from what is now enacted, that in this case the time during which X. has occupied is not available to Y., for during a distinct and definite period there was no person against whom the person

---

[1] *Moses* v. *Lovegrove*, [1953] 2 Q. B. 533 ; [1952] 1 All E. R. 1279. The mere fact that the premises become subject to the Rent Restriction Acts, so that possession cannot be recovered without a court order, does not prevent the tenant's possession from being adverse.

[2] *Asher* v. *Whitlock* (1865), L. R. 1 Q. B. 1.

[3] *Trustees, Executors and Agency Co., Ltd.* v. *Short* (1888), 13 App. Cas. 793, at p. 798 ; explained by PARKER, J., in *Samuel Johnson and Sons, Ltd.* v. *Brock*, [1907] 2 Ch. 533, 538 ; criticized by A. D. Hargreaves, 19 *M.L.R.* p. 22, note 11.

[4] Limitation Act, 1939, s 10 (2).

ousted by X. could bring an action for the recovery of the land. Y. is not a successor in title of X., and his intrusion causes a fresh right of action to accrue in favour of the person dispossessed by X.

(*d*) X. loses possession and is followed by a succession of trespassers each claiming adversely to the others.

(d) Continuous adverse possession by several persons.

Here there is no distinct interval of time during which the possession is vacant. X., for instance, ejects V., Y. ejects X., Z. ejects Y., and is in actual possession when the statutory period of twelve years has run from the time of V.'s ejectment. Who is entitled to succeed in an action to recover the land ? [1] Objection may be taken to the title of each of these persons, for V. has been out of possession for more than twelve years, and yet none of the trespassers has been in possession for that period. Nevertheless, V. is barred.

" A *continuous* adverse possession for the statutory period, though
" by a succession of persons not claiming under one another, does,
" in my opinion, bar the true owner." [2]

As for the trespassers, something might be said by the moralist for the earliest possessor, also for the one who has possessed for the longest period, and again for the latest possessor,[3] but it is clear that these conflicting claims must be decided in accordance with the general principle that possession is evidence of title.[4] X., while in possession, is ejected by Y. His possession, therefore, entitles him to recover the land from the wrongdoer, Y. If he takes no proceedings, then Y., upon being ejected by Z., may recover upon the strength of his existing possession.

" Possession being once admitted to be a root of title, every posses-
" sion must create a title which, as against all subsequent intruders,
" has all the incidents and advantages of a true title." [5]

We are now in a position to deal with the accrual of the cause of action in the different cases described by the statute.

(A) PRESENT INTERESTS.

Time does not begin to run against a person in present possession of land until possession has been taken by another person. The Act states the rule in this way [6] :

Accrual at dispossession or discontinuance.

" Where the person bringing an action to recover land, or some per-
" son though whom he claims, has been in possession thereof, and

---

[1] See Pollock and Wright, *Possession in the Common Law,* pp. 95 *et seq.*; Lightwood, *Possession of Land,* pp. 275 *et seq.*
[2] *Willis* v. *Howe,* [1893] 2 Ch. 545, 553, KAY, L.J.
[3] *Dixon* v. *Gayfere* (No. 1) (1853), 17 Beav. 421, 430 ; Lord ROMILLY.
[4] *Asher* v. *Whitlock* (1865), L. R. 1 Q. B. 1, at p. 6 ; approved, *Perry* v. *Clissold,* [1907] A. C. 73 ; Pollock and Wright, *supra,* p. 98.
[5] Pollock and Wright, *Possession in the Common Law,* p. 95.
[6] S. 5 (1).

" has while entitled thereto been *dispossessed* or *discontinued his*
" *possession*, the right of action shall be deemed to have accrued on
" the date of the dispossession or discontinuance."

This language is not altogether happy, for, unless the true
meaning of " discontinuance " is appreciated, it might be thought
that a mere abandonment of possession is sufficient to set time
running.[1] This is not so, however, for the factor common to dispossession and discontinuance is entry upon the land by a stranger.

" The difference," said FRY, J., " between dispossession and the dis-
" continuance of possession might be expressed in this way : the one
" is where a person comes in and drives out the others from possession,
" the other case is where the person in possession goes out and is
" followed in by others." [2]

Dispossession. The question whether a person has been
dispossessed so as to set time running against him does not always
admit of a ready answer. Some cases, of course, are obvious,
as for instance where a stranger occupies the house of another
or encloses and cultivates a strip of his neighbour's land.[3] In
a doubtful case, however, the acts claimed to constitute possession, whether by the plaintiff or the defendant, must be considered relatively to the nature of the land.[4] Regard must be
had, in other words, both to the kind of enjoyment that is possible
and to the intention of the owner. The mere fact that X. has
interfered in some way with the land of A. is not enough to show
adverse possession in him ; he must go further and prove some
act which is inconsistent with the form of enjoyment that is
available to, or intended by, A. If the act of interference precludes A. from exploiting the land in the manner he intended,
there is dispossession, otherwise not. The leading case on the
subject is *Leigh* v. *Jack*,[5] where the facts were these :

> In 1854 the plaintiff conveyed to the defendant a plot of land on
> the south side of a strip of land which it was intended to make into a
> street. In 1872 the defendant took a conveyance of the land to the
> north of the strip. The strip was never dedicated by the plaintiff to
> the public as a highway, and the defendant used it for various pur-
> poses connected with his own property. For instance, from 1854 he
> regularly encumbered it with materials used at his factory so as to
> close it to all except pedestrians; in 1865 he enclosed an oblong
> portion of it; and in 1872 he fenced in the ends. Within a few years
> of the action the plaintiff had repaired the fence.

It was held that the plaintiff had not lost his title to the land.
His intention was to dedicate it to the use of the public, and
therefore his failure to exploit it for his own advantage was con-

(marginal note: What constitutes
adverse
possession.*)*

---

[1] Preston and Newsom, *op. cit.*, p. 83.
[2] *Rains* v. *Buxton* (1880), 14 Ch. D. 537, 539–40.
[3] *Marshall* v. *Taylor*, [1895] 1 Ch. 641.
[4] Preston and Newsom, *Limitation of Actions* (2nd Edn.), pp. 85–6.
[5] (1879), 5 Ex. D. 264; followed in *Littledale* v. *Liverpool College*, [1900]
1 Ch. 19; *Williams Brothers Direct Supply, Ltd.* v. *Raftery*, [1958] 1 Q. B. 159;
[1957] 3 All E. R. 593 (C. A.). *George Wimpey & Co., Ltd.* v. *Sohn*, [1966]
1 All E. R. 232; *West Bank Estates, Ltd.* v. *Arthur*, [1966] 3 W. L. R. 750.

sistent with that intention and therefore did not constitute a discontinuance of possession. Neither had he been dispossessed by the acts of the defendant, for these were not inconsistent with the ultimate use of the land as a public way. They were not done *animo possidendi, i.e.* with the intention of excluding the plaintiff and all other persons.

Deceased person in possession at death. When X., the person entitled to land, dies while still in possession, and a stranger seizes possession after his death, time begins to run from the date of his death, not from the wrongful seizure, against those who claim under his will or upon his intestacy.[1] The same rule applies to a rentcharge created by will or taking effect upon death.[2]

(margin) Failure to acquire possession on death.

Grant of present interest. Where an interest in possession has been granted to X., or where the land has been charged in his favour with the payment of a rentcharge, and he has not taken possession or has not received the rent, time begins to run against him from the date of the grant.[3]

(margin) Failure to acquire possession under a grant.

So far as a rentcharge is concerned this rule meets the case where the chargor has never made a payment of the money due.

(margin) Rentcharge.

Another case that requires attention is where he wrongfully makes payment to a stranger.[4] The statutory rule here is that time shall begin to run against the chargee from " the date of the last receipt of rent " by him.[5] The result of this is to reduce the limitation period of twelve years, for normally a right of action would accrue and time would begin to run, not from the last receipt of rent, but from the date when the rent again became due.

If, for example, the rent is payable annually on September 29, and payment is duly made on that date in 1967, no *right of action or of distraint* accrues until September 29, 1968.

Nevertheless time begins to run under the statute on September 29, 1967, so that in effect the period of limitation is reduced to eleven years.[6]

(B) FUTURE INTERESTS.

The date upon which time begins to run against the owner of a future interest depends upon whether the person entitled to the preceding estate was in possession when it came to an end. Suppose, for instance, that there is a

(margin) Accrual depends upon whether preceding owner continues in possession.

---

[1] Limitation Act, 1939, s. 5 (2), replaci ng Real Property Limitation Act 1833, s. 3, second branch.
[2] *Ibid.*
[3] *Ibid.*, s. 5 (3), replacing Real Property Limitation Act, s. 3, third branch.
[4] See generally Preston and Newsom, *Limitation of Actions* (2nd Edn.), pp. 124 *et seq.*
[5] Limitation Act, 1939, s. 31 (6).
[6] *Owen* v. *De Beauvoir* (1847), 16 M. & W. 547.

grant to A. for life, remainder to B. in fee simple,

and that B. fails to take possession on the death of A. In such a case the statute enacts alternative rules.

> (i) If A. dies while still possessed of the land, B.'s right of action accrues upon the determination of the life interest, *i.e.* he must sue within twelve years from the death of A.[1]

> (ii) If A. is not in possession at death, *e.g.* where he has been dispossessed by a stranger, B. has the longer of two alternative periods within which he may bring his action, namely, twelve years from the time when the cause of action accrued to A., or six years from the death of A.[2]

This second rule does not apply where the preceding estate is a term of years absolute.[3] Thus time does not begin to run against a landlord until the lease determines, even though the tenant may have been ejected before that date.[4]

Future interests expectant upon entailed interest. Neither rule applies to an interest limited after an entailed interest which is capable of being barred by the tenant in tail.[5] In this case the remainderman " claims through " the tenant in tail, so that if time has commenced running against the latter it continues to run against the remainderman, and does not start afresh upon the determination of the entail.

Settlement made by person against whom time is already running. Future interests created by a settlor after time has commenced to run against him are subject to a different rule. The second case given above contemplates that *after* the settlement in favour of B. has been made, a right of action accrues to A., the owner of the preceding estate, against an adverse possessor. In those circumstances, as we have seen, B. may recover the land within six years from the death of A., though it may be more than twelve years since A. was wrongfully dispossessed. But if time once begins to run against a settlor, no *subsequent* alteration in his title, *e.g.* by the later creation of future interests, will prevent the bar from operating after the lapse of twelve years. The persons deriving title from the settlor cannot be in a better position than he is.[6]

> " Thus if A., seised in fee in possession, were dispossessed by B., " and were afterwards to settle the estate upon C. for life, remainder " to D. in fee, the time would run from the dispossession in the " same manner as if no such settlement had been made." [7]

One person entitled to successive interests. Where a person is entitled to successive interests in land, one

---

[1] Limitation Act, 1939, s. 6 (1).
[2] *Ibid.*, s. 6 (2). The corresponding periods are thirty years and twelve years where the Crown or a spiritual or eleemosynary corporation is entitled to the future interest. [3] *Ibid.*
[4] *Infra*, p. 818.
[5] Limitation Act, 1939, s. 6 (3).   [6] *Ibid.*, s. 6 (4).
[7] Hayes, *Introduction to Conveyancing* (5th Edn.), p. 257.

present the other future, the general principle is that, if his present interest is barred, the bar shall extend also to his future right.[1] Thus if land stands limited,

> to A. for life, remainder to B. for life, remainder to A. in fee simple,

and A. is dispossessed for twelve years, he and those claiming under him lose the right to recover both the life interest and the fee simple in remainder. The right to recover the fee simple, however, is not barred if, to quote the words of the Act, " possession has been recovered by a person entitled to an intermediate estate or interest." [2]

> If, for instance, in the example just given, B. were to recover possession after A. had been dispossessed for twelve years, a right of recovery in respect of the fee simple would accrue to A., and those claiming under him, upon the death of B.

(C) FORFEITURE OR BREACH OF CONDITION.

A right of action to recover land by virtue of a forfeiture or breach of condition accrues on the date on which the forfeiture was incurred or the condition broken. If, however, a reversioner or remainderman fails to take advantage of the forfeiture or breach of condition he still retains the right of recovery that accrues to him when his estate falls into possession.[3]

Time runs from breach of condition.

> " So if A., lessee for years, subject to a condition of re-entry,
> " breaks the condition, the time runs against the reversioner in
> " respect of his right of entry for the breach from its occurrence ;
> " but a bar to such right of entry will not affect his right to enter
> " on the expiration of the lease by effluxion of time." [4]

(D) SETTLED LAND AND LAND HELD ON TRUST.

Equitable interests in land, such as a life interest under a settlement and equitable interests in the proceeds of sale of land held upon trust for sale, are " land " within the meaning of the Limitation Act, 1939.[5] In general, the provisions of the Act apply to these interests in like manner as they apply to legal estates, and the right to sue for the recovery of the land is deemed to accrue to the person entitled in possession on the date on which it would accrue if his interest were a legal estate.[6] Where such equitable interests exist the legal estate

Application of the statute to equitable interests.

---

[1] Limitation Act, 1939, s. 6 (5).
[2] *Ibid.*, replacing Real Property Limitation Act, 1833, s. 20.
[3] *Ibid.*, s. 8, replacing Real Property Limitation Act, 1833, s. 3, fifth branch, and s. 4.
[4] Hayes, *Introduction to Conveyancing* (5th Edn.), p. 252.
[5] Limitation Act, 1939, s. 31 (1).
[6] *Ibid.*, s. 7 (1).

will, according to the circumstances, be vested in a tenant for life or statutory owner, or in personal representatives or in trustees for sale, all of whom are trustees for the purposes of the Act.[1]

There are two circumstances in which the beneficiaries entitled to the equitable interests may be affected by wrongful possession.

First, the trustee in possession may disregard the rights of the beneficiaries.

Secondly, a stranger may seize possession and hold it adversely to the beneficiaries.

Statute does not run in favour of trustee.
The first case raises no difficulty, for a trustee cannot possess the land adversely to the beneficiaries. It is expressly enacted that no period of limitation shall apply to an action brought by a beneficiary,

> (*a*) in respect of any fraud or fraudulent breach of trust to which the trustee was a party or privy ; or
>
> (*b*) *to recover from the trustee trust property or the proceeds thereof in his possession* or previously received by him and converted to his use.[2]

Thus, if a person, who is in possession of land as trustee for A. and B., pays the whole of the profits to A., time does not run against B.[3] Even a notional receipt of property may come within this enactment. Thus, a trustee who remains in occupation of trust land for his own benefit is deemed to have received profits belonging to the beneficiaries, since in the circumstances he is chargeable with an occupation rent. Therefore, he can never escape liability for payment of this by pleading lapse of time, unless, indeed, under the equitable doctrine of laches, a beneficiary has been so tardy in bringing his action that it would be practically unjust to grant him relief.[4]

Effect upon tenancies in common.
The statutory provision (*b*) has an important effect upon tenancies in common. Where land is limited to A. and B. as tenants in common in fee, the beneficiaries become, as we have seen,[5] joint tenants and trustees of the legal estate upon trust to sell the land and to give effect to their own beneficial interests. If, therefore, A. appropriates the whole of the rents and profits to himself for many years, he does not acquire a title against B., for, since the land is in his possession as trustee, time does not run in his favour.[6]

---

[1] Limitation Act, 1939, s. 31 (1).
[2] *Ibid.*, s. 19 (1).
[3] *Knight* v. *Bowyer* (1858), 2 De G. & J. 421 ; see Preston and Newsom, *Limitation of Actions* (2nd Edn.), pp. 133, 158.
[4] *Re Howlett, Howlett* v. *Howlett*, [1949] Ch. 767 ; [1949] 2 All E. R. 490.
[5] *Supra*, p. 312.
[6] *Re Landi*, [1939] Ch. 828 ; *Re Milkin ? Pail Farm Trusts*, [1940] Ch. 996 ; Preston and Newsom, *op. cit.*, p. 134. See 57 *L.Q.R.*, pp. 26–9.

Where the claim is not comprised in classes (*a*) and (*b*), as for instance where it concerns an unauthorized investment, the beneficiary must sue the trustee within six years from the accrual of his cause of action.[1]

As regards the second class of wrong, where a stranger seizes possession, the rule stated above, that the statutory provisions apply to equitable interests as well as to legal estates, if it stood alone, would mean that twelve years' possession held by the stranger adversely to the trustee would extinguish the legal estate and bar the remedy of the beneficiaries. This, however, is not so. It is provided by another section that [2] :

Time does not run against trustee until beneficiary is barred.

> Where possession of land has been held for twelve years adversely to the trustee (*i.e.* adversely to a tenant for life or statutory owner of settled land, or to trustees for sale), the legal estate shall not be extinguished so long as the right of a beneficiary to recover the land has not accrued or has not been barred.

Thus the legal estate is not extinguished until the right of action of the *beneficiary* is barred. There is a further provision that a statutory owner or a trustee may sue for the recovery of the land on behalf of a beneficiary whose title to the equitable interest has not been barred.[3] By way of illustration :

> Suppose that land is settled upon A. for life with remainder to B. in fee simple, and that a stranger seizes the land in A's. lifetime and remains in adverse possession for twelve years.

In these circumstances the *beneficial* life interest of A. is extinguished, with the result that the adverse possessor acquires an equitable interest *pur autre vie*. Nevertheless the *legal fee simple*, held by A. under the provisions of the Settled Land Act, remains intact, and therefore B., as the owner of a future interest, will be able to enforce his right of action when it accrues to him upon the death of A. When that event occurs, the representatives of A., upon whom his legal fee simple devolves, may recover the land on behalf of B.[4]

The only case remaining for consideration is where a *beneficiary* claims title by virtue of adverse possession for twelve years. Under the law as it stood before 1940 such a person, although he was ordinarily regarded as tenant at will of the trustee, acquired a title by twelve years' possession if he occupied the land to the exclusion of the trustees and the other beneficiaries.[5] Now,

Time does not run against trustee in favour of beneficiary.

---

[1] Limitation Act, 1939, s. 19 (2).
[2] *Ibid.*, s. 7 (2), (3).   [3] *Ibid.*, s. 7 (4).
[4] See generally Preston and Newsom, *Limitation of Actions* (2nd Edn.), pp. 128–30.
[5] *Burroughs* v. *M'Creight* (1844), 1 Jo. & Lat. 290 (Ireland).

however, his possession cannot be adverse to these persons, for it is enacted that during his occupation of the land time shall not run against a tenant for life, statutory owner, trustee or beneficiary.[1]

(E) TENANCIES.

Lessor's
right
against
tenant
accrues at
end of lease.

Recovery of possession from the tenant.   The right of action of a lessor to recover the land from the tenant accrues when the lease determines by effluxion of time.[2]   He must, therefore, sue within twelve years from this date.   The mere fact that he has received no rent for many years does not affect his right to recover the land within this period.[3]

Lessor's
right to
enforce a
forfeiture.

If the lease contains a clause providing for the forfeiture of the premises upon non-payment of the rent, and if the rent is not paid within the stipulated period, the landlord acquires by virtue of this clause a right to recover the land during the continuance of the tenancy.[4]   This right accrues to him, as we have seen, when the forfeiture is incurred,[5] but the fact that he fails to enforce it does not affect his right to recover the land within twelve years after the determination of the term.   Moreover, his failure to enforce one forfeiture does not prejudice him with regard to the future.   A fresh right of re-entry accrues to him on each occasion that the tenant defaults in payment.[6]

Rights of
lessor and
tenant
against
stranger.

Recovery of possession from a stranger.   If a stranger enters upon land which is held by lease, time begins to run in his favour against the *tenant* from the moment when the latter is dispossessed ; but it does not begin to run against the *landlord* until the end of the lease, for it is only then that the landlord's right of action arises.   The landlord must sue within the next twelve years, even though the existing lease is renewed in favour of the lessee while the stranger is still in possession.[7]

Time runs
against
lessor
from adverse
receipt of
rent.

But since the receipt of rent is the only fact that symbolizes the landlord's title to the land, and since an adverse receipt by a stranger is really tantamount to dispossession, it is enacted that [8]:

Where any person is in possession of land by virtue of a *written lease*, under which a yearly rent of *twenty shillings or upwards* is

---

[1] Limitation Act, 1939, s. 7 (5).   But see Preston and Newsom, *op. cit.* (2nd Edn.), p. 133.
[2] *Ibid.*, s. 6 (1).
[3] *Doe d. Davy v. Oxenham* (1840), 7 M. & W. 131.
[4] *Supra*, pp. 414–6.
[5] *Supra*, p. 815.
[6] *Barratt* v. *Richardson and Cresswell*, [1930] 1 K. B. 686.
[7] *Ecclesiastical Commissioners of England and Wales* v. *Rowe* (1880), 5 App. Cas. 736.
[8] Limitation Act, 1939, s. 9 (3) ; re-enacting Real Property Limitation Act, 1833, s. 9.

reserved, and the rent is received by some person wrongfully claiming to be entitled to the reversion, the landlord's right of action shall be deemed to have accrued at the time of the first wrongful receipt of rent, and not at the date of the determination of the lease.

Thus, if the rent is wrongfully received by a stranger for twelve years, both the right of action and the title of the landlord are irretrievably barred, but if before the twelve years have elapsed rent is once more received by him, his right of action revives.[1] If the lease is not in writing or if the annual rent is less than twenty shillings, adverse receipt of the rent does not set time running against the landlord.

Tenancies at will and from year to year have received special treatment.

1. **Tenancy at will.** Time begins to run against the lessor in either of two events.

Time runs from determination or from end of first year.

First, from the determination of the tenancy.[2] The landlord may determine the tenancy either by demanding possession or by exercising some act of ownership on the land which is inconsistent with the right of the tenant.

Secondly, in the absence of determination, time begins to run against the lessor at the end of one year from the beginning of the tenancy.[3] The object of this enactment is to make the possession of the tenant adverse at an early date, for otherwise he might remain in occupation for an indefinite period, making no payment and giving no acknowledgment of the lessor's title, without ever being able to acquire a valid and transferable title.

If, therefore, the lessor does nothing that constitutes a positive determination, his title is extinguished in thirteen years from the commencement of the tenancy, though a written and signed acknowledgment of his title given by the tenant before the expiration of thirteen years, will revive his cause of action.[4] Similarly, the determination of the old tenancy and the creation of a new one before the expiration of the thirteen years, will cause time to run afresh.[5] The payment of rent by the tenant does not *per se* prevent time running against the landlord, but if it is payable on a yearly basis the tenancy is converted into one from year to year.

These rules are confined to a tenancy at will properly so called. If, for instance, A. is given exclusive occupation of the land of B. for an indefinite period and the circumstances show that all that is intended is that he shall have a personal privilege with no interest in the land, he is not a tenant at will, but a licensee, and time does not run against B. under the Act.[6]

Licence distinguished from tenancy.

---

[1] Limitation Act, 1939, ss. 16, 23 (4).   [2] *Ibid.*, s. 9 (1).
[3] *Ibid.*   [4] *Ibid.*, ss. 23 (1) ; 24 (1).
[5] *Doe d. Groves* v. *Groves* (1847), 10 Q. B. 486.
[6] *Cobb* v. *Lane*, [1952] 1 All E. R. 1199 ; *supra*, pp. 338–9.

Oral lease.

2. Tenancy from year to year.   In the case of a tenancy from year to year or other period *without a lease in writing*,[1] the right of the lessor to recover the land accrues either at the end of the first of such years or other period, or at the last receipt of rent, whichever shall last occur.[2]   If the tenant remains in possession without paying rent for twelve years after the right of action has arisen, and without giving a written acknowledgment of the lessor's title, the cause of action is effectually barred, and a subsequent acknowledgment or payment of rent does not start time running afresh.[3]

Written lease.

If the lease is in writing the present rule does not apply, and the lessor's right of action accrues when he determines the tenancy by notice to quit.

Certain equitable claims subject to no statutory bar.

The doctrine of laches.   Despite the general rule that the provisions of the Limitation Act apply to equitable interests in land,[4] there are certain cases in which an equitable claim is unaffected by the statutory bars just discussed.   Thus, as we have seen, a claim by a beneficiary to recover trust property retained by a trustee or to recover damages from a fraudulent trustee is subject to no period of limitation.[5]   Again, the statutory bars do not apply to any claim for specific performance, an injunction or other equitable relief, except in so far as they may be applied by analogy to the Act.[6]

Effect of the equitable doctrine of laches.

Nevertheless, whenever a plaintiff seeks to enforce an equitable right to which no statute of limitation applies or to obtain a form of relief unknown to the common law, courts of equity have always required him to prosecute his claim with due diligence.   In pursuance of the maxim—*vigilantibus non dormientibus aequitas solverit*—they discourage what is called *laches*, a word that signifies the negligent failure of a plaintiff to take proceedings for the enforcement of his claim within a reasonable time after he has become aware of his rights.[7]   But the application of the doctrine of laches has always depended upon whether or not the suit in equity corresponds to an action at law that is within a statute of limitation.

(1) Effect where correspondent remedy at common law.

If the equitable claim is substantially similar to a legal right that is subject to a statutory bar, the courts act by analogy to the statute and enforce the same bar upon the equitable right of action.[8]   Thus an action by a widow for the assignment to her of specific land in satisfaction of her right to dower, which lay in Chancery

---

[1] The possession by the tenant of a rent book does not convert an oral into a written lease, *Moses* v. *Lovegrove*, [1953] 2 Q. B. 533 ; [1952] 1 All E. R. 1279.

[2] Limitation Act, 1939, s. 9 (2) ; re-enacting Real Property Limitation Act, 1833, s. 8 ; *Re Jolly, Gathercole* v. *Norfolk*, [1900] 2 Ch. 616, 619.

[3] *Nicholson* v. *England*, [1926] 2 K. B. 93.

[4] Limitation Act, 1939, s. 7 (1).

[5] *Ibid.*, s. 19 (1); *supra*, p. 816.   [6] *Ibid.*, s. 2 (7).

[7] For a detailed discussion, see Preston & Newsom, *op. cit.*, pp. 236–43.

[8] *Knox* v. *Gye* (1872), L. R. 5 H. L. 656, at p. 674, *per* Lord WESTBURY.

before the abolition of dower, would fail unless she started proceedings within the statutory period prescribed for an action of ejectment.[1] The court, however, will not adopt the analogous statutory bar if the equitable claim has been deliberately omitted from the Act as a matter of policy. Relevant examples are the right of a mortgagor to redeem a mortgage of personalty,[2] or of a beneficiary to recover trust property retained by a trustee.

This principle of analogous application is now of much diminished importance, for the legislation of the 19th century, fortified by the Limitation Act, 1939, has imposed a statutory bar upon most equitable claims.

If there is no correspondent claim or remedy at common law, or if, despite such correspondence, the equitable claim has been omitted from the statutory limitation as a matter of policy, equity applies its own test of unreasonable delay. Mere delay is seldom sufficient to constitute laches. It must be considered in the light of the circumstances. (2) Effect where no correspondent remedy at law.

> "A defence based on staleness of demand renders it necessary to
> "consider the time which has elapsed and the balance of justice and
> "injustice in affording or refusing relief."[3]

At bottom, the enquiry is whether the reasonable inference from the delay and the attendant circumstances is that the plaintiff has acquiesced in the violation of his right, once it has become known to him, and thereby has in effect waived his claim against the defendant.[4] A further factor is whether the defendant has altered his position to his prejudice in the belief that the claim has been abandoned.[5]

Such will be the nature of the enquiry if laches is pleaded as a defence to an action by a *cestui que trust* to recover property retained by a trustee; by a mortgagor to redeem a mortgage of personalty;[6] or by a mortgagee to foreclose an equitable mortgage of an advowson.[7]

This doctrine of laches, which is of ancient origin, is preserved by the following provision of the Limitation Act, 1939: Doctrine of laches still enforced.

> "Nothing in this Act shall affect any equitable jurisdiction to refuse
> "relief on the ground of acquiescence or otherwise."[7]

---

[1] *Williams* v. *Thomas*, [1909] 1 Ch. 713.

[2] Waldock, *The Law of Mortgages*, p. 199. An action to foreclose a mortgage of personalty is barred by the Limitation Act after twelve years, but not an action to redeem such a mortgage.

[3] *Re Sharpe, Re Bennett, Masonic and General Life Assurance Co.* v. *Sharpe*, [1892] 1 Ch. 154, at p. 168, *per* LINDLEY, L.J.

[4] See *Lindsay Petroleum Co.* v. *Hurd* (1874), L. R. 5 P. C. 221, at p. 239; approved in *Erlanger* v. *New Sombrero Phosphate Co.* (1878), 3 App. Cas. 1218, at p. 1279.

[5] *Allcard* v. *Skinner* (1887), 36 Ch. D. 145, at p. 192, *per* BOWEN, L.J.

[6] *Brooks* v. *Muckleston*, [1909] 2 Ch. 519. Such an action of foreclosure is subject to no statutory bar, since an advowson, an incorporeal interest, is not "land" within the meaning of the Limitation Act, 1939. Distinguish an action to enforce an advowson which is barred after the expiration of the relevant period prescribed by the Limitation Act, 1939, s. 14.   [7] S. 29.

SECTION IV.   THE NATURE OF THE TITLE ACQUIRED UNDER THE STATUTE.

It is necessary to consider what effect the expiration of the statutory period produces upon the title to the land.

What is the effect upon the legal position, first, of the person dispossessed, secondly of the person who has held adverse possession for twelve years?

Remedy and title of former owner extinguished. 1. When time has run against a claimant, the effect in every case, no matter whether his claim is founded on tort, breach of contract, dispossession of land or some other wrong, is to bar his *remedy*. As a general rule, however, his *right* is not barred. He is precluded by the extinction of his remedy from a resort to legal proceedings, but he is free to enforce his still existent right by any other method that may be available.   Before 1833 this was the effect of adverse possession of land for the required period, but the Real Property Limitation Act of that year provided that at the end of the statutory period the right, as well as the remedy, of the dispossessed owner should be extinguished.[1] This rule is retained by the Limitation Act, 1939, in a section which runs as follows [2] :

> At the expiration of the period prescribed by this Act for any person to bring an action to recover land (including a redemption action), or an action to enforce an advowson, the title of that person to the land or advowson shall be extinguished.

Two exceptions. There are, however, two exceptions.

(i) Settled land. First, in the case of settled land and land held on trust, as we have already seen, the title of the trustee to the legal estate is not extinguished until all the beneficiaries have been barred.[3]

(ii) Registered land. Secondly, where a person registered as owner under the Land Registration Act, 1925, is dispossessed for twelve years, his title is not forthwith extinguished, but he is deemed to hold the land upon trust for the adverse possessor.[4] The register may be rectified in favour of the latter if he makes application to that end, but no rectification will prejudice any other person interested in the land whose right has not been extinguished by lapse of time.[5]

In considering the extent to which the *status quo ante* of the parties is affected by the statutory extinguishment of the right of action, we will deal first with the former possessor and then with the squatter.

---

[1] S. 34.
[2] S. 16.   S. 3 (2) has now extended the rule to conversion and detinue of chattels.
[3] *Supra*, p. 817.
[4] Land Registration Act, 1925, s. 75 (1).
[5] *Ibid.*, s. 75 (2), (3).

What the dispossessed person loses. The dispossessed person and those who claim through him lose the title to possession that he could previously have enforced against the squatter. To that extent, his title is finally destroyed and there is no method by which it can be revived, not even by a written acknowledgment given by the squatter.[1]

But the restricted effect of the extinguishment must be realized. It extinguishes nothing more than the title of the dispossessed *against the squatter*.[2] Thus, the dispossession of a lessee does not destroy his lease. His title against the lessor remains good, so that, for instance, he is entitled to resume possession if the land is vacated by the squatter. Likewise, the lessor remains entitled to sue the lessee on the covenants or indeed to re-enter the land for a forfeiture committed by the squatter if the lease contains a proviso for forefeiture.[3]

A fortiori, the titles of third parties who have enforceable interests in the land, such as those entitled to the benefit of a restrictive covenant, are unaffected by the adverse possession of the land, for no remedy accrues to them until *their* rights have been infringed.[4]

What the squatter acquires. It follows from what has been said, that the sole, though substantial, privilege acquired by a squatter is immunity from interference by the person dispossessed. In other words, the statutory effect of twelve years' adverse possession is merely negative; not, as Baron Parke once said, "to make a parliamentary conveyance to the person in possession."[5] This judicial heresy has long been exploded and it is now recognised that:

"we must not confound the negative effect of the statute with the "positive effect of a conveyance."[6]

There is no transfer, statutory or otherwise, to the squatter of the very title held by the dispossessed person.

"He is not at any stage of his possession a successor to the title of the "man he has dispossessed. He comes in and remains in always by "right of possession, which in due course becomes incapable of "disturbance as time exhausts the one or more periods allowed by "statute for successful intervention. His title, therefore, is never "derived through but arises always in spite of the dispossessed "owner."[7]

Thus if a man ejects a tenant for years and remains in possession

Side notes:
Title of dispossessed person against squatter alone extinguished.

Squatter acquires the right not to be disturbed by dispossessed person.

The effect of the Limitation Act is merely negative.

---

[1] *Nicholson* v. *England*, [1926] 2 K. B. 93.
[2] *Fairweather* v. *St. Marylebone Property Co., Ltd.*, [1963] A. C. 510, at p. 539; [1962] 2 All E. R. 288, *per* Lord RADCLIFFE.
[3] *Ibid.*, at p. 545, *per* Lord DENNING.
[4] *Re Nisbet and Pott's Contract*, [1905] 1 Ch. 391; *supra*, pp. 551–2.
[5] *Doe d. Jukes* v. *Sumner* (1845), 14 M. & W. 39, at p. 42.
[6] Hayes, *Introduction to Conveyancing*, vol. i, p. 269.
[7] *Fairweather* v. *St. Marylebone Property Co., Ltd.*, [1963] A. C. 510, at p. 535; [1962] 2 All E. R. 288, *per* Lord RADCLIFFE.

for the statutory period, he cannot be sued for breach of a repairing covenant contained in the lease, for there has been no transfer to him of the tenant's estate.[1]   Again, any right enjoyed by the dispossessed person that is based upon an implied grant, such as a way of necessity, will not avail an adverse possessor, for the doctrine of implication cannot be imported into a statutory provision that is purely negative.[2]

Negative effect illustrated by dispossession of a lessee.

The decision of the House of Lords in *Fairweather* v. *St. Marylebone Property Co., Ltd.,*[3] is a further illustration of the rule that there is no transfer to a squatter of an interest commensurate with that held by the person dispossessed.   The facts relevant to the present enquiry may be stated in a much simplified form as follows:

> A house and garden containing a shed were leased by X. to Y. for 99 years.   The shed was occupied by a neighbour, Z., for more than twelve years adversely to Y.   While the lease was still running, Y. surrendered it to the freeholder, X.
>
> The question was whether X., *qua* freeholder, could resume possession immediately or whether he had no such right until the lease determined by effluxion of time.

The majority of the House of Lords, overruling *Walter* v. *Yalden,*[4] gave judgment for X.   Despite the title acquired by the squatter against Y. the lessee, the relationship between X. and Y. still continued with all its implications, including the right of Y. to retain possession as against X.   By surrendering the lease, Y. had abandoned the right to possession, with the result that his tenancy had merged in the freehold and had disappeared.   Therefore, the landlord could recover the shed on the strength of his own right to immediate possession of the freehold.[5]

The earlier decision of *Taylor* v. *Twinberrow*[6] was approved. In that case, the facts were in effect as follows:

> X., a yearly tenant, allowed Y. to occupy a cottage for more than thirteen years as a tenant at will.   X. then bought the fee simple, with the result that the yearly tenancy was determined by its merger in the freehold.   It was argued that the title acquired by Y. was commensurate with that lost by X. and that therefore he was entitled to the half a year's notice to quit appropriate to a yearly tenancy.

This argument was fallacious.   All that the squatter had acquired

---

[1] *Tichborne* v. *Weir* (1892), 67 L. T. 735; *supra,* p. 415.
[2] *Wilkes* v. *Greenway* (1890), 6 T. L. R. 449.
[3] [1963] A. C. 510; [1962] 2 All E. R. 288.   [4] [1902] 2 K. B. 304.
[5] Lord MORRIS dissented.   He took the view that the tenant could not surrender what he had not himself got, namely, a right to immediate possession. *Nemo dat quod non habet.*   For a criticism of the decision, see 78 *L.Q.R.,* pp. 541–59 (H. W. R. Wade).   For a discussion of the difficulty of terminology in this context, see 90 *L.Q.R.,* pp. 63–72 (Bernard Rudden).
[6] [1930] 2 K. B. 16.

was a title to possession indefeasible by the yearly tenant. With the disappearance of the yearly tenancy, the former yearly tenant had become the freeholder, and as such he had an immediate right to recover possession.

One effect of these decisions is that the lessor and lessee can combine to defeat the squatter. If the lessor accepts a surrender of the term, he is then able to grant a new lease to the tenant.[1]

Nevertheless, despite the negative operation of the Limitation Act, the title to possession acquired by a squatter against the person dispossessed may ultimately ripen into a title to the fee simple.

Adverse title may ripen into absolute title to fee simple.

> "Whenever you find a person in possession of property, that posess-
> "sion is *prima facie* evidence of ownership in fee, and that *prima facie*
> "evidence becomes absolute when once you have extinguished the
> "right of every other person to challenge it."[2]

In other words, a squatter, though a wrongdoer, acquires by virtue of his possession a new independent title to the fee simple which prevails against all persons except those who can rely on an earlier and therefore a better title. Moreover, it is a title that will prevail against those with better titles if they fail to assert their rights within the period prescribed by the Limitation Act. Thus, a title originally defeasible may in course of time become indefeasible.[3]

For instance,

> X. dispossesses W., the fee simple owner of Blackacre, and remains in possession for eight years when he himself is dispossessed by Y.

As between X. and Y., X.'s is the earlier and therefore the stronger title of the two, but he must assert it against the weaker within the statutory period. If Y. is allowed to remain in possession for twelve years without being challenged either by W. or X., his title to possession of the fee simple becomes indefeasible. It rests on the infirmity of the right of other to eject him.[4]

Again, if some lesser title than that to the fee simple is destroyed, as when a tenant for years is ejected, the squatter may still be challenged by the landlord, the freeholder. So, if the lease terminates by effluxion of time or becomes forfeitable for breach of condition,[5] the freeholder's right to recover possession accrues and prevails over that of the squatter. Relatively to the tenant, the squatter's right is the stronger; relatively to the freeholder, it is the weaker. But if the freeholder does not pursue his remedy with-

---

[1] *Fairweather* v. *St. Marylebone Property Co., Ltd.*, [1963] A. C. 510, at p. 457; *per* Lord DENNING; [1962] 2 All E. R. 288.
[2] *Re Atkinson and Horsell's Contract*, [1912] 2 Ch. 1, at p. 9.
[3] *St. Marylebone Property Co., Ltd.* v. *Fairweather*, [1962] 1 Q. B. 498, at p. 513; *per* HOLROYD PEARCE, L.J.; [1961] 3 All E. R. 560.
[4] Darby and Bosanquet, *Statutes of Limitation* (2nd Edn.), p. 493, adopted by BOWEN, L.J., in *Tichborne* v. *Weir* (1892), 67 L. T. 735.
[5] *Tickner* v. *Buzzacott*, [1965] Ch. 426; [1965] 1 All E. R. 131.

in six years from the end of the lease, the squatter's title to the fee simple becomes indefeasible.

SECTION V.   CIRCUMSTANCES IN WHICH THE STATUTORY PERIOD IS EXTENDED.

In three cases, namely,

1. where the person entitled to recover land is under a disability ;

2. where a cause of action has been fraudulently concealed ; and

3. where a person seeks relief from the consequences of a mistake,

the period of twelve years within which an action must normally be brought is lengthened.

Persons under a disability.

1. **Disabilities.**   A person is deemed to be under a disability for the purposes of the Act while he is an infant or of unsound mind.[1]

Six years from cessation of disability or from death.

If, on the date when a right of action for the recovery of land accrues, the person to whom it has accrued is under a disability, the action may be brought at any time within six years from the removal of the disability or from his death, whichever event first occurs, notwithstanding that the normal period of limitation has expired.[2]   No action, however, to recover land or money charged on land may be brought after the expiration of thirty years from the date on which the right accrued.[3]   A disability which begins *after* the accrual of a right of action does not prevent time from continuing to run against the disabled person.[4]

Successive disabilities.

If before the cessation of one disability another one supervenes, time does not begin to run until both have ceased.[5]   For instance :

A. dispossesses B., an infant six years of age.   When nineteen years old B. becomes of unsound mind, and is still in this state upon the attainment of his majority.   Time does not begin to run until he recovers his sanity.

---

[1] Limitation Act, 1939, s. 31 (2), (3).   For definition of " person of unsound mind " in this context, see Mental Health Act, 1959, Sch. 7. S. 31 (2) of the Limitation Act, 1939 also provides that the like consequences shall ensue where a person is sentenced to death or penal servitude for treason or felony, if no administrator has been appointed for him under the Forfeiture Act, 1870. Penal servitude is abolished and the provisions in that Act for appointing administrators are repealed by the Criminal Justice Act, 1948, ss. 1, 70, 83, and 10th Sched; and s. 8 of the Forfeiture Act, 1870, imposing contractual incapacity on a " convict " is also so repealed.

[2] Limitation Act, 1939, s. 22 (1).

[3] *Ibid.*, s. 22 (1) (c).   [4] *Ibid.*, s. 22 (1) (b).

[5] *Borrows* v. *Ellison* (1871), L. R. 6 Exch. 128.

If the person entitled to the right of action dies while still under a disability, his successor in title must sue within six years even though he himself is under a disability.[1]

2. Fraudulent concealment of causes of action. It is enacted that when a right of action is concealed by the fraud of the defendant or his agent, or of any person through whom he claims or his agent, time shall not begin to run until the plaintiff has discovered, or could with reasonable diligence have discovered, the fraud.[2] There is, however, a saving clause which provides that the enactment shall not enable a person to recover the land from a purchaser for valuable consideration who was not a party to the fraud, and who at the time of the purchase did not know and had no reason to believe that a fraud had been committed.

> *Right accrues on discovery of fraud.*

Wrongfully to enter land without the knowledge of the owner does not constitute concealed fraud.[3] The fraud contemplated by the statute is not restricted to what common law regards as deceit, but comprises any unconscionable conduct stigmatized as equitable fraud by the old Court of Chancery.[4] At any rate, it clearly covers a case in the context of adverse possession where a person, knowing that the land belongs to X., conceals from X. the circumstances which confer the right upon him, and thus enables himself to enter and hold.[5] Examples are the destruction of title deeds,[6] the intentional concealment of a voluntary conveyance to the plaintiff,[7] the passing off of a bastard as the eldest legitimate son,[8] and procuring a conveyance from a person of unsound mind.[9]

> *Meaning of " concealed fraud."*

3. Mistake. There was a conflict between common law and equity before the Limitation Act, 1939, with regard to mistake. In equity time ran against a plaintiff only from the date on which the mistake was, or could with reasonable diligence have been, discovered; but at law, in the case of an action to recover money paid by mistake, time ran from the date of payment.[10] The equitable doctrine is now, however, extended to all cases where a period of limitation is prescribed by the Act.[11] This extension does not enable an action to be brought for the recovery of property that has been purchased for valuable consideration, after the transaction in which the mistake was made,

> *Right accrues upon discovery of mistake.*

---

[1] Limitation Act, 1939, s. 22 (1) (b).
[2] *Ibid.*, s. 26, extending Real Property Limitation Act, 1833, s. 26, to all actions.
[3] *Rains* v. *Buxton* (1880), 14 Ch. D. 537.
[4] *Clark* v. *Woor*, [1965] 2 All E. R. 353, at p. 356; [1965] 1 W. L. R. 650, 654.
[5] *Petre* v. *Petre* (1853), 1 Drew. 371 at p. 397, *per* KINDERSLEY, V.-C.
[6] *Lawrance* v. *Norreys (Lord)* (1890), 15 App. Cas. 210.
[7] *Re McCallum, McCallum* v. *McCallum*, [1901] 1 Ch. 143.
[8] *Vane* v. *Vane* (1873), 8 Ch. App. 383.
[9] *Lewis* v. *Thomas* (1843), 3 Hare, 26.
[10] Fifth Interim Report of Law Revision Committee, pp. 31–2.
[11] Limitation Act, 1939, s. 26 (c).

by a person who neither knew nor had reason to believe that there had been a mistake.[1]

SECTION VI.   THE METHODS BY WHICH TIME MAY BE PREVENTED FROM RUNNING.

Assertion by owner of his right.
Time which has begun to run under the Act is stopped, either when the owner asserts his right or when his right is admitted by the adverse possessor.

Assertion of right occurs when the owner takes legal proceedings or makes an effective entry into the land. The old rule was that a merely formal entry was sufficient to vest possession in the true owner and to prevent time from running against him. Such a nominal entry, even though it was secret, entitled him to bring an action within a year afterwards, and as it was possible to make such an entry every year, in this case called *continual claim*, the title to land might be in doubt for longer than the period of limitation. It was therefore provided by the Real Property Limitation Act, 1833,[2] in a section which has been repeated in the Limitation Act, 1939,[3] that a person shall not be deemed to have been in possession merely because he has made an entry on the land. He must either make a peaceable and effective entry, or sue for the recovery of the land.

Admission of owner's right.
An admission of the right of the person entitled occurs where the adverse possessor acknowledges the right, or, if the right is to the payment of money, where he makes a part payment.

Acknowledgment.
Acknowledgment. Where a right of action to recover land or an advowson or to foreclose a mortgage has already accrued to X. and his title is later acknowledged by the person in possession, his right shall be deemed to have accrued on and not before the date of the acknowledgment.[4] The effect is that the owner's right of action recommences, not only against the person who makes the admission, but also against all later possessors, and remains effective until there has been adverse possession for a further period of twelve years.[5] An acknowledgment, however, has no effect if it is given after the period of limitation has run its full course.[6]

Acknowledgment must be in writing and signed.
Every acknowledgment must be in writing and signed by the person by whom it is made.[7] It must be made to the person whose title or claim is being acknowledged or to his agent.[8] Any written statement is sufficient that implicitly recognizes the title of the person to whom it is made, as for instance an offer by a

---

[1] Limitation Act, 1939, s. 26 (ii).
[2] Ss. 10, 11.   [3] S. 13.
[4] Limitation Act, 1939, s. 23 (1).   [5] *Ibid.*, s. 25 (1).
[6] *Sanders* v. *Sanders* (1881), 19 Ch. D. 373.
[7] Limitation Act, 1939, s. 24 (1).   [8] *Ibid.*, s. 24 (2).

squatter to purchase the land from the freeholder;[1] or a request for further time within which to pay made by the possessor of land in response to a demand for rent.[2]

Part payment. If, after a right of foreclosure or other cause of action has accrued to a mortgagee, the possessor of the land or the person liable for the mortgage debt makes a payment of principal or interest, there is a fresh accrual of the right of action from the date of payment.[3]

Part payment: foreclosure action.

Where a right of action has accrued to recover any debt or other liquidated pecuniary claim, as for instance rent due under a lease, and the person liable acknowledges the claim or makes any payment in respect thereof, the right is deemed to accrue on and not before the date of the acknowledgment or last payment.[4] A payment of part only of rent does not, however, enable the remainder then due to be recovered more than six years after it became due.[5]

Part payment and acknowledgment: rent.

An acknowledgment to be effective for this purpose must admit the existence of the debt, but it need not state its precise amount, provided that this is ascertainable by extrinsic evidence.[6]

Persons bound by acknowledgment and part payment. There is a distinction between acknowledgments and part payments with regard to the persons upon whom they are binding. An acknowledgment binds only the acknowledgor and his successors,[7] *i.e.* persons who claim through him, such as a trustee in bankruptcy or an executor.[8] A part payment of a debt or other liquidated money claim, on the other hand, binds all persons liable in respect thereof,[9] for since they derive advantage from the payment it is only just that they should share the disadvantage of a fresh accrual of a right of action to the creditor. Thus a part payment of rent by a tenant revives the landlord's right of action against a surety.

Part payment binds more persons than an acknowledgment.

We have already seen that in the case of an action to recover land an acknowledgment given *after* the period of limitation has run is ineffective. The reason is that, since the right as well as the remedy is barred, there is nothing left to acknowledge. In other cases, however, where the remedy alone is barred, the established principle is that an acknowledgment or part payment is effective though given after the period has elapsed. The

Acknowledgment and part payment after period has run.

---

[1] *Edginton* v. *Clark*, [1964] 1 Q. B. 367; [1963] 3 All E. R. 468.
[2] *Fursdon* v. *Clogg* (1842), 10 M. & W. 257.
[3] Limitation Act, 1939, s. 23 (1) (b).
[4] *Ibid.*, s. 23 (4).
[5] *Ibid.*, proviso.
[6] *Dungate* v. *Dungate*, [1965] 3 All E. R. 393; [1965] 1 W. L. R. 1477, explaining *Good* v. *Parry*, [1963] 2 Q. B. 418; [1963] 2 All E. R. 59.
[7] Limitation Act, 1939, s. 25 (5).
[8] *Ibid.*, s. 25 (8).   [9] *Ibid.*, s. 25 (6).

Limitation Act, 1939, preserves this rule but restricts the binding effect of either form of admission to the person who makes the acknowledgment or part payment and his successors.[1] There is, however, a particular case in which a " successor " is not bound, *i.e.* where the tenant for life of land, which is mortgaged or charged with the payment of money, makes an acknowledgment or a part payment to the creditor after the period has elapsed. In this case the admission of liability, though binding on the life tenant, does not bind the remainderman.[2]

---

[1] S. 25 (5), (6).   [2] S. 25 (5) proviso, (6) proviso.

CHAPTER II.

MERGER.

The term *merger* means that, where a lesser and a greater estate in the same land come together and vest, without any intermediate estate, in the same person and in the same right, the lesser is immediately annihilated by operation of law. It is said to be " merged," *i.e.* sunk or drowned, in the greater estate.[1]

For example :

> If land is limited to A. for life, remainder to B. in fee simple, merger will result from any event which produces the union in one person of the life interest and the remainder in fee. Thus if A. conveys his life interest to B., or if B. conveys his remainder to A., there is in each case a merger. Again, a term of years may merge in a life interest, and an estate *pur autre vie* may merge in the interest held by a tenant for his own life.

At common law the doctrine of merger has nothing to do with the intention of the parties, and provided that certain essentials are satisfied, the effect is automatically to annihilate the smaller estate.

The essentials are that the estates shall unite in the same person without any intervening estate, and that the person in whom they unite shall hold them both in the same right.

To illustrate the first essential, if A., who is tenant for life, with remainder to B. for life, remainder to C. in fee, purchases and takes a conveyance of C.'s fee, the intervening life interest of B., since it is vested, excludes the possibility of merger.

As regards the second essential, if an executor takes, under the Administration of Estates Act, a term of years which belonged to the testator, and then purchases the reversion in fee on his own behalf, the term which the executor holds for the purposes of

---

[1] Blackstone, vol. ii. p. 177; Cruise, Digest, Tit. xxxix. s. 1

administration does not merge in the fee which he owns beneficially.[1]

No merger of entailed interest.

Entailed interests. The exception to the doctrine of merger at common law is that an entailed interest does not merge in the fee simple in reversion or remainder, for the intention of the Statute *de Donis* is that such an interest shall descend to the issue of the tenant in tail. If, for instance, where lands are limited to A. in tail, remainder to B. in fee simple, A. were able by a purchase of the reversion in fee to extinguish his entailed interest under the doctrine of merger, a simple method of defeating the issue would be thrown open. It has therefore been the rule since the sixteenth century that in such a case no merger results.[2]

Effect of merger of term of years.

One effect of the common law doctrine was that the merger of a term of years in the reversion destroyed the covenants contained in any sub-lease that had been carved out of the term.

> Suppose, for instance, that A., seised in fee, leased the land to T. who sub-leased it to U. T. If T. were to surrender his interest to A., the covenants contained in the sub-lease would become un-enforceable, since the reversion to which they were formerly attached no longer existed.[3]

To remedy this, it was enacted in effect by the Real Property Act, 1845,[4] in a section reproduced in the Law of Property Act, 1925,[5] that where the reversion on a lease is destroyed by surrender or merger, the next vested interest in the land shall be deemed to be the reversion for the purpose of preserving the incidents and obligations of the defunct reversion.

> Thus, in the example given above, the covenants entered into between T. and U. T. are enforceable by and against A. and U. T. respectively.

Merger in equity.

View of Equity. Equity has taken a different view of merger. At common law merger results automatically from the union of two estates in the circumstances we have mentioned, and intention does not affect the result. But Equity looks to the intention and to the duties of the parties. If an intention is expressly declared to the effect that the lesser estate shall be kept alive, there is no difficulty; but even in the absence of such an express declaration Equity will presume an intention against merger if it is clearly advantageous to the person in whom the estates are united, or if it is consistent with his duty, that the lesser interest shall not be destroyed.[6] This view now prevails, for it was enacted by the Judicature Act, 1873, that there should be no merger by operation of law of any estate the beneficial interest in which would not be

---

[1] *Chambers* v. *Kingham* (1878), 10 Ch. D. 743.
[2] *Wiscot's Case* (1599), 2 Co. Rep. 60*b*, 61*a*.
[3] *Webb* v. *Russell* (1789), 3 Term Rep. 393.
[4] S. 9.   [5] S. 139.
[6] *Ingle* v. *Vaughan Jenkins*, [1900] 2 Ch. 368; *Re Fletcher*, [1917] 1 Ch. 330.

deemed to be merged or extinguished in equity.[1]

In one case, for instance,[2]

> land was limited to A. for life, remainder to B. for life. A., being too old to manage the property, conveyed the land to B. for the rest of her life to the use that B. should pay her £400 a year out of the profits. The effect of this was that an estate *pur autre vie* and an estate for his own life vested in B., so that at common law the estate *pur autre vie* was destroyed by merger. B. died in the lifetime of A., and the question arose whether A.'s life estate had been destroyed so as to let in the estates which were limited to take effect after B.'s life estate. It was held that there was no merger *in equity*, and therefore no such destruction, for the parties could not have intended to create an interest *pur autre vie* in order that it should be immediately swallowed up in an existing life interest and thereby lost.

In another case :   *Ingle* v.
                                                         Vaughan
                                                         Jenkins.

> X., the first tenant for life under a settlement, agreed to let three acres of the land for 99 years to Y., the second tenant for life, at an annual ground rent of £9, in consideration that Y. would erect thereon a house at a cost of £1,500. After the house had been erected, X. died, with the result that at common law Y's term of years was merged in the life interest to which he now became entitled.

On the death of Y., the remainderman contended that Y's executor was prevented by this merger from claiming any further leasehold interest in the land. The contention failed. The court's one concern is the benefit of the person in whom the two interests unite, and in the instant circumstances it was obviously to the advantage of Y. that the term of years should be kept separate from the life interest.[3]

---

[1] Section 25 (4) ; reproduced in Law of Property Act, 1925, s. 185.
[2] *Snow* v. *Boycott*, [1892] 3 Ch. 110.
[3] *Ingle* v. *Vaughan Jenkins*, [1900] 2 Ch. 368.

BOOK III.

THE TRANSFER AND EXTINCTION OF ESTATES AND INTERESTS.

PART VI.

REGISTERED CONVEYANCING.

SUMMARY.

SECTION I.

THE PRINCIPLE OF REGISTERED CONVEYANCING

The conveyancing of unregistered land depends upon the production by a vendor of a series of documents which recount previous transactions affecting the land and demonstrate to a purchaser the ability of a vendor to convey what he has agreed to convey. "Title" to the interest to be conveyed is thus something deduced from evidence. It has to be proved afresh each time a disposition of land is made. The conveyancing of registered land is different in principle and in practice. Once the title to land is registered, its past history is irrelevant. The title thenceforth is guaranteed by the State, and a purchaser can do no other than rely on it. "Title" has now become something more than evidence. In a sense, it is itself the subject matter of the conveyance. Transfer of land becomes the substitution of one person's name for another's in a registry. That transfer necessarily shifts the whole title registered in the former proprietor's name. Words of limitation do not occur. *Contrast with private conveyancing.*

Registered conveyancing is not, however, a new system of land law. It is based on the familiar concepts of estates and interests for periods of time, leases, mortgages, covenants, settlements, etc. Moreover title to land, though state guaranteed, is still less than absolute. Registered conveyancing is also very firmly a part of the 1925 legislation. The only freehold estate the title to which can be *registered* is the fee simple absolute in possession. Lesser interests are protected in other ways, the most obvious being by *entry* in the register. (This distinction between registration, and an entry in the register, is basic to an understanding of the system.) It follows too that the "curtain principle" is retained. "References to trusts shall, so far as possible, be excluded from the register",[1] though, as we shall see, a notice of their existence has to be entered. Again, following s. 1 of the Law of Property Act, 1925, any incorporeal hereditament in which a legal interest may subsist, e.g. an easement or a rentcharge, is regarded as land for the purposes of registration.[2] *Based on existing land law.*

---

[1] Land Registration Act, hereinafter referred to as L. R. A., 1925, s. 74. Cf. s. 88(1), and *Abigail* v. *Lapin*, [1934] A. C. 491, at p. 500.

[2] If incorporeal, they are protected by entry, and by registration. See Land Registration Rules, hereinafter referred to as L. R. R. 252-7 for the registration of legal easements only as appurtenant to the title to the dominant tenement.

But neither must it be concluded that registered conveyancing is only concerned with transfer, and never affects the substance of land law. This is to give too restricted a meaning to "substance". The difference is due principally to different methods of protecting limited interests; mortgages are protected in a way that avoids the doubts and complexities of their priority in unregistered conveyancing; beneficial interests under settlements are protected in a way that ensures that problems such as those in *Weston* v. *Henshaw*[1] are unlikely to recur. But more fundamental principles are also affected. The *bona fide* purchaser of the legal estate has no special place in registered conveyancing[2] and, furthermore, a person with no title who nevertheless succeeds in getting one registered can transfer it to a purchaser.[3]

The Act[4] lays down precise rules for dealings in the land, and attempts an enumeration of the powers of an owner under the Act.[5]

> "The powers of disposition possessed by a registered proprietor are those expressly conferred on him by the Land Registration Act, 1925, and he has no others."[6]

This rule affects not only the legal title, but also the creation of other rights, such as easements and mortgages. But there remains, of course, a residual power[7] to negotiate and bring into existence equitable rights,[8] though these will in the main stand in need of protection through entry in the register. Obviously, then, a rule of fundamental importance is that the legal title can be affected only by observing the proper requirements. For this reason, it has been suggested[9] that the Act really provides a new statutory title to land, one that is not the fee simple, but a new fee

---

[1] [1950] Ch. 510. *Supra*, p. 715. Possibly also those that occur when a tenant for life's beneficial interest comes to an end secretly, behind the curtain.

[2] For a residual reference to general principle see *Strand Securities, Ltd.* v. *Caswell*, [1965] Ch. 958, at p. 991 *per* RUSSELL, L. J.; [1965] 1 All E. R. 820; and *Abigail* v. *Lapin*, [1934] A. C. 491, at p. 502.

[3] See *Morelle, Ltd.* v. *Wakeling*, [1955] 2 Q. B. 379, at p. 416, per EVERSHED M. R., [1955] 1 All E. R. 708; *A. G.* v. *Parsons* [1956] A. C. 421 at p. 441; *per* Earl JOWITT, [1956] 1 All E. R. 65; and L. R. A., s. 114. See also *infra*, p. 853.

[4] "The Act" is now the Land Registration Acts (L. R. A.) of 1925, 1936, and 1966, implemented by the Land Registration Rules of 1925, 1930, 1936, 1956, and 1964. The authoritative account is Curtis and Ruoff, *Registered Conveyancing* (2nd Edn., 1965). The Act and Rules are not as accurately drafted as could be wished and there are numerous inconsistencies, see for example note 6 on p. 840, *infra*. The courts have taken a fairly robust view in construing the Act so as to give due weight to its overall intent: see *Grace Rymer Investments, Ltd.* v. *Waite*, [1958] Ch. 831; [1958] 2 All E. R. 777.

[5] L. R. A., ss. 18, 19, 21, 22, 69 (4), 108, 109; L. R. R. 74.

[6] Curtis and Ruoff, p. 141.

[7] L. R. A. ss. 101, 107. A contract of sale is an obvious example.

[8] Leases for 21 years or less are not created or noted on the register.

[9] See the controversy between Professor Potter and Professor Hargreaves 1949, 12 M. L. R. at 139, 205 and 477. For other discussions see Connell in (1947), 11 Conv. 184 and 232, and Farrand, *Conveyancing Contracts* (1st Edn., 1964) at p. 186–9.

based on it. But the argument is really a verbal one as to how the consequences of registration affect the character of what is registered. Sections 5 and 69(1) of the Act refer to a registered proprietor as having a fee simple absolute in possession vested in him and it seems only a complication to depart from this terminology.

Registration of title was introduced into England over a century ago, but only on a voluntary basis. It was based on the system which Sir Robert Torrens had invented in Australia.[1] First made compulsory (for the City of London only) in 1897,[2] it is now in the process of being extended on a compulsory basis to all parts of England and Wales, a process that should be complete by 1980.[3] An area is declared to be an area of compulsory registration by Order in Council; until 1966 this was done on the application of the county or county borough concerned, but responsibility for extension is now vested in the central government.[4]

Registration need not be effected immediately an area is made an area of compulsory registration. Title to freehold land (this includes the legal title held by trustees or held under the Settled Land Act) must be registered on its first *sale* after the relevant date, while for registrable leaseholds the rule is that every *grant* of a leasehold for forty years or more, and every assignment on *sale* of a lease with forty or more years still to run, must be registered.[5] If registration is not applied for within two months, the legal estate will not be regarded as vesting in the transferee. Until 1966 it was possible for any title to land in England and Wales to be registered voluntarily, but this is now possible only in special cases.[6] Where voluntary registration occurs, the important rule is that all further dealings with the title attracts the mandatory requirements of the registration system. Though the register is not open to the public, it is possible to discover whether or not a particular plot of land has been registered.

The register is a register of title to land, not a register of deeds

Margin notes:
Extension of registered conveyancing.

Distinction between registration and entry.

---

[1] But our system diverges widely from the Torrens system, which is not a system of insurance, and which presupposes a changed land law. Our system of registered conveyancing must also be kept wholly apart from the system of registration of assurances practised in Yorkshire and Kingston-upon-Hull, which merely records conveyances and devises in a public register.

[2] Land Transfer Act, 1897. For earlier ideas on the subject see Walker in 55 *L. Q. R.*, p. 547, and the Appendix to the Report of R. P. Commissioners (1830), p. 97. See also Scott Cttee. Report, 1919 (Cmd 424); Scott Cttee. Report, 1942 (Cmd 6378); esp. para 238; Rushcliffe Cttee. Report, 1943, (Cmd 6467), and Roxburgh Cttee. Report, 1956 (Cmd 9825).

[3] It is hoped to extend it to all built-up areas by the mid-nineteen-seventies. See 1966 New Law Journal p. 1681 for the position at the end of 1966.

[4] L. R. A., ss. 120-5 as amended by L. R. A., 1936 s. 1, and L. R. A., 1966, s. 1 (1).

[5] L. R. A., s. 123.

[6] L. R. A., 1966, s. 1 (2). The purpose of this restriction is to concentrate on extending compulsory registration. A special case would be a new town, or other large building development, or certain cases of lost deeds.

or charges. Only legal interests in land can be registered,[1] i.e. the fee simple absolute in possession and the term of years absolute. The position in relation to leaseholds is complicated, but the general effect of the legislation is that only leases with more than 21 years to run are to be registered, (but not a mortgage term).[2] Other interests in land, or claimed against or over land, are either protected by entry in the register or (and the best example is leases for not more than 21 years) they take effect as over-riding interests. This is a subject to which we must return later. At the present stage it may be said that, since not all claims against land are registrable, searches of the old kind must still be made.[3] The provisions of the Land Charges Act, 1925 are, however, excluded.[4] We must now look more closely at the registration of the title itself.

SECTION II. THE REGISTER

(A) THE TITLE.

Form of the register.

    The register is divided into three parts, a property register, a proprietorship register, and a charges register.[5] It was intended that the register should "mirror" the title, though, as we shall see, it does so in only a qualified manner. The register is kept on a card index system, and each of its three parts relating to any given title are filed on a separate single card. The register is a register of title, so that where there is more than one legal title subsisting in one piece of land (the obvious case is that of a long leasehold) there will be two cards. A copy of the various entries, called a Land Certificate, is given to the registered proprietor of a title, and can be retained by him or deposited in the registry, but the title itself is not the certificate but the registration in the registry.

Property register.

    The property register describes and identifies the land, and the interest in the land, which is the subject matter of the title, e.g. a fee simple absolute in possession of Blackacre. The interest must, as we have said already, be a legal one. The property register will also mention specific benefits capable of subsisting as legal interests, such as legal easements,[6] and the effect will be to create

---

[1] L. R. A., 2 (1).

[2] L. R. A., s. 8; and see Burford (1937), 1 Conv. (N. S.) at p. 344.

[3] For this and other reasons, it is still necessary (the early view was more optimistic) to proceed by way of contract preliminaries: see Farrand, *Conveyancing Contracts*, at p. 174, *et seq.*

[4] L. R. A., s. 59; see also *Webb* v. *Pollmount, Ltd.*, [1966] Ch. 584; [1966] 1 All E. R. 481, at p. 487, *per* Ungoed-Thomas, J.

[5] L. R. R. 2–12. The register is kept on a geographical basis.

[6] L. R. R. 3 (2)(c) and 254–7. See also L. R. A., s. 19 (2), 72 and *infra*, p. 844. The Registrar has a discretion here, but all *expressly* created easements should appear somewhere on the register. The position in relation to the benefit of covenants is less satisfactory, for the Registrar, due to the complicated

a registered title in them. There may also be a reference to other benefits, for instance the benefit of covenants, and this may extend to the freedom of the land from specific interests such as easements or tithe annuities.[1]

The proprietorship register states the nature of the title, e.g. absolute or qualified, the name of the proprietor, and also the nature of any restrictions that concern the disposition of the land. The charges register contains entries of incumbrances which burden the land, e.g. covenants and mortgages. We will return to these matters later.

Protection of any lesser interests.

There are four different kinds of title, absolute title, possessory title, good leasehold title (for a lessee only) and, finally, qualified title, which cannot be the subject of an application but may be granted by the Registrar.

An absolute title is what the vast majority of applicants obtain. It cannot be registered until it has been approved by the Registrar,[2] who will carry out a full investigation of the title and who can compel the production of deeds and other evidence of title.[3] Opportunity is given to anyone wishing to object, and objections are heard and determined by the Registrar, subject to an appeal to the court.[4] An applicant who has a title which professional opinion would regard as good under private conveyancing may expect to be registered with an absolute title, for the Registrar seems "to occupy the position of a willing but prudent purchaser",[5] and is willing to overlook technical defects in a title if he is satisfied that there is no-one who can impugn the title. A title registered in this way is actually improved by registration. The technical defect is cured, for no-one can subsequently raise it, save in the exceptional case of a rectification action.

Absolute title.

In the case of a leasehold interest,[6] an absolute title may be

---

rules governing covenants, is reluctant to enter on the register a note that a particular piece of land is entitled to a covenant running with that land. He is not bound to, as the property register is only concerned with legal interests, which covenants are not: Curtis and Ruoff, at p, 19. Cf. however the mandatory language of s. 40 (3). The Registrar may, however, note that a particular covenant is *claimed*, and this indulgence is extended to some postive covenants, even though the burden of them does not run with land. See L. R. A., ss. 40 (3), 50, and L. R. R. 78, 199, and 212, and generally 1 Conv. (N. S.) 326, 16 Conv. (N. S.) 38, and Farrand, *Contents of a Conveyance,* at pp. 184–8.

[1] L. R. R. 197, and see *Re Dances Way, West Town, Hayling Island,* [1962] Ch. 490. The dictum of DIPLOCK, L. J., at p. 510 of that case that jurisdiction under this rule is restricted to an interest previously on the register seems unwarranted: see Curtis and Ruoff, at pp. 135–6

[2] L. R. A., s. 4.   [3] L. R. A., s. 15.

[4] L. R. A. s. 13; L. R. R. 31–3, and 298–9. See too s. 14 and the discussion on procedure in *Re Dances Way, West Town, Hayling Island,* [1962] Ch. 490.

[5] Hargreaves in *Stephens' Commentaries* (21st Ed.) vol. i. p. 624. See also Curtis and Ruoff, at pp. 75–7, and Ruoff in 1963 Law Society Gazette 345, and 18 Conv. 130. The Registrar relies on the language of L. R. A., s. 13, proviso (c).

[6] The provisions relating to leaseholds are contained in L. R. A., ss. 8–12. "Lease" includes underlease: L. R. A., s. 3 (x).

2E*

registered only if the Registrar approves not only the title to the leasehold itself, but also the titles to the freehold and to any intermediate leaseholds that may exist. If an absolute title to a leasehold is registered, it vests the leasehold in the first proprietor subject to the same rights, interests and incumbrances as in the case of a freehold registered with an absolute title, but subject to all implied and express covenants, obligations and liabilities incident to the registered land. Where, as under an open contract,[1] a leaseholder is precluded from investigating title to the freehold, he may be registered as the owner of a good leasehold title. This will not protect him if his lease fails owing to some flaw in the freehold interest, as for instance where the lessor is not entitled to grant a lease.

Good leasehold title.

Possessory title.

The Act admits the registration of a possessory title as an inferior but speedy alternative to absolute and good leasehold titles. It depends upon satisfying the Registrar that the applicant is in possession of the land or receipt of rents and profits. There is no examination of title and, as might be expected, the guarantee is a limited one. The registration does not affect or prejudice the enforcement of any estate, right or interest adverse to or in derogation of the title of the first proprietor and subsisting or capable of arising at the time of the first registration.[2] In the case of a freehold or leasehold interest registered with a possessory title the guarantee covers, therefore, only dealings which take place after the registration and does not extend to the title prior to registration.

Qualified title.

Where an application is made to register a freehold with an absolute title and the Registrar comes to the conclusion on the examination of title that it can be established only for a limited period or subject to certain reservations, he may, at the applicant's request, register a qualified title. This title may except from the effect of registration any estate, right or interest arising before a specified date, or arising under a specified instrument, or otherwise described in the register, and has the same effect as an absolute title save for the estate, right or interest excepted.[3] A qualified title may also be registered in respect of a leasehold when the examination of the title either of the lessor to the reversion, or of the lessee to the leasehold interest, discloses similar problems to those described above. It has the same effect as a good leasehold title, subject to the exception of the specified interests.[4]

Conversion of titles.

The Act provides for the conversion of inferior titles to absolute or good leasehold titles.[5] Possessory titles, if for no other reason than the effect of the Limitation Act, cannot remain so per-

---

[1] Law of Property Act, 1925, s. 44; *supra*, p. 659. The Registrar cannot insist on production of the lessor's land certificate unless the lessee could: *Strand Securities, Ltd.* v. *Caswell*, [1965] Ch. 958; [1965] 1 All E. R. 820.

[2] L. R. A., ss. 6 and 11. There is also provision for a transitional possessory title, while further enquiries are carried out: L. R. R. 36.

[3] L. R. A., s. 7.   [4] L. R. A., s. 12.   [5] L. R. A., s. 77.

manently. The Registrar, after due enquiry, must convert possessory titles of freehold land to absolute where the title has been registered for fifteen years, and possessory titles of leasehold to good leasehold where registered for ten years, but he must be satisfied that the proprietor is in possession. The Registrar also has an option to convert into absolute (or good leasehold) title in two cases: firstly, if land has been registered with a qualified, good leasehold or possessory title and is subsequently transferred for value; secondly, if land has been registered as good leasehold and the first proprietor or his successors have been in possession for ten years.

(B). THIRD PARTY RIGHTS.

Third party rights and claims on the register may be protected in four different ways, namely, by the entry on the register of a restriction, a caution, an inhibition or a notice.[1]

A restriction is an entry which prevents dealings in registered land until certain specified conditions or requirements have been complied with.[2] Its object is thus to record, on the proprietorship register, any impediment to the proprietor's freedom of disposal. A restriction can only be entered on the register with the concurrence of the proprietor and, once entered, no transaction will be permitted except in conformity with its terms, although the Registrar must not enter any restriction which he considers to be "unreasonable or calculated to cause inconvenience". Restrictions are employed *inter alia* to give effect to strict settlements and trusts for sale of registered land. Thus, if X is the tenant for life and Y and Z are the trustees of a settlement, X will be the registered proprietor of the fee simple of the settled land and the register will contain two restrictions, the first preventing the registration of any disposition under which capital money arises unless the money is paid to Y and Z, and the second preventing the registration of any disposition not authorized by the Settled Land Act, 1925. In the same way, when land is held upon trust for sale, restrictions ensure that capital money arising is paid to at least two trustees or to a trust corporation or into court. By this means, the trusts of a strict settlement or trust for sale are protected without their details being brought onto the register. There is still a curtain.[3] Similarly with co-ownership, a restriction is obligatory unless the proprietors are entitled for their own benefit or can give valid receipts for the capital money, or unless one of them is a trust corporation.[4]

Restrictions.

Protection of equitable interests.

Co-ownership.

---

[1] See generally Crane (1958), 22 Conv. 14 and Ruoff, 17 Conv. 105, 18 Conv. 130. For mortgages, see *infra* p. 848.

[2] L. R. A., s. 58.

[3] L. R. A., ss. 86, 91 (2), 94, 95, and L. R. R. 56–59 and 104 (1), and Forms 9 and 10.

[4] L. R. A., s. 58 (3), L. R. R. 213, Form 62.

Cautions.   A caution,[1] unlike a restriction, is often hostile. It too is entered in the proprietorship register, but without the proprietor's concurrence. The Registrar must warn a cautioner if an application is made to register any dealing with, or make any entry to protect any interest in, the land. The effect is to give the cautioner a certain amount of time in which to protest.

A caution may be lodged at the time of first registration. For instance, anyone who claims that he has such an interest in land (not already registered) as entitles him to object to any disposition of it being made without his consent, may lodge a caution against a first registration; this will secure him an opportunity of opposing it.[2] This is available for example to a person who has agreed to purchase the land. But a caution may also be lodged subsequently. Anyone with an interest in land (already registered in the name of another) may lodge a caution if his interest is unprotected by a notice or restriction.[3] But anyone who lodges a caution without reasonable cause will be liable to pay compensation for any damage sustained.[4]

Inhibitions.   An inhibition is also hostile, and is entered on the proprietorship register, upon the application of a person interested.[5] Such an entry prevents any dealings with the registered land, either generally or for a given time or until the occurrence of an event named in the order. This is a residual provision and is intended to be employed primarily where, for reasons of urgency or otherwise, the other methods of protection cannot be used.[6]

Notices.   A notice may be entered to protect any of a number of lesser interests and rights affecting the land.[7] It will only protect an interest that is valid and effective independently of the register for, unlike registration of title, notice is incapable of converting an invalid interest into a potentially valid one.[8] Nor does entry of a covenant guarantee that it will run with land. Notice may also be entered of a *claim* to a right or interest.[9] But subject to these reservations, entry by way of a notice gives protection to and information about important rights adverse to land like easements,[10] covenants, long leases[11] and estate contracts. Noting of adverse

---

[1] L. R. A. s. 55.   [2] L. R. A., s. 53 (1).
[3] L. R. A., s. 54 (1).   [4] L. R. A., s. 56 (3).
[5] L. R. A., s. 57. The court, or the registrar, must agree to its entry.
[6] For an instance where it is used as a matter of ordinary procedure, see bankruptcy, *infra*, p. 852.
[7] L. R. A., ss. 48–53, 59, and L. R. R. 190. For the residual character of notices, see particularly ss. 49 (1) (f) and 59 (1) and (5).
[8] *Cator* v. *Newton and Bates*, [1940] 1 K. B. 415; [1939] 4 All E. R. 457; L. R. A., s. 52.
[9] L. R. A., s. 52 (2).
[10] The Registrar must enter on the register all adverse easements shown to exist in the documents produced at the time of first registration: s. 70 (2). Thereafter, adverse easements may be entered by him, in his discretion: L. R. R. 41 (1). The difficulties in determining, from available evidence, the nature and extent of easements is considerable. See generally *Re Dances Way, West Town, Hayling Island*, [1962] Ch. 490.
[11] Leases for 21 years or less are overriding interests and, despite the

interests is quite separate, of course, from the *registration* of lease-holds and easements and the noting of the *benefit* of covenants in the property register; though there will frequently be cross references. For instance, registration of a lease will always be accompanied by a note of it on the title out of which it is carved.[1]

Notice in the register has, in general, the same function that registration in the Land Charges Register has in unregistered conveyancing. Subsequent dispositions of the land are subject to those interests capable of affecting a transferee as are the subject of a notice, while *purchasers* take free of interests requiring a notice for protection if they are not so protected.[2]

The availability of protection by way of a notice does not exclude protection under other parts of the registration machinery, if relevant, a factor which places flexibility above symmetry. Thus, an option in a lease to purchase the freehold can both be protected by a notice and, independently of the register, may constitute an overriding interest;[3] again, a deposit of a land certificate as security for a loan can be the subject of protection in several different ways.[4]

Overriding and Minor Interests. We must at this stage consider the distinction between overriding and minor interests. This is the most difficult and unsatisfactory part of the whole system of registration of title in its present form. The basic idea is simple enough. Some interests require protection on the register; others do not. Overriding interests are those interests that bind a registered proprietor and his transferees, irrespective of entry on the register.[5] The main examples are profits à prendre, legal easements, leases for not more than 21 years, local land charges, rights acquired or being acquired under the Limitation Act, and the

Overriding interests.

> "rights of every person in actual occupation of the land or in receipt of the rents and profits thereof, save where enquiry is made of such person and the rights are not disclosed."

generous wording of L. R. A., s. 70 (3), never appear on the register, but are protected only as overriding interests. See L. R. A., ss. 19 (2), 48 (1). Generally on the subject of leases and underleases, see *Strand Securities, Ltd.* v. *Caswell*, [1965] Ch. 958, [1965] 1 All E. R. 820.

[1] Lease includes underlease: s. 3 (x). Accordingly, underleases are properly noted on the title of the head-lease.

[2] L. R. A., ss. 20, 23, 48, 50, 52 (1), 101; *White* v. *Bijou Mansions*, [1937] Ch. 610; [1937] 3 All E. R. 269. The sections refer to " valuable consideration", and nowhere is there the reference that one would expect to s. 3 (xxi), defining "purchaser" as *bona fide* purchaser for value. See also *Jones* v. *Lipman*, [1962] 1 W. L. R. 832.

[3] *Webb* v. *Pollmount, Ltd.*, [1966] 1 All E. R. 481, interpreting L. R. A., s. 59 (1). Again, L. R. A., s. 48 makes provision for notice, on the superior title, of leases that do not constitute overriding interests *as such* (i.e. leases for more than 21 years), but in fact most lessees and lessors can claim the protection given to an overriding interest under s. 70 (1) (g): see *infra*, p. 847.

[4] *Re White Rose Cottage*, [1965] Ch. 940, especially *per* Lord DENNING, M. R., at pp. 949–50.

[5] L. R. A., s. 70, which contains a complete list, and s. 3 (xvi).

Even the Chief Land Registrar is compelled to call this assortment "an unholy jumble".[1]

Minor interests.

Minor interests, on the other hand, are interests needing protection on the register.[2] Some of them are incapable of binding a purchaser even if registered, but nevertheless affect the method of disposing of land. Thus, in the case of beneficial interests under a settlement or trust for sale that will be overreached on a sale of the land, a restriction will be entered on the proprietorship register indicating that the proprietor of the legal title is limited in his powers. But other minor interests do bind purchasers for valuable consideration,[3] if protected by entry in the register. Conversely, a purchaser will take free from them (unless, as happens quite frequently, they are protected in other ways[4]) if they are not so protected by entry. A donee, however, will be bound by them even if they are not so protected. In this category come covenants, equitable easements, legal and equitable rentcharges, and estate contracts.

Difficulties of overriding interests.

Three points must now be made.

Firstly, the distinction between overriding and minor interests is not the same as that between legal and equitable interests. Equitable profits are overriding while equitable easements and legal rentcharges are minor interests (though a legal rentcharge is itself an incorporeal hereditament!). These statutory provisions replace the old rule in equity of the *bona fide* purchaser for value of the legal estate.

Secondly, it does not follow, as one would at first sight think that it would, that overriding interests do not appear on the register. They do appear frequently, but their capacity to override is not dependent on the register.[5] If on the register, however, they are not regarded as overriding.[6] It is convenient that some should appear on the register, and under some circumstances it is obligatory that they should; expressly created legal easements provide an example when this is both convenient and obligatory.[7]

Thirdly, some interests which can and should be protected as minor interests are capable of constituting overriding interests. There is a sad overlap here, due in some degree to classifying the

[1] Ruoff, *Concise Land Registration Act*, at p. 34.

[2] L. R. A., ss. 3 (xv), 20, 23, 48, 50, 52, 59, 101. As with unregistered land (L. P. A., 1925, s. 199), express notice of what should be protected in the register but is not, is immaterial: *Hodges* v. *Jones*, [1935] Ch. 657, at p. 671, *per* LUXMOORE, J, and s. 59 (6).

[3] See note 2, *supra*, p. 845.

[4] See note 3, *supra*, p. 845.

[5] *Re Dances Way, West Town, Hayling Island*, [1962] Ch. 490, at p. 507, *per* UPJOHN, L. J.

[6] *Webb* v. *Pollmount, Ltd.*, [1966] Ch. 584; [1966] 1 All E. R. 481, at p. 484, *per* UNGOED-THOMAS, J.; L. R. A., s. 3 (xvi). The relevant statutory protections then apply.

[7] L. R. A., ss. 19 (2), 70 (2) (3); L. R. R. 41 (1), 252–7; see *supra*, p. 840, esp. note 6 and p. 844, esp. note 10.

rights of those in actual occupation as overriding.[1] Thus a contract for the sale or lease[2] of registered land should be protected by notice as a minor interest, but if the purchaser or lessee is let into occupation before formal transfer *and* there is no note on the register of his interest, the mere fact of his occupation turns his minor interest into an overriding one.[3] The weight attached to occupation is most significant and unbalancing. Nor is the problem confined to the single right to occupy, for it extends to the *rights of those in* occupation, which includes options to purchase the freehold contained in a lease[4] and rights being acquired under the Limitation Act.[5] In its effect on leases, occupation has the most remarkable consequences; it would seem that a lessee in occupation (irrespective of the length of the lease) can always rely on just his occupation for protection—a result which can not have been intended. A lessor in receipt of rent, or in occupation through a servant or agent is also protected in this way. As Lord DENNING, M.R., put it in the leading case:[6]

> " Section 70 (1) (g) is an important provision. Fundamentally, its object is to protect a person in actual occupation of land from having his rights lost in the welter of registration. He can stay there and do nothing. Yet he will be protected. No one can buy the land over his head and thereby take away or diminish his rights. It is up to every purchaser before he buys to make inquiry on the premises. If he fails to do so, it is at his own risk. He must take subject to whatever rights the occupier may have. Such is the doctrine of *Hunt* v. *Luck*, for unregistered land. Section 70 (1) (g) carries the same doctrine forward into registered land . . . ".

It must be emphasized, however, that it is the *rights* of the occupier that are crucial. As RUSSELL, L. J., put it:[7]

---

[1] L. R. A., s. 70 (1) (g), quoted *supra*, p. 845. See also *Bridges* v. *Mees*, [1957] Ch. 475, at p. 487, *per* HARMAN J.; [1957] 2 All. E. R. 577.

[2] A contract for the grant of a lease (for 21 years or less) is not an overriding interest under L. R. A., s. 70 (1) (k), as there has been no "grant"; *Walsh* v. *Lonsdale* is of no assistance: *City Permanent Building Society* v. *Miller*, [1952] Ch. 840; [1952] 2 All E. R. 621. S. 3 (x), taken by itself, is misleading on this point.

[3] *Woolwich Equitable Building Society* v. *Marshall*, [1952] Ch. 1; [1951] 2 All E. R. 769; *Mornington Permanent Building Society* v. *Kenway*, [1953] Ch. 382; [1953] 1 All E. R. 951. It has even been suggested that, since possession plus a valid contract for sale constitutes an overriding interest, there is little point in registration itself—a suggestion which, though cogent, is too destructive!

[4] *Webb* v. *Pollmount, Ltd.*, [1966] Ch. 584; [1966] 1 All E. R. 481.

[5] *Bridges* v. *Mees*, [1957] Ch. 475.

[6] *Strand Securities, Ltd.* v. *Caswell*, [1965] Ch. 958 at 979–80; see also *per* RUSSELL, L. J., at p. 984; [1965] 1 All. E. R. 820. The facts of this case showed that the only person in occupation (a step-daughter who had been deserted by her husband) was a rent-free licensee not acting as an agent. But this is a most exceptional situation.

[7] *National Provincial Bank, Ltd.* v. *Hastings Car Mart, Ltd.*, [1964] Ch. 665, at p. 696; [1964] 3 All E. R. 93; a dissenting judgment which was upheld (with special reference to this passage) in the House of Lords: [1965] A. C. 1175 at 1226, 1228, 1240 and 1261–2. *Quaere* whether this analysis helps in solving the perplexing problem of whether beneficiaries under a trust for sale (settled land is provided for by L. R. A., s. 86 (2)) are protected under s. 70. See 22 Conv., at p. 24.

"It seems to me that section 70 in all its parts is dealing with rights in reference to land which have the quality of being capable of enduring through different ownerships of the land, according to normal conceptions of title to real property. . . . It is the rights of such a person which constitute the overriding interest and must be examined, not his occupation."

Thus the deserted wife in occupation of the matrimonial home has no right affecting property entitling her to claim an overriding interest,[1] while the owner of an option to purchase a freehold contained in a lease does, since it "affects the reversion . . . and subsists in reference to the registered land".[2]

Need for reform.   It has to be concluded that a severe measure of reform is needed to avoid this needless confusion.[3] The registration system, being dependent on statute, is itself dependent on the vagaries of statutory interpretation. But criticism goes further than that. The basic idea of overriding interests seems to have been to save from registration those interests which any prudent purchaser could discover by inspection of the land itself. But though this is convenient to the person enjoying the interest, one must set against it the inconvenience to purchasers, who frequently have to proceed *via* the older methods of investigation.[4] Those who find the latter factor the more persuasive would counsel not the tidying up of overriding interests, but as complete an abolition of them as is feasible.[5]

(C). MORTGAGES.

A mortgage of registered land may be created (i) by registered charge (ii) by unregistered mortgage and (iii) by deposit of the land certificate.

Registered charge.   (i) A registered charge must be created by deed but may be in any form, provided that the land is described by reference to the register or in some other way that will enable the land to be identified without reference to any other document. A registered charge must not refer to any other interest or charge which (a) would have priority over it and is not registered or protected in the register and (b) is not an overriding interest.[6] A chargee is registered as the proprietor of the charge, and a charge certificate

---

[1] *National Provincial Bank, Ltd.,* v. *Ainsworth,* [1965] A. C. 1175; [1965] 2 All E. R. 472. *Quaere* does this affect the position of the wife who has no title to the matrimonial home but who contributed to its purchase: see Rudden, 27 Conv. 51.

[2] *Webb* v. *Pollmount Estates,* [1966] Ch. 584; [1966] 1 All E. R. 481 at p. 485 and pp. 486–7, *per* Ungoed-Thomas, J.

[3] See also (1952), 16 Conv, at p. 187.

[4] There is, on general principle, a duty to declare any overriding interest that is not obvious.

[5] See the matter discussed at (1961) 24 M. L. R. 136, and also by Farrand, *Conveyancing Contracts,* at p. 193, *et seq.*

[6] L. R. A., s. 25.

is then issued to him, the land certificate being deposited at the registry until the charge is cancelled.[1] The registered charge takes effect as a charge by way of legal mortgage, but it may include a demise or sub-demise.[2]

Covenants are implied to pay principal and interest and, where the charge is created on a leasehold, to pay rent, observe covenants and conditions and to indemnify the proprietor.[3] Registered charges rank for priority according to the order in which they are entered on the register, not according to the order in which they are created, unless an entry on the register provides otherwise.[4] The proprietor has all the powers conferred by law on the owner of a legal mortgage,[5] and he may therefore take possession, foreclose and sell. Upon foreclosure the proprietor of the charge is registered as proprietor of the land, and the charge and all incumbrances and entries inferior to it are cancelled. In the same way, a sale will be completed by registration which will transfer the legal estate to the purchaser, once again cancelling the charge and all incumbrances and entries inferior to it.[6]

Rights of chargees.

Tacking is only possible (*a*) if the registered proprietor is under an obligation to make further advances or (*b*) where a registered charge is made for securing further advances. In this case the Registrar must, before making any entry in the register which would prejudicially affect the priority of any further advances, give notice by registered post to the proprietor of the charge, who may tack any advances made by him up to the time when he receives or ought to have received the notice in due course of post.[7]

Tacking.

(ii) A proprietor of registered land may mortgage the land as if it were unregistered, and the mortgage so created may be protected by a caution in special form.[8] This form of mortgage is rarely employed, for unless a mortgage of both registered and unregistered land is created, it has no advantages over the registered charge.

Unregistered mortgage.

(iii) The proprietor of registered land or of a registered charge may create a lien by deposit of the land or charge certificate. The lien is similar to a mortgage by deposit of title deeds of unregistered land, and takes effect subject to overriding interests, registered interests and any entries then upon the register.[9] The mortgagee by deposit should give written notice to the Registrar,

Mortgage by deposit.

---

[1] *Ibid.*, s. 26`(1), s. 63. *Grace Rymer Investments, Ltd.* v. *Waite*, [1958] 1 Ch. 831. The charge is entered on the charges register.
[2] *Ibid.*, s. 27 (2).   [3] *Ibid.*, s. 28.
[4] *Ibid.*, s. 29. L. R. R. 160–1.   [5] L. R. A., s. 34.
[6] The legal estate may in certain circumstances be transferrable by a mere equitable mortgagee: *Re White Rose Cottage*, [1965] Ch. 940.
[7] *Ibid.*, s. 30 (1) (3), added by Law of Property (Amendment) Act, 1926, s. 5.
[8] L. R. A., s. 106; L. R. R. 223 (a mortgage caution).
[9] *Ibid.*, s. 66; *Re White Rose Cottage*, [1965] Ch. 940; [1965] 1 All E. R. 11.

who will enter on the charges register a notice that will operate as a caution.[1]

Lodging of cautions and inhibitions governs priority of equitable interests.

Priority of mortgages of equitable interests. It will be recalled that, in unregistered land, priorities of equitable interests are governed by the rule in *Dearle* v. *Hall* as extended by s. 137 of the Law of Property Act, 1925.[2] In registered land, such priorities are governed by special rules and not by the giving of notice to trustees. A mortgagee or other assignee of an equitable interest will obtain priority by lodging a priority inhibition (used in the case of an absolute assignment) or a priority caution (used in all other cases). Priorities are determined by the order in which these inhibitions and cautions are lodged. They are entered in the " Index of Minor Interests ",[3] a misleading name, for it is not a register of minor interests at all but a register of *dealings* in minor interests. A purchaser of the legal estate will not be concerned with it, for its purpose is solely to determine the priority of dealings with minor interests which are not on the register and which will be overreached. A priority caution or inhibition once lodged differs in an important respect from notice given to trustees in the case of unregistered land, for a mortgagee who protects himself by an entry will obtain priority over an earlier unprotected mortgage, even if he knows of its existence.

SECTION III. DEALINGS WITH REGISTERED LAND

(A). TRANSFER INTER VIVOS.

The preliminary enquiries and the contract of sale[4] follow the pattern of unregistered conveyancing, but the investigation of the title is radically different. No longer does the vendor need to trace the history of the transactions in which the estate has been involved, for the register is conclusive on the question of ownership. The register is, however, private and the vendor must

Duties of vendor.

give the purchaser authority to inspect it and, in lieu of an abstract of title, supply him with a copy of the entries and of any filed plans and copies or abstracts of any documents noted on the register. The register is, however, not conclusive as to third party rights and a vendor is therefore required to provide a purchaser with copies, abstracts and evidence of all rights and interests appurtenant to the registered land, as to which the register is not conclusive.[5]

---

[1] L. R. R. 239. There may also be a notice of intent to deposit: L. R. R. 240–1.

[2] *Supra*, p. 637.

[3] The index is not of course confined to mortgages. See generally L. R. A., s. 102 and L. R. R. 229.

[4] Which can, of course, pass an equitable interest.

[5] L. R. A., s. 110.

Requisitions on title follow the usual form but are limited to overriding interests and interests protected by an entry. Searches must be made of local land charges registers, for local land charges are overriding interests. But it will not be necessary to search the charges register under the Land Charges Act, 1925, as third party rights which would appear there if the land were unregistered will appear on the register of title. The main search will therefore be of the register itself. This may be undertaken either personally or by an official search. The official search has a considerable advantage, for once a purchaser has obtained a certificate of such a search any entry made after the date of the certificate and before an application is made by the purchaser for registration is postponed to the purchaser's application, provided that his application is delivered, together with the certificate, at the registry before the office is opened or deemed to be open on the fifteenth day after the date of the certificate.[1]

Requisitions and searches.

The transfer must be on one of the forms set out in the Rules. It will be deemed to contain the general words implied by s. 62 of the Law of Property Act, 1925, so far as they are appropriate.[2] The usual covenants for title may be incorporated, it is thought, by inserting the appropriate words whereby a person is expressed to convey "as beneficial owner", "as settlor", "as trustee", etc., as the case may be. The transfer must be executed by deed in the same way as a conveyance under the Law of Property Act, stamped with the appropriate Inland Revenue Stamp, and sent to the registry together with the Land Certificate. The Registrar will then send a notice to the transferor and, if no objection is made within three days, the transferee will be registered as the proprietor. Registration of the transferee's name completes the transfer and terminates the legal ownership of the transferor.[3]

Form of transfer.

(B). TRANSFER ON DEATH.

Personal representatives of a sole registered proprietor or of the survivor of two or more joint proprietors are entitled to be registered as proprietors in place of the deceased proprietor on the production to the Registrar of the grant of probate or letters of administration.[4] There is, however, an alternative procedure which is more frequently adopted, for the personal representatives need not themselves be registered but may have the land transferred direct to the devisee, legatee or purchaser, who will be registered in place of the deceased proprietor on production of the

---

[1] L. R. R. 290, *et seq.*, L. R. R., 1930, r. 1; L. R. R. 1936, r. 1. There are provisions for obtaining priority for 14 days for specified applications; L. R. R. 10, 71, 88. See also *Strand Securities, Ltd.* v. *Caswell*, [1965] Ch. 958; [1965] 1 All E. R. 820; and Ruoff, 1965 Law Society's Gazette 507.

[2] L. R. A., s. 19 (3); *supra*, p. 485. See also Curtis and Ruoff, at p. 115.

[3] Registration takes effect as from the day on which a completed application is delivered: L. R. R. 83.

[4] L. R. A., s. 41.

instrument of assent or transfer together with the grant of probate or letters of administration.[1]

(C). TRANSFER ON BANKRUPTCY.

If a registered proprietor is adjudicated bankrupt, his estate vests in his trustee in bankruptcy who may be registered in his place.[2] At the earlier stages, creditors are protected by a creditor's notice and a bankruptcy inhibition. The Registrar will enter a creditor's notice as soon as a bankruptcy petition is presented. This prevents the land being sold free from the creditor's claims and remains effective until a bankruptcy inhibition is entered or the trustee in bankruptcy is registered as proprietor. The bankruptcy inhibition is entered on the proprietorship register when a receiving order is made, and this ensures that no dealing with the registered land can take place until the inhibition is vacated.[3]

(D). LIMITATION AND PRESCRIPTION.

Adverse possession.

The Limitation Act, 1939 applies to registered land, and a title to a registered estate may be acquired by adverse possession.[4] There is, however, an interesting difference which springs from the mechanics of registration. When a squatter acquires a legal title to unregistered land by adverse possession, the former owner's estate is automatically extinguished. With registered land however, there is no automatic extinction of the proprietor's title but it is deemed to be held by the proprietor on trust for the squatter, though without prejudice to the rights of any other person interested in the land whose estate or interest is not extinguished by the Act of 1939. Anyone claiming to have acquired a title to registered land under the Limitation Act may apply to be registered as proprietor and he may be registered with an absolute, good leasehold, qualified or possessory title, as the case may be, but his estate will be a completely new one and the registration will be treated as that of a first proprietor.[5]

Easements.

An easement, right or privilege may be acquired by prescription over registered land in the same way as it can over unregistered land. It takes effect in equity unless it is capable of subsisting as a legal estate, in which case it also takes effect at law. It then becomes an overriding interest and notice of it may be entered on the register if the Registrar thinks fit.[6]

---

[1] L. R. A., s. 37.
[2] L. R. A., ss. 42 (1), 61 (5). Until the appointment of a trustee, the official receiver is entitled to be registered.   [3] L. R. A., s. 61.
[4] See L. R. A., s. 70 (1) (f) for the connection of this subject with overriding interests: *Bridges* v. *Mees*, [1957] Ch. 475; [1957] 2 All E. R. 577 and cf. *National Provincial Bank, Ltd.* v. *Hastings Car Mart Ltd.*, [1964] Ch. 665 at p. 696, *per* Russell, L. J.; [1964] 3 All E. R. 93.
[5] L. R. A., s. 75; *St. Marylebone Property, Co., Ltd.* v. *Fairweather*, [1963] A. C. 510, at pp. 541 and 548; [1962] 2 All E. R. 288. Cf. *supra*, p. 822.
[6] L. R. A. s. 75 (2); L. R. R. 250. See *supra*, p. 840, and Curtis and Ruoff, pp. 116 and 742–3.

SECTION IV. RECTIFICATION AND INDEMNITIES.

Title to land, once registered, is thenceforth guaranteed by the State. The Land Registration system is to some extent an insurance system, and is backed by an Insurance Fund, out of which compensation is payable in certain circumstances. It is this which makes it so different from the Torrens system.[1] We have also seen that the title may be expressly registered as qualified or only possessory, and that overriding interests are excluded.

We must now go a further stage and note that there is an internal qualification to the title written in by the Acts themselves, for s. 82 enables the register to be rectified. Section 83, however, provides for an indemnity for those who have suffered loss through errors in the register.

Under Section 82, a proprietor's name may be removed when an entry has been obtained by fraud, when he would not have become an estate owner had the land not been registered in his name, and when, because of any error or omission in the register it would be just to rectify it. But the section protects a *proprietor in possession* by providing that rectification may only take place against him if:

Rectification of register.

(*a*)   it is to give effect to an overriding interest, or

(*b*)   he is a party or privy, or has caused or substantially contributed by his act, neglect or default to the fraud, mistake or omission which needs to be rectified,[2] or

(*c*)   the immediate disposition to him was void, or the disposition of any person through whom he claims otherwise than for value was void, or

(*d*)   for any other reason, it would be unjust not to rectify against him.

The principle which emerges is that a *purchaser* who buys registered land and remains in *possession* of it is guaranteed his possession, and rectification will not be ordered against him except to give effect to an overriding interest. If, however, he has contributed to the error, rectification may be ordered against him. An applicant for registration will be regarded as having contributed to a mistaken registration if, however innocently, the description of the property in an application leads to other property

---

[1] In over 50 years, claims for indemnity have only amounted to a little over £20,000. Curtis and Ruoff, p. 12. Title insurance as practised in America is of course something even more different. See 27 Conv. 240 (Roberts), and also 30 Conv. 194 (Payne).

[2] *Re Deptford High Street, No.* 139, [1951] Ch. 884; [1951] 1 All E. R. 950, following *Chowood, Ltd.* v *Lybil* (No. 2), [1930] 2 Ch. 156; *Re Seaview Gardens, Claridge* v. *Tingey*, [1966] 3 All E. R. 935; [1967] 1 W. L. R. 134. But rectification is only likely to be ordered against a *first* purchaser: see *supra*, p. 838 n. 3, for the principle that then applies, see also Farrand, *Conveyancing Contracts*, pp. 233-5.

being included in the area of which the applicant is eventually registered as first proprietor. There is a discretionary element in the jurisdiction, however, and rectification may not be ordered in favour of an owner who has stood by and has watched a defendant build on the land before intervening.[1]

Right of indemnity.   A right of indemnity is available under section 83 to anyone suffering loss by reason of:

(*a*) any rectification of the register,

(*b*) an error or omission on the register which is not rectified,

(*c*) the loss or destruction of any document lodged at the registry for inspection or safe custody, or an error in any official search.

Apart from (*c*), compensation is paid only when someone *suffers loss by reason of* a rectification or a mistake that has been made on the register, which is not to be rectified. Hence, when a purchaser bought registered land on part of which, unknown to the purchaser, a squatter had already established a title by possession and rectification was ordered (because the right was an overriding interest), the purchaser was unable to obtain an indemnity because his loss was not "by reason of the rectification" but had resulted from the purchase itself.[2] If, however, a proprietor of registered land claims in good faith under a disposition which is forged and the register is rectified against him, he is deemed to have suffered loss by reason of the rectification.[3] But compensation is never payable if the applicant has caused or substantially contributed to the loss by his own acts, neglects, defaults or fraud, or if he derives title (otherwise than under a disposition for valuable consideration which is registered or protected on the register) from someone who has behaved likewise.[4] An extreme example is provided by the case of the acid bath murderer, Haigh.[5] Haigh forged the signature of a registered proprietor, was registered in his name and then, in that name, sold to a purchaser for value. This last disposition was held to protect the purchaser from rectification. But the personal representatives of the real proprietor were compensated in full.

[1] *Re Sea View Gardens, supra,* at pp. 941 and 141, respectively, *per* PENNYCUICK, J.

[2] In *Re Chowood's Registered Land,* [1933] Ch. 574; followed in *Re Boyle's Claim,* [1961] 1 All E. R. 620; [1961] 1 W. L. R. 339.

[3] L. R. A. s. 83 (4).

[4] S. 83 (5) (a) as amended by L. R. A., 1966, s. 1 (4). Only fraud affects compensation for losses incurred before 1967.

[5] Recounted in Curtis and Ruoff, p. 74.

BOOK III.

THE TRANSFER AND EXTINCTION OF ESTATES AND INTERESTS.

PART VII.

INCAPACITIES AND DISABILITIES WITH REGARD TO THE HOLDING AND TRANSFER OF ESTATES AND INTERESTS.

SUMMARY.

or voluntarily it may be said in general that he is prohibited from

1. the acquisition by an infant of interests in land;
2. the alienation by an infant of interests in land; and
3. the management of an infant's property.

CHAPTER I.

INFANTS.

SUMMARY.

SECTION I. INTRODUCTORY NOTE.

An infant is a person, whether male or female, who has not
reached the age of twenty-one years. This age was in the earliest
times adopted to mark the termination of a tenant's minority in
the case of the military tenures, though a tenant who held by
some other tenure apparently attained his majority at fifteen.
This divergence, however, gradually fell into desuetude, and
as long ago as the time of Littleton the age of twenty-one years
was said to constitute full age for both males and females in all
cases.[1] A person who has not attained that age is held by English
law to require special protection, and as regards the ownership

marginal note: What is full age.

---

[1] Litt., s. 104.   See generally, Holdsworth, *History of English Law*, vol. iii.
pp. 510 *et seq*.

of property, it may be said in general that he is prohibited from exercising those powers of management and alienation which, in the case of a person of full age, are the necessary incidents of ownership. There are no gradations of infancy according to English law, and so a person of twenty years of age is, for the most part, subject to the same incapacities as a child in arms.[1]

Our task in the present chapter is to deal with three aspects of infancy, namely :

1. the acquisition by an infant of interests in land ;
2. the alienation by an infant of interests in land ; and
3. the management of an infant's property.

SECTION II. ACQUISITION BY AN INFANT OF INTERESTS IN LAND.

Infant cannot be estate owner.

The fundamental principle of the legislation of 1925 is that an infant can never hold a *legal estate* in land.[2] He cannot be an estate owner.[3] This restriction, which is imposed in the interests of a simplified system of conveyancing, does not mean that he cannot hold and enjoy beneficially an equitable interest, and there is nothing to prevent land being transferred to him by

If beneficially entitled is tenant for life.

way of gift, sale or settlement. In such a case, the statutory policy is to put him in the position of a beneficial tenant for life and during his minority to vest the legal estate in trustees whose identity will depend upon whether he comes to his interest as grantee, devisee, heir on intestacy, beneficiary under a settlement, mortgagee, or trustee of the land for the benefit of another person.

(A) GRANT *INTER VIVOS* TO AN INFANT.

Grant operates as contract to settle.

It is enacted that a conveyance of a legal estate in land to an infant alone, or to two or more persons jointly, both or all of whom are infants, for his or their own benefit, shall operate only as an agreement for valuable consideration to execute a settlement in his or their favour.[4] This means that the grantor must as soon as possible execute a principal vesting deed and a trust instrument,[5] meanwhile holding the land in trust for the infant. In this case, however, the legal estate will be transferred by the vesting deed not to the infant as tenant for life, but to the trustees when they are appointed, who then become the " statutory owners."[6]

---

[1] A male of fourteen or a female of twelve could contract a valid marriage; Comyn's Digest, Baron & Feme, B. 5 ; but now, by the Age of Marriage Act, 1929 (s. 1 (1)), a marriage between persons either of whom is under 16 is void.
[2] Law of Property Act, 1925, s. 1 (6).
[3] *Ibid.*, s. 205 (2).
[4] *Ibid.*, s. 19 (1) ; Settled Land Act, 1925, s. 27 (1).
[5] *Supra*, pp. 705 *et seq.*   [6] *Supra*, p. 701.

If a legal estate is conveyed to an infant jointly with one or more other persons of full age, the person or persons of full age take the legal estate on trust for sale.[1]   In this case the persons of full age hold upon the *statutory trusts* applicable to a joint tenancy, *i.e.* upon trust to sell the land and to hold the proceeds and the interim profits for the benefit of themselves and the infant.[2]   If, however, life interests are given, there is a settlement and the adults are tenants for life under the Settled Land Act, 1925.[3]

Grant to infant jointly with adult.

(B) DEVISE TO AN INFANT.

In the case of a devise to an infant the legal estate vests at first in the personal representatives by virtue of the Administration of Estates Act, 1925, but in considering the ultimate destination of the legal estate we must distinguish between a devise of an absolute interest, and a devise by way of settlement in which trustees of the settlement have been appointed.

Representatives take legal estate.

Where the land is devised to the infant for an estate in fee simple or for a term of years absolute, or where it is settled upon him for life and no trustees are appointed, the personal representatives can retain the land until the infant attains his majority, and until that time they possess all the powers of a tenant for life under a settlement,[4] and also the powers of trustees for sale.[5]   If, however, they do not desire to retain the land, they may appoint trustees to be trustees of the land for the purposes of the Settled Land Act and for the purposes of the statutory provisions relating to the management of land during a minority.[6]

Where the land is devised by way of settlement to an infant for a limited interest and the testator has appointed trustees of the settlement, the Act directs that the personal representatives shall, when their administration duties are completed, transfer the legal estate to the trustees if they are required to do so.[7]

(C) DESCENT OF LAND TO AN INFANT.

In the case of deaths occurring after 1925 it is impossible for an infant to become entitled to a fee simple estate by descent, for primogeniture has been abolished, and the residuary estate of the intestate, as we have seen,[8] is held by the administrator upon trust to sell and to divide the proceeds among the relatives entitled under the Administration of Estates Act.   Even if an infant is the

Fee simple estate.

---

[1] Law of Property Act, 1925, s. 19 (2).
[2] *Ibid.*, s. 35.   [3] S. 19 (3).
[4] Settled Land Act, 1925, s. 26 (1).
[5] Administration of Estates Act, 1925, s. 39 (1).   [6] *Ibid.*, s. 42.
[7] Settled Land Act, 1925, ss. 6, 26.
[8] *Supra*, pp. 793 *et seq.*

sole relative so entitled, he does not take an absolute interest until he either marries or attains his majority.[1]

Entailed interests.

The old law of descent, however, still applies to the entailed interest, but if the heir is an infant the legal estate must be vested in the trustees of the settlement until he attains his majority. If money is required during his minority for his maintenance, education or benefit, the court if necessary may make an order under the Trustee Act, 1925,[2] appointing a person to execute a disentailing assurance which will bar the issue and remaindermen as completely as if it were effected by the infant after attaining his majority.[3]

(D) SETTLEMENT OF LAND IN FAVOUR OF AN INFANT.

Two methods of effecting settlement.

A person who desires to settle land in favour of an infant has an alternative, for he may create either a settlement under the Settled Land Act or a trust for sale.

In the case of a settlement, the statutory powers of a tenant for life, together with any additional powers that may be conferred by the settlement, become exercisable by the trustees,[4] who, in their capacity as " statutory owners," [5] are entitled to have the legal estate transferred to them by a vesting deed. If the settlor adopts the method of a trust for sale, the trustees not only obtain the legal estate but they also possess all the powers of a tenant for life under the Settled Land Act, so long as the land remains unsold.[6]

Infant tenant for life.

If a tenant for life under an existing settlement is succeeded by an infant tenant for life, the latter is not entitled to the legal estate until he attains his majority. In the meantime the legal estate and the statutory powers will be possessed by the trustees of the settlement.[7]

Infant becoming absolutely entitled.

Where an infant becomes absolutely entitled under a settlement, as, for example, where there is a grant or a devise

> to A. for life, remainder to B. in fee simple, and A. dies during the minority of B.,

the settlement continues until B. attains his majority,[8] the legal estate in the meantime being vested in the trustees of the settlement. In a case such as this, statutory provision is made to meet the contingency of the infant dying under age, for it is enacted that unless he marries before reaching his majority he shall be

---

[1] Administration of Estates Act, 1925, s. 47, *supra*, p. 798.
[2] Trustee Act, 1925, s. 53.
[3] *Re Gower's Settlement,* [1934] Ch. 365.
[4] Settled Land Act, s. 26 (1) (*b*).   [5] *Ibid.,* s. 117 (1) (xxvi).
[6] Law of Property Act, 1925, s. 28 (1).
[7] Settled Land Act, 1925, s. 26 (1).
[8] *Ibid.,* s. 3 (*b*).

deemed to have had an entailed interest at the time of his death.[1] In other words, the fee simple of the infant B., in the above example, though potentially absolute,[2] is cut down to an entail until he marries or reaches twenty-one. Therefore, if he is an unmarried infant at his death, the estate will revert to the settlor if the settlement was by deed, or will pass to the residuary devisee in the case of a testamentary settlement, for an infant cannot make a valid will, and if unmarried cannot have heirs capable of taking the estate tail. It is better that there should be this reversion to the settlor, rather than that the estate should enure for the benefit of some distant relative of the infant, which would be the result if he were to die owning an absolute interest.

(E) MORTGAGE TO AN INFANT.

It is expressly enacted that a legal estate cannot be conveyed to an infant by way of mortgage. A grant of a legal mortgage of land to an infant merely operates as an agreement for valuable consideration that the grantor will execute a proper conveyance when the infant attains full age, and that in the meantime he will hold the beneficial interest on trust for the infant. If, however, the conveyance is made to the infant and to another person of full age, it operates as if the infant had not been named, though of course his beneficial interest is not prejudiced.[3]

Mortgage operates as contract to convey.

(F) CONVEYANCE TO AN INFANT AS TRUSTEE.

An infant cannot be appointed a trustee.[4] A conveyance which purports to convey land to an infant as trustee does not transfer the legal estate, but operates as a declaration of trust in favour of the beneficiaries designated.[5] In such a case the person who is empowered by the trust instrument to appoint new trustees may make a new appointment,[6] or, if there is no such person, the court may do so.[7]

Infant cannot be trustee.

We have already seen that the legal estate cannot pass to an infant who is appointed executor by the will of a testator.[8]

SECTION III. ACQUISITION AND ALIENATION OF EQUITABLE INTERESTS IN LAND BY AN INFANT.

An equitable interest, as distinct from a legal estate, may be effectively transferred to an infant, but since the ownership of an interest in land may occasionally prove to be more of a burden than a benefit, especially in the case of a leasehold containing

Conveyance to infant voidable.

---

[1] Administration of Estates Act, 1925, s. 51 (3).
[2] *Re Taylor, Pullan* v. *Taylor*, [1931] 2 Ch. 243, 246.
[3] Law of Property Act, 1925, s. 19 (6).
[4] *Ibid.*, s. 20. [5] *Ibid.*, s. 19 (4).
[6] Trustee Act, 1925, s. 36.
[7] *Ibid.*, s. 41. [8] Judicature Act, 1925, s. 165.

onerous covenants, the long established rule is that the transfer is voidable at the option of the infant, either at any time during minority or within a reasonable time after the attainment of his majority. In the event of his death the same power is exercisable by his successors.[1] But repudiation must not be unduly delayed. Thus where an infant bought land at a price payable by instalments, and continued to pay them for some time after he reached full age, it was held that his procrastination had defeated his right of avoidance and that he must pay the instalments which remained due.[2]

Conveyance by infant voidable.

Apart from the Infant Settlements Act, 1855, which will be described below, an infant cannot make an irrevocable disposition of his interest, for the rule is that any disposition is voidable and can be repudiated by him during his minority or within a reasonable time after he attains full age.[3] So the disability is not absolute. It goes no further than is necessary for the protection of the infant. It leaves him the power to act during infancy, but in order that he may have protection, it permits him to avoid the transaction when he comes of age if he finds it right and proper to do so.[4] The tendency of the courts, however, is to regard very slight acts, such as the receipt of rent in the case of a lease, as amounting to a ratification of the conveyance.[5]

Wills of infants.

An infant cannot make a will, either of real or of personal property,[6] unless he is a person entitled to the privileges granted by the Wills Act, 1837, and Wills (Soldiers and Sailors) Act, 1918.[7]

Settlements by infants.

In accordance with the principle applicable to alienation in general, a settlement made by an infant in contemplation of marriage is voidable, but it becomes binding upon him or her unless it is repudiated within a reasonable time after the attainment of majority.[8] The reasonable time is calculated from the attainment of majority, and not, as was once thought, from the moment when the property falls into possession.[9] If, for instance,

> an infant settles a reversionary interest, consisting of a fee simple estate which will come to him on the death of his mother, he will lose his right to repudiate unless he takes the necessary steps soon after he reaches full age, notwithstanding

---

[1] Blackstone, vol. ii. p. 292 ; *North Western Rly. Co.* v. *McMichael* (1850), 5 Ex. 114, 123.

[2] *Whittingham* v. *Murdy* (1889), 60 L. T. 956.

[3] Co. Litt., 171*b*.

[4] *Burnaby* v. *Equitable Reversionary Interest Society* (1885), 28 Ch. D. 416, 424.

[5] *Slator* v. *Brady* (1863), 14 Ir. C. L. R. 61.

[6] Wills Act, 1837, s. 7.

[7] *Ibid.*, s. 11 ; Wills (Soldiers and Sailors) Act, 1918, s. 3 (1) ; *supra*, pp. 764-7.

[8] *Edwards* v. *Carter*, [1893] A. C. 360.

[9] *Carnell* v. *Harrison*, [1916] 1 Ch. 328.

that it may be many years before possession of the land becomes available by the death of his mother.

His ignorance of the right of repudiation does not absolve him from the obligation to take steps within a reasonable time.[1]

In order, however, to enable an infant to make a binding settlement *in contemplation of marriage*, the Infant Settlements Act, 1855, has removed the disability of infancy in this particular case, provided that the consent of the court is obtained and that the infant, if a male is over twenty years of age, or if a female is over seventeen years of age. Subject to this requirement as to age the Act provides that it shall be lawful for every infant upon or in contemplation of his or her marriage, with the sanction of the Court of Chancery, to make a valid and binding settlement or contract for a settlement, of all his or her property, whether real or personal and whether in possession or in expectancy, including property over which he or she has any power of appointment. A post-nuptial settlement comes within the terms of the statute.[2] The statute is not affected by the legislation of 1925, but it is provided that a settlement must not be made which will have the effect of vesting a legal estate in an infant.[3]

Infant Settlements Act, 1855.

SECTION IV. MANAGEMENT OF AN INFANT'S PROPERTY.

Land to which an infant is beneficially entitled, either absolutely or as tenant for life, is, as we have seen, deemed to be settled land. This involves the existence of trustees, and wide powers of management have been conferred upon them by statute. Thus they have all the ordinary powers conferred on a tenant for life and upon settlement trustees by the Settled Land Act, 1925.[4] They may enter into and continue in possession of the land on behalf of the infant, and if they do, they are directed to manage or superintend the management of the land, with full power, *inter alia* :

Powers of trustees.

1. to fell timber in the usual course for sale or for repairs ;
2. to erect, pull down, rebuild and repair buildings ;
3. to work mines which have usually been worked ;
4. to drain or otherwise improve the land ;
5. to deal generally with the land in a proper and due course of management. [5]

These powers are also exercisable, subject to any prior interests or charges, where an infant is contingently entitled to land.[6]

---

[1] *Carnell* v. *Harrison*, [1916] 1 Ch. 328.
[2] *Re A. B. (An Infant)*, [1914] W. N. 140.
[3] Settled Land Act, 1925, s. 27 (3).
[4] *Ibid.*, s. 26 ; *supra*, pp. 131 *et seq.*; 151.
[5] Settled Land Act, 1925, s. 102.   [6] *Ibid.*, s. 102 (5).

Application
of surplus
income.

As regards the use which must be made of surplus income during the minority, it is provided [1] that the trustees may, at their sole discretion, apply a reasonable part of the income of the property for the maintenance, education or benefit of the infant, notwithstanding that some other fund may be applicable to those purposes, or that some other person, such as a parent, may be legally bound to provide for the infant's maintenance or education. But in deciding whether income shall be used for such purposes, the trustees must have regard to the age and requirements of the infant and to the circumstances of the case in general. In particular they must, in spite of the latitude allowed them, take into account whether some other fund may be used for the purpose.

The residue of the income is to be accumulated by way of compound interest, and the accumulations are to be paid over to the infant when he attains twenty-one years or marries under that age, provided that his interest is vested. If the infant has a merely contingent interest, or if he dies under twenty-one years of age and without having married, the accumulations must be added to capital.[2] Where land to which an infant is entitled is subject to a trust for sale, the trustees are empowered to use the capital to an amount not exceeding one-half of his presumptive or vested share for his advancement or benefit.[3]

---

[1] Trustee Act, 1925, s. 31.   [2] *Ibid.*, s. 31 (2).
[3] *Ibid.*, s. 32.

CHAPTER II.

MARRIED WOMEN AND PERSONS SUF-
FERING FROM MENTAL DISORDER.

SUMMARY.

SECTION I. MARRIED WOMEN.

History. Married women have at last emerged from that ⟶ Married
bondage which formerly characterized their status. The history of ⟶ women at
their proprietary disabilities forms an illuminating chapter in the ⟶ common
growth of English law. At common law husband and wife were one ⟶ law.
person. The general result of this merger of the wife's status in
that of her husband was that he became absolute owner of her
personal chattels, he might dispose of her leaseholds and take the
proceeds, and he had the sole right of controlling and managing her
freehold estates. If she predeceased him, he became absolutely
entitled to any personal property of which she died possessed,
and to a life estate by curtesy in her freehold estates of inheritance
provided that a child had been born.[1] Again, a man could not
make a grant to his wife directly or enter into a covenant with her,
for to allow either of these things would have been to suppose her
separate existence. In short, the effect of marriage at common
law was to make a man complete master of his wife's property
and to deprive her of contractual capacity.

Gradually, however, and quite apart from legislation, wives ⟶ Introduction
were placed by the courts of equity in an even more favourable ⟶ of separate
position than men or unmarried women, a result that was ⟶ property.
due to the invention by the Court of Chancery of the doctrine
of *equitable separate estate*. If property was given to a married

---

[1] *Supra*, p. 161.

woman by words which indicated either expressly or by implication that she was to enjoy it *for her sole and separate use*,
equity removed that property from the control of the husband
by regarding him as a trustee, and conferred upon the wife full
powers of enjoyment and disposition. But equity went even
further than this, for, perceiving the danger that a husband might
over-persuade his wife to sell her separate property and hand the
proceeds to him, it permitted the insertion in marriage settlements
of what was known as a *restraint upon anticipation*. The effect of
such a restraint was that a woman, while possessing full enjoyment of the income, was prevented during her coverture from
alienating or charging the corpus of the property. She could
devise, but could not sell or mortgage it.

Statutory separate property.

The next step in the emancipation of married women came
with the enactment from 1870 onwards of various Married
Women's Property Acts.[1] The principle of these was not
to let the existence of separate property depend upon the intention of the donor, but to provide that in all cases property
of married women should be separate property. Thus the
intervention of the court of equity was no longer needed, for all
property belonging to a married woman became her *statutory
separate property* over which she had sole control and power of
disposition.

Woman's proprietary rights now unaffected by marriage.

The final stage in the emancipation of married women came
with the Law Reform (Married Women and Tortfeasors) Act,
1935. This provides that so far as concerns the acquisition,
holding and disposition of any property a married woman shall
be in the same position as if she were a *feme sole*. This Act also
forbade the imposition of restraints upon anticipation after 1935,
while preserving those already in existence, but in 1949 all
restrictions upon anticipation or alienation, whether already
imposed or not, were totally abolished.[2] Thus in future any
restriction which it is proposed to place upon the enjoyment of
property by a married woman must take the form of a protective
trust, which is the only form of restriction applicable to a man or a
feme sole.[3]

Married Women's Property Act, 1964.

The position of a married woman has, indeed, been improved
in a more positive sense by a statute which entitles her to a half
share in any property acquired out of money given to her for
household expenses.[4]

---

[1] S. 1.
[2] Married Women (Restraint upon Anticipation) Act, 1949.
[3] *Supra*, p. 148.
[4] Married Woman's Property Act, 1964, s. 1.

SECTION II.

PERSONS SUFFERING FROM MENTAL DISORDER.

The law relating to mentally incompetent persons, originally styled " lunatics " by the legislature, then " persons of unsound mind " and now " mental patients," has been codified and radically altered by the Mental Health Act, 1959. There is no longer any distinction between lunatics *so found* and lunatics *not so found,* for the former practice under which, after a formal inquiry (" inquisition "), a patient could be declared to be of unsound mind and the management of his property be entrusted to a person called a " committee " has been abolished. Moreover, there are no longer different categories of patients, but only one, namely, a person who is suffering from " mental disorder " as defined by the Act.[1] The jurisdiction relating to the property of a patient, the only matter relevant to the present book, is vested in the Lord Chancellor, three judges of the Chancery Division, called " nominated judges " and in the Master (replacing the former Master in Lunacy) and Deputy Master of the Court of Protection. When exercising the statutory powers of management, such a person is referred to as " the judge."[2]

Mental Health Act, 1959.

This jurisdiction is exercisable where, after considering medical evidence, the judge is satisfied that a person is incapable by reason of mental disorder of managing and administering his property and affairs,[3] though in a case of emergency the judge may exercise his powers pending the determination of mental incapacity.[4] The jurisdiction is very wide.

Wide powers of management vested in the judge.

" The general scheme of the new code is to confer on the judge a wide power in general terms to do anything expedient for the benefit of the patient or members of his family or other persons for whom he might be expected to provide, followed by certain express powers which are to be without prejudice to the overriding general power. In fact, it is difficult to think of any power which the judge would want to exercise which is not to be found in the specific powers."[5]

Thus, in pursuance of his specific powers, the judge may make such orders as he thinks fit for the sale, exchange, lease or other disposition of the patient's property,[6] and for the acquisition or the settlement of any property.[7] For instance in order to fill the void caused by a patient's lack of testamentary capacity, a settlement may be framed containing the provisions that would normally be made by a sane testator in the interests of his wife and family, and further a will made by a testator when he was *compos mentis*

---

[1] Mental Health Act, 1959, s. 4.
[2] *Ibid.,* s. 100, 119 (1).
[3] *Ibid.,* s. 101.
[4] *Ibid.,* s. 104.
[5] 23 *Modern Law Review,* p. 423 (Raymond Jennings).
[6] Mental Health Act, 1959, s. 103 (1), (b).
[7] *Ibid.,* s. 103 (1) (c), (d).

may be modified to meet the exigencies of a changed situation. In one case, for instance:

> A testator, some forty years before his mental powers failed, made a will disposing of his residuary estate equally between his wife and children as a class. His wife and one of his four children predeceased him, with the result that according to the terms of the will each of the surviving children would take a third of the residue and the issue of the deceased child would take nothing.

It was therefore directed that a settlement should be made under which the issue of the deceased child were to take the one-fourth share of the residue that the testator, were he still of full capacity, would no doubt wish them to have .[1]

Appointment of a receiver.

The judge may also appoint as receiver a specified person or the holder of a specified office and may authorize him to do all such things in relation to the property of a patient as he himself is empowered to do by the Act.[2]

Preservation of interests in property disposed of.

The paramount consideration of the judge in his exercise of these powers is the interest of the patient, even though this may mean changing the nature of his property to the detriment of those who would otherwise have been entitled to it on his death. The Act, therefore, includes provisions designed to preserve the interests of such persons. It provides in effect that where the patient's property has been disposed of by sale, exchange, charging or other disposition or where money has been spent on the purchase of property, then the proprietary rights of the persons entitled under his will or intestacy shall attach to that property in its new form. If the property was real property, any property representing it shall so long as it remains part of his estate be treated as real property.[3]

Conveyances of legal estate.

As regards conveyances of property, it is enacted that when a legal estate in land (whether settled or not) is vested in a person suffering from mental disorder, the judge may order his receiver or some other authorized person to make all requisite dispositions for conveying or creating a legal estate on his behalf.[4] Again, if land is vested in such a person on trust for sale, a new trustee must be appointed in his place.[5]

Intestacy in case of freehold held before 1926.

As regards the descent of land on intestacy, the rule under the Administration of Estates Act, 1925, is that where a person of unsound mind was alive on 1st January, 1926 and was before that date entitled to a beneficial interest in freehold property, such interest shall in the event of his intestacy descend according to the old canons of descent applicable to freeholds of inheritance before 1926.[6]

---

[1] *In re E.A.*, [1928] Ch. 528; [1928] All E. R. 664. See also *Re T. B.*, [1966] 3 All E. R. 509; [1967] 2 W. L. R. 15.
[2] Mental Health Act, 1959, s. 105 (1).   [3] *Ibid.* 1959, s. 107 (1).
[4] Law of Property Act, 1925, s. 22 (1), as substituted by Mental Health Act, 1959, s. 149 (1), Sch. 7, Part 1.   [5] *Ibid.*
[6] Administration of Estates Act, 1925, s. 51 (2).

CHAPTER III.

CORPORATIONS AND CHARITIES.

SUMMARY.

SECTION I.   CORPORATIONS.

Necessity for incorporation. One of the reasons for the existence of corporations is the principle of law that rights of property can be vested only in definite persons. It frequently occurs that a body of persons desires to hold and enjoy land, but apart from the case where a fluctuating class of persons acquires rights in the nature of easements by the method known as custom,[1] there are only two methods by which effect can be given to the desire. Either the land must be vested in trustees upon trust to hold and manage the land for the benefit of the proposed beneficiaries, or else an Act of Parliament or a charter must be procured that turns the indefinite body of persons into a definite, though artificial, person called a corporation. The effect of this latter method is that the corporation becomes in the eye of the law a separate person, distinct from the members of which it is formed, and capable of acquiring, holding and alienating land.

Nature of corporations.

Effect of incorporation.

Thus the modern limited liability company is not, like a partnership, a mere collection or aggregate of the shareholders, but is a metaphysical entity, a legal *persona* with many of the rights and powers of a human person.

Classifications of Corporations. Corporations may be classified in several ways. The first classification is into aggregate and sole.

Classifications.

A corporation aggregate is a collection of several persons who

Corporations aggregate.

---

[1] *Supra*, pp. 527 *et seq.*

are united together into one society and who are followed by a perpetual succession of members, so that the corporation is capable of existing for ever.[1]   Examples are:

> the head and fellows of a college,
> the dean and chapter of a cathedral,
> the mayor and corporation of a city, and
> a limited liability company incorporated under the Companies Act, 1948.

Corporations sole.

A corporation sole consists of a single person occupying a particular office and each and several of the persons in perpetuity who succeed him in that office, as, for instance, the rector or vicar of a parish, a bishop and the Postmaster-General.

Another division of corporations is into ecclesiastical and lay.

Ecclesiastical corporations.

Ecclesiastical corporations are those which exist for upholding religion and perpetuating the rights of the Church, such as bishops, parsons, and deans and chapters, and the abbot and monks of an earlier age.

Lay corporations.

Lay corporations may be either trading or non-trading corporations.

Trading.

Trading corporations are those which have been incorporated by charter, by special Act of Parliament or under the provisions of the Companies Act, 1948, and whose main object is trade.

Non-trading.

Non-trading corporations are those which have no concern with commerce, but which exist either for the better government of a town or district, such as urban district councils and municipal corporations, or for eleemosynary purposes, such as St. Thomas's Hospital and the colleges of Oxford and Cambridge.

Methods of creation.

A corporation can in general exist only if it has been formed under the authority of the State, and the two methods of creation in use at the present day are a charter from the Crown and an Act of Parliament. If, for instance, a town wishes to become a borough, application must be made for a charter; while persons who wish to form themselves into a trading corporation must either secure the passing of a private Act of Parliament or take advantage of the Companies Act, which contains provisions enabling companies to be formed without the necessity of a special statute.

But in addition to those that are incorporated by charter or by statute, corporations may also exist by common law and prescription.

Examples of common law corporations are a parson, a bishop, and the Crown. Corporations by prescription are those which have existed so long that the law presumes that they received from the Crown a grant or charter that has been lost.[2]

---

[1] Blackstone, vol. i. p. 469.
[2] *Re Free Fishermen of Faversham* (1887), 36 Ch. D. 329, *supra*, p. 531.

Doctrine of *Ultra Vires.* Statutory corporations are subject to the *ultra vires* doctrine. At common law a corporation that has been created by charter has power to deal with its property and to bind itself by contract to the same extent as a private person, and even if the charter imposes some direction which would have the effect of limiting its natural capacity, the legal power of the corporation is not affected, though the direction may be enforced by the Attorney-General.[1]

Ultra vires doctrine.

But the case of a statutory corporation is very different. Such a body exists for certain purposes which are defined in the statute to which it owes its origin, and no rule is more inviolable than that which ordains that the powers of a statutory corporation are limited to those which are reasonably necessary to the realization of the purposes for which it is incorporated. The corporation possesses its own constitution (called, in the case of a trading company, the memorandum of association), which has statutory effect. Anything that the constitution authorizes, either expressly or by implication, can be done, but what is not so authorized cannot be done.

Lord CAIRNS said in *Ashbury Ry. Carriage and Iron Co.* v. *Riche*[2] :—

> " Now, my Lords, if that is so—if that is the condition upon which
> " the corporation is established—it is a mode of incorporation which
> " contains in it both that which is affirmative and that which is
> " negative. It states affirmatively the ambit and extent of vitality
> " and power which by law are given to the corporation, and it states
> " . . . negatively that nothing shall be done beyond that ambit, and
> " that no attempt shall be made to use the corporate life for any other
> " purpose than that which is so specified."

It is, for instance,[3] *ultra vires* for a railway company which has statutory power of taking and using land for the purposes of the railway to grant a right of way over its land, if the way is unconnected with railway purposes.

Acquisition of land. Corporations, whether aggregate or sole, have the same capacity as natural persons to acquire land and to hold the same to them and their successors,[4] and any conveyancing difficulties to which they were subject at common law in this respect were removed by the Law of Property Act, 1925. Two rules which formerly raised difficulties were that leaseholds could not be granted to a corporation *sole* in such a way as to make them vest in the successive holders of the office; and that a grant of land to a corporation sole made at a time when the office was vacant was

Abolition of certain technicalities.

---

[1] *Baroness Wenlock* v. *River Dee Co.* (1887), 36 Ch. D. 674, 684 ; BOWEN, L.J.

[2] *Ashbury Ry. Carriage and Iron Co.* v. *Riche* (1875), L. R. 7 H. L. 653, 670.

[3] *Mulliner* v. *Midland Rly. Co.* (1879), 11 Ch. D. 611.

[4] *Sutton's Hospital Case* (1612), 10 Rep. 23a.

void.   If leaseholds were granted to a person *qua* parson, and he
died before the term had run out, his personal representatives and
not his successor in the office became entitled to the residue of the
lease.[1]

It is now, however, enacted [2] that where any property or *any
interest* therein is or has been vested in a corporation sole, whether
before or after 1926, it shall pass to the successors from time to
time of such corporation.   Again, it is enacted [3] that where
property is granted to a corporation sole during a vacancy of the
office, or to a corporation aggregate during a vacancy of the
headship, the property shall, notwithstanding such vacancy, vest
in the successor of the corporation sole, or in the corporation
aggregate, as the case may be.

**Words of
limitation.**
Again, the rule formerly was that, unless a grant was made to a
corporation sole *and his successors*, the grant operated to confer
a life estate upon the actual holder of the office in his natural
capacity ; but now, as we have already seen, a conveyance of
freehold land to a corporation sole by his corporate designation
even without the word " successors " passes to the corporation the
fee simple or other the whole interest which the grantor has power
to convey in such land, unless a contrary intention appears in the
conveyance.[4]

**Dissolution
of corpora-
tion.**
The rule at common law is that when a corporation is dissolved,
any land which it may have held does not escheat to the Crown,
but reverts to the original donor,[5] but since January 1, 1926,
when a legal estate determines for this reason, the court is empowered to vest a corresponding estate in the person who would
have been entitled to the estate had it not determined.[6]   This
power is apparently meant to be used when the corporation has
been holding land as a trustee.

NOTE ON THE LAW OF MORTMAIN.

**History of
Mortmain
Statutes.**
Until 1st January, 1961, when the Charities Act, 1960, came into force,
the long established rule was that no land could be assured to or for the
benefit of, or acquired by or on behalf of, any corporation unless the
corporation was authorized, either by some statute or by a licence from
the Crown, to hold land.   If land was transferred by way of gift, sale,
mortgage, settlement or devise to a corporation which had no such
authority, the land was forfeited to the Crown.[7]   The explanation of this
disability lies far back in history and is to be found in the exigencies of the
feudal system.

---

[1] Co. Litt., 46*b*.
[2] Law of Property Act, 1925, s. 180 (1).
[3] *Ibid.*, s. 180 (2).
[4] *Supra*, p. 115.
[5] Co. Litt., 13*b* ; Blackstone, vol. i. pp. 484–5 ; *Hastings Corpn.* v. *Letton.*
[1908] 1 K. B. 378 ; *Re Woking U.D.C.*, [1914] 1 Ch. 300, at p. 310.
[6] Law of Property Act, 1925, s. 181.
[7] Mortmain and Charitable Uses Act, 1888, s. 1.

We have seen that the chief advantage in early days of feudal lordship was the right to claim those tenurial incidents which, though bearing hardly upon the tenant, were of great profit to the lord. But the most valuable of these incidents, such as escheat, wardship, marriage, relief and so on, matured upon the death, minority and marriage of the tenant. It is clear, therefore, that a lord would not unnaturally feel himself aggrieved if a tenant were foisted upon him who was immune from these common phenomena of life. This is just what occurred when the land was vested in a *dead hand*, that is, in a corporation which by its very nature is never under age, never marries and may never die. Hence from an early date a series of statutes, generally called the Mortmain Statutes, was passed requiring the authority either of a statute or of a Crown licence before land could be vested in a corporation.

It was enacted by Magna Carta and by the Provisions of Westminster, 1252, that gifts to corporations should be void and any land so given forfeited to the superior lord, but as this enactment extended only to ecclesiastical corporations aggregate, and as even they found subtle means of evasion, it was followed in 1279 by a more comprehensive enactment, which is known as the Statute *De viris religiosis*. This provided **Magna Carta.**

> that *no person*, religious or other, should buy, or sell, or lease, nor should by any art or ingenuity appropriate to himself, any lands or tenements in mortmain; upon pain that the immediate lord of the fee, or, on his default for one year, the lords paramount, and, in default of all of them, the king, should enter and take the land by way of forfeiture **De viris religiosis.**

Even this statute was not a sufficient protection against gifts in mortmain, for the religious houses, by collusion with landowners, brought fictitious actions (common recoveries) and through the default of the defendants succeeded in recovering by process of law land to which in fact they had no title. This device was stopped in 1285 by the Statute of Westminster the Second. Yet it was still found difficult to thwart ecclesiastical ingenuity, for when the religious houses were driven out of all their former holds, they devised a new method of conveyance by which the lands were granted, not to themselves directly, but to nominal feoffees *to the use of* the religious houses.[1] **Statute Westminster II.**

This practice was stopped in 1392 by the Statute 15 Ric. II, which also extended the Mortmain Statutes to all corporations, such as city and borough corporate bodies. **Statute 15 Ric. II.**

Nevertheless during all this time it was lawful for the Crown to remit the forfeiture by granting a licence of mortmain, and to allow any corporation, whether ecclesiastical or lay, to acquire and hold land in perpetuity, and in 1697 it was expressly enacted that the Crown at its own discretion might grant licences to alienees to take in mortmain, of whomsoever the land might be held.

This doctrine of mortmain was confirmed by the Mortmain and Charitable Uses Act, 1888, which provided as follows:— **Mortmain and Charitable Uses Act, 1888.**

> Land shall not be assured to or for the benefit of, or acquired by or on behalf of, any corporation in mortmain, otherwise than under the authority of a licence from Her Majesty the Queen, or of a statute for the time being in force, and if any land is so assured otherwise than as aforesaid the land shall be forfeited to Her Majesty from the date of the assurance, and Her Majesty may enter on and hold the land accordingly. . . .[2]

In this Act, unless the context otherwise requires, "Assurance "

---

[1] Blackstone, vol. ii. p. 271.   [2] S. 1 (1).

2F*

includes a gift, conveyance, appointment, lease, transfer, settlement, mortgage, charge, incumbrance, devise, bequest, and every other assurance by deed, will or other instrument. . . .[1]

Land that was assured in mortmain contrary to this Act was not automatically forfeited to the Crown. The word " forfeited " in the section cited above, when construed in the light of the subsequent words, meant " liable to be forfeited," and therefore if the Crown took no steps to enforce its rights the corporation was not deprived of the land.

Repeal of law of mortmain. With the progress of time the restrictions imposed by the Act had become of little significance, for the vast majority of corporations were for one reason or another exempt from the necessity to obtain a licence from the Crown. The subject, however, requires no further elaboration, for the Act was repealed by the Charities Act, 1960,[2] and thus the law of mortmain is now defunct.

SECTION II. CHARITIES.

Abolition of restrictions upon charitable gifts of land. **Assurances of land to a charity.** The right of a charity to acquire land was until recently severely restricted by the Mortmain and Charitable Uses Acts of 1888 and 1891, which dealt separately with assurances *inter vivos* and devises. Subject to many exceptions, the statutory rule broadly speaking was that an assurance of land *inter vivos* was void unless it was irrevocable and gave the charity the right to take immediate possession; and, if not made for valuable consideration, unless it was executed at least twelve months before the death of the alienor.

On the other hand, charitable devises, which generally speaking were not permitted until 1891, were declared to be valid by the Act of that year, subject however to the proviso that the land must be sold within one year from the testator's death unless the High Court or the Charity Commissioners decided otherwise.[3]

These restrictions, however, have now disappeared with the repeal of the Acts of 1888 and 1891 by the Charities Act, 1960.[4]

Charities not free to deal with their land. **Alienation of land by a charity.** The freedom of charities to alienate or deal with their land has long been restricted by a series of Charitable Trusts Act and now by the Charities Act, 1960. The latter, replacing the former statutes, provides that no property forming part of the permanent endowment of a charity shall, without an order of the court or of the Charity Commissioners, be mortgaged or charged by way of security for the repayment of money borrowed, nor, in the case of land in England and Wales, be sold, leased or otherwise disposed of.[5] Thus, a lease made contrary to the Act is utterly void, not merely voidable.[6] By way of exception, however, it is permissible for a charity to grant a lease for a term ending not more than twenty-two years after it is

---

[1] S. 10.   [2] S. 38.
[3] Mortmain and Charitable Uses Act, 1891, s. 5.
[4] S. 38.
[5] Charities Act, 1960, s. 29 (1).
[6] *Bangor (Bishop)* v. *Parry,* [1891] 2 Q. B. 277.

granted, provided that it is not granted wholly or partly in consideration of a fine.[1]

" Permanent endowment " means property held subject to the restriction that in its expenditure regard must be had to the distinction between capital and income.[2]

These restrictions upon alienation do not affect " exempt charities," a list of which is given in the Act.[3] The list includes, *inter alia*, the universities of Oxford, Cambridge, London and Durham; the colleges and halls in Oxford, Cambridge and Durham; any university or similar institution declared by an Order in Council to be an exempt charity; the British Museum and the Church Commissioners.

Exempt charities.

---

[1] Charities Act, 1960, s. 29 (3) (b).
[2] *Ibid.*, s. 45 (3).
[3] *Ibid.*, s. 29 (4); Sch. 2.

BOOK IV.

TOWN AND COUNTRY PLANNING.

SUMMARY.

TOWN AND COUNTRY PLANNING.

SECTION I. INTRODUCTION.

As we have already seen, it gradually became necessary to control the right of an owner to exploit his land.[1] Such control, which had its beginnings more than a hundred years ago, came to be imposed mainly by three statutory codes dealing with health, housing and town planning. Statutory precursors of planning.

The conditions produced by the Industrial Revolution when the new workers moved into towns from the country and were accommodated in hastily constructed and insanitary dwellings inevitably led to the control of land. England in the 1840's, alarmed by the constant recurrent outbreaks of cholera, turned away from the *laissez faire* of Bentham and it was Ernest Chadwick, Bentham's disciple and literary editor, who laid the foundations of the present system. Some 1,500 local authorities were placed under a Central Board, public health became an acknowledged service of local government and inevitably the control of land became accepted as an essential administrative service on this overcrowded island. In 1845 and 1847 a series of Clauses Acts provided codes of powers which local authorities could incorporate in their local private Acts if they wished and it was, of course, no accident that the Land Clauses Consolidation Act, 1845, dealing with procedures on compulsory purchase of land, should have been among the first to be passed. In 1848 the first general act dealing with health was placed upon the statute book, the Public Health Act, and this was followed by others culminating in the Public Health Act of 1875, as a result of which the whole country was divided into sanitary districts responsible for all matters of public health. Amending legislation, which was in whole or part adoptive, was passed in 1890, 1907 and 1925, and in 1936 a large part of the public health legislation was consolidated in the Public Public Health legislation.

---

[1] *Supra,* pp. 121–2.

879

Health Act, 1936. A further Public Health Act was passed in 1961.[1] Public health legislation is concerned with a vital but restricted sphere of activity, for, although it can certainly prevent a repetition of the building confusion produced by the Industrial Revolution, it is concerned with each building or plot of land as an isolated unit and not with the optimum use of land in the country as a whole.

Housing legislation.

Housing legislation dealt with another sphere of land control. Congested houses and overcrowded slums had been the subject of some earlier statutes,[2] but the first comprehensive piece of legislation to remove slums and replace them by decent houses was the Housing of the Working Classes Act, 1890. A series of enactments dealing with housing followed, of which the principal consolidation measures were the Housing Acts of 1925 and 1936. Between 1936 and 1957 a change in political consciousness was reflected in the elimination from this legislation of all reference to "the working classes" and the present code, which is contained in the Housing Acts 1957–65,[3] is intended to have general application. Its main object is to empower local authorities to ensure that all houses attain a reasonable standard of fitness. Houses falling below this standard must either be repaired or subjected to a demolition or closure order, and where an area comprises a number of unfit houses the local authority may provide for its clearance (slum clearance) or redevelopment. Local authorities are also under a duty to prevent over-crowding and may themselves provide housing accommodation either by building, by acquisition, by conversion or by alterations; they can also lend money to enable persons to buy houses and make grants (improvement grants) towards the cost of reconditioning existing houses.

Early planning legislation.

The Housing Acts deal with slums and the standards of housing but neither this legislation nor the Health Acts tackle the main problem of town and country planning. Town planning powers were first included in a housing statute as Part II of the Housing, Town Planning &c. Act of 1909, which enabled local authorities to make planning schemes for land that was in the course of development or likely to be used for building purposes. By an amending Act of 1919,[4] a local authority whose district comprised more than 20,000 people was compelled to submit a scheme for the approval of the Local Government Board by a specified date. The next stage came with the Town and Country Planning Act, 1932, which enabled but did not compel schemes to be prepared for any land, whether already built upon or not. Schemes, after

---

[1] See S. I. 1965, No. 1373 and 1966, No. 1144 for the important Building Regulations made under this Act.

[2] The Artizans' and Labourers' Dwellings Act, 1868, the Artizans' and Labourers' Dwellings Improvement Acts, 1875 and 1879.

[3] See also the Local Authorities (Land) Act, 1963, the Housing (Slum Clearance Compensations) Act, 1965, and Circular 24/66.

[4] Housing, Town Planning &c. Act, 1919.

approval by the Minister of Health, were laid before both Houses of Parliament and became operative if not suspended by Parliament and not challenged in the High Court. Compensation was payable by the local authority to an owner of property injuriously affected by the scheme, but if his property were increased in value the authority could recover from him 75% of this "betterment". In fact very few of these schemes ever came into force, probably because compensation was a charge upon the rates. But development in the thirties, ribbon and otherwise, made clear the need for some compulsory scheme under which compensation would be a national charge.

In 1943 the whole of the country was put under interim development control by an Act[1] which subjected all land to a scheme deemed to have been passed by the local authority concerned and approved by the Minister. The Minister, now the Minister of Housing and Local Government, was then and still is charged

> " with the duty of securing consistency and continuity in the framing
> " and execution of a national policy with respect to the use and
> " development of land throughout England and Wales."[2]

With the wide powers heaped upon him by subsequent legislation, the Minister is a powerful residual authority in the crystallization of the whole policy of land use in town and country.[3]

The present planning law depends upon a series of statutes commencing with the Town and Country Planning Act, 1947. This was a far more drastic and comprehensive measure than any previous measure. This parent Act was added to and amended by Acts of 1953, 1954, 1959 and 1960, but most of the provisions of these Acts are now contained in the consolidating Act of 1962[4] which, together with the accumulation of statutory rules, orders and instruments made under them, comprise the planning code for the control of land use in England and Wales today.[5] *The present planning code.*

The local planning authorities are, ordinarily, the county *The local planning authorities.*

---

[1] Town and Country Planning (Interim Development) Act, 1943.

[2] Minister of Town and Country Planning Act, 1943. See, for his present wide juridiction, Hansard Vol. 728 (1966) Col. 1127.

[3] The exercise by the Minister of these powers was considered in *Robinson* v. *Minister of Town and Country Planning*, [1947] K. B. 702; [1947] 1 All E. R. 851 and of similar powers under the New Towns Act, 1946, in *Fletcher* v. *Minister of Town and Country Planning*, [1947] 2 All E. R. 496; *Rollo* v. *Minister of Town and Country Planning*, [1948] 1 All E. R. 13 and *Franklin* v. *Minister of Town and Country Planning*, [1948] A. C. 87; [1947] 2 All E. R. 289.

[4] Town and Country Planning Act, 1962, hereafter referred to as the 1962 Act. There is a further amending Act in 1963.

[5] There are, of course, special controls such as those contained in the New Towns Act, 1965, the Control of Office and Industrial Development Act, 1965, and the Building Control Act, 1966. It is not possible to discuss detailed legislation of this sort in a general account of the law of property, but the significance of their combined effect should be appreciated. See *infra*, p. 899, for a discussion of the Land Commission.

councils and county borough councils.[1] It is, therefore, not every local authority that constitutes a local planning authority. County district councils, however, with a population of 60,000 or more can now claim as of right to have delegated to them considerable planning powers under the Act, and a county district council with a population under 60,000 may obtain such delegation if the Minister agrees that there are special circumstances to justify it.[2] In all other cases county councils if they wish may delegate these functions. On the other hand, a local planning authority is never allowed to delegate its responsibility for the making of a development plan but must consult district councils so far as its development plan will affect their areas.[3]

Objectives
of the
1947 Act.
The 1947 Act had two main objectives, the first was to create a system to control the future planning of land use and the second, to nationalize all future uses of land. The provisions of the Act designed to achieve the first objective are still the basis of our planning law, but it has been found necessary to repeal the more controversial nationalization provisions, and these will be dealt with later.[4]

Nature of
the system.
The system emerging from the planning acts and from rules and orders and ministerial circulars is very different from the normal process of law making and its administration. This is doubtless inevitable, for effective planning is only possible if the widest discretions are conferred, first upon the planning authorities and then upon the Minister. But the result is that through the circulars in which the Minister explains to planning authorities how they should exercise their discretion and how he intends to exercise his own, the citizen's rights are being moulded. A new land ownership is being fashioned by administrative trial and error.

SECTION II. THE DEVELOPMENT PLAN.

The
development
plan.
The planning provisions of the 1947 Act have created an extensive system of control which operates in the opposite way to that obtaining under the earlier Acts. While those Acts gave an owner complete freedom of action provided that he did not infringe a scheme already made by the local authority, the basic principle of the 1947 Act is that, apart from trifling exceptions, no development may be effected without the permission of the local planning authority. The broad policy of a planning authority is set out in the development plan which it is required to produce for its own area. This plan must contain proposals show-

---

[1] 1962 Act, s. 2. There are special authorities for the Lake and Peak Districts. See S. I. 1966, No. 48 for London. The local government system is at present being reviewed by a Royal Commission.
[2] S. I. 1964, No. 1382.
[3] 1962 Act, s. 10.
[4] *Infra*, p. 895.

ing the uses to which the land in that area should be put. It
should define the sites of proposed roads, buildings and open
spaces, allocate areas for agricultural, residential, commercial
and industrial purposes and designate land for compulsory
purchase. It should indicate the stages by which these developments are to be carried out.[1]

Once a development plan has been prepared, it must be
published and submitted to the Minister for his approval, which
may be given with or without modification. Objectors must be
given an opportunity of being heard but, in deciding whether to
approve the plan, the Minister is acting administratively and not
quasi-judicially, and the Act expressly permits him to consult the
local planning authority or any other authority or person before
reaching his decision and without affording objectors a further
opportunity of being heard.[2] Anyone aggrieved by a development
plan may resist its validity in the High Court on the ground that it
is *ultra vires* or that he has been substantially prejudiced by a
failure to secure the procedural provisions of the Act, but once
published, a development plan gives no rights to individual
citizens.[3]

Minister's approval of development plan.

Once every five years the plan must be reviewed.[4] The underlying intention is that it should be altered to reflect the influence of
the best current ideas on planning. In 1948 planning authorities
were advised that in making their development plans, they should
plan for twenty years ahead.[5] But despite good intentions, it is
doubtful if planning has kept pace with the times and the future of
development plans is now under review.[6]

Review of development plan.

If any system is to be successful, the planning authority must
be in a position to secure adherence to its development plan and
this requires positive as well as negative action. Thus one of the
most important consequential statutory powers is that which
provides for the acquisition of land, by having it designated in
the development plan for compulsory acquisition. The Act
contains extensive powers[7] for land to be so designated, whether
for direct use by local or governmental authorities or to further
the development plan itself. These powers are of particular
significance in respect of areas of "comprehensive development"
and town centres.[8] But before such designation can take place the
Minister must be satisfied that actual acquisition is likely to be

Compulsory acquisitions of land for planning purposes.

---

[1] 1962 Act, s. 4. S. I. 1965, No. 1483.
[2] 1962 Act, s. 10 (3): the principle of *Errington* v. *Minister of Health*, [1935]
1 K.B. 249 does not therefore apply. Cf. the procedure on appeals, *infra*, p. 884.
[3] 1962 Act, s. 178: *Gregory* v. *London Borough of Camden*, [1966] 2 All E. R.
196; [1966] 1 W. L. R. 899.
[4] 1962 Act, s. 6. See also *infra*, pp. 891–2.
[5] Circulars 59/48 and 37/60.
[6] "The Future of Development Plans", H.M.S.O. 1965. See also Heap in
Journal of Planning Law 1965, pp. 591 *et seq.*
[7] 1962 Act, ss. 4, 67 *et seq.*
[8] H.M.S.O. Planning Bulletin No. 1: Town Centres; Circular 38/62.

made within ten years (or seven years in the case of agricultural land).[1] Local authorities who have acquired land in this way are empowered, with the Minister's consent, to make it available to persons who wish to undertake some development but are unable to obtain land zoned for that type of development.[2] What interest in land the local authority and the Minister might be prepared to convey is not altogether clear, but practice reflects the planning principle adopted by the Uthwatt Committee,[3] that "once any interest has passed into public ownership it should be disposed of by way of lease only and not by way of sale." These general powers of compulsory acquisition are wider than any powers previously conferred by a general enactment upon public authorities and are, of course, additional to powers of compulsory acquisition which Ministers and local authorities possess under particular statutes, such as Housing and Highways Acts.[4] Apart from these particular statutes, the development plan itself is subject to amendment every five years by a full dress review, and at any time if the planning authority and Minister consider it to be necessary.[5] If land designated for compulsory purchase is not in fact acquired within twelve years (eight years if it is agricultural land) from the date on which the designation becomes effective, the owner may require the land to be dealt with within six months, and if it is not, the land is automatically freed from its designation.[6] But this would not, of course, prevent its redesignation at a later date.

Planning blight.

Land which is designated in a development plan as allocated to a governmental or local authority for its functions or for eventual compulsory purchase for other objects cannot, for obvious reasons, be sold save at a greatly reduced price. Local authorities have power to make purchases in advance of their requirements, but it is doubtful if these are frequently exercised.[7] But a remedy for this "planning blight", as it is termed, is available.[8] Where reasonable efforts to sell the land have been made and only a price substantially lower than that which might otherwise have been expected could be obtained, a notice may be served requiring the appropriate authority to purchase the land. The purchase price

---

[1] 1962 Act, s. 5.

[2] 1962 Act, s. 78

[3] Cmd. 6386 (1942) Para. 147.

[4] Many of the provisions respecting Compulsory Purchase are consolidated in the Compulsory Purchase Act 1965 and S. I. 1962, No. 1424: see 1966 Jo. Planning Law 18. The compensation payable is now mainly dealt with in the Land Compensation Act, 1961 (as amended in 1965): see also S. I. 1963, Nos. 483, 749 and 798. Compensation may extend to the "injurious affection" of adjacent land—a remedy deriving from the Land Clauses Consolidation Act, 1845.

[5] See S. I. 1964, No. 1382, reg. 35 for concurrent amendment and purchase.

[6] 1962 Act, s. 9.

[7] Circular 48/59; 1966 Journal of Planning Law 327.

[8] 1962 Act, ss. 138–151. The remedy is aptly described by Heap, *Outline of Planning Law* (4th Edn.), p. 160, as "compulsory purchase in reverse". S. 138 lists the precise circumstances in which a remedy is available.

will be based on the "unblighted" value,[1] and any dispute will be settled by the Lands Tribunal.

This remedy exists as of right, but is restricted in its scope. It is available only to the resident owner-occupier of a dwelling house, and the owner-occupier of a farm or small business.[2] Moreover, the owner-occupier must have been in occupation for six months before making his claim, and this requirement is strictly construed.[3] There is no remedy for loss due to the possibility of neighbouring land being compulsorily acquired. Finally, land is not regarded as allocated to a local government "function" merely by being marked in the development plan as ripe for clearance and redevelopment.[4] It is obvious that there are many forms of actual blight that are quite outside the remedy which the Act provides.

SECTION III. DEVELOPMENT.

The control[5] of the use of land is ensured by requiring the owner, in all but a few instances, to obtain permission from the local planning authority for any *development* of his land, but the vast extent of the control does not become apparent until it is seen what a very wide meaning is given to the word " development ". The statutory definition is as follows: *(Wide definition of development.)*

> " 'Development' means the carrying out of building, engineering,
> " mining and other operations in, on, over or under land or the
> " making of any material change in the use of any buildings or other
> " land."[6]

Moreover, the individual words used by the statute are each given a wide meaning.[7] The first part of the definition refers to positive operations on the land or buildings, whilst the second part is concerned with changes which may be made in the use of land or buildings.

In the first part, building operations include rebuilding, alterations of or additions to buildings and other operations normally undertaken by a builder. Thus the demolition of a *(Positive operations which constitute development.)*

---

[1] Land Compensation Act, 1961, s. 9.

[2] "Small" business means of an annual value not exceeding £250: S. I. 1959, No. 1318. But "owner-occupier" includes a lessee with at least three years to run.

[3] *Ministry of Transport* v. *Holland*, (1963), 61 L. G. R. 134.

[4] *Bolton Corpn.* v. *Owen* [1962] 1 Q. B. 470, [1962] 1 All E. R. 101.

[5] There are special controls in addition to the general law, e.g. in relation to advertisements, buildings of special interest, trees, and caravan sites. There is also power to require the proper maintenance of "waste land": 1962 Act, ss. 36 and 57. See *Stephens* v. *Cuckfield Rural District Council*, [1960] 2 Q. B. 373; [1960] 2 All E. R. 716 on the definition of "waste land", and also *Britt* v. *Buckinghamshire County Council*, [1964] 1 Q. B. 77; [1963] 2 All E. R. 175.

[6] 1962 Act, s. 12 (1). The distinction between "new" development and "existing rights user" is important for compensation, not permission: *infra*, pp. 897–8.

[7] 1962 Act, ss. 12 (2) and 221 (1).

building does not, of itself, involve development, although it may do so if it forms part of a building operation or leads to a natural change of use of the land on which it stood.   On the other hand, the Act provides that *internal work* in a building, such as an internal conversion, which does not naturally affect the external appearance of the building would not amount to development. " Engineering operations " include the formation of means of access to highways.   Any means of access to any street therefore amounts to development and requires the consent of the planning authority.

Changes of use which constitute development.   Turning to the second part of the definition which is concerned with the use being made of land and buildings, as distinct from active operations upon them, it provides that a change in the use[1] of land or buildings is development if it is a " material change ". This expression is not defined and raises frequent difficulties, but it is basically a factual question, and one on which the courts are not too ready to intervene on an appeal.[2]   But there must be a *substantial* difference between the existing use and what is proposed.   Moreover, in deciding whether a change is material, the governing factor is its comparison with the previous use of the land or buildings taken as a whole, not its effect on the surrounding neighbourhood.[3]   Thus, when an owner proposed to use the cellar of his house for storing wines and spirits in connection with his wine and spirit business, the Minister considered this to be development.[4]   A change in *kind*, for instance from house to shop or shop to factory, would require permission; so would a change in the *degree* of existing use if it were very marked.[5]   Thus, taking in lodgers would not normally amount to a material change of use of a house, but running it as a guest house would.   For the avoidance of doubt the Act expressly declares that a material change is involved if a single dwelling-house is converted into two or more houses or if advertisements are displayed on any external part of a building which is not normally used for that purpose.[6]

The Act also provides that the use of any land or buildings

---

[1] This is, of course, a different issue from that which arises if a development ment is refused which restricts "existing rights"; this is a matter for compensation, see *infra*, p. 898. Existing use rights have been considered recently in relation to what constitutes sufficient previous user of caravan sites: see *Biss* v. *Smallburgh Rural District Council* [1965] Ch. 335 especially *per* Russell, L. J., at pp. 370–2.

[2] *Bendles Motors, Ltd.* v. *Bristol Corpn.* [1963] 1 All E. R. 578; [1963] 1 W. L. R. 247.

[3] Circular 67/49. *G. Percy Trentham, Ltd.* v. *Gloucestershire County Council,* [1966] 1 All E. R. 701; [1966] 1 W. L. R. 506.

[4] Bulletin of Selected Appeal Decisions VII, No. 21.

[5] Intensification of use raises great problems: see note 1, *supra*, and *Guildford Rural District Council* v. *Fortescue,* [1959] 2 Q. B. 112, especially *per* Lord Evershed, M. R., at p. 125.

[6] 1962 Act, ss. 12 (3) (a) and 12 (4): *Birmingham Corpn.* v. *Minister of Housing and Local Government,* [1964] 1 Q. B. 178: [1963] 3 All E. R. 668; *Ealing B.C.* v. *Ryan* [1965] 2 Q. B. 486; [1965] 1 All E. R. 137.

within the curtilage[1] of a dwelling house for purposes incidental to its enjoyment is not development. New building within the curtilage would, of course, be development, although, as we shall see, if it is incidental to the enjoyment of a dwelling house, it will frequently amount to what is called " permitted development " for which permission is not required.[2]

Many cases of change of use are dealt with by the Town and Country Planning (Use Classes) Order, 1963.[3] This Order classifies buildings or other land into nineteen different classes according to the purposes for which they are used, and provides that buildings or land used for a purpose in one class may be used for any other purpose in the same class without involving development. The order is intended to be facultative, not restrictive; it is intended to release controls imposed by the Act and does not itself impose any control. Thus, a change from a use in one class to another use in the same class is never development; on the other hand, a change[4] from a use in one class to a use in another class is not automatically development, but only if it involves a material change. Only a few examples of the operation of the order can be given. Under Class I, planning permission is not normally required when there is a change in the type of commodity sold at a shop, as when a grocery stores is converted into a furniture shop, but exceptionally permission must be obtained before the existing trade is changed into selling fried fish, tripe, cats meat, pet animals or birds. Under Class II an office may be used for any purpose, so that for instance, a solicitor's office may be converted to a surveyor's office without the need for planning permission. Classes III to IX deal with different types of industrial buildings.[5] Thus, a building used for light industrial purposes (defined as one in which the processes carried on or the machinery installed are such as could be carried on or installed in any residential area without detriment to the amenity of the area) could be used for any other type of light industrial activity without permission being obtained. Similarly, a hospital may be converted into a mental institution without permission, for these are both Class XVI uses, but if it is

The Use Classes Order.

---

[1] See *Sinclair-Lockhart's Trustees* v. *Central Land Board* (1950), 1. P. & C. R. 195, affirmed (1951) 1 P. & C. R. 320, for a definition of curtilage, " the ground which is used for the comfortable enjoyment of a house or other building . . . although it has not been marked off or enclosed in any way ".

[2] *Infra*, p. 888.

[3] S. I. 1963, No. 708 as amended by S. I. 1965, No. 229. Circulars 42/48, 94/50 and 10/60.

[4] For a different view of the Order see 1966 Jo. Planning Law 504 *et seq.*

[5] It may be mentioned here that industrial and office building is subject to the Board of Trade, which is concerned with unemployment and distribution of industry issues. Under ss. 38 and 39 of the 1962 Act, industrial development certificates are required for buildings involving more that 5,000 sq. ft. of industrial floor space, as well as planning permission. The Control of Office and Industrial Development Act, 1965 reduces this figure to 1,000 sq. ft. in specified areas of the country, and provides for office development permits, again in specified areas, where new office floor space is to exceed 3,000 sq. ft.

to become a health centre, a Class XV use, planning permission would be required if it were judged to be a material change.

Procedure for determining what amounts to development.

When a question arises as to whether a particular operation or change of use amounts to development, an application may be made to the local planning authority requiring it to decide whether permission is required and from their decision an appeal will lie to the Minister.[1]   A further appeal is possible to the High Court on a point of law but, apart from this, the Minister's decision would seem to be final.   Nothing in this statutory procedure, however, prohibits a developer from applying to the High Court for a judicial declaration as to whether in given circumstances development is involved.[2]   Such an application must be made before any appeal to the Minister is lodged; on the other hand, once a declaration is made by the Court, the Minister would doubtless regard it as binding.

The General Development Order.

An owner,[3] then, who wishes to embark on what is technically development, must obtain planning permission from the local planning authority.   If, however, the development falls within one of the classes of development set out in the General Development Order, 1963[4], he is allowed to undertake it without obtaining permission.   These relaxations, which are known as "permitted development", are often made subject to special conditions and two standard conditions apply generally; the projected development must not involve the creation or widening of a means of access to a classified road and must not create a dangerous obstruction at any corner or intersection.

Permitted development.

One important class of permitted development is that occurring within the curtilage of a dwelling-house.[5]   The house may be enlarged or improved, and even a garage may be erected, so long as the cubic content of the original dwelling house is not exceeded by more than 1,750 cubic feet or one tenth, whichever is the greater, subject to a maximum of 4,000 cubic feet.   The alterations must not, however, result in raising the height of the original dwelling house and there must be no projection beyond its forwardmost part.   This enables many minor operations to be carried out without consuming time and manpower out of all proportion to their importance.   For the same reason, the owner

---

[1] 1962 Act, ss. 43 and 181. S. I. 1963, No. 709, art. 5. S. 43 must not be used as generally applicable appeal machinery: *Edgewarebury Park Investments, Ltd.* v. *Ministry of Housing*, [1963] 2 Q. B. 408; [1963] 1 All E. R., 124.

[2] *Pyx Granite Co.* v. *Minister of Housing and Local Government*, [1960] A. C. 260; [1959] 3 All E. R. 1 (H. L.).

[3] 1962 Act, s. 13. The Crown does not require planning permission: *Ministry of Agriculture, Fisheries and Food* v. *Jenkins*, [1963] 2 Q. B. 317; [1963] 2 All E. R. 147. Local authorities may or may not require it: 1965 Jo. Planning Law 142.

[4] S. I. 1963, No. 709. Circulars 87/50 and 10/60. A planning authority may, with the Minister's approval, limit the operation of the Order within a special area: S. I. 1963, No. 709, art. 4.

[5] See 1964 Jo. Planning Law 462.

of a dwelling house is permitted to erect, within the curtilage, a building (other than another dwelling house or a garage) for any purpose incidental to the enjoyment of his house, provided that the building does not exceed ten feet or, if it has a rigid roof, twelve feet in height. Again, farmers and those engaged in forestry are released from the necessity of obtaining planning permission if they wish to erect certain buildings or plant for the purpose of agriculture or forestry. Another class of permitted development benefits industrialists, who are permitted to extend industrial buildings by one-tenth or by so much as does not require a Board of Trade certificate,[1] whichever is the less, subject to an overriding maximum. The additional buildings may be extensions to existing buildings or new buildings but there must be no marked change in the appearance of the premises from the outside. Many of the classes of the Order exempt development undertaken by local authorities and other public bodies, such as river boards and the National Coal Board.

SECTION IV. APPLICATION FOR PLANNING PERMISSION.

The outline application.

Development therefore needs the permission of the local planning authority unless it is permitted by the General Development Order. If the development involves the erection of a new building, the developer may find it convenient to make an "outline application" for planning permission.[2] The applicant, who need not be the owner of the land, may by this means ascertain whether his proposals will be acceptable in principle, before incurring the expense of detailed plans. Only a site plan needs to be submitted with such an application, indicating the character and approximate size of the building and the use to which it is to be put, for example a three bedroomed house. Such an application is less suitable where the siting, design or outward appearance of the development, or the means of access, are relevant. In such a case the authority may ask for whatever detail it needs to decide the application, and the applicant may either provide the information or appeal immediately to the Minister. Outline applications could result in an accumulation of permissions for which no detailed plans had been submitted for approval and hence it is customary for planning authorities to attach a condition requiring plans to be submitted within a stated period, say, three years. A permission, once granted upon an outline application, however general its terms, is as complete a planning permission as one granted on the fullest information and, therefore, any matters

---

[1] *Supra* p. 887. In some areas, industrial buildings are further controlled by the Control of Office and Industrial Development Act, 1965.

[2] See S. I. 1963, No. 709, art 5. Advice given by an officer of a local authority creates no estoppel and, in a doubtful case, is better not given: *Southend-on-Sea Corpn.* v. *Hodgson (Wickford), Ltd.*, [1962] 1 Q. B. 416; [1961] 2 All E. R. 46.

which an authority wishes to reserve for subsequent approval must be expressly reserved. If approval is withheld or granted subject to conditions an appeal will lie to the Minister against the authority's decision.

Owners and agricultural tenants to be notified.   An applicant for planning permission need not have an interest in land that is the subject matter of the application. An application could even be made without the knowledge of the owner of the land until the 1959 Act took steps to ensure that owners and agricultural tenants are notified when applications are made to develop their land.[1] No planning application may now be entertained unless it is accompanied by a certificate showing that the applicant is either the owner of the freehold, or has a tenancy of all the land concerned, or has given appropriate notice of his application. The applicant must also certify that he has given an individual notice to any agricultural tenant. Owners and agricultural tenants are then entitled to twenty-one days within which to make representations to the planning authority, who must take them into account in reaching a decision. The planning authority must give notice of its decision not only to the applicant but also to anyone whose representations it was required to consider.

General notice in some cases.   There are certain developments which can only be undertaken after the applicant has published a notice in the local newspaper.[2] Examples are the disposal of waste, and buildings such as cinemas. In these cases, *but only in these cases*, neighbours have an opportunity of expressing their views to the planning authority before it deals with the application. The planning authority is bound to consider any representations received, but the objector has no right of personal appearance. Quite independently of these rules however, a planning authority must keep a register of all applications for development and their outcome.[3]

Timetable for a decision.   Once an application for planning permission has been made the planning authority must deal with it within two months, or three months in the case of an application affecting a trunk road, although these periods may be extended by written agreement between the parties; an applicant who does not hear from the authority within these periods may appeal to the Minister as if his application has been rejected.[4] Permission may be granted, refused, or granted subject to conditions.[5] The imposition of conditions is a source of difficulty. A condition must not be

Permissions subject to conditions.

---

[1] S. 37. Now see ss. 15–17 of the 1962 Act.

[2] 1962 Act, s. 15; S. I. 1963 No. 709 art. 6.

[3] 1962 Act, s. 19 (5); S. I. 1963, No. 709, art. 14. An application must be noted in the register within 14 days of its receipt.

[4] S. I. 1963, No. 709, art. 5. See *James v. Minister of Housing and Local Government*, [1966] 1 W. L. R. 135 (C. A.) at p. 142 *per* Lord DENNING, M. R.; [1967] 1 W. L. R. 171 (H. L.] at p. 203, *per* Lord WILBERFORCE.

[5] 1962 Act, s. 17. If reasons are not given, *mandamus* lies to obtain them: *Brayhead (Ascot), Ltd.* v. *Berkshire County Council*, [1964] 2 Q. B. 303, at p. 313; [1964] 1 All E. R. 149.

seriously uncertain in its meaning,[1] nor must it have the effect of levying a charge or depriving owners of rights, such as existing use rights, of which they cannot be dispossessed without offer of compensation.[2] Furthermore, as Lord DENNING put it, "Conditions, to be valid, must fairly and reasonably relate to the permitted development".[3] Conditions relating to type and extent of use, including use by specific classes of person e.g. agricultural workers, do relate to development;[4] but not conditions which, for instance, purport to confer Rent Act protection on caravan dwellers[5] or which seek to perform the task of other legislation.[6] A planning authority which imposes conditions on irrelevant considerations may be held to have acted beyond the four corners of its powers.[7] But an applicant who succeeds in an action for a declaration of the invalidity of such a condition may nevertheless have won a pyrrhic victory. Unless the condition was "trivial or at least unimportant",[8] its invalidity will cause the whole permission to be void.[9] For this reason, disappointed applicants may be better advised to appeal to the Minister, who can treat the appeal as if it were an application and so amend it.[10]

The planning authority will normally follow its development plan in reaching a decision, but it may also take into account any other material considerations.[11] But a permission which is contrary to the provisions of the development plan may be given.[12]

Departure from development plan.

---

[1] *Fawcett Properties, Ltd.* v. *Buckinghamshire County Council,* [1961] A. C. 636; [1960] 3 All E. R. 503. The onus is on those alleging the uncertainty: *Hall & Co., Ltd.* v. *Shoreham-by-Sea Urban District Council,* [1964] 1 All E. R. 1, at pp. 5–6, *per* WILLMER, L. J.; [1964] 1 W. L. R. 240.

[2] *Hall & Co. Ltd.* v. *Shoreham-by-Sea Urban District Council, supra; Minister of Housing and Local Government* v. *Hartnell,* [1965] A. C. 1134; [1965] 1 All E. R. 490, a case on the Caravan Sites and Control of Development Act, 1960, an Act which subjects caravan sites to special rules in addition to those under the general planning Acts and which leads to great difficulties: see *Esdell Caravan Parks, Ltd.* v. *Hemel Hempstead Rural District Council,* [1966] 1 Q. B. 895; [1965] 2 All E. R. 1011 (C. A.)

[3] *Pyx Granite Co., Ltd.* v. *Ministry of Housing and Local Government,* [1958] 1 Q. B. 554 at p. 572; [1958] 1 All E.R. 625, a dictum approved by the House of Lords in the *Fawcett* and *Mixnam's Properties* cases.

[4] *Fawcett Properties, Ltd.* v. *Buckinghamshire County Council, supra.*

[5] *Mixnam's Properties, Ltd.* v. *Chertsey Urban District Council,* [1965] A. C. 735, another case arising under the 1960 Act,, *supra,* note 2.

[6] E.g. Highways Acts: *Hall & Co., Ltd.* v. *Shoreham-by-Sea Urban District Council, supra.*

[7] *Associated Provincial Picture Houses, Ltd.* v. *Wednesbury Corpn.,* [1948] 1. K.B. 223; [1947] 2 All E. R. 680.

[8] *Hall & Co., Ltd.* v. *Shoreham-by-Sea Urban District Council, supra* at p. 261, *per* PEARSON, L. J.

[9] This consequence may not follow if the permission makes clear sense without the condition, as where the authority considered all the relevant matters in giving permission, and imposed conditions after considering irrelevant matters: *Allnatt London Properties, Ltd.* v. *Middlesex County Council,* [1964] L. G. R. 304.

[10] *Infra,* p. 892. Alternatively, the matter may be dealt with by way of appeal from an enforcement notice, *infra,* pp. 894–5.

[11] 1962 Act, s. 17. S. I. 1963, No. 709, articles 9 and 11 provide for consulting other interested authorities, such as the Minister of Transport.

[12] S. I. 1963, No 709, art. 10; Circular 70/65.

Substantial variations must be preceded by local advertisement and the Minister given an opportunity to consider the case; while really serious variations must be referred to the Minister for a decision by him. It is clear, then, that the Development Plan is only a general indication of policy, and gives no guarantee.

Effect of permission.

Once a permission has been granted it will, unless revoked or modified, enure for the benefit of the land and of all persons interested in it.[1] But a planning authority may by an order revoke or modify it, subject to confirmation by the Minister. This order must be made before building operations, authorized by the original permission, have been carried out or before an authorized change of use has actually taken place.[2]

Appeals.

Local planning authorities, in refusing an application or granting permission subject to conditions, should state their reasons; nor would it suffice to say that the development is "injurious to amenity", without particularizing the amenity.[3] The applicant will then decide whether or not to appeal.[4] He and the local authority must be given an opportunity of appearing before a person specially appointed by the Minister to hear the case, but appeals by way of written submissions are encouraged in suitable cases.[5] Once the applicant has given notice that he intends to appeal, the local planning authority must ensure that he knows the case he has to meet. If reliance is placed on any Ministerial statement of policy or departmental circular, the applicant should be informed of it. Moreover, should there be brought to the Minister's attention after the inquiry, new evidence which, in his view, may be a material factor in the decision, the parties will be given an opportunity of commenting upon it and, if necessary, the inquiry will be reopened. The Minister must, in particular, not depart from his inspector's recommendation without observing this rule.[6] In reaching his decision, three courses are open to the Minister; he may allow or dismiss the appeal or vary *any part of the decision*, whether or not the appeal relates to that part, and deal with the application as if it had been made to him in the first instance. Thus, an applicant, appealing because of an objectionable condition, exposes himself to the possibility that the Minister, if he decides against him, may not merely reject the appeal but add further conditions. The Minister communicates his decision[7] to the parties by a letter, summarizing the main

[1] 1962 Act, s. 21. A permission may, of course, be limited as to time.

[2] 1962 Act, s. 27. Such a revocation or modification will generally entail the payment of compensation which is dealt with *infra*, p. 899. S. 179 provides for an appeal to the High Court.

[3] S. I. 1963, No. 709, art. 5 (10). Failure to give reasons does not make the decision void, however: *Brayhead (Ascot), Ltd.* v. *Berkshire County Council*, [1964] 2 Q. B. 303; [1964] 1 All E. R. 149.

[4] 1962 Act, s. 23. Notice to appeal should be given within 28 days. The procedure governing appeals in contained in S. I. 1965, No. 473.

[5] Circular 32/65.

[6] *Lord Luke of Pavenham* v. *Minister of Housing* [1967] 1 All E. R. 351.

[7] *Givaudan & Co., Ltd.* v. *Minister of Housing* [1966] 3 All E. R. 696.

points at the inquiry and setting out the Inspector's findings and recommendation. Finally, the letter will give the reasons for the Minister's decision.

The 1947 Act provided that the decision of the Minister should be final but the 1959 Act enabled a decision of the Minister to be challenged on the ground that it is not within his statutory powers, or that the correct procedures were not observed.[1] But it is not a re-hearing.[2] Furthermore, the word final only means that there is no normal appeal. Certiorari is available[3] if an error of law is apparent on the face of the Minister's decision. A declaration is also available in appropriate cases.[4] Application to High Court.

The Minister is empowered to take a particular application for permission to develop land or a whole class of such applications out of the hands of the local planning authority and to deal with the matter himself.[5] If this exceptional course is adopted and a case is "called in" for decision by the Minister, the applicant must be informed and both he and the local planning authority given an opportunity of being heard by an inspector. This entitles the applicant to argue his case, a right that he does not enjoy if his application were being dealt with by the local planning authority. "Calling in."

When a permission is refused or granted subject to conditions, the owner may in certain circumstances require the land to be purchased.[6] The matter is ordinarily one for confirmation by the Minister, who must be satisfied that the land is incapable in its existing state or subject to the imposed conditions of reasonably beneficial use and is not susceptible to reasonably beneficial use by any development for which permission would be granted. The issue turns, then, on the land *in its existing state* and with its existing permissions. Thus, if permission is refused for the development of land which is on the edge of a town but in a green belt, it would not be permissible to take into account that at some time the green belt might be redrawn to permit urban development taking place there. Only potentially existing uses should be taken into account.[7] A purchase notice is, therefore, not a remedy for an owner whose Purchase notices.

---

[1] 1947 Act, ss. 15 (3), 16 (2); 1959 Act, s. 31; see now s. 179 of the 1962 Act.
[2] Cf. *Rhodes* v. *Minister of Housing,* [1963] 1 All E.R. 300; [1963] 1 W. L. R. 208; *Green* v. *Minister of Housing and Local Government,* [1967] 2 W. L. R. 192.
[3] *R.* v. *Northumberland Compensation Appeal Tribunal, ex parte Shaw,* [1952] 1 K. B. 338; [1952] 1 All E. R. 122; *R.* v. *Medical Appeal Tribunal, ex parte Gilmore,* [1957] 1 Q. B. 574; [1957] 1 All E. R. 796, C. A: and cf. *Associated Provincial Picture Houses* v. *Wednesbury Corporation,* [1948] 1 Q. B. 223.
[4] *Pyx Granite Co. Ltd.* v. *Ministry of Housing and Local Government,* [1960] A. C. 260; [1959] 3 All E. R. 1 and cf. *Munnich* v. *Godstone Rural District Council,* [1966] 1 All E. R. 930, at pp. 932–3, *per* Lord DENNING, M. R., and SALMON, L. J. at pp 935–6, (a case on enforcement notices, *infra,* p. 894), and *Biss* v. *Smallburgh Rural District Council,* [1965] Ch. 335 at 361, *per* HARMAN, L. J.
[5] 1962 Act, s. 22: S. I. 1965, No. 473, art. 2 (1)(a).
[6] 1962 Act, ss. 129–133. S. I. 1963, No. 709, Sched 2, Pt. II, para (2).
[7] Circular 49/59: "A use of relatively low value may be reasonably beneficial if such a use is common for similar land in the neighbourhood and a small area of land may in some circumstances be capable of reasonably beneficial use in conjunction with a wider area."

complaint is that he is unable to realize the *full* development value of his land.

Action of Minister where owner serves a purchase notice.

The Minister may confirm a purchase notice, grant permission for the development in respect of which the application was originally made, or amend any condition attached to it. Furthermore, if he considers that the land could be capable of reasonably beneficial use within a reasonable time by the carrying out of some other development, he may direct that permission be granted for that development, if the developer makes application.[1] He may also rule that another authority should acquire the land in place of the authority on whom the purchase notice was served.

SECTION V. ENFORCEMENT.

Requirements of enforcement notices.

A planning authority may serve an enforcement notice if development is carried out without permission or in defiance of a condition imposed.[2] But such a notice must be served within four years of the development being carried out. To that extent a limitation period works against planning authorities. The notice may require the restoration of the land or buildings to its former state, but must specify the steps to be taken and give reasonable time for their accomplishment.[3] The notice must be served on all affected parties and must specify the period at the end of which it is to become effective (which must be at least 28 days) and the period within which reinstatement is to be carried out.[4] The notice must tell the offender "fairly what he has done wrong and what he must do to remedy it".[5] If there is an obvious defect on the face of the notice, it will be a nullity,[6] but otherwise the only procedure for challenging a notice is by appeal to the Minister.[7] The appellant may challenge its validity on a wide variety of grounds; that planning permission ought to be granted, has been granted, is not required, or on procedural grounds. If, for instance, it fails to make clear what the real nature of the offence is, so that the

---

[1] Compensation may be recoverable in such a case, see *infra*, p. 898–9.

[2] 1962 Act, s. 45.

[3] A planning authority can, if necessary, carry out the work itself and recover the cost from the owner: 1962 Act, s. 48.

[4] These requirements are mandatory: *Mead* v. *Chelmsford Rural District Council*, [1953] 1 Q. B. 32; [1952] 2 All E. R. 723; *Bambury* v. *London Borough of Hounslow*, [1966] 2 All E. R. 532.

[5] *Per* UPJOHN, L. J., in *Miller-Mead* v. *Minister of Housing and Local Government*, [1963] 2 Q. B. 196 at 232; [1963] 1 All E. R. 459.

[6] *Per* UPJOHN, L. J., in *Miller-Mead* v. *Minister of Housing and Local Government*, *supra*, at pp. 226–7, and cf. *per* Lord DENNING, M. R., at p. 219 and DIPLOCK, L. J., at p. 238.

[7] 1962 Act, ss. 46 and 177. These provisions derive from the 1960 Act, which abolished a former appeal to justices. The distinction drawn between invalidity and nullity is not easy: the Court of Appeal reviewed the whole matter in *Miller-Mead* v. *Minister of Housing and Local Government*, *supra*.

offender is in peril on an ambiguity, the order will be quashed.[1] But an order will not be quashed because of any error or slight ambiguity, but only if they go to the substance of the matter.[2] Indeed, the Minister has express power to amend errors that are not material.[3] There is an appeal from the Minister to the High Court on points of law.[4] It is obvious then that many matters of importance will arise for decision in this way.

SECTION VI. DEVELOPMENT CHARGES AND COMPENSATION.

The intention of the 1947 Act was to restrict the owner of land to the enjoyment of its existing use upon the 1st July, 1948, and to pay him compensation for all the other uses of which the land was potentially capable (out of a central fund of £300,000,000 that was established for the purpose).[5] The scheme envisaged that, for the future, an owner who wished to carry out some new development must first obtain planning permission from the local planning authority and then pay a development charge to the State. The Central Land Board was created to administer the compensation fund and levy development charges.

Owner restricted to existing uses.

Under this Act therefore an owner, say of a farm, was entitled to devote it to its existing use as agricultural land, but if he wished to develop it in some way, as for example by the erection of a housing estate on fields adjacent to a nearby town, he would be required to obtain permission and to pay a development charge representing the increase in land value attributable to the more gainful use of the property. If, however, land increased in value for some reason unconnected with its development, as for instance where a house which cost £7,000 to build became more valuable because of the scarcity of that type of house in the neighbourhood and was sold for £10,000, there would be no question of any development charge being payable.[6]

The development charge.

In making his claim against the compensation fund, the owner[7] was allowed to claim for the difference between what was called the *restricted* and *unrestricted* value of the land as at 1st July, 1948. The unrestricted value of the land was its value on that date without any of the restrictions introduced by the 1947 Act. The restricted value was its value after the restrictions had been

The measure of compensation.

---

[1] *Francis* v. *Yiewsley and West Drayton Urban District Council*, [1958] 1 Q. B. 478; [1957] 3 All E. R. 529.
[2] *Miller-Mead* v. *Minister of Housing and Local Government, supra.* cf. *Bambury* v. *London Borough of Hounslow.* See also 1963 Jo. Planning Law 151.
[3] 1962 Act, s. 46 (4).   [4] 1962 Act, s. 180; R. S. C. Order 94, *r.* 12.
[5] See the speech of Lord Reid in *Hartnell* v. *Minister of Housing and Local Government,* [1965] A. C. 1134, and Heap 1964 Jo. Planning Law, at p. 6. and p. 645.
[6] Cf. *infra*, p. 899.   [7] 1947 Act, ss. 60 (3) and 119 (1).

imposed by the Act. Although these calculations were based upon the condition and state of the land on 1st July, 1948, they were made with reference to prices current immediately before 7th January, 1947.

Failure of the scheme.

The payment of compensation for the future uses of land and the collection of development charges for betterment were clearly complementary, and were intended to implement the recommendations of the Uthwatt Committee in 1942 that the successful control of land depended upon tackling the compensation or betterment problem.[1] But in 1952 the Government decided to abandon the betterment side of the scheme altogether, since it had become clear that the financial provisions of the 1947 Act were neither understood nor likely to be successful. The intention of the Act was that a man who bought land for building purposes should pay no more for it than would have been paid before the Act. He was to buy the existing use from the owner (who had already received compensation from the fund) and then pay a development charge to the State, representing the increased value of the land once development permission had been given. Landowners generally failed to realize the fundamental change in their position. The land was still there and to all outward appearances the owner was just as much in control of it as he was before. The subtlety of the fundamental change wrought by the Act largely contributed to its failure.[2] For the most part owners were unwilling to sell land at its existing use value. Purchasers, who paid more, were in effect paying twice for the right to develop—once to the owner and again to the State by way of development charge. Further, those owners who appreciated the true position refrained from selling, with the result that little land was offered for development. To the extent, therefore, that the existing use basis was effective, it tended to keep land off the market; to the extent that it was ignored, the cost of development rose. The Central Land Board threatened to make wider use of certain powers of compulsory purchase with which it had been armed and thus compel observance of the general scheme by acquiring land at its existing use value from unwilling sellers, and then reconveying it to developers. But it was to no avail. In 1953 an Act was passed which abolished development charges,[3] thereby restoring to owners the full value of their land. The Act also provided that the distribution of the £300,000,000 fund should not take place.[4] Nevertheless, claims against the fund continued to be of the greatest importance for, in 1954, a further Act was passed with two objectives that concern us here.

---

[1] Cmd. 6386.

[2] E. H. Scammell, *The Development of Land under the Planning Acts,* 1953, C. L. P., p. 135.

[3] For all development on or after 18th November, 1952; 1953 Act, s. 1.

[4] 1953 Act, s. 3.

First, between 1947 and 1953 many landowners had ordered their affairs on the assumption that the £300,000,000 fund would be distributed. Special "unscrambling provisions" had to be passed to deal with such cases.

Secondly it was necessary to provide compensation for some cases[1] where planning permission was refused. Although the financial provisions of the 1947 Act had been repealed, the scheme of planning control introduced by that Act remained and, once the full use of his land had been restored to an owner, he might justifiably expect to receive compensation if he applied to carry out some development and was refused planning consent. Such an owner was, accordingly, enabled to receive compensation if, but only if, he *had already* established a claim against the £300,000,000 fund in respect of the land which he wishes to develop—the "claim holding".[2] To the claim holding one-seventh of its value was added (representing interest less tax) and the resulting sum was known as "the original unexpended balance of established development value"[3]. While, under the 1947 Act, the established claim was a piece of personal property which an owner could dispose of, its successor, the unexpended balance of established development value, is not personal and disposable but is attached to the land. It fixed for all time the *upper* limit of compensation to be paid when an owner, seeking to develop his land, is refused planning consent. It was also used to fix the maximum compensation payable for compulsory acquisition, but the 1959 Act restored market value as the basis of compensation.[4]

When therefore, permission for the carrying out of some *new development* is refused or only granted subject to conditions, anyone with a sufficient interest in the land may claim compensation, but the amount which he *may* receive will be the amount by which the value of his interest has been depreciated by the decision or the amount of the unexpended balance of established development value immediately before the decision, whichever is the less.[5] The unexpended balance attached to the land is

Compensation for refusal of planning permission.

---

[1] See *infra*, p. 898. It is not possible to go into this complex subject in a book of this nature. Basically, what is being discussed at this stage is compensation for "new development" (as defined in s. 12 (5) of the 1962 Act) under what is now Part VI of that Act. Compensation for loss of "existing use rights" (sometimes known as "Third Schedule Development," since it derived from that Schedule in the 1947 Act) is based upon different considerations and does not depend on the claim holding being discussed here. See *infra*, p. 899 for compensation in respect of this and other special cases.

[2] 1954 Act, s. 2 (1).   [3] 1954 Act, s. 17.

[4] Land Compensation Act, 1961, s. 5. Ss. 14, 15, and 16 of this Act contain complicated provisions whereby the market value is assessed. Specific assumptions have to be made concerning planning permission. S. 17 provides that, if asked, a planning authority must certify the nature of the development that would have been allowed if compulsory purchase was not taking place.

[5] 1962 Act, ss, 88, 89, 90, 106, 107. The matter is one for the Minister: ss. 108–111. The Minister, after giving notice and hearing representations, may review the planning decision so as to avoid the payment of compensation: s. 26.

reduced accordingly, as it also is by any new development which takes place after 1st July, 1948, unless it was the subject matter of a development charge.[1]

Cases where compensation is not allowed.

But in addition to the above limitations, the Act in many cases specifically excludes the payment of compensation altogether.[2] This applies particularly where the refusal of permission limits, controls or postpones development but does not prevent development altogether. Hence, in respect of many matters, the planning authority may exercise considerable control, without involving the payment of compensation. But to grant a permission subject to a condition which would in practice nullify the permission is not proper.[3] In such circumstances, a planning authority should give a plain refusal, as a result of which the applicant would be entitled to compensation. The principle is that, so long as an owner is allowed some reasonably remunerative development, he should not be entitled to compensation merely because the maximum exploitation of the development possibilities of his land is denied to him.[4] Thus, the restrictions upon the payment of compensation are severe; and even when it is allowed, its distribution depends upon an unrealistic and arbitrary basis.

Compensation payable by local authority.

We have, in the preceding paragraphs, been concerned with the general scheme of compensation established by the 1954 Act, when planning permission has been refused for *new development*. There are in addition a group of cases (derived from the 1947 Act) where compensation is payable not by the State but by the local authority and, moreover, is payable whether or not the land carries an unexpended balance of established development value.[5] The foremost among these cases is the case where planning permission to develop the *existing use* of land or buildings is refused or granted subject to conditions.[6] The circumstances in which compensation is payable for the loss of such rights are set out in Part II of the Third Schedule of the 1962 Act,[7] but to establish his right to compensation, the applicant must first have appealed to the Minister against the decision. Compensation is also payable by a local authority under Schedule VII of the 1962 Act if the Minister, in refusing to confirm a purchase notice, directs that permission be granted (if the applicant asks for it) for a develop-

---

[1] See *supra*, p. 896. Compensation received may be repayable in certain cases where a new development is subsequently permitted: 1962 Act, ss. 113, 114. A purchaser of land should always ascertain from the local land charges register whether compensation has been paid.

[2] 1962 Act, ss. 101–103.   [3] Circular 40/55.

[4] See the Minister of Housing's reply in Hansard, vol. 525 (1954) col. 56.

[5] This is compensation under Schedule VII of the 1962 Act. Compensation is again determined by the Land Compensation Act, 1961, and, if necessary, by a reference to the Lands Tribunal: 1962 Act, ss. 110 and 117.

[6] 1962 Act, s. 123; s. 26 of the 1947 Act established the principle that compensation was payable for the loss, or enforced discontinuance, of existing rights.

[7] As amended by the Town and Country Planning Act, 1963. This is so-called "Third Schedule Development."

ment, the development value of which is less than what is termed "existing use value".[1] Yet another example occurs where the quinquennial reviews of the development plan produce changes in the planning of particular areas and these conflict with developments which have already taken place. If the planning authority wishes to remove or alter some building, the erection of which has been duly authorized, it may issue an order (which must be confirmed by the Minister), but anyone who suffers loss by such an order may obtain compensation.[2] A final example[3] of Schedule VII compensation is provided by that following revocation or modification of a planning permission already granted and acted on.[4] It is probably invalid for a planning authority to exact, in return for permission, an undertaking not to ask for compensation in the event of its being revoked.[5]

SECTION VII. THE LAND COMMISSION.

Recent legislation is again changing the implications of land ownership. The imposition of a capital gains tax on profits made on dispositions of property applies to land, save land (of up to one acre) with a dwelling house on it which is the owner's home.[6] Thus profits ascribable to the natural growth of land values are no longer immune from fiscal legislation. The owner-occupier is further privileged in that he, unlike a landlord, is now exempt from taxation under Schedule A.[7] But this is far from being the end of the matter. Land is now thought of as being too valuable a community asset for undue profit to be made from it by anyone; and the central issue of betterment values[8] has been raised and dealt with afresh by the creation of the Land Commission, from which not even an owner-occupier is exempt. This drastic new legislation is concerned not with the natural growth of land values but with increases in value due to development or potential development. When land is disposed of, the vendor will retain only part of the purchase price he receives, namely that part representing (i) its current use value and (ii) a proportion (60% at present but probably less in forthcoming years) of its realised development value; the remaining 40% (or more) will go to the State. This levy will also be exacted in certain cases where an actual development occurs without a disposition taking place.[9]

Taxation of Land Values.

---

[1] 1962 Act, s. 134; see *supra*, p. 894.

[2] 1962 Act, ss. 28 and 124; *supra*, p. 883.

[3] Ss. 124 and 125 of the 1962 Act deal with other special cases.

[4] 1962 Act, ss. 28 and 118; *supra*, p. 892. *Holmes* v. *Bradfield Rural District Council*, [1949] 2 K. B. 1; [1949] 1 All E. R. 381.

[5] See 1965 Jo. Planning Law 641.

[6] Finance Act, 1965, ss. 19 and 29.

[7] Finance Act, 1963, s. 14.

[8] See, for a discussion of the term, its history and meaning, Heap in 1964 Jo. Planning Law 6 and 645 and Parker in *Land Values* (ed. Hall), p. 53.

[9] The Land Commission Act, 1967 (see, for a discussion, Heap, *Introducing the Land Commission Act*) contains in Part III a list of six events on the occurrence

This levy is a tax on the vendor, and is different from the development charge of the 1947 Act, which rested on the developer. It is also different from the 1947 Act in that it is not a nationalization of land uses with immediate effect (subject to the possibility of compensation), but is a tax (at less than 100%) levied on the occurrence of certain events. Nevertheless the proposals are, partly at least, a return to the betterment proposals of the Uthwatt Committee in 1942. The intention is that the purchaser will pay no more for the land than hitherto, but that the vendor will retain only a proportion of that part of his profit which is ascribable to development value.[1] Whether the financial inducement of 60% (or less) will succeed in tempting owners to sell land, or whether land will be kept from the market remains to be seen. The present Conservative opposition contend that, as after 1947, it will lead to vendors demanding higher prices to offset the levy and a renewed shortage of land on the market; and they have pledged themselves to repeal the legislation at the earliest opportunity. But in the meanwhile, the legislation is backed up by considerable powers of enforcement, far greater than those available to the old Central Land Board. In fact, these powers could presage more significant developments than the levy.

New principle of land acquisition.

The legislation sets up a Land Commission. But the commission will not just collect the levy. It is given wide powers, in Part II, to make compulsory purchases of land that, in its view, should be available for development.[2] On a first look it seems that the commission must act within the ambit of and subject to each individual planning authority; for the powers of compulsory purchase are to be exercised only in respect of land which is already defined in the development plan or designated for compulsory purchase or already possessed of permission for material development. It is thus rightly said that the commission is not a planning authority or an organ of local government. But equally rightly it is an organ of central government, and as such it is responsible for the availability of land for the community generally. A second look reveals that, as from a date yet to be announced,[3] the commission will not be restricted to the purposes for which it

---

of which a levy is to be made; the levy will be assessed on the difference between what is called "base value" and "market value," and these terms are defined in the immensely complicated Schedules 4 and 5 so as to achieve the objects of the legislation: sometimes the profit will be subject to levy before it is actually realised.

[1] In practice, owner-occupiers will only be leviable if they own developable land along with their house: but this raises problems, see 1966 Jo. Planning Law 133-4. Liability to capital gains tax will be taken into account so as to prevent a double levy.

[2] The technical phrase is "material development", which excludes "permitted development "under the General Development Order and Third Schedule Development. The commission must have more in mind than what is covered by these exceptions.

[3] This is the "second appointed day"; the first appointed day, 6th April, 1967, brings the commission into being with less than its full eventual powers.

wishes to acquire land, but may dispose of land for purposes other than the purposes for which it acquired it, and may effect compulsory purchase by a greatly accelerated procedure.[1] Indeed, the commission can itself apply for planning permission in respect of any land, and thus if granted permission, bring its own compulsory purchasing powers into operation. It is clear that, in the long run, these powers will enable the commission to take comprehensive planning decisions untrammelled by local considerations or by the need to relate compulsory purchase to particular purposes.[2] It is, accordingly, a much more powerful instrument in the building up, for the community, of a "land bank"[3] than any that has been available hitherto. And that, clearly, is the object that the present government has it in mind for the commission to achieve.

> "The Commission will often be acquiring land in advance of need—both undeveloped land and developed land in need of redevelopment."[4]

The commission may dispose of land by selling or leasing it, but selling should be restricted to sales to public bodies. The really unusual feature of this part, Part II, of the 1967 Act however, is the proposal for "crownhold". Crownhold is a form of disposition which restricts the powers of the holder, in that he may be prevented from carrying out any development of the land, and may be prevented from leasing it for a period exceeding two years. The commission will have a right of pre-emption in the event of an attempted sale, and considerable powers of enforcing forfeitures by the direct means of a vesting declaration. Crownhold covenants are not subject to modification by the Lands Tribunal, and are immune from the rule against perpetuities; they will run with the land, and will be registrable under the Land Charges Act and the Land Registration Act.

Crownhold.

A "crownhold disposition " may be by way of sale or lease; it is not a new form of conveyance or a startling new alternative to freehold and leasehold. "Crownhold interest", as a description of the holder's limited rights, provides a better insight into this new device, which is really a means of reserving development rights for the state while leaving actual development to private hands. An owner of a crownhold interest is simply an owner whose rights over the land are circumscribed in a manner incompatible with freehold and difficult to effectuate within the law relating to leasehold.

---

[1] See Heap in 1966 Jo. Planning Law 65, *et seq.*

[2] As under the provisions of the Acquisition of Land (Authorisation Procedure) Act, 1946. It must be remembered also that development plans and the whole of the present local government structure are under review.

[3] See Lichfield in *Land Values* (ed. Hall), 107.

[4] "The Land Commission", Cmnd. 2771, para 21; cf. Cmnd. 2838 (Housing), para. 26.

INDEX

INDEX

A

ABSOLUTE TITLE,
    registration with, 841
ABSTRACT OF TITLE,
    contents, verification, 65
    delivery, 658
    perusal, 658, 664
        cost, 664
    preparation, 64
    root of title, 660, 661
    sale of settled land after 1882 and before 1926, on, 78
ACCOUNT,
    guardian in socage, by, 22
ACCUMULATIONS,
    excessive, effect, 279
    land, for purpose of buying, 278
    minorities, during, 279
    payment of debts, for, 270, 280
    portions, raising, for, 280
    right to stop, 279
    rule against, 277
            exceptions, 280
            origin, 277
            periods allowed, 277
    timber, 281
ACTION,
    arrears of rent, for, 390
    corporation sole, by, limitation, 807
    damages, for, 396
        breach of contract, for, 652, 653
    debt, of, rentcharge, to recover, 563
    foreclosure, 605–607
    limitation of. *See* LIMITATION OF ACTIONS.
    mortgagor's covenant on, 600
    pending, registration, 665
    real and personal contrasted, 37-
        common recovery, 157
        freeholder only, lay against, 215
    recovery of land, for. *See* RECOVERY OF LAND.
    redemption, 594
    specific performance, for. *See* SPECIFIC PERFORMANCE.
ADMINISTRATION OF ESTATES. *And see* ADMINISTRATORS, EXECUTORS *and*
    PERSONAL REPRESENTATIVES.
    assets, application order of, 89
        equitable, 742
            and legal distinguished, 743
       land as, 741, 742, 744
           formerly not, 741
       personalty as, 740
       property now available as, 744
    beneficiaries, priority, 749–751
            variation by testator, 751
    debts, payment, property available for, 749–751
    following property, creditors' rights, 770
    grant of, right to, order of priority, 763 n.
    in court, 745
    insolvent estates, 746–751
            bankruptcy rules apply, 746.
            creditors, priority, 747
            preferential creditors, 748
    letters of administration. *See* LETTERS OF ADMINISTRATION.
    modes, 745
    out of court, 745
    solvent estates, order of application of assets, 749.

2G*   [I]

[3]

[7]

[8]

Index.

[19]

[23]

Index.

Index.

2H*

[33]

Index.

Index.

Index.

SETTLEMENT—*continued*

[46]

Index.

TITLE,
    abstract of, 64, 65
        delivery, 658
        perusal, 658, 664
            cost, 664
    administrator, of, 786
    adverse possessor, acquired by, 823–826
        to landlord, setting up, 397 n.
    adverse title,
        absolute title, when develops into, 825
    advowson, to, 661
    beneficiary under will, of, 692
    deeds, abstraction, 661
        delivery to purchaser, 674
        deposit, mortgage by, 581
        examination, 65
        mortgagee's right to, 607
        production, 65
            cost, 664
    defect in, vendor unable to complete owing to, 653
    equities overreached not abstracted, 661
    evidence of, nature, 711
    executors, of, 769
    freehold, not abstracted on sale of leaseholds, 662
    investigation, 91, 665
        matters kept off, 96
        meaning, 63
        notice from failure to make, 63–65
        sale by tenant for life before 1926, on, 96
    leaseholds, to, 661
    length, 64, 660
        open contract, under, 659
        special condition as to, 675
    possession as evidence of, 659
    proof of, 63
    registration. *See* REGISTERED CONVEYANCING.
    reversionary interests, to, 661
    root of, 64, 660
    settled land to, investigation, 712
    trust for sale, land held on, 80
TOWN AND COUNTRY PLANNING,
    Acts in force, 881
    advertisements, control of, 885 n.
    appeals, 888, 892, 893
        enforcement notices, as to, 894
    "calling in", 893
    compensation,
        fund, 895
        local authority, payable by, 898
        measure, 895, 897
        not allowed, where, 898
        planning decisions, for, 897
    compulsory acquisition, designation for, 883
    control, enforcement, 894–895
        extent, 885
        present object of, 882
    development charges, 895–899
        abolition of, 896
    development, curtilage, within, 887, 888
        definition, 885, 886
        operations amounting to, 885–889
        permission for, 885
        permitted, 888, 889
        plan. *See* DEVELOPMENT PLAN.
    enforcement notices, 894–895
    General Development Order, 888, 889
    interim development control, 881
    Land Commission. *See* LAND COMMISSION.
    local planning authorities, 881, 882
    Minister, powers of, 881, 894, 895
    necessity, 122
    planning blight, 884
    planning permission, outline of application, 889
        effect, 892
    present law, 881
    purchase notice, 893

Index.

TRUST FOR SALE—*continued*
    overreaching of equities, 718
    personalty settlement, 79
    power of sale distinguished, 149
    settlement by, advantages, 152
                subject-matter, usual, 147
                " trader's settlement," 149
    special, 719
    statutory, conveyance on, 314
            when arising, 718, 719
    strict settlement distinguished, 126
    trust deed, 79
    trustees on. *See* TRUSTEES FOR SALE.
    two deeds usual, 79
    undivided shares exist behind, 312

TRUST INSTRUMENT,
    function, 97, 706
    precedent, 707
    title, does not appear on, 712, 713

TRUSTEES,
    administrative powers of, 262, 276
    appointment, additional, 330
            court, by, 331
            maximum number, 329
            new, 329
            original, 329
    approved, 719
    bankruptcy in. *See under* BANKRUPTCY.
    beneficiaries under will may be declared to be, 692, 771
    compound, 702–704
    estate, devolution, 331
    infants cannot be, 861
    joint tenants, 331
    lease to, rentcharge in arrear, where, 562
    limitation of actions against, 816
                 by, 817
    mortgage to, 301
    new, appointment, 329
            by court, 331
      powers, 330
      vesting in, 330
    notice to, dealings with equitable interests, of, 637
    number, maximum, 329
    origin, 57
    original, appointment, 329
    protection by advertisement, 771
    qualified, 651
    retirement, 330
    securities, 144
    tenants for life as, 142
    vendors as, 650

TRUSTEES FOR SALE,
    administrators as, 786, 793
    management powers, 151
    postponement of sale, 149
    powers, 151
        delegation, 151
        pending sale, 151
    purchases from, 717
    receipt by, 80
    sale by, 717
    title of, proof, 717
    trust property transferred to, 147

TURBARY,
    common of, 518

U.

ULTRA VIRES,
    doctrine of, 871

UNBORN PERSON
    child of, limitation to, 236, 237
                validation, 240
    general power of appointment given to, 250

[53]

Index.